Lecture Notes in Computer Science 12952

More information about this subseries at http://www.springer.com/series/7407

Osvaldo Gervasi · Beniamino Murgante ·
Sanjay Misra · Chiara Garau ·
Ivan Blečić · David Taniar ·
Bernady O. Apduhan · Ana Maria A. C. Rocha ·
Eufemia Tarantino · Carmelo Maria Torre (Eds.)

Computational Science and Its Applications – ICCSA 2021

21st International Conference
Cagliari, Italy, September 13–16, 2021
Proceedings, Part IV

Springer

Editors
Osvaldo Gervasi
University of Perugia
Perugia, Italy

Sanjay Misra
Covenant University
Ota, Nigeria

Ivan Blečić
University of Cagliari
Cagliari, Italy

Bernady O. Apduhan
Kyushu Sangyo University
Fukuoka, Japan

Eufemia Tarantino
Polytechnic University of Bari
Bari, Italy

Beniamino Murgante
University of Basilicata
Potenza, Potenza, Italy

Chiara Garau
University of Cagliari
Cagliari, Italy

David Taniar
Monash University
Clayton, VIC, Australia

Ana Maria A. C. Rocha
University of Minho
Braga, Portugal

Carmelo Maria Torre
Polytechnic University of Bari
Bari, Italy

ISSN 0302-9743 ISSN 1611-3349 (electronic)
Lecture Notes in Computer Science
ISBN 978-3-030-86972-4 ISBN 978-3-030-86973-1 (eBook)
https://doi.org/10.1007/978-3-030-86973-1

LNCS Sublibrary: SL1 – Theoretical Computer Science and General Issues

This Springer imprint is published by the registered company Springer Nature Switzerland AG
The registered company address is: Gewerbestrasse 11, 6330 Cham, Switzerland

Preface

These 10 volumes (LNCS volumes 12949–12958) consist of the peer-reviewed papers from the 21st International Conference on Computational Science and Its Applications (ICCSA 2021) which took place during September 13–16, 2021. By virtue of the vaccination campaign conducted in various countries around the world, we decided to try a hybrid conference, with some of the delegates attending in person at the University of Cagliari and others attending in virtual mode, reproducing the infrastructure established last year.

This year's edition was a successful continuation of the ICCSA conference series, which was also held as a virtual event in 2020, and previously held in Saint Petersburg, Russia (2019), Melbourne, Australia (2018), Trieste, Italy (2017), Beijing. China (2016), Banff, Canada (2015), Guimaraes, Portugal (2014), Ho Chi Minh City, Vietnam (2013), Salvador, Brazil (2012), Santander, Spain (2011), Fukuoka, Japan (2010), Suwon, South Korea (2009), Perugia, Italy (2008), Kuala Lumpur, Malaysia (2007), Glasgow, UK (2006), Singapore (2005), Assisi, Italy (2004), Montreal, Canada (2003), and (as ICCS) Amsterdam, The Netherlands (2002) and San Francisco, USA (2001).

Computational science is the main pillar of most of the present research on understanding and solving complex problems. It plays a unique role in exploiting innovative ICT technologies and in the development of industrial and commercial applications. The ICCSA conference series provides a venue for researchers and industry practitioners to discuss new ideas, to share complex problems and their solutions, and to shape new trends in computational science.

Apart from the six main conference tracks, ICCSA 2021 also included 52 workshops in various areas of computational sciences, ranging from computational science technologies to specific areas of computational sciences, such as software engineering, security, machine learning and artificial intelligence, blockchain technologies, and applications in many fields. In total, we accepted 494 papers, giving an acceptance rate of 30%, of which 18 papers were short papers and 6 were published open access. We would like to express our appreciation for the workshop chairs and co-chairs for their hard work and dedication.

The success of the ICCSA conference series in general, and of ICCSA 2021 in particular, vitally depends on the support of many people: authors, presenters, participants, keynote speakers, workshop chairs, session chairs, organizing committee members, student volunteers, Program Committee members, advisory committee members, international liaison chairs, reviewers, and others in various roles. We take this opportunity to wholehartedly thank them all.

We also wish to thank Springer for publishing the proceedings, for sponsoring some of the best paper awards, and for their kind assistance and cooperation during the editing process.

We cordially invite you to visit the ICCSA website https://iccsa.org where you can find all the relevant information about this interesting and exciting event.

September 2021

Osvaldo Gervasi
Beniamino Murgante
Sanjay Misra

Welcome Message from the Organizers

COVID-19 has continued to alter our plans for organizing the ICCSA 2021 conference, so although vaccination plans are progressing worldwide, the spread of virus variants still forces us into a period of profound uncertainty. Only a very limited number of participants were able to enjoy the beauty of Sardinia and Cagliari in particular, rediscovering the immense pleasure of meeting again, albeit safely spaced out. The social events, in which we rediscovered the ancient values that abound on this wonderful island and in this city, gave us even more strength and hope for the future. For the management of the virtual part of the conference, we consolidated the methods, organization, and infrastructure of ICCSA 2020.

The technological infrastructure was based on open source software, with the addition of the streaming channels on YouTube. In particular, we used Jitsi (jitsi.org) for videoconferencing, Riot (riot.im) together with Matrix (matrix.org) for chat and ansynchronous communication, and Jibri (github.com/jitsi/jibri) for streaming live sessions to YouTube.

Seven Jitsi servers were set up, one for each parallel session. The participants of the sessions were helped and assisted by eight student volunteers (from the universities of Cagliari, Florence, Perugia, and Bari), who provided technical support and ensured smooth running of the conference proceedings.

The implementation of the software infrastructure and the technical coordination of the volunteers were carried out by Damiano Perri and Marco Simonetti.

Our warmest thanks go to all the student volunteers, to the technical coordinators, and to the development communities of Jitsi, Jibri, Riot, and Matrix, who made their terrific platforms available as open source software.

A big thank you goes to all of the 450 speakers, many of whom showed an enormous collaborative spirit, sometimes participating and presenting at almost prohibitive times of the day, given that the participants of this year's conference came from 58 countries scattered over many time zones of the globe.

Finally, we would like to thank Google for letting us stream all the live events via YouTube. In addition to lightening the load of our Jitsi servers, this allowed us to record the event and to be able to review the most exciting moments of the conference.

Ivan Blečić
Chiara Garau

Organization

ICCSA 2021 was organized by the University of Cagliari (Italy), the University of Perugia (Italy), the University of Basilicata (Italy), Monash University (Australia), Kyushu Sangyo University (Japan), and the University of Minho (Portugal).

Honorary General Chairs

Norio Shiratori	Chuo University, Japan
Kenneth C. J. Tan	Sardina Systems, UK
Corrado Zoppi	University of Cagliari, Italy

General Chairs

Osvaldo Gervasi	University of Perugia, Italy
Ivan Blečić	University of Cagliari, Italy
David Taniar	Monash University, Australia

Program Committee Chairs

Beniamino Murgante	University of Basilicata, Italy
Bernady O. Apduhan	Kyushu Sangyo University, Japan
Chiara Garau	University of Cagliari, Italy
Ana Maria A. C. Rocha	University of Minho, Portugal

International Advisory Committee

Jemal Abawajy	Deakin University, Australia
Dharma P. Agarwal	University of Cincinnati, USA
Rajkumar Buyya	University of Melbourne, Australia
Claudia Bauzer Medeiros	University of Campinas, Brazil
Manfred M. Fisher	Vienna University of Economics and Business, Austria
Marina L. Gavrilova	University of Calgary, Canada
Yee Leung	Chinese University of Hong Kong, China

International Liaison Chairs

Giuseppe Borruso	University of Trieste, Italy
Elise De Donker	Western Michigan University, USA
Maria Irene Falcão	University of Minho, Portugal
Robert C. H. Hsu	Chung Hua University, Taiwan
Tai-Hoon Kim	Beijing Jaotong University, China

Vladimir Korkhov	St. Petersburg University, Russia
Sanjay Misra	Covenant University, Nigeria
Takashi Naka	Kyushu Sangyo University, Japan
Rafael D. C. Santos	National Institute for Space Research, Brazil
Maribel Yasmina Santos	University of Minho, Portugal
Elena Stankova	St. Petersburg University, Russia

Workshop and Session Chairs

Beniamino Murgante	University of Basilicata, Italy
Sanjay Misra	Covenant University, Nigeria
Jorge Gustavo Rocha	University of Minho, Portugal

Awards Chair

Wenny Rahayu	La Trobe University, Australia

Publicity Committee Chairs

Elmer Dadios	De La Salle University, Philippines
Nataliia Kulabukhova	St. Petersburg University, Russia
Daisuke Takahashi	Tsukuba University, Japan
Shangwang Wang	Beijing University of Posts and Telecommunications, China

Technology Chairs

Damiano Perri	University of Florence, Italy
Marco Simonetti	University of Florence, Italy

Local Arrangement Chairs

Ivan Blečić	University of Cagliari, Italy
Chiara Garau	University of Cagliari, Italy
Alfonso Annunziata	University of Cagliari, Italy
Ginevra Balletto	University of Cagliari, Italy
Giuseppe Borruso	University of Trieste, Italy
Alessandro Buccini	University of Cagliari, Italy
Michele Campagna	University of Cagliari, Italy
Mauro Coni	University of Cagliari, Italy
Anna Maria Colavitti	University of Cagliari, Italy
Giulia Desogus	University of Cagliari, Italy
Caterina Fenu	University of Cagliari, Italy
Sabrina Lai	University of Cagliari, Italy
Francesca Maltinti	University of Cagliari, Italy
Pasquale Mistretta	University of Cagliari, Italy

Augusto Montisci	University of Cagliari, Italy
Francesco Pinna	University of Cagliari, Italy
Davide Spano	University of Cagliari, Italy
Giuseppe A. Trunfio	University of Sassari, Italy
Corrado Zoppi	University of Cagliari, Italy

Program Committee

Vera Afreixo	University of Aveiro, Portugal
Filipe Alvelos	University of Minho, Portugal
Hartmut Asche	University of Potsdam, Germany
Ginevra Balletto	University of Cagliari, Italy
Michela Bertolotto	University College Dublin, Ireland
Sandro Bimonte	INRAE-TSCF, France
Rod Blais	University of Calgary, Canada
Ivan Blečić	University of Sassari, Italy
Giuseppe Borruso	University of Trieste, Italy
Ana Cristina Braga	University of Minho, Portugal
Massimo Cafaro	University of Salento, Italy
Yves Caniou	University of Lyon, France
José A. Cardoso e Cunha	Universidade Nova de Lisboa, Portugal
Rui Cardoso	University of Beira Interior, Portugal
Leocadio G. Casado	University of Almeria, Spain
Carlo Cattani	University of Salerno, Italy
Mete Celik	Erciyes University, Turkey
Maria Cerreta	University of Naples "Federico II", Italy
Hyunseung Choo	Sungkyunkwan University, South Korea
Chien-Sing Lee	Sunway University, Malaysia
Min Young Chung	Sungkyunkwan University, South Korea
Florbela Maria da Cruz Domingues Correia	Polytechnic Institute of Viana do Castelo, Portugal
Gilberto Corso Pereira	Federal University of Bahia, Brazil
Fernanda Costa	University of Minho, Portugal
Alessandro Costantini	INFN, Italy
Carla Dal Sasso Freitas	Universidade Federal do Rio Grande do Sul, Brazil
Pradesh Debba	The Council for Scientific and Industrial Research (CSIR), South Africa
Hendrik Decker	Instituto Tecnolčgico de Informática, Spain
Robertas Damaševičius	Kausan University of Technology, Lithuania
Frank Devai	London South Bank University, UK
Rodolphe Devillers	Memorial University of Newfoundland, Canada
Joana Matos Dias	University of Coimbra, Portugal
Paolino Di Felice	University of L'Aquila, Italy
Prabu Dorairaj	NetApp, India/USA
Noelia Faginas Lago	University of Perugia, Italy
M. Irene Falcao	University of Minho, Portugal

Tinghuai Ma	Nanjing University of Information Science and Technology, China
Ernesto Marcheggiani	Katholieke Universiteit Leuven, Belgium
Antonino Marvuglia	Research Centre Henri Tudor, Luxembourg
Nicola Masini	National Research Council, Italy
Ilaria Matteucci	National Research Council, Italy
Eric Medvet	University of Trieste, Italy
Nirvana Meratnia	University of Twente, The Netherlands
Giuseppe Modica	University of Reggio Calabria, Italy
Josè Luis Montaña	University of Cantabria, Spain
Maria Filipa Mourão	Instituto Politécnico de Viana do Castelo, Portugal
Louiza de Macedo Mourelle	State University of Rio de Janeiro, Brazil
Nadia Nedjah	State University of Rio de Janeiro, Brazil
Laszlo Neumann	University of Girona, Spain
Kok-Leong Ong	Deakin University, Australia
Belen Palop	Universidad de Valladolid, Spain
Marcin Paprzycki	Polish Academy of Sciences, Poland
Eric Pardede	La Trobe University, Australia
Kwangjin Park	Wonkwang University, South Korea
Ana Isabel Pereira	Polytechnic Institute of Bragança, Portugal
Massimiliano Petri	University of Pisa, Italy
Telmo Pinto	University of Coimbra, Portugal
Maurizio Pollino	Italian National Agency for New Technologies, Energy and Sustainable Economic Development, Italy
Alenka Poplin	University of Hamburg, Germany
Vidyasagar Potdar	Curtin University of Technology, Australia
David C. Prosperi	Florida Atlantic University, USA
Wenny Rahayu	La Trobe University, Australia
Jerzy Respondek	Silesian University of Technology Poland
Humberto Rocha	INESC-Coimbra, Portugal
Jon Rokne	University of Calgary, Canada
Octavio Roncero	CSIC, Spain
Maytham Safar	Kuwait University, Kuwait
Francesco Santini	University of Perugia, Italy
Chiara Saracino	A.O. Ospedale Niguarda Ca' Granda, Italy
Haiduke Sarafian	Pennsylvania State University, USA
Marco Paulo Seabra dos Reis	University of Coimbra, Portugal
Jie Shen	University of Michigan, USA
Qi Shi	Liverpool John Moores University, UK
Dale Shires	U.S. Army Research Laboratory, USA
Inês Soares	University of Coimbra, Portugal
Elena Stankova	St. Petersburg University, Russia
Takuo Suganuma	Tohoku University, Japan
Eufemia Tarantino	Polytechnic University of Bari, Italy
Sergio Tasso	University of Perugia, Italy

Ana Paula Teixeira	University of Trás-os-Montes and Alto Douro, Portugal
Senhorinha Teixeira	University of Minho, Portugal
M. Filomena Teodoro	Portuguese Naval Academy/University of Lisbon, Portugal
Parimala Thulasiraman	University of Manitoba, Canada
Carmelo Torre	Polytechnic University of Bari, Italy
Javier Martinez Torres	Centro Universitario de la Defensa Zaragoza, Spain
Giuseppe A. Trunfio	University of Sassari, Italy
Pablo Vanegas	University of Cuenca, Equador
Marco Vizzari	University of Perugia, Italy
Varun Vohra	Merck Inc., USA
Koichi Wada	University of Tsukuba, Japan
Krzysztof Walkowiak	Wroclaw University of Technology, Poland
Zequn Wang	Intelligent Automation Inc, USA
Robert Weibel	University of Zurich, Switzerland
Frank Westad	Norwegian University of Science and Technology, Norway
Roland Wismüller	Universität Siegen, Germany
Mudasser Wyne	National University, USA
Chung-Huang Yang	National Kaohsiung Normal University, Taiwan
Xin-She Yang	National Physical Laboratory, UK
Salim Zabir	National Institute of Technology, Tsuruoka, Japan
Haifeng Zhao	University of California, Davis, USA
Fabiana Zollo	University of Venice "Cà Foscari", Italy
Albert Y. Zomaya	University of Sydney, Australia

Workshop Organizers

Advanced Transport Tools and Methods (A2TM 2021)

Massimiliano Petri	University of Pisa, Italy
Antonio Pratelli	University of Pisa, Italy

Advances in Artificial Intelligence Learning Technologies: Blended Learning, STEM, Computational Thinking and Coding (AAILT 2021)

Alfredo Milani	University of Perugia, Italy
Giulio Biondi	University of Florence, Italy
Sergio Tasso	University of Perugia, Italy

Workshop on Advancements in Applied Machine Learning and Data Analytics (AAMDA 2021)

Alessandro Costantini	INFN, Italy
Davide Salomoni	INFN, Italy
Doina Cristina Duma	INFN, Italy
Daniele Cesini	INFN, Italy

Automatic Landform Classification: Spatial Methods and Applications (ALCSMA 2021)

Maria Danese	ISPC, National Research Council, Italy
Dario Gioia	ISPC, National Research Council, Italy

Application of Numerical Analysis to Imaging Science (ANAIS 2021)

Caterina Fenu	University of Cagliari, Italy
Alessandro Buccini	University of Cagliari, Italy

Advances in Information Systems and Technologies for Emergency Management, Risk Assessment and Mitigation Based on the Resilience Concepts (ASTER 2021)

Maurizio Pollino	ENEA, Italy
Marco Vona	University of Basilicata, Italy
Amedeo Flora	University of Basilicata, Italy
Chiara Iacovino	University of Basilicata, Italy
Beniamino Murgante	University of Basilicata, Italy

Advances in Web Based Learning (AWBL 2021)

Birol Ciloglugil	Ege University, Turkey
Mustafa Murat Inceoglu	Ege University, Turkey

Blockchain and Distributed Ledgers: Technologies and Applications (BDLTA 2021)

Vladimir Korkhov	St. Petersburg University, Russia
Elena Stankova	St. Petersburg University, Russia
Nataliia Kulabukhova	St. Petersburg University, Russia

Bio and Neuro Inspired Computing and Applications (BIONCA 2021)

Nadia Nedjah	State University of Rio de Janeiro, Brazil
Luiza De Macedo Mourelle	State University of Rio de Janeiro, Brazil

Computational and Applied Mathematics (CAM 2021)

Maria Irene Falcão	University of Minho, Portugal
Fernando Miranda	University of Minho, Portugal

Computational and Applied Statistics (CAS 2021)

Ana Cristina Braga	University of Minho, Portugal

Computerized Evaluation of Economic Activities: Urban Spaces (CEEA 2021)

Diego Altafini	Università di Pisa, Italy
Valerio Cutini	Università di Pisa, Italy

Computational Geometry and Applications (CGA 2021)

Marina Gavrilova	University of Calgary, Canada

Collaborative Intelligence in Multimodal Applications (CIMA 2021)

Robertas Damasevicius	Kaunas University of Technology, Lithuania
Rytis Maskeliunas	Kaunas University of Technology, Lithuania

Computational Optimization and Applications (COA 2021)

Ana Rocha	University of Minho, Portugal
Humberto Rocha	University of Coimbra, Portugal

Computational Astrochemistry (CompAstro 2021)

Marzio Rosi	University of Perugia, Italy
Cecilia Ceccarelli	University of Grenoble, France
Stefano Falcinelli	University of Perugia, Italy
Dimitrios Skouteris	Master-Up, Italy

Computational Science and HPC (CSHPC 2021)

Elise de Doncker	Western Michigan University, USA
Fukuko Yuasa	High Energy Accelerator Research Organization (KEK), Japan
Hideo Matsufuru	High Energy Accelerator Research Organization (KEK), Japan

Cities, Technologies and Planning (CTP 2021)

Malgorzata Hanzl	University of Łódż, Poland
Beniamino Murgante	University of Basilicata, Italy
Ljiljana Zivkovic	Ministry of Construction, Transport and Infrastructure/Institute of Architecture and Urban and Spatial Planning of Serbia, Serbia
Anastasia Stratigea	National Technical University of Athens, Greece
Giuseppe Borruso	University of Trieste, Italy
Ginevra Balletto	University of Cagliari, Italy

Advanced Modeling E-Mobility in Urban Spaces (DEMOS 2021)

Tiziana Campisi	Kore University of Enna, Italy
Socrates Basbas	Aristotle University of Thessaloniki, Greece
Ioannis Politis	Aristotle University of Thessaloniki, Greece
Florin Nemtanu	Polytechnic University of Bucharest, Romania
Giovanna Acampa	Kore University of Enna, Italy
Wolfgang Schulz	Zeppelin University, Germany

Digital Transformation and Smart City (DIGISMART 2021)

Mauro Mazzei	National Research Council, Italy

Econometric and Multidimensional Evaluation in Urban Environment (EMEUE 2021)

Carmelo Maria Torre	Polytechnic University of Bari, Italy
Maria Cerreta	University “Federico II” of Naples, Italy
Pierluigi Morano	Polytechnic University of Bari, Italy
Simona Panaro	University of Portsmouth, UK
Francesco Tajani	Sapienza University of Rome, Italy
Marco Locurcio	Polytechnic University of Bari, Italy

The 11th International Workshop on Future Computing System Technologies and Applications (FiSTA 2021)

Bernady Apduhan	Kyushu Sangyo University, Japan
Rafael Santos	Brazilian National Institute for Space Research, Brazil

Transformational Urban Mobility: Challenges and Opportunities During and Post COVID Era (FURTHER 2021)

Tiziana Campisi	Kore University of Enna, Italy
Socrates Basbas	Aristotle University of Thessaloniki, Greece
Dilum Dissanayake	Newcastle University, UK
Kh Md Nahiduzzaman	University of British Columbia, Canada
Nurten Akgün Tanbay	Bursa Technical University, Turkey
Khaled J. Assi	King Fahd University of Petroleum and Minerals, Saudi Arabia
Giovanni Tesoriere	Kore University of Enna, Italy
Motasem Darwish	Middle East University, Jordan

Geodesign in Decision Making: Meta Planning and Collaborative Design for Sustainable and Inclusive Development (GDM 2021)

Francesco Scorza	University of Basilicata, Italy
Michele Campagna	University of Cagliari, Italy
Ana Clara Mourao Moura	Federal University of Minas Gerais, Brazil

Geomatics in Forestry and Agriculture: New Advances and Perspectives (GeoForAgr 2021)

Maurizio Pollino	ENEA, Italy
Giuseppe Modica	University of Reggio Calabria, Italy
Marco Vizzari	University of Perugia, Italy

Geographical Analysis, Urban Modeling, Spatial Statistics (GEOG-AND-MOD 2021)

Beniamino Murgante	University of Basilicata, Italy
Giuseppe Borruso	University of Trieste, Italy
Hartmut Asche	University of Potsdam, Germany

Geomatics for Resource Monitoring and Management (GRMM 2021)

Eufemia Tarantino	Polytechnic University of Bari, Italy
Enrico Borgogno Mondino	University of Turin, Italy
Alessandra Capolupo	Polytechnic University of Bari, Italy
Mirko Saponaro	Polytechnic University of Bari, Italy

12th International Symposium on Software Quality (ISSQ 2021)

Sanjay Misra	Covenant University, Nigeria

10th International Workshop on Collective, Massive and Evolutionary Systems (IWCES 2021)

Alfredo Milani	University of Perugia, Italy
Rajdeep Niyogi	Indian Institute of Technology, Roorkee, India

Land Use Monitoring for Sustainability (LUMS 2021)

Carmelo Maria Torre	Polytechnic University of Bari, Italy
Maria Cerreta	University "Federico II" of Naples, Italy
Massimiliano Bencardino	University of Salerno, Italy
Alessandro Bonifazi	Polytechnic University of Bari, Italy
Pasquale Balena	Polytechnic University of Bari, Italy
Giuliano Poli	University "Federico II" of Naples, Italy

Machine Learning for Space and Earth Observation Data (MALSEOD 2021)

Rafael Santos	Instituto Nacional de Pesquisas Espaciais, Brazil
Karine Ferreira	Instituto Nacional de Pesquisas Espaciais, Brazil

Building Multi-dimensional Models for Assessing Complex Environmental Systems (MES 2021)

Marta Dell'Ovo	Polytechnic University of Milan, Italy
Vanessa Assumma	Polytechnic University of Turin, Italy
Caterina Caprioli	Polytechnic University of Turin, Italy
Giulia Datola	Polytechnic University of Turin, Italy
Federico dell'Anna	Polytechnic University of Turin, Italy

Ecosystem Services: Nature's Contribution to People in Practice. Assessment Frameworks, Models, Mapping, and Implications (NC2P 2021)

Francesco Scorza	University of Basilicata, Italy
Sabrina Lai	University of Cagliari, Italy
Ana Clara Mourao Moura	Federal University of Minas Gerais, Brazil
Corrado Zoppi	University of Cagliari, Italy
Dani Broitman	Technion, Israel Institute of Technology, Israel

Privacy in the Cloud/Edge/IoT World (PCEIoT 2021)

Michele Mastroianni	University of Campania Luigi Vanvitelli, Italy
Lelio Campanile	University of Campania Luigi Vanvitelli, Italy
Mauro Iacono	University of Campania Luigi Vanvitelli, Italy

Processes, Methods and Tools Towards RESilient Cities and Cultural Heritage Prone to SOD and ROD Disasters (RES 2021)

Elena Cantatore	Polytechnic University of Bari, Italy
Alberico Sonnessa	Polytechnic University of Bari, Italy
Dario Esposito	Polytechnic University of Bari, Italy

Risk, Resilience and Sustainability in the Efficient Management of Water Resources: Approaches, Tools, Methodologies and Multidisciplinary Integrated Applications (RRS 2021)

Maria Macchiaroli	University of Salerno, Italy
Chiara D'Alpaos	Università degli Studi di Padova, Italy
Mirka Mobilia	Università degli Studi di Salerno, Italy
Antonia Longobardi	Università degli Studi di Salerno, Italy
Grazia Fattoruso	ENEA Research Center, Italy
Vincenzo Pellecchia	Ente Idrico Campano, Italy

Scientific Computing Infrastructure (SCI 2021)

Elena Stankova	St. Petersburg University, Russia
Vladimir Korkhov	St. Petersburg University, Russia
Natalia Kulabukhova	St. Petersburg University, Russia

Smart Cities and User Data Management (SCIDAM 2021)

Chiara Garau	University of Cagliari, Italy
Luigi Mundula	University of Cagliari, Italy
Gianni Fenu	University of Cagliari, Italy
Paolo Nesi	University of Florence, Italy
Paola Zamperlin	University of Pisa, Italy

13th International Symposium on Software Engineering Processes and Applications (SEPA 2021)

Sanjay Misra	Covenant University, Nigeria

Ports of the Future - Smartness and Sustainability (SmartPorts 2021)

Patrizia Serra	University of Cagliari, Italy
Gianfranco Fancello	University of Cagliari, Italy
Ginevra Balletto	University of Cagliari, Italy
Luigi Mundula	University of Cagliari, Italy
Marco Mazzarino	University of Venice, Italy
Giuseppe Borruso	University of Trieste, Italy
Maria del Mar Munoz Leonisio	Universidad de Cádiz, Spain

Smart Tourism (SmartTourism 2021)

Giuseppe Borruso	University of Trieste, Italy
Silvia Battino	University of Sassari, Italy
Ginevra Balletto	University of Cagliari, Italy
Maria del Mar Munoz Leonisio	Universidad de Cádiz, Spain
Ainhoa Amaro Garcia	Universidad de Alcalà/Universidad de Las Palmas, Spain
Francesca Krasna	University of Trieste, Italy

Sustainability Performance Assessment: Models, Approaches and Applications toward Interdisciplinary and Integrated Solutions (SPA 2021)

Francesco Scorza	University of Basilicata, Italy
Sabrina Lai	University of Cagliari, Italy
Jolanta Dvarioniene	Kaunas University of Technology, Lithuania
Valentin Grecu	Lucian Blaga University, Romania
Corrado Zoppi	University of Cagliari, Italy
Iole Cerminara	University of Basilicata, Italy

Smart and Sustainable Island Communities (SSIC 2021)

Chiara Garau	University of Cagliari, Italy
Anastasia Stratigea	National Technical University of Athens, Greece
Paola Zamperlin	University of Pisa, Italy
Francesco Scorza	University of Basilicata, Italy

Science, Technologies and Policies to Innovate Spatial Planning (STP4P 2021)

Chiara Garau	University of Cagliari, Italy
Daniele La Rosa	University of Catania, Italy
Francesco Scorza	University of Basilicata, Italy

Anna Maria Colavitti	University of Cagliari, Italy
Beniamino Murgante	University of Basilicata, Italy
Paolo La Greca	University of Catania, Italy

Sustainable Urban Energy Systems (SURENSYS 2021)

Luigi Mundula	University of Cagliari, Italy
Emilio Ghiani	University of Cagliari, Italy

Space Syntax for Cities in Theory and Practice (Syntax_City 2021)

Claudia Yamu	University of Groningen, The Netherlands
Akkelies van Nes	Western Norway University of Applied Sciences, Norway
Chiara Garau	University of Cagliari, Italy

Theoretical and Computational Chemistry and Its Applications (TCCMA 2021)

Noelia Faginas-Lago	University of Perugia, Italy

13th International Workshop on Tools and Techniques in Software Development Process (TTSDP 2021)

Sanjay Misra	Covenant University, Nigeria

Urban Form Studies (UForm 2021)

Malgorzata Hanzl	Łódź University of Technology, Poland
Beniamino Murgante	University of Basilicata, Italy
Eufemia Tarantino	Polytechnic University of Bari, Italy
Irena Itova	University of Westminster, UK

Urban Space Accessibility and Safety (USAS 2021)

Chiara Garau	University of Cagliari, Italy
Francesco Pinna	University of Cagliari, Italy
Claudia Yamu	University of Groningen, The Netherlands
Vincenza Torrisi	University of Catania, Italy
Matteo Ignaccolo	University of Catania, Italy
Michela Tiboni	University of Brescia, Italy
Silvia Rossetti	University of Parma, Italy

Virtual and Augmented Reality and Applications (VRA 2021)

Osvaldo Gervasi	University of Perugia, Italy
Damiano Perri	University of Perugia, Italy
Marco Simonetti	University of Perugia, Italy
Sergio Tasso	University of Perugia, Italy

Workshop on Advanced and Computational Methods for Earth Science Applications (WACM4ES 2021)

Luca Piroddi	University of Cagliari, Italy
Laura Foddis	University of Cagliari, Italy
Augusto Montisci	University of Cagliari, Italy
Sergio Vincenzo Calcina	University of Cagliari, Italy
Sebastiano D'Amico	University of Malta, Malta
Giovanni Martinelli	Istituto Nazionale di Geofisica e Vulcanologia, Italy/Chinese Academy of Sciences, China

Sponsoring Organizations

ICCSA 2021 would not have been possible without the tremendous support of many organizations and institutions, for which all organizers and participants of ICCSA 2021 express their sincere gratitude:

Springer International Publishing AG, Germany
(https://www.springer.com)

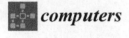

Computers Open Access Journal
(https://www.mdpi.com/journal/computers)

IEEE Italy Section, Italy
(https://italy.ieeer8.org/)

Centre-North Italy Chapter IEEE GRSS, Italy
(https://cispio.diet.uniroma1.it/marzano/ieee-grs/index.html)

Italy Section of the Computer Society, Italy
(https://site.ieee.org/italy-cs/)

University of Perugia, Italy
(https://www.unipg.it)

University of Cagliari, Italy
(https://unica.it/)

University of Basilicata, Italy
(http://www.unibas.it)

Monash University, Australia
(https://www.monash.edu/)

Kyushu Sangyo University, Japan
(https://www.kyusan-u.ac.jp/)

University of Minho, Portugal
(https://www.uminho.pt/)

Scientific Association Transport Infrastructures, Italy
(https://www.stradeeautostrade.it/associazioni-e-organizzazioni/asit-associazione-scientifica-infrastrutture-trasporto/)

Regione Sardegna, Italy
(https://regione.sardegna.it/)

Comune di Cagliari, Italy
(https://www.comune.cagliari.it/)

Città Metropolitana di Cagliari

Cagliari Accessibility Lab (CAL)
(https://www.unica.it/unica/it/cagliari_accessibility_lab.page/)

Referees

Nicodemo Abate	IMAA, National Research Council, Italy
Andre Ricardo Abed Grégio	Federal University of Paraná State, Brazil
Nasser Abu Zeid	Università di Ferrara, Italy
Lidia Aceto	Università del Piemonte Orientale, Italy
Nurten Akgün Tanbay	Bursa Technical University, Turkey
Filipe Alvelos	Universidade do Minho, Portugal
Paula Amaral	Universidade Nova de Lisboa, Portugal
Federico Amato	University of Lausanne, Switzerland
Marina Alexandra Pedro Andrade	ISCTE-IUL, Portugal
Debora Anelli	Sapienza University of Rome, Italy
Alfonso Annunziata	University of Cagliari, Italy
Fahim Anzum	University of Calgary, Canada
Tatsumi Aoyama	High Energy Accelerator Research Organization, Japan
Bernady Apduhan	Kyushu Sangyo University, Japan
Jonathan Apeh	Covenant University, Nigeria
Vasilike Argyropoulos	University of West Attica, Greece
Giuseppe Aronica	Università di Messina, Italy
Daniela Ascenzi	Università degli Studi di Trento, Italy
Vanessa Assumma	Politecnico di Torino, Italy
Muhammad Attique Khan	HITEC University Taxila, Pakistan
Vecdi Aytaç	Ege University, Turkey
Alina Elena Baia	University of Perugia, Italy
Ginevra Balletto	University of Cagliari, Italy
Marialaura Bancheri	ISAFOM, National Research Council, Italy
Benedetto Barabino	University of Brescia, Italy
Simona Barbaro	Università degli Studi di Palermo, Italy
Enrico Barbierato	Università Cattolica del Sacro Cuore di Milano, Italy
Jeniffer Barreto	Istituto Superior Técnico, Lisboa, Portugal
Michele Bartalini	TAGES, Italy
Socrates Basbas	Aristotle University of Thessaloniki, Greece
Silvia Battino	University of Sassari, Italy
Marcelo Becerra Rozas	Pontificia Universidad Católica de Valparaíso, Chile
Ranjan Kumar Behera	National Institute of Technology, Rourkela, India
Emanuele Bellini	University of Campania Luigi Vanvitelli, Italy
Massimo Bilancia	University of Bari Aldo Moro, Italy
Giulio Biondi	University of Firenze, Italy
Adriano Bisello	Eurac Research, Italy
Ignacio Blanquer	Universitat Politècnica de València, Spain
Semen Bochkov	Ulyanovsk State Technical University, Russia
Alexander Bogdanov	St. Petersburg University, Russia
Silvia Bonettini	University of Modena and Reggio Emilia, Italy
Enrico Borgogno Mondino	Università di Torino, Italy
Giuseppe Borruso	University of Trieste, Italy

Michele Bottazzi	University of Trento, Italy
Rahma Bouaziz	Taibah University, Saudi Arabia
Ouafik Boulariah	University of Salerno, Italy
Tulin Boyar	Yildiz Technical University, Turkey
Ana Cristina Braga	University of Minho, Portugal
Paolo Bragolusi	University of Padova, Italy
Luca Braidotti	University of Trieste, Italy
Alessandro Buccini	University of Cagliari, Italy
Jorge Buele	Universidad Tecnológica Indoamérica, Ecuador
Andrea Buffoni	TAGES, Italy
Sergio Vincenzo Calcina	University of Cagliari, Italy
Michele Campagna	University of Cagliari, Italy
Lelio Campanile	Università degli Studi della Campania Luigi Vanvitelli, Italy
Tiziana Campisi	Kore University of Enna, Italy
Antonino Canale	Kore University of Enna, Italy
Elena Cantatore	DICATECh, Polytechnic University of Bari, Italy
Pasquale Cantiello	Istituto Nazionale di Geofisica e Vulcanologia, Italy
Alessandra Capolupo	Polytechnic University of Bari, Italy
David Michele Cappelletti	University of Perugia, Italy
Caterina Caprioli	Politecnico di Torino, Italy
Sara Carcangiu	University of Cagliari, Italy
Pedro Carrasqueira	INESC Coimbra, Portugal
Arcangelo Castiglione	University of Salerno, Italy
Giulio Cavana	Politecnico di Torino, Italy
Davide Cerati	Politecnico di Milano, Italy
Maria Cerreta	University of Naples Federico II, Italy
Daniele Cesini	INFN-CNAF, Italy
Jabed Chowdhury	La Trobe University, Australia
Gennaro Ciccarelli	Iuav University of Venice, Italy
Birol Ciloglugil	Ege University, Turkey
Elena Cocuzza	Univesity of Catania, Italy
Anna Maria Colavitt	University of Cagliari, Italy
Cecilia Coletti	Università "G. d'Annunzio" di Chieti-Pescara, Italy
Alberto Collu	Independent Researcher, Italy
Anna Concas	University of Basilicata, Italy
Mauro Coni	University of Cagliari, Italy
Melchiorre Contino	Università di Palermo, Italy
Antonella Cornelio	Università degli Studi di Brescia, Italy
Aldina Correia	Politécnico do Porto, Portugal
Elisete Correia	Universidade de Trás-os-Montes e Alto Douro, Portugal
Florbela Correia	Polytechnic Institute of Viana do Castelo, Portugal
Stefano Corsi	Università degli Studi di Milano, Italy
Alberto Cortez	Polytechnic of University Coimbra, Portugal
Lino Costa	Universidade do Minho, Portugal

Alessandro Costantini	INFN, Italy
Marilena Cozzolino	Università del Molise, Italy
Giulia Crespi	Politecnico di Torino, Italy
Maurizio Crispino	Politecnico di Milano, Italy
Chiara D'Alpaos	University of Padova, Italy
Roberta D'Ambrosio	Università di Salerno, Italy
Sebastiano D'Amico	University of Malta, Malta
Hiroshi Daisaka	Hitotsubashi University, Japan
Gaia Daldanise	Italian National Research Council, Italy
Robertas Damasevicius	Silesian University of Technology, Poland
Maria Danese	ISPC, National Research Council, Italy
Bartoli Daniele	University of Perugia, Italy
Motasem Darwish	Middle East University, Jordan
Giulia Datola	Politecnico di Torino, Italy
Regina de Almeida	UTAD, Portugal
Elise de Doncker	Western Michigan University, USA
Mariella De Fino	Politecnico di Bari, Italy
Giandomenico De Luca	Mediterranean University of Reggio Calabria, Italy
Luiza de Macedo Mourelle	State University of Rio de Janeiro, Brazil
Gianluigi De Mare	University of Salerno, Italy
Itamir de Morais Barroca Filho	Federal University of Rio Grande do Norte, Brazil
Samuele De Petris	Università di Torino, Italy
Marcilio de Souto	LIFO, University of Orléans, France
Alexander Degtyarev	St. Petersburg University, Russia
Federico Dell'Anna	Politecnico di Torino, Italy
Marta Dell'Ovo	Politecnico di Milano, Italy
Fernanda Della Mura	University of Naples "Federico II", Italy
Ahu Dereli Dursun	Istanbul Commerce University, Turkey
Bashir Derradji	University of Sfax, Tunisia
Giulia Desogus	Università degli Studi di Cagliari, Italy
Marco Dettori	Università degli Studi di Sassari, Italy
Frank Devai	London South Bank University, UK
Felicia Di Liddo	Polytechnic University of Bari, Italy
Valerio Di Pinto	University of Naples "Federico II", Italy
Joana Dias	University of Coimbra, Portugal
Luis Dias	University of Minho, Portugal
Patricia Diaz de Alba	Gran Sasso Science Institute, Italy
Isabel Dimas	University of Coimbra, Portugal
Aleksandra Djordjevic	University of Belgrade, Serbia
Luigi Dolores	Università degli Studi di Salerno, Italy
Marco Donatelli	University of Insubria, Italy
Doina Cristina Duma	INFN-CNAF, Italy
Fabio Durastante	University of Pisa, Italy
Aziz Dursun	Virginia Tech University, USA
Juan Enrique-Romero	Université Grenoble Alpes, France

Annunziata Esposito Amideo	University College Dublin, Ireland
Dario Esposito	Polytechnic University of Bari, Italy
Claudio Estatico	University of Genova, Italy
Noelia Faginas-Lago	Università di Perugia, Italy
Maria Irene Falcão	University of Minho, Portugal
Stefano Falcinelli	University of Perugia, Italy
Alessandro Farina	University of Pisa, Italy
Grazia Fattoruso	ENEA, Italy
Caterina Fenu	University of Cagliari, Italy
Luisa Fermo	University of Cagliari, Italy
Florbela Fernandes	Instituto Politecnico de Braganca, Portugal
Rosário Fernandes	University of Minho, Portugal
Luis Fernandez-Sanz	University of Alcala, Spain
Alessia Ferrari	Università di Parma, Italy
Luís Ferrás	University of Minho, Portugal
Ângela Ferreira	Instituto Politécnico de Bragança, Portugal
Flora Ferreira	University of Minho, Portugal
Manuel Carlos Figueiredo	University of Minho, Portugal
Ugo Fiore	University of Naples "Parthenope", Italy
Amedeo Flora	University of Basilicata, Italy
Hector Florez	Universidad Distrital Francisco Jose de Caldas, Colombia
Maria Laura Foddis	University of Cagliari, Italy
Valentina Franzoni	Perugia University, Italy
Adelaide Freitas	University of Aveiro, Portugal
Samuel Frimpong	Durban University of Technology, South Africa
Ioannis Fyrogenis	Aristotle University of Thessaloniki, Greece
Marika Gaballo	Politecnico di Torino, Italy
Laura Gabrielli	Iuav University of Venice, Italy
Ivan Gankevich	St. Petersburg University, Russia
Chiara Garau	University of Cagliari, Italy
Ernesto Garcia Para	Universidad del País Vasco, Spain,
Fernando Garrido	Universidad Técnica del Norte, Ecuador
Marina Gavrilova	University of Calgary, Canada
Silvia Gazzola	University of Bath, UK
Georgios Georgiadis	Aristotle University of Thessaloniki, Greece
Osvaldo Gervasi	University of Perugia, Italy
Andrea Gioia	Polytechnic University of Bari, Italy
Dario Gioia	ISPC-CNT, Italy
Raffaele Giordano	IRSS, National Research Council, Italy
Giacomo Giorgi	University of Perugia, Italy
Eleonora Giovene di Girasole	IRISS, National Research Council, Italy
Salvatore Giuffrida	Università di Catania, Italy
Marco Gola	Politecnico di Milano, Italy

A. Manuela Gonçalves	University of Minho, Portugal
Yuriy Gorbachev	Coddan Technologies LLC, Russia
Angela Gorgoglione	Universidad de la República, Uruguay
Yusuke Gotoh	Okayama University, Japan
Anestis Gourgiotis	University of Thessaly, Greece
Valery Grishkin	St. Petersburg University, Russia
Alessandro Grottesi	CINECA, Italy
Eduardo Guerra	Free University of Bozen-Bolzano, Italy
Ayse Giz Gulnerman	Ankara HBV University, Turkey
Sevin Gümgüm	Izmir University of Economics, Turkey
Himanshu Gupta	BITS Pilani, Hyderabad, India
Sandra Haddad	Arab Academy for Science, Egypt
Malgorzata Hanzl	Lodz University of Technology, Poland
Shoji Hashimoto	KEK, Japan
Peter Hegedus	University of Szeged, Hungary
Eligius M. T. Hendrix	Universidad de Málaga, Spain
Edmond Ho	Northumbria University, UK
Guan Yue Hong	Western Michigan University, USA
Vito Iacobellis	Polytechnic University of Bari, Italy
Mauro Iacono	Università degli Studi della Campania, Italy
Chiara Iacovino	University of Basilicata, Italy
Antonino Iannuzzo	ETH Zurich, Switzerland
Ali Idri	University Mohammed V, Morocco
Oana-Ramona Ilovan	Babeş-Bolyai University, Romania
Mustafa Inceoglu	Ege University, Turkey
Tadashi Ishikawa	KEK, Japan
Federica Isola	University of Cagliari, Italy
Irena Itova	University of Westminster, UK
Edgar David de Izeppi	VTTI, USA
Marija Jankovic	CERTH, Greece
Adrian Jaramillo	Universidad Tecnológica Metropolitana, Chile
Monalisa Jena	Fakir Mohan University, India
Dorota Kamrowska-Załuska	Gdansk University of Technology, Poland
Issaku Kanamori	RIKEN Center for Computational Science, Japan
Korhan Karabulut	Yasar University, Turkey
Yeliz Karaca	University of Massachusetts Medical School, USA
Vicky Katsoni	University of West Attica, Greece
Dimitris Kavroudakis	University of the Aegean, Greece
Shuhei Kimura	Okayama University, Japan
Joanna Kolozej	Cracow University of Technology, Poland
Vladimir Korkhov	St. Petersburg University, Russia
Thales Körting	INPE, Brazil
Tomonori Kouya	Shizuoka Institute of Science and Technology, Japan
Sylwia Krzysztofik	Lodz University of Technology, Poland
Nataliia Kulabukhova	St. Petersburg University, Russia
Shrinivas B. Kulkarni	SDM College of Engineering and Technology, India

Pavan Kumar	University of Calgary, Canada
Anisha Kumari	National Institute of Technology, Rourkela, India
Ludovica La Rocca	University of Naples "Federico II", Italy
Daniele La Rosa	University of Catania, Italy
Sabrina Lai	University of Cagliari, Italy
Giuseppe Francesco Cesare Lama	University of Naples "Federico II", Italy
Mariusz Lamprecht	University of Lodz, Poland
Vincenzo Laporta	National Research Council, Italy
Chien-Sing Lee	Sunway University, Malaysia
José Isaac Lemus Romani	Pontifical Catholic University of Valparaíso, Chile
Federica Leone	University of Cagliari, Italy
Alexander H. Levis	George Mason University, USA
Carola Lingua	Polytechnic University of Turin, Italy
Marco Locurcio	Polytechnic University of Bari, Italy
Andrea Lombardi	University of Perugia, Italy
Savino Longo	University of Bari, Italy
Fernando Lopez Gayarre	University of Oviedo, Spain
Yan Lu	Western Michigan University, USA
Maria Macchiaroli	University of Salerno, Italy
Helmuth Malonek	University of Aveiro, Portugal
Francesca Maltinti	University of Cagliari, Italy
Luca Mancini	University of Perugia, Italy
Marcos Mandado	University of Vigo, Spain
Ernesto Marcheggiani	Università Politecnica delle Marche, Italy
Krassimir Markov	University of Telecommunications and Post, Bulgaria
Giovanni Martinelli	INGV, Italy
Alessandro Marucci	University of L'Aquila, Italy
Fiammetta Marulli	University of Campania Luigi Vanvitelli, Italy
Gabriella Maselli	University of Salerno, Italy
Rytis Maskeliunas	Kaunas University of Technology, Lithuania
Michele Mastroianni	University of Campania Luigi Vanvitelli, Italy
Cristian Mateos	Universidad Nacional del Centro de la Provincia de Buenos Aires, Argentina
Hideo Matsufuru	High Energy Accelerator Research Organization (KEK), Japan
D'Apuzzo Mauro	University of Cassino and Southern Lazio, Italy
Chiara Mazzarella	University Federico II, Italy
Marco Mazzarino	University of Venice, Italy
Giovanni Mei	University of Cagliari, Italy
Mário Melo	Federal Institute of Rio Grande do Norte, Brazil
Francesco Mercaldo	University of Molise, Italy
Alfredo Milani	University of Perugia, Italy
Alessandra Milesi	University of Cagliari, Italy
Antonio Minervino	ISPC, National Research Council, Italy
Fernando Miranda	Universidade do Minho, Portugal

B. Mishra	University of Szeged, Hungary
Sanjay Misra	Covenant University, Nigeria
Mirka Mobilia	University of Salerno, Italy
Giuseppe Modica	Università degli Studi di Reggio Calabria, Italy
Mohammadsadegh Mohagheghi	Vali-e-Asr University of Rafsanjan, Iran
Mohamad Molaei Qelichi	University of Tehran, Iran
Mario Molinara	University of Cassino and Southern Lazio, Italy
Augusto Montisci	Università degli Studi di Cagliari, Italy
Pierluigi Morano	Polytechnic University of Bari, Italy
Ricardo Moura	Universidade Nova de Lisboa, Portugal
Ana Clara Mourao Moura	Federal University of Minas Gerais, Brazil
Maria Mourao	Polytechnic Institute of Viana do Castelo, Portugal
Daichi Mukunoki	RIKEN Center for Computational Science, Japan
Beniamino Murgante	University of Basilicata, Italy
Naohito Nakasato	University of Aizu, Japan
Grazia Napoli	Università degli Studi di Palermo, Italy
Isabel Cristina Natário	Universidade Nova de Lisboa, Portugal
Nadia Nedjah	State University of Rio de Janeiro, Brazil
Antonio Nesticò	University of Salerno, Italy
Andreas Nikiforiadis	Aristotle University of Thessaloniki, Greece
Keigo Nitadori	RIKEN Center for Computational Science, Japan
Silvio Nocera	Iuav University of Venice, Italy
Giuseppina Oliva	University of Salerno, Italy
Arogundade Oluwasefunmi	Academy of Mathematics and System Science, China
Ken-ichi Oohara	University of Tokyo, Japan
Tommaso Orusa	University of Turin, Italy
M. Fernanda P. Costa	University of Minho, Portugal
Roberta Padulano	Centro Euro-Mediterraneo sui Cambiamenti Climatici, Italy
Maria Panagiotopoulou	National Technical University of Athens, Greece
Jay Pancham	Durban University of Technology, South Africa
Gianni Pantaleo	University of Florence, Italy
Dimos Pantazis	University of West Attica, Greece
Michela Paolucci	University of Florence, Italy
Eric Pardede	La Trobe University, Australia
Olivier Parisot	Luxembourg Institute of Science and Technology, Luxembourg
Vincenzo Pellecchia	Ente Idrico Campano, Italy
Anna Pelosi	University of Salerno, Italy
Edit Pengő	University of Szeged, Hungary
Marco Pepe	University of Salerno, Italy
Paola Perchinunno	University of Cagliari, Italy
Ana Pereira	Polytechnic Institute of Bragança, Portugal
Mariano Pernetti	University of Campania, Italy
Damiano Perri	University of Perugia, Italy

Federica Pes	University of Cagliari, Italy
Marco Petrelli	Roma Tre University, Italy
Massimiliano Petri	University of Pisa, Italy
Khiem Phan	Duy Tan University, Vietnam
Alberto Ferruccio Piccinni	Polytechnic of Bari, Italy
Angela Pilogallo	University of Basilicata, Italy
Francesco Pinna	University of Cagliari, Italy
Telmo Pinto	University of Coimbra, Portugal
Luca Piroddi	University of Cagliari, Italy
Darius Plonis	Vilnius Gediminas Technical University, Lithuania
Giuliano Poli	University of Naples "Federico II", Italy
Maria João Polidoro	Polytecnic Institute of Porto, Portugal
Ioannis Politis	Aristotle University of Thessaloniki, Greece
Maurizio Pollino	ENEA, Italy
Antonio Pratelli	University of Pisa, Italy
Salvatore Praticò	Mediterranean University of Reggio Calabria, Italy
Marco Prato	University of Modena and Reggio Emilia, Italy
Carlotta Quagliolo	Polytechnic University of Turin, Italy
Emanuela Quaquero	Univesity of Cagliari, Italy
Garrisi Raffaele	Polizia postale e delle Comunicazioni, Italy
Nicoletta Rassu	University of Cagliari, Italy
Hafiz Tayyab Rauf	University of Bradford, UK
Michela Ravanelli	Sapienza University of Rome, Italy
Roberta Ravanelli	Sapienza University of Rome, Italy
Alfredo Reder	Centro Euro-Mediterraneo sui Cambiamenti Climatici, Italy
Stefania Regalbuto	University of Naples "Federico II", Italy
Rommel Regis	Saint Joseph's University, USA
Lothar Reichel	Kent State University, USA
Marco Reis	University of Coimbra, Portugal
Maria Reitano	University of Naples "Federico II", Italy
Jerzy Respondek	Silesian University of Technology, Poland
Elisa Riccietti	École Normale Supérieure de Lyon, France
Albert Rimola	Universitat Autònoma de Barcelona, Spain
Angela Rizzo	University of Bari, Italy
Ana Maria A. C. Rocha	University of Minho, Portugal
Fabio Rocha	Institute of Technology and Research, Brazil
Humberto Rocha	University of Coimbra, Portugal
Maria Clara Rocha	Polytechnic Institute of Coimbra, Portugal
Miguel Rocha	University of Minho, Portugal
Giuseppe Rodriguez	University of Cagliari, Italy
Guillermo Rodriguez	UNICEN, Argentina
Elisabetta Ronchieri	INFN, Italy
Marzio Rosi	University of Perugia, Italy
Silvia Rossetti	University of Parma, Italy
Marco Rossitti	Polytechnic University of Milan, Italy

Francesco Rotondo	Marche Polytechnic University, Italy
Irene Rubino	Polytechnic University of Turin, Italy
Agustín Salas	Pontifical Catholic University of Valparaíso, Chile
Juan Pablo Sandoval Alcocer	Universidad Católica Boliviana "San Pablo", Bolivia
Luigi Santopietro	University of Basilicata, Italy
Rafael Santos	National Institute for Space Research, Brazil
Valentino Santucci	Università per Stranieri di Perugia, Italy
Mirko Saponaro	Polytechnic University of Bari, Italy
Filippo Sarvia	University of Turin, Italy
Marco Scaioni	Polytechnic University of Milan, Italy
Rafal Scherer	Częstochowa University of Technology, Poland
Francesco Scorza	University of Basilicata, Italy
Ester Scotto di Perta	University of Napoli "Federico II", Italy
Monica Sebillo	University of Salerno, Italy
Patrizia Serra	University of Cagliari, Italy
Ricardo Severino	University of Minho, Portugal
Jie Shen	University of Michigan, USA
Huahao Shou	Zhejiang University of Technology, China
Miltiadis Siavvas	Centre for Research and Technology Hellas, Greece
Brandon Sieu	University of Calgary, Canada
Ângela Silva	Instituto Politécnico de Viana do Castelo, Portugal
Carina Silva	Polytechic Institute of Lisbon, Portugal
Joao Carlos Silva	Polytechnic Institute of Cavado and Ave, Portugal
Fabio Silveira	Federal University of Sao Paulo, Brazil
Marco Simonetti	University of Florence, Italy
Ana Jacinta Soares	University of Minho, Portugal
Maria Joana Soares	University of Minho, Portugal
Michel Soares	Federal University of Sergipe, Brazil
George Somarakis	Foundation for Research and Technology Hellas, Greece
Maria Somma	University of Naples "Federico II", Italy
Alberico Sonnessa	Polytechnic University of Bari, Italy
Elena Stankova	St. Petersburg University, Russia
Flavio Stochino	University of Cagliari, Italy
Anastasia Stratigea	National Technical University of Athens, Greece
Yasuaki Sumida	Kyushu Sangyo University, Japan
Yue Sun	European X-Ray Free-Electron Laser Facility, Germany
Kirill Sviatov	Ulyanovsk State Technical University, Russia
Daisuke Takahashi	University of Tsukuba, Japan
Aladics Tamás	University of Szeged, Hungary
David Taniar	Monash University, Australia
Rodrigo Tapia McClung	Centro de Investigación en Ciencias de Información Geoespacial, Mexico
Eufemia Tarantino	Polytechnic University of Bari, Italy

Sergio Tasso	University of Perugia, Italy
Ana Paula Teixeira	Universidade de Trás-os-Montes e Alto Douro, Portugal
Senhorinha Teixeira	University of Minho, Portugal
Tengku Adil Tengku Izhar	Universiti Teknologi MARA, Malaysia
Maria Filomena Teodoro	University of Lisbon/Portuguese Naval Academy, Portugal
Giovanni Tesoriere	Kore University of Enna, Italy
Yiota Theodora	National Technical Univeristy of Athens, Greece
Graça Tomaz	Polytechnic Institute of Guarda, Portugal
Carmelo Maria Torre	Polytechnic University of Bari, Italy
Francesca Torrieri	University of Naples "Federico II", Italy
Vincenza Torrisi	University of Catania, Italy
Vincenzo Totaro	Polytechnic University of Bari, Italy
Pham Trung	Ho Chi Minh City University of Technology, Vietnam
Dimitrios Tsoukalas	Centre of Research and Technology Hellas (CERTH), Greece
Sanjida Tumpa	University of Calgary, Canada
Iñaki Tuñon	Universidad de Valencia, Spain
Takahiro Ueda	Seikei University, Japan
Piero Ugliengo	University of Turin, Italy
Abdi Usman	Haramaya University, Ethiopia
Ettore Valente	University of Naples "Federico II", Italy
Jordi Vallverdu	Universitat Autònoma de Barcelona, Spain
Cornelis Van Der Mee	University of Cagliari, Italy
José Varela-Aldás	Universidad Tecnológica Indoamérica, Ecuador
Fanny Vazart	University of Grenoble Alpes, France
Franco Vecchiocattivi	University of Perugia, Italy
Laura Verde	University of Campania Luigi Vanvitelli, Italy
Giulia Vergerio	Polytechnic University of Turin, Italy
Jos Vermaseren	Nikhef, The Netherlands
Giacomo Viccione	University of Salerno, Italy
Marco Vizzari	University of Perugia, Italy
Corrado Vizzarri	Polytechnic University of Bari, Italy
Alexander Vodyaho	St. Petersburg State Electrotechnical University "LETI", Russia
Nikolay N. Voit	Ulyanovsk State Technical University, Russia
Marco Vona	University of Basilicata, Italy
Agustinus Borgy Waluyo	Monash University, Australia
Fernando Wanderley	Catholic University of Pernambuco, Brazil
Chao Wang	University of Science and Technology of China, China
Marcin Wozniak	Silesian University of Technology, Poland
Tiang Xian	Nathong University, China
Rekha Yadav	KL University, India
Claudia Yamu	University of Groningen, The Netherlands
Fenghui Yao	Tennessee State University, USA

Fukuko Yuasa	KEK, Japan
Moayid Ali Zaidi	Ostfold University College Norway, Norway
Paola Zamperlin	University of Pisa, Italy
Peter Zeile	Karlsruhe Institute of Technology, Germany
Milliam Maxime Zekeng Ndadji	University of Dschang, Cameroon
Nataly Zhukova	ITMO University, Russia
Ljiljiana Zivkovic	Ministry of Construction, Transport and Infrastructure/Institute of Architecture and Urban and Spatial Planning of Serbia, Serbia

Contents – Part IV

International Workshop on Blockchain and Distributed Ledgers: Technologies and Applications (BDLTA 2021)

Vulnerabilities and Open Issues of Smart Contracts: A Systematic Mapping

Gabriel de Sousa Matsumura[1(✉)], Luciana Brasil Rebelo dos Santos[1(✉)], Arlindo Flavio da Conceição[2(✉)], and Nandamudi Lankalapalli Vijaykumar[2,3(✉)]

[1] Federal Institute of Education, Science and Technology of São Paulo, São Paulo, Brazil
lurebelo@ifsp.edu.br

[2] Federal University of São Paulo, São Paulo, Brazil
{arlindo.conceicao,vijaykumar}@unifesp.br

[3] National Institute for Space Research, São José dos Campos, Brazil

Abstract. Smart Contracts (SCs) are programs stored in a Blockchain to ensure agreements between two or more parties. The combination of factors like the newness of the field, with less than a decade of practical use, and a high and growing popularity in industry, leads to an increase in the possibility of severe security issues occurrence. Even though, systems based on Blockchain and SCs technologies inherit several benefits, like a tamper-proof decentralized ledger and anonymous transactions. This way, even with security issues, the trend is that its popularity will increase. Due the unchangeable essence of Blockchain, failures or errors in SCs become perpetual once published, being critical to mitigate them, since the involvement of huge economic assets are common. To handle this, the academic and industrial communities have been expanding their efforts in this field, with a growth in research publications similar to exponential. Aiming at reasoning about the current state-of-art in vulnerabilities and open issues over Blockchain SCs, we conducted a systematic literature mapping over 32 primary and 18 secondary selected articles. As contribution, this work discusses and relates the selected papers, identifying gaps that may lead to research topics for future work.

Keywords: Blockchain · Smart Contracts · Systematic mapping · Tertiary study · Vulnerabilities · Security

1 Introduction

Software reliability is highly relevant given the dependence that modern society has on software systems. Defects can result in minor annoyances, such as not accessing social networks for a while. They may become serious, leading to severe financial losses. Amid advances in software technology, the idea of digital financial transactions emerges, to facilitate money transactions between people anywhere in the world, without the need for mediators, such as banks or brokers.

O. Gervasi et al. (Eds.): ICCSA 2021, LNCS 12952, pp. 3–18, 2021.
https://doi.org/10.1007/978-3-030-86973-1_1

Blockchain [14] is a technology to make these financial operations viable. It is a distributed ledger that records all transactions of a digital currency, so it is constantly updated. In 2015, the introduction of Smart Contracts (SCs) extended the functionality of Blockchain.

An SC is a program designed to guarantee the execution of a transaction between two or more parties. There are fundamental differences between SC and standard software, and these differences introduce new vulnerabilities and concerns. SCs are immutable computer programs stored in a Blockchain and verified and executed by some of its nodes in a distributed manner [@13][1].

Notice that the code of an SC cannot be modified to correct defects [19], i.e., once implanted, it cannot be updated. Thus, the correctness and security of SCs are necessary, as failures can cause millionaire losses, as already extensively reported in the literature [19].

There is an extensive number of cases where bugs and breaches in SCs led to severe economic losses. In 2016, an attack stole approximately $50 million worth of Ether by exploiting a flaw in the Distributed Autonomous Organization (DAO) source code [5][@13]. In 2017, the multi-signature wallet Parity had embezzlement of about $30 million as a consequence of an attack on Ethereum. In 2018, about $900 million was stolen due to the BEC (BeautyChain) token attack [@13]. Also in 2018, researchers performed a security analysis of nearly a million SCs using the MAIAN tool, resulting in 34,200 SCs flagged as vulnerable [13]. Then, with a random sample of 3,759 contracts obtained from the vulnerable contracts set, they found that 3,686 SCs had an 89% probability of vulnerability [13][@5].

Although recent studies have proposed a huge number of tools and techniques to detect bugs in SCs, the literature shows that the development of SCs needs to be improved in many ways, in order to minimize the problems detected so far. A possible reason for this situation is the lack of a comprehensive mapping of all the existing bugs [7] and how to deal with each of them. The present paper carried out a systematic literature mapping to characterize the techniques, methods, and tools that deal with SCs' vulnerabilities and showing recent advances in this area. Thus, the results can identify eventual gaps and use this information to mitigate problems in future research.

While conducting the study, in the stage of Data Extraction and Synthesis, we have noticed that a relevant number of secondary studies were returned. So, to make a more comprehensive contribution, we have decided to include them as part of the mapping, presenting also a tertiary study. In this way, the answers to the research questions consider both primary and secondary studies.

This paper is organized as follows. Section 2 shows the background to this paper. The secondary studies related to this mapping are commented in Sect. 3. Section 4 describes the research questions and research methods adopted.

[1] In this text, for a question of space and simplicity, we differentiate among *0)* regular references, *1)* primary studies (denoted with #) and *2)* secondary studies (written with @). Regular references are available at the end of the text. In order to have access to the aforementioned primary and secondary studies, the reader must check the list of papers in https://bit.ly/3tNkIG6 [11].

Section 5 presents the results obtained, making considerations and discussions about the outcomes. Section 6 discusses the potential threats to the research validity. Finally, Sect. 7 presents final remarks about the mapping conducted.

2 Background

This section address needed concepts for understanding this work.

2.1 Blockchain

A Blockchain platform is a decentralized ledger. It stores transactions permanently, in a secure and auditable way [3]. Blockchain technology was popularized by Bitcoin in 2008 [12], enabling reliable digital financial transactions without a trusted third party between anonymous entities. Bitcoin merged the qualities of cryptography techniques and peer-to-peer networks. In this network, miners verify transactions as they occur, checking signatures and balances. Then, a distributed consensus algorithm is used to create a block with the validated transactions. The block is broadcasted to the entire network so that all nodes can, after validating its correctness, add the new blocks to their copy of the ledger [1]. The consensus algorithm maintains a trusted network without the need to trust any node in particular [@5].

2.2 Smart Contracts

A Smart Contract (SC) is software that runs on the Blockchain and represents an agreement between non-trusting participants [1]. The most popular Blockchain platform that supports SCs is Ethereum [4,18]. However, the development of complex SCs is not trivial [1]. For example, the Ethereum platform uses a network of Turing complete virtual machines to validate transactions [1]. In Ethereum, the programmer uses a high-level programming language (e.g., Solidity) to write the SCs. The interaction between users and SCs occurs by sending a transaction to the contract address. An SC can call other SCs during its execution and can pass data as parameters, making it possible to execute untrusted code [2]. So there is a need to ensure the correctness of the executable codes, but that is a challenging task [@13].

Before the Blockchain technology arising, although the concept of SCs already existed [16], they were not well developed [@5]. The participation of central authorities or resource managers was a requirement at the time, limiting strongly the usefulness of smart contracts since these third parties are able to handle agreements themselves [@10, @13]. Since there is no need for a trusted third party in the Blockchain, smart contracts can be advantageously employed.

3 Related Literature

In this section, we provide a concise overview of the main secondary studies related to our systematic mapping. Regarding publication sources, Table 1 shows that journals are composed of the following study types: systematic reviews, surveys (37.5% each), and systematic mappings (25%). Regarding the conference publications, there was a multivocal review, a systematic review (11.11% each) and surveys (77.78%). Also, we have an e-print survey publication. So, in journals, systematic approaches are more often, while surveys are more often in conferences. Even though the e-print survey is not yet published in a journal or conference, it is worth mentioning that it was included since it has rich information for our paper.

For the classification of the secondary papers, we not only consider the types defined by the authors, but also the definition of each type. Systematic approaches have a precise methodology, like the one we present in the next section to minimize subjectivity and maximize reproducibility. Systematic mappings and reviews utilize a similar methodology, the main difference is the scope. Mappings are more likely to be high-level, having a broader view about a topic and a review is more likely to be low-level, aiming at a specific perspective of a subject, often comparing two specific topics. The multivocal literature review can also have a systematic methodology, but it includes in its scope gray literature, for instance, technical reports, thesis, dissertations, etc. Finally, a survey does not utilize a precise methodology to select their primary papers. They have the tendency to have more subjectivity, increasing the odds that relevant articles may have been left behind.

Table 1. Related secondary papers types and publication sources

Sources and secondary type	Journal	Conference	E-Print	Total
Multivocal literature review	0	1	0	1
Survey	3	7	1	11
Systematic literature mapping	2	0	0	2
Systematic literature review	3	1	0	4
Total	8	9	1	18

Table 2. Focus areas identified in the related secondary papers

Areas		@Secondary articles	Total (%)
Issues	Vulnerability	1, 3, 4, 6, 7, 11, 14, 15, 17	38.89
	Attacks	1, 7, 12, 13, 15, 17	33.33
	External data	8, 9, 17	16.67
Solutions	Design	4, 6, 9, 17, 18	27.78
	Implementation	2, 4, 5, 6, 7, 8, 12, 17, 18	50.00
	Software testing	3, 5, 13, 14, 16, 17, 18	38.89
	Formal methods	4, 5, 6, 9, 10, 13, 14, 16, 17, 18	55.56
	Machine learning	11, 12, 17, 18	22.22
	Tools	3, 4, 5, 6, 9, 10, 13, 14, 16	50.00
	Monitoring	4, 9, 12, 17, 18	27.78
Blockchain platform		11, 12, 14, 16	22.22

In Table 2, we provide a simple categorization of the related secondary articles concerning the kind of their contributions, being common the availability of some kind of classifications and, sometimes, a taxonomy. In these issues, among papers in vulnerability scope, all of them, except [@17], mention vulnerabilities related to programming languages. Also all, but [@15] and [@17], mention vulnerabilities related to Blockchain platform and virtual machine. Considering the papers on vulnerability, we can highlight that [@15] provides a great systematization of Ethereum vulnerabilities based on the Common Weakness Enumeration that may probably be extended to other platforms. About the external data scope, all of them mention oracles, and [@17] mentions verifiable third-party and cryptography technology as possible solutions for off-chain interactions.

For solutions concerning design, we selected papers that handle modeling or specifications. For the case of implementation, solutions like design patterns [@2, @4, @8, @17], templates [@4, @17], standards [@5], more secure domain-specific languages [@5, @9, @17] and code generation [@12] are mentioned. In relation to software testing, all of the selected papers mention fuzzing test, being that [@16] also mentions test case generation. Considering the papers that mention machine learning we highlight [@12], that, unlike others, focuses on Blockchain and machine learning and, therefore, handles them more deeply, with less emphasis on SCs. With respect to monitoring SCs after deployment, papers mention runtime monitoring [@4], bug bounty [@4, @9, @17], and monitoring strategies [@18], being also worthy to mention that monitoring is often related to the update of SCs [@12, @17].

4 Research Method

The research method adopted in this Systematic Literature Mapping (SLM) is defined based on the guidelines [9], involving three main phases: (i) Planning: referring to the pre-review activities, aiming to define the research questions, inclusion and exclusion criteria, study sources, research string, and mapping procedures to establish a protocol review; (ii) Realization: search and selection of studies, aiming at extracting and synthesizing their data; (iii) Report: final phase whose objective is to write the results and disseminate them to potentially interested parties, using the results to answer the research questions.

The research questions are listed in next section. The study selection is explained in Sect. 4.2, and data extraction is presented in Sect. 4.3.

4.1 Research Questions

This mapping presents an overview of the current state of research on the problems/issues directly involved with SCs in the Blockchain context. Table 3 shows the Research Questions (RQ) and the rationales considering them in this SLM.

Table 3. Research questions and their rationales

N°	Research question	Rationale
RQ1	When and where have the studies on vulnerabilities and open issues on SCs been published?	This question is to understand whether there are specific Publication sources for these studies, and when they have been published
RQ2	What are the problems/issues with respect to SCs?	This question identifies what are the problems/issues directly related to the use of SCs in the Blockchain context
RQ3	How are the problems/issues categorized or classified?	This question investigates how the problems/issues related to the use and development of SCs have been categorized/classified, checking if there is a proper taxonomy
RQ4	What are the proposed solutions to the problems/issues identified within the context of SCs?	The aim is to determine what are the proposed solutions to the problems/issues identified in RQ2
RQ5	Are there methods and tools available for the identified solutions?	This question verifies, among the methods and tools identified in RQ4, what are the limits of using each one in terms of practical purposes

4.2 Study Selection

Source and Search String. The search was performed in the Scopus[2] repository. We chose this database because, in the initial searches, Scopus returned a larger set of results compared to others. It was also noted that many papers found on other platforms were also returned in Scopus, considering the same search string. Finally, we defined the following search string for this mapping:

TITLE-ABS-KEY("smart contract" w/12 (problem OR issue))

The main focus of the search was to identify papers that addressed problems/issues about smart contracts used in the Blockchain context. During the test of search strings, it was clear that the results of the string *("smart contract" AND (problem OR issue))* contemplated the papers being looked for. With the goal of narrow the resulting papers to our scope, we used the proximity operator available in Scopus, expressed by w/x, where x is the maximum number acceptable of words between two terms, regardless of the order of the terms. Using $x{=}12$ it was possible find previously defined control papers.

Inclusion and Exclusion Criteria. The selection criteria are organized into two inclusion criteria (IC) and eight exclusion criteria (EC). The inclusion criteria are: (IC1) Study must include the use of smart contracts in Blockchain

[2] http://www.scopus.com.

context; and (IC2) Study must include problems or solutions related to the use of smart contracts. The exclusion criteria are: (EC1) Study has no abstract; (EC2) Study is just an abstract or extended abstract without full text; (EC3) Study is not a primary study, such as editorials, summaries of keynotes, and tutorials; (EC4) Study is not written in English; (EC5) Study is a copy or an older version of another publication already considered; (EC6) No access to the full paper; (EC7) Study with a publication date prior to 2015; and (EC8) Study should contain problems related to smart contracts itself, problems about smart contract applications aren't enough.

Data Storage. We used a spreadsheet to gather all the relevant data from the returned studies in the searching phase (e.g., id, title and bibliographic reference), cataloging and storing each publication appropriately.

Assessment. Before conducting the mapping, we checked our protocol. We defined a pre-selected set of papers, which should be present in the returned set of studies. Regarding the review process, stage 1 was conducted by one of the authors, and the papers not excluded were validated by the other authors. Stage 2 was conducted by all authors, and we equally divided the remaining papers. Throughout the review process, in cases of doubt, the papers were not excluded, and, in a meeting, the authors reached a consensus on whether or not to include the studies.

4.3 Data Extraction and Synthesis

The search resulted in 341 publications from Scopus. We followed a selection process with 2 main stages in this SLM (Fig. 1).

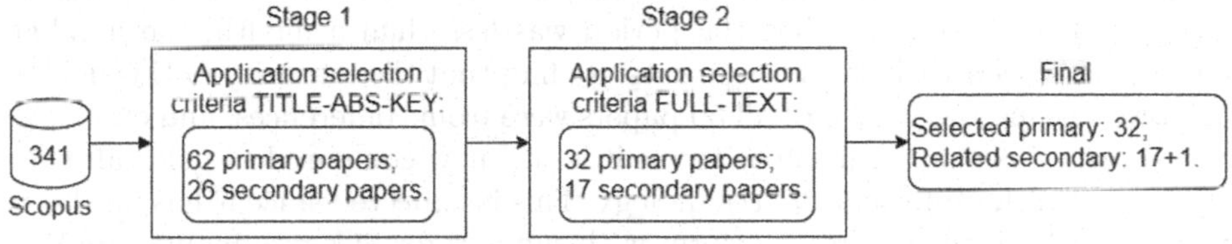

Fig. 1. Search and selection SLM process

In stage 1, we applied the selection criteria (inclusion and exclusion criteria) over title, abstract and keywords, resulting in 62 papers (reduction of approximately 82%). 1 paper was eliminated by EC1 (Study has no abstract); 10 by EC2 (Study without full text); 34 by EC3 (Study is not a primary study); 8 by EC4 (Study is not written in English) 3 by EC5 (Study is a copy or an older version of another study already considered); 2 by EC7 (Study with publication date prior to 2015); and 221 by EC8 (Study should contain problems related to smart contracts itself, problems about smart contract applications aren't enough). In stage 2, we applied the selection criteria considering the full text, resulting in 32 studies (a reduction of approximately 48%). 1 paper was eliminated by EC2, EC3 and EC5; and 26 by EC8. From the first stage on, secondary works were also selected among the EC3 excluded papers. We separated those that didn't fit other exclusion criteria, obtaining 17 papers at the end of the 2nd stage. One more was included outside the search results because it was indicated by an expert due to its relevance, totaling 18 papers. The related work supported the determination of answers to our research questions through taxonomies, classifications and other contributions.

5 Results and Discussions

The SLM study was carried out according to Sect. 4. Here we show the results for each of the research questions and discuss them. To answer the questions, an id was determined for each of the articles, as in [11].

To assist in the analysis and systematize the extracted data, categories for classifying the studies were defined, one for each research question. We considered the characteristics of the selected studies, both reusing categories already considered in the literature and defining new categories when necessary. It is possible that the same paper fits multiple categories. In cases of doubts about whether an article belongs to a certain category, we simply didn't include it.

5.1 Question 1: When and Where Have the Studies Been Published?

Over the years, publications on smart contracts for Blockchain, had a growth similar to quadratic for both the primary and secondary papers, as presented in Fig. 2. We conducted our search in January 2021. So, we have only two papers this year, but considering that the period was less than a month, the number was not bad. Even with this growth rate, we find that the maturity of this field is still low. The majority, 72% of all 50 papers were from conferences, and only 26% from journals, is that in absolute terms it is still new compared to fields already established in the Information Technology. This is expected since it has not been even a decade since the first platform with support for SCs was inaugurated.

We count the frequency of the countries from where the papers were written. They are shown in Fig. 3. Countries that appeared only once (3.67% each) were Italy, Malta, Saudi Arabia, Hong Kong, Thailand, Qatar and Morocco; twice (6.67% each) were Austria, Switzerland, United Kingdom, France, Japan and Russia; three times (10%) was Germany; four times (13.33% each) were Singapore and Australia; seven times (23.33%) was the USA; and eleven times (36.67%) was China.

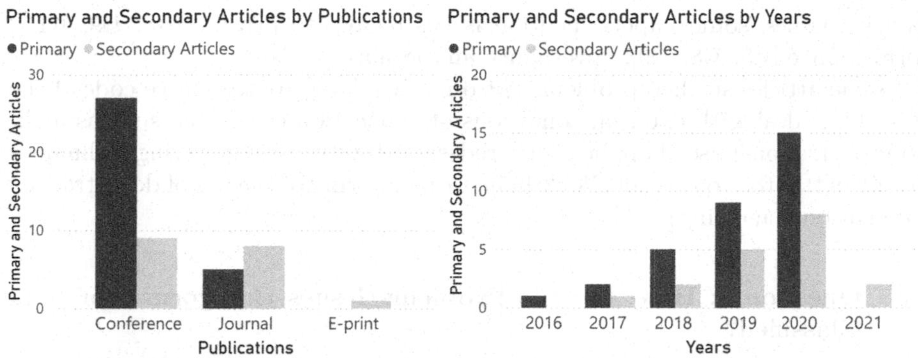

Fig. 2. Frequency of year and source of publications of primary and secondary papers

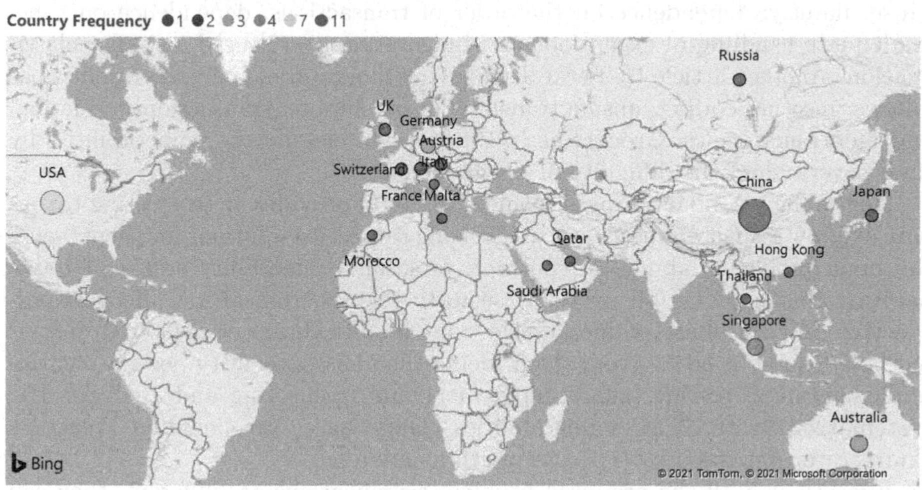

Fig. 3. Countries of institutions where the authors of the primary papers are affiliated

5.2 Question 2: What Are the Problems/Issues with Respect to Smart Contracts?

Most of the problems/issues pointed out in the literature were the exploitation of specific vulnerabilities in Ethereum. Solidity, the most used language in Ethereum, has several known problems[3].

In general, the articles seek to automatically find vulnerabilities by analyzing the source code, identifying the use of critical instructions (e.g., transfer funds), and analyzing the possibility of the code reaching these critical instructions.

The most common critical instructions mentioned were reentrancy, integer overflow, withdrawn and unprotected SELFDESTRUCT instruction. Besides

[3] The address https://swcregistry.io/ has an updated list of known vulnerabilities.

security issues, some papers mention issues related to privacy [@8, @9, @11], performance [@5, @8, @9], governance and legality [@11].

Some articles studied problems not directly related to the source code of the SCs. They deal with external conditions of application execution, such as malicious or irrational use of applications, redesign of software engineering techniques to suit better the context of Blockchain, or monitoring of the use of decentralized applications (auditing).

5.3 Question 3: How Are the Problems/Issues Categorized or Classified?

There was no common proposal to classify problems. Among primary papers, Luu*et al.* [#1], for example, organized vulnerabilities based on their origin or cause, namely: dependence on the order of transactions, dependence on time, inadequate handling of exceptions and indentation. [#15] used a similar classification. Another article by Petar Tsankov [#4] organized the vulnerabilities as follows: insecure coding, unsafe transfers, unsafe inputs, transaction reordering, and reentrancy issues. Groce*et al.* [#19] prefer to classify the vulnerabilities by their severity and the difficulty of being exploited.

Regarding secondary papers, Wang*et al.* [@17] provides an interesting taxonomy over SC security issues, also categorizing respective solutions for them, being the main problems: abnormal contract, program vulnerability and exploitable habitat. Huang*et al.* [@4] overview security themes from an SC lifecycle perspective. In each phase, vulnerabilities may be introduced or exploited, just as methods can be used to avoid them, being the phases: security design, security implementation, testing before deployment and monitoring and analysis. The systematization of 10 SC vulnerabilities classes based on Common Weakness Enumerator, provided by [@15], is worth mentioning.

Even though all the proposed problem classifications are different, they can be the basis to design a more complete taxonomy for the critical issues in SC. Also, there are examples where that issue and solution classifications fit well together [@17]. It might be worth considering combining them.

5.4 Question 4: What Are the Proposed Solutions to the Problems/Issues Identified Within the Context of Smart Contracts?

The material extracted for this question was organized considering related work that had categories or taxonomies for solutions [17] [@4, @13, @17]. Based on the resulting papers, we defined the categories as in Table 4, showing their distribution.

Table 4. Distribution over the proposed solutions to the problems/issues identified

Methods		#Primary articles	Total (%)
Design	Modeling	1, 2, 3, 4, 5, 7, 8, 10, 12, 14, 15,16, 20, 24, 25, 28, 29, 31, 32	59.38
	Specification	4, 7, 14, 15, 16, 18, 24, 25	25.00
Implementation	Design pattern	6, 8, 11, 17	12.50
Verification	Theorem proving	1, 5, 10, 18, 26, 27, 30	21.88
	Model checking	7, 15, 31	9.38
	Abstract interpretation	2, 24	6.25
	Symbolic execution	1, 5, 10, 13, 14, 16, 18, 19, 26, 30	31.25
	Runtime verification	8	3.13
	Software testing	6, 16, 19, 21, 32	15.62
	Machine learning	9, 16, 22, 23	12.50
	Manual auditing	19	3.13

Regarding the proposed solutions, we only included papers that were certain of their classifications. The dominant category was Design Modeling with 19 papers, among them: Event-B, a set-based method [#31]; State-Transition Systems like Colored Petri nets [#28], Markov decision processes [#16], Kripke structure [#15], Dynamic Automata with Events [#8] and state machines [#7]; Abstract Syntax Tree-Level Analysis [#12, #25, #29]; Control Flow Graph [#1, #2, #4, #5, #10, #12, #14, #16, #20, #24, #32]; and Agent-based model [#3], borrowed from Game Theory. Yet in Design realm, Specification has 8 papers, among them: logic like Computation Tree Logic [#7] and Linear Temporal Logic [#15]; Horn Clauses [#24]; Hoare-Style Properties [#25]; and Program Path-Level Patterns like execution traces [#14, #16, #18] and datalog [#4].

In the Verification aspect, the most often approach is Symbolic Execution with 10 articles [#1; #5, #10, #13, #14, #16, #18, #19, #26, #30] followed by: Theorem Proving like Z3 [#1, #5, #10, #18], Isabelle/HOL [#27] and Yices2 [#30], with 7 articles in total; Software Testing, with approaches like unit testing [#19], fuzzing [#16, #19], mutation testing [#21] and Test Case Generation [#32], with 5 papers; Machine Learning, among the approaches there are Random Forest [#9], Imitation Learning [#16], degree-free graph convolutional neural network [#22], temporal message propagation network [#22] and bidirectional long-short term memory with attention mechanism [#23], totaling 4 papers; Model Checking, leveraging tools like NuSMV [#7, #15] and ProB [#31], with 3 papers in total; Abstract Interpretation with 2 papers [#2, #24]; Runtime Verification [#8] and Manual Auditing [#19], each of them with 1 paper.

Note that it is common for Symbolic Execution approaches to leverage a satisfiability modulo theories solver, from the Theorem Prover category. Another consideration is that not only proposals for approaches were included in Table 4. We also include leveraged methods and tools used with experimental proposals. Hence, the Verification category contains 23 (71.875%) papers, Design has 20

(62.5%) and Implementation 4 (12.5%) papers [#6, #8, #11, #17], all belonging to its only subcategory, the Design Pattern.

5.5 Question 5: Are There Methods and Tools Available for the Identified Solutions?

The material extracted for this question was schematized considering that the tool(s)/method(s): (i) are proposed; (ii) have implementation available (studies that no mention how to access or obtain the implementation, even if it exists, wasn't included); (iii) even if not proposed in the paper, are evaluated in experiments (reproducible cases will be mentioned); (iv) aren't proposed, but have relevant contributions; and (v) the possibility of conflict of interest is considerable (studies with less than half of the authors being part of a for-profit organization wasn't included). Table 5 shows the distribution over this scheme.

Table 5. Distribution over methods and tools available for the identified solutions

ID	#Primary articles	Total (%)
(i)	1, 2, 3, 4, 5, 7, 8, 9, 10, 11, 12, 13, 14, 15, 16, 17, 20, 21, 22, 23, 24, 25, 26, 27, 28, 30, 31, 32	87.50
(ii)	1, 4, 5, 12, 16, 23, 24, 26, 30	28.13
(iii)	1, 2, 5, 8, 9, 10, 12, 13, 14, 16, 17, 18, 19, 21, 22, 23, 24, 28, 30, 32	62.50
(iv)	6, 18, 19, 29	12.50
(v)	7, 9, 12, 19, 29	15.63

As category (i) has a dominant frequency, with 29 papers (87.50%), the category (iv) has the lowest representativeness, with only four papers (12.50%). Even though the proposal for solutions is a category with a larger number, there are considerably fewer papers with available implementations, with only nine articles (28.13%) in that category. About category (iii), it's worth mentioning papers that facilitate the reproduction of experiments/analyses [#1, #5, #12, #16, #18, #23, #24, #28]. We emphasize that we consider only those papers that have made available/indicated a dataset and tools/methods used to allow public access, being potentially reproducible.

Regarding the contributions presented in (iv) we highlight: the importance of Software Engineering in the area of Blockchain and SCs, being mentioned testing, design patterns and best development practices [#6]. Regarding software testing, an important limitation pointed out in SC are the few options for execution environments for testing. In the case of the Ethereum platform there are only the main (the real), test (for developers) and simulation (local) networks [#6]; In [#18], we mention as the main contributions the security analysis framework to classify security issues in on-chain wallet contracts and the reproducible experiments; and, in [#19], a very interesting flaws categorization, involving 22 categories, is used to outline 246 flaws found in audits. In addition, each of the flaws found is classified according to its severity (potential impact) and difficulty of exploitation. After an in-depth examination of empirical evidence, the authors came to interesting conclusions, such as: unit tests are ineffective in identifying failures, as the correlation between the number of pre-existing unit tests and the audit results was weak; there's a trade-off between cost/degree of automation and flaws detection with the exploitation of high severity and low difficulty; and many failures can be solved by adopting the ERC20 standard.

In relation to category (v), it is clear that identifying cases of conflict of interest having as criterion that at least half of the authors of an article are part of a for-profit organization is not really a good decisive criterion. Identifying cases like these is not a simple task, after all, conflicting interests are not necessarily financial, even though the existence of a conflict of interest in some cases may be evident. On the other hand, how much this affects the content is generally not clear. Then, category (v) indicates only the possibility of conflict of interest and might be worth remembering this detail during reading.

5.6 Discussion

Summarizing what was seen in the studies addressed, we can understand that the observed vulnerabilities have as common cause the difficulty of detecting incompatibilities between the intended and the real behavior. This is largely due to the platform's immaturity, which still has high-level resources with complicated and unexpected low-level behaviors for conventional developers. But the technology is considerably new, and it is expected to mature.

Beyond this scenario, in which there is an increase in attacks exploiting vulnerabilities in SCs, and the existence of already published vulnerable contracts is known, Almakhour *et al.* [@13] mention three reasons to apply formal specification and verification to SCs before their deployment: once an SC is published, any vulnerabilities in its code will become permanent; programmers' lack of knowledge about proper programming semantics to reflect high-level workflow may lead to misconception issues, resulting in "unfair contracts"; and, many programming paradigms used to develop SCs were not designed to be used in the context of the Blockchain environment [8] [@13]. Besides, Liu and Liu [@5] recommended carrying out more research to design more complete formal verification tools, combining formal verification methods with vulnerability analysis methods that complement each other. Observing the results presented in Table 4, Modeling and Specification have been extensively studied. The solutions least explored in the research, that were related to Formal Verification are: Runtime Verification (3.13%), Abstract Interpretation (6.25%), and Model Checking (9.38%). It's an indicative that little was exploited of such techniques to deal with vulnerabilities in SCs, which points us to a direction to be investigated.

A limitation often mentioned in relation to some methods, e.g. symbolic execution and model checking, is path/state explosion [@13, @18], a situation predominantly caused by unbounded iterations. It's important to remember that, in practice, there are no unbounded iterations because there is a well-defined limit: the gas. Therefore, an adequate modeling of the gas usage by SCs is a promising way to mitigate this limitation of the methods. In this case, simple heuristics can be applied to define values for variables such as the balance of SCs and the cost per instruction.

Regarding to software testing approaches, a considerable part of them have a dynamic nature, requiring the execution of system under test. We known that there is no suitable environment for dynamic analysis. Those that are available range from simulated or real network environments, but each of them with own drawbacks. The resulting papers that mention software testing often wasn't clear if the context was static or dynamic, so we suggest that future work in this topic should address these details.

With respect to reasoning on security vulnerabilities, attacks often are based on exploitation of more than one vulnerability. In this sense there is a certain similarity between the attacks and the propagation [@15]. In addition, it is highly likely that new vulnerabilities will be discovered only after they have already been exploited, and only after that, low-level properties may be defined to mitigation. So, one may consider anticipating new attacks to handle them. One possibility may be to consider the issue of finding new attacks as an optimization problem where the search space are the infinite combinations of vulnerabilities, applying some metrics, like gas cost.

6 Threats to Validity

We clarify some of the possible limitations of this mapping. During the process of selecting studies and extracting data, there was the matter of subjectivity. One of the solutions to avoid subjectivity was that all the authors participated in defining the search string. When the papers were selected to be fully read, the authors conducted a check by reading full papers of the other three authors.

The use of only one electronic database causes a limitation in the set of relevant papers that can be obtained as a result. However, as mentioned previously, Scopus has been selected as it also contains most of the publications from other databases. One other limitation is the lack of snowballing (forward and backward) [6] which could have brought some more relevant publications to complement and to bring a more qualified analysis. Looking directly at the publications of some research groups also is a valid search to enhance our process. These two aspects might have limited the input of more papers. Also, regarding the tertiary analysis provided, a limitation is the fact that we did not use specific strings to find secondary papers, so some relevant articles may have been left out. However, this is the initial study being performed and definitely these aspects will be considered in the continuity of this mapping.

7 Conclusions

A mapping study gives an idea, in the early phases, of shortcomings in existing evidence, which becomes a basis for future investigations [10]. This paper presented a systematic mapping on vulnerabilities and open issues of Smart Contracts in the Blockchain context. We have analyzed 32 primary references and 18 secondary articles. The findings from this study are expected to contribute to the existing knowledge about the vulnerabilities of SCs. In summary, we concluded that: (i) critical instructions that lead to problems directly related to the correct writing of contracts are: reentrancy, integer overflow, withdrawn and unprotected SELFDESTRUCT instruction; (ii) It was not possible to identify a standard proposal for classification of problems, both in primary and secondary works. Even though the classification is different, it is possible to use them as a basis to design a complete taxonomy regarding the critical issues in SCs; (iii) the papers showed that the proposed solutions to the identified problems are: Design, Implementation, and Verification, the most used methods, Modeling (present in 59.38% of the papers), which belongs to the Design category and Symbolic Execution (present in 31.25% of the papers), which belongs to Verification. Also, some studies point to the need for more research to design formal verification tools, combining formal verification methods with vulnerability analysis.

Thus, as future work, we intend to update this SLM to include more electronic databases and include more stages in the selection process, such as snowballing and research groups. Furthermore, extending the scope of the mapping to more categories related to SCs security problems/issues, as in the categorizations proposed by works like [@16, @17] and traditional software vulnerability analysis [7,15] is a promising path. As future work, we can also suggest: research in the perspective of machine learning on the application of automatic vulnerability detection for SCs, since it is a promising vulnerability detection technique even for traditional software [7,15], does not rely heavily on rules defined by human experts and has obtained competitive results; research proposing solutions involving dynamic analysis or software testing, seeking to deal with the limitations of the execution environment.

Conflicts of Interest. The authors declare that they have no conflicts of interest.

References

1. Alharby, M., Aldweesh, A., van Moorsel, A.: Blockchain-based smart contracts: a systematic mapping study of academic research (2018). In: 2018 International Conference on Cloud Computing, Big Data and Blockchain (ICCBB), pp. 1–6. IEEE (2018)
2. Alt, L., Reitwiessner, C.: SMT-based verification of solidity smart contracts. In: Margaria, T., Steffen, B. (eds.) ISoLA 2018. LNCS, vol. 11247, pp. 376–388. Springer, Cham (2018). https://doi.org/10.1007/978-3-030-03427-6_28
3. Argañaraz, M., Berón, M., Pereira, M.J., Henriques, P.: Detection of vulnerabilities in smart contracts specifications in ethereum platforms. In: 9th Symposium on Languages, Applications and Technologies (SLATE 2020), vol. 83, pp. 1–16. Schloss Dagstuhl-Leibniz-Zentrum fuer Informatik (2020)
4. Buterin, V., et al.: Ethereum: a next-generation smart contract and decentralized application platform. https://github.com/ethereum/wiki/wiki/%5BEnglish%5D-White-Paper7 (2014)

5. Gelvez, M.: Explaining the DAO exploit for beginners in solidity (2016)
6. Jalali, S., Wohlin, C.: Systematic literature studies: database searches vs. backward snowballing. In: Proceedings of the 2012 ACM-IEEE International Symposium on Empirical Software Engineering and Measurement, pp. 29–38. IEEE (2012)
7. Ji, T., Wu, Y., Wang, C., Zhang, X., Wang, Z.: The coming era of alphahacking? A survey of automatic software vulnerability detection, exploitation and patching techniques. In: 2018 IEEE third international conference on data science in cyberspace (DSC), pp. 53–60. IEEE (2018)
8. Kalra, S., Goel, S., Dhawan, M., Sharma, S.: Zeus: analyzing safety of smart contracts. In: Ndss, pp. 1–12 (2018)
9. Keele, S., et al.: Guidelines for performing systematic literature reviews in software engineering. Tech. rep, Citeseer (2007)
10. Kitchenham, B.A., Budgen, D., Brereton, O.P.: Using mapping studies as the basis for further research-a participant-observer case study. Inf. Softw. Technol. **53**(6), 638–651 (2011)
11. Matsumura, G.d.S., dos Santos, L.B.R., da Conceição, A.F., Vijaykumar, N.L.: Resulting articles: selected primary and related secondary papers. https://bit.ly/3tNkIG6 (2021)
12. Nakamoto, S.: Bitcoin: a peer-to-peer electronic cash system. Tech. rep, Manubot (2019)
13. Nikolić, I., Kolluri, A., Sergey, I., Saxena, P., Hobor, A.: Finding the greedy, prodigal, and suicidal contracts at scale. In: Proceedings of the 34th Annual Computer Security Applications Conference, pp. 653–663 (2018)
14. Schueffel, P., Groeneweg, N., Baldegger, R.: The crypto encyclopedia. Growth publisher, Tech. rep. (2019)
15. Shen, Z., Chen, S.: A survey of automatic software vulnerability detection, program repair, and defect prediction techniques. Security and Communication Networks v2020 (2020)
16. Szabo, N.: Formalizing and securing relationships on public networks. First monday (1997)
17. Tolmach, P., Li, Y., Lin, S.W., Liu, Y., Li, Z.: A survey of smart contract formal specification and verification. arXiv preprint arXiv:2008.02712 (2020)
18. Wood, G., et al.: Ethereum: a secure decentralised generalised transaction ledger. Ethereum Project Yellow Pap. **151**(2014), 1–32 (2014)
19. Zhang, P., Xiao, F., Luo, X.: A framework and dataset for bugs in ethereum smart contracts. In: 2020 IEEE International Conference on Software Maintenance and Evolution (ICSME), pp. 139–150. IEEE (2020)

Comparison of Deterministic, Stochastic, and Mixed Approaches to Cryptocurrency Dynamics Analysis

Victor Dostov[1,2(✉)], Pavel Pimenov[1,2], and Pavel Shoust[1,2]

[1] Federal State Budgetary Educational Institution of Higher Education, Saint-Petersburg State University, 7-9 Universitetskaya Emb., St Petersburg 199034, Russia
dostov@npaed.ru

[2] Russian Electronic Money and Remittance Association, 5/2 Orlikov per, Moscow 107078, Russia

Abstract. Two approaches are most frequently used to predict the development of cryptocurrency market: deterministic and stochastic. The deterministic approach seeks to explain the development of cryptocurrencies through the relationship of several indicators. A stochastic approach (such as ARIMA) seeks to optimize the parameters of a statistical model. This article aims to compare approaches to the assessing cryptocurrencies development using the number of active Bitcoin and Ethereum wallets. For this purpose, a deterministic model based on the Verhulst equation, and a stochastic model based on ARIMA was formulated. The results show that the usage of relative differences wins over absolute ones. At the same time, the predictive value of a purely deterministic model on short segments is not very high, but it has the advantage in analytical form. Further will focus on the combination of a deterministic Bass-type model and statistical methods with stochastic analysis tools.

Keywords: Cryptocurrency dynamics analysis · ARIMA · Deterministic approach · Stochastic approach · Bitcoin · Ethereum

1 Introduction

Over the past five years, cryptocurrencies have become an integral part of the exchange trading, banking, and financial markets. Central banks in many countries are conducting experiments to create national cryptocurrencies-CBDC. Ripple digital currency has become an important factor in the development of the interbank payments market. In such conditions, the analysis of the dynamics of cryptocurrencies development takes on high practical and theoretical significance.

In modern studies of the dynamics of cryptocurrencies, two approaches dominate: deterministic (averaging and inferring the determinant component) [4, 6] and stochastic (using modern regression methods – for example, ARIMA) [15, 18]. Each of these approaches has both undeniable advantages and significant disadvantages. This article

O. Gervasi et al. (Eds.): ICCSA 2021, LNCS 12952, pp. 19–30, 2021.
https://doi.org/10.1007/978-3-030-86973-1_2

aims to conduct a comparative analysis of the application of both approaches to identify these advantages and disadvantages, the level of their reliability and effectiveness in describing the processes in the cryptocurrency market, as well as to consider the possibility and prospects of combined analysis using both stochastic and deterministic models.

The paper will be divided into four parts. In the first section, we look at the main aspects of the concept of "payment system", its classification into C2B and P2P, and the place of cryptocurrencies in this classification. In the second part, we consider the main idea of the deterministic approach, give successful examples of its implementation, and offer our own research on this issue. In the third part, we consider the stochastic approach and examples of its application. We present the authors' approach to predicting the dynamics of the number of wallets in major cryptocurrencies systems using ARIMA methods. Finally, we compare the results of the analysis and draw some conclusions about the choice between approaches, as well as the prospects for applying a mixed strategy.

2 Methodology

For this study, we selected two of the most famous cryptocurrencies – Bitcoin (hereinafter referred to as BTC) and Ethereum (hereinafter referred to as ETH). These cryptocurrencies are perfectly suitable for research purposes, because of a long history of development and a large number of active addresses.

In addition, we believe that these cryptocurrencies can be considered as a "payment system". For the purposes of the article, we will define the payment system as a set of tools, banking procedures and interbank money transfer systems that provide money circulation [8].

Considering Bitcoin and Ethereum as payment systems allows us to apply deterministic approaches to evaluate classical payment systems. This will be demonstrated in the next part of the article. It should be noted that these approaches may differ significantly depending on the payment system in the payment system. There are two models-P2P (payment from person to person) [16] and C2B (client for business) [8]. In C2B payments, a limited number of clients make payments to a company with an infinite capacity [13]. P2P payments are made between individuals within a closed community.

P2P transactions dominate in cryptocurrency schemes, therefore, when considering the degree of accuracy of the analysis, we suggest relying on studies focused on the analysis of P2P payment systems.

3 Deterministic Approach

The generally accepted approach to describing the diffusion of innovations relies on the assumption that it is possible to empirically describe the behavior of complex systems with a small number of parameters [18]. The essence of the approach is the construction of various analytical models, which include the assumption about the mechanisms that determine the behaviour of the system. The models are constructed either by using computer modelling, in which mechanisms determine the rules of model dynamics or by using differential, less often integral, equations of model dynamics, in which these mechanisms are represented as a mathematical relationship between the states of the system in the present or past.

Often, studies that use a deterministic approach set an ambitious goal of predicting the dynamics of cryptocurrency prices for the needs of technical analysis. For example, Stephen Dipple, Abhishek Choudhary, James Flamino, Boleslaw K. Szymanski & G. Korniss [4] use standard geometric Brownian motion to model cryptocurrency rates. For social media activity and cryptocurrency trading volume, the authors use the Ornstein-Uhlenbeck geometric process. The researchers propose their own model of the correlation between different stochastic variables, which occur through the noise in the corresponding stochastic differential equation.

In our previous works, we have studied the application of a deterministic approach to the study of the behaviour of payment systems [6]. We did not try to create an algorithm for predicting the price, as the high influence of the randomness factor and hype will limit the practical significance of such a model. On the other hand, predicting the number of clients is of more practical value. We assumed that there are payment systems with binary behaviour, where the client's decision to use the system is significantly affected by the presence of other customers in this system.

To predict the dynamics of cryptocurrencies, we used the modified Bass [18] and Verhulst [14] equations. We adapted Bass' idea of interpreting the appearance of a quadratic multiplier because of the simulation effect. In P2P payment systems, you cannot make a transfer if your recipient is not included to the system.

In our calculations, we assumed that when forecasting the P2P market, the relationship between the following parameters should be considered:

- current number of users x.
- the maximum number of users, for example, the entire audience of a given country N. Therefore, the number of potential users not currently participating in the system is N-x.
- audience capture rate, which reflects the probability that a given user will start using the service: a > 0 (the reverse time of the decision) within a given period.
- number of new customers (registrations) R per unit of time.
- fatigue coefficient from system b.
- In addition, we considered the fatigue effect, which means the user can stop using the system at any time, which is not in the original Bass model.

As a result, to predict the P2P market, we proposed the Eq. (1):

$$\frac{dx}{dt} = a(N - x)x - bx \tag{1}$$

The model was used to predict the dynamics of changes in the number of active wallets (addresses) of the most popular cryptocurrencies – Bitcoin [1] and Ethereum [1].

The results of the study are shown in Fig. 1.

The usage of a deterministic approach has shown that due to the complex nature of cryptocurrencies (they are both a means of payment and an investment tool) [10], qualitative and quantitative analysis become more complex. To compensate the investment

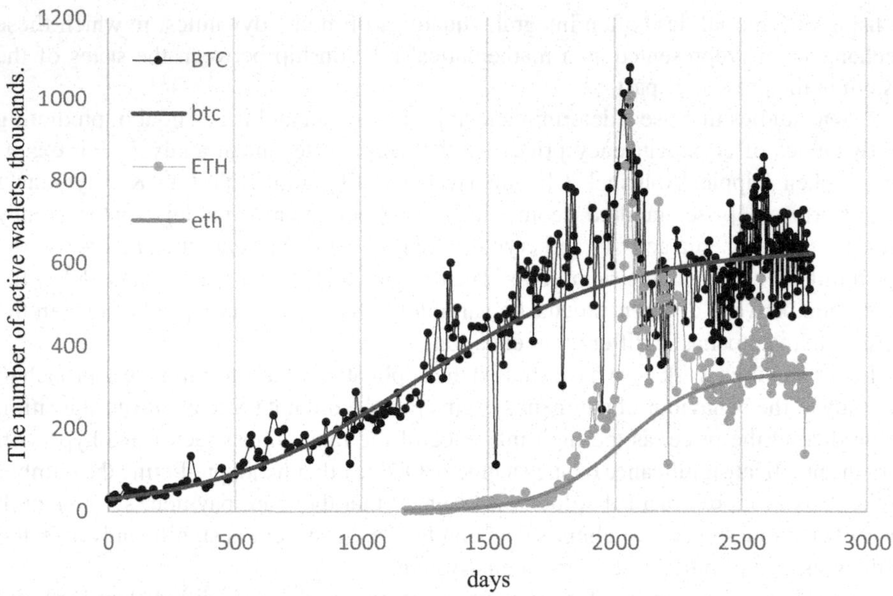

Fig. 1. Statistics of active wallets (addresses) Bitcoin and Ethereum 20.05.2012–27.12.2019

behavior of cryptocurrencies and get the correct overall trend, we used the interpolation method. For the purpose of simplifying the problem, we applied the method of the smallest SPO to the initial sample, summed by years. To do this, we obtained an interpolation with an average deviation of 5% (Fig. 2), introduced mainly by one period of speculative cryptocurrencies of 2017–2018 [17]. We excluded these anomalous points from the STR calculation by further refining the coefficients. Then we superimposed the resulting function on the full source data, as shown in Fig. 2. For this combination, the SPO is about 20%, which is quite expected in case of the initial noise level of the curve.

Similar calculations were carried out for Ethereum (ETH), for which the STR is 27%, also due to one anomalous value (Fig. 2).

Figure 1 and Fig. 2 demonstrate that our equation describes the behavior of both cryptocurrencies well. The exception is the period of 2017–2018, when the growth in the number of wallets was determined not by real transactions, but by speculative behavior. However, we believe that the deterministic approach, if applied to payment systems based on cryptocurrencies, is limited. This is because of two aspects that affect on the behavior of cryptocurrencies. First, the payment functionality, according to our assumption, is quite deterministic. Secondly, the investment component provides high volatility of the cryptocurrency exchange rate in competition with fiat currencies. This leads to a higher noise level of data in comparison with classical payment systems.

As shown in [6], equation coefficients (1) can be considered as constant for a limited period, since the natural development of services and markets in the long term inevitably leads to their change. The rapid growth in the popularity of bitcoin at the beginning of 2021 was because of speculative investments and is not a sign of the inefficiency of the model. During such periods, the model deviations become large, and the quality of the

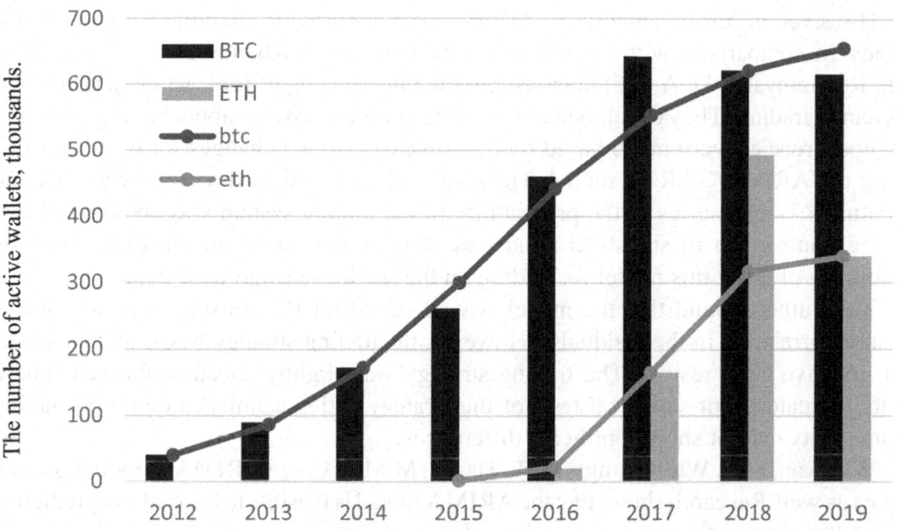

Fig. 2. Statistics of active Bitcoin and Ethereum wallets per day, thousands, averaged over years, actual (histograms) and calculated values.

forecast temporarily decreases. We expect to see a decrease in the exchange rate and a stabilization of user activity, after which the model can be reinterpreted considering new statistics.

4 Stochastic Approach

For the stochastic approach, a set of existing data is considered, and the parameters of the statistical model are optimized, which gives optimal results for the available data and for extrapolation of these data for future periods. The most effective methods at the moment are based on the theory of time series [11] and implemented in the form of algorithms of the ARIMA family [2]. A big advantage of these algorithms is the consideration of random, noise factors in the behaviour of the simulated systems, as well as some secondary systematic, for example, seasonal trends. At the same time, models do not include the available information about the nature of the simulated systems, often have weak explanatory power, require a large amount of data for training, and often poorly describe the behaviour of systems with long-term changing trends.

The application of ARIMA on the example of the cryptocurrency market is studied in detail in many academic works. of Russian authors. In this study, we present the results M. R. Safiullin, A. A. Abdukayev, L. A. Elshin [14] research where the authors suggested that stochastic models in the absence of effective tools for predicting exchange rate fluctuations of cryptocurrencies should show themselves most effectively.

The reliability and adequacy of the results were confirmed by comparing the actual and predictive parameters of the bitcoin exchange rate and based on a high R-square value. The research suggests big promise for using ARIMA in business process modelling based on usage of crypto transactions, including prediction of cryptocurrency price to minimize losses induced by high volatility rates.

However, in certain conditions, ARIMA does not provide an initial increase in efficiency in comparison with other forecasting methods. Sukhanov E. I., Shirnaeva S. Yu., Kozhemyakin D. A. [15] demonstrate the imperfection of forecasting in relation to exchange trading. They developed a special algorithm: decisions about buying or selling cryptocurrencies were made based on the forecast of price changes for each next day using the ARIMA/GARCH model. The results of each trading day were recorded, and eventually, a time series of the profitability of the trading system was obtained. Based on the comparison of statistical indicators of two-time series, conclusions about the feasibility of using this model for trading on the stock exchange were made.

The authors found that the model is well suited for the considered data (there is no autocorrelation in the residuals). However, the trading strategy based on this model did not give good results. The trading strategy was slightly ahead of the benchmark in its indicators, but statistical tests of the strategy and benchmark in case of making profitability did not show significant differences.

Wirawan, I.M., Widiyaningtyas, T., Hasan, M.M. [19] use ARIMA to model Bitcoin prices as well. Research shows that the ARIMA model is feasible to be used as a predictive method of Bitcoin for one to seven days ahead.

In our paper, to obtain an objective comparison of the stochastic and deterministic approaches, we propose to compare the effectiveness of using both approaches. For this purpose, we will analyze the data used in our previous work [6] using the ARIMA method.

In our study, the pmdarima and statsmodels.tsa packages of the Python programming language were used to build ARIMA. The R programming language tools were also used. The usage of the models considered in the work assumed the implementation of five main iterations:

1. Building a time series.
2. Checking the series for stationarity (as a result, the class of the used model is determined-ARMA or ARIMA).
3. The model parameters were selected by using auto-ARIMA. Auto-ARIMA works by conducting differencing tests (i.e., Kwiatkowski–Phillips–Schmidt–Shin, Augmented Dickey-Fuller or Phillips–Perron) to determine the order of differencing, d, and then fitting models within ranges.
4. Assessment of the reliability and adequacy of the constructed model.
5. Development of predictive parameters of the time series under study.

The task of defining criteria for a deterministic model applied to highly noisy data is not trivial, because direct formal comparison of a purely deterministic model with a model that includes random components does not seem correct to us. Considering the question of the significance of the deterministic model for a strongly stochastic process, we take as a basis the approach to the theory of time series described in the article by Kantorovich [11]. In his research, various trends and random components are distinguished in the data sample. Further, as a null hypothesis, we assume that the developed model closely describes the trend, and a noticeable further improvement is possible only taking into account random components that exist beyond this model. Let's also assume that the autoregressive integrated moving average model (ARIMA) is fairly accurate. Therefore, we will propose the following criterion for the quality of our model as a correct description of the trend:

1. The remainder of the optimal model (relative BTC-btc or absolute (BTC-btc)/btc) give a stationary process.
2. Applying the ARIMA model to the time series obtained at the first step, respectively, gives a model with parameters (p, 0, q), where p and q are the order of the AR - and MA-components of the econometric model.
3. ARIMA estimated on the residuals of the model predicts better than the model applied to the original series.
4. We should make a special condition to implement this approach:
5. A deterministic model is trained by minimizing absolute deviations (or by another classical criterion).
6. The residuals of the deterministic model (relative and absolute) are calculated.
7. The stationarity criterion is applied to the remainders: the Dickey-Fuller test [9] or the CPSS test [12]. If the stationarity hypothesis is accepted, we presume that the model correctly describes the deterministic trend.
8. To determine the predictive strength of a deterministic trend, we apply various ARIMA modifications to the initial data and model residuals and compare the prediction accuracy for both cases.

The results are shown in Table 1. As data for ARIMA, we used 1) the first differences of the original series, 2) the BTC-btc differences, 3) the relative differences of the original data, and 4) the relative differences (BTC-btc)/BTC. The model was trained on 1 365 values, after which a sample of 30 values was predicted.

5 Comparison of Deterministic, Stochastic, and Mixed Approaches

The assumption that the trend is stationary for the BTC-btc differences and ETH-eth differences is confirmed by the behaviour of auto-ARIMA. For both Bitcoin and Ethereum, we observe the smallest prediction error for most of the metrics used in the latest model – ARIMA for relative differences with a deterministic trend. The order of integration of the series is determined based on the KPSS test. The use of the alternative Dickey-Fuller criterion does not change the conclusion in favour of the third model. The residuals from the ARIMA model are white noise, as indicated by the high P-values in the corresponding tests.

It should be noted that at a small interval and under the condition of the relative stability of the source data, the predictive power of ARIMA on real data and ARIMA on the differences between real data and the deterministic model is approximately the same, with a small advantage of the model on the BTC-btc differences. However, because this paper aims to identify trends in the cryptocurrencies' development, and not to create a tool for technical analysis, the most important issue is the functioning of ARIMA over long periods. We expect that in this case, the differences will be more significant. The above-mentioned research by Wirawan, I. M., Widiyaningtyas, T., Hasan, M. M. shows that ARIMA loses its effectiveness on the seventh day of the observations period. For

Table 1. The value of forecast error metrics for different ARIMA models

Bitcoin		Error metrics				P-value of the Box-Pierce and Lewing-Box tests
		RMSE	MSE	MAE	MAPE	
1	ARIMA in differences (4, 1, 2)	0.133	0.018	0.105	0.008	0.122 0.121
2	ARIMA for BTC-btc (4, 1, 2)	0.157	0.025	0.134	1.194	0.126 0.124
3	ARIMA in relative differences (5, 0, 3)	0.163	0.027	0.137	0.990	0.207 0.204
4	ARIMA for (BTC-btc)/btc (1, 0, 0)	0.021	0.0005	0.019	3.107	0.409 0.408
Ethereum		RMSE	MSE	MAE	MAPE	
1	ARIMA in differences (3, 2, 1)	0.292	0.085	0.273	0.021	0.967 0.966
2	ARIMA for ETH-eth (2, 1, 1)	0.299	0.089	0.279	1.015	0.962 0.961
3	ARIMA in relative differences (3, 1, 1)	0.139	0.019	0.104	1.023	0.968 0.968
4	ARIMA for (ETH-eth)/eth (2, 1, 1)	0.024	0.001	0.022	1.035	0.878 0.877

the purposes of our paper, we performed the ARIMA calculation on a smaller amount of data to increase the number of test data. The predicted data for ARIMA based on real data (1, 1, 2) and ARIMA based on BTC-btc differences (2, 0, 2) is shown in Fig. 3.

Both models, after a period of confidently following the real data, demonstrate stationarity in the long term. This situation is typical for ARIMA. Nevertheless, it should be noted that data from the deterministic ARIMA model demonstrates a more adequate trend prediction. MAPE for ARIMA with BTC-btc differences is better than for ARIMA based on real data (0.1609 vs. 0.1716). Thus, the effectiveness of ARIMA with the usage of BTC-btc differences and ETH-eth differences strongly depends on the correctness of the expert assessment of the deterministic model.

Table 1 shows that using the difference with the model gives better results than differentiating. On the other hand, the usage of relative differences wins over absolute ones because of the high volatility of the source data. Therefore, we can conclude that: 1) in the above sense, the deterministic model is reliable and 2) the combination of the deterministic model and the ARIMA methodology is a promising direction for the study of highly volatile payment systems [3]. At the same time, the predictive value of a purely deterministic model on short segments is not very high, but it has the advantage in analytical form. We suppose that other criteria of optimization of parameters of the

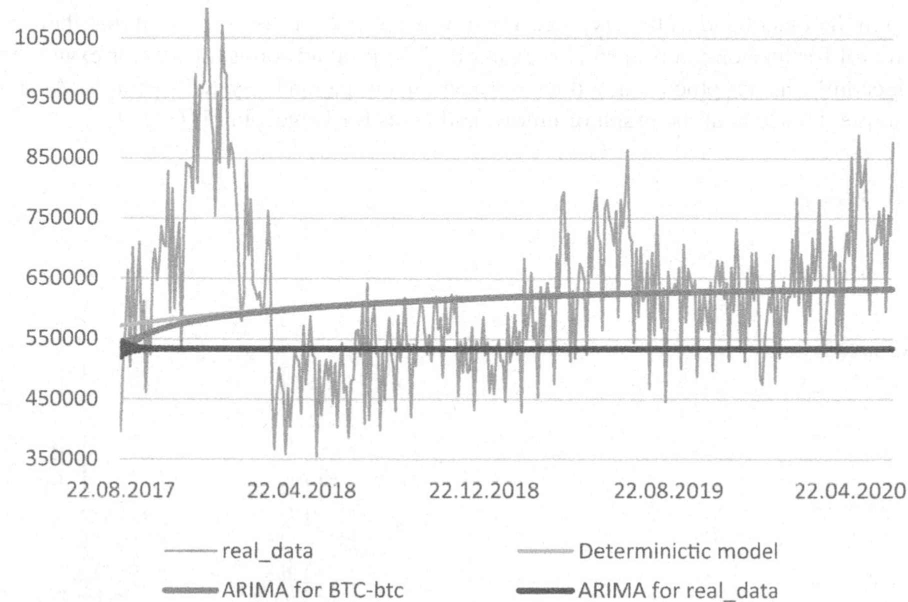

Fig. 3. ARIMA Prediction Charts

deterministic model can be tested to improve the quality of the mixed approach and we are planning to do this in future. We also see that for the BTC model, the parameter d = 0, which indicates that our model takes the trend into account qualitatively. For other models, d = 1. This may indicate the presence of small unrecorded, for example, seasonal trends, higher stationarity requirements in the ARIMA implementation, or the need for more careful parameters' selection of our model in order to increase stationarity, for example, based on the Dickey-Fuller criterion.

6 Using Mixed Approach to Analyze the Dynamics of Other Cryptocurrencies

It is necessary to note that the effectiveness of using a combination of stochastic and deterministic approaches in configuration of combining ARIMA methods and the Bass equation may differ depending on the nature of the cryptocurrency and the initial idea of their positioning.

Both Bitcoin and Ethereum were initially positioned as an alternative payment system to fiat money. It was assumed that cryptocurrencies would become a faster and safer way to pay for goods and services. Nevertheless, the regulatory barriers of many countries make cryptocurrencies as volatile speculative trading instruments.

Some cryptocurrencies in these conditions have retained the features of payment systems and are used for their intended purpose (for example, Bitcoin and Ethereum). This is reflected in the presence of a characteristic periodization of the growth of the number of wallets, explained by the Bass equation.

On the other hand, if the cryptocurrency was created for the purpose of distribution as a tool for financing a project (for example, ICO product) or as a joke (for example, Dogecoin), this cryptocurrency does not have many payment system features. As an example, let's look at the graph of unique addresses for Dogecoin [5] (Fig, 4).

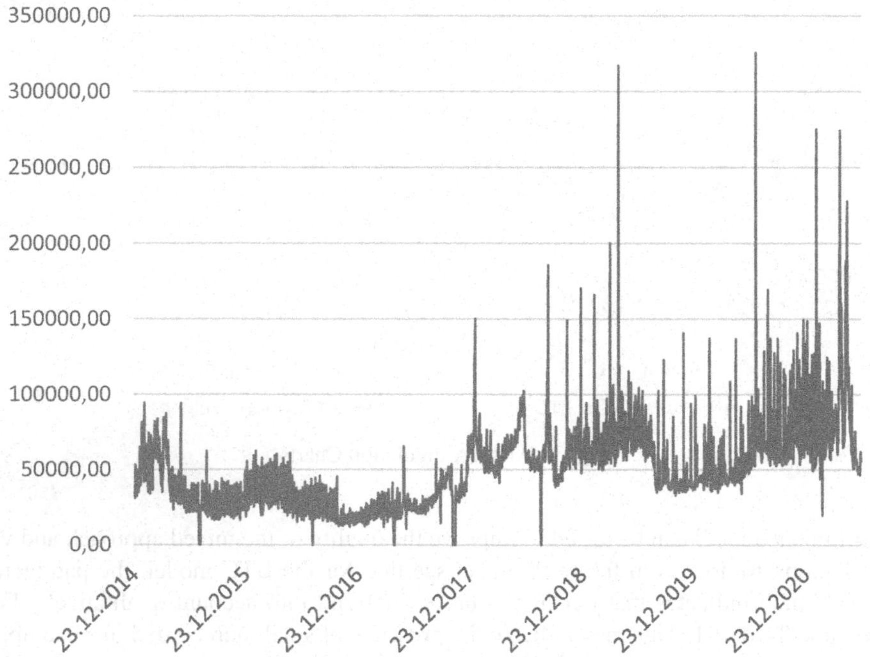

Fig. 4. Number of active Dogecoin wallets

Dogecoin is named after the Internet meme, which demonstrates the frivolity of this coin. It should be noted that the graph of the number of addresses does not have the typical inflection that is observed in the Bitcoin or Ethereum charts. Number of active Dogecoin wallets is feint. This growth is provided not by real demands, but by series of twitters by one of cryptocurrency opinion leaders, E.Mask [7] and therefore are not stochastic in sense of [3] and not deterministic [18]. That's why it can be assumed that the application of the approach described in this paper in case of predicting the number of unique wallets for such cryptocurrency is difficult.

On the other hand, we assume that the model can be quite accurate if it is used to predict the development of Central Bank Digital Currencies (CBDC). Indeed, CBDC is essentially the same cryptocurrency – a distributed ledger, the usage of tokens, a similar level of security. However, unlike existing cryptocurrencies, the price of CBDC and its security will be guaranteed by the state regulator. In fact, CBDC will be a classic payment system. We are confident that for this type of cryptocurrency mixed approach can become an effective tool for predicting scalability. We propose to test this hypothesis when at least one CBDC starts functioning, and the regulator starts to publish statistics on its development.

7 Conclusions

The study shows that the application of both a deterministic and stochastic model to such strongly stochastic systems as cryptocurrencies, in general, has a positive result. It was shown that using the result of the model as a trend can improve the quality of such models forecast.

We have shown the advantages and disadvantages of both a deterministic and stochastic approach to predicting the dynamics of the development of cryptocurrencies. In particular, we found that deterministic models show low efficiency over brief time segments; however, they are sufficiently efficient in general trend forecasts, although the efficiency decays in the period of active growth over a long period of time. On the other hand, stochastic (in particular, ARIMA) forecasting methods show excellent results in short-term periods but cannot effectively predict the behaviour of a P2P system over long distances because of insufficient emphasis on non-numeric factors.

In this regard, the combination of a deterministic Bass-type model and statistical methods with stochastic analysis tools seems to be a prospective direction and will be the subject of further research.

References

1. Bitcoin Active Addresses historical chart. https://bitinfocharts.com/comparison/bitcoin-activeaddresses.html. Accessed 13 Mar 2021
2. Box, G.E.P., Jenkins, G.M.: Time Series Analysis: Forecasting and Control, 575 p. Holden-Day, San Francisco (1970)
3. Christodoulos, C., Michalakelis, C., Varoutas, D.: Forecasting with limited data: combining ARIMA and diffusion models. Technol. Forecast. Soc. Change **77**(4), 558–565 (2010)
4. Dipple, S., Choudhary, A., Flamino, J., Szymanski, B.K., Korniss, G.: Using correlated stochastic differential equations to forecast cryptocurrency rates and social media activities. Appl. Netw. Sci. **5**(1), 1–30 (2020). https://doi.org/10.1007/s41109-020-00259-1
5. Dogecoin Active Addresses historical chart. Homepage https://bitinfocharts.com/comparison/activeaddresses-doge.html
6. Dostov, V., Shoust, P., Popova, E.: Using mathematical models to describe the dynamics of the spread of traditional and cryptocurrency payment systems. In: Misra, S., et al. (eds.) ICCSA 2019. LNCS, vol. 11620, pp. 457–471. Springer, Cham (2019). https://doi.org/10.1007/978-3-030-24296-1_36
7. Elon Musk's Bitcoin Fun Continues. Bloomberg. https://www.bloomberg.com/opinion/articles/2021-05-17/elon-musk-controls-bitcoin-and-dogecoin-prices-with-pure-magic
8. Four Different Types of Services. Homepage https://localfirstbank.com/content/different-types-of-banking-services/. Accessed 10 Mar 2021
9. Fuller W. A.: Introduction to Statistical Time Series. Wiley (2009)
10. Genkin, A., Micheev, A.: Blockchain. How it Works and What Awaits Us Tomorrow, 592 p. Alpina Publisher (2018)
11. Kantorovich, G.G.: Time series analysis. HSE Econ. J. **2020**(1), 85–116 (2006)
12. Kwiatkowski, D., Phillips, P.C.B., Schmidt, P., Shin, Y.: Testing the null hypothesis of stationarity against the alternative of a unit root. J. Econometrics **54**(1–3), 159–178 (1992)
13. Laffont, J.-J.: Regulation and Development, 440 p. Cambridge University Press (2005)

14. Recherches mathématiques sur la loi d'accroissement de la population, dans Nouveaux Mémoires de l'Académie Royale des Sciences et Belles-Lettres de Bruxelles. 1845. № 18, pp. 1–42
15. Safiullin, M.R., Abdukaeva, A.A., El'shin, L.A.: Methodological approaches to forecasting dynamics of cryptocurrencies exchange rate using stochastic analysis tools (on the example of bitcoin). Finan. Theor. Pract. **22**(4), 38–51 (2018). https://doi.org/10.26794/2587-5671-2018-22-4-38-51
16. Takako, F.-G.: Non-cooperative Game Theory, 260 p. Springer, Japan (2015). https://doi.org/10.1007/978-4-431-55645-9
17. The annual cryptocurrency market review: what's left after the hype. Bitnews Today (2019). https://bitnewstoday.com/news/the-annual-cryptocurrency-market-review-what-s-left-after-the-hype. Accessed 19 Mar 2021
18. The Bass Model Homepage. http://bassbasement.org/BassModel/Default.aspx. Accessed 15 Mar 2021
19. Wirawan, I.M., Widiyaningtyas, T., Hasan, M.M.: Short Term prediction on bitcoin price using ARIMA method. In: International Seminar on Application for Technology of Information and Communication (iSemantic), Semarang, Indonesia, pp. 260–265 (2019). https://doi.org/10.1109/ISEMANTIC.2019.8884257

Testing and Comparative Analysis of the F-BFT-based DLT Solution

Alexander Bogdanov[1], Nadezhda Shchegoleva[1(✉)], Vladimir Korkhov[1,4], Valery Khvatov[2], Nodir Zaynalov[3], Jasur Kiyamov[1], Aleksandr Dik[1], and Anar Faradzhov[1]

[1] Saint Petersburg State University, St. Petersburg, Russia
{a.v.bogdanov,n.shchegoleva,v.korkhov}@spbu.ru,
{st087383,st087383,st069744}@student.spbu.ru
[2] DGT Technologies AG, Toronto, Canada
[3] Samarkand branch Tashkent University of Information Technologies named after Muhammad al-Khwarizmi, Samarkand, Uzbekistan
nodirz@mail.ru
[4] Plekhanov Russian University of Economics, Moscow, Russia

Abstract. Consensus algorithm is a crucial part of a blockchain system. In particular, in any blockchain-based Distributed Ledger Technology (DLT) solution the consensus algorithm plays the key role in maintaining consistency of databases. The choice of consensus type during design of the distributed system will inevitably and significantly affect such characteristics as throughput and network load what in turn can impose serious restrictions on functionality or applicability of the whole system. In this research paper we overview the most commonly used algorithms and approaches, the highest attention is paid to those based on the solution of the Byzantine Fault Tolerance problem (BFT). One of the best-known algorithms of that type is the Practical Byzantine Fault Tolerance (PBFT) which has become the basis and the benchmark for a plenty of different BFT algorithms. The focus of this paper is sharpened on a particular PBFT modification known as the Federalized BFT. The aim of this study is to investigate a particular F-BFT-based DLT solution, to compare it with the other systems of that type and to determine areas of its applicability.

Keywords: Blockchain · Distributed ledger technology · Smart contracts

1 Introduction

1.1 Background

The modern business trends are directed towards integration and further complication of the IT environments. In these circumstances the need in universal solutions which could be compliment with higher security requirements and, at the same time, could be universal and flexible has risen as much as never before.

O. Gervasi et al. (Eds.): ICCSA 2021, LNCS 12952, pp. 31–41, 2021.
https://doi.org/10.1007/978-3-030-86973-1_3

The situation is aggravated by the fact that today businesses have a tendency to move their infrastructure into clouds. It is understandable, despite all the complications that migration to cloud environment entails, it helps to optimize operational expenses, deployment costs, and costs of exploitation quite effectively [1,2]. Fast spreading of cloud-based services has inspired interest to highly-scalable blockchain systems, their possibilities and applicability in different business environments.

Unfortunately, there are still a lot of obstacles for blockchain deployment in the cloud. The most notable one is performance instability of blockchain based solutions in dynamic cloud environments which is also worsened by complications of influence factors identification.

A key role in controlling this instability plays the choice of consensus algorithm that would be most appropriate for the purpose in consideration.

Nowadays there are plenty of different approaches to designing consensus algorithms. For instance, in Bitcoin and Ethereum Proof-of-Work [4] protocol is implemented. The main idea of this algorithm is based on the idea that only those nodes who have done some computational work are allowed to create a new block in the blockchain. Another well-known specimen is Proof-of-Stake [5] protocol implemented in Nxt [6] and many other cryptocurrencies. The idea of this one is in giving the right for creating a new block to the stakeholders of a currency only.

Even though the diversity of different consensus algorithms is high, they all impose different expenditures and restrictions on participants. One of well researched approaches to construction consensus protocols is based on Byzantine Fault Tolerance problem [9] solution. The BFT-based algorithms family includes: DBFT [10], FBFT [11], RBFT [12], PBFT [13] and many others. This study is focused on comparison of two DLT-products based on different BFT algorithms: Hyperledger Sawtooth [17] and BGX/DGT [16], which are highly similar, but use different BFT-based consensus protocols.

1.2 BGX/DGT

BGX/DGT is the DLT solution based on Hyperledger Sawtooth framework. It inherits most of the architectural and technological concepts applied in Sawtooth of version 1.1. Nevertheless, BGX/DGT differs from the original Sawtooth in the most crucial parts. Unlike Sawtooth, BGX/DGT is not a p2p network, it is based on the federated structure of clusters—separated p2p networks, and the ring of arbiters—the second layer which connects clusters with each other. Therefore, p2p based consensus protocols are incompatible with such a network structure, that is one of the reasons why BGX/DGT uses two-layered F-BFT consensus [8] to keep its database consistent (see Fig. 1).

As in Sawtooth, the node in BGX/DGT consists of several components that communicate with each other using TCP protocol. The central component of any node is the validator, which functions are: providing interoperability for other modules on the particular node, communicating with other nodes, authenticating and identity checking for nodes in the network.

Another important component is the REST-API module— it provides an interface for users to interact with the system. REST-API allows users to access the validator using simple HTTP queries.

The consensus engine in BGX/DGT is also presented as the separated module.

Besides these three components, this product uses different transaction processors to set up and sustain the environment as well as to implement user-defined business-logic.

Several distinguishing features should be emphasized [7]:

- The storage system in BGX/DGT has a structure of Directed Acyclic Graph what makes it similar with IOTA, Hedera Hashgraph, Orumesh, DagCoin, Byteball, Nano. But unlike aforementioned platforms, BGX/DGT is designed in the way that allows voting in federalized networks with dynamic topology.
- There are several solutions that use similar federative approach e.g. Ripple, Stellar. The combination of DAG and federative voting methods together with leaders rotation and dynamic topologies makes BGX/DGT notably more horizontally scalable, but not less secure.
- Consortium based consensus helps to preserve flexibility along with not losing interoperability. In comparison with, for instance, Hyperledger Fabric which is designed to be used in private networks only and ICON which have to use a special Loopchain Fault Tolerance mechanism to interact with networks on the side, usage of dynamic topologies together with DAG-based storage in BGX/DGT provides a significant asynchronicity. This fact ensures a significant level of interoperability (Table 1).

1.3 F-BFT Algorithm Description

When the system is up, it should choose the higher rank nodes - Leaders and Arbiters. In each cluster there should be exactly one Leader (see Fig. 2, I).

Once the transaction is initiated by any node, the initiator's node publishes this transaction to the whole network, unless the transaction is incorrect (Fig. 2, II). When initiator's cluster nodes receive the transaction, they verify it and, in case everything is correct, they commit it using PBFT consensus algorithm. Meanwhile the rest of the nodes should receive that transaction too, but they have to verify it only, keeping committing pending until they receive the permission from arbiters. The next phase of the algorithm comes up when the leader of the initiator's cluster receives $\frac{2n+1}{3}$ confirmation messages, where n is the number of nodes in initiator's cluster. At that moment the leader sends a special message to arbiters (Fig. 2.2, III) who in turn, in case the corresponding transaction have been verified successfully, send permission for committing to other nodes(Fig. 2, IV).

Table 1. Blockchain platforms' functionality comparison

Parameter	Ethereum	Stellar	Hyperledger fabric	BGX/DGT
Purpose	Distributed processing, cryptocurrencies	Payment system	Data exchange within corporate environment	Real time data integration, ecosystems
Networking	P2P, public	Federated, public	P2P, public	Federated, consortium based
Cryptocurrency supported	Yes	Yes	No	Optional
Consensus	PoW	FBA	PBFT	F-BFT
Data storage	Blocks	Blocks	Blocks	DAG
Tokenization	Yes	No	No	Yes
Smart contract	Yes	Yes	Yes	Yes
Encryption	ECDSA	Asymmetric, Ed25519	PKCS11, pluggable	Asymmetric, ECDSA curve secp256k1
Programming language	GO	Java	Java, JavaScript (Node.js), GO	C++, Python

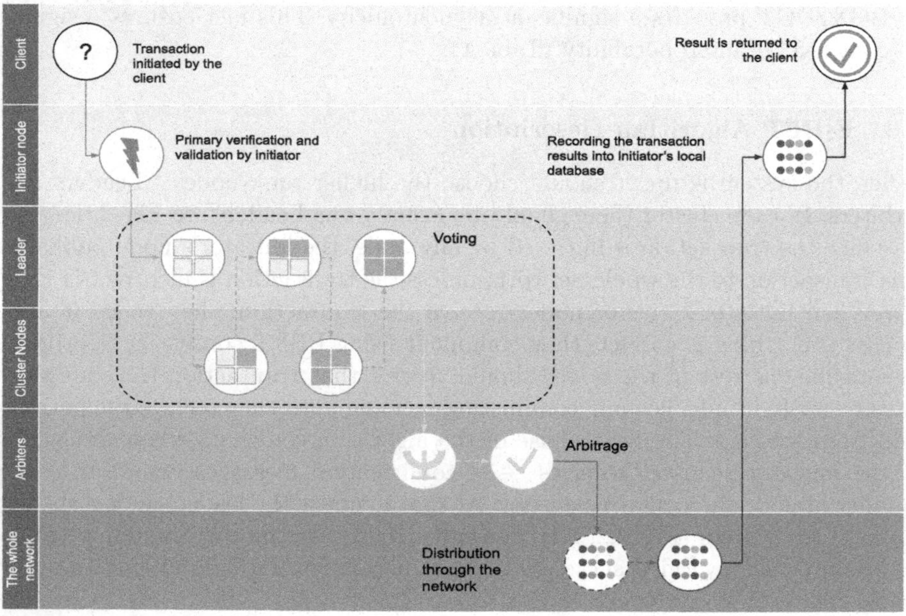

Fig. 1. Transaction committing in BGX/DGT

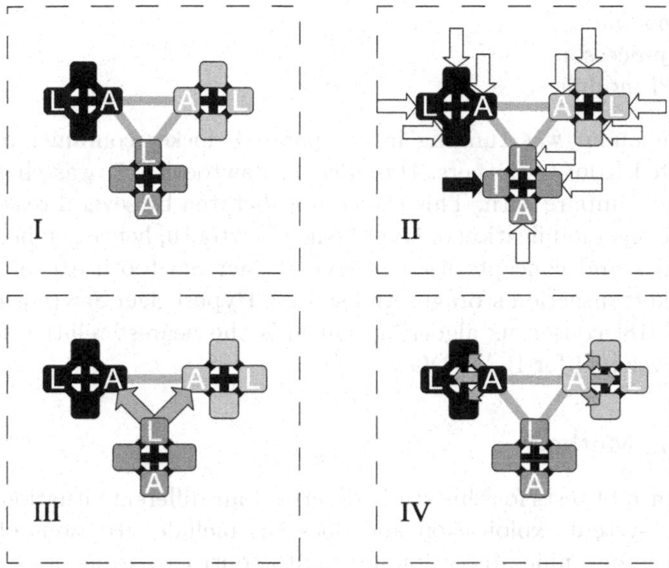

Fig. 2. F-BFT consensus illustration

2 Testing

The following section contains the testing results for several scenarios which will inevitably occur during exploitation of the system. The testing was conducted to examine weaknesses of the current version of BGX/DGT in cases unspecific for different applicability areas, as well to assess competitiveness of it in the current stage of development.

2.1 Testing Environment

The environment configuration was used for testing is listed below:

- OS: Fedora 28
- CPU: Intel(R) Xeon(R) CPU E5-2690 v4, 2.60 GHz
- RAM: 255 GB

Tests were conducted using Docker [14] and Docker-compose [15] for creating test networks. All the measurements were taken using Docker tools, vnStat and embedded tools of Hyperledger Sawtooth.

Tested version of the product was Kawartha [16].

A typical node in BGX/DGT network consists of several components:

- transactions processor
- validator module
- shell module
- consensus module

- settings module
- topology processor
- REST API module

Each component was running in a separated docker container in order to remain isolated from the others. Hyperledger Sawtooth [17] was chosen as the benchmark to compare with. This choice was dictated by several reasons. First, BGX/DGT is the modification of Hyperledger Sawtooth, hence it inherits almost all technologies and concepts used in Hyperledger Sawtooth except consensus algorithm and transaction storage. And second, Hyperledger Sawtooth has pluggable PBFT [18] consensus algorithm which is the nearest relative for F-BFT consensus developed for BGX/DGT.

2.2 Testing Method

Tests. A bunch of tests for this study describe four different situations that can occur during system exploitation and does not include situations of intended attacks on cryptographic protection nor taking control over one or several nodes of the network by intruder:

1. Single transactions committing. During this test transactions were made one at a time from each node. The next transaction was not sent until the previous had been committed.
2. Asynchronous streams of transactions committing. Transactions were sent in bunches of 100 from different nodes in different clusters (through one node in cluster at the same time).
3. Simultaneous transactions committing test I. As in the second, transactions were sent in bunches of 100 from different nodes in different clusters, but this time streams were synchronized – transactions were sent simultaneously.
4. Simultaneous transactions committing test II. A bunch of 100 transactions was sent simultaneously from every node.

Tests were taken in five different configurations:

1. One cluster of 6 nodes,
2. Two clusters of 6 nodes,
3. Two clusters of 6 nodes and one cluster of 3,
4. Two clusters of 6 nodes and two clusters of 3,
5. Two clusters of 6 nodes and three clusters of 3.

It should be kept in mind that the first and the second clusters had 6 nodes, while the third, fourth and fifth consisted of 3 only—this configuration was static and had never been changed during testing.

The explanation of why only those five configurations were chosen to conduct tests is due to several technical issues of BGX/DGT which impose restrictions on scalability of the network. The second reason is the fact that such a size of the network and its scaling dynamics was enough to see differences between

BGX/DGT and the benchmark, and to establish the most crucial shortcomings of the current version (Kawartha) of the product in consideration.

In order to unify terminology we assume that the benchmark also has the federated structure, therefore in new terms the first six nodes will belong to the first cluster, the second six to the second cluster, 13, 14, 15 nodes—to the third, and the last 6 nodes will compose the fourth and the fifth clusters correspondingly.

Metrics. The benchmark and BGX/DGT were compared using two main metrics: committed transactions per second (CTPS) and the average volume of network traffic on validator per transaction (VONT):

$$\text{CTPS} = \frac{\text{committed transactions}}{\text{time elapsed}},$$

$$\text{VONT} = \frac{\text{average input volume + average output volume}}{\text{committed transactions}}.$$

Committed transactions are transactions included in databases in ALL nodes.

Elapsed time is the time elapsed since sending the first transaction until all transactions are committed.

Input/output volume was measured within the same period as the number of committed transactions.

In order to make results more precise we took two additional metrics: average resting state volume (ARSV) – an average volume of network traffic for sustaining network (without committing transactions), and committing rate (CR):

$$\text{ARSV} = \frac{\text{60 sec. average input + 60 sec. average output}}{\text{60 sec.}}$$

$$\text{CR} = \frac{\text{transactions committed}}{\text{transactions sent}},$$

Here, 60 s time interval was chosen as it ensures that no unique message will remain unaccounted, at the same time, it is short enough for the test to be conducted several times.

As BGX/DGT is not a p2p network, ARSV was calculated separately for two kinds of nodes—leader nodes and ordinary nodes. On the contrary, Sawtooth PBFT builds up a p2p network, hence there is no need in calculation of two different ARSV values.

3 Results

Testing results are shown in the following tables (see Tables 2, 3).

The results of Test 1 show that the speed of committing standalone transactions for BGX/DGT is considerably higher then for Sawtooth PBFT, moreover, the dynamics of the traffic volume ingested by a single node for BGX/DGT is much flatter than for Sawtooth PBFT.

Table 2. Testing results

Num. of nodes	Sawtooth PBFT			**BGX/DGT**		
Test 1. Single transactions committing.						
	CTPS, tps	VONT, kb/tr	CR	CTPS, tps	VONT, kb/tr	CR
6	0.85	81.2	1	0.62	226	1
12	0.8	168	1	1.2	162.7	1
15	0.83	212.8	1	1.07	207	1
18	0.62	293.1	1	1.09	234.9	1
21	0.87	340	1	1.18	206	1
Test 2. Asynchronous streams of transactions committing						
6	0.74	66	1	1.23	180.8	1
12	1.85	109.2	1	1.49	185	0.57
15	2.43	121.6	1	1.72	142.6	0.49
18	4.54	108.8	1	1.09	209	0.36
21	5.55	115	1	0.81	232.7	0.28
Test 3. Simultaneous transactions commiting test I.						
12	0.8	109.2	1	–	–	0
15	3.13	110	1	–	–	0
18	3.8	123.4	1	–	–	0
21	4.76	112.6	1	–	–	0
Test 4. Simultaneous transactions commiting test II.						
6	0.87	42.5	1	–	–	0
12	1.18	101.6	1	–	–	0
15	2.78	75.8	1	–	–	0
18	3.45	103.8	1	–	–	0
21	3.85	129.9	0.95	–	–	0

Table 3. Testing results

Num. of nodes	Sawtooth PBFT	BGX/DGT	
	ARSV, kb/sec.	ARSV Lead, kb/sec.	ARSV Ord., kb/sec.
6	1.59	32.42	10.08
12	1.59	25.26	8.53
15	1.43	26.28	15
18	1.59	24.9	17.06
21	1.36	21.16	17.07

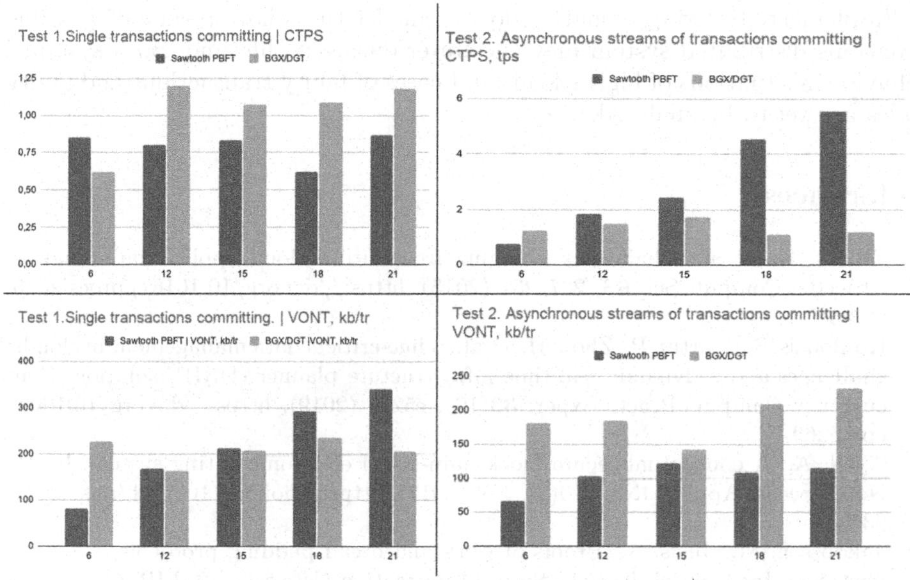

Fig. 3. Results of tests 1 and 2

In higher loads, with the presence of several parallel transaction streams, results shown by BGX/DGT are much more ambiguous. CTPS shows that the throughput of the system does not rise when the load increases, while Sawtooth shows quite a steady rising dynamics. Also, Sawtooth works much more efficient in terms of VONT when the load increases. It might be happening due to different storage models that BGX/DGT and Sawtooth use to store transactions. While Sawtooth unites simultaneous transactions in blocks and stores blocks, BGX/DGT stores standalone transactions in its databases so it is unable to process more then one transaction at the same time. This hypothesis is supported also by the dynamics of CR in Test 2: as streaming density increases, more transaction collisions happen and more of them left unprocessed. Results of Tests 3 and 4 speak in favor of this hypothesis too.

4 Conclusion and Future Work

In this paper, we presented results of implementing several testing scenarios of BGX/DGT and Hyperledger Sawtooth DLT platforms with comparable consensus algorithms used. Regarding the results, it is possible to surmise the main areas of applicability for BGX/DGT Kawartha. For now it might be applied to highly distributed but low loaded systems. For systems of higher reliability Sawtooth PBFT is more preferable.

Even though the current version of BGX/DGT performs poorly in dealing with parallel workloads, it remains effective in terms of horizontal scalability, what is a promising result in the current development stage.

Implemented testing scenarios do not model the whole plenty of possible situations distributed system may encounter during its lifetime. Both systems' behavior in situations of higher loads and cases of faulty transactions and faulty nodes are yet to be analysed.

References

1. Jeffery, K., et al.: Challenges emerging from future cloud application scenarios. Procedia Comput. Sci. **68**, 227–237 (2015). https://doi.org/10.1016/j.procs.2015.09.238
2. Koulouzis, S., Martin, P., Zhou, H., et al.: Time-critical data management in clouds: challenges and a dynamic real-time infrastructure planner (DRIP) solution. Concurrency Comput. Pract. Exper. **32**(16), e5269 (2019). https://doi.org/10.1002/cpe.5269
3. Ayed, A.: A conceptual secure blockchain-based electronic voting system. Int. J. Netw. Secur. Appl. (IJNSA) **9**(3), 1–9 (2017). https://doi.org/10.5121/ijnsa.2017.9301
4. Jakobsson, M., Juels, A.: Proofs of work and bread pudding protocols (extended abstract). In: Preneel, B. (ed.) Secure Information Networks. ITIFIP, vol. 23, pp. 258–272. Springer, Boston (1999). https://doi.org/10.1007/978-0-387-35568-9_18
5. Li, W., Andreina, S., Bohli, J.-M., Karame, G.: Securing proof-of-stake blockchain protocols. In: Garcia-Alfaro, J., Navarro-Arribas, G., Hartenstein, H., Herrera-Joancomartí, J. (eds.) ESORICS/DPM/CBT -2017. LNCS, vol. 10436, pp. 297–315. Springer, Cham (2017). https://doi.org/10.1007/978-3-319-67816-0_17
6. Nxt technical documentation: https://nxtdocs.jelurida.com Accessed 11 May 2021
7. Bogdanov, A., Degtyarev, A., Uteshev, A., Shchegoleva, N., Khvatov, V., Zvyagintsev, M.: A DLT based innovative investment platform. In: Gervasi, O., et al. (eds.) ICCSA 2020. LNCS, vol. 12251, pp. 72–86. Springer, Cham (2020). https://doi.org/10.1007/978-3-030-58808-3_7
8. Bogdanov, A., Uteshev, A., Khvatov, V.: Error detection in the decentralized voting protocol. In: Misra, S., et al. (eds.) ICCSA 2019. LNCS, vol. 11620, pp. 485–494. Springer, Cham (2019). https://doi.org/10.1007/978-3-030-24296-1_38
9. Lamport, L., Shostak, R., Pease, M.: The Byzantine general problem. ACM Trans. Programm. Lang. Syst. **4**, 382–401 (1982)
10. Wang, Q., Yu, J., Peng, Z., Bui, V.C., Chen, S., Ding, Y., Xiang, Y.: Security analysis on dBFT protocol of NEO. In: Bonneau, J., Heninger, N. (eds.) FC 2020. LNCS, vol. 12059, pp. 20–31. Springer, Cham (2020). https://doi.org/10.1007/978-3-030-51280-4_2
11. Malkhi, D., Nayak, K., Ren, L.: Flexible Byzantine fault tolerance. In: Proceedings of the 2019 ACM SIGSAC Conference on Computer and Communications Security, pp. 1041–1053 (2019). https://doi.org/10.1145/3319535.3354225
12. Aublin, P., Mokhtar, S., Quéma, V.: RBFT: redundant byzantine fault tolerance. In: Proceedings - International Conference on Distributed Computing Systems, pp. 297–306 (2013). https://doi.org/10.1109/ICDCS.2013.53
13. Castro, M., Liskov, B.: Practical Byzantine fault tolerance. In: Proceedings of the third symposium on Operating systems design and implementation (OSDI 1999), pp. 173–186. USENIX Association, USA (1999)
14. Overview of Docker Engine. https://docs.docker.com/engine/ Accessed 15 Mar 2021

15. Overview of Docker Compose. https://docs.docker.com/compose/ Accessed 15 Mar 2021
16. BGX/DGT repository. https://github.com/DGT-Network/DGT-Kawartha Accessed 17 Mar 2021
17. Hyperledger Sawtooth repository. https://github.com/hyperledger/sawtooth-core Accessed 15 Mar 2021
18. Introduction to Sawtooth PBFT. https://sawtooth.hyperledger.org/docs/pbft/releases/latest/introduction-to-sawtooth-pbft.html Accessed 15 Mar 2021

Implementation of the Cross-Blockchain Interacting Protocol

Rita Tsepeleva and Vladimir Korkhov(✉)

Saint Petersburg State University, St. Petersburg, Russia
st062153@student.spbu.ru, v.korkhov@spbu.ru

Abstract. Blockchain is a developing and promising technology that can provide users with such advantages as decentralization, data security and transparency of transactions. Blockchain has many applications, one of them is the decentralized finance (DeFi) industry which is growing more and more recently. The concept of decentralized finance involves the creation of a single ecosystem of many blockchains that interact with each other. The problem of combining and interacting blockchains becomes crucial to enable DeFi. In this paper, we look at the essence of the DeFi industry, the possibilities of overcoming the problem of cross-blockchain interaction, present our approach, and analyze the results of the proposed solution.

Keywords: Blockchain · Distributed ledger technologies · Solidity · Smart-contracts · Decentralized finances

1 Introduction

Blockchain is a modern technology that is a huge distributed database, i.e. a database whose components are placed in various nodes of a computer network in accordance with certain criteria. They reflect the transfer of information from one user to another. This database is stored on a large number of computers and has a decentralized character. It means that there is no central node that manages everything. It is a great advantage, because if there is a failure of one machine in the system, the entire system will continue to work properly and the information will not be lost. The data is organized into chain of blocks, each new block contains encrypted information from the previous block. Such an organization ensures that no data can be replaced, corrected or deleted. Accordingly, the information is as reliable and secure as possible.

Thanks to these advantages, blockchain is popular in the field of finance and in other spheres. In addition to the obvious advantages of blockchain in the form of reliability, transparency and etc., blockchain technology provides another very important thing. This is the ability to write smart contracts, i.e. executable code that helps users manage their finances independently, without resorting to the help of third parties (for example, the banking sector). However, there is an indisputable fact that smart contracts are not completely safe to use, because a

O. Gervasi et al. (Eds.): ICCSA 2021, LNCS 12952, pp. 42–55, 2021.
https://doi.org/10.1007/978-3-030-86973-1_4

mistake in the code can cost a lot of money. Despite this fact, the industry of decentralized finance is becoming more and more popular.

Next, we will take a closer look at decentralized finances concept, will talk about the most important problem in this area, which in a certain way restricts the use of its tools. We will discuss possible solutions of the problem and will analyze them, as well as give our own version of the solution and compare the results.

The rest of this paper is organized as follows. Section 2 describes the essence of decentralized finance, as well as the problems that need to be solved. Section 3 describes the existing methods and solutions. Section 4 describes the idea of our solution and its implementation. And in Sect. 5, the resulting solution is analyzed in comparison with the existing ones. Section 6 concludes the paper and points out directions of future work.

2 Decentralized Finances and Its Problems

Decentralized Finances (DeFi [1]) is an independent financial ecosystem that gives users a full control over their money without the involvement of governments and banks. Blockchain technologies have played a key role in the implementation of this industry.

2.1 The Essence of DeFi

Interaction in decentralized ecosystems occurs without intermediaries according to the P2P scheme, that is, market participants independently cope with making transactions. It:

1. Saves your time;
2. Saves your money;
3. Allows you to keep your privacy.

What is the reason for the active popularization of DeFi and why are projects increasingly integrating them into their systems? The monetary monopoly of the state is a problem that is quite difficult to solve. The control that we have over our own savings is only relative, and in recent years this has been felt especially acutely. In many European countries, the population is gradually abandoning cash and switching to electronic payments. Banks, constant monitoring, and lack of anonymity are nuances that are absent in DeFi. App developers cannot influence the money of the participants, and the latter manage their own budget. The main advantages of decentralized finance are:

1. Simplicity and accessibility of technology for ordinary people;
2. Scalability and distribution of the registry; as a result, system is more secure and resistant to technical errors;
3. Lower system maintenance costs and lower fees (or no fees);
4. Versability - DeFi can be used in almost any area of our life.

2.2 Usability of DeFi

Developers have already offered quite a lot of options for using decentralized financing. First of all, of course, in the field of banking services.

Mortgages and Insurance. The absence of intermediaries and transparency are the optimal conditions for issuing mortgage loans and insurance, including medical insurance. This category could include social benefits – such as pensions.

Lending. Classical lending is primarily a mass of restrictions. Salary requirements, sureties, and the many certifications that need to be obtained make these services inaccessible to a whole category of people. A person spent his time for making all of documents well, but still waiting for the result, which can be negative, too. DeFi should solve this problem. Moreover, without intermediaries, lending should be cheaper and more reliable. Instant transactions, transparency and security – what is so lacking in this area.

Trading. Cryptocurrency trading has remained popular for quite a long time, and the world knows dozens of trading platforms with different currencies in the listing and trading instruments. Most exchanges are centralized, i.e. they work according to the classical scheme. Decentralized exchanges or DEX operate without the participation of the administration, i.e. traders enter into a P2P relationship. The funds are not stored in the platform's wallets, which is also very important.

2.3 DeFi and Smart-Contracts

Decentralized finance is inextricably linked to smart contracts. Smart contracts are programs written in Turing-complete, modern, high-level programming languages (Solidity, for example). The main difference of such program code is that after its publication in the blockchain, the contract not only begins its autonomous work, but also loses an ability to edit or change the code. Also it is necessary to say that smart-contracts are not available in all of the blockchain platforms. For example, the most popular platform for developing and deploying such contracts is an Ethereum [2]. The Binance Smart Chain [3] and Matic [4] also provide such an opportunity. But such popular network as the Bitcoin does not provide smart contracts. Smart contracts are used in DeFi, because they help to fully automate the process, save time and avoid paperwork.

2.4 The Main Problem of DeFi

The concept of decentralized finance involves the creation of a single ecosystem in which there are many blockchains that interact with each other. However, each blockchain network was originally created and conceived as an independent, autonomous unit. In our opinion, it is the main problem of DeFi. User's funds have been "locked up" for a very long time. Users do not have an ability to transfer their digital assets to another network, and this is a serious restriction on the mobility of their funds. In addition, blockchain developers, while choosing one of the platforms, today have to give up the advantages of using other platforms. They could use several blockchains in their project at once, along with their qualities. Instead of this, they should sacrifice such important development indicators as scalability, speed, low fees and so on. That is why the issue of combining and interacting blockchain networks has been relevant for recent years.

3 Related Work

As already mentioned, the problem of combining and interacting blockchains is of interest today. That is why at the moment there are already completed or relatively completed projects in the world which solve it. Let's look at them in more detail.

3.1 Polkadot Ecosystem and Polkadot Projects

Polkadot [5] is a new-generation blockchain protocol that greatly simplifies cross-chain communication and interoperability by bringing multiple blockchains into one network. This network is going to be secured by a GRANDPA consensus algorithm [6], tailored for the Polkadot (a flavor of a Proof of Stake). The most critical parts of the Polkadot network are Relay Chain, Parachains, Parathreads, and Bridges.

Relay chain is the backbone of Polkadot's network and it is the main communication hub between parachains. Validators on this chain are accepting blocks from all parachains and thus provide security for the whole network.

Parachains are independent blockchains that run on top of the Relay Chain and provide chain-specific features to the Polkadot network. Each parachain serves a specialized purpose in the network – think of having a fine-tuned chain for smart contracts, another chain that provides a stable coin for payments between chains or a parachain which brings a decentralized energy industry to the network. Each parachain is maintained by the collator which is responsible for producing chain blocks. Parachains also benefit from a shared security model provided by the Relay Chain so they are already secured against 51% attacks or similar. However, there is only a limited amount of parachains in the network (and the number will be increasing in the future) so there is a system of public auctions where parachain candidates have to compete in order to obtain their own slot.

Parathreads are very similar to parachains from a technical point of view, however, they are very different from an economical standpoint. As we said in the previous paragraph, parachains have to compete in auctions in order to become part of the network. On the other hand, the parathread slot can be leased almost instantly and for only a short period of time. This provides a different way to run projects on the Polkadot – some of those projects can benefit from trying out the network before purchasing an expensive parachain slot, others can run as a parathreads before they win an auction for a slot.

Bridges are a special kind of parachain. Bridges connect other already running blockchains into the ecosystem (like a BTC or ETH) and allow for transfers of tokens between Polkadot and outside networks.

The peculiarity of the system is that transactions can be carried out simultaneously and distributed between blockchains. The main goal of the Polkadot ecosystem is to make sure that all participating blockchains remain secure and transactions are carried out in good faith.

The two issues most blockchain-based systems need to solve are scalability: the number of transactions per second the network can handle, and governance: how the community manages protocol upgrades and changes. Polkadot aims to solve both of these problems.

Many different projects are based on the Polkadot technology. Some of them coincide in their essence and purpose with our goals. For example, Polkaswap. Polkaswap is a decentralized exchange for the Polkadot ecosystem. It provides a framework that allows users to connect multiple blockchains using bridges and become an exchange for connecting Polkadot participants and other blockchains for efficient asset trading. The principle of operation and implementation of this project is that Polkadot simplifies the process of combining many assets from as many chains as possible by providing a Host relay chain, a cross-chain message transfer protocol XCMP and a SPREE module (Shared Protected Runtime Execution Enclaves). In addition to this project, there are several similar ones.

The disadvantages of projects based on Polkadot are as follows. Firstly, the analysis showed that all similar and interesting projects are stuck in the development stage and do not develop further. The second disadvantage is more significant and weighty. It is about security. In projects on Polkadot the exchange process is implemented as follows:

- To make the transfer of tokens from one blockchain network to another, the process of freezing tokens takes place;
- The freezing of tokens implies the transfer by the user of his funds, which he wants to exchange, to the "storage";
- Next, the logic should be implemented: if the tokens come to the storage, then hold them, and an equivalent amount of them should be credited to the specified address in the target network.

The security issue is that the storage is just an address, not a smart-contract. Accordingly, there are no guarantees and protection of users from fraud or technical failure. It can easily happen that the user will send the tokens that will remain in the storage, and the equivalent amount will not come to him.

3.2 Bridges

A blockchain bridge is an interconnected link that provides communication and interaction between two blockchain systems. By connecting two blockchain networks, blockchain bridges help decentralized applications take advantage of both systems, not just their host platform. For example, an application hosted on Ethereum and linked to the EOS blockchain can use the functionality of Ethereum smart contracts, as well as the scalability of EOS. Thanks to blockchain bridges, any data, information and tokens can be transferred between two blockchain platforms. These bridges are regulated by the mint-and-burn protocol. The token transfer does not take place literally; rather, when a token is needed to transfer from one blockchain to another, it is burned on the first, and the equivalent token is minted on the other.

An example of such bridge is the Panama Bridge [7], a new solution that allows users to transfer their cross-chain assets from centralized or decentralized wallets to the Binance Smart Chain (BSC). Panama Bridge provides an API. This means that we can use the Panama Bridge on our platform to exchange the tokens. We can collect POST or GET requests through the form and send them to the bridge. The disadvantage of this approach is its limitation. The Panama Bridge, like the other bridges, connects only two blockchains (in this case, Ethereum and Binance Smart Chain). Thus, it is not possible to talk about a single ecosystem using only one bridge.

4 The "Wish Swap" Project Idea

The Wish token [8] has the BEP2 format [9] and is placed in the Binance [3] blockchain, which limits its use. It is necessary to develop a mechanism for exchanging tokens:

- BEP2 Wish to Ethereum tokens ERC-20 and Binance Smart Chain tokens BEP-20;
- Ethereum Tokens ERC-20 and Binance Smart Chain Tokens BEP-20 to BEP2 Wish;
- Ethereum ERC-20 Tokens to Binance Smart Chain BEP-20 Tokens;
- Binance Smart Chain BEP-20 Tokens to Ethereum ERC-20 Tokens.

5 Implementation

5.1 Token Smart Contracts

In order to exchange the Wish token, it was decided to implement the contracts of the token analogues in the Binance Smart Chain (BEP20) and Ethereum [2] (ERC-20) networks, with the names BWish and WWish, respectively. All project contracts were developed in the Solidity language. Solidity is a JavaScript-like object-oriented language for developing smart contracts. It is cross-platform, so it was easy to generalize the task of writing tokens to two platforms. The token contracts, in addition to the standard functions and fields, had to contain the functions and events (events reflected in the transaction log) transferToEthereum/transferToBSC (transfer function to the Ethereum network, or

Binance Smart Chain; depending on the network) and transferToBC (transfer of tokens to Binance Chain), as well as the mint and burn functions. These functions allow you to issue/burn tokens and are only available to the contract owner (in our case, the backend) to prevent uncontrolled issue/burning of tokens.

In addition to token contracts, a Python backend and scanner were implemented.

5.2 Exchange Process with Binance Chain Network

In the Binance Chain network was created an address for exchange with the Ethereum and Binance Smart Chain blockchains. The address is a "swap contract", and the scanner has to catch transfers to it. Transactions on the Binance network contain a Memo field, which may contain additional information. A user who wants to exchange Wish tokens from the Binance Chain network, via the frontend (Django+React), or via binance.org, or via Binance Chain Wallet sends its BEP2 Wish tokens to this address, filling in the memo field according to the rules. The memo field must contain the name of the network to which the user wants to transfer tokens, as well as their number. The scanner scans operations with the BEP2 Wish token. When a transaction is detected to the exchange address, it sends it to the backend via RabbitMQ. The backend accesses the BEP20 BWish token contract and issues tokens to the user's address minus the set commission (a commission is provided for the transfer in the target network tokens). Tokens in the Binance network cannot be destroyed and they remain on the exchange address, only the backend has access to sending from the exchange address, so the number of tokens on the exchange address corresponds to the number of tokens in the Binance Smart Chain and Ethereum networks.

5.3 Exchange Process with Binance Smart Chain and Ethereum Networks

The exchange of tokens carried out from these networks is almost similar. The difference is that:

- here users interact not with the address, but with the smart contract;
- when tokens are transferred to the contract and successfully credited to the target account, they are burned.

The Exchange Process from Binance Smart Chain to Binance. A smart contract has been created in the Binance Smart Chain network for exchange with other blockchains. The procedure for exchanging **BEP 20 BWish** tokens for tokens in **the Binance Chain** network will be as follows:

- the user specifies the parameters on the page:
    1. the network to which the tokens changes (Binance Chain);
    2. receiver address;
    3. the amount of exchanged tokens.

- the user calls the transferToBC function of the BWish contract (the frontend forms a transaction);
- when calling the transaction function, the BEP20 tokens are burned;
- the scanner catches the event of the BWish contract and sends it to the backend;
- the backend makes a Wish transfer to the user's address in the Binance Chain

Only the backend has the right to access the token sending function, which protects against uncontrolled token issuance. All operations with the token are performed within a single transaction, if it was successful, the tokens are burned.

The Exchange Process from Ethereum to Binance Chain. For the Ethereum network, the exchange process is similar to the exchange from Binance Smart Chain to Binance Chain. A smart contract has been created in the Ethereum network for exchange with other blockchains. The procedure for exchanging **ERC 20 WWish** tokens for tokens in **the Binance Chain** network will be as follows:

- the user specifies the parameters on the page:
  1. the network to which the tokens are exchanged (Binance Chain);
  2. receiver address;
  3. the amount of exchanged tokens.
- the user calls the transferToBC function of the WWish contract (the frontend forms a transaction);
- when calling the transaction function, the ERC20 tokens are burned;
- the scanner catches the event of the WWish contract and sends it to the backend;
- the back makes a Wish transfer to the user's address in the Binance Chain

Only the backend has the right to access the token sending function, which protects against uncontrolled token issuance. All operations with the token are performed within a single transaction, if it was successful, the tokens are burned.

The Exchange Process Between Ethereum and Binance Smart Chain Networks. The procedure for exchanging BEP 20 BWish tokens for tokens in the Ethereum network will be as follows:

- the user specifies the following parameters:
  1. the network to which the tokens are exchanged (Binance Chain);
  2. receiver address;
  3. the amount of exchanged tokens.
- the user calls the transferToEthereum function of the BWish contract or transferToBSC function of the WWish contract(the frontend forms a transaction);
- when calling the transaction function, the BEP20 or ERC20 tokens are burned;

- the scanner catches an event on the BWish or WWish contract and sends it to the backend via RabbitMQ;
- the backend address call to WWish token or BWish token to mint tokens to the user's address in current network.

Similarly, only the backend has the right to access the token sending function, which protects against uncontrolled token issuance and all operations with the token are performed within a single transaction. If it was successful, the tokens are burned.

5.4 Project Architecture

The final architecture of the project is shown in Fig. 1:

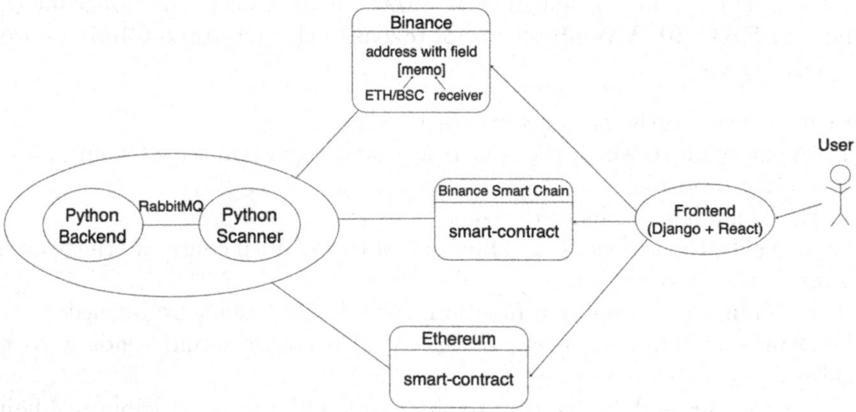

Fig. 1. Project architecture.

The Solidity Token smart contract template includes the following features:

- transferToBC and transferToBSC/transferToEthereum functions (depending on the network) - transfer of tokens in the Binance Chain and Binance Smart Chain/Ethereum networks;
- mint function - a function that is available only to the contract owner, in our case, it is the backend; mint function is necessary to charge tokens to a specific address;
- burn function - it is also used by the backend in the Ethereum and Binance Smart Chain networks after the transfer function; it burns tokens;
- other ERC-20/BEP-20 standart functions.

The Django + React web application performs the following tasks:

- collecting information from the user;
- generating transactions;
- calling contract functions (mint, transfers, burn);
- calculating transaction fees.

Ethereum and Binance Smart Chain Network Scanners and Binance Chain Network Scanner:

It is important to note that the scanners for the Ethereum and Binance Smart Chain networks are identical, they are configured to check a specific token, token contract, and event. That is, in order for our application to be able to see the call of the functions of our contracts coming from the frontend, we just need to use the API provided by Etherscan [10] (The Ethereum Blockchain Explorer) or BscScan [11] (Binance Smart Chain Explorer) (block-observers). And the scanner for the Binance Chain network works in a unique way due to the high frequency of transactions in the Binance Chain. Instead of parsing all blocks in a row, a list of transactions involving the address for the last day is requested with some frequency. When you restart the first request, the data for the week is returned. Network registry scanners scan all transactions in an open registry to send confirmation messages to the backend via a queue (RabbitMQ).

5.5 Security

The current backend has the following architecture: there are N networks/blockchains in which the exchange takes place, each of them has a contract/address that can mint tokens to the addresses of end users. Such a contract/address has an owner who has access, and accordingly, the owner has a private key for such operations.

In fact, we have a small number of private keys (for example, 3 contracts = 3 keys), which in some way makes the task easier, unlike if there were an ever-growing set of private keys needed.

It is not a good idea to store private keys in a database in a pure form. The options for avoiding the problem are as follows.

Refuse to Store the Private Key in Pure Text in the Database Field. There is an option to use Encrypted Field/Symmetric Field/PGP Encrypted Field. Such fields work on the principle that the data stored in the field is encrypted, and cannot be obtained in the absence of the correct password/passphrase/secret key required for decryption (such a key is stored separately, and for example, if you get the database, but do not have such a key, it will be impossible to decrypt the table field).

Advantages of this option: even if someone takes possession of the table, he will not be able to see the keys. Even if you dump the table and pull it out from somewhere, you won't be able to decrypt it either. Also, this practice can be freely combined with other options for strengthening the security of the backend, and it almost never hurts.

Disadvantages of this option: we still have some key on the server/in the settings, but this can not be avoided with other options.

Do Not Store the Key in the Backend Database at All Option 1: It is a good practice to divide the logic of working with the private key and working directly with the rest of the backend into two indirectly dependent components. Since in the current stages and architectures, the backend is already essentially multi-component (scanners, receivers, deferred tasks, web handler), it will not be difficult to make another microservice that would work directly with keys and their receipt/issuance, and keep the rest of the logic in the main part of the backend.

- Such a service should be separated from the backend, but it can be located as a separate subservice in the Docker-Compose backend, or it can be put in a separate application running on its own, perhaps even on a separate server;
- Such a service must communicate with bacon necessarily with encryption, but it can be either an HTTP or a RabbitMQ channel;
- Such a service must have verification of everything that comes to it for the correctness of the sender. The API key or the secret message being transmitted. Perhaps even one-time, according to this scheme:
  1. The main backend requests a secret message from the private backend;
  2. receives the message and encodes it in a certain way;
  3. sends the encoded and initial message to the private backend;
  4. private backend will check whether it is encoded correctly and if everything is in order will give the private key.

Option 2

This option is more suitable for networks similar to the Ethereum network. And for networks like Binance Chain, it is not quite suitable. The idea is that the main backend does not sign anything at all, which means that it will not need private keys. The very same transaction signature would occur on a separate backend/service that accepts the signature parameters, and gives the already signed message:

- The main backend sends parameters to the signature backend;
- The signature backend signs the transaction and gives it to the main backend.
- Such a service must have verification of everything that comes to it for the correctness of the sender. The API key or the secret message being transmitted. Perhaps even one-time, according to this scheme

The provisions on API keys and encrypted requests from the previous version also apply here.

Keep Private Keys Normally, if Everything Else Is Secure. Necessary to understand that to achieve perfection in not storing private keys at all is a little possible technique, but no methods will save you if you make everything super-secure, but forget any obvious thing that will put everything in question. It is impossible to get a black box that will save all the private keys, because we need to get them back. Anyway, the level of security should be not only in the logic of the backend, but also in everything around it. There are many points here, but the main ones are:

1. Web Server Security:
   - Imperative HTTPS;
   - Imperative firewall, with only port 443 open to the outside, not counting SSH;
   - Strict request policy (e.g. Fail2ban and other request limits);
   - Proxy servers, Cloudflare - required. If the main server is flooded with HTTP Bandwidth attack or DDoS-obviously everything will fall, and no one knows how to use it;
   - Perhaps you should consider Heroku/Kubernetes/Docker Swarm in order to make the so-called scalability for the backend and reduce the number of fail-places (as, for example, only one backend instance).
2. Security of the server:
   - Imperative firewall again;
   - SSH connection ports can be reassigned and it is a good practice to use it. Obviously, half of the Internet uses port 22, why not put another one?
   - Access to the server is NOT by password. The RSA and ECDSA algorithms exist for a reason, and this also needs to be used. No one will get in without a key, unless you will approve it.

Security Implementation. After studying all the above methods and options for protecting private keys, it was decided to implement a combined solution that would contain the maximum number of the listed protection methods.

6 Analysis of the Results Obtained

Comparing the resulting solution with similar projects:

	Wish swap	PolkaSwap	Panama bridge
Security	Yes	No	Yes
Implementation	Yes	In future	Yes
Versatility	No	Yes	No
Scalability	Yes	Yes	No
Fees	100 WWish or 5 Wish/BWish	0.3%	0.001 BNB

For greater clarity, Fig. 2 shows histograms that display quantitative estimates of the performance of the compared services.

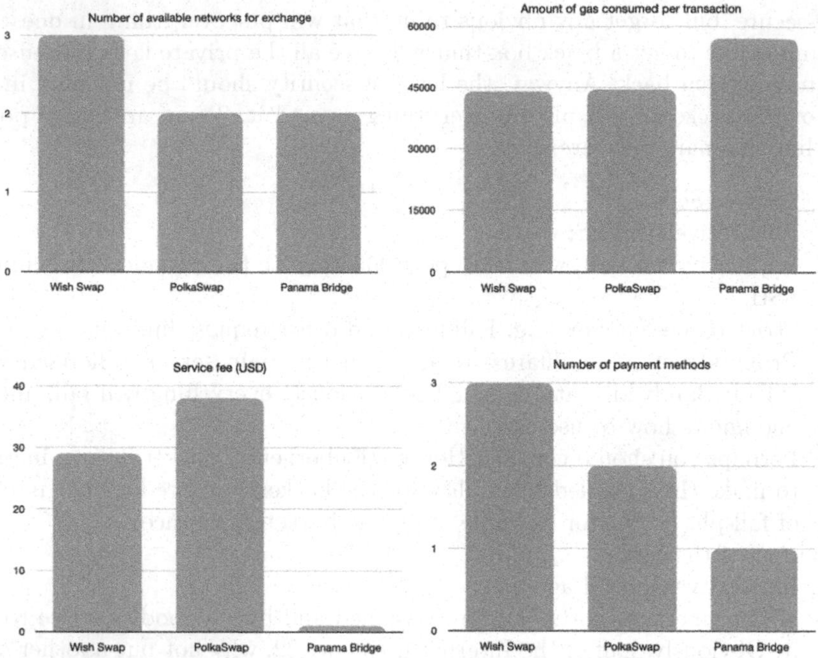

Fig. 2. Comparison wish swap with other projects.

Finally it is clear that our solution meets the security requirements, and also has prospects for development when adding new blockchains, such as, for example, Tron, Neo, Waves, and others.

7 Conclusion

A few years ago, the transfer of tokens and any other information from one network to another was absolutely not possible. However, today, we have proved from our experience that in this direction it is possible and necessary to build useful and completely secure solutions to provide users with as much freedom as possible and remove all possible boundaries in the use of blockchain technology.

The service is planned to be developed further by connecting more and more new networks.

References

1. Zetzsche, D.A., Arner, D.W., Buckley, R.P.: Blockchain disruption and decentralized finance: the rise of decentralized business models. J. Financ. Regul. **6**(2), 172–203 (2020)
2. Ethereum [Electronic resource]. https://ethereum.org (date of the application: 11.03.2021)

3. Binance [Electronic resource]. https://docs.binance.org (date of the application: 11.03.2021)
4. Matic [Electronic resource]. https://matic.network/ (date of the application: 11.03.2021)
5. Polkadot [Electronic resource]. https://wiki.polkadot.network/docs (date of the application: 11.03.2021)
6. Stewart, A., Kokoris-Kogia, E.: GRANDPA: a Byzantie finality gadget (2020)
7. Official Binance Panama Bridge Webpage. https://www.binance.org/en/bridge (date of the application: 11.03.2021)
8. Wish BEP2 Token [Electronic resource]. https://explorer.binance.org/asset/WISH-2D5 (date of the application: 11.03.2021)
9. The definition of BEP2 token standard by Binance Academy [Electronic resource]. https://academy.binance.com/en/glossary/bep-2 (date of the application: 11.03.2021)
10. Etherscan (Ethereum Explorer) [Electronic resource]. https://etherscan.io/ (date of the application: 11.03.2021)
11. BscScan (Binance Smart Chain Explorer) [Electronic resource]. https://bscscan.com/ (date of the application: 11.03.2021)

Evaluation of the Neo P2P Blockchain Network Protocol Efficiency

Anna Shaleva and Vladimir Korkhov(✉)

Saint Petersburg State University, St. Petersburg, Russia
st050450@student.spbu.ru, v.korkhov@spbu.ru

Abstract. P2P networks along with the other distributed systems need to satisfy the strict requirement of efficiency in terms of the information propagation process. Fast message transmission affects the whole network functionality which includes data processing, attacks robustness, topology changes, etc. In this paper we consider the most wide-spread gossip-based network protocols, explore and compare several approaches to improve the information dissemination model. We describe the Neo blockchain network protocol which extends gossip algorithms for message propagation over the P2P network. Based on the imitation modelling results, we build a network protocol model of the Neo blockchain and evaluate the Neo network protocol efficiency in terms of reactive message processing in several scenarios, propose protocol enhancements and evaluate resulting performance gain.

Keywords: Gossip protocol · P2P network · Blockchain

1 Introduction

Distributed peer-to-peer systems offer a trustful, scalable and powerful alternative to the traditional client-server architecture. This model assumes that end-users act both like a client and server, sharing resources in a peer style. The P2P approach is devoid the central server failures and performance bottleneck as far as the load balancing issues. However, building efficient, scalable and cheap P2P application level protocol still represents a non-trivial task. At the current moment, the most effective and reliable solution to design P2P protocols for information dissemination in a large dynamic systems is epidemic algorithms. These algorithms are based on the idea of contagious disease spreading and used in a variety set of purposes from distributed systems monitoring to the usage in blockchain broadcasting protocols.

One of the crucial factors for P2P distributed networks functioning which affects the network efficiency is the delay during network messages propagation [7]. This includes message processing delays as far as delays during message broadcasting. Delays have a direct impact on the frame non-delivery probability [5] which is the key performance measure in the distributed P2P networks.

O. Gervasi et al. (Eds.): ICCSA 2021, LNCS 12952, pp. 56–71, 2021.
https://doi.org/10.1007/978-3-030-86973-1_5

Another vital issue is a problem of flooding network with network-wide broadcast messages [5] or the problem of a high traffic load. A plenty of synchronisation-related information in the network results in a low bandwidth protocol utilization efficiency which may slow down the data processing. Consider the case of blockhain networks, where producing a large number of duplicated messages increases block-acceptance time which directly affects transaction processing delays.

Motivation. Epidemic algorithms are widely explored for the case of trustful environments. However assuming that peers may behave arbitrary makes a large part of well-studied algorithms inapplicable which is the case of blockchain networks. Consider the case of blockchain systems, while consensus protocols efficiency and reliability receives a lot of attention, the performance and scalability of broadcast network protocols remain poorly explored. However, the efficiency, fairness and cost of the network protocol directly affects not only the key metrics described above, but also the consensus algorithm operation and even the functionality of the whole blockchain network. In this article we study the main features of the gossip broadcast algorithm which affect the efficiency of the network protocol, and try to improve them.

Paper Outline. Section 2 contains a brief introduction to the gossip-family algorithms classification and several known theoretical results for algorithms complexity and performance related to the subject of study. In Sect. 3 we describe the network protocol used in the Neo blockchain and propose an assumption on the ways it may be improved. Section 4 summarizes several papers related to the push-gossip imitation algorithm modelling. Based on these works we propose an enhanced model of the Neo network protocol which reflects the aspects needed to analyze the protocol efficiency. Section 5 contains the modelling results for both original and enhanced protocols and points out the original protocol weaknesses as far as the enhanced protocol advantages. Based on the modelling information we evaluate the enhanced Neo network protocol efficiency for scenario of blocks propagation over the network. The analysis includes comparing delays during specified message propagation and evaluation of the network bandwidth utilisation used to keep all the participants in sync. We use the data collected to propose several fields for further research in Sect. 6.

2 Related Work

Gossip-based algorithms are well-known and widely explored field of study. One of the most recent works that summarizes known theoretical results for different gossip-based protocols is described in [1]. The study investigates a knowledge-based approach to the gossip problem in a multi-agent system and results in a reach epistemic gossip protocols theoretical basis. Need to mention that gossip algorithms are highly reliable in a probabilistic sense. Paper [7] briefly summarizes known mathematical evaluations of basic gossiping models which includes probability of atomic infection, proportion of infected process and latency of infection evaluation.

A wide set of approaches for gossip algorithms optimisation can be analyzed. Our study is inspired by the ideas presented in [3–5]. Paper [5] proposes a novel protocol for real-time N-to-N group communication achieving a considerably lower traffic load with higher performance gain in networks with smaller delays. Paper [3] describes simulation model for push-gossip protocol efficiency evaluation. Based on the modelling results the optimal number of peers the current peer should forward the message to (also known as $fan - out$) is calculated as a function of the number of nodes in the network. Paper [4] proposes a robust and fast protocol for weakly-consistent knowledge of process group membership information at all participating processes.

Consider the case of untrustful environment and, more specifically, blockchain networks, the performance and scalability of broadcast network protocols remain poorly explored. The inspiring study of the Hyperledger Fabric gossip layer is presented in [2], taking into account several significant features of messaging in an untrustful environment. However, the field of study still needs to be investigated, and one of the most significant reasons for that is presented below.

Aggregation Problem. Most of the gossip optimisation algorithms (e.g. ones presented in [2] and [3]) require local peer access to the global information about the network. This is a separate problem which is known as the task of aggregation [8] and refers to a set of functions providing access to such distributed system components as network size, average load and uptime, network map, etc. There is a set of existing approaches for gossip-based information aggregation over distributed P2P networks which can be divided into two groups. The first one uses epoch-based solution to calculate a global estimation from the initial set of predefined local values [8]. Network members are exchanging with the aggregated information by iterating over aggregation epochs; once the estimation converges system-wide, a new epoch is started with fresh initial values which makes the algorithm robust to the dynamic estimations aging. The other approach uses continuous epoch-less data aggregation [10] and considers the local measurements of the nodes in every round. This approach does not require initial measurements and performs aggregation and inter-node exchange rounds continuously.

However, these approaches rely on the information veracity and are not able to cope with Byzantine failures with nodes behaving arbitrarily [8]. Thus, some extra assumptions and constraints are needed to apply these algorithms in untrustful distributed systems. One of the ways to handle this problem is malicious nodes detecting [9] and excluding their data from the aggregation service results. However, this issue is outside of the paper scope, but should be taken into account while applying mentioned algorithms in untrustful distributed systems.

3 Neo Network Protocol

Neo is an open-source community driven blockchain platform [12]. It was founded by Da Hongfei and Erik Zhang in 2014 under the name Antshares and then has grown into a first-class smart contract platform. The Neo blockchain is based on the dBFT consensus algorithm providing one block finality and broadcast network protocol based on the gossip model. In this section we describe the current implementation of the Neo blockchain epidemic network protocol. We also summarize the impact of the gossip protocol to a consensus protocol functionality and the whole network operation.

Gossip protocol is used in Neo for a set of purposes: building and maintaining local peer view on a network structure, consensus-related message exchange, new peers discovering, network metadata exchange (i.e. current chain height and etc.) and, finally, blocks, transactions and other payloads dissemination. In this study we mostly focus on the blocks propagation from the consensus service to all peers because the network protocol mechanism is almost the same for all payload messages.

3.1 Gossip Protocol Description

Consider the case of blocks propagation, the beginning of block dissemination process is the moment of block's appliance by the consensus service. Consensus nodes then receive, validate and store the block built by a consensus service and forward it to a set of connected peers. There are three main phases in the Neo gossip algorithm which define the rules of blocks propagation over network: *push*, *pull* and *recovery*. Below we describe these phases with focus on their strengths and weaknesses.

Push. Neo uses infect-and-die push model [7] in which peer tries to contaminate others for only one gossip round and then stops. Speaking more technically, the new block is firstly being put into the queue, validated and stored in a local database. And only after the new block is persisted to a local storage iterating over all peers with sending them the new block digest occurs. Current protocol implementation does not have $fan - out$ setting, instead peer either forward messages to all connected peers or does not forward at all. The number of peers to keep an open connection with can be configured by min_{peers} and max_{peers} settings. Thus, these settings directly affect not only the network connectivity level, but also the traffic load which can definitely be improved.

It should also be mentioned that Neo uses "Inv-GetData" model for all payload-related messages including blocks. It assumes that push phase has three steps: firstly, the payload hash (the short unique payload digest) is sent to a connected peer with the help of Inventory command which contains the hash (or hashes). Then if the peer doesn't yet have the payload with the digest specified it responds with the GetData command containing the requested hashes. Finally, the peer that initiates dissemination forwards the payload itself. Such push model allows to avoid unacceptable communication overhead while passing heavy payloads, e.g. blocks, allowing to ensure that large payload messages will be passed only $n + o(n)$ times.

Pull. The pull phase is used by peers to receive the blocks they didn't receive during the push phase. At each time interval t_{ping} a peer sends Ping message containing current local chain's height to all its connected peers. The Pong response contains a connected peer's height, so if some of the peers are higher than the pull phase initiator, then the new blocks will be requested by the GetBlockByIndex command. A default t_{ping} interval is set to be 30 s. If the peer receives a new block via the pull request, it will be handled as described in the push phase (the Inventory command containing the block hash will be set to all connected peers after the block is successful persisted to a local storage).

Recovery. Peers use the recovery phase to restore the chain after a long out-of-sync period or for the first time they join the network. During this phase peers exchange meta information including the network magic and current chain's height and request batches of missing blocks by GetBlockByIndex command from those peers which have the latest chain state. This mechanism is running at the very beginning of the connection establishment and is similar to the pull phase. Consider the real stable network functioning, this phase does not affect blocks propagation latency, thus won't be taken into account.

3.2 Impact on the Network Operation

The network protocol described above has a large impact on the whole network operation process which can be described in two ways. Firstly, the protocol directly affects network bandwidth consumption level which is one of the key metrics for network efficiency evaluation. Heavy payloads and a lot of sync-related messages result in a high traffic load which creates load-balancing issues and contention. Moreover, a plenty of large payloads in the network results in a higher broadcast protocol operation cost.

Another vital aspect concerns the byzantine fault-tolerant consensus protocol. The dBFT consensus protocol Neo is operating on requires all consensus nodes to have the same set of transactions to accept a new block. Thus, one of the most priority task of the network protocol is to keep all the consensus nodes in sync. However, the consequence of a high network traffic load is a slow transaction dissemination process which leads to delays and timeouts in the consensus service, i.e. slower blocks producing.

While a lot of attention is payed to the consensus protocol performance improvements, the performance and scalability of the network protocol remain poorly explored. We have showed that the broadcast protocol directly affects overall blockchain network operation, so it's important to keep an eye on the efficiency and cost of the gossip protocol used for peers communication.

4 Enhanced Protocol

One of the main advantages of the Neo broadcast model is that all phases are decoupled from each other and can be modified independently. It also allows to completely resynchronize pull, push and recovery so that cheaper push operations can be run more frequently than expensive pulls.

From the other hand, the Neo push model has several significant drawbacks. Inability to tune f_{out} without affecting the network connectivity level results in an unwanted overhead of the network utilisation level. Infect-and-die algorithm has relatively low probability of delivering block to all peers, which also results in a high bandwidth consumption.

Considering the network aggregation problem and assuming the presence of malicious nodes in the network, the ways of protocol optimisation are desired to improve information dissemination process with the minimal membership maintenance and without an assumption on the underlying network structure.

4.1 Proposed Improvements

Based on the Neo protocol drawbacks described above along with the most effective ways to optimise the gossip protocol from related works, we propose several protocol enhancements described in the next subsections.

Introducing f_{out} Setting: Current Neo protocol scheme assumes that peer either transmits received blocks to all peers it's connected to or doesn't transmit blocks at all. Although maximum and minimum peers number can be configured for Neo node, it still lacks the f_{out} setting, i.e. the number of randomly selected peers the current peer should forward the message to. Missing f_{out} setting leads to network flooding with the sync-related messages for large max_{peers} values and a lack of connectivity resulting in a slower block processing for small max_{peers} values. At the same time, proposed f_{out} setting can have considerably lower value than the node's maximum connected peers constraint, which allows to vary network traffic load irrespective to the nodes connectivity rate. As shown in the [2], given a relatively small f_{out} it is possible to provide the desired level of frame non-delivery probability for a fixed number of gossip rounds. This improvement allows to decrease the traffic utilisation level keeping probabilistic reliable frame non-delivery rate at the low level.

Randomisation of the Source Gossiper: According to the Neo consensus protocol, blocks produced by consensus service are firstly passed to nodes picked from the standby committee list which has quite a limited capacity. These leader nodes are those who start the dissemination, thus their network utilisation is up to max_{peers} times higher then that of regular peers. To smooth this difference out, we'll set $f_{out}^{leader} = 1$. We expect this improvement to distribute the initial dissemination load over all regular peers.

Using Infect-Forever Model for the Push-Phase: Neo protocol currently uses infect-and-die model for the push-phase of the gossip algorithm. We propose to replace it with the infect-forever model [6] modified to use a stop condition. It assumes that peers forward blocks whenever they receive them until the stop condition is satisfied. To implement the stop condition, the counter r initialized to 0 is attached to each new block. For the first time peer receives this block, it increments the counter and continues block transmission with the incremented counter in a standard way. When the peer receives the same block next time, it just forwards the block to f_{out} peers selected randomly from a set of the connected peers. Dissemination of the block stops when r reaches preconfigured time-to-live TTL value which is the same for all peers in the network. This improvement is highly dependant on the f_{out} parameter and in combination with f_{out} is expected to balance load between peers initiating gossip rounds and the others.

To summarize, the proposed improvements are presented in Table 1.

4.2 Choosing the Parameters

Given a fixed probability of imperfect dissemination p_e, i.e. the probability that block does not reach all peers during the push phase, depends on n, f_{out} and TTL, these parameters can be calculated very precisely. According to estimations for p_e, n, f_{out} and TTL presented in the [2], for our experiments with $n = 100$ peers and target $p_e = 10^{-6}$ we set up a configuration with $f_{out} = \lfloor \ln(n) \rfloor = 4$ and $TTL = 9$.

Table 1. Proposed protocol improvements.

Improvement	Explanation	Effect
Introducing f_{out} setting	Transmitting messages to a predefined number of peers instead of sending it to all the connected peers	Ability to control network bandwidth consumption and decrease the number of messages in the network
Randomisation of the source gossiper	Restrict $f_{out}^{leader} = 1$ to randomise peer initiating gossip round	Alleviation of the leader peers traffic burden
Using infect-forever model for the push-phase	Forward blocks whenever they are received until the stop condition is met	Load balancing over all peers in the network

5 Experiments and Evaluation

We evaluate proposed NeoGo gossip module improvements and compare the results with the original version of module implementation. Inspired by the [2] we are mostly focusing our evaluation on the three key metrics described above: block non-delivery probability, blocks propagation latency and traffic load (also called the bandwidth utilisation) and how these metrics correlate with each other.

5.1 Setups

As many other Neo projects, NeoGo currently is on its way to Neo 3.0 - the next evolution of the blockchain with new architecture, native contracts, and an improved economic model. While developing is continuing, it's important to reveal places to be improved and optimized, thus we use latest intermediate Neo3 release of NeoGo v0.91.0 for experiments and evaluation.

We base our experiment environment on the NeoBench [11] - an open-source benchmark tool for Neo nodes stress testing. We set up a network of 101 peers where one peer is an RPC node accepting transactions from the client, four peers are consensus nodes building and approving blocks, and the rest of peers are regular nodes storing blocks and disseminating network messages. All nodes are deployed on a cluster equipped with 2 x Intel® Xeon® CPU E5-2690 v4 at 2.60 GHz and 256 GB of RAM and running inside Docker containers sharing the same proportion of CPU cycles and grouped into the network. Benchmark tool with an RPC client concurrently sending pre-generated transactions to the RPC node and gathering statistics is running inside a separate Docker container.

As a default node setup for each experiment we use blocks dump moving all NEO and almost all GAS tokens from default multisignature account to a simple one. We use the following network configuration settings for the experiments: each block contains 50 transactions at max, the interval which should pass between two successive blocks equals 2 s. For each experiment we generate and concurrently push to the network 50,000 transactions, each of them transfers one NEO from the simple account back to the same account. As a result, a full block containing 50 transactions is created about every 2 s which results in 1,000 blocks of 4320 byte per block.

5.2 Original Protocol Evaluation

To compare proposed protocol improvements with the current implementation, we firstly have tested the original NeoGo protocol with the $max_{peers} = 10$ for each node. This value is considered to be optimal for the experimental network of 100 peers because too large values lead to the network flooding with synchronisation-related messages and traffic wasting; too small values are impractical for real networks due to the lack of connectivity between peers.

Figure 1 shows the latency at the peer level (LPL) by measuring the time peer takes to receive each block starting from the beginning of its dissemination. The start time is defined by the moment when block is received by one of the consensus nodes from the consensus service. Thin lines correspond to peers; colored markers highlight the slowest, the fastest and median peers, i.e. peers received all the blocks with highest/lowest/median overall latency respectively. Figure 2 illustrates the latency at the block level (LBL) by showing how much time block takes to reach each peer starting from the beginning of block's dissemination defined by the same value as the one calculated for LPL. Each thin lines corresponds to a separate block; the slowest, fastest and median blocks are highlighted with colored markers, where the block delivered to all the peers with the highest latency considered to be slowest and vice versa. Both figures are probability plots and shown in a logarithmic scale based on logistic distribution for OY axis for better tails latency focusing.

From Fig. 1 we can say that about 94% of the blocks were delivered to peers for less than 2 s after the beginning. However, things get more interesting at the upper part of the plot where some peers take up to 160 s to receive the rest 6% of the blocks. Likely, these are the most remote from the consensus nodes peers which use pull-phase of the gossip algorithm to fetch missing blocks. The similar summary can be drawn from the block-level latency analysis of the Fig. 2. Up to 65% of all peers have insignificant latency during blocks receiving, but a set of the slowest blocks takes quite a long time (up to 160 s) to reach the rest 35% of all peers. That is the first field for the future research: try to make the block dissemination process more uniform and accelerate transmission of the backward blocks.

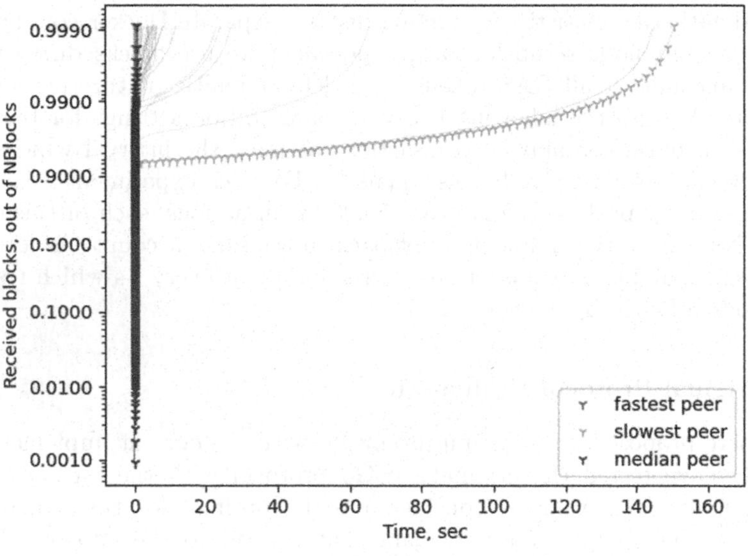

Fig. 1. Latency at the peer level using the original gossip module of NeoGo.

Figure 3 illustrates the network traffic load not only throughout the whole experiment, but also a few moments before and after it. That's done to compare the network utilisation in the ideal state with the overloaded one. Two lines correspond with the average consensus and regular peers bandwidth consumption measured by the size of sent messages per second. For readability purposes the bandwidth consumption was gathered only for blocks-related messages with an interval of 10 s. The benchmark service has started pushing transactions to the network since $\approx$ 400 s from the start and ends after $\approx$ 2400 s from the start. Thus, the figure shows significantly low block-related traffic load $\approx$ 0.7 KB/s for

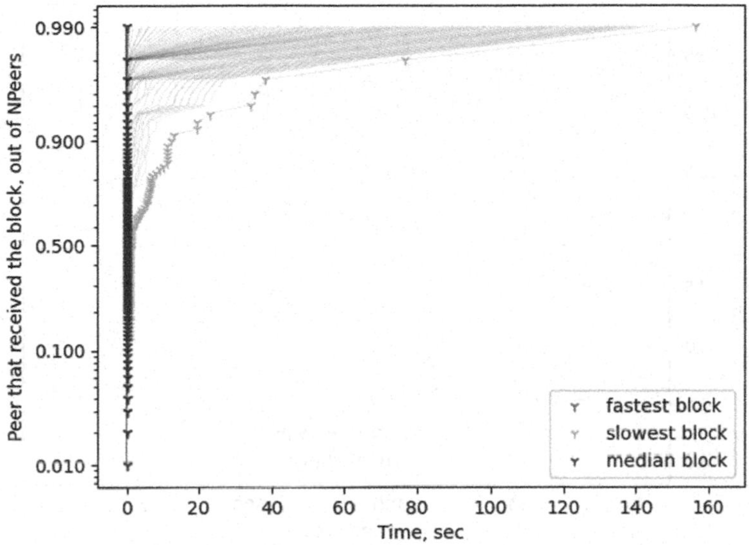

Fig. 2. Latency at the block level using the original gossip module of NeoGo.

regular peers and ≈ 2.7 KB/s for consensus peers when the network is in an ideal state during empty blocks processing. During the experiment average consensus peer bandwidth consumption oscillates from 15 to 18 KB/s which is about 6 times higher than the network load of the regular peer. It occurs because once the consensus node receives a new block from the consensus module, it transmits the block to all connected peers while regular nodes follow infect-and-die dissemination scheme. Such a considerable difference illustrates an importance of gossip-based protocols bandwidth consumption optimisation, which is the other field for optimisation-related research. It includes decreasing the number of messages in the network and balancing the network bandwidth load.

5.3 Proposed Changes Efficiency Evaluation

We tested the performance of the improved protocol and compared it to the original results. Each of the proposed improvements was tested separately as far as the combination of the infect-forever model for the push phase and introducing f_{out} parameter (as mentioned in Sect. 4.2, these settings are highly connected).

Firstly, the protocol with $f_{out}^{leader} = 1$ improvement was evaluated. Figures 4, 5 and 6 respectively show the latency at the peer level, latency at the block level and bandwidth consumption for the enhanced protocol. While the original protocol takes up to 160 s to deliver last 6% of blocks to all peers, the proposed improvement shows twice times better result for LPL metric (Fig. 4) and takes ≈ 74 s to disseminate 3% of the slowest blocks to all peers while the rest 97% of blocks are delivered for less than two seconds. As for the bandwidth utilisation, significant improvement was reached for the consensus peers traffic load

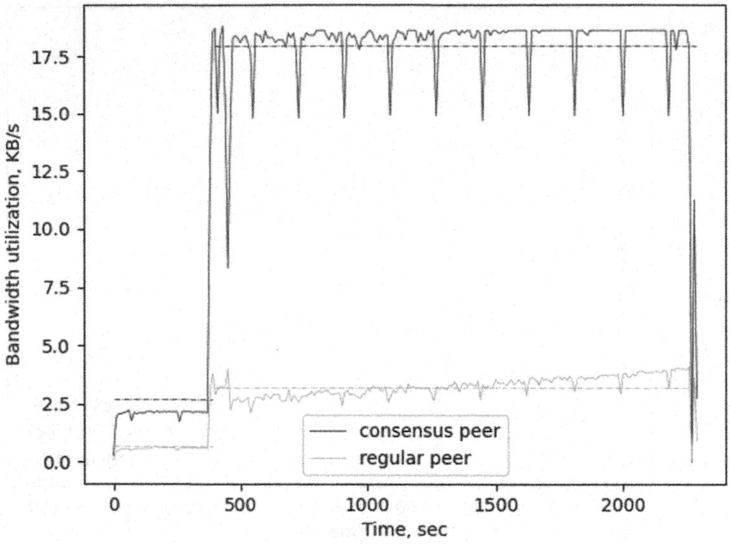

Fig. 3. Bandwidth utilisation using the original gossip module of NeoGo.

shown in Fig. 6 which is decreased by more than 80% and is even lower than the regular peers bandwidth consumption. At the same time, network utilisation of the regular peers remains almost the same as with the original protocol and oscillates around 2.7 KB/s value. We expect this improvement to become more significant with larger block size, as blocks-related traffic predominates over other sync-related messages.

We evaluated the performance gain of introducing f_{out} parameter and infect-forever model for the push phase applied separately. However, the results of these experiments are quite controversial. Applying the $f_{out} = 4$ setting allows to decrease both consensus and regular peers average bandwidth utilisation to ≈ 16.3 and 2.3 KB/s respectively which is about 9% and 28% lower than the reference values. At the same time, maximum latency at both peer and block level was decreased by less then 30 s from 162 to 138 s while median latency remains almost the same. Experiment with infect-forever model for the push phase with $TTL = 9$ didn't show the substantial LPL and LBL efficiency gain. Moreover, without proper f_{out} setting this improvement significantly increases average network traffic utilisation, so that f_{out} limitation expected to compensate this effect.

Finally, we tested the enhanced protocol with combination of $f_{out} = 4$ and $TTL = 9$ settings. Figures 7 and 8 are LPL and LBL plots respectively. The enhanced protocol allows to reach significant median latency decrease from 1.13 to 0.47 s for peer-level latency and from 0.19 to 0.15 s for block-level latency which is even better than source gossiper randomisation shows. At the same time, average network traffic utilisation was decreased down to 11.3 and 2.7 KB/s for consensus and regular peers respectively, which is effectively $\approx 36\%$ and 15%

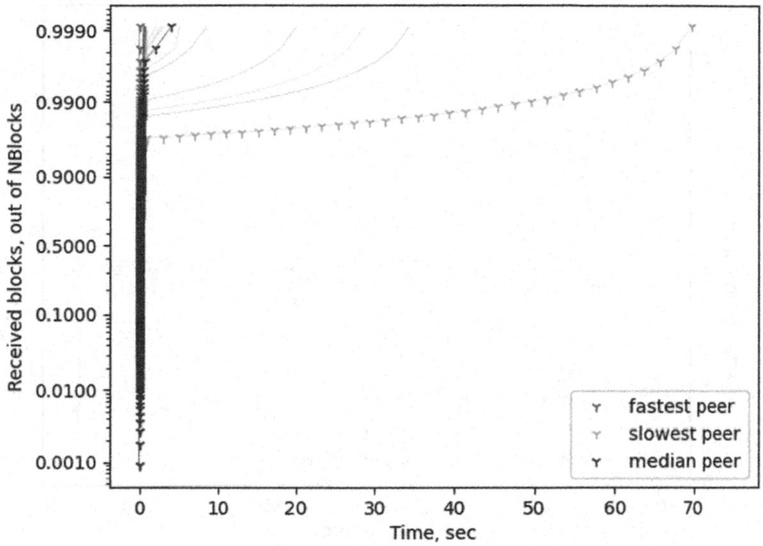

Fig. 4. Latency at the peer level using NeoGo module with the source gossiper randomisation.

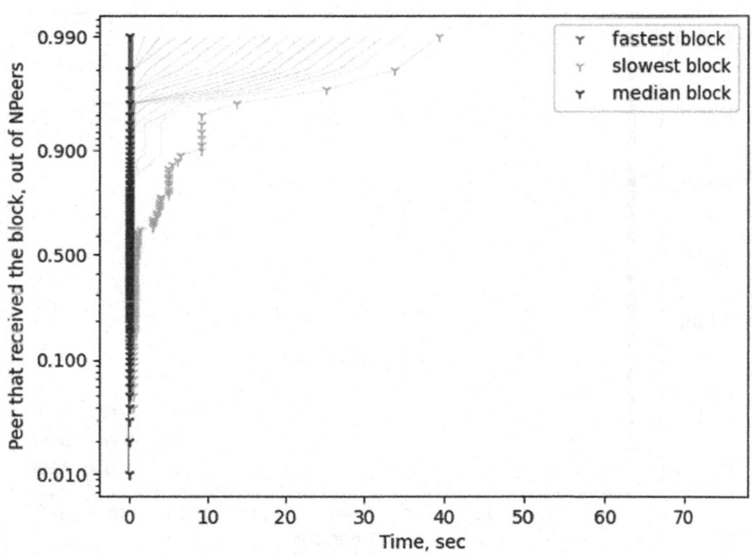

Fig. 5. Latency at the block level using NeoGo module with the source gossiper randomisation.

lower than the reference values. So the combination of the infect-forever model for the push phase and introducing f_{out} parameter results in a more uniform network traffic distribution over the set of regular peers and noticeably lower bandwidth utilisation by the consensus peers (Fig. 9).

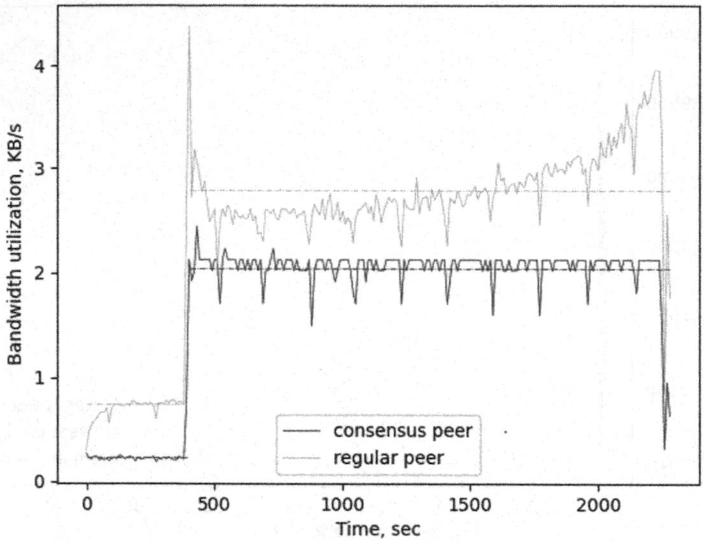

Fig. 6. Bandwidth utilisation using NeoGo module with the source gossiper randomisation.

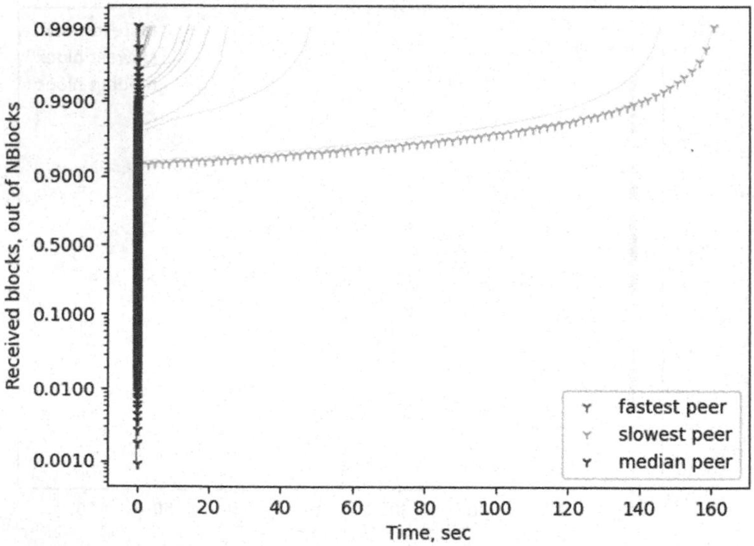

Fig. 7. Latency at the peer level using NeoGo module with $f_{out} = 4$ and $TTL = 9$.

Although the efficiency gain obtained from the last experiment is not such substantial as the one got from the initial gossiper randomisation enhancement, it still perfectly balances network traffic load between regular and consensus peers and reduces median block-level and peer-level latency. Thus, set of protocol enhancements considered in the work, should be combined together to achieve better efficiency improvement in both terms of message delivery latency and bandwidth utilisation balancing.

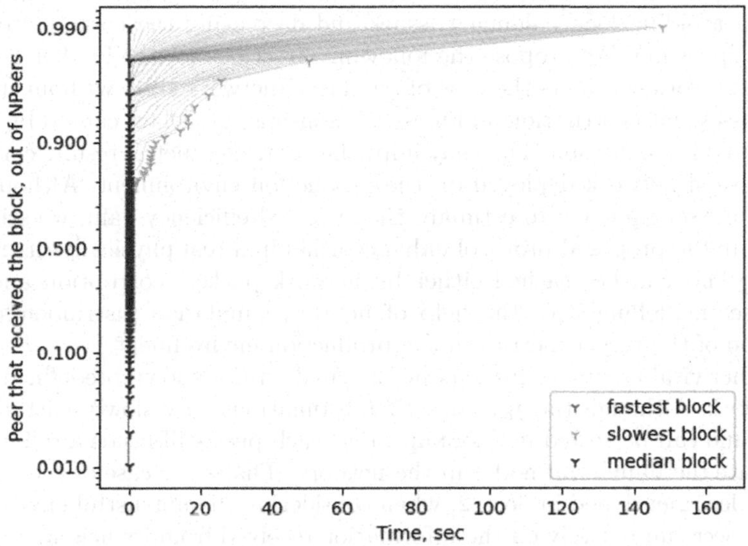

Fig. 8. Latency at the block level using NeoGo module with $f_{out} = 4$ and $TTL = 9$.

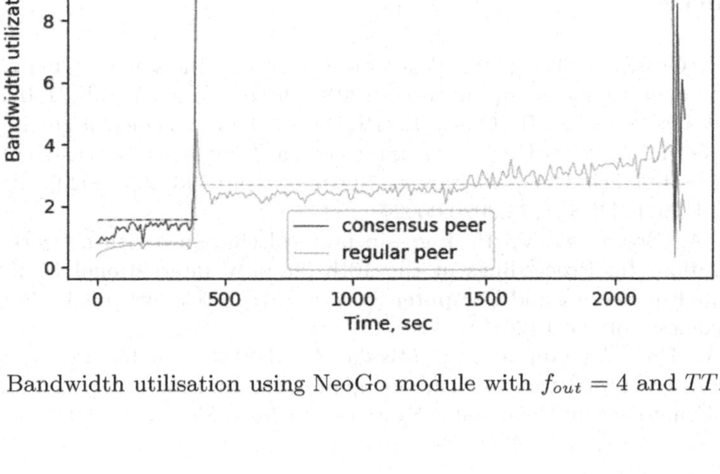

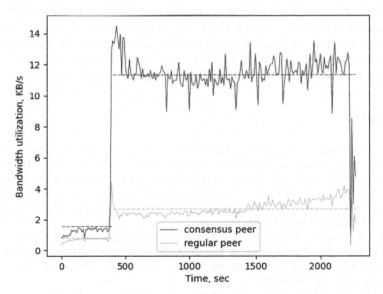

Fig. 9. Bandwidth utilisation using NeoGo module with $f_{out} = 4$ and $TTL = 9$.

6 Conclusion and Future Work

In this work, we enhanced the Neo gossip layer. Decreasing its latency allowed to maintain a reliable basis for consensus protocol functioning. The enhanced protocol also shows significant network bandwidth consumption improvement which results in avoiding load-balancing issues and decreasing the cost of broadcast protocol operation. We propose the following directions for the further research.

Current work considers the case of an "ideal" network state without network packet losses, data corruption and message transmission delays caused by imperfect inter-node connection. This may imply better target metric results compared to the case of network deployed on the production environment. Although the experiments set up allow to estimate the expected efficiency gain, we still need to evaluate the proposed protocol enhancements in a real physically-distributed network. This can be reached either by network packets corruption and message losses modelling with the help of network simulation instruments or by evaluation of the target metrics in the production environment.

Another vital assumption the paper is based on is a known predefined size of the network. Although the f_{out} and TTL estimations vary slowly with number of peers and can be stored in a lookup table, each peer still needs a reliable way to estimate the number of nodes in the network. That's the case of the aggregation problem mentioned in Sect. 2, when considering the untrustful environment factor, a peer can not rely on the information received from its neighbours, thus standard aggregation algorithms are not applicable.

Finally, we did not consider malicious nodes trying, for instance, to inhibit the dissemination process by dropping blocks received from the other peers. The enhancements robustness to such behavior still needs to be evaluated, although given relatively low probability of imperfect dissemination, it shouldn't be a problem for the proposed algorithms to cope with adversarial peers. So the impact analysis and possible countermeasures are to be investigated.

References

1. Apt, K., Grossi, D., Hoek, W.: When are two gossips the same? Types of communication in epistemic gossip protocols (2018). http://arxiv.org/abs/1807.05283
2. Berendea, N., Mercier, H., Onica, E., Riviere, E.: Fair and efficient gossip in hyperledger fabric. In: 2020 IEEE 40th International Conference on Distributed Computing Systems (ICDCS), Singapore, Singapore, pp. 190–200 (2020). https://doi.org/10.1109/ICDCS47774.2020.00027
3. Vanin, A., Bogatyrev, V.: Push-gossip protocol efficiency with network topology propagation. In: Proceedings of the 10th Majorov International Conference on Software Engineering and Computer Systems (MICSECS-2018), CEUR Workshop Proceedings, vol. 2344 (2019)
4. Das, A., Das, A., Gupta, I., Motivala, A.: SWIM: scalable weakly-consistent infection-style process group membership protocol. In: Proceedings of 2002 International Conference on Dependable Systems and Networks (DSN 2002), pp. 303–312 (2002)

5. Luk, V.W.H., Wong, A.K.S., Lea, C.T. et al.: RRG: redundancy reduced gossip protocol for real-time N-to-N dynamic group communication. J Internet Serv. Appl. **4**, 14 (2013). https://doi.org/10.1186/1869-0238-4-14
6. Koldehofe, B.: Simple gossiping with balls and bins. Studia Informatica Universalis. **3**, 43–60 (2004)
7. Eugster, P.T., Guerraoui, R., Kermarrec, A., Massoulie, L.: Epidemic information dissemination in distributed systems. Computer **37**(5), 60–67 (2004). https://doi.org/10.1109/MC.2004.1297243
8. Jelasity, M., Montresor, A., Babaoglu, 0.: Gossip-based aggregation in large dynamic networks. ACM Trans. Comput. Syst. **23**(3), 219–252 (2005). https://doi.org/10.1145/1082469.1082470
9. Jelasity, M., Montresor, A., Babaoglu, O.: Detection and removal of malicious peers in gossip-based protocols. S.O.S., Bertinoro, Italy, InFuDiCo II (2004)
10. Rapp V., Graffi K.: Continuous gossip-based aggregation through dynamic information aging. In: 22nd International Conference on Computer Communication and Networks (ICCCN), pp. 1–7 (2013). https://doi.org/10.1109/ICCCN.2013.6614118
11. NeoBench. https://github.com/nspcc-dev/neo-bench
12. Neo blockchain platform. https://neo.org/

General Track 6: Urban and Regional Planning

Spatial Automated Valuation Model (sAVM) – From the Notion of Space to the Design of an Evaluation Tool

João Lourenço Marques[1(✉)], Paulo Batista[1], Eduardo Anselmo Castro[1], and Arnab Bhattacharjee[2]

[1] GOVCOPP, Department of Social, Political and Territorial Sciences, University of Aveiro, Campus Universitário de Santiago, Aveiro, Portugal
jjmarques@ua.pt
[2] Heriot-Watt University, Edinburgh, UK

Abstract. Assuming that it is not possible to detach a dwelling from its location, this article highlights the relevance of space in the context of housing market analysis and the challenge of capturing the key elements of spatial structure in an automated valuation model: location attributes, heterogeneity, dependence and scale. Thus, the aim is to present a spatial automated valuation model (sAVM) prototype, which uses spatial econometric models to determine the value of a residential property, based on identification of eight housing characteristics (seven are physical attributes of a dwelling, and one is its location; once this spatial data is known, dozens of new variables are automatically associated with the model, producing new and valuable information to estimate the price of a housing unit). This prototype was developed in a successful cooperation between an academic institution (University of Aveiro) and a business company (PrimeYield SA), resulting the Prime AVM & Analytics product/service. This collaboration has provided an opportunity to materialize some of fundamental knowledge and research produced in the field of spatial econometric models over the last 15 years into decision support tools.

Keywords: Spatial automated valuation model · Housing market analysis · Spatial econometric models

1 Introduction

Housing can be understood in the strict sense as "… *the stock of houses, apartments, and other shelters that provide the usual residences of persons, families, and households*" [1], but could be more than that. More generally it is: i) a physical facility unit, used and appropriate by an individual or household; ii) a social or collective good that works as a public policy mechanism of social inclusion; iii) a package of services, since one of the fundamental characteristics of a dwelling is its location and in turn all the urban amenities that are located in the neighbourhood; and iv) an economic good, subject to market mechanisms in which there is supply and demand [2]. For these reasons, housing,

O. Gervasi et al. (Eds.): ICCSA 2021, LNCS 12952, pp. 75–90, 2021.
https://doi.org/10.1007/978-3-030-86973-1_6

or more broadly the housing market, plays a central role in modern societies, being closely related to the socio-economic system, to the quality of life of each individual and to the structure of the territory [3, 4]. Housing is a commodity in the usual sense but has some distinguishing features that separate it from other commodity markets [1, 2, 5]. It is characterized by: i) being heterogeneous, in terms of the typology of construction, infrastructure and accessibility; ii) being rigid, since it is a fixed asset in space and has long durability; iii) providing shelter, security and well-being; iv) being an instrument of social distinction, associated with the status image; and v) involving massive collective and private investments [6, 7].

The multiplicity of agents involved in the process of urban transformation, and more precisely in the housing market, with different and contradictory objectives and needs, explains the complexity associated with market operations [8]. This complexity is also compounded by the volatility of exogenous factors that the housing market depends on and by the lack of transparency which results from scarce and asymmetrically distributed information among agents, as well as the inability to use it; this fact leads to a biased price formation mechanism and it is somewhat difficult to explain it rationally and explicitly. In short, it is necessary to provide more information, but most of all it must be better organized to be incorporated into different decision support models.

In order to overcome some of these challenges, particularly the lack of transparency in real estate valuation, automated valuation models (AVM) have been developed and used to more accurately assess the real value of a property. These tools produce objective estimates of market value, based on database and statistical methods, and are designed to perform the same function as manual appraisals (see [9, 10]. Despite some limitations stressed by several authors, essentially related to the unavailability of information, these computational tools are currently popular systems in property analyses [11, 12]. Since the spatial dimension is a determinant component in the estimation of the price of a dwelling (as will be argued in Sect. 3) and captures significant intangible information housing preferences, the aim of this article is to present a spatial automated valuation model (sAVM), which uses spatial econometric models and dozens of housing attributes to determine the value of a residential property. Thus, this article presents a sAVM prototype where the value of a housing unit is estimated (high level of accuracy) using a reduced number of attributes (eight).

In addition to the introduction, this article is organized in four more sections: the second section presents the challenges of having reliable information in the context of housing market analysis; in the third section the relevance and challenges in modelling the spatial component in the real estate market are emphasized; in section four the sAVM and the indicators (housing attributes) behind the spatial model of this prototype are presented; and section five provides conclusions.

2 Data and Information Required

An important consideration highlighted in the previous section is that housing is a heterogenous good that can be defined by a bundle of characteristics, both locational and physical, and that vary in space and also in time. Thus, the availability of reliable and relevant housing data which allows an appropriate analysis on the complexities of the urban housing theme is a central question to monitoring and forecasting housing market dynamics.

In addition to the physical characteristics (intrinsic), the location and all the attributes associated to the spatial environmental are crucial dimensions in housing market analysis [8]. Each individual has specific interests, preferences and economic capabilities, and these thus tend be organized into a complex territorial pattern (heterogeneity) and relations (interactions and spillovers), which are sometimes not easily explained by simple geometric measures (see [7, 8, 13]).

Thus, one of the critical aspects for the success of housing market analysis is the capability to integrate location attributes that can influence the price of a dwelling directly (distances to any specific urban amenity) and indirectly (spatial heterogeneity and dependence). Advances in statistics and spatial econometrics provide valuable contributions to the analysis and understanding of spatial phenomena; however, the methods developed in theses scientific domains depend on the consistency and completeness of the initial information. If a close connection is not ensured between data source, methods and objectives, the results produced may be unreliable [14].

An empirical study of housing can include a multitude of aspects and, depending on the goals of the research, each set of housing attributes can assume different levels of importance; thus, a relevant and corresponding database should be used.

Depending on the purpose of the analysis, various types of data can be used, which can range over different level of spatial disaggregation. However, to take advantage of the potential of spatial econometric techniques, the level of detail of the geographical information must be adequate to capture the particularities of the territory in terms of housing preferences. At the micro scale level, in the particular case of Portugal, three different sources of housing data can be used. First, and the most commonly used, is statistical information provided by the National Institute of Statistics (INE) and the Local Tax on Real Estate database (IMI – Imposto Municipal sobre Imóveis). The former makes a wide range of indicators available on construction and housing in Portugal, while the latter is a database of the Ministry of Finance, in which detailed information of property attributes for all housing that has been traded on the market since 2004 is available. Despite the rich information provided, these data are confidential and the values of the prices shared have a tendency to be significantly below market – both buyer and seller have incentives to declare the minimum value for the transaction to avoid paying higher taxes. These disparities are adjusted by local expert committees, which assess the real price of the dwellings in loco. However, the quality of these adjustments is questionable because the homogeneity of appreciation is not guaranteed.

Real estate agencies are other possible data sources. These private institutions (individually or organized in a group) collect housing market data resulting from their business activity. One of the problems identified in these data sources is the level of territorial coverage. Since each agency has its own niche market, the information is partial and often unrepresentative of the market as a whole, both in sold or rented dwellings.

Another alternative is the data gathered by loan associations and mortgage banks. Some limitations are also to be found in this type of data: one is that housing values are truncated at maximum price, because of the upper limit on conventional mortgage lending amounts; and also properties transacted that are not subject to a mortgage are not included.

This non-exhaustive systematization of data sources that can be used in the context of housing market analysis to illustrate the difficulty in producing data on the real estate market; however, its importance to monitoring the market dynamics is absolutely crucial.

3 Spatial Analysis and Modelling

As mentioned before, the critical challenge for the success of housing market analysis is the ability to incorporate a set of location attributes able which are to explain housing price and capture the (in)tangible spatial elements (in)directly related to a dwelling.

Based on the seminal work of [16] and on revealed preference theory, the use hedonic models is a common approach to decomposing a heterogenous good, based on the idea that a specific good derives from its properties. In the context of housing, the properties are the characteristics, both physical (buildings and typological characteristics of the lot) or location (proximity effect to surrounding neighbourhoods and accessibility to goods and services) that can influence the price of a dwelling. As an dependent variable, we have the dwelling unit values (or proxies such as price or rents) that are regressed on a bundle of housing characteristics (independent variables) which are considered most relevant in the explanation of the house price value.

Despite the challenges in coupling territorial attributes in these models [17], as highlighted before, additional efforts are needed to incorporate this dimension into housing market analysis.

Hedonic pricing models, proposed by [18], allow the price of an item, in this case a house, to be decomposed into separate components that determine its unit values (P), or proxies such as price or rents. In the specific application of housing, the price of a dwelling is regressed on a bundle of characteristics (H) with their respective shadow prices (v), which are normally unknown. The following equation represents the hedonic model in a reduced form [19, 20]:

$$ln\mathrm{p} = f(\mathrm{H}, v) + \varepsilon \tag{1}$$

Housing attributes (H) can typically be organized in two groups: i) structural attributes or intrinsic characteristics and ii) location, neighbourhood attributes or extrinsic characteristics; ε is the vector of regression errors. As the spatial dimension is the focus of this article, we assume that the physical attributes are given by the real estate agencies and are representative of the main intrinsic characteristics.

The integration of spatial attributes faces important challenges [21, 22]. Apart from the choice of explanatory variables and functional specification of the model, the validity of the econometric estimation depends on restrictive assumptions that do not necessarily hold in a housing market context. Spatial homogeneity is a strong assumption in the hedonic housing price context, and if not analysed appropriately' it can be a potential source of specification errors (3).

From urban studies disciplines, a clear statement emerges that the assumption of (bi-dimensional) Euclidean geometric space is quite limited in capturing the abovementioned spatial complexity [3, 13]. Thus, the notion of space evolved from a concept of absolute space, defined by traditional notions of physical or geographical distances (exogenously given), to a relational space, in which space is socially produced by people – multi-dimensional non-Euclidean space (endogenously produced and spatially organized as a social product). While the former is a reductionist perspective, in which space is socially structured in terms of classes accurately defined (labour and capital), the former is a non-reductionist view of space, in which boundaries and interactions that occur in such space cannot be precisely defined or captured by multiple geometries [8, 23, 24].

Spatial analysis (and consequently, the analysis of the housing market), has been a fast development, and has made considerable efforts to contribute to understanding permanent urban transformations. However, there is still an unsatisfactory connection between spatial analysis and spatial theory, i.e. the conceptual assumptions to support the analytical mechanisms [25]. Theoretical contributions developed in geography, sociology or other social sciences (the "soft sciences"), reject statistical approaches on the grounds that they are incapable of coping with the complexity of the real world and provide misleading generalizations that do not reflect the uniqueness of places and interaction processes. On the other hand, spatial analysis/econometrics (the "hard sciences") are used to include the spatial components as a way to increase the efficiency of their models or to not violate any "sacrosanct" model assumption. Considerable effort has been expended in the spatial econometric field to overcome several statistical problems associated with non-stationarity, normality and homoscedasticity of the errors; however, rather less attention seems to have been paid to the role of these approaches in the interpretation of spatial structures [8]. A brief contextualization of the understanding of space in the urban studies literature (geography, economy and sociology) can be found in [3, 25].

In general, analyses of spatial structures (should) involve four distinctive but interdependent aspects: i) the definition and calculation of location attributes (influences and distances to different territorial amenities); ii) spatial heterogeneity (related to the structural differences between spatial units, regarding their characteristics), iii) spatial dependence (representing the spatial interactions across spatial units) and spatial scale (the territorial level where these phenomena occur); and iv) spatial scale (the level of granularity/disaggregation at which phenomena are described – type of the lens and zoom).

i) *(Proximity to) Location attributes*

Different geographical distances are identified in the literature to capture the explanatory variables of location (environmental and neighbourhood attributes; proximity to urban amenities; and public service characteristics [20, 26], which can contribute to a better capture of the housing value. For instance, [27] suggest three types of geographical distances: i) *global distances*, measured by counting the number of abstract units of length between two objects (kilometres); ii) *effort distances*, related to the effort that someone expends when moving from one point in space to another (travel time, monetary costs, or stress caused by traffic congestion, speed limits, or road quality); and iii) *metaphorical distances*, regarding the process of social cognition – meaning that two objects which are geographically close can be considered to be very distant.

For the location attributes, they can be defined combining the location of each house and the influence of different urban amenities. These geographic influences can be computed according to the classification and principles illustrated in Fig. 1: i) the intensity of use – which can vary from occasional to intensive; ii) the scale and level of influence – which can be local, resulting from the precise location of a dwelling, parishes or any other administrative boundary, or global, involving the influence of external factors; and iii) type of measurements – which can be nominal, measuring if it is under certain influences; ordinal, measuring the level of proximity; or scalar, measuring the proximity of the objects.

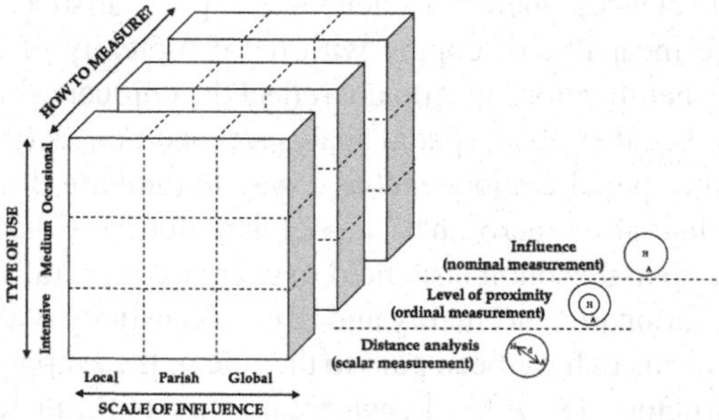

Fig. 1. Three dimensions to build location attributes H_L

It is possible to associate these perspectives, respectively, with Harvey's tripartite notion of absolute, relative and relational space [23], as shown in Table 1.

Table 1. Notions of space and types of distances

Notions of space	Type of distance (and space)
Bi-dimensional Euclidean space	Global distances (absolute space)
Multi-dimensional non-Euclidean space	Effort distances (relative space)
	Metaphorical distances (relational space)

ii) Locality – Spatial Heterogeneity

The relevance and the difficulty in defining submarkets (heterogeneity) is broadly discussed in the literature, as are methods to analyse this aspect of spatial structure [28–31]. Housing prices and attributes, the interests and the preferences of households are not expected to be constant over space. Thus, if not analysed appropriately, it may be a source of specification errors.

The definition of housing sub-market areas has also proved a difficult problem. Nevertheless, some common definitions of a housing sub-market can be found in the literature linked to the concept of substitutability. It comprises dwellings in which, independent of their location, share a set of characteristics that can be considered as substitutes for the potential purchasers. In line with this idea, [28, 29] pointed out that sub-markets are distinctive because houses within them are viewed (more or less) as perfect substitutes by the households. More recently, the same economic concept of substitution has been followed by many works [30, 32].

The early empirical works on sub-markets tended to be segmented into two perspectives, considering that a set of socio-economic and physical characteristics of the territory are acceptable criteria to define housing submarkets; those studies adopt: i) a supply side determinant, including structural and neighbourhood characteristics of dwellings [33], and ii) a focus on demand side determinants, based on household incomes or other demographic and socioeconomic characteristics [34, 35].

Conceptually, submarkets can be defined based on three major perspectives [30]: i) similarity in hedonic housing characteristics', when the submarket is characterized as a collection of locations, or housing units located therein, that have a similar bundle quality; ii) similarity in hedonic prices, when submarkets are characterized as locations where hedonic prices are homogeneous; iii) substitutability of housing units, when submarkets are defined by similarity in house prices. In which circumstance are these approaches equivalent? A comprehensive discussion of this issue is beyond the scope of this article, but it is possible to envisage situations where homogeneity in hedonic characteristics does not imply a close substitutability, for example, two locations with similar houses inhabited by two different social groups (however, different tastes and different responses to fashion are expected to generate a local branding effect in the medium term). Nevertheless, two locations with similar houses and hedonic prices must be good substitutes and it is very difficult to make a distinction between them. Therefore, similarity in hedonic prices and characteristics is a sufficient condition for substitutability, but it is not a necessary condition – for example, two houses with very different hedonic characteristics can be good substitutes: a flat in the centre or a house on the periphery.

There is substantial literature that presents appropriate methods for defining housing markets, following: i) an inductive perspective, in which pre-existing geographic administrative boundaries [36] or a subjective knowledge and expertise of the real estate agents [37] are assumed as a proxy of homogeneous units and used to define submarkets – these procedures are based on a priori judgement, and are subject to a posteriori validation; ii) a deductive and analytical perspective in which several statistical methods are applied, for instance, geographically weighted regression (GWR) [36] and functional data analysis (FDA) [30]. Examples of the use of the hedonic approach to identify space heterogeneity can be found in [39] (see Table 2).

Table 2. Notions of space and sub-markets

Notions of space	Approaches to define submarkets
Bi-dimensional Euclidean space	Inductive perspective (administrative boundaries and expert knowledge) and Deductive and perspective (statistical methods)
Multi-dimensional non-Euclidean space	

iii) Interaction – Spatial dependence

Spatial dependence (or interaction, or spillover, or externalities or spatial autocorrelation) is related to the level of mutual connection of two objects in space, i.e. it occurs when observations at a specific location *i* depend on other observations at a different location *j*. A major challenge here is how to describe the interaction between spatial units, or in other words, to know how individuals or sets of individuals interact. These principles of spatial dependence are closely related to Waldo Tobler's first law of geography, which states "everything is related to everything else, but nearer things are more related than distant things" [40]. But what is the meaning of "near" and what is the notion of space (absolute, relative or relational) on which we base our concept of neighbourhood?

Spatial econometric literature makes a major contribution in this context, describing the interactions between spatial units through a spatial weights matrix (W) [41]. Accordingly, spatial weights are closely related to distances and the challenge lies in the measurement of such distances. There are two distinctive philosophical perspectives in which spatial interaction can be modelled.

One of them largely follows the traditional assumption of an ad hoc predefined matrix W, using geometric distances, both spatial contiguity and geographic, to measure the weights (a deductive approach). Based on this assumed W, global tests for spatial autocorrelation (Moran's index and LISA indicator) and more specific tests of spatial autocorrelation, such as spatial error dependence (SED) and spatial lag dependence (SLD) are used [41].

An inductivist alternative is to move away from the usual practice of an ex-ante definition of spatial interactions, considering that the spatial weights matrix is unknown but can be estimated under some structural constraint (refs). These assumptions are necessary to fully identify W. From this inductive approach, a third challenge emerges, concerning the theoretical background which sustains the assumptions required for identification. Two main alternatives can be formulated:

i) the symmetrical (anti-symmetrical) assumption, considering that $I_{ij} = I_{ji}$ or $I_{ij} = -I_{ji}$, assuming that the phenomenon under analysis describes fluxes between pairs of places. The results are typically represented by topological pattern (e.g. neighbourhoods, graphs – such as communication networks, or space syntax, where the notion of symmetry (or anti-symmetry) can be assumed [3, 13].
ii) a hierarchical diffusion, where the focus is on understanding the spatial diffusion of a shock (e.g. spread of ideas, innovations, trends). The results are usually described

by the amount of "information" spread in the system. In this context, social networks principles suggest a system of hierarchical triangular relations as a plausible structural assumption [15] (see Table 3).

Table 3. Notions of space and sub-markets

Notions of space	Approaches to define spatial dependence
Bi-dimensional Euclidean space	A priori assumption of geographical distances (known weighting matrices)
Multi-dimensional non-Euclidean space	Distances determined by socio-economic relations (unknown weighting matrices)

iv) Scale

Definition of (housing) submarkets and spatial interactions is important and challenging at both conceptual and empirical levels. One of the difficulties in accurately capturing these two spatial features is the definition of the "right zoom" in which these phenomena occur, and consequently the availability of disaggregated data to analyse them [3, 13].

In line with some consideration of the previous theoretical background, the next section presents the model, both the specification and the dimensions, used in the context of the prototype sAVM PrimeYield – UA Tool.

4 sAVM PrimeYield – UA

The sAVM PRIMEYIELD-UA tool was developed to provide real estate property valuation using a spatial econometric model and a restricted number of housing attributes. This tool uses three different data sources: i) data accumulated by PrimeYield (www.prime-yield.com), derived from its real estate evaluation services; ii) statistical data from the National Statistical Institute of Portugal (Instituto Nacional de Estatística - https://www.ine.pt/); and the European Environmental Agency – Corine Land Cover (https://www.eea.europa.eu). More than 120 variables representing the main housing characteristics are used, divided into three main categories: i) physical/intrinsic (such as, dimension, preservation); ii) location (accessibility to several urban amenities) and iii) neighbourhood (socioeconomic and urban characteristics of the territory).

The spatial econometric models were developed considering a database with 625 cases which covered the main urban areas of the municipality of Sintra, located in the metropolitan area of Lisbon – Portugal (see Fig. 2), for a time-period of seven years.

The value of each property, used in these econometric models, refers to the evaluation value given by expert appraisers in their evaluation process. In this context, the results represent the estimations of the possible evaluation value, simulating the (recent past) accumulated behaviour and knowledge of PrimeYield's expert appraisers.

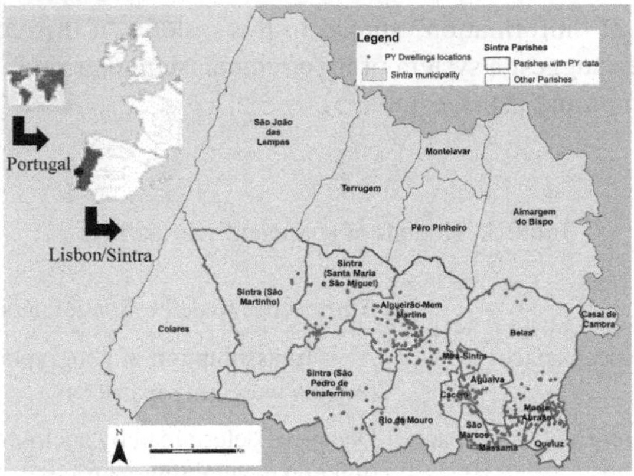

Fig. 2. Location of housing in the municipality of Sintra – Portugal

4.1 sAVM Dimensions and Attributes

The tool AVM-PRIMEYIELD-UA requires an initial identification of eight housing characteristics: 1. Type (flats or single-family houses); 2. Level of conservation (new or used); 3. Net area (m^2); 4. Land area[1] (m^2); 5. Typology (number of rooms). 6. Quality of the property[2] (NA/From 1 to 3); 7; Year of construction; 8. Location (GPS coordinates of the property).

These data inputs are automatically processed by the tool, providing the set of housing variables necessary for correctly estimating the value of a house. It should be noted that, for example, since the precise location of a dwelling is introduced, more than 40 housing dimensions are automatically associated and considered in the model. The detailed information considered in the model is described below.

The specification of the sAVM PRIMEYIELD-UA spatial econometric model follows Eq. 1, defined previously:

$$P = f(v, F; L; T; \varepsilon) \tag{2}$$

where: P is the housing value (in euros with logarithmic transformation); F is the intrinsic (physical) characteristics of housing; L is the extrinsic characteristics (location and neighbourhood) of housing; T is the temporal dimension; υ is the regression coefficients of the model (weights of each attribute in the value of the dwelling); and finally, ε is the stochastic component of the model.

i) Specification of dimension F [Intrinsic (physical) characteristics of housing]

$$\mathrm{H} = \mathrm{f}(T; C; S; A; Q) \tag{3}$$

where: **T** is the typology of housing (T = 1,…,N, with 1 corresponding to T0 and so on); **C** is the level of conservation (new dwellings; dwellings used up to 15 years; dwellings

[1] Only for single-family houses.

[2] The variable related to the level of conservation refers to a qualitative classification provided by PrimeYield's expert appraisers. Based on the available data, only two classifications were incorporated – good and fair; for new properties this classification is not applicable.

used between 15 and 30 years); **S** is the size of a dwelling (small size flats [until 95 m^2], large size flats [more than 95 m^2], small single-family houses [up to 190 m^2], medium-size single family houses [between 190 m^2 and 323 m^2], large single family houses [more than 323 m^2], **A** is the property area (total and land [lnA_i (m^2); lnA_{at} (m^2)]; and **Q** is the quality of the dwelling[3] (1 – Fair, 3 – Good).

In the definition of the categorical variables related to the physical dimension of flats and single-family houses, multivariate analysis statistical techniques – principal component analysis and cluster analysis techniques – were used. This approach is justified by the need to avoid multicollinearity and to capture market segmentation effects (spatial heterogeneity), emphasized in Sect. 3, both in terms of the value and of the size of dwellings.

ii) Specification of dimension L [Extrinsic characteristics (location and neighbourhood) of housing]

$$L = f(IDU; ISE; IAP; IIP, IEP; ITI; IAI; IAN; IAS, D_{zi}) \quad (4)$$

where:

IDU –Indicator for urban density
This includes % of buildings with 1 or 2 floors, % of buildings with five or more floors, % of dwellings with an area between 30 m^2 and 100 m^2, % urban area of continuous urban fabric.
ISE – Indicator for socioeconomic characteristics (qualifications and housing characteristics)
This includes % of buildings built in the 70s, % of buildings built between 2000 and 2005, % of dwellings with an area between 50 m^2 and 100 m^2, % of dwellings with an area less than 200 m^2, % of rented dwellings, % of resident individuals with the first cycle of basic education, % of resident individuals with the second cycle of basic education and % of resident individuals with higher education.
IAP – Indicator for professional activity
This includes % of residents aged between 25 and 65 years, % of residents with the third cycle of basic education, % of residents with secondary education, % of residents employed in the tertiary sector.
IIP – Indicator for the typo morphology and age of the housing stock
This includes % of building blocks, % of buildings built before 1920, % of buildings built between 1920 and 1945, % of buildings built between 1945 and 1960, % of buildings built in the 70s, % of rented dwellings.
IEP – Indicator for the buildings and population age
This includes % of residents aged over 65, % of buildings built between 1945 and 1960, % of buildings built in the 60 s, % of buildings built between 1995 and 2000.
ITI – Indicator for the typo-morphology and age of population

[3] Anticipating possible data collection problems related to this variable, the tool provides an alternative econometric model, which does not use this attribute. As this specification alternative proved to be consistent with the general specification (only a slight decrease in explanatory capacity is noted), it was decided to omit references to this alternative model throughout the following sections.

This includes % of buildings built between 2000 and 2005, % of buildings built between 2005 and 2010, % of residents aged up to four years, % of residents aged between four and five years and % of urban area of medium-continuous urban fabric.
IAI – Indicator for internal global accessibility of the urban area

This includes a measure of accessibility to a set of urban amenities, such as: train stations, schools (kindergarten, primary school (first to third cycles, secondary school), health care facilities (health centre, hospital, pharmacies and diagnostic centres), other shops and services (shopping centres, hypermarkets, grocery stores, markets, ATMs & post offices, restaurants, entertainment facilities and sports facilities).
IAN – Indicator to measure accessibility of municipalities located in the north to the municipality of Sintra.
IAS – Indicator to measure the accessibility of municipalities located in east and south to the municipality of Sintra.
D_{zi} – Dummy to identify zones (Zi = 1,…, 31)
These zones correspond to a spatial disaggregation lower than the administrative delimitation of the parishes. When the zones had a reduced number of cases they were grouped, using a combination of georeferenced information methods and multivariate analysis.

iii) Specification of dimension T

$$T = f(D_{ti}) \tag{5}$$

D_{t1} -Dummy for the year of time i = 1,…,7

4.2 sAVMs Assessment

As discussed above, the adequacy (and the efficiency of the evaluation model) is conditioned by the information provided by the initial data set. Thus, the validation of the estimates is reported under a qualitative index of reliability. The notion of reliability used here refers to a verification of the characteristics introduced for a property and the characteristics (sample) of the supporting data of similar properties. In this version, the verification procedure is applied for two characteristics: the location of the property and its dimensional characteristics, which is based on the following criteria:

Property with parameters within sampling limits
Property with parameters partially out of the sampling limits
Property out of the geographic sample

For the two last classifications it is possible to identify which are the variables where the sample limits are exceeded: **A** - Land area of the property is out of sample; **B** - Housing net area is out of the sample; **C** - Flat net area is out of the sample; **D** – The number of properties of the sample in this zone is reduced (less than 9 records); **E** – In this zone there are no new properties in the sample; **F** – In this zone there are no used in the sample.

The tool implemented a statistical routine for the estimation of confidence intervals. In this context, the confidence intervals aim at providing a concrete indication of the reasonableness of the point estimate – given the unexplained variability embedded in the sample data.

As the use of parametric statistical techniques may be problematic in this context (requiring more demanding statistical assumptions), a non-parametric mechanism of estimation of value ranges predicted by the econometric model was used. Thus, the routine implements a successive sampling scheme, named bootstrapping. In this routine, 500 estimates of the housing value are generated, which are obtained by defining a specific econometric model, generated for a set of 500 subsamples (obtained through replacement based on the original sample data set).

Figure 3 presents the layout of the AVM PRIMEYIELD-UA PROTOTYPE I Version 1.0.

Fig. 3. Interfaces of AVM PRIMEYIELD-UA prototype

5 Conclusions

The main purpose of this article was to explore spatial analysis techniques to be incorporated into a property valuation tool. A spatial automated valuation model (sAVM) was presented, in which the role of space was assumed as a fundamental aspect. Despite the complexity and difficulties of analysing space, four key elements were emphasized: i) location housing attributes, ii) spatial heterogeneity (structural differences between housing markets or housings) and iii) spatial interaction (spatial interactions across submarkets or housings). The scale is a fourth crucial element that makes the process of understanding the relative location (influence of the neighbourhoods), absolute location, the spatial patterns and the spillovers more complex.

The results show different strategies for dealing with spatial heterogeneity across housing submarkets, and independent of the methodology used, the shadow prices and willingness-to-pay for different housing characteristics are different in the selected housing submarkets. In this study no major development of spatial interaction analysis has been presented. However, it can be assumed that an adequate treatment of spatial heterogeneity could considerably reduce the presence of spatial dependence effects, even though the two problems are theoretically distinct [42].

This work was an opportunity to apply some fundamental research, developed in an academic context, in the business world. This was a good example of cooperation, contributing to a more transparent and objective analysis of the real estate market.

Acknowledgements. The authors are grateful to the two reviewers for many helpful comments and suggestions which helped us improve upon the paper. The usual disclaimer applies. This work is an output of the research project DRIVIT-UP - DRIVIng forces of urban Transformation: assessing pUblic Policies, Grant/Award Number: POCI-01–0145-FEDER-031905; Research Unit on Governance, Competitiveness and Public Policy (GOVCOPP), Grant/Award Number: UID/CPO/04058/2019.

References

1. Adams, J.S.: Housing America in the 1980s. Russell Sage Foundation (1988)
2. Bourne, L.S.: The Geography of Housing. Edward Arnold, London (1981)
3. Marques, J.L.: The notion of space in urban housing markets, Doctoral dissertation, Universidade de Aveiro, Portugal (2012)
4. Leung, C.K.Y., Ng, C.Y.J.: Macroeconomic aspects of housing. In: Oxford Research Encyclopedia of Economics and Finance (2019)
5. Bramley, G., Bartlett, W., Lambert, C.: Planning, the Market and Private Housebuilding. UCL Press Ltd, London (1995)
6. Adams, J.S.: The meaning of housing in America. Ann. Assoc. Am. Geogr. **74**(4), 515–526 (1984)
7. Berridge, G.R., Lloyd, L.: In: Barder, R.B., Pope, L.E., Rana, K.S. (eds.) The Palgrave Macmillan Dictionary of Diplomacy, pp. 309–329. Palgrave Macmillan UK, London (2012). https://doi.org/10.1057/9781137017611_18
8. Marques, J.L., Batista, P., Castro, E.A., Bhattacharjee, A.: Housing consumption: a territorial analysis of housing market drivers. In: Anthropological Approaches to Understanding Consumption Patterns and Consumer Behavior, pp. 265–285. IGI Global (2020)
9. d'Amato, M., Kauko, T.: Advances in Automated Valuation Modeling. Springer International Publishing AG, 10, 978-983 (2017)
10. Metzner, S., Kindt, A.: Determination of the parameters of automated valuation models for the hedonic property valuation of residential properties: a literature-based approach. Int. J. Hous. Markets Anal. (2018)
11. Renigier-Bilozor, M., Janowski, A., Walacik, M.: Geoscience methods in real estate market analyses subjectivity decrease. Geosciences **9**(3), 130 (2019)
12. European AVM Alliance: Standards for statistical valuation methods for residential properties in Europe. London (UK). http://www.europeanavmalliance.org/. Accessed 28 Mar 2021 (2017)
13. Bhattacharjee, A., Castro, E., Marques, J.L.: Spatial interactions in hedonic pricing models: the urban housing market of Aveiro, Portugal. Spat. Econ. Anal. **7**(1), 133–167 (2012)
14. Pollakowski, H.O.: Data sources for measuring house price changes. J. Hous. Res., 377–387 (1995)
15. Batista, P.R.L.: The Interaction Structure of E-Territorial Systems: Territory, Housing Market and Spatial Econometrics, Doctoral dissertation, Universidade de Aveiro, Portugal (2019)
16. Lancaster, K.J.: A new approach to consumer theory. J. Polit. Econ. **74**(2), 132–157 (1966)

17. Hasanzadeh, K., Kyttä, M., Brown, G.: Beyond housing preferences: urban structure and actualisation of residential area preferences. Urban Sci. **3**(1), 21 (2019)
18. Rosen, S.: Hedonic prices and implicit markets: product differentiation in pure competition. J. Polit. Econ. **82**(1), 35–55 (1974)
19. Maclennan, D.: Some thoughts on the nature and purpose of house price studies. Urban Stud. **14**(1), 59–71 (1977)
20. Malpezzi, S.: Hedonic pricing model: a selective and applied review. In: O'Sullivan, T., Gibb, K. (eds.) Housing Economics and Public Policy. Blackwell Science Ltd (2003)
21. Straszheim, M.: An econometric analyis of the urban housing market (N. B. of E. Research (Ed.)). Cambridge MA (1975)
22. Freeman, A.M.: The hedonic price approach to measuring demand for neighborhood characteristics. In: Segal, D. (ed.) The economics of neighborhood, pp. 191–217. Elsevier (1979)
23. Harvey, D.: Space as a keyword. In: Castree, N., Gregory, D. (eds.) David Harvey: A Critical Reader, pp. 270–293. Blackwell Publishing Ltd (2006)
24. Lefebvre, H.: The Production of Space. John Wiley & Sons Ltd (1991)
25. Marques, J.L., Batista, P., Castro, E.A.: A noção de espaço em ciência regional. In: Marques, J.L., Carballo, F. (eds.) Ciência Regional em Perspetiva, pp. 11–46. Almedina (2021)
26. Stull, W.J.: Community environment, zoning, and the market value of single-family homes. J. Law Econ. **18**(2), 535–557 (1975)
27. Falk, T., Abler, R.: Intercommunications, distance, and geographical theory. Geografiska Annaler: Series B, Human Geography **62**(2), 59–67 (1980)
28. Grigsby, W.: Housing Markets and Public Policy. University of Pennsylvania Press, Philadelphia (1963)
29. Rapkin, C., Winnick, L., Blank, D.: Housing market analysis. A study of theory and methods. Housing and Home Finance Agency, Division of Housing Research.
30. Bhattacharjee, A., Castro, E., Maiti, T., Marques, J.L.: Endogenous spatial regression and delineation of submarkets: a new framework with application to housing markets. J. Appl. Economet. **31**(1), 32–57 (2016)
31. Marques, J.L., Castro, E., Bhattacharjee, A.: Os padrões espaciais do mercado da habitação: uma noção multidimensional não euclideana do espaço. Revista Portuguesa de Estudos Regionais **32**, 5–23 (2013)
32. Pryce, G.: Housing submarkets and the lattice of substitution. Urban Stud. **50**(13), 2682–2699 (2013)
33. Galster, G.C.: Residential segregation and interracial economic disparities: a simultaneous-equations approach. J. Urban Econ. **21**(1), 22–44 (1987)
34. Adair, A.S., Berry, J.N., McGreal, W.S.: Hedonic modelling, housing submarkets and residential valuation. J. Prop. Res. **13**(1), 67–83 (1996)
35. Maclennan, D., Tu, Y.: Economic perspectives on the structure of local housing systems. Hous. Stud. **11**(3), 387–406 (1996)
36. Straszheim, M.: Hedonic estimation of housing market prices: a further comment. Rev. Econ. Stat., 404–406 (1974)
37. Palm, R.: Spatial segmentation of the urban housing market. Econ. Geogr. **54**(3), 210–221 (1978)
38. Manganelli, B., Pontrandolfi, P., Azzato, A., Murgante, B.: Using geographically weighted regression for housing market segmentation. Int. J. Bus. Intell. Data Min. 13 **9**(2), 161–177 (2014)
39. Goodman, A.C.: Housing submarkets within urban areas: definitions and evidence. J. Reg. Sci. **21**(2), 175–185 (1981)
40. Tobler, W.R.: A computer movie simulating urban growth in the Detroit region. Econ. Geogr. **46**(sup1), 234–240 (1970)

41. Anselin, L.: Spatial Econometrics: Methods and Models. Kluwer Academic Publishers, Dordrecht, The Netherlands (1988)
42. Se Can, A., Megbolugbe, I.: Spatial dependence and house price index construction. J. Real Estate Finan. Econ. **14**(1), 203–222 (1997)

Sustainable Optimization Model for Routing the Process of Distribution of Products, Pickup and Transport of Waste in the Context of Urban Logistics

José Rodriguez-Melquiades[1(✉)], Edwar Lujan[2], and Flabio Gutierrez Segura[3]

[1] Departamento de informática, Universidad Nacional de Trujillo, Trujillo, Peru
jrodriguez@unitru.edu.pe
[2] Escuela de posgrado, Universidad Nacional de Trujillo, Trujillo, Peru
elujans@unitru.edu.pe
[3] Departamento de matemática, Universidad Nacional de Piura, Piura, Peru
flabio@unp.edu.pe

Abstract. Literature research urban logistics has shown us the growing interest in sustainable supply chain serving the population, which must necessarily be based on location and routing of vehicles in order, using the integer linear programming methodology, to model these cases. This study presents a sustainable four-level bi-objective model to optimize economic costs and measure the amount of carbon dioxide generated by the transportation process. The process consists of a provider that supplies a distribution center or warehouse, which also serves a group of facilities located by a group of customers who expect to receive attention to their two orders, one for the purchase of the acquired product and the other for the delivery of the waste generated. Finally, the waste is transported to specialized centers. The model implemented with CLPK obtained optimal results for small and medium-sized instances. For scenarios with more than 40 customers, it was not possible to find solutions, as the computational processing time limit was exceeded by 7 200 s, for these scenarios it is recommended to solve the model using metaheuristics.

Keywords: Sustainability · Location · Vehicle routing

1 Introduction

In the cities, there are activities such as the purchase and sale of food products, home appliances, cargo and passenger transportation, etc.; as well as waste collection services, transportation of products to areas affected by natural disasters,

Our gratitude to the Fondo Nacional de Desarrollo Científico, Tecnológico y de Innovación Tecnológica - Fondecyt, for financing the research in progress.

O. Gervasi et al. (Eds.): ICCSA 2021, LNCS 12952, pp. 91–106, 2021.
https://doi.org/10.1007/978-3-030-86973-1_7

firefighting services etc. In the case of food support for citizens, it is necessary to distribute products coming from the producing companies, which after use must be collected and transported to specialized centers to follow a process of reuse, recycling or rejection in case they no longer have value.

Faced with this situation and in a competitive world, companies have strategies that respond to the dynamic environment of the urban sector. Therefore, an adequate location of suppliers and facilities is necessary, as well as the distribution of products by means of a transportation system and their collection after use. This is achieved by developing and implementing an optimization model through which the logistics system of a city is reorganized in such a way as to achieve a better dimensioning of the transportation network, with the consequent reduction in the number of vehicles circulating in the city, providing an optimized solution for the distribution of products and the pickup-transportation of solid waste in the context of urban logistics.

This study presents a sustainable four-level bi-objective model in the urban context, where the facilities initially locate a warehouse or distribution center that supplies them with products through a vehicle routing process, according to the demand generated by a group of customers. The suppliers in turn supply the warehouse, thus forming three levels. Customers are served through a routing of delivery and pickup vehicles starting and ending at the selected facility. The pickup consists of obtaining waste, which are concentrated in the facility and then transported to the specialized centers in a fourth level as shown in Fig. 1. This article, in addition to optimizing economic costs based on the distance traveled by vehicles, measures the amount of CO2 emissions generated in the routing process, therefore the importance of this article to contribute to the preservation of people's health and the protection of the environment.

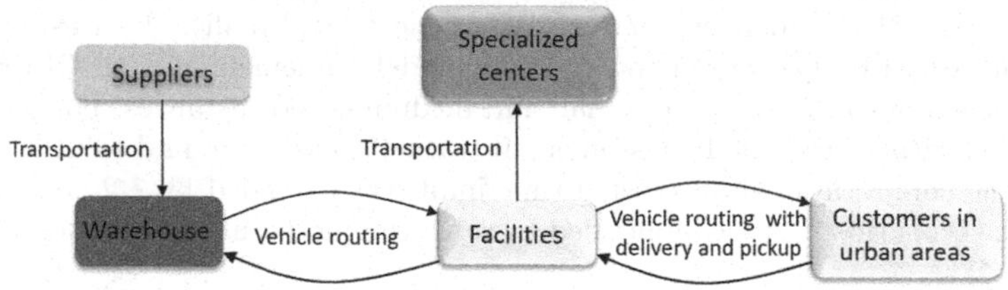

Fig. 1. Diagram of a four-level logistics system.

The article is organized as follows: Sect. 2 comprises a review of the literature related to the research. Section 3 discusses the problem through a description and formulation of a new four-level mixed integer linear programming model. Section 4, shows the results and discussions. Finally, conclusions are presented in Sect. 5

2 Review of the Literature

2.1 Sustainability

Cities are systems that interact continuously and constantly with their environment, being the means of transportation very important for their development. In this dynamic, in the process of supply and demand of various products for the well-being of the citizen, waste of all types is generated, whether industrial, chemical, pharmaceutical, construction, food, hospitals, etc. Waste that for many decades was indiscriminately dumped into the environment without proper supervision and oversight by local governments. Thus, the waste generated in addition to the depletion of natural resources and the lack of environmental preservation, increased the crisis of sustainability of the urban and rural environment in various areas of several countries.

In [8] the notion of sustainability is an important concept, since reducing the greenhouse gas effect, pollution, economic sustainability and social impacts must be taken into account in fields such as production, distribution, logistics, energy or transportation of people and/or cargo. In the opinion of [22] the meaning and importance of sustainable development of cities is great, the objective being to seek the welfare of citizens through the optimal management of the resources that nature and the industrial sector offer. See Fig. 2 due [22].

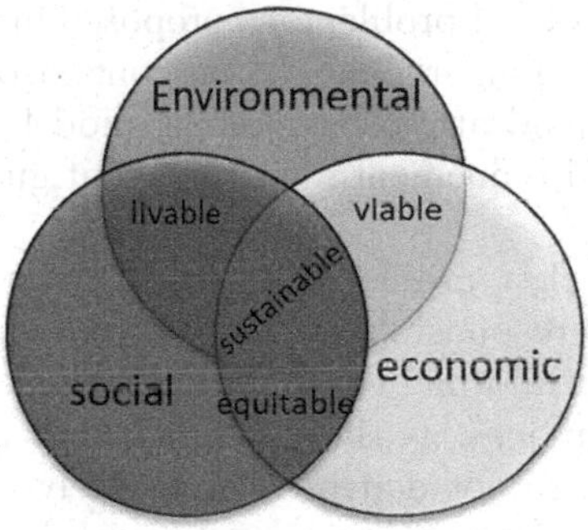

Fig. 2. Key aspects for sustainable development.

Therefore, it becomes necessary as already emphasized in [2], the use of a sustainable supply chain with successful operations and strategies to maintain environmental sustainability.

Recently [24] report that transportation provides a quarter of the total amount of carbon emissions and the proportion continues to grow due to the widespread demand for products from an ever-increasing population. Therefore, it is necessary to implement logistic systems so that the activities of transporting products for their use, pickup, classification and processing, guarantee a sustainable recovery and thus preserve the health of people and the protection of the environment.

In [11] present awareness level for environmental sustainability and economic security as a stochastic optimization. Due to the large amount of related data that exists, [12] presents an advisory framework based on deep neural networks for the achievement of sustainable development goals.

2.2 Localization from the Perspective of Sustainability

The urban population growth brings as a consequence greater needs to be satisfied, therefore, requiring speed and quality in meeting the demands, has determined that there is a change on the part of companies who to maintain urban sustainability have the commitment to use new strategies, in other words, it is necessary the integration of the supply chain and the business sector responsible for the supply of cities under the sustainable approach [2]. Therefore, as indicated by [4], sustainability is an important issue for locating facilities, as environmental, social and economic perspectives are identified.

An interesting application to reduce pollution is presented in [19] who solve the problem of designing a network for a sustainable supply chain. The model presented is based on the binary integer programming methodology, which determines a number of facilities that are located at sites chosen from a set of candidates; in addition to a genetic algorithm for its solution given the complexity of the problem.

Capacitated facility localization in [5] has been extended to the multi-product capacitated facility localization problem, as proposed in [1], who solve the problem with branch-and-bound algorithms. In the context of sustainability [10] formulate a mixed integer quadratic programming model with equilibrium conditions and a branching and refinement algorithm that guarantees convergence to the desired solutions.

Recently [7] indicate that problems in health, safety and environment are issues of concern to those responsible for sustainable supply chain management, since newly established or informal companies can affect the reputation of other formally established companies, as there is a risk that the products offered are not of good quality and are not delivered in a timely manner, in other words, not complying with the logistics principle.

2.3 Sustainable Vehicle Routing

Throughout the historical process of the vehicle routing problem, and in order to be closer to the reality under study, it has been classified into variants such as: capacitated vehicle routing, routing with time windows, routing with simultaneous pickup and delivery and open routing are discussed in [9,13,20,21]. These variants have been applied to distribute products through the supply chain, however, they have focused on optimizing economic logistics costs.

In recent decades, taking into account the pollution generated by transportation, new proposals are framed in the preservation of the environment, in other words sustainability, which is an important issue to preserve the health of the population and all living beings that inhabit the earth. In this context, [6] establish that environmental objectives should be added to economic objectives, extending the classical definition of logistics in green logistics and propose a variant of heterogeneous fleet vehicle routing whose solution is given by a mixed integer linear programming model and a heuristic.

[18] presents a solution for the sustainable vehicle routing problem using a heterogeneous vehicle fleet by developing a mixed integer linear programming model with three different objective functions which model the economic, environmental and social aspects considered simultaneously. Recently [15] discuss the impact on the environment of carbon dioxide emissions in multi-tank vehicle routing.

2.4 Sustainable Location-Routing

In the research of [16], it is stated that the location of facilities is solved at the level of strategic decisions to be used in the location of factories, warehouses and distribution centers, and the routing of vehicles is used at the tactical or operational level as it is about offering or providing a service to customers, likewise, they analyze, discuss new variants and classify the location-routing problems.

Under the view of sustainability and considering the commitment that the consumer must have with the environment, [23] design an optimization model involving location, routing and inventories; in addition to a particle swarm optimization algorithm for sustainable supply chain. Facility location and decision making for sustainable freight distribution in urban areas through vehicle routing was proposed in [14] which aims to minimize costs and CO2 emissions. A new variation for location-routing is presented in [17], who through a new transport-location-routing model succeed in designing a network for sustainable distribution that minimizes distribution costs, fuel consumption, and CO2 emissions.

3 Formulation of the Integrated Model

Based on the knowledge discussed in Sect. 2, a new integrated four-level model combining transport, location and routing is presented as shown in Fig. 1.

Sets
S: Set of suppliers.
P: Set of warehouses.
F: Set of facilities.
C: Set of customers in urban areas.
CE: Set of specialized centers.
$N2 = P \cup F$: Set of nodes forming the warehouses-facility network.
$N3 = F \cup C$: Set of nodes forming the customer-facility network.
$N4 = F \cup CE$: Set of nodes forming the network facility-specialized centers.

Constant
CC: Fuel consumption in litre per kilometre.

Level 1: Set, Parameters and variables
$K1$: Set of large vehicles.
$d1_{s,p}$: Distance between suppliers and warehouses.
$EM1_{k1}$: CO2 emission of large vehicles in grams per liter.
ggg: Number of large vehicles.
$q1_{k1}$: Capacity of large vehicles.
CP_s: Supplier fixed cost.
$Z1_{s,p,k1}$: Quantity transported from suppliers to warehouses.
$X1_s$: Binary variable, the value 1 denotes a provider located to provide a service.

Level 2: Sets, Parameters and variables
$K2$: Set of medium vehicles.
$d2_{p,f}$: Distance between warehouses and facilities.
$EM2_{k2}$: CO2 emissions by medium-sized vehicles in grams per liter.
g: Number of medium vehicles.
$q2_{k2}$: Capacity of medium vehicles.
ff_p: Fixed cost for the operation of the warehouses.
t_p: Warehouse capacity.
fff_f: Fixed cost for the operation of the facility.
dd_f: Demand for warehouses.
$Z2_{p,f}$: Binary variable, the value 1 denotes supplier's attention to the facility.
$X2_p$: Binary variable, the value 1 denotes depots located to provide a service.
$Y2_{f,p}$: Binary variable, where the value 1 denotes facility served by a warehouse.
$U_{i,j}$: Variable representing delivery of products from the warehouse to the facilities.

Level 3: Sets, Parameters and Variables
$K3$: Set of urban vehicles to serve customers.
$d3_{f,c}$: Distance between facilities and customers.
$EM3_{k3}$: CO2 emissions generated by urban vehicles in grams per liter.
gg: Number of urban vehicles.
$q3_{k3}$: Capacity of urban vehicles.
ddd_c: Customer demand for the delivery of a requested product.
pp_c: Customer demand for the pickup of their waste.
$Z3_{f,c}$: Binary variable, where value 1 denotes attention to customer by facilities.
$X3_f$: Binary variable, the value 1 denotes localized facility to provide a service.
$Y3_{c,f}$: Binary variable, where the value 1 denotes customer served by a facility.
$UU_{i,j}$: Variable denoting delivery of product from the facility to the customer.

Level 4: Sets, Parameters and Variables
KB: Set of waste transport vehicles or compactors.
$d4_{i,j}$: Distance between the facility and specialized centers.
QB: Number of transport vehicles or compactors.
d_i: Demand from specialized centers.
qB_k: Capacity of transport vehicles or compactors.
$XB_{i,j}$: Binary variable, where the value 1 indicates attention from the specialized center.

$DD_{i,j}$: Variable denoting delivery of the waste to the specialized center.

The bi-objective mixed integer linear programming model are:

$$Minimize: \sum_{s\in S} CP_s X1_s + \sum_{s\in S, p\in P, k1\in K1} d1_{s,p} Z1_{s,p,k1} + \sum_{p\in P} ff_p X2_p + \sum_{i,j\in N2} d2_{i,j} Z2_{i,j} + \sum_{f\in F} fff_f X3_f + \sum_{i,j\in N3} d3_{i,j} Z3_{i,j} + \sum_{i,j\in N4} d4_{i,j} XB_{i,j} \quad (1)$$

$$Minimize: \sum_{s\in S, p\in P, k1\in K1: s\neq p} CC\left(\frac{EM1_{k1}}{q1_{k1}}\right)\left(\frac{d1_{sp}}{ggg}\right) Z1_{s,p,k1} + \sum_{i,j\in N2, k2\in K2: i\neq j} CC\left(\frac{EM2_{k2}}{q2_{k2}}\right)\left(\frac{d2_{i,j}}{g}\right) Z2_{i,j} + \sum_{i,j\in N3, k3\in K3: i\neq j} CC\left(\frac{EM3_{k3}}{q3_{k3}}\right)\left(\frac{d3_{i,j}}{gg}\right) Z3_{i,j} \quad (2)$$

s.t.

$$\sum_{s\in S, k1\in K1} Z1_{s,j,k1} - \sum_{f\in F} dd_f Y2_{f,p} = 0, \forall p \in P \quad (3)$$

$$\sum_{s\in S, k1\in K1} Z1_{s,p,k1} \leq t_p X2_p, \forall p \in P \quad (4)$$

$$\sum_{p\in N2: f\neq p} Z2_{f,p} = 1, \forall f \in F \quad (5)$$

$$\sum_{f\in F, p\in P} Z2_{f,p} \leq 1 \quad (6)$$

$$\sum_{j\in N2: i\neq j} Z2_{i,j} - \sum_{j\in N2: i\neq j} Z2_{j,i} = 0, \forall i \in N2 \quad (7)$$

$$\sum_{m\in N2: f\neq m} Z2_{f,m} + \sum_{n\in N2: n\neq p} Z2_{p,n} - Y2_{f,p} \leq 1, \forall f \in F, p \in P \quad (8)$$

$$\sum_{i\in N2, p\in P: i\neq p} Z2_{i,p} \leq g \quad (9)$$

$$\sum_{j\in N2: f\neq j} U_{j,f} - \sum_{j\in N2: f\neq j} U_{f,j} - dd_f = dd_f, \forall f \in F \quad (10)$$

$$U_{i,j} \leq q2_{k2} Z2_{i,j}, \forall i,j \in N2 : i \neq j, k2 \in K2 \quad (11)$$

$$\sum_{f\in N3: c\neq f} Z3_{c,f} = 1, \forall c \in C \quad (12)$$

$$\sum_{c\in C, f\in F} Z3_{c,f} \leq 1 \quad (13)$$

$$\sum_{j \in N3: i \neq j} Z3_{i,j} - \sum_{j \in N3: i \neq j} Z3_{j,i} = 0, \forall i \in N3 \tag{14}$$

$$\sum_{m \in N3: c \neq m} Z3_{c,m} + \sum_{n \in N3: n \neq f} Z3_{f,n} - Y3_{c,f} \leq 1, \forall c \in C, f \in F : c \neq f \tag{15}$$

$$\sum_{i \in N3, f \in F: i \neq f} Z3_{i,j} \leq gg \tag{16}$$

$$\sum_{j \in N3: c \neq j} UU_{j,c} - \sum_{j \in N3: c \neq j} UU_{c,j} = ddd_c, \forall c \in C \tag{17}$$

$$\sum_{j \in N3: c \neq j} VV_{c,j} - \sum_{j \in N3: c \neq j} VV_{j,c} = pp_c, \forall c \in C \tag{18}$$

$$UU_{i,j} + VV_{i,j} \leq q3_{k3} Z3_{i,j}, \forall i, j \in N3 : i \neq j, k3 \in K3 \tag{19}$$

$$\sum_{j \in N4} XB_{i,j} = 1, \forall i \in N4 : i \neq j \tag{20}$$

$$\sum_{j \in N4} XB_{j,i} = 1, \forall i \in N4 : i \neq j \tag{21}$$

$$\sum_{i,j \in N4: i = \text{facilidad}: i \neq j} XB_{i,j} \leq QB \tag{22}$$

$$\sum_{j \in N4} DD_{j,i} - \sum_{j \in N4} DD_{i,j} = d_i, \forall i \in N4 : i \neq \text{facilidad seleccionada} \tag{23}$$

$$DD_{i,j} \leq qB_k XB_{i,j}, \forall i, j \in N4, k \in KB \tag{24}$$

The objective function (1) minimizes the costs of supplier location, supplier to warehouse transportation, warehouse location, warehouse to facility transportation, facility location, vehicle routing from facility to customer, finally the transportation of waste from the facility to the specialized centers. Objective function (2) minimize amount CO2 emissions at each of the first three levels. Constraint (3) models the flow coming into a facility from a supplier in terms of the total demand that is served by the facility

Constraint (4) states that the supplier supplies the warehouse as long as the capacity of the warehouse is not exceeded and it is operating. Constraint (5) formalizes the process that each facility is assigned a route. In constraint (6), a route operated with only one warehouse. Constraint (7) models the arrival and departure of the medium vehicle of a certain facility, in other words equilibrium condition. Constraint (8) indicates that a facility is assigned to the warehouse. Constraint (9) establishes that service to the facilities is possible if there are medium vehicles. The equilibrium condition to meet the demand of the facilities is given in constraint (10). The final level two constraint is given by (11) whose equation models the attention to the facilities, provided that the capacity of the medium vehicles is not exceed.

At level three, constraint (12) states that each customer is assigned a route. In constraint (13) a route can operate with only one facility. Constraint (14) indicates that a vehicle, after serving a customer, continues its journey in search of another customer to serve. It is also called equilibrium condition. Constraint (15) a customer is assigned to a facility that will provide a service. Constraint (16) states that the customer is served as long as there are vehicles available. The constraint that guarantees attention to all customers, also called equilibrium, is given in (17). With constraint (18) it is guaranteed that all waste will be collected. Finally, constraint (19) models that facilities are served as long as they do not exceed the capacity of urban vehicles.

At level four, vehicle routing is also applied, starting from the facility whose collection vehicle will deliver the waste to the specialized centers according to the demand requested by them. A specialized center is a factory, recycling center or sanitary landfill. The constraint (20) establishes that each specialized center is visited once by the transporting vehicle. Constraint (21) a specialized center is visited exactly once. Constraint (22) establishes that the vehicle begins transporting the collect waste, starting at the facility selected by the customers for their attention, taking into account the number of available transport vehicles. The equilibrium condition for meeting the demand of specialized centers is given in constraint (23). Finally, in constraint (24), service to specialized centers is possible depending on the capacity of the transport vehicles.

4 Results and Discussion

A Core (TM) i7-8550U CPU @ 1.80 GHz with 8.00 GB of RAM was used to evaluate the model. The optimization software used to solve the scenarios was GLPK (GNU Linear Programming Kit). In addition, considering that it is an integrated four-level vehicle location and routing model, a time limit of 7 200 s was set for processing to obtain solutions in the scenarios considered.

Cases with Simulated Data

Case 1: Three suppliers, two warehouses, five facilities and three specialized centers with their respective geographic locations were considered as shown in Table 1 and Table 2. Two large vehicles, one medium vehicle and one urban vehicle with their respective capacities were considered as means of transportation to serve the warehouse, facilities and customers.

Table 1. Location of suppliers, warehouses and specialized centres.

Suppliers: Location	Warehouse : Location	Specialized centres
s1: (35,15)	p1: (3,25)	C. Transformation: (120,120)
s2: (100,65)	p2: (20,61)	R. Sanitary landfill: (80, 170)
s3: (7,59)		Factory: (55,135)

Table 2. Facility location and demands.

Facility	Location	Demands
f1	(10,15)	4
f2	(20,50)	3
f3	(30,70)	3
f4	(55,105)	1
f5	(80,40)	3

Table 3 shows the customers, their geographic locations, quantities of products requested and quantities of waste to be collected for further processing, which can be reused or recycled or discarded because they have no value.

Table 3. Customers, location, quantities of products purchased and waste quantities.

Customers	Location coordinates	Number of products purchased	Quantity of waste
c1	(80,120)	2	1
c2	(100,40)	1	1
c3	(78,100)	4	1
c4	(70,90)	2	0
c5	(120,50)	2	2

With these data, the model implemented reported results for each of the four levels. In level 1, Table 4, supplier s3 was located to supply products to warehouse p2 with 14 units of products, which will be transported to the facilities in level 2, being the distance traveled 13.15 km and 1.46 of CO2 generated in this route.

Table 4. Transportation of products from selected supplier to warehouse.

Supplier	Warehouse	Ordered products	Distance (km)	CO2 (kg/ton-km)
s3	p2	14	13.15	1.46

In level 2, Table 5, following a vehicle routing process, the facilities are served, starting and ending at the p2 warehouse selected in level 1. The table shows that the number of products decreases as the demand of the respective facility is met. In addition, during the transportation process, this table shows the distances traveled and the amounts of CO2 generated.

Table 5. Transportation of products from selected warehouse to facilities.

Origin	Destination	Delivery	Distance (km)	CO2 (kg/ton-km)
p2	f3	14	14.45	0.34
f3	f4	11	43.01	1.09
f4	f5	10	69.64	1.77
f5	f1	7	74.33	1.89
f1	f2	3	36.4	0.92
f2	p2	0	11	0.28

Following the same methodology shown in Table 5; the Table 6 shows the results when using routing of delivery vehicles for requested products and pickup of waste delivered by customers. In addition, the distances traveled and carbon dioxide emitted.

Table 6. Delivery of products and pickup waste from customers.

Origin	Destination	Delivery	Pickup	Distance (km)	CO2 (kg/ton-km)
f5	c2	11	0	20	0.05
c2	c5	10	1	22.36	0.06
c5	c1	8	3	80.62	0.24
c1	c3	6	4	20.09	0.05
c3	c4	2	5	12.8	0.03
c4	f5	0	5	50.99	0.15

Finally, level 4 is based on the demand generated by the specialized centers according to their requirements. In this case, it was considered that the transformation center (TC) requires 5 tons of waste that can be recycled, and the factory (FA) requires 4 tons of products that will be reused. See Fig. 3 where it can be seen that the warehouse p2 was chosen to supply the facilities located on the way of the route with blue lines. Customers can locate facility f5 which serves through the route with the green lines. Last but not least, regarding level 4 with red lines, it is clear that all the waste will be used and will not need to be transported to the sanitary landfill (RS).

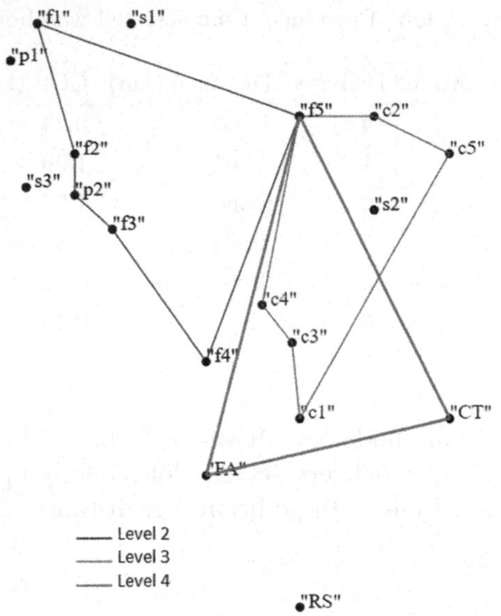

Fig. 3. Attention to specialized centers. (Color figure online)

Case 2: The proposed model was tested in other scenarios formed in customer groups. In this case, the quantities and geographic locations of suppliers, warehouses and facilities remained fixed (see Tables 1 and 2). The number of vehicles was also the same, only their capacities changed according to the demand determined by the customers. Data related to customers is shown in Table 7.

Table 8 shows the results of the model implemented for ten scenarios. The table also shows the time taken to obtain the results, which increases when working with more customers. In addition, the total travel in the four levels of the model, as well as the total amount of CO2 generated in the first three levels. CO2 generation was not evaluated at level 4. A special situation occurred in scenario 8 (35 customers), as the execution time increased greatly, then in scenario 9 (37 customers), this process time decreased. It was concluded that it was due to how close some customers are to others. For scenarios larger than 40 customers, no response was obtained within the time limit. This limitation is due to the computational complexity of vehicle routing from facility to customer.

Table 7. Location of customers and their demands.

Customers	Geographical location	Products purchased	Waste to be pickup
c1	(31,6)	2	1
c2	(36,20)	1	1
c3	(9,19)	4	1
c4	(47,42)	2	0
c5	(28,20)	2	2
c6	(38,43)	1	1
c7	(41,4)	4	0
c8	(36,30)	2	1
c9	(4,10)	3	2
c10	(43,16)	3	1
c11	(26,40)	1	0
c12	(39,57)	2	1
c13	(4,40)	1	2
c14	(55,20)	3	0
c15	(65,10)	1	0
c16	(70,20)	2	1
c17	(53, 5)	1	1
c18	(22,14)	4	2
c19	(30,55)	2	0
c20	(21,35)	1	0
c21	(34,11)	2	1
c22	(41,34)	5	1
c23	(46,48)	3	0
c24	(28,48)	1	2
c25	(4,35)	2	0
c26	(64,32)	2	1
c27	(50,27)	1	0
c28	(36,26)	3	2
c29	(80,16)	2	1
c30	(14,7)	5	0
c31	(18,30)	3	0
c32	(50,30)	1	1
c33	(28,60)	1	1
c34	(26,65)	1	0
c35	(47,50)	2	1
c36	(45,48)	1	0
c37	(73,20)	1	1
c38	(5,43)	2	0
c39	(65,15)	1	1
c40	(80,20)	1	1

Table 8. Results obtained for each of the scenarios considered.

Scenarios	Customers	Time (secs)	Distance traveled (km.)	CO2 (kg/ton-km)
1	5	0.1	762.77	7.69
2	10	10.8	795.38	7.76
3	15	35.3	881.34	8.01
4	20	221.1	903.66	8.04
5	25	184.0	909.39	8.02
6	30	261.9	949.87	8.12
7	33	4094.3	965.03	8.15
8	35	–	–	–
9	37	5693.6	975.23	8.16
10	40	–	–	–

5 Conclusions

The results show that the sustainable four-level bi-objective mixed integer linear programming model, in the context of urban logistics, integrates transportation to service warehouses from the selected supplier; location of warehouses by facilities and routing of vehicles for their supply; location of facilities by customers and their routing of vehicles for delivery of requested products and pickup of waste which will be transported to specialized centers. CO2 emissions are also measured at levels 1, 2 and 3.

The proposal is based on the premise of two demands generated by customers to the facilities, one for products to be used and the other to pickup waste to be collected and subsequently transported to specialized centers. This premise determines the timely attention since the facilities will be supplied from a warehouse, thus reducing transportation costs as observed in the tests carried out in the scenarios presented. Therefore, the vehicles used in the four levels travel along the best routes determined by the model through vehicle routing.

The results of the cases presented show the potential of the proposed model obtaining optimal solutions quickly in scenarios with up to 30 customers. From 33 customers the processing time starts to increase, obtaining optimal solutions up to 37 customers. A critical aspect is from 40 customers onwards no response was obtained within the time limit. Given the difficulty of the problem, a new perspective recommended is the use of metaheuristics for higher dimensional scenarios to obtain good solutions in reasonable times.

References

1. Akyüz, M.H., Öncan, T., Altınel, İK.: Branch and bound algorithms for solving the multi-commodity capacitated multi-facility Weber problem. Ann. Oper. Res., 1–42 (2018). https://doi.org/10.1007/s10479-018-3026-5

2. Bouchery, Y., Corbett, C.J., Fransoo, J.C., Tan, T. (eds.): Sustainable Supply Chains. SSSCM, vol. 4. Springer, Cham (2017). https://doi.org/10.1007/978-3-319-29791-0
3. Bugliarello, G.: Urban sustainability: Dilemas, challenges and paradigms. Technol. Soc. **28**(1–2), 19–26 (2006). https://doi.org/10.1016/j.techsoc.2005.10.018
4. Chen, L., Olhager, J., Tang, O.: Manufacturing facility location and sustainability: a literature review and research agenda. Int. J. Prod. Econ. **149**, 154–163 (2014). https://doi.org/10.1016/j.ijpe.2013.05.013
5. Daskin, M. S., Snyder, L V., Berger, R. T.: Facility Location in Supply Chain Design, chapter 2. Logistics systems: Design and optimization. In: Langevin , A., Riopel, D. (eds.) GERAD & École Polytechnique de Montréal Montréal Canada. Springer, Boston, MA (2005). https://doi.org/10.1007/0-387-24977-X_2
6. Eguia, I., Racero, J., Molina, J. C., Guerrero, F.: Environmental Issues in Vehicle Routing Problems. In: Erechtchoukova M., Khaiter P., Golinska P. (eds) Sustainability Appraisal: Quantitative Methods and Mathematical Techniques for Environmental Performance Evaluation. EcoProduction (Environmental Issues in Logistics and Manufacturing). Springer, Hidelberg (2013). https://doi.org/10.1007/978-3-642-32081-1_10
7. Fan, D., Lo, C.K.Y., Zhou, Y.: Sustainability risk in supply bases: the role of complexity and coupling. Transp. Res. Part E **145**(2021) (2021). https://doi.org/10.1016/j.tre.2020.102175
8. Gonzales-Feliu, J., Morana, J.: Are city logistics solutions sustainable? the city-porto case. J. Land Use Mob. Environ. **3**(2), 55–64 (2010)
9. Li, F., Golden, B., Wasil, E.: The open vehicle routing problema: algorithms, large-scale test problems, and computational results. Comput. Oper. Res. **34**(10), 2918–2930 (2007). https://doi.org/10.1016/j.cor.2005.11.018
10. Liu, W., Kong, N., Wang, M., Zhang, L.: Sustainable multi-commodity capacitated facility location problem with complementary demand functions. Transp. Res. Part E **145**(2) (2021). https://doi.org/10.1016/j.tre.2020.102165
11. Okewu, E., Misra, S., Maskeliūnas, R., Damaševičius, R., Fernández-Sanz, L.: Optimizing green computing awareness for environmental sustainability and economic security as a stochastic optimization problem. Sustainability, MDPI 9(10) (2017). https://doi.org/10.3390/su9101857
12. Okewu, E., Ananya, M., Misra, S., Koyuncu, M.: A deep neural network-based advisory framework for attainment of sustainable development goals 1–6. Sustainability, MDPI 12(24) (2020). https://doi.org/10.3390/su122410524
13. Ombuki, B., Ross, B., Hanshar, F.T.: Multi-objetive genetic algorithms for vehicle routing problem with time windows. Appl. Intell. **24**(1), 17–30 (2006). https://doi.org/10.1007/s10489-006-6926-z
14. Ouhader, H., El Kyal, M.: Combining facility location and routing decisions in sustainable urban freight distribution under horizontal collaboration: how can shippers be benefited? Math. Probl. Eng. Hindawi **2017**, 1–18 (2017). https://doi.org/10.1155/2017/8687515
15. Peng, B., Wu, L., Yi, Y., Chen, X.: Solving the multi-depot Green vehicle routing problem by a hybrid evolutionary algorithm. Sustainability, MDPI 12(5) (2020). https://doi.org/10.3390/su12052127
16. Prodhon, C., Prins, C.: A survey of recent research on location-routing problems. Europ. J. Oper. Res. **238**(1), 1–17 (2014). https://doi.org/10.1016/j.ejor.2014.01.005

17. Rabbani, M., Navazi, F., Farrokhi-Asl, H., Balali, M.H.: A sustainable transportation-location-routing problem with soft time windows for distribution systems. Uncertain Supply Chain Management, Publishers of distinguished academic and professional journals **6**(3), 229–254 (2018). https://doi.org/10.5267/j.uscm.2017.12.002
18. Rabbani, M., Taghi-Molla, A., Farrokhi-Asl, H., Mobini, M.: Sustainable vehicle-routing problem with time Windows by heterogeneous fleet of vehicle and separated compartments: application in waste collection problem. Int. J. Transp. Eng. **7**(2), 195–216 (2019). https://doi.org/10.22119/IJTE.2019.94586.1361
19. Santibañez, E. D. R., Mateus, G. R., Luna, H. P. L.: Solving a public sector sustainable supply chain problem: a genetic algorithm approach. In: WCAMA Brazilian Computer Society Proceedings, pp. 19–22. Publisher, Natal, RN, Brazil (2011)
20. Subramanian, A., Uchoa, E., Ochi, L.S.: New lower bounds for the vehicle routing problem with simultaneous pickup and delivery. In: Festa, P. (ed.) SEA 2010. LNCS, vol. 6049, pp. 276–287. Springer, Heidelberg (2010). https://doi.org/10.1007/978-3-642-13193-6_24
21. Sungur, I., Ordoñez, F., Dessouky, M.: A robust optimization approach for the capacitated vehicle routing problem with demand uncertainty. IIE Trans. **40**(5), 509–523 (2008). https://doi.org/10.1080/07408170701745378
22. Tanguay, G.A., Rajaonson, J., Lefevre, J., Lanoie, P.: Measuring the sustainability of cities: an analysis of the use of local indicators. Ecological Indiators **10**(2), 407–418 (2010). https://doi.org/10.1016/j.ecolind.2009.07.013
23. Tang, J., Ji, S., Jiang, L.: The design of a sustainable location-routing-inventory model considering consumer environmental behavior. Sustainability, MDPI 8(3) (2016). https://doi.org/10.3390/su8030211
24. Tsao, Y., Thanh, V.: A multi-objective mixed robust possibilistic flexible programming approach for sustainable seaport-dry port network design under an uncertain environment. Transp. Res. Part E: Logistics Transp. Rev. **124**, 13–39 (2019). https://doi.org/10.1016/j.tre.2019.02.006

A Random Forest Regression Model for Predicting the Movement of Horseshoe Crabs in Long Island Sound

Samah Senbel[1](✉), Jo-Marie Elisha Kasinak[2], and Jennifer Mattei[2]

[1] School of Computer Science and Engineering, Welch College of Business and Technology, Sacred Heart University, Connecticut, USA
senbels@sacredheart.edu

[2] Department of Biology, College of Arts and Science, Sacred Heart University, Connecticut, USA
{kasinakj,matteij}@sacredheart.edu

Abstract. Developing models to predict animal movement patterns is an important area of study in ecology and wildlife management. Project *Limulus,* a community research program, has been tracking the movement of tagged American horseshoe crabs (*Limulus polyphemus*) in Long Island Sound since 1998. During the spawning season, horseshoe crabs are captured by hand, tagged and then released. Recaptured horseshoe crabs give valuable information about their behavior and movement patterns. In this paper, we tested various models to find the best predictor for the movement of horseshoe crabs based on the observed movement activity in previous years. We experimented with three different models: Linear Regression, Decision Tree, and Random Forest Regression models. We used the data for 2018 as our test set and the data of all previous 19 years as our training set (19,219 records). The Random Forest Regression model proved to be the best predictive model and resulted in the smallest RMSE and MAE, as well as the smallest maximum error in prediction. The predicted horseshoe crab locations can be targeted in the next season for recapturing tagged horseshoe crabs. It also concentrates the scientists' effort and time to find the maximum number of horseshoe crabs.

Keywords: Prediction model · Random forest · Horseshoe crabs · Animal tracking · Movement prediction · Long Island Sound

1 Introduction and Literature Review

The study and understanding of the movement of animals is a long-standing area of scientific interest. Movement ecology has been practiced for hundreds of years by farmers tracking locust outbreaks, to migratory bird counts organized by non-profit groups starting at the turn of the twentieth century [1]. Animal movement studies provide in-depth knowledge of animal behavior, when and where animals move, and in some cases, why they move (e.g. for food or reproduction) [2]. The technology to track animals

O. Gervasi et al. (Eds.): ICCSA 2021, LNCS 12952, pp. 107–119, 2021.
https://doi.org/10.1007/978-3-030-86973-1_8

has changed vastly over the years, but the goals are unchanged and remains critically important for wildlife conservation.

In the 1990s, Global Positioning Systems (GPS) and satellite technology became a popular, albeit invasive, way to perform animal tracking. A radio frequency identification (RFID) tag or a GPS devise (e.g. radio collar) is physically attached to the animal, and its location is transmitted periodically to a central monitoring location [3]. This method is the current favorite of researchers due to the continuous data locations being sent on a regular basis. However, it is an expensive option and the tags are usually heavy making them more suitable for larger animals [4]. Another invasive but much less harmful method is the use of externally applied, traditional plastic or metal tags with unique identification numbers on them that are attached to a large group of animals. They are later recaptured and their location, health, and mates noted. This methods works best with smaller animals, insects, and birds. Typically, as many animals as possible are tagged to increase the probability of recapture. This method depends heavily on citizen scientists or community volunteers [5] and researchers to report any sightings or recaptures of these animals.

The American horseshoe crab, *Limulus polyphemus*, can be found along the Atlantic coast of the United States from Maine to Florida and in parts of the Gulf Coast. This study concentrated on Long Island Sound (LIS) which is bounded by the coasts of CT and Long Island, New York. Horseshoe crabs move to find food in the coastal benthic zone and during the spawning season to find nesting sites along shorelines. The horseshoe crabs in LIS come to shore from mid-May through June for the spawning season. Horseshoe crabs play a key role in the eel and whelk fishing industry as bait and an unparalleled, integral part in ensuring the safety of vaccines and medical devices as products from their blood are used for bacterial toxin testing [6, 7, and 8].

Fig. 1. A tagged horseshoe crab

Project *Limulus* [9], a community research program, at Sacred Heart University focuses on the ecology and population dynamics of horseshoe crabs in LIS since 1998. It is run as a research and educational tool to increase public awareness of the horseshoe crab and its connection to the LIS ecosystem and human health. It is also a data-gathering and analyzing network to help state managers direct conservation programs for the horseshoe crab population in LIS, to allow for its sustainable harvest. Their movement pattern over the seasons is of particular interest as individuals of the population frequently cross State boundaries with very different management programs [10, 11]. Figure 1 shows a tagged horseshoe crab. The tag has a unique ID number and a website to visit for reporting recaptures.

Three research projects also concentrate on the study of the movement of horseshoe crabs in particular. A study in New England [12] uses both acoustic telemetry and tagging to study the movement of horseshoe crabs on Pleasant bay in Cape Cod, Massachusetts, USA. They tagged and followed the movement of 70 crabs over a period of two years using acoustics and 2000 horseshoe crabs using tagging similar to our project. Their results are very interesting, but we note the limitation of the study due to its short time period and small horseshoe crab population test set. Another project was conducted on the Asian horseshoe crabs [13] in the south of Japan. A group of 20 horseshoe crabs were fitted with electronic tags and their movement was tracked for two years. Their mating habits were also studied. Although it is a useful and informative study, the small set of horseshoe crabs that were tagged and studied does not give a complete picture of the movement of the Asian horseshoe crabs. Closer to LIS, Bopp et al. [11] conducted a study on the movement pattern and survival rates of horseshoe crabs in NY State waters. They divided the NY coastal area into three parts: Jamaica bay, south shore of Long Island, and North shore of Long Island. They conclude that the survival rate is highest in the northern part of Long Island for both male and female horseshoe crabs. And, there is a trend of movement towards the north shore of Long Island as well. They limited their work to New York City shores. Their results supports the findings of our previous work, where we observed a trend for horseshoe crabs to move towards the shores of CT from the NY metropolitan region [14].

This prediction model focuses on the population dynamics of horseshoe crabs in LIS. The study of the movement of horseshoe crabs is an important part of Project *Limulus*. With 20 years of accumulated movement data, it is possible to paint a fairly accurate picture of their travel behavior both in the short term and over the years19. Our analysis showed an interesting trend in movement: horseshoe crabs are mostly static, but when they do move, there is a tendency to move towards the northern part of LIS. The data shows that horseshoe crabs from Rhode Island rarely travel west to the LIS, and that those from the northern part of the Sound rarely travel west or south. Meanwhile, there is a slight tendency for horseshoe crabs from the western New York City part of LIS to travel northeast, and horseshoe crabs from the south shores of LIS also show a tendency to move northeast [14].

Building on this collection of work on the horseshoe crab population in LIS, it was imperative to have a good estimate of the best locations to capture horseshoe crabs in the future and to predict the possible movement of crabs that have not been recaptured based on the general movement of the population. We experimented with three different models: Linear Regression, Decision Tree, and Random Forest Regression models. We used the data for 2018 as our test set and the data of all previous 19 years as our training set (19,219 records).

In this paper, we present a prediction model for finding the best horseshoe tagging locations using three different methods, and compare their performances. In Sect. 2, we describe the dataset characteristics, performance measures, and the prediction models. Section 3 presents our implementation results and conclusion.

2 Prediction Model

Our three models were coded using the Python coding language [15] on a regular Intel i5 laptop. The dataset was divided into two parts, a training set ("train") for building our models and a testing set ("test") for measuring their performance. Each set is further divided into the 5 input fields: initial longitude, initial latitude, initial date, is Male, and is Female, (used in X_train and X_test) and the two output fields, final longitude and final latitude (used in Y_train and Y_test). Figure 2 shows how the dataset was split into those 4 subsets.

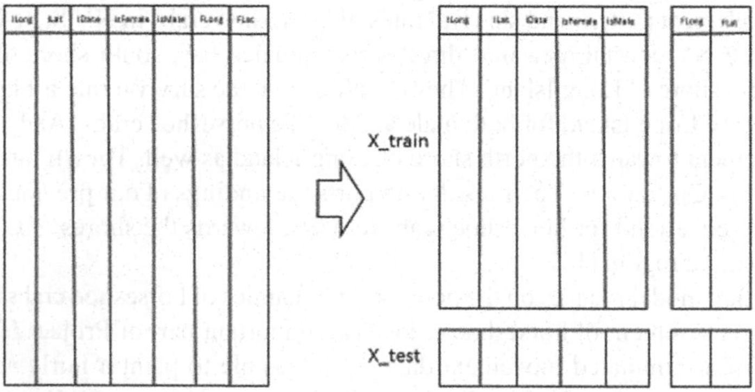

Fig. 2. An illustration of how the dataset was split into X_train, Y_train, X_test, and Y_test.

Performance Measure: For continuous-valued estimation problems, two performance measures are typically used to measure the accuracy of a model's prediction: the root mean squared error (RMSE) and the mean absolute error (MAE). RMSE measures the root of the average squared error of our predictions. The smaller the MSE, the better. Equation 1 shows the MSE calculation. RMSE is simply the root of the MSE.

$$\text{MSE} = \frac{1}{N}\sum_{i=1}^{N}\left(y_i - \hat{y}_i\right)^2 \tag{1}$$

The MAE is another popular measure: the error is calculated as an average of absolute differences between the target values and the predictions. Equation 2 shows how to calculate the MAE.

$$\text{MAE} = \frac{1}{N}\sum_{i=1}^{N}\left|y_i - \hat{y}_i\right| \tag{2}$$

An important distinction between this metric and the RMSE is that MAE does not penalizes huge errors as much as MSE does. Thus, it is not as sensitive to outliers compared to the mean square error. We used both metrics and they gave similar results.

The Movement Dataset and Its Features: Our dataset consists of a large repository of 19,219 movements of horseshoe crabs throughout the LIS area collected between 1998 and 2019. Each record consists of the horseshoe crab tag number, sex, initial latitude and longitude, initial capture (tagging) date, final latitude and longitude, and final recapture date. In the early years of Project *Limulus* (1998–2008), the data collection was mainly in the south-central CT area (between longitudes −72.5 and −73.5 and between latitude 41.1 and 41.3 approximately) and on a relatively small-scale. 2009 to 2013 were years of large-scale data collection as well as a great expansion in the collection area to cover all of LIS. From 2014 to 2018, the data collection size was stabilized and still covers the entire LIS area, however the data collection size was smaller due to less funding for the project. Figure 3 shows the number of recaptured horseshoe crabs, respectively from 2000–2018.

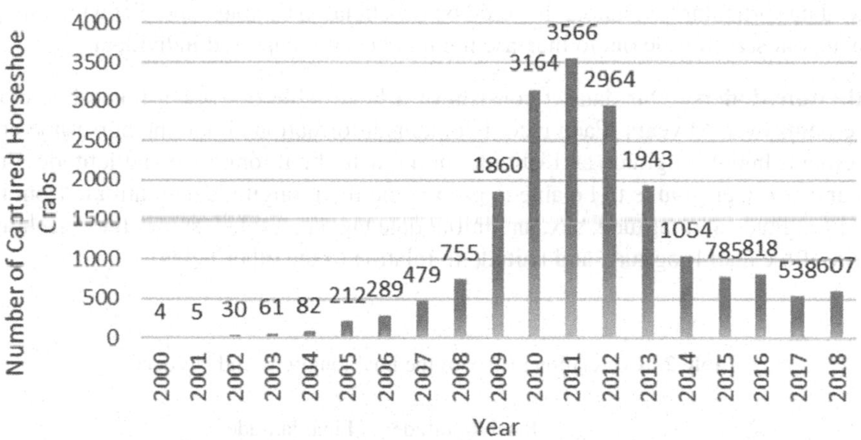

Fig. 3. Number of recaptured horseshoe crabs from 2000–2018.

The nature of capture-and-release animal tracking means that only a small percentage of the tagged animals are recaptured. In Project *Limulus*, about 17% of all tagged horseshoe crabs were ever re-captured, and the majority of crabs are only recaptured once (Table 1).

Table 1. Number of horseshoe crabs recaptures

Number of recaptures	Number of crabs
0	~37,000
1	12364
2	2544
3	564
4	131
5	43
6	6
7	1 (Horseshoe Crab ID 172143)
8	1 (Horseshoe Crab ID 192594)
9	1 (Horseshoe Crab ID 182857)

Our prediction model would generate a list of target beaches to be visited by community volunteers in the expectation of capturing previously tagged horseshoe crabs. This would hopefully lead to a rise in the number of recaptures, thereby providing more information about the movement of the horseshoe crabs. Some particular crabs have been captured multiple times over the years, making their movement, growth and health status data particularly valuable. It would be beneficial to be able to predict which beach to focus our search time on, to increase the number of recaptured individuals.

Prediction Models: Our dataset consists of a large table of 19,219 horseshoe crabs movements over 20 years. Each record contains information about one horseshoe crab movement: Initial longitude and latitude, initial date, final longitude and latitude, final date and sex. Our goal is to be able to predict the final longitude and latitude from the initial longitude and latitude, sex, and initial date tagged. Table 2 shows the correlation matrix of the final longitude and latitude in relation to the other fields.

Table 2. Correlation matrix of the final longitude and latitude.

	Final longitude	Final latitude
Initial longitude	0.9408	0.7755
Initial latitude	0.8008	0.8722
Initial date	0.1146	0.0973
Is male	−0.0907	−0.0617
Is female	0.0963	0.0667

The table shows a high correlation between the final location and the initial location data and a weak correlation with the initial date and gender (~0.1). This implies that our prediction model will heavily rely on these two fields (initial longitude and initial latitude) and we can ignore the other fields with little change in results.

Three different regression models were experimented with for our dataset: Linear Regression, Decision Trees and Random Forests. Ordinary Least Squares Linear Regression [17] is the simplest regression model as it assumes a simple direct linear relationship between the output data (Final longitude and latitude) and the input variables, and aims to minimize the square error between the prediction line and the input data.

A decision tree predictor [18] is another popular technique based on recursively building a decision tree by selecting the best attribute to split the data into two parts. Then it recursively repeats the process on each part until either the data size is zero or all tuples belong to one group, or there are no more attributes to split on. This tree is then used to predict the new data instance values. Figure 4 shows a 3-level decision tree for prediction the final longitude, and it shows clearly that the preferred splitting attribute is the Initial Longitude (ILong) as expected from the correlation matrix (Table 2). A typical decision tree would have tens of levels for good accuracy. We show a 3-level decision tree just for clarity. Although simple and clear to trace decision trees are not optimal due to several factors: decision trees are sensitive to the specific data on which they are trained. So, they tend to over-fit the training data and a small change in the training data would result in a different decision tree and a different prediction. Also, decision trees are computationally expensive to train, carry a big risk of overfitting, and tend to find local optima because they cannot go back after they have made a split.

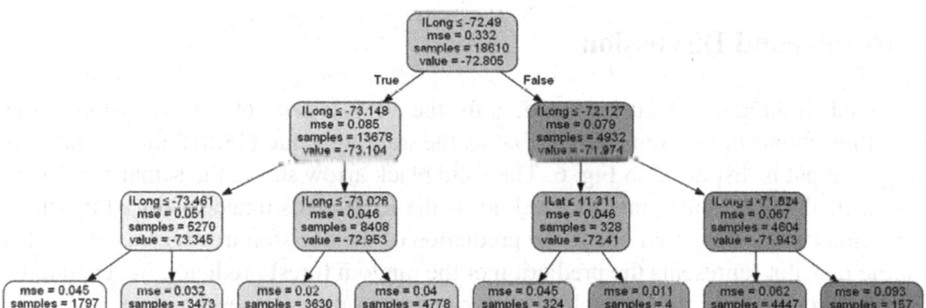

Fig. 4. A small 3-level decision tree regression model.

The third technique we used is the Random Forest Ensemble Regression model [19]. An Ensemble method aggregates the output of several similar or different machine learning techniques to produce an output that is better than using any individual method. A random forest regression ensemble is a meta-estimator which aggregates many decision trees. It operates by constructing a multitude of decision trees at training time and outputting the class that is the mean prediction of the individual trees, as shown in Fig. 5.

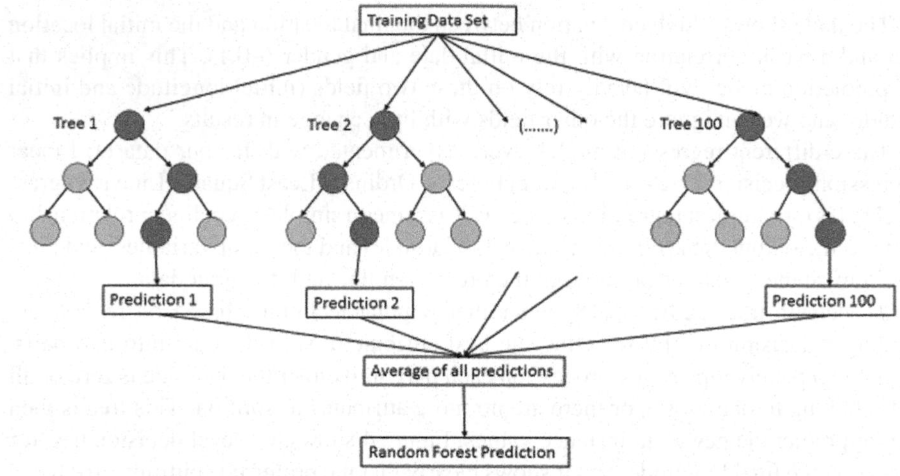

Fig. 5. A simplified version of the random forest regression model.

Two modifications are made to keep the individual decision trees from being too similar: First, the number of features that can be split on at each node is limited to some percentage of the total. This ensures that the ensemble model does not rely too heavily on any individual feature, and makes fair use of all potentially predictive features. Second, each tree draws a random sample from the original data set when generating its splits, adding a further element of randomness that prevents overfitting.

3 Results and Discussion

We tested all three models using the data for the 2018 season (607 movements) as our test value and all the seasons before that as the training value (18,612 movements). A sample output is displayed in Fig. 6. The solid black arrow shows the actual movement of a particular horseshoe crab. The red dot is the location estimate produced by linear regression model, the green one is the prediction of the decision tree regression model, and the blue dot represents the prediction of the random forest predictor. In general, the random forest predictor gave the best performance for most horseshoe crabs.

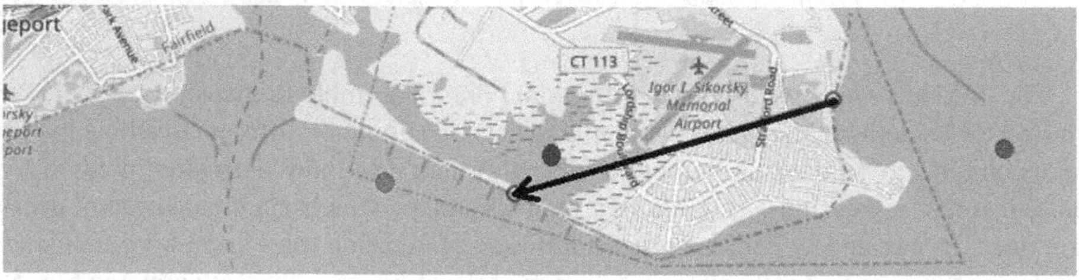

Fig. 6. Sample prediction output. (Color figure online)

A model would be very useful to predict the approximate area where horseshoe crabs would be found, but would not accurately predict the location of a particular horseshoe crab. Figure 7 shows the predictor results for all 607 horseshoe crabs in the test set. The black dots represents the actual final locations of the horseshoe crabs. The Red dots represent the linear regression, the green dots represent the decision tree predictor, and the blue dots represent the results of the random forest predictor. All three predictors did not perform well with the data points on the south side of the Sound (i.e. Long Island's North shore). This is due to a general lack of data points there in both the training and test sets.

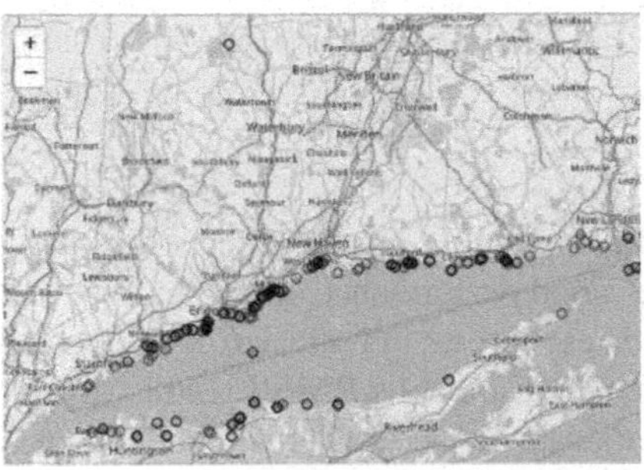

a) Actual Horseshoe crab location

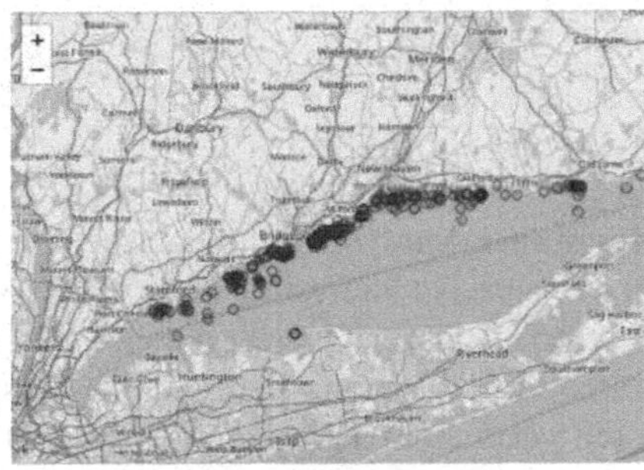

b) Random Forest model

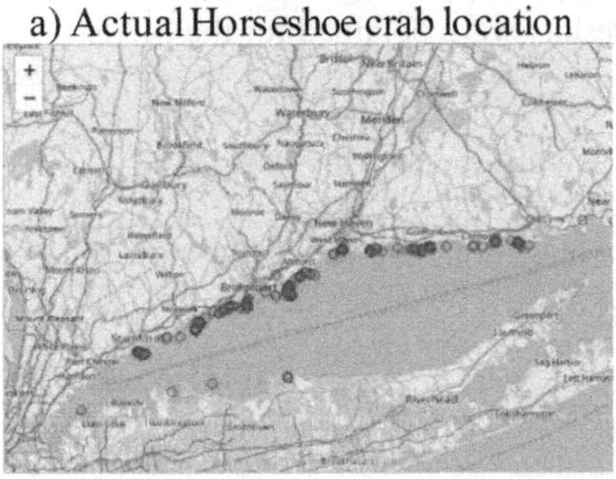

c) Linear Regression model

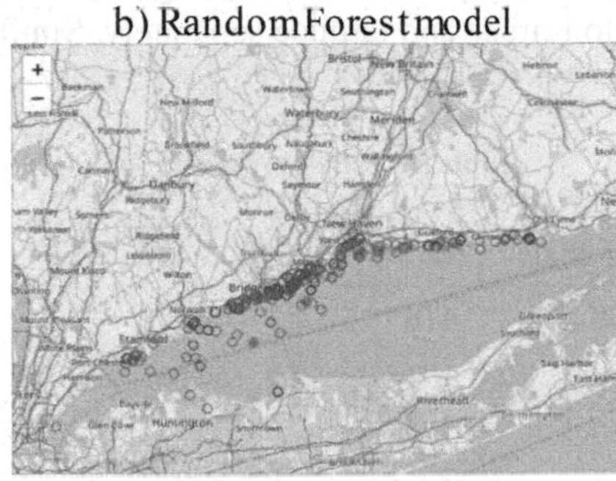

d) Decision tree model

Fig. 7. Collective result of prediction for all three models. (Color figure online)

Table 3 shows the results for the 2018 season prediction based on all previous seasons. We tried two different methods: predict both final longitude and latitude together, or predict each one alone and average the error. An interesting observation is that all techniques performed better in predicting the latitude, compared to the longitude. This is due to the fact that the latitude range is much smaller than the longitude range for the LIS region. Also, we observe that we get better results when we predict the longitude and latitude separately. The least error was obtained when using the Random forest regression model and when predicting the longitude and latitude separately. Based on these results, we conclude that the random forest regression model is the most suitable for our prediction model, and predicting the longitude and latitude individually is slightly better than running the model on them both together.

Table 3. Performance results for the three prediction models.

	Least square linear regression model		Decision tree regression model		Random forest regression model with 100 estimators	
	Max error	MAE	Max error	MAE	Max error	MAE
Predict longitude and latitude together	1.555	0.098	1.616	0.099	1.433	0.097
Predict longitude only	2.399	0.143	2.487	0.163	2.270	0.141
Predict latitude only	0.712	0.053	0.746	0.055	0.662	0.050
Average of both	1.555	0.098	1.616	0.109	**1.466**	**0.096**

Performance Analysis: The dataset size and composition greatly affects the performance results. An interesting observation is the varied performance of the random forest prediction model results over the years, as the dataset grows in both size and geographical area. Table 4 shows the random forest prediction model's RMSE results over the past ten years. For each year, we used that year's data as the test set and the data of all the previous years as the training data. The RMSE is the average RMSE for predicting the longitude and latitude separately. Similar results were obtained for the MAE.

Table 4. Random forest prediction model results for the years 2008–2018.

Test year	Train set size	Test set size	Percentage of testing set	RMSE	MAE
2008	1163	755	39%	0.146	0.068
2009	1918	1860	49%	0.121	0.049
2010	3778	3164	46%	0.097	0.043
2011	6942	3566	34%	0.103	0.045
2012	10508	2964	22%	0.112	0.055
2013	13472	1943	13%	0.156	0.077
2014	15415	1054	6%	0.194	0.113
2015	16469	785	5%	0.204	0.116
2016	17254	818	5%	0.187	0.110
2017	18071	538	3%	0.173	0.103
2018	18609	607	3%	0.183	0.096

Interestingly, the table could be divided into three areas with different prediction results: 2008–2010 the prediction error decreases steadily, 2011–2015 the prediction error increases, and then in 2016–2018 the prediction error showed a gradual descent over time.

The prediction error was decreasing from 2008 to 2010 as expected, as the tagging/recapture activity was mainly concentrated on the north central part of LIS. However, as the dataset changed over time by having a larger geographical area to cover all of the LIS region after 2011, the prediction results had a larger error, as the training set mainly contained data from the northern shores of LIS area and the testing sets started to have more data from the western and southern shores. Those new data points had no similar movement history in the training set and therefore most of them were predicted with a huge error (2011–2015). Then, as more and more data points in the western and southern parts of LIS were added, we observed a decrease in the prediction error (2015 - present), as the training set gets more varied year after year to cover the entire LIS area. We expect their prediction error to decrease in future seasons as more data is added. Also, we recommend more capture activity in the southern and western parts of the Sound to be able to gather more movement data there.

Based upon our experimental results, we conclude that the best prediction model for horseshoe crab movement in LIS is the random forest prediction model with 100 estimators. Also, the results have shown that performance is expected to improve over the years as more data points are added over the seasons.

4 Discussion

The prediction model would be used for two purposes: First, to determine the best locations for the tagging/recapture teams to search for horseshoe crabs, thus saving their time and effort. Also, particular horseshoe crabs are of interest, those who have been tracked for the longest time, or have traveled long distances, or have a particular interesting feature. The model can predict the best location to find that individual horseshoe crab as shown in Figs. 6 and 7.

A weakness of the prediction model is its dependency on the dataset being used, as is common with all machine learning techniques. The more data that is available, the better the prediction. There has been higher tagging/recapture activity on the CT or north shore of LIS than the NY or south shore. This easily explains why the model prediction rate is better in CT. We recommend an increased tagging/recapture effort in the south on Long Island to get a better picture of the movement of horseshoe crabs there and improve our predictions for all of LIS.

While movement inside LIS is a useful ecological study for the management of horseshoe crabs, a wider look at the movement of horseshoe crabs in New England would be extremely useful in the study of the mortality and movement of the American horseshoe crab. Currently, research into the movement of horseshoe crabs in this area is plentiful but highly localized [7, 11, 12, and 16].

5 Conclusion

Animal movement prediction is a vital aspect of animal tracking using tags. It enables researchers to predict an approximate location they are expected to be in, thus enabling a better chance of re-capture of the tagged animals, and locating more members of the general population. Project *Limulus* has been monitoring and studying the population of horseshoe crabs in Long Island Sound since 1998. Predicting the optimal beaches to target for tagging horseshoe crabs would be useful for the project to enable the capture of more horseshoe crabs per season. Also, some horseshoe crabs have been captured multiple times over several years and are of particular interest for revealing movement patterns over time. Therefore, it is of great value to recapture those particular crabs.

In this paper, we present a horseshoe crab location predictor for estimating the locations of horseshoe crabs for the next season, based on previously observed movements over the years. We tried three different regression models: Ordinary Least Square Linear regression, Decision Tree regression, and Random Forest Ensemble regression. Based on our results, we recommend the Random Forest regression model with 100 estimators as it gave the best predictions compared to the others. The measure of accuracy used were the root mean squared error (RMSE) and the mean absolute error (MAE). The prediction model proved accurate when the 2018 summer capture season was used as a test set. The expectation is that the predictions will get more accurate as the data set grows over the seasons.

Acknowledgment. We thank the US Fish & Wildlife Service for their support with the tagging program, CT Sea Grant, Disney Conservation Fund, The Nature Conservancy, Audubon CT, CT Audubon Society, Sacred Heart University undergraduate Biology Majors, and the College of Arts and Sciences for funding and time supporting this project.

References

1. Allen, A., Singh, N.: Linking movement ecology with wildlife management and conservation. Front. Ecol. Evol. **3**, 155 (2016). https://doi.org/10.3389/fevo.2015.00155
2. Fraser, K., Davies, K., Davy, C., Ford, A., Flockhart, D., Martins, E.: Tracking the conservation promise of movement ecology. Front. Ecol. Evol. **6**(150), 1–8 (2018)
3. Benson, E.: Wired Wilderness: Technologies of Tracking and the Making of Modern Wildlife. The Johns Hopkins University Press, Baltimore (2010)
4. Peniche, G., Vaughan-Higgins, R., Carter, I., Pocknell, A., Simpson, D., Sainsbury, A.: Long-term health effects of harness-mounted radio transmitters in red kites (Milvus milvus) in England. Vet. Rec. **169**, 311 (2011)
5. Li, Z.: MoveMine: mining moving object data for discovery of animal movement patterns. ACM Trans. Intell. Syst. Technol. (TIST) **2**(4), 1–32 (2011). Article no. 37
6. Krisfalusi-Gannon, J., et al.: The role of horseshoe crabs in the biomedical industry and recent trends impacting species sustainability. J. Front. Mar. Sci. **5**, 185 (2018)
7. Mattei, J., Kasinak, J., Senbel, S., Bartholomew, K.: The power of citizen science: 20 years of horseshoe crab community research merging conservation, education and management. In: Tanacredi, J.T., et al. (eds.) 4th Proceedings of Horseshoe crab Conservation and Biology, Springer-NATURE (2021, in press)
8. Beekey, M., Mattei, J., Pierce, B.: Horseshoe crab eggs: a rare resource for predators in Long Island Sound. J. Exp. Mar. Biol. Ecol. **439**, 152–159 (2013)
9. Project *Limulus*. www.projectlimulus.org. Accessed 30th Aug 2020
10. Bakibayev, T., Kulzhanova, A.: Common movement prediction using polynomial regression. In: 2018 IEEE 12th International Conference on Application of Information and Communication Technologies (AICT), Almaty, Kazakhstan, pp. 1–4 (2018)

11. Bopp, J., Sclafani, M., Smith, D., et al.: Geographic-specific capture-recapture models reveal contrasting migration and survival rates of adult horseshoe crabs (*Limulus polyphemus*). Estuaries Coasts **42**, 1570–1585 (2019)
12. James-Pirri, M.: Seasonal movement of the American horseshoe crab Limulus polyphemus in a semi-enclosed bay on Cape Cod, Massachusetts (USA) as determined by acoustic telemetry. Curr. Zool. **56**(5), 575–586 (2010)
13. Wada, T., Mitsushio, T., Inoue, S., Kioke, H., Kawabe, R.: Movement patterns and residency of the critically endangered horseshoe crab Tachypleus tridentatus in a semi-enclosed bay determined using acoustic telemetry. PLoS ONE **11**(2), e0147429 (2016)
14. Youssef, I., Senbel, S., Kasinak, J.E., Mattei, J.: RCrab: an R analytics tool to visualize and analyze the movement of horseshoe crabs in long island sound. In: 2019 IEEE Long Island Systems, Applications and Technology Conference, NY, USA, pp. 1–6 (2019)
15. Van Rossum, G.: Python tutorial, Technical Report CS-R9526. Centrum voor Wiskunde en Informatica (CWI), Amsterdam, May 1995. http://www.python.org. Accessed 5th Sep 2020
16. Swan, B.: Migrations of adult horseshoe crabs, Limulus polyphemus, in the middle Atlantic bight: a 17-year tagging study. Estuaries **28**, 28–40 (2005)
17. Goldstein, H.: Multilevel mixed linear model analysis using iterative generalized least squares. Biometrika **73**(1), 43–56 (1986)
18. Shalev-Shwartz, S., Ben-David, S.: Chapter 18. Decision trees. In: Understanding Machine Learning. Cambridge University Press (2014)
19. Ho, T.: Random decision forests. In: Proceedings of the 3rd International Conference on Document Analysis and Recognition, Montreal, QC, pp. 278–282, August 1995

Low-Cost Smart Indoor Greenhouse for Urban Farming

Melisa Acosta-Coll[1](✉), Daniel Anaya[1], Luis Ojeda-Field[1], and Ronald Zamora-Musa[2]

[1] Universidad de la Costa, Barranquilla, Colombia
macosta10@cuc.edu.co
[2] Universidad Cooperativa de Colombia UCC, Bucaramanga, Colombia

Abstract. Currently, people want to take control of what they consume as well as the local authorities pursue to implement measures to improve sustainability, food security, and living standards. Indoor urban farming initiatives provide an opportunity to grow their own and obtain fresher food with fewer transportation emissions, likewise, it is a strategy to lift people out of food poverty, reduce environmental impact since the use of herbicides and pesticides is minimal and helps to reduce food waste. However, factors such as the time dedicated to the cultivation of plants, and the adequate space inside their houses prevents them from carrying out this activity.

This project presents the design of a low cost smart indoor greenhouse design to cultivate herbs and vegetables with minimum human intervention monitored by a web application. The prototype has three systems to control and monitor the main variables involved in the plant's growth such as soil moisture, temperature, and solar light intensity. Likewise, it is suitable for a home with little space and it is easily installable, has low energy consumption, and is cost-efficient.

Keywords: Indoor greenhouse · Smart greenhouse · Urban farming

1 Introduction

The global food crisis has brought the attention of many governments about food supply and security, especially in the cities since most of them import more than 90% of its food. Urban farming arises in this time as an alternative to local produce, and by 2030 it could produce 30% of the food supply in cities [1]. Highly populated cities worldwide are placing enormous demands on urban food supply systems and raise concerns about food security and unemployment [2]. Urban and Peri-Urban agriculture (UPA) arise as a strategy to supply the food consumption for city dwellers and at the same, generates employment, provide training opportunities for disadvantaged and marginalized groups, enhanced access to fresh fruit and vegetables [3, 4]. Likewise, it reduces environmental impacts through less transport, packaging, and storage and strengthens cities' resilience to climate change [5].

This type of farming includes the growth of agricultural products and the raising of animals within and around cities. It can be in indoor or outdoor environments and

O. Gervasi et al. (Eds.): ICCSA 2021, LNCS 12952, pp. 120–132, 2021.
https://doi.org/10.1007/978-3-030-86973-1_9

developed by small-specialized producers or large scale farming in the urban areas [6, 7].

Farming in outdoor environments is susceptible to significant risks such as attacks from pests, droughts, floods, and high winds. It also requires the use of pesticides that can introduce real health risks [8]. However, cultivation under controlled indoor environments constitutes a more efficient option for the production of edible products since it will not require the use of pesticides and allows only the amount of water and nutrients needed by the plants to be applied [9].

Most of the indoor urban farming projects worldwide use technology to provide optimal growing conditions of crops or plants in indoor environments and optimize the use of resources such as water, energy, nutrients, and space [10] and there are two main viable options, vertical farming, and greenhouse. The primary function of a greenhouse is to recreate the appropriate conditions to give life and generate the reproduction of plants, whether they are edible (such as fruit and vegetables), or for medicinal purposes, simulating optimal physicochemical conditions of temperature, carbon dioxide, and humidity (among others) for the proper care and growth that these plants require [11].

On the other hand, vertical farming consists of growing crops in a controlled environment based on vertically stacked layers design [12]. Greenhouses and vertical farms have different benefits for indoor urban farming and should be selected according to available space, product type, human resources, and other requirements [13].

This project presents the design of an indoor greenhouse for the cultivation of herbs and vegetables that automatically monitors and controls the main variables related to the plant's growth. This greenhouse is ideal for homes with little space due to its size and portability, also for users with little knowledge in plant cultivation and who have no time for it.

Below we review some indoor greenhouse system architectures for urban farming identifying the sensors and actuators to monitor and control the environment.

In Indonesia, Kaburuan *et. al* developed a system for monitoring the performance of indoor micro-climate that can help farmers grow crops using electronic sensors connected to an Internet-of-Things (IoT) board [9]. Figure 1 illustrates the architecture system.

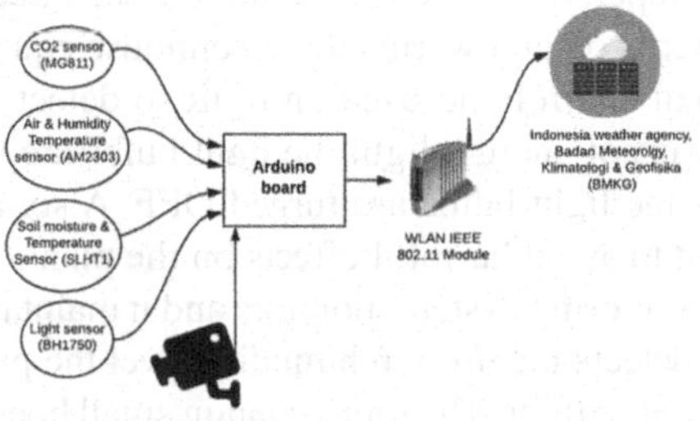

Fig. 1. IoT-based indoor greenhouse

The CO2 sensor (MG811) is a low-cost sensor used as an air pollution detector, the air humidity temperature sensor (AM2303) measures the temperature and humidity every 2 s and the light sensor (BH1750) provides high-resolution reading with small measurement variation. Likewise, the soil sensor module is a low-cost protected built-in soil temperature and humidity sensor and the OV767 camera module is s a single-chip 640 × 480 that can capture good still image. Furthermore, an Arduino board equipped with a WLAN IEEE 802.11 module with full TCP/IP to transmit all the sensors reading to the server controls the greenhouse. As future work, it will be implemented actuators such as fan and air conditioning for temperature control and an automated watering system for dehydration and humidity. Likewise, it will be implemented an automated fertilizer and lighting system that will use a machine-learning algorithm to automated control of the horticulture process.

A project developed in India by Pandit and Mancharkar measures and automatically controls conditions of a greenhouse environment conditions such as temperature, humidity, light intensity, and soil moisture by using different types of sensors [14]. Figure 2 shows the general system architecture.

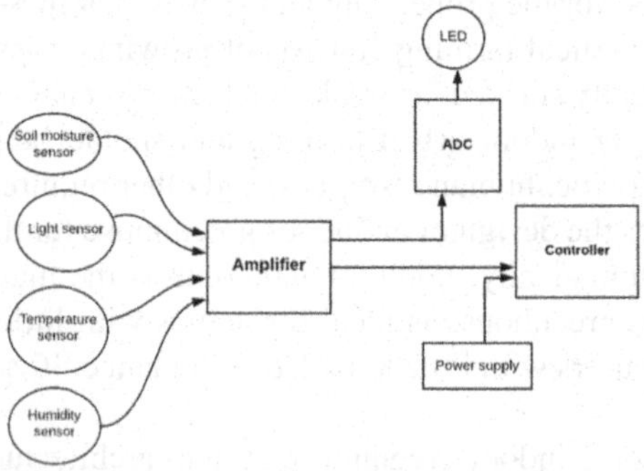

Fig. 2. Greenhouse environment conditions system monitoring

The system monitors and controls the greenhouse temperature according to a value set by the user and displays the information on an LED screen. When the temperature exceeds the value set, a fan placed inside of the greenhouse turns on and reduces the temperature. When the temperature decreases under the set value, a heater placed at the floor of the greenhouse turns on and warms the greenhouse equally.

The system has a light control and used an LDR to detect the light falling on the greenhouse. When there is not enough light the light bulbs are switched ON and turns off when there is lighter the light bulbs are turned OFF. Also, a switch was placed to turn off the lights at night to avoid harmful effects on the plants.

The humidity level monitoring system monitors and it maintains around a predefined value. When the system detects the drop in humidity level the pipelines installed inside the greenhouse allows water to floor. The pipes contain small hoes and hence allow water to reach the soil quickly. When the humidity level reaches the correct value the system OFFS the motor and flow of water stops.

In Indonesia, Chitti and Ktha developed a greenhouse gases and energy monitoring system integrating into an ARM logically small scale controller a CO2 sensor (MG-811), a CO sensor (MG-7), temperature sensor (LM-35) and humidity sensor (Sy-Sh-220) [15].

An XBee pro remote module connected to the ARM controller sends the acquired data to a base station that uses another Xbee Pro to get the data. Figure 3 shows the system architecture.

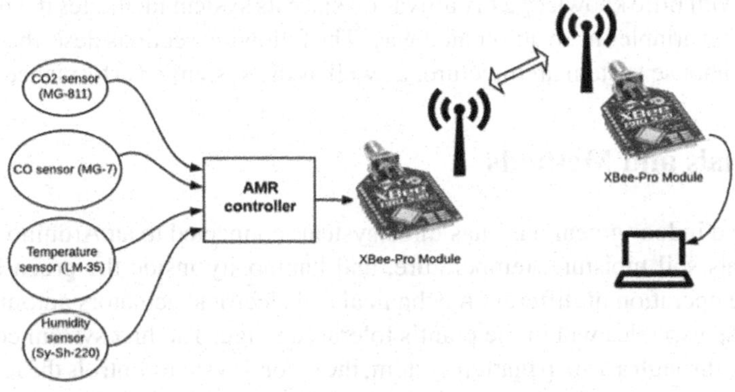

Fig. 3. Greenhouse gases and energy monitoring system

Another automated greenhouse for small-scale cultivation developed in Mexico by Salazar-Aguilar, used five different sensors connected to an Arduino controller to monitor and control the greenhouse environmental conditions [16]. The system has a humidity and temperature sensor (DHT 11, DHT22), an LDR as a light sensor, a hygrometer (FC-28) to measure the soil moisture and, a barometric sensor (BMP280) to measure atmospheric pressure. Figure 4 shows the automated greenhouse.

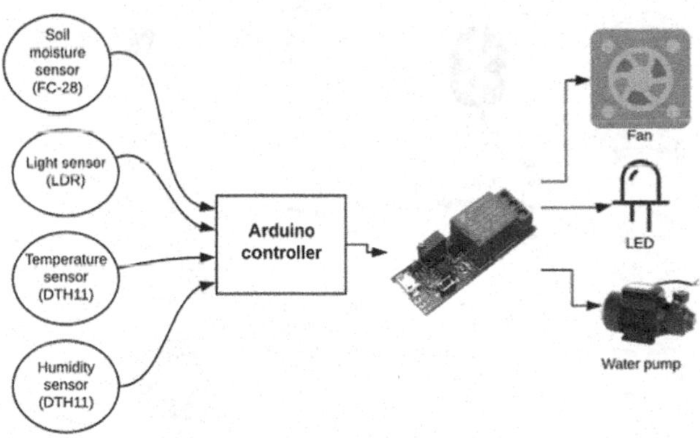

Fig. 4. Automated greenhouse for small-scale cultivation

For this system, when the temperature exceeds the temperature range, the relay will activate the fan; conversely, when the temperature is below the set temperature range, the relay turns on the led lamp. On the other hand, to maintain the desired humidity levels, the system activates a water pump when the humidity sensor (hygrometer) is removed from the soil and begins to water the plant.

Considering the reviewed projects and identifying the sensors and actuators to monitor and controlled the most important environmental variables that influence plant growth, a low-cost smart indoor greenhouse for growing herbs and small vegetables were developed. This indoor greenhouse is suitable for houses with little space, as well as for users with little knowledge in cultivation since its system facilitates the monitoring and control of variables in an automated way. The following sections describe the design and the greenhouse system architecture, as well as the system's performance.

2 Materials and Methods

The presented indoor greenhouse has three systems connected to an Arduino board that measurements soil moisture, temperature, and luminosity inside the green-house and manages the operation of different mechanical and electrical actuators automatically to controls these variables within the plant's tolerance range. The first system controls the soil moisture through a drip irrigation system; the second system controls the temperature inside the greenhouse and activates a ventilation system when it is necessary. The third system measures the light intensity activating a lighting system when the solar light is not good enough for the plant. Finally, a web app allows users to monitor remotely the variables and receive alerts. Figure 5 illustrates the general system architecture.

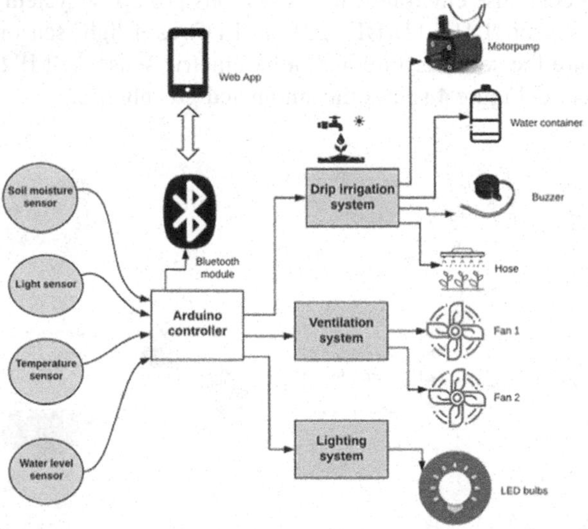

Fig. 5. Indoor greenhouse general system architecture

The control system follows a cyclic control logic programmed in ARDUINO to perform all the necessary actions for greenhouse automation. The central control system receives all the measurements and manages the operation of the different mechanical and electrical actuators. Through this primary system, the orders for each of the subsystems are established. In this particular case, it uses a feedback control system or closed circuit, where the output signals of the different sensors can modify the signals emitted by the ARDUINO.

The greenhouse control system aims to preserve the integrity of the crop, as well as promotes the energy efficiency of the final prototype and activates the subsystems in a range of 7 am-7 pm; if in that time range any need is detected by the crop, the corresponding subsystem will act, outside this range it will not execute any action.

This measure does not affect any of the variables involved in plant growth since the crops need only approximately 12 h of sunlight for optimal development. Also, the supply of artificial light higher than necessary could cause irreparable damage to the crop [17]. In the case of irrigation and ventilation subsystems, it will prevent the wear of mechanical actuators such as relays, motor pumps, among others.

The first action the system executes is to read the time; if the time is within the activation range (7 am – 7 pm), read the temperature sensor measurement. When the temperature measurement is above the plant's tolerance range, the control system activates the fans and proceeds to read the light intensity measurement.

If the light intensity value is below the set range, it activates the lighting system and proceeds to read the soil moisture. When the soil moisture is lower than the set value, it enables the drip irrigation system.

The ventilation system will be deactivated when the temperature inside the greenhouse is within the tolerance range of the plant, also, the lighting system will turn off the bulbs when the entire system is deactivated or the plant receives the amount of light it needs. Finally, the irrigation system will be deactivated when the substrate reaches the desired humidity.

Following, it will be described the physical construction of the greenhouse and the operation of each of the systems.

2.1 Greenhouse Physical Design

The main physical characteristics of this indoor greenhouse are that it is easy to move due to its weight; also, its size is suitable for the growing of herbs and small vegetables in places with little space. The structure has dimensions of 60 cm × 60 cm with a

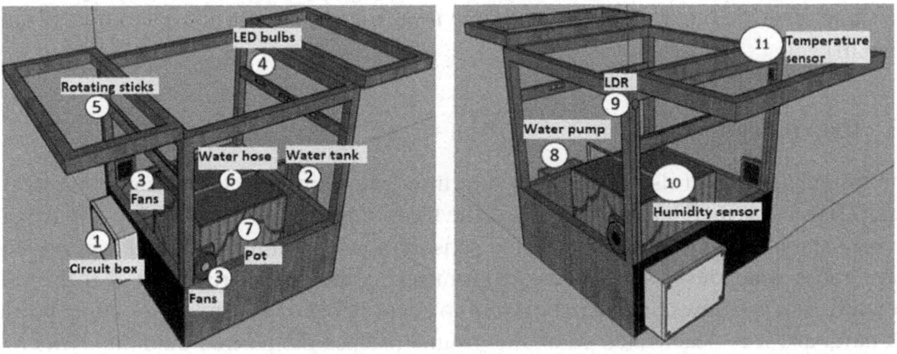

Fig. 6. A Greenhouse prototype parts B Prototype Model

superior opening system that allows the user easy access to the crop. Figure 6 shows the greenhouse prototype parts and Fig. 7 the greenhouse prototype.

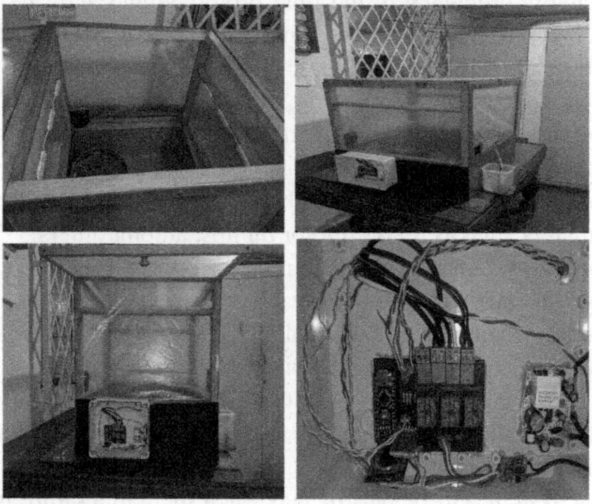

Fig. 7. Greenhouse prototype

2.2 Lighting System

The lighting system has an LDR (light dependent resistance) that measures the amount of light that falls on the greenhouse and a set of LED bulbs installed on two rotating sticks. The control system compares the measured value with a value set by programming that allows the optimal plant growth with the amount of light the plant needs daily; if the obtained measurement is below the established range, activates the set of LED bulbs. To increase the incidence intensity and improve photosynthesis, the LED lights are installed on two rotating sticks that varies the light exposure angle in a range of 0° – 180°. The lighting system deactivates the light bulbs when the light intensity value is higher than the value set in the control system or when it is outside the system activation time (7 a.m – 7 p.m).

2.3 Drip Irrigation System

The greenhouse controls the soil moisture through a drip irrigation system that helps water, fertilizers, and nutrients can reach the roots of plants effectively. This drip irrigation system has a hygrometer (humidity sensor), a motor pump, a plastichose, a water tank, and a water level sensor. The hygrometer module measures every 4 h the soil moisture, if it is below the range, the Arduino controller activates the motor pump inside the tank, and it is deactivated when the ground reaches the desired humidity. Water is pumped from the tank to the plant roots using a fish pump and to prevent damages, the greenhouse has a water level system constituted by an integrated ULN2803 whose terminals are inside the tank. If the water level is below 15 cm, a buzzer emits a warning sound and will be deactivated when the tank is full again.

2.4 Ventilation System

The ventilation system measures the temperature and air humidity inside the greenhouse using a DTH11 sensor that measures the temperature each hour, and two fans installed whose purpose is to recirculate the air inside the greenhouse. This system is not designed for massive temperature decrement, but to recirculate the air inside the greenhouse. If the temperature exceeds the tolerance range, the control system activates the fans, one fan drives air into the interior and the other pulls it out, that is, a mechanical ventilation-extraction ventilation system.

2.5 Remote Warning System

A web application visualizes in the temperature, air humidity, soil moisture, and the light intensity of the greenhouse. This application was designed and compiled on the free APP INVENTOR website initially for Android. If the temperature inside the greenhouse exceeds the set range, the temperature module turns red and indicates the user should relocate the greenhouse to a colder place. Likewise, when the water tank is low, the soil moisture module turns red and shows the user to fill up the tank. If the light intensity is higher than the plant's needs, the light intensity module turns red indicating the user to relocate the greenhouse.

3 Results and Discussion

For each of the systems, measurements are made separately and in conjunction with the prototype. The tests and measurements obtained for each system are described below.

3.1 Lighting System Test

The measurements of the lighting system were made in inside and outside a house in Barranquilla (Colombia) to be able to set the light intensity threshold. This city is located in the Caribbean region of the Colombia, and during the course of the year, the temperature generally ranges from 24 °C to 32 °C and rarely drops below 23 °C or rises above 34 °C.

These measurements were performed with a sunny sky from 8 am to 5 pm with a temporal resolution of 20 min. Figure 8 shows the measurements inside and outside the house.

Considering the data obtained from Fig. 8, an optimum light intensity range for the plant was set between 15% – 82%; if the system measures values lower than 15%, it activates the artificial lighting system. This criterion was used to choose the characteristics of artificial lights, where the light intensity provided by artificial lights will not exceed 25% of the values obtained in broad daylight.

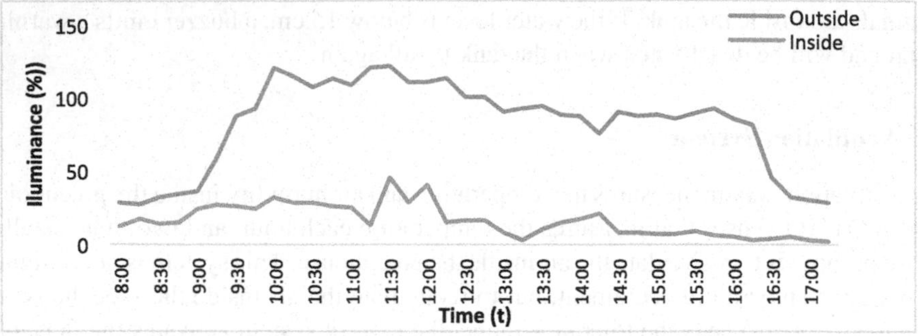

Fig. 8. Light intensity measurements inside the house.

3.2 Drip Irrigation System Test

The drip irrigation system tests were performed for three consecutive days in a round pot with an area of 0.4 m^2 to measure the relative soil moisture (RSM) before introducing the hygrometer tip inside a black sand substrate. A plastic hose with diffusion points was placed superficially on a substrate of black sand and connected to a plastic bottle filled with 500 ml of water and raised manually so that by gravity the water would lower. Figures 9 shows the results of measurements of days 1, 2 and 3, respectively.

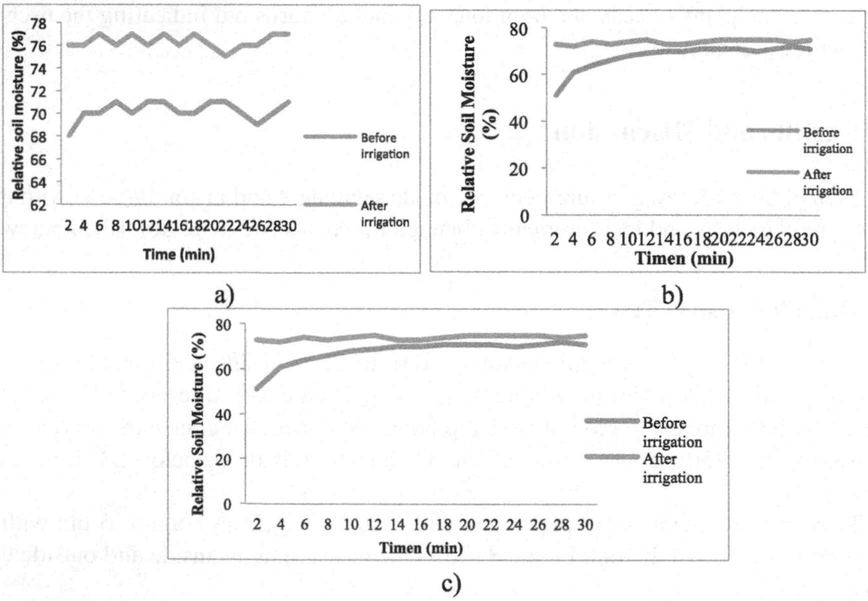

Fig. 9. Relative soil moisture measurements a) Day 1. b) Day 2. c) Day 3

From Fig. 9, it was established that when the soil moisture is below 70%, the irrigation system is activated and deactivated when it reaches a humidity of 76%. Also, the system will be deactivated when it is outside the operating range.

3.3 Ventilation System Test

The greenhouse ventilation system is associated with the measurement of temperature inside it. For two consecutive days, the temperature was measured to observe the behavior of the thermal load inside it, and to determine the forced ventilation requirements. Figure 10 shows the temperature measurements inside the greenhouse.

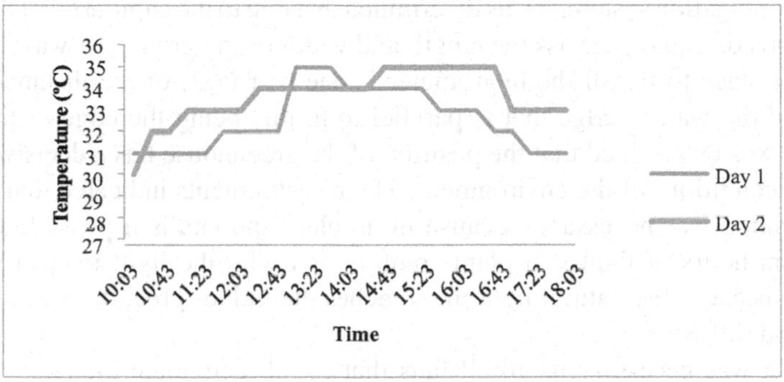

Fig. 10. Ventilation system test results

Although the previous measurements were made inside the house and in a place in the shade, the acquired temperature values are high and without proper air circulation, can damage the plant. Therefore, it is necessary to use fans to recirculate the air, with this; the objective is to avoid suffocation of the plant if there is a temperature spike that could negatively affect the development of the plant. With forced ventilation, air recirculation is also sought to remove CO2.

This prototype of indoor greenhouse is an efficient solution for people who do not have a large space at home, who have little knowledge and who do not have much time to care for the crop since the greenhouse automatically performs all the vital functions of care that a crop requires and it only needs human intervention to fill the water tank. Likewise, the system design allows better use of water and nutrients through the irrigation system, increases photosynthesis with the lighting system, and maintains the proper temperature for plant growth. As future work, the aim is to improve the structural design using lighter and more weather-resistant materials and implement a photovoltaic system for power supply.

4 Conclusions

Currently, governments and institutions around the world are investing millions in indoor urban farms projects, since it can produce more food with less impact. Likewise, the global food crisis has sparked citizens' interest in growing their food but many face obstacles such as costs, space limitations, and time dedicated to cultivation. To provide an optimum solution, this manuscript presents the design of an automated low-cost indoor greenhouse prototype for urban farming suitable for little space homes. Unlike other indoor greenhouse prototypes, this system automatically monitors and controls the main variables involved in plants growth with the least user intervention since it a plug and play design.

The system monitors and controls the temperature and lighting that the plant needs inside the greenhouse, as well as the soil moisture through a drip irrigation system where the user through a web application can monitor these actions, as it can be easily programmed with the ARDUINO board.

From the irrigation system, it was determined that due to the capillarity of the ground, the water spreads equally across the length and width of the ground. It was determined that the best place to install the hygrometer is one half (1/2) of the distance between the hose and the wall or edge that is parallel to it, this being the edge of the planter. Likewise, it was determined that the position of the greenhouse has a decisive factor in the lighting conditions of the environment. The measurements indicated that the use of artificial lighting was necessary, because in no place indoors is it possible to provide the minimum hours of light that plants require and with the light intensity that they also require because the natural light that reaches the indoor green-house is always by reflection and diffusion.

Finally, it was necessary to install fans that could recirculate the air in the room, with this it was sought to avoid suffocating the plant; additionally, forced ventilation also seeks to renew the air since the plants emanate CO2 and it is necessary that they have fresh air for their breathing.

As future work, the aim is to improve the structural design using lighter and more weather-resistant materials and implement a photovoltaic system for power supply.

References

1. Thompson Reuters Foundation: ANALYSIS-Urban farms to traffic bans: cities prep for post-coronavirus future. Thompson Reuters Foundation News, 21 April 2020
2. De Bon, H., Parrot, L., Moustier, P.: Sustainable urban agriculture in developing countries. A review. Agron. Sustain. Dev. **30**, 21–32 (2010)
3. Farhangi, M., Turvani, M., Van der Valk, A., Carsjens, G.: High-tech urban agriculture in Amsterdam: an actor network analysis. Sustainability **12**(10) (2020). https://doi.org/10.3390/su12103955
4. Zanele Khumalo, N., Sibanda, M.: Does urban and peri-urban agriculture contribute to household food security? An assessment of the food security status of households in Tongaat, eThekwini Municipality. Sustainability **11**(14) (2019). https://doi.org/10.3390/su11041082
5. Zasad, I.: Multifunctional peri-urban agriculture—a review of societal demands and the provision of goods and services by farming. Land Use Policy **28**(4), 639–648 (2011)
6. Orsini, F., Kahane, R., Nono-Womdim, R., Gianquinto, G.: Urban agriculture in the developing world: a review. Agron. Sustain. Dev. **33** (2013)
7. Pearson, L.J., Pearson, L., Pearson, C.J.: Sustainable urban agriculture: stocktake and opportunities. Int. J. Agric. Sustain. (2010). https://doi.org/10.3763/ijas.2009.0468
8. Pinstrup-Andersen, P.: Is it time to take vertical indoor farming seriously?. Glob. Food Secur. **17**, 233–235 (2018)
9. Kaburuan, E.R., Jayadi, R., Harisno: A design of IoT-based monitoring system for intelligence indoor micro-climate horticulture farming in Indonesia. In: Procedia Computer Science, pp. 459–464 (2019)

10. Goodman, W., Minner, J.: Will the urban agricultural revolution be vertical and soilless? A case study of controlled environment agriculture in New York City. Land Use Policy **83**, 160–173 (2019)
11. Sammons, P.J., Furukawua, T., Bulgin, A.: Autonomous pesticide spraying robot for use in a greenhouse. ISBN 0–9587583–7–9 (2005)
12. Benke, K., Tomkins, B.: Future food-production systems: vertical farming and controlled-environment agriculture. Sustain. Sci. Pract. Policy **13**(1) (2017). https://doi.org/10.1080/15487733.2017.1394054
13. Martin, M., Molin, E.: Environmental assessment of an urban vertical hydroponic farming system in Sweden. Sustainability **11**(15) (2019). https://doi.org/10.3390/su11154124
14. Pandit, A.A., Mancharkar, A.V.: Green house environment monitoring and control system. Int. J. Sci. Eng. Res. **7**(8) (2016)
15. Chitti, S., Ktha, L.S.: Data acquisition of green house gases and energy monitoring system using GSM technology. Int. J. Innov. Technol. Explor. Eng. IJITEE **8** (2019)
16. Salazar-Aguilar, N.: Diseño de un Sistema Inteligente para el Control Automa-tizado de Invernaderos. Universidad Autónoma del Estado de More-los, México, Maestría (2020)
17. Moliner, R., Marsh, H., Heinz, E.: Del carbón activo al grafeno : Evolución de los materiales de carbono. In: Grupo de conversion de combustibles. ICB-CSIC, pp. 2–5 (2016)
18. Richard, M.: El carbón activo ya se fabrica con una estructura diseñada a medida, MIT Technol. Rev. 12 junio (2015)
19. Omo-Okoro, P.N., Daso, A.P., Okonkwo, J.O.: A review of the application of agricultural wastes as precursor materials for the adsorption of per- and polyfluoroalkyl substances: A focus on current approaches and methodologies. Environ. Technol. Innov. **9**, 100–114 (2018). https://doi.org/10.1016/j.eti.2017.11.005
20. Palansooriya, K.N., et al.: Impacts of biochar application on upland agriculture: a review. J. Environ. Manage. **234**(December 2018), 52–64 (2019). https://doi.org/10.1016/j.jenvman.2018.12.085
21. Green Power: Eco friendly technology. El uso de carbón vegetal como fertilizante, 27 July 2018
22. C. Jacobo Mendez Alzamora Consultor Eco-Agricultura. (PGSJ): Carbón en Agricultura – Engormix, 11 septiembre 2017
23. Yuan, C., Feng, S., Huo, Z., Ji, Q.: Effects of deficit irrigation with saline water on soil water-salt distribution and water use efficiency of maize for seed production in arid Northwest China. Agric. Water Manag. **212**(September 2018), 424–432 (2019). https://doi.org/10.1016/j.agwat.2018.09.019
24. Kamcev, J., et al.: Author's accepted manuscript salt concentration dependence of ionic conductivity in ion exchange membranes. J. Membr. Sci. **547**(October 2017), 123–133 (2017). https://doi.org/10.1016/j.memsci.2017.10.024
25. Sadiku, M.N.O., Alexander, C.K.: Fundamentals of Electric Circuits, Third Ed. vol. 91, Bookman (2017)
26. Cotching, W.E., Kögel-Knabner, I.: Organic matter in the agricultural soils of Tasmania, Australia-a review A R T I C L E I N F O, Geoderma **312**(October 2017), 170–182 (2018). https://doi.org/10.1016/j.geoderma.2017.10.006
27. Frouz, J.: Effects of soil macro- and mesofauna on litter decomposition and soil organic matter stabilization. Geoderma **332**(September 2017), 161–172 (2018). https://doi.org/10.1016/j.geoderma.2017.08.039
28. Rostami, S., Azhdarpoor, A.: The application of plant growth regulators to improve phytoremediation of contaminated soils: a review. Chemosphere **220**, 818–827 (2019). https://doi.org/10.1016/j.chemosphere.2018.12.203

29. Piyare, R., Murphy, A.L., Tosato, P., Brunelli, D.: Plug into a plant: using a plant microbial fuel cell and a wake-up radio for an energy neutral sensing system. Proc. - 2017 IEEE 42nd Conf. Local Comput. Netw. Workshop LCN Workshop, pp. 18–25, 2017 (2017). https://doi.org/10.1109/LCN.Workshops.2017.60
30. Hubenova, Y., Mitov, M.: Conversion of solar energy into electricity by using duckweed in direct photosynthetic plant fuel cell. Bioelectrochemistry **87**, 185–191 (2012). https://doi.org/10.1016/j.bioelechem.2012.02.008
31. Atzori, G., Mancuso, S., Masi, E.: Seawater potential use in soilless culture: a review. Sci. Hortic. **249**(January), 199–207 (2019). https://doi.org/10.1016/j.scienta.2019.01.035
32. Yang, S., Wang, Z., Han, Z., Pan, X.: Performance modelling of seawater electrolysis in an undivided cell: Effects of current density and seawater salinity. Chem. Eng. Res. Des. **143**(1037), 79–89 (2019). https://doi.org/10.1016/j.cherd.2019.01.009
33. CANNA Research: Influencia de la temperatura ambiental en las plantas, CANNA España. 15 de marzo (2017)
34. Olubode, O.O.: Influence of seasonal variability of precipitation and temperature on performances of pawpaw varieties intercropped with cucumber. Sci. Hortic. **243**(February 2018), 622–644 (2019). https://doi.org/10.1016/j.scienta.2018.06.007
35. Sánchez-Lucas, R., Fernández-Escobar, R., Suárez, M.P., Benlloch, M., Benlloch-González, M., Quintero, J.M.: Effect of moderate high temperature on the vegetative growth and potassium allocation in olive plants. J. Plant Physiol. **207**, 22–29 (2016). https://doi.org/10.1016/j.jplph.2016.10.001
36. Vegas, J.: Qué ocurre al regar las plantas con agua caliente?, 3 de abril (2016)
37. Ni, J., Cheng, Y., Wang, Q., Ng, C.W.W., Garg, A.: Effects of vegetation on soil temperature and water content: field monitoring and numerical modelling. J. Hydrol. **571**(November 2018), 494–502 (2019). https://doi.org/10.1016/j.jhydrol.2019.02.009

Competitiveness Analysis of the Georgian Transport and Logistics System in the Black Sea Region: Challenges and Perspectives

George Abuselidze(✉)

Batumi Shota Rustaveli State University, Ninoshvili, 35, 6010 Batumi, Georgia
george.abuselidze@bsu.edu.ge

Abstract. We have discussed transit potential as the actor of the regional development and Georgia as the transit hub in this piece of work. Performing the function of transit hub represents an important economic and political aspiration for Georgia's integration into the world economy. Effective use of transit potential in global economy conditions guarantees the achievement of success. As a result of the formation of new forms of economic relations, Georgia's function as a Transcaucasia corridor is expanding. The present paper aims to study and analyze the potential of Georgia's transit capabilities and to determine its influence on the financial and economic development of the country. The object of research is the transport and logistics sector of Georgia in terms of transit. The subject of the research is the comparative analysis of the targeted and consequential indicators of the potential of Georgia's transit capabilities. The main results and recommendations of the research, the implementation of which will promote the socio-economic development of Georgia, increase competitiveness and effective use of transit potential are presented in the conclusion part of this paper. In particular, when trying to reveal the problems related to the transit flows of Georgia, it turned out that the favorable geographical location cannot ensure the realization of Georgia's transit capabilities and its formation as a transit hub; The Europe-Caucasus-Asia transport corridor is characterized by low competitiveness both in terms of shipping costs and transit time; The necessity of complex development of the transport system of Georgia and completion of the Anaklia Deep Sea Port Project is substantiated.

Keywords: Transit flows · Transit hub · Caucasus transit corridor · TRACECA · Logistics · Competition · Economic development · Black sea region

1 Introduction

Georgia, as a transit area connecting Europe and Asia, is an attractive short-distance hub for international shipping. Due to its convenient location, Georgia can become a major logistics hub in the Europe-Caucasus-Asia (TRACECA) transport corridor. Utilization of transit potential requires increasing the efficiency of the transport complex, which is related to the need to build multimodal logistics centers. Establishment of logistics centers in Georgia will be an important determinant of the growth of cargo flows in the

O. Gervasi et al. (Eds.): ICCSA 2021, LNCS 12952, pp. 133–148, 2021.
https://doi.org/10.1007/978-3-030-86973-1_10

transit corridor and the competitiveness of the country's transit function. In addition, the logistics infrastructure significantly attracts foreign investment. The development of the transport sector is essential for the performance of the transit function, as well as for the development of all priority sectors in Georgia. Transit flows are one of the major components of the budget revenues of Georgia. Therefore, taking effective measures in this direction is an important precondition for the economic prosperity of the country. The difficulties associated with attracting and handling transit cargo flows are increasing. This is caused, on the one hand, by the activation of competing corridors and, on the other hand, by the lack of internal transport infrastructure. The study and analysis of these issues determines the urgency of the given topic. As Georgia is a low-productivity country and therefore the share of exports in total shipping is very low, attracting transit flows is vital for the country's financial and economic development. The problems existing in this regard hinder the performance of Georgia's transit function. Therefore, research and complex analysis of the existing problems in this direction is necessary for the development of Georgia's transit potential.

2 Research Methods

The theoretical basis of the research is the papers of various sciences on the research problem. Out of those, it is significant to analyze the spillover effects of the Logistical Trends in Eurasia at the domestic level, practice and theory on New Silk Road [1–11]. The conducted research is based on the reports of the National Statistics Office of Georgia, Ministries, Eurostat, World Bank, World Economic Forum, Sea ports of Georgia and railway operators, as well as legislative acts related to the research issue.

The research was conducted by using various methods. In particular, the economic activity in the field of transport was studied by the method of analysis and synthesis; Quantitative and qualitative methods were used to determine the volume of revenues received from the fees of road use and cargo turnover of Ports of Georgia. The Logistics Performance Index was calculated by grouping and index method; The competitiveness of the corridors of the Black Sea Region was determined by the method of comparative analysis; The sectorial structure of Gross Domestic Product (GDP) and the share of transport in economic growth were presented using the graphic representation method.

3 Results and Discussion

3.1 Caucasus Transit Corridor and Perspectives of a Logistics Hub in Georgia

In the Modern Global Competitive Environment, transit creates additional capabilities for achieving success in the international market and for the financial and economic development of the country. Using the transit potential to full gives certain advantages to the region, such as: increasing competitiveness; Deepening foreign economic relations; Involvement in international cargo flows; Forming an additional source of filling the country's budget; Promoting socio-economic development. Only economic benefits, which are received from transit flows are not sufficient, each country should develop appropriate approaches and methods to prevent the following threats that accompany the movement of these flows: wrongful activities, illegal migration, spreading various diseases, vibration and dust caused by the movement of long vehicles. Exactly, to this end, an ECP action plan is developed, which is based on the processing of world practice and forecast data. Regional ECP seminars were conducted in all WCO regions by WCO. It was noted that the exchange of innovative practices among members is favorable means for the development of transit [12].

Competitive transit corridors for Georgia are [13]:

- Northern Maritime Corridor;
- Southern Maritime Corridor;
- Trans-Siberian Railway transit Corridor;
- South Land Transport Corridor;

The New Silk Road (by railway route) is the shortest distance for China to transport cargo to Europe. Despite its short transit time, China prefers a southern maritime corridor which has a flexible tariff policy. There is no unified pricing system in the conditions of the New Silk Road. Tariffs are very expensive due to the fact that it combines all transport nodes. In relation to Chinese cargo, the main competitor is the South Maritime route, which passes through Iran. The Port of Bandar Abbas (Iran), after lifting the sanctions of the West, operates successfully and competes greatly with the ports of Poti and Batumi. Cargo shipping from China via Bandar Abbas port to Azerbaijan is much cheaper than in case of Poti port, the reason for which are high tariffs imposed on services.

Another expression of interest towards the Caucasus region is a project ratified by the European Union. The main goal of the TRACECA project is to create the shortest transport corridor connecting Europe and Asia, which will ensure the development of economic, political and cultural relations among the countries of this region. The Europe-Caucasus-Asia transport corridor represents a precondition for the restoration of the "Great Silk Road". Despite the short transit time and the shortest distance, the disadvantage of this corridor is the multimodal shipments, which increases the cost of shipping. In addition, it is less competitive due to the lack of a unified tariff policy. Georgia's competitors are the ports of Russia, Turkey and Ukraine, which have highly developed and arranged port infrastructure and optimal transit times. In the research of 2012, the recommendations are developed on how the Caucasus Transit Corridor can increase competitiveness compared to alternative corridors. In particular, if the Caucasus transit corridor becomes 10% cheaper, transit time will be reduced by one week, Georgia's railway infrastructure will be improved and reliability will be increases when crossing the Caspian Sea, the abovementioned corridor will carry out unprecedented transit shipments and contribute to the increase of the country's GDP [14]. The modern Silk Road will increase the revenues of all participating parties, including Georgia, in the form of transit taxes. The transit corridor will create real potential for Georgia to become a logistics "hub" and easily connect to all parts of the world. This will be an important stimulus to encourage production development and investment in the country. Georgia has been given the opportunity to play an important role in the transport corridor serving cargo turnover between Europe and Asia, to create transit services for intercontinental passenger flows and to serve the cargo shipment market in the region. The implementation of the Europe-Caucasus-Asia project is of strategic importance for

Georgia. The development of transit shipments through the TRACECA corridor is a task of state importance, which will greatly promote the growth of production and job creation in our country.

The power of states is determined by the perfect realization of all economic capabilities. Militaristic capabilities are gradually losing their role of the main determinant of maintaining a leading position in the world economic system. In the real world, success is achieved through geo-economic war.

The South Caucasus is not only an economically but also a geopolitically important region for both the East and the West, as well as for the modern world. Georgia holds a key place in this region. As well as, our country has the potential capability to become a connecting country between the North and the East.

Georgia is one of the countries in Eurasia that came closer to the EU regions and became involved in its integration processes [15]. Georgia, as an arena of conflict zones and its difficult relations with Russia expresses the difficult nature of the region's development, which significantly hinders the development of the transport corridor from north to south in the direction of Russia-Armenia-Iran. Georgia represents important state for the European Union with the function of a transport bridge connecting Europe-Caucasus-Asia. Georgia, as one of the important participants of this corridor, can play a crucial role in increasing overall efficiency.

The node to strengthening Georgia's transit function is the development of all transit highway, all port, railway and road infrastructure passing on its territory. As well as, the introduction of flexible customs control mechanisms, the implementation of a common European transport strategy and the development of other necessary measures, which are related to the proper functioning of the corridor. Port systems and its geographical regularities of its development play a major role in the development of the global economy. A seaport is a major transportation node through which goods of world importance and passengers are transported from one point to another. More than 70% of world production is shipped by sea and ocean through containers. According to the cargo turnover pursuant to the data of 2018, among the major seaports of the world, the Ports of China are leading ones, which is explained by the fact that the number of exports from Asia to other countries are quite large [16]. Seaports represent not only an instrument for the use of transit potential and socio-economic development of the country, but also a prerequisite for the successful operation of the international transport corridor TRACECA. Maritime transport represents the backbone of the global economy. One of the main components of the logistics chain system is the Georgian ports. They play a major role in the socio-economic development of the country. Transport-transit infrastructure of Georgia is significantly related to the development of seaports. The seaport system of Georgia is currently represented by the ports of Batumi, Poti, Supsa, Kulevi and constructing Anaklia, through which transit cargos (see Fig. 1) passing on Georgia are transported – to the direction of Varna, Constanza, Novorossiysk, Odessa and Istanbul [17].

The Georgian Railway is an important niche in the Eurasian Transport Corridor, connecting Europe with Central Asia and then China with the shortest route. The implementation of the TRACECA project has significantly promoted the increase of the volume of railway shipping. The most cost-effective direction of Georgian Railway is cargo

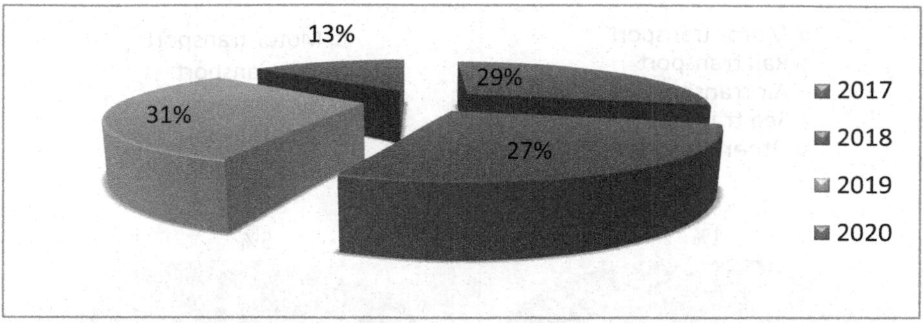

Fig. 1. Georgia Cargo Turnover of Georgia 2017–2020 (I-IV 2020). Source: Compiled by the authors based on the information of the Ministry of Economic and Sustainable Development

shipments. It is linked to the ports of Batumi, Poti and Kulevi, from where cargo is transported directly to the ports of Bulgaria, Romania, Ukraine, Russia and Turkey.

As we can see (see Table 1) in the total cargo turnover of the railway, transit have the leading place, therefore taking effective measures in this direction are required [18].

Table 1. Volume of cargo according to the transport conditions on the Georgian Railway, in tons (during I-III months) 2019–2020.

Volume of Cargo according to the transport conditions	2019	2020
Export	340 956.0	316 031.0
Import	552 720.0	603 942.0
Local	390 607.0	340 002.0
Transit	1 236 224.2	1 514 180.0

Source: Compiled by the authors based on the data of the Georgian Railway

Road transport holds an important place in the structure of the Georgian transport system. About 43–44% comes to road transport (see Fig. 2). After the opening of the border with Turkey, the scale of road transport activities has reached to a maximum. Cargo turnover indicators have also increased accordingly. Almost 17.2 million tons of cargo are transported annually. The automotive sector has an increasing character in recent years. The peak rate was observed in 2015, when the amount of cargo handled on it reached to 47 million ton. By 2018, it has reduced to 31 million tons [19]. Transit from Turkey is characterized by a growing trend, which causes serious delays in traffic. This problem should be solved through the Batumi bypass road, through which ecologic condition wiil be significantly improved in the resort area and international transit traffic will be simplified [7].

When shipping transit cargo directly, the road use fee is accumulated in the budget in the amount of GEL 200, which is provided for the for the utilization of transit infrastructure on the territory of Georgia [20]. In addition, additional benefits for the country during the transit process is obtained from the costs of fuel, food products, maintenance,

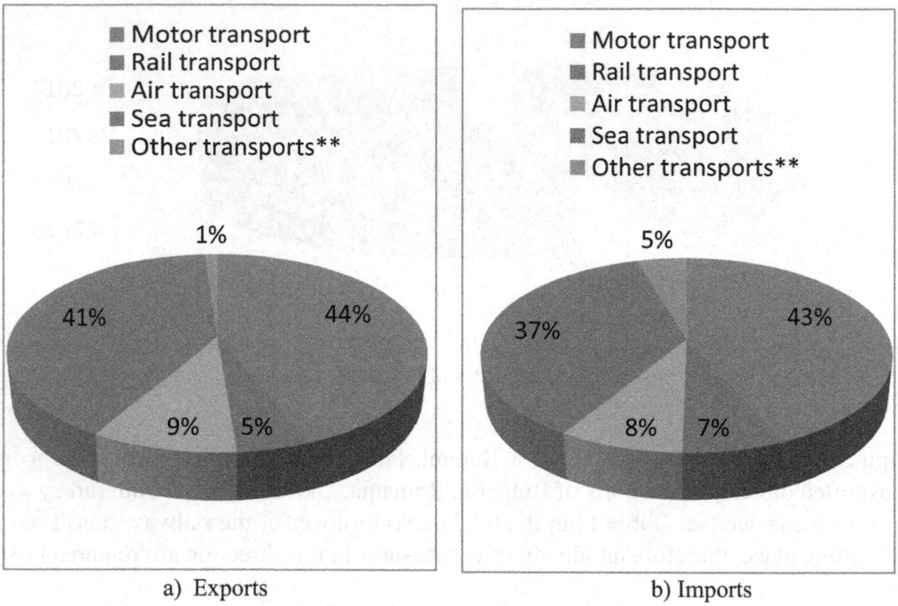

Fig. 2. Exports-Imports of Georgia by Mode of Transport (2016–2021). Source: Compiled based on the information of the National Statistics Office of Georgia [25]

fines and other services. In the case of increased transit cargo flows, significant funds are flowed into the budget (see Fig. 3).

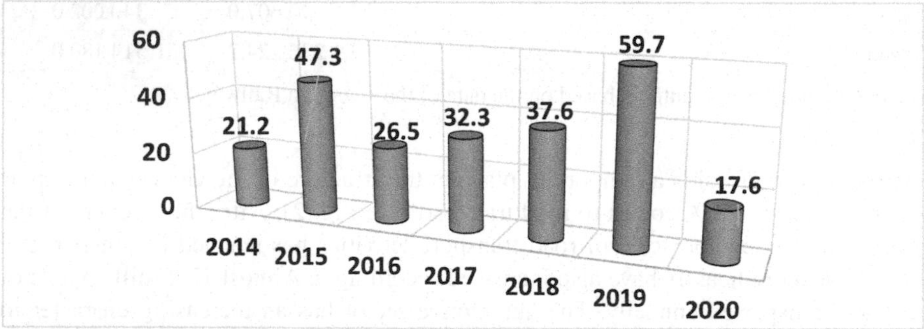

Fig. 3. Revenues received from the Road Use Fees 2014 – 2020 years (million GEL). Source: Compiled based on the information of the Ministry of Finance of Georgia [21]

The increase in road transit shipment from Armenia through Larsi to Russia is conditioned by the increase in the number of vehicles moving by transit. As well as, high road taxes imposed between Turkey and Iran are pushing Turkish cargo owners to carry out the shipment through the transport corridor of Georgia.

The volume of cargo transported by vehicles is characterized by a decreasing trend. In 2018, it was decreased by 0.4 million tons compared to the previous year. In 2019, a small increase was observed - 42.3 million tons [22]. Despite the decrease in cargo turnover volume, the role and function of the transport sector on the country's economy is still large. Such a trend is caused by foreign or domestic factors. Since we have to function in a dynamically changeable environment we cannot draw conclusions explicitly. Salary levels in this sector are characterized by an increasing trend from year to year (maneuvering within 1300 million Gel), which increases the potential for development. As we can see, transit flows have a great impact on the socio-economic growth of the country. By realizing the transit function, Georgia can promote the growth of cargo transportation, increase the level of employment and achieve common welfare. Increasing investment in this area and strengthening government policy are crucial cornerstones.

Relative share of logistic sector amounts to about 12% of Gross Domestic Product of the Country. The quality and competitiveness of the transport-logistics system represents an important factor in the process of making a decision regarding the investment of capital by an investor in a potential investment country. Georgia is the carrier of LPI low indicator (2.44) compared to its competitive transport corridors (see Fig. 4). It holds 119th place out of 160 countries [23]. The cost of logistics services and shipping is non-competitive. As well as, Georgia lags behind Armenia with LPI indicator of 2018 (2.61 points/rating - 92), which does not even have exit to the sea.

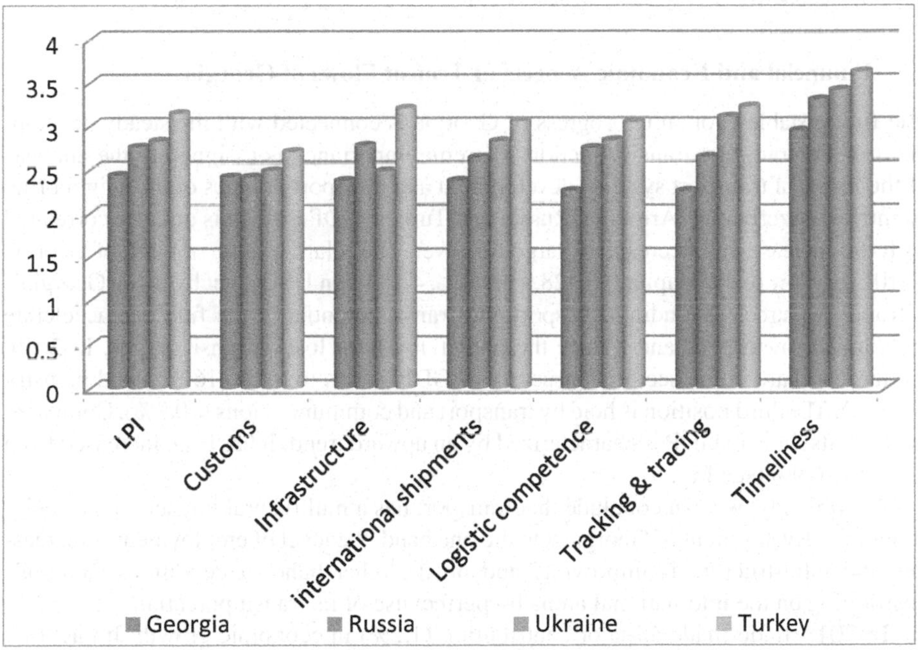

Fig. 4. Logistics Performance Index 2018. Source: Compiled by the authors based on the information of the World Bank [11, 23]

There are no logistic centers in the country that meet modern requirements, which would allow the country to make the most of its transit and trade potential. Georgia will not become a transport hub in the region until the transport corridor infrastructure is improved.

The Turkish logistics industry holds about 10–15% in GDP, which indicates on a fairly good state of the transport system. There are flexible domestic and international transport networks in Turkey. Large share comes to road transport in domestic transportation, while international shipping is dominated by maritime transport, which amounts to 85% of total shipments. It is the owner of the largest cargo fleet in Europe. The Turkish government hopes, that the indicator of foreign trading will increase to $ 1.1 trillion by 2023. Half of this indicator is export, which will influence on the transport and logistics sector. As for the railway network, the situation is not so favorable, only 5% of the cargo is transported by railway, although it is supposed to increase up to 15% by 2023 [24]. Turkey Logistics Performance Index amounts to 3.15. It overtakes Georgia, Russia and Azerbaijan in all components of this index. Due to Turkey's favorable location, the country actively cooperates with China in domestic and international railway projects. In the direction of Asia, it performs the function of railway gate. Transport and logistics are the main priority directions of Turkey and a large share of investments comes to this field. According to 2018 data, transport amounts to 73% of total exports and 38.8% of total imports. Currently, the epidemiological situation in Turkey is difficult, the cargos are moving, but with great delays. A number of ports are either closed or operating at 20–30% capacity.

3.2 Financial and Economic Aspects of Transit Flows of Georgia

The future stable economic progress of Georgia is connected with the steady development of the transport-transit function. Extreme importance is assigned to the analysis of the levels of transport systems development and transport policies of the neighboring countries - Azerbaijan, Armenia, Russia and Turkey. GDP growth is directly correlated with the increase and decrease in cargo turnover. The relative share of GDP of Georgia is still very low on per capita (13 428.9 in GEL, 4,763.5 in USD), but by using Georgia's national resources, including transport and transit potential to the full, can accelerate economic growth pace and reduce the potential risk of losing transit cargos. In 2019, the largest share in the sectorial structure of GDP comes to trade (16.8%) and industry (16.6%). The third position is held by transport and communications (10.9%). Compared to 2018, its share in GDP is characterized by an upward trend. It has been increased from 9.2% to 10.9% (see Fig. 5).

Accordingly, we can conclude that transport has a multilateral impact on the socio-economic development of Georgia. On the one hand, the level of employment is increasing, the infrastructure is improving, and on the other hand, it conditions Georgia's positioning on the international arena by perfect use of its transit potential.

In 2018, trade made a major contribution (1.2%) in economic growth. It has been increased by 8.3% compared to the previous year. The share of transport in economic growth is 0.8% (see Fig. 6).

According to BIA Business Catalog, 2,410 companies are registered in the field of transport and shipment in Georgia, from which 76.2% are small, 18.7% are medium, and 4.9% are large [27]. Given the diversity of these organizations, we can say that the market is quite competitive. The results of each company's activities have a direct

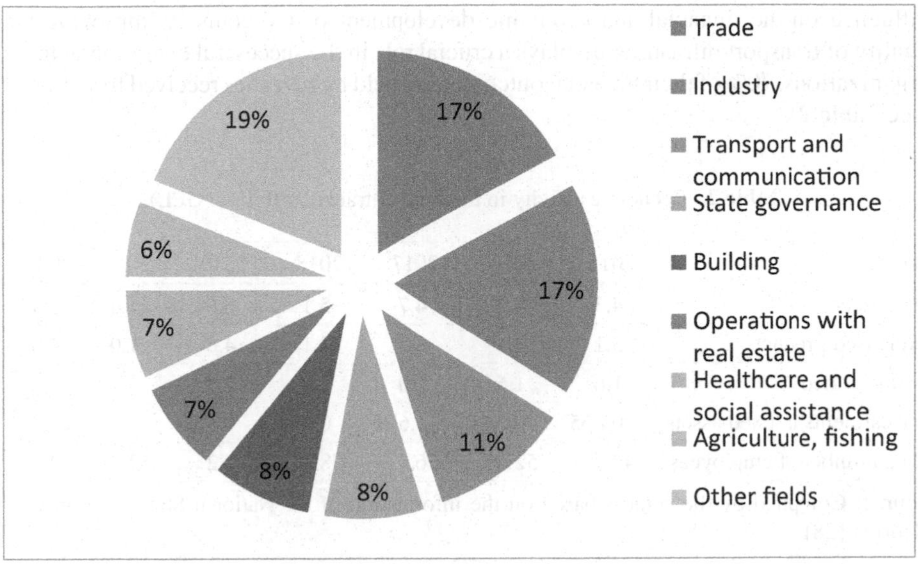

Fig. 5. Sectoral structure of gross domestic product, 2019. Source: Compiled by the authors based on the information of the National Statistics Office of Georgia [25]

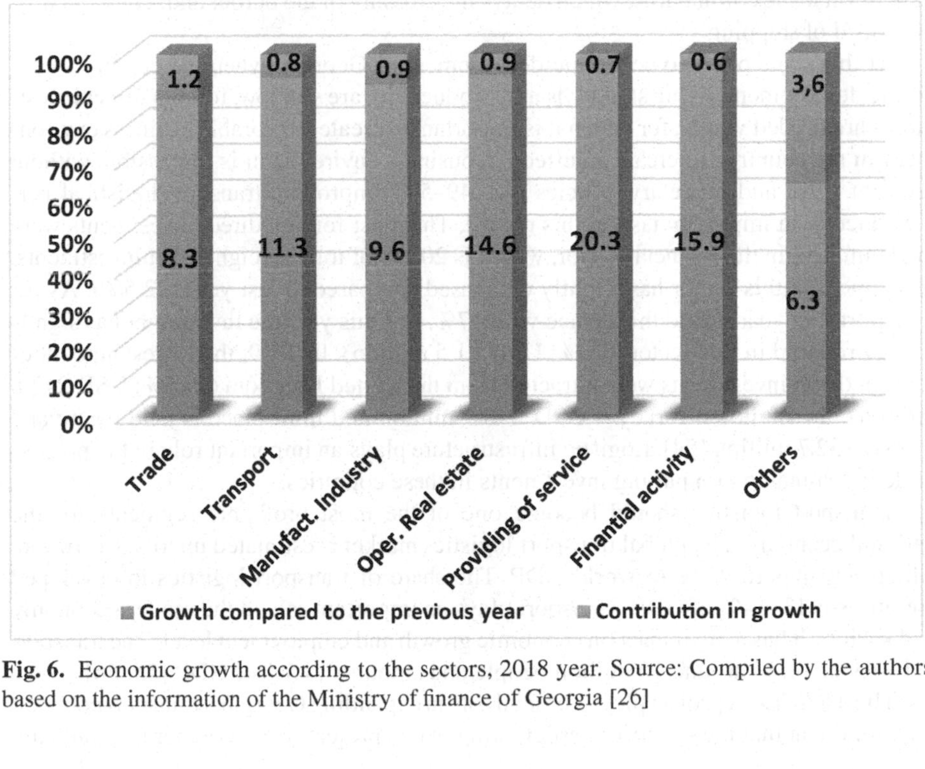

Fig. 6. Economic growth according to the sectors, 2018 year. Source: Compiled by the authors based on the information of the Ministry of finance of Georgia [26]

influence on the financial and economic development of the country. Improving the quality of transport infrastructure plays a crucial role in the successful operation of these organizations. 70% of their financial outcomes are held by revenues received from transit (see Table 2).

Table 2. Economic activity in the field of transport (billion GEL)

Year	2015	2016	2017	2018	2019	2020	2021
Turnover	4.3	4.2	4.7	5.1	6.0	1.4	1.4
Released products	3.1	3.1	3.7	4.1	4.6	1.0	1.0
Value added	1.6	1.6	2.0	2.1	2.3	-	-
Investments in fixed assets	0.665	0.644	1.672	0.597	0.362	-	-
The number of employees	48.7	52.8	56.5	58.1	61.2	52.3	49.6

Source: Compiled by the authors based on the information of the National Statistics Office of Georgia [28]

COVID-19 restrictions [29–48] did not affect transit shipments, although shipping activities were still reduced. There are a number of measures at the border checkpoints in relation to the coronavirus, which delays the crossing of the border and, consequently, the speed of shipping.

At this stage of socio-economic development of Georgia, when the country's economic development, living standards and productivity are still low, foreign direct investments are needed vitally, for which it is important to create a favorable business environment in the country. To create an effective business environment is impossible without relevant fiscal and monetary policies [40, 49–53]. Improving transport-logistical performance is an important task in this regard. The most foreign direct investments were made in 2019 in the financial sector, which is 20.6% of total foreign direct investments. Investment in this sector has slightly decreased compared to last year (22.5%). As for transport, last year it held third place with 17%, and this year the investment has significantly reduced in this sector (5.6%; USD 71.5 million). In 2019, the largest amount of foreign direct investments were attracted from the United Kingdom (19.5%; USD 247.8 million), then follows Turkey – USD 236.5 million and third place is held by Ireland – USD 132.7 million [54]. Logistic infrastructure plays an important role in the process of decision-making on putting investments in these countries.

Transport logistics should become one of the most profitable segments for the national economy. The global transport logistics market is estimated up to $ 3.1 trillion, which amounts to 7.1% of world GDP. The share of transport logistics in developed countries is 13–14% of GDP. Transport plays an important role in the modern economy and society. It has a big impact on economic growth and employment level. The transport industry employs around 10 million people and amounts to 5% of GDP [55, 56].

The TRACECA project plays a crucial role in expanding Georgia's transport corridor. It is important that the countries participating in this project work together in a mutually agreed and consistent manner in order to gain common benefits in this transit corridor. For which the proper conduct of economic diplomacy is essential.

The New Silk Road (by railway route) is the shortest distance for China to transport cargo to Europe. Despite its short transit time, China prefers a Southern Maritime Corridor, which has a flexible tariff policy. There is no unified pricing system in the new Silk Road conditions. Tariffs are very expensive due to the fact that it combines all transport nodes. The main competitor in terms of Chinese cargo is the South Sea route, which passes through Iran. The Port of Bandar Abbas (Iran), after lifting the sanctions of the West, operates successfully and competes greatly with the ports of Poti and Batumi. Cargo shipping from China via Bandar Abbas port to Azerbaijan is much cheaper than in case of Poti port, the reason for which are high tariffs imposed on services. Given the cost of shipping, this port creates a competitive position for cargo owners. Poti port has the highest tariffs in the Black Sea basin, which is explained by its natural monopoly. The pricing of APM terminal is an independent process. Georgia is losing large and scaled military cargos, coming from the port of Bandar Abbas. It is necessary to increase state regulation (in terms of non-tariff) in the activities of Poti port. Poti port offers consolidated services to its customers, which further aggravates the overall picture. Logistics centers remain "out of the game". Due to its monopoly nature, Poti port does not incur any financial costs to improve the port infrastructure. Due to bad maintenance, ships often have to stand on the raid. In case of excessive cargo flows, it cannot ensure timely and safe handling of cargo. Batumi port cannot play the role of an alternative due to its geographical location, it is ingrown into the city and at the same time, has no carrying capacity. The Anaklia port project is the best lever in this regard. Completion of the Anaklia port project means that Georgia will have a 16-m-deep port that can receive Panamax and Post-Panamax type vessels. The port will also be able to handle about 100 million tons of cargo during the planned 9 phases, which is a very high figure for Georgia. The port of Anaklia provides services to at least 900,000 containers per year [57]. At the same time, the port of Anaklia represents the guarantee of employment for thousands of people. The port of Anaklia is still an unfinished project, which means a significant loss of revenue for the country. The transport networks of Georgia are almost all alienated, except for railway transport, which's 100% is owned by Georgia. Therefore, the state should promote the stimulation of the private sector and imperceptibly "force" them to take care of the infrastructure development. International rating company "Fitch" downgraded the rating of the Georgian Railways from BB minus to BB plus in 2017. As a result, cargo turnover decreased by 21% and revenues by 25%. The main reason for the decrease in cargo turnover was the shift of Kazakh crude oil to the pipeline transport. It filled rail cargo turnover by 50%. As well as, high tariffs are named as the reason for downgrading the rating, even though it operates in highly competitive conditions. With the effective actuation of the Karsi-Akhalkalaki railway line, it is possible to attract additional cargo [58].

Baku-Tbilisi-Karsi railway allows attracting potential cargo flows. The project will be able to employ 2,500 people after putting into operation, herewith it is supposed that the volume of cargo flows will increase from 5 million tons to 15 million tons. Along with China, Russia is also showing great interest towards this project, which will be able to carry out large-scale shipments to Turkey through this railway line. This will be an additional lever for Georgia. It will be possible to handle more than 6–8% of cargo with the participation of Russia [59].

In order to use Georgia's transit capabilities to the full, it is necessary to assess the monetary and fiscal policies of those states that affect Georgia's transit function. The development of the transit corridor is not limited to the success of any certain state. It is necessary for all countries participating in this corridor to make joint efforts to achieve a unified result. Each country should be interested in raising all components of the logistics performance index, as this index is the carrier of key meaning for using transit potential to the full, including increasing regional competitiveness and increasing the reliability quality towards corridor.

4 Conclusions

Georgia's geopolitical location is the main point of departure for its formation as a transit hub. Georgia's transport capabilities and transit function has been the subject of the interest to international players for a long time. The analysis reflected in the paper shows that cargo turnover in Georgia varies according to the means of transport and is characterized by a decreasing trend in recent years, which is mainly the result of increased competition, infrastructural and technical capabilities and the lack of agreed pricing policies. One of the directions is the identification of each transport sector for shipments of different types of cargo, so that cargo turnover is not reduced as a result of internal competition. The problems of transit corridor of Georgia are growing due to high competition from competing corridors. Interest towards the new Silk Road, especially towards Chinese cargo, is very high, although the multimodality of the corridor hinders the process of transporting Chinese cargo to Europe. The port of Badar Abbas is considered as an alternative route, despite the short distance and short transit time of the New Silk Road.

The analysis of Logistics Performance Index developed by the World Bank revealed that Georgia's LPI indicator among neighboring countries in the region has deteriorated. It is overtaken even by Armenia, which does not have even the exit to the Sea. It is necessary to take practical steps in this direction. Increased investments in the field of logistics will be reflected both on the improvement of the index and the overall economic development of the country.

As the analysis showed, transit flows have a great influence on the socio-economic development of Georgia. Transit is one of the main mechanisms for filling the state budget of Georgia.

In order to increase the competitiveness of the transport-logistics system and the transit corridor of the country, the following recommendations need to be considered:

- Implementing infrastructural projects - completion of the Anaklia project at the planned pace and provision of technical capabilities of Panamax type vessels;
- Increasing the number of its own containers by the Georgian Railway, creating new locomotives;
- Developing a targeted state policy in the process of transport-logistics decisions;
- Introducing an effective system of state governance;

- Implementing training and skills development support projects, for the formation of the right personnel policy in the field of transport logistics;
- Flexible (unified) tariff policy;
- Building modern logistics centers;
- Establishing Transit Shipment Coordination Council (if we take the example of Azerbaijan, the volume of shipments has increased by 7–8% due to the effective measures taken by the above mentioned Council);
- Forming common conditions for customs procedures in the states along the Silk Road (harmonization of border-crossing legislation) in order to simplify the transportation of transit cargo;
- Improving the operation of transit cargo services;
- Supporting the activities of forwarding and logistics companies to ensure a high level of service;
- Continuous monitoring of transit traffic to eliminate obstacles;
- Developing financial support mechanisms on transport-logistics projects by the state.

References

1. Audonin, A., Turginbayeva, A., Askerov, A., Yergobek, D.: Modern economic and logistical trends in Eurasia: how do new trans-eurasian mega-projects influent to national economic growth. In: E3S Web of Conferences, vol. 159, p. 06009 (2020). https://doi.org/10.1051/e3sconf/202015906009
2. Barisitz, S.: New silk road—a geo-economic assessment with a focus on the European region. In: Pechlaner, H., Erschbamer, G., Thees, H., Gruber, M. (eds.) China and the New Silk Road, pp. 53–67. Springer, Cham (2020). https://doi.org/10.1007/978-3-030-43399-4_5
3. Diener, A.C.: Parsing mobilities in central Eurasia: border management and new silk roads. Eurasian Geogr. Econ. **56**(4), 376–404 (2015). https://doi.org/10.1080/15387216.2015.1078736
4. Janić, M.: Multicriteria evaluation of intermodal (rail/road) freight transport corridors. Logistics Sustain. Trans. **11**(1), 1–23 (2020). https://doi.org/10.2478/jlst-2020-0001
5. Kovács, G., Kot, S.: New logistics and production trends as the effect of global economy changes. Polish J. Manage. Stud. **14**(2), 115–126 (2016)
6. Payne, R.E.: The silk road and the Iranian political economy in late antiquity: Iran, the silk road, and the problem of aristocratic empire. Bull. Sch. Orient. Afr. Stud. **81**(2), 227–250 (2018). https://doi.org/10.1017/S0041977X18000459
7. Putkaradze, M., Abuselidze, G., Phagava, N., Chichileishvili, Kh., Kamadadze, T.: Economic and ecological issues related to construction of Batumi city bypass road of Traceca: transport corridor Europe-CAucasus-Asia. In: 20th International Multidisciplinary Scientific GeoConference: SGEM 2020, vol. **20**, pp. 275–282 (2020). https://doi.org/10.5593/sgem2020/5.1/s20.035
8. Romanov, M.T., Romanova, I.M.: About Eurasian transcontinental transport corridors and economic axes. Mediterr. J. Soc. Sci. **6**(5), 328 (2015). https://doi.org/10.5901/mjss.2015.v6n5s2p328
9. Vinokurov, E., Tsukarev, T.: The belt and road initiative and the transit countries: an economic assessment of land transport corridors. Area Dev. Policy, 1–21 (2017). https://doi.org/10.1080/23792949.2017.1385406

10. Ji, Z., Abuselidze, G., Lymar, V.: Problems and perspectives of sustainable trade development in China under the one belt one road initiative. In: E3S Web of Conferences, vol. 258, p. 06050 (2021). https://doi.org/10.1051/e3sconf/202125806050
11. Aragones, V.A., Valiyev, N., Mutyaba, R., Aliyev, S.: Improving freight transit and logistics performance of the trans-caucasus transit corridor: strategy and action plan. The World Bank **147325**, 1–49 (2020). http://documents1.worldbank.org/curated/en/701831585898113781/pdf/Improving-Freight-Transit-and-Logistics-Performance-of-the-Trans-Caucasus-Transit-Corridor-Strategy-and-Action-Plan.pdf
12. Turner, B.: World customs organization. In: Turner, B. (ed.) The Statesman's Yearbook, pp. 58–58. Palgrave Macmillan UK, London (2014). https://doi.org/10.1007/978-1-349-67278-3_57
13. Transport and logistics sector in Georgia: key challenges and development prospects. Center for Business and Economics. The Parliament of Georgia, pp. 3–7 (2017).
14. Competitiveness Analysis of the Caucasus Transit corridor: Improving Transit Potencial for Central Asia-Europe-Traffic (USAID), p. 1 (2012)
15. Abuselidze, G.: European integration of Georgia and financial-economic condition: achievements and challenges. Eur. J. Sustain. Develop. **8**(1), 53–68 (2019). https://doi.org/10.14207/ejsd.2019.v8n1p53
16. The world's largest ports: world economic forum (2016). https://www.weforum.org/agenda/2019/02/visualizing-the-world-s-busiest-ports
17. Ministry of economy and sustainable development: economic overview (2020). http://www.economy.ge/?page=ecoreview&s=26
18. Official web-portal of Georgian Railway (2020): http://cdn4.grmedia.com.ge/app/uploads/2019/03/gad_saxeobis_mixedvit_GE-2.pdf
19. Transport-logistics sector in Georgia: key challenges and development prospects, pp. 13–14. Business and Economic Center, The parliament of Georgia (2017)
20. Resolution of the Government of Georgia on determining the procedures and conditions related to the road use fees and its payment. https://matsne.gov.ge/ka/document/view/1025879?publication=0
21. State Treasury of the Ministry of Finance of Georgia (2020). http://treasury.ge/5669
22. Ministry of Economy and Sustainable Development of Georgia (2019). http://www.economy.ge/?page=ecoreview&s=26
23. Logistics Performance Index: International LPI. The World Bank (2018). https://lpi.worldbank.org/international/global
24. Turkey's transport and logistics industry (2015). https://www.transport-exhibitions.com/Market-Insights/Cold-Chain/A-guide-to-Turkey%E2%80%99s-transport-logistics-industry
25. National Statistics Office of Georgia (2019). https://www.geostat.ge/media/24610/Mtliani-shida-produqti-2019-I-kvartali-%28geo%29.pdf
26. Ministry of Finance of Georgia: Current economic trends. (2019). https://mof.ge/images/File/2019-publikaciebi/Outlook-April-2019_GEO.pdf
27. Bia. Transport and shipping: https://www.bia.ge/Company/IndustryCategory/77.
28. National Statistics Office of Georgia (2019). https://www.geostat.ge/ka/modules/categories/395/transporti307
29. Abuselidze, G., Mamaladze, L.: The impact of the COVID-19 outbreak on the socio-economic issues of the black sea region countries. In: Gervasi, O., et al. (eds.) ICCSA 2020. LNCS, vol. 12253, pp. 453–467. Springer, Cham (2020). https://doi.org/10.1007/978-3-030-58814-4_32
30. Abuselidze, G., Slobodianyk, A.: Pandeconomic crisis and its impact on small open economies: a case study of COVID-19. Adv. Intell. Syst. Comput. **1258**, 718–728 (2021). Springer, Cham. https://doi.org/10.1007/978-3-03057450-5_61

31. Orlik, T., Rush, J., Cousin, M., Hong, J.: Coronavirus could cost the global economy $2.7 Trillion (2020). https://www.bloomberg.com/graphics/2020-coronavirus-pandemic-global-economic-risk/
32. Glodowska, K., Owczarek, P.: Effect of Covid-19 pandemic on the safety of transport companies operation. Eur. Res. Stud. J. **23**(SI 3), 439–452 (2020). https://doi.org/10.35808/ersj/1919
33. UNCTAD: The coronavirus shock: a story of another global crisis foretold and what policy makers should be doing about it (2020). https://bit.ly/2WwcW5O
34. Visan, G.: The black sea and COVID-19. Middle East Institute (2020). https://www.mei.edu/publications/black-sea-and-covid-19
35. Economic Policy Research Center: COVID-19: Economic Consequences of the World and for Georgia (2020). http://eprc.ge/uploads/brosh/COVID__fin-geo.pdf
36. Emerging europe: postcard from Romania: the most gentle of lockdowns, and Easter, make me anxious (2020). https://emerging-europe.com/from-the-editor/postcard-from-romania-the-most-gentle-of-lockdowns-and-easter-make-me-anxious/
37. Fair wear: Covid-19 impact and responses: Romania (2020). https://www.fairwear.org/covid-19-dossier/covid-19-guidance-for-production-countries/covid-19-impact-and-responses-romania/
38. Euractiv: Romania still establishing how best to lift lock-down measures (2020). https://www.euractiv.com/section/coronavirus/short_news/romania-update-covid-19/
39. Business review: Coronavirus to take high toll on Romanian economy (2020). https://business-review.eu/money/finance/br-analysis-coronavirus-to-take-high-toll-on-romanian-economy-209743
40. Abuselidze, G.: The Influence of Covid-19 on the public debt growth and default risk: a fiscal sustainability analysis. In: Proceedings of the International Scientific and Practical Conference on Sustainable Development of Regional Infrastructure - ISSDRI, pp. 151–159, SciTePress (2021). https://doi.org/10.5220/0010587501510159
41. Dizikes, P.: The data speak: stronger pandemic response yields better economic recovery, MIT News Office (2020). http://news.mit.edu/2020/pandemic-health-response-economic-recovery-0401
42. EPC: Consequences of Coronavirus Pandemic on Turkish Economy (2020). https://epc.ae/topic/consequences-of-coronavirus-pandemic-on-turkish-economy
43. TRT world: In pictures: Turkey's booming tourism sector takes a hit from coronavirus (2020). https://www.trtworld.com/turkey/in-pictures-turkey-s-booming-tourism-sector-takes-a-hit-from-coronavirus-34845
44. Foreign Policy: The Coronavirus will destroy Turkey's economy (2020). https://foreignpolicy.com/2020/04/08/the-coronavirus-will-destroy-turkeys-economy/
45. Willson Center: Projected impact of COVID-19 on Ukraine's economy. (2020). https://www.wilsoncenter.org/blog-post/projected-impact-covid-19-ukraines-economy
46. Bulgaria: Economic and political overview (2020). https://www.nordeatrade.com/no/explore-new-market/bulgaria/economical-context
47. BalkanInsight: Bulgaria prepares for worst-case economic scenario (2020). https://balkaninsight.com/2020/03/31/bulgaria-prepares-for-worst-case-economic-scenario/
48. Osinska, M., Zalewski, W.: Effectiveness of the anti-crisis policy in the period of COVID-19 pandemic in the road transport industry. Eur. Res. Stud. J. **23**(SI 2), 40–57 (2020). https://doi.org/10.35808/ersj/1807
49. Abuselidze, G.: Modern challenges of monetary policy strategies: inflation and devaluation influence on economic development of the country. Acad. Strateg. Manag. J. **18**(4), 1–10 (2019)

50. Abuselidze, G.: Optimality of tax policy on the basis of comparative analysis of income taxation. Eur. J. Sustain. Dev. **9**(1), 272–293 (2020). https://doi.org/10.14207/ejsd.2020.v9n1p272
51. Abuselidze, G., Gogitidze, I.: Tax policy for business entities under the conditions of association with the European union: features and optimization directions. In: E3S Web of Conferences, vol. 166, pp. 13013 (2020). https://doi.org/10.1051/e3sconf/202016613013
52. Pirogova, O., Zasenko, V., Medvednikova, D.: Development of digital tax services in the transport industry in the Russian Federation. In: IOP Conference Series: Materials Science and Engineering, vol. 918, pp. 012191 (2020). https://doi.org/10.1088/1757-899X/918/1/012191
53. Abuselidze, G.: The impact of banking competition on economic growth and financial stability: an empirical investigation. Eur. J. Sustain. Dev. **10**(1), 203–220 (2021). https://doi.org/10.14207/ejsd.2021.v10n1p203
54. National Statistics Office of Georgia: Foreign direct investment in Georgia 2018 (2020). https://www.geostat.ge/media/25519/ucxouri-investiciebi-2018-celi-%28geo%29.pdf
55. Davydenko, N., Dibrova, A., Onishko, S., Fedoryshyna, L.: The influence of the gross regional product on the formation of the financial potential of the region. J. Optim. Ind. Eng. **14**(1), 177–181 (2021). https://doi.org/10.22094/JOIE.2020.677843
56. European commission: EU Sciense Hub. Research Topic. Transport sector economic analysis. https://ec.europa.eu/jrc/en/research-topic/transport-sector-economic-analysis
57. Official web-portal of Anaklia Development Consortium. http://anakliadevelopment.com/ka/info/
58. Danelia, I.: Fitch downgraded the raiting of Georgian Railway (2017). https://www.youtube.com/watch?v=povSGaT-07c
59. Georgia, B.P.: Baku-Tbilisi-Ceyhan pipeline (2020). https://www.bp.com/ka_ge/georgia/home/who-we-are/_-_-_-_.html

Structural Analysis of Bituminous Road Pavements Embedding Charging Units for Electric Vehicles

Claudia Nodari[1](✉), Maurizio Crispino[1], Mariano Pernetti[2], and Emanuele Toraldo[1]

[1] Department of Civil and Environmental Engineering, Politecnico di Milano, Piazza Leonardo da Vinci 32, 20133 Milan, Italy
claudia.nodari@polimi.it

[2] Department of Engineering, Università Della Campania "Luigi Vanvitelli", via Roma 29, 81031 Aversa, Caserta, Italy

Abstract. Among the arising technologies for electric mobility, the *on-the-road* (dynamic) vehicle charging appears to be a promising solution in order to overcome the current limitations of the electric vehicles' batteries. For achieving this purpose, the use of Charging Units (CUs) embedded into the road pavements is needed. These CU are made of a cement concrete box in which the electric technologies are allocated. However, the CUs have not to be detrimental for the structural behavior of the pavements, including their load resistance performances.

The lack of scientific studies in the available literature demonstrate that the topic is not fully investigated. Moreover, the available scientific papers assume the CU as a solid, not considering it as a box (having a void for the electric technologies). However, it is a key factor for the pavements' structural response.

This is the reason why this research was devoted to assess the structural response of electrified roads (*e-roads*), in which the CUs are embedded, compared to the traditional roads (*t-roads*), using a Finite Element Modelling (FEM) approach. Therefore, the main scope of this study is the optimization of the void dimensions into CU from a pavement structural performances point of view. The optimization included different cross-sectional geometries and load positions. As a result of these FEM investigations, a first set of interesting outcomes were obtained, as shown and discussed in the paper.

Keywords: Electrified road · Dynamic charging · Charging Unit (CU) · Finite Element Modelling (FEM) · Structural analysis · Bituminous pavements

1 Introduction

As the European Commission report 2019 shown, in the EU-28 transport generates 32.1% of the total Green House Gases (GHG) emissions and road transport is responsible for 71.7% of the sector's emissions [1]. In this framework and in line with EU policy to climate neutrality by 2050 [2], the electrification of vehicles is a possible solution to enhancing road sector environmental sustainability [3–5].

O. Gervasi et al. (Eds.): ICCSA 2021, LNCS 12952, pp. 149–162, 2021.
https://doi.org/10.1007/978-3-030-86973-1_11

In this view, several environmental benefits can be obtained by the use of Electric Vehicles, this is the reason why this technology is becoming very much attractive [4, 6]. In particular, Battery Electric Vehicles (BEV) are entirely powered by batteries, without any internal combustion engine (ICE) [7]. However, some handicaps restrain their potential application [4, 5, 8]: high initial cost, long waiting time and short range, better known as *range anxiety* (i.e. an EV driver's fear of running out of electricity before reaching another available charging station [9]). Therefore, on-the-road (dynamic) charging appears to be a promising solution to overcome the current limitations [4, 8, 10], but it requires a proper charging infrastructure network [11]. Thus, traditional road (*t-road*) becomes electrified road (*e-road*) if it is able to deliver the electrical power to charge the EV efficiently using specific conductive or contactless charging systems, as stated in [4].

2 Literature Review

According to the available literature, two charging methods are nowadays considering a promising option: conductive and contactless technologies [4, 5]. In the first case, a practical connection mode is used to link vehicle to the charging infrastructure. Some examples are overhead pantograph or conductive track mounted on the road surface, as shown in Fig. 1a and Fig. 1b, respectively. As regards contactless charging, Wireless Power Transmission (WPT) system is adopted to deliver electrical energy to the electric vehicle at a gap distance. Being a near-field WPT charging technology, the Inductive Power Transfer (IPT) charging has shown good performance [4].

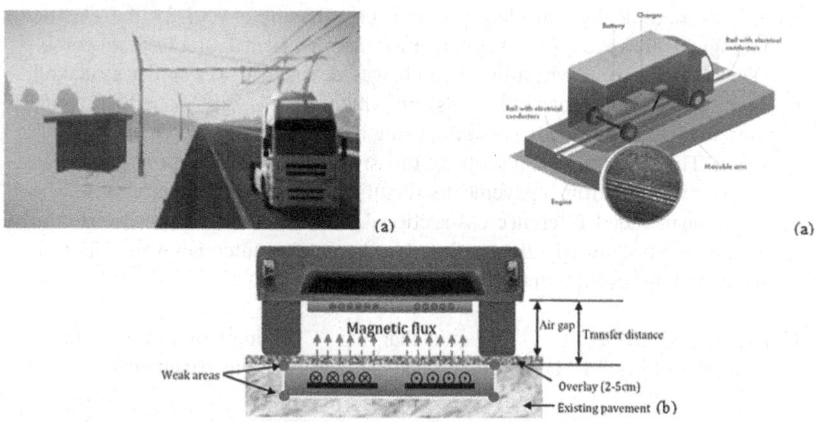

Fig. 1. Examples of charging systems (a) conductive [12, 13] (b) contactless [4]

Considering dynamic inductive charging technology, the use of prefabricated Charging Unit (CU) embedded into flexible pavement is a possible solution, as suggested by the available scientific literature [5, 14]. As presented in [5], it is possible to classify construction technologies of embedded charging systems into two categories: prefabrication-based construction method and on-site construction method. In the first case, CU are built in the factory as prefabricated modulus and then embedded on-site in short period. In the second one, all the facilities are prepared and installed on-site.

CU normally is composed of power electronic device protected by a concrete slab from traffic-induced damages [15] and water aggression [4, 15]: CU is a concrete box in which the electric technologies are allocated.

Currently, contactless charging has shown good performance as a battery charging technology [4]. However, there are few studies in literature on the structural behavior of this type of composite pavement. In other words, the available scientific literature is not able to demonstrate the effects of the CU on the pavement structural response and how it affects the pavement lifetime. Thus, the research described in this paper focuses on the aforementioned topics, particularly focusing on the structural response of *e-road*, evaluating the effects of CU in comparison with a standard *t-road* solution. It was performed by developing a Finite Element Model (FEM). Therefore, the novelty is not the model, since it is well known at the state of the art of pavement structural calculations, but the road pavement itself, in which CUs are embedded for electric vehicles charging. Moreover, the aforementioned scientific papers assume the CU as a solid, not considering it as a box (having a void for allocating the electric technologies). Therefore, to be a step ahead of the current *e-road* state of art, the FEM calculations consider the prefabricated concrete CU both as a solid box (solid CU) and as a hollow box (void CU). Consequently, the present study has two stages. In the first phase, structural behaviors of *t-road* and *e-road* with solid box (*e-road_solid CU*) are compared to evaluate solid CU effect. In the second step, a void CU is studied in order to optimize the dimension of the void from a pavement structural response point of view. Thus, to gain the optimum void CU geometry, several simulations are performed progressively increasing hollow dimension. Finally, a comparison between *e-road_solid CU* and different *e-road_void CU* geometries is made, considering the effects of the voids into the CU on the pavement stress-strain.

The paper is planned as follows. The adopted methodology is detailed in Sect. 3. Section 4 shows the effect of solid CU into the road pavement, in terms of stresses, for different load positions. Section 5 analyses the effect of void CU, considering various void dimensions and load positions. In Sect. 6 the procedure for void CU optimization is described. Finally, conclusions and future studies are drawn in Sect. 7.

3 Methodology

As mentioned above, the research is divided in two stages, in which different cross-sectional geometries are studied (Sect. 3.1). Moreover, three different load positions are evaluated for considering the absence of drivers' physical constraints in choosing their road paths. In fact, vehicles can move along road cross direction with a certain wander distance. Considering these conditions, 15 simulations are carried out using a FEM software to calculate stresses and strains throughout the domain.

A 2D model is built for simulating the structural behavior of pavements (*t-road* and *e-road)* subjected to traffic. For the sake of simplicity, an elastic model is assumed to be acceptable for all materials, even if more precise models have been developed as viscoelastic-viscoplastic one with damage coupled for asphalt materials [16]. Each layer is defined as isotropic-linear-elastic material, so marked by thickness, Young's modulus, and Poisson's Ratio. Such a model has been implemented by using COMSOL Multiphysics 5.5. The equations used are shown below: equilibrium Eq. (1), constitutive equation based on Hooke's law (2) and strain-displacement (6) equations.

$$div\sigma + F_v = 0 \tag{1}$$

$$\sigma = \sigma_{ex} + \mathbb{D} \cdot \varepsilon_{el} \tag{2}$$

$$\varepsilon_{el} = \varepsilon - \varepsilon_{inel} \tag{3}$$

$$\varepsilon_{inel} = \varepsilon_0 + \varepsilon_{ext} + \varepsilon_{th} + \varepsilon_{hs} + \varepsilon_{pl} + \varepsilon_{cr} + \varepsilon_{vp} \tag{4}$$

$$\sigma_{ex} = \sigma_0 + \sigma_{ext} + \sigma_q \tag{5}$$

$$\varepsilon = 1/2 \cdot \left(\nabla u + \nabla u^T\right) \tag{6}$$

$$\mathbb{D} = \mathbb{D}(E, \nu) \tag{7}$$

Where:
σ = stress tensor;
F_v = Volume force vector;
$\mathbb{D}$ = 4th order elasticity tensor;
ε = strain tensor;
ε_{el} = elastic strain tensor;
ε_{inel} = inelastic strain tensor; inelastic strain tensor contributions: ε_0 = initial strain; ε_{ext} = external strain; ε_{th} = thermal strain; ε_{hs} = hygroscopic strain; ε_{pl} = plastic strain; ε_{cr} = creep strain; ε_{vp} = viscoplastic strain;
σ_{ex} = extra stress tensor; extra stress tensor contributions: σ_0 = initial stress; σ_{ext} = external stress; σ_q = extra stress caused by viscous damping;
∇u = displacement gradient tensor;
E = Young's modulus;
ν = Poisson's Ratio.

3.1 Geometry and Materials

As already stated, various cross-sectional geometries were analyzed for *t-road* and *e-road*. Figure 2 shows the geometries considered in this study. Figure 2a describes a *t-road* as a semi-rigid pavement. Thickness of wearing course is selected in the typical reference range of 40-50 mm [17] to reduce the energy transfer distance, with better results in battery charging [4]. Based on this sketch, prefabricated CU is embedded in the middle of the lane within a single asphalt layer, obtaining a composite pavement cross section. CU is assumed to have a size of 0.14 m in height and 0.8 m in width, as introduced in Chen's study [4]. In Fig. 2b, CU is considered as a solid box, as the current state of art [4, 5]. Figure 2c, Fig. 2d and Fig. 2e, instead, suggest new *e-road* cross-sectional geometries in which the prefabricated CU has an opening in the middle with different void dimensions (more details are given in Sect. 6).

The characteristics of each layer and/or material are reported in Table 1, based on typical material properties. As regard asphalt, Young's modulus refers to mean value of stiffness modulus evaluated at a temperature of 20 °C and load frequency equal to 2 Hz. As mentioned before the CU is made of cement concrete and an isotropic behavior [15] is assumed.

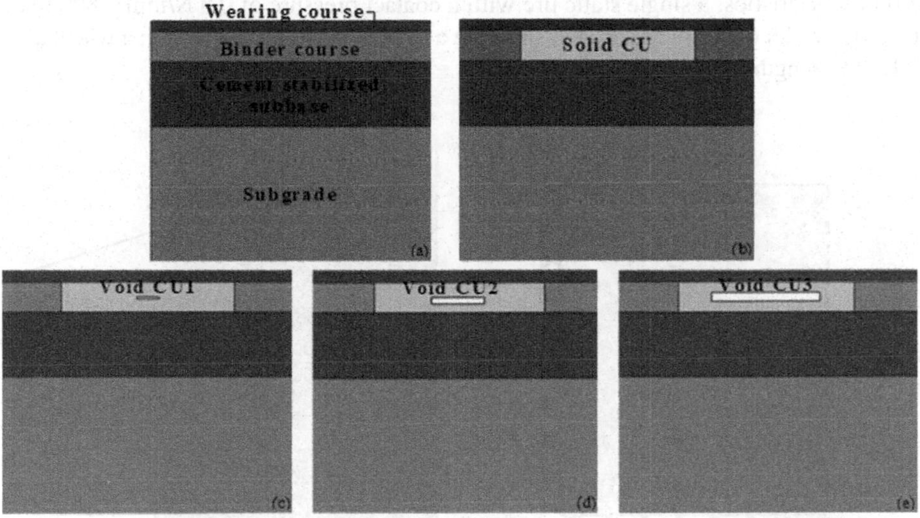

Fig. 2. Cross-sectional geometry (a) *t-road* (b) *e-road_solid CU* (c-e) *e-road_void CU*

Table 1. Key material main characteristics

	Thickness [m]	Bulk density [N/m^3]	Young's modulus [N/mm^2]	Poisson's ratio [-]
Wearing course	0.05	24,000	5,500	0.35
Binder course	0.14	23,500	3,500	0.35
Cement stabilized subbase	0.30	23,000	2,000	0.20
Subgrade	6.00	21,000	800	0.30
Concrete CU	0.14	23,000	25,000	0.20

3.2 Loads and Boundary Conditions

Model boundary conditions are shown in Fig. 3. The 2D model is assumed to be symmetric, along the road symmetry axis. A roller constraint is used at the bottom of the thick subgrade and on the right of the model, to put equal to zero the displacement in the direction perpendicular (normal) to the boundary. The default boundary condition is free on the surface, except for the area in which the load acts. As shown in Fig. 3(b), a total number of 7,456 triangular elements are built and finer elements are established around CU corners. Three different load positions are considered to explain cross wander distance compared to CU location, as reported in Fig. 4. In the first one, the load is centered on CU (Fig. 4a). The lateral displacements are also considered: left wheel is on the CU left edge (Fig. 4b), left wheel is located at the CU center (Fig. 4c). Concerning load characteristics, a single static tire with a contact pressure of 0.8 N/mm^2 (800 kPa) and a tire width of 0.2 m are used to simulate a road heavy vehicle loading; a wheel axis of 1.56 m length is assumed [5].

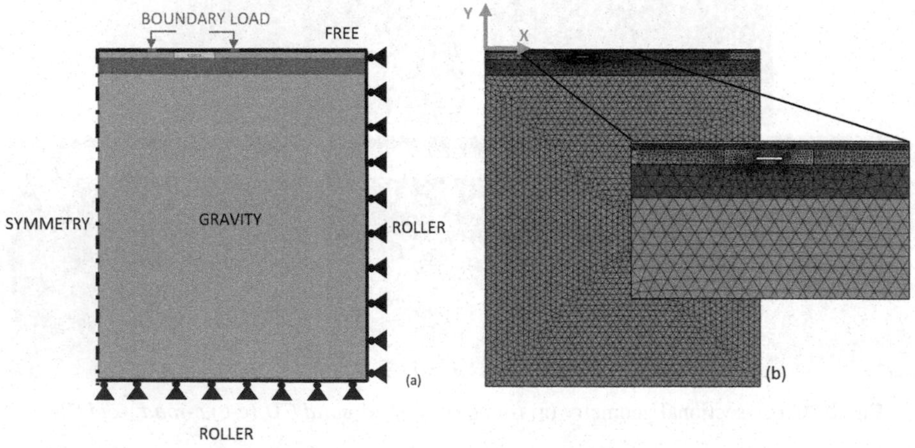

Fig. 3. (a) Loads and boundary conditions (b) FE mesh

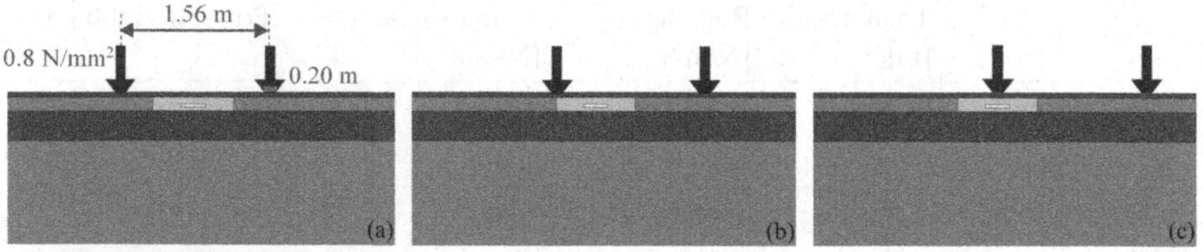

Fig. 4. Load positions (a) centered on CU (b) CU edge (c) CU center

4 Effects of Solid CU into the Road Pavements

Among the several outputs of the FEM calculations, the stresses are considered in this study. In Fig. 5 and in Fig. 6 the stress FEM results are shown for both *t-road* and *e-road_solid CU*, according to the three load positions previously described.

Focusing on Fig. 5, the FEM results reveal that the vertical stress σ_{yy} is close to the applied load, which penetrates and vanish gradually downward, according to the results obtained in the Chen's study [5]. As regard *e-road_solid CU*, when load is centered on CU or on CU center, a similar stress distribution can be seen. When load is located on the CU edge, instead, stress distribution changes near CU left edge. At the left margin out of CU, stress in compression decreases of 60% compared to *t-road*; in the middle of CU, compression stress increases by more than 55% respect to *t-road*. In the last load position, along CU center, it is possible to observe a decrease of stress in compression of 66% compared to *t-road*. Moreover, stress increases in the area outside CU lateral edge by 130% compared to the traditional pavement.

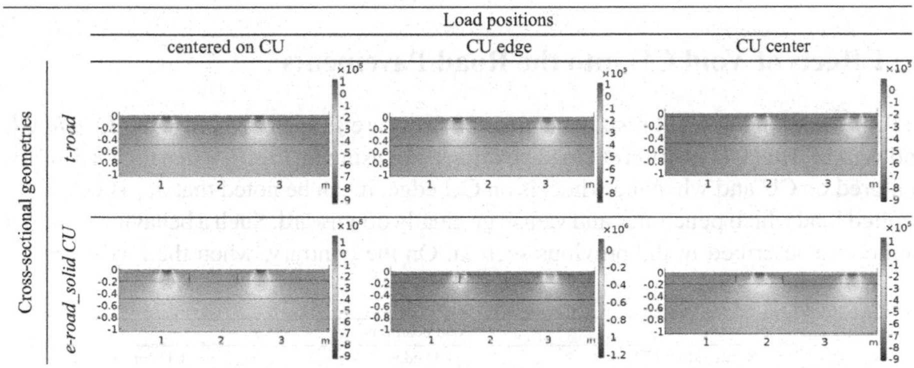

Fig. 5. Distribution of vertical stress σ_{yy} at different cross-sectional geometries and different load positions

As regard horizontal stress (Fig. 6), it can be observed that stress field mostly changes according to cross-sectional geometry and load position. The FEM outputs show that

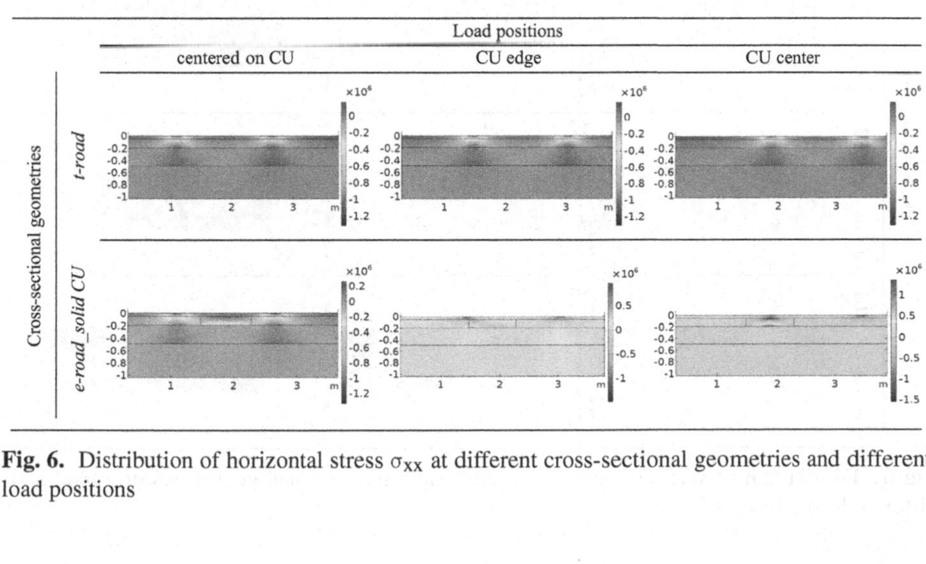

Fig. 6. Distribution of horizontal stress σ_{xx} at different cross-sectional geometries and different load positions

significant horizontal stresses σ_{xx} in compression appears on the pavement surface close to the area of load application, confirming the results reported in [5].

Moreover, tensile stresses are concentrated at the bottom of cement stabilized subbase layer of the *t-road*. Considering the *e-road*, when load is centered on CU, compressive stresses arise at the bottom of CU (an increase of four time is observed in comparison with the *t-road* results). If the load is on CU edge, *e-road* results show tensile stresses at the CU left edge bottom corner. In detail, considering left edge out, stress increases by 230% compared to the *t-road*. In the last load position (CU center) stress concentration rises in CU: at the CU top it is possible to note an increase of compression stress (270% compared to the *t-road* outputs), at CU bottom, the tensile stress can be evaluated 13 times higher than the *t-road* results.

5 Effects of Void CU into the Road Pavements

In Fig. 7 and Fig. 8, FEM results in terms of stress are shown for both *e-road_solid CU* and *e-road_void CU* at different load positions. Focusing on Fig. 7, when the load axle is centered on CU and when the wheel is on CU edge, it can be noted that σ_{yy} is below the applied load which penetrates and vanish gradually downward. Such a behavior is similar to the one described in the previous section. On the contrary, when the load is on the

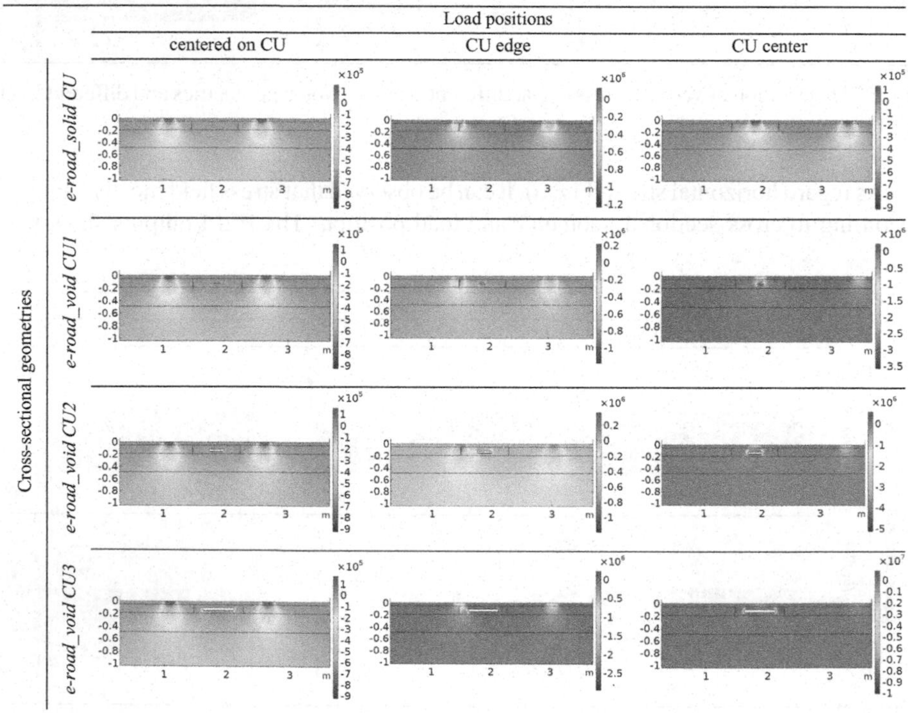

Fig. 7. Distribution of vertical stress σ_{yy} at different cross-sectional geometries of *e-road* and different load positions

CU center, stress distribution changes compared to *e-road_solid CU*. It is still possible to observe light stress under load, but there is a compressive stress concentration around CU void, that increases with void dimension. In particular, stress in compression at the top left corner of cavity increases by 72% (*e-road_void CU2*) and by 234% (*e-road_void CU3*) compared to *e-road_void CU1*.

As regard horizontal stress (Fig. 8), it can be observed that stress field mostly changes according to load position. All the FEM simulations reveal that significant σ_{XX} in compression appears on the pavement surface close to the applied load, as presented in the previous section. When load is centered on CU, some compressive stresses arise at the bottom of CU itself. Moreover, tensile stresses concentrate at the bottom of cement stabilized subbase layer.

If the load is on CU edge, tensile stresses grow at left bottom corner of the CU, an increase of 10% for both *e-road_void CU1* and *e-road_void CU2* in comparation with the solid CU results; in the case of *e-road_void CU3* it increases up to 36%. Further, at left top corner of the cavity, it is possible to note the arising of tensile stresses according to the cavity dimension increase. It can be estimated at a magnitude of 330% for *e-road_void CU2* and more than 740% for *e-road_void CU3*, once again in comparation to *e-road_void CU1* results. At left bottom corners of cavity, the compression stresses also arise (an increase of 208% and 572% is found, respectively).

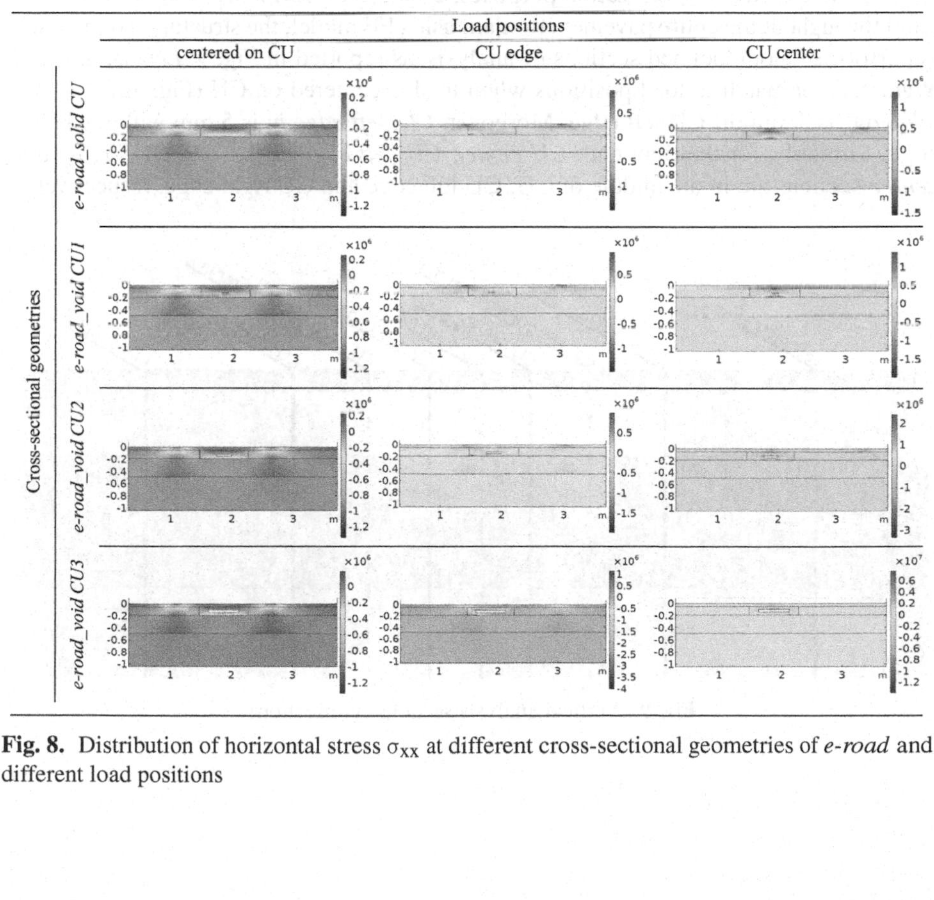

Fig. 8. Distribution of horizontal stress σ_{XX} at different cross-sectional geometries of *e-road* and different load positions

In the last load position (CU center), a stress concentration rising on the CU is appreciable. In detail, at the CU top the compression stress arise according to the cavity dimension, passing from 27% for the *e-road_void CU3*, to the 85% for the *e-road_void CU2* and exceeding the 240% for the *e-road_void CU1*. Moreover, tensile stresses can be observed at the bottom of the CU, such stresses increase according to the cavity dimension: by 13%, 35% and 128% compared to solid CU outputs, respectively.

In addition, it can be observed that some tensile stresses rise on the top and on the bottom of CU cavity. In the first case, an increase of more than 725% (*e-road*_void CU3) and 160% (*e-road_void CU2*) compared to *e-road_void CU1* is recorded. In the second case, stresses gain 113% and 157%, respectively, compared to *e-road_void CU1*.

6 Optimization of *Void CU* Dimension

As already stated, in order to achieve the optimum void CU geometry, several FEM simulations are performed progressively increasing void dimension. A comparison between different *e-road_void CU* geometries is made, as described in Sect. 5. The cavity dimension into the CU is optimized comparing the FEM stress outputs with the failure tensile/compression stresses of the materials of both layers and charging unit (Table 2).

For the CU cavity optimization purposes, even if the FEM stress outputs are calculated throughout the entire pavement domain using FE model, the structural comparison is performed along defined sections of analysis, as reported in Fig. 9. *Left section* and *Right section* match to load positions when load is centered on CU (Fig. 4a). *CU_left edge out* is 5 mm off CU left edge. Moreover, *CU_left edge in* is 5 mm within CU left edge. Similarly, for the right end. *CU center, CU_left edge center* and *CU_right edge center* sections are in the middle of CU, CU left edge and CU right edge, respectively.

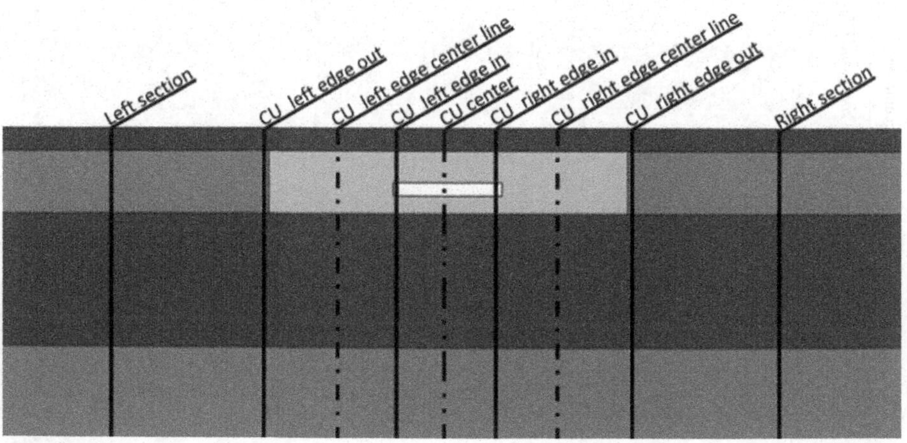

Fig. 9. Vertical analysis sections (y-direction)

The horizontal analysis is performed on the layers' interfaces, as shown in Fig. 10. Two sections are evaluated per each interface, at +1 mm (top) and −1 mm (down) from the interface. The surface of wearing course is also analyzed.

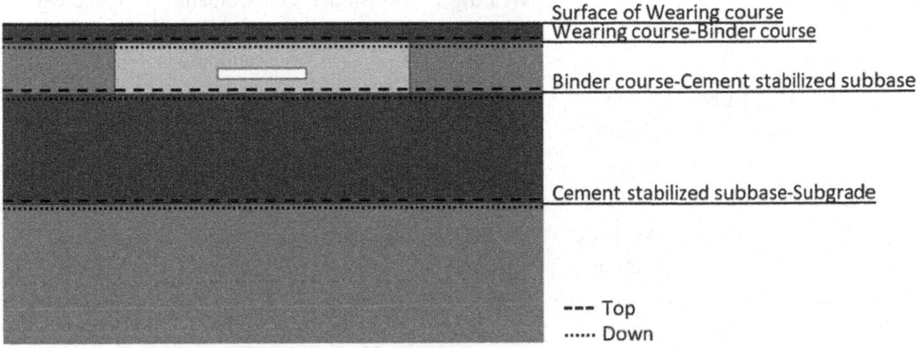

Fig. 10. Horizontal analysis sections (x-direction)

Therefore, the FEM stress outputs along these sections are compared with the failure tensile/compression stresses of the materials composing each layer. Acceptable results are achieved for *e-road_void CU1* and *e-road_void CU2*, instead *e-road_void CU3* failed, as suggested by the results discussed in the previous Sect. 5.

The final choice falls on *e-road_void CU2*, since it is the solution that maximize the cavity dimension maintaining the stress levels of the whole pavement lower than the failure stresses of the component materials. In Fig. 11 the details of the selected void CU are given.

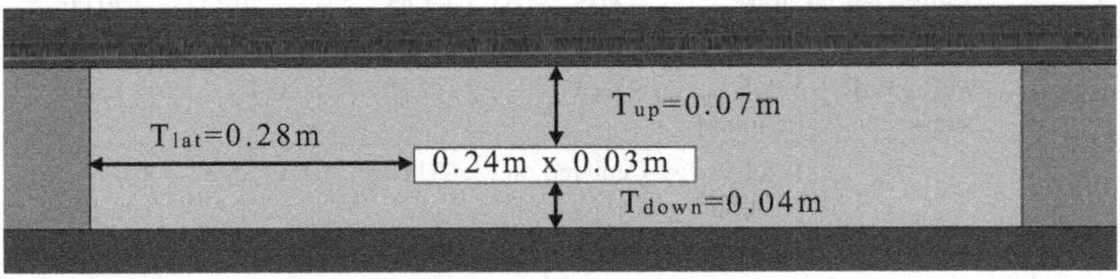

Fig. 11. Void CU details

Table 2 shows the comparison between the maximum FEM stress outputs, calculated in the optimized void CU, and failure tensile/compression stresses of the materials of both layers and charging unit.

Table 2. Comparison between maximum FEM stresses in optimized void CU and failure tensile/compression stresses

			Materials			
			Wearing course	Binder course	Cement stabilized subbase	Concrete
$\sigma_{xx,tens}$	Max FEM stress	Value [N/mm^2]	0.18	0.31	0.15	2.20
		Load position	CU center	CU edge	CU edge	CU center
		Analysis section	Surface of wearing course	Binder course - cem.stab subb._ Top	Binder course - cem.stab subb._ Down	Binder course - cem.stab subb._ Top
	Failure tensile stress [N/mm^2]		1.25[a]	1.55[b]	0.50[c]	2.21
$\sigma_{xx,comp}$	Max FEM stress	Value [N/mm^2]	−1.58	−0.56	−0.14	−3.15
		Load position	CU center	CU edge	CU center	CU center
		Analysis section	CU center	Wearing course - binder course_ Down	Binder course - cem.stab subb._ Down	CU_left edge in
	Failure tensile stress [N/mm^2]		−3.75	−4.65	−1.50	−20.00
$\sigma_{yy,comp}$	Max FEM stress	Value [N/mm^2]	−1.13	−0.76	−0.46	−1.30
		Load position	Centered on CU	CU edge	CU edge	CU center
		Analysis section	Surface of wearing course	Wearing course - binder course_ Down	Binder course - cem.stab subb._ Down	CU_right edge in
	Failure tensile stress [N/mm^2]		−6.25	−7.75	−4.00	−20.00[d]

[a]Value in the interval 1.11–1.67 MPa [18]
[b]Value in the interval 1.20–1.55 MPa [19]
[c]Value in the interval 0.43–0.55 MPa [20]
[d]Considering C20/25 [21]

7 Conclusions

The electrification of vehicles is a possible solution to enhancing road sector environmental sustainability. On-the-road charging appears to be a promising solution to overcome the current limitations of batteries, but it requires a proper charging infrastructure network. For this purpose, traditional road needs to be converted in electrified road. This research focuses on structural response of electrified road pavement compared to the traditional one, using a Finite Element Modelling approach, considering both the charging unit a solid box, as suggested by the available scientific literature, and a void box for allocating the electronic devices.

As a summary of the obtained results, the following conclusions can be drawn.

Considering the Charging Unit as a Solid Box, the results previously described suggest that small differences exist between *t-road* and *e-road*, considering the stresses to which the pavement is subjected on the vertical direction. On the contrary, considering the horizontal direction, an increase of stresses on the pavement close to the CU can be expected; thus, the CU changes the pavement stress distribution.

The results about the Void Charging Unit reveal that it has a non-negligible impact on the structural response, making the pavement more vulnerable to load position effects. Furthermore, the stresses to which both the CU and the pavement are subjected increase according to the cavity dimension. However, these stresses can be managed, optimizing the CU cavity dimension, in order to maintain them lower than the failure tensile/compression stresses of the materials composing the pavement layers (including the CU).

Obviously, the results reported in the paper can be considered as a first step in the comprehension of the CU structural effects on road pavements. Some issues remain still open (e.g. the effects of temperature changing, fatigue and rutting on the bituminous layers behavior, surface distresses) and must be optimized (e.g. the charging unit shape considering a fillet-shaped exterior corner) in further studies.

References

1. Commission, E.: EU Transport in figures - Statistical Pocketbook 2019 (2018). https://doi.org/10.2832/017172
2. Commission, E.: The European Green Deal (2019)
3. Nicolaides, D., Cebon, D., Miles, J.: An urban charging infrastructure for electric road freight operations: a case study for Cambridge UK. IEEE Syst. J. **13**, 2057–2068 (2019). https://doi.org/10.1109/JSYST.2018.2864693
4. Chen, F., Kringos, N.: Towards new infrastructure materials for on-the-road charging. In: 2014 IEEE Int. Electr. Veh. Conf. IEVC 2014, pp. 1–5 (2015). https://doi.org/10.1109/IEVC.2014.7056235
5. Chen, F., Balieu, R., Córdoba, E., Kringos, N.: Towards an understanding of the structural performance of future electrified roads: a finite element simulation study. Int. J. Pavement Eng. **20**, 204–215 (2019). https://doi.org/10.1080/10298436.2017.1279487
6. Karmaker, A.K., Roy, S., Ahmed, M.R.: Analysis of the impact of electric vehicle charging station on power quality issues. In: 2nd Int. Conf. Electr. Comput. Commun. Eng. ECCE 2019, pp. 7–9 (2019). https://doi.org/10.1109/ECACE.2019.8679164

7. Ajanovic, A.: The future of electric vehicles: prospects and impediments. Wiley Interdiscip. Rev. Energy Environ. **4**, 521–536 (2015). https://doi.org/10.1002/wene.160
8. Gill, J.S., Bhavsar, P., Chowdhury, M., Johnson, J., Taiber, J., Fries, R.: Infrastructure cost issues related to inductively coupled power transfer for electric vehicles. Procedia Comput. Sci. **32**, 545–552 (2014). https://doi.org/10.1016/j.procs.2014.05.459
9. Pevec, D., Babic, J., Carvalho, A., Ghiassi-Farrokhfal, Y., Ketter, W., Podobnik, V.: A survey-based assessment of how existing and potential electric vehicle owners perceive range anxiety. J. Clean. Prod. **276** (2020). https://doi.org/10.1016/j.jclepro.2020.122779
10. Venugopal, P., et al.: Roadway to self-healing highways with integrated wireless electric vehicle charging and sustainable energy harvesting technologies. Appl. Energy. **212**, 1226–1239 (2018). https://doi.org/10.1016/j.apenergy.2017.12.108
11. Throngnumchai, K., Hanamura, A., Naruse, Y., Takeda, K.: Design and evaluation of a wireless power transfer system with road embedded transmitter coils for dynamic charging of electric vehicles. In: 2013 World Electr. Veh. Symp. Exhib. EVS 2014, pp. 1–10 (2014). https://doi.org/10.1109/EVS.2013.6914937
12. Chairman, F.B.– B.S. p. A.: eHighway - per il trasporto elettrico delle merci. http://www.brebemi.it/site/wp-content/uploads/2019/03/A35Brebemi_EMotorway_Francoforte.pdf. Accessed 23 Nov 2020
13. eRoadArlanda. https://eroadarlanda.com/the-technology/. Accessed 23 Nov 2020
14. Chabot, A., Deep, P.: 2D Multilayer solution for an electrified road with a built-in charging box. Road Mater. Pavement Des. **20**, S590–S603 (2019). https://doi.org/10.1080/14680629.2019.1621445
15. Chen, F., Coronado, C.F., Balieu, R., Kringos, N.: Structural performance of electrified roads: a computational analysis. J. Clean. Prod. **195**, 1338–1349 (2018). https://doi.org/10.1016/j.jclepro.2018.05.273
16. Chen, F., Balieu, R., Kringos, N.: Thermodynamics-based finite strain viscoelastic-viscoplastic model coupled with damage for asphalt material. Int. J. Solids Struct. **129**, 61–73 (2017). https://doi.org/10.1016/j.ijsolstr.2017.09.014
17. Ceravolo, R., Miraglia, G., Surace, C., Zanotti Fragonara, L.: A computational methodology for assessing the time-dependent structural performance of electric road infrastructures. Comput. Civ. Infrastruct. Eng. **31**, 701–716 (2016). https://doi.org/10.1111/mice.12199
18. Zemedkun, B.S., Takahashi, O.: Demarcation study on reclaimed asphalt pavement contents in recycled hot mix asphalt mixtures for wearing course in asphalt pavements. Int. J. Adv. Sci. Eng. Inf. Technol. **10**, 1571–1577 (2020). https://doi.org/10.18517/ijaseit.10.4.3946
19. Topini, D., Toraldo, E., Andena, L., Mariani, E.: Use of recycled fillers in bituminous mixtures for road pavements. Constr. Build. Mater. **159**, 189–197 (2018). https://doi.org/10.1016/j.conbuildmat.2017.10.105
20. Toraldo, E., Mariani, E., Crispino, M.: Laboratory investigation into the effects of fibres and bituminous emulsion on cement-treated recycled materials for road pavements. Eur. J. Environ. Civ. Eng. **20**, 725–736 (2016). https://doi.org/10.1080/19648189.2015.1061460
21. European Commission: Concrete - Part 1: Specification, performance, production and conformity. EN 206–1

A Proposal for Viewing Government Open Data Information, Based on User Profiles

César Alencar Assumpção(✉) and José Remo Ferreira Brega

Computer Science, Paulista State University "Júlio de Mesquita Filho" – UNESP, Bauru, SP 17033-360, Brazil

{cesar.assumpcao,remo.brega}@unesp.br

Abstract. There is a global movement for the democratization of access to open government data, for the free use of society. This movement should enable greater participation by society in the development of a more efficient State, with the provision of public utility services, making wide use of technologies. To make this understanding clearer, a Systematic Literature Review (SLR) was carried out, which sought to reveal strategies for the use of open data, tools and techniques of Information Visualization. In Brazil, the municipalities are inspected by the State Audit Courts, and the São Paulo State Court of Auditors provides an open database of more than 600 municipalities. From this open database, complemented by other data sources and performance indicators, based on SLR results, the work presented in this article shows that with the correct application of Information Visualization techniques, it facilitates the understanding of public management. The public service is an important source of data, as it contains information that can have a direct impact on each citizen's life and compromise essential services such as health, safety and education. What is intended again is to structure specialized presentations according to the user's profile. The proposal is presented in the form of specific dashboards according to the user's profile, which proved to be essential to add value to the information and improve the understanding of the interested parties.

Keywords: Visualization · Information visualization techniques · Open data · OGD - Open Government Data

1 Introduction

Public Transparency in Brazil is provided by law, which guarantees citizens access to public data generated and maintained by any sphere of government, including the legislative and judicial powers.

Law 12,527 of 2011 [1] is one of the legal provisions that regulate access to information provided for in the Constitution [2], it is known as the Law of Access to Information (LAI).

Article 5 of the LAI states that it is the duty of the State to guarantee the right of access to information in an objective, agile manner and using clear and accessible language.

O. Gervasi et al. (Eds.): ICCSA 2021, LNCS 12952, pp. 163–182, 2021.
https://doi.org/10.1007/978-3-030-86973-1_12

With this, LAI and the Public Transparency Law complement each other as important instruments to fight corruption and control State activities, making it easier to monitor the acts of the Legislative and the Executive.

Brazil is a member and co-founder of the Open Government Partneship (OGP), created in 2011 and which includes 60 countries. This initiative is proof of the interest that open government is increasing worldwide [3]. It is an open, permanent and bidirectional form of communication between the administration and its managers, citizens, companies and civil society. The three pillars that define it are participation, collaboration and responsibility (publication of information).

The Brazilian Government has a data portal open since 2012, where it centralizes the search and access to data and public information. The creation of the portal is part of the actions determined in the First Open Government Action Plan, launched in 2011.

The publication of open data provides us with some benefits, such as increasing transparency and reducing corruption by political agents, empowering citizens who can better interpret information and encouraging innovation, promoting economic development. The development of applications based on open data benefits citizens in the form of providing services, accessing public services and assessing problems of public interest [4].

It also contributes to the measurement of the impact of public policies and the creation of new knowledge, based on the combination of data and information sources.

David Weinberger, one of the co-authors of "The Cluetrain Manifesto" [5], notes that "there is an inverse relationship between control and trust". Governments may want to negotiate a loss of control, offering more transparency and openness, hoping to receive in return an increase in public confidence.

The São Paulo State Court of Auditors [6] receives detailed data from 645 municipalities on a monthly basis, the vast majority of which are small municipalities. The data collected from the municipalities in CSV format are available on its portal, starting in 2014.

In Brazil, public transparency refers to fighting corruption, but the interest in government data must go further, where we can identify some classes of stakeholders with different views on the same mass of data.

In addition to the citizen, who is primarily interested in government actions, social organizations may be interested in government resources for social assistance, while businesspeople in the region want to know consumption data and government investment plans.

Members of the legislature and inspection auditors need to know whether the government is investing resources in accordance with legal limits and parameters. The municipal manager himself and his advisers are often unaware of fundamental information about his management, due to the absence of an information visualization tool, which could be useful in supporting decision making.

The main objective of this article is precisely to present a proposal for structuring the visualization of government data by user profile. In view of the large volume of data available and the variety and complexity of this data, it is very difficult to create a single dashboard with visualizations covering all the information.

The motivation for conducting the research and development of a visualization tool for government information is due to the large amount of published open data and the lack of a specific visualization application.

Society's role is to use the data made available in order to increase its participation and interaction with public policies, obtaining a better understanding of government actions [7].

The execution of the work was concentrated on the publication of open data for the municipalities of the State of São Paulo, related to budget execution, however, the legal requirements in relation to budget execution, public accounting and transparency are the same for all Brazilian municipalities. The result of the work, therefore, can be useful to any Brazilian municipality.

The article is structured in eight sections: after this introduction, Sect. 2 deals with concepts related to Open Data, followed by Sect. 3 which deals with Information Visualization concepts, complemented by Sect. 4 which describes the construction process of the information visualization. Subsequently, Sect. 5 presents the methodology and results of the Systematic Literature Review carried out. In Sect. 6 the structure of the proposed solution is demonstrated, followed by Sect. 7 which presents the application's functionalities, the identification of user profiles and some visualization techniques used. Finally, Sect. 8 contains final considerations and future work.

2 Open Data

The Brazilian Open Data Portal [4] defines and characterizes what Open Data represents.

According to the definition of Open Knowledge International [8], data are open when anyone can freely access, use, modify and share them for any purpose, being subject to, at most, requirements that aim to preserve its provenance and its openness. Open Knowledge International is an international non-profit organization that promotes information sharing and the creation of free knowledge.

This is generally satisfied by publishing the data in an open format and under an open license.

Open data is also governed by three laws and eight principles.

The three laws were proposed by David Eaves [9], a public policy expert, open data activist and public policy speaker at the Harvard Kennedy School of Government. Are they:

- If the data cannot be found and indexed on the Web, it does not exist;
- If it is not open and available in a machine-understandable format, it cannot be reused; and
- If a legal device does not allow it to be replicated, it is not useful.

The laws were proposed for open government data, but it can be said that they apply to open data in general, even outside government environments.

According to OpenGovData [10], a working group of 30 people met in California, United States of America, to define the principles of Government Open Data.

They reached consensus on the following eight principles for open government data:

- **Complete**: All public data in electronic format are made available;
- **Primary**: Data are published in the form collected at the source;
- **Current**: Available quickly;
- **Accessible**: Available to the widest possible audience and varied purposes;
- **Processable by machine**: The data is reasonably structured;
- **Non-discriminatory access**: No identification or registration is required;
- **Non-proprietary formats**: No entity can have exclusive control over the data; and
- **Free licenses**: Free from restrictions by copyright regulations.

The next section deals with Information Visualization concepts, another important foundation for this work.

3 Information Views

To access open data and understand it, in the format that is published, it is necessary to have technical knowledge. The concept of open data is to share it as widely as possible. With the help of tools and applications for data analysis and information visualization, innovative solutions for society's problems that would never have been imagined by the data owner emerge.

Even so, it is important to share the perspectives brought by these visualizations, applications and infographics so that everyone can access the data, without having to have the technical knowledge to use the data directly.

When information is made available on the Web using appropriate open standards, it can be used over and over again in new, unforeseen and imaginative ways, capable of greatly increasing the value of the data through its reuse and combination, with greater automation and better interoperability. As the Many Minds Principle document, "The Many Minds Principle," says [11]: the coolest thing to do with your data will be imagined by someone else.

Information visualization is the presentation of quantitative data in a graphical form. In other words, information visualizations turn large and small data sets into visuals that are easier for the human brain to understand and process.

According to Yamaguchi [12], one of the factors to be considered for choosing the most appropriate information visualization technique is the type of data to be manipulated.

As an example, Yamaguchi [12] points out that visualizations of information can be used to discover unknown facts and trends. You can have presentations in the form of line charts to show changes over time. Bar and column charts are useful when looking at relationships and making comparisons. Pie charts are a great way to show parts-of-a-whole. And maps are the best way to visually share geographic data.

Taking into account that 90% of the information that passes through our brain is visual, according to Dagostin [13], Information Visualization through graphics ends up becoming the fastest and most direct way to disseminate information. In addition, the graphical visualization is shared much faster than any written content.

Organizations are making use of visualizations of information to support decision making. With the aid of data analysis software and visual statement generators, it is easier to understand the reality of the business, offering better conditions for decisions based on data.

The next section complements the Information Visualization concept, presenting the information visualization construction process.

4 Information Visualization Construction Process

Card and others [14] define Information Visualization as "the use of visual representations of abstract data supported by computer and interactive to increase cognition". It is important to highlight the inclusion of the computational factor as a support for visual representations, which allows for possibilities of interaction and increases the power of cognition.

The objective is to facilitate the observer to see a certain phenomenon, through visualizations. Visualizations amplify cognition because almost half of the human brain is focused on the visual sense - we are good at interpreting graphic patterns and discovering trends, according to Ware [15]. This cognition capacity is enhanced by the advances in new technologies, which allow the creation of interactive, dynamic, animated and real-time visualizations [15].

To create visualizations that amplify cognition, it is necessary to think about the data to be presented, how to extract them, organize them and how to represent them to the user, in a way that helps him to perform one or more tasks. CARD and others [14] proposed a model that details the steps for creating visualizations.

Figure 1 illustrates a reference model for the information visualization process, presented by Card and others [14], which is formed by three stages.

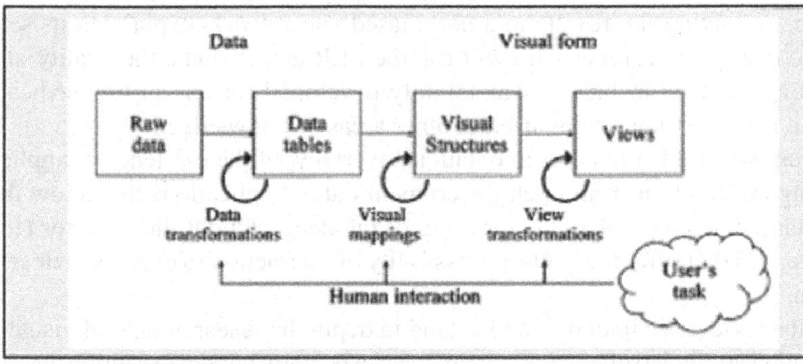

Fig. 1. Card et al. reference visualization model (Source: adapted from Card et al. 1999.)

The first step is called Data Transformations. In this step, a set of raw data is processed and structured, usually in the form of one or more tables. The processing seeks to perform data cleaning, elimination of redundancies, filtering, groupings and totalizations in categories and other classifications.

The second step is Visual Mapping, which involves building a structure that visually represents the data in the table. Usually represented by axes, such as the X and Y axes of the Cartesian plane.

The third stage of the visualization process is that of Visual Transformations, in which it is possible to modify and extend visual structures with the insertion of interaction resources. The interaction mechanisms allow the user to explore different scenarios for a better understanding of the visualized data.

According to Kirk [16] the data classification methods for viewing the information are: comparing categories; evaluation of hierarchies and relation parts of a whole, showing changes over time; plotting connections and relationships; and mapping of geospatial data.

According to Kirk [16], the criteria for building a consistent visualization are: data with statistical precision; precision in visualization; functional precision; visual inference; precision formatting; and accuracy in annotation. It is necessary to be rigorous with all the details, accurate and true in the representation of the data to obtain visualizations that are functional, effective and do not deceive the reader.

The next section presents the methodology and results of the Systematic Literature Review. Government areas of interest, tools, visual techniques and purpose of the applications present in the studies.

5 Systematic Literature Review (SLR)

SLR is a type of scientific research that aims to gather, critically evaluate and conduct a synthesis of the results of multiple primary studies [17]. It also aims to answer a clearly formulated question, using systematic and explicit methods to identify, select and evaluate relevant research, collect and analyze data from studies included in the SLR [18].

SLR is a technique that seeks to carry out comprehensive reviews of the literature on a topic, evaluating the results in a non-biased way, always explaining its selection criteria, so that the researcher who will use the SLR can evaluate the quality of it and execute it again. This technique was initially developed for use in the medical field, however, it is increasingly being used in other areas of knowledge [19].

The purpose of this review is to obtain an overview of the existence of applications for viewing information from open government data. Applications that allow the user to understand in a simple way the meaning of the data, without the need for technical knowledge, and that offer the user the possibility of interaction to express their criticism or opinion.

With the review, we intend to understand in depth the research field of visualization of information applied to open government data, especially budget execution data (public revenues and expenditures).

After a careful evaluation based on previous research, the following main research question was defined:

What information visualization tools and techniques are being applied to Government Open Data, seeking to facilitate the understanding of information to interested users, and what is the main purpose of these applications?

This main question can be expanded on to the following questions:

1) What is the governmental area, of open government data available?
2) What technologies are used for accessing and manipulating open government data, generating graphical visualizations and developing applications?
3) What information visualization techniques are explored by these applications?
4) What is the specific purpose of the application and what type of user is it intended for?

The searches were carried out in the ACM Digital Library, IEEE Xplore Digital Library and Scopus databases.

76 (seventy-six) studies were identified in the researched databases, and after the selection process, 38 (thirty-eight) studies for the extraction phase were included.

Several trends could be investigated during the execution of this review, among them, can be cited:

- **Governmental area**: the public area involves a multitude of services and administrative functions, and its management produces a huge amount of information with very different contents. In the analysis of the studies, it can be seen that the areas of greatest interest, referenced in the studies, are related to Finance/Public Budget and Public Health. In a second block, we have data on Education, Transport and Socioeconomic;
- **Tools for manipulating open data**: what has been observed as a trend is the use of data analysis tools, which allow importing data of different formats, defining data structures, establishing relationships between data sets, including those collected from different sources, being able to apply selections, filters and summaries;
- **Tools for generating graphical visualizations**: the observed trend is that the choice of a specific graphic resource is related to the type of visualization of the desired information;
- **Visual techniques**: the selected studies point to a clear trend of use in the application of visualization techniques on maps, followed by visualizations in graphs. Applications aimed at the area of public health and urban services, explore geolocation as the main information visualization technique; and
- **Main purpose of applications**: the most common trend is the classic purpose of demonstrating information, of giving publicity, also called public transparency. The goal is to make use of graphical visualizations to make it easier for users to understand the information. There is also a tendency to create applications that are useful or offer some service to the user. Other applications seek to provide the user with the power to inspect public administration and even interact, being able to participate in debates and decision-making.

In Fig. 2, it is possible to observe the classification of studies according to the purpose of the application.

In general, there is a trend in the development of common applications to improve the understanding of information using graphics, and applications that offer urban or public utility services using maps. It is noticed an increasing number of data sets published by

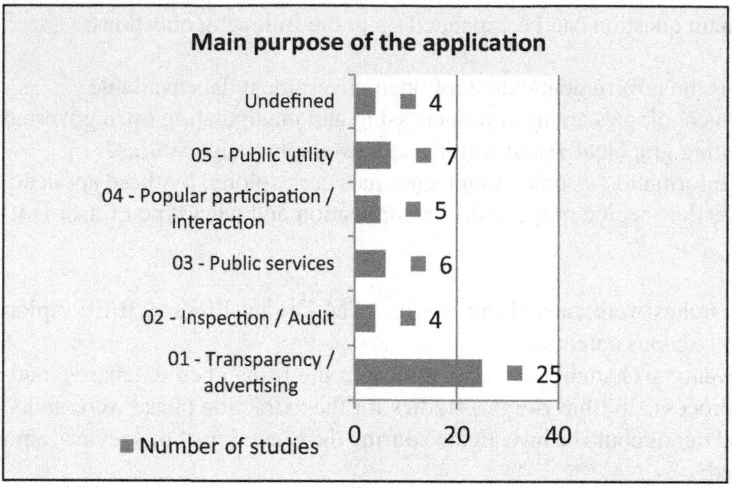

Fig. 2. Main purpose of the application (Source: produced by the author)

public agencies and the concern of many studies in finding a more adequate model for the process of accessing the data, preparation and visualization of the information of the same.

Among the studies, it is possible to highlight some that seek to create visualizations based on open government data:

1. In their study, Joohee Choi and Yla Tausczik [20], conclude that open government data analysis is expected to encourage citizens to participate in government, as well as to improve transparency and efficiency in government processes;
2. Maria Sokhn et al. [21], proposes in their study the display of information on panels, where the panels could be offered to citizens before public meetings so that they can have full knowledge of the administrative situation. Subsequently, citizens would have the means to contribute to political implementation, taking advantage of open data, in order to propose services and improvements. In the discussion of a particular problem, users could send comments, photos and videos to enrich their considerations to provoke a debate among the participants;
3. D. Burkhardt et al. [22], reports in his study on the possibility of adding indicators to open data, to improve understanding. Open data can only indicate a possible problem through deviations from the normal level, for example, if the unemployment rate has increased significantly within a short period of time. In fact, the information alone does not explain why there was a certain deviation. It is necessary to add other information (indicators) and relate to the data to better understand the deviation detected in the data. This allows for a much higher quality in the analysis and inspection of the information; and
4. Gebetsroither-Geringer, Stollnberger and Peters-Anders [23], designed to develop a web platform that can be used as a system of dialogue between participatory citizens. The platform must be flexible and generic to provide a basis for different topics to

be addressed within a city. In this way, citizens should be able to share their ideas in the decision-making process.

Among the technological resources highlighted in the studies we have the CSV data format and the graphic library D3.JS among the most cited.

In the next section, the structure of the proposed solution is demonstrated, from access to open data, data preparation and subsequent visualization.

6 Structure of the Solution

The main objective of the proposed solution is to view information on the budgetary execution of municipal administrations, through graphics organized on information display panels in the WEB environment, in specific formats according to the group of users.

With the help of the SLR results, the following requirements were raised to achieve the intended objective:

1. Data entry must provide access to more than one open data source and allow the relationship between them;
2. It must enable the insertion of performance indicators that allow a better interpretation of the calculated values;
3. The application must allow filters by categories, by government area, and other classifications;
4. It must make it possible to select the data by period ranges and value ranges; and
5. The data output must be structured according to the user's profile. The visualization of the information must have more than one format, to attend different groups of users.

Figure 3 shows the complete structure of the solution.

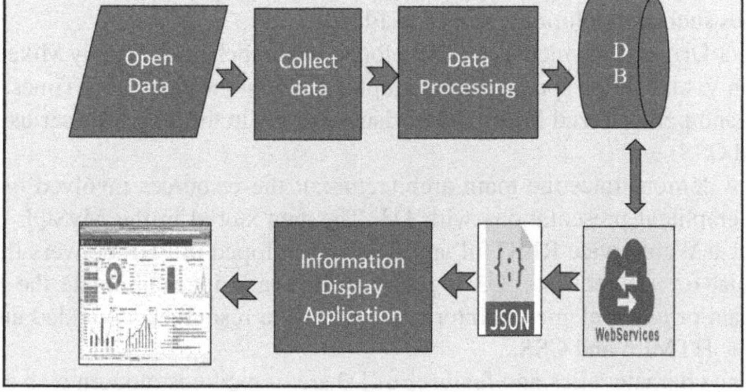

Fig. 3. Structure of the proposed solution (Source: produced by the author)

The structure presented can be divided into two parts, the first being responsible for the collection, processing of data and storage in a database and the second refers to the application of visualization of information based on data requested from this database through a WebService API.

The data collection provides access to more than one open data source, including data from the municipality itself, and the possibility of inserting performance indicators, while the visualization application must allow different formats of dashboards for different user profiles.

The main source of data for the application is available on the São Paulo Court of Auditors portal [6]. The portal provides data in the CSV format of budget revenues and expenses and debt data for municipalities in the State of São Paulo as of 2014. Access is via the address https://transparencia.tce.sp.gov.br, making it possible to choose the desired municipality and financial year.

The application performs data import in CSV format into SQL database. The relational database manager MySQL was used, created in a WEB environment.

A RESTful WebService application with PHP language and the SLIM Framework was developed especially to meet the data requests of the application.

Based on the user's choices, the application will be responsible for requesting the necessary data through a WebService application. The application will receive the data requested in JSON format in return and will be responsible for rendering the graphics that will be displayed in a panel of information visualizations.

For the development of the information visualization application, to make graphical presentations of data received in a WEB environment, the graphic library D3.JS was used, together with HTML5, CSS and JavaScript, non-proprietary resources.

The graphic library D3.js is among the main technological resources for creating information visualizations, according to the SLR. D3.js was the main resource used in the development of this application.

D3.js is a free-to-use JavaScript library, with incredible resources for creating dynamic and interactive visualizations, and has a lot of content on the internet and several galleries with templates ready for reuse. One of the galleries is available at https://www.d3-graph-gallery.com/, and has several models of graphic visualizations organized in categories such as Evolution, Maps and Flow.

D3 (Data-Driven Documents) was developed and launched in 2011 by Mike Bostock, Information Visualization specialist and graphic editor at the New York Times, to create interactive and personalized information visualizations in the web browser using SVG, HTML and CSS.

Figure 4 demonstrates the main architecture of the resources involved in the generation of graphical presentations with D3. The data stored in the MySQL database, accessed by a WebService RESTful application developed in PHP delivers the data in JSON format for D3 requests. D3 together with JavaScript manipulate the DOM by inserting data-oriented elements. Interaction and style resources are added and finally presented by HTML5 and CSS.

The main characteristics and features of D3 are: it explores modern web standards: SVG, HTML5 and CSS; data oriented in CSV, JSON and XML formats; allows you to manipulate the DOM (Document Object Model) based on your data; allows you to

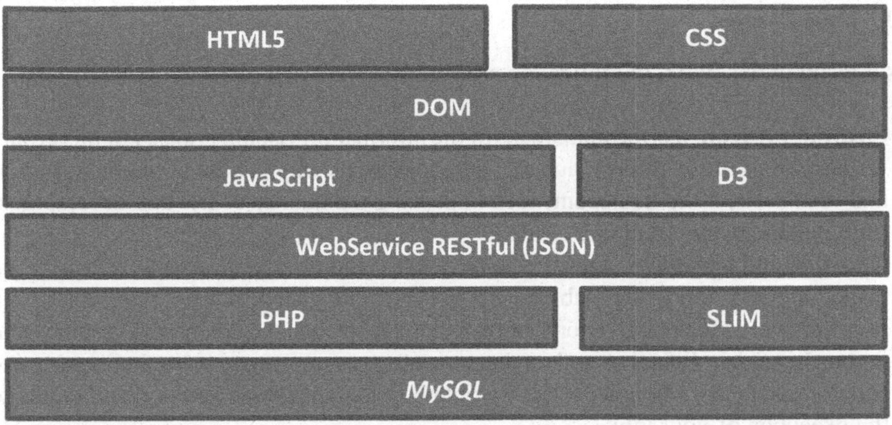

Fig. 4. Architecture of the information visualization application (Source: produced by the author)

dynamically generate new HTML elements and apply styles based on your data; dynamic properties: data can direct its styles and attributes; allows you to create graphic elements such as tables, pie charts or bars to geospatial maps; custom views with full control over your viewing capabilities; provides very powerful transition features; and great support for interaction and animation features.

The following web standards are widely used in D3: HTML5, DOM, CSS, SVG and JavaScript.

SVG (Scalable Vector Graphics) is an XML language to describe two-dimensional drawings and graphics in a vector way, either static, dynamic or animated.

One of the main characteristics of vector graphics is that they do not lose quality when they are enlarged.

The next section presents the application's features, the identification of user profiles and some visualization techniques used.

7 Application Features

In addition to the technological resources, it is necessary to define the scope of the proposed solution. Some questions need to be answered in relation to the target audience and the type of visualization desired.

For which audience do you want to make the application available? To create visualizations of functional information, it is necessary to know your target audience, to support project decisions and develop an application that meets the user's needs.

One of the main points of this work was the specification of the different user profiles, according to the participation of each element in public management. It was observed the role of each group in the municipal administration, their needs and what type of information they are interested in. This definition was fundamental for the development of the application and planning of the necessary visualizations.

7.1 User Profiles

As a result of this work, the following user profiles were identified:

- **Ordinary citizen**: it is the main focus of the information visualizations. For this group, visualizations of the information that demonstrate the application of public resources and results of public management in improving the quality of life and development of the municipality would be created;
- **Auditors and legislative agents**: responsible for authorizing the executive's projects, inspecting and approving public accounts. For this group that normally analyze a large amount of technical reports and copy of documents, the creation of graphics that demonstrate the allocation and application of approved resources in their respective categories and government projects, would be a tool that would support and facilitate the execution of your job;
- **Executive managers and public agents**: responsible for the application of public resources. For this group, it is important to create graphs that demonstrate the evolution of budgetary execution within the year, compliance with mandatory investments and respect for the limits imposed by legislation. Another need for the public manager is to assess how much has been invested in the development of the city and to monitor the evolution of the public debt;
- **Non-governmental entities, Social Organizations and the press**: entities that seek information from the government to inform and defend the interests of society. This group resembles ordinary citizens, but needs more elaborate and more detailed views; and
- **Entrepreneurs and public sector suppliers**: companies that seek information on consumption patterns and investments from the government. As it is a local database, it is important that businesspeople in the region are able to visualize the consumption needs of the local government to guide their sales strategies.

Thinking about the visualization needs for different profiles makes it possible to better plan the visualization of the information. It is important to put yourself in the shoes of a particular user and think about what would be important to them.

What about the type of information display? What you want to convey to the reader?

The intention regarding the function of the information visualizations is that it is more focused on "explaining" and "exploring". Transmit information to the reader in a specific and focused narrative, and allow discoveries free of interest and check patterns. The visualizations of the information will have a pragmatic and analytical tone, with more open and less conclusive content for an audience that seeks to interpret the information and reach their own conclusions.

It is not intended to impose an emotional and abstract tone, aiming to impress and impact readers.

These are important factors for an information visualization project. When establishing the purpose of the information visualization project, the desired tone and its function are defined.

7.2 Using the Stacked Area Visualization Technique

Stacked area graph resembles a line graph, but it presents a colored area below the line, and each series starts at the top of the previous series, and compare historical trends showing the proportion of the total that each category represents at any given time. It indicates general trends rather than individual values when comparing multiple data sets, showing how each category contributes to the cumulative total over time.

With the application of this technique, it is possible to demonstrate the evolution of income or expenses for several years, grouped into categories.

In Fig. 5, it is possible to observe the visualization in D3 using the stacked area technique. The categories can be activated or deactivated by the corresponding buttons, by the user's interaction, and the visualization is updated automatically, without the need to search for the data again. The user also has the possibility to select the type of display, for stacked area, flow chart or 100% stacked area. A table with information for each exercise is displayed when the mouse is placed over the image at the points corresponding to the X coordinate.

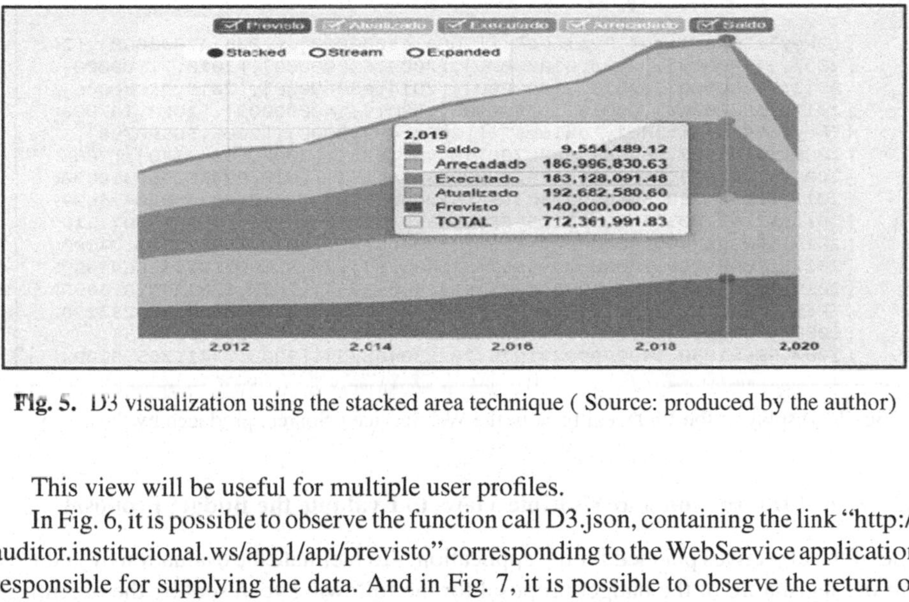

Fig. 5. D3 visualization using the stacked area technique (Source: produced by the author)

This view will be useful for multiple user profiles.

In Fig. 6, it is possible to observe the function call D3.json, containing the link "http://auditor.institucional.ws/app1/api/previsto" corresponding to the WebService application responsible for supplying the data. And in Fig. 7, it is possible to observe the return of data in JSON format related to the WebService call.

With this sequence of images, it was possible to demonstrate the operation of the application with the visualization of an interactive graphic, generated with resources from the D3.js library, the request for data through a WebService API and the return of the data in JSON format.

This information visualization using the stacked area technique was based on a model from the NVD3 library, which is a JavaScript library containing a set of components coded from the D3.js library. NVD3 allows developers to create reusable graphics, from a wide variety of models and codes that can be explored on the library's website (https://nvd3.org/).

```
d3.json("http://auditor.institucional.ws/app1/api/previsto",
        function(error, data) {
    d3.select('#chart1')
        .datum(data)
        .transition().duration(1000)
        .call(chart)
        .each('start', function() {
            setTimeout(function() {
                d3.selectAll('#chart1 *').each(function() {
                    if(this.__transition__)
                        this.__transition__.duration = 1;
                })
            }, 0)
        });
});
```

Fig. 6. Code snippet with the call from D3 to the WebService (Source: produced by the author)

Não seguro | auditor.institucional.ws/app1/api/previsto

[{"key":"Previsto","values":[[2004,43000000],[2005,47000000],[20
[2007,54500000],[2008,61000000],[2009,63000000],[2010,71500000],
[2012,78000000],[2013,81000000],[2014,85000000],[2015,93000000],
[2017,115000000],[2018,133500000],[2019,140000000],[2020,147000
{"key":"Atualizado","values":[[2004,49303000],[2005,56590798],
[2006,54791487.96999999880790710449218750],[2007,60847340],[2008,
[2009,81561023.28000000119209289550781250],[2010,99438296.310000
[2011,120104783.34999999403953552246093750],[2012,131430204.4699
[2013,127622803.54000000655651092529296875],[2014,145325007.319
[2015,160320740.18000000715255737304687500],[2016,159480727.77000
[2017,170909868.74000000953674316406250],[2018,199759753.669999
[2019,192682580.59999999403953552246093750],[2020,176139918.8899
{"key":"Executado","values":[[2004,44117231.8200000002980232238
[2005,49992988],[2006,53914896.259999997913837432861328125],
[2007,58681850.54999999701976776123046875],[2008,73415365.51999

Fig. 7. Display of the JSON callback to the WebService (Source: produced by the author)

7.3 Use of Interaction and Multiple Views to Evaluate the Budget Proposal

One of the objectives planned for the application is to facilitate the evaluation by auditors and the legislature of the budget proposal for the following year, sent by the executive. This moment occurs once a year, between August and October of each year. The chief executive submits the budget proposal, which comprises a set of annexes with detailed statements of the values classified into categories and government projects distributed in the various budget units.

The evaluation of these documents first passes through the analysis of technicians and then goes on to debates and voting in plenary.

To facilitate the discussion around the proposal and support the speech and presentation of each councilor, the interesting thing is that a graphic presentation is prepared to facilitate understanding. Considering that the majority of the City Councils do not have advisers for their Councilors, being in charge of preparing their exposition, normally their speech is not supported by a facilitating presentation.

This moment is of great importance for public administration, where the allocation of public resources for the next financial year will be defined. Which government projects will be carried out and the source of their funding.

For this moment, a visualization was planned that demonstrates the application of general resources and for each budgetary unit (Secretariats and Departments), and the amount applied in each unit can be evaluated. It will also be possible to make a comparison of the current proposal with the proposal approved in the previous year, in order to verify which Departments had an increase or reduction in the budget. Another possibility is the classification of the values into categories, which in this case divides the values proposed by the Public Agency (Legislative and Executive).

To develop this visualization, the bubble model was chosen from a gallery of models with D3 code, available on GITHUB.COM, on the page "https://github.com/d3/d3/wiki/Gallery". This model was used in 2013 by the New York Times in the newspaper's article about the American government's budget proposal for that year.

Figure 8 and Fig. 9 are the information visualization using different bubble grouping by size and colors, and show the budget proposal grouped by Management Area (Secretaries) and in General.

Fig. 8. Visualization in D3 with departments grouped into management area (Source: produced by the author)

Figure 8 shows visualization in D3 with the budget proposal grouped by Secretaries (Management Area). Each bubble represents a department that is part of a Secretariat. A Secretariat has at least one Department, and some Secretariats have up to five Departments. The size of the bubble indicates the value of the budget, on a scale of 1 to 90 pixels to determine the radius of the bubble, for a range of values from 0 to 50 million reais. The color of the bubble is defined by a gradient of shades of green for budgets with an increase in relation to the previous year and a gradient of shades of red for budgets with a reduction in relation to the previous year.

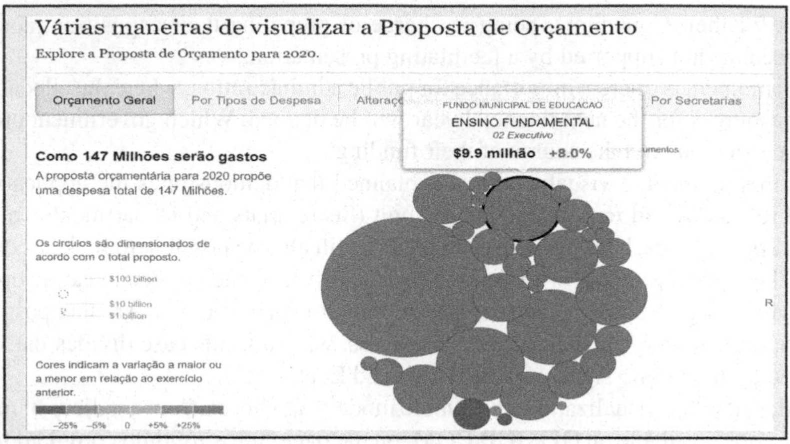

Fig. 9. D3 visualization of the general budget (Source: produced by the author)

A box with information from the Department is displayed when the mouse is placed over a certain bubble in the image.

Figure 9 shows visualization in D3 with the total of the budget proposal, and also contains the same characteristics of the grouping by Secretariats.

The same data can be evaluated in four different ways, totaled, by Secretariat, by Agency and by variation in relation to the previous year. The transition between the visualizations of the information occurs only by changing the position of the coordinates of each bubble in the image. The loading of the data with information from each Department (bubble) occurs only once, and the positioning of the bubbles is determined with D3 transition features and dynamic properties, adding interaction and animation to the visualization.

Despite starting from a ready-made model, available for use and reuse, this model is very complex with more than 10,000 lines, and had to have its structure modified according to the data structure, scale and X coordinate calculation strategy, Y, for positioning the bubbles in the image.

7.4 Using the Treemap Technique to Assess Budget Execution Within the year

In order to display the values executed at a certain point in the exercise, important information for the public manager, the visualization technique with hierarchical data and structured in a tree (treemap) was selected. This model initially allows the visualization of the total executed for each Secretariat. The size of the rectangle indicates the total value executed, ordered from largest to smallest value. The starting line of the table contains the total value executed in the exercise, and is used as the title of the path taken in the tree.

When clicking with the mouse on a particular Secretariat, the Secretariat expands into Departments. Each rectangle of the image contains its title and executed value, in addition to the total value of items subordinate to this item.

When clicking with the mouse on a specific Department, the Department expands to expense categories of this Department, such as Personnel Expenses, Services, Consumables, Permanent Material and Investment in Works/Installation.

The visualization therefore contains three levels of hierarchy, without considering the City Hall as a whole. The first level is the separation into Secretaries. The second level is separation of the Secretariat into Departments and the third level is the classification of the Department's executed values into Expense Categories.

For this visualization, a model was chosen from the D3 graphics gallery on the page "https://www.d3-graph-gallery.com". This gallery contains models with the basic structure of each type of chart, with some variations for each type.

Figure 10 shows the model with hierarchical data and structured in a tree.

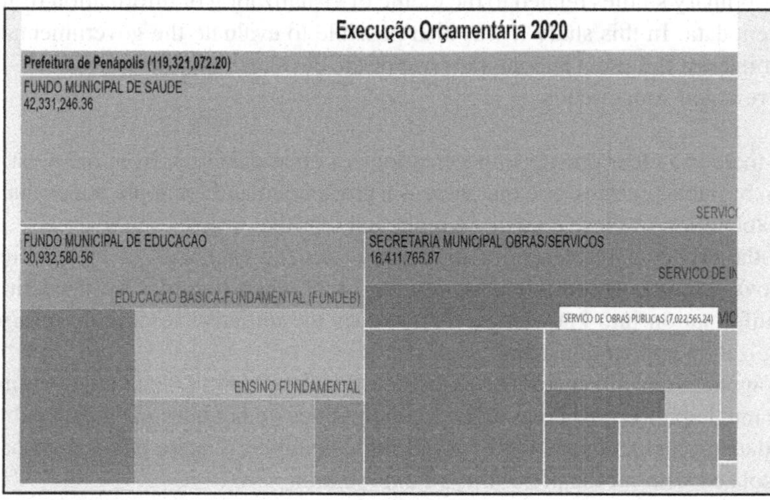

Fig. 10. View with hierarchical and tree-structured data – Treemap (Source: produced by the author)

It is important to highlight that three different approaches were used for the codification of D3. One approach was to make use of the NVD3 library, which contains several ready-made D3 models, available for reuse, exploring various visualization and interaction techniques. A second approach is related to the use of ready-made codes, previously used in a specific event or publication and made available by the authors to be modified and reused. These ready-made codes are usually available in D3 galleries on the internet. A third approach is related to the coding of D3 based on minimal structures, available in tutorials or on the library portal itself, at the address "https://d3js.org". In this case, development requires a greater coding effort, and a greater dependence on the programmer's knowledge and creativity.

The D3 library allows the free creation of new models with incredible visualization and interaction resources, being able to combine code reuse and new implementations.

The next section presents the final considerations and future work.

8 Conclusion and Future Work

The development of this work sought to present a development strategy for the application of information visualization for open government data from small municipalities.

The main data source used was the open data provided by the São Paulo State Court of Auditors [6], which is responsible for supervising the municipalities, complemented by other sources, including data from the municipality itself. The insertion of performance indicators allows the reader to better assess possible deviations from standards, such as whether the amount of investment in the educational area is related to the variation in the literacy rate.

The technological resources used and the information visualization techniques adopted were based on the SLR previously carried out, which resulted in the selection of 38 primary studies related to the theme of visualization of information from open government data. In this study it was also possible to evaluate the governmental areas that most interest the users and the purpose of the developed applications.

SLR revealed some trends:

1. That there is a clear growth in publications of open data sets, from the most varied areas, by public entities, and that there is a greater demand for applications that allow the exploration of these data in a simple and intuitive way;
2. That the proper presentation of data, motivates the exchange of information and improves communication. It is an essential tool when it comes to translating data and information into knowledge. This values the initiative to develop information visualization applications; and
3. That applications in general are based on open data from the federal government or large municipalities, whereas small municipalities do not have open data published. The data on budget execution of small municipalities, despite public transparency, are isolated without the possibility of exploitation.

In this work, it seeks to assist users with visualization of information from small municipalities, based on open data from the State and the municipality itself.

The presentation of the visualizations was also planned to be structured in user categories, with exclusive dashboards. The visualization and interaction techniques were selected according to the data set and needs for understanding the information, of interest to each user profile. The views are more attractive and interesting, for each category of users, because they are planned according to their interests.

For future work, we intend to make the application available for evaluating users of different profiles in order to improve the views of each category.

It is also intended for future work, considering that the open database contains information from all municipalities in the State, the possibility of creating views comparing data from different municipalities. It would be possible to compare income and expenses for a group of similar municipalities or even evaluate some information in the region or in the State using geolocation techniques.

Innumerable situations could be assessed using data from all municipalities in the State, such as investment in education per student, or health expenses per person. The performance of the same supplier could be evaluated in several cities, including trying to find out if the values practiced in similar acquisitions are consistent.

Finally, this work sought to demonstrate that the development of a government data visualization application meets a current reality, the publication of an infinity of government data and information due to the legal obligation of public transparency, and the absence of a application of reading and presentation of these data, mainly for small municipalities. And implemented a new proposal for visualizations based on user profiles, seeking to serve different audiences, with different objectives in the analysis of the same database.

References

1. Brazil: Law 12.527, of November 18, 2011. Regulates access to information provided for in item XXXIII of article 5, in item II of & 3rd of art. 37 and in the 2nd of art.216 of the Federal Constitution; amends Law No. 8,112, of December 11, 1990; repeals Law No. 11,111, of May 5, 2005, and provisions of Law No. 8,159, of January 8, 1991; and make other arrangements. Federal Official Gazette, Brasilia, 19 November 2011. http://www.planalto.gov.br/ccivil_03/_ato2011-2014/2011/lei/l12527.htm
2. Brazil: [Constitution (1988)]. Constitution of the Federative Republic of Brazil. Presidency of the Republic, Brasília, DF (1988). http://www.planalto.gov.br/ccivil_03/constituicao/constituicao.htm
3. Ramírez-Alujas, Á., Dassen, N.: Exchange rate: the advance of open government policies in Latin America and the Caribbean, Inter-American Development Bank, Technical note # idb-tn-629 (2014). https://publications.iadb.org/es/publicacion/16833/vientos-de-cambio-el-avance-de-las-politicas-de-gobierno-abierto-en-america
4. DADOS.GOV.BR. Portal: Brazilian Open Data Portal (2019). http://dados.gov.br/
5. Levine, R., et al.: The Cluetrain Manifesto. The End of Business as Usual, (The Cluetrain manifesto. The end of normal business), Reading: Perseus Book (2001)
6. TCE-SP: Court of auditors of the state of São Paulo (2020). https://www.tce.sp.gov.br/
7. EGOV-IMPROVING: Improving access to government through better use to the web. Accar, S., Alonso, J., Novak, K. (eds.) W3C Group Note (2009)
8. OKFN - Open Knowledge Foundation: Free knowledge network (2019). https://br.okfn.org/
9. Eaves, D.: The three laws of open government data (2009). https://eaves.ca/2009/09/30/three-law-of-open-government-data/
10. OpenGovData: 8 Principles of open government data (2007). https://public.resource.org/8_principles.html
11. Walsh, J., Pollock, R.: The many minds principle. Open Data and Componentization, XTech (2007), 17 May 2007. https://rufuspollock.com/many-minds/
12. Yamaguchi, J.K.: Guidelines for choosing visualization techniques applied to the knowledge extraction process. Master's Dissertation in Computer Science. State University of Maringá, Maringá.41 (2010)
13. Dagostin, D.: The use of tdics as an interactive tool in the teaching - learning process of chemical discipline in higher education. In: International Distance Education Symposium, São Carlos, Anais, São Carlos, UFSCAR (2014)
14. Card, S.K., Ackinlay, J.D., Shneiderman, B., Card, M.: Readings in information visualization: using vision to think. Morgan Kaufmann Series in Interactive Technologies, Academic Press (1999)
15. Ware, C.: Information visualization: perception for design. 3rd edition, Morgan Kaufmann Interactive Technologies Series (2012)

16. Kirk, A.: Data visualization: a sucessful design process, 1st. Ed, Packt Publishing Ltd, p. 206 (2012)
17. Cook, D.J., Mulrow, C.D., Haynes, R.B.: Systematic reviews: synthesis of best evidence for clinical decisions. Ann Intern Med. **126**(5), 376–380 (1997)
18. Clarke, M., Horton, R.: Bringing it all together: Lancet-Cochrane collaborate on systematic reviews. Lancet **2**(357), 1728 (2001)
19. Brereton, P., et al.: Lessons from applying the systematic literature review process within the software engineering domain. J. Syst. Softw. Elsevier Sci. Inc. **80**(4), 571–583, April 2007, ISSN 01641212. https://www.sciencedirect.com/science/article/pii/S016412120600197X?via%3Dihub
20. Choi, J., Tausczik, Y.: Characteristics of collaboration in the emerging practice of open data analysis. In: Proceedings of the 2017 ACM Conference on Computer Supported Cooperative Work and Social Computing (CSCW 2017), pp. 835–846. ACM, New York, NY, USA (2017). https://doi.org/10.1145/2998181.2998265
21. Sokhn, M., et al.: From data to decisions. In: Proceedings of the 9th International Conference on Theory and Practice of Electronic Governance (ICEGOV 2015 - 2016), pp. 361–362. ACM, New York, NY, USA (2016). https://doi.org/10.1145/2910019.2910032
22. Burkhardt, D., Nazemi, K., Retz, W., Kohlhammer, J.: Visual explanation of government-data for policy making through open-data inclusion. In: The 9th International Conference for Internet Technology and Secured Transactions (ICITST-2014), pp. 83–89. London (2014). https://doi.org/10.1109/ICITST.2014.7038782
23. Gebetsroither-Geringer, E., Stollnberger, R., Peters-Anders, J.: Interactive spatial web-applications as new means of support for urban decision-making processes. ISPRS Ann. Photogrammetry, Remote Sens. Spat. Inf. Sci. **4**(4/W7), 59–66 (2018). https://doi.org/10.5194/isprs-annals-IV-4-W7-59-2018

Extended Maturity Model for Digital Transformation

Nuno Soares[1,2(✉)], Paula Monteiro[1,2], Francisco J. Duarte[1], and Ricardo J. Machado[1]

[1] ALGORITMI Research Centre, University of Minho, Campus de Azurém, 4800-058 Guimarães, Portugal
{nuno.soares,paula.monteiro}@ccg.pt, {francisco.duarte, rmac}@dsi.uminho.pt

[2] CCG/ZGDV Institute, Campus de Azurém Edifício 14, 4800-058 Guimarães, Portugal

Abstract. The integration of disruptive technologies into the industrial value chain has built the foundation for the fourth industrial revolution. For a company that wants to embark in this digital transformation, a set of issues remain doubtful, uncertain and unsolved. Thus, is essential to assist companies in transitioning to digital transformation technologies and practices. Maturity models (MMs) aim to assist organizations by providing comprehensive guidance towards the improvement of their capabilities in a standardized, objective, and repeatable way. This study pretends to adjust and extend the MM that seems to be more used by the Portuguese companies, with components and requirements which can overcome its gaps, thus suggesting ways for it completion and enrichment. Consequently, the literature is reviewed systematically to identify existing studies proposing MMs in the context of Industry 4.0 (I4.0). Twenty-one identified MMs are analysed by comparing their dimensions, context, purpose, wholeness, objectivity, and assessment type. Great variability was found which was reconciled in order to build a perspective as holistic as possible for the phenomenon of digital transformation. The proposed MM with an all-inclusive approach pretends to assess digital transformation through the appraisal of 28 dimensions organized in six categories. In addition to the dimensions, the framework to assist the assessment of the I4.0 practices is completed with a questionnaire that evaluates the fulfilment of the requirement of each dimension by maturity level and evidence that can confirm that evaluation.

Keywords: Digital transformation · Industry 4.0 readiness · Digital maturity model · Roadmap for Industry 4.0

1 Introduction

The materialization of the digital transformation on value chains across industries is made through several initiatives around the world. The increasing integration of the Internet of Everything (IoE) and disruptive technologies into the industrial value chain has built the foundation for the 4th industrial revolution. The designations differ but the one that has the most impact and perhaps best describes the use of Internet technologies in industrial

O. Gervasi et al. (Eds.): ICCSA 2021, LNCS 12952, pp. 183–200, 2021.
https://doi.org/10.1007/978-3-030-86973-1_13

value chain organization is the I4.0. However, Smart Manufacturing, Industrial Internet, Intelligent Manufacturing, Industrial Value Chain, are analogous terms that describe somewhat the same movement.

With I4.0 becoming a top priority for many research centres, universities, and companies, the manifold contributions from academics and practitioners have made the meaning of the term more unclear than solid [1]. Even the key promoters of the idea, the I4.0 Working Group [2] only describe the vision, the basic technologies the idea aims at, and selected scenarios, but do not provide a clear definition. As a result, a generally accepted understanding of I4.0 and a straight roadmap towards it, has not been published so far, hindering transformation efforts, causing indecision and uncertainty. The same can be observed about the other initiatives that under other designations and resulting from the efforts of other groups and institutions, contribute to the same result: smarter digital factories.

Thus, from the point of view of a company that wants to embark in this digital transformation, a set of issues remain doubtful, uncertain and unsolved. It is essential to assist companies in transitioning to digital transformation technologies and practices. Maturity Models (MMs) aim to assist organizations by providing comprehensive guidance towards the improvement of their capabilities in a standardized, objective, and repeatable way. MMs provide organisations with measuring for auditing and benchmarking, a measuring of progress assessment against well-known objectives, and an understanding of current strengths, weaknesses and opportunities, which can support informed decision making concerning strategy and organisation management.

The IMPULS Readiness Model, commissioned by the IMPULS Foundation of the German Engineering Federation (VDMA) carried out by IW Consult and the Institute for Industrial Management at RWTH Aachen University, was aligned closely with I4.0. It seemed to be at the outset, and the study confirmed it, the most popular model, possibly to which more merits are recognized according to the number of references stated in the literature. SHIFTo4.0 is the Portuguese equivalent to IMPULS and is based on it, suffering from the same virtues and limitations. Given the influence of the SHIFTo4.0 promoters, it will be expected that it will become the model adopted to measure the maturity of the digital transformation of Portuguese companies.

This paper describes our effort to complete and enrich IMPULS, thus SHIFTo4.0, with extra dimensions, components and requirements which can overcome the flaws that are pointed out to it, obtaining a more holistic model that addresses all the components of evaluating the maturity of the digital transformation in industrial organisations.

The remainder of the paper is structured as follows. Starting by establishing some theoretical background, Sect. 2 summarizes the motivation for this work, recognising the problem, defining the restrictions, structuring and describing the research method. Section 3 describes the selected MMs distinguishing them from their origin: industry and academia. Section 4 explains the analysis performed for the selected MMs and the development of the proposed model. Finally, Sect. 5 concludes with remarks about the undertaken study and some considerations for future work.

2 Methodology

Paulk et al. [3] define maturity as a specific process for explicitly defining, managing, measuring, and controlling the evolutionary growth of an entity. A maturity model consists of a sequence of maturity levels for a class of objects. It represents an anticipated, desired, or typical evolution path of these objects shaped as discrete stages [4]. Typically, these objects are organizations or processes. Maturity models, as a technique, has been proven to be valuable in measuring different aspects of such processes or organizations. The bottom stage stands for an initial state that can be by an organization or process having little capabilities in the present domain. In contrast, the highest stage represents a notion of complete maturity.

Practitioners and academics have developed numerous maturity models for many domains to measure competency, influenced by SEI Capability Maturity Model's pioneering spirit. Some of them become a standard like current CMMI itself [5] and Software Process Improvement and Capability Determination (SPICE) [6].

According to [7], the IMPULS Readiness Model, was aligned closely with the four dimensions of Industrie 4.0 (I4.0): smart factory, smart products, smart operations and data-driven services, and two additional universally applicable dimensions: strategy and organization, and employees. SHIFTo4.0 is the Portuguese self-diagnosis tool that allows companies to assess their state of digital maturity, obtaining guidelines to improve the way forward towards I4.0. Promoted by the Portuguese Institute to Support SMEs (IAPMEI), the design of SHIFTo4.0 was based on IMPULS, having been adapted to the Portuguese reality predominantly by ISQ, an influential institution on the Portuguese industrial environment with a history of standardization contributions. But SHIFTo4.0 does not go one step further than IMPULS and suffers from the same gaps that can be pointed out to the model commissioned by the IMPULS Foundation.

A maturity model is a very important technique for Industry 4.0 in terms of companies seeking for assessing their processes, products and organizations [8]. The better the model, the more complete that diagnosis will be. Despite the reasonable number of I4.0-related maturity models, gaps in the existing models continue to be identified in the literature. Gracel and Lebkowsk [9] state that some areas in the models should be extended, e.g., deep technology insights. In the opposite direction, Schumacher et al. [10] proposed an empirically grounded novel model where the main goal was extending, which according to the authors, was the dominating technology focus of developed models, by the inclusion of lacking organizational aspects.

Given the national strength of the organizations promoting SHIFTo4.0 and realizing the usage already made of the model, it was understood that this work which aims to arrive at a model as complete as possible, capable of addressing all the challenges and I4.0 hurdles, should not start from scratch. This study will take IMPULS as a starting point and will look for other models, on one hand for bridge the breaches identified in IMPULS and on the other hand, striving for alternative components and requirements which can overcome deficiencies, thus suggesting ways of complementing and enriching a model that is already been used by the Portuguese industry.

A systematic literature review according to the guidelines proposed by Kitchenham [11] was applied to find existing maturity models for digital transformation. Literature was surveyed taking into account the identification of all the maturity models that could contribute to complement IMPULS's approach.

Databases like Scopus, Web of Science, IEEE Xplore; ACM Digital Library; Springer Link and Google Scholar were surveyed with variations of similar terms and expressions around Industry 4.0 maturity model, Industry 4.0 capability maturity, Industry 4.0 readiness, digital transformation maturity model, among others. Article search was performed since the year of 2011, the appearance of the Industry 4.0 concept, to late 2020. Immediate duplicates removal based on titles was performed and also exclusion based on titles and abstracts for papers that notoriously did not present a MM. This research work refers to surveying maturity models and not papers describing them. So, hundreds of sources and articles were found, which together refer to only a limited set of different MMs. A great diversity can be seen in the nature of the proposals, some influenced by other MMs, others with a disparate number of maturity levels, as well others not providing the dimensions of the model neither their items and yet others that refer to non-academic initiatives. The goal here was to select different MMs for digital transformation that reflects the most diverse approaches. As part of the second elimination phase, the studies were evaluated in terms of their suitability by examining their keywords, titles, and abstracts, before reading the papers fully. The search resulted in an initial set of more than a hundred papers, of which the references were analysed and selected, if relevant. This snowballing process was essential to identify industry-driven MMs about which there is no published academic work. Three more MMs were identified by reviewing references. We arrived at a set of 21 maturity models, represented by the respective papers or technical reports that define and characterize them.

3 Maturity Models for Digital Transformation

However, there are no standard or published evaluation criteria for maturity models in the domain of Digital Transformation, a set of assessment criteria is identified based on CMMI [5] and SPICE [6] in order to objectively analyse these 21 models. They are summarized in Table 1. Models were studied to try to break them down into their constituent parts and systematically assess the strengths and weaknesses of each one. The literature sources used in Table 1 can be classified into two basic categories: academic literature, and non-academic literature.

The number of maturity stages, the number of the categories of dimensions, the research context as stated by the authors, the source of the assessment data, and the granularity of the dimensions (the level of detail with which dimensions and their attributes are described and characterized), are depicted for each MM on Table 1.

3.1 Models Developed by Practitioners

The IMPULS MM [7] proposes six maturity levels that measure I4.0 readiness. It contains an action plan to boost the readiness of the organisations. According to the model, the level of maturity of a given dimension is defined by the lower level of maturity of the respective areas of interest that compose it. According to the level of maturity obtained by the model, organizations can be classified into three types: Newcomers (level 0 and

Table 1. Category-organized dimensions for model propositions for smart factories.

Maturity model	Origin	Stages	Cat.	Research context as stated by the authors	Assessment data	Granularity	Agg.
IMPULS [7]	Industry	6	6	I4.0 readiness	Questionnaire	Requirements of each dimension by maturity level	No
PWC [12]	Industry	5	6	Digital readiness for I4.0	Questionnaire	Textual description of the dimensions by maturity level	No
Schumacher [10]	Academia	5	9	I4.0 maturity	Questionnaire	Only item names and incomplete	Yes
METI [13]	Academia	6	5	I4.0 capability maturity model	n.a	Textual description of the stages	Yes
Deloitte [14]	Industry	n.a	5	Digital maturity model	n.a	Undescribed dimensions without items list	No
SIMMI4.0 [15]	Academia	5	4	I4.0 maturity	Interview/self-assess	Textual description of the dimensions by maturity level	No
Forrester Rch [16]	Industry	4	4	Digital maturity model	Paid assessment tool	Brief affirmations checklist under each dimension	No
Acatech [17]	Industry	6	4	I4.0 maturity index	n.a	Textual description for each capability	No
DREAMY [18]	Academia	5	4	Digital readiness assessment maturity model	n.a	No detail beyond the designation of the dimensions	No
Canetta [19]	Academia	4	5	Digitalization maturity model	Interviews	No detail beyond the designation of the dimensions	Yes
Sjödin [20]	Academia	4	3	Maturity model for smart factory	n.a	2 items list for each dimension by maturity level	No
Pessl [21]	Academia	5	5	Roadmap for I4.0	On-site approach	Only details the human dimension	Yes
ManuTech [9]	Academia	4	8	Manufacturing technology maturity model	n.a	Textual description of each dimension	Yes

(*continued*)

Table 1. (*continued*)

Maturity model	Origin	Stages	Cat.	Research context as stated by the authors	Assessment data	Granularity	Agg.
Scremin [22]	Academia	5	3	Maturity of manufacturing companies	n.a	Textual description for each indicator	No
Akdil [8]	Academia	4	3	Maturity and readiness model for I4.0	Assessment survey	Textual description of the dimensions by maturity level	Yes
M2DDM [23]	Academia	6	6	Maturity model for data-driven manufacturing	n.a	Textual description of the features	Yes
Defence Sector [24]	Academia	4	3	I4.0 maturity levels	Questionnaire	Textual description of each dimension	No
WMG [25]	Industry	4	6	I4.0 readiness assessment	Questionnaire	Requirements of each dimension by maturity level	No
Almamalik [26]	Academia	6	5	Maturity model for I4.0	Surveys	Undescribed dimensions without items list	Yes
Betrieb [27]	Industry	5	4	I4.0 self-check	Questionnaire	Requirements of each dimension by maturity level	No
Rockwell [28]	Industry	5	n.a	IT readiness	n.a	No dimensions identification	No

1), Learners (level 2), and Leaders (level 3 and 4). The PricewaterhouseCoopers (PWC) MM [12] has online self-assessment in six practical steps that a company needs to take to lead tomorrow's competitive digital landscape. The emphasis is on digital maturity in five levels per phase. The application as a consulting tool for assessment is required in three of the six dimensions. The MM no details items neither the development process offered Forrester Research MM [16] defines four maturity levels and includes the same number of dimensions: culture, technology, organization, and insights.

Acatech, the German Academy of Science and Engineering [17] proposes an I4.0 maturity index based on two main pillars: corporate structure (4 dimensions) and corporate processes (5 dimensions), within the company in which the maturity model is going to be used. Each one of the four structural dimensions has two main principles, and the company's maturity of that dimension is related to a combination of both. The dimensions contain altogether 8 sub-dimensions and 27 maturity topics. Based on research at the University of Warwick (WMG), in conjunction with our industrial collaborators Crimson & Co and Pinsent Masons, an Industry 4 readiness assessment tool has been developed [25]. The MM considers six core dimensions, with 37 sub-dimensions that determine four readiness stages. The MM can be used for self-assessment and provides a benchmark of current I4.0 readiness across a group of 53 companies from 22 countries. Betrieb Machen 4.0 [27], from Mittelstand Kompetenzzentrum Chemnitz is an I4.0 self-check that appears to have been elaborated grounded on VDMA Guideline Industrie 4.0. The Guideline Industrie 4.0 [29] - Guiding principles for the implementation of I4.0 in small and medium-sized businesses, is not a MM, but resembles one since the toolbox it presents classifies five different steps, which can be perceived as maturity stages. Betrieb MM [27] appears to extend these guidelines, maintaining five steps/maturity levels and adding two new dimensions to product and production, the two only dimensions considered in the original toolbox. With the addition of the two new dimensions Work (People) and Organisation (Company), the Betrieb MM [27] ends up structuring its maturity assessment approach in four dimensions and eleven sub-dimensions. Rockwell Automation [28] in a partnership with other major technology companies such as Microsoft, Cisco and Panduit, presents a MM with five stages of measures and best practices for changing technology and organisational culture with the aim of developing a connected company. Although Rockwell MM is widely mentioned by the authors of other models, it does not give any description of the dimensions.

3.2 Models Developed by Academia

Schumacher et al. [10] developed a MM based on 62 items of maturity concerning technology and organization. These items are grouped into nine company dimensions each being evaluated within five levels of maturity. The MM developed by academics of the Middle East Technical University METI [13] are based on SPICE, and has a succession of six capability stages: incomplete, performed, managed, established, predictable, optimizing, based on five areas: process transformation, application management, data governance, asset management, and organizational alignment. SIMMI4.0 [15] consists of five maturity levels with four dimensions: vertical integration, horizontal integration, digital product development, and cross-sectional technology criteria. The digital readiness assessment maturity model (DREAMY) [18] guides manufacturing companies toward digitalization. The MM consists of five maturity levels and four dimensions: processes; control and monitoring; technology; and organization. The MM proposed by Canetta et al. [19] is based on 36 questions divided into five areas: strategy, processes, products and services, technology, and human resources. Based on the questions, four different levels of maturity are derived. Sjödin et al. [20] build their MM on three principles: people, introduction of agile processes and configuration of modular technologies. These principles are classified into four maturity levels. Pessl et al. [21] propose a model with five unnamed maturity stages and five dimensions or fields of action: purchasing, production, intralogistics, sales, and human. The authors only detail the human dimension.

The ManuTech Maturity Model (MTMM) [9] was conducted in Polish manufacturing companies and prescribes a lower number of maturity stages than the average – only four, and eight dimensions: core technologies, people & culture, knowledge management, real-time integration, infrastructure, strategic awareness & alignment, process excellence, and cybersecurity. Scholars of the Politecnico di Milano and Polytechnique

Montréal developed a framework for assessing the maturity of manufacturing companies in I4.0 adoption (Scremin et al.) [22]. The framework delineates maturity in five stages per indicator, taking into account three dimensions with eight indicators: analytic skills, infrastructure for IIoT, absorptive capacity, business strategy, networking and integration, technology strategy, impact on efficiency, and benefits for IIoT adoption. Akdil et al. [8] propose The Maturity and Readiness Model which considers four maturity stages determined by three major dimensions: smart products and services, Smart business processes, and strategy and organization. Dimensions are organized in 13 associated fields. The Maturity Model for Data-Driven Manufacturing (M2DDM) [23] is a MM that solely target IT architectures for data-driven manufacturing. It only analyses the IT architecture of manufacturing companies, in deep, to provide a development path toward servitization. There are six maturity stages and six features: real-time capabilities, digital twin, advanced analytics, information integration, service-oriented architecture, data storage and compute. Bibby and Dehe [24] designed a MM to be applied to 12 companies in the defence sector. It has four maturity levels and only three dimensions, but each dimension has its sub-dimensions. Each sub-dimension needs to have a minimum score to be positioned in each maturity stage. Almamalik [26] developed a MM using a multi-mixed methodology, combining systematic literature study analysis, semi-structured interviews with experts, and surveys for validation. The MM consists of five dimensions and 34 sub-dimensions of analysis to evaluate the Indonesian manufacturing companies in six stages of I4.0 readiness.

Some of the academic MMs are built on aggregation analysis of other models, mainly non-academic models. In addition to widespread recognition and spread across several models, influences from CMMI [5] and SPICE [6], some models testify that part of their structure came explicitly from other models in the selected list. For instance, in the aggregation analysis of the Akdil et al. MM [8], IMPULS [7] is used together with PWC [12], Rockwell Automation [28], and the academic MM of Schumacher et al. [10]. Figure 1 illustrates all the aggregation linkages identified in the selected MM. Some of the models refer to some of the most well-known reference architectures for factories, like RAMI4.0 [30] and IIRA [31].

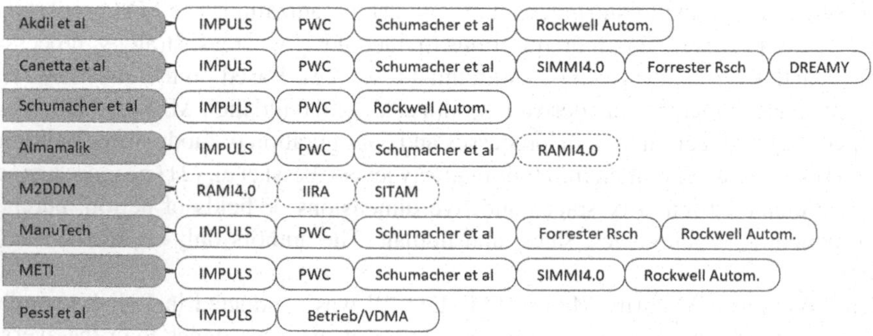

Fig. 1. Selected MMs that are built on an aggregation of other models.

4 Proposed Maturity Model

The whole procedure of the comparative analysis consists of four phases. After having identified the maturity models from previous research, we deeply analyse and characterize them based on the different dimensions and requirements. We use the available literature and summarize the required data in an Excel sheet in the format of a large matrix. Since the main objective of the study is to complement IMPULS [7], the comparative analysis started from it to identify and organize the dimensions of the other models selected in the literature review. We used the available literature and summarize the required data in Excel in the format of a large matrix. The spreadsheet was used to display the categories of dimensions and the dimensions of the IMPULS MM and to identify and associate similar or closer dimensions from the other studied models.

4.1 Phase 1

The categories were organized based on the meta-categories presented by IMPULS: Universal, Virtual and Physical, although the distinction between virtual and physical is somewhat childish when it comes to a by nature hybrid context where cyber-physical systems are increasingly most frequent and important. It is difficult to disassociate the physical from the virtual.

Most MM have dimensions and corresponding sub-dimensions. With some heterogeneity, always according to the objectives of the study, these dimensions and /or their sub-dimensions, which in some models are very high in number, were placed in the spreadsheet, to be aligned with the equivalent dimensions of IMPULS. Four different circumstances emerged from this attempt:

1. The dimension analysed is circumscribed or equivalent to a similar dimension in IMPULS. In these cases, the dimension is displayed in the respective MM column and the same row as the equivalent IMPULS dimension. For example, *Strategy: Implementation I4.0 roadmap* [10] is equivalent to IMPULS's *Strategy* dimension.
2. The dimension is agglutinating and generic to a whole category of IMPULS dimensions. In this case, the dimension is shown in the category title row. E.g. *Products and Services* [19] was in the title row of the IMPULS Smart Products category.
3. The dimension is circumscribed to one of the IMPULS dimension categories, but it is distinct from all the dimensions that IMPULS defines as being part of that category. In these cases, the dimension is enclosed in the respective category, not being aligned with any IMPULS dimension. For instance, *Organizational Structure: Agile management* [17] is confined to the *Smart Factory* category but has no equivalent IMPULS dimension.
4. The dimension is not equivalent to any IMPULS dimension, nor is it circumscribed to one of the IMPULS dimension categories. In these cases, the dimension is kept apart from the existing categories, without belonging to any. E.g., *Sales and Distribution channels* [8] was not included in any of the categories established in IMPULS.

The process described above resulted in new rows in the spreadsheet, meaning new dimensions beyond IMPULS in which, instances of dimensions proposed by the various

MMs have accumulated. These new rows were created by affinity in the rows immediately adjacent to the respective existing dimensions. E.g. *Operations: Automated Resource Management* [14] and *Manufacturing and Operations: Automation* [25] were placed together on an adjacent row to IMPULS' *Distributed Control*. (Fig. 2).

	IMPULS	PWC	Deloitte		Schumacher et al.	
Universal	Strategy & Organization		S: Brand Management	S: Strategic Management		
	strategy		S: Ecosystem Management		S: Implementation I4.0 roadmap	
	Definition of indicators					
	investments		S: Finance & Investment		S: Available resources for realization	
	innovation management	Organization & Culture		S: Stakeholder Management	Cult: Open-innovation and cross company	L: Management competences and methods
		Business Models, Product & Service	S: Portfolio, Ideation & Innovation	OC: Leadership & Governance	L: Willingness of leaders	S: Adaption of business models
		Compliance, Legal, Risk, Security & Tax			G: Labour regulations for I4.0	G: Protection of intellectual property
			OC: Culture			
	Employees				L: Central coordination for I4.0	
	skill sets		OC: Organisational Design & Talent		Peo: ICT competences of employees	
	skill acquisition		OC: Workforce Enablement		Peo: Openness of employees to new	
					Cult: Knowledge sharing	Cult: Value of ICT in company
					Peo: Autonomy of employees	
Virtual	Smart Operations	Value Chains & Processes	O: Agile Change Management			
	Vert and Hor integration				O: Interdisciplinary, interdepartmental	
	Distributed control		(1)O: Real-time Insights & Analytics;	O: Smart and Adaptive Process Management	G: Suitability of technological standards	O: Decentralization of processes
			O: Automated Resource Management			
	IT Security		T: Security			
	Cloud usage					
			O: Integrated Service Management			
			O: Standards & Governance Automation			
	Data-driven					
	data-driven services					
	share of revenues					
Physical	Smart Factory		T: Applications		T: Utilization of mobile devices	
	Equipment Infrastructure		T: Connected Things		T: Utilization of M2M communication	
	Digital Modelling				O: Modelling and simulation	
	data collection					
	data usage		T: Data & Analytics			
	IT systems	IT Architecture	T: Technology Architecture		T: Existence of modern ICT	
	Smart Products				P: Digitalization of products	
	ICT add-on functionalities				P: Product integration into other systems	
	Data analytics usage phase					
					P: Individualization of products	
	Market	Market & Customer Access	C: Customer Engagement	C: Customer Trust & Perception	C: Customer's Digital media competence	
			C: Customer Experience	S: Market & Customer	C: Digitalization of sales/services	
			C: Customer Insights &		C: Utilization of	

Fig. 2. Excerpt of the large matrix built for the comparative process.

The procedure just described is subject to some subjectivity, so the descriptions of the dimensions were permanently invoked in the judgment on what is the best alignment for each one. In this sense, the more information each author added to the definition of their dimensions, the greater the level of objectivity is. The column granularity, in Table 1 records the level of detail and information about each MM.

Simultaneously, to deal with the most ambiguous decisions regarding the definition and placement of dimensions, a symmetric matrix was created to annotate the proximity relations between dimensions. A table where all dimensions appear both as rows and as columns, to be able to point out the eventual closest relationships between them. For example, there is some overlap between the *Data Collection* dimension of the *Smart Factory* category and the *Product Data* dimension of the *Smart Products* category, which leads to highlight this relationship in that table.

4.2 Phase 2

The previous procedure resulted in a very extensive spreadsheet with some complexity that does not facilitate reasoning and decision making. Several spreadsheets were then created to deal with each category of dimensions separately, and an additional spreadsheet to deal with the dimensions that were left out of these categories.

Categories of dimensions were analysed separately, even if some decisions taken in phase 1 concerning the placement of the dimensions have been reverted. In these cases, all spreadsheets were kept consistent, with the Phase 1 spreadsheet being altered and the dimensions moved between different Phase 2 spreadsheets. The symmetric matrix played a key role in helping to maintain consistency. The dimensions that were left out of the categories, because didn't fit into any, began to form what we designated as *Market & Network* category, containing the dimensions *Cooperation within the network* [17], *Pricing/Promotion* [8], *Integrated marketing channels* [25], etc.

In each category sheet, the dimensions were rearranged. Firstly, the dimensions with IMPULS twin-dimensions. Secondly, the generic dimensions. Those, that were identified in situation 2 of phase 1 as being generic to the category itself. In the description of these dimensions, information can be found to help better characterize any of the more specific dimensions of the same category. Thirdly, the dimensions that IMPULS does not contemplate and that are replicated more than once in the various models. For example, in *Strategy & Organisation* there are 13 dimensions related to the topic of *Leadership/Structure*.

Finally, the dimensions with singular instances that do not have within the category, a similar or equivalent dimension, are left apart. For instance, *Organizational Structure: Agile management* [17] in category *Smart Factory*.

This way, some new dimensions for our MM have been drawn, particularly those that have a high cardinality. As for the aforementioned dimension *Leadership/Structure* it became clear that there would have to be a new dimension regarding the aspects of *knowledge creation and management* since among the selected models were realized the alignment of eight dimensions with this subject.

Altogether, eleven new dimensions were created. Table 2 shows the final roll of dimensions established at the end of the process for the MM we are proposing. Shaded are the new dimensions.

- Three new dimensions included in Strategy & Organization: Leadership & structure, Business Models, Compliance & Legal;
- One new dimension comprised in Smart Operations: Control and Monitoring;
- Two new dimensions built-in Smart Products: Products' digital connectivity, Customization/Individualisation;

Table 2. The final cast of dimensions that resulted from the study.

Strategy & organization	Employees	Market & network	Smart operations	Smart factory	Smart products & services
Strategy Investments Innovation Leadership & structure Business model Compliance & Legal	Skills Skill Acquisition Knowledge Autonomy/ Flexibility	Digital Channels Sales Communication & Collaboration	Integration Autonomous Processes Control & Monitoring IT Security Cloud usage	Equipment Infrastructure Digital Model Data Collection and Usage IT Systems	ICT Add-Ons Products' digital connectivity Product Data Customisation/Individualisation Data-driven Services DDS Share

- Two new dimensions included in Employees: Knowledge, Autonomy/Flexibility
- Three new dimensions for the new Market & Network category: Digital Channels, Sales Services, Communication.

4.3 Phase 3

This phase aimed to verify the feasibility of the new dimensions that emerged from the previous phase. The maturity levels were added to the discussion and it was decided to choose five different levels, although IMPULS, the starting model, defines six. There is great variability in the number of levels proposed by the MMs, as can be seen in Table 1. It was understood that five is the ideal number of levels, based mostly on the CMMI [5] inspiring maturity model. Efforts were made to transform the IMPULS requirements defined to six levels, into only five. In some dimensions, it even seemed to make more sense than the original.

The next step was to evaluate if these requirements could be improved by the contributions of the other models that were understood to have equivalent dimensions. The adjustments were performed with punctual amendments and it was concluded that for the dimensions already defined by the IMPULS, the requirements of the various levels are relatively consensual. Adjustments were made to *Smart Factory: Digital modelling*; *Smart Operations: IT Security*; *Smart Operations: Cloud usage*; *Smart Product: Product data.* Table 3 shows the requirements for the five maturity levels of *Smart Operations: IT Security*, complemented with the help of the following dimensions: *Manufacturing and operations: IT and data security* (WMG [25]), *Information Systems: IT security* (Acatech [17]), *Cybersecurity* (ManuTech [9]), *Technology: Security* (Deloitte [14]), *Technology: IT & data security* (Almamalik [26]).

Table 3. Requirements for the five maturity levels of the dimension Smart Operations: IT Security.

Level 1	Level 2	Level 3	Level 4	Level 5
No, or initial IT security solutions planned (IMPULS [7]). No base practice is performed. Ad-hoc reactively application and implementation of IT (Schumacher et al. [10], WMG [25], Acatech [17])	Multiple IT security solutions are planned or initial solutions are in development (IMPULS [7]). Although there is a concern to normalize IT governance activities, they are erratic (Schumacher et al. [10], WMG [25], Acatech [17])	IT security solutions have been partially implemented (IMPULS [7]). There is a written standard for IT governance activities currently being internalized (Schumacher et al. [10], WMG [25], Acatech [17])	Comprehensive IT security solutions have been implemented, existing gaps are being closed (IMPULS [7]). There are performance targets for every IT application (Schumacher et al. [10], WMG [25], Acatech [17])	IT security solutions have been implemented for all relevant areas (IMPULS [7]) and are reviewed frequently to ensure compliance (WMG [25]). IT governance is fully implemented (Schumacher [10], Acatech [17])

For the new dimensions that were intended to be created, the requirements had to be completely defined and for that it was useful to understand where better contributions could be sought. Once again, we reported the degree of detail (column granularity) of each MM in Table 1. Then, the requirements of the new dimensions were built using the MMs best described.

Table 4 shows the requirements for the five maturity levels of the *Digital Channels* dimension, from the new category *Market & Network*, built based on the following dimensions: *Market & Customer Access* (PWC [12]), *Business model: Integrated marketing channels* (WMG [25]), *Smart marketing and Sales operations*, and *Sales and Distribution channels - Campaign systems and sales channels* (Akdil et al. [8]), *Customers: Customer's Digital media competence* (Schumacher et al. [10]).

The symmetric matrix signalized that the dimensions *Data-driven Services: Share of data used* and *Smart Products: Data usage* are deeply related. As such, it was intended to merge the two dimensions and position the resulting dimension under *Smart Products* which is more representative. Consequently, we also incorporated the remaining two dimensions of *Data-Driven Services* into the *Smart Products* category, establishing a unique category named *Smart Products and Services.*

Table 4. Requirements for the 5 maturity levels of Market & Network: Digital Channels.

Level 1	Level 2	Level 3	Level 4	Level 5
Online presence, if present, is separated from offline channels (WMG [25])	At least one channel beside the classical sales force is used for customer interaction (typically a website and shop). First steps are done to increase customer insight (PWC [12]). Online presence is separated from offline channels (WMG [25])	There is already a multi or omnichannel approach for customer access (PWC [12]). Integration within the online and offline channels but not between them (WMG [25]). Campaign systems and sales channels have low-level integration and data analytics tools are not in use to measure campaign performances (Akdil et al. [8])	Multiple channels are used for customer interaction. Data is used extensively to increase customer insight (PWC [12]). Integrated channels and individualised customer approach (WMG [25]). Campaign systems and sales channels have medium level integration and data analytics tools are in use to measure campaign performances (Akdil et al. [8])	Multiple channels (site, social, mobile devices) are leveraged to sell products and services (PWC [12]). Integrated customer experience management across all channels (WMG [25]). Campaign systems and sales channels have high integration and data analytics are in use to measure campaign performances (Akdil et al. [8])

4.4 Phase 4

Although the big majority of the MMs studied have a self-assessment questionnaire and have been designed to be used without the intervention of an appraiser, it was understood that the role of such a facilitator is not negligible. The appraiser can disambiguate any question, translating the spirit of the question into terms closer to the company's culture, can ensure that the questions are understood and the answers are given full awareness and can validate responses by collecting pieces of evidence.

We chose to extend the questionnaire that accompanies the model with the suggestion of some artefacts that can be collected to gather evidence about the company's real state of maturity.

The model was completed with the alteration of the IMPULS questions for the dimensions being adjusted and with the creation of new questions for the new dimensions introduced. As the model is intended to be used to assess the digital maturity of the Portuguese companies, the questions were simultaneously translated into Portuguese. Each question was complemented with an indication of the artefacts that can confirm a rigorous answer. Case of modelling artefacts like technical documentation as functional diagrams, plant diagrams, product descriptions, procedural descriptions; and operative plans as production plans and project plans. Physical artefacts like products, resources, production systems like equipment, sensors, actuators, and IT systems and control systems, may constitute the desired evidence to confirm the situations reported in the responses to the questionnaire.

Table 5 shows the questions that allow assessing the level of maturity regarding dimension *Knowledge*, as well as the type of evidence that can confirm the responses.

Table 5. Compound question to assess the dimension Knowledge of the category Employees.

E.3 How do People deal with the Information System, processes and transmission of knowledge?		
☐ Distrust the Information System	☐ Distrust processes	☐ Mouth to mouth
☐ Trust the core Information Systems	☐ Follow unstructured paper based processes	☐ In meetings
☐ Trust less conventional IS applications	☐ Follow structured paper based processes	☐ Using a Knowledge MIS
	☐ Follow digital structured workflows	☐ Using a Knowledge MIS integrated on corporate's IS
Hypothetical evidence:		
– Affirmations – Example of non-mainstream IS application – Example of a structured process workflow sheet	– Knowledge Management Information System – Workflow Software Application	

5 Conclusion

Companies need assistance in the path to digital transformation. The overall idea of I4.0 is not completely understood by many companies. The implementation and gradual adoption of the industrial internet, accompanying disruptive technologies and related business models can be a very complex and extensive process of change. MMs are useful instruments to assist organizations by providing comprehensive guidance, paving the way towards I4.0 technologies/practices fulfilment.

This study aims to adjust and extend the MM that seems to be more used by the Portuguese companies, with components and requirements which can overcome its pointed-out breeches, thus suggesting ways for it completion and enrichment. Twenty-one MMs in the context of I4.0 were analysed, compared and reconciled to build an embracing perspective of digital transformation. The result is a MM with the appraisal of 28 dimensions organized in six categories. The framework to assess the maturity concerning I4.0 practices involves also a questionnaire that evaluates the fulfilment of the requirements of each dimension by maturity level, types of evidence that can confirm the evaluation, and a set of maturity requirements whose incremental satisfaction can serve as a roadmap for companies towards higher compliance with I4.0.

This work has some limitations. The first constraint concerns the fact that this study started from an existing MM without questioning it completely, although it has refined it in some aspects, changed the number of maturity levels, re-arranged dimensions in different categories, and even extending it with new categories and dimensions. The second limitation will be the subject of future work: the absence of an exploratory case study to validate the usefulness and applicability of the proposed MM. In the immediate future, we will conduct a set of test cases in industrial partner companies of a major Portuguese Interface Centre that develops and fosters research and innovation processes. Finally, how the company's overall maturity level is calculated stills a matter not properly addressed. Data from the exploratory test cases will play an important role in the definition of a weighted average that adjusts and quantifies the importance of each dimension according to the industrial sector, size and scope of the organizations.

Acknowledgements. This work has been supported by FCT – Fundação para a Ciência e Tecnologia within the R&D Units Project Scope: UIDB/00319/2020 and by the Doctoral scholarship PDE/BDE/114567/2016 funded by FCT, the Portuguese Ministry of Science, Technology and Higher Education, through national funds, and co-financed by the European Social Fund (ESF) through the Operational Programme for Human Capital (POCH).

References

1. Hermann, M., Pentek, T., Otto, B.: Design principles for industrie 4.0 scenarios. In: Proceedings of the Annual Hawaii International Conference on System Science, March 2016, pp. 3928–3937 (2016). https://doi.org/10.1109/HICSS.2016.488
2. Kagermann, H., Wahlster, W., Johannes, H.: Recommendations for implementing the strategic initiative INDUSTRIE 4.0: Final report of the Industrie 4.0 working group. Acatech, Frankfurt (2013)

3. Paulk, M.C., Curtis, B., Chrissis, M.B., Weber, C.V.: Capability Maturity Model for Software, Version 1.1. Carnegie Mellon University (1993)
4. Becker, J., Knackstedt, R., Pöppelbuß, J.: Developing maturity models for IT management. Bus. Inf. Syst. Eng. **1**, 213–222 (2009). https://doi.org/10.1007/s12599-009-0044-5
5. CMMI Product Team: CMMI for Development, Version 1.3 CMMI-DEV, V1.3 (2010)
6. ISO/IEC: ISO/IEC 33004:2015 - Information technology — Process assessment — Requirements for process reference, process assessment and maturity models
7. Lichtblau, K., et al.: IMPULS - Industrie 4.0 -Readiness (2015)
8. Akdil, K., Ustundag, A., Cevikcan, E.: Maturity and readiness model for industry 4.0 strategy. In: Industry 4.0: Managing The Digital Transformation. SSAM, pp. 61–94. Springer, Cham (2018). https://doi.org/10.1007/978-3-319-57870-5_4
9. Gracel, J., Łebkowski, P.: The concept of Industry 4.0 related manufacturing technology maturity model (ManuTech Maturity Model, MTMM). Decis. Mak. Manuf. Serv. **12**, 17–31 (2017)
10. Schumacher, A., Erol, S., Sihn, W.: A maturity model for assessing industry 4.0 readiness and maturity of manufacturing enterprises. Procedia CIRP **52**, 161–166 (2016). https://doi.org/10.1016/j.procir.2016.07.040
11. Kitchenham, B., Charters, S.: Procedures for performing systematic literature reviews in software engineering. EBSE Technical Report, Software Engineering Group, School of Computer Science and Mathematics, Keele University, UK and Department of Computer Science, University of Durham. Presented at the (2007)
12. Griessbauer, R., Vedso, J., Schrauf, S.: Industry 4.0: Building the digital enterprise. 2016 Global Industry 4.0 Survey, pp. 1–39 (2016)
13. Gökalp, E., Şener, U., Eren, P.E.: Development of an assessment model for industry 4.0: industry 4.0-MM. In: Mas, A., Mesquida, A., O'Connor, R.V., Rout, T., Dorling, A. (eds.) SPICE 2017. CCIS, vol. 770, pp. 128–142. Springer, Cham (2017). https://doi.org/10.1007/978-3-319-67383-7_10
14. Anderson, C., Ellerby, W.: Digital Maturity Model. Deloitte. 9–12 (2018)
15. Leyh, C., Bley, K., Schäffer, T., Forstenhäusler, S.: SIMMI 4.0-a maturity model for classifying the enterprise-wide it and software landscape focusing on Industry 4.0. In: 2016 Federated Conference on Computer Science and Information Systems (FedCSIS), pp. 1297–1302 (2016)
16. Gill, M., VanBoskirk, S.: The Digital Maturity Model 4.0. Forrester. 0–17 (2016)
17. Schuh, G., Anderl, R., Gausemeier, J., ten Hompel, M., Wahlster, W.: Industrie 4.0 Maturity Index (2017)
18. De Carolis, A., Macchi, M., Negri, E., Terzi, S.: A maturity model for assessing the digital readiness of manufacturing companies. In: Lödding, H., Riedel, R., Thoben, K.-D., von Cieminski, G., Kiritsis, D. (eds.) APMS 2017. IAICT, vol. 513, pp. 13–20. Springer, Cham (2017). https://doi.org/10.1007/978-3-319-66923-6_2
19. Canetta, L., Barni, A., Montini, E.: Development of a digitalization maturity model for the manufacturing sector. In: 2018 IEEE International Conference on Engineering, Technology and Innovation ICE/ITMC 2018 - Proceedings (2018). https://doi.org/10.1109/ICE.2018.8436292
20. Sjödin, D.R., Parida, V., Leksell, M., Petrovic, A.: Smart factory implementation and process innovation: a preliminary maturity model for leveraging digitalization in manufacturing moving to smart factories presents specific challenges that can be addressed through a structured approach focused on people. Res. Technol. Manag. **61**, 22–31 (2018). https://doi.org/10.1080/08956308.2018.1471277
21. Pessl, E., Sorko, S.R., Mayer, B.: Roadmap industry 4.0 - implementation guideline for enterprises. In: 26th International Association for Management and Technology Conference IAMOT 2017, vol. 5, pp. 1728–1743 (2020). https://doi.org/10.11648/j.ijsts.20170506.14

22. Scremin, L., Armellini, F., Brun, A., Solar-Pelletier, L., Beaudry, C.: Towards a framework for assessing the maturity of manufacturing companies in industry 4.0 adoption (2018)
23. Weber, C., Königsberger, J., Kassner, L., Mitschang, B.: M2DDM - a maturity model for data-driven manufacturing. Procedia CIRP **63**, 173–178 (2017). https://doi.org/10.1016/j.procir.2017.03.309
24. Bibby, L., Dehe, B.: Defining and assessing industry 4.0 maturity levels–case of the defence sector. Prod. Plan. Control. **29**, 1030–1043 (2018). https://doi.org/10.1080/09537287.2018.1503355
25. Agca, O., Gibson, J., Godsell, J., Ignatius, J., Wyn Davies, C., Xu, O.: An industry 4 readiness assessment tool. International Institute of Product and Service Innovation, pp. 1–19 (2017)
26. Almamalik, L.: The development of the maturity model to assess the smart Indonesia manufacturing companies 4.0 readiness, vol. 123, pp. 103–107 (2020). https://doi.org/10.2991/aebmr.k.200305.026
27. Mittelstand 4.0 Kompetenzzentrum Chemnitz: Betrieb machen 4.0. https://betrieb-machen.de/selbstcheck/
28. Allen-Bradley: The Connected Enterprise Maturity Model. Ind. Conectada 4.0. 1–12 (2014)
29. Anderl, R., Fleischer, J.: Guideline Industrie 4.0 - Guiding principles for the implementation of Industrie 4.0 in small and medium sized businesses. VDMA Verlag. 32 (2015)
30. Adolphs, P., et al.: Reference Architecture Model Industrie 4.0 (RAMI4.0). VDI/VDE/ZVEI, Frankfurt am Main, Germany (2015)
31. Shi-Wan, L., et al.: The industrial Internet of Things volume G1: reference architecture. Industrial Internet Consortium, White Paper Version 1., 58 Seiten (2017)

Non-cooperative Vehicular Density Prediction in VANETs

Lourdes Portugal-Poma Costa[1], Cesar A. C. Marcondes[2], and Hermes Senger[1(✉)]

[1] Computer Science Department, Federal University of São Carlos – UFSCar, São Carlos, SP 13565-905, Brazil
hermes@ufscar.br

[2] Computer Science Division, Aeronautics Institute of Technology – ITA, São José dos Campos, SP 12228-900, Brazil
cmarcondes@ita.br

Abstract. In large urban spaces, like cities, VANETs are formed by vehicles of highly variable speed and uneven geographic node distribution. Due to the ad-hoc nature of such environments, communication systems must seamlessly adapt to abrupt topology changes to keep the vehicular network organized. Maintain connectivity is hard; a possible naive strategy is based upon expensive on-demand reconnections. Another approach relies on controlled message epidemics. Both of them need to adjust communication behavior under different density situations. Thus, infrastructure-free density estimation methods are becoming popular solutions for this problem. Our paper contributes to this area using a unique density estimation method, independent of beaconing and neighbor discovery (which might generate network congestion), free of cooperative orchestration and based on long-term stability metrics. Our method is validated using vehicular mobility traces, showing outstanding group prediction and stability.

Keywords: VANETs communication · Density estimation · Clustering

1 Introduction

Estimates reveal that the total number of vehicles worldwide reached more than 1.4 billion, including cars, trucks, buses, and others [5]. Some forecasts estimate that this number can reach nearly 2.8 billion vehicles by 2036 [26]. Modern intelligent transport system (ITS) applications will be increasingly necessary to improve safety, efficiency, and comfort in traffic. Last decade, to support novel applications and innovation, the automotive sector promoted dramatic evolution in hardware, software, and sensor technologies incorporated into vehicles [13].

This scenario creates an opportunity for innovation and many new applications and services focusing on road safety, traffic management, smart cities, information services, and entertainment. Besides sensors and computational resources incorporated into vehicles, communication is the basic underlying technology

O. Gervasi et al. (Eds.): ICCSA 2021, LNCS 12952, pp. 201–217, 2021.
https://doi.org/10.1007/978-3-030-86973-1_14

that can enable integration to support new applications and information services. Aiming to support messaging and information propagation among vehicles, information services, and applications in Vehicular Adhoc Networks (VANETS), communication has been studied under different approaches including Vehicle-to-Vehicle (V2V) [25], Vehicle-to-Infrastructure (V2I) [14], Vehicle-to-Everything (V2X) [22] and Vehicle-to-Pedestrian (V2P) [7]. On the other hand, cloud computing and related approaches such as fog computing have also been addressed for the integration of VANETS applications [13].

In VANET, many conditions that affect communication can change over time, such as vehicle location, speed, and time between encounters. A major challenge is the vehicular density, which may be defined as the number of vehicles per measurement unit in a defined area [6]. Vehicular density information is not only important to prevent vehicular traffic congestion, it is also the primer to make VANETs communication possible. For example, message broadcasting must be avoided in dense regions, while it can be useful in low-density regions where scarce communication opportunities can disrupt the spreading of messages.

In order to make vehicles aware of the local density, density estimation algorithms can be used. Those that are infrastructure-free, like V2V based algorithms, are of particular interest in VANETs since they do not depend on network infrastructure (for sensing and gathering of information), have lower cost, and cover great areas. However, infrastructure-free density estimation approaches still present performance challenges to be addressed. Mostly, because the algorithms require information gathered by the neighbor discovery (ND), which could be expensive depending on the vehicular density and how frequently the vehicles update their local knowledge base [21]. During the neighborhood discovery (ND), each vehicle broadcasts short messages with its ID and some useful metadata to the directly connected vehicles. The means such messages are transmitted are the base of these algorithms, and currently, a research topic in MANETs [4].

Because VANETs do not have rigorous power constraints, Global Navigation Satellite Systems (GNSS) can help the ND process create collaborative and synchronized solutions. The gathering of information by cooperative effort allows vehicles to update their local knowledge-base with information obtained by themselves and nearest neighbors. Once that information is processed (e.g., aggregation or summarization), it could be propagated in a recurrent process, allowing vehicles to be aware of the density after more than one-hop of connectivity. But, VANETs are highly dynamic networks, vehicles' knowledge could be outdated or misinformed rapidly. That is because any orchestration in the collaborative process could be interrupted under intermittent connectivity conditions. Thus, vehicles could not update their local knowledge-base and keep outdated information, which could be shared on opportunistic occasions (e.g., store-and-forward), leading the system to make wrong decisions.

Another problem in a collaborative information gathering process is information privacy. Neighboring vehicles share location, speed or even travel routes. So, it is necessary a scheme that considers vehicles' identification, anonymity, trusted authorities (TA), and other privacy issues. Relying on vehicles to execute security tasks could overload VANETs with different responsibilities that are difficult to perform effectively in a VANET environment. Because of that,

VANETs should leverage other technologies, such as Cloud Computing, which is an important component for IoT to succeed. Vehicular using Clouds (VuC) [1] is being recently considered as an extension of VANETs to facilitate the sharing and processing of information [20], relieving VANETs from the active management effort, improving performance, and decreasing privacy risks.

This paper presents a novel density estimation proposal based on Machine Learning (ML) to be supported by Cloud Computing (CC) for decoupling processing and storage from on-board units. Differently from common density measures: based on connectivity (e.g., node degree, two-hops measures [15]), speed properties (e.g., average velocity, speed direction), average fraction of vehicle stop time [19], we used group stability metrics that describe long time properties. Our method allows vehicles to detect changes in density (without on-edge cooperative effort), suggesting if vehicles tend to be alone or in groups in specific places and times. We reason that particular group behavior is related to specific city places, and consequently, it is predictive. We simulate our novel method using real taxi trace replays and epidemic communication patterns to show the method's benefits. We present results that our method was able to find great cluster stability related to each group behavior. Finally, we limit our study and do not approach privacy issues since Physical VuC architecture is out of scope, but we suggest [1] and [18] for more details.

The rest of the paper is organized as follows. In Sect. 2 we present background and literature review on density estimation. Our novel method for density estimation is presented in Sect. 3, while experiments that validate the proposal are presented in Sect. 4. Section 5 has a discussion on results, and our concluding remarks are presented in Sect. 6.

2 Background and Related Work

Vehicular distribution is not uniform in urban scenarios due to the topology of the cities, traffic regulation, time influence, the interaction between vehicles, among other factors. Because of that, the communication systems require to adapt their operation according to the form of communication. Beaconing, geocasting -or multicasting- and unicast routing are basic communication forms that could support VANETs applications. Beaconing is used among all neighboring nodes to announce their presence (e.g., in the ND process) or continuously update information. Geocasting is advertising information inside a target area and is used by many safety applications to send high priority warnings triggered by external events. Finally, unicast routing is the transmission of messages through the ad-hoc network to a specific destination.

Despite these, VANETs communication systems could be further improved when informed about vehicular density. Under high-density conditions, beaconing messages can be lost, erroneous, or higher latency beacon reception. To solve these beaconing problems, one could adapt MAC/PHY layer related parameters (e.g., message frequency, transmission power [11]) according to the region's density. Density estimation aims to reduce beaconing loads under high-density scenarios, increasing reliability of beacon delivery, and reducing application degradation.

There is no guarantee that vehicles within the target area will receive the message in *geocasting* on low-density vehicular scenarios. Under that condition, vehicles could apply flooding-based, static-nodes assistance, message replication, and caching techniques. On the other hand, under high vehicular density, data redundancy and overhead problems are likely to happen. In that condition, farthest vehicle selection, probability-based, timer-based, and priority-based mechanisms could be applied to make communication effective. In terms of routing and connectivity, with high density, *unicast* routing may present transmission collisions and errors. While, under lower density and faster mobility, end-to-end connectivity is more intermittent or even absent. Thus, if routing algorithms were augmented with density information, there is an opportunity to choose between different routing paradigms, such as Store Carry and Forward (SCF) paradigm [24], cluster-based routing [17] or even hybrid routing [16].

2.1 Density Estimation Algorithms

Density algorithms' performance is influenced by two main elements: which information is used to represent density and how it is gathered and processed to recognize a dense region. Throughout literature, most proposals regarding density estimation can be organized depending on the information used. Some use metrics of the transmission medium (e.g., channel busy ratio, bit error rate, interference level, number of received beacons [2]). Moreover, mobility information from vehicles as individual nodes (e.g., velocity, movement direction, acceleration) or from the vehicular traffic as a whole (e.g., traffic flow, traffic stream speed, road density) can also be used. Ultimately, some proposals use graph-based connectivity information (e.g., node degree, link duration, and cluster coefficient).

Nevertheless, these parameters' measurements change rapidly in VANETs, so it is important to update these parameters frequently or use predictive algorithms to estimate their future values. That is the reason why an adequate infrastructure for gathering and process that information is important. Thus, if we focus our attention on how density algorithms gather and process the information, infrastructure-free density estimation approaches are preferred because of the lower cost and greater coverage area. According to [6], infrastructure-free density estimation algorithms are classified into three types. The first category includes the algorithms that use *statistical modeling*, which could be applied when specific requirements are fulfilled (e.g., exponential vehicles inter-arrival times [10]). However, such algorithms are not suitable for complex urban VANETs (whose vehicles follow many mobility patterns) and their performance depends on the sampling process, being difficult to apply in low-density regions with a low amount of collected samples. The second category includes the algorithms that use VANETs and traffic flow information for density estimation. They employ V2V (vehicle-to-vehicle) communications [21] and also could work collaboratively with RSUs (roadside nits). In addition, these RSUs can support the collection and distribution of information and provide access to external infrastructure with data aggregation and processing services.

Finally, a third category considered in [6] includes the *group or cluster-based density estimation algorithms*. The detection of clusters of vehicles is a current research topic not only in density estimation but also in vehicular communication, to improve performance using load balance and message aggregation. In density estimation and once the clusters are detected, the members entrust the density estimation to a specific node (Cluster Head - CH), which will aggregate and process the gathered information inside the cluster and propagate the density results to the members. In this category, the main challenge is to form and maintain the clusters, based on the connectivity stability which is determined by the similarity of the members' behavior (e.g. pairwise link duration, movement direction, and velocities ratio [9]). Thus, the processes of cluster formation, its maintenance, the allocation of the CH and member roles, have an additional cost due to the transmission of control messages and metadata with information that could even outdated, because of the VANET dynamic behavior.

2.2 The Role of Cloud Computing

Given that vehicular density recognition is challenging to be performed in a cooperative and pure VANET manner, the gathering and processing of information could be supported by services on the cloud. Vehicles could access Cloud Computing services through RSUs or other network devices and inter-networking technologies. Cloud Computing in VANETs has two major research lines, Vehicular cloud computing (VCC) and Vehicle using Cloud (VuC). VCC includes VANETs as an extension of the Cloud services (e.g., for data storage or VANETs as networking service), VuC is the efficient use of cloud resources to support VANETs. Vehicles using Clouds (VuC) can enable applications that are unlikely to be developed in a pure VANETs, such as smart ITS applications including real-time traffic and predictive capabilities. Thus, we can consider VANETs as part of a perception layer [1] that gather density related parameters and take them to the cloud, without on-edge data sharing and using more advanced and self-controlled resources on the cloud. Also, as the work in [20] propose, we can make use of Cloud resources for the sharing of sensitive information (e.g., vehicles trajectories), which will not only be protected by on-edge privacy schemes (e.g., RSUs recognized by a trusted authority) but also by additional elements on the cloud that ensure that this information will not be compromised.

3 Non-cooperative Density Category Prediction

In this section, we propose a novel method based on machine learning (ML) and Vehicles using the Cloud (VuC) to predict when and where vehicles tend to form groups and how stables are those. That information alone can support different communication forms (i.e., beaconing, geocasting, unicasting) to improve their performance.

Our method is based on a VuC architecture, as shown in Fig. 1. The lowest/first layer, or the perception layer, includes all devices involved in gathering

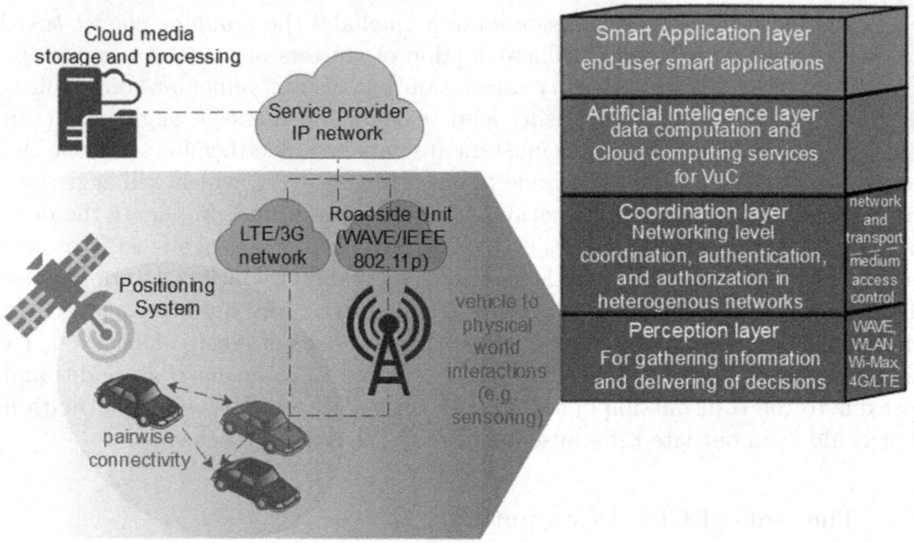

Fig. 1. Architecture for our method (based on the layered VuC structure in [1])

information such as in-vehicle sensors, GPS receivers, and RSU collecting traffic and environmental data. The second layer represents all the coordination for the transmission and hand-off of heterogeneous networks that support VANETs. However, as we modify how VANETs transmission is performed, second layer's devices would act as *networking actuators*. Hence, networking devices that modify the beaconing, geocaching, or unicasting normal behavior according to the vehicular density by using a produced model in upper/third layer (or Intelligence layer). The third layer is where the entire machine learning is executed to recognize groups of vehicles. It includes conventional Cloud Computing devices for storage and processing (e.g., location and temporal information). Finally, the highest layer, or Smart Application layer, includes end-user smart applications such as safety, efficient-driven, and infotainment, supported by beaconing, geocasting, or unicasting communications.

Our proposal consists of using a traditional VuC architecture, where the actuators will be located on the second layer or Coordination layer, which will use density inference rules produced by a trained model to modify beaconing, geocaching, or unicasting behavior. We assume that vehicles can transmit GPS coordinates and temporal data to the cloud through a car-to-cloud communication system. Once the data is stored on the cloud, and with the Cloud resources in the artificial intelligence layer, we can apply our method in three main key steps: *i*) the detection of moving groups and isolated nodes, *ii*) the clustering of groups of vehicles, which establish density categories using hierarchical clustering, and *iii*) training and prediction of group density conditions, using a model based on ensemble learning of the Random Forest algorithm.

3.1 Step 1 - Moving Groups and Isolated Nodes Detection

In the first step, we use the positioning and temporal information, stored in the cloud, to identify vehicle groups that existed before, at different places and times. Once the groups are identified, we detect moving groups using snapshots information. At first, we interpolated the reported temporal and GPS data, so we can reconstruct vehicles' trajectories and produce snapshots of their locations at a fixed interval of time. Thus, beginning at the moment of time i and interpolating at a time interval of h seconds, we obtain a set of n snapshots $S = \{S_i, S_{i+h}, S_{i+2h}, \cdots, S_{i+nh}\}$, where each snapshot S_j is the set of locations and time information tuples $((time, coordinate_x, coordinate_y))$ of the m vehicles that are transiting at the moment of time j, that is

$$S_j = \{(time_j, v1_x, v1_y), (time_j, v2_x, v2_y), \cdots, (time_j, vm_x, vm_y)\} \quad (1)$$

Once vehicles' trajectories are timestamped, we detect moving groups of vehicles doing the following: *i*) the detection of isolated vehicles and groups in every single snapshot, and *ii*) recognition of moving groups of vehicles by observing consecutive snapshots.

Detection of Isolated Vehicles and Groups: Our method can process the locations of a specific snapshot S_i to detect groups of vehicles by using density-based clustering algorithms. These algorithms "classify" clusters as dense areas in the data space, where the observations are close to each other and separate from regions of low density. To detect groups of connected vehicles (that sustain pairwise connectivity) and isolated vehicles, we employ a simplification of the DBSCAN algorithm (Density-based spatial clustering with noise)[1]. Our simplified DBSCAN is based on two main parameters: the *neighborhood* and a *minimum number of observations* inside the neighborhood, that is necessary to consider the neighborhood as dense (or as a group) ($MinPts$). We can express the neighborhood of a vehicle like this:

Definition 1. *The ξ-Neighborhood of a vehicle v ($N_\xi(v)$) is the subset of vehicles inside its neighborhood of radius ξ, from the set D of vehicles in the scenario:*

$$N_\xi(v) = \{q \in D | distance(v, q) <= \xi\} \quad (2)$$

Once defined the neighborhood, the next definition is related to reachability:

Definition 2. *A vehicle v is Directly density reachable from another vehicle q, with respect to ξ and $MinPts$, if:*

- *$v \in N_\xi(q)$ and,*
- *$|N_\xi(q)| \geqslant MinPts$.*

[1] Because in pairwise connectivity two is the minimum number of points to form a group, so there will be no difference between core and border nodes (see [8]).

Considering the *directly density reachable* definition, two vehicles p and q are *density-connected* if there is a vehicle o such that both p and q are directly density reachable from o. Thus, all density-connected vehicles are members of the cluster, and any other connected to them will also be part of it. Hence, as we can see, vehicle group connectivity can be captured using DBSCAN if we set the parameters $MinPts$ to two (for representing pairwise connectivity) and ξ to an approximate value of the effective transmission rate in V2V communication.

Detection of Moving Group of Vehicles: A moving cluster is a set of entities that move together and closely for some time. The entities do not need to remain together, as nodes can join or leave the group during their lifetime. For instance, a movement cluster is a convoy of vehicles, whose movement is restricted by the roads and traffic signs in a city. Having identified all groups of vehicles in each snapshot S_i using DBSCAN, we can consider a threshold of the minimum percentage of vehicles that should remain in a group to be considered as a moving cluster. Thus we can define a moving cluster formally as follows:

Definition 3. *Let* $S = \{S_1, S_2, \cdots, S_n\}$ *be a sequence of snapshots, and let* $C = \{C_1, C_2, \cdots, C_n\}$ *be a set of* C_i*s, where each* C_i *is a set of clusters found at snapshot* S_i*. Then,* m *is a moving cluster with respect to a threshold* θ*, where* $0 < \theta \leq 1$*, if:*

$$\frac{|c_i \cap c_{i+1}|}{|c_i \cup c_{i+1}|} > \theta \, , \textit{ where } c_i \in C_i \textit{ and } c_{i+1} \in C_{i+1} \tag{3}$$

Finally, we obtain as the result of this step the moving groups of vehicles already identified, the list of their members, and the isolated vehicles (not members of any DBSCAN cluster) with temporal and geographic information.

3.2 Step 2 - Clustering of Groups of Vehicles

Given the moving groups of vehicles, already identified in the previous step, our objective is to describe their stability and use ML clustering techniques to cluster those groups into similar stability categories. Thus, this step is performed in two parts: *i*) describing vehicle group behaviors, using a good set of features, and *ii*) clustering vehicle groups' behaviors. Also, from now on, and to avoid misunderstandings, we use the term "group" to refer to each group of vehicles found in the previous step, and "cluster" refers to each cluster (in the machine learning function) composed of groups of vehicles with similar stability.

Afterwards, to describe the stability of vehicles' groups, we use *long-time cluster stability* measurements, calculated to represent the survival of vehicles as a group, and as members of any group in consecutive snapshots. These measurements are: *cluster lifetime*, which is the time that a group of vehicles existed according to Eq. 3, the *average membership time*, and the *average number of members* that a vehicle group had during its existence. We only use information about the groups of vehicles that have disappeared (dead groups) to include complete information. Hierarchical clustering with complete linkage is used in the clustering of the vehicle groups, based on their stability metrics. As a result, we obtained clusters of vehicle groups with similar stability behavior.

3.3 Step 3 - Training and Prediction of Group Density Condition

The last part of our method is based on the following insight: *Group motion and their properties are closely related to specific regions and times of the day.* Thus, only geographic and temporal information can be enough to predict the categories of groups of vehicles found by hierarchical clustering.

To test our hypothesis and allow vehicles to recognize how the group behavior is in a specific place and time, we could label each cluster of the hierarchical clustering result and train an ML classifier to predict these categories in the future. We use Random Forest classifier, with the following attributes: (*i*) the number of the day (from 1 to 5, meaning Monday to Friday), (*ii*) time of the day in seconds, (*iii*) x-coordinate, (*iv*) y-coordinate, and (*v*) the cluster label.

The cluster label is our target feature, which would indicate a particular cluster behavior. In Table 1, we show an example of the dataset used for training. The dataset also includes observations that belong to isolated vehicles (i.e., identified as noise in Step-1) in moments where vehicles cannot form groups. Isolated vehicles are labeled with "−1". As we can observe, the stability metric used for clustering were excluded from the classification dataset. While, the cluster label represents the vehicle groups' behavior based on these metrics, and it is the target feature of the classifier predictions.

Table 1. Entries of hierarchical clustering and classification observations.

Samples of observations used for the clustering				
Time of life	Avg. membership time		Avg. Num. of members	
840	435		2.1	
1860	1470		2.4	
Samples of observations used for classification (class label: cluster ID)				
Day	Time of day	x-coordinate	y-coordinate	Cluster ID
5	32490	292275.2	4641412	−1
2	14940	292329.1	4642126	1

4 Case Study and Experimental Validation

This section explains how our method could be applied using a simulated scenario based on real traces of taxis from the city of Rome [3]. The simulation performed stands as a method validation approach since it augments other proposals. Hence it is not comparable directly to other proposals of message delivery improvement.

Then, the Rome traces are used as input into the Opportunistic Networking Environment (ONE) simulator [12] which is designed for evaluating DTN routing and application protocols. We simulate a VANET transmitting messages using the naive Epidemic algorithm. Epidemic [23] performs routing under the Store-Carry-Forward paradigm and message replication. Once a message is created in the epidemic, each vehicle transmits a copy of each neighbor's message in opportunistic contacts. The general idea is that some vehicle finds the destination and delivers a copy to it. As in other VANETs routing algorithms, Epidemic routing performance is affected by vehicular density, so it is expected that our density predictions will be related to the Epidemic performance.

Initially, we interpolate the movement traces to obtain snapshots of the locations of the vehicles. Next, we applied our method to produce a Random Forest (RF) model that will be executed throughout the simulation. To query the RF trained classifier, we create an interface between the ONE simulator (made in Java) and R. It allows us to execute scripts with the necessary programming code to receive the vehicles' geographic and temporal information in the simulator. Thus, each vehicle queries the classifier every 15 s and starts from its first movement. As a result, the classifier returns a predicted value, indicating the region's group density category where the vehicle is located.

4.1 VANETs Scenario and Communication

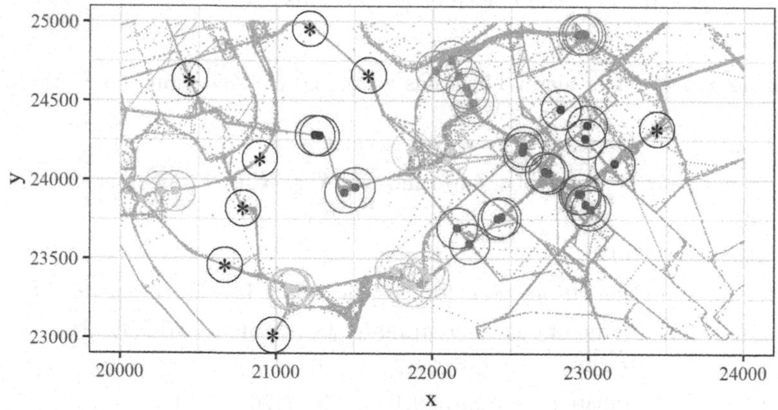

Fig. 2. Groups of vehicles reconigzed by DBSCAN (isolated vehicles in black).

We cleanse the data by pre-processing the Rome traces to remove GPS misreadings, exclude incomplete short trajectories, and interpolate and complete partitioned trajectories applying a map-based approach. The number of active taxis in our dataset depends on the time of the day. The number of taxis from Monday to Friday is plotted in Fig. 3. We observe three peaks of activity: one in the early hours, another in the morning, and the last at night. Our final dataset includes movement traces of twelve hours, from 7 a.m. to 7 p.m. Then, we simulate a VANET transmitting messages using the Epidemic algorithm.

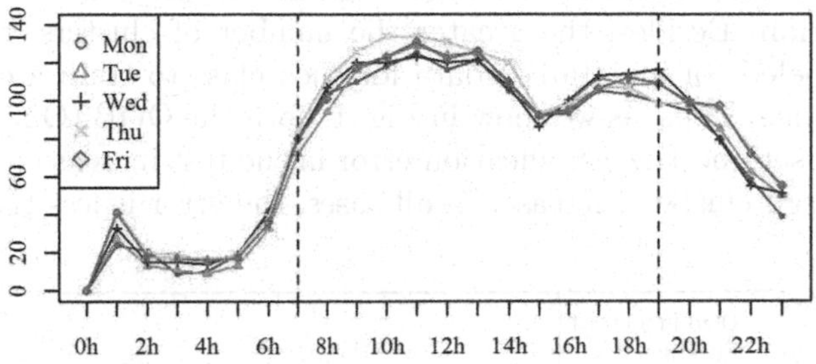

Fig. 3. Number of vehicles from Monday to Friday in different times of the day.

Regarding which vehicles were considered as source and destination of messages, we aim to select (randomly) between vehicles with long times of activity (according to the traces dataset). New messages are generated only from 7 a.m. to 2 p.m. Afterwards, throughout simulation, only copies of the messages created initially will be transmitted. Also, Epidemic flooding of copies is not restricted as we show in Table 2 where we also include other simulation parameters.

Table 2. Simulation parameters.

Transmission rate	5 Mpbs	Transmission range	250 m
Storage capacity	Unlimited	Message size	128 KB
Message creation	≈ each 60 s	Number of nodes	Variable

4.2 Settings and Method Application

We set the DBSCAN parameters ξ and $MinPts$ of 200 m and 2 units, respectively. Therefore, it allows us to identify vehicles connected inside a transmission range of 200 m as a group. In Fig. 2 we show, as an example, a region of the city of Rome with isolated and group of vehicles identified by DBSCAN in a single snapshot. To detect moving clusters, we set the θ value to 0.5 so that the required quantity of common vehicles (in two consecutive snapshots) be at least half of all the vehicles in the snapshots. After the moving clusters have been identified, we measure how stable are those using the metrics of *cluster lifetime*, *average membership time*, and the *average number of members*. Subsequently, on the obtained dataset, we proceed to perform hierarchical clustering and, we finish the pipeline by including a cluster identifier (or category), which will be the target variable of the RF classifier.

Depending on the number of categories that we obtained in the clustering of vehicle groups, it will be more difficult to distinguish which cluster (or category) has certain properties and how stable they are. For that reason, we choose to cut the hierarchical structure into three clusters, which are three categories or stability behaviors influenced by the vehicular density, as we report in the discussion section. Besides, the greater the number of clusters, the lower the quantity of labeled (or annotated) data for each class to train a classifier with good performance. Thus, as we show in Fig. 4, both the OOB (Out-of-bag) error in the training set and the classification error in the test increase (slowly) as the number of chosen clusters increase. In all cases, the error is less than 16%.

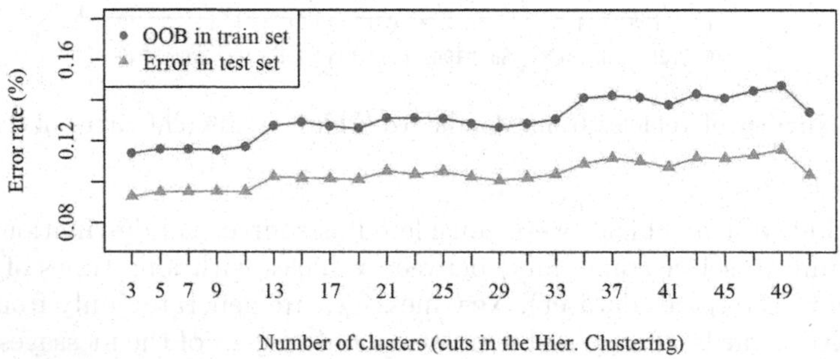

Fig. 4. Error rate in training and testing sets per number of categories for Random Forest with ten trees. The OOB is the "Out Of the Bag" error in the train set.

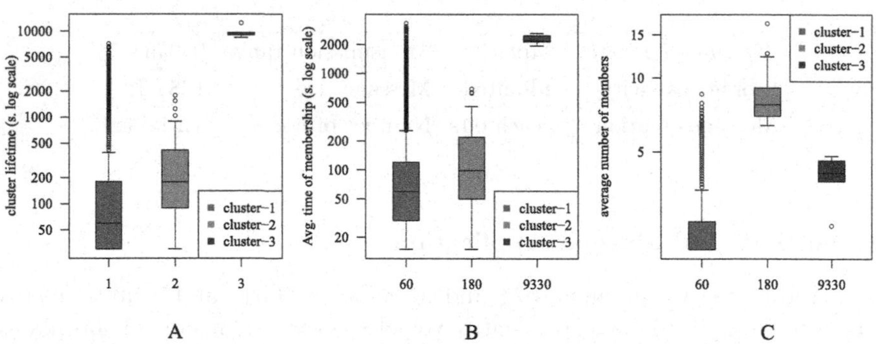

Fig. 5. Clusters of vehicles. (A) Clusters' lifetime. (B) Time of membership per cluster.(C) Average number of members in each cluster type, versus average clusters lifetime.

4.3 Simulation Reports and Evaluation

In our VANET simulations using traces from Monday to Friday, vehicles save all the predicted group density category values, connectivity measurements, and message transmission information for evaluation purposes. Those values are reported at the simulation end, with the proper timestamp. The purpose is to discover if the predictions have a logical relation with the connectivity properties and the message transmission performance. The reported measures are collected by each vehicle, and the values are obtained every time vehicles perceive (through the classifier) that the group density category has changed. After reporting its measurements, each vehicle resets its variables to perform new measurements for the new group density category detected. In Table 3 showed below, on the left side of the table, the connectivity and message transmission measurements gathered during the simulation. While, on the right side, we include what we want to represent or know with each of the measurements.

Table 3. Measurements from simulation

Variable from simulation	Aim of representing
Same category prediction interval time ($TinC_i$)	Membership time
Average node degree during ($TinC_i$)	Avg. number of members
Avg. connection duration during ($TinC_i$)	Membership time
Number of received messages during ($TinC_i$)	Transmission performance
Number of initiated connections during ($TinC_i$)	Overhead existence or absence

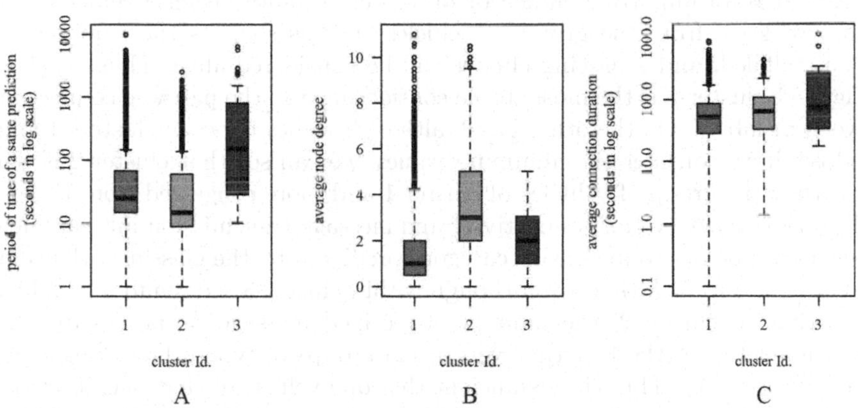

Fig. 6. The classifier's predictions. (A) Duration of a condition group per classifier. (B) Average number of neighbors during time that a vehicle remains in group condition. (C) Average times connections keep stable, when vehicle was under group condition.

5 Analysis of Results

Before showing our validation results, notice that group density conditions were categorized according to group stability metrics. That information was not used to train our classifier. In this way, it is important to see how coherent the connectivity and message transmission measurements are from the simulation itself, using the classifier's predictions. In Fig. 6-A, we show the prediction interval time variability ($TinC_i$) within same category. That is, the period of time in which the classifier did not return a different group density (within the *cluster* $-$ *ID*-C_i-). As expected, $TinC_i$ is related to the membership time attribute used for hierarchical clustering in Step-2. Thus, it was designed to work like that. Since a vehicle receives the same $cluster - ID$ from the classifier, it is probably that the vehicle is part of that group's underlying connectivity properties. Hence the classifier assumes that it is of category C_i. The clearest relationship here happens between the prediction of C_i and the categorization, like the case of category number 3. The category with $cluster - ID$ 3 is, in fact, the most stable density group category; thus, as expected, the membership time is higher. The result highlights the outstanding performance of group stability of our method. In Fig. 6-B, we get other accurate results. If we consider that the average node degree of a vehicle is related to the average number of members that a group has (see Fig. 5-C). Thus, if a vehicle's classifier predicts a density group category C_i, its average number of members should be related to the average number of neighbors that the vehicle has during $TinC_i$. Hence, as we can observe in Fig. 6-B, cluster-2 values are higher than those of cluster-3, which in turn, are higher than the cluster-1 values. Therefore, even though cluster-3 is more stable among all (see Fig. 6-A), clearly cluster-2 was detected in places of more congestion. Finally, in Fig. 6-C, we plot average connection duration between pairs of vehicles. It is an important indicator of cluster stability because vehicles could remain or leave from the group of vehicles and, as soon as the expression in Eq. 3 is fulfilled, and a moving cluster will be considered alive. Thus, as shown in Fig. 6-C, cluster-3 is the most stable considering also the pairwise connectivity between members. On the other hand, although values between clusters 1 and 2 are close, if we consider the minimum values, we can see that cluster-2 is more stable than the group of vehicles of cluster-1 and more congested from Fig. 6-B.

Figure 7 shows overall connectivity and message transmission measurements under each type of group density category predicted by the classifier. Hence, we can verify, in Fig. 7-A that, even though within cluster-3 the number of vehicles is less than in cluster-2, the number of received messages is far greater. The reason is related to the fact that vehicles in groups of type 3 have longer periods of connectivity. Thus, it is sufficient that one vehicle of that pack to receive a message to share it with the group. Moreover, Fig. 7-B shows the number of initiated connections of vehicles under each group density category. For this particular result, We also include the measurements from vehicles whose classifier predicted as isolated vehicles or in a "non-group category. The horizontal labels mean that one vehicle's average time remains in a specific condition (average $TinC_i$ determines it is isolated or in a group of type 1, 2, or 3). We can verify that most observations were classified when vehicles required it. The most classification errors happen between the "non-group" and cluster-1 categories. That is because groups of cluster-1 include very unstable vehicle groups. Besides, due

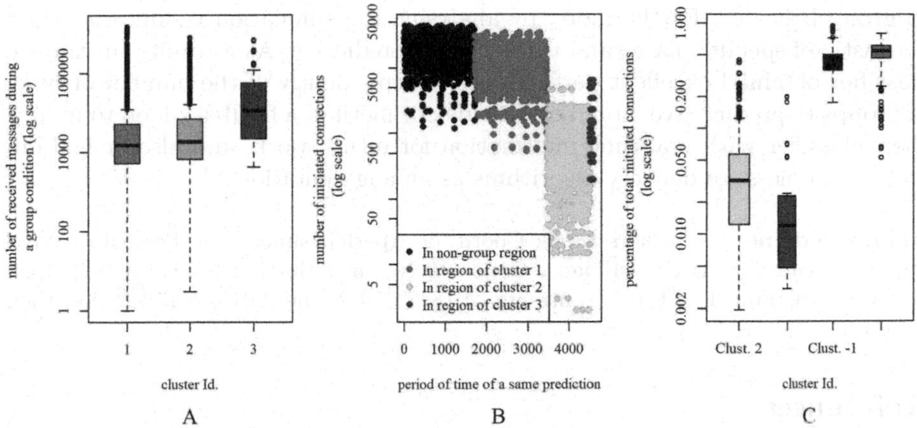

Fig. 7. Connectivity and transmission behavior for each group. (A) Messages received when vehicles remain in the same condition. (B) Average number of neighbors of each vehicle. (C) Percentage of connections that a vehicle establishes under a group.

to the nature of our 30 s snapshots interval, if vehicles' group did not survive such a lower period of time, they were automatically considered as isolate nodes.

Finally, we can observe that more unstable types of clusters established a higher number of connections. The cause of this instability can be interpreted as intermittent connections. These tend to break and establish again among the same vehicles. On the other hand, regarding the more stable category (cluster-3), the classifier can recognize it, despite using an unbalanced dataset for classification. Moreover, Fig. 7-C shows the percentage representing the number of connections under each group density category from the total number of connections established during the simulation. This metric reveals that most of the connections established by vehicles are under unstable conditions. Such finding is consistent with our taxi scenario of Rome.

6 Conclusions and Future Work

Density estimation algorithms could support communication systems to adapt under different connectivity situations. However, collective connectivity awareness is costly and might be inaccurate after a short time, thus density estimation algorithms independent of V2V communication are needed. Therefore, we propose a method that can categorize vehicular density according to long-time stability metrics related to connectivity properties and message transmission performance. This improvement is achieved by using the vehicular location information and identifying a group of vehicles through density-based clustering. Afterward, we categorize the identified groups using group stability measures and hierarchical clustering. We demonstrated using extensive simulations based on real traces, that cluster stability measures capture relevant information related to group behavior. Furthermore, by analysing the simulation results that characteristic of specific places and times can be predictive. As a result, our trained classifier obtained excellent performance, independently of the number of types of groups to predict. We intend to provide our method a feedback loop to update their classifier with real-time information for future work, and also embed our method in message delivery algorithms as an augmentation.

Acknowledgment. Authors thank Coord. de Aperfeiçoamento de Pessoal de Nível Superior - Brasil (CAPES) - Finance Code 001. H.S. also thanks Stic-AMSUD (project 20-STIC-09), and FAPESP (contracts 2018/22979-2 and 2015/24461-2) for their support.

References

1. Aliyu, A., et al.: Cloud computing in VANETs: architecture, taxonomy, and challenges. IETE Tech. Rev. **35**(5), 523–547 (2018)
2. Barrachina, J., et al.: I-VDE: a novel approach to estimate vehicular density by using vehicular networks. In: Cichoń, J., Gębala, M., Klonowski, M. (eds.) ADHOC-NOW 2013. LNCS, vol. 7960, pp. 63–74. Springer, Heidelberg (2013). https://doi.org/10.1007/978-3-642-39247-4_6
3. Bracciale, L., Bonola, M., Loreti, P., Bianchi, G., Amici, R., Rabuffi, A.: CRAWDAD dataset roma/taxi (v. 2014-07-17), July 2014. https://crawdad.org/roma/taxi/20140717
4. Chen, L., Bian, K.: Neighbor discovery in mobile sensing applications: a comprehensive survey. Ad Hoc Netw. **48**, 38–52 (2016)
5. Chesterton, A.: How many cars are there in the world? (2018). https://www.carsguide.com.au/car-advice/how-many-cars-are-there-in-the-world-70629
6. Darwish, T., Bakar, K.A.: Traffic density estimation in vehicular ad hoc networks: a review. Ad Hoc Netw. **24**, 337–351 (2015)
7. Doone, M.G., Cotton, S.L., Matolak, D.W., Oestges, C., Heaney, S.F., Scanlon, W.G.: Pedestrian-to-vehicle communications in an urban environment: channel measurements and modeling. IEEE Trans. Antennas Propag. **67**(3), 1790–1803 (2018)
8. Ester, M., Kriegel, H.P., Sander, J., Xu, X.: A density-based algorithm for discovering clusters in large spatial databases with noise. In: International Conference on Knowledge Discovery and Data Mining, KDD 1996, pp. 226–231 (1996)
9. Grzybek, A., Seredynski, M., Danoy, G., Bouvry, P.: Detection of stable mobile communities in vehicular ad hoc networks. In: IEEE International Conference on Intelligent Transportation Systems (ITSC), pp. 1172–1178 (2014)
10. He, J., Cai, L., Pan, J., Cheng, P.: Delay analysis and routing for two-dimensional VANETs using carry-and-forward mechanism. IEEE Trans. Mobile Comput. **16**(7), 1830–1841 (2017)
11. Jabbarpour, M.R., Noor, R.M., Khokhar, R.H., Ke, C.H.: Cross-layer congestion control model for urban vehicular environments. J. Netw. Comput. Appl. **44**, 1–16 (2014)
12. Keränen, A., Kärkkäinen, T., Ott, J.: Simulating mobility and DTNs with the one. J. Commun. **5**, 92–105 (2010)
13. Kim, T., Min, H., Choi, E., Jung, J.: Optimal job partitioning and allocation for vehicular cloud computing. Future Gener. Comput. Syst. **108**, 82–96 (2020)

14. Kimura, T., Saito, H., Honda, H.: Optimal transmission range for v2i communications on congested highways. In: IEEE Annual International Symposium on Personal, Indoor, and Mobile Radio Communications (PIMRC), pp. 1–7 (2017)
15. Korn, A., Schubert, A., Telcs, A.: Lobby index in networks. Phys. A **388**(11), 2221–2226 (2009)
16. Lakkakorpi, J., Pitkänen, M., Ott, J.: Adaptive routing in mobile opportunistic networks. In: 13th ACM International Conference on Modeling, Analysis, and Simulation of Wireless and Mobile Systems, MSWIM 2010, pp. 101–109. ACM (2010)
17. Liu, X.: A survey on clustering routing protocols in wireless sensor networks. Sensors **12**(8), 11113–11153 (2012)
18. Pan, J., Cui, J., Wei, L., Xu, Y., Zhong, H.: Secure data sharing scheme for VANETs based on edge computing. EURASIP J. Wireless Comm. Netw. **2019** (2019)
19. Panichpapiboon, S., Pattara-atikom, W.: Exploiting wireless communication in vehicle density estimation. IEEE Trans. Veh. Technol. **60**(6), 2742–2751 (2011)
20. Park, Y., Sur, C., Noh, S.W., Rhee, K.H.: Self-controllable secure location sharing for trajectory-based message delivery on cloud-assisted VANETs. Sensors **18**(7), 2112 (2018)
21. Sun, Y., Luo, S., Dai, Q., Ji, Y.: An adaptive routing protocol based on QoS and vehicular density in urban VANETs. Int. J. Distrib. Sensor Netw. **2015**, 5:5 (2015)
22. Toghi, B., Saifuddin, M., Mughal, M., Fallah, Y.P.: Spatio-temporal dynamics of cellular v2x communication in dense vehicular networks. In: IEEE Connected and Automated Vehicles Symposium (CAVS), pp. 1–5. IEEE (2019)
23. Vahdat, A., Becker, D.: Epidemic routing for partially-connected ad hoc networks. Technical report, Duke University (2000)
24. Vasilakos, A.V., Zhang, Y., Spyropoulos, T.: Delay Tolerant Networks: Protocols and Applications. Wireless Networks and Mobile Communications. CRC Press, Hoboken (2011)
25. Wang, J., Peeta, S., Lu, L., Li, T.: Multiclass information flow propagation control under vehicle-to-vehicle communication environments. Transp. Res. Part B Methodol. **129**, 96–121 (2019)
26. Zeadally, S., Guerrero, J., Contreras, J.: A tutorial survey on vehicle-to-vehicle communications. Telecommun. Syst. **73**(3), 469–489 (2019). https://doi.org/10.1007/s11235-019-00639-8

Resistance and Resilience. A Methodological Approach for Cities and Territories in Italy

Ginevra Balletto[1(✉)], Giuseppe Borruso[2], Beniamino Murgante[3], Alessandra Milesi[1], and Mara Ladu[1]

[1] DICAAR - Department of Civil and Environmental Engineering and Architecture, University of Cagliari, 09100 Cagliari, Italy
{balletto,mara.ladu}@unica.it

[2] DEAMS - Department of Economics, Business, Mathematics and Statistics Sciences "Bruno de Finetti", University of Trieste, 34127 Trieste, Italy
giuseppe.borruso@deams.units.it

[3] School of Engineering, University of Basilicata, Viale dell'Ateneo Lucano, 10, 85100 Potenza, Italy
beniamino.murgante@unibas.it

Abstract. The recent pandemic has affected health and lifestyles, highlighting the vulnerability of cities and territories, such as the ecological-environmental and climatic crisis, as a result of the progressive urbanization-urban connections. The prevalence of CoViD-19 cases was recorded in highly connected urban contexts with poor air quality. The entire health emergency was governed in the absence of geographical-territorial references, generalizing limitations and actions to contain the spread of the Sars-Cov2 virus. In this framework, a methodological approach to policy for cities and territories is proposed, for multi-risk management (environment-health) and to formulate responses to change, as part of the completion of the reform of intermediate bodies in Italy also with reference to the National Plan Resistance and Resilience.

Keywords: Multi-risk management · Environment and health · Metropolitan cities

1 Introduction

Before the CoViD-19 epidemic the health risk was considered a second degree one, closely related to a different type of disaster [1]. The recent epidemic highlighted how environmental, geographical and socio-economic factors contribute to delineating different levels of health incidence and severity, due to the spatial distribution of cases and deaths [2]. Known and often neglected aspects in economic planning and urban

This study was supported by the research grant for the project "Investigating the relationships between knowledge-building and design and decision-making in spatial planning with geodesign" funded by Fondazione di Sardegna (2018).

O. Gervasi et al. (Eds.): ICCSA 2021, LNCS 12952, pp. 218–229, 2021.
https://doi.org/10.1007/978-3-030-86973-1_15

and territorial planning were highlighted, including the conjuncture of the ecological-environmental and climate crisis that requires coordinated responses 'from local to global', according to a multi- risk, as a result of progressive urbanization-urban connections [3]. From the ecological and pandemic crisis, it is necessary to act to increase the resilience of the territorial system, also due to the greater frequency and speed of spread of epidemics that confirm the urgent need for an international - and national vision between: quality of life, health-well-being and natural and urban environment [4, 5] which can be monitored through the main indicators: BES (Equitable and sustainable well-being) and URBES (well-being and natural and urban environment) on which economic planning is also based national [6, 7].

In other words, convergence is necessary between 'Smart City' and 'Healthy City', made favorable by the sharing of their main objectives [8], such as improving the quality of life: in particular air quality, ecosystem services urban, lifestyle and urban green development [9, 10] and social participation and involvement.

The natural disasters that have repeatedly hit the country, from earthquakes to events also induced by climate change, such as landslides and floods, call for the need to improve the resilience of infrastructures, focusing on extraordinary maintenance, prevention and civil protection [11, 12].

Even the multiform Italian territorial and urban system, evolution and transformation of the historic city, confirms the need for a multidimensional approach to the concept of risk, also given by the temporal interrelation, with combined, cumulative and simultaneous effects. In this sense, the metropolitan city/province, due to the initiation of the reform with Law 56/2014, represents the optimal territorial dimension, for the evaluation of phenomena and for the construction of vision to increase resilience, through the Strategic Plan Metropolitan, which constitutes the main act of orientation for the promotion and integrated management of services (education, infrastructure and mobility) and protection (well-being, ecosystem services and civil protection). From the experience of the management of the health emergency, faced mainly by the Government through the Civil Protection and by means of the DPCM (Decree of the President of the Council of Ministers), through a direct State-Regions relationship, actually temporarily modifying the normal institutional balance, it clearly emerges that the reform should begin of intermediate territorial bodies to ensure the necessary subsidiarity and optimal social cohesion [13].

In this framework, the paper is divided into the following parts:

- Section 2, which focuses on territorial competencies and health emergency;
- Section 3, which focuses on the role for the provinces and metropolitan cities;
- Section 4, which proposes a methodology to define an operational theoretical-practical progress to support governance in the construction-revision phase of the Strategic Planning of metropolitan cities/provinces;
- Section 5, dedicated to discussion and conclusions.

2 Territorial Competencies and Health Emergency

One of the issues that went through the period of the CoViD-19 explosion, following the spread of the Sars-Cov2 virus in Italy, concerns the division of competences and powers between the central State and the administrative units of which it is composed, regions and provinces. autonomous in particular.

Throughout the pandemic period, the discussion on which bodies had the last say on operational aspects related to the health emergency, the closures/openings of commercial activities and local public transport remained in the background. These are undoubtedly aspects of regional competence, subordinated to what has been established, in an emergency, by the government structures. The regional dimension has prevailed in terms of assessments, roles, functions and often with an apparent homogeneity that has led to various restrictions on mobility and the exercise of economic and social activities (e.g. regional subdivisions in colors: yellow - orange - red).

The 'empirical' observations of the crisis by CoViD-19, and the analysis carried out, from the health, territorial and environmental point of view [2, 14], have highlighted how the regional level of administrative units appears unsuitable for a more detailed understanding of local phenomena, as well as too stringent for the application of rapid intervention actions (e.g., limitations to mobility and the performance of economic activities), the extent of which often interrupts the relationships and interactions in spatial areas of supra-regional scope. The case of the Milanese metropolitan area, the area most affected by the spread of the Sars-Cov2 virus since February 2020, is emblematic. On the one hand, the analysis of the phenomenon, in the explosive and diffusion phases, had to be based on a narrative mainly on the provincial scale, followed by restrictions and initiatives on the regional scale.

The provincial area was found, as per the analyzes developed, to be the most suitable for observation and a series of considerations on local trends, without going down to the municipal scale, more difficult in terms of data retrieval and representativeness because it is less aggregated [2]. In fact, the analyzes developed have highlighted homogeneity of behavior and diffusion processes that can be explained more easily at the provincial scale which, very often, go beyond regional administrative borders. From the analysis of the standardized CoViD-19 excess mortality as of March 31, 2020 (Fig. 1) referring to the provincial level, it is evident that the most affected area is the 'core' of the Po Valley and the Milanese metropolitan area, which is an area straddling three distinct regions: Lombardy, Emilia Romagna and Piedmont. In particular, the phenomenon that can be identified more markedly especially in the southern and eastern provinces of Lombardy, as well as in those of Emilia.

Considerable parts of the Piedmont and Romagna territory seemed, in the first phase, to be less affected by the phenomenon, highlighting a rather high spatial variability within the individual regional contexts. On the other hand, the containment policies are aimed at individual regional contexts.

3 What Role for Provinces and Metropolitan Cities?

With reference to the complexity of the Italian administrative question, referring above all to the transformation of the intermediate territorial realities, some ideas for the proposals

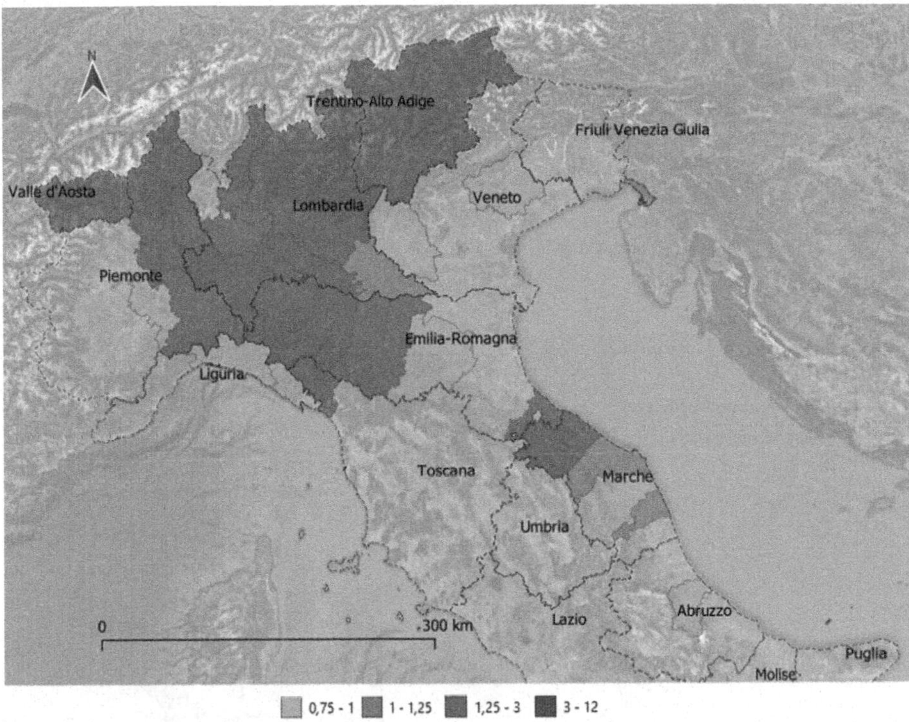

Fig. 1. Standardized CoViD-19 mortality (SMR) and administrative contexts of northern Italy.

that will be explained later are important. Referring to the extensive and in-depth works developed on the subject [15–19], we can recall some specificities that characterize this level of governance intermediate, especially from the metropolitan point of view, such as, in particular, the drafting of the Strategic Plan.

Figure 2 highlights the current supra-municipal (and sub-regional) administrative structure into which the Italian state is divided. We note the presence of metropolitan cities, the latest system resulting from the 'Del Rio' law (Law 56/2014), alongside the provinces, the autonomous provinces (Trento and Bolzano, equated in roles and functions to real regions with statute special), to the free consortia of municipalities (launched only in the case of the Sicily Region) and to units, in fact, purely statistical where these realities are, at the moment, no longer active.

These intermediate territorial administrative units have different characteristics and functions, and the focus is on the metropolitan cities established by national law (and by the autonomous regions). With Law 142/90 and up to the current legislative structure, these are configured as 'super provinces', whose spatial structuring is conforming to administrative aspects, rather than geographic-functional, characterized, however, by an important role of territorial planning.

The territorial extensions of the metropolitan cities - apart from the case of the metropolitan city of Cagliari, correspond to those of the previous provinces, not being connected to the concept of metropolitan area, whose conformation derives, instead,

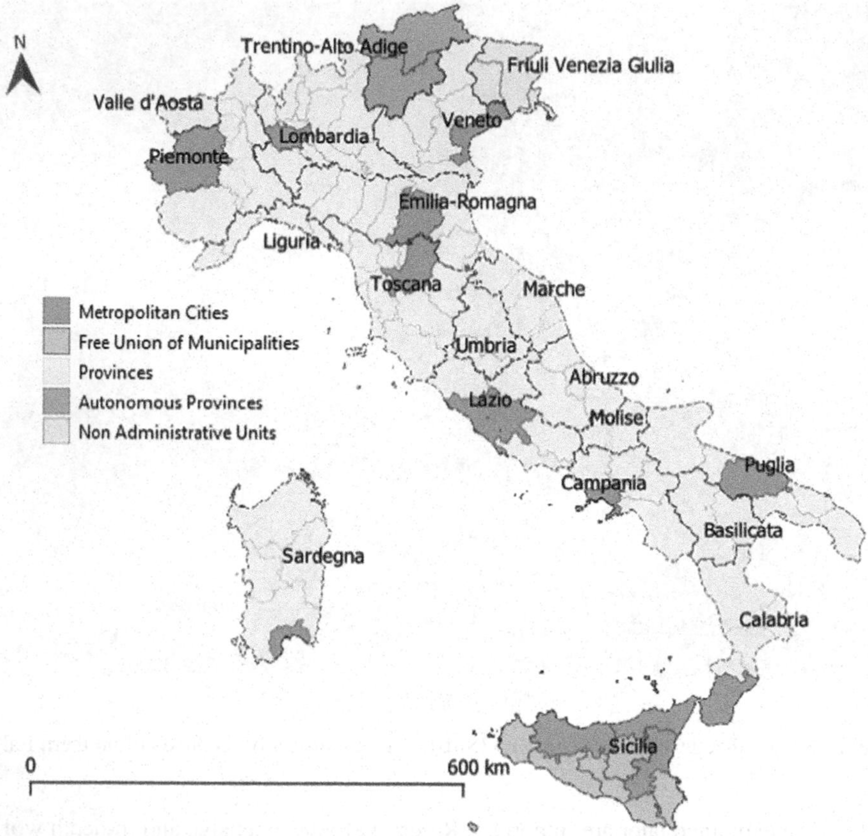

Fig. 2. Intermediate administrative units in Italy

from spatial interaction processes linked above all to mobility for reasons work and the presence of superior services in the central places of the same areas, with a range of action often more extended not only than the provincial, but also the regional delimitation.

The *Next Generation Italy* fits into this framework in response to delicate environmental issues and health protection.

Although the reform is not completed, this intermediate territorial dimension is also the most coherent also for the activation of governance policies in relation to the recent PNRR National Recovery and Resilience Plan (Next Generation Italy), which intends to link well-being, health, territory, environment and climate in the direction of greater sustainability, equity, inclusiveness and resilience.

The PNRR is also a Reform Plan, because the investment lines must be accompanied by the adoption of a set of reforms, as an 'enabling' element, in line with the European Commission's (Country Specific Recommendations. CSR) [20]. In addition, Italy also intends to accelerate the pursuit of the 17 Sustainable Development Goals (SDGs) signed by the UN Agenda 2030 with the related monitoring through the indicators of Wellness, Fair and Sustainable (Bes) already introduced in the economic-financial planning. There is talk of three strategic axes: digitization and innovation, ecological transition and social inclusion which decline six missions, necessary to intercept the growth drivers of the next decade (Fig. 3).

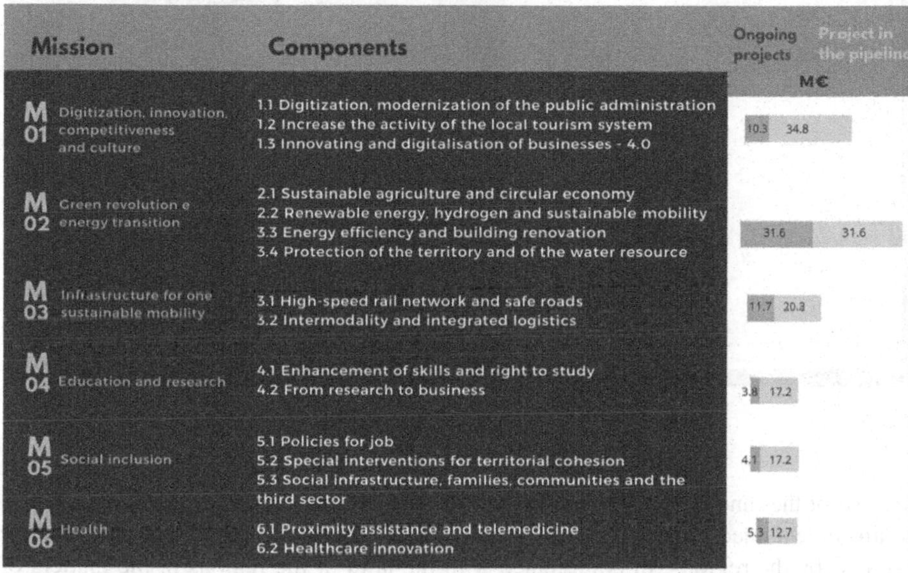

Mission
Components
Ongoing projects
Project in the pipeline
M€
M 01 Digitization, innovation, competitiveness and culture
1.1 Digitization, modernization of the public administration
1.2 Increase the activity of the local tourism system
1.3 Innovating and digitalisation of businesses - 4.0
10.3
34.8
M 02 Green revolution e energy transition
2.1 Sustainable agriculture and circular economy
2.2 Renewable energy, hydrogen and sustainable mobility
3.3 Energy efficiency and building renovation
3.4 Protection of the territory and of the water resource
31.6
31.6
M 03 Infrastructure for one sustainable mobility
3.1 High-speed rail network and safe roads
3.2 Intermodality and integrated logistics
11.7
20.3
M 04 Education and research
4.1 Enhancement of skills and right to study
4.2 From research to business
3.8
17.2
M 05 Social inclusion
5.1 Policies for job
5.2 Special interventions for territorial cohesion
5.3 Social infrastructure, families, communities and the third sector
4.1
17.2
M 06 Health
6.1 Proximity assistance and telemedicine
6.2 Healthcare innovation
5.3
12.7

Fig. 3. Summary of the PNRR- National Recovery and Resilience Plan.

In this sense, the authors, agreeing how the disciplines relating to territorial analysis and planning can contribute to the development of new models of territorial governance and for the formulation of useful tools for decision-making in the direction of greater sustainability, equity, inclusiveness and resilience [21], believe that the six missions find the optimal city/land size in the intermediate dimension of the metropolitan city/province [22]. The strategic planning of metropolitan cities is in fact an indispensable process for addressing the progressive urban, environmental and social complexity (Fig. 4). The necessary ecological transition outlined in the PNRR requires, firstly, the drastic reduction of climate-altering gas emissions in line with the objectives of the Paris Agreement and the European Green Deal, secondly, urban regeneration [23–25] and the improvement of urban energy efficiency, the prevention and contrast to the instability of the territory also with actions to reverse the decline of biodiversity and the degradation of the territory [26–28] and an effective and integrated management of the waste cycle to enhance the circular economy [29], require a representative territorial dimension.

It is a multi-risk management that finds functional representativeness in the metropolitan dimension, both to more adequately recognize the interdependence between territories (clusters of municipalities), and to respond to the specific needs of the same territories, regardless of administrative borders, and finally, certainly not least, to make the distribution of investments more equitable [22].

In this context, the "Adoption and annual update of a three-year strategic plan for the metropolitan area, which constitutes an act of guidance for the body and for the

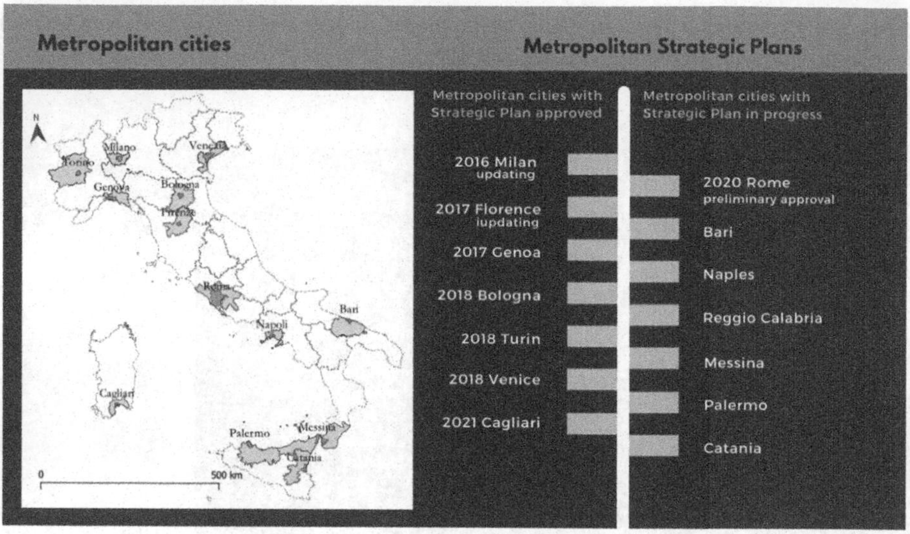

Fig. 4. State of metropolitan strategic planning in Italy

exercise of the functions of the municipalities and unions of municipalities included in the aforementioned territory, also in relation to the exercise of functions delegated or assigned by the regions, in compliance with the laws of the regions in the matters of their competence "(Law no. 56/2014 art. 1, c. 44, lett. a) the pandemic must be added, to which we intend to respond through the PNRR.

4 Methods

The health crisis invites us to reflect on the territorial dimension and on new and possible development models, not only based on financial and productive balance, but also on collective and individual well-being, health, respect for the natural environment, cooperation and solidarity, social belonging and community, just to name the most important.

The emergency experience confirms how the fundamental components of well-being, if neglected, increase the fragility of the social and economic system. In other words, the capacity of urban communities and the support of institutions must be aligned to ensure real change. In this sense, a methodology is proposed to define an operational theoretical-practical progress to support governance in the construction-revision phase of the Strategic Planning of metropolitan cities / provinces in response to multi-risk phenomena between environment, climate and health, both to define actions of prevention and both to facilitate a harmonious recovery. It is believed that by focusing on Strategic Planning, by aggregating university institutions, companies, and with civil society organizations [22, 23], it is possible to link forces coming from below by integrating them with the recent PNRR. The Strategic Plan is configured as a guiding tool for territorial planning, as well as the main planning act for the economic, social and environmental development of the metropolitan area: it defines the general, sectoral and transversal development objectives for the metropolitan area identifying priorities for intervention, in compliance with the principles of environmental sustainability.

Due to its characteristics, it also supports the formulation of the Single Programming Document - Documento Unico di Programmazione - DUP (for the Strategic and Operational part) for each of the individual municipalities of the cluster (from Article n. 151 of Legislative Decree No. 267/2000 - Testo Unico sugli Enti Locali), guaranteeing the principle of coordination and coherence of the budget documents [31], which constitutes the necessary prerequisite for all other local level planning documents (Fig. 5).

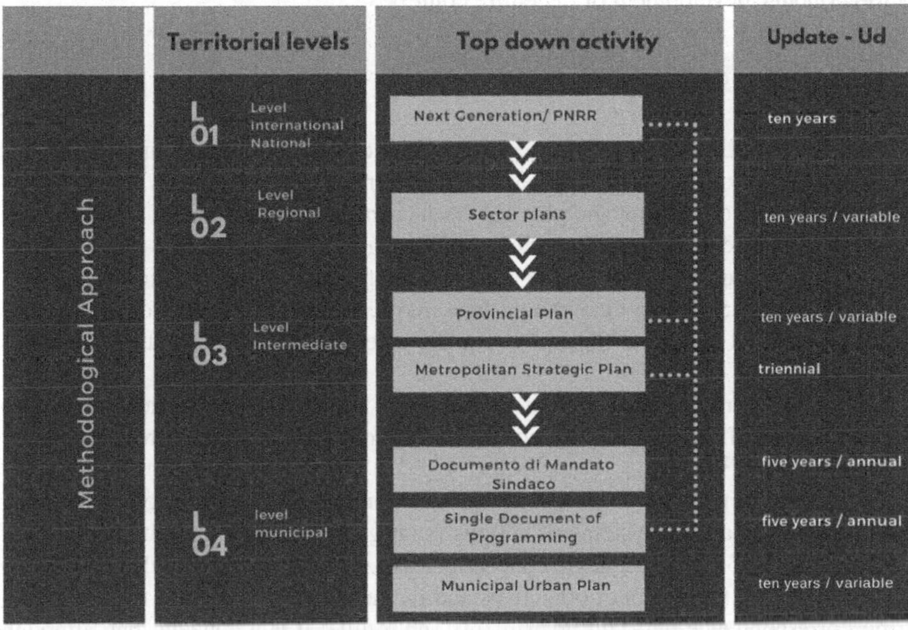

Fig. 5. Framework of methodological approach

The proposed methodology responds to stability needs, associated with the uncertainty of regulatory scenarios, often contradictory, which impose predetermined rules of conduct capable of responding in time to collective needs also in relation to the recent health crisis through the political program of the mayors.

The DUP constitutes the link between the objectives of the political program and the accounting documents of the budget and the executive management plan, with the desire to build a constantly updated and updatable management system, also due to the environmental-health crisis.

In fact, the goal is to always guarantee real-time programming (essential in the emergency phases and transition to normality) and its necessary management control.

The DUP therefore allows the strategic and operational guidance of the planning of the municipalities, for the implementation of the political program and to locally transfer the actions of Strategic Planning. In this sense, Strategic Planning is understood as the result of interactions between institutions both to prevent and to govern multi-risks, recovery and resilience.

Finally, this proposed method finds concreteness also due to the recent formulation of the Council of State (Second Section, sentence no. 6263 of 15 October 2020) which interprets as: "the system of urban territorial planning subsequent to the constitutional reform of 2001 less 'hierarchical' and more harmonious vision. Supra-municipal planning is characterized by a 'mixed' nature and flexibility in relations with the instruments below. Municipal planning presents an articulation in acts, distinct between the structural and operational profile, aimed at a general planning that has as its objective the socio-economic development of the entire context".

5 Discussion and Conclusions

In Italy, in the last twenty years there has been little attention to planning with strong resistance in applying strategic approaches in governance models [22, 31, 32].

Often the role of the strategic plan has been connected to the concept of a structural plan, but in most experiences the latter was lacking in strategy, lacking reflections on economic, social and political factors that, in fact, affect its implementation [23, 27].

A performing Strategic Plan should take into account the structural characteristics and to make good structural plans it is equally essential to include strategic elements [24, 28, 33–35].

The word 'strategic' is unanimously used as an adjective that qualifies the choices of the plan, underlining the importance of the repercussions in a structured framework of objectives [26, 37].

From this point of view, the definition of an organized system of objectives that gives meaning to all the systems of actions (strategies) to which one intends to think becomes central [38]. The strategic concept consists, in fact, precisely in the care for the reorganization of the system of objectives and for the careful research of the evaluation of the correspondence between investments and results. It is a concept that, although apparently elementary, is often lost when it is considered important to create a work that has not been preceded by adequate reflection on the reasons that made it necessary, without being able to evaluate other alternative solutions [39].

In this sense, it becomes essential to compare the National Recovery and Resilience Plan (PNRR) and the Next Generation Italy with all the components of the territory, infrastructures, physical, social and economic space, activities and organizations, analyzing both strategic and structural aspects. Not considering these aspects would lead the PNRR to be a single list of interventions disconnected from each other, because they are not connected to the geographical-territorial contexts.

In fact, although the health emergency was governed in the absence of geographical-territorial references, it highlighted several and interesting issues. It was possible to observe the national territory differently than before, with a clear separation between north, center and south for once not dependent on the polarization dynamics of economic development. The fragility of the industrious North, air pollution in areas with greater industrial development and the spread of the virus, spatial distribution of health services, infrastructural connections, were some of the main aspects neglected during the emergency. The complexity of the situation has resulted in a dimensionless approach that must necessarily be eliminated as soon as possible, also to formulate a concrete multi-risk and recovery management [22, 40].

References

1. Protezione Civile Nazionale, Il rischio sanitario. http://www.protezionecivile.gov.it/attivita-rischi/rischio-sanitario. Accessed 03 Feb 2021
2. Murgante, B., Balletto, G., Borruso, G., Las Casas, G., Castiglia, P., Dettori, M.: Geographical analyses of CoViD-19 's spreading contagion in the challenge of global health risks. TeMA (Special Issue), 283–304 (2020)
3. De Lotto, R., et al.: Exposure and risk reduction strategy: the role of functional change. In: Margani, G., et al. (eds.) Proceedings of the International Conference on Seismic and Energy Renovation for Sustainable Cities (SER4SC 2018), Catania, Italy, 1–3 Febbraio 2018, pp. 319–330 (2018)
4. Barton, H., Grant, M.: Urban planning for healthy cities. J. Urban Health **90**(1), 129–141 (2011). https://doi.org/10.1007/s11524-011-9649-3
5. Salmond, J.A., et al.: Health and climate related ecosystem services provided by street trees in the urban environment. Environ. Health **15**, 36 (2016). https://doi.org/10.1186/s12940-016-0103-6
6. La Torre, M., Semplici, L., Zapata, J.D.S.: Un Modello di Impact Finance per i Comuni: il Piano Strategico di Mandato BES-Oriented. In: Corporate Governance and Research & Development studies-Open Access, vol. 2, pp. 141–170 (2020)
7. Krasna, F., Borruso, G., Mauro, G., Zaccomer, G.P.: Green economy as a new pathway to development (and cohesion)? Place evidence analysis in the North-Eastern Italy: first findings of an ongoing research project. Bollettino della Società Geografica Italiana serie **14**(2), Special Issue, 143–153 (2019). https://doi.org/10.13128/bsgi.v2i3.820
8. Alves, L.A.: Healthy cities and smart cities: a comparative approach. Sociedade Natureza **31**, e47004 (2019)
9. Dettori, M., et al.: Air pollutants and risk of death due to COVID-19 in Italy. Environ. Res. **192**, 110459 (2021)
10. Murgante, B., Borruso, G., Balletto, G., Castiglia, P., Dettori, M.: Why Italy first? Health, geographical and planning aspects of the COVID-19 outbreak. Sustainability **12**, 5064 (2020)
11. Komendantova, N., Scolobig, A., Garcia-Aristizabal, A., Monfort, D., Fleming, K.: Multi-risk approach and urban resilience. Int. J. Disaster Resilience Built Environ. **7**, 114–132 (2016)
12. Zhao, L., et al.: Global multi-model projections of local urban climates. Nat. Clim. Change **11**, 152–157 (2021)
13. Fera, G., Lombardo, M.T.: La città metropolitana come opportunità per promuovere lo sviluppo integrato tra aree centrali e aree marginali: Il Caso di Studio di Reggio Calabria. LaborEst (20), 30–36 (2020). https://doi.org/10.19254/LaborEst.20.05
14. Borruso, G., Balletto, G., Murgante, B., Castiglia, P., Dettori, M.: CoViD-19. Diffusione spaziale e aspetti ambientali del caso italiano. Semestrale di studi e ricerche di geografia **32**(2), 39–56 (2020). https://doi.org/10.13133/1125-5218.17031
15. Gasparini, A.: Città metropolitana di Trieste, città metropolitana transfrontaliera di Trieste-Capodistria. Possibilità, probabilità, desiderabilità, Regione Autonoma Friuli Venezia Giulia – Relazioni Internazionali e Comunitarie. ISIG, Istituto di Sociologia Internazionale di Gorizia, Gorizia (2010)
16. Galluccio, F.: Una o divisibile? La questione regionale e il nodo del federalismo in Italia. Semestrale di Studi e Ricerche di Geografia **31**(2), 71–93 (2011)

17. AA. VV.: Il riordino territoriale dello Stato. Scenari italiani 2014. Rapporto annuale della Società Geografica Italiana Onlus, Roma, Società Geografica Italiana Onlus (2015)
18. Riboldazzi, R.: Local government innovation in Italy and its impact on urban and regional planning with a focus on the Milanese context. In: Nunes Silva, C., Buček, J. (eds.) Local Government and Urban Governance in Europe. TUBS, pp. 89–109. Springer, Cham (2017). https://doi.org/10.1007/978-3-319-43979-2_5
19. Dini, F., Zilli, S.: Introduzione. In: Cerutti, S., Tadini, M. Mosaico/Mosaic, Società di Studi Geografici. Memorie Geografiche NS 17, pp. 549–555 (2019)
20. Messori, M.: The 'Next Generation – EU' breakthrough: Opportunities and risks for Italy. SEP Policy Brief, June, n. 31; trad.it. 'La svolta 'Next Generation – EU': Opportunità e rischi per l'Italia' (2020)
21. Morri, R.: A question of geography literacy: geographical studies on Covid Sars 2 and lifelong education. J-READING **2**(9), 5–9 (2020). https://doi.org/10.4458/3617-01
22. Balletto, G., Mundula, L., Milesi, A., Ladu, M.: Cohesion policies in Italian metropolitan cities. Evaluation and challenges. In: Gervasi, O., et al. (eds.) ICCSA 2020. LNCS, vol. 12255, pp. 441–455. Springer, Cham (2020). https://doi.org/10.1007/978-3-030-58820-5_33
23. Ladu, M., Balletto, G., Milesi, A., Mundula, L., Borruso, G.: Public real estate assets and the metropolitan strategic plan in Italy. The two cases of Milan and Cagliari. In: Gervasi, O., et al. (eds.) ICCSA 2020. LNCS, vol. 12255, pp. 472–486. Springer, Cham (2020). https://doi.org/10.1007/978-3-030-58820-5_35
24. Balletto, G., Ladu, M., Milesi, A., Borruso, G.: A methodological approach on disused public properties in the 15-minute city perspective. Sustainability **13**(2), 593 (2021)
25. Balletto, G., Milesi, A., Fenu, N., Borruso, G., Mundula, L.: Military training areas as semicommons: the territorial valorization of Quirra (Sardinia) from easements to ecosystem services. Sustainability **12**(2), 622 (2020)
26. Capotorti, G., et al.: More nature in the city. Plant Biosyst.-Int. J. Dealing Aspects Plant Biol. **154**(6), 1003–1006 (2020)
27. Palumbo, M., Mundula, L., Balletto, G., Bazzato, E., Marignani, M.: Environmental dimension into strategic planning. The case of metropolitan city of Cagliari. In: Gervasi, O., et al. (eds.) ICCSA 2020. LNCS, vol. 12255, pp. 456–471. Springer, Cham (2020). https://doi.org/10.1007/978-3-030-58820-5_34
28. Balletto, G., Milesi, A., Ladu, M., Borruso, G.: A dashboard for supporting slow tourism in green infrastructures. A methodological proposal in Sardinia (Italy). Sustainability **12**(9), 3579 (2020)
29. Balletto, G., Borruso, G., Mei, G.: Location theory and circular economy. Demolition, constructions and spatial organization of firms – an applied model to Sardinia Region. The case study of the New Cagliari Stadium. In: Misra, S., et al. (eds.) ICCSA 2019. LNCS, vol. 11621, pp. 535–550. Springer, Cham (2019). https://doi.org/10.1007/978-3-030-24302-9_38
30. Albrechts, L., Balducci, A., Hillier, J. (eds.): Situated Practices of Strategic Planning: An International Perspective. Routledge (2016). https://doi.org/10.4324/9781315679181
31. Balletto, G., Borruso, G., Donato, C.: City dashboards and the Achilles' heel of smart cities: putting governance in action and in space. In: Gervasi, O., et al. (eds.) ICCSA 2018. LNCS, vol. 10962, pp. 654–668. Springer, Cham (2018). https://doi.org/10.1007/978-3-319-95168-3_44
32. Moccia, F.D.: Resistenze alla pianificazione strategica: una analisi trans-culturale della ricezione ed uso della pianificazione strategica nella pianificazione integrata italiana. In Archibugi, F., Saturnino, A. (eds.) Pianificazione strategica e governabilità ambientale. Alinea editrice, Firenze (2004)
33. Archibugi, F.: La Città Ecologica Urbanistica e sostenibilità. Torino, Bollati Boringhieri (2002)

34. Mundula, L., Ladu, M., Balletto, G., Milesi, A.: Smart marinas. The case of metropolitan city of Cagliari. In: Gervasi, O., et al. (eds.) ICCSA 2020. LNCS, vol. 12255, pp. 51–66. Springer, Cham (2020). https://doi.org/10.1007/978-3-030-58820-5_5
35. Balletto, G., Borruso, G., Mei, G., Milesi, A.: Recycled aggregates in constructions. A case of circular economy in Sardinia (Italy). TeMA – J. Land Use Mobility Environ. **14**(1), 51–68 (2021). https://doi.org/10.6092/1970-9870/7354
36. Cicerchia, A.: Pianificazione Strategica e Ambiente: teorie, metodi, strumenti ed esperienze internazionali. Franco Angeli, Milano (2000)
37. Balletto, G., Mundula, L., Milesi, A., Ladu, M.: Ex post evaluation of cohesion policies in the strategic planning of Italian metropolitan cities: analysis for the development of new strategies. In: La Rosa, D., Privitera, R. (eds.) INPUT 2021. LNCE, vol. 146, pp. 329–337. Springer, Cham (2021). https://doi.org/10.1007/978-3-030-68824-0_36
38. Archibugi, F.: Introduzione alla pianificazione strategica in ambito pubblico. Alinea Editrice, Firenze (2005)
39. Las Casas, G., Murgante, B.: Il Documento preliminare al Piano strutturale della Provincia di Potenza: i termini di un approccio strategico». Archivio di studi urbani e regionali edizioni Franco Angeli Milano **37**, 199–211 (2006)
40. Marzocchi, W., Garcia-Aristizabal, A., Gasparini, P., Mastellone, M.L., Di Ruocco, A.: Basic principles of multi-risk assessment: a case study in Italy. Nat. Hazards **62**(2), 551–573 (2012)

Towards a Semantic 3D Model of Sofia City

Dessislava Petrova-Antonova[1,2](✉) and Angel Spasov[1]

[1] Sofia University "St. Kliment Ohridski", GATE Institute, 1113 Sofia, Bulgaria
{dessislava.petrova,angel.spasov}@gate-ai.eu
[2] Sofia University "St. Kliment Ohridski", FMI, 1164 Sofia, Bulgaria

Abstract. More and more cities worldwide are working on their digital transformation in order to deliver better living environment for citizens. Over the last decades, a lot of research efforts are dedicated to development of semantic 3D city models, covering variety city dimensions based on standards such as CityGML. The complexity of cities' processes, the heterogeneity of data they produced and different special scale requirements for planning and managing urban environment bring emerging challenges to implementation of semantic 3D city models. In order to address these challenges, this paper presents the process of development a semantic 3D model of the city of Sofia and its visual representation through a simple web application. As a pilot area, District "Vazrajdane" is selected, consisting of several neighbourhoods close to the center of the city. The 3D transformation of proprietary geospatial data into CityGML schema, covering building and terrain modules, is described. Further, the implementation of the web application for user interaction with the semantic 3D city model is presented. Its main features include silhouetting a single building on handling mouse events and showing relevant overlay content, displaying shadows and styling of buildings depending on their data attributes.

Keywords: Semantic 3D city model · CityGML · Buildings and terrain · FME · Cesium

1 Introduction

The semantic 3D models of cities have significantly advanced recently, especially with the adoption of the Digital Twin's concept. They provide a solid foundation for a wide range of urban analysis and simulations. Since such models go far beyond the simple visualisation, they are used for a variety of applications such as disaster management, urban planning and design, solar potential analysis, air pollution simulation, etc. [1, 2].

Currently, more than a thousand city models exist worldwide [3]. The majority of them are implemented using either the CityGML or IFC standard [4, 5]. A number of techniques can be applied for their development such as aerial photographs and laser scanning [6, 7], extrusion from 2D footprints [8], airborne point clouds [9–11], architectural drawings and plans [12, 13], procedural modelling [14, 15], and open street map [16, 17]. The 3D models, based on CityGML, represent the cityscape with respect to geometry, topology, semantics and appearance of common urban objects. They can be

O. Gervasi et al. (Eds.): ICCSA 2021, LNCS 12952, pp. 230–241, 2021.
https://doi.org/10.1007/978-3-030-86973-1_16

modelled in five different Levels of Detail (LOD) with respect to their geometry and spatial accuracy [18]. As a widely adopted standard, CityGML enables reusability and interoperability of 3D models over different applications. Till now, it is mostly used for modelling of the buildings due to their dominant role within the urban environment and lack of data for other thematic objects such as road infrastructure, underground networks and utilities, water bodies, etc. [19]. CityGML influenced the INSPIRE Directive of the European Commission (EC), which aims at the creation of a European Union spatial data infrastructure providing public sector data in an interoperable way [20]. In addition, a lot of commercial and open-source tools provide support for CityGML standard. For example, citygml4j is a Java class library for processing CityGML models developed by the Technische Universität Berlin. The 3D City Database is a free 3D geo-database to store and manage 3D city models on top of Oracle Spatial or PostgreSQL/PostGIS database management systems [21]. FME (Feature Manipulation Engine) from Safe Software Inc. provides a rich functionality for transformation of city data in a variety of formats in CityGML [22]. Bentley Map combines the strengths of CAD and traditional GIS providing capabilities for 2D or 3D analysis and visualizations [23]. Solar3Dcity, a simple tool developed by TU Delft, assesses the yearly solar irradiation of buildings modeled in CityGML [24]. Cesium Ion and CesiumJS enable a CityGML upload and visualization in the Cesium Globe. Another tool for visualization of 3D models is FZKViewer from Karlsruhe Institute of Technology, supporting both for IFC and CityGML standards [25]. The number of such tools is steadily growing, especially in the context of rapid development of city digital twin platforms.

This paper presents the preliminary results from creating a CityGML-compliant semantic 3D model of the city of Sofia. It explains the 3D transformation of proprietary geospatial data into CityGML schema and its further visualization in a web application. First, a semantic 3D model of buildings and terrain at district scale is created. It covers the territory of District "Vazrajdane" of Sofia, which almost entirely belongs to the city centre. Next, a simple web application is developed for visualisation and user interaction with the 3D model of the buildings. The semantic 3D city model and its visual representation are the first step towards building of a digital twin platform, which will be used for planning, design, exploration, experimentation and optimization of urban processes and services.

The rest of the paper is organised as follows. Section 2 points out data used and describes the process of model creation in the current use case. Section 3 explains in detail workflow and implementation for visualization. Section 4 summarizes the paper and extends on future work.

2 3D Modelling

This section describes geospatial data transformation with the help of FME software, which is a widely used tool for data elevation by extruding 2D geometry to 3D models [26]. It provides pre-built transformation components that accelerate the process of workflow creation. The goal of the transformation is to produce 3D city model compliant with CityGML standard in LOD1.

2.1 Data Sources

The geospatial data were provided for research purposes by Sofiaplan, which is a municipal enterprise responsible for the spatial and strategic planning of Sofia Municipality. Table 1 provides description of the data sources.

Table 1. Description of data sources

Type object	File type	File size	Number of objects	Description
Buildings	.SHP	1063 KB	5090	Building footprints, floor count and function
Digital terrain	.TIF	953 KB	1	Digital terrain

The buildings' data is stored in PostGIS database and exported in.shp format. In addition, a digital terrain model was provided in.tif format. Figure 1 shows the visualisation of source data in QGIS. The relief is presented with grey colour, while the buildings' footprints are coloured in blue. The coordinate reference system of source data is BGS2005/CCS2005 (Bulgaria Geodetic System 2005, EPSG: 7801).

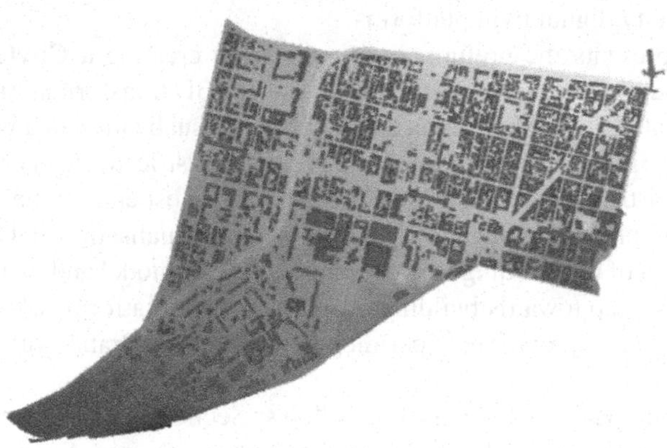

Fig. 1. Visualisation of source data.

2.2 Building Modelling

Each LOD defined in CityGML standard is characterized by differing accuracies and minimal dimensions of the corresponding objects. The buildings are modelled based on the thematic module Building. In contrast to higher level of details, in LOD1 buildings are represented as a general geometry of the outer shell where volume and surface are identical. Furthermore, different structural parts are combined into a simple block [18], including roofs which receive a flat representation. The absolute 3D point accuracy is required to be 5/5 m. The interior structure of the buildings is not part of the LOD1 model.

The geometric representation can be implemented by only one of the properties *lod1Solid* and *lod1MultiSurface*. For the current model lod1Solid property was selected to be implemented, including the following building's attributes: *class, function, measuredHeight* and *storeysAboveGround*. The CityGML class and function attributes of the buildings are obtained from their function property in the dataset. The function code types of the building in the dataset are mapped to the function and class code types in the CityGML standard. As a result, an additional.xlsx file is created, which contains the CityGML function and class attributes of the buildings.

The CityGML standard does not provide specifications and instructions how objects can be geometrically modelled [27]. The *measuredHeight* attribute of the building is the measured or computed difference between the lowest terrain intersection point and the highest roof point. Figure 2 shows different valid heights for different roof overhangs. Since the roof could overhang, roof edges could have a lower elevation than the highest point of the walls. The current implementation of the model considers heights at the roof eaves.

Fig. 2. Different valid representations of building height in LOD1 [28].

The heights of the buildings are not presented in the dataset and therefore the footprints are extruded to their respective heights from the number of floors, depending on the class attribute. Based on this logic *measuredHeight* attribute is preliminary calculated and included in.xlsx file. For example, a building having three floors and a CityGML class "habitation" has received a value of nine meters for *measuredHeight* attribute. Consequently, the 2D footprints can be transformed into 3D solid geometries.

The input data, delivered in.shp and.xlsx files, is merged and transformed in several steps. The FME workflow is depicted in the Fig. 3.

The input data is joined using *FeatureJoiner* transformer. The join is based on the Id property, which matches both input files in one-to-one relation. Next, the Extruder transformer is used to create solid geometries, based on the approximated building heights. In this way, the 2D data is extruded into 3D. Unnecessary attributes in the input data are cleaned using *AttributeKeeper* transformer. Thus, only CityGML relevant data is passed to the next step. FME allows for simple sampling with the Sampler transformer. Within the implemented workflow, it is used to speed up testing. Further, a new attribute "*gml:id*" is added. This is accomplished using the "*AttributeCreator*" transformer, which assigns unique identifiers based on the Id attribute. Next, the buildings' geometries are

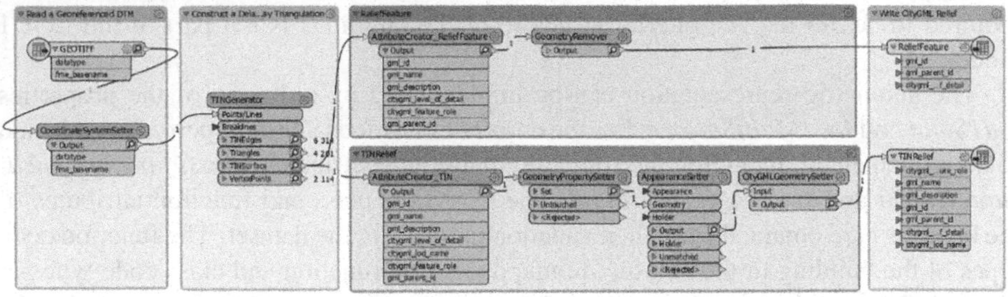

Fig. 3. FME workflow for building modelling.

set up using the *CityGMLGeometrySetter* transformer. The CityGML LOD name is set to "*lod1Solid*" and the feature role is set to "*cityObjectMember*".

The last step of the workflow is the reprojection of the geometries to the desired coordinate system. This is needed since the local footprint polygons are usually projected in a different coordinate system than the base map used for visualisation. Finally, a Writer is used to generate CityGML output for the buildings. A 3D view of the obtained result is shown in Fig. 4.

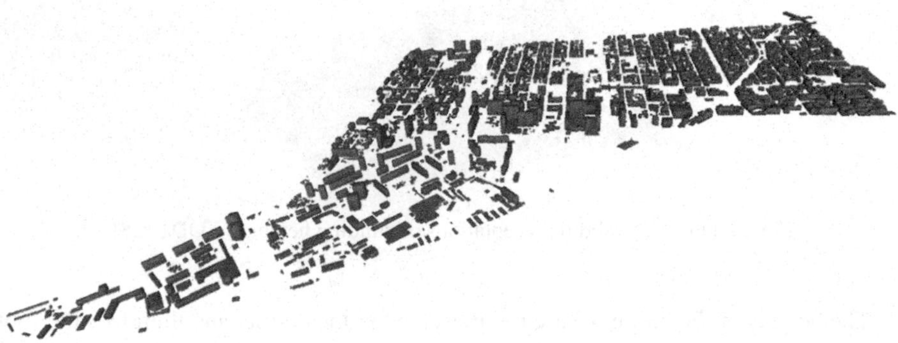

Fig. 4. A 3D view of the buildings.

2.3 Terrain Modelling

CityGML standard supports Digital Terrain Model (DTM) through the thematic module *Relief*. The terrain is modelled using *ReliefFeature* class and could be represented with different concepts – a regular raster or grid, break lines, a Triangular Irregular Network (TIN) or mass points. For the current model the TIN concept is selected, which represents the relief as triangles, implemented by the *TinRelief* class.

The FME workflow for generation of CityGML compliant relief model is shown in Fig. 5. The input data is provided in.tiff format. The transformation starts with construction of a Delaunay triangulation using *TINGenerator* transformer. Next, it is split into two chains. The first chain produces an instance of *ReliefFeature* class. The *AttributeCreator* transformer is used for generation of gml_id, gml_name, gml_description, city_gml_level_of_detail, citygml_feature_role and gml_parent_id attributes for *ReliefFeature*. The *GeometryRemover* transformer uses the gml:id attribute of *ReliefFeature* for aggregation of all geometries from the input file.

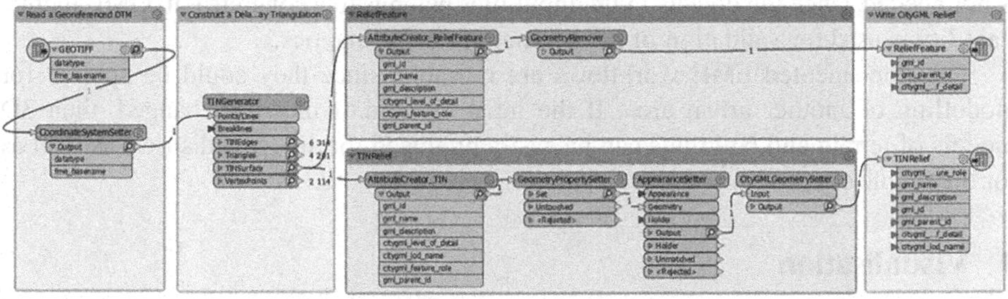

Fig. 5. FME workflow for terrain modelling

The second chain produces an instance of *TinRelief* class. The *AttributeCreator* transformer is used again to set values for gml_id, gml_name, gml_description, city_gml_level_of_detail, citygml_lod_name, city_gml_feature_role and gml_parent_id attributes. The relation between *ReliefFeature* and *TinRelief* instances is specified through gml_id and gml_parent_id attributes. The citygml_lod_name attribute is used to set a trait by *GeometryPropertySetter* transformer. The *AppearanceSetter* transformer sets appearance style of geometries. The *CityGMLGeometrySetter* transformer sets the CityGML LOD name to "tin" and the feature role to "ReliefComponent". Finally, a Writer is used to generate CityGML output for the buildings. A 3D view of the obtained result is shown in Fig. 6.

Fig. 6. A 3D view of relief.

2.4 Validation

The quality of semantic 3D models is essential, especially when they will be used for analysis and simulations. The presented semantic 3D models of the buildings and terrain are validated by open-source tools. 3DCityDB Importer/Exporter is used to check whether the models are actually compliant with CityGML 2.0 schema and can be further imported into 3DCityDB on top of PostGIS. FZK Viewer is useful to check if the 3D models are delivered to the correct CityGML theme. In the current case, such validation is not needed, since the objects in the input files belongs to a concrete CityGML theme. Val3dity is used for validation of the geometries and semantics.

The implemented FME workflows are reusable, since they could be applied for modelling of another urban area. If the input.shp and.tif files are changed, then 3D models of terrain and buildings can be easily produced for different districts as well as for the whole city.

3 Visualisation

A web application is developed for visualizing the CityGML buildings model of district "Vazrajdane". Cesium ion platform is used for streaming and hosting the 3D content, namely the CityGML building model. The hosted 3D content is accessed through its AssetId. CesiumJS is used to visualize the 3D content that is loaded by Cesium ion platform. The web application is hosted on a local web server, which is set up with Node.js – an asynchronous event-driven JavaScript runtime [29]. It is developed as a single HTML page as follows. First, a Cesium Widget is implemented using an ordinary div element (see Listing 1).

Listing 1

```
<div id="cesiumContainer" class="fullSize"></div>
```

Next, an instance Cesium Viewer is created (see Listing 2) and attached to the Cesium Widget. Cesium Viewer provides an interactive 3D globe with rich functionality.

Listing 2

```
var viewer = new Cesium.Viewer("cesiumContainer");
```

In order to visualize the 3D content in the Cesium Viewer, an instance of Cesium3DTileset is created and initialized with the AssetId of the 3D content hosted on Cesium ion platform as it is shown in Listing 3.

Listing 3

```
var tileset = viewer.scene.primitives.add(
  new Cesium.Cesium3DTileset({
    url: Cesium.IonResource.fromAssetId(155869),
  })
)
```

The following functionality is implemented for user interaction:

- Silhouette a building on mouseover and show its class as overlay content;
- Silhouette a building on selection and show its class, function, floor count and height in an information box;

- Show shadows depending on the current time;
- Show buildings in different colours depending on their height, class and latitude;
- Show buildings in transparent style;
- Show buildings with height over 50 m.

A HTML overlay for showing building's class on mouseover is created and appended to the Cesium Viewer. The corresponding code is shown in Listing 4.

Listing 4

```
var nameOverlay = document.createElement("div");
viewer.container.appendChild(nameOverlay);
var name = pickedFeature.getProperty("citygml_class_description");
nameOverlay.textContent = name;
```

In order to silhouette a building, a post-process stage that detects edges is created. The length in pixels and colour of edge are initialised as it is shown in Listing 5.

Listing 5

```
var silhouetteBlue = Cesium.PostProcessStageLibrary.
                              createEdgeDetectionStage();
silhouetteBlue.uniforms.color =
                            Cesium.Color.MEDIUMSLATEBLUE;
silhouetteBlue.uniforms.length = 0.01;
```

The styles of the buildings are implemented through instances of the Cesium3DTileStyle. When default style is applied, the buildings are coloured in white (see Listing 6).

Listing 6

```
var defaultStyle = new Cesium.Cesium3DTileStyle({
        color : "color('white')",
        show : true
    });
```

Additional 3 instances of Cesium3DTileStyle are created for colouring the building by height, by class and by latitude. A separate instance of Cesium3DTileStyle is created for transparent style of the buildings (see Listing 7).

Listing 7

```
var transparentStyle = new Cesium.Cesium3DTileStyle({
        color : "color('white', 0.3)",
        show : true
    });
```

In order to show the buildings with heigh over 50 m, a conditional style is defined as it is shown in Listing 8.

Listing 8

```
var hideStyle = new Cesium.Cesium3DTileStyle({
      show: "${Height} > 50"
   });
```

The shadows if the buildings are shown through setting the *shadow* property of the Cesium Viewer (see Listing 9).

Listing 9

```
var shadowsElement = document.getElementById('shadows');
 shadowsElement.addEventListener('change', function (e) {
      viewer.shadows = e.target.checked;
   });
```

Figure 7 shows the web application for visualization of the buildings' model.

Fig. 7. Buildings' model visualization.

The web application is designed to work independently of the actual CityGML buildings model. If the same model is implemented for another urban area, the only the AssetId of the 3D content hosted on Cesium ion platform needs to be changed. Since

Cesium ion is built on a modern cloud architecture, large datasets can be efficiently streamed into the web application. Thus, the proposed solution could be easily scaled at city level.

4 Conclusions and Future Work

The paper presents the process of creating a semantic 3D city model and its visual representation. The transformation workflow of proprietary data into a CityGML schema using FME was described in detail. The semantic 3D city model covers the buildings and relief thematic modules of CityGML standard. It is hosted on Cesium ion platform and visualized through a simple web application, developed with CesiumJS. The web application provides functionality for user interaction, including silhouetting a building on mouse hover and mouse click and showing overlay content, displaying shadows and styling of buildings.

As a standard CityGML is applicable for areas with various size, and can represent 3D urban objects and terrain in different levels of detail simultaneously. The 3D models, based on CityGML could be simple, single scale models as those presented in the paper as well as very complex multi-scale models. Since, CityGML standardizes the representation of 3D urban objects, providing data consistency, the respective 3D city models could be used in various application domains such as urban and landscape planning, disaster management, environment simulations, vehicle and pedestrian navigation, etc. For example, the 3D city models in high level of detail deliver true picture and real scene of the urban environment, enabling urban planners explore the 3D urban objects in an intuitive and user-friendly way as well as to simulate different planning and design scenarios.

In future work, a computation of *Terrain Intersection Curve* (TIC) is considered. The most commonly used method, including buildings' footprints and DTM, will be applied. A special attention should be given on parts of the terrain without having enough points in between footprints. In such cases, the terrain could be refined through additional terrain points obtained from the original terrain or by integrating footprints of new objects such as trees and streets [30].

Acknowledgement. This work has been supported by GATE project, funded by the Horizon 2020 WIDESPREAD-2018-2020 TEAMING Phase 2 programme under grant agreement no. 857155, by Operational Programme Science and Education for Smart Growth under Grant Agreement No. BG05M2OP001-1.003-0002-C01 and by the Bulgarian National Science fund under project Big4Smart agreement no. DN12/9.

References

1. Biljecki, F., Stoter, J., Ledoux, H., Zlatanova, S., Çöltekin, A.: Applications of 3D city models: state of the art review. ISPRS Int. J. Geo-Information **4**, 2842–2889 (2015)
2. Julin, A., et al.: Characterizing 3D city modeling projects: towards a harmonized interoperable system. ISPRS Int. J. Geo-Information **7**, 55 (2018)

3. Morton, P., Horne, M., Dalton, R., Thompson, E.: Virtual city models: avoidance of obsolescence. In: Proceedings of the 30th eCAADe Conference In Digital Physicality, Prague (2012)
4. Li, W., Zlatanova, S., Diakite, A., Aleksandrov, M., Yan, J.: Towards integrating heterogeneous data: a spatial DBMS solution from a CRC-LCL project in Australia. ISPRS Int. J. Geo-Information **9**, 63 (2020)
5. Arroyo Ohori, K., Biljecki, F., Kumar, K., Ledoux, H., Stoter, J.: Modeling cities and landscapes in 3D with CityGML. In: Borrmann, A., König, M., Koch, C., Beetz, J. (eds.) Building Information Modeling, pp. 199–215. Springer, Cham (2018). https://doi.org/10.1007/978-3-319-92862-3_11
6. Blaschke, T.: Object based image analysis for remote sensing. ISPRS J. Photogramm. Remote Sens. **65**, 2–16 (2010)
7. Tomljenovic, I., Höfle, B., Tiede, D., Blaschke, T.: Building extraction from airborne laser scanning data: an analysis of the state of the art. Remote Sens. **7**, 3826–3862 (2015)
8. Arroyo Ohori, K., Ledoux, H., Stoter, J.: A dimension-independent extrusion algorithm using generalised maps. Int. J. Geogr. Inf. Sci. **29**, 1166–1186 (2015)
9. Shahzad, M., Zhu, X.: Robust reconstruction of building facades for large areas using spaceborne TomoSAR point clouds. IEEE J. Sel. Top. Appl. Earth Obs. Remote Sens. **53**, 752–769 (2015)
10. Soon, H., Khoo, V.H.S.: Citygml modelling for singapore 3D national mapping. ISPRS – Int. Arch. Photogramm. Remote Sens. Spat. Inf. Sci. **42**, 37–42 (2017)
11. Wang, Y., Cheng, Y., Zlatanova, S., Palazzo, E.: Identification of physical and visual enclosure of landscape space units with the help of point clouds. Spat. Cogn. Comput. **20**(3), 257–279 (2020)
12. Yin, X., Wonka, P., Razdan, A.: Generating 3D building models from architectural drawings: a survey. IEEE Comput. Graph. Appl. **29**, 20–30 (2009)
13. Lewis, R., Séquin, C.: Generation of 3D building models from 2D architectural plans. Comput. Aided Des. **30**, 765–779 (1998)
14. Smelik, R., Tutenel, T., Bidarra, R., Benes, B.: A Survey on procedural modelling for virtual worlds. IEEE Comput. Graph. Appl. **33**, 31–50 (2014)
15. Besuievsky, G., Patow, G.: Recent advances on LoD for procedural urban models. In: Proceedings of the 2014 Workshop on Processing Large Geospatial Data, Cardiff, UK (2014)
16. Goetz, M.: Towards generating highly detailed 3D CityGML models from OpenStreetMap. Int. J. Geogr. Inf. Sci. **27**, 845–865 (2013)
17. Over, M., Schilling, A., Neubauer, S., Zipf, A.: Generating web-based 3D city models from OpenStreetMap: the current situation in Germany. Comput. Environ. Urban Syst. **34**, 496–507 (2010)
18. Gröger, G., Kolbe, T., Nagel, C., Häfele, K.: OGC City Geography Markup Language (CityGML) Encoding Standard. Open Geospatial Consortium, Wayland, MA, USA (2012)
19. Beil, C., Kolbe, T.H.: Citygml and the streets of New York - a proposal for detailed street space modelling. ISPRS Ann. Photogramm. Remote Sens. Spat. Inf. Sci. **44**, 9–16 (2017)
20. European Commission: INSPIRE Directive. https://inspire.ec.europa.eu/about-inspire/563. Accessed 20 Mar 2021
21. Yao, Z., Nagel, C., Kunde, F., et. al.: 3DCityDB - a 3D geodatabase solution for the management, analysis, and visualization of semantic 3D city models based on CityGML. Open Geospatial Data Softw. Stand. **3**, 1–26 (2018). https://opengeospatialdata.springeropen.com/track/pdf/10.1186/s40965-018-0046-7.pdf
22. Safe Software: FME Desktop. https://www.safe.com/fme/fme-desktop/. Accessed 22 Jan 2021
23. Bentley OpenCities Map 2D/3D Desktop GIS and Mapping Software. https://www.bentley.com/en/products/product-line/asset-performance/opencities-map. Accessed 22 Jan 2021

24. TU Delft: Solar3Dcity GitHub repository. https://github.com/tudelft3d/Solar3Dcity. Accessed 22 Jan 2021
25. Karlsruhe Institute of Technology: FZKViewer details. https://www.iai.kit.edu/english/1648.php. Accessed 22 Jan 2021
26. Safe Software: FME Software. https://www.safe.com/fme/. Accessed 22 Jan 2021
27. Biljecki, F., Ledoux, H., Stoter, J., Zhao, J.: Formalisation of the level of detail in 3D city modelling. Comput. Environ. Urban Syst. **48**, 1–15 (2014)
28. F. Biljecki, H. Ledoux, Stoter, J.: Height references of CityGML LOD1 buildings and their influence on applications. In: Breunig, M., et al. (eds.) Proceedings of the ISPRS 3D GeoInfo 2014 Conference, November 2014
29. OpenJS Foundation: "Node.js main page,". https://nodejs.org/en/. Accessed 22 Jan 2021
30. Yan, J., Zlatanova, S., Aleksandrov, M., Diakite, A.A., Pettit, C.: Integration of 3D objects and terrain for 3D modelling supporting the digital twin. ISPRS Ann. Photogramm. Remote Sens. Spat. Inf. Sci. **44**, 147–154 (2019)

The Impacts of High-Speed Rail on Territorial Accessibility: A Comparison Among Some European Countries

Francesca Pagliara(✉) and Ilaria Henke

Department of Civil, Architectural and Environmental Engineering, University of Naples Federico II, Naples, Italy
{fpagliar,Ilaria.henke}@unina.it

Abstract. Over the centuries, the means of transport have changed due to the technological development, and one of the most interesting sectors is that of rail, which has experienced a real revolution. Indeed, investments in High Speed Rail (HSR) have been significant and new projects are going to be built around the world. Fast trains represent comfortable, safe, flexible and eco-sustainable means of transport both for people and goods. There is a classification of the effects induced by HSR services, according to which they can be grouped into: impacts on the transport system (internal), socio-economic impacts (external) and environmental impacts (external). Much less studied, however, are the impacts on accessibility. Users living in a given area, characterized by low accessibility to transport, will consequently have low accessibility to job opportunities, health and educational facilities, services, etc. Based on the previous considerations, the purpose of this paper is to study and analyze the impacts on accessibility induced by the introduction of HSR services in four European countries, i.e. Spain, France, Germany and Italy. The main findings show that HSR has brought an increase of accessibility.

Keywords: High Speed Rail · Accessibility measures · European countries

1 Introduction

Over the centuries, the means of transport have changed due to the technological development, and one of the most revolutionized sectors is that of rail transport, which has experienced significant changes in recent years. The revolution in this sector has been represented by the High Speed Rail (HSR). Indeed, significant expansion and new projects have been built and new ones are in the pipeline around the world. Fast trains represent a comfortable, safe, flexible and eco-sustainable means of transport both for people and goods. Major investments in this sector have significantly expanded the length of the European rail network, which in 2016 was more than 8,100 km long and is expected to reach more than 22,000 km by 2025 [1]. In the world, however, at the beginning of 2008, 20,000 km of lines dedicated to the provision of HSR services were in operation

O. Gervasi et al. (Eds.): ICCSA 2021, LNCS 12952, pp. 242–254, 2021.
https://doi.org/10.1007/978-3-030-86973-1_17

for passengers willing to pay for shorter travel times and for an improvement in the quality of rail transport. In the USA, the only HS service is the one that connects Boston to Washington and has been operational since 2001. In the USA, as well as for all of North America, HS is currently underdeveloped, but a large number of projects are going to be promoted. Around 763 km are under construction and more than 2000 km are planned. In Canada and Mexico, where at the moment there is no operational line, about 500 km are planned. In Latin America, no HSR are currently in operation, but approximately 500 km are planned in Brazil. In Africa, only in Morocco there is an operational HSR line, about 200 km long. In the next few years there will be an increase in the extension of the HS lines in the African continent. Indeed, approximately 4,700 km of new lines are planned, 1100 in Morocco, 1,200 in Egypt and 2,400 in South Africa.

A similar case to Africa concerns the Oceanic continent. There is currently no HSR line in operation but approximately 1,750 km are planned in Australia. Significant investments are expected in several Middle Eastern countries in the coming years. Turkey, which currently has about 600 km of operational lines, has planned an extension to 7,400 km. In Iran, between lines under construction and planned, approximately new 3,000 km will be reached. In China, the national railway operating mileage is over 139,000 km, of which 35,000 km is of HSR. China has the largest HSR network in the world, alone accounting for two-thirds of the world's HSR network. The first fully HS line was inaugurated in 2008 between Beijing and Tianjin, coinciding with the Olympic Games. Japan developed the world's first HSR with the Shinkansen line opened in 1964. In this country there are more than 2,000 km of railway line and others are under construction.

A classification of the effects produced by HSR services can be identified, according to which they can be grouped into impacts on the transport system (internal), socio-economic impacts (external) and environmental impacts (external). Much less studied, however, are the impacts on accessibility. The user who lives in a given area characterized by low accessibility to transport will consequently have low accessibility to job opportunities, health and education facilities, services, etc. The purpose of this paper is to study and analyze the impacts on accessibility produced by the introduction of HSR services in four European countries, i.e. Spain, France, Germany and Italy. The manuscript is organized as follows. In Sect. 2 the case studies are described. In Sect. 3 a review of accessibility measures is reported; while Sect. 4 deals with the methodology. Finally, conclusions are described in Sect. 5.

2 The Case Studies

2.1 France

France was the first European nation to enter the high speed era and has the second largest HSR network in Europe after Spain (2814 km compared to almost 2852 km in Spain) but with higher traffic (54 billion of passenger-km compared to 12 billion passenger-km in Spain) (Crozet, 2014). The acronym LGV indicates high-speed lines (Lignes à Grande Vitesse), with TGV instead refers to high-speed trains (Train à Grande Vitesse). In 1975 the first Lyon-Paris high-speed line (TGV South-East) was approved, the opening took place in two stages, the southern section Lyon Sathonay-Saint Florentin, 275 km long, was opened in September 1981 and the 142 km long northern section Combs la Ville (Paris)-Saint Florentin was opened in September 1983 [2, 3]. The success of this line provided the basis for extending the network. In 1989 the Bagneux (Paris)–Connerré Junction (Le Mans) section of the TGV Atlantique line was inaugurated, which was then extended by 101 km in 1990 with the Courtalain Junction - Monts Junction (Tours) section.

In 1992 he opened the Rhône-Alpes TGV line that connects Montanay Junction station to Satolas airport, which was extended in 1994 by 84 km, connecting Satolas airport to St Marcel les Valence. The TGV North Europe line was inaugurated in 1993, is 333 km long and connects Paris to Lille and Lille to Calais. In 1994 the TGV Paris interconnection was opened which allows high-speed trains to serve all French regions without passing through Paris, which ended in 1996 with a 17 km extension link connecting the Northern Europe, South East and Atlantique lines. In 2001 the TGV Méditerranée line (also called LN5 or New Line 5) was inaugurated, connecting Valence to Marseille, 251 km long, the project had started in 1989 but following a series of disputes on the route and anti-TGV protests the works have been delayed [4]. In 2007 the TGV Est line was opened that connects Paris to Strasbourg, passing through Luxembourg, Switzerland and Germany, with a length of 406 km, the first 300 km (connecting Vaires-sur-Marne near Paris to Baudrecourt in the Moselle) can be traveled with a speed of 350 km/h, the remaining 106 instead can support a speed of 320 km. This line forms a commercial network connecting 26 French cities and 11 European cities.

In 2011 the first section of the Rhine-Rhone line was opened which is not directly connected to Paris. In 2017, several LGV lines were inaugurated, one of which, Contournement Nîmes - Montpellier, is the first high-speed line in France built for mixed traffic (goods and passengers), in December 2017 the first freight train crossed the route and, in the July 2018, the first passenger services began. In July 2017, the 340 km long LGV Sud Europe Atlantique line (extension of the Atlantique line) connecting Tours to Bordeaux, the Bretagne-Pays de la Loire line, an extension of the TGV Atlantique, entered into service on the same day. 182 km plus 32 km of connections with the existing network which led to an improvement in the rail service in the countries served.

All French TGV lines are interconnected, today it is possible to go from Calais in the far north to Marseille in the far south of France in just over 3 h with a train traveling at 300 km/h. The LGV network has a star structure (Fig. 1), radiates from Paris and aims to connect the capital with the main cities in order to allow users to move and re-enter during the day. The TGV in France and neighboring countries (including Eurostar and Thalys services) is managed by the SNCF (Société Nationale des Chemins de fer Français) and offers a service dedicated exclusively to passengers. The trains are able to use both dedicated high-speed lines and conventional lines as long as they are electrified, thus serving around 200 French cities, some of which are distant from the LGV lines [3]; Performance in France: From appraisal methodologies to ex-post evaluation]. In addition, TGV trains can serve the UK, Belgium, the Netherlands, Germany, Switzerland and Italy directly [3]. The frequency of services is very high, just think that between Paris and Lyon or Paris and Nantes there are 23 round trips per day. The TGV service is aimed at users who can afford to pay only about 10–15% of the French population use high speed on a regular basis (Crozet, 2013).

Roissy Charles de Gaulle (CDG) airports near Paris and Lyon Saint Exupéry (LYS) are served by TGV stations inside the airport itself, both stations were inaugurated in 1994. The TGV Air service combines international flights, operated by many airlines, with high-speed travel in a single ticket thus allowing you to reach several French cities [3]. A characteristic of the French TGV are the relatively low construction costs, just think that the first South-East TGV cost 4 million per km, the lowest value in the world. In 2013, annual TGV traffic amounted to 90 million passengers.

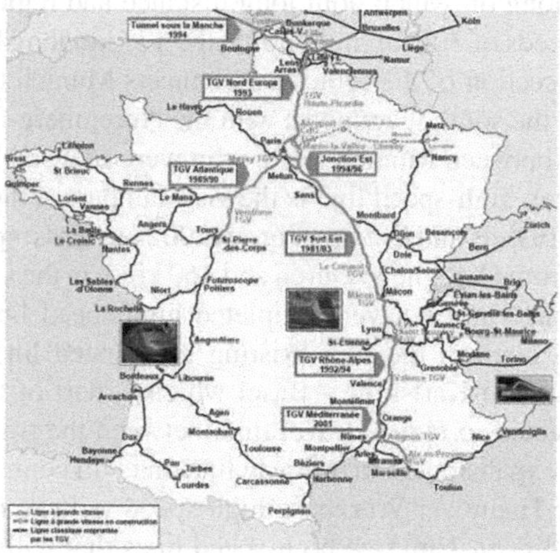

Fig. 1. HSR in France. *Source:* www.evasion-online.com

2.2 Germany

Germany was one of the first European countries to invest in high speed but due to legal disputes the first high speed line was inaugurated after the French LGV lines. The German HSR network was built and extended in two main waves which are structurally very different [5]. During the first wave, which ran from 1991 to 1998, about all the major cities of Germany were connected by the HSR but, being the largest cities distributed unevenly across the territory, the 46 stations existing in 1998 were found only in 3 of the 16 German states (Baden-Württemberg, Hesse, North Rhine-Westphalia). The second wave led to the construction of HSR stations also in the smaller cities located along the ICE connections previously built between two metropolitan areas, during this period 34 medium and small cities were annexed to the network. The reason why even smaller cities have been added to the network is that these cities have been obliged to contribute to the costs of updating the network for the use of high-speed trains, in return stops have been scheduled on their territory. Construction of the first 327 km long high-speed line linking Hanover in Saxony to Wàrzburg in Bavaria began in August 1973 and the line, built section by section between 1988 and 1991, was fully opened in June. in 1991, although the Würzburg-Fulda section was used by InterCity trains as early as 1988 [6]. In 1988 the construction of the Mannheim-Stuttgart line which has a length of 99 km was completed, the line was officially opened in May 1991 and the passenger service began in June of the same year at the same time as the one on the Hannover-Würzburg line.

In 1998 the Berlin-Hanover line was opened consisting of five sections consisting of new and upgraded lines and in 2002 the 182 km long link between the cities of Cologne and Frankfurt was opened and traveled at a speed of 300 km/h, which has alleviated the congestion on the two existing railway lines that bordered the Rhine, this line also allows access to the airports of the two cities. In 2006 the Nuremberg-Munich line was inaugurated, 90.1 km long on which both long-distance and regional services operate, the ICE trains reach speeds of 300 km/h. In 2015, the 123 km long Erfurt - Leipzig/Halle section was opened, a section of the route that connects Munich to Berlin of the trans-European networks, to the south it connects with the Nuremberg-Erfur high-speed line, opened in 2017. travel between Munich and Berlin were reduced by about 4 h.

The Cologne-Aachen high-speed line is the German part of the high-speed network project linking Paris, Brussels and Cologne. From 2002 onwards, speeds of 250 km/h can be reached on the line from Cologne to Düren and 160 km/h in the section between Düren and Aachen. The planned and not yet completed high-speed lines are: 1) Frankfurt-Mannheim which will connect the two existing high-speed lines Cologne-Frankfurt and Mannheim-Stuttgart; 2) Karlsruhe - Basel which is part of the Rotterdam-Genoa corridor, which is expected to reduce travel time between the two cities by 31 min; 3) Hanau-Gelnhausen an expansion of the railway line that will connect the cities of Hanau and Gelnhausen to the Hannover-Würzburg high-speed railway network; 4) Stuttgart-Wendlingen and Wendlingen-Ulm two high-speed lines that will be connected to each other, are part of the Paris-Budapest axis of the trans-European network, once opened the travel time between Stuttgart and Ulm will be only 28 min instead of 54.

To date, the German network extends for 1658 km (Fig. 2). German high-speed trains, InterCityExpress (ICE) do not travel on reserved tracks but use conventional

Fig. 2. HSR in Germany. *Source:* www.forsal.pl

railway lines serving other passenger and freight trains called Ausbaustrecken (ABS) (Barrón et al., 2009), reaching lower speeds, only on short sections the trains travel on dedicated and newly built tracks called Neubaustrecken (NBS). The idea was to use ICE high-speed trains for both passenger and freight transport, but since its introduction, ICE has been used only for passenger transport [7]. The opening and expansion of the HSR network has reduced travel times on average by 9.5% on relationships with a direct connection, leading to an increase in the number of commuters. Between 1996 and 2004 the number of passengers increased by 132.8% [8]. The trains currently in use by the German state railway Deutsche Bahn are 259, which can travel up to a speed of 320 km/h, have a very high level of comfort and the rates are not calculated based on the km but are at fixed prices for connections from station to station.

2.3 Spain

Spain with 2852 km is the second nation in the world, after China, in terms of length of the HSR network (Fig. 3) [9, 10], but relative to the number of trips it ranks after France, Germany and Italy despite their more limited networks. The number of passengers of the HSR service in 2014 in France, Germany and Italy was respectively 5, 4.4 and 2.6 times greater than in Spain. The main purpose of the high-speed train is to build a rapid link between all the provincial capitals of the country and the political capital Madrid [11–13]. The structure of the network gives priority to the connections between Madrid and the provincial capitals over the development of the country's transversal corridors or those that connect tourist destinations along the Mediterranean and the Cantabrian Sea respectively to the east and north of Spain. Spain has made HSR networks a priority in its transport policy, one third of all investments in the country's Transport Infrastructure Strategic Plan (PEIT) are dedicated to HSR [14]. Spain is the only country that starts building high-speed corridors to connect its most populated cities rather than introducing high-speed corridors into the more congested corridors. The first Spanish high-speed connection is the one between Madrid and Seville, with intermediate stations in Ciudad

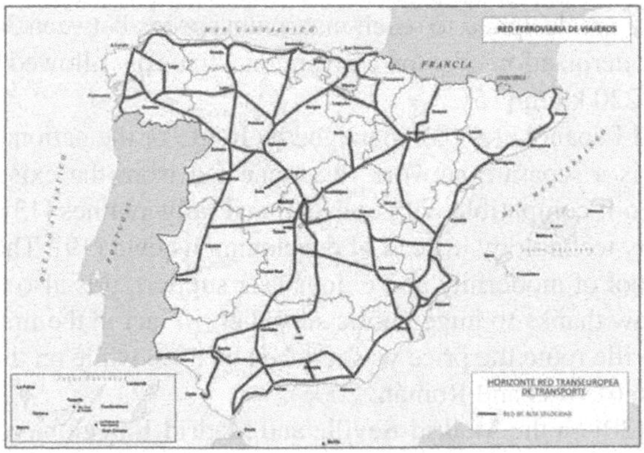

Fig. 3. HSR in Spain. *Source:* https://www.vozpopuli.com/upload/Pablo_Garcia/aveespana-2.jpg

Real, Puertollano and Cordova, which began in 1988 and inaugurated in 1992 on the occasion of the Universal Exhibition held in Seville [15]. The train travels 471.8 km in 2 h and 15 min (direct service train). Traditional rail services have lost a large part of the traffic in this section, but the absence of a complementary freight service has ensured that conventional rail networks remain operational [16].

The construction of the Madrid-Barcelona-France line began in 1998, in 2003 the first 300 km long section connecting Madrid to Zaragoza/Lleida was opened, the second Madrid-Tarragona section was opened three years later and only in February 2008 the line, 621 km long, reached Barcelona [13, 17]. Thus connecting the two largest cities of Spain in 2 h and 30 min by direct train or in 3 h and 10 min with the train that stops at all the stations. In 2013, the Spanish high-speed train was connected to France through direct services on the high-speed network. In January 2001, work began on the infrastructure that connects Madrid to Montilla de Palancar and then divides into two different routes, one that reaches Valencia (inaugurated in 2010) and one that arrives in Alicante (inaugurated in 2013) [17]. In 2002 construction began on the line connecting Madrid to Valladolid via Segovia, inaugurated in 2008 and extended in 2015 to the city of Leon in northern Spain. In 2003 the Zaragoza-Huesca line branch of the Madrid-Barcelona-France line was inaugurated and in 2004 the Madrid-Toledo line was opened, a branch of the Madrid-Seville line that allows to travel between the two cities with a travel time less than 30 min.

In 2008, the Madrid-Malaga line was opened, which in the first 345 km, that is, up to the city of Cordoba, is in common with the Madrid-Seville line, the Cordoba-Malaga connection is 155 km long. The Madrid-Seville and Madrid-Malaga corridors are also used to connect Barcelona to the two cities of Andalucia. In 2015, the extension of the Madrid-Seville section to Cadiz was completed and put into service, and in 2019 the line connecting Antequera to Granada was opened. Not all regions are still connected and some important provinces, in particular the industrial Atlantic coastal regions, the northern and western regions, remain unconnected. New investments are planned in connections with other peripheral regions on the north and west limits of Spain [18]. At the end of the construction of all the high-speed lines, Spain will have 7000 km of lines that will allow you to connect Madrid in 4 h and Barcelona in 6 h to all the provincial capitals. Most lines are designed to reach maximum speeds between 300 and 350 km/h. In addition, the modernization of some conventional lines has allowed high-speed trains to operate at 200–220 km/h [15].

Alta Velocidad Española (AVE), managed by Renfe or the national company of the Iberian railways, is a separate network, disconnected from the existing conventional infrastructure, even if compatible with conventional railway lines [13]. Spain has opted to purchase railway technology instead of developing its own [19]. The Spanish HSR is considered a symbol of modernity and enjoys user support, this also because the high-speed prices are low thanks to huge public subsidies, in fact in the first year of activity, on the Madrid-Seville route the price was reduced by 30% while on the Madrid-Ciudad Real route by 50% (de Rus and Román, 2006).

According to [20] on the Madrid-Seville and Madrid-Barcelona routes there are no significant differences between the emissions of high-speed services and conventional services, for the Madrid-Toledo connection instead the emissions of the HSR service are

50% higher. It should be considered that the first two routes are medium-distance connections while Madrid-Toledo is a short-distance connection and this seems to influence its performance.

2.4 Italy

In Italy the history of the high-speed rail network began in 1975 with the construction of the Rome-Florence line which ended in 1992, on which speeds exceeding 250 km/h were reached [21].The goal was to connect two main cities without intermediate stops. In 1996 the National General Transport Plan establishes high-speed lines as one of the main interventions capable of relaunching rail transport and hence the decision-making and implementation process of the Italian HSR network. In 2005 the second section of the network connecting Naples and Rome was completed and in 2009 the entire Turin-Salerno line was completed [21, 22]. On this line, the speed of 300 km/h is reached except on the Florence-Rome and Naples-Salerno routes where the speed does not exceed 250 km/h. In 2007 the Padua-Mestre high-speed line was completed, a 24 km route alongside the traditional railway, and entry into operation dates back to 2010. In 2016 the entire Milan-Brescia line, 39.6 km long in length, came into operation, which is made up of two lots, the first Milan-Treviglio lot which started operating in 2007 and the second Treviglio-Brescia lot completed in December 2016. The number of high-speed connections is small, only a few cities are served by the HSR. There are several high-speed lines currently under construction: Brescia-Padua, Milan-Genoa, Naples-Bari and Palermo-Catania-Messina. Today in Italy the entire high-speed network is 1,467 km

Fig. 4. HSR in Italy

long (Fig. 4) and only 34% of Italian citizens (20 million inhabitants) are directly served by an HSR station. The objective of the national general transport plan was to build a high-speed network for both passengers and freight trains, to date freight trains have not yet transited on the Italian high-speed network but their transit should start in 2020.

In 2012 a new railway transport operator, NTV-Nuovo Trasporto Viaggiatori, entered the Italian HSR market, bringing Italy to be the only country with competition in the market, this also led to a drop in ticket prices thus making the service accessible to several people.

From 2009 to 2017 the number of travellers using HSR increased by 169% in 8 years, limiting the reference period from 2013 to 2016, there was an increase in demand for AV services of around 40%, compared 8% and only 1.2% for auto and airplane modes. High speed now serves 43 million travellers, of which 7 million represent a demand diverted from the traditional railway network and 19 million are diverted from other modes of transport (for example, private cars). From 2010 to 2017, the demand induced by HSR services in Italy was about 17 million passengers/year, equal to 40% of the total annual demand [21] HSR services in Italy allow people to work in cities other than home, maintaining a "commuter" working model, in particular for the cities of Rome and Naples [23].

The internal impacts due to high-speed trains are: an increase in speed of about 32% compared to the traditional railway, considering also the stop time at the intermediate stops, an average effective speed of 164 km/h is reached, thus reducing the travel time between major cities; greater services offered to HSR travellers rather than traditional users (wi-fi network, waiting rooms, dedicated ticket offices, free newspapers, etc.); high frequency (34 trains travelled on the Naples-Rome route before the HSR on a weekday, but today about 94 trains travel with a train rush hour every 6 min).

The external impacts produced by the HSR are visible on the tourism market and on the environmental system. the external cost of the HSR is 70% lower than that of a car and 59% less than that of the airplane. The amount of CO2 saved for people who travel with the HSR service compared to cars and planes is about 700 thousand tons/year, an amount equivalent to the emissions produced by urban travel in a metropolis in a year.

The goal of the Italian government is to extend high speed to the whole peninsula, serving the main Italian cities. For the moment, the cities served by high speed are still few, it will take several years before the Italian subway is completed.

3 Transport Accessibility Measures

In the last century, transport has changed the space-time conception of the individual, guaranteeing accessibility to services, goods and opportunities never reached before. The concept of accessibility has long been discussed in the research on transportation planning as a measure of "*the extent and quality of the interaction between land development patterns of a given area and the transportation systems serving it*" [24] The very definition of accessibility can boast numerous and different interpretations, each representative of the approach followed and, therefore, poorly suited to having a general character. The evolution of interpretations is closely linked to the evolution over time of the purposes of accessibility studies.

The first ever who presented a first attempt to define accessibility is Reilly [25], who demonstrates an analogy with the universal gravitational law. For Shimble [26] accessibility is defined in a simplified form, in practice it is represented as the sum of the distances of zone j from all other zones of the study area. With Hansen [27] accessibility varies directly with the size of place j and inversely with an attribute of spatial separation between the two areas.

Ten years later, Wilson (1967), starting from Hansen's accessibility measure, proposed an impedance function in which the generalized cost appears as a linear combination by means of the homogenization coefficients of a cost attribute and a travel time attribute.

In 1971, Ingram [28] expressed the accessibility of an area simply as a function of spatial impedance. Starting from Shimble [26], an index was proposed based on an impedance function averaged over all the areas with respect to which the accessibility itself is calculated.

In 1971, however, Wickstram [29] highlighted that accessibility should be a function of the opportunities present in the territory and the time needed to reach them and expressed accessibility as a cumulative function of opportunities that could be achieved in a given time frame.

From 1975 to 1979 the indices based on gravitational analogy, although powerful tools, did not allow highlighting the direct relationship between accessibility and the choices made by users. As a consequence, users residing in the same area perceived the same accessibility, regardless the socio-economic class to which they belonged to, the modes of transport available and their travel choices. For this reason, the studies led to the development of the concept of accessibility in the light of the theory of random utility.

Burns et al. [30] introduced a behavioural approach, which provided a new and interesting definition of accessibility, associating it with the freedom of users to decide whether or not to participate in different activities in the area. Utility measures tried to best represent the choices of individuals with respect to possible paths to reach a given destination by identifying that path minimizes utility but actually maximizing accessibility.

Papaioannou and Martinez [31] introduced a new definition of accessibility, tackling the problem from an economic point of view by defining accessibility as the set of economic benefits deriving from the interaction between two activities for a specific purpose. The economic benefits are obtained from the difference between the benefits deriving from the contact between the two entities minus the cost of the interaction.

Monzón et al. [32] defined numerous accessibility indicators, based on the travel time of a network, i.e. the cost/time represented along the transport infrastructures.

The methodological contribution of this paper is twofold. Firstly, a general index is designed to assess the complete connectivity and accessibility levels of the HSR network. Secondly, this paper investigates how to quantify the impact of the future HSR network on the different levels of the cities over different time periods based on the change in the overall connectivity/accessibility index.

4 The Impact of HSR on Accessibility

HSR significantly reduces travel time between cities compared to the speed of a conventional line, the rapid development of HSR has raised questions about its implications for accessibility. In this paper the focus is on the main European countries above described. The variation in accessibility induced by the introduction of HSR over the years has been analysed, starting from the year 2000 till 2018. For Spain, 46 provinces have been considered; for Italy 102 provinces have been considered, for France 99 cities for the Germany 47 cities have been taken into account.

To evaluate the accessibility variations induced by the AV in the case studies considered, an accessibility measure has been proposed, based on the variation of the generalized cost expressed with the following equation:

$$A = \Delta CG = \Delta[(\sum_{o=1}^{N} CG_{od} * Addd)/(\sum_{o=1}^{N} Ad_o)]$$

where:

CG_{od} is the generalised travel cost between two zones;

Add_d is the number of jobs (number of opportunities available in a given zone d).

The cost of the trip is calculated based on the Value Of Time. The reference VOT values (€/hour) considered for the estimates are those proposed by the European Commission in the "Mobility and Transport" section (2016) which results in a value of 19 €/h for extra-urban trips in Spain, 27 €/h in France, € 31/h in Germany and € 22/h in Italy.

To estimate the variation of the generalized cost for each country OD matrices related to travel times with the fastest railway service and the relative ticket cost to and from the cities considered have been estimated.

The results obtained show that in Spain, taking into account only OD pairs served by HSR (where the path is on a HSR section), the variation in 18 years (2018–2000) of the generalised cost is equal to −29% and for a traditional line is of −19%, therefore, on average on the network there has been an increase in accessibility with a reduction in the generalized cost on average of −24%. This happens because even the cities, the areas, not located on the HSR network have benefited from the service, in fact from the traditional service it is possible to switch to the fastest one. In Germany, on average on the network there has been an increase in accessibility with a reduction in the average generalized cost of −12%. This result is similar to the Spanish one but with a slighter decrease caused by the fact that the German network is not very extended in addition to the fact that the HS lines are already existing lines, renewed with a lower commercial speed.

Finally, similar conclusions also emerge from the studies carried out on all the French provinces. From Table 1 it can be seen that for France an overall reduction of −14% is reported, a result that would apparently be odd as the railway network is very capillary but it has been noted that the monetary cost over time increases a lot compared to the other countries considered. The accessibility measure in Italy as well has been calculated from the year 2000 to 2018. The results (consistent with the results of Cascetta et al. [33]) show that the introduction of the HSR service has produced a very significant increase in accessibility caused by the decrease of the generalised cost for long-distance areas.

Table 1. Results

	Δ (2018–2000) HSR network generalised cost	Δ (2018–2000) No HSR network generalised cost	Δ (2018–2000) Network generalised cost
Spagna	−29%	−19%	−24%
Germania	−14%	−10%	−12%
Francia	−18%	−9%	−14%
Italy	−26%	−3%	−9%

5 Conclusions and Further Perspectives

Similarly, to the construction of a new airport or the opening of a new motorway to traffic, the construction of a new HSR line falls within the typology of interventions on the transport system that generally introduces significant changes in the transport supply with inevitable social, economic and environmental impacts for the areas involved. For this reason, the impacts induced by the HSR infrastructures and the related services have been extensively studied in many countries in relation to the specific socio-economic and territorial characteristics, as well as at different levels of service variables (e.g. average speed, frequencies, etc.).

These results are relevant from an operational practical point of view, as they suggest significant insights in the context of transport planning. Transport policies and investments should aim at increasing accessibility, but often transport infrastructures and services are implemented precisely where there are more transport opportunities and demands to justify them. This is partly due to the fact that social justice considerations are much more difficult to measure than other factors relating to, for example, traffic speed or environmental pollution. In the future, more could potentially be done to make accessibility a less "intangible" aspect of transport planning.

Furthermore, it is important to emphasize that the accessibility measure used in this work could be enriched with many other variables in order to be able to carry out a broader and more complete analysis of this problem.

References

1. Cascetta, E.: Perché TAV. Risultati, prospettive e rischi di un Progetto Paese. Edited by Il sole 24 ore (2019)
2. Bonnafous, A.: The regional impact of the TGV. Transportation **14**, 127–137 (1987)
3. Arduin, J.-P., Ni, J.: French TGV network development. Japan Railway Transp. Rev. **40**, 22–28 (2005)
4. Leheis, S.: High-speed train planning in France: lessons from the Mediterranean TGV-line. Transp. Policy **21**, 37–44 (2012)
5. Heuermann, D.F., Schmieder, J.F.: The effect of infrastructure on worker mobility: evidence from high-speed rail expansion in Germany. J. Econ. Geogr. **19**, 335–372 (2019)
6. Ebeling, K.: High speed railway in Germany. Japan Railway Transp. Rev. **40**, 36–45 (2005)
7. Deutsche Bahn (2016). https://www.bahn.de/

8. Lee, Y.S.: A study of the development and issues concerning high speed rail (HSR). Transport Studies Unit, Oxford University Center for the Environment (2007)
9. Albalate, D., Bel, G.: Cuando la economía no importa: auge y esplendor de la alta velocidad en españa. Revista de Economía Aplicada **19**(55), 171–190 (2011)
10. Albalate, D., Fageda, X.: High speed rail and tourism: empirical evidence from Spain. Transp. Res. Part A **85**, 174–185 (2016)
11. Bel, G.: Infrastructure and nation building: the regulation and financing of network transport infrastructures in Spain (1720–2010). Bus. Hist. **53**(5), 688–705 (2011)
12. Bel, G.: Infrastructure and the Political Economy of Nation Building in Spain, 1720–2010. Sussex Academic Press, Eastbourne (2012)
13. Albalate, D., Bel, G.: High-speed rail: lessons for policy makers from experiences abroad. Public Adm. Rev. **72**(3), 336–349 (2012)
14. Bel, G.: Transport policy: more investment or better management? Economistas **111**, 279–284 (2007)
15. Beria, P., Grimaldi, R., Albalate, D., Bel, G.: Delusions of success: costs and demand of high-speed rail in Italy and Spain. Transp. Policy **68**, 63–79 (2018)
16. de Rus, G., Nash, C.: In what circumstances is investment in HSR worthwhile? ITS Working Paper, 590, University of Leeds (2007)
17. Betancor, O., Llobet, G.: Estudios sobre la economía española, Contabilidad Financiera y Social de la Alta Velocidad en España (2015)
18. Campa, J.L., Arce, R., López-Lambas, M.E., Guirao, B.: Can HSR improve the mobility of international tourists visiting Spain? Territorial evidence derived from the Spanish experience. J. Transp. Geogr. **73**, 94–107 (2018)
19. Vickerman, R.: High-speed rail in Europe: experience and issues for future development. Ann. Reg. Sci. **31**(1), 21–38 (1997)
20. García Alvarez, A.: Energy consumption and high-speed train emissions compared with other transportation modes. Anales de Mecánica y Electricidad **84**(5), 26–34 (2007)
21. Cascetta, E., Coppola, P.: Evidence from the Italian high-speed rail market: competition between modes and between HSR operators. In: High-Speed Rail and Sustainability (2017)
22. Cascetta, E., Coppola, P.: High Speed Rail (HSR) induced demand models. Procedia – Soc. Behav. Sci. **111**, 147–156 (2014)
23. Cascetta, E., Papola, A., Pagliara, F., Marzano, V.: Analysis of mobility impacts of the high speed Rome-Naples rail link using withinday dynamic mode service choice models. J. Transp. Geogr. **19**, 635–643 (2011)
24. Cascetta, E., Cartenì, A., Montanino, M.: A behavioral model of accessibility based on the number of available opportunities. J. Transp. Geogr. **51**, 45–58 (2016)
25. Reilly, W.J.: The Law of Retail Gravitation. Knickerbocker Press, New York (1931)
26. Shimble, A.: Structural parameters of communication networks. Bull. Math. Biophys. **15**, 501–507 (1953). https://doi.org/10.1007/BF02476438
27. Hansen, W.G.: How accessibility shapes land use. J. Am. Inst. Planners **25**(2), 73–76 (1959)
28. Ingram, D.R.: The concept of accessibility: a search for an operational form. Reg. Stud. **5**(2), 101–107 (1971)
29. Wickstram, C.E.: The Credibility Gap and the Ecology Reaction (1971)
30. Burns, R.B.: The Self Concept in Theory, Measurement, Development, and Behaviour. Addison-Wesley Longman Limited (1979)
31. Papaioannou, D., Martinez, L.M.: The role of accessibility and connectivity in mode choice. A structural equation modeling approach. Transp. Res. Procedia **10**, 831–839 (2015)
32. Monzón, A., Ortega, E., López, E.: Efficiency and spatial equity impacts of high-speed rail extensions in urban areas. Cities **30**, 18–30 (2013)
33. Cascetta, E., Cartenì, A., Henke, I., Pagliara, F.: Economic growth, transport accessibility and regional equity impacts of high-speed railways in Italy: ten years ex post evaluation and future perspectives. Transp. Res. Part A **139**, 412–428 (2020)

Sport-City Planning. A Proposal for an Index to Support Decision-Making Practice: Principles and Strategies

Ginevra Balletto[1(✉)], Giuseppe Borruso[2], Alessandra Milesi[1], Mara Ladu[1], Paolo Castiglia[3], Marco Dettori[3], and Antonella Arghittu[3]

[1] DICAAR - Department of Civil and Environmental Engineering and Architecture, University of Cagliari, 09100 Cagliari, Italy
{balletto,mara.ladu}@unica.it

[2] DEAMS - Department of Economics, Business, Mathematics and Statistics Sciences "Bruno de Finetti", University of Trieste, 34127 Trieste, Italy
giuseppe.borruso@deams.units.it

[3] DMCS - Department of Medical, Surgical and Experimental Sciences, University of Sassari, Sassari, Italy
{paolo.castiglia,madettori}@uniss.it

Abstract. Currently more than half of the world population - between formal and informal urban settlements - has been affected by the health crisis. In cities there are great difficulties in facing the new challenges that are intertwined between urban-environmental and economic aspects. Cities were among the first and most affected areas hit by the epidemic, however they have always been places of maximum creativity and innovation, deriving precisely from the aggregation processes of social and economic networks. These same networks actually favored the spread of the health crisis. In recent months, many scenarios have been advanced for a renewed urban development, to favor the reduction of contacts, including the idea of 'villages' and the "city of 15 min". In this framework, some questions arise: what are the multi-sectoral policies that can make cities more inclusive, sustainable, reducing vulnerability and health risks? What individual commitment can cities make into a model of health promotion? These questions guided the authors in evaluating the role of the Sport-city in the research of the post-pandemic city through qualitative/quantitative indicators in the main Italian provinces and metropolitan cities, between health and well-being and environment, proposing a specific index (UPA - Urban Physical Activity Index) to support Sport-city planning initiatives aimed at the health-well-being of communities through urban design.

The paper is part of the activities of the Interdepartmental Center "Cagliari Accessibility Lab" of the University of Cagliari. This study was supported by the research grant for the project "Investigating the relationships between knowledge-building and design and decision-making in spatial planning with geodesign" funded by Fondazione di Sardegna (2018).
This paper is the result of the joint work of the authors. In particular: Sect. 1 has been written by G. Balletto. Sect. 2 has been written by P. Castiglia, M. Dettori, A. Arghittu; Sect. 3.1 by A. Milesi, M. Ladu; Sect. 3.2 by G. Balletto, Sect. 3.3 by A. Milesi, M. Ladu; Sect. 4 by G. Balletto; Sect. 5 by A. Milesi, M. Ladu; Sect. 6 by Ginevra Balletto and Sect. 7 by G. Borruso.

O. Gervasi et al. (Eds.): ICCSA 2021, LNCS 12952, pp. 255–269, 2021.
https://doi.org/10.1007/978-3-030-86973-1_18

Keywords: Health city · Sport city · Metropolitan cities · Urban planning · Post pandemic city

1 Introduction

The research hereby presented is part of a wider, multidisciplinary project the authors have been carried on since the recent Covid-19 outbreak, aware that the topics related to planning at urban and regional level need an integrated and multifaceted approach and a particular care and attention towards health issues. The paper, in particular, was aimed at stressing the importance of physical activity in improving the quality of life and health. In such a sense, the attention has been on analyzing the performances of Sardinian provinces and the metropolitan city in terms of the parameters that are more likely to positively affect human health from the planning point of view.

To do that, a novel approach was adopted, as that of considering in a combined index the performances that characterize the different areas considered – provinces and the metropolitan city of Cagliari in the Sardinia region and island – considering the structured and unstructured activities that can be addressed to sport and other "healthy" activities. The attention in particular was on urban planning and therefore on how such indicators can be used both as a means to evaluate the effect of a set of actions put in place by local governments, and as a suggestion for future policies for improving the quality of urban life.

This contribution is divided into the following parts:

- Background of health aspects (Sect. 2), which focuses on health aspects referred to the city;
- Materials (Sect. 3), which focuses on the urban and geographic aspects (Sect. 3.1), on the recent advances in the scientific debate relating to the identification of indicators to measure the health-well-being of communities (Sect. 3.2), with particular reference to regional and intermediate level indicators to support Sport-city planning in Sardinia (Sect. 3.3);
- Methods (Sect. 4) in which a method is proposed for the determination of an Urban Physical Activity index (UPA Index);
- Case study (Sect. 5).
- Results and Discussion (Sect. 6) which analyzes the results obtained;
- Conclusions (Sect. 7).

2 Background of Health Aspects

Regular physical activity (PA) is one of the major lever factors in general health prevention. It has been demonstrated that it reduces morbidity and mortality by decreasing heart disease, diabetes, high blood pressure, colon cancer, feelings of depression/anxiety and weight, building and maintaining healthy bones, muscles, and joints [1–9]. It has been demonstrated that 30 min of moderate PA, such as daily walking, is recommended to obtain significant health benefits [10, 11]. Despite the well-known benefits for health, large proportions of the population in many developed countries are physically inactive. Today the insufficient PA is a growing global concern, with estimates ranging from 33% of adults worldwide who are physically inactive [12]. Globally, approximately 9% of premature mortality is attributable to insufficient PA [13, 14]. In Europe, a sedentary lifestyle is assumed to be responsible for about 600,000 deaths per year, with a percentage between 5 and 10% of total mortality by country, and the loss of 5.3 million years of life in good health. In addition, PA tends to decrease with increasing urbanization [15]. This is the reason why today an effective collaboration between public health professionals, sociologists, psychologists, economists, urban planners, architects, and public safety officers is needed to design feasible interventions, both physical and intangible, that support an enhancement of PA level [1]. In Italy, the situation is similar and many observational epidemiological studies offer an indicative framework of the reality. According to the Cardiovascular Epidemiological Observatory, on average, 34% of men and 46% of women aged 35–74 do not perform any PA during leisure time. Among them, the elderly population (men and women aged 65–74) amounts to 31% of men and 51% of women [16]. The national survey of the Health Surveillance System, labelled "OKkio alla salute 2019", on eating habits and PA of primary school children of 6–10 years, shows that 20.3% of children play sport for no more than one hour per week and did not exercise the day before the interview. Only 1 out of 4 children went to school on foot or by bicycle [17]. Another national survey, named "Health Behaviour in School-aged Children - Italy", regards children aged 11, 13, and 15 years old, and it shows that the fifteen-agers do less PA (47.5% of males and 26.6% of females) than the thirteen-agers (50.9% males and 33.7% females) and that females perform less physical activity than their peers in all three age groups examined during the investigation [18]. Data obtained from the national surveillance system "PASSI" ("Progressi delle Aziende Sanitarie per la Salute in Italia"), which monitors the health of the adult Italian population of 18–69 years, showed that during the period 2013–2016 about 32.5% of interviewees were completely sedentary [19]. The habit of PA is not the same in all Italian regions and the analysis of local data shows a North-South gradient. In particular, in the Sardinia Region, it is estimated that 26% of the population can be considered completely sedentary. There is also a distorted perception of the PA: 12% of sedentary people believed to practice enough. The percentage of sedentary remains very high even in subgroups of the population that could benefit most thereof (particularly people with symptoms of depression, hypertensive, obese or overweight). It should be reported that the operators in the health sector do not yet sufficiently promote active lifestyles among their patients, although this data varies among Local Health Agencies. The positive effects of PA are evident both socially and economically. Strategies to increase active living are receiving widespread attention and support across several sectors. Indeed, this important goal can only be achieved with the application of cross-sectorial strategies, with interventions on the environmental, social, and economic factors that together influence the adoption of active lifestyles [19].

The idea that a walkable environment may function as an important vector for health promotion in urban areas is widely accepted and sustained among scholars and professionals of social health and planning domains. A social-ecological perspective on health suggests that social and environmental factors play an important role in increasing physical activity [20]. There is growing scientific evidence that urban design features at the neighborhood level such as green spaces, parks, pedestrian areas, etc., are associated with an increased PA and with beneficial health impacts on the population [21–24]. As a consequence, environmental and policy approaches to promote physical activity, such as walking trail construction and promotion, sustainable mobility policies, environment, and urban design favoring walking and cycling and physical activity in general, are being widely recommended, yet sparse data exist on their effectiveness [25–27].

3 Materials

3.1 Materials: Urban Geographic Aspects

The link between the physical characteristics of urban contexts and public health impacts open new scenarios between Urban Health [23] and Sport-city (Spatial integration of sports facilities and mixing sport (structured and/or unstructured) [28]. Furthermore, since 54% of the world population lives in urban areas, with a forecast of 70% by 2050, it follows the strategic and decisive role of jointly planning built environments and open spaces, such as: pedestrian areas, cycle paths, parks and environmental ecosystem services [29–31]. The risk factors related to urbanization include the following macro-categories: urban heat islands [32, 33] and air pollution [34], apparently disjoint, but at present related to each other [35, 36]. In this sense, scientific knowledge and design practice identify health-sport urban planning and design strategies, through: green infrastructures, cycle and pedestrian areas [30]; and more generally a social and functional mix derived from urban and environmental regeneration [37–40] according to the principle - Design for All [41]. Furthermore, although the sport industry is criticized, because it is often incompatible with the principles of sustainability [42, 43], on the contrary, interventions aimed at community sport - open to all by age and status, help to enhance the strategic role of public space outdoor [44] on individual and collective health [45]. In this sense, in Italy, PA increases from generation to generation [46, 47], stabilizing around the age of 50. This increase is influenced by the level of education (52% of those who practice PA are graduates). In Italy, more than four out of ten people practice PA in a completely unstructured way, that is, in full autonomy, preferring open spaces and not always equipped [48]. The health crisis, like all previous epidemics, has recalled the need to combine: community, health and urban design. In this sense we intend to evaluate in qualitative and quantitative terms the role of the Sport-city for a renewed urban development in the light of the recent health emergency, proposing a specific index (UPA Urban Physical Activity) to support the post-pandemic city.

3.2 Fair and Sustainable Well-Being (Bes) Index

In the last twenty years, the scientific debate on measuring the health-well-being of communities has developed a lot [49]. The international crises (energy-environmental, financial-real estate, economic-social and recently also health) have made it urgent to develop new parameters capable of supporting political decision-makers in defining new scenarios. In particular, with the "Fair and Sustainable Well-being (Bes)" index, the National Council for Economy and Labor (CNEL) and the National Statistical Institute (ISTAT) responded to the need to identify indicators on the state of health and well-being in Italy [50]. The report on Fair and Sustainable Wellbeing (published annually, Italy) is at the forefront of the international scene in terms of development of indicators (regional and sometimes provincial level) and aims to integrate GDP (gross domestic product), not more sufficient to represent the complexity of contemporary society. The set of indicators proposed for about a decade express the multidimensionality of health-well-being and the numerous aspects that contribute to the quality of life of the community. Over the years, new indicators have been introduced, collected in 12 domains. Since 2016, some Bes indicators have become part of the national economic planning process (Law 163/2016), used in the Economics and Finance Document, to assess the impact of the proposed policies. According to the latest Bes 2020 report [51] - due to the health emergency - the following synthetic picture emerged in Italy (Table 1):

Table 1. The Italian condition according to the Bes Report 2020. Authors: A. Milesi and M. Ladu

Object	Year	↑ ↓	Value (%)
Sedentary people	2020		34%
Sedentary lifestyle_Gap women – men	2010–2020	↓	7,8%–6,3% (women are more sedentary than men)
Sedentary lifestyle_Age	2020		20% (from adolescents to people aged 24) 70% (people aged 75 and over)
Sedentary lifestyle_ Central IT	2019–2020	↓	35,1%–30,2%
People who practiced physical activity for 1 average day	2020 (1st lockdown)		22,7% (people aged 18 and over)
Overweight people	2020	↑	45,5%
Overweight people_men	2020		54,7%
Overweight people_women	2020		36,9%
Overweight people_ Northern IT	2019–2020	↑	42,1%–43,4%
Overweight people_ Southern IT	2019–2020	↑	49,3%–50,4%
Overweight people_ Central IT	2019–2020	↓	43,7%–42,2%

In particular, with the health emergency in Italy in 2020 there was:

- an expectation life of 82.3 years (down by 0.9 years compared to 2019 data); this was especially evident in Northern Italy and is more evident in Lombardy, where there was a decrease of 2.4 years compared to 2019;
- a difficulty in accessing health care: in fact, 1 in 10 citizens did not use it even if they needed it. Furthermore, the health emergency pushes to accelerate the implementation

of the 2030 Agenda in a logic of transformative resilience: not by going back to the pre-crisis situation, but to boost a decisive change in urban development models based on sustainability, locally and globally, of territories and communities jointly [52]. In fact, the health crisis has highlighted the need for a change of perspective through territorial and urban design approaches that put the health and well-being of the community at the center.

3.3 Regional and Intermediate Indicators to Support Sport-City Planning. The Sardinia Case

The Sardinia Region has geographical and climatic characteristics that allows practicing a significant variety of outdoor sports - hiking, swimming, running, sailing. In particular, in the city of Cagliari, the regional capital, as well as a metropolitan city, the PA (structured and unstructured) has been enhanced in the last 10 years [30]. With the recognition of "European City of Sport" for 2017 (European City of Sport) by ACES Europe, Federation of Capitals and European Cities of Sport, in the city of Cagliari it has been established that all the PA constitutes a fundamental part for the health-well-being of the community, promoting socialization and social inclusion, as well as the dissemination of civic and ethical values [53].

Table 2. Bes indicators for main factors correlated to the PA, referring to the Sardinia Region (SAR) and the national context (IT). Authors: A. Milesi and M. Ladu

		2018		2019		2020	
		SAR	IT	SAR	IT	SAR	IT
Health	Bes_1.11	38.2	44.8	39.7	44.9	42.5	45.5
	Bes_1.14	33.8	35.7	34.6	35.5	31	33.8
Education and training	Bes_2.2	51.5	61.7	54.2	62.2	53.7	62.6
	Bes_2.3	21.5	27.8	21.6	27.6	–	–
Job and reconciliation of lifetime	Bes_3.1	56.1	63	57.3	63.5	55.4	62
Economic well-being	Bes_4.9	19.3	11.3	15.6	10	–	–
Social relations	Bes_5.9	17	21	20.1	23.9	23.4	23.7
Subjective well-being	Bes_8.2	63.6	66.2	63.7	68	69.6	69.4
Environment	Bes_10.8	78.6	70.1	73.2	69	76.2	70.1

where: Bes_1.11: Excess weight (Standardized rates per 100 people); Bes_1.14: Sedentary lifestyle (Standardized rates per 100 people); Bes_2.2: People with at least a high school diploma (25–64 anni); Bes_2.3: Graduates and similar (30–34 years); Bes_3.1: Employment rate (20–64 years); Bes_4.9: Low labor intensity (%); Bes_5.9: Generalized trust (%); Bes_8.2: Leisure satisfaction (%); Bes_10.8: Satisfaction with the environmental situation (%).

The important recognition comes from the enhancement and promotion of the PA in programs and projects for the transformation and regeneration of entire urban areas, both on a local scale and of supra-local and territorial interest [28]. Among the most important public initiatives of strategic importance, some already completed, others in the construction phase or planned, are the recovery project of the Lungomare Poetto (about 10 km) and the project for the new stadium (30,000 seats) [54]. Following the assessments developed previously, some Bes indicators were selected for the case of the Region of Sardinia on the basis of the main factors related to the PA: health, education and training, work and reconciliation of life times, economic well-being, social relations, well-being and subjective environment (Table 2) [55]. From Table 2 it emerges that Sardinia always presents values very close to the Italian average. On the other hand, they are higher in relation to the low intensity of work (Bes_4.9) and satisfaction with the environmental situation (Bes_10.8). Also the indicator on subjective well-being (Bes_8.2) slightly exceeds the Italian average for the year 2020. Furthermore, the data on excess weight (Bes_1.11), shows a constantly increasing trend both in Sardinia and in Italy, although sedentary lifestyle decreases slightly (Bes_1.14). This analysis, however, is based on data referring to the years prior to the spread of the Covid-19 pandemic and, therefore, to the restrictions that in fact limited the free movement of people, modifying lifestyles, also in reference to PA. To complete the representation of the PA in the urban environment, the two parts that make it up were then evaluated: structured and de-structured activity. By structured activity we mean activities related to sports federations, managed by specific subjects (public or private), while by de-structured activity we mean all those activities carried out outdoors individually and/or collectively, in a self-managed manner. In particular, the structured activity was represented by the sportsmanship index proposed by 'Il Sole 24 ore' [56] which, for the year 2020, considered the effect on sport deriving from the health emergency. Below the summary of the data relating to the position (Ranking) and the sportsmanship index (Score) attributed to each province of the Sardinia Region in the three-year period 2018, 2019 and 2020 is shown (Table 3). The data reveal how the metropolitan city of Cagliari always holds high positions in the national ranking, strongly detaching itself from the positions held by the other provinces of the Region, starting with the one closest to it, the province of Southern Sardinia, confirming the central role that the metropolitan area continues to perform with respect to its immediate territorial context. Since 2018, the year following the achievement of the title of European City of Sport, Cagliari has stood in third place in Italy, falling to ninth place in 2019 and fifteenth in 2020, according to a downward trend due, for this last year, the restrictions due to the spread of the COVID-19 pandemic, which resulted in the closure of sports facilities, the interruption and postponement of a series of amateur and competitive sporting events.If it is true that the province of Southern Sardinia recorded a sharp decline in 2020, the provinces of Oristano and Nuoro, in central Sardinia, record positions among the last in the national rankings in all three years analyzed in this study. It could therefore be argued that the COVID-19 effect has generated more evident negative impacts in the metropolitan city of Cagliari and in the province of Southern Sardinia. The de-structured sporting activity required a specific elaboration, proposed by the authors, based on the quantitative evaluation of pedestrian areas, cycle paths and parks [57, 58] closely linked to urban design.

Table 3. Sport index score (S) and ranking (R) assigned to the provinces of the Sardinia Region in 2018, 2019 and 2020. Authors: A. Milesi and M. Ladu

	2018		2019		2020	
Provinces	S	R	S	R	S	R
Cagliari	828.79	3	773.61	9	790.24	15
Sud Sardegna	228.97	71	202.7	79	180.41	104
Oristano	205.68	97	217.7	97	270.07	91
Nuoro	167.63	103	158	105	163.22	105
Sassari	395.46	60	426.01	58	477.48	56

Figure 1 compares the data relating to structured and de-structured sporting activity in the provinces of Sardinia and the metropolitan city of Cagliari for the three-year period 2018, 2019 and 2020.

				2018	2019	2020
CAGLIARI						
	SPORT	structured	sportsmanship index	828.79	773.61	790.24
		unstructured	Pedestrian areas (sqm/inh)	0.5	0.5	0.2
			bicycle-line (sqm/100 inh)	4.5	4.4	3.4
			Urban green (sqm/inh)	54.8	54.9	54.8
SUD Sardegna						
	SPORT	structured	sportsmanship index	228.97	202.7	180.41
		unstructured	Pedestrian areas (sqm/inh)	0.5	0.5	0.2
			bicycle-line (sqm/100 inh)	4.5	4.4	3.4
			Urban green (sqm/inh)	54.8	54.9	54.8
ORISTANO						
	SPORT	structured	sportsmanship index	205.68	217.7	270.07
		unstructured	Pedestrian areas (sqm/inh)	-	0.1	0.1
			bicycle-line (sqm/100 inh)	-	-	-
			Urban green (sqm/inh)	47.5	47.5	47.4
NUORO						
	SPORT	structured	sportsmanship index	167.63	158	163.22
		unstructured	Pedestrian areas (sqm/inh)	0.1	0.1	0.1
			bicycle-line (sqm/100 inh)	0.3	0.3	0.3
			Urban green (sqm/inh)	32.7	31.8	32.7
SASSARI						
	SPORT	structured	sportsmanship index	395.46	426.01	477.48
		unstructured	Pedestrian areas (sqm/inh)	0.1	-	-
			bicycle-line (sqm/100 inh)	0.4	0.4	0.4
			Urban green (sqm/inh)	14.3	16.9	14.3

Fig. 1. Values recognized for structured and unstructured sport in the Sardinia Region for the three-year period 2018, 2019, 2020 (Please note that Cagliari and South Sardinia hold the same values for unstructured activities, as data are referred to their aggregation). Authors: A. Milesi and M. Ladu.

The metropolitan city of Cagliari and the province of Southern Sardinia are considered together as the sources are often not updated to the current administrative spatial structure, although from 2016. This performance is due not only to the presence of sports services and equipment but also to a series of urban facilities - pedestrian areas, cycling and urban green.In particular, the province of Oristano records low values for pedestrian areas, no value for cycling, against a good endowment of urban green. On the contrary, the province of Sassari records values similar to the Cagliari context as regards cycling, compared to a less significant amount of urban green. The same province records an average value, in regional reference, as regards the services in support of the structured PA.

4 Methods

The proposed method consists in determining an Urban Physical Activity index (UPA Index), in order to quantitatively represent the unstructured PA, connected to the urban design of pedestrian areas, cycling and urban green areas. Based on the previous paragraphs, the UPA index can be represented as follow:

$$UPAIndex = \frac{\sum_{i=1}^{n} i * W_i}{\sum_{i=1}^{n} W_i}$$

where:
i_1 = pedestrian areas/100 inhabitants
i_2 = cycling/100 inhabitants
i_3 = urban green/100 inhabitants
W_1 pedestrian areas = 1/n_1 * EUL
W_2 cycling = 1/n_2 * EUL
W_3 urban green = 1/n_3 * EUL
and EUL (Efficient Use of Land) = efficient use of land which represents the synthetic index (score 0–10) of the trend of land consumption/residents and the level of urbanization/residents and 1/n 1–3 represents the incidence factor respectively for pedestrian areas, cycling and urban green areas on EUL. In summary, the proposed UPA index referring to PA de-structured by using the incidence of EUL, allows you to connect land use efficiency and urban design, obtaining a representative index also in terms of urban ecologies [37, 59, 60].

5 The Case Study

The UPA index was applied to the Sardinia case for each province for the three-year period 2018, 2019, 2020.

In particular, $1/n_1 = 0.075$; $1/n_2 = 0.025$; $1/n_3 = 0.15$ were determined empirically from the evaluation of the urban and territorial context of the province and the Public Works Plans.

Table 4 shows the input data (i_1, i_2, i_3; W_1, W_2, W_3) and output of the proposed method for the evaluation of UPA index.

Table 4. Input and output data (UPA Index) by province of the Sardinia Region for the three-year period 2018, 2019, 2020. Authors: A. Milesi and M. Ladu.

	i_1	i_2	i_3	EUL	W_1	W_2	W_3	UPA index
2018								
Cagliari + Sud Sardegna	0.5	4.5	54.8	9.2	0.69	0.23	1.38	**33.48**
Oristano			47.5	4	0.30	0.1	0.6	**28.50**
Nuoro	0.1	0.3	32.7	5.2	0.39	0.13	0.78	**19.68**
Sassari	0.1	0.4	14.3	4	0.30	0.1	0.6	**8.65**
2019								
Cagliari + Sud Sardegna	0.5	4.4	54.9	8.6	0.65	0.215	1.29	**33.53**
Oristano	0.1		47.5	5.4	0.41	0.135	0.81	**28.53**
Nuoro	0.1	0.3	31.8	3.9	0.29	0.0975	0.585	**19.14**
Sassari		0.4	16.9	3.2	0.24	0.08	0.48	**10.18**
2020								
Cagliari + Sud Sardegna	0.2	3.4	54.8	7.8	0.59	0.195	1.17	**33.28**
Oristano	0.1		47.4	3.8	0.29	0.095	0.57	**28.47**
Nuoro	0.1	0.3	32.7	3.6	0.27	0.09	0.54	**19.68**
Sassari		0.4	14.3	3	0.23	0.075	0.45	**8.62**

Figure 2 shows the related UPAs in Sardinia by intermediate territorial area.

The results of the proposed method were presented and discussed in Sect. 4 and Section.

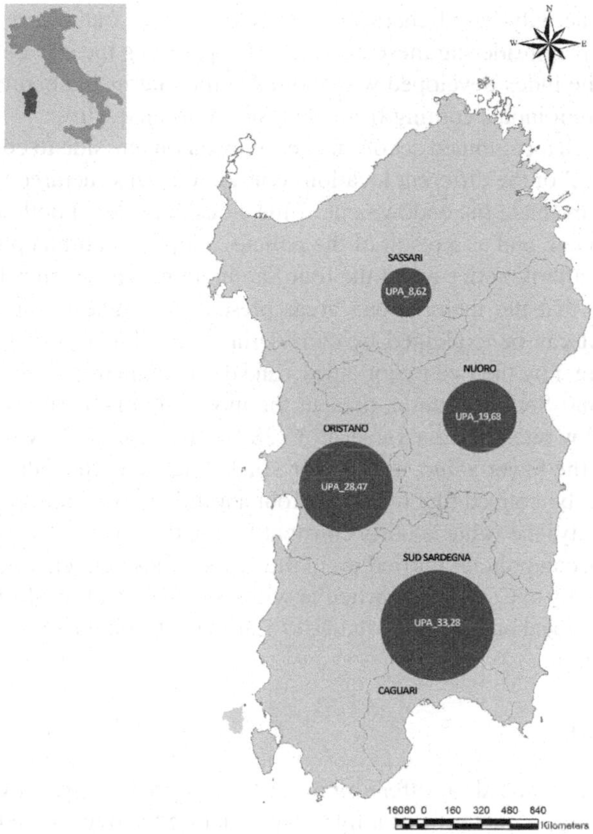

Fig. 2. The UPA Index in Sardinia. Authors: A. Milesi and M. Ladu.

6 Results and Discussion

The research hereby developed and proposed was aimed at proposing a novel approach in addressing issues related to health in its consideration with PA (Physical Activities, including sport ones) and the relation they can have with city planning. The approach led to the development to a suited-for-purpose index capable of combining de facto existing sport activities and practices, particularly at urban level, both related to structured and unstructured solutions. In a real world scenario, such combination seems to be the most natural one, as physical activities and active life are both related to structured practices, as in terms of sport associations, clubs, gyms, playing courts and grounds, etc., so as in terms of the spontaneous and unstructured ones, let us think about walking, running, cycling, swimming, as doable without the registration or belonging to groups or associations. Not all the 'active people', in fact, structure their activities in official manners. Nonetheless, usual and typical indexes and indicators focus on the structured supply of sport clubs and facilities for classifying cities and evaluating their performance as healthy and sport-oriented ones. As said, the approach here is that of inserting the sport-based and activity-based characters of the city into a framework of the 'healthy city' and therefore considering these characters for planning the city of the future.

The composite index developed was applied to the intermediate, province level and considered different inputs coming from analysis on urban quality.

The use of such a combined set of indexes allowed on one side to consider a kind of official 'Sportness' of the different locations considered - in structured terms - while on the other side to evaluate the endowment of the cities considered both in terms of their 'natural' component, and as a result of the policies adopted on urban planning.

We can particularly notice as, of the four Sardinian provinces plus the metropolitan city of Cagliari, that the major urban areas present the highest values of structured endowment, as it can be explained by considering their 'higher order role' played in the regional context by the two major cities - and de facto metropolitan areas. Southern areas, Cagliari and South Sardinia, present the most important values in terms of the unstructured endowment. with a value of 33.28 for the year 2020, while the province of Sassari holds the lower value, as 8.62 for 2020. Analysing the values for the period 2018–2020 it can be noticed that for all the four administrative aggregations (provinces + metropolitan city) the value is fairly constant for the three years. That possibly comes down from the urban policies carried on in the years, whose effects can be observed in such values. The city of Cagliari in particular witnessed the major results from the actions performed by the local authority for the 2017 European Capital of Sport as certified by the European Union.

7 Conclusions

The research so far carried on offered a multi-faceted view of the different areas considered, showing, as a matter of example, that structured activities are more present in major urban areas. This can be considered the effect of a higher presence of services – associations, clubs, etc. - related to sport and physical activities can be related to the proper urban, higher role played by such places. Unstructured activities appear more concentrated on the Southern part of the regions, particularly in the aggregation of the province of South Sardinia and the metropolitan city of Cagliari. Here, investments in bicycle and walking lanes, green spaces, etc., considered as indicators of an attention towards the unstructured activities, appear more present than in the other provinces considered. An observation on a time series analyzed is that investment in such a sense was boosted particularly before the year 2017, when Cagliari was nominated European Capital of sport. In the coming years, the endowments related to these elements remained constant.

Further evolutions of this research imply considering other elements to enrich the composite indicator of structured and unstructured physical activity, other than modeling such index in order to be considered into, and as an effect of, the urban policies adopted. A more refined spatial scale of analysis will also be considered.

References

1. Bedimo-Rung, A.L., Mowen, A.J., Cohen, D.A.: The significance of parks to physical activity and public health. A conceptual model. Am. J. Prev. Med. **28**(22), 159–168 (2005)

2. Ballor, D.L., Keesey, R.E.: A meta-analysis of the factors affecting exercise induced changes in body mass, fat mass, and fat-free mass in males and females. Int. J. Obesity **15**, 717–726 (1991)
3. Hovell, M.F., Sallis, J.F., Hofstetter, C.R., Spry, V.M., Faucher, P., Caspersen, C.J.: Identifying correlates of walking for exercise: an epidemiologic prerequisite for physical activity promotion. Prev. Med. **18**, 856–866 (1989)
4. Phillips, W.T., Pruitt, L.A., King, A.C.: Lifestyle activity. Current recommendations. Sports Med. **22**, 1–7 (1996)
5. Dunn, A.L., Marcus, B.H., Kampert, J.B., Garcia, M.E., Kohl, H.W., Blair, S.N.: Comparison of lifestyle and structured interventions to increase physical activity and cardiorespiratory fitness: a randomized trial. JAMA **281**, 327–334 (1994)
6. Hakim, A.A., Petrovitch, H., Burchfiel, C.M., et al.: Effects of walking on mortality among nonsmoking retired men. NE J. Med. **338**, 94–99 (1998)
7. Manson, J.E., Hu, F.B., Rich-Edwards, J.W., et al.: A prospective study of walking as compared with vigorous exercise in the prevention of coronary heart disease in women. NE J. Med. **341**, 650–658 (1999)
8. Siegel, P., Brackbill, R., Heath, G.: The epidemiology of walking for exercise: implications for promoting activity among sedentary groups. Am. J. Public Health **85**, 706–710 (1995)
9. Brownson, R.C., et al.: Promoting physical activity in rural communities. Walking trail access, use, and effects. Am. J. Prev. Med. **18**(3), 235–241 (2000)
10. Pate, R.R.P.M., Blair, S.N., Haskell, W.L., Macera, C.A., Bouchard, C., et al.: Physical activity and public health. A recommendation from the Centers for Disease Control and Prevention and the American College of Sports Medicine. JAMA **273**, 402–407 (1995)
11. Baerta, V., Gorusa, E., Metsa, T., Geertsa, C., Bautmans, I.: Motivators and barriers for physical activity in the oldest old: a systematic review. Ageing Res. Rev. **10**, 464–474 (2011)
12. Hallal, P.C., Andersen, L.B., Bull, F.C., Guthold, R., Haskell, W., Ekelund, U.: Global physical activity levels: surveillance progress, pitfalls, and prospects. Lancet **380**, 247–257 (2012)
13. Lee, I.M., Shiroma, E.J., Lobelo, F., Puska, P., Blair, S.N., Katzmarzyk, P.T.: Effect of physical inactivity on major non-communicable diseases worldwide: an analysis of burden of disease and life expectancy. Lancet **380**, 219–229 (2012)
14. Linke, S.E., Ussher, M.: Exercise-based treatments for substance use disorders: evidence, theory, and practicality. Am. J. Drug Alcohol Abuse **41**(1), 7–15 (2015)
15. World Health Organization: The European Health Report 2009. Health and health systems. http://www.euro.who.int/__data/assets/pdf_file/0009/82386/E93103.pdf. Accessed 20 May 2021
16. Epicentro: Il portale dell'epidemiologia per la sanità pubblica a cura del Centro Nazionale di Epidemiologia, Sorveglianza e Promozione della Salute. http://www.epicentro.iss.it/problemi/attivita_fisica/fisica.asp. Accessed 20 May 2021
17. Istituto Superiore della Sanità (ISS): Centro nazionale di epidemiologia, sorveglianza e promozione della salute (Cnesps): OKkio alla salute: sintesi dei risultati 2019. In: collaborazione con Centro per la prevenzione e il controllo delle malattie (Ccm) del Ministero della Salute e le Regioni
18. Cavallo, F., et al. (eds.): Studio HBSC-Italia (Health Behaviour in School-aged Children): rapporto sui dati 2010. Istituto Superiore di Sanità, Roma (Rapporti ISTISAN 13/5) (2013)
19. Epicentro. Il portale dell'epidemiologia per la sanità pubblica a cura del Centro Nazionale di Epidemiologia, Sorveglianza e Promozione della Salute. La sorveglianza PASSI (Progressi delle Aziende Sanitarie per la Salute in Italia). http://www.epicentro.iss.it/passi/. Accessed 20 May 2021
20. Sallis, J., et al.: An ecological approach to creating active living communities. Annu. Rev. Public Health **27**, 297–322 (2006). https://doi.org/10.1146/annurev.publhealth.27.021405.102100

21. Rebecchi, A., et al.: Walkable environments and healthy urban moves: urban context features assessment framework experienced in Milan. Sustainability **11**, 2778 (2019)
22. Congiu, T., et al.: Built environment features and pedestrian accidents: an Italian retrospective study. Sustainability **11**, 1064 (2019)
23. D'Alessandro, D., et al.: Strategies for disease prevention and health promotion in urban areas. In: The Erice 50 Charter. Ann. Ig. **29**, 481–493 (2017). https://doi.org/10.7416/ai.2017.2179. ISSN: 1120-9135
24. Capolongo, S., et al.: Healthy design and urban planning strategies, actions, and policy to achieve salutogenic cities. Int. J. Environ. Res. Public Health **15**, 2698 (2018)
25. Rydin, Y., et al.: Shaping cities for health: complexity and the planning of urban environments in the 21st century. Lancet **379**, 2079–2108 (2012)
26. Addy, C.L., Wilson, D.K., Kirtland, K.A., Ainsworth, B.E., Sharpe, P., Kimsey, D.: Associations of perceived social and physical environmental supports with physical activity and walking behavior. Am. J. Public Health **94**(3), 440–443 (2004)
27. Bauman, A., Smith, B., Stoker, L., Bellew, B., Booth, M.: Geographical influence upon physical activity participation: evidence of a "coastal effect." ANZJPH **23**(3), 322–324 (1999)
28. Ladu, M., Balletto, G., Borruso, G.: Sport and the city, between urban regeneration and sustainable development. TeMA-J. Land Use Mobility Environ. **12**(2), 157–164 (2019)
29. Capotorti, G., et al.: More nature in the city. Plant Biosyst.-Int. J. Dealing Aspects Plant Biol. **154**(6), 1003–1006 (2020)
30. Ladu, M., Balletto, G., Borruso, G.: Sport and smart communities. Assessing the sporting attractiveness and community perceptions of Cagliari (Sardinia, Italy). In: Misra, S., et al. (eds.) ICCSA 2019. LNCS, vol. 11624, pp. 200–215. Springer, Cham (2019). https://doi.org/10.1007/978-3-030-24311-1_14
31. Balletto, G., Milesi, A., Ladu, M., Borruso, G.: A dashboard for supporting slow tourism in green infrastructures. A methodological proposal in Sardinia (Italy). Sustainability **12**(9), 3579 (2020)
32. Macintyre, H.L., Heaviside, C., Cai, X., Phalkey, R.: Comparing temperature-related mortality impacts of cool roofs in winter and summer in a highly urbanized European region for present and future climate. Environ. Int. **154**, 106606 (2021)
33. Lehnert, M., Savić, S., Milošević, D., Dunjić, J., Geletič, J.: Mapping local climate zones and their applications in European urban environments: a systematic literature review and future development trends. ISPRS Int. J. Geo-Information **10**(4), 260 (2021)
34. Dettori, M., et al.: Air pollutants and risk of death due to COVID-19 in Italy. Environ. Res. **192**, 110459 (2021)
35. Ulpiani, G.: On the linkage between urban heat island and urban pollution island: three-decade literature review towards a conceptual framework. Sci. Total Environ. **751**, 141727 (2020)
36. Maragno, D., Pozzer, G., Musco, F.: Multi-risk climate mapping for the adaptation of the Venice metropolitan area. Sustainability **13**(3), 1334 (2021)
37. Balletto, G., Ladu, M., Milesi, A., Borruso, G.: A methodological approach on disused public properties in the 15-minute city perspective. Sustainability **13**, 593 (2021). https://doi.org/10.3390/su13020593
38. Balletto, G., Milesi, A., Fenu, N., Borruso, G., Mundula, L.: Military training areas as semicommons: The territorial valorization of Quirra (Sardinia) from easements to ecosystem services. Sustainability **12**(2), 622 (2020)
39. Balletto, G., Borruso, G., Tajani, F., Torre, C.: Gentrification and sport. Football stadiums and changes in the urban rent. In: Gervasi, O., et al. (eds.) ICCSA 2018. LNCS, vol. 10964, pp. 58–74. Springer, Cham (2018). https://doi.org/10.1007/978-3-319-95174-4_5
40. Balletto, G., Borruso, G., Mei, G.: Location theory and circular economy. Demolition, constructions and spatial organization of firms – an applied model to Sardinia Region. The case

study of the New Cagliari Stadium. In: Misra, S., et al. (eds.) ICCSA 2019. LNCS, vol. 11621, pp. 535–550. Springer, Cham (2019). https://doi.org/10.1007/978-3-030-24302-9_38
41. Carmona, M.: Public Places, Urban Spaces: The Dimensions of Urban Design. Routledge, Milton Park (2021)
42. Kellison, T.B., McCullough, B.P.: A pragmatic perspective on the future of sustainability in sport. In: Routledge Handbook of Sport and the Environment, pp. 445–455. Routledge (2017)
43. Camerin, F., Gastaldi, F.: Il ruolo dei fondi di investimento immobiliare nella riconversione del patrimonio immobiliare pubblico in Italia. Urban@ it Background Papers Rapporto sulle città 2018 IL GOVERNO DEBOLE DELLE ECONOMIE URBANE 2/2018, pp. 1–13 (2018)
44. Pedersen, P.M., Ruihley, B.J., Li, B. (eds.): Sport and the Pandemic: Perspectives on Covid-19's Impact on the Sport Industry. Routledge, Milton Park (2020)
45. Di Caro, P., Pagliara, F.: Sportcity. Viaggio nello sport che cambia le città. Malcor D' (2020)
46. ISTAT: Rapporto Bes 2019. Il Benessere Equo e sostenibile in Italia (2019)
47. ISTAT: Rapporto Bes 2020. Il Benessere Equo e sostenibile in Italia (2020)
48. Ronchetti, P.: Regole e numeri dello sport. Zanichelli (2019)
49. Scally, G., Black, D., Pilkington, P., Williams, B., Ige-Elegbede, J., Prestwood, E.: The application of 'elite interviewing' methodology in transdisciplinary research: a record of process and lessons learned during a 3-year pilot in urban planetary health research. J. Urban Health **98**, 404–414 (2021). https://doi.org/10.1007/s11524-021-00542-1
50. ISTAT. https://www.istat.it/it/benessere-e-sostenibilit%C3%A0/la-misurazione-del-benessere-(bes)/gli-indicatori-del-bes. Accessed 27 May 2021
51. ISTAT. https://www.istat.it/it/archivio/254761. Accessed 27 May 2021
52. ASviS. https://asvis.it/public/asvis2/files/Pubblicazioni/RAPPORTO_ASviS_TERRITORI_2020.pdf. Accessed 27 May 2021
53. Kiuppis, F.: Inclusion in sport: Disability and participation. Taylor & Francis Online (2018)
54. Balletto, G., Borruso, G.: Sport and city. The case of Cagliari's new stadium (Sardinia – Italy). In: Proceedings of the 22nd IPSAPA/ISPALEM International Scientific Conference Aversa/Caserta (Italy), 2nd–3rd July 2018, pp. 231–240 (2018)
55. Moeinaddini, M., Asadi-Shekari, Z., Aghaabbasi, M., Saadi, I., Shah, M.Z., Cools, M.: Applying non-parametric models to explore urban life satisfaction in European cities. Cities **105**, 102851 (2020)
56. Il Sole 24 Ore. https://lab24.ilsole24ore.com/indiceSportivita/index.php. Accessed 27 May 2021
57. Il Sole 24 Ore. https://lab24.ilsole24ore.com/ecosistema-urbano/index.php. Accessed 27 May 2021
58. Legambiente. https://www.legambiente.it/wp-content/uploads/2020/11/Ecosistema-Urbano-2020.pdf. Accessed 27 May 2021
59. Romano, B., Zullo, F., Marucci, A., Fiorini, L.: Vintage urban planning in Italy: land management with the tools of the mid-twentieth century. Sustainability **10**, 4125 (2018). https://doi.org/10.3390/su10114125
60. Fabris, L.M.F., Balzarotti, R.M., Semprebon, G., Camerin, F.: New healthy settlements responding to pandemic outbreaks. Approaches from and for the global city (2020)

A Decision Support System for Tuberculosis Prevalence in South Africa

Mulalo Razwiedani[1] and Okuthe P. Kogeda[2(✉)]

[1] Tshwane University of Technology, Pretoria 0001, South Africa
razwiedanims@tut.ac.za
[2] University of the Free State, Bloemfontein 9300, South Africa
kogedapo@ufs.ac.za

Abstract. Tuberculosis is one of the most prevalent diseases, which is a threat to the lives of many South Africans. The disease has been spreading at a high rate in the past years. World health organization reported that South Africa is amongst 22 countries most burdened by the disease that has around 80% of the total global Tuberculosis cases. Despite the fact that the South African government is undertaking Tuberculosis campaigns, there is still a challenge in the control of the spread of Tuberculosis. The lack of awareness and access to information further contributes to the high rate at which Tuberculosis is spreading. Therefore, we developed a decision support system for Tuberculosis prevalence in South Africa. We used Bayesian network to aggregate, analyse and mine data received from health department of Mpumalanga province. The data is stored in MySQL database. We used WampServer environment, which enabled us to develop a web application. The proposed model educates, informs, and prescribes measures to take when visiting a high prevalence location. We then tested the system developed with data from Mpumalanga provincial health department showing that males are more at risk with prevalence rate of 53%, 0–35 age group are the most affected at 50%, Ehlanzeni location in Mpumalanga province is the most affected at 47%, pulmonary Tuberculosis is the most prevalence at 90% and the survival rate is at 87%. We evaluated the model achieving a utility of 88.2%. We believe this utility can be improved with more training and accurate data.

Keywords: Bayesian network · Decision support system · Tuberculosis · Data mining · ICT4D · Probability · Mobile health

1 Introduction

Tuberculosis (TB) is an airborne disease caused by a bacterium that mostly affects the lungs. It is highly infectious and can affect anybody exposed to the bacteria. The spread of the disease has been growing at an alarming rate. Globally about 9 million people got infected with TB in 2013 and about 16% of them died WHO [1]. South Africa is amongst the countries with a high prevalence rate and recorded approximately 320 000 infected people in 2013.

O. Gervasi et al. (Eds.): ICCSA 2021, LNCS 12952, pp. 270–284, 2021.
https://doi.org/10.1007/978-3-030-86973-1_19

In South Africa, TB kills people who are mostly in the productive age of their employment and parenting lives, therefore, the country is losing members of the workforce, which is impacting negatively on the economy of the country. Children grow up without parents increasing the levels of the needy people without income, and the lack of income means that education is no longer a priority for them. The elderly are also affected as they lose those who support and care for them. Further, the productivity of the country drops resulting in a slowdown of development and growth, and the spread of the disease costs the country as more money has to be allocated to the health budget. Finally, the factors mentioned above discourage investors thereby affecting business and government revenues. This means that South Africa is in dire need of an effective TB epidemic control programme. This programme should have accurate information on prevalence of and the measures necessary in dealing with the epidemic. This can be achieved by creating a TB epidemic model.

In this study, we focused on predicting the chances of someone being infected if they visit an area with a high prevalence of TB. This prediction is done based on demographic data. Ultimately the study assists people to make a decision on what precautionary measures to take based on the prediction obtained. In this study, we used Bayesian networks to compute the probability of getting infected with TB.

This paper is organized as follows. In Sect. 2, we present related works. In Sect. 3, we present Bayesian network including reasons why we chose it. In Sect. 4, we provide system design and architecture. In Sect. 5, we provide implementation. Testing and results are presented in Sect. 6 with conclusion being presented in Sect. 7.

2 Related Works

There are a number of researchers who have done some work in this area. They are summarised as follows. Kumari, Rajan & Anshul [2] presented a prediction of diabetes using Bayesian network. The main objective of their work was to help in predicting diabetes by applying data mining. The discovery of knowledge from the medical data set was done in order to make effective medical diagnosis. They proposed the Bayesian network methodology to predict whether the person has diabetes or not. In their results they found that Bayesian network gave the prediction accuracy of 99.5%. This study is similar to ours as it uses the same methodology that we are using in our study, but they used it to predict whether the person has diabetes or not.

Thakkar *et al.* [3] presents a health care decision support system for swine flu prediction using Naive Bayes classifier. In their study, Naïve Bayes classifier was used to classify the patient of swine flu in three categories. Their research focused on medical diagnosis by learning pattern through the collected data for Swine Flu. They claimed that Naïve Bayes could identify all the significant medical predictors and had the accuracy rate of 63.33%. Though the approach of this study is similar to ours as we also used collected historical data to implement our system, however, they used Naïve Bayes classifier in predicting swine flu.

Palaniappan & Rafiah [4] presents intelligent heart disease prediction system using data mining techniques. Their research developed a prototype intelligent heart disease prediction system using data mining techniques, namely, Decision Trees, Naïve Bayes and Neural Network. They used medical profiles such as age, sex, blood pressure and blood sugar to predict the likelihood of patients getting a heart disease. Their results showed that the most effective model to predict patients with heart disease appears to be Naïve Bayes followed by Neural Network and Decision Trees. Their study is similar to ours as it focuses on prediction. Our study focuses on the chances of contracting Tuberculosis but theirs was mainly focused on predicting the chances of having a heart disease.

Sharareh, Niakan & Xiao-Jun [5] present evaluation and comparison of different machine learning methods to predict outcome of Tuberculosis treatment course with the aim to provide prediction on the outcome of Tuberculosis treatment to the World Health Organisation. Their methodology involves the collection of Tuberculosis data from Tuberculosis control centres throughout Iran in 2005. They developed and evaluated models by six algorithms including decision tree, artificial neural network, logical regression, radial basis function, Bayesian networks and support vector machine. They used a dataset of 6450 patients with 4515 patients used for training and 1935 patients used for testing the models. Decision tree was found to be the best algorithm with 74.21% prediction accuracy. Their study is similar and related to the one we are doing as it uses the same methodology that we followed. The methodology that they used is similar to the one we are using of collecting historical data and constructing a model for prediction, however, their study is different to our study as they predict the outcome of the Tuberculosis treatment course.

Kogeda, Agbinya & Omlin [6] present a probabilistic approach to faults prediction in cellular networks. They derived probabilistic models of cellular network systems in which the independence between the relations between the variables of interest are represented explicitly. The methodology they used involved constructing a structure of a Bayesian network. They further evaluated the Bayesian network showing the causal relationship between variables with a belief factor. Their experimental results showed a fault prediction model. While they used Bayesian networks and looks at cellular network systems, in our study we are looking at Tuberculosis prevalence.

Ogutu, Kogeda & Lall [10] present a probabilistic assessment of location dependent failure trends in South Africa water distribution networks. Their work evaluated failure trends of pipelines in a region characterised by dolomitic grounds, outlining how the different soil tyes affect water pipeline failures. They used data from a selected metropolitan region in South Africa and applied Bayesian networks to accommodate inherent data uncertainty while modelling failure causal properties. While they used Bayesian networks and historical data to evaluate water pipeline failure trends, in our study we used the same method to model Tuberculosis prevalence in South Africa.

Kgoete & Kogeda [11] present a prediction model for mitigating Tuberculosis infection for HIV patients at greater Tubatse local municipality in South Africa. They developed a windows mobile application system using Visual Basic.NET to predict Tuberculosis prevalence in Tubatse area using Bayesian network model. They collected, aggregated and analysed data and developed a system infusing Bayesian network model. Their system showed a prediction rate of 98% utility. Though their work used the same methodology as ours, their work majored on HIV patients and their system was targeted towards the HIV patients.

Kogeda & Dladlu [12] present a decision support system for Cancer prevalence in South Africa. They collected data of Cancer patients from major hospitals in Eastern Cape Province of South Africa, then aggregated, classified and analysed using Bayesian network model. They attained accuracy of 97%. While they also used Bayesian network and historical data, their study majored on Cancer patients.

3 Bayesian Networks

A Bayesian Network also known as Bayes network is a probabilistic graphical model that represents a set of random variables and their conditional dependencies via a Directed Acyclic Graph (DAG) [7]. A Bayesian Network is defined by a directed network structure in the form of a DAG and a set of the local probability distributions (local pdfs), one for each node. A Bayesian Network shows conditional probability and causality relationships between variables. Conditional probability is the probability of an event happening given that another event has already happened. Probability (or likelihood) is a measure or estimation of how likely it is that something occurs or that a statement is true. The Bayesian network efficiently expresses the Joint Probability Distribution (JPD) of a set of variables. A Bayesian Network is made up of nodes that represent random variables and events, while arcs or arrows represent the probabilistic relationships between these variables. Each arrow starts at the parent node and ends at the child node, with the parent influencing the child in one way or another. Each node in the network has its conditional probability table computed from the dataset.

The joint probability distribution of random variable S $= \{X_i \ldots, X\}$ in a Bayesian network is calculated by the product of the local conditional probabilities of all the nodes. Let a node X_i in S denote the random variable X_i, and let $Pa(X_i)$ denote the parent nodes of X_i. Then, the joint probability distribution of S $= \{X_i \ldots, X\}$ is given by Eq. (1):

$$P(X_1, X_2, \ldots, X_n) = \prod_{i=0}^{n} P(X_i|Pa(X_i)) \tag{1}$$

Bayesian Networks have been used in the areas including: Medical diagnosis, Decision-making, Adaptive testing, Decision centric troubleshooting, Data mining, Pattern recognition, Bioinformatics/computational biology, Weather forecasting, etc.

Bayes theorem was originally developed by Thomas Bayes, a theologian and mathematician in the 18th century. Bayes is the theory that gave rise to Bayesian networks. The theorem was first published in 1763 and is stated as:

$$P(A|B) = \frac{P(B|A)P(A)}{P(B)} \tag{2}$$

Where:

- P(A) is the prior probability of the event A, without any information about the event B,
- P(A/B) is the conditional probability of the event A, given the event B,
- P(B/A) is the conditional probability of the event B, given the event A,
- P(B) is the marginal probability of the event B, acting like a normalizing constant.

Bayesian network is defined by:

- a directed cyclic graph in which each node denotes a random variable, either discrete or continuous values
- a set of conditional probability tables (CPT) for each node [5].

3.1 Why Bayesian Networks?

Classical statistics do not handle uncertainty well. For this reason, some of the grounds for using a Bayesian Network to tackle this problem included:

- They are graphical models and can represent relationships clearly and easily.
- They clearly depict the direction, thereby showing the cause-effect relationship which other Artificial Intelligence domains (decision trees, artificial neural networks, mixtures of basic functions, Markov networks, etc.) are not able to represent.
- They are able to handle uncertainty.
- They handle uncertainty using the theory of probability [8].

A Bayesian Network was the best algorithm to use as it relies on a well-established theoretical or mathematical base and it is very simple to understand and use.

4 System Design and Architecture

The main system requirement of this study is to create a prototype that computes the probability of getting infected with Tuberculosis using Bayesian network. The Mobile Health Decision Support System (MHDSS) was constructed according to the following functional requirements:

- Allow user to query for the probability of getting infected with Tuberculosis based on their age group, gender, location and type of Tuberculosis.
- Allow user to view the precautionary measures to avoid being infected with Tuberculosis.
- Allow health practitioner to add more patient records on the system.

4.1 Object-Oriented Requirements Analysis

An object-oriented approach with Unified Modelling Language (UML) has been used in the design of the MHDSS. UML is the standard language for modelling software systems [9]. The UML has several types of diagrams in order to model the static and dynamic behaviour of a system. The use cases of the MHDSS are presented. Figure 1, shows user use case diagram. The diagram illustrates that the user is able to request for the probability of getting infected with Tuberculosis in the location of interest by selecting and submitting information about their location, age group, gender and type of Tuberculosis. The system employs the Bayesian Network to compute the probability of getting infected with Tuberculosis. The system then presents the user with the probability of getting infected with Tuberculosis. The user is able to view precautionary measures to take when avoiding being infected with Tuberculosis.

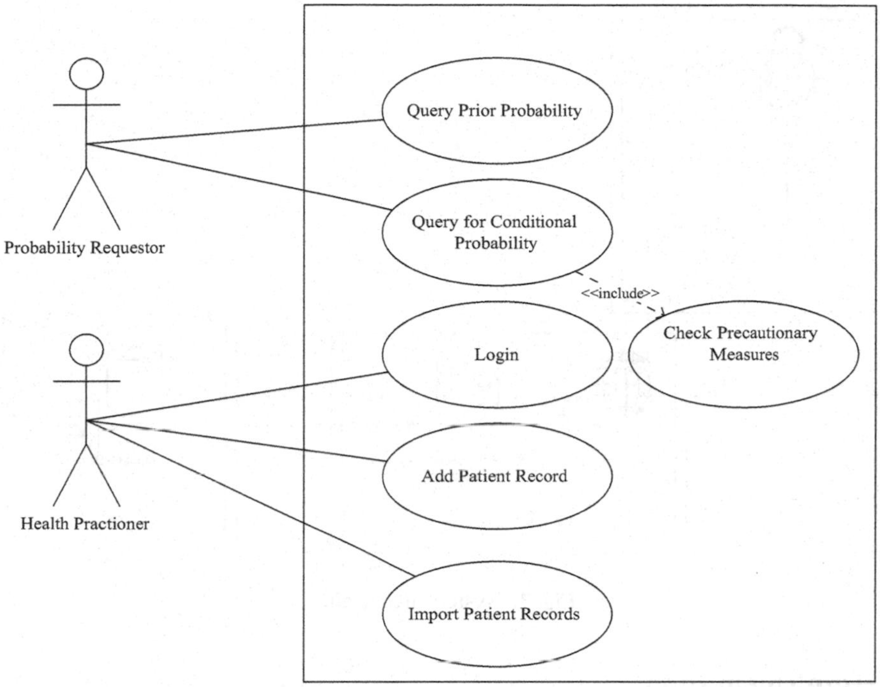

Fig. 1. Top level use case diagram

4.2 System Architecture

The MHDSS architecture is based on a three-tier architecture (see Fig. 2). This system architecture approach was chosen as it brought with it system robustness, flexibility and resistance to potential change. A three-tier architecture provides the following benefits: scalability, maintainability, reliability, availability, extensibility, performance, manageability, and security. The chosen architecture is composed of three layers: the user interface layer, the application logic layer and the data layer.

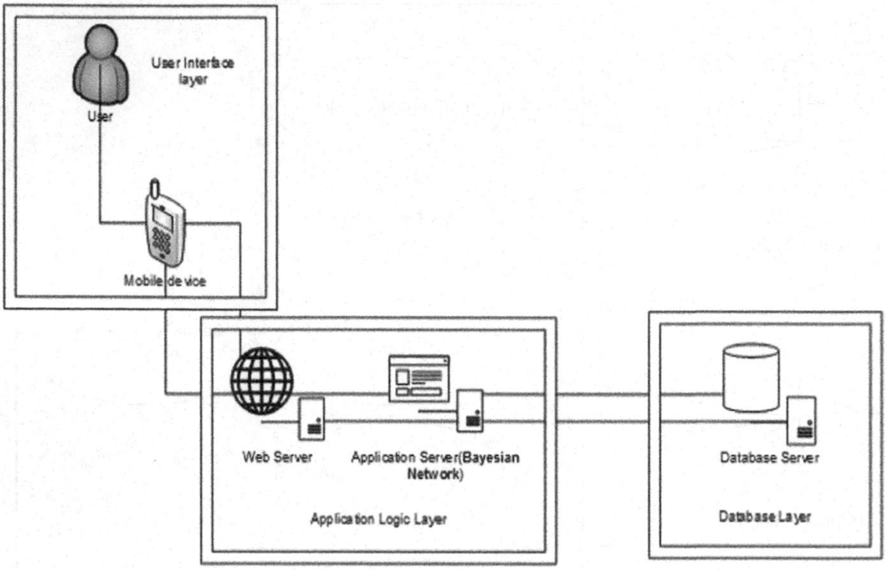

Fig. 2. System architecture

5 Implementation

The research implementation involved developing the mobile health decision support system for Tuberculosis prevalence. The data collected were stored in a database and the model designed during the modelling stage was then implemented. The implementation involved designing the software system, reusing software components e.g., MySQL, and choosing appropriate programming language. The mobile graphical user interface was then developed for the system. After testing, a system evaluation was conducted to ensure that the system implemented was as designed. The evaluation process also assisted to make sure that all the system requirements were achieved.

From literature review, we have learned that Tuberculosis is caused by breathing in an air droplet that contains a Tuberculosis bacterium. The bacterium spreads when an infected person coughs, spits, sneezes or shouts. This means that being in an area where there is a high prevalence of Tuberculosis, your chance of contracting the disease increases. There are a number of stages that we are going to take in order to build a Bayesian Network.

5.1 The Database

The available dataset has been collected from gathered records by health practitioners, nurses, and doctors at local Clinics and hospitals throughout Mpumalanga in 2012. Table 1 presents a sample from the dataset from Mpumalanga health department.

Table 1. Sample of TB patient dataset

Location	Agegroup	Gender	Classification	Outcome
Ehlanzeni	35 to 65	Male	Pulmonary	Died
Ehlanzeni	0 to 35	Female	Extra-Pulmonary	Died
Gert Sibande	35 to 65	Female	Pulmonary	Died
Ehlanzeni	35 to 65	Male	Pulmonary	Died
Nkangala	35 to 65	Male	Pulmonary	Died
Nkangala	35 to 65	Male	Extra-Pulmonary	Alive
Nkangala	0 to 35	Male	Pulmonary	Alive
Ehlanzeni	0 to 35	Male	Pulmonary	Alive
Nkangala	35 to 65	Male	Pulmonary	Alive
Ehlanzeni	65+	Female	Pulmonary	Alive

The Tuberculosis patient dataset consist of Location (i.e., District in Mpumalanga shown in Fig. 3), Agegroup, Gender, Tuberculosis classification and Treatment outcome. Table 2 presents the variables and their possible states.

Table 2. Definition of the possible states of variables TB, L, A, G and TO

Types of TB (TB)	Location (L)	Age group (A)	Gender (G)	Treatment outcome (TO)
Pulmonary = p	Nkangala = n	0 to 35	Male = m	Alive = a
Extra-Pulmonary = xp	Gert Sibande = g	35 to 65	Female = f	Died = d
	Ehlanzeni = e	65+		

5.2 Network Structure

The structure of the network captures the relationships between the variables. In our problem the factors that affect a user's chance of having Tuberculosis are Age group, Location and Gender. Then we add arcs from Age group, Location and Gender to Tuberculosis (TB) to show the cause effect relationship of TB. Similarly, having a particular type of TB affects the Treatment outcome of TB. So we then add arcs from TB to Treatment outcome. The resultant structure is shown in Fig. 4.

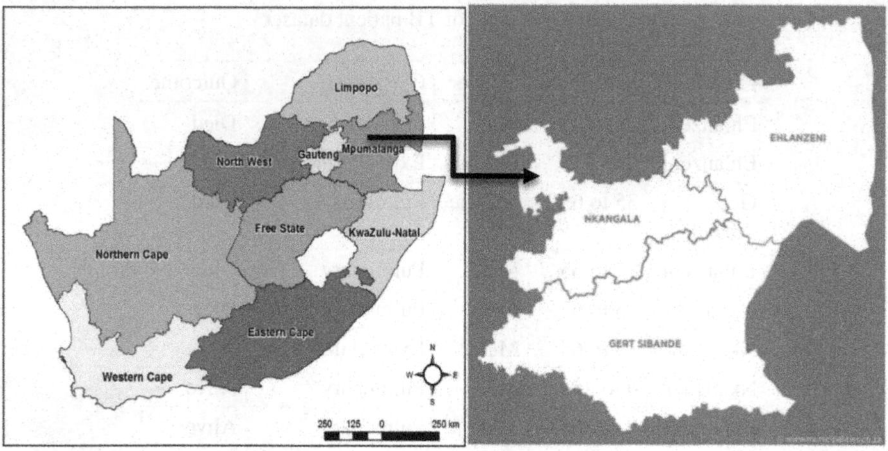

Fig. 3. Mpumalanga districts

5.3 Joint Probabilities Distribution

Figure 4 shows the construction of a Bayesian network that predicts the Tuberculosis prevalence. The joint probability distribution for a Bayesian network is obtained by the product of the local probabilities distributions for each node. Then the joint probability of our Bayesian network may be calculated as given by Eq. (3):

$$P(A, L, G, TB, TO) = P(A) \times P(L) \times P(G) \times P(TB|A, L, G) \times P(TO|TB) \quad (3)$$

For example, we can calculate joint probability using Eq. (3):
P(L = Nkangala, A = 0 to 35, G = Male, TB = Pulmonary, TO = Alive)
= P(L = Nkangala) × P(A = 0 to 35) × P(G = Male)
× P(TB = Pulmonary| L = Nkangala, A = 0 to 35, G = Male)
× P(TO = Alive| TB = Pulmonary)
= 0,53685 * 0,50279 * 0,28141 * 0,87179 * 0,86811 = 0.05749.

5.4 Conditional Probabilities

Given the prior probability, the conditional probability distribution for each types of TB given the state of Location, Gender and Age group can be computed. Then having TB causes the patient to go through the TB treatment thereby affecting the treatment outcome.

Given variable A and variable B are independent on each other. Then conditional probability can be computed using Eq. (2). The probability of A occurring given that B has already occurred is given by Eq. (2).

Suppose we want to calculate the probability of a female of age 0 to 35 living in Nkangala district of getting infected with Pulmonary TB. The conditional probability is calculated below:

P(TB = p⊣ |A = 0–35, G = f, L = n) = P(TB = p, A = 0–35, G = f, L = n)/P(A = 0–35, G = f, A = n).

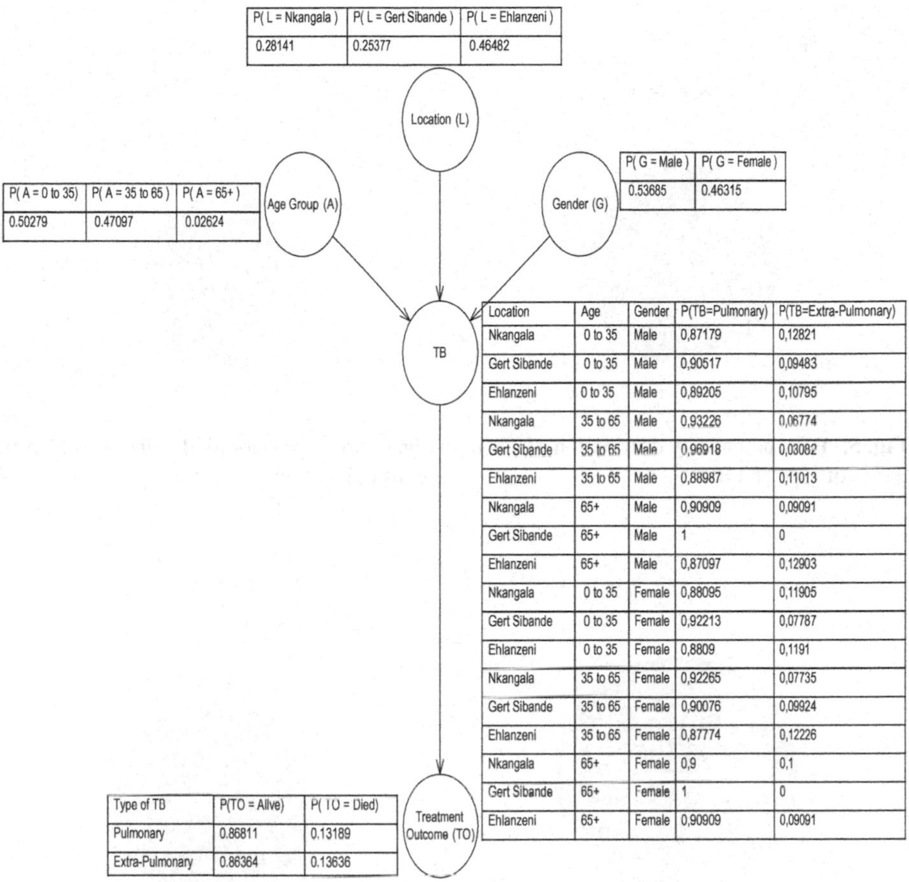

Fig. 4. Bayesian network for the tuberculosis example.

$P(TB = p \mid A = 0\text{–}35, G = f, L = n) = 0.05773/0.065531 = 0.88095.$

Therefore, the probability of a female of age group 0 to 35 in Nkangala district getting infected with Pulmonary TB is 88.095%.

6 Testing and Results

The results show that Pulmonary TB is the most prevalent and make more than 90% of the TB cases in Mpumalanga Province. Figure 5 shows the prior probability distribution of the types of TB.

Ehlanzeni district has the most cases of TB as shown in Fig. 6. Figure 7 shows that males are the most infected with TB in Mpumalanga as compared to females. The prevalence of TB across age group showed that age group 0 to 35 and 35 to 65 are the most vulnerable groups. The older groups of 65+ are less vulnerable as shown in Fig. 8. The rate of patients being cured and alive is high according to our results. However, more than 10% of the patient's treatment outcomes show that they have died. This is

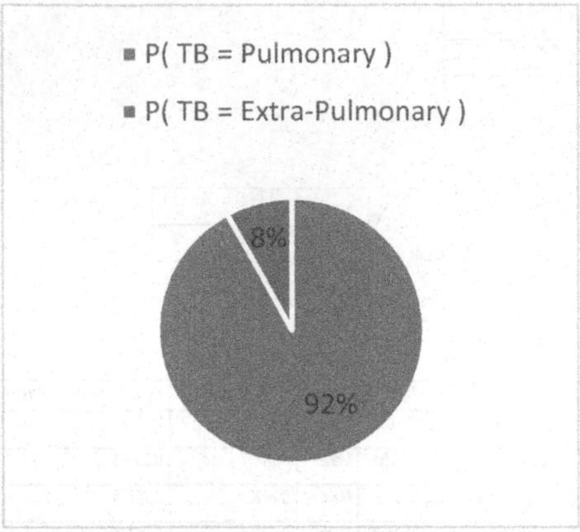

Fig. 5. Prior probability distribution of TB in terms of type of TB

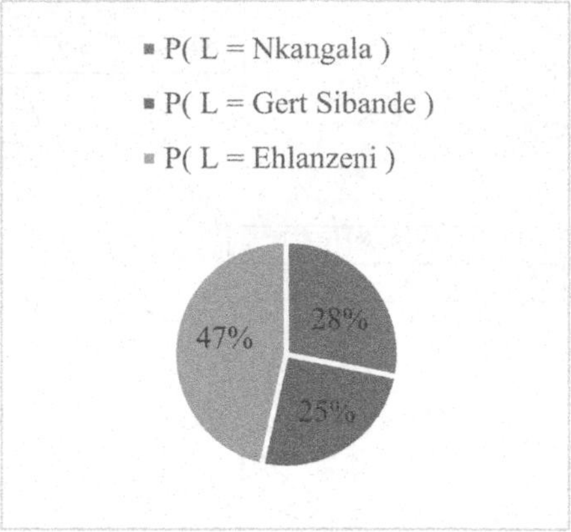

Fig. 6. Prior probability distribution of TB in terms of location

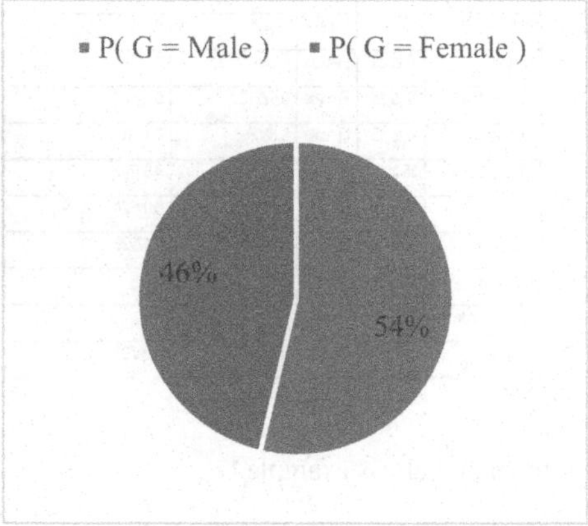

Fig. 7. Prior probability distribution of TB in terms of gender

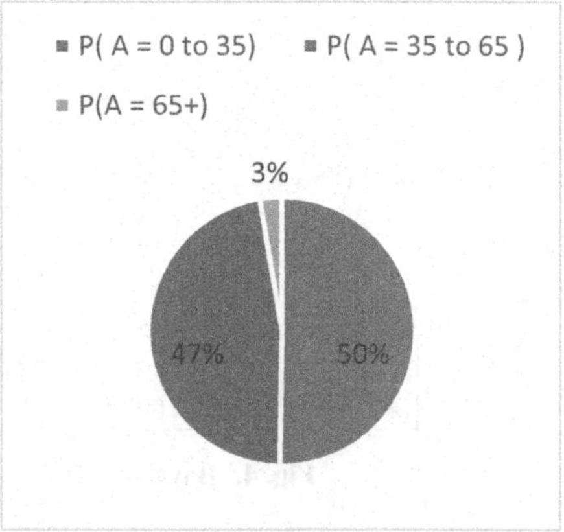

Fig. 8. Prior probability distribution of TB in terms of type of TB

shown in Fig. 9. The conditional probability distribution results for Treatment outcome, TO shown in Table 3.

Testing was done to validate and verify that the system is implemented correctly and according to the functional requirements. The following scenarios were used during testing.

In training the model, five different cases from doctors were injected to test the quality of the MHDSS developed. Each time a case was injected, a calculation was conducted to verify if the MHDSS system has predicted correctly. Let us examine one of the cases injected to the system. To calculate, we used probabilities from Table 3.

To Predict Treatment Outcome of new sample X:

L = Nkangala, A = 0 to 35, G = male, TB = Pulmonary.

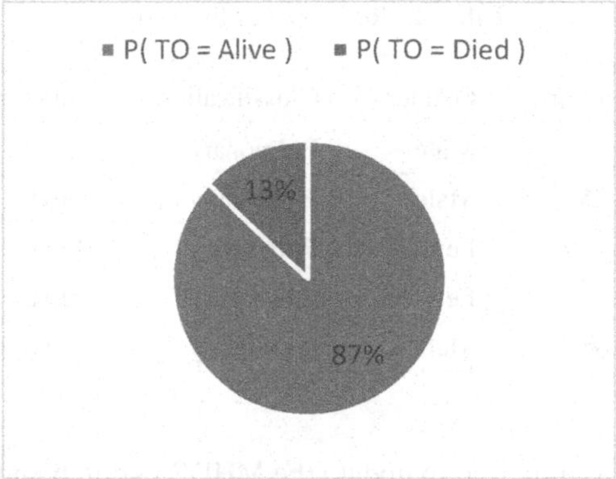

Fig. 9. Prior probability distribution of TB in terms of type of TB

Table 3. Probability distribution for node TO

P(TO = a)	0.86998	P(TO = d)	0.13002
P(L = n | TO = a)	0.28498	P(L = n | TO = d)	0.25751
P(L = g | TO = a)	0.2516	P(L = g | TO = d)	0.26824
P(L = e | TO = a)	0.46341	P(L = e | TO = d)	0.47425
P(A = 0 to 35 | TO = a)	0.52985	P(A = 0 to 35 | TO = d)	0.32189
P(A = 35 to 65 | TO = a)	0.44961	P(A = 35 to 65 | TO = d)	0.61373
P(A = 65 + | TO = a)	0.02054	P(A = 65 + | TO = d)	0.06438
P(G = m | TO = a)	0.53273	P(G = m | TO = d)	0.56438
P(G = f | TO = a)	0.46727	P(G = f | TO = d)	0.43562
P(TB = p | TO = a)	0.89987	P(TB = p | TO = d)	0.91416
P(TB = xp | TO = a)	0.07927	P(TB = xp | TO = d)	0.08369

P(TO = a | X) = P(TO = a) * P(L = n | TO = a) * P(A = 0 to 35 | TO = a) * P(G = m | TO = a) * P(TB = p | TO = a) = 0.86998 * 0.28498 * 0.52985 * 0.532738 * 0.89987 = 0.062975.

P(TO-d | X) = P(TO = d) * P(L = n | TO = d) * P(A = 0 to 35 | TO = d) * P(G = m | TO = d) * P(TB = p | TO = d) = 0.13002 * 0.25751 * 0.32189 * 0.56438 * 0.91416 = 0.00556.

The highest probability is for treatment outcome being alive. To evaluate if the system has predicted correctly, we compute the utility of the system. Table 4 shows that the system was able to correctly predict 3 out the five cases. So it showed a utility of 60%. However, we performed further training with data we got from the hospitals.

The system showed good performance as it could execute a probability results in about 0.15 μs. Further training of the proposed system was done to get the utility of the model. New hourly data was further collected from the department of health. The

Table 4. Results after five tests

Location	Agegroup	Gender	Classification	Outcome	Prediction
Nkangala	0 to 35	Male	Pulmonary	Alive	Alive
Gert Sibande	0 to 35	Male	Pulmonary	Died	Alive
Nkangala	35 to 65	Female	Pulmonary	Alive	Alive
Ehlanzeni	0 to 35	Female	Pulmonary	Alive	Died
Gert Sibande	0 to 35	Male	Pulmonary	Alive	Alive

first hour, new data was imported to update the MHDSS system and new 'belief' would be computed for each and every variable. This further trained the Bayesian Network, resulting in improved accuracy of the model. After each and every hour data was updated, the conditional probability of a person contracting Tuberculosis was computed and prediction calculation similar to the one shown above was done for each case in the new hourly dataset batch. We then compared the prediction with the data that we received from the department to confirm if the system has been predicted correctly or incorrectly. This was then done 63 times (runs) by feeding the system with hourly updated data and each time a percentage of correctly and incorrectly predicted cases were recorded to produce the utility graph of the MHDSS shown in Fig. 10. It shows utility of 88.2% which can be improved by further training of the MHDSS with new data when it becomes available.

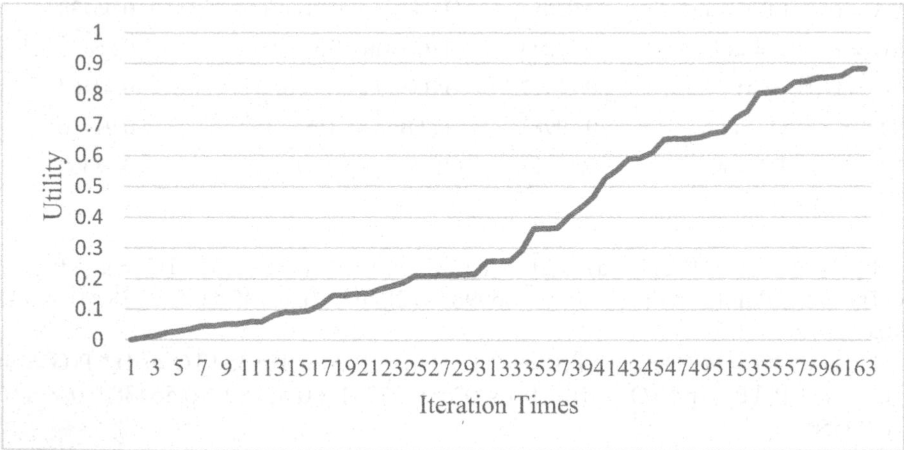

Fig. 10. MHDSS utility

7 Conclusion

Upon testing the model, it predicted the probability of getting infected with Tuberculosis given location, age group and gender. We then did system training, making 63 runs of tests, getting a utility of 88.2%. The MHDSS was scalable, robust and efficient. Bayesian Networks are suitable for use in problems that require reasoning and decision-making under uncertain conditions. Because of their strong mathematical base they handle uncertainty very well using probabilities, and are also simple to build and easy to use. The Bayesian networks thus provide a probability of a specific event occurring. Further research is required to enhance the response of the system. The scalability, security and interoperability of the system could be areas of further research. It can be thought provoking to investigate on how the performance can be improved perhaps by using other models (i.e., neural network, genetic algorithm, etc.) instead of Bayesian Network. Predict the prevalence of Tuberculosis given the rate at which the population is growing. This could be used by government health departments for the control of Tuberculosis. Adoption of the system by the users, government and health practitioners in decision making could be investigated further.

Acknowledgement. The authors would like to acknowledge Tshwane University of Technology for financial support, Mpumalanga provincial health department for data and Tshwane University of Technology ethics committee for ethical approval (Ref. REC2014/01/002) of this project.

References

1. WHO: Tuberculosis Prevalence Surveys. World Health Organisation, New York (2014)
2. Kumari, M., Rajan, V., Anshul, A.: Prediction of diabetes using Bayesian network. Int. J. Comput. Sci. Inf. Technol. **30**(4), 5174–5178 (2014)
3. Thakkar, B.A., Hasan, M.I., Desai, M.A.: Health care decision support system for swine flu prediction using Naives Bayes classifier, Spain (2010)
4. Palaniappan, S., Rafiah, A.: Intelligent heart disease prediction system using data mining techniques. In: IEEE/ACS International Conference, Doha, pp. 108–115 (2008)
5. Sharareh, R., Niakan, K., Xiao-Jun, Z.: Evaluation and comparison of different machine learning methods to predict outcome of tuberculosis treatment course. J. Intell. Learn. Syst. Appl. Suzhou **2013**, 184–193 (2013)
6. Kogeda, O.P., Agbinya, J.I., Omlin, C.W.: A probabilistic approach to faults prediction in cellular networks. In: International Conference on Systems and International Conference on Mobile Communications and Learning Technologies, Sydney (2006)
7. Horvatovich, P., Bischoff, R.: Comprehensive Biomarker Discovery and Validation for Clinical Application. Royal Society of Chemistry, Cambridge (2013)
8. Margaritis, D.: Learning Bayesian Network Model Structure from Data. Carnegie Mellon University, Pittsburgh (2003)
9. Booch, G., Jocobson, I., Rumbaugh, J.: The Unified Modeling Language User Guide. Addison-Wesley, Boston (1999)
10. Achieng, O.G., Kogeda, O.P., Lall, M.: A review of probabilistic modelling of pipeline leakage using Bayesian networks. J. Eng. Appl. Sci. **12**(12), 3163–3173 (2017)

11. Kgoete, S.F., Kogeda, O.P.: A prediction model for mitigating tuberculosis infection for HIV patients at greater Tubatse local municipality in South Africa. In: The Proceedings of Southern Africa Telecommunication Networks and Applications Conference (SATNAC), Fairmont, Zimbali Resort in Ballito, KwaZulu-Natal, South Africa, 1–4 September 2019, pp. 240–247 (2019)
12. Dladlu, N., Kogeda, O.P.: A decision support system for cancer prevalence in South Africa. In: The Proceedings of IEEE 8th International Conference on Computing Technology and Information Management (NCM & ICNIT), vol. 1: NCM Track, Grand Hilton Hotel, Seoul, Korea, 24–26 April 2012, pp. 532–537 (2012)

Origin-Destination Matrix Estimation Using Bush-Based User Equilibrium Algorithms

František Kolovský[1(✉)] and Ivana Kolingerová[2]

[1] Department of Geomatics, University of West Bohemia, Univerzitní 2732/8, 301 00 Pilsen, Czech Republic
kolovsky@kgm.zcu.cz

[2] Department of Computer Science and Engineering, University of West Bohemia, Univerzitní 2732/8, 301 00 Pilsen, Czech Republic
kolinger@kiv.zcu.cz

Abstract. This paper deals with origin-destination matrix estimation using traffic counts where the traffic assignment subproblem is solved using modern bush-based algorithms that are very powerful. The proposed algorithm for the origin-destination matrix estimation uses the well-known advantages of bushes (the origin-rooted acyclic subgraph) so that the algorithm does not need to enumerate the paths between origins and destinations. The proposed approach saves 5%–17% of the computation time compared to the methods that enumerate the paths and also is less memory demanding. The algorithm especially speeds up the origin-destination matrix estimation on high congested road networks.

Keywords: Origin-destination matrix estimation · Traffic assignment problem · Maximum entropy user equilibrium · Bush-based solution · Assignment matrix

1 Introduction

The origin-destination matrix (ODM) estimation (also called calibration) is a very important step in transportation modeling. Unfortunately, it is also a very time-consuming step. There is a lot of methods how to estimate the matrix, e.g., using speed data, traffic counts, and partial path data (license plates). In this paper, we deal with ODM estimation using traffic counts. The input is observed traffic flow on selected links and an initial ODM. The output is the calibrated matrix.

The work was supported by TRAFFO: Innovative Approaches to Mathematical Traffic Modelling for Sustainable Development of Cities and Regions. The Technology Agency of the Czech Republic. Programme: DOPRAVA 2020+. Grant agreement no: CK01000096 and by project SGS-2019-015 ("Application of Mathematics and Informatics in Geomatics IV").

O. Gervasi et al. (Eds.): ICCSA 2021, LNCS 12952, pp. 285–294, 2021.
https://doi.org/10.1007/978-3-030-86973-1_20

After the year 2000, the bush-based algorithms for solving user equilibrium (UE) came. These algorithms provide the equilibrated flow on acyclic subgraphs called bushes so these algorithms compute the UE implicitly without path enumeration and they seem the most powerful class of algorithms for solving UE [13].

In the classic formulations of ODM estimation, the flows on paths between origin-destination pairs are needed to compute the search direction during the matrix estimation. It is well-known that the solution of UE in the path space is not unique and the maximum entropy UE (MEUE) should be computed [19]. The best-known method for solving MEUE is also bush-based and computes the solution without the path enumeration.

Our proposed method builds on bush-based methods and estimates the ODM also without path-enumeration and thus saves the memory and computational time.

In Sect. 2 there are definitions of the problem and all subproblems with a literature survey. Section 3 introduces the proposed method for the determination of the assignment matrix. The numerical tests are described in Sect. 4.

2 Problem Definition and State-of-the-Art

The task is to estimate (calibrate) the origin-destination matrix using the traffic counts. The inputs are non-calibrated (target or initial) ODM and traffic counts on selected edges in the road network.

Let $G = (N, A)$ be a directed graph that represents the road network, where N is a set of nodes and A is a set of edges. The set of zones $Z \subset N$ contains all nodes where the vehicles enter/leave the road network. The $g = \{g_{ij} : ij \in W\}$ is the origin-destination matrix (ODM) containing the number of trips between all zones, where W is a set of all origin-destination (OD) pairs. The g_{ij} is the number of trips between the origin zone $i \in Z$ and the destination zone $j \in Z$. The $Q = \{g : g_{ij} \geq 0\}$ is a set of all feasible ODMs.

2.1 Origin-Destination Matrix Estimation

Let $\widehat{v} = (\widehat{v_a} : a \in \widehat{A})$ be a vector of observed traffic flows where $\widehat{A} \subset A$ is a set of edges where the traffic flow was measured. According to [10] the origin-destination matrix estimation problem is defined as bi-level optimization problem as

$$\min_{g} F(g) = \gamma_1 F_1(g, \widehat{g}) + \gamma_2 F_2(v(g), \widehat{v}) \tag{1}$$

where $\widehat{g}$ is the initial (target) ODM and $v(g)$ is a function that assigns the ODM to the road network. This function provides the static user equilibrium (see next section). The functions F_1 and F_2 return the distance between vectors and can be defined in various way.

The formulation of the objective function F based on entropy maximization was published by Henk [18,22]. The maximum likelihood approach was presented by [16]. Cascetta used the objective functions based on generalized least squares [4]. The Bayesian inference approach provides a method for combining of two sources of information [6,11]. Solution based on classic least squares was published in [10,14,17].

For the purpose of this paper, we simply choose $\gamma_1 = 0$ and

$$F = F_2 = \frac{1}{2} \sum_{a \in \widehat{A}} (v_a - \widehat{v_a})^2 \tag{2}$$

as in [17]. There is a lot of methods how to solve this bi-level problem. The general approach is to use the steepest decedent with a long step [10,17]. A general solution strategy consists from three steps:

- Compute search direction. The simplest method is to take the negative value of the gradient.
- Determine the size of a step so that the objective function is minimized.
- Update the ODM using the search direction and the step size.

The most difficult task is to compute the gradient of F_2, namely, the value of $\frac{\partial v_a}{\partial g_{ij}}$ [10]. For computation of these values there is several heuristic methods (see [10]). A common feature of these methods is that they need the *assignment matrix*. The assignment matrix expresses the relationship between the edge flow v_a and OD flow g_{ij}.

In this paper we present an effective way how to compute the assignment matrix implicitly without path enumeration. For this purpose, the origin-rooted flow provided by bush-based algorithms, are used.

2.2 User Equilibrium

Let the cost c_a of the edge $a \in A$ is dependent on the traffic flow v_a

$$c_a = c_a(v_a) \tag{3}$$

It is assumed that the cost function $c_a(v_a)$ is monotonically increasing and convex. The user's route choice is dependent on travel costs. It follows that equilibrium must be found. The user equilibrium is the state where every used path from the source zone i to the destination zone j has an equal (minimal) cost. The problem of searching user equilibrium is called Traffic Assignment Problem (TAP) and can be defined as Variational Inequality problem (VI) [5,15]. The optimal solution v_p^* must satisfy

$$\sum_{p \in P} c_p(v_p^*)(v_p - v_p^*) \geq 0, \quad \forall u \in \Lambda \tag{4}$$

where v_p is the flow on the path p, P is the set of all used paths in the road network, c_p is the cost of path p, $u = (v_p : p \in P)$ is a vector of all path flows, and Λ is the set of all feasible solutions in the space of paths

$$\Lambda = \left\{ u > 0 : \sum_{p \in P_{ij}} v_p = g_{ij} \quad \forall ij \in W \right\} \tag{5}$$

where $P_{ij} \subset P$ is a set of used paths for OD pair $ij \in W$. The relationship between the solution in the path space and the edge space is

$$v_a = \sum_{p \in P} \delta_{ap} v_p \tag{6}$$

where $\delta_{ap} \in \{0, 1\}$ is equal to one if the edge a lies on the path p otherwise the δ_{ap} is zero. It should be noted that there is only one solution in edge space. In contrast with this the solution in path space is not unique [19].

There are three basic groups of algorithms for solving TAP [13]:

- *Link-based* algorithms compute the solution in the edge space. They have low memory requirements but very poor convergence rate. A classic representative of this group is Frank-Wolfe algorithm (FW). e.g., [9]
- *Path-based* algorithms search the solution in the path space. They are much faster than the link-based algorithms but generally need a lot of memory for the path enumeration. e.g., [1,20]
- *Bush-based* algorithms decompose the problem to acyclic sub-graphs called *bushes*. These algorithms are fast and do not need to enumerate the paths. e.g., [2,3,7,8].

As was shown by Perederieieva in [13], the bushed-based algorithms generally provide good performance.

2.3 Maximum Entropy User Equilibrium

As mentioned above, the assignment matrix and the flow on paths are necessary for ODM estimation, but the solution in path space is not unique. We must choose the solution with the most likely realization that is generally understood in terms of maximum entropy. The maximum entropy user equilibrium (MEUE) is defined as [19]

$$\max_{v_p} = - \sum_{ij \in W} \sum_{p \in P_{ij}} v_p \log\left(\frac{v_p}{g_{ij}}\right) \tag{7}$$

subject to

$$\sum_{p \in P_{ij}} v_p = g_{ij}, \quad \forall ij \in W \tag{8}$$

$$\sum_{p \in P} \delta_{ap} v_p = v_a, \quad \forall a \in A \tag{9}$$

$$v_p \geq 0, \quad \forall p \in P \tag{10}$$

In literature, two methods can solve the MEUE problem for real size networks. The first method by Xie [21] uses the *paired alternative segments* that are provided by TAPAS algorithm [3]. The second method, also by Xie [19] uses the flow on bushes and maximizes entropy on them so the method does not enumerate the paths. As was shown in [19], the second method provides better results.

3 Proposed Solution

In this section, the implicit method for computing the assignment matrix is introduced. For this purpose, the flow on bushes is used. This bush-based flow has to fulfill the user equilibrium and maximizes the entropy. In this paper, the B-algorithm by Dial [7] is used for providing the equilibrated bash-based flow. For entropy maximization, the algorithm by Xie [19] was implemented.

For purpose of this paper, we build on the estimation approaches according to Spiess [17] because it is simple and effective for large networks [10]. However, the idea of assignment matrix computation can be applied to various estimation methods.

According to [17] the gradient is computed as

$$\frac{\partial F(g)}{\partial g_{ij}} = \sum_{k \in P_{ij}} p_k \sum_{a \in \widehat{A}} \delta_{ak}(v_a - \widehat{v_a}) \tag{11}$$

$$= \sum_{a \in \widehat{A}} (v_a - \widehat{v_a}) \sum_{k \in P_{ij}} p_k \delta_{ak} \tag{12}$$

where $p_k = \frac{v_k}{g_{ij}}$ is probability that user chooses the path k on the trip between origin i and destination j. The $\delta_{ap} \in \{0, 1\}$ is one if the edge a lies on path p else is zero. Let us set

$$p_{ij}^a = \sum_{k \in P_{ij}} p_k \delta_{ak} \tag{13}$$

where p_{ij}^a is the probability that the user crosses the edge a on the trip between origin i and destination j. The $\mathbb{P} = \{p_{ij}^a : ij \in W, a \in A\}$ is the assignment matrix. By substitution (13) to (11) we obtain the negative value of search direction

$$d_{ij} = \sum_{a \in \widehat{A}} (v_a - \widehat{v_a}) p_{ij}^a \tag{14}$$

According to [17] the ODM update is performed as

$$g_{ij} = g_{ij}(1 - \lambda d_{ij}) \tag{15}$$

where λ is the length of the step. Using the assignment matrix $\mathbb{P}$, the optimal step length can be rewritten as

$$\lambda = \frac{\sum_{a \in \widehat{A}} v_a'(\widehat{v_a} - v_a)}{\sum_{a \in \widehat{A}} (v_a')^2} \tag{16}$$

where

$$v_a' = \frac{\partial v_a}{\partial \lambda} = -\sum_{ij \in W} g_{ij} d_{ij} p_{ij}^a \tag{17}$$

3.1 The Implicit Computation of Assignment Matrix

Let v_a^i be the flow on the edge $a \in A$ that starts in the origin $i \in Z$. The edges where $v_a^i > 0$ creates the acyclic sub-graph called a bush. For more precise definition see [12]. The source node of the edge a is noted as $s(a)$ and the target node $t(a)$.

According to [19], the path flow can be computed as

$$v_k = g_{ij} \prod_{a \in k} \phi_a^i \tag{18}$$

where

$$\phi_a^i = \frac{v_a^i}{\sum_{e \in I(t(a))} v_e^i} \tag{19}$$

where $I(n)$ is a set of incoming edges to the node $n \in N$. The ϕ_a^i represents the proportion of all bush flow inflowing to the target node $t(a)$ of the edge a. The $s(a)$ is the source node of the edge a. Combining (13) and (19) we have

$$p_{ij}^a = \sum_{k \in P_{ij}} \delta_{ak} \prod_{e \in k} \phi_e^i \tag{20}$$

The implicit computation of the assignment matrix p_{ij}^a is based on Breadth First Search (BFS). Let κ_n be a node label representing the probability that a driver crosses the node n on the trip between zones i and j. It follows, that

$$p_{ij}^a = \kappa_{t(a)} \phi_a^i \tag{21}$$

and

$$\kappa_n = \sum_{a \in O(n)} p_{ij}^a \tag{22}$$

where $O(n)$ is a set of outgoing edges from node n. Using the Eqs. (21) and (22) p_{ij}^a can be determined sequentially for all used edges a corresponding with the OD pair ij.

In Algorithm 1 there is a pseudo-code that computes the assignment matrix for one OD pair. The input of the algorithm is the origin node $i \in Z$, destination node $j \in Z$ and the feasible flow v_a^i on the bush originated at i. For whole assignment matrix, the Algorithm 1 must be run for every OD pair.

First, it is necessary to determine how many outgoing edges from the node n lead to the destination j. The edges with $p_{ij}^a = 0$ do not lead to the destination j. For this purpose, the BFS on the reverse graph is used. The searching starts at the destination node j. In Algorithm 1, the searching is represented by lines 4–10.

The second part of the algorithm sequentially determines p_{ij}^a values. The BFS started at the destination node j is also used for this purpose. The origin and destination node must cross all vehicles so $\kappa_i = \kappa_j = 1.0$. In every edge relaxation p_{ij}^a is determined and the node label $\kappa_{s(a)}$ is updated. The node $s(a)$

Algorithm 1: Implicit computation of the assignment matrix. The input is the OD pair $ij \in W$ and the feasible flow v_a^i on bush originated at i.

1 $o_n = 0 \quad \forall n \in N$
2 U is the FIFO queue of nodes
3 $U.add(j)$
4 **while** $|U| > 0$ **do** // compute the number of outgoing edges o_n
5     $n = U.remove()$
6   **foreach** $e \in I(n)$ **do**
7   **if** $v_e^i > 0$ **then**
8   **if** $o_{s(e)} = 0$ **then**
9                 $U.add(s(e))$
10             $o_{s(e)} = o_{s(e)} + 1$
11 $\kappa_n = 0 \quad \forall n \in N$
12 $\kappa_j = 1.0$ // probability at destination node
13 $U.add(j)$
14 **while** $|U| > 0$ **do** // determine the p_{ij}^e for every link in the bush
15     $n = U.remove()$
16   compute $\phi_e^i \quad \forall e \in I(n)$
17   **foreach** $e \in I(n)$ **do**
18   **if** $\phi_e^i > 0$ **then**
19             $p_{ij}^e = \kappa_n \phi_e^i$
20             $\kappa_{s(e)} = \kappa_{s(e)} + p_{ij}^e$
21             $o_{s(e)} = o_{s(e)} - 1$
22   **if** $o_{s(e)} = 0$ **then**
23                 $U.add(s(e))$

is added to the queue only if $\kappa_{s(a)}$ was updated by all outgoing edges leading to the destination. In Algorithm 1, this procedure is represented by lines 14–23.

In Fig. 1 you can see an example bush with ϕ_a^i that are computed from the bush flow and the result probability values p_{ij}^a. The dashed lines represent the edges leading to other destinations. These edges are eliminated by the first part of the algorithm.

4 Numerical Tests

The proposed method and the original method by [17] for ODM estimation were implemented in the Java programming language. The B-algorithm [7] for solving UE and the algorithm by [19] for determining the MEUE were also implemented in Java. All tests were performed on a laptop with four core processor Intel(R) Core(TM) i5-8250U CPU @ 1.60 GHz and with 16 GB RAM. For testing, the real model of Pilsen (the city in the Czech Republic) was used. The model has 9036 edges, 3727 nodes, 316 zones, and 65411 OD pairs. The relative gap

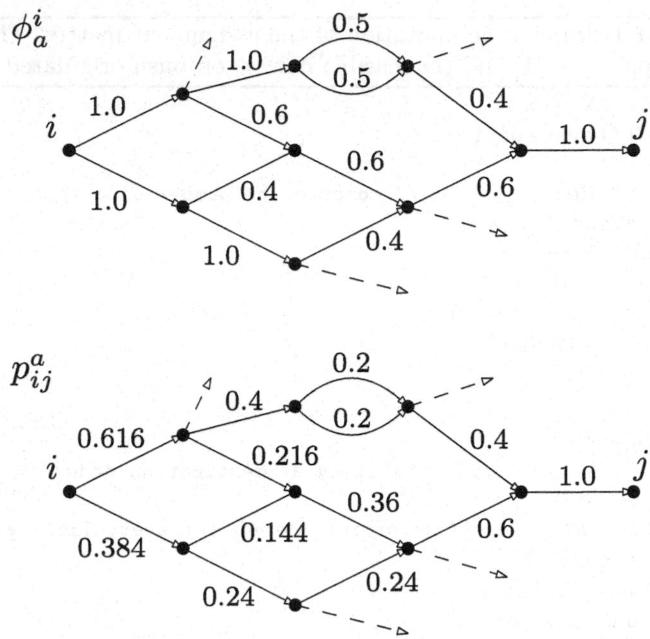

Fig. 1. Example bush with ϕ_a^i and p_{ij}^a values

for B-algorithm was set to 10^{-10}. For a simulation of the high-congested (HC) situation, the original ODM was multiplied by 2.0.

Table 1. Testing results

Model	Number of paths		Update runtime [ms]		Savings [%]
	Initial	Target	Explicit	Implicit	
Pilsen	66 109	69 179	19 467	9 691	50
Pilsen HC	71 083	124 346	26 241	10 041	62

In Table 1 there are results of the tests. The *update runtime* column represents the time that the algorithm spends in the ODM update procedure. The initial number of paths is counted before entropy maximization and the target is measured after entropy maximization. In the case of the original model, there are only 1.06 paths for one OD pair in average. Despite that, the time-savings in the update procedure compared to the original method by [17] are 50%. In high-congested case, there are 1.9 paths for one OD pair in average and the time-savings increase to 62%. It follows that the proposed method is suitable in cases, where there is a lot of route choices.

The most time-consuming part of the ODM estimation is the computation of MEUE so the total time savings are only 6% in the HC case. In most state-of-the-art approaches, the entropy maximization is not taken into account. In this case, the time-savings are 17% for the HC model.

5 Conclusion

The method that computes the assignment matrix implicitly from bush-based flows was introduced. This method does not need to enumerate the paths so the computation of the search direction and the optimal step length is more effective. The tests show that the proposed method saves more than 50% of the time that is needed for ODM updates. In the total computation time, the savings are in the order of percent.

The most time-consuming part is the computation of MEUE. It would be interesting to determine how the precision of the MEUE solution influences the quality of ODM estimation and possibly decreases the accuracy of MEUE computation.

References

1. Babazadeh, A., Javani, B., Gentile, G., Florian, M.: Reduced gradient algorithm for user equilibrium traffic assignment problem. Transportmetrica A Transp. Sci. **16**(3), 1111–1135 (2020). https://doi.org/10.1080/23249935.2020.1722279
2. Bar-Gera, H.: Origin-based algorithm for the traffic assignment problem. Transp. Sci. **36**(4), 398–417 (2002). https://doi.org/10.1287/trsc.36.4.398.549
3. Bar-Gera, H.: Traffic assignment by paired alternative segments. Transp. Res. Part B Methodol. **44**(8-9), 1022–1046 (2010). https://doi.org/10.1016/j.trb.2009.11.004. http://linkinghub.elsevier.com/retrieve/pii/S0191261509001350
4. Cascetta, E.: Estimation of trip matrices from traffic counts and survey data: a generalized least squares estimator. Transp. Res. Part B Methodol. **18**(4–5), 289–299 (1984)
5. Dafermos, S.: Traffic equilibrium and variational inequalities. Transp. Sci. **14**(1), 42–54 (1980)
6. Dey, S.S., Fricker, J.D.: Bayesian updating of trip generation data: combining national trip generation rates with local data. Transportation **21**(4), 393–403 (1994)
7. Dial, R.B.: A path-based user-equilibrium traffic assignment algorithm that obviates path storage and enumeration. Transp. Res. Part B Methodol. **40**(10), 917–936 (2006)
8. Gentile, G.: Local user cost equilibrium: a bush-based algorithm for traffic assignment. Transportmetrica A Transp. Sci. **10**(1), 15–54 (2014). https://doi.org/10.1080/18128602.2012.691911
9. LeBlanc, L.J., Helgason, R.V., Boyce, D.E.: Improved efficiency of the Frank-Wolfe algorithm for convex network programs. Transp. Sci. **19**(4), 445–462 (1985). https://doi.org/10.1287/trsc.19.4.445

10. Lundgren, J.T., Peterson, A.: A heuristic for the bilevel origin–destination-matrix estimation problem. Transp. Res. Part B Methodol. **42**(4), 339–354 (2008). https://doi.org/10.1016/j.trb.2007.09.005. http://www.sciencedirect.com/science/article/pii/S019126150700080X
11. Maher, M.: Inferences on trip matrices from observations on link volumes: a Bayesian statistical approach. Transp. Res. Part B Methodol. **17**(6), 435–447 (1983)
12. Nie, Y.M.: A class of bush-based algorithms for the traffic assignment problem. Transp. Res. Part B Methodol. **44**(1), 73–89 (2010). https://doi.org/10.1016/j.trb.2009.06.005. http://linkinghub.elsevier.com/retrieve/pii/S0191261509000769
13. Perederieieva, O., Ehrgott, M., Raith, A., Wang, J.Y.: A framework for and empirical study of algorithms for traffic assignment. Comput. Oper. Res. **54**, 90–107 (2015). https://doi.org/10.1016/j.cor.2014.08.024. http://linkinghub.elsevier.com/retrieve/pii/S0305054814002354
14. Rostami Nasab, M., Shafahi, Y.: Estimation of origin-destination matrices using link counts and partial path data. Transportation **47**(6), 2923–2950 (2020). https://doi.org/10.1007/s11116-019-09999-1
15. Smith, M.J.: The existence, uniqueness and stability of traffic equilibria. Transp. Res. Part B Methodol. **13**(4), 295–304 (1979)
16. Spiess, H.: A maximum likelihood model for estimating origin-destination matrices. Transp. Res. Part B Methodol. **21**(5), 395–412 (1987)
17. Spiess, H.: A gradient approach for the O-D matrix adjustment problem. EMME/2 Support Center, CH-2558 Aegerten, Switzerland (1990)
18. Van Zuylen, H.J., Willumsen, L.G.: The most likely trip matrix estimated from traffic counts. Transp. Res. Part B Methodol. **14**(3), 281–293 (1980)
19. Xie, J., Nie, Y.M.: A new algorithm for achieving proportionality in user equilibrium traffic assignment. Transp. Sci. **53**(2), 566–584 (2019). https://doi.org/10.1287/trsc.2018.0845
20. Xie, J., Nie, Y.M., Liu, X.: A greedy path-based algorithm for traffic assignment. Transp. Res. Rec. **2672**(48), 36–44 (2018). https://doi.org/10.1177/0361198118774236
21. Xie, J., Xie, C.: New insights and improvements of using paired alternative segments for traffic assignment. Transp. Res. Part B Methodol. **93**, 406–424 (2016). https://doi.org/10.1016/j.trb.2016.08.009. https://www.sciencedirect.com/science/article/pii/S0191261516305902
22. van Zuylen, H.J., Branston, D.M.: Consistent link flow estimation from counts. Transp. Res. Part B Methodol. **16**(6), 473–476 (1982)

The Role of the Smart Citizen in Smart Cities

Mariana Magalhães[1,3], Rui P. Duarte[1,2(✉)], Cátia Oliveira[3], and Filipe C. Pinto[2,3]

[1] Polytechnic of Viseu, Viseu, Portugal
[2] CISeD – Research Centre in Digital Services, Viseu, Portugal
{pduarte,fcpinto}@estgv.ipv.pt
[3] Altice Labs, Aveiro, Portugal
catia-r-oliveira@alticelabs.com

Abstract. The exponential growth of the urban population made cities to feel the obligation to guarantee liveable conditions for all citizens who seek them. The creation of new models of cities and the interconnection between the services they offer became a pressing need. With the technological advancements, all this integration lead cities to scale to the concept of Smart City. This paper focuses on the perspective of the citizen. When asked about how smart the cities where they live, few citizens know it, and, even more, when asked about how participative they are, the answer is null or ineffective. Their perspective is being neglected in public matters, either governmental or environmental. Therefore, it is essential to carry out a comprehensive study that allows understanding how the citizen becomes an integral element of the city where he lives, studies, works, or visits. Inclusive cities use technological platforms that motivate citizens to stay or visit the city, thus contributing to citizen inclusion. It is crucial to understand the best digital approach to meet citizens' needs in the city to take advantage of what the city has to offer.

Keywords: Smart cities · Smart citizens · User experience · Human behavior · Social impact

1 Introduction

Due to the rapid growth of the urban population and the lack of natural resources, cities face several challenges that can range from technical, material, social to organizational, thus influencing citizens' quality of life. It is of most importance to develop logistical measures for the proper functioning of cities and at the same time guarantee livable conditions for all citizens. In this sense, new models of interconnection of services have become a pressing need. With the exponential evolution of technology in the recent years, cities tend to use Information and Communication Technologies (ICT) to become more attractive, sustainable, interactive, and accessible, which lead to the concept of Smart City (SC).

O. Gervasi et al. (Eds.): ICCSA 2021, LNCS 12952, pp. 295–310, 2021.
https://doi.org/10.1007/978-3-030-86973-1_21

According to Zubizarreta et al. [1], a SC is a constantly evolving city, using technology in its different areas of application such as economy, people, housing, governance, environment, and mobility. Moreover, a SC requires the active involvement and participation of the citizen. Although the definition of a SC is well established in the literature, there is no clear definition of smart citizens. According to Yonezawa et al. [2], an attractive city focuses on the citizen who is a crucial component to the city since he consumes what the city provides. However, it is imperative to facilitate the citizen's participation process. Mellouli et al. [3] refer that the citizen's opinion has a significant contribution to public issues, such as the development of society, the design and implementation of public policies, and decisions transparently and responsibly. Cities need to show the citizen that their involvement is relevant and positively impacts the community. To achieve this, it is also necessary to provide the citizen useful, relevant, and complete information.

1.1 Smart Cities

Citizens increasingly switch from rural to urban areas, causing rapid population growth. This implies that cities need to face issues related to governance and deficit of natural resources, which influence the future of cities and citizens.

Pellicer et al. [4] refer that, currently, the concept of SC is widely used, influencing the analysis of its meaning in different perspectives. Although there are multiple definitions, the authors state that a SC is an urban system that uses ICT to make its infrastructures and public services more interactive, accessible, and efficient, so it must be able to efficiently manage its infrastructure and services, taking into account the needs of the cities and their citizens. Kumar and Dahiya [5] state that SC are composed of six fundamental areas: smart people, smart economy, smart mobility, smart environment, smart housing, and smart governance. Intelligent people are the critical element of cities because their participation is essential for a sustainable development. Joss et al. [6] believe that it is not enough to make incremental improvements in the management of cities, and claim that city leaders should identify and implement radical and transformative solutions. They describe new approaches to the city management and consider that the development of technologies provides new and useful tools, creating more significant opportunities for citizens, companies, and other organizations to implement the required changes. Examples of these management tools include parking, traffic, air quality, water consumption, and urban waste. In terms of parking management, Lu et al. [7] developed an intelligent parking system (SPARK) which provides information to the user in real-time of empty parking lots. The system also provides an anti-theft protection service, by detecting if the vehicle leaves the parking area illegally. Another system implemented in this area is the Khanna and Anand project [8]. Their smart parking system indicates available spaces in real-time, and allows the user to reserve a parking space for a period of time.

The increasing number of vehicles circulating in cities causes traffic congestion, an increase in the number of accidents, and high fuel consumption.

Kanungo et al. [9] calculated traffic density in real-time using cameras to allow the automatic management of traffic lights, improving the fluidity of traffic. In this context, Ghazal et al. [10] developed a system that allows the traffic lights to be switched depending on the traffic density. This system complements with a portable controller for priority vehicles stuck in traffic. The vehicles communicate through a wireless system, XBee, to activate the emergency mode. Air pollution is a global concern in the management of air quality due to citizens' exposition to air pollutants. AirSense is an air quality detection system presented by Dutta et al. [11] consisting in the aggregation of data from sensors to infer air quality. Through a heat map, citizens can view the city's air pollution and the air quality index of his location. The captured data can alert the citizen to make decisions about how to improve the environment. Regarding water, within cities, there is a growing concern for its efficient management. To ensure that water is properly supervised, Shahanas and Sivakumar [12] propose an intelligent water management system using IoT. It includes sensors that measure several tanks' water level in real-time, with observable information generated on a web platform. Also, the system allows the reception of alerts through SMS or email. Finally, at the level of urban waste management, there is a pressing need to reduce the stench on city streets, spread of diseases, and the reproduction of insects in the garbage due to the overflow of the containers. Sharma et al. [13] monitor the degree of filling of the garbage containers in real-time. They verify when they are full and act quickly and efficiently in their emptying. Considering the diverse works presented in the different areas of a SC, there are multiple platforms developed that help SC provide responsive services to improve their governance and citizens' quality of life. However, it is essential to have the vision of citizen participation.

1.2 Citizen Participation

According to Degbelo et al. [14], cities need to gather macro (aggregate data) and micro (citizen generated data) observations to discover how global phenomena (transport, mobility, energy, etc.) relate to the observations of citizens. It is essential to listen to citizens' opinions, understand and act in accordance to improve the quality of life in cities. Neirotti et al. [15] claim that the population of cities with more advanced internet services makes citizens more active in launching and participating in initiatives in areas such as government and economy.

Citizen participation can provide multiple benefits to cities, such as more significant contribution to education and socialization processes, better political decisions, producing better social and environmental results [16]. However, the citizen must receive useful, relevant, and complete information to give their opinion in a meaningful way. According to Caragliu et al. [17], a way to reach out to citizens is through ICT, since they enable sustainable economic growth and high quality of life, with intelligent management of natural resources, through participatory governance. ICTs can energize the citizen so that they have direct participation in the city's sustainable growth. According to Granier and Kudo

[18], some students consider ICT a powerful means of promoting and improving public participation. These can reduce participation costs, allowing citizens to participate through their mobile devices at any time and place. The authors consider the means of expression and communication provided by ICTs as objects that allow new citizens to have an interest and legitimacy in participating in public affairs. Both students and professionals emphasize that citizens play a crucial role in SC, not only for their appropriate behavior but also for their governance participation.

This paper focuses on the citizen's perspective to improve the quality of his experience in the city. Moreover, it is measured how the different means of communication can be used to better establish a communication between the city and the citizen.

2 Materials and Methods

This section identifies the objectives and research hypothesis. Moreover, the methodological approach implemented in the different stages of the investigation, as well as exploratory research and qualitative research, is presented.

2.1 Research Goals and Hypothesis

The research goals define what is to be achieved with the research to be carried out. They are declarative statements that clarify the keywords, the target population, and the research's orientation [19]. Thus, the research goals of this paper are: (1) understand how the digital means can be used to improve the citizen experience; and (2) define the digital model that enhances the improvement of the citizen's experience in the city.

The research hypotheses are constructed to explain or understand a specific phenomenon and are guidelines for the problem to be demonstrated [20]. Notwithstanding its formulation tries to answer the formulated problem, they are assumptions as they may not be confirmed with the research results. However, they provide the research a guiding thread and criteria to select relevant data. Following the objectives of the research work, the research hypotheses are:

- H_A: The way the city communicates with the citizen influences their participation in the city
- H_B: A mobile application is a suitable digital means for citizens to communicate with the city and encourage their participation
- H_C: The type of information that the citizen seeks depends on several characteristics, such as age, profession, means of travel, and the region where he lives

2.2 Qualitative Analysis

Qualitative research is a methodology based on samples that provide an understanding of the problem context [21], and to answer research questions [22].

According to the qualitative research and the research hypotheses, the elaboration of a questionnaire is an adequate procedure to collect feedback from the target audience [20]. Wolniak and Jonek-Kowalska [23] refer that the city's quality of life is measured by implementing the ISO 37120 standard of the International Organization for Standardization that evaluates cities' performance and consists of a list of indicators. Hajduk [24] states that the ISO 37120 standard is the most practical method for measuring the city's performance.

For the formulation of the questionnaire, several research questions are defined: *Q1*: What type of information citizens look for?; *Q2*: Which means of communication influence the citizen?; *Q3*: Are citizens aware that cities are smart cities?; *Q4*: How information in public spaces influences the citizen?; *Q5*: Is environment information important for citizens?; *Q6*: Active participation rewards are important for the citizen?

3 Results

This section aims to present the results obtained from the qualitative analysis resulting from the responses achieved by disseminating the questionnaire. The study is divided into three phases: the characterization of the sample profile, the analysis of the main results, and the validation of the research hypotheses.

3.1 Sample Characterization

This section characterizes socio-demographic characteristics of the sample made of 387 valid answers from portuguese citizens; 55% of participants are females, and the overall ages vary from 15 to 79 years, and the most representative is between 19 to 24 years (average age of the sample is 31 years). 61% of the citizens live in the urban space and 39% in rural areas. Most citizens (91.6%) live with other people in their household. Moreover, 50.4% are employed, while 32.6% are students and 17% are retired or unemployed. The preferred means of transport is personal transport (72.6%), and the rest use public transportation or shared transport.

3.2 Influence of Information

There is a lot of information available to citizens, however not all of that information is relevant. Generally, a young citizen does not have the same interests as an older citizen. To understand these differences, Fig. 1 presents the information that groups of citizens look for according to their ages, and three major groups can be identified: under 25 years old (given by Fig. (1a) and Fig. (1b)), a transition group between 26 and 39 (Fig. (1c)), and over 40 (Fig. (1d) and Fig. (1e)). Results show that citizens have a great interest in social media, films, news, and products. Although social networks are influencers in all age groups, it tends to reduce for older citizens, as well as films. On the other hand, news and services' influence increases for older citizens.

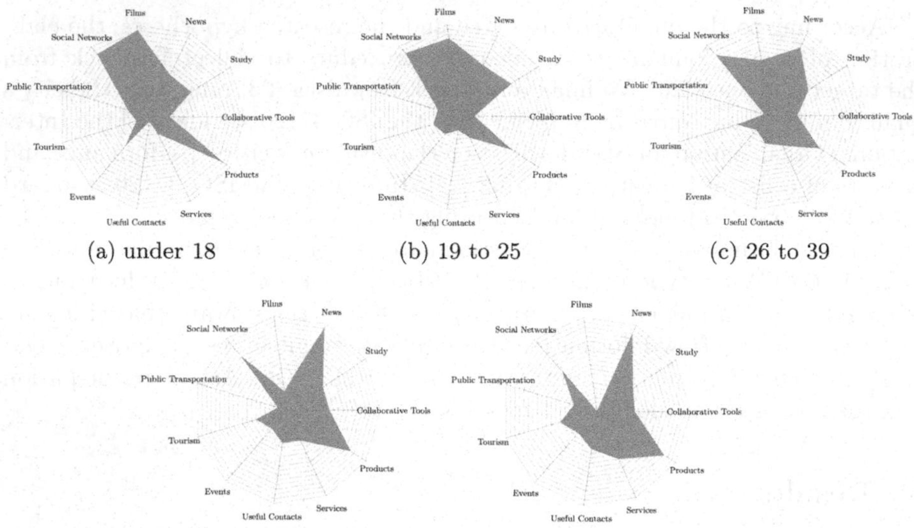

(a) under 18 (b) 19 to 25 (c) 26 to 39

(d) 40 to 59 (e) over 60

Fig. 1. Distribution of influence of information into age groups.

Considering the region where the citizen lives (Fig. (2a)), there are no representative differences regarding the interest in information. The most valued information is social media, news, buying products, studying, and watching films or series. At the gender level (Fig. (2b)), similar interests are identified. Both genders are interested in products, news, studying, and social networks. This analysis is concordant with the information inquired by citizens living in rural or urban areas, by their occupation, and age groups.

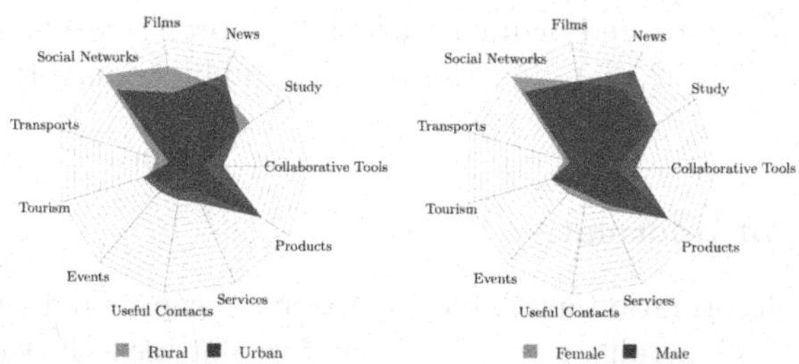

(a) Region (b) Gender

Fig. 2. Distribution of influence of information considering regions and gender.

3.3 Influence of Means of Communication

The means of communication aim to disseminate information, so cities should consider them a form of communication with the citizen. In this sense,for cities to captivate the citizen's interests, it is crucial to consider which means of communication are best received by the citizen. The means that most influences the citizens are social networks, television, websites, and mobile applications, as shown in Fig. 3.

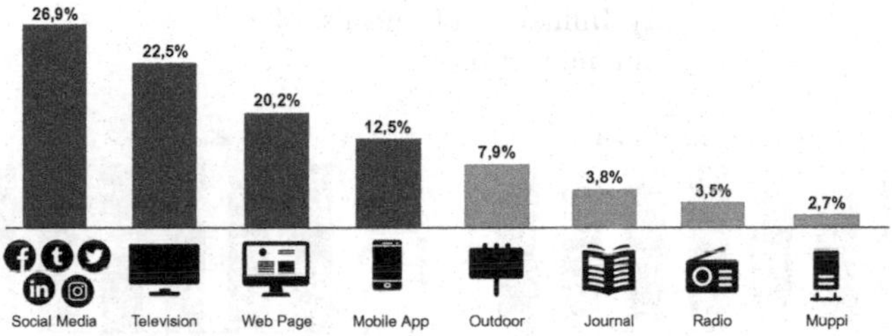

Fig. 3. Influence of different means of communication.

By considering the analysis of the region where the citizen lives, there are no significant differences. Social networks have more influence in rural areas, and the remaining media in urban areas (Fig. (4a)). When incorporating the age range, and the region where the citizen lives, it is noticeable the difference in the values. While in the rural area, television, social media, websites, and mobile apps have great influence in under 25 years old citizens. On the other hand, these values decrease in this age range and increase for other age ranges, as presented in Fig. (4b) and Fig. (4c).

3.4 Citizen Awareness of Living in a Smart City

Due to the continuous increase in the population in cities, which makes their management difficult, they tend to use technology to guarantee a better quality of life for citizens and provide them better services [25]. With this, cities tend to become more intelligent; however, this intelligence does not always reach the citizens' knowledge. This is aligned with the results obtained in this paper, since 56% of citizens are not aware of the use of technology in cities (from these, 57% live in urban areas).

Thus, nevertheless some technologies are incorporated in cities, they do not reach public knowledge, and, thus, do not have the expected impact on citizen's lives.

3.5 Impact of Information in Public Spaces in the Citizen

This paper aims at investigating if the means that exist in a city can influence the citizen to engage with the city. If this occurs, cites are able to capture citizen attention to promote the concept of SC. Several aspects are taken

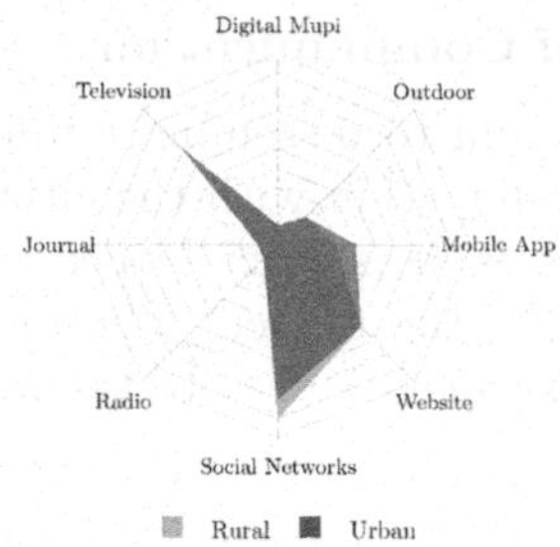

(a) Influence of means of communication

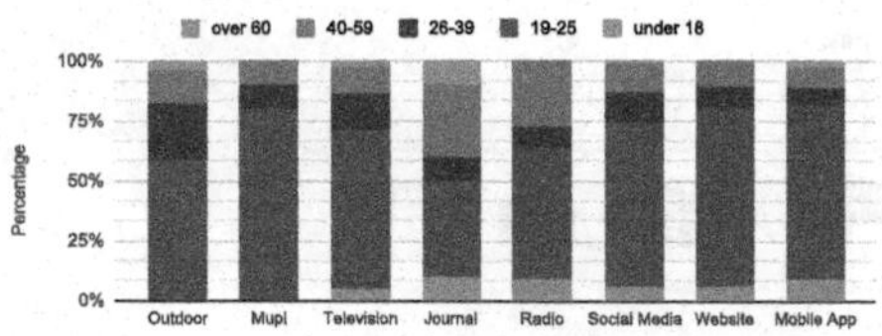

(b) Rural age distribution

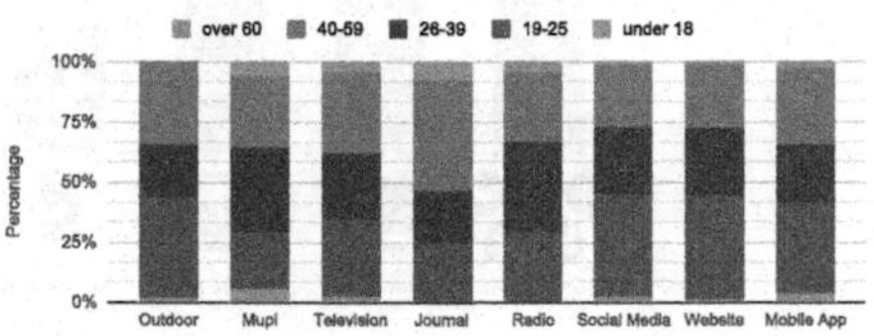

(c) Urban age distribution

Fig. 4. Means of communication in rural and urban areas.

into account: public transportation, road work, charity actions, municipality discounts or investments, with special focus on their environmental concerns. Results show that citizens are aware and interested, as presented in Fig. 5.

Due to the excessive population in cities there is an increase in waste production and resources become limited, making recycling a growing concern [26]. It is essential to raise awareness among citizens to act differently. This section examines the citizen's interest obtaining discounts for recycling actions. Figure (5a) shows that the information is considered attractive regarding discounts in municipality taxes, except for citizens up to 18 years old. The use of alternative transport is one of the environmental concerns of cities since by reducing car traffic, CO2 emissions into the atmosphere are also reduced. This study variable measures the impact on the citizens when receiving discounts by using an alternative transport. According to Fig. (5b), this information is considered important for the citizen. At another level, public transport is a means of transport used by citizens in various activities, typically managed by schedules and routes, which may change. Citizens up to the age of 59 are interested in obtaining information about public transport changes (Fig. (5c)). Citizens over 60 years of age have different opinions, which is related to the region they live in (less interest in urban citizens). Regarding the road work scenario, depicted in Fig. (5d), this information is considered of interest in all age ranges. At the donations level, it is common to see cities ask for donations to assist several charity associations. Although citizens under 25 are neutral about this subject, all the other citizens consider this information interesting, as shown in Fig. (5e). Within the scope of citizen participation in city governance, there has been a significant increase in Participatory Budgets' participation, promoted by cities. According to Fig. (5f), citizens measured their interest in information related to the city's intervention, resulting from their action. Thus, most citizens find this information interesting at the investment level, emphasizing citizens over 60 years of age. The opinion of citizens under the age of 18 is divided.

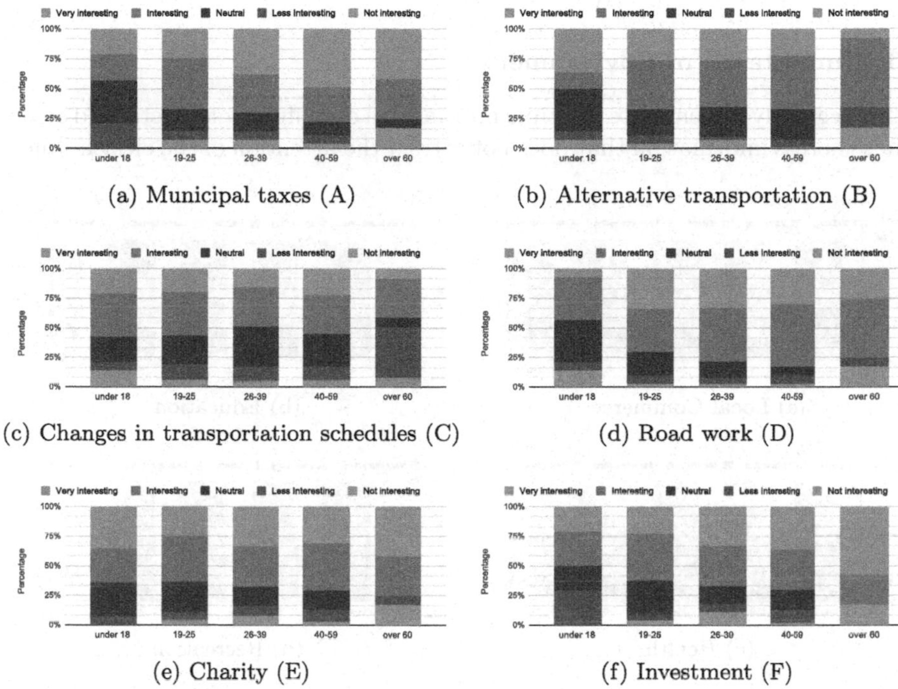

(a) Municipal taxes (A)

(b) Alternative transportation (B)

(c) Changes in transportation schedules (C)

(d) Road work (D)

(e) Charity (E)

(f) Investment (F)

Fig. 5. Impact of information in public spaces.

In addition to the scenarios presented above, this study also considers a set of interest areas to the citizen, presented in Fig. 6. The areas of health and recreation are those that capture the attention of citizens. Advertising is the type of information that they find less interesting or feel neutral. In general terms, the traditional use of outdoors for advertising has little impact on the citizen, in this context.

When refining this analysis related to the age ranges, different results are obtained (Fig. 7). With the exception of advertising, all age ranges consider each type of information as interesting in all age ranges, with the exceptions of under 18 citizens in information regarding health (Fig. (7c)) and municipality services (Fig. (7e)). On the other extreme, information regarding sports is considered neutral for citizens above 60 years old (Fig. (7f)).

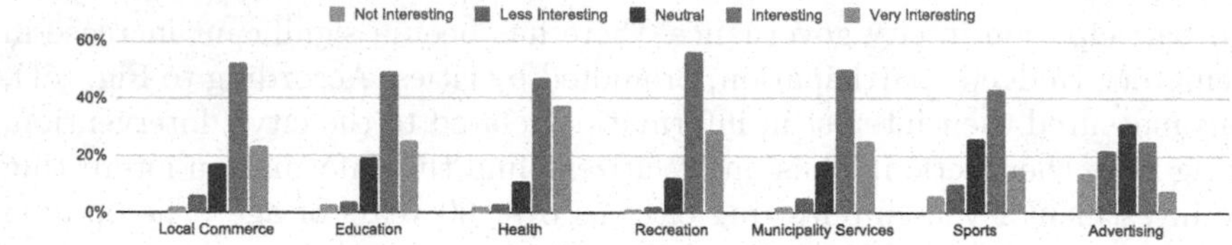

Fig. 6. Information exhibited in outdoor means of communication.

3.6 Importance of Environment

Cities regularly disseminate multiple information on different subjects, and sometimes there is information that does not attract the attention of the citizen. Infor-

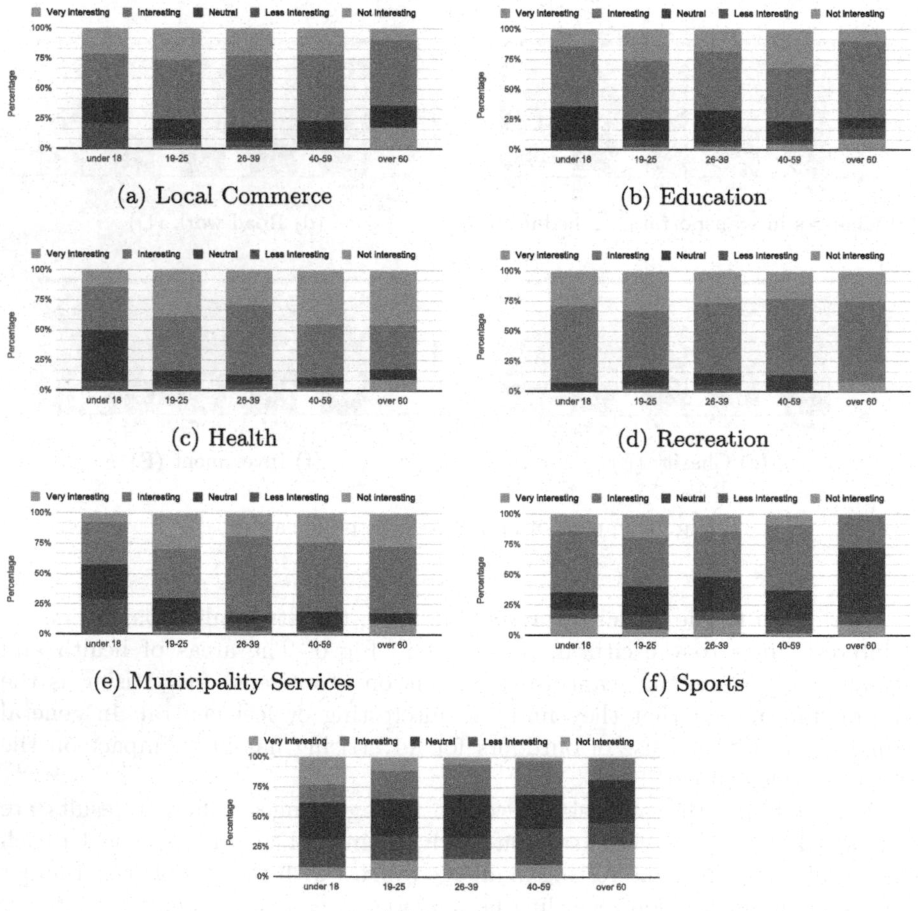

(a) Local Commerce

(b) Education

(c) Health

(d) Recreation

(e) Municipality Services

(f) Sports

(g) Advertising

Fig. 7. Areas of interest for the citizen by age range.

mation about the environment sometimes appears to be unappealing information due to a lack of regular dissemination. Thus, according to Fig. 8, all information is considered important, despite the significant interest in civil warnings. The detailed analysis of the interest of citizens does not vary when considering the region where the citizen lives and the age range. As a consequence of the citizen interest in environment, becomes clear that cities must take this into account. Thus, according to the qualitative research, cities tend to invest in projects that involve taking care of the environment. However, it also appears that cities need to motivate citizens to participate. Thus, the interest of offering rewards to citizens is analyzed if they perform a specific action. According to Fig. 9, rewards are a good way to captivate the citizen to this concern.

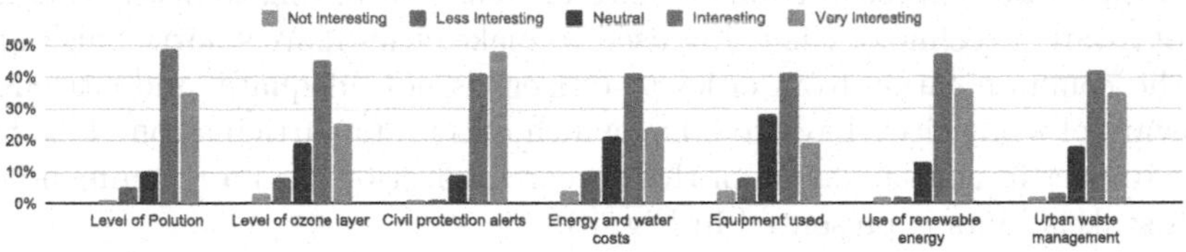

Fig. 8. Importance of environmental information.

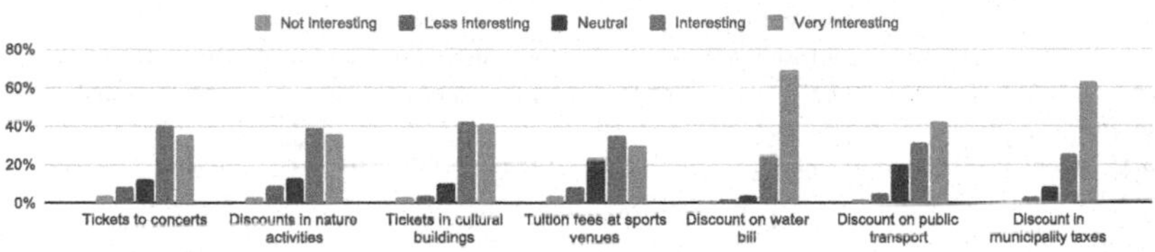

Fig. 9. Importance of rewards.

3.7 Validation of the Research Questions

After characterizing the sample and analyzing the main results, it is essential to determine the research hypotheses' integrity by executing statistical tests, ANOVA, and Chi-square, to compare the hypothesis variables and their dependence and association relationship.

***H_A* - The Way the City Communicates with the Citizen Influences their Participation in the City:** As previously referred, it is important to listen to the citizen so that the city can act to improve its life quality. For that, it is important that citizens obtain useful information so that they feel as an integral member of it. Two hypothesis have been defined: *H0*: The citizen is not interested in participating in the city through the means of communication, and *H1*: The citizen is interested in participating in the city through the means of communication. According to Table 1, the citizen is interested in participating in the city, since multiple solutions reject *H0*. To understand the communication from the city to the citizen, the impact of the means of communication in the citizen participation is tested with the following hypothesis: *H0*: The mean of technological communication do not influence the citizen participation, and *H1*: The means of technological communication influence the citizen participation. ANOVA Results show that the outdoor is the only mean that rejects *H0* ($\sigma = 0.049 < 0.05$). Since citizens are not aware that the city uses technology to make it a SC, this is an indicator that the communication is not adequate. This way, *H1* has to be considered, since communication is of major importance in a city. In this context, citizens need to be informed about the use of technology, and the development of applications for citizens has to be preceded by a different communicational approach from cities to citizens. According to Sect. 3.4 citizens are not aware if technology is being used to make cities more smart. This implies that the communication from cities to citizens is not adequate, and citizens are not aware of what cities have to offer, which affects its participation. This has a major impact in the validation of this research question, and a recommendation for all stakeholders is presented in Fig. 10.

Table 1. ANOVA test with citizen participation and means of communication.

Solutions	ANOVA (sig. Value)							
	Outdoor	Digital Mupi	Television	Journal	Radio	Social media	Websites	Mobile apps
Register problems of the city	0.04	0.574	0.05	0.297	0.091	0.008	0.03	0.07
Report problematic locations in the city	0.880	0.550	0.418	0.138	0.143	0.01	0.049	0.096
Share information about events in open spaces	0.276	0.195	0.023	0.210	0.309	<0.001	0.077	0.047
Report Level of occupation of public trash deposits	0.032	0.043	0.024	0.789	0.347	<0.001	0.022	0.028
Share or rent non-polluent transports	0.264	<0.001	0.027	0.311	0.274	<0.001	0.081	0.088

H_B: A Mobile Application is a Suitable Digital Mean for Citizens to Communicate with the City and Encourage Participation: According to Sect. 3.3, there are several means of communication that are well received by the citizen, and the mobile application is within the top means. W have tested if the other means of communication are influencers of using mobile applications. The following hypothesis were formulated: *H0*: The use of mobile application is not influenced by other means of communication, and *H1*: The use of mobile application is influenced by other means of communication.

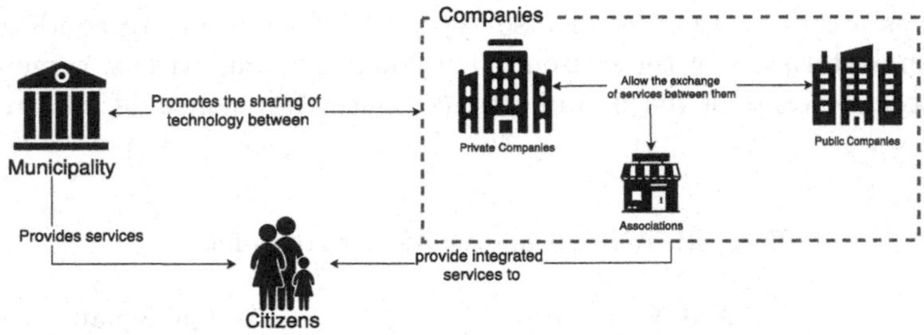

Fig. 10. Recommendation for stakeholders in a SC environment.

ANOVA results show that only radio ($\sigma = 0.585$) and journals ($\sigma = 0.228$) accept *H0*, that is, they are not influencers for the use of mobile applications. All the other means are important influencers for the use of mobile applications to generate communication between the city and the citizen. Thus, the use of a mobile application is an adequate mean to establish a communication between the city and the citizen, and H_B is accepted. Figure 11 illustrates how the means can be used to influence the acceptance of mobile applications as means of communication.

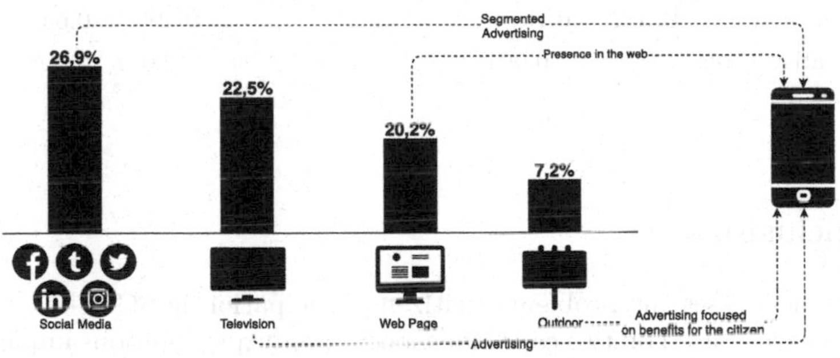

Fig. 11. Distribution of the means of communication as influencers to the use of mobile applications.

H_C: The Type of Information that the Citizen Seeks Depends on Several Characteristics, Such as Age, Profession, Means of travel, and the Region where he Lives: The citizens' interest on specific information is segmented in several groups as age, gender, mean of transportation, and rural or urban. To determine if different groups of citizens have different interests, two types of tests were carried out: ANOVA and Qui-square for the following hypothesis: *H0*: The type of information citizens are interested is not related to the characteristics of the citizen, and *H1*: The type of information citizens are interested depends on the characteristics of the citizen. Results are presented in Table 2, and *H1* is accepted for most cases, indicating that the H_C research question is accepted and the diverse types of information are conditioned by several characteristics of the citizen. Therefore, to reach citizens, targeted marketing approaches is of major importance, since they consume information in different ways.

Table 2. ANOVA and Qui-Square tests for H_C.

Activity	ANOVA			Qui-Square	
	σ				
	Age	Occupation	Mean transport	Gender	Rural/Urban
Study	0.012	<0.001	<0.001	0.423	0.171
Read news	<0.001	<0.001	0.073	0.003	0.002
Watch movies	<0.001	<0.001	0.174	0.844	<0.001
Social media	0.003	0.005	0.002	<0.001	0.003
Public transports	0.001	0.004	<0.001	0.008	0.017
Touristic points	0.375	0.008	0.014	0.838	0.068
Search for events	0.668	0.603	0.842	0.273	0.286
Usefull contacts	0.012	0.007	<0.001	0.047	0.199
Available services	0.102	0.158	0.011	0.321	0.008
Products	0.012	0.167	0.302	0.496	0.636
Collaborative tools	<0.001	<0.001	0.057	<0.001	0.008

4 Conclusions

This paper addresses the problem of citizen participation in SC. The methodology followed was based on two essential aspects: analyzing solutions implemented in other SC and understanding the citizen. In the latter, more than knowing what the city has to offer, it explored the citizen's opinion about what interests him, understanding the way he sees the city and whether it influences his participation. This work allowed us to realize that cities tend to take advantage of technology. Still, they do not always communicate correctly, as most citizens are not aware of the technology used in cities, affecting their participation.

When analyzing the research hypotheses, citizens have different interests according to their characteristics, such as age, gender, the location where they live, and means of transport used. Based on this, it was also studied that the type of information that captivates the citizen's interest the most is the information that influences their daily lives and rewards them for their attitudes. Then, based on the integrity of the research hypotheses, it is concluded that the digital medium that the citizen best receives is the mobile application, taking into account the means of communication used in the city as influencers of the application. Results show that the way the city communicates is of major importance since, without communication, the citizen does not obtain information about the city. For example, when verifying that the mobile application is the best way received by the citizen, citizens must know about their existence to enjoy the application and participate in the city. Therefore, nevertheless a user-centered mobile application becomes an asset for citizen participation in the city, it is necessary to bear in mind that the stakeholders in a city need to communicate between them and with the citizen so that he becomes an active member of the city.

Acknowledgements. This work is funded by National Funds through the FCT - Foundation for Science and Technology, I.P., within the scope of the project Ref. UIDB/05583/2020. Furthermore, we would like to thank the Research Centre in Digital Services (CISeD) and the Polytechnic of Viseu for their support.

References

1. Zubizarreta, I., Seravalli, A., Arrizabalaga, S.: Smart city concept: what it is and what it should be. J. Urban Plan. Dev. **142**(1), 04015005 (2016)
2. Yonezawa, T., Matranga, I., Galache, J.A., Maeomichi, H., Gurgen, L., Shibuya, T.: A citizen-centric approach towards global-scale smart city platform. In: 2015 International Conference on Recent Advances in Internet of Things (RIoT), pp. 1–6. IEEE (2015)
3. Mellouli, S., Luna-Reyes, L.F., Zhang, J.: Smart government, citizen participation and open data. Inf. Polity **19**(1,2), 1–4 (2014)
4. Pellicer, S., Santa, G., Bleda, A.L., Maestre, R., Jara, A.J., Skarmeta, A.G.: A global perspective of smart cities: a survey. In: 2013 Seventh International Conference on Innovative Mobile and Internet Services in Ubiquitous Computing, pp. 439–444. IEEE (2013)
5. Vinod Kumar, T.M., Dahiya, B.: Smart economy in smart cities. In: Vinod Kumar, T.M. (ed.) Smart Economy in Smart Cities. ACHS, pp. 3–76. Springer, Singapore (2017). https://doi.org/10.1007/978-981-10-1610-3_1
6. Joss, S., Cook, M., Dayot, Y.: Smart cities: towards a new citizenship regime? a discourse analysis of the british smart city standard. J. Urban Technol. **24**(4), 29–49 (2017)
7. Lu, R., Lin, X., Zhu, H., Shen, X.: Spark: a new vanet-based smart parking scheme for large parking lots. IEEE INFOCOM **2009**, 1413–1421 (2009)
8. Khanna, A., Anand, R.: Iot based smart parking system. In: 2016 International Conference on Internet of Things and Applications (IOTA), pp. 266–270 (2016)
9. Kanungo, A., Sharma, A., Singla, C.: Smart traffic lights switching and traffic density calculation using video processing. In: 2014 Recent Advances in Engineering and Computational Sciences (RAECS), pp. 1–6 (2014)
10. Ghazal, B., ElKhatib, K., Chahine, K., Kherfan, M.: Smart traffic light control system. In: 2016 Third International Conference on Electrical, Electronics, Computer Engineering and their Applications (EECEA), pp. 140–145 (2016)
11. Dutta, J., Gazi, F., Roy, S., Chowdhury, C.: Airsense: opportunistic crowd-sensing based air quality monitoring system for smart city. In: 2016 IEEE SENSORS, pp. 1–3 (2016)

12. Mohammed Shahanas, K., Bagavathi Sivakumar, P.: Framework for a smart water management system in the context of smart city initiatives in India. Procedia Comput. Sci. **92**, 142–147 (2016). 2nd International Conference on Intelligent Computing, Communication & Convergence, ICCC 2016, 24–25 January 2016, Bhubaneswar, Odisha, India
13. Singh, M.S., Singh, K.M., Ranjeet, R.K., Shukla, K.K.: Smart bin implementation for smart city. Int. J. Adv. Res. Comput. Eng. Commun. Eng. **6**(4), 765–769 (2017)
14. Degbelo, A., Granell, C., Trilles, S., Bhattacharya, D., Casteleyn, S., Kray, C.: Opening up smart cities: citizen-centric challenges and opportunities from giscience. ISPRS Int. J. Geo-Inf. **5**(2), 16 (2016)
15. Neirotti, P., De Marco, A., Cagliano, A.C., Mangano, G., Scorrano, F.: Current trends in smart city initiatives: some stylised facts. Cities **38**, 25–36 (2014)
16. Irvin, R.A., Stansbury, J.: Citizen participation in decision making: is it worth the effort? Public Adm. Rev. **64**(1), 55–65 (2004)
17. Caragliu, A., Bo, C.D., Nijkamp, P.: Smart cities in europe. J. Urban Technol. **18**(2), 65–82 (2011)
18. Granier, B., Kudo, H.: How are citizens involved in smart cities? analysing citizen participation in Japanese "smart communities". Inf. Polity **21**(1), 61–76 (2016)
19. O'Leary, Z.: The Essential Guide to Doing Your Research Project. Sage, Thousand Oaks (2017)
20. De Vaus, D., de Vaus, D.: Surveys in Social Research. Routledge, Abingdon (2013)
21. Churchill, G.A., Iacobucci, D.: Marketing research: methodological foundations (2006)
22. Miles, M.B., Huberman, A.M.: Qualitative Data Analysis: An Expanded Sourcebook. Sage, Thousand Oaks (1994)
23. Wolniak, R., Jonek-Kowalska, I.: The level of the quality of life in the city and its monitoring. Innov. Eur. J. Social Sci. Res., 1–23 (2020)
24. Hajduk, S., et al.: The concept of a smart city in urban management. Bus. Manag. Educ. **14**(1), 34–49 (2016)
25. Dameri, R.: Searching for smart city definition: a comprehensive proposal. In: BIOINFORMATICS 2013 (2013)
26. Pelonero, L., Fornaia, A., Tramontana, E.: From smart city to smart citizen: rewarding waste recycle by designing a data-centric iot based garbage collection service. In: 2020 IEEE International Conference on Smart Computing (SMARTCOMP), pp. 380–385 (2020)

A MCDA/GIS-Based Approach for Evaluating Accessibility to Health Facilities

D. F. Lopes(✉), J. L. Marques, and E. A. Castro

GOVCOPP, DCSPT, University of Aveiro, Aveiro, Portugal
lopesdiana@ua.pt

Abstract. Access to health care services is a key concept in the formulation of health policies to improve the population's health status and to mitigate inequities in health. Previous studies have significantly enhanced our understanding and knowledge of the role played by spatial distribution of health facilities in sustaining population health, with extensive research being devoted to the place-based accessibility theory, with special focus on the gravity-based methods. Although they represent a good starting point to analyse disparities across different regions, the results are not intelligible for policy-making purposes. Given the weaknesses of these methods and the multidimensional nature of the topic, this study intends to: (i) highlight the main measurements of access and their major challenges; and (ii) propose a framework based on multiple criteria decision analysis methods and GIS to appraise the population's accessibility to health facilities. In particular, this framework is based on a new variant of the UTASTAR method, which requires decision makers and/or experts preference information, in the form of an ordinal ranking, similarly to the UTASTAR method, but to which cardinal information is also added. A numerical example is presented to illustrate the application of the proposed methodology.

Keywords: Accessibility analysis · Accessibility monitoring · Multiple Criteria Decision Analysis (MCDA) · UTASTAR · Health facilities

1 Introduction

Although health access is not a recent issue in Portugal's policy [1], only in the last decade has been an increasing effort to achieve the promotion and monitoring of this objective. This situation is transversal to other countries, with the European Commission, the European Council and the European Parliament recognizing access to health care as one of the pillars of social rights in Europe [2]. Within this context, it is critical to have a correct identification of the spatial accessibility to health facilities and having tools to assist analysing how to mitigate spatial inequalities. The inherent complexity given the multidimensional nature of access, as well as the scarcity of information seems to contribute to the weaknesses still present in this topic.

Previous studies have significantly enhanced our understanding of the role played by geographic distribution of healthcare facilities in sustaining population health, with

O. Gervasi et al. (Eds.): ICCSA 2021, LNCS 12952, pp. 311–322, 2021.
https://doi.org/10.1007/978-3-030-86973-1_22

extensive research being devoted to the place-based accessibility theory, with special focus on the gravity-based methods, including the two-step floating catchment area (2SFCA) method. In particular, these models (2SFCA) create an index for each territorial unit, based on a predefined catchment area for health facility and a specific travel time (distance), considering the availability of human resources in health and population contained therein [3]. The incorporation of this type of models in Geographic Information Systems (GIS) – e.g. ArcGIS software – contributed significantly to its dissemination [3]. However, despite being a good starting point for the study of spatial inequalities, many authors argue that the results are not intelligible [4]. As such, the topic remains on the list of priorities for several countries. Thus, this study proposes and describes how the articulation of the Multiple Criteria Decision Analysis (MCDA) methods with the GIS can support in the evaluation of the population's access to health facilities. In particular, the proposed methodology follows the logic of addressing some weaknesses of the mentioned models, exploiting the application of the combined approach of a new variant of the UTA (UTilités Additives) method with the ArcGIS software, to evaluate the spatial accessibility to Primary Health Care (PHC) facilities.

This paper is structured as follows: Sect. 2 presents a brief review of related literature. Section 3 contains the proposed methodology. Section 4 shows an example of application of the proposed methodology, followed by the concluding remarks.

2 Literature Review

The evaluation of geographic healthcare accessibility provides valuable information to public policy. Previous studies on this topic had focused on two dimensions: availability of human resources in health and/or proximity to health facilities [5]. In particular, several national and international studies have shown an uneven distribution of health facilities [2, 3, 6], in which GIS play a key role in the impacts' measurement of geographic accessibility.

GIS are a spatial analysis tool that allows not only to identify spatial patterns, but also to provide an integrative view of the territory, helping to make more informed decisions. Recent developments in the scope of spatial access have focused on gravitational models, which provide a joint measure of two components of access [5]: (i) the volume of services provided or human resources considering the population they serve; and (ii) proximity to the healthcare offer points, taking into account the population's location. These models result from a modified version of Newton's Law of Gravity, representing the potential interaction of a population point i to a provider j within a certain distance [7]. Given the computational and programming efforts that this model requires, simpler versions have emerged, such as the 2SFCA models, which generate an index through the definition of the service area of human health resources by a threshold travel time/distance while taking into account the availability of these professionals (e.g. physicians) by their surrounded requirements [8].

The incorporation of this type of models in a GIS environment contributed significantly to its dissemination and use [3]. The scope of these studies mainly focused on the dimensions of availability of human resources and proximity to health facilities [3, 5, 8], however some studies incorporated other dimensions [9, 10]. Although these models serve as a basis for assessing the population's access to health facilities and measuring geographic inequalities, their results, reported as an index, are pointed out as unintuitive and unintelligible [4]. In addition, their users should be aware that they do not respect important theoretical properties and they might generate inconsistencies in the management and planning of the healthcare network, given that:

1. Gravity-based models do not include all the dimensions of access, which make any recommendation unsuitable, no matter how sophisticated the mathematical formulation and analytical assessment tools are. To be useful, the set of criteria/dimensions should be exhaustive, measurable, non-redundant, consensual and as concise as possible [11, 12]. For this reason, structuring the problem is paramount, that is, to identify the criteria on which accessibility should be evaluated according to the literature in the area, knowledge and experience of decision makers (DMs) and other relevant actors. Otherwise, the problem is formulated as if there were only one DM;
2. The scores generated by the index are devoid of absolute meaning, as it is not possible to identify the intrinsic value of the population's accessibility at location *i* to the health facility *j*, being just possible to relatively compare the accessibility's values in locations *i* and *t* [13]. In this sense, it does not reveal, for example, the threshold from which accessibility is recommended;
3. Impact (e.g. travel time, patients per physician, among others) is not the same as value [11]. For instance, the difference between 10 and 20 minutes of travel time between population and physician locations may not have the same meaning as the difference between 20 and 30 min. Although, in terms of impact, the difference is the same (10 min), the perception or value may not be equivalent, depending on subjective information coming from experts, citizens and other relevant actors. This conversion of impact into value should not be carried out on an *ad hoc* basis, and it is essential to collect subjective information through the use of participatory methods [14];
4. There is no reflection about the aggregation mechanism (compensatory *versus* non-compensatory) of the different criteria, that is, the trade-offs between different criteria are grounded on simplistic mechanisms without discussing the rationale behind them;
5. And above all, the use of these methods can lead to suboptimal resource allocation (e.g., low accessibility's values typically receive higher priority for treatment and mitigation, which might be inadequate), and there has been little rigorous empirical or theoretical evidence on how well these accessibility's indices succeed in improving the population's accessibility to health facilities.

In short, despite an increasing interest from academia and organizations in the properly evaluation of the population's accessibility to health facilities, further theoretical and applied research is needed.

3 Methodological Framework

This study proposes and describes how the articulation of MCDA methods with GIS can be used to improve the evaluation and monitoring of the population's accessibility to PHC units. Although the articulation of MCDA methods with GIS has been little explored in the context of the population's accessibility to health facilities, in recent years several theoretical and empirical studies have recognized the potential of combining these systems in different sectors [15–18]. The GIS, in particular ArcGIS 10.5, plays a fundamental role both in the spatial representation of the problem, and in the determination of travel times (or physical distances) between demand and supply points, considering different means of transport. MCDA provides a set of methods with sound theoretical foundations [19] that can be used to evaluate the population's accessibility to health facilities and help to overcome the weaknesses of gravity-based indices identified in the literature. First, MCDA methods allow for accounting multiple accessibility's dimensions (proximity, availability, among others). Secondly, they allow for accounting different levels of quantitative and qualitative information of access, as well as for subjective preferences of DMs, which are key features in any evaluation process [19].

The mostly used MCDA methods (e.g. AHP, MACBETH, TOPSIS) are based on direct preferences information which requires from DM a huge amount of subjective preferences. Given the current pandemic context and the limited availability of DM and experts involved in this context, (i.e. health administrators and health professionals with limited availability as frontline soldiers against COVID-19), a novel approach based on a disaggregation model is proposed, requiring a reduced number of judgments from DMs. We believe that this will avoid the risk of triggering rejection by DM, without compromising the model accuracy and quality. Inspired by the UTASTAR method [20], the proposed approach is based on a preference disaggregation model and aims to assess decision models from preference data regarding a list of alternatives.

The methodology proposed in this article consists of the activities presented in Fig. 1, with the evaluation activity described in the next section in greater detail.

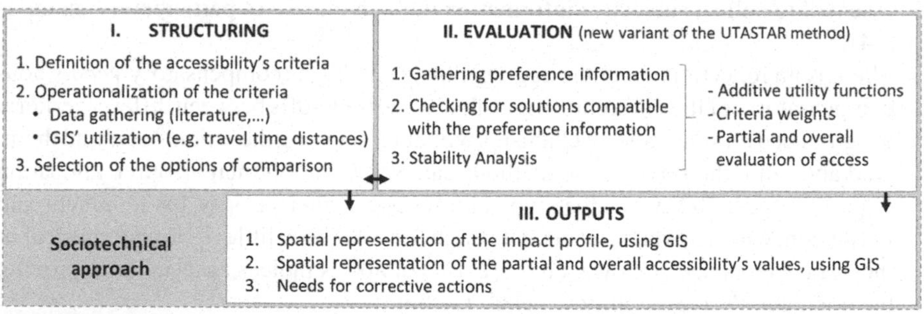

Fig. 1. Activities involved in the evaluation of the population's accessibility to health facilities.

3.1 Model Structuring

This activity consists of an interactive learning process between the DMs (health professionals, health administrators, policy makers, among others) in order to: (1) specify the relevant criteria for the DMs; (2) operationalize each criterion; and (3) define the alternatives of comparison. Regarding the former, different strategies and techniques can be used and developed with the DMs (such as cognitive maps and Delphi technique [14]), to identify and describe the relevant criteria for evaluating the population's accessibility. Secondly, a descriptor of impacts is assigned to each criterion in which is defined a set of plausible impact levels (g), intended to serve as a basis to appraise, as much possible objectively, PHC units' impact on each criterion. Since this is not the focus of this paper, further details can be consulted in [11].

3.2 Evaluation Model

Main Concepts and Notation. Consider a MCDA problem characterized by a set of alternatives a, which is valued by a family of criteria $C = \{C_1,\ldots,C_n\}$. The following notation will be used in the remaining paper:

- $A = \{a_1,\ldots,a_m\}$ is the finite set of alternatives;
- A_R is the reference set of alternatives ($A_R \subseteq A$);
- $A_H = \{a_{H0}, a_{H1},\ldots a_{Hn}\}$ is a set of hypothetical alternatives, where a_0 is an hypothetical alternative with the worst impacts in all criteria, and $a_{Hi}(i = 1,2,\ldots,n)$ an hypothetical alternative with the best impact in the *i*th criterion and the worst impacts in all the other criteria, where *n* is the number of criteria under analysis;
- a_{HB} is an hypothetical alternative with the best impact in all criteria;
- The impact scale of the *i*th criterion varies between g_{i*}, the worst impact level, and g_i^*, the best impact level;
- The utility function for the *i*th criterion, u_i, converts impacts (g_i) into value $u_i(g_i)$ in a non-decreasing form, being assigned the value 0 to the worst level and 1 to the best level on each criterion (1). These utility functions are assumed to be piecewise linear, being necessary to divide the interval $[g_{i*}, g_i^*]$ into α_i-*1* equal sub-intervals, such that each criterion level g_i^j and $u_i(g_i(a))$ are given by (2) and (3), respectively.

$$u_i(g_{i*}) = 0;\ u_i\left(g_i^*\right), \forall i = 1, 2, \ldots, n \tag{1}$$

$$g_i^j - g_{i*} + (j-1)/(\alpha_i - 1) \times \left(g_i^* - g_{i*}\right), \forall j = 1, 2, \ldots, \alpha_i \tag{2}$$

$$u_i(g_i(a)) = u_i\left(g_i^j\right) + \left(g_i(a) - g_i^j\right)/\left(g_i^{j+1} - g_i^j\right) \times [u_i\left(g_i^{j+1}\right) - u_i\left(g_i^j\right)] \tag{3}$$

- Assuming an additive value model, the aggregated value of an alternative, $u(g)$, is given by the expression (4) in which p_i is the weight of criterion *i*.

$$u(g) = \sum\nolimits_i p_i u_i(g_i),\ \sum\nolimits_i p_i = 1 \tag{4}$$

- Let us assume that the reference set of alternatives $A_R = \{a_{R1}\ldots a_{Rm}\}$ is ordered so as a_{R1} is the best alternative and a_{Rm} the worst alternative. The difference of attractiveness between alternatives a_k and a_{k+1}, $\Delta(a_k, a_{k+1})$, that could be of preference ($a_k \succ a_{k+1}$) or indifference ($a_k \sim a_{k+1}$), is given by:

$$\Delta(a_k, a_{k+1}) = \sum\nolimits_i^n \{u_i[g_i(a_k)] - u_i[g_i(a_{k+1})] - \sigma^+(a_k) + \sigma^-(a_k) + \sigma^+(a_{k+1}) - \sigma^-(a_{k+1})\} \tag{5}$$

– The monotonicity condition is required (6–7), in which ε is a non-negative indifference threshold to avoid phenomena such as $u_i(g_i^{j+1}) = u_i(g_i^j)$ when $g_i^{j+1} \succ g_i^j$.

$$u_i\left(g_i^1\right) = 0, u_i\left(g_i^j\right) = \sum_{t=1}^{j-1} w_{it}, \forall i = 1, \ldots n \tag{6}$$

$$w_{ij} = u_i\left(g_i^{j+1}\right) - u_i\left(g_i^j\right) \geq \varepsilon, \forall i = 1, \ldots nandj = 1, \ldots, \alpha_i - 1 \tag{7}$$

New Variant of the UTASTAR Algorithm. Our proposed algorithm is an improvement of the original UTASTAR method, composed by the following activities:

Activity 1: Gathering the Preference Information. In the UTASTAR method, the preference information given by the DM is elicited in the form of a ranked list of a reference set of alternatives, A_R (ordinal information) [20]. Following the suggestion from a previous study, recommending "some additional judgements to perform a number of consistency checks" [21] (p. 228) and with the aim of increasing the model robustness so as to better reflect the DMs' preferences, this study proposes the use of both ordinal and cardinal information in two steps:

– In the comparison of the reference set of alternatives A_R and a_{HB}, in which the DMs are invited to order and to semantically judge the differences of attractiveness between two consecutive ordered alternatives, based on the seven qualitative categories (null, very weak, weak, moderate, strong, very strong and extreme) proposed in [22];
– In the comparison of a set of hypothetical alternatives A_H to determine the criteria weights, following the MACBETH procedure [22]. This step consists in asking the DMs to (i) order the hypothetical alternatives; and (ii) qualitatively judge the differences of attractiveness between any two consecutive ordered alternatives.

The latter adds to the model more information and concomitantly it is expected that the results will better reflect the DMs' perspectives and preferences, compared to the ones provided by the UTASTAR model.

Activity 2: Testing for Existing Solutions Compatible with the Preference Information. The judgments collected in the previous activity are introduced in the algorithm, with the compatibility being verified by means of the linear program 1 (LP1) – Eq. system (8) - represented by an Objective Function (OF), that aims to minimize the sum of overestimation and underestimation errors ($\sigma^-(a_k)$ and $\sigma^+(a_k)$, respectively) between the calculated and the real utility functions, under constraints that provides enforced properties of the additive utility function:

$$\begin{cases} \min z = \sum_{k=1} \left[\sigma^+(a_k) + \sigma^-(a_k)\right] \\ subject\ to: \Delta(a_k, a_{k+1}) \geq C\delta, if\ a_k \succ a_{k+1}, \forall k \in \{A_R, A_H\} \\ \Delta(a_k, a_{k+1}) = 0, if\ a_k \sim a_{k+1}, \forall k\, \forall k\ \in \{A_R, A_H\} \\ \sum_i^n \sum_j^{\alpha i=1} w_{ij} = 1 \\ w_{ij} \geq \varepsilon; \sigma^+(a_k) \geq 0; \sigma^-(a_k) \geq 0,\ \forall i, j, k \end{cases} \tag{8}$$

In which δ represents a small positive number and C a semantic category of difference in attractiveness (with 'null' = 0, 'very weak' = 1, 'weak' = 2, 'moderate' = 3, 'strong' = 4, 'very strong' = 5 and 'extreme' = 6).

If the OF is null, there is at least one solution that leads to a perfect representation of the preference information given by the DMs. In the case of a positive OF, other solutions, less good, can improve other relevant criteria, such as Kendall's [20]. When no solution is found, this is the case of incompatibility, as no value function is compatible with the preference information. In such cases, we recommend the revision of some comparisons in order to obtain a compatible value function, as discussed by Greco [23].

Activity 3: Stability Analysis. This activity consists on a post-optimality analysis problem of the UTASTAR algorithm that aims to exploit the existence of multiple or near solutions of LP1. In particular, it aims to maximize each criterion weight, through the implementation of n objective functions:

$$max\, u_i(g_i^*) = \sum_j^{\alpha i-1} w_{ij}, \forall i = 1, 2, \ldots, n \tag{9}$$

grounded by the constraints of the LP1 and bounded by a new constraint:

$$\sum_{k=1} [\sigma^+(a_k) + \sigma^-(a_k)] \leq z^* + \gamma \tag{10}$$

where γ is a very small positive number and z^* is the optimal value of the LP1. The average of the results may be considered as the final solution of the problem.

4 Illustrative Example

In this section, we present a numerical example to illustrate the application of the proposed methodology in the evaluation of the population's accessibility to PHC units (with focus on the evaluation activities previously described). In particular, this study considers PHC units from Portugal mainland, in which the reference set of alternatives, A_R, is composed by four PHC units. Suppose that the DM is interested only in the following criteria of spatial accessibility: (i) General Practitioners (GP) per 10 000 patients; (ii) nurses per 10 000 patients, and (iii) travel time between population and GP locations.

For the illustration of the first activity of the evaluation process, consider Table 1 that reunite data concerning: (i) the impacts of the reference and hypothetical sets of PHC units (A_R and A_H, respectively) and a_{HB} and (ii) the preference information on the referred sets. For instance, in the comparison of the PHC units from the set A_R, the most preferred alternative is A followed by B, C and D. The difference of attractiveness between the considered desirable PHC unit (a_{HB} or I) and A is 'very weak', and the difference between A and B is 'weak'. Regarding the comparison between PHC units from the set A_H, three comparisons were elicited between each pair of consecutive ordered alternatives. The data shows that GP per 10 000 patients is the most important criteria, followed by the travel time and nurses per 10 000 patients.

For each criterion, we considered the following breakpoints ordered from the least to the most preferred impact levels.

– Criterion 1 (GP per 10 000 patients): [1, 2.4, 3.8, 5.2];
– Criterion 2 (Nurses per 10 000 patients): [1, 2.4, 3.8, 5.2];
– Criterion 3 (Travel time/ minutes): [61, 41, 21, 1].

Given these impact scales, the utility/value of the PHC units can be determined by linear interpolation (4). For instance:

$$\begin{cases} u(g(A) = 4/7u_1(3.8) + 3/7u_1(5.2) + 4/7u_2(3.8) + 3/7u_2(5.2) + 1/2u_3(21) + 1/2u_3(1) \\ u(g(B) = 1/2u_1(3.8) + 1/2u_1(5.2) + 6/7u_2(2.4) + 1/20u_3(21) + 19/20u_3(1) \\ u(g(C) = 5/7u_1(2.4) + 2/7u_1(3.8) + u_2(5.2) + 7/10u_3(41) + 3/10u_3(21) \\ u(g(D) = 1/14u_1(2.4) + 2/7u_2(2.4) + 5/7u_2(3.8) + 3/20u_3(21) + 17/20u_3(1) \end{cases} \quad (11)$$

Table 1. Criteria impacts of a_{HB} and of the alternatives from the sets A_R and A_H, as well as the preference information used to illustrate the proposed method. Note that 'GP' and 'nurses' stands for GP and nurses per 10 000 patients, respectively.

Alternatives		Impacts in each criterion			Preference information	
		GP	Nurses	Travel time	Ranking	Qualitative judgment
a_{HB}	I	5.2	5.2	1	1	Very weak
A_R	A	4.4	4.4	11	2	Weak
	B	4.5	2.2	2	3	Very strong
	C	2.8	5.2	35	4	Moderate
	D	1.1	3.4	4	5	
A_H	A_{H1}	5.2	1	61	1	Very weak
	A_{H3}	1	1	1	2	Weak
	A_{H2}	1	5.2	61	3	Weak
	A_{H0}	1	1	61	4	

Then, through the transformation of variables (6), we are able to check for existing solutions compatible with the preference information, by applying LP1 (Table 2) – activity 2.

The results are consistent with the DM's preferences, with a null OF and concomitantly null over- and underestimation errors. Since the solution is not unique (OF = 0), we proceed to the post-optimality analysis (activity 3) to search for more characteristic solutions, which maximizes the weights of each criterion (10) – LP2. The solutions are present in Table 3, being the average of the three results taken as the most representative solution of the problem.

Table 2. Linear programming formulation (activity 2), in which the monitonicity condition-based constraints are not shown.

Restriction type		w_{11}	w_{12}	w_{13}	w_{21}	w_{22}	w_{23}	w_{31}	w_{32}	w_{33}	δ	RHS
Preference information	Δ(I,A)	0	0	0.57	0	0	0.57	0	0	0.5	-1	≥ 0
	Δ(A,B)	0	0	-0.07	0.14	1	0.43	0	0	-0.45	-2	≥ 0
	Δ(B,C)	0	0.71	0.5	-0.14	-1	-1	0	0.7	0.95	-5	≥ 0
	Δ(C,D)	0.93	0.29	0	0	0.29	1	0	-0.7	-0.85	-3	≥ 0
	$\Delta(A_{H1},A_{H3})$	1	1	1	0	0	0	-1	-1	-1	-1	≥ 0
	$\Delta(A_{H3},A_{H2})$	0	0	0	-1	-1	-1	1	1	1	-2	≥ 0
	$\Delta(A_{H2},A_{H0})$	0	0	0	1	1	1	0	0	0	-2	≥ 0
Normalization		1	1	1	1	1	1	1	1	1	0	= 1

The final solution leads to the (normalized) utility functions, criteria weights and the aggregated utilities of the PHC units (A-D) presented in Fig. 2. Based on this information, we are able to estimate the aggregated value of the remaining PHC units from Portugal mainland and to spatial represent the results, by using GIS.

Table 3. Results from LP1, LP2 and the final solution (average LP2)

		w_{11}	w_{12}	w_{13}	w_{21}	w_{22}	w_{23}	w_{31}	w_{32}	w_{33}
LP1	Initial solution	0,005	0,336	0,277	0,005	0,110	0,026	0,231	0,005	0,005
LP2	[max] $u_1(g_1^*)$	0,005	0,587	0,078	0,005	0,105	0,005	0,134	0,076	0,005
	[max] $u_2(g_2^*)$	0,005	0,396	0,005	0,005	0,005	0,237	0,056	0,276	0,016
	[max] $u_3(g_3^*)$	0,005	0,442	0,005	0,005	0,068	0,078	0,285	0,106	0,005
Average (LP2)		0,005	0,475	0,029	0,005	0,059	0,107	0,158	0,153	0,009

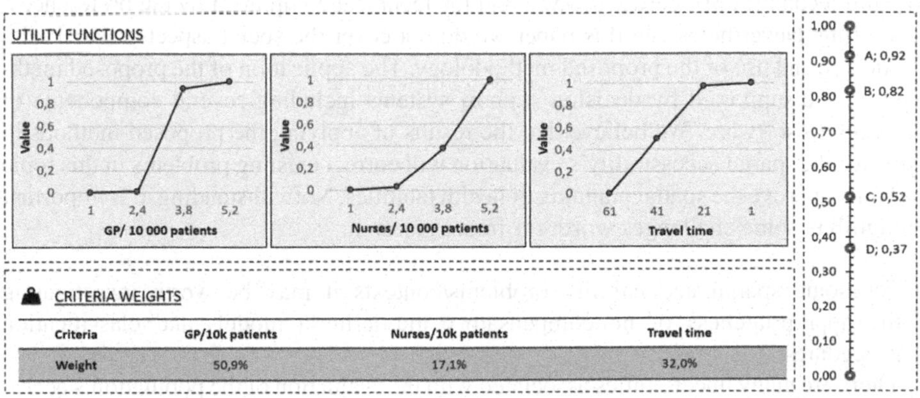

Fig. 2. Utility functions, criteria weights and the aggregated values of the PHC units A-D.

5 Concluding Remarks

Evaluation of the spatial accessibility is an under-researched subject, with the complexities involved in the spatial planning and management of health facilities growing as fast or faster than the development of tools and methodologies to manage these challenges in real contexts. This is particularly relevant considering the spread and utilization of gravity-based models, which do not respect important theoretical properties. This study aims to bridge that gap by proposing a novel methodology to improve the evaluation and monitoring of the population's accessibility to PHC units. In particular, this study proposes a MCDA/GIS-based approach, in which the proposed MCDA method consists on a new variant of the UTASTAR approach.

Compared to other MCDA methods, UTASTAR-based methods are less time-consuming as they require from DMs a lower number of subjective preferences, without compromising the model's accuracy and quality. This is even more critical considering the current pandemic situation and the limited availability of DMs and experts involved in the context.

The proposed new variant adopts all features of the UTASTAR algorithm and takes additional information into account, in the form of comparisons of intensities of preference between alternatives (cardinal information). Furthermore, the process of gathering the preference information follows the logical of comparing not only a reference set of alternatives, but also a hypothetical set of alternatives in order to determine the criteria weights, according to the MACBETH procedure as suggested by Bana e Costa *et al.* [22]. Altogether, these will lead to a higher robustness of the model, better reflecting the DMs' preferences and perspectives, compared to the results provided by the UTASTAR approach.

Within the DRIVIT-UP (DRIVIng forces of urban Transformation: assessing pUblic Policies) project, we are developing the proposed methods, as well as we are applying them to the evaluation of the population's spatial accessibility to PHC units in Portugal mainland. The proposed methods follow a socio-technical approach, with the social component being defined by the use of participatory methods to gather preferences and to build a compromise between DMs; and the technical component by the preferences' modelling. Nevertheless, in this paper we do not cover the social aspects related with the design and use of the proposed methodology. The application of the proposed methods will be supported by decision support systems including several components of the ArcGIS software. We believe that the results of applying the proposed methods to improve the spatial accessibility's evaluation will correct existing problems in this topic and thus improve the spatial planning of health facilities. Notwithstanding, it is important to highlight some challenges worth for future research:

- For some spatial accessibility problems/contexts it may be worth investigating the appropriateness of noncompensatory multicriteria models and classification procedures;
- There are many uncertainties associated with the evaluation of the population's accessibility, such as uncertainties regarding the measurement of impacts (e.g., imprecise measurement) and of DMs preferences. Few studies have discussed these issues within this context;

– Finally, it is important to apply the proposed methodology to other contexts (e.g. school accessibility) and to study the extent to which its application translates into better spatial planning and management of the health network, in comparison to the use of gravity-based models.

Acknowledgments. This work is based on the PhD thesis in progress (SFRH/BD/133124/2017), funded by FCT, I.P. (Fundação para a Ciência e a Tecnologia). This work has also been supported by Portuguese national and EU funds through FCT, I.P., in the context of the JUST_PLAN project (PTDC/GES-OUT/2662/20) and the DRIVIT-UP project (POCI-01-0145-FEDER-031905).

References

1. Assembleia da República. Lei n.º 48/1990: Lei de Bases da Saúde. Diário da República. Série I-:3452–9 (1990)
2. OECD/European Observatory on Health Systems and Policies. Portugal: Perfil de Saúde do País. Paris: OECD Publishing (2017). https://doi.org/10.1787/9789264285385-pt
3. Luo, W., Whippo, T.: Variable catchment sizes for the two-step floating catchment area (2SFCA) method. Health Place **18**, 789–795 (2012). https://doi.org/10.1016/j.healthplace.2012.04.002
4. Lopes, H.S., Ribeiro, V., Remoaldo, P.C.: Spatial accessibility and social inclusion: the impact of Portugal's last health reform. Geohealth **3**, 356–368 (2019). https://doi.org/10.1029/2018GH000165
5. Gao, F., Kihal, W., Souris, M., Deguen, S.: Assessment of the spatial accessibility to health professionals at French census block level. Int. J. Equity Health **15**, 1–14 (2016). https://doi.org/10.1186/s12939-016-0411-z
6. Ribeiro, V., Remoaldo, P., Gutiérrez, J., Ribeiro, J.C.: Accessibility and GIS on health planning. An approach based on location-allocation models. Acessibilidade e SIG no planeamento em saúde: uma abordagem baseada em modelos de alocação-localização. Rev Port Estud Reg 38 (2015)
7. Joseph, E., Bantock, P.: Measuring potential physical accessibility to general practitioners in rural areas: a method and case study. Soc. Sci. Med. **16**, 85–90 (1982). https://doi.org/10.1016/0277-9536(82)90428-2
8. Luo, W., Wang, F.: Measures of spatial accessibility to health care in a GIS environment: synthesis and a case study in the Chicago region. Environ. Plan. B Plan. Des. **30**, 865–884 (2003). https://doi.org/10.1068/b29120
9. Dai, D., Wang, F.: Geographic disparities in accessibility to food stores in southwest Mississippi. Environ. Plan. B Plan. Des. **38**, 659–677 (2011)
10. Polzin, P., Borges, J., Coelho, A.: An extended kernel density two-step floating catchment area method to analyze access to health care. Environ. Plan. B Plan. Des. **41**, 717–735 (2014). https://doi.org/10.1068/b120050p
11. Keeney, R.L.: Value-Focused Thinking: A Path to Creative Decision making. Harvard University Press, Cambridge (1992)
12. Bana e Costa, C.A., Beinat, E.: Model-structuring in public decision-aiding, vol. 05.79-Lo (2005)
13. Blumenthal, A.L.: The Process of Cognition. Prenctice-Hall, Upper Saddle River (1977)

14. Marttunen, M., Lienert, J., Belton, V.: Structuring problems for multi-criteria decision analysis in practice: a literature review of method combinations. Eur. J. Oper. Res. **263** (2017). https://doi.org/10.1016/j.ejor.2017.04.041
15. Alzouby, A.M., Nusair, A.A., Taha, L.M.: GIS based multi criteria decision analysis for analyzing accessibility of the disabled in the greater irbid municipality area, Irbid, Jordan. Alexandria Eng. J. **58**, 689–698 (2019). https://doi.org/10.1016/j.aej.2019.05.015
16. Malczewski, J.: Multiple criteria decision analysis and geographic information systems. In: Ehrgott, Matthias, Figueira, José Rui., Greco, Salvatore (eds.) Trends in Multiple Criteria Decision Analysis, pp. 369–395. Springer US, Boston, MA (2010). https://doi.org/10.1007/978-1-4419-5904-1_13
17. Zucca, A., Sharifi, M., Fabbri, A.: Application of spatial multi-criteria analysis to site selection for a local park: A case study in the Bergamo Province, Italy. J Environ. Manag. **88**, 752–769 (2008). https://doi.org/10.1016/j.jenvman.2007.04.026
18. Cerreta, M., Panaro, S., Poli, G.: A spatial decision support system for multifunctional landscape assessment: A transformative resilience perspective for vulnerable inland areas. Sustainability **13** (2021). https://doi.org/10.3390/su13052748
19. Belton, V., Stewart, T.: Multiple Criteria Decision Analysis. Springer, Boston (2002). https://doi.org/10.1007/978-1-4615-1495-4
20. Siskos, Y., Grigoroudis, E., Matsatsinis, N.: UTA methods. Mult. Criteria Decis. Anal. State Art Surv. Int. Ser. Oper. Res. Manag. Sci., pp. 297–343. Springer, New York (2005). https://doi.org/10.1007/0-387-23081-5_8
21. von Winterfeldt, D., Edwards, W.: Decision Analysis and Behavioral Research. Cambridge University Press, New York (1986)
22. Bana e Costa, C.A., De Corte, J.M., Vansnick, J.C.: On the mathematical foundation of MACBETH. In: Figueira, J., Greco, S., Ehrogott, M. (eds.) Multiple Criteria Decision Analysis: State of the Art Surveys, pp. 409–437. Springer New York, New York, NY (2005). https://doi.org/10.1007/0-387-23081-5_10
23. Greco, S., Mousseau, V., Slowinski, R.: Ordinal regression revisited: multiple criteria ranking using a set of additive value functions. Eur. J. Oper. Res. **191**, 416–436 (2008). https://doi.org/10.1016/j.ejor.2007.08.013

An Integrated Model for Locating-Routing in the Goods Delivery and Simultaneous Pickup in the Urban Context

José Rodriguez-Melquiades[1(✉)], Edwar Lujan[2], and Flabio Gutierrez Segura[3]

[1] Departamento de Informática, Universidad Nacional de Trujillo, Trujillo, Peru
jrodriguez@unitru.edu.pe

[2] Escuela de posgrado, Universidad Nacional de Trujillo, Trujillo, Peru
elujans@unitru.edu.pe

[3] Departamento de matemática, Universidad Nacional de Piura, Piura, Peru
flabio@unp.edu.pe

Abstract. Bibliographic research on facilities location and vehicle routing shows interest in the academic community and contributes to the welfare in cities. In this sense a Mixed Integer linear new Programming model is presented to optimise cost by integrating location and routing. This process is about delivering and collecting goods and wastes at the same time in order to maintain urban sustainability. It also determines the consumption of the used fuel and measures the C02 generation in the routing. This model was implemented by GLPK which obtained results in small simulated scenarios. For sceneries between 21 and 25 customers, optimal solutions were not found in 7200 s despite the timeout.

Keywords: Location · Vehicle routing · Urban sustainability

1 Introduction

Locating a production or distribution centre called facility, is an activity very important in the logistics systems such as the design of a net for a supply network since location is known in a geographic space where it will be possible to choose a centre that is nearer the customers who are the locators. After such localization it is possible to obtain a service for each customer by following a routing plan that starts and ends in the distribution centre, that is to say a vehicle routing. It is crucially important to integrate the facility location problems and vehicle routing but also considers the environment in the process of the logistic network routing. This can be done by integrating the values of cost and C02 emissions

Our gratitude to the Fondo Nacional de Desarrollo Científico, Tecnológico y de Innovación Tecnológica - FONDECYT.

O. Gervasi et al. (Eds.): ICCSA 2021, LNCS 12952, pp. 323–336, 2021.
https://doi.org/10.1007/978-3-030-86973-1_23

generated by the vehicles [2]. Facilities location and vehicle routing are two NP-hard problems [10,15], of the combinatorial optimization, for which it is possible to build linear programming models and solution techniques in the context of urban logistics [21].

In [15], examples of applications are presented in the regional planification, telecommunications and transportation as well the energy management. In [6], it is stated that vehicle routing has gained much attention with the distribution and logistic management. According to [13], this kind of problem is a research area that is considered within the locating analysis with emphasis on vehicle routing. This term is not well defined nevertheless it is considered within the location theory which models and solves location problems. It is being applied to food distribution, soda and goods consumption, location of blood banks besides factories and military equipment, delivery of newspapers, collecting wastes, designs of networks and telecommunications and so on. In [13], a review on location-routing is found, a more recent review is presented in [4].

Some models of location-routing have been focused on optimizing economic costs in [3,8], very few proposals have considered urban protection as in the case of transportation that is a great pollution agent [24].

In this work a location–routing model is presented in the urban context that besides optimizing economic costs according to distance travelled by the vehicles measures the amount of fuel that the vehicle is consuming and measures the quantity of C02 emissions generated in the routing process. In the model, the facilities initially locate a group of suppliers who meet your demands. These facilities in turn are located by a group of customers to whom a delivery service of their bought goods is provided and their wastes are collected, that is to say a process of two levels. The process starts and ends in the selected facility by the model according to the geographic location, the vehicle returns with the collected wastes from the customers. (See Fig. 1)

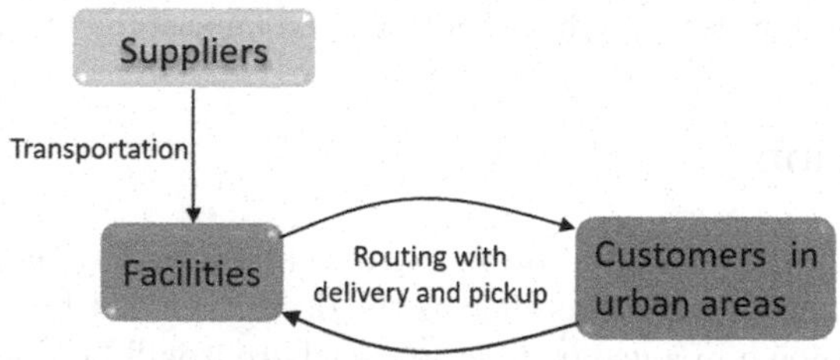

Fig. 1. Location-routing scheme with simultaneous delivery and pickup.

The paper consists of the following points: Sect. 2, this work is underpinned over this section. It is about a revision of the literature related to research. Section 3, the problem is discussed through a description and formulation of a mixed integer linear programming new model with two functions objectives. Section 4, the results and discussions are presented in this section. Section 5, the conclusions.

2 Review of the Literature

With the purpose of getting an integrated location-routing model, a revision of the location-routing literature is made and then experiments with some of these models are carried out but considering the environmental part.

2.1 Location

Four components should be taken into consideration for locating problems: The customers who are located in a geographic zone; the facilities that will be located to give a service; a geographic space where the customers and facilities are. Finally a metric that indicates the distances or time between customers and facilities [5]. From what has been said it follows, network planification integrates the decisions of locating facilities to others relevant in order to set up a logistic net.

The classical problem of facilities location presented in [3], has been very used in the design of supply chains. The problem refers to finding the locations of such facilities and a service they give the customers in such a way as to minimize the costs according to a set of conditions. For this problem, given a set of customers I and other facilities J, at least one solution involves serving the request of each customer $i \in I$ by $j \in J$ facility who will give a service.

A variation of the facility location model which is capacitated and presented in [3], can be seen in (1), it determines the quantity of CO2 generated by the vehicles in the process of serving the customers requests, that is to say quantifying the C02 emitted by the vehicles of transportation, as can be observed in the third sum of function objective. This formula is obtained by the Volvo Trucks Corporation, being X_{ijk} the variable of serving the customer i through the k vehicle whose capacity is q_k.

The two first summations of this variation of the model minimize the fixed costs of locating the facilities $f_j Y_j$ and transportation $c_{ij} X_{ijk}$ being f_j the parameter of fixed cost in the facilities location and Y_j the binary variable that represents location or no location of a better facility, besides c_{ij} that is the transportation cost between the customer and the facility. The third sum has been added to obtain such variation.

$$Minimize\ : \sum_{j \in J} f_j Y_j + \sum_{j \in J, i \in I} c_{ij} X_{ijk} + \sum_{j \in J, i \in I} cc \left(\frac{em_k}{q_k} \right) X_{ijk} \qquad (1)$$

Results of the computational experiments for this variation of the locating model are shown in the Fig. 2, where the capacitated location optimizes the costs since the customers of a total of five applicant facilities, $f_i, \forall i = 1, \ldots, 5$, only located the f_1 and f_3 facilities which are necessaries to give the service.

Discussions related to the facilities location with mathematical rigour are presented in [11], where differences between uncapacitated location and capacitated location are established. In the first case the customers are assigned to the nearer factories; in the second case the customers may not be assigned to the

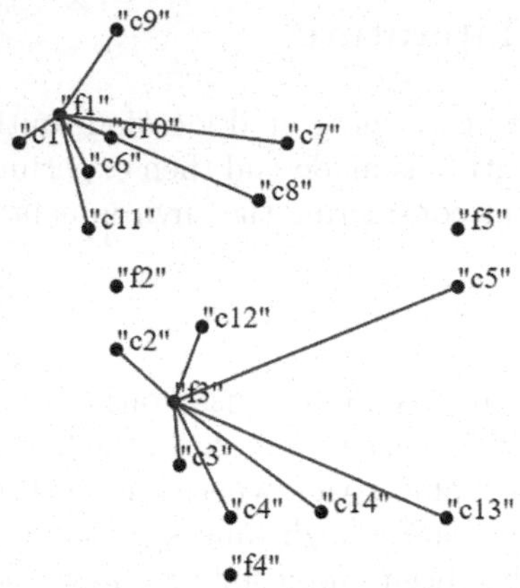

Fig. 2. Network for capacitated localization.

nearer Factory. Recently in [17], present optimization models and heuristics for locating capacited mobile facilities.

2.2 Location and Sustainability

In the current context of cities where the environmental and social objectives rely on the proper use of the natural resources earth provides us. Location becomes more important since it contributes to maintaining the sustainability of cities. The notion of sustainability is an important concept since it reduces the effect of greenhouses, pollution, economic sustainability and social impacts. For this reason it has been taken into account for its evaluation and for the production, distribution, logistics, energy or transportation of people and load. Otherwise they can affect the health in cities [7]. A study undertaken by the European commission results in the urban cargo transportation which generates 21% in C02 emissions whereas other smaller vehicles generate 10% in C02 emissions.

In [19] an interesting proposal was made in order to reduce pollution. This proposal gives a solution for the network design problem of a sustainable supply chain. This model is based on the methodology of binary integer programming that determines the quantities of facilities located in selected areas among a set of candidates besides a genetic algorithm which gives a solution to the complexity of the problem.

These discussions lead to the so-called locating problem of sustainable facilities as [23] mentions. This location has made progress in such a way that the economic criterium is not only important to take into account but the social and environmental ones as well. As can be discussed in [1]. Recently the location of sustainable facilities is discussed in [22], for decision-making in the energy generation.

2.3 Vehicle Routing

The vehicle routing (in Fig. 3 shows three routes), has been presented in various versions in order that they will be used in some applications. The most known are capacitated routing, routing with time windows, routing with delivery and pickup at the same time, open routing, fleet of homogenous and heterogenous vehicles and so on. For each variation, optimization models have been built besides metaheuristic in order to be solved, as discussed in [9,12].

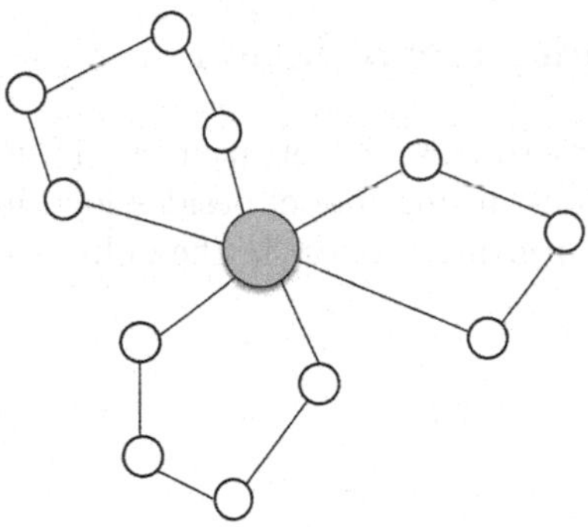

Fig. 3. Vehicle routing.

2.4 Location-Routing

Location–routing from the practical point of view is part of the distribution management of goods. A proposal was presented in [8]. It refers that an application is established on a network and the process of delivery and pickup are made simultaneously to minimise the cost of locating and at the same time assigning vehicles for the routing by meeting the demand of each customer. Research about the state of the art in location-routing and new applications are found in [20], who classify the various contributions published in the specialized literature. An expanded location of sustainable facilities and routing of sustainable vehicles is discussed in [16]. Similarly another sustainable proposal on location–routing that works with a two-compartment vehicle through delivery and pickup at the same time in the service of perishable goods, is presented in [14].

The reference [3] also presents an integrated model of integer programming to locate production facilities and through a routing process meets the requests. For being of interest in the development of the work this last model has been modified by adding to the Z_{ij} transportation variable an additional component related to the use of a vehicle $k \in K$ that means Z_{ijk}. In this way, a new objective function (2) is obtained which quantifies the C02 emissions generated by the vehicles that minimizes the fixed costs of facilities location, freight transportation costs, cost of assigning the facility to the customer, routing cost, and

C02 quantification generated during the trip. The computing experiments show results up to certain quantities of data from which the use of some metaheuristic may be necessary.

$$Minimize : \sum_{j \in J} f_j X_j + \sum_{s \in S, j \in J} c_{sj} W_{sj} + \sum_{i \in I, j \in J} v_j h_i Y_{ij}$$
$$+ \sum_{i,j \in P, k \in K} g_k d_{ij} Z_{ijk} + \sum_{j \in J, i \in I} cc \left(\frac{em_k}{q_k} \right) Z_{ijk} \quad (2)$$

3 Integrated Model Formulation

It is based on [8], the experiments undertaken by (1) in [3] and in [18], present an integrated new location-routing model besides locating suppliers and serving the customers through a routing process in the delivery and pickup of waste, as shown in Fig. 1.

Sets
S: Suppliers.
J: Facilities.
I: Customers.
KK: Big vehicles serving facilities.
K: Urban vehicles serving facilities.
$SF = S \cup J$: Network formed by suppliers and facilities.
$P = J \cup I$: Network formed by facilities and customers.

Parameters
cs_s: Supplier capacity. $s \in S$.
$dist1_{sj}$: Distance between suppliers $s \in S$ and facilities $j \in J$.
$c_{sj} = f1 \times dist1_{sj}/100$: Transportation cost from $s \in S$ to $j \in J$, with freightage $f1$.
qq_{kk}: Big vehicle capacity $kk \in KK$.
t_j: Facilities capacity $j \in J$.
f_j: Fixed cost for the operation of facility $j \in J$.
$dist2_{ij}$: Distance between facility $j \in J$ and customer $i \in I$.
$d_{ij} = f2 \times dist2_{ij}/100$: Transportation cost from $j \in J$ to $i \in I$, with freighge $f2$.
cf_k: Fixed cost for the operation of the urban vehicle $k \in K$.
q_k: Urban vehicle capacity $k \in K$.
g: Number of urban vehicles $k \in K$.
CC: Fuel consumption in litre per kilometre.
EM_k: CO2 emission in grams per litre of the urban vehicle $k \in K$.
T_k: Maximum fuel tank capacity of urban vehicle.
p_i: Pickup of customer waste $i \in I$.
dd_i: Delivery of the product to the customer $i \in I$.

Decision Variables
XX_s: Binary variable that denotes attention or not attention of the $s \in S$.
$W_{sj,kk}$: Transportation from supplier to facility using the $kk \in KK$ vehicle.
X_j: Binary variable that indicates if facility $j \in J$ is open or closed.
Y_{ij}: Binary variable indicating assignment of customer $i \in I$ to facility $j \in J$.
Z_{ijk}: Routing binary variable, indicating attention from $j \in J$ to $i \in I$, with vehicle k.
U_{ij}: Product delivery to customers.
V_{ij}: Collect customer waste if any.
M_k: Binary variable that indicates if urban vehicle $k \in K$ is used.
G_{ik}: Amount of fuel used when vehicle to visit at customer.

The bi-objective mixed integer linear programming model is:

$$Min: \sum_{s\in S, j\in J, kk\in KK} c_{sj} W_{sj,kk} + \sum_{j\in J} f_j X_j + \sum_{i,j\in P, k\in K} d_{ij} Z_{ijk} + \sum_{k\in K} cf_k M_k \quad (3)$$

$$Min: \sum_{i,j\in P, k\in K} CC\left(\frac{EM_k}{q_k}\right) d_{ij} Z_{ijk} \quad (4)$$

s.t.

$$\sum_{j\in J, kk\in KK} W_{sj,kk} \leq cs_s XX_s, \forall s \in S \quad (5)$$

$$\sum_{s\in S, kk\in KK} W_{sj,kk} - \sum_{i\in I} dd_i Y_{ij} = 0, \forall j \in J \quad (6)$$

$$\sum_{s\in S, kk\in KK} W_{sj,kk} \leq t_j X_j, \forall j \in J \quad (7)$$

$$\sum_{s\in S, j\in J} W_{sj,kk} \leq qq_{kk}, \forall kk \in KK \quad (8)$$

$$\sum_{j\in P} Z_{ijk} = 1, \forall i \in I, k \in K \quad (9)$$

$$\sum_{i\in I, j\in J} Z_{ijk} \leq 1, \forall k \in K \quad (10)$$

$$\sum_{j\in P} Z_{ijk} - \sum_{j\in P} Z_{jik} = 0, \forall i \in P, k \in K \quad (11)$$

$$\sum_{m\in P} Z_{imk} + \sum_{n\in P} Z_{jnk} - Y_{ij} \leq 1, \forall i \in I, j \in J, k \in K \quad (12)$$

$$\sum_{i,j\in I} Z_{ijk} \leq q_k M_k, \forall k \in K \quad (13)$$

$$\sum_{i\in I, j\in J} Z_{ijk} \leq g, \forall k \in K \tag{14}$$

$$\sum_{j\in P} U_{ji} - \sum_{j\in P} U_{ij} = dd_i, \forall i \in I \tag{15}$$

$$\sum_{j\in P} V_{ij} - \sum_{j\in P} V_{ji} = p_i, \forall i \in I \tag{16}$$

$$U_{ij} + V_{ij} \leq q_k Z_{ijk}, \forall i, j \in P, k \in K \tag{17}$$

$$G_{jk} \leq G_{ik} - 0.35\left(\frac{EM_k}{q_k}\right) dist2_{ij} Z_{ijk} + T_k\left(1 - Z_{ijk}\right), \forall i \in P, j \in I, k \in K \tag{18}$$

$$G_{ik} = T_k \sum_{j\in I} Z_{ijk}, \forall i \in P, k \in K \tag{19}$$

The objective function (3) optimizes the transportation cost from the suppliers to the facilities besides the facilities location costs, the routing costs from the facilities to the customers and the use of the vehicles. The generated C02 pollution is measured section by section for the objective function (4) during the routing process in order to meet the customers on the part of the selected facility by the model.

The Eq. (5) indicates that the supplier can supply the facility goods as long as it does not exceed its own capacity and will be available to give a service. Condition (6) models the service of the supplier to the facility and according to the customer's demand it will be met by the selected facility. Condition (7) models the supplier who can provide the facility as long as it does not exceed the capacity of the facility and will be available to receive the supply. Equation (8) indicates that each big vehicle carries a cargo of goods according to its allowance capacity. In (9), refers to the routing that is assigned to each customer.

The fact that a routing can work with only one facility it is modelled in (10), the constraint (11) indicates that every urban vehicle that arrives and meets a customer should go to look for the next customer in order to provide a service, that is, an equilibrium condition.

The Eq. (12), is an assignment and routing condition which assigns a vehicle to service the customer. The constraint (13), it is established that each vehicle carries a load of products according to its capacity. The condition (14) models the fact that the service of the customer is possible as long as there is a vehicle availability. In the conditions (15) and (16) show two simultaneous activities of service to the customer, that is to say the delivery of goods and pickup of wastes will be for free. The Eq. (17) indicates that the customer service is possible as long as it does not exceed the capacity of the urban vehicle when there is a journey. In (18) models the level of the fuel tank and the urban vehicle is in the j customer. Finally, the condition (19) refers to the full tank before starting the process of routing.

4 Results and Discussion

To the evaluation we have used a personal computer equipped with a Core (TM) i7-8550U CPU 1.8 Ghz with 8.00 GB RAM. The optimization software GLPK (GNU Linear Programming Kit) was used to solve the considered scenarios. The experiments were performed with a timeout of 7200 segundos.

Cases with Simulated Data

Case 1: Three suppliers and five facilities with their respective geographic location are considered as a case study, as shown in Table 1. Four big vehicles (kk) with a capacity of 30 tons. to serve the facilities, and three urban vehicles (k) with a capacity of 30 kg. to serve customers.

Table 1. Location of suppliers and facilities.

Suppliers : Location	Facilities : Location
s1 : (35,15)	f1 : (3,13)
s2 : (100,65)	f2 : (50,10)
s3 : (7,59)	f3 : (22,9)
	f4 : (15, 22)
	f5 : (3, 37)

Table 2, shows the location of the customers and their respectives purchase demands as well as the delivery of waste for free.

Table 2. Location of customers and their demands.

Customers	Location	Delivery demand	Demand to collect
c1	(3,25)	4	2
c2	(20,61)	3	2
c3	(31,81)	3	2
c4	(40,90)	2	2
c5	(65,50)	3	2
c6	(15,30)	3	2

Results were obtained for the two levels. The results of the Table 3, shows in level 1, in response to demand for some goods, the model located the supplier s1 who provides to the f3 facility for a value of 18 units of goods by using the kk1 vehicle that runs a distance of 14 km.

Table 3. Transportation from supplier to select facility.

Supplier	Facility	Ordered products	Big vehicle	Distance (km)
s1	f3	18	kk1	14

In level 2, Table 4, shows the results of the process through a vehicle routing that any of the three vehicles can service the customers, starting and ending the tour in the f3 facility. Delivered quantities and picked up wastes from the customers are seen in this level, in addition to the travelled distances by the urban vehicles in km. and the quantity of fuel in litres L, used in the routing process. The vehicle has the tank with 20 L, which is going to be reduced during the tour and in every road section. Finally the C02 emission in kg/ton-km.

Table 4. Delivery of demands products and waste collection.

Origin	Destination	Delivery	Pickup	Distance (km)	Fuel consumption	CO2
f3	c1	18	0	25	20	0.39
c1	c6	14	2	13	18.6	0.2
c6	c2	11	4	31	18	0.49
c2	c3	8	6	23	16.3	0.35
c3	c4	5	8	13	15.1	0.2
c4	c5	3	10	47	14.4	0.74
c5	f3	0	12	59	12	0.93

Case 2: The proposal model was also tested in other sceneries. For this purpose the quantity of suppliers and their locations remained fixed. The quantity of facilities are the same but the location of three of them were modified. See Table 5.

Table 5. Location of suppliers and facilities.

Suppliers : Location	Facilities : Location
s1 : (35,15)	f1 : (1,13)
s2 : (100,65)	f2 : (46,4)
s3 : (7,59)	f3 : (2,3)
	f4 : (15,22)
	f5 : (3,37)

The kind of vehicles for both levels as it was established above are the same but the capacities of the urban vehicles increase and the more customers are the more quantities of demands increase as well. Other information such as the total quantity of customers, their locations and demands are shown in Table 6.

Table 6. Location of customers and their demands.

Customers	Location	Delivery demand	Demand to collect
c1	(31,6)	6	2
c2	(36,20)	6	4
c3	(9,19)	3	3
c4	(47,42)	5	4
c5	(28,20)	4	5
c6	(38,43)	2	4
c7	(41,4)	9	7
c8	(36,30)	3	5
c9	(4,10)	8	10
c10	(43,16)	7	8
c11	(33,45)	9	8
c12	(39,30)	4	5
c13	(6,40)	1	3
c14	(50,20)	2	4
c15	(48,14)	5	7
c16	(34,34)	2	5
c17	(49, 3)	6	7
c18	(26,14)	9	9
c19	(28,44)	5	7
c20	(21,38)	1	3
c21	(15,11)	2	0
c22	(31,22)	3	2
c23	(24,36)	2	1
c24	(24,28)	2	2
c25	(2,23)	3	1

With these pieces of information, Table 7 shows the results of the model when it was implemented in four sceneries. Each one is formed by groups of five, ten, fifteen and twenty customers. The table also shows the time used to obtain computing results which increase as there are more customers, and therefore also the costs and the distances traveled. A fact that drew attention was related to the C02 generation. The work reached the conclusion that this emission was reduced since some customers have a nearer location among them.

Table 7. Results obtained by the model in four scenarios.

Scenarios	Customers	Time (secs)	Cost of tour	Distance (km)	CO2 (kg/ton-km)
1	5	1.2	103	114	1.076
2	10	34.1	132	146	0.691
3	15	157.4	170	189	0.668
4	20	361.3	184	205	0.527
5	21	7 871	–	–	–
6	25	8 812.6	–	–	–

For each one of these scenarios, the model estimates the quantity of fuel used during the formation of the tour such as it was presented in Table 4.

For sceneries greater than 21 customers, a solution was not found in the timeout used in the experiments.

5 Conclusions

The paper show a mixed integer linear programming model new integrated facilities location and vehicle routing in the urban context. In the routing activity goods are delivered and wastes are pickup. It also models situations such as the fuel consumption and measures the C02 emission in every road section during the process of the customer service, that is to say the model can be used in the environment sustainability in cities.

The proposal is based on the premise that there is a set of customers who previously make known their needs. For example: Electrical appliances, computer equipment or some other delivery services whose wastes are also demanded for their pickup. This premise reduces the service and transportation costs such as it was shown in the tests performed. Therefore, the use of vehicle feet that travels by the best selected routes that are part of the urban ways is also reduced.

The results presented show the potential aspect of the new model proposed, for a smaller number of customers quickly finds optimal solutions, however a critical aspect solutions are not found for sceneries with more than 21 customers within the time limit of 7200 s, because the problem is NP-Hard. For medium and big sceneries it is recommended the use of metaheuristics that gives good solutions at reasonable times.

References

1. Anvari, S., Turkay, M.: The facility location problem from the perspective of triple bottom accounting of sustainability. Int. J. Prod. Res. **55**(21), 6266–6287 (2017). https://doi.org/10.1080/00207543.2017.1341064
2. Chen, C., Qiu, R., Hu, X.: The location-routing problem with full truckloads in low-carbon supply chain network designing. Math. Prob. Eng. **2018**, 13 (2018). Article ID 6315631 https://doi.org/10.1155/2018/6315631

3. Daskin, M.S., Snyder, L.V., Berger, R.T.: Facility location in supply chain design, chapter 2. logistics systems: design and optimization. In: Langevin, A., Riopel, D., (eds.) GERAD & École Polytechnique de Montréal Montréal Canada. Springer, Boston (2005). https://doi.org/10.1007/0-387-24977-X_2
4. Drexl, M., Schneider, M.: A survey of variants and extensions of the location-routing problem. Eur. J. Oper. Res. **241**(2), 283–308 (2015). https://doi.org/10.1016/j.ejor.2014.08.030
5. Zanjirani Farahani, R., Hekmatfar, M. (eds.): Facility Location. CMS, Physica-Verlag HD, Heidelberg (2009). https://doi.org/10.1007/978-3-7908-2151-2
6. Feng, Y., Zhang, R., Jia, G.: Vehicle routing problems with fuel consumption and stochastic travel speeds. Math. Prob. Eng. **2017**, 16 (2017) Article ID 6329203. https://doi.org/10.1155/2017/6329203
7. Gonzales-Feliu, J., Morana, J.: Are city logistics solutions sustainable? The city-porto case. J. Land Use Mob. Environ. **3**(2), 55–64 (2010)
8. Karaoglan, I., Altiparmak, I., Kara, F., Dengiz, B.: The location-routing problem with simultaneous pickup and delivery: formulations and a heuristic approach. Omega **40**(4), 465–477 (2012). https://doi.org/10.1016/j.omega.2011.09.002
9. Kumar, S.N., Panneerselvam, R.: A survey on the vehicle routing problem and its variants. Intell. Inf. Manage. **4**(3), 66–74 (2012). https://doi.org/10.4236/iim.2012.43010
10. Lenstra, J.K., Rinnooy Kam, A.H.G.: Complexity of vehicles routing and scheduling problems. Netw. Int. J. **11**(2), 221–227 (1981). https://doi.org/10.1002/net.3230110211
11. Liu, B.: Facility location problem. In: Theory and Practice of Uncertain Programming. Studies in Fuzziness and Soft Computing, vol. 239, pp. 157-165. Springer, Berlin (2009). https://doi.org/10.1007/978-3-540-89484-1_11
12. Marinakis, Y., Marinaki, M., Migdalas, A.: Variants and formulations of the vehicle routing problem. In: Pardalos, P.M., Migdalas, A. (eds.) Open Problems in Optimization and Data Analysis. SOIA, vol. 141, pp. 91–127. Springer, Cham (2018). https://doi.org/10.1007/978-3-319-99142-9_7
13. Nagy, G., Salhi, S.: Location-routing: Issues, models and methods. Eur. J. Oper. Res. **177**(2), 649–672 (2007). https://doi.org/10.1016/j.ejor.2006.04.004
14. Navazi, F., Sedaghat, A., Tavakkoli-Moghaddam, R.: A new sustainable location-routing problem with simultaneous pickup and delivery by two-compartment vehicles for a perishable product considering circular economy. IFAC-PapersOnLine **52**(13), 790–795 (2019). https://doi.org/10.1016/j.ifacol.2019.11.212
15. Qin, J., Xiang, X., Ye, Y., Ni, L.: A simulated annealing methodology to multi-product capacitated facility location with stochastic demand. Sci. World J. **2015**, 9 (2015), Article ID 826363. https://doi.org/10.1155/2015/826363
16. Rabbani, M., Navazi, F., Farrokhi-Asl, H., Balali, M.H.: A sustainable transportation-location-routing problem with soft time windows for distribution systems. Uncertain Supply Chain Manage. **6**(3), 229–254 (2018). https://doi.org/10.5267/j.uscm.2017.12.002
17. Raghavan, S., Sahin, M., Salman, F.S.: The capacitated mobile facility location problem. Research **277**(2), 507–520 (2019). https://doi.org/10.1016/j.ejor.2019.02.055
18. Rezaei, N., Ebrahimnejad, S., Moosavi, A., Nikfarjam, A.: A green vehicle routing problem with time windows considering the heterogeneous fleet of vehicles: two metaheuristic algorithms. Eur. J. Ind. Eng. **13**(4), 507–535 (2019). https://doi.org/10.1504/EJIE.2019.100919

19. Santibañez, E.D.R., Mateus, G.R., Luna, H.P.L.: Solving a public sector sustainable supply chain problem: a genetic algorithm approach. In: WCAMA Brazilian Computer Society Proceedings, pp. 19–22. Publisher, Natal, RN, Brazil (2011)
20. Schneider, M., Drexl, M.: A survey of the standard location-routing problem. Ann. Oper. Res. **259**, 389–414 (2017). https://doi.org/10.1007/s10479-017-2509-0
21. Stopka, O., Jerábek, K., Stopkova, M.: Using the operations research methods to address distribution tasks at a city logistics scale. In: Stopkova, M., Bartuska, L., Stopka, O., (eds.) LOGI 2019 - Horizons of autonomous mobility in Europe, vol. 44, pp. 348–355. Transportation research procedia, ScienceDirect, Elsevier (2020). https://doi.org/10.1016/j.trpro.2020.02.032
22. Tajbakhsh, A., Sahmsi, A.: A facility location problem for sustainability-conscious power generation decision makers. J. Environ. Manage. **230**, 319–334 (2019). https://doi.org/10.1016/j.jenvman.2018.09.066
23. Terouhid, S.A., Ries, R., Fard, M.M.: Towards sustainable facility location-a literature review. J. Sustainable Dev. **5**(7), 507–535 (2012). https://doi.org/10.5539/jsd.v5n7p18
24. UNITED STATES ENVIRONMENTAL PROTECTION AGENCY - EPA. https://www.epa.gov/ghgemissions/overview-greenhouse-gases. Accessed 10 Mar 2021

Towards Endowing Intelligent Cars with the Ability to Learn the Routines of Multiple Drivers: A Dynamic Neural Field Model

Weronika Wojtak[1,2], Flora Ferreira[1], Pedro Guimarães[1,2], Paulo Barbosa[1,2(✉)], Sérgio Monteiro[2], Wolfram Erlhagen[1], and Estela Bicho[2]

[1] Research Centre of Mathematics, University of Minho, 4800-058 Guimarães, Portugal
{fjferreira,wolfram.erlhagen}@math.uminho.pt, pauloricardolb@ua.pt
[2] Research Centre Algoritmi, University of Minho, 4800-058 Guimarães, Portugal
{w.wojtak,estela.bicho}@dei.uminho.pt

Abstract. Driving a car is often a routine activity that includes visiting the same locations at about the same time on a certain day of the week. Here, we present a learning system based on Dynamic Neural Fields that allows an intelligent vehicle to acquire sequential and temporal information about daily driving routines. Learning is fast, implicit (no need to specify destinations in advance), continuous, and can be adapted to different temporal scales. The learned information can be recalled to predict the driver's destination intention, when to arrive at a specific location and when to leave there. Importantly, the system allows to learn and recall multiple routines corresponding to different drivers and different days. This personalized information can be used for planning the next trip for every user of a shared vehicle.

Keywords: Neurocomputational model · Learning driver routines · Space and time prediction · Dynamic neural field

1 Introduction

Advances in technology used in the vehicle's cockpit systems have contributed to the increase of spatiotemporal information on human mobility, opening new opportunities in the research topic of human-machine interaction. For a convenient human-machine interaction, an intelligent system such as a smart vehicle

The work received financial support from European Structural and Investment Funds in the FEDER component, through the Operational Competitiveness and Internationalization Programme (COMPETE 2020) and national funds, through FCT (Project **"Neurofield"**, ref POCI01-0145FEDER-031393) and ADI (Project **"Easy Ride:Experience is everything"**, ref POCI-01-0247-FEDER-039334), FCT PhD fellowship PD/BD/128183/2016, and R&D Units Project Scope: UIDB/00319/2020 and UIDB/00013/2020.

O. Gervasi et al. (Eds.): ICCSA 2021, LNCS 12952, pp. 337–349, 2021.
https://doi.org/10.1007/978-3-030-86973-1_24

must be able to learn and make decisions based on the received data. Nowadays, the Global Positioning System (GPS) is often used to guide a driver to a destination that he/she enters into the system. Future vehicles might be able to predict where a specific driver wishes to go as well as the time the driver should arrive or depart [13]. Human mobility is characterized by a high level of spatial-temporal regularity [3,11,21], a tendency to visit specific locations at specific times [11,12,15,20], and a significant tendency to spend most of the time in a few locations [20]. Driving a car is typically coupled with daily routines such as going to work every weekday or routines across other temporal scales such as going to the gym on specific days of the week. Profiling the mobility routine of a specific driver can be used by intelligent navigation systems to support individual traveling by for instance warning the driver about traffic conditions that might cause a late arrival at the specific destination. Since a car might be shared by several users, it is important to keep in mind that the system should be able to make predictions according to the learned routines of different drivers.

Several different approaches, most of them statistical models based on big data [2,18], have been proposed for predicting the next location in human mobility. Traditional Markov models work well for a specific set of behaviors but destinations need to be fixed in advance. Recently deep learning techniques have been applied for an accurate prediction of user destination [5,22]. In [5] a Long Short-Term Memory recurrent neural network is used not only to predict drivers' destinations but also respective departure times. In this framework, the destinations (places visited by a driver with significant frequency) are first identified using a clustering algorithm, and the updating of new destinations requires the learning system to be restarted. The deep learning approach in [22] is based on a division of the spatial map in grids, each with a specific ID number, and the IDs of all possible destinations are predefined at the beginning of the learning process. Although the model takes into account the temporal characteristics of the GPS trajectories, this information is not used to predict departure or arrival times.

In [8] a model based on the theoretical framework of Dynamic Neural Fields (DNFs) was proposed that is able to learn ordinal and temporal aspects of a daily driver routine. The learning is implicit (driver does not need to be asked for his/her destinations), continuous, and can be adapted to different temporal scales. The theoretical framework of DNFs has been proven to provide key brain-inspired processing mechanisms to implement working memory, decision making, and prediction in cognitive systems (e.g. [16,17]), including the learning of the temporal and ordinal properties of sequential tasks [7,10], and in recent work, the temporal integration of GPS coordinates for the identification of stop locations [9]. The central idea of DNF models is that continuous-valued information, such as for example position in space, is represented by localized activity patterns (or bumps) in a network of recurrently connected neurons tuned to the continuous dimension. Initially driven by transient input signals, a bump becomes self-sustained due to the recurrent interactions within the network. The bump attractor thus encodes in its position the memory of a specific input value. An additional threshold accommodation dynamics ensures that the bump amplitude increases monotonically with elapsed time since input onset. In response to an entire input sequence, the field dynamics develops a multi-bump pattern with an activation gradient over neural subpopulations which carries the information about the temporal order and relative timing of the sequential events.

In this paper, we present an extension of our previous DNF model of learning daily routines [8]. The most significant advances are the integration of a long-term memory that supports the continuous up-dating and consolidation over weeks of the memory of driving experiences at a specific weekday, and the capacity to learn and distinguish the routines of different drivers. The proposed mechanism supports 1) the encoding and recall of different routines according to the driver and the day, 2) the continuous adaptation of these routines (e.g., a destination can be added or deleted without the need to restart the system), 3) the prediction of the driver's destination intention, 4) the prediction when she/he intends to arrive, and 5) the prediction how long the stay duration will be.

In what follows, we begin with a description of the DNF model and its mathematical details in Sect. 2. The results of model simulations of the routine learning and prediction processes based on recorded real-world GPS trajectories are discussed in Sect. 3. Conclusions and future work are presented in Sect. 4.

2 The Model

2.1 Model Description

Dynamic neural fields (DNFs) have been first proposed as the theoretical framework to analyze the dynamics of pattern formation in neuronal populations [1]. They have been later used to model cognitive functions such as working memory, decision making or motor planning and to synthesize these functions in autonomous robots [4]. Neural field models, formalized by integro-differential equations, represent a specific class of recurrent neural networks with a connectivity function depending on the distance in parametric space between neurons tuned to continuous metric dimensions. In the present application, the dynamic fields are spanned over the two spatial GPS coordinates latitude and longitude. The recurrent excitatory and inhibitory interactions within the network support the existence of self-stabilized bumps of activity which are initially triggered by sufficiently strong inputs. The bump position represents the memory of the GPS coordinates of a stop location of a given driver. A *stop* here stands for a visited location where the car arrived at time t_{off} and left at time t_{on}, $S = (lat, long, t_{off}, t_{on})$, where $(lat, long)$ represent the latitude and longitude coordinates corresponding to the centroid of the respective bump. Let S_i and S_k be two stops where the index indicates different days, then $i = k$ (that is, S_i and S_k represent a stop at about the same location and time of the day) if the haversine distance between the two sets of coordinates are below a distance threshold δ_d, that is, $dist_{ik} = dist_{haversine}(lat_i, long_i, long_k, lat_k) < \delta_d$, and $|t_{off_i} - t_{off_k}| < \delta_t$, where δ_t represents a time threshold. The haversine distance [19] between two points, p_1 and p_2, with coordinates $(lat_1, long_1)$ and $(lat_2, long_2)$, respectively, is defined as

$$dist_{haversine}(p_1, p_2) = 2R\left(\sqrt{\frac{a(p_1, p_2)}{a(p_1, p_2) - 1}}\right), \tag{1}$$

where R is the Earth's radius and

$$a(p_1, p_2) = \sin^2\left(\frac{lat_2 - lat_1}{2}\right) + \cos(lat_1)\cos(lat_2)\sin^2\left(\frac{long_2 - long_1}{2}\right). \tag{2}$$

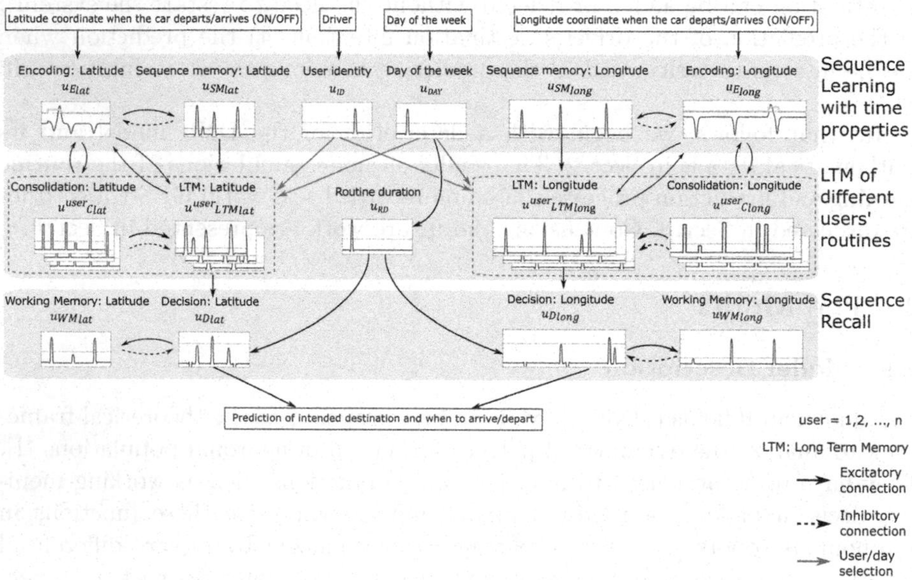

Fig. 1. Schematic view of the model architecture with several interconnected neural fields implementing sequence learning, long term memory and sequence recall. For details see the text.

Figure 1 illustrates an overview of the model architecture consisting of several interconnected neural fields. The architecture can be divided into three functionally different parts running in parallel: sequence learning, long term memory and sequence recall.

The *Sequence learning* part processes incoming GPS inputs and memorizes the stop locations of a certain driver at a specific weekday. The inputs are given by the GPS coordinates (latitude and longitude) when the vehicle is switched off or on, representing the coordinates of a destination at the time of the car's arrival or departure, respectively. We further assume that additional inputs identify the specific user and the day of the week. For consistency, we also use bumps to store this discrete information in an user identity field, u_{ID} and a weekday field, u_{DAY}. The fields are divided in several distinct regions which receive localized input in form of a Gaussian carrying the user and weekday information.

To simplify the following model description, we refer to the "arrival" signal only. At the moment when the driver switches off the car at a specific location, the GPS input drives the evolution of a bump in the latitude field $u_{E_{lat}}$ and the longitude field $u_{E_{long}}$. Each of these bumps triggers through excitatory connections the evolution of a localized activity pattern at the corresponding sites in the latitude and longitude sequence memory fields, $u_{SM_{lat}}$ and $u_{SM_{long}}$, respectively. Inhibitory feedback from $u_{SM_{lat}}$ to $u_{E_{lat}}$ (from $u_{SM_{long}}$ to $u_{E_{long}}$) destabilizes the existing bump in the encoding field. This ensures that newly arrived localized input to $u_{E_{lat}}$ ($u_{E_{long}}$) will automatically create a bump at a different field location even if the position information is repeated during the course of the day. A series of GPS coordinates at the moments when the car is switched off creates a multi-bump pattern in $u_{SM_{lat}}$ and in $u_{SM_{long}}$ with the strength of activation decreasing from bump to bump as a function of elapsed time since the start of the routine. This activation gradient over subpopulations is achieved by applying a threshold accommodation dynamics to the self-sustained activity patterns which lead to a continuous increase of the bump amplitude as a function of elapsed time [10].

The *Long Term Memory (LTM)* part stores in separate fields multiple memories of daily routines corresponding to different drivers and different days of the week. According to the information represented by a bump in the user detection and weekday fields, the corresponding consolidation fields, $u^{user}_{C_{lat}}$ and $u^{user}_{C_{long}}$, and the associated LTM fields, $u^{user}_{LTM_{lat}}$ and $u^{user}_{LTM_{long}}$, receive excitatory input from u_E and u_{SM}. The consolidation field controls whether a new stop location becomes stored in LTM as part of a daily routine or whether a memorized stop location will be forgotten since the driver has changed the routine. When a stop event occurred with a certain frequency, the accumulated localized activity in $u^{user}_{C_{lat}}$ ($u^{user}_{C_{long}}$) is above threshold. The combined excitatory input from $u^{user}_{C_{lat}}$ ($u^{user}_{C_{long}}$), $u_{E_{lat}}$ ($u_{E_{long}}$) and $u_{SM_{lat}}$ ($u_{SM_{long}}$) is then able to create a memory bump in the LTM fields. If on the other hand a bump exists in $u^{user}_{LTM_{lat}}$ ($u^{user}_{LTM_{long}}$) but the activity in $u^{user}_{C_{lat}}$ ($u^{user}_{C_{long}}$) is subthreshold due to a continuous activity decay without excitation from the encoding field $u_{E_{lat}}$ ($u_{E_{long}}$), the LTM bump becomes suppressed mediated by inhibition. There exist also excitatory connections from the memory fields back to $u_{E_{lat}}$ and $u_{E_{long}}$. This feedback excitation causes a pre-activation of neural populations in the encoding fields representing previously visited locations. Functionally, this pre-shaping mechanisms increases the robustness of the encoding process in the face of noisy and potentially incomplete GPS inputs. The routine duration field, u_{RD}, receives excitatory input from the weekday field, u_{DAY}, at the beginning of the day. The amplitude of the resulting self-sustained activity pattern increases continuously due to applied threshold accommodation dynamics. At the end of the day, the bump amplitude represents a time span of 24 h. The amplitude value is used to define the baseline activity level in the decision fields.

In the *Sequence Recall* phase, the stored information is used to make predictions about the driver's intended destinations and the time of arrival. The decision field $u_{D_{lat}}$ ($u_{D_{long}}$) receives the activation gradient stored in $u^{user}_{LTM_{lat}}$ ($u^{user}_{LTM_{long}}$) as subthreshold input. A continuous increase of the baseline activity in $u_{D_{lat}}$ ($u_{D_{long}}$) brings all subpopulations closer to the threshold for the evolution of a self-stabilized bump. The moment when the activity of the population with the highest pre-activation in the decision field reaches threshold is used to predict the location and arrival time of the first destination. Excitatory-inhibitory connections between associated populations in $u_{D_{lat}}$ ($u_{D_{long}}$) and the working memory field $u_{WM_{lat}}$ ($u_{WM_{long}}$) guarantee that a bump representing the coordinate of a predicted stop event evolve in the working memory field which then suppresses the suprathreshold activity in the decision field. This dynamic process continuous until the population with the lowest pre-activation has reached threshold and the prediction about the last stop event has been stored in working memory.

2.2 Model Equations

The population dynamics in each field is governed by an integro-differential equation first proposed and analyzed by Amari [1]

$$\tau \frac{\partial u(x,t)}{\partial t} = -u(x,t) - h + I(x,t) + \int_{\Omega} w(|x-x'|) f(u(x',t)-\theta) \mathrm{d}x' + \epsilon^{1/2} \mathrm{d}W(x,t). \tag{3}$$

The variable $u(x,t)$ represents the activity at time t of a neuron at field position x in a spatial domain $\Omega \subset \mathbb{R}$. The constant $\tau > 0$ defines the time scale of the field dynamics. Term $I(x,t)$ represents a time-dependent, localized input centered at site x, and $h > 0$ defines the stable resting state of a field without external input. The distance-dependent connectivity function $w(|x-x'|)$ determines the interaction strength between neurons at positions x and x'. An example is a kernel of lateral inhibition type given by a Gaussian function minus a constant

$$w_{lat}(x) = A_{lat} e^{(-x^2/2\sigma_{lat}^2)} - g_{lat}, \tag{4}$$

with $A_{lat} > g_{lat} > 0$ and $\sigma_{lat} > 0$. We use the lateral inhibition kernel in the fields in which only one bump at a time should evolve (e.g., u_E and u_R) [1]. To enable stable multi-bump solutions in the memory fields, an oscillatory connectivity function [6, 14] is used:

$$w_{osc}(x) = A_{osc} e^{-b|x|} (b \sin|\alpha x| + \cos(\alpha x)), \tag{5}$$

where A_{osc} controls the amplitude and parameters $b < \alpha \leq 1$ control the rate at which the oscillations decay with distance and the zero crossings of w, respectively.

The firing rate function $f(u)$ is taken here as the Heaviside step function with threshold $\theta = 0$. Finally, the additive noise term $\mathrm{d}W(x,t)$ describes the increment of a spatially dependent Wiener process with amplitude $\epsilon \ll 1$.

The activation gradients in $u_{SM_{lat}}$ and $u_{SM_{long}}$ encode the serial order of visited locations, that is, the earlier a certain location was visited, the higher is its memory bump. Since the bump amplitude increases as a function of elapsed time, the difference in bump amplitude of two successive destinations represents the temporal interval separating the two visits. To establish the activation gradient, we consider the following state-dependent dynamics [7,10]

$$\tau_h \frac{\partial h_{SM}(x,t)}{\partial t} = \kappa f(u_{SM}(x,t)) + (1 - f(u_{SM}(x,t)))(-h_{SM}(x,t) + h_{SM_0}) \quad (6)$$

where h_{SM_0} defines the baseline activation to which h_{SM} relaxes without suprathreshold activity at position x, $\kappa > 0$ is the growth rate when it is present and τ_h is time scale of the dynamics. The time window for the buildup is proportional to the total routine time, which in the present example is assumed as 24 h. The h-level accommodation dynamics begins at $t = t_{start}$ (here, at 0:00) and ends at $t = t_{end}$ (here, at 24:00).

To ensure that only the places visited with some minimal frequency are memorized and that the places no longer visited are forgotten, the consolidation field u_C governed by Eq. (7) integrates the input from u_E with a simple linear dynamics. It approaches with the growth rate λ_{build} the value $a > 0$, representing the maximum level of activation in u_C. When there is no suprathreshold activity in u_E, the activity of excited neurons decays with a slower rate λ_{decay} towards the resting level $h_c < 0$:

$$\begin{aligned} \frac{\partial u_C(x,t)}{\partial t} &= \lambda_{build}(-u_C(x,t) + a) f(u_E(x,t)) \\ &+ \lambda_{decay}(-u_C(x,t) + h_c)(1 - f(u_E(x,t))). \end{aligned} \quad (7)$$

In the examples of user and weekday specific routines presented here, the growth and decay rates are chosen in such a way that 1) accumulated localized activity in u_C is above threshold when a certain stop point has been visited in two consecutive weeks, and that 2) the activity falls below threshold when the predicted visit has not been realized in two consecutive weeks at the specific weekday. Note that longer integration and forgetting periods could be realized by adapting the parameters λ_{build} and λ_{decay} accordingly.

A dynamic build-up of a long term memory of routines is performed in $u^{user}_{LTM_{lat}}$ ($u^{user}_{LTM_{long}}$) through excitatory connections from $u_{SM_{lat}}$ ($u_{SM_{long}}$), $u_{E_{lat}}$ ($u_{E_{long}}$) and $u_{C_{lat}}$ ($u_{C_{long}}$). The LTM fields receive the following input:

$$I_{user}(x,t) = D_{user} f(u_C(x,t)) f(u_E(x,t)) u_{SM}(x,t) \quad (8)$$

where

$$D_{user} = \max_{A_{ID}}(f(u_{ID}(x,t) - \theta)) \times \max_{A_{DAY}}(f(u_{DAY}(x,t) - \theta)), \quad user = 1, 2, \ldots, n, \quad (9)$$

and A_{ID} and A_{DAY} represent the regions in the fields u_{ID} and u_{DAY} which receive the information about the user identity and the working day, respectively.

Since $D_{user} = 1$ when bumps exist in both fields and 0 otherwise, the parameter D_{user} acts as a multiplicative signal that gates the input from the encoding and sequence memory fields to the associated LTM fields.

The gradient in the LTM fields is established by the following state-dependent dynamics:

$$\begin{aligned} \tau_h \frac{\partial h_{LTM}(x,t)}{\partial t} &= (1 - f(u_{LTM}(x,t)))\,(-h_{LTM}(x,t) + h_{LTM_0}) \\ +f(u_{LTM}(x,t)) f(u_C(x,t)) & f(u_{SM}(x,t))(-h_{LTM}(x,t) + h_{SM}(x,t)) \\ +f(u_{LTM}(x,t))&(1 - f(u_C(x,t)))(-h_{LTM}(x,t) + h_{LTM_{inih}}) \end{aligned} \tag{10}$$

where $h_{LTM_0} < 0$ is the baseline activity to which h_{LTM} converges without suprathreshold activity at position x. The negative constant $h_{LTM_{inih}} < 0$ represents the stable state to which h_{LTM} converges at sites with a bump in $u_{LTM}(x,t)$ and no suprathreshold activity in $u_C(x,t)$. This ensures that the memory of a stop location that is not part of the daily routine anymore will be erased. At positions x with subthreshold activation in the three fields $u_C(x,t)$, $u_{LTM}(x,t)$ and $u_{SM}(x,t)$, the h-value $h_{LTM}(x,t)$ tends to $h_{SM}(x,t)$. The bump amplitude in $u_{LTM}(x,t)$ thus equals the corresponding bump amplitude in $u_{SM}(x,t)$. This means that the relative timing information recorded during the last routine execution is preserved in long term memory.

The recall of the learned routine is performed by the four fields shown on bottom of Fig. 1. The decision field $u_{D_{lat}}$ ($u_{D_{long}}$) receives the multi-bump patterns from $u^{user}_{LTM_{lat}}$ ($u^{user}_{LTM_{long}}$) as subthreshold input

$$I_{user}(x) = \sum_{user=1}^{n} D_{user} u^{user}_{LTM}(x). \tag{11}$$

The coefficient D_{user} given by (9) ensures again that only the gradient that corresponds to the current driver and day of the week contributes to this input.

To recall the order and timing information stored in the activation gradients, we apply a linear dynamics for the resting level h_D in $u_{D_{lat}}$ ($u_{D_{long}}$) which brings all pre-activated subpopulations closer to the threshold 0:

$$\frac{\mathrm{d}h_D(t)}{\mathrm{d}t} = \kappa_D, \quad h_D(t_0) = h_{D_0} < 0, \tag{12}$$

where κ_D defines the constant growth rate.

The initial value h_{D_0} is chosen equal to the amplitude of the bump in the duration field, u_{RD}, from the last routine execution. Since the amplitude of this bump represents a routine time span of 24 h, the representation of the stop events reaches the threshold 0 exactly at the predicted event time. The initial resting state could be chosen slightly larger to ensure that the diver assistant anticipates (e.g., by $t_a = 10$ min) the true arrival time. Note that we have proposed in our previous work a learning mechanism that allows the system to autonomously adapt its internal event timing encoded in the bump amplitudes based on environmental feedback [10].

Numerical simulations of the model were performed in MATLAB using a forward Euler method. To compute the spatial convolution of w and f we employ a fast Fourier transform (FFT), using MATLAB's in-built functions `fft` and `ifft` to perform the Fourier transform and the inverse Fourier transform, respectively.

3 Results

To test the proposed model, we consider a previously recorded dataset consisting of 11 consecutive weeks of a real-world driving scenario. It represents the routines of two different drivers from the Portuguese city Guimarães sharing the same car. To identify distinct stop locations in the dataset, we apply threshold values for the location radius ($\delta_d = 200$ m) and the stay duration ($\delta_t = 30$ min). Furthermore, we assume that a stop event is part of daily routine if it happens at least twice in consecutive weeks and that the location is forgotten when a prediction is not confirmed twice in a row. To generate predictions, a routine for each day and each driver has to be executed at least three times. To directly compare the real with the predicted arrival times, we do not apply any forecast period, that is, a perfect prediction matches the exact arrival time.

As an example of a daily routine of one of the drivers, Fig. 2(A) shows a map with a series of five destinations where the car was switched off, one place (the school) was visited twice. The memories of the GPS coordinates, latitude and longitude, are represented in the activation gradients in $u_{SM_{lat}}$ (left) and $u_{SM_{long}}$ (top), respectively. Supposing that this daily routine does not change in space and time, running the routine three times results in long term memories (not shown) reflecting the order and the timing of the arrival/departure destinations. Figure 2(B) compares the exact point in time in which the driver arrives at and departures from a specific destination (vertical lines) with the time course of the maximal activation of the corresponding population representation in the decision fields, where $u_{D_{long}}$ is taken as example. As can be seen when considering the reaching of the threshold as read-out time, there is a perfect match. The temporal difference between successive time courses indicates the interval timing between successive arrivals or departures. The information about the stay duration at a specific destination can be extracted by comparing the respective time courses of arrival and departure. In the specific example considered in Fig. 2(B), the stay duration predictions at stops S_1 to S_5 are: S_1: 21 min, S_2: 7 h and 54 min, S_3: 20 min, S_4: 60 min and S_5: 24 min.

As an example to compare daily routines of the two drivers, we consider 11 Monday trajectories of driver A and 8 Friday trajectories of driver B. Looking at the time t_{off} when the driver has switched off the car, Table 1 compares the real and predicted arrival times of each stop for both driver routines. Driver A stops at locations S_1, S_3, S_4 and S_5 on all Mondays. From the third Monday on, the stops are correctly predicted and the foreseen arrival times over the weeks closely follow the observed variations in timing of the driver trajectories. For stop locations such as S_1 with a relatively small variation of real stop times, the differences between predicted and realized arrival time is small (Fig. 3(A)). Adding a fixed

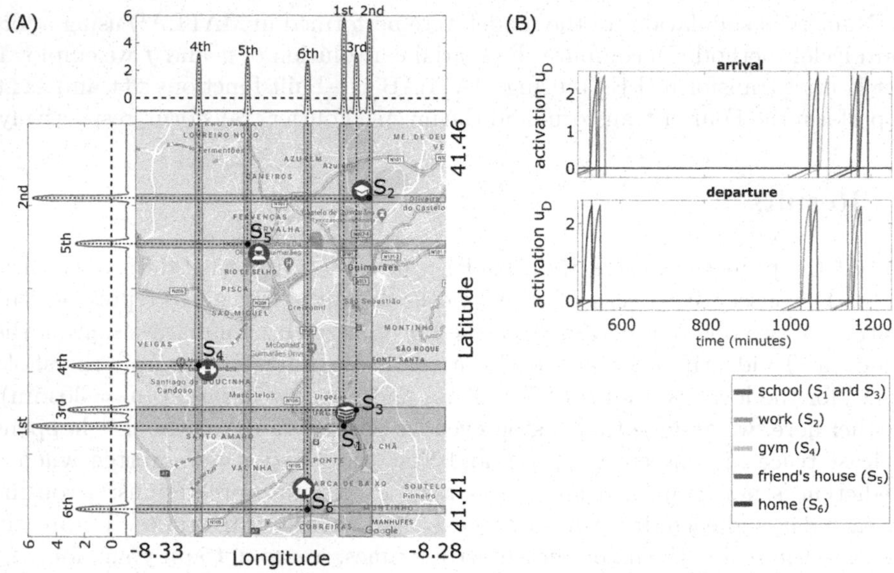

Fig. 2. (A) Map of part of Portugal generated from Google Maps showing a sequence of arrivals of Driver A and the respective activation gradients in the memory fields $u_{SM_{lat}}$ (left) and $u_{SM_{long}}$ (top). (B) Time courses of the activation at the bump centers in the decision field $u_{D_{long}}$.

forecast period that takes into account this variability would guarantee that a driver assistant anticipates in all cases the real stop event. Stop location S_6 is an example in which the arrival time appears to be significantly delayed in one week compared to the habitual timing pattern (compare Mondays 4 and 5 in Fig. 3(C)). Since the arrival delay does not represent a consistent change in the routine and the timing of the current prediction reflects the observed timing of the preceding routine execution, a relatively large prediction delay manifests in the following week. Stop S_2 did not occur on all Mondays, but this stop location was not completely forgotten since its memory is refreshed in the week directly following a trajectory without visit (e.g., weeks 6 and 7 in Fig. 3(B)). Driver A stopped at S_5 only twice in different weeks. This stop event thus does not enter the long term routine memory and no prediction is made. Driver B stops at locations S_1, S_2, S_3, and S_5 on all Fridays. From the third Friday on, these four stops are correctly predicted with a timing pattern that closely matches the mean and standard deviation of the observed pattern. Implementing a short forecast period in the field dynamics would again ensure that the prediction anticipates in all cases the real arrival time. Stop S_4 happened only on the first three Fridays (Fig. 3(D)). From the third to the fifth Friday the systems incorrectly predicts this location as being part of a routine, and in the sixth week it appears to be forgotten.

Table 1. Real and predicted times in minutes of two different day routines from two different drivers.

Monday routine of driver A (11 weeks)					Friday routine of driver B (8 weeks)				
Stops	NS	Real time	NP	Predicted time	Stops	NS	Real time	NP	Predicted time
S_1	11	526.5 (±1.81)	9	525.8 (±1.97)	S_1	8	520.0 (±4.11)	6	518.3 (±5.16)
S_2	7	542.1 (±2.19)	9	541.1 (±2.66)	S_2	8	539.5 (±5.88)	6	537.0 (±6.95)
S_3	11	550.1 (±6.45)	9	549.2 (±7.18)	S_3	8	1116.3 (±8.40)	6	1117.0 (±9.67)
S_4	11	1113.1 (±2.07)	9	1112.8 (±2.87)	S_4	3	1132.0 (±3.61)	3	1133.4 (±3.64)
S_5	2	1129.5 (±12.02)	0	–	S_5	8	1261.6 (±5.21)	6	1262.5 (±5.48)
S_6	11	1134.0 (±7.35)	9	1134.0 (±7.67)	–				

Data is presented as mean (± standard deviation). NS and NP are the number of weeks that the location at about the same period of the day was visited and predicted, respectively.

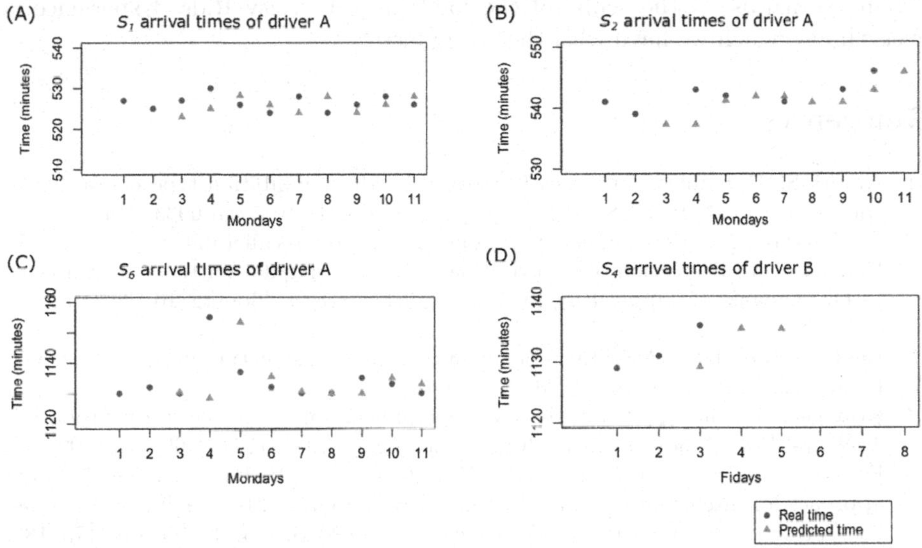

Fig. 3. Real and predicted arrival times in minutes of several stops from 11 Monday trajectories of driver A (A-C), and from 8 Friday trajectories of driver B (D).

4 Conclusion

In this paper, we have presented a Dynamic Neural Field approach to learning and memorizing ordinal and temporal properties of different driver routines. The learning is continuous starting with the first driving trajectory, happens implicitly without direct driver feedback, and can be scaled to different time periods (e.g., hours, days or weeks). The experiments with real GPS trajectory data validate the model architecture for two drivers sharing the car at different weekdays. The results confirm that the system correctly predicts in most cases the where and when of driver destinations. Prediction errors happen in cases of an exceptional, one-time deviation from the routine behavior. The activation-based learning mechanism implemented in the neural network also supports a fast adaption to consistent changes in the routines when predictions fail more than once or new destinations should be integrated in an existing routine. This contrast with many other neural network approaches (e.g., deep learning [5,22]) to learning sequential tasks which store the acquired information in synaptic weights. Weight-based learning typically requires large training sets and can be computationally very heavy.

The integration of the long term memory with other factors such as traffic conditions in GPS-based navigation systems could be used to smarter route selection/recommendation without requiring input from the driver. Furthermore, the driver could benefit from advanced warnings about the possibility of arriving late at the next destination.

In future work will test the proposed model architecture in more complex driving scenarios, in the scope of the joint project "Easy Ride: Experience is everything" which we have with the car industry.

References

1. Amari, S.: Dynamics of pattern formation in lateral-inhibition type neural fields. Biol. Cybern. **27**(2), 77–87 (1977). https://doi.org/10.1007/BF00337259
2. Boukhechba, M., Bouzouane, A., Gaboury, S., Gouin-Vallerand, C., Giroux, S., Bouchard, B.: Prediction of next destinations from irregular patterns. J. Ambient. Intell. Humaniz. Comput. **9**(5), 1345–1357 (2017). https://doi.org/10.1007/s12652-017-0519-z
3. Eagle, N., Pentland, A.S.: Eigenbehaviors: identifying structure in routine. Behav. Ecol. Sociobiol. **63**(7), 1057–1066 (2009)
4. Erlhagen, W., Bicho, E.: The dynamic neural field approach to cognitive robotics. J. Neural Eng. **3**, 36–54 (2006). https://doi.org/10.1088/1741-2560/3/3/R02
5. Fernandes, C., Ferreira, F., Erlhagen, W., Monteiro, S., Bicho, E.: A deep learning approach for intelligent cockpits: learning drivers routines. In: Analide, C., Novais, P., Camacho, D., Yin, H. (eds.) IDEAL 2020. LNCS, vol. 12490, pp. 173–183. Springer, Cham (2020). https://doi.org/10.1007/978-3-030-62365-4_17
6. Ferreira, F., Erlhagen, W., Bicho, E.: Multi-bump solutions in a neural field model with external inputs. Physica D Nonlinear Phenomena **326**, 32–51 (2016). https://doi.org/10.1016/j.physd.2016.01.009
7. Ferreira, F., Erlhagen, W., Sousa, E., Louro, L., Bicho, E.: Learning a musical sequence by observation: a robotics implementation of a dynamic neural field model. In: 4th International Conference on Development and Learning and on Epigenetic Robotics, pp. 157–162. IEEE (2014)
8. Ferreira, F., et al.: A dynamic neural model for endowing intelligent cars with the ability to learn driver routines: where to go, when to arrive and how long to stay there. In: Towards Cognitive Vehicles Workshop (TCV2019), IROS2019, pp. 15–18 (2019)
9. Ferreira, F., et al.: Dynamic identification of stop locations from GPS trajectories based on their temporal and spatial characteristics (2021, under review)
10. Ferreira, F., Wojtak, W., Sousa, E., Louro, L., Bicho, E., Erlhagen, W.: Rapid learning of complex sequences with time constraints: a dynamic neural field model. IEEE Trans. Cogn. Dev. Syst. (2020). https://doi.org/10.1109/TCDS.2020.2991789

11. Gonzalez, M.C., Hidalgo, C.A., Barabasi, A.L.: Understanding individual human mobility patterns. Nature **453**(7196), 779–782 (2008)
12. Jiang, S., Ferreira, J., González, M.C.: Clustering daily patterns of human activities in the city. Data Min. Knowl. Disc. **25**(3), 478–510 (2012)
13. Kun, A.L., et al.: Human-machine interaction for vehicles: review and outlook. Found. Trends® Hum.-Comput. Interact. **11**(4), 201–293 (2018)
14. Laing, C.R., Troy, W.C., Gutkin, B., Ermentrout, G.B.: Multiple bumps in a neuronal model of working memory. SIAM J. Appl. Math. **63**(1), 62–97 (2002). https://doi.org/10.1137/S0036139901389495
15. Rinzivillo, S., Gabrielli, L., Nanni, M., Pappalardo, L., Pedreschi, D., Giannotti, F.: The purpose of motion: learning activities from individual mobility networks. In: 2014 International Conference on Data Science and Advanced Analytics (DSAA), pp. 312–318. IEEE (2014)
16. Sandamirskaya, Y., Zibner, S.K., Schneegans, S., Schöner, G.: Using dynamic field theory to extend the embodiment stance toward higher cognition. New Ideas Psychol. **31**(3), 322–339 (2013)
17. Schöner, G.: Dynamical systems approaches to cognition. In: Cambridge Handbook of Computational Cognitive Modeling, pp. 101–126 (2008)
18. Simmons, R., Browning, B., Zhang, Y., Sadekar, V.: Learning to predict driver route and destination intent. In: 2006 IEEE Intelligent Transportation Systems Conference, pp. 127–132. IEEE (2006)
19. Sinnott, R.W.: Virtues of the haversine. S&T **68**(2), 158 (1984)
20. Song, C., Koren, T., Wang, P., Barabási, A.L.: Modelling the scaling properties of human mobility. Nat. Phys. **6**(10), 818–823 (2010)
21. Song, C., Qu, Z., Blumm, N., Barabási, A.L.: Limits of predictability in human mobility. Science **327**(5968), 1018–1021 (2010)
22. Xu, J., Zhao, J., Zhou, R., Liu, C., Zhao, P., Zhao, L.: Predicting destinations by a deep learning based approach. IEEE Trans. Knowl. Data Eng. **33**(2), 651–666 (2021)

Bio-Inspired Scan Matching for Efficient Simultaneous Localization and Mapping

Nadia Nedjah[1(✉)], Luiza de Macedo Mourelle[2], and Pedro Jorge Albuquerque de Oliveira[1]

[1] Department of Electronics Engineering and Telecommunications, State University of Rio de Janeiro, Rio de Janeiro, Brazil
{nadia,pedrojorge}@eng.uerj.br

[2] Department of Systems Engineering and Computation, State University of Rio de Janeiro, Rio de Janeiro, Brazil
ldmm@eng.uerj.br

Abstract. Simultaneous Localization And Mapping (SLAM) is a fundamental problem in robotic systems. In this work, we apply a derivative free bio-inspired techniques to the scan-matching step, which is a the main step in the SLAM problem based on the exploitation of swarm intelligence. For this purpose, we have explore the swarm intelligence optimization meta-heuristics based on the firefly behavior. Aiming at reducing further the translational and rotational scan alignment errors, the proposed scan matching proceeds in two main steps, namely scan-to-scan and scan-to-map matching. The proposed firefly-based implementation of the SLAM provides a good trade-off regarding accuracy and execution efficiency.

Keywords: SLAM · Scan matching · Swarm intelligence · Firefly algorithm

1 Introduction

The Simultaneous Localization And Mapping (SLAM) problem deals with the intertwined tasks of estimating the trajectory of a moving agent and a map of the environment in which it takes place. One of the basic steps in SLAM is the scan matching.

Scan matching and the closely related image registration problem are a fundamental part of many methods developed to address the problems of simultaneous localization and mapping, structure from motion, object recognition, image fusion and 3D modeling. In most cases, the goal is to find a transformation that leads to maximum overlap between two sets of measurements taken from different viewpoints, or perhaps, from a single vantage point at two different instants in time or even between a set of measurements and a *global model* being constructed. In the context of SLAM, such a procedure is usually employed either to recover, or to enhance a gross estimate of the relative motion observed between

O. Gervasi et al. (Eds.): ICCSA 2021, LNCS 12952, pp. 350–365, 2021.
https://doi.org/10.1007/978-3-030-86973-1_25

two data frames. In the specific case of laser range data, the problem of aligning measurements is often called *scan alignment* or *scan matching*. There are many different formulations of the scan-matching problem, as touching the form taken by the data and the pattern to be aligned. The most commonly encountered such variations are: scan-to-scan; scan-to-line; line-to-line; scan-to-map; map-to-map. The distinction between these formulations, and especially their reason for being, is but one of type, and level of complexity, of the pre-processing performed on the sensed data. It is thus sufficient to note that each one tries to exploit a particular characteristic of the data in order to get a better result under a specific set of conditions. For instance, the scan-to-line formulation is expected to have a better performance than the simple alignment of raw scan data, if the data in question has a strong linear trend, but may perform poorly if the entries of the covariance matrix of the scan data are of similar magnitude. The map-to-map approach tries to exploit all of the available data and is usually seen in the form of correlative matching [19]. Nonetheless, for all its advantages, like less sensitivity to outliers and more effective usage of past information, the large number of floating point operations it requires, makes it computationally expensive to perform, in some cases prohibitively so. This is said, it is of utmost importance to emphasize that the performance of the implementation of the scan-matching step is the main bottleneck for any SLAM solution. Hence, it is safe to establish that any improvement in terms of accuracy and/or execution speed regarding scan matching is most welcome in any SLAM system.

In this paper we propose a solution to the SLAM problem that is based on scan matching through Firefly bio-inspired meta-heuristic. The advantage of such an approach is apparent from the well-known multi-modality of the scan-matching problem. As far as we are concerned, this approach has not been investigated before. Furthermore, we have employed a graph-based back-end to allow this system to be consistent in exploration sessions that are either too long or cover too large an area. In both cases, a solution based exclusively on scan matching is known to fail due to the incremental nature of the estimation error.

The rest of this paper is organized in sections. First, in Sect. 2, we give a general overview of the slam problem and related challenges, including localization and mapping. After that, in Sect. 3, we describe the main steps of the firefly algorithm (FA). Subsequently, in Sect. 4, we explain the proposed method to perform robot SLAM efficiently yet accurately using the bio-inspired technique. Then, in Sect. 5, we present the performance results and their analysis. Finally, in Sect. 6, we draw some conclusions of the described works and point out some promising future directions to improve the proposed methodology.

2 The SLAM Problem

The SLAM problem consists of the concurrent estimation of the robot trajectory and a map of the environment in which a robotic entity moves in the course of its operation. A solution to this problem is required in situations in which a robot has no access to its trajectory and/or to a map of the environment wherein it moves. Any SLAM system needs to provide a solution to the trajectory estimation, *i.e.* solve the localization problem, and to the approximate environment map building, *i.e.* solve the mapping problem. We assume that the required concepts to tackle the localization problem. We first define the necessary elements to approach the mapping problem. In Sect. 2.1, we describe the scan matching technique and in Sect. 2.2, we describe the main basic technique that have been applied later to form the basis concepts for understanding the proposed SLAM implementation, described in Sect. 4.

The concept of pose is well known and refers to a set of coordinates that are sufficient to determine the location and orientation of the robot in relation to the environment. In the case of confined systems moving in a two-dimensional $\mathbb{R}^3$ subspace, the pose must contain three coordinates. All definition of operations on poses are well defined [17].

The methods used to solve the SLAM problem that are take advantage of a pose graph are based on a formulation of the SLAM problem in terms of a graph of relationships between various frames in which the robot has met over time. These methods address the problem of state estimation as an optimization problem [9,10,13,15]. We also take advantage of the graph-based SLAM method contributed in [9].

2.1 Scan Matching

Because scan matching is at the heart of this work, we dedicate this section to explaining the idea behind such a process and its functionality as well as the different methodologies taken to approach it. It is noteworthy to point out that here we use a Light Detection And Ranging device (LiDAR). The scan-matching process aims to determine the best transformation between two point clouds obtained by some sensing instrument. Scan-matching usage, as a way of estimating the movement between two poses, from which measurements were taken, is effective as long as we can rely on the accuracy of both measurements and on the convergence of the underlying optimization process, within a reasonable time.

Existing scan-matching algorithms, although reasonably efficient, they are very sensitive to initialization. Given the advantages of applying techniques that are not only able to fully exploit the search space but also to exploit the solution space independently of function derivatives, and taking into account the fact that different heuristics present characteristics that make them better suited to solving particular types of problems, we decided that it would be advantageous and positively contributive for our work to investigate swarm optimization techniques to implement the scan-matching problem. In line with the objective of comparing the performance of swarm optimization meta-heuristics, we selected the part of the system, which is responsible for scan alignment to be implemented in such a way in order to allow the interchangeable application of any selected techniques. In this work, a map representation is used as an occupancy grid, and the scans are represented as point clouds.

Occupancy maps are a form of spatial representation based on space discretization *i.e.* associates one cell to each space region, each of which can be classified either as *full* or *empty* [17]. This type of spatial representation is based on the hypotheses of world staticity, independence between random variables that represent the map, and the fact that a cell can be completely full or completely empty. In other words, the presence of an obstacle in a part of a given space region makes one consider the region as entirely filled and what is estimated is the probability that this fact is true. The hypothesis of independence between the various cells is based on the probability distribution of the map given by the product of the probabilities of all its cells [19]. In this work, we will adopt the convention used in [19], wherein the algorithm that allows to perform cells mapping in this kinds of representation can be found.

2.2 Nearest Neighbor Search

A fundamental part of several of the steps of this work consists of searching for the nearest neighbors to a given point in a set of points. In order to give a formal definition of the problem, let $P = \{p_1, p_2, \cdots, p_N\}$ a set of points in $\mathbb{R}^2$, and a point q. The problem of searching for the nearest neighbor of point q in P is to find point $p \in P$, such that p is the closest to q. The simplest way to accomplish such a task would be to perform an exhaustive search computing the distance between any point of P to q and choosing the one that occasion the smallest distance. However, this approach is the least efficient and it is evident when the cardinality of P is large. In the proposed SLAM system, we are led to perform multiple searches for nearest neighbors, each with neighbors of entire point sets in a counterpart set, we proposed to store P in a structure of data that facilitates a fast search. The usage of KD-trees reduces significantly the time required to find a closer set of neighbors [5]. One of the most traditional algorithms this task is called Iterative Closest Point (ICP) [5]. The main advantages of ICP-based methods are their simplicity of implementation and agility when implemented using KD-Trees [3,4,8,20]. In the proposed implementation, several changes have been proposed which range from suggestions of point association heuristics to the implementation of hybrid methods that employ global optimization techniques to provide a version of ICP with the best initial estimate. Algorithm 1 presents the steps of the canonical method, whereing two sets of points A and B are aligned and T_i is a the initial pre-defined transformation matrix, w_i are the weighing coefficients for each deviation and d_{max} is the acceptable error threshold [5].

In general terms, the underlying operation can be viewed as an iteration of the following steps:

1. Matching: Associates to each pose in the source dataset its nearest neighbor in the destination set.
2. Minimization: Minimizes the error measure according to the cost function used.
3. Transformation: Transforms the poses in the source dataset using the result of the minimization process.

Algorithm 1. Steps of the canonical version of ICP

Require: N; T_i
$A = \{a_1, a_2, \cdots, a_i, \cdots, a_N\}$;
$B = \{b_1, b_2, \cdots, b_i, \cdots, b_N\}$;
$T = T_i$
repeat
  for $i = 1 \cdots N$ **do**
    $p_i = FindNearestNeighbor(a_i, T \cdot B)$
    if $\|p_i - T \cdot B\| < d_{max}$ **then**
      $w_i = 1$
    else
      $w_i = 0$
    end if
  end for
  $T = \min_{T} \sum_{i=1}^{N} w_i \cdot \|p_i - T \cdot b_i\|^2$
until Stopping condition
return T

3 Firefly Based Optimization

The FA is swarm intelligence method [7]. The inspiration of FA comes from the bio-luminescence of fireflies. In fact, it is precisely the periodic flickering of lights, a striking feature of these insects, which, together with the physical characteristic of the decay of light intensity, was used to elaborate this optimization strategy. In [7], it is shown that the decay of the luminous intensity I follows a relation of the type $I \propto \frac{1}{r^2}$, where r indicates the distance to the source of luminescence. The communication between social insects has been successfully used several times as an inspiration for the development of optimization techniques, such as in the cases of ants and bees [1,6].

The parameters of the FA are β_0, γ and n. The coefficient β_0 is the attractiveness of a firefly when the distance to it is zero. The constant γ determines the decay rate of the attractiveness of a firefly in terms of the distance to it. In the Algorithm 2, each firefly was denoted by s and the objective function by f.

The main operation is the combination of random motion with the attraction of each firefly by the other brighter members of the swarm. In fact, firefly s_j is attracted to the firefly s_i and its motion is defined by Eq. 1:

$$s_i^{t+1} = s_i^{t} + \beta_0 \cdot \exp(-\gamma \cdot r_{ij}^2) \cdot (s_j - s_i) + \alpha \cdot \epsilon_i, \tag{1}$$

wherein γ represents the light absorption factor, that is how light diffuses through the medium in which it propagates between one firefly and another. The parameter $\alpha \in [0, 1]$ is responsible for the random term $\alpha \cdot \epsilon_i$ of Eq. 1, and is sampled from a uniform distribution in that interval. The value ϵ_i is sampled from a Gaussian distribution. The value of r_{ij} is the distance between the fireflies s_i and s_j, as defined by the two-dimensional Euclidean distance r_{ij} between s_j and s_i

Algorithm 2. FA

Require: β_0,γ,n
Initialize the swarm
repeat
    $\alpha^{(t)} = newAlfa()$
    for $i := 1, 2, \ldots, n$ **do**
        Compute $f(s_i)$
    end for
    Sort the fireflies s of the swarm according to their quality $f(s)$.
    Assign the fittest firefly to s^*.
    Move the fireflies according to Equation 1.
until Stopping criteria are met
return s^*

4 Proposed Solution

The proposed solution to the SLAM problem consists of four parts: (i) a scan matcher; (ii) a pose-graph updating system; (iii) a pose-graph optimization system; and (iv) a loop closure detection system. Algorithm 3 shows the macro-architecture of the proposed method.

Algorithm 3. Proposed SLAM Solution

$G := \emptyset$; $l_v := \emptyset$
$\mu_\lambda := 0$; $\sigma_\lambda := 0$;$\lambda := 0$
$\Delta P := [0\,0\,0]^T$
$l_v(0) :=$ **Acquire_Scan**()
$t := 1$
repeat
    $l_v(t) :=$ **Acquire_Scan**()
    $\Delta P :=$ **Align_Scans**($l_v(t), l_v(t-1)$)
    $G :=$ **Update_Graph**($G, \Delta P, t-1, t$)
    $G :=$ **Seek_Loop_Closure**(G, l_v)
    $G :=$ **Optimize_Graph**(G)
    $t := t + 1$
until Halt command is received.
$M :=$ **Generate_Global_Map** (G, l_v))
return M

4.1 The Scan Matcher

The scan matcher role, in the proposed system, is to determine the relationship that exists between pairs of LiDAR scans.

The proposed scan matcher, whose main steps are given in Algorithm 4, is designed to operate on two different, and complementary, modes. The first mode of operation is a scan-to-scan alignment based on a point-to-point distance metric. Its operation is dependent on the minimization of the used distance metric, and it operates on a pair of scans by first determining a set of correspondences between them, based on a nearest neighbor criteria. The second mode is a scan-to-map alignment and consists of minimizing the distance between the pairs of corresponding points. The result of the aforementioned procedure is a transformation that leads to a maximal alignment between the input scans. So, the scan matcher works in two modes in an attempt to reduce uncertainties of scan matching. Hence, when the scan-to-scan mode fails to achieve an acceptable alignment (*i.e.* alignment error is above a threshold), the scan-to-map is executed, attempting to fine tune the relative position found by the scan-to-scan alignment in order to hopefully reduce the alignment error.

Algorithm 4. Align_Scans(v, v_r)

Require: t, μ_λ, σ_λ, ϵ
l_c := **Seek_Correspondences**(v, v_r)
$[\Delta P\ \lambda]^T$:= **Minimize** Equation 2
if $\lambda > \epsilon$ **then**
  m := **Renderize_Local_Map** (v_r)
  $[\Delta P\ \lambda]^T$:= **Minimize** Equation 4 with arguments (v, m)
  λ := **Calculate** the new λ using Equation 2 with ΔP as its argument.
end if
$\mu_\lambda := \frac{1}{t}(\lambda + (t-1)\mu_\lambda)$
$\sigma_\lambda := \left[\frac{t-1}{t}\left(\sigma_\lambda^2 + (\lambda - \mu_\lambda)^2\right)\right]^{\frac{1}{2}}$
$\epsilon := \mu_\lambda + \sigma_\lambda$
return ΔP

The objective function used for the scan-to-scan alignment, which evaluates the quadratic distance between the points of scan v and those of scan v_r in the coordinate system centered in pose ΔP, is specified by Eq. 2:

$$f(\Delta P) = \log\left(1 + \sum_{i=1}^{N}\left\|\left(\Delta P \oplus \begin{bmatrix} v_{x_i} \\ v_{y_i} \end{bmatrix}\right) - \begin{bmatrix} v_{rx_i} \\ v_{ry_i} \end{bmatrix}\right\|^2\right), \tag{2}$$

where ΔP is a relative pose and $\oplus$ is the operation of composition between a pose and a point. This composition allows us to express the points in v in the same coordinate system as the points in v_r centered at new pose ΔP. Note that the log function is computed in order to limit the wide variation of the used comparison function f. So, we impose the $\log(1 + x)$ re-scale transformation [2]. Constant 1 is added to avoid the non-definition of the logarithm function on 0.

The scan-to-map alignment allows us to correct the robot pose estimation exploiting three facts: *(i)* all beams of a scan must end at obstacles; *(ii)* the robot estimated position must be empty in the current occupancy map; and *(iii)* robot must be able to reach that position in the map and continue its mapping from thereon. The objective function for this second mode of scan-to-map matching is inspired by these two facts. The minimization of the proposed objective function attempts to find the best matching that minimizes any breach of these two facts. Moreover, the scan-to-map alignment is performed in the manner previously described via a minimization process using the swarm-based optimization meta-heuristic. In this case, the objective function takes on the form described in Eq. 3 [18]. Namely, let v_{x_i} and v_{y_i} be the Cartesian coordinates of the obstacle detected by the i-th beam of scan v and let ΔP be a relative pose. The result of the composition operation between the point (v_{x_i}, v_{y_i}) and the relative pose ΔP, in the coordinates of the local occupancy grid map, is denoted (ξ_i, ζ_i) and defined by Eq. 3:

$$\begin{bmatrix} \xi_i \\ \zeta_i \end{bmatrix} = \Delta P \oplus \begin{bmatrix} v_{x_i} \\ v_{y_i} \end{bmatrix}. \tag{3}$$

The process of scan-to-map alignment is then reduced to the minimization of the objective function g defined in Eq. 4:

$$g(\xi_i, \zeta_i) = \sum_{i=1}^{n} \frac{255 - m(\xi_i, \zeta_i)}{255} + \frac{1}{9} \sum_{k=-1}^{1} \sum_{\ell=-1}^{1} \frac{m(x_r + k, y_r + \ell)}{255}, \tag{4}$$

wherein n is the number of beams within the current scan, x_r and y_r represent the position of the robot in the local map. Variable m represents the local occupancy grid map as a matrix of unsigned eight bit integer numbers that codify the occupancy probabilities from 0 to 100% by mapping them linearly to the range from 255 to 0, respectively. So, it is established that value 0 indicates an entry in the map of 100% probability of being occupied while value 255 denotes an entry of 100% probability of being empty.

It is noteworthy to emphasize that the first summation term in Eq. 4 is with respect to all n beams within the scan one wishes to localize and thus evaluates the veracity of the first fact (*i.e.* scan beams must end at obstacles), and the second summation term is employed to penalize the presence of occupied cells in the $(\varrho + 2)^2$ adjacent cells of the robot location, taking into account the robot's size and map cell size, and thus verifying the veracity of the second fact (*i.e.* robot estimate position must be empty in the map), augmented by the extra cells around the robot location, thus guaranteeing the veracity of the third fact (*i.e.* robot must be able to reach the position and continue its trajectory from it). In both modes of operation three halting conditions have been imposed upon the optimization procedure: a limit of 1000 maximum iterations performed by each technique, a stagnation limit of 50 iterations, wherein the difference between the best and the worst solution within the swarm does not vary by more than 10^{-6}, and a tolerance threshold, whereby a solution whose corresponding objective function value is inferior to 10^{-6} is immediately accepted.

Aiming to evaluate the performance, from a mostly a qualitative point of view, of the FA meta-heuristic, we carried out an preliminary test, in which we used the map of Fig. 1 as the test-object and evaluated the mean square error as a way of check the quality of the solutions provided. Figure 1 shows the interest region while Fig. 1(b) the details of this interest region.

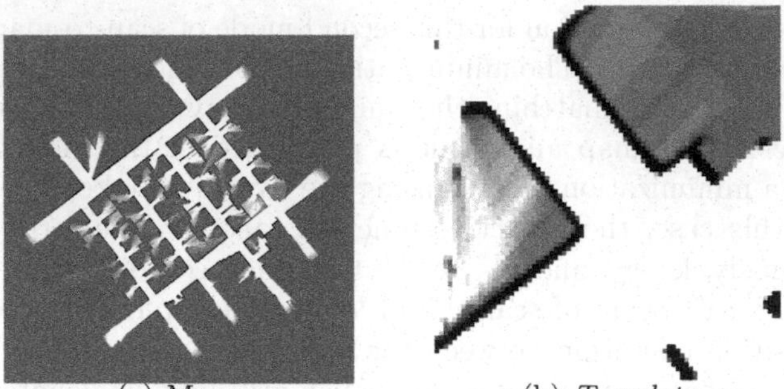

(a) Mapa (b) *Template*

Fig. 1. Map and template used for a preliminary evaluation of the FA meta-heuristic in the SLAM context

During the test execution, we used a limit of 1000 iterations. We performed the computational experiment with 20 fireflies with $\alpha = 0.5$, $\beta = 0.2$ and $\gamma = 1.0$, which are the default values in the code provided by the author. The number of assessments of the objective function throughout the test are shown in the histogram of Fig. 2. It presents the distribution of the number of calls to the objective function until convergence is reached.

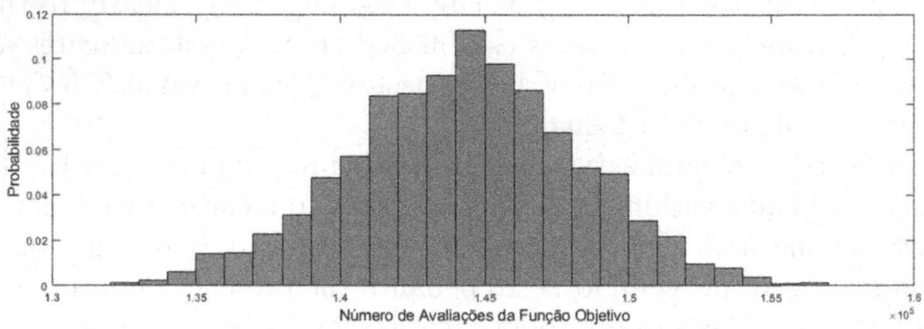

Fig. 2. Overall number of evaluation of the objective function during the test

The average number of calls observed is 1.4408×10^5, with a standard deviation of 4126.5. The overall accuracy is succinctly illustrated in the boxplot shown in Fig. 3, where it can be seen that under the imposed conditions the FA obtained a median of coordinates x, y and θ of 459.0; 547.0 and 0.0, respectively. This indicates that the FA achieved an average absolute error of 0.0% regarding coordinate x, 21.0670% regarding coordinate y and an absolute error of 0.0 radians regarding angle θ.

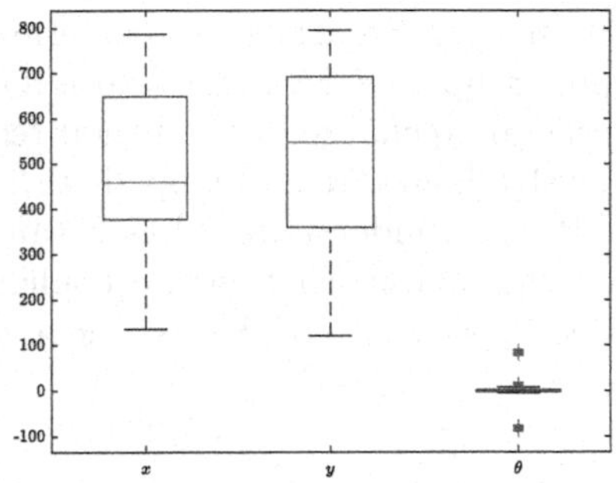

Fig. 3. *Boxplot* of the roto-translational as estimated by FA.

5 Performance Evaluation

We have performed tests using the mobile robot P3DX [16] to evaluate our system based on its accuracy and the overall speed of execution. About the accuracy, we have employed the method described in [14].

5.1 Robot Characteristics

In the performed experiments, we used the P3DX robot from Mobile Robots. The P3DX is a robot with a differential engine that weighs 9 kg, has a body composed of 1.6 mm aluminum plates, is capable of carrying a payload of up to 17 kg and has foam-filled rubber tires. The manufacturer's manual provides diagrams that specify the dimensions of the robot, one of which we reproduce in Fig. 4, where all measurements are expressed in millimeters.

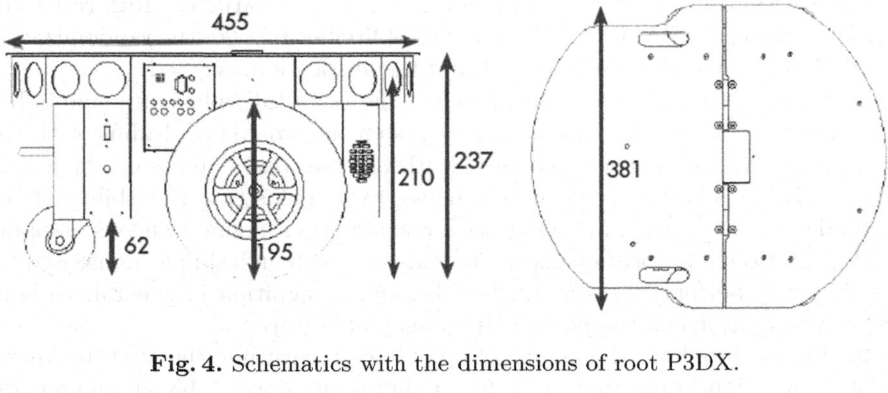

Fig. 4. Schematics with the dimensions of root P3DX.

According to the manufacturer, the robot motor is capable of reaching translational speeds of up to 1.2 m/s and angular speeds of up to 300°/s. The engine, together with all robot components and accessories, are powered by a battery bank. The P3DX has the capacity to carry three batteries with a voltage of 12V that are capable of supplying up to 7.2Ah and whose lifespan is between eight and ten hours. The batteries are rechargeable and their recharge time is specified by the manufacturer as twelve hours. It is equipped with a SICK LMS100 laser range finder. The Laser Range Finder (LRF) has a range of 20m and sweeps a 270° circular sector in such a way that in the configuration used, 541 distance readings are returned in each sweep, that is, one measurement at each half degree.

5.2 Performance Results

The results we obtained with robot P3DX are satisfactory, as will be shown later in this section. Indeed, even though the data collection occurred along trajectories that we had not planned, the system was able to obtain results of good accuracy in a reasonably short processing time. It is noteworthy to mention that the datasets used in the experiments, called COPA and CPSL, are of our authorship and did not have any pre-established references. This said, and with the intention of enabling an evaluation of the results presented here, we carried out an automatic and incremental alignment process combined with evaluation to build a pattern, similarly to that described in [14], which we consider the groundtruth for the obtained results.

Regarding the optimization process, the parameters of the meta-heuristics were adjusted empirically based on 30 repeated alignment tests per scenario regarding each of the used meta-heuristics. Each case was constructed based on a scan of one of the data sets that we selected for random experimentation (a random number generator was used so that the selection could take place without any human bias). We selected 10 scans and applied 3 transformation types to each scan: a pure rotation, a pure translation and a roto-translation. From the resulting 30 scenarios, two variants were generated: one without noise and one with zero mean Gaussian noise and a unit variance. Regarding the hyperparameters of FA, we set the number of fireflies $n = 20$, the randomization $\alpha = 0.75$, the attractiveness $\beta_0 = 0.2$ and the absorption as $\gamma = 1$.

The trajectory and environment where the tests take place are simple but long enough to show that the proposed system is capable of dealing with the complexity imposed by environments with diverse, and extensive, ambiguous characteristics. Through these experiments, we demonstrate the ability of the exposed system to cope, in practice with real scenarios of simultaneous mapping and localization. The location chosen for this test, although simple, demonstrates the ability to perform measurement tasks, and recognition in general, without major interventions on the part of the human operator.

In Fig. 5, we show the maps obtained by measuring the first region in a data collection stage that in a few minutes obtained 1665 measurements. The occasioned translational error is 0.75 ± 0.009 while the rotational error is 0.164 ± 0.019. Figure 6 shows some critical regions in details.

Region A presents a corner with failed alignment and the consequent replication of a section of the two walls that constitute it. This defect is observable

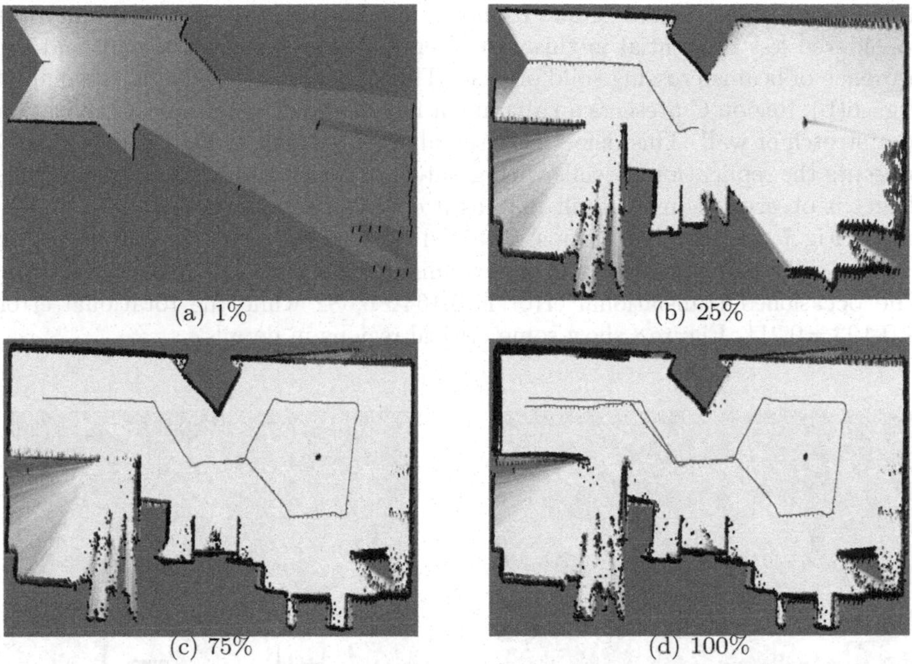

(a) 1% (b) 25% (c) 75% (d) 100%

Fig. 5. The generated maps during the performed tests regarding the dataset COPA.

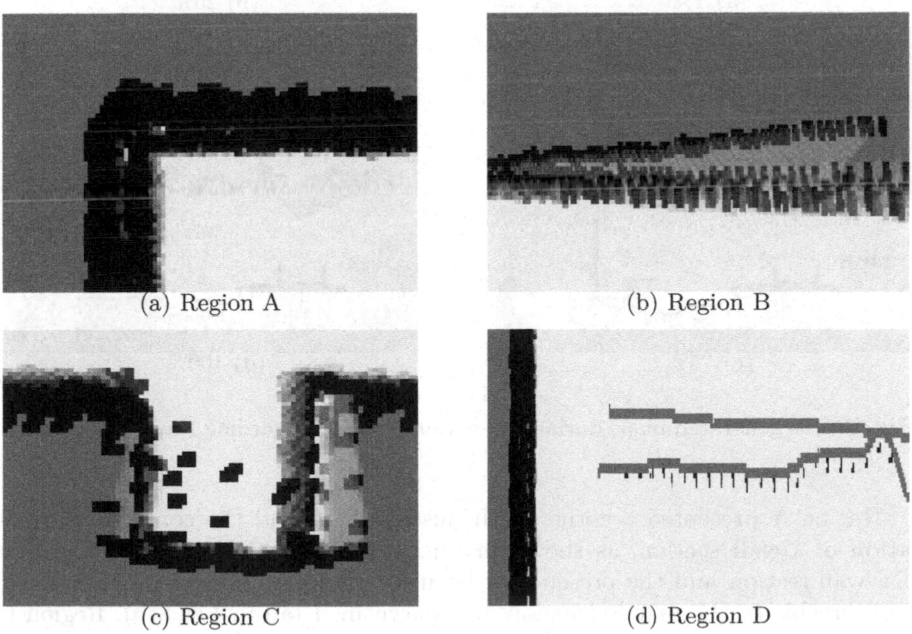

(a) Region A (b) Region B (c) Region C (d) Region D

Fig. 6. Comparison of the four regions of interest in the built map regarding the dataset COPA.

in the built maps. The first one is shown in details in Fig. 6(a). The failure is considered less influential in this case. Region B has a stretch of wall and the presence of beams crossing solid objects. This defect is observable in the map of Figs. 6(b). Region C presents an alignment failure and the consequent replication of a stretch of wall. This defect is observable in the map of Fig. 6(c). Region D presents the replication of walls with great proximity between the replicas. This defect is observable in the built map as it can be seen in Figs. 6(d).

In Fig. 7, we show the maps obtained by measuring the second region in a data collection stage that in a few minutes obtained 1576 measurements. The occasioned translational error is 0.164 ± 0.082 while the rotational error is 0.193 ± 0.211. Figure 8 show some critical regions in details.

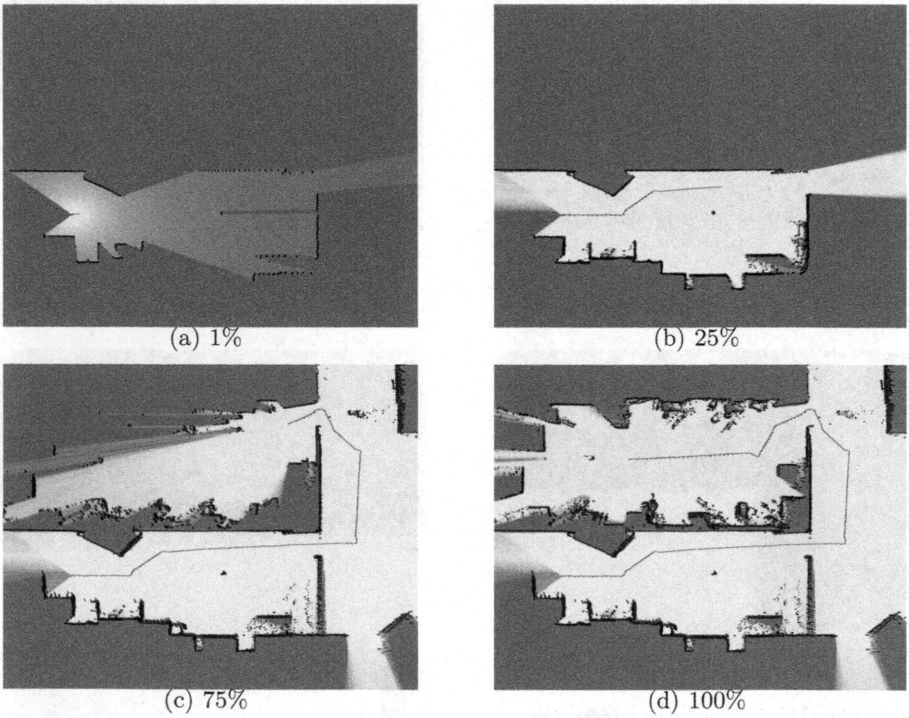

(a) 1%

(b) 25%

(c) 75%

(d) 100%

Fig. 7. The generated maps during the performed tests regarding the dataset CPSL

Region A presented a corner with misalignment and the consequent replication of a wall section, as shown in Fig. 8(a). Region B presents replication of a wall section and the presence of beams crossing solid objects. This defect is observable in the mapped region and shown in detail in Fig. 8(b). Region C presents beams that cross solid objects. This defect is observable in built map, as shown in Figs. 8(c). Region D presents the replication of walls and a clear imprecision in the rotational component of the poses from which the visible scans were

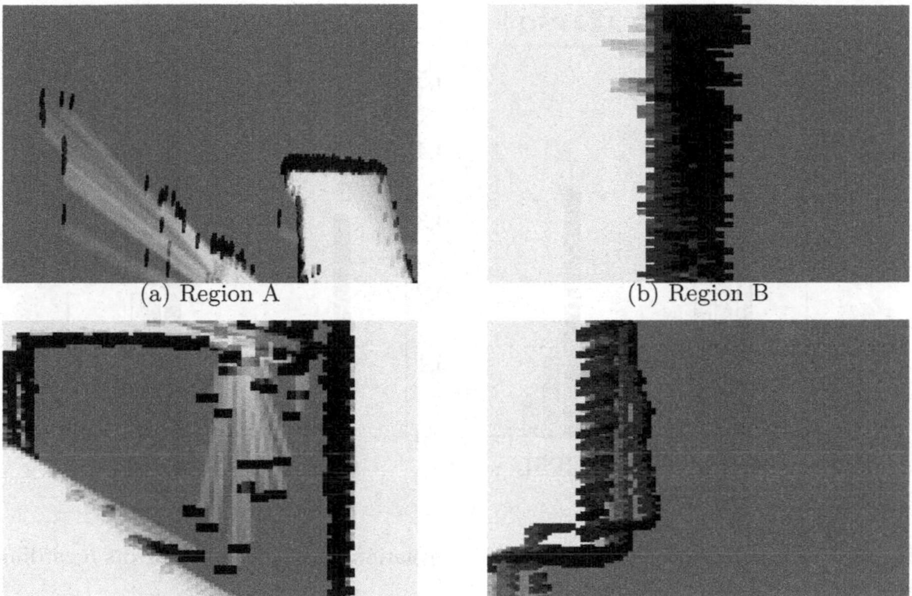

(a) Region A (b) Region B

(c) Region C (d) Region D

Fig. 8. Comparison of the four regions of interest in the built map regarding dataset CPSL.

performed in this region. This defect is observable in the built map, as shown in Figs. 8(d)

The results of the experiments conducted with the P3DX compared with those obtained when using Particle Swam Optimization (PSO) [12] and Artificial Bee Colony (ABC) [11] are shown in Fig. 9 and the corresponding data for the COPA and CPSL sets are presented in Table 1.

Table 1. Values of the absolute translational and rotational errors regarding the dataset COPA and CPSL.

Dataset	Type of error	ABC	FA	PSO
COPA	Translation	0.511 ± 0.164	0.164 ± 0.082	0.0721 ± 0.159
	Rotation	0.937 ± 1.124	0.193 ± 0.221	0.157 ± 0.044
CPSL	Translation	0.5 ± 0.07	0.759 ± 0.2	0.607 ± 0.159
	Rotation	0.956 ± 0.432	1.319 ± 0.279	1.043 ± 0.544

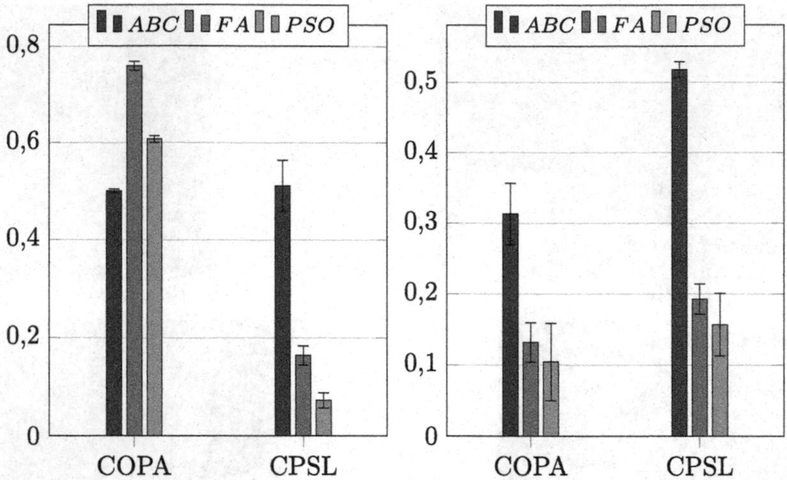

(a) Translation (b) Rotation

Fig. 9. Visual comparison of the absolute translational and rotational errors regarding the dataset COPA and CPSL.

6 Conclusions

In this paper, we investigated the development of a solution to the simultaneous localization and mapping problem using the swarm intelligence technique that is inspired by the firefly behaviors. The proposed scan-matching step proceeds into two main steps, aiming at further reducing the alignment error: The scan-to-scan alignment and the scan-to-map alignment. Both steps are achieved using the same swarm-based optimization meta-heuristics.

As future work, we plan to use an adaptive parameter configuration during the SLAM actual operation. Moreover, we intend to provide a parallel GPU-based implementation in order to reduce the execution time during scan alignments.

Acknowledgments. This study is financed in part by the *Coordenação de Aperfeicoiamento de Pessoal de Nível Superior*, Brasil (CAPES), Finance Code 001.

References

1. Akbari, R., Mohammadi, A., Ziarati, K.: A powerful bee swarm optimization algorithm. In: 2009 IEEE 13th International Multitopic Conference, pp. 1–6 (2009). https://doi.org/10.1109/INMIC.2009.5383155
2. Baeck, T., Fogel, D., Michalewicz, Z.: Evolutionary Computation 1: Basic Algorithms and Operators (Chapter 23). Taylor & Francis, Oxon, OX (2000)
3. Bentley, J.L.: Multidimensional divide-and-conquer. Commun. ACM **23**(4), 214–229 (1980)

4. Bentley, J.L., Friedman, J.H.: Data structures for range searching. ACM Comput. Surv. **11**(4), 397–409 (1979)
5. Besl, P., McKay, N.: A method for registration of 3-d shapes. IEEE Trans. Pattern Anal. Mach. Intell. **14**(2), 239–256 (1992)
6. Dorigo, M., Caro, G.D., Gambardella, L.M.: Ant algorithms for discrete optimization. Artif. Life **5**, 137–172 (1999)
7. Fister, I., Yang, X.S., Brest, J.: A comprehensive review of firefly algorithms. Swarm Evol. Comput. **13**, 34–46 (2013)
8. Friedman, J.H., Bentley, J.L., Finkel, R.A.: An algorithm for finding best matches in logarithmic expected time. ACM Trans. Math. Softw. **3**(3), 209–226 (1977)
9. Grisetti, G., Kummerle, R., Stachniss, C., Burgard, W.: A tutorial on graph-based SLAM. IEEE Intell. Transp. Syst. Mag. **2**(4), 31–43 (12 2010)
10. Kaess, M., Ranganathan, A., Dellaert, F.: iSAM: incremental smoothing and mapping. IEEE Trans. Rob. **24**, 1365–1378 (2008)
11. Karaboga, D., Basturk, B.: A powerful and efficient algorithm for numerical function optimization: artificial bee colony ABC algorithm. J. Global Optim. **39**(3), 459–471 (2007)
12. Kennedy, J., Eberhart, R.: Particle swarm optimization. In: Proceedings IEEE International Conference on Neural Networks, vol. 4, pp. 1942–1948. IEEE, Perth, WA, Australia, November 1995
13. Kümmerle, R., Grisetti, G., Strasdat, H., Konolige, K., Burgard, W.: G2O: a general framework for graph optimization. In: Proceedings - IEEE International Conference on Robotics and Automation, pp. 3607–3613. IEEE, Shanghai, China (2011)
14. Kümmerle, R.e.: On measuring the accuracy of SLAM algorithms. Autonomous Robots **27**(4), 387 (2009)
15. Lu, F., Milios, E.: Globally consistent range scan alignment for environment mapping. Auton. Robot. **4**(4), 333–349 (1997)
16. Mobile Robot: Pioneer 3dx robot (2011). https://www.generationrobots.com/media/Pioneer3DX-P3DX-RevA.pdf
17. Nedjah, N., Macedo Mourelle, L., Albuquerque de Oliveira, P.J.: Simultaneous localization and mapping using swarm intelligence based methods. Expert Syst. Appl. **159**, 113547 (2020). https://doi.org/10.1016/j.eswa.2020.113547
18. Oliveira, P.J.A., Nedjah, N., Mourelle, L.M.: SLAM baseado em scan-matching com otimização por enxame de partículas. In: Proceedings of the XIII Brazilian Congress on Computational Intelligence. Curitiba, Brazil (2017). https://doi.org/10.21528/CBIC2017-96
19. Thrun, S., Burgard, W., Fox, D.: Probabilistic robotics (Chapters 6 and 10), 1 edn. The MIT Press, Cambridge (2005)
20. Zhang, Z.: Iterative point matching for registration of free-form curves. Int. J. Comput. Vision **13**(2), 119–152 (1994)

Automated Housing Price Valuation and Spatial Data

Paulo Batista(✉) and João Lourenço Marques

Universidade de Aveiro – GOVCOPP, Campus universitário de Santiago, Aveiro, Portugal
pauloricardolb@ua.pt

Abstract. The demand for automated, reliable and understandable housing price valuation mechanisms is increasing. Most efforts have been made to improve model accuracy and prediction power through the well-established standard econometric models based on regression techniques. However, the modelling of the spatial attributes of housing through mass appraisal tools has been given less attention. Incorporating spatial modelling approaches through econometrics frameworks opens new opportunities for improving automated valuation tools.

This work presents an exploratory analysis of different approaches to incorporating spatial data into AVM tools, taking advantage of the potential of spatial (big) data, stored on different sources – census data, open street maps and public administration data.

Improvement of the standard housing price models embedded in a Portuguese housing appraisal decision system (held by PrimeYield SA) will be presented. Different strategies to incorporate spatial data from public sources are analysed, taking the Sintra municipality and PrimeYield data on this territory as a case study. The focus is the mitigation of the well-known pitfalls of spatial models, such as spatial heterogeneity and spatial dependence.

The results show the potential added-value of collecting and (pre)processing a different set of territorial variables – socioeconomic, accessibility, and land use – to improve the explanation power, parsimony and understanding of housing price models. Geographic weight regression models can be a balanced compromise to achieve those objectives which will be investigated.

Keywords: AVM · The housing market · Spatial econometric models

1 Introduction

In Portugal, as in most European countries, the free market is the primary gatekeeper for accessing housing. At the time of the 2011 Census, Portugal had 73% of families as owners of their residential dwellings, with 31% of Portuguese families ensuring their residential property through mortgage mechanisms. The characteristics of housing set it apart from more traditional assets concepts in economic theory [1], mainly due to its i) heterogeneity and singularity, ii) immobility and iii) durability.

The original version of this chapter was revised: It has been changed to open access and the copyright holder is now "The Author(s)". The correction to this chapter is available at https://doi.org/10.1007/978-3-030-86973-1_51

O. Gervasi et al. (Eds.): ICCSA 2021, LNCS 12952, pp. 366–381, 2021.
https://doi.org/10.1007/978-3-030-86973-1_26

Some distinct elements of housing prices related to the territorial features of its location are well-known [2–4]. However, in some way, these elements are challenging to fully measure in housing markets. Their role as market drivers prevails, codified for the multiple market agents, including mediators such as house value appraisal agents [5].

New financial regulations, new tax policy requirements and an increasing demand from investors for more accurate price valuations have resulted in the adoption of more sophisticated approaches to appraisals in housing valuation support systems [6, 7]. As data on house transactions is growing and the demand for mass appraisals of housing assets is rising, the adoption of machine learning models has been gaining a central role despite questions remaining related to the role of space in these models.

As housing data and information on spatial features are expanding, efforts to adequately process and combine these different datasets need to be investigated. Appraisals agents should pay attention to the notion of space in housing market analysis as a spatially fixed good: the concept remains of paramount debate in housing economics, urban and regional sciences [8–10] and it is recognized that an inaccurate understanding of its role in housing market mechanisms can lead to incomplete identification of the housing price drivers [11]. Despite this, the segmentation in housing markets, specifically the emergence of spatial submarkets and their spatial interlinkages, is a well-known issue. Empirical observations based on exploratory statistical measures, such as the Moran index (Moran I) indicator of (global) spatial dependence [12] and the local indicators of spatial association [13], confirm the extension of this challenge.

In short, the specification of reliable housing market price models is essential to ensure the (partial) automation of valuation processes usually adopted by appraisal agents. More information needs to be provided, particularly related to the role of spatial features in housing prices. This data should also be incorporated into the usual decision support models. This paper intends to contribute to this emerging debate – see, for example, the chapter "AVM Methodological Challenges: Dealing with the Spatial Issue" in the book *Advances in Automated Valuation Modelling* [6]. Moreover, the general objective here is motivated by the efforts of PrimeYield S.A. (PY) – an official real estate appraisal operator in Portugal – to implement a more accurate (semi-)automated valuation model in its operations. Specifically, the intention of this work is to i) explore different ways to enhance housing price models with spatial data with different types and resolutions – such as spatial data specified as spatial points or as spatial polygons; ii) analyse the added-value of enhancing housing price models with indicators which measure territorial features; and iii) examine a different set of standard specification techniques of the standard housing price models to embed spatial data.

The paper is organized as follows. The following Sect. 2 presents the theoretical background on the standard econometric model framework to analyse housing price and its drivers – the hedonic approach – and the significant light which this framework sheds on dealing with spatial pitfalls – particularly, the understanding of spatial dependence and spatial heterogeneity. Proposed solutions in the literature will be highlighted. The Sect. 3 provides the case study data and the methods suggested in this exploratory work to incorporate data about spatial features, taking advantage of new open data sources. The Sect. 4 presents the significant findings and the validation of the methods proposed, with a brief discussion on the relevance of incorporating the new data for better modelling parsimony. The paper finishes with the major highlights of these work contributions to the debate and a brief comment on the next necessary steps.

2 Theoretical Background

2.1 Housing Valuation, Housing Hedonic Price Models and Spatial Modelling Challenges

The hedonic housing pricing model (HHPM) [14] is a well-known modelling framework and is widely used in decision support systems for housing appraisal processes. Its technical simplicity – as models can be deployed through the standard OLS regression approach – and its anchorage in rational economic theory leads to HHPM being chosen to ensure the reliable and understandable role of the housing price drivers.

Housing is defined as a heterogeneous good for which a complex set of attributes should be selected to describe it, namely, intrinsic (physical) and spatial (neighbourhood) characteristics. The estimations of HHPM can be obtained through the traditional regression model [15], which assumes a reduced-form econometric model, such that:

$$\boldsymbol{P} = \alpha + \beta H + \varepsilon \tag{1}$$

where P is the vector of prices (or prices by square meter) for each one of the n dwellings; and β is a vector of hedonic (or shadow) prices to be estimated, describing the value of each one the k dwelling attributes H. This is a reduced form of the model where the reliability of estimations is linked to the theoretical assumption of a competitive market in equilibrium. Finally, ε is the stochastic model error.

Grounded on the categorization proposed by Stull [16] and the open debate on what features to include to describe spatial (territorial) features (see Galster [3]), the matrix H that quantifies the attributes of a dwelling can be decomposed into a set of four subcategories: F, E, L and S, plus time (T) – in order to fix time effects (such as inflation or other macro-economic time-dependent phenomena); F denotes structural characteristics of the dwelling; E, L, S[1] are environmental and neighbourhood characteristics, the location within the territorial system (or the housing market delimitation considered) and other spatial characteristics (access to utilities and public services, such as transport nodes, working place poles, schools, etc.).

2.2 Challenges Related to the Spatial Features of Residential Dwellings

Well-known social and economic phenomena supported the rise of spatial econometrics [17, 18], which combined the knowledge produced in economics, geography and other spatial sciences. These joint efforts have resulted in new light being shed on the nature of spatial phenomena, the challenges of modelling them and the tools concerned with

[1] In this work L will be used as a reference to all E, L and S types of spatial features.

fixing the models' spatial pitfalls. Two significant spatial challenges to producing reliable models are identified: the rise of heterogeneity and spatial dependence.

Spatial Dependence

Spatial dependence is a well-known phenomenon in a wide range of empirical studies in different fields. It can be observed on different spatial scales of analysis or other spatial (geographic) features – polygons or points as references to territorial attributes embedded in the modelling process.

The complexity behind the concept of territoriality is related to locality, urbanity, socioeconomic characteristics and other features. This has resulted in substantial uncertainties over model specifications. Spatial econometrics has developed several spatial interaction models where theoretical assumptions mainly guide the choices through economic mechanisms [19, 20]; however these models are focused on estimate average (global) spatial interaction effects rather than obtain point estimates (the spatial effects in each dwelling unit).

The spatial dependence usually requires both the spatial unit and its W to be known a priori [20]. Following a business-as-usual approach, W is usually defined as the neighbourhoods' relations through a Euclidian geometrical reference frame, using a specific Euclidian distance threshold or the topological relations between geographical units (polygons). Landry & Chakraborty's work [21] adopted a function of (Euclidian) distance between spatial units, allowing for a more geographically coherent definition of neighbourhoods when the geographic units (polygons) are not regular (which is usual, for example, in administrative unit settings). An interesting lesson from the attempts to define W is the tendency to decrease spatial autocorrelation with increasing distance (see Getis and Aldstadt [22]). This can be understood as an expression of Tobler's law, according to which the closest things are more related than distant things [23].

The above observation can be used to introduce another modelling alternative: geographically weighted regression (GWR) [24, 25]. GWR focuses on obtaining spatially located parameter estimates through a relaxation of the theoretical assumptions usually imposed through W. The primary mechanism of GWR relies on the assumption that contextual, spatial factors may modify the strength and direction of the relationship between a dependent variable and its predictors. Estimations for each geographic data point are then obtained locally using a kernel function centred on that point and adapted so that neighbouring data points (in Euclidian space) are considered as weights based on a distance decay function. In short, the regression framework is adapted to allow spatial variation of the regression coefficients across space; different (kernel) functions can be used. The GWR regression model can be written as:

$$Y = \alpha(u, v) + \sum_{s=1}^{S} X_s \beta_s(u, v) + \varepsilon \quad (2)$$

where Y is the target variable (in this work P – the housing price) at location (u, v), X is the set of explanatory variables (the H characteristics of each dwelling), and $\beta_s(u, v)$ are the parameters for the regression coefficient β, obtained through a weighting scheme w_{ij} applied to take into account (u, v). The weighting scheme is based on the kernel function, such as a Gaussian kernel (as adopted later in this work); specifically, this function incorporates a distance decay mechanism which allocates more weight to dwellings closer to a regression point than dwellings farther away, as follows:

$$w_{ij} = \exp\left(-\left({}^{d_{ij}}/_{b}\right)^2\right) \quad (3)$$

Here, d_{ij} is the (Euclidean) distance[2] between dwelling i and the neighbourhood dwelling j, and b is the bandwidth, the distance where searching for dwellings is considered used in the weight estimation mechanism.

One critical assumption of GWR is that all dwelling transactions occur simultaneously, or, at the very least, that the time of transaction is not a crucial factor to consider. In standard HHPM, time non-stationarity can be addressed simply by including time fixed effects. Recently developments in the GWR framework lead to the adaptation of the kernel function to take into account local effects in both space and time dimensions. Fotheringham et al. [26] propose the GTWR model and demonstrate the increasing accuracy of that approach compared to standard models in time non-stationarity settings.

Spatial Heterogeneity

In another direction, the emergence of spatial dependence can be pinpointed to the heterogeneous nature of spatial phenomena. The distinction between both phenomena is not total. For example, the concept of substitutability (in economics) supports this close connection between both spatial phenomena: the work of Bourassa et al. [27] points that substitutability in housing markets is mainly related to location and neighbourhood attributes. Despite the induced spatial delimitation of such a concept, empirical approaches remain challenging [28].

As described for spatial dependence, a standard approach usually assumes the territorial units' boundaries a priori, and that they are reasonably homogenous. A typical straight path is the use of administrative units or other known spatial partitions. Alternatives may be to previously produce spatial clusters following the knowledge developed in geography, urban studies or regional science; moreover, places can be identified by local communities or can be defined as the zones adopted by housing market agents. In their PhD theses [8, 9], the authors of this work argued that these different approaches call for a conception of space beyond the classic, geometric and dimensional notions of space usually embedded in spatial sciences, HHPM in particular.

The diversity of solutions and the absence of an unequivocal consensus have led to adopting different solutions, usually constrained by data availability. Here two approaches will be followed: a) the use of pre-existing territorial areas (political-administrative boundaries and identifiable "neighbourhoods"); b) the use of a set of measured spatial variables (such as, for example, indicators retrieved from census data or accessibility indexes) as proxies to fix the effects of neighbourhood characteristics.

[2] Although other distance measures can be used.

3 Data and Methods

3.1 Processing and Combining Data from Different Sources

As argued before, HHHP analysis should incorporate spatial information on order to be reliable. Housing market databases usually include some spatial data: the zone/neighbourhood/administrative unit assigned (a spatial polygon that contains the dwelling) or the specific housing address (which will define a particular spatial point through geocoding tools[3]). Each type of spatial feature encodes different information details, which should be decoded. Also, the data type conditions the information precision that it will be possible to retrieve.

This work uses three different data sources: i) data accumulated by PY, which describes physical housing attributes, housing price and its geographic location (geographic coordinates); the data is referenced to PY's appraisal service; ii) territorial data will be collected from three different open data sources, namely, the Portuguese statistical authority, the government spatial planning department (for land use data) and, the SapoMapas geoservices (http://api.mapas.sapo.pt/) to retrieve a collection of points of interest (POIs) and distance matrix between the different spatial points.

Decoding spatial information usually requires processing data produced by different sources. This data typically presents significant modelling challenges, namely: geographically, different polygons may be topologically inconsistent; thematically, other datasets may have diverse attributes or coding typification; and methodologically, as a different type of geometries are used to represent spatial data (points, lines, polygons), it can result in imprecisions or inconsistencies.

In the following two sections, the details of the data available on these different sources and the most important pre-processing steps will be presented.

Dwelling Data

For this study, PY provided a dataset with 625 housing transaction records (based on data for the Sintra municipality) and comprising a period of 7 years (between 2008 and 2015). The available target variable (price) is derived from the PY appraisal auditions – which adopted certified appraisal processes such as the RICS [29] and TEGOVA [30] guidelines. Only a small number of variables are available from the original dataset after data cleaning steps (such as dropping variables with missing values). The dataset provides each dwelling's geographical location (address or x, y coordinates provided on WGS84 coordinates system), which was matched with the external geographic datasets (administrative units, locality, census tracts and the regular geographic grid used to produce the accessibility index). Summary statistics are provided in Table 2.

Territorial Data

Combining the dwellings' precise location with spatial data on the additional data sources will provide an enrichment of the dataset with territorial information.

This information can be divided into three types: a) the geographic boundaries of the smaller administrative units (the parishes), b) the geographic boundaries of familiar

[3] Sometimes that spatial point is given through precise geographic latitude and longitude coordinates – this is the case in the database used here.

distinct urban places (localities) and c) a set of indicators that can be derived from i) processing census data and ii) the distribution of POIs across the territory and the accessibility to them via the road network.

The set of indicators described in (c) are obtained from a pre-processing step where retrieved open data is subject to a variable reduction modelling approach (principal component factor analysis – PCA-FA) to i) obtain summary (reduced) data (described by the scores of FA) and ii) ensure a better match with statistical assumptions of the HHPM and the OLS in particular (such as avoiding collinearity). The PCA-FA was applied separately to i) the socioeconomic, housing stock characteristics[4] and the land-use coverage[5] (retrieved from the INE and DGOTDU data sources, for each census tract polygons[6]) and ii) the accessibility index obtained by the data processing of the POIs' geographic location and distance matrix through the road network obtained for the regular square grid where each square has sides of 600 m; the accessibility index base at each census tract is an average of the accessibility index on the original grid. Moreover, the accessibility index is calculated for each POI category described in Table 1.

The summary statistics for spatial data and PY data is described in Table 2; the column notes include a short description of the meaning of positive values associated with the component scores resulting from the PCA-FA pre-processing.

Table 1. Collected geographic data – themes

Census tract data		POIs data		
Thematic categories	N. of classes	Thematic categories	N. of classes	N. of POIs
Type of building	2	Workplace poles (1)	1	21
Number of floors in building	2	Transportation (2)	4	38
Dwelling size	2	Education (3)	6	110
Building age	9	Health (5)	4	30
Dwelling type of occupation	2	Food stores and basic services (6)	4	223
Population age	4	Leisure (7)	3	449
Population education	5			
Population work place location (outside the municipality)	1			
Population work sector (tertiary only)	1			
Land use (urban category only)	3			

[4] This data is referenced to the public Census 2011 dataset, available at https://bit.ly/3ssuqNj.

[5] This data is referenced to the 2010 land use coverage – COS2010, available at https://bit.ly/3tSS99M.

[6] The statistical subsection is a georeferenced polygon which is closely similar to the urbanistic concept of a city block – more information on: https://smi.ine.pt/Conceito/Detalhes/1926.

Table 2. Data summary statistics

	Avg	Std. Dev	Min	Max	Notes
Price (€)	120,215	123,534	14,000	988,930	
Area (m2)	110.82	76.21	22.00	915.77	
Age (years)	26.42	11.00	4.00	78.00	
Backyard/land area (ratio)	0.26	1.02	0.00	14.24	
Type (categorical) (n. of records by class)	Flats (1) = 557, Single house (0) = 68				
Scores PCA-FA – A1	−0.85	0.87	−2.61	1.70	Low density land occupation
Scores PCA-FA – A2	0.42	0.71	−1.64	2.32	Prevalence of low qualified pop
Scores PCA-FA – A3	−0.01	0.94	−4.04	1.93	Prevalence of employed pop. with basic classifications and working in tertiary sector
Scores PCA-FA – A4	−0.17	0.84	−2.45	4.49	High urban density associated with old buildings
Scores PCA-FA – A5	−0.31	1.25	−2.43	2.74	Prevalence of old, non-active pop. and buildings built on the 60s and 70s
Scores PCA-FA – A6	−0.06	1.01	−3.39	4.93	Prevalence of younger pop. and buildings built in the 00s
Scores PCA-FA (accessibility) – B1	0.76	0.96	−1.69	3.98	Close to train stations, basic schools, ATM & postal services and leisure facilities
Scores PCA-FA (accessibility) – B2	0.30	1.03	−1.52	3.37	Close to main highway nodes and to the townhall (Sintra city centre)
Scores PCA-FA (accessibility) – B3	0.19	0.93	−2.51	2.01	Close to principal itineraries nodes
Parishes (categorical) (statistics about the n. of records)	48.08	40.96	4.00	172.00	13 parishes of 20 Sintra municipality parishes
Locality (categorical) (statistics about the n. of records)	20.16	18.37	2.00	54.00	31 localities of 163 Sintra municipality localities

3.2 Case Study and Spatial Data

Sintra is one of the most densely populated Portuguese municipalities. It is part of the Lisbon Metropolitan Area, and large parts of the territory are dominated by suburban settlements – mainly across the Lisbon–Sintra train line. As the spatial variables described in Table 2 can anticipate, this is a territory characterized by compelling territorial patterns. Here it is possible to find small neighbourhoods where discrepant spatial characteristics can be seen at different territorial dimensions – social, economic, land use, historical landmarks and geomorphological, among others. This makes this case study interesting for this work. It clearly emphasizes the modelling challenges as spatial data can be essential elements to understand housing price drivers.

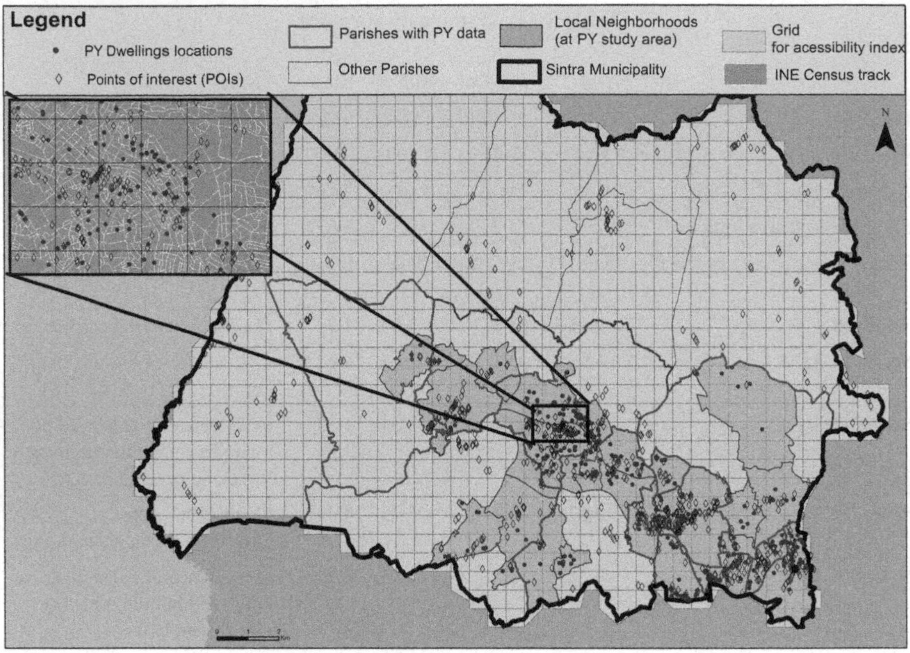

Fig. 1. PY Dataset and spatial data of Sintra municipality. The maps show the multiple spatial georeferentiation and resolution available. (Color figure online)

However, it is essential to highlight that PY data is not fully representative of all the Sintra municipality territory. PY data is concentrated in the high-density locations, namely the parishes crossed by the train line and most relevant road networks (highways), plus the city centre parish (where the train line ends). Rural areas and historical places are absent from the PY data. However, as can be anticipated from Table 2, the physical attributes of the dwellings present a high dispersion, showing that dwellings on the data revealed the great diversity of the Sintra municipality. The diversity reinforces the idea of a territory where high levels of heterogeneity can be observed. In fact, in a small area, it is possible to find housing complexes with characteristics close to slums side by side with housing complexes of very high quality, occupied by some of the wealthiest families living in Portugal. Figure 1 shows Sintra municipality and some spatial data features, which were retrieved to be combined with the PY dataset.

Observing the PY data (red dots), it can be identified that the spatial data distribution is not uniform. In fact, it is concentrated in well-known, highly populated places with a suburban nature.

3.3 Estimation Framework

Basic Specification of HHPM

Despite the diversity of available model specifications, one important point is to correctly and completely identify the relevant explanatory variables. As argued before, this is a particular challenge and remains naturally uncertain, given the enormous spatial challenges related to HHPM. The spatial data enhancement presented before will be adopted here as an answer to achieve this model assumption.

Another important point in model specification is the nature of the functional relation between dependent (Y, the price or, in this study, the price per square metre) and independent variables (X). Further studies have shown that the housing market implies a non-linear pricing structure [31]. As standard regression models assume linearity, then a variable transformation will be performed. The Box-Cox transformation toolbox is the usual approach; in housing market models a strictly log-log or semi-log specification is commonly used – an option which will be followed here.

Specification of Dimension F and T

The available intrinsic attributes of the PY dataset are reduced, but they correspond to the usual main physical dwelling characteristics. It will be assumed that the potential effects of missing attributes will be negligible for the objectives of this work. Thus, the specifications follow including variable transformations such:

$$H = \beta_1 lnArea_{Dwel.} + \beta_2 lnAge_{Dwel.} + \beta_3 D_{DwellingType} + \beta_4 Ratio_{DwArea/LandArea} \quad (4)$$

where $lnArea_{Dwel.}$ is the dwelling area (m^2) transformed into a natural logarithm, $Age_{Dwel.}$, is the dwelling age transformed into a natural logarithm, $D_{DwellingType}$ is a dummy variable identifying a single-house (1) or a flat (0) and $Ratio_{DwArea/LandArea}$ is the ratio between dwelling area and the open or backyard area. β_i are the hedonic prices of each variable to be estimated.

Time stationarity of PY data will be achieved through a standard time fixed effect specification, as follows:

$$H = \sum_{i=2007}^{2014} \beta_i D_{Ti}$$

where D_i is the dummy variable identifying the year when the dwelling price was stored in the database. It comprises dummies for the years between 2008 and 2014. The 2015 year dummy is dropped to avoid the dummy trap [32].

Specification of Dimension S

The focus of this work is to present an exploratory analysis of the spatial modelling challenges related to the two usual spatial model pitfalls: a) the statistical difficulties of dealing with the heterogeneity and correlation of spatial data, and b) the different detail (precision) related with the type of spatial representation (points or polygons), the kind of georeferenced detail (such as census tracks, administrative boundaries or regular spatial grids) and the compatibility between different spatial data sources (for example, how to merge diverse spatial representation or spatial data resolutions).

Thus, in addition to an initial (benchmark) model (without spatial data – M0), five models were investigated (see Table 3 to a general overview). In detail, each model comprises:

- **M1:** Spatial features are considered as captured by the assignment of each dwelling to its corresponding parish. In this model, spatial effects are captured through the classical approach of fixed effects: dummy variables for each parish (minus one, to avoid the dummy trap) will be accomplished to the model.

- **M2:** This model is similar to M1 but the territorial unit considered is the locality[7] (neighbourhood) information provided by INE. With this model, it is possible to compare different spatial resolutions (parishes and neighbourhoods) for similar spatial data types (polygons).
- **M3:** The third model specification intends to analyse the effect of use quantitative variables measuring the spatial features of the dwelling's surroundings rather than an explicit assignment of a dwelling to a territorial unit (which is exogenously defined).
- **M4:** This model will introduce the geographic weight regression (GWR) framework – namely in its recently time-space variant (GTWR) as referenced before – to include time non-stationarity presented in PY data. In this (and next model, M5), the time effects dummy are dropped. The GWR approach is selected because its focus is on producing reliable point estimates, which relax the need for a priori and strong assumptions on the territorial partitions to considered. Moreover, GWR has gained relevance in appraisal decision support systems.
- **M5:** Finally, the intention of the fifth model is to explore if GTWR will benefit from spatial data enhancement, namely, including explanatory variables whose parameters estimations will be obtained by a similar spatial (geographic) weighted scheme .

Table 3. General overview of the spatial modelling specification strategies adopted

Models	Spatial components specifications
M2; M3;	$H = \sum_{i=1}^{S} \beta_i D_{Si}$ Where D_{Si} is a dummy for each parish (M2) or each locality (M3)
M4; M5;	$\sum_{s=1}^{S} X_s \beta_s(u, v)$ Where X_s are each intrinsic attribute (M4) or each intrinsic attribute plus each one of the PCA-FA territorial indicators (M5)

Note that in GWR the Gaussian kernels with fixed bandwidths are adopted, chosen following a cross-validation (CV) process for each of the models M4 and M5, respectively. All data processing and modelling steps are performed in R language; for GTWR modelling, the GWmodel R library was selected [33].

4 Results

4.1 Model Validation and Comparison

Model comparison and basic model validation is performed through two types of model performance assessment approach: a) the standard classical statistical indicators – adjusted R2 and AIC – and b) the standard indicators advocated by guidelines on property valuation performance [34] – the coefficient of dispersion (COD) and price-related differential (PRD) (see Table 4).

[7] See INE for further description https://smi.ine.pt/Conceito/Detalhes/2990.

Table 4. Selected model evaluation indicators

Statistical measures	Real estate appraisal measures
$R^2 = 1 - \frac{\sum_{i=1}^{n}(y_i - \hat{y}_i)^2}{\sum_{i=1}^{n}(y_i - \bar{y}_i)^2}$ $AdjR^2 = 1 - \left(\frac{n-1}{n-k}\right)\left(1 - R^2\right)$	$COD = \frac{100}{n}\frac{\sum_{i=1}^{n}\left\lvert\frac{\hat{y}_i}{y_i} - Median\left(\frac{\hat{y}_i}{y_i}\right)\right\rvert}{Median\left(\frac{\hat{y}_i}{y_i}\right)}$
$AIC = -2\log(L) + 2K$	$PRD = \frac{Mean\left(\frac{\hat{y}_i}{y_i}\right)}{\sum_i^n \hat{y}_i / \sum_i^n y_i}$

The statistical approach follows the well-established model fit evaluation measures: the adjusted coefficient of determinations. R^2 provides a straightforward interpretation: the amount of variation accounted for in the fitted model. A pitfall of this measure is that R^2 always increases with the model size; the adjusted R^2 tries to limit this effect by adding a penalization to the coefficient estimation based on the number of variables. The Akaike information criteria (AIC) are usually assumed to be more robust to the effect of increasing model size, although the value calculated is less meaningful for non-statistical experts. Both measures are well-known in model evaluation and model comparison settings.

As one focus of this work is on the appraiser's needs for reliable models to help the valuation process, it is valuable to introduce two evaluation indicators advocated by real estate appraisal guidelines, which ensures model estimates will follow the uniformity and equity guidelines of the valuation process. COD is a dispersion coefficient focused on the uniformity of the set of evaluations performed, and PRD is concentrated in vertical equity across the set of valuations. In IAAO guidelines, the acceptability threshold for single-family homes is set to COD value between 5 and 15. PRD threshold is set between 0.98 and 1.03, with values above (below) this range providing evidence of regressivity (progressivity).

4.2 Modelling Results and Discussion

Table 5 shows the results obtained, where M4 and M5 can be identified as producing the best performance in all of the validation and comparison indicators. This performance is easily explained by the GWR/GTWR model's specificities reported in the theoretical review section: the GWR/GTWR model allows a local adjustment of the model which results in greater flexibility concerning the spatial specification. The presence of non-uniform phenomena of heterogeneity and spatial dependence in space naturally hinders the capacity for specifications that limit the scope of these effects a priori, to adjust correctly to local peculiarities. The difference in performance between models M4 and M5 and model M3 also highlights the role of this greater flexibility. By restricting the estimates to the observation (spatial) points, the M3 model is more vulnerable to the spatial pitfalls effects, particularly spatial correlation; this can explain the lower comparative performance.

Table 5. Results

	M0 (F)	M1 (F + parish)	M2 (F + places)	M3 (F + L)	M4 (F GTWR)	M5 (F + L GTWR)
N. of var	4 + 7	4 + 7 + 12	4 + 7 + 30	4 + 7 + 6 + 3	4	4 + 6 + 3
Adj. R2	0.840	0.867	0.888	0.869	0.881	0.878
AIC	−73.879	−179.493	−266.022	−190.548	−322.783	−318.029
COD	13.485	12.454	11.252	12.803	12.281	12.188
PRD	1.058	1.049	1.038	1.049	1.038	1.036

As concerns GWR/GTWR, it is essential to highlight some possible general drawbacks. First, it needs to be borne in mind that as GWR/GTWR models focus on local estimations, they are more susceptible to data quality and spatial data representativeness; these issues can induce various model pitfalls – such as model overfitting or the small area estimation traps [35].

Another critical point in GWR/GTWR is the need to include high-resolution spatial data. One of the interesting features of the model is that it takes advantage of the geographic coordinates to implement a weighting scheme in the process of parameter estimation. This is usual with data that is not fully compatible with the best resolution (as is the case with M5, where additional spatial variables are defined not for each dwelling's exact point but the centroid of the tract census).

Although the M5 model presents a lower level of performance than the M4 model on the statistical indicators, note that it offers slightly superior performance in terms of the remaining two appraisal performance indicators. Given the minor differences between the performance of M4 and M5, a simple possible explanation is that the statistical measures selected tend to penalize models with more variables. Moreover, the M4 model may present a tendency towards overfitting the data sample.

Finally, one of the weaknesses of the GWR is its lower capacity to provide the evaluating agent with an immediate perception of the contribution of tangible spatial characteristics to the price estimation (although, in the M5 model, when evaluating the contribution of spatial variables, this weakness is mitigated).

Models M1 and M2 should not be forgotten in this discussion. They reveal the determining role that coherent territorial partitions can play as explanatory drivers of dwelling prices. Moreover, spatial data resolution is sometimes limited (for example, see the real estate listing portals in Portugal, such as Casa Sapo or Imovirtual), which means these model specifications remain an adequate model approach' Moreover, this type of specification also has the advantage of adapting more effectively to the tacit knowledge of the expert in the local housing market, for which these spatial partitions encode a remarkable amount of information (about their characteristics).

The results obtained underline the need to develop a more sophisticated validation scheme. It should be noted that schemes such as bootstrap or cross-validation have not yet been implemented but are under development: they have specific challenges, such as the need to ensure sampling consistency (for example, in models of type M1 and M2, it should be necessary to ensure that sampling will provide the spatial stratification associated the records in each spatial unit). Moreover, the information revealed by COD and PRD indicators points to values outside acceptable thresholds. This needs further investigation.

5 Conclusions

For an applied case study, this work shows the contributions of spatial data enhancement to the efforts to deploy reliable housing price models to be embedded on housing appraisal support systems – such as AVMs. The results show that spatial data can be incorporated through different specifications which support complementary notions on the role of space as a driver of housing prices. Further, the other model specifications can offer practitioners the flexibility to adapt their models to the spatial extent, spatial data types and spatial compatibility of the different datasets. Data analysts will be aware of the strengths and weaknesses of each model specification.

From a general point of view, this work highlights the complexity of space in the housing market model. It identifies its known (spatial) pitfalls on empirical applications – heterogeneity and spatial dependence. Moreover, it reveals the challenges that emerge both in econometric terms (including the model's theoretical assumptions) and the necessary interpretation of model results – as required by the appraisal activities' codes.

Although considerable uncertainty prevails about the interchange between spatial heterogeneity and spatial dependence, this work reinforces flexible but remaining simple modelling approaches regarding these theoretical and technical debates and offers a reasonable and reliable solution to the real estate appraisal agent. Thus, comprehensible and parsimonious appraisal support models are a crucial feature advocated by international guidelines. Despite the increasing use of machine learning model approaches, this work points to the need to avoid hidden spatial challenges by increasing black-box adoptions, despite the better performance in predicting house prices.

The housing market has undergone profound transformations in societies; demographic dynamics, social modifications of the population, lifestyle changes and families' preferences have led to new housing demands and requirements. Thus, it is expected that improving housing appraisal support systems will help its role in supporting market agents to produce more informed investment decisions. Moreover, a transparent appraise support model on its spatial features will help market agents and policymakers (or spatial planners) better understand the potential interplays between changes in the territorial systems and housing market behaviour.

Funding Information:. This work has been financially supported by the project "Drivers of urban transformation – DRIVIT-UP (POCI-01–0145-FEDER-031905) funded by FCT - Fundação para a Ciência e a Tecnologia and co-funded by FEDER through COMPETE2020 - Programa Operacional Competitividade e Internacionalização (POCI).

References

1. Bourne, L.S.: The Geography of Housing. Edward Arnold, London (1981)
2. Can, A.: The measurement of neighborhood dynamics in urban house prices. Econ. Geogr. **66**(3), 254–272 (1990). https://doi.org/10.2307/143400
3. Galster, G.: On the nature of neighbourhood. Urban Stud. **38**(12), 2111–2124 (2001). https://doi.org/10.1080/00420980120087072
4. Palm, R.: Spatial segmentation of the urban housing market. J. Econ. Geogr. **54**, 210–221 (1978)
5. Pagourtzi, E., Assimakopoulos, V., Hatzichristos, T., French, N.: Real estate appraisal: a review of valuation methods. J. Property Investment Financ. **21**(4), 383–401 (2003). https://doi.org/10.1108/14635780310483656
6. d'Amato, M., Kauko, T.: Appraisal methods and the non-agency mortgage crisis. In: d'Amato, M., Kauko, T. (eds.) Advances in Automated Valuation Modeling, pp. 23–32. Springer, Cham (2017). https://doi.org/10.1007/978-3-319-49746-4_2
7. Wang, D., Li, V.J.: Mass appraisal models of real estate in the 21st century: a systematic literature review. Sustainability **11**(24), 7006 (2019). https://doi.org/10.3390/su11247006
8. Marques, J.: The Notion of Space in Urban Housing Markets. Universidade de Aveiro (2012)
9. Batista, P.: The interaction structure of e-territorial systems: territory, housing market and spatial econometrics/A estrutura de interação de um sistema e-territorial. Território, mercado de habitação e econometria espacial. Universidade de Aveiro (2019)
10. Marques, J.L., Batista, P., Castro, E.A.: Espaço e território no contexto do desenvolvimento regional. In: Marques, J.L., Carballo-Cruz, F. (eds.) 30 anos de ciência regional em perspetiva, Almedina, Coimbra, Portugal, pp. 11–46 (2021)
11. Marques, J.L., Batista, P., Castro, E.A., Bhattacharjee, A.: Housing consumption. In: Chkoniya, V., Madsen, A.O., Bukhrashvili, P. (eds.) Anthropological Approaches to Understanding Consumption Patterns and Consumer Behavior, pp. 265–285. IGI Global (2020)
12. Moran, P.A.P.: A test for the serial independence of residuals. Biometrika **37**(1/2), 178–181 (1950). https://doi.org/10.2307/2332162
13. Anselin, L.: Local indicators of spatial association-LISA. Geogr. Anal. **27**(2), 93–115 (2010). https://doi.org/10.1111/j.1538-4632.1995.tb00338.x
14. Rosen, S.: Hedonic prices and implicit markets: product differentiation in pure competition. J. Polit. Econ. **82**(1), 35–55 (1974)
15. Malpezzi, S.: Hedonic pricing models: a selective and applied review. In: Gibb, K., O'Sullivan, A. (eds.) Housing Economics and Public Policy: Essays in Honour of Duncan Maclennan, pp. 67–89. Blackwell Science, Oxford (UK) (2003)
16. Stull, W.J.: Community environment, zoning, and the market value of single-family homes. J. Law Econ. **18**(2), 535–557 (1975)
17. Paelinck, J.H.P.: Spatial econometrics: a personal overview. Stud. Ekon. **152**, 106–118 (2013)
18. Pace, R.K., LeSage, J.: Spatial econometrics and real estate. J. Real Estate Financ. Econ. **29**(2), 147–148 (2004)
19. Corrado, L., Fingleton, B.: Where is the economics in spatial econometrics. J. Reg. Sci. **52**(2), 210–239 (2012)
20. Elhorst, J.P.: Spatial Econometrics: From Cross-Sectional Data to Spatial Panels. Springer, Heidelberg (2014). https://doi.org/10.1007/978-3-642-40340-8
21. Landry, S.M., Chakraborty, J.: Street trees and equity: evaluating the spatial distribution of an urban amenity. Environ. Plan. A Econ. Sp. **41**(11), 2651–2670 (2009). https://doi.org/10.1068/a41236
22. Getis, A., Aldstadt, J.: Constructing the spatial weights matrix using a local statistic. Geogr. Anal. **36**(2), 90–104 (2004). https://doi.org/10.1111/j.1538-4632.2004.tb01127.x

23. Anselin, L., Li, X.: Tobler's law in a multivariate world. Geogr. Anal. **52**(4), 494–510 (2020). https://doi.org/10.1111/gean.12237
24. Brunsdon, C., Fotheringham, A.S., Charlton, M.E.: Geographically weighted regression: a method for exploring spatial nonstationarity. Geogr. Anal. **28**(4), 281–298 (2010). https://doi.org/10.1111/j.1538-4632.1996.tb00936.x
25. Cleveland, W.S., Devlin, S.J.: Locally weighted regression: an approach to regression analysis by local fitting. J. Am. Stat. Assoc. **83**(403), 596–610 (1988). https://doi.org/10.1080/01621459.1988.10478639
26. Fotheringham, A.S., Crespo, R., Yao, J.: Geographical and temporal weighted regression (GTWR). Geogr. Anal. **47**(4), 431–452 (2015). https://doi.org/10.1111/gean.12071
27. Bourassa, S., Hamelink, F., Hoesli, M.: Defining housing markets. J. Hous. Econ. **8**, 160–183 (1999)
28. Meen, G.: Modelling Spatial Housing Markets: Theory, Analysis, and Policy, vol. 2. Springer, Boston (2001). https://doi.org/10.1007/978-1-4615-1673-6
29. RICS Valuation – Global Standards (2019)
30. European Valuation Standards 2020 (2020)
31. Sheppard, S.: Hedonic analysis of housing markets. In: Cheshire, P.C., Mills, E.S. (eds.) Handbook of Regional and Urban Economics, vol. 3, pp. 1595–1635. Elsevier, Amesterdam, The Netherlands (1999)
32. Wooldridge, J.: Introductory Econometrics: A Modern Approach, 4th edn. Cengage Learning, Mason, USA (2008)
33. Gollini, I., Lu, B., Charlton, M., Brunsdon, C., Harris, P.: GWmodel: an R package for exploring spatial heterogeneity using geographically weighted models. J. Stat. Softw. **63**(17), 1–50 (2013). http://arxiv.org/abs/1306.0413. Accessed 28 Mar 2021
34. Standard on Automated Valuation Models (AVMs) (2018)
35. Openshaw, S.: Ecological fallacies and the analysis of areal census data. Environ. Plan. A **16**(1), 17–31 (1984). https://doi.org/10.1068/a160017

International Workshop on Computational and Applied Mathematics (CAM 2021)

Solving Differential Equations Using Feedforward Neural Networks

Wilson Guasti Junior[2(✉)] and Isaac P. Santos[1,2]

[1] Department of Applied Mathematics, Federal University of Espírito Santo, São Mateus, ES, Brazil
isaac.santos@ufes.br

[2] Graduate Program in Informatics, Federal University of Espírito Santo, Vitória, ES, Brazil

Abstract. In this work we explore the use of deep learning models based on deep feedforward neural networks to solve ordinary and partial differential equations. The illustration of this methodology is given by solving a variety of initial and boundary value problems. The numerical results, obtained based on different feedforward neural networks structures, activation functions and minimization methods, were compared to each other and to the exact solutions. The neural network was implemented using the Python language, with the Tensorflow library.

Keywords: Artificial neural networks · Differential equations · Deep learning · TensorFlow

1 Introduction

Differential equations play an important role in various fields of science and technology, modeling real-world problems of great interest in society. In fact, a variety of problems present in engineering, physics, economics, biology, epidemiology, etc. can be described using differential equations. Analytical solutions for mathematical models governed by differential equations are given only for simple problems. Thus, numerical methods are widely employed in the solution of this kind of problem. Classical numerical methods are based on the discretization of the domain at a finite number of points or elements, so that the approximate solution is defined at these points. Approximate solutions between these points must be interpolated. A drawback of the traditional methods, such as finite difference and standard finite element methods, is the need to use well-refined meshes to obtain better solutions. The computational cost of this strategy can grow a lot, preventing its use in high-dimensional problems [2,9,17].

Artificial neural networks (NNs) are models of machine learning, which works like neurons in the human brain. NNs have received a lot of attention in recent years, due to their success in numerous important applications. Mathematically, an ANN can be defined as a directed graph, where the vertices represent

The original version of this chapter was revised: It has been changed to non-open access and the copyright holder is now "Springer Nature Switzerland AG". The correction to this chapter is available at https://doi.org/10.1007/978-3-030-86973-1_51

O. Gervasi et al. (Eds.): ICCSA 2021, LNCS 12952, pp. 385–399, 2021.
https://doi.org/10.1007/978-3-030-86973-1_27

the neurons and the edges represent the connections between them. There are many variants of neural networks that differ in their architecture (how neurons are connected). Deep neural networks and deep learning models refer to neural networks with many hidden layers hidden in the context of machine learning. One of the advantages of adding hidden layers to a neural network is the exponential reduction in computational cost in some applications and the exponential decrease in the amount of training data needed in the network learning process [3].

Since the nineties, many studies have been dedicated to the application of NN in solving differential equations. In [15,19] the authors highlighted some properties of the NN solution in comparison with conventional numerical methods, such as: the solution is continuous and differentiable over all the domain; the propagation of rounding errors, common in classic numerical methods, does not affect the solution; the computational complexity does not increase considerably with the number of discretization points and with the number of dimensions; the method can be applied in the solution of linear, nonlinear, steady or unsteady ordinary or partial equations. Another motivation in using neural networks to solve differential equations is its property of approximating continuous functions. The universal approximation theorem [7,13] states that NN feedforward can approximate any continuous function in a compact set. According to [13], neural networks feedforward are universal approximators, so, at least in theory, these networks can provide a solution to any differential equation, with an arbitrarily small margin of error. In [8] the author pointed out some benefits and drawbacks of solving partial differential equations with neural networks.

In the last four years, several works have appeared in the literature addressing solutions of differential equations through deep neural networks or deep learning models [5,11,20,23,24]. Deep learning-based methods have been shown to be effective in solving mathematical models involving differential equations, especially high-dimensional problems. The success of deep learning in important learning tasks may be related to the development of efficient computational tools, such as the Tensorflow library [1], which provides some facilities, such as automatic differentiation, activation functions and minimization methods.

In the present work we explore the use of feedforward neural networks in the solution of boundary and initial value problems, involving ordinary and partial differential equations. The neural networks were implemented using the Python language, with the Tensorflow library. We applied this methodology in the solution of some problems to evaluate the quality of the solutions obtained. In the first experiment we compare the NN solution of an ordinary differential equation with the finite difference methods, Explicit Euler and second order Runge-Kutta, and with the exact solution. Then, we apply different feedforward neural networks structures, activation functions and minimization methods for solving a elliptic problem (a two-dimensional Poisson equation) and a parabolic problem (a Heat equation), comparing its result to each other and to the exact solutions. The remainder of this work is organized as follows. In Sect. 2 we present the definition of feedforward neural networks. The methodology studied is briefly addressed in Sect. 3 and the numerical experiments are presented in Sect. 4. Finally, the conclusions are presented in Sect. 5.

2 Feedforward Neural Networks

Feedforward neural networks offer a promising approach for solving differential equations. Consider a deep neural network composed of $L+1$ layers, where the input layer is denoted by 0 and the output layer is L. The intermediate layers between the input and the output layers are the so called hidden layers. The ℓ-th layer, $\ell = 0, 1, \cdots, L$, contains N_ℓ neurons. In particular, $N_L = 1$, that is, the output layer has only one neuron. Each neuron in the current layer ℓ receives each output from layer $\ell - 1$ as input and forwards its own output to each neuron in the next layer. The weighted input in each neuron j, $j = 1, \cdots, N_\ell$, in layer ℓ, for $\ell = 1, \cdots, L$, is given by the recursive expression

$$z_j^\ell = \sum_{i=1}^{N_{\ell-1}} w_{ji}^\ell \phi_{\ell-1}(z_i^{\ell-1}) + b_j^\ell, \tag{1}$$

where w_{ji}^ℓ is the weight between neuron i in layer $\ell - 1$ and neuron j in layer ℓ, b_j^ℓ is the bias of neuron j in layer ℓ and $\phi_\ell : \mathbb{R} \longrightarrow \mathbb{R}$ denotes the activation function of layer ℓ. For simplicity, we write n instead of N_0. If $\boldsymbol{x} = (x_1, \cdots, x_n) \in \mathbb{R}^n$ is the vector input, then

$$\phi_0(z_i^0) = x_i, \quad i = 1, \cdots, n.$$

Thus, the output of the neural network is given by

$$y = N(\boldsymbol{x}, \boldsymbol{p}) = z^L(\boldsymbol{x}, \boldsymbol{p}), \tag{2}$$

where z^L is obtained from Eq. (1) and $\boldsymbol{p} \in \mathbb{R}^{n_p}$ is the vector of all adjustable parameters, w_{ij}^ℓ and b_i^ℓ, with n_p denoting the total number of parameters. Figure 1 shows a neural network with one input layer with N_0 units, a unique hidden layer with N_1 neurons and one output layer with only one unit.

In Eq. (1) we assumed that a single activation function is used in ℓ-th layer, $\ell = 1, \cdots, L-1$. The activation function of a node defines the output of that node given an input or set of inputs. A neural network without the activation function would be just a linear transformation. There are several types of activation functions, for example, the sigmoid, the hyperbolic tangent and the Rectified Linear Unit (RELU) functions [16].

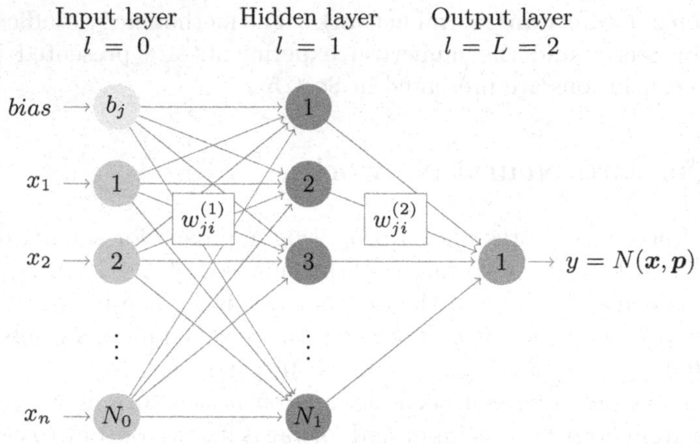

Fig. 1. Feedforward neural network with one hidden layer.

3 Description of the Method

The process of solving differential equations via artificial neural networks consists of transforming the original model into a quadratic functional (loss function), associated to the residual of the equation (and boundary and initial conditions), that is minimized using techniques of unrestricted optimization in terms of the weights and biases of the neural network [15].

Consider a mathematical model, described by a parabolic partial differential equation with Dirichlet boundary condition, that consists in finding a scalar function $u : \Omega \times (0, T_f] \longrightarrow \mathbb{R}$, such that,

$$\frac{\partial u(\boldsymbol{x},t)}{\partial t} + \mathcal{L}u(\boldsymbol{x},t) = f(\boldsymbol{x},t), \quad \forall(\boldsymbol{x},t) \in \Omega \times (0,T_f], \tag{3}$$

$$u(\boldsymbol{x},t) = g(\boldsymbol{x},t), \quad \forall(\boldsymbol{x},t) \in \Gamma \times (0,T_f], \tag{4}$$

$$u(\boldsymbol{x},0) = u_0(\boldsymbol{x}), \quad \forall \boldsymbol{x} \in \Omega, \tag{5}$$

where $\Omega \subset \mathbb{R}^d$ is a rectangular domain with boundary Γ, $(0, T_f]$ is the time interval, with $T_f > 0$, $\boldsymbol{x} = (x_1, \cdots, x_n) \in \Omega$, f and g are given functions (f represents the source/sink term and g the Dirichlet boundary condition), u_0 is the initial solution and $\mathcal{L}(\cdot)$ is a second order differential operator.

The NN method for solving (3)–(5) seeks a function u_{NN} that approximates the exact solution u, minimizing a loss function defined by

$$L(\boldsymbol{p}) = \sum_{\boldsymbol{x}_i \in \mathcal{P}_\Omega} \sum_{t_j \in \mathcal{P}_t} \Big(\frac{\partial u_{NN}(\boldsymbol{x}_i, t_j, \boldsymbol{p})}{\partial t} + \mathcal{L}(u_{NN}(\boldsymbol{x}_i, t_j, \boldsymbol{p})) - f(\boldsymbol{x}_i, t_j) \Big)^2, \tag{6}$$

where $\mathcal{P}_\Omega = \{\boldsymbol{x}_i \in \Omega; i = 1, \cdots, n_\Omega\}$ and $\mathcal{P}_t = \{t_j \in [0, T_f]; j = 1, \cdots, n_t\}$ are discretizations of the spatial and temporal domains, respectively, and $\boldsymbol{p} \in \mathbb{R}^{n_p}$ is the vector of adjustable parameters (weights and biases) of the neural network. The approximate solution u_{NN} is written as

$$u_{NN}(\boldsymbol{x}, t, \boldsymbol{p}) = G(\boldsymbol{x}, t) + Q(\boldsymbol{x}, t, N(\boldsymbol{x}, t, \boldsymbol{p})),$$

where the function $G(\boldsymbol{x}, t)$ is defined a priori in order to satisfy the boundary and initial conditions, that is,

$$G(\boldsymbol{x}, t) = g(\boldsymbol{x}, t), \quad \forall (\boldsymbol{x}, t) \in \Gamma \times (0, T_f], \tag{7}$$

$$G(\boldsymbol{x}, 0) = u_0(\boldsymbol{x}), \quad \forall \boldsymbol{x} \in \Omega. \tag{8}$$

In general, the function Q is written as

$$Q(\boldsymbol{x}, t, N(\boldsymbol{x}, t, \boldsymbol{p})) = \Phi(\boldsymbol{x}, t) N(\boldsymbol{x}, t, \boldsymbol{p}),$$

where $\Phi(\boldsymbol{x}, t) = 0$, for all $(\boldsymbol{x}, t) \in (\Omega \times \{0\}) \cup (\Gamma \times [0, T_f])$ and $N(\boldsymbol{x}, t, \boldsymbol{p})$ is a feedforward neural network with parameters $\boldsymbol{p}$ (see Eq. 2). For a given problem, there are various ways to construct the functions $G(\boldsymbol{x}, t)$ and $\Phi(\boldsymbol{x}, t)$ (see [15]).

The derivatives of the function u_{NN} in relation to the network inputs are calculated via backpropagation algorithm [22], a special automatic differentiation technique. TensorFlow includes a reverse-mode automatic differentiation library that calculates all derivatives of the loss function, producing a new symbolic expression representing the gradients [1,25].

The goal is to find $\boldsymbol{p}^* = \arg \min_{\boldsymbol{p} \in \mathbb{R}^{n_p}} L(\boldsymbol{p})$, so that $u_{NN}(\boldsymbol{x}, t, \boldsymbol{p}^*)$ is the NN solution of (3)–(5). Several optimization methods can be used to minimize the loss function (6), such as, Gradient Descent [6], Stochastic Gradient Descent (SGD) [21], Levenberg-Marquardt [12], Broyden-Fletcher-Goldfarb-Shanno (BFGS) [10], Limited-memory Broyden-Fletcher-Goldfarb-Shanno (L-BFGS) [18], ADAM (adaptive moment estimation) [14], etc. A review about optimization methods for machine learning is presented in [4]. Several of these methods are implemented in TensorFlow.

4 Numerical Experiments

In this section we study three problems: an initial value problem, the Poisson problem and the Heat equation using the methodology presented in this work. The approximation results of the neural networks are compared with the true solutions. The neural networks has been implemented using the open-source TensorFlow framework. In all experiments we used the learning rate $\eta = 0,001$, the hyperbolic tangent (Tanh) activation function and the minimization method ADAM [14], with 10000 iterations. In the text, N_x, N_y and N_t stand for the number of partition points of the domain on directions x, y and t, respectively.

4.1 Ordinary Differential Equation (ODE)

We consider the following linear initial value problem (described in [15]) consisting of finding $u : [0,1] \to \mathbb{R}$, satisfying

$$\frac{du(x)}{dx} + g(x)u(x) = q(x), \quad x \in (0,1], \tag{9}$$

$$u(0) = 1, \tag{10}$$

with $g(x) = \left(x + \frac{1+3x^2}{1+x+x^3}\right)$, $q(x) = x^3 + 2x + x^2\left(\frac{1+3x^2}{1+x+x^3}\right)$, whose exact solution is

$$u(x) = \frac{-e^{\frac{x^2}{2}}}{(1+x+x^3)+x^2}.$$

The approximate solution for this problem is defined as

$$u_{NN}(x) = u_{NN}(x, \boldsymbol{p}) = u_0 + (x - x_0)N(x, \boldsymbol{p}) = 1 + xN(x, \boldsymbol{p})$$

and the loss function,

$$L(\boldsymbol{p}) = \sum_{x_j \in \mathcal{P}_x} \left[\frac{du_{NN}(x_j, \boldsymbol{p})}{dx} + g(x_j)u_{NN}(x_j, \boldsymbol{p}) - q(x_j)\right]^2,$$

where $\mathcal{P}_x$ is a uniform discretization grid of the interval $[0, 1]$.

The Table 1 presents the errors $e = u - u_{NN}$, in the infinity and $L^2(0,1)$ norms, as well as the minimal value of the loss function. We used an NN with one hidden layer with six different numbers of neurons (5, 10, 30, 50, 100, 500) and two discretization grids, with $N_x = 10$ and $N_x = 20$. Using $N_x = 10$, the minimum error in both norms were obtained with 30 neurons in the hidden layer. Increasing the number of training points to $N_x = 20$ the errors do not decrease substantially. In this case, the minimum error was obtained with 10 neurons in the hidden layer. The Table 2 considers two hidden layers with the same number of neurons in each one. We observed that the increase in the number of hidden layers resulted in a decrease in the error. The minimum errors in both discretization grids were obtained with 10 neurons in each hidden layer.

In order to compare the NN solution with the Explicit Euler (EE) and second order Runge-Kutta (RK2) methods, the Table 3 presents the errors in the infinity norm for these three methodologies. We used a network with two hidden layers with 50 neurons each one, and three discretization grids, with $N_x = 10, 20, 40$. The results show that the quality of the NN solution is compared to the RK2 solution, as pointed out in Fig. 2.

Table 1. Errors ($e = u - u_{RN}$) using the infinity and the $L^2(0,1)$ norms and minimum value of the loss function J_R, considering 6 different numbers of neurons in one hidden layer and two discretization grids, with $N_x = 10$ e $N_x = 20$.

Neurons	$N_x = 10$			$N_x = 20$		
	$\|e\|_\infty$	$\|e\|_{L^2(0,1)}$	min J_R	$\|e\|_\infty$	$\|e\|_{L^2(0,1)}$	min J_R
5	$3,773 \times 10^{-3}$	$5,951 \times 10^{-3}$	$5,366 \times 10^{-7}$	$2,851 \times 10^{-3}$	$6,361 \times 10^{-3}$	$1,878 \times 10^{-6}$
10	$2,320 \times 10^{-3}$	$3,880 \times 10^{-3}$	$1,052 \times 10^{-6}$	$1,673 \times 10^{-3}$	$3,785 \times 10^{-3}$	$3,645 \times 10^{-7}$
30	$1,673 \times 10^{-3}$	$3,785 \times 10^{-3}$	$3,645 \times 10^{-7}$	$2,676 \times 10^{-3}$	$5,820 \times 10^{-3}$	$6,203 \times 10^{-8}$
50	$4,025 \times 10^{-3}$	$6,161 \times 10^{-3}$	$2,300 \times 10^{-5}$	$2,703 \times 10^{-3}$	$5,861 \times 10^{-3}$	$3,875 \times 10^{-7}$
100	$4,461 \times 10^{-3}$	$6,954 \times 10^{-3}$	$9,293 \times 10^{-8}$	$3,026 \times 10^{-3}$	$6,570 \times 10^{-3}$	$2,687 \times 10^{-6}$
500	$4,356 \times 10^{-3}$	$6,767 \times 10^{-3}$	$4,939 \times 10^{-8}$	$3,002 \times 10^{-3}$	$6,515 \times 10^{-3}$	$2,755 \times 10^{-6}$

Table 2. Errors ($e = u - u_{RN}$) using the infinity and the $L^2(0,1)$ norms and minimum value of the loss function J_R, considering 6 different numbers of neurons in two hidden layers and two discretization grids, with $N_x = 10$ e $N_x = 20$.

Neurons	$N_x = 10$			$N_x = 20$		
	$\|e\|_\infty$	$\|e\|_{L^2(0,1)}$	min J_R	$\|e\|_\infty$	$\|e\|_{L^2(0,1)}$	min J_R
5	$5,787 \times 10^{-4}$	$9,235 \times 10^{-4}$	$7,188 \times 10^{-8}$	$4,685 \times 10^{-4}$	$1,023 \times 10^{-3}$	$9,328 \times 10^{-9}$
10	$3,191 \times 10^{-4}$	$5,077 \times 10^{-4}$	$7,875 \times 10^{-10}$	$2,370 \times 10^{-4}$	$5,387 \times 10^{-4}$	$1,015 \times 10^{-9}$
30	$3,502 \times 10^{-3}$	$5,355 \times 10^{-3}$	$9,980 \times 10^{-6}$	$2,486 \times 10^{-3}$	$5,385 \times 10^{-3}$	$3,681 \times 10^{-7}$
50	$1,372 \times 10^{-3}$	$2,079 \times 10^{-3}$	$4,952 \times 10^{-7}$	$1,006 \times 10^{-3}$	$2,151 \times 10^{-3}$	$4,173 \times 10^{-7}$
100	$1,231 \times 10^{-3}$	$1,839 \times 10^{-3}$	$2,398 \times 10^{-7}$	$7,456 \times 10^{-4}$	$1,518 \times 10^{-3}$	$2,369 \times 10^{-8}$
500	$1,208 \times 10^{-3}$	$1,821 \times 10^{-3}$	$1,719 \times 10^{-7}$	$9,276 \times 10^{-4}$	$2,008 \times 10^{-3}$	$4,899 \times 10^{-9}$

Table 3. Errors in the infinite norm for the Explicit Euler, RK2 and NN methods.

Method	Discretization grids		
	$N_x = 10$	$N_x = 20$	$N_x = 40$
Explicit Euler	$1,359 \times 10^{-1}$	$6,214 \times 10^{-2}$	$2,979 \times 10^{-2}$
RK2	$3,614 \times 10^{-3}$	$7,698 \times 10^{-4}$	$1,783 \times 10^{-4}$
NN	$1,372 \times 10^{-3}$	$1,006 \times 10^{-4}$	$7,783 \times 10^{-4}$

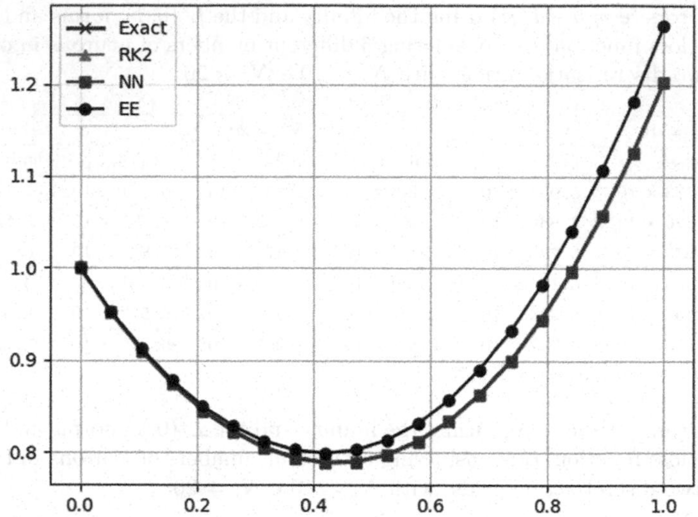

Fig. 2. Explicit Euler (EE), RK2 and NN (2 layers with 50 neurons each one) solutions, using $N_x = 20$.

4.2 The Poisson Problem

Consider the Poisson problem, consisting of finding $u : \Omega \longrightarrow \mathbb{R}$, such that,

$$-\Delta u(x,y) = f(x,y), \quad (x,y) \in \Omega, \tag{11}$$
$$u(x,y) = g(x,y), \quad (x,y) \in \Gamma, \tag{12}$$

where

$$\Delta u(x,y) = \left(\frac{\partial^2 u}{\partial x^2} + \frac{\partial^2 u}{\partial y^2}\right),$$

$\Omega = (0,1) \times (0,1)$, Γ is the boundary of Ω, f and g are given functions.

This problem is one of the most used in the numerical study of elliptic boundary value problems. Choosing the functions $f(x,y) = 2\pi^2 \sin(\pi x)\sin(\pi y)$ in Ω and $g(x,y) = \sin(\pi x)\sin(\pi y)$ on Γ, the exact solution of (11)–(12) is

$$u(x,y) = \sin(\pi x)\sin(\pi y).$$

The approximate solution for this problem is defined as

$$u_{NN}(x,y) = u_{NN}(x,y,\boldsymbol{p}) = G(x,y) + \Phi(x,y)N(x,y,\boldsymbol{p}),$$

where

$$G(x,y) = (1-x)g(0,y) + xg(1,y) + (1-y)\Big(g(x,0) - (1-x)g(0,0) - xg(1,0)\Big)$$
$$+y\Big(g(x,1) - (1-x)g(0,1) - xg(1,1)\Big),$$
$$\Phi(x,y) = x(1-x)y(1-y).$$

The loss function is given by

$$L(\mathbf{p}) = \sum_{(x_i,y_i)\in \mathcal{P}_\Omega} \Big[-\Delta u_{NN}(x_i, y_i, \mathbf{p}) - f(x_i, y_i) \Big]^2.$$

where $\mathcal{P}_\Omega$ is a uniform discretization grid of Ω, with N_x and N_y partition points on directions x and y, respectively.

Figure 3 presents the loss function training (log scale) for the following three activation functions, sigmoid, RELU and hyperbolic tangent (Tanh), and two minimization methods, the Descent Gradient and ADAM, using $N_x = N_y = 50$ and two hidden layers with 40 neurons each one. The combination of the minimization method, ADAM, with the activation function, Tanh, obtained the best result, justifying their use in the numerical simulations. The Fig. 4 shows the exact (left) and NN (right) solutions for this Poisson problem, using a discretization grid with $N_x = N_y = 50$. The network was configured with one hidden layer and 10 neurons. Visually, the NN solution is well represented. In order to measure the quality of the NN solution, the errors in the infinite norm for several configurations of the neural network are presented as follows.

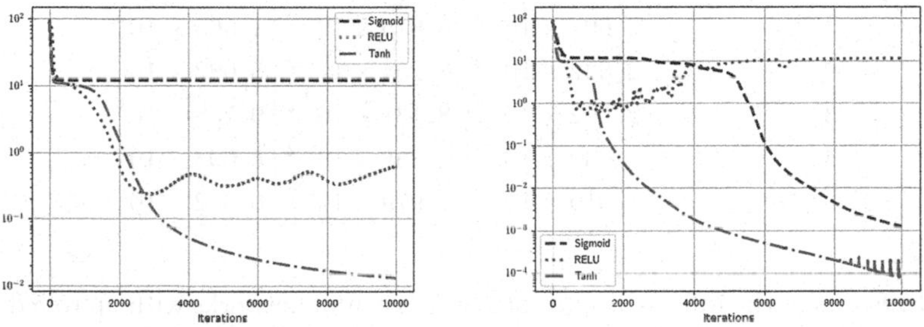

Fig. 3. Loss function training (log scale) for three activation functions and two minimization methods: Descent Gradient (left) and ADAM (right).

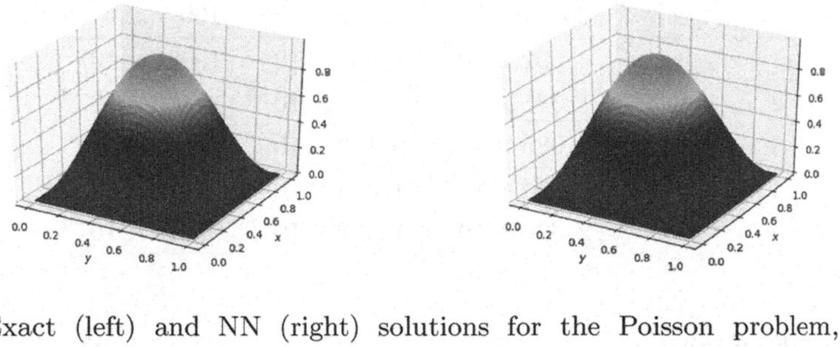

Fig. 4. Exact (left) and NN (right) solutions for the Poisson problem, using a discretization grid with $N_x = N_y = 50$. The network was configured with one hidden layer and 10 neurons.

Table 4 shows the errors in the infinite norm for different networks, all of them trained in a set of 100 points ($N_x = N_y = 10$). We consider 5 different hidden layers and an amount of neurons (in each one) equal to 10, 20 and 40. The errors obtained with 10 or 20 neurons are of order 10^{-2}, and by adding hidden layers (up to 5) in the network, the error does not decrease. For the case of 40 neurons, using more than one hidden layer causes the error to be of order 10^{-3}. The best result is achieved for the neural network with two hidden layers and 40 neurons in each one.

We made a second experiment on the same problem, considering a set of training with 2500 points ($N_x = N_y = 50$) and an amount of neurons in each layer equal to 20, 50 and 100. The numerical results are exposed in Table 5. As expected, increasing the number of training points the error decreases (see the case with 20 neurons). The best result was an error of order 10^4, achieved for the neural network with four hidden layers and 1000 neurons in each one.

Table 4. Errors in the infinite norm, considering neural networks with up to 5 different hidden layers and a number of neurons (in each one) equal to 10, 20, 40. The training of the network was performed with $N_x = N_y = 10$ (100 points).

Hidden layers	Neurons		
	10	20	40
1	$2,601 \times 10^{-2}$	$8,075 \times 10^{-2}$	$1,563 \times 10^{-2}$
2	$2,632 \times 10^{-2}$	$8,254 \times 10^{-2}$	$5,082 \times 10^{-3}$
3	$2,592 \times 10^{-2}$	$8,131 \times 10^{-2}$	$9,738 \times 10^{-3}$
4	$2,632 \times 10^{-2}$	$8,258 \times 10^{-2}$	$5,093 \times 10^{-3}$
5	$2,510 \times 10^{-2}$	$7,979 \times 10^{-2}$	$6,382 \times 10^{-3}$

Table 5. Errors in the infinite norm, considering neural networks with up to 5 different hidden layers and a number of neurons (in each one) equal to 20, 50, 100. The training of the network was performed with $N_x = N_y = 50$ (2500 points).

Hidden layers	Neurons		
	20	50	100
1	$4,692 \times 10^{-3}$	$8,439 \times 10^{-3}$	$1,061 \times 10^{-2}$
2	$\underline{1,575 \times 10^{-3}}$	$1,251 \times 10^{-3}$	$2,380 \times 10^{-3}$
3	$1,985 \times 10^{-3}$	$\underline{8,183 \times 10^{-4}}$	$6,724 \times 10^{-4}$
4	$1,660 \times 10^{-3}$	$1,038 \times 10^{-3}$	$\underline{6,185 \times 10^{-4}}$
5	$2,326 \times 10^{-3}$	$1,362 \times 10^{-3}$	$9,118 \times 10^{-4}$

4.3 Heat Equation

In this experiment we consider an evolutionary partial differential equation, the heat equation,

$$\frac{\partial u}{\partial t}(x,t) - \alpha \frac{\partial^2 u}{\partial x^2}(x,t) = f(x,t), \quad x \in (0,\ell),\ t > 0, \tag{13}$$

subject to Dirichlet boundary conditions,

$$u(0,t) = u_0^0(t), \quad u(\ell,t) = u_\ell^0(t), \quad \forall t > 0 \tag{14}$$

and initial condition,

$$u(x,0) = u_0(x), \quad \forall x \in [0,\ell]. \tag{15}$$

In (13), f is a given function (source term) and $\alpha > 0$ is the thermal diffusivity coefficient. Equation (13) models the temperature distribution in the one-dimensional region (a beam, for example) $[0,\ell]$, with boundary and initial conditions given by (14) and (15). Function $u(x,t)$ represents the temperature at point $x \in [0,\ell]$ and time $t \geq 0$.

Considering $f = 0$, $u_0^0(t) = u_\ell^0(t) = 0$, for all $t > 0$ and initial condition,

$$u_0(x) = \sin\left(\frac{\pi x}{\ell}\right), \quad \forall x \in [0,\ell], \tag{16}$$

the exact solution of (13), (14) and (15) is given by

$$u(x,t) = e^{\frac{-\alpha\pi^2 t}{\ell}} \sin\left(\frac{\pi x}{\ell}\right). \tag{17}$$

We solve the problem considering the space-time domain $\Omega = (0,\ell) \times (0, T_f]$, where $T_f > 0$ is the final time, so that the initial condition is treated as a boundary condition. The approximate solution is defined as

$$u_{NN}(x,t,\boldsymbol{p}) = G(x,t) + \Phi(x,t)N(x,t,\boldsymbol{p}),$$

where $G(x,t) = \frac{(\ell-t)}{\ell}u_0(x)$ and $\Phi(x,t) = x(\ell-x)t$, and the loss function is described by

$$L(\boldsymbol{p}) = \sum_{(x_i,t_i)\in\mathcal{P}_\Omega} \left[\frac{\partial u_{NN}(x_i,t_i,\boldsymbol{p})}{\partial t} - \alpha\frac{\partial^2 u_{NN}(x_i,t_i,\boldsymbol{p})}{\partial x^2} - f(x_i,t_i)\right]^2. \tag{18}$$

Considering $\ell = \alpha = 1$, the Fig. 5 shows the exact (left) and NN (right) solutions for this Heat problem, using a discretization grid with $N_x = N_t = 50$. The network was configured with two hidden layers and 20 neurons. Visually, the NN solution is well represented. Figure 7 shows the NN (in blue) and true (in red) solutions in four points in time. At t = 0, the temperature is given by the initial condition. As the time approaches to $t = 0.5$, it gradually spreads tending to zero over the whole spatial domain. Figure 6 presents the loss function training (log scale) for the activation functions, sigmoid, RELU and hyperbolic tangent (Tanh), and the minimization methods, the Descent Gradient and ADAM, using $N_x = N_t = 50$ and four hidden layers with 20 neurons each one. The minimization method, ADAM, and the activation function, Tanh, provided the best result.

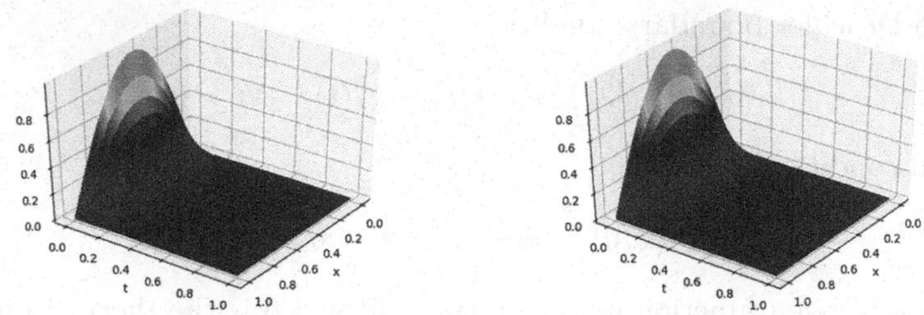

Fig. 5. Exact (left) and NN (right) solutions for the Heat problem, using a discretization grid with $N_x = N_t = 50$. The network was configured with two hidden layer and 20 neurons in each one.

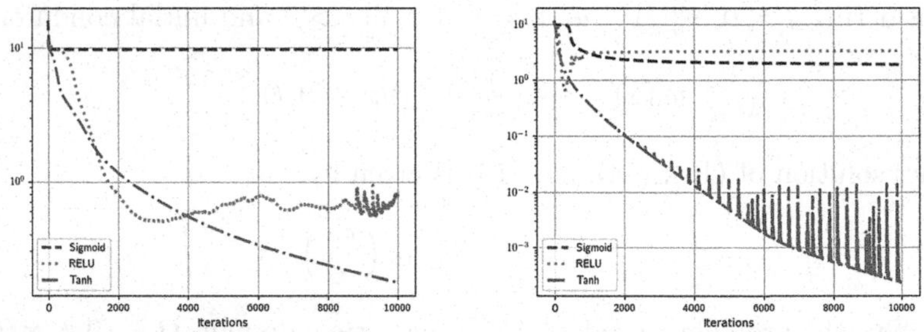

Fig. 6. Loss function training (log scale) for three activation functions and two minimization methods: Descent Gradient (left) and ADAM (right).

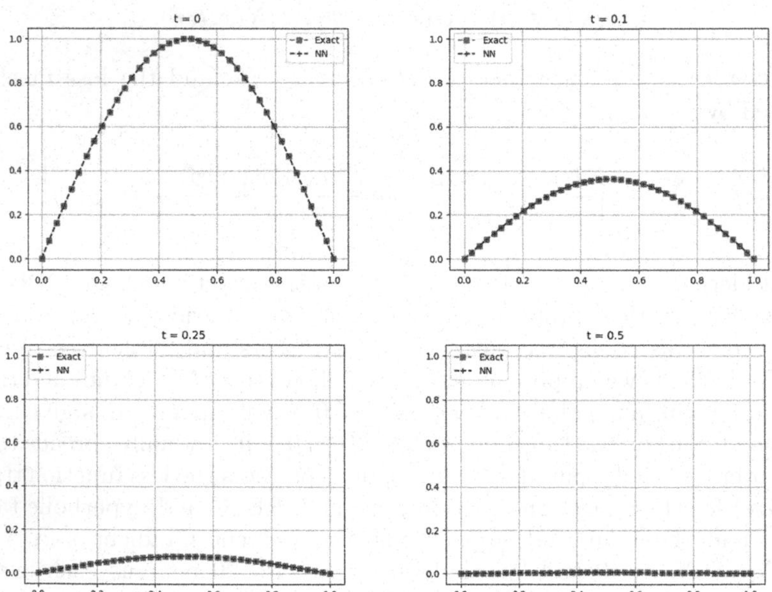

Fig. 7. Exact (in red) and NN (in blue) solutions of (13) in four points in time. (Color figure online)

In order to measure the quality of the NN solution, the errors in the infinite norm for several configurations of the neural network are presented as follows. Table 6 shows the errors in the infinite norm for various neural network configurations (hidden layers and neurons per layer). We observe that the addition of more neurons or more hidden layers did not reduce significantly the error. Using three hidden layers with twenty neurons each one is sufficient to obtain a solution with an error of order 10^{-4}.

Table 6. Infinity norm errors, considering $N_x = N_t = 50$.

Hidden layers	Neurons		
	10	20	40
1	6.982×10^{-2}	4.261×10^{-2}	3.109×10^{-2}
2	3.568×10^{-2}	2.063×10^{-3}	1.301×10^{-3}
3	1.012×10^{-3}	9.519×10^{-4}	8.899×10^{-4}
4	3.586×10^{-3}	9.418×10^{-4}	9.934×10^{-4}
5	2.567×10^{-3}	9.749×10^{-4}	9.380×10^{-4}

5 Conclusions

In this work we presented a study about solutions of differential equations using a method based on deep learning models, more specifically, feedforward deep neural networks. Numerical experiments were carried out to evaluate the efficiency of the methodology, comparing its results with the exact solutions and calculating the errors in the infinite norm. The method achieved good results due to the powerful function approximation ability of neural networks. The neural networks were implemented using the open-source TensorFlow framework.

The method proved to be a promising methodology for solving initial and boundary value problems. However, more numerical experiments need to be carried out in order to strengthen our conclusions. As future work, we plan to explore other network topologies and apply them for solving problems with curved or irregular boundaries and 3D unsteady transport problems, including the Euler and the Navier-Stokes equations.

Despite the success of these new approaches based on deep learning to solve differential equations, there are many important points involving theoretical and practical issues that deserve discussions and further investigations.

References

1. Abadi, M., et al.: TensorFlow: a system for large-scale machine learning. In: OSDI 2016, pp. 265–283. USENIX Association, USA (2016)
2. Bellman, R.: Dynamic Programming. Princeton University Press (1957)

3. Bengio, Y., Simard, P., Frasconi, P.: Learning long-term dependencies with gradient descent is difficult. IEEE Trans. Neural Netw. **5**, 157–166 (1994). https://doi.org/10.1109/72.279181
4. Bottou, L., Curtis, E.F., Nocedal, J.: Optimization methods for large-scale machine learning. SIAM Rev. **60**(2), 223–311 (2018). https://doi.org/10.1137/16M1080173
5. Chaudhari, P., Oberman, A., Osher, S., Soatto, S., Carlier, G.: Deep relaxation: partial differential equations for optimizing deep neural networks. Res. Math. Sci. **5**(3), 1–30 (2018). https://doi.org/10.1007/s40687-018-0148-y
6. Curry, H.B.: The method of steepest descent for non-linear minimization problems. Quart. Appl. Math. **2**, 258–261 (1944). https://doi.org/10.1090/qam/10667
7. Cybenko, G.: Approximation by superposition of a sigmoidal function. Math. Control Sig. Syst. **2**, 303–314 (1989)
8. Dockhorn, T.: A discussion on solving partial differential equations using neural networks. arXiv:1904.07200 (2019)
9. Weinan, E., Han, J., Jentzen, A.: Algorithms for solving high dimensional PDEs: from nonlinear Monte Carlo to machine learning. CoRR abs/2008.13333 (2020). https://arxiv.org/abs/2008.13333
10. Guo, Q., Liu, J.G., Wang, D.H.: A modified BFGS method and its superlinear convergence in nonconvex minimization with general line search rule. J. Appl. Math. Comput. **28**, 435–446 (2008). https://doi.org/10.1007/s12190-008-0117-5
11. Guo, Y., Cao, X., Bainian, L., Gao, M.: Solving partial differential equations using deep learning and physical constraints. Appl. Sci. **10**, 5917 (2020). https://doi.org/10.3390/app10175917
12. Hagan, M.T., Menhaj, M.B.: Training feedforward networks with the Marquardt algorithm. IEEE Trans. Neural Netw. **5**(6), 989–993 (1994). https://doi.org/10.1109/72.329697
13. Hornik, K., Stinchcombe, M., White, H.: Multilayer feedforward networks are universal approximators. Neural Netw. **2**(5), 359–366 (1989). https://doi.org/10.1016/0893-6080(89)90020-8
14. Kingma, D.P., Ba, J.: Adam: a method for stochastic optimization (2017)
15. Lagaris, I.E., Likas, A., Fotiadis, D.I.: Artificial neural networks for solving ordinary and partial differential equations. IEEE Trans. Neural Netw. **9**(5), 987–1000 (1998). https://doi.org/10.1109/72.712178
16. Lau, M.M., Hann Lim, K.: Review of adaptive activation function in deep neural network. In: 2018 IEEE-EMBS Conference on Biomedical Engineering and Sciences (IECBES), pp. 686–690 (2018). https://doi.org/10.1109/IECBES.2018.8626714
17. Leake, C., Mortari, D.: Deep theory of functional connections: a new method for estimating the solutions of partial differential equations. Mach. Learn. Knowl. Extr. **2**(1), 37–55 (2020). https://doi.org/10.3390/make2010004
18. Liu, D.C., Nocedal, J.: On the limited memory BFGS method for large scale optimization. Math. Program. **45**, 503–528 (1989)
19. Parisi, D.R., Mariani, M.C., Laborde, M.A.: Solving differential equations with unsupervised neural networks. Chem. Eng. Process. Process Intensif. **42**(8), 715–721 (2003). https://doi.org/10.1016/S0255-2701(02)00207-6
20. Raissi, M., Karniadakis, G.E.: Hidden physics models: machine learning of nonlinear partial differential equations. J. Comput. Phys. **357**, 125–141 (2018). https://doi.org/10.1016/j.jcp.2017.11.039
21. Robbins, H., Monro, S.: A stochastic approximation method. Ann. Math. Stat. **22**(3), 400–407 (1951). https://doi.org/10.1214/aoms/1177729586

22. Rumelhart, D.E., Willians, G.E., Williams, R.J.: Learning representations by back-propagating errors. Nature **323**, 533–536 (1986). https://doi.org/10.1038/323533a0
23. Samaniego, E., et al.: An energy approach to the solution of partial differential equations in computational mechanics via machine learning: concepts, implementation and applications. Comput. Meth. Appl. Mech. Eng. **362**, 112790 (2020). https://doi.org/10.1016/j.cma.2019.112790
24. Sirignano, J., Spiliopoulos, K.: DGM: a deep learning algorithm for solving partial differential equations. J. Comput. Phys. **375**, 1339–1364 (2018). https://doi.org/10.1016/j.jcp.2018.08.029
25. Yu, Y., et al.: Dynamic control flow in large-scale machine learning. In: Proceedings of the 13th EuroSys Conference, EuroSys 2018, Association for Computing Machinery, New York (2018)

An Application of Genetic Algorithms to Estimate both the Blood Perfusion and Geometric Parameters of Breast Tumors by Thermal Analysis

Antônio Márcio Gonçalo Filho[1,2(✉)], Michelli Marlane Silva Loureiro[1(✉)], and Felipe Santos Loureiro[1(✉)]

[1] Federal University of São João del Rei, Av. Visconde do Rio Preto, s/no Colônia do Bengo, São João del Rei 36301-360, Brazil
{michelli.loureiro,felipe.loureiro}@ufsj.edu.br
[2] Accenture, Dublin, Ireland
antonio.marcio.filho@accenture.com
http://www.ufsj.edu.br

Abstract. This work presents the application of a genetic algorithm (GA) for solving the inverse bioheat transfer problem to estimate the position, as well as the blood perfusion of a breast tumor based on the skin temperature. A multi-layered breast cancer model is employed with the Pennes' bioheat equation being discretized by the finite element method. The input data consist of the skin temperature of the target breast tumor. The evolution process generates a set of meshes for representing the breast with the tumor and tries to minimize the temperature difference on the skin surface between the target model and the model generated from the GA. Three different GA strategies were tested, and the results were satisfactory and reached a model close to the expected target.

Keywords: Genetic algorithms · Bio-heat transfer · Inverse problem · Finite elements method

1 Introduction

Tumor detection is a common problem in computational applications. After collecting patient data, it is possible to apply a wide range of search algorithms to locate the tumor position within the tissue. Many machine learning algorithms have been applied to solve such a problem, e.g., neural networks, support vector machines, Bayesian networks, clustering, fuzzy logic and decision trees [1,8]. This work aims at applying a genetic algorithm (GA) to estimate the position (center and radius) and the blood perfusion of a circular tumor within the

Supported by Federal University of São João del Rei and CNPq and FAPEMIG.

O. Gervasi et al. (Eds.): ICCSA 2021, LNCS 12952, pp. 400–410, 2021.
https://doi.org/10.1007/978-3-030-86973-1_28

modelled breast tissue, proposed by [13]. This work is based on the methodology presented in [6], that used genetic algorithm in a rectangular shaped tissue model, and the one presented in [5]. The temperature field, collected at the outer portion of the tissue, is calculated via the Penne's Bio-Heat Transfer Equation (acronym PBHTE). The genetic algorithm then tries to estimate the aforementioned parameters within the tissue by generating a population of cancerous breast models that can fit within the expected target model. Those populations are evolved, and after a number of generations, the model that most approaches to the target model is then returned.

Wahab's breast cancer model describes the breast as a semicircle with an underlying circular tumor. This model has three different layers of tissue, representing fat, mammary gland and muscular tissue. Here, the open-source finite-element mesh generator software Gmsh [4] is used to create the mesh of each GA individual model. Afterwards, the temperature field of each individual is computed by the finite element method through an in-house code. The objective function minimizes the temperature difference on the skin surface between the GA model to the target model. Continuous operators are applied during the evolutionary process, and individuals with most resemblance to the target model are selected with both generating offsprings, proceeding to the next generation via elitism.

2 Related Work

This work applies the methodology of Gonçalo et al. [6] and Gonçalo [5] in the Wahab's [13] breast cancer model. Gonçalo et al. work uses a steady-state genetic algorithm to estimate a tumor within a simple rectangular cancerous tissue model. In this model, the temperature field is calculated by the PBHTE, described by Harry H. Pennes in [11], which can be stated as: given Ω as the tissue domain; k as the thermal conductivity; ρ_b as the density of the blood; c_b as specific heat of the blood; ω_b as the blood perfusion and Q_m as the metabolic heat generation, find the tissue temperature T such that

$$\nabla \cdot k\nabla T + \omega_b \rho_b c_b (T_a - T) + Q_m = 0, \text{in } \Omega, \tag{1}$$

where T_a is the arterial temperature. This equation is used to calculate the temperature in the computational domain of the model.

In the work of Gonçalo et al. [6], each individual created by the GA was evaluated taking into account the difference between the target temperature on the skin surface used as reference and the respective skin temperature calculated within the model. This objective function can be stated as

$$J(\mathbf{x}_r, r) = \frac{1}{2} \sum_{i \in \eta_{\Gamma_S}} (\hat{T}_i - T_i(\mathbf{x}_r, r))^2 \tag{2}$$

where J is the error of each individual; $\mathbf{x}_r$ is the center of the circular tumor in the two-dimensional space, and r its radius; T_i is the computed temperature of the node i on the skin surface labeled as Γ_S, and $\hat{T}_i$ is the target temperature of the model in the same node. The model used is based on [13], which describes a three-layered breast cancer model, with fat, mammary gland and muscular tissue.

Other works, including [10] utilizes dual reciprocity, combined with genetic algorithms, to estimate the location of a tumor using the skin temperature analysis through an inverse methodology considering the PBHTE. [2] utilizes curve fitting techniques to estimate the position of a breast cancer by non-invasive means. 2D and 3D breast models taking into account the PBHTE are discretized by the finite volume method. Das's model only has a single healthy tissue and the breast tumor. The referred work's algorithm tries to estimate the depth, in centimeters, the size and the blood perfusion through the solution of the inverse bio-heat transfer problem. This work is further expanded in [3], where the analysis also tries to find the angular and radial position of the breast model tumor. Melo et al. [9] employed a binary-coded GA to estimate the blood perfusion of a rectangular tumor considering the PBHTE and the finite element method. A detailed study on the effect of the GA parameters into the analyzed problem was also presented.

2.1 Breast Cancer Model

A breast cancer geometric model, based on Wahab's model, was created to be employed as a guideline for the mesh generator. The model is described in [13] as a semi-circle with four distinct tissue layers, namely: fat, mammary gland, muscle, and the tumor considered as a circle inside the gland layer. This model is used as a reference to the Gmsh to create a mesh of the model. In his work, Wahab proposed three different models of breast cancer, while referencing Sudharsan [12] with his own proposed model for the composition percentage of each tissue layer. Each of the models has the composition percentage as described by Table 1. This work uses the extremely dense model of breast cancer as reference.

Table 1. Composition of each healthy tissue in Wahab's breast cancer model, using Sudharsan's model as a reference for comparison.

Tissue composition (%)	Muscle (D_1)	Gland (D_2)	Fat (D_3)
Extremely dense (ED)	20	70	10
Heterogeneously dense (HD)	20	60	20
Scattered fibroglandular (SF)	20	40	40
Predominantly fatty (PF)	10	20	70
Sudharsan's model	26.5	54.1	19.4

The physical properties of each layer, as described by Wahab, are shown at Table 2. Those properties are considered in the PBHTE to calculate the temperature field in the model through the finite element method.

Table 2. Physical properties of each tissue layer, as described by Wahab.

Physical properties	Muscle (D_1)	Gland (D_2)	Fat (D_3)	Tumor (T_1)
Thermal conductivity (W/m °C)	0.48	0.48	0.21	0.48
Metabolic heat generation (W/m^3)	700	700	400	8720
Blood perfusion (1/s)	0.8e−3	0.5e−3	0.2e−3	0.1e−1
Blood specific heat (J/kg °C)	4200	4200	4200	4200
Blood density (kg/m^3)	1060	1060	1060	1060

3 Methodology

This work follows the one in Gonçalo et al. [6] to calculate the temperature raise through the modelled tissue. The problem is formulated as an inverse problem, where the temperature measured on the skin surface is used to determine how parameters of the input model should be in order to estimate both center and radius, and the blood perfusion of the yet unknown breast tumor. To estimate such parameters, this work uses a Genetic Algorithm (GA) in which each genotype is comprised of the radius r of the tumor, its center x_r and y_r, and its blood perfusion ω. The target of the function is a set of calculated skin temperature of a reference model, and the objective is to minimize the temperature difference on the skin surface between each individual model generated and the target model through Eq. 2.

3.1 Model Generation Through Gmsh

To generate Wahab's breast cancer model mesh, the open-source software Gmsh was used. To create the mesh, the geometric model, represented in Fig. 1, is defined as described below:

- An outer semi-circle of diameter 14.4 cm defines the outermost boundary (skin surface) of the model.
- An inner semi-circle of diameter 13.4 cm, separates the fat outer layer D_3 from the inner mammary gland layer D_2.
- The innermost ellipse defines the muscle layer and has 2.2 cm y-radius and 6.7 cm x-radius.
- A circle inside the middle layer, defined as the mammary gland layer, represents the tumor. Its radius is variable, though the target (reference) model uses it as having 1 cm radius.

Each layer with its own physical properties is defined as a separate group that, during the evaluation process, will receive different levels of refinement in the mesh. The input model for each mesh is represented in Fig. 2, which is also the target model for the GA. After processing by Gmsh, the final generated mesh is represented in Fig. 3(a).

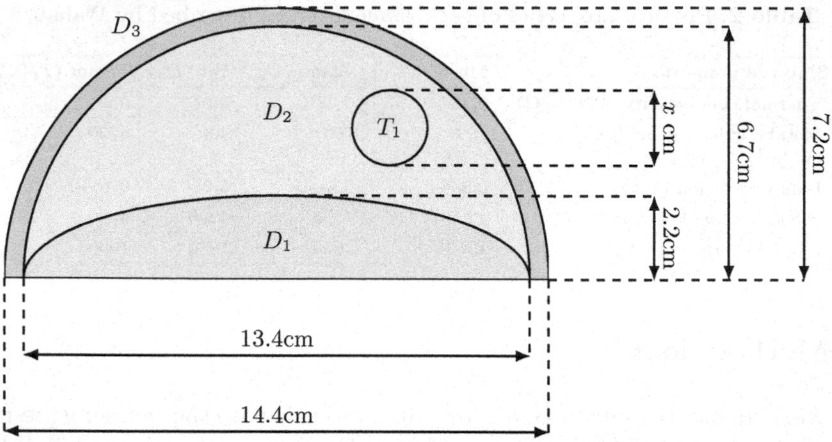

Fig. 1. Breast cancer model based on Wahab's model used as mesh generation reference. D_1 is the muscular layer; D_2, the mammary gland; D_3 the fat layer; and T_1 the tumor.

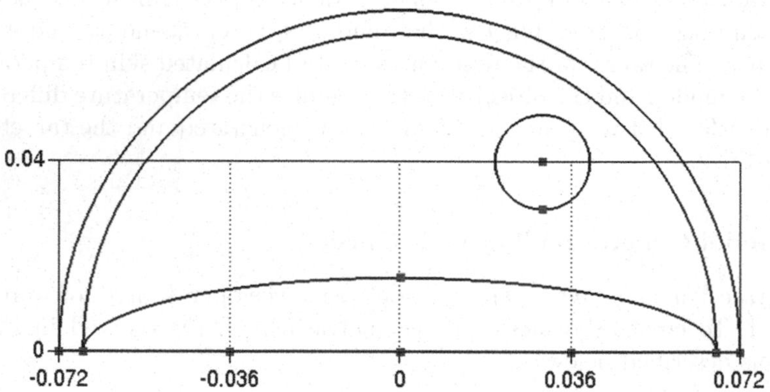

Fig. 2. Geometric model used as input for mesh generation on Gmsh. This model is also the reference model for the objective function on the GA.

3.2 Genetic Algorithm

Three different strategies of GA were used on this work: a classic generational GA; a steady-state algorithm; and an operator-independent strategy, developed for this problem. All of them use the same objective function, defined by Eq. 6, which will be discussed on Sect. 3.3. Each individual in the GA has its genotype defined by the tumor radius, its respective centre on a bi-dimensional plane and its blood perfusion. Each strategy can be described as follows:

- Generational GAs are the most traditional form of GA and use a random set of individuals that evolve, based on the Darwin's evolution theory, by selecting

the best individuals of each generation and applying a set of operators to pass the best genotypes to the next generation.
- Steady-state GAs do not apply the concept of "generations" between populations of generated individuals. All the operators are applied within the same population, and each new generated individual substitutes the worst ones.
- A third strategy, developed and based on the generational GA, create different groups of individuals based on the operator applied to create each individual, then merge all those groups to create a new generation. This method isolates the effect of each operator in the process, making easier to determine the influence of each operator within the population. This strategy was developed due to the heavy influence of the crossover over the mutation in this real inverse problem.

Other techniques, applied on all three strategies, include elitism, which tries to keep the best individuals for the next generation, and it is a default method in steady-state GAs, where most of the population, except the very worst individuals, is within the elitism margin; and partial re-initialization of the population, which creates random individuals on-the-fly for some of the generations. Both strategies can be described as tools that help the algorithm's performance [7].

All the GAs used in this current work are real GAs and use real numbers on the genotype of the individuals. As such, the operators used to solve the problem also considers the rational nature of the problem. The arithmetic crossover generates a couple of individuals y_1 and y_2 based on the Eq. 3, where x_1 and x_2 are the selected parents, and α is an uniformly distributed random value between x_1 and x_2, weighting randomly which parent will have more influence on each offspring value.

$$\begin{aligned} y_1 &= \alpha x_1 + (1-\alpha)x_2 \\ y_2 &= \alpha x_2 + (1-\alpha)x_1 \end{aligned} \tag{3}$$

Similarly, the mutation also uses a randomly uniform value around the value of the x_i parent genotype to generate the y_i value, as shown in Eq. 4. This value limited by γ_i, which varies differently for the centre, the blood perfusion and for the radius.

$$y_i = y_i + \alpha, \quad \alpha \in [-\gamma_i, \gamma_i] \tag{4}$$

The selection for the next generation in the generational and operator independent strategies is carried out by tournament, which chooses an n number of random individuals, then selects the one of those for the next generation with probability of p_1 for the best evaluated individual, then consecutively decreasing probability p_i for the rest of the individuals, following Eq. 5.

$$p_i = p((1-p)^{i-1}) \tag{5}$$

3.3 Evaluation

The evaluation process uses a modified version of Eq. 2, with the addition of the blood perfusion variable ω as input for the skin temperature calculation, and compares the skin surface temperature of the target model with the one of each generated individual model as represented by Eq. 6.

$$J(\mathbf{x}_r, r, \omega) = \frac{1}{2} \sum_{i \in \eta_{\Gamma_S}} (\hat{T}_i - T_i(\mathbf{x}_r, r, \omega))^2 \tag{6}$$

Each individual generated by the AG has its own temperature field computed on the nodes of the mesh through the PBHTE, described by Eq. 1, using the finite element method. The individuals that approaches the most from the target model's skin surface temperature curve are considered the best, thus having better chance of being selected for the next generations and to generate offspring through the operators.

4 Testing and Experimental Results

Using the model represented in Fig. 3(a) as the target model and the parameters described at Table 3, each GA strategy was tested in order to find evidence that the method could estimate the centre and the radius, as well as the blood perfusion of the tumor inside Wahab's model. Table 3 shows the parameter configuration for each of the algorithms tested. The method was developed under OCTAVE software and ran on a Intel® Core i7-4790 at 3.60 GHz, with 16 GB DDR3 RAM memory.

Table 3. Final parameter configuration used for the testing of each GA strategy.

Parameter	Generational	Steady-state	Operator-independent
Number of executions	15	15	15
Number of iterations	200	5000	200
Population size	200	200	200
Crossover rate	0.8	0.8	0.8
Mutation rate	0.01	0.1	0.1
Elitism rate	0.1	-*	0.1

*Steady-state algorithm does not have elitism rate.

Table 4 shows the resulting model characteristics generated by each strategy, its genotype for centre, radius and blood perfusion, and its respective objective function. All three strategies generated individuals very close to the target model, with the objective function value varying between 2.3456e−08 and 2.7460e−09, and the operator independent GA performing a little better than the others. Each generated best model for each strategy is represented at Fig. 3.

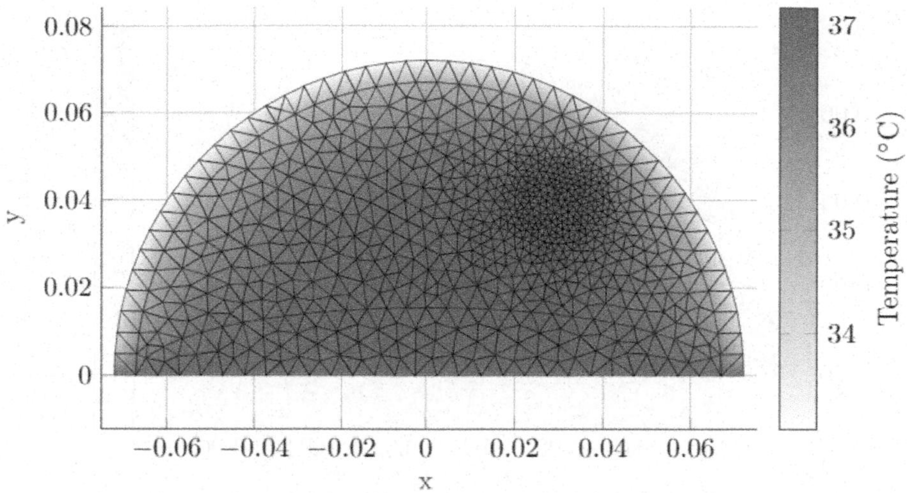

(a) Target model

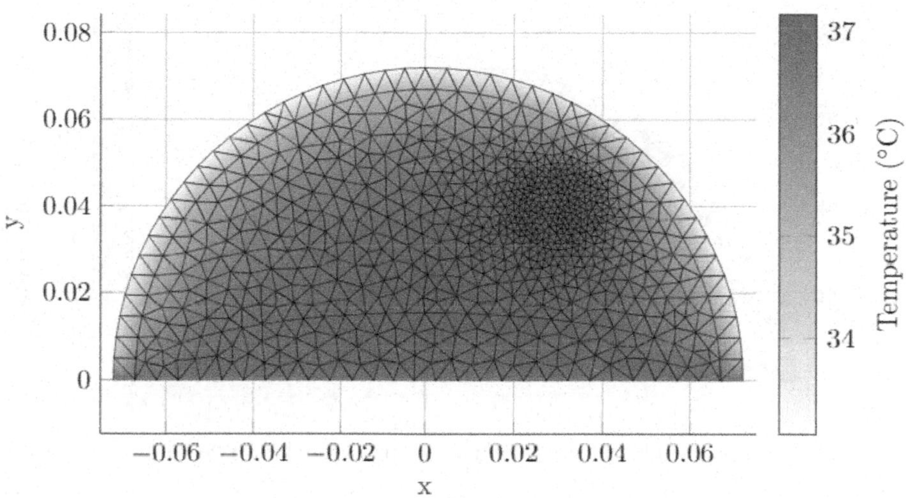

(b) Generational GA

Fig. 3. The target model used for reference and each generated model temperature map by different strategies used in this work.

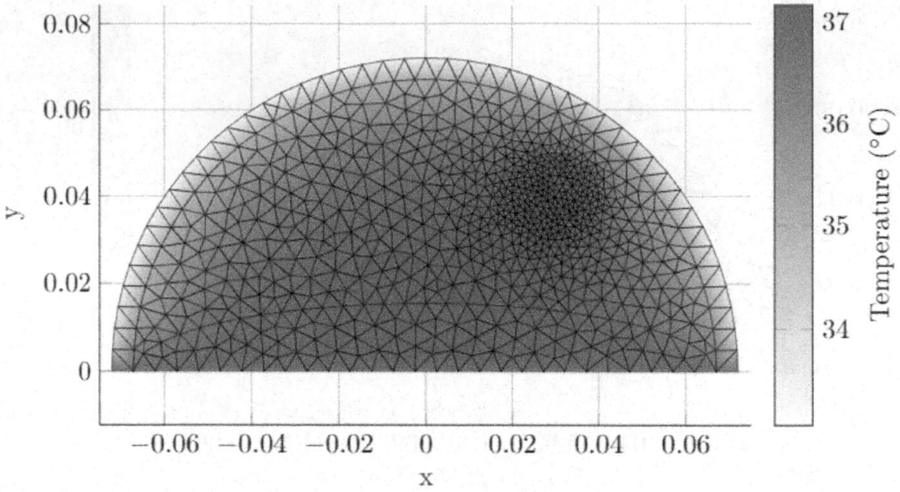

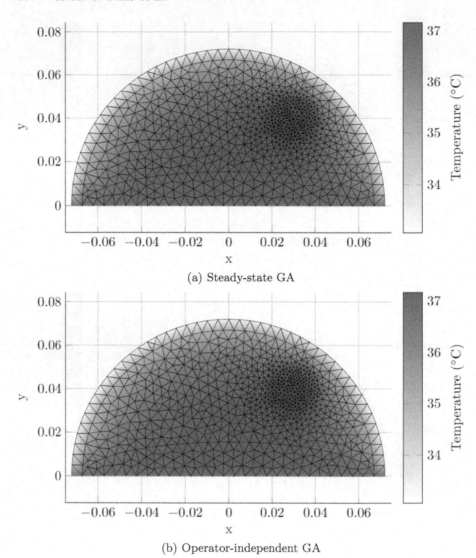

(a) Steady-state GA

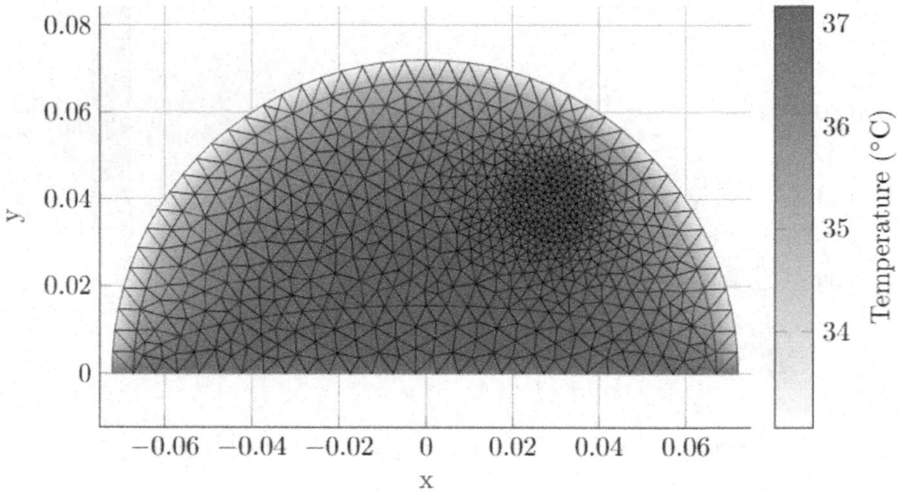

(b) Operator-independent GA

Fig. 3. (*continued*)

Table 4. Results for the three GA strategies in comparison to the target model used as reference for the objective function. r is the radius, x_r and y_r defines its centre and ω indicates the blood perfusion.

Model	r	x_r	y_r	ω	$J(\mathbf{x}_r, r, \omega)$
Target	1.0000e−03	3.0000e−02	4.0000e−02	1.0000e−02	–
Operator independent GA	9.9980e−03	3.0001e−02	4.0001e−02	1.0022e−02	2.7460e−09
Steady-state GA	9.9976e−03	3.0006e−02	4.0010e−02	9.8934e−03	1.6576e−09
Generational GA	9.9991e−03	3.0014e−02	4.0022e−02	9.6939e−03	2.3456e−08

5 Conclusion

The application of three different GA strategies on the inverse problem showed some evidence that the method could potentially work on tumor detection. The used breast cancer model, being more complex than other similar works, approaches more of a real problem than more simple and geometric abstract models. The solution of the PBHTE through FEM permits the GA to have precise metrics on determining simultaneously the geometric parameters and the blood perfusion of the tumor in the 2D model, and could as well help doctors to develop protocols for the detection of tumors based on thermal analysis.

6 Future Work

Future works that include the application of the current methodology on more realistic models, as well as 3D models, could determine real applications of the methodology proposed by this present work. The number of physical properties, layers of tissues, and other variables could also be increased to reach even more precise models.

References

1. Cruz, J.A., Wishart, D.S.: Applications of machine learning in cancer prediction and prognosis. Cancer Inf. **2**, 117693510600200030 (2006)
2. Das, K., Mishra, S.C.: Non-invasive estimation of size and location of a tumor in a human breast using a curve fitting technique. Int. Commun. Heat Mass Transf. **56**, 63–70 (2014)
3. Das, K., Mishra, S.C.: Simultaneous estimation of size, radial and angular locations of a malignant tumor in a 3-d human breast-a numerical study. J. Therm. Biol. **52**, 147–156 (2015)
4. Geuzaine, C., Remacle, J.F.: Gmsh: a 3-d finite element mesh generator with built-in pre-and post-processing facilities. Int. J. Numer. Meth. Eng. **79**(11), 1309–1331 (2009)
5. Gonçalo, A: Application of genetic algorithms for the solution of the inverse bioheat transfer problem for the detection of breast tumors (2018). Graduation final project (in Portuguese)

6. Gonçalo Filho, A.M., Nogueira, L.L., Silveira, J.V.C., Loureiro, M.M.S., dos Santos Loureiro, F.: Solution of the inverse bioheat transfer problem for the detection of tumors by genetic algorithms. In: Gervasi, O., et al. (eds.) ICCSA 2017. LNCS, vol. 10405, pp. 441–452. Springer, Cham (2017). https://doi.org/10.1007/978-3-319-62395-5_30
7. Kora, P., Yadlapalli, P.: Crossover Operators in Genetic Algorithms: A Review (2006)
8. Kourou, K., Exarchos, T.P., Exarchos, K.P., Karamouzis, M.V., Fotiadis, D.I.: Machine learning applications in cancer prognosis and prediction. Comput. Struct. Biotechnol. J. **13**, 8–17 (2015)
9. Melo, A.R., Loureiro, M.M.S., Loureiro, F.S.: Blood perfusion parameter estimation in tumors by means of a genetic algorithm. Procedia Comput. Sci. **108**, 1384–1393 (2017)
10. Partridge, P., Wrobel, L.: An inverse geometry problem for the localisation of skin tumours by thermal analysis. Eng. Anal. Boundary Elem. **31**(10), 803–811 (2007)
11. Pennes, H.H.: Analysis of tissue and arterial blood temperatures in the resting human forearm. J. Appl. Physiol. **1**(2), 93–122 (1948)
12. Sudharsan, N., Ng, E., Teh, S.: Surface temperature distribution of a breast with and without tumour. Comput. Meth. Biomech. Biomed. Eng. **2**(3), 187–199 (1999)
13. Wahab, A.A., Salim, M.I.M., Ahamat, M.A., Manaf, N.A., Yunus, J., Lai, K.W.: Thermal distribution analysis of three-dimensional tumor-embedded breast models with different breast density compositions. Med. Biol. Eng. Comput. **54**(9), 1363–1373 (2015). https://doi.org/10.1007/s11517-015-1403-7

A Numerical Method for the Transient Couette Flow of a Distributed-Order Viscoelastic Fluid

Luis L. Ferrás[1(✉)], M. L. Morgado[2,3], and Magda Rebelo[4]

[1] Centro de Matemática, Departamento de Matemática, Universidade do Minho, Campus de Azurém, 4800-058 Guimarães, Portugal
llima@math.uminho.pt
[2] Center for Computational and Stochastic Mathematics (CEMAT), Instituto Superior Técnico, Universidade de Lisboa, Lisboa, Portugal
[3] Department of Mathematics, University of Trás-os-Montes e Alto Douro, UTAD, Vila Real, Portugal
luisam@utad.pt
[4] Centro de Matemática e Aplicações (CMA) and Departamento de Matemática, Faculdade de Ciências e Tecnologia, Universidade NOVA de Lisboa, Quinta da Torre, 2829-516 Caparica, Portugal
msjr@fct.unl.pt
https://www.cmat.uminho.pt, http://cemat.ist.utl.pt/, http://matematica.utad.pt/, https://www.cma.fct.unl.pt/, https://www.dm.fct.unl.pt/

Abstract. This work presents a numerical method for the solution of two coupled distributed-order fractional differential equations, that appear in the pure tangential flow of fluids modelled by the Distributed-Order Viscoelastic Model. We prove the solvability of the method, and, perform numerical simulations of relaxation tests.

Keywords: Distributed-order fractional derivatives · Numerical methods · Finite differences · Viscoelasticity

1 Introduction

The word polymers comes from the Greek poly, meaning "many," and mere, meaning "parts," because the macromolecules of these compounds are formed by joining several units of small molecules called monomers.

Supported by FCT - Fundação para a Ciência e a Tecnologia, through projects: UIDB/00013/2020 and UIDP/00013/2020 (CMAT - Centre of Mathematics - University of Minho); UIDB/04621/2020 and UIDP/04621/2020 (CEMAT/IST-ID, Center for Computational and Stochastic Mathematics, Instituto Superior Técnico, University of Lisbon). This work was also partially supported by FCT through the project UIDB/00297/2020 (Centro de Matemática e Aplicações).

O. Gervasi et al. (Eds.): ICCSA 2021, LNCS 12952, pp. 411–421, 2021.
https://doi.org/10.1007/978-3-030-86973-1_29

Polymers were not invented by man, they already existed in nature. Some examples of macromolecules that have been used by man for thousands of years are in cotton, wool, silk, animal hooves, ivory and starch (which is found in vegetables and in the form of grains from seeds and roots of various plants, such as: Potato, wheat, rice, corn and cassava).

With the industrial revolution, the need to understand the behaviour of such complex materials increased, and several researchers began to develop experiments and theoretical models to understand this behaviour.

In the literature one can find several differential and integral models that can mimic the behaviour of complex material (such as polymers) under different deformations [1–10]. Each model has its own advantages and disadvantages when compared to others.

Recently, the research group devised a generalised viscoelastic model based on distributed-order derivatives of the Caputo type [11]. The model is able to fit well experimental rheological data obtained in the linear regime for food products (that behave as critical gels [12]).

To better understand the model behaviour, one can derive either analytical solutions or numerical methods. Since analytical solutions are difficult to obtain for such complex models (they are restricted to limited flows and geometries), numerical methods seem to be the only and best choice.

In this work we develop a numerical method for the solution of the 1D transient Couette flow of a Distributed-Order Viscoelastic Model (DOVM). The method is based on finite differences [8,13].

The remaining of this work is organised as follows. In Sect. 2 the DOVM is introduced together with some basic definitions. The governing equations are presented in Sect. 3. Section 4 is devoted to the development of a numerical method and its validation. The numerical results are presented in Sect. 5. The work ends with the conclusions in Sect. 6.

2 The Distributed-Order Viscoelastic Model (DOVM)

In order to introduce the DOVM, some basic definitions are needed first.

Definition 1. *The* ***single order fractional derivative*** *in the* ***Caputo*** *sense* $(0 < \alpha < 1)$ *is given by [14]:*

$$ {}_0^C D_t^{\alpha} f(t) = \frac{1}{\Gamma(1-\alpha)} \int_0^t (t-t')^{-\alpha} \frac{df(t')}{dt'} dt'. \tag{1} $$

Definition 2. *The* ***Caputo Distributed-Order Fractional Derivative*** $({}_0^C\mathbb{D}_t)$ *of a general function* f *is given by:*

$$ {}_0^C\mathbb{D}_t f(t) = \int_0^1 c(\alpha) {}_0^C D_t^{\alpha} f(t)\, d\alpha = \int_0^1 c(\alpha) \frac{1}{\Gamma(1-\alpha)} \int_0^t (t-t')^{-\alpha} \frac{df(t')}{dt'} dt'\, d\alpha \tag{2} $$

where the function $c(\alpha)$ *(acting as weight for the order of differentiation) is such that* $c(\alpha) \geq 0$ *and* $\int_0^1 c(\alpha)\, d\alpha = C > 0$ *([15, 16]).*

The function $c(\alpha)$ is used to represent mathematically the presence of multiple memory formalisms. If $c(\alpha) = \delta(\alpha - \beta)$, where $\delta(\cdot)$ is the delta Dirac function, then (2) reduces to the Caputo derivative ${}_0^C D_t^{\beta} f\,(t)$.

The Distributed-Order Fractional Viscoelastic Model (DOVM) is given by

$$\sigma\,(t) = {}_0^C\, \mathbb{D}_t \gamma(t). \tag{3}$$

were ${}_0^C \mathbb{D}_t$ is the distributed-order derivative of the Caputo type, $\sigma(t)$ is the stress and $\gamma(t)$ the strain or deformation.

The model can be seen as the classical Boltzmann model,

$$\sigma\,(t) = \int_0^t G(t-t')\frac{d\gamma(t')}{dt'}dt' \tag{4}$$

with the relaxation modulus $G(t)$ given in the form:

$$G\,(t) = \int_0^1 \frac{c(\alpha)}{\Gamma(1-\alpha)} t^{-\alpha}\, d\alpha. \tag{5}$$

Fore more details on the derivation of the DOVM model please consult the reference [11].

3 Governing Equations for a 1D Transient Couette Flow

In fluid mechanics, Couette flow refers to the laminar flow of a viscous fluid in the space between two parallel planes (plates), one of which is moving relative to the other (Fig. 1).

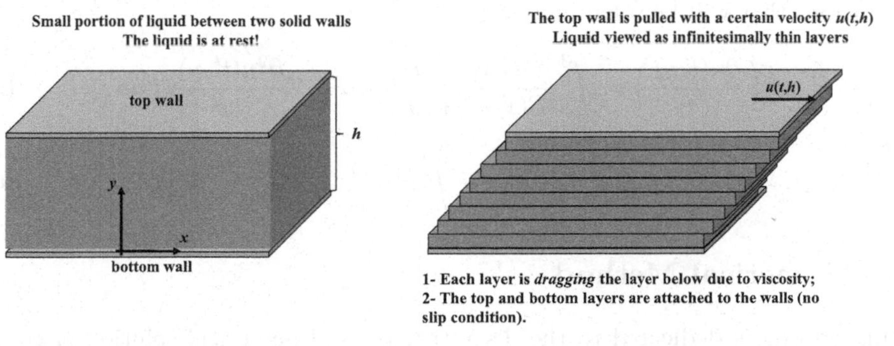

Fig. 1. Illustration of a Couette flow. A certain velocity $u(t, h)$ is imposed at the resting upper wall. As this wall moves along time, the displacement information travels along the different layers of fluid until it reaches the bottom wall. Note that these layers are merely illustrative.

The flow is driven by the drag force acting on it. This type of fluid is named after Maurice Marie Alfred Couette, a physics professor at the French University of Angers in the late 19th century.

The equations governing the 1D transient Couette flow are obtained from a simplification of the Navier-Stokes equations, together with an extra equation for the stress, given (in this case) by the DOVM. Note that we consider a small transient deformation, so that the DOVM (which is not invariant [9]) can be used (only invariant models can be used for large deformations).

We saw before that the stress was only a function of time, because, it was being measured at a specific point in space. In the 1D case, the stress $\sigma(t, y)$ and velocity $u(t, y)$ (that is obtained from the rate of deformation $d\gamma(t)/dt$ [9]) also vary in space (along y). In this particular flow, the stress has more than one component, being the one of interest denoted by σ_{xy} (shear stress). The governing equations are given by:

$$\rho\left(\frac{\partial u(t,y)}{\partial t}\right) = \frac{\partial \sigma_{xy}(t,y)}{\partial y} \tag{6}$$

$$\sigma_{xy}(t,y) = \int_0^t G(t-t')\frac{\partial u(t',y)}{\partial y}dt' \tag{7}$$

were ρ is the fluid density, and, it was assumed that only tangential movement exists. The velocity profile is given by $(u, v) = (u, 0)$. This means that, for a fixed t, we can only see changes in velocity when moving in the transverse direction.

To solve this system of equations we do the following. First, we substitute (7) into (6), resulting in an integro-differential equation for the velocity:

$$\rho\left(\frac{\partial u(t,y)}{\partial t}\right) = \frac{\partial}{\partial y}\left(\int_0^t \int_0^1 \frac{c(\alpha)}{\Gamma(1-\alpha)}(t-t')^{-\alpha} d\alpha \frac{\partial u(t',y)}{\partial y} dt'\right). \tag{8}$$

Second, with the velocity profile obtained from solving (8) we can easily calculate the stress from (7). (8) can be rewritten by changing the integration and differentiation order. This results in the following system of integro-differential equations that will be solved numerically:

$$\rho\left(\frac{\partial u(t,y)}{\partial t}\right) = \int_0^1 \frac{c(\alpha)}{\Gamma(1-\alpha)} \int_0^t (t-t')^{-\alpha} \frac{\partial^2 u(t',y)}{\partial y^2} dt' d\alpha, \tag{9}$$

$$\sigma_{xy}(t,y) = \int_0^1 \frac{c(\alpha)}{\Gamma(1-\alpha)} \int_0^t (t-t')^{-\alpha} \frac{\partial u(t',y)}{\partial y} dt' d\alpha. \tag{10}$$

4 Numerical Method

This Section is dedicated to the discretisation and numerical solution of equations (9) and (10). To test the convergence of the method we analyse the precision of the numerical scheme by comparing the numerical results with generalised analytical solutions.

4.1 Discretisation of the Velocity and Shear Stress Equations

We will now derive a numerical method for the solution of the system (9)–(10), with boundary and initial conditions of Dirichlet type:

$$u(t,0)=0,\ u(t,h)=\phi_h(t),\quad 0<t<T, \tag{11}$$

$$u(0,y)=\frac{\partial u(0,y)}{\partial t}=0,\ \sigma_{x,y}(0,y)=0,\qquad y\in[0,h],\ h>0 \tag{12}$$

Note that the viscoelastic fluid is at rest and fully relaxed at $t=0^-$.

Numerically, we need to obtain an approximation for all the operators (time and spatial derivatives). For that, we consider a uniform space mesh on the interval $[0,h]$, defined by the gridpoints $y_i=i\Delta y$, $i=0,\ldots,N$, where $\Delta y=\frac{h}{N}$. For the discretisation of the fractional time derivative we also assume a uniform mesh, with a time step $\Delta t=T/S$ and time gridpoints $t_s=s\Delta t$, $s=0,1,\ldots,S$.

At $t=t_s$ the integral on the right-hand side of the momentum equation can be written as,

$$\begin{aligned}&\int_0^1\frac{c(\alpha)}{\Gamma(1-\alpha)}\int_0^{t_s}(t_s-t')^{-\alpha}\frac{\partial^2u(t',y)}{\partial y^2}dt'd\alpha\\&=\int_0^1\frac{c(\alpha)}{\Gamma(1-\alpha)}\sum_{j=0}^{s-1}\int_{t_j}^{t_{j+1}}(t_s-t')^{-\alpha}\frac{\partial^2u(t',y)}{\partial y^2}dt'd\alpha\end{aligned} \tag{13}$$

for $s=1,\ldots,S$. We define u_i^s as the approximation of $u(t_s,y_i)$, $i=1,\ldots,N-1$, $s=1,\ldots,S$. The following approximation is considered for the integration in time:

$$\begin{aligned}\int_{t_j}^{t_{j+1}}(t_s-t')^{-\alpha}\frac{\partial^2u(t',y)}{\partial y^2}dt'&\approx\frac{u_{i+1}^{j+1}-2u_i^{j+1}+u_{i-1}^{j+1}}{(\Delta y)^2}\int_{t_j}^{t_{j+1}}(t_s-t')^{-\alpha}dt'\\&=\frac{u_{i+1}^{j+1}-2u_i^{j+1}+u_{i-1}^{j+1}}{(\Delta y)^2}\frac{\Delta t^{1-\alpha}d_{sj}(\alpha)}{1-\alpha}\end{aligned} \tag{14}$$

with $d_{sj}(\alpha)=(s-j)^{1-\alpha}-(s-(j+1))^{1-\alpha}$.

This results in the following discretized equation:

$$\rho\frac{\partial u(t,y)}{\partial t}=\int_0^1F(\alpha)d\alpha \tag{15}$$

with

$$F(\alpha)=\frac{c(\alpha)(\Delta t)^{1-\alpha}}{\Gamma(2-\alpha)(\Delta y)^2}\sum_{j=0}^{s-1}(u_{i+1}^{j+1}-2u_i^{j+1}+u_{i-1}^{j+1})d_{sj}(\alpha). \tag{16}$$

A simple first order approximation for the time derivative, and the use of the midpoint rule to approximate the integral in the interval [0, 1] considering the gridpoints $\alpha_l = (l-1/2)\Delta\alpha$, $l = 1,\ldots,P$, $\Delta\alpha = 1/P$, leads to the following discretized velocity equation:

$$\begin{aligned}\rho\frac{u_i^s - u_i^{s-1}}{\Delta t} &= \Delta\alpha\sum_{l=1}^{P} F(\alpha_l)\\ &= \Delta\alpha\sum_{l=1}^{P}\frac{c(\alpha_l)(\Delta t)^{1-\alpha_l}}{\Gamma(2-\alpha_l)(\Delta y)^2}\sum_{j=0}^{s-1}(u_{i+1}^{j+1} - 2u_i^{j+1} + u_{i-1}^{j+1})d_{sj}(\alpha_l)\end{aligned} \tag{17}$$

for $i = 1,\ldots,N-1$ and $s = 1,\ldots,S$ (for each time step we need to solve a system of equations).

After solving each system of equations, an approximation of velocity at time and space mesh points is known, and, the evolution of the shear stress, equation (10), can be easily obtained for the same time and space mesh points using:

$$\sigma_{xy_i}^s = \Delta\alpha\sum_{l=1}^{P}\frac{c(\alpha_l)(\Delta t)^{1-\alpha_l}}{2\Gamma(2-\alpha_l)\Delta y}\sum_{j=0}^{s-1}(u_{i+1}^{j+1} - u_{i-1}^{j+1})d_{sj}(\alpha_l) \tag{18}$$

where $\sigma_{xy_i}^s$ is the approximation of $\sigma_{xy}(t_s, y_i)$, $i = 1,\ldots,N-1$, $s = 1,\ldots,S$.

4.2 Solvability

In the matrix form, (9) writes:

$$AU^s = \rho U^{s-1} + \sum_{j=0}^{s-2} B_j U^{j+1} + \sum_{j=0}^{s-2} C_j,\quad s = 1,2,\ldots,S \tag{19}$$

where

$$U^j = [u_1^j,\, u_2^j,\, \ldots,\, u_N^j]^T, \tag{20}$$

$$B_j = \begin{pmatrix} 2Q & -Q & & & \\ -Q & 2Q & Q & & \\ & -Q & 2Q & Q & \\ & & \ddots & \ddots & \ddots \\ & & & & \\ & & -Q & 2Q & Q \\ & & & -Q & 2Q \end{pmatrix}, \tag{21}$$

with

$$Q = \Delta\alpha\Delta t\sum_{l=1}^{P}\frac{c(\alpha_l)(\Delta t)^{1-\alpha_l}}{\Gamma(2-\alpha_l)\Delta y^2}d_{sj}(\alpha_l). \tag{22}$$

C_j is given by,

$$C_j = \begin{pmatrix} 0 \\ 0 \\ \vdots \\ \\ Q\phi_h(t_{j+1}) \end{pmatrix}. \tag{23}$$

A is a tridiagonal matrix

$$A = \begin{pmatrix} \rho+2M & -M & & & & \\ -M & \rho+2M & -M & & & \\ & -M & \rho+2M & -M & & \\ & \ddots & \ddots & \ddots & & \\ & & & & & \\ & & & -M & \rho+2M & -M \\ & & & & -M & \rho+2M \end{pmatrix}$$

with

$$M \equiv M(\Delta\alpha, \Delta t, \Delta y) = \Delta\alpha\Delta t \sum_{l=1}^{P} \frac{c(\alpha_l)(\Delta t)^{1-\alpha_l}}{\Gamma(2-\alpha_l)(\Delta y)^2}. \tag{24}$$

A is a strictly diagonal dominant matrix and therefore the system is uniquely solved.

4.3 Validation

To assess the robustness of the numerical method, we developed a non-smooth analytical solution (for the velocity equation), by imposing a certain velocity profile, through the inclusion of correcting source terms, $f(t, y)$.

We consider the following problem:

$$\begin{cases} \rho\dfrac{\partial u(x,t)}{\partial t} - _0^1 \dfrac{\Gamma(5/2-\alpha)}{\Gamma(1-\alpha)} \displaystyle\int_0^t (t-s)^{-\alpha} \dfrac{\partial^2 u(x,t)}{\partial y^2} ds = \dfrac{x^3 \log(t) - 6\sqrt{\pi}(t-1)tx}{2\sqrt{t}\log(t)} \\ u(0,y) = 0, \ 0 < y < h \\ u(t,0) = 0, \ u(t,L) = t^{1/2}h^3 \ 0 < t \leq 1 \end{cases} \tag{25}$$

with analytical solution $u(t, y) = t^{1/2}y^3$.

To evaluate the accuracy of the numerical predictions, we define:

$$\varepsilon_{\Delta t,\Delta y} = \max_{k=1,\dots,N-1} \left| u\left(t_i, y_k\right) - u^{num}\left(t_i, y_k\right)\right|, \; i = 1, 2, \dots, S \tag{26}$$

Figure 2 shows the 3D plot of the analytical solution and the results obtained numerically for $h = 0.1$, $t = 0.5$, $\Delta\alpha = 0.1$, $\Delta t = 0.01$ and $\Delta y = 0.002$. This resulted in $\varepsilon_{\Delta t,\Delta y} = 1.40337\times10^{-6}$. For a courser mesh with $\Delta\alpha = 0.2$, $\Delta t = 0.1$ and $\Delta x = 0.02$ we still obtained a small error $\varepsilon_{\Delta t,\Delta y} = 1.41838 \times 10^{-5}$.

We can therefore conclude that the numerical method converges easily to the singular analytical solution, illustrating the robustness of the numerical scheme.

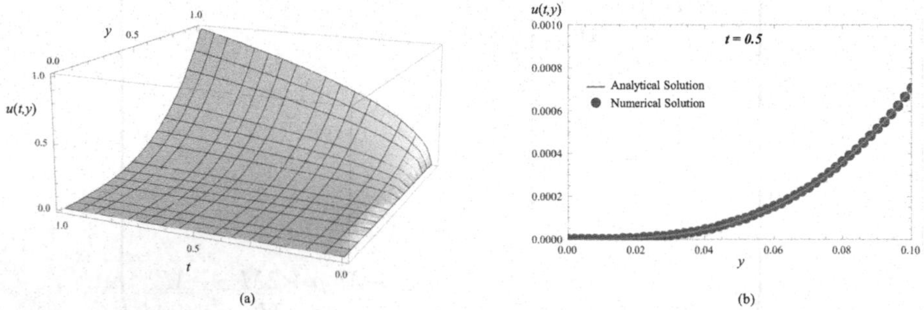

Fig. 2. (a) 3D plot of the analytical solution given by $u(t, y) = t^{1/2}y^3$. (b) Comparison between the analytical and numerical solutions for $h = 0.1$, $t = 0.5$, $\Delta\alpha = 0.1$, $\Delta t = 0.01$ and $\Delta y = 0.002$ ($\varepsilon_{\Delta t,\Delta y} = 1.40337 \times 10^{-6}$).

5 Numerical Results

One way to experimentally characterise viscoelastic fluids is to perform a relaxation test, i.e., we impose a step displacement given by $\gamma = \gamma_0 H(t - a)$ (with $H(t)$ the Heaviside function) and measure the stress response to this deformation. At time $t = a$ we impose a constant deformation, and we observe that the stress relaxes until it becomes zero (Fig. 3).

To mimic the step-strain test illustrated in Fig. 3, the upper wall suddenly starts moving at $t = 0^+$ with a tangential velocity given by,

$$u\left(t, h\right) = \frac{\Delta_{wall}}{\psi\sqrt{\pi}} e^{-\frac{(t-t_d)^2}{\psi^2}}. \tag{27}$$

and then stops (after a period of $\Delta t_{exp} \approx 50\,\text{ms}$). Then we observe how the tangential stress in the fluid relaxes.

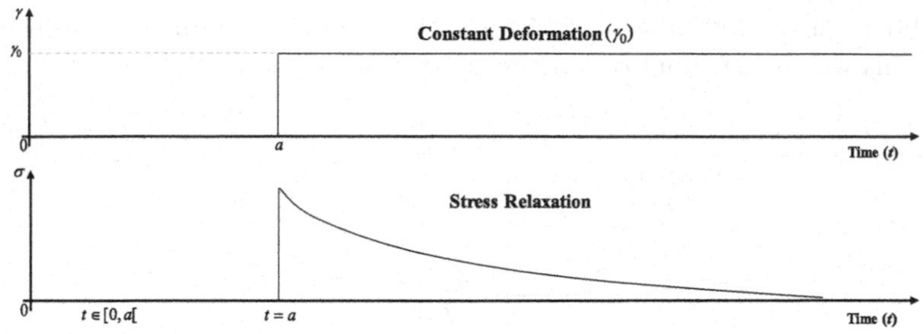

Fig. 3. Stress relaxation of a viscoelastic material after a step displacement.

As $\psi \to 0$, the velocity converges to the Dirac delta function multiplied by the displacement of the upper wall, $\Delta_{wall}\delta(t)$ (assuming $t_d = 0$). The need for the delay time, t_d, comes from the initial condition $\frac{du(0,h)}{dt} = 0$. This step-strain is illustrated in Fig. 4.

Figure 4 (a) shows the initial and final state of the deformation. After 50 ms the upper wall stops moving (the displacement is Δ_{wall}). Figure 4 (b) shows the variation of the upper wall velocity along the 50 ms. For this case we considered a deformation ($\gamma_0 = \Delta_{wall}/h$) of 100%.

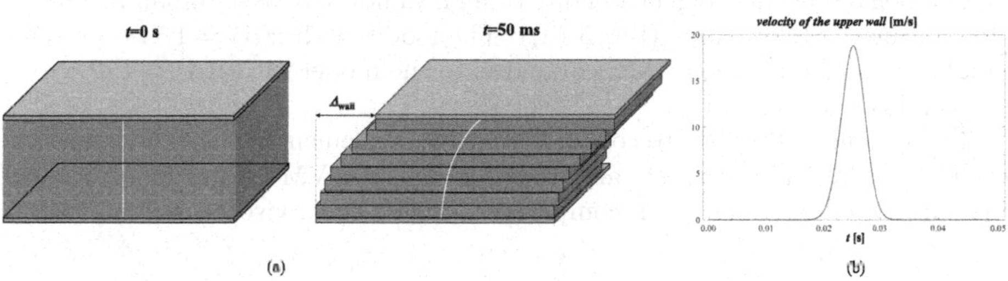

Fig. 4. Step displacement. (a) Initial and final state of the deformation. After 50 ms the upper wall stops moving (the displacement is Δ_{wall}). (b) Variation of the upper wall velocity along the 50 ms. The deformation ($\gamma_0 = \Delta_{wall}/h$) is 100%, $\psi = 0.003$ and the delay (t_d) is 0.025 s.

5.1 Case Study

After some preliminary experiments with the step-strain problem, the trade-off between simulation time and accuracy resulted in a mesh size of $\Delta t = 2 \times 10^{-3}$, $\Delta y = 2.5 \times 10^{-3}$ and $\Delta \alpha = 0.1$. Note that these parameters are dimensional and not scaled with the relaxation of the fluid. This happens because the DOVM represents an infinite set of relaxations weighted by the function $c(\alpha)$.

Figure 5 shows the stress relaxation test in a narrow gap Couette cell following a sudden straining deformation (the upper wall moves) for $\gamma_0 = 100\%$, $\psi = 0.003$ and $t_d = 0.025$ s.

We have considered different $c(\alpha)$ functions in order to understand the influence of this weighting function on the relaxation of the DOVM.

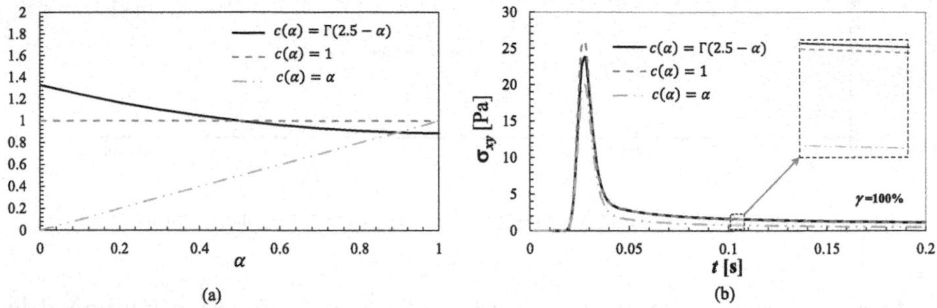

Fig. 5. (a) Three different functions $c(\alpha)$. (b) Stress relaxation test in a narrow gap Couette cell following a sudden straining deformation (the upper wall moves) for $\gamma_0 = 100\%$) and different functions $c(\alpha)$.

As expected, for the case $c(\alpha) = \alpha$ we obtained a higher rate of relaxation when compared to $c(\alpha) = 1$ or $c(\alpha) = \Gamma(2.5 - \alpha)$ (Fig. 5 (a) and (b)). This happens because for $c(\alpha) = \alpha$ we attribute smaller weights to low values of α (elastic behaviour) and bigger weights to high values of α (Newtonian behaviour - instantaneous relaxation) (Fig. 5 (a)). The model with $c(\alpha) = 1$ also presents a higher rate of relaxation when compared to the model with $c(\alpha) = \Gamma(2.5 - \alpha)$ (see the inset in Fig. 5 (b)).

These results allow one to conclude that the implementation of the numerical method is physically correct, and that the new DOVM allows for a broader spectrum of relaxations, when compared to the classical viscoelastic models.

6 Conclusions

A new numerical method for solving the 1D Couette flow of a Distributed-Order Viscoelastic Model has been developed. We proved the solvability of the numerical scheme and analysed its convergence considering a non-smooth solution. The numerical method was used to study the relaxation of fluids (governed by the DOVM) under a step-strain.

This prototype numerical scheme can be improved by considering high order approximations in its derivation. This is an ongoing work, where we also analyse the convergence and stability of the fully discretized family of numerical schemes for this kind of problems.

References

1. Bird, R.B., Armstrong, R.C., Hassager, O.: Dynamics of Polymeric Liquids. Fluid Mechanics, 2nd edn., vol. I. Wiley (1987)

2. Boltzmann, L.: Zur Theorie der elastischen Nachwirkungen, Sitzungsber. Kaiserlich Akad. Wiss. (Wien) Math. Naturwiss. Classe **70**(II), 275 (1874)
3. Markovitz, H.: Boltzmann and the beginnings of linear viscoelasticity. Trans. Soc. Rheol. **21**, 381–398 (1977)
4. Maxwell, J.C.: On the dynamical theory of gases. Philos. Trans. R. Soc. Lond. **157**, 49–88 (1867)
5. Ferrás, L.L., et al.: Recent advances in complex fluids modeling. In: Fluid Flow Problems (2019)
6. Ferrás, L.L., Ford, N., Morgado, M.L., Rebelo, M., Mckinley, G.H., Nobrega, J.M.: A primer on experimental and computational rheology with fractional viscoelastic constitutive models. AIP Conf. Proc. **1843**, 020002 (2017). https://doi.org/10.1063/1.4982977
7. Ferrás, L.L., Morgado, M.L., Rebelo, M., Mckinley, G.H., Afonso, A.: A generalized Phan-Thien–Tanner model. J. Nonnewton. Fluid Mech. **269**, 88–99 (2019)
8. Ferrás, L.L., Ford, N., Morgado, M.L., Rebelo, M., Mckinley, G.H., Nobrega, J.M.: Theoretical and numerical analysis of unsteady fractional viscoelastic flows in simple geometries. Comput. Fluids **174**, 14–33 (2018)
9. Huilgol, R.R., Phan-Thien, N.: Fluid Mechanics of Viscoelasticity: General Principles, Constitutive Modelling and Numerical Techniques. Rheology Series, vol. 6 (1997)
10. Larson, R.G.: The Structure and Rheology of Complex Fluids, vol. 150. Oxford University Press, New York (1999)
11. Ferrás, L.L., Morgado, M.L., Rebelo, M.: A distributed order viscoelastic model for small deformations. In: 5th International Conference on Numerical and Symbolic Computation: Developments and Applications, SYMCOMP 2021 (2021). ISBN 978-989-99410-6-9
12. Keshavarz, B., Divoux, T., Manneville, S., McKinley, G.H.: Nonlinear viscoelasticity and generalized failure criterion for biopolymer gels. ACS Macro Lett. **6**(7), 663–667 (2017)
13. LeVeque, R.J.: Finite Difference Methods for Ordinary and Partial Differential Equations: Steady-State and Time-Dependent Problems. Society for Industrial and Applied Mathematics (2007)
14. Caputo, M.: Elasticità e Dissipazione. Zanichelli, Bologna, Italy (1969)
15. Gorenflo, R., Luchko, Y., Stojanovic, M.: Fundamental solution of a distributed order time-fractional diffusion-wave equation as probability density. Fract. Calc. Appl. Anal. **16**, 297–316 (2013)
16. Mainardi, F., Pagnini, G., Mura, A., Gorenflo, R.: Time-fractional diffusion of distributed order. J. Vib. Control **14**, 1267–1290 (2008)

Simulated Annealing and Iterated Local Search Approaches to the Aircraft Refueling Problem

Karyne Alves Zampirolli(✉) and André Renato Sales Amaral

Graduate School of Computer Science (PPGI), Federal University of Espírito Santo, UFES, Vitória 29075-910, Brazil
karyne.zampirolli@edu.ufes.br, amaral@inf.ufes.br

Abstract. In this paper, we present the Aircraft Refueling Problem (ARP), whose objective is to find the shortest distance traveled by tank trucks to meet fuel demands requested by aircraft at an airport. We describe a mixed-integer linear programming (MILP) model to represent this problem. Besides MILP, Simulated Annealing (SA) and Iterated Local Search (ILS) algorithms were implemented to solve the problem. We provide computational experiments with adapted instances representing a real airport to validate the model. The results show that SA and ILS were able to schedule refueling well.

Keywords: Aircraft refueling problem · Mixed-integer linear programming · Simulated annealing · Iterated local search

1 Introduction

At an airport, after an aircraft's arrival, ground services are provided to prepare the aircraft for its next departure. Ground services include unloading/loading baggage, cleaning toilets, loading catering supplies, and refueling.

Refueling would normally begin not long after landing because it requires some time to complete. Depending on the airport, aircraft might be refueled by means of hydrant systems and/or tank trucks. Small to medium airports usually utilize tank trucks. It is widely recognized that achieving efficiency in refueling operations is necessary for aircraft to land and take off without delay. Therefore, it is important to study the aircraft refueling activity. However, few studies have been found in the literature.

The objective of this work is to study the aircraft refueling problem (ARP) using tank trucks. The Aircraft Refueling Problem (ARP) can be formulated as a Vehicle Routing Problem with Time Windows (VRPTW), which is NP-hard. In the literature, the VRPTW has been studied by many authors such as [2,3,6] and [10]. However, among the many studies published in this field, there is little research that specifically addresses the topic of aircraft refueling. As far as we know, the first paper that presented a model for the aircraft refueling process is that by Babić [1].

O. Gervasi et al. (Eds.): ICCSA 2021, LNCS 12952, pp. 422–438, 2021.
https://doi.org/10.1007/978-3-030-86973-1_30

Babić [1] studied the ARP with two objectives: minimizing the number of refuelling trucks and minimizing the truck's total travelling distance. In his study, the former objective is assumed to be more important than the latter. He developed a solution approach based on branch-and-bound and solved a real case in which eight aircraft need to be refuelled.

Du et al. [4] solved the aircraft refueling problem using an Ant Colony Optimization (ACO) algorithm with MAX-MIN and Rankbased Ant System. They considered three objectives in order of importance. First: minimizing the number of vehicles; second: minimizing the sum of the service start time for each flight; and third: minimizing the total flow time of trucks. Their study also uses Non-Homogeneous vehicles.

Wang et al. [12] considered a mathematical model with time windows for the airport refueling vehicle scheduling problem (ARVSP). An evaluation function was devised to minimize the distance travelled by the vehicles and the number of vehicles utilized. A greedy algorithm was presented for the ARVSP and a practical example was solved.

Gamayanti et al. [5] examined the problem of refueling aircraft using refuelling trucks at Juanda Airport, Surabaya. The problem was formulated as the Vehicle Routing Problem with Short Time Windows, Short Travel Time and Reused Vehicles (VRPTSR). The objective was to determine the minimum number of trucks. By applying Ant Colony Optimization, they were able to reduce the number of trucks operating in DPPU Juanda Terminal 2.

Given the related works, we incorporated some different conditions to address the problem. Aircraft are located in a straight line. Refueling trucks approach the aircraft from the beginning of this line. To construct the route, it is not mandatory that aircraft i is served before aircraft $i+1$, if $a_i \leq a_{i+1}$, where a_i is the earliest moment at which refueling can start. The papers mentioned above require that refueling of aircraft i must occur before aircraft $i+1$.

We describe a mixed-integer linear programming (MILP) model and implemented Simulated Annealing (SA) and Iterated Local Search (ILS) algorithms for the ARP. The model defined for the ARP is adapted from a VRPTW model to incorporate real characteristics of the aircraft refueling process. Thus, the ARP model considers the refueling rate of an aircraft to calculate the service time. The ARP model also considers the average velocity of the refueling truck to travel from one aircraft to another. So far, no SA and ILS heuristics have been proposed to solve the ARP. We provide computational experiments with adapted instances representing a real airport to validate the model. The paper is structured as follows. We provide an overview of the problem in Sect. 2 and describe the proposed MILP model in Sect. 3. In Sect. 4, the SA and ILS algorithms are presented. Section 5 reports the performance of the proposed model and algorithms using a set of instances representing a real airport, followed by our conclusions in Sect. 6.

2 Problem Description

The ARP can be described as follows. Let N_A be a set of aircraft and K a set of non-homogeneous tank trucks such that $n = |N_A|$ and $\bar{k} = |K|$. Each aircraft i requests a quantity of fuel c_i, $i \in N_A$. Each truck k has a capacity Q_k, $k \in K$. Each truck starts at the storage area (depot) serves some aircraft and returns to the depot. It is considered that for each aircraft $i \in N_A$ the refueling activity begins during a predetermined period of time $[a_i, b_i]$. A truck cannot arrive and refuel aircraft i after moment b_i and if the truck arrives before moment a_i, it must wait to start its service at a_i.

Let us consider an airport where the refueling process assumes the following premises: at the beginning of a certain operational period, all refuelers are in the storage area and each used truck k is filled with its full capacity Q_k; each aircraft $i \in N_A$ is served using a single truck; to construct the route, it is not mandatory that aircraft i is served before aircraft $i+1$, if $a_i \leq a_{i+1}$; the number $\bar{k}$ of available trucks is sufficient for refueling; aircraft i with $c_i > Q_k$ are not considered here; the reason for this is that most of the aircraft with high fuel demands are serviced by refueling using underground piping systems, known as hydrant refueling; aircraft are located in a straight line; refueling trucks approach the aircraft from the beginning of this line; the fleet used is heterogeneous, that is, the capacity of each truck is different. The ability of scheduling trucks with different capacities makes the model more applicable under real circumstances. Thus, the aim of ARP is to find the shortest distance traveled by tank trucks to meet fuel demands requested by aircraft at an airport.

3 Mathematical Model

We describe a MILP model for the ARP. The problem can be represented by a complete graph $G(N, A)$ where $N = N_A \cup \{0, n+1\}$ and $N_A = \{1, 2, ..., n\}$. The graph consists of $|N_A|+2$ vertices, where the storage area (depot) is represented by vertexes 0 and $n+1$.

The set of arcs denoted by $A = \{(i,j) : i,j \in N, i \neq j, i \neq n+1, j \neq 0\}$ represents connections between the depot and the aircraft and among the aircraft. No arc terminates in vertex 0, and no arc originates from vertex $n+1$. Table 1 shows the list of parameters for each node i, where the column *Par* designates the name of the parameter. The depot is associated with a time window: trucks may not leave the depot before a_0 and must be back before or at time b_{n+1}. Table 2 shows the list of parameters defined for each truck $k \in K$. It is assumed that Q_k, a_i, b_i, c_i, d_i and $D_{i,j}$ are non-negative integers, while the displacement time of each truck is assumed to be a positive integer. The decision variables used in the proposed model are described in Table 3.

We want to find minimal cost routes, one for each truck, where each aircraft will be visited only once. Every route originates at vertex 0 and ends at vertex $n+1$, and the time windows and capacity constraints must be observed. Based on the previous definitions, the proposed mathematical model for the problem is defined as follows:

Table 1. List of parameters for each node.

Par	Description	*Par*	Description
$D_{i,j}$	Distance between nodes $i, j \in N$	c_i	Fuel quantity requested by aircraft i
a_i	Earliest moment at which refueling can start	b_i	Latest possible starting time for refueling
d_i	Distance between parked aircraft i and the storage area	q_i	Refueling rate for aircraft i

Table 2. List of parameters for each truck $k \in K$.

Par	Description
V_k	Average velocity of truck k
Q_k	Maximum fuel capacity of truck k

$$min: \sum_{k \in K} \sum_{i \in N} \sum_{j \in N, j \neq i} D_{i,j} X_{i,j,k} \tag{1}$$

subject to:

$$\sum_{k \in K} \sum_{j \in N, j \neq i} X_{i,j,k} = 1 \quad i \in N_A \tag{2}$$

$$\sum_{i \in N_A} \sum_{j \in N, j \neq i} c_i X_{i,j,k} \leq Q_k Z_k \quad k \in K \tag{3}$$

$$\sum_{j \in N} X_{0,j,k} = Z_k \quad k \subset K \tag{4}$$

$$\sum_{i \in N, h \neq i} X_{i,h,k} - \sum_{j \in N, j \neq h} X_{h,j,k} = 0 \quad h \in N_A, k \in K \tag{5}$$

$$\sum_{i \in N} X_{i,n+1,k} = Z_k \quad k \in K \tag{6}$$

Table 3. List from decision variables.

Decision variable	Description
$X_{i,j,k}$	Binary variable equal to 1 if truck $k \in K$ moves from node $i \in N$ to node $j \in N$, $i \neq j$. Otherwise, it is equal to 0
$T_{i,k}$	Indicates the time when truck $k \in K$ starts serving node $i \in N$
Z_k	Binary variable equal to 1 if truck $k \in K$ is used to meet any request. Otherwise, it is equal to 0
$TotalDis_k$	Indicates total distance traveled by each truck $k \in K$

$$\sum_{i \in N} \sum_{j \in N, j \neq i} D_{i,j} X_{i,j,k} = TotalDis_k \quad k \in K \tag{7}$$

$$T_{j,k} \geq T_{i,k} + \frac{c_i}{q_i} + \frac{d_{i,j}}{V_k} - M(1 - X_{i,j,k}) \quad i, j \in N, k \in K \tag{8}$$

$$a_i \leq T_{i,k} \leq b_i \quad k \in K \tag{9}$$

$$X_{i,j,k} \in \{0, 1\} \quad i, j \in N, k \in K \tag{10}$$

$$Z_k \in \{0, 1\} \quad k \in K \tag{11}$$

The objective function (1) is to minimize the distance traveled by the trucks to perform the refueling process. The $D_{i,j}$ parameter is calculated as the absolute difference between d_i and d_j, i.e. $|d_i - d_j|$. Parameter d_i is the distance between parked aircraft i and the depot. It is only possible to calculate $D_{i,j}$ in this way because the aircraft are parked in a straight line. The deposit is located in the same direction as the aircraft. Constraint (2) states that each aircraft will be visited only once.

Constraint (3) ensures that no truck is loaded with more than its capacity allows it to. The next three Eqs. (4), (5), and (6) ensure that each truck used leaves depot 0. After arriving at an aircraft, the vehicle leaves again and finally arrives at the depot $n + 1$. Constraint (7) counts the total distance traveled by each truck.

Inequality (8) states that a truck k cannot arrive at aircraft j before $T_{i,k} + c_i/q_i + d_{i,j}/V_k$ if it is traveling from i to j, where the service time to refuel the aircraft i is represented by the amount of fuel requested divided by the refueling rate (c_i/q_i); and the time to travel from i to j is represented by the distance between nodes i, j divided by the average velocity of the refueling truck $(d_{i,j}/V_k)$. Refueling rate and average velocity are also considered in [1]. Here M is a large scalar. The slack in Constraint (8) corresponds to the waiting time of the vehicle serving aircraft j, that is, the time spent between the moment the vehicle arrives at the aircraft destination and the start of service. Finally, Constraint (9) ensures that refueling time windows are observed and (10)–(11) are the integrality constraints. Note that an unused truck k ($Z_k = 0$) is modeled by driving the empty route $(0, n + 1)$.

4 Simulated Annealing and Iterated Local Search Approaches to the Problem

In this section, we present how a solution to the problem is represented, how the initial solutions are generated, the types of moves used to explore the solution space, the evaluation function used to guide the search and the detailed description of the proposed algorithms.

4.1 Solution Representation

A solution to the problem can be represented by multiple routes, each followed by a copy of the depot. Each copy of the depot is a separator between routes. For example, a solution representation as shown in Table 4 would correspond to a problem solution made of three routes. The first route contains aircraft (customers) 12, 4, 1, 6 and 10, the second route contains aircraft 2, 11, 9 and 3, the third route contains aircraft 8, 5 and 7. Each route starts at the depot, visiting aircraft and ends at the depot. Other authors have also used this representation (e.g. [8]).

Table 4. An example of the solution representation.

12	4	1	6	10	0	2	11	9	3	0	8	5	7

4.2 Initial Solution

To determine a feasible initial solution for the application of the algorithms, two methods were defined in order to analyze the behavior of the algorithm when subjected to different initial solutions. The first approach considered a Random Constructive Heuristic, and the second uses the Nearest-Neighbor Heuristic proposed by Salomon [11], as described below.

Random Constructive Heuristic (RCH). The initial solution to the problem was generated through a procedure that, starting from the depot, inserts a single aircraft on a route at each iteration. This insertion is done by analyzing the time window of each aircraft and the capacity limit of the refueling truck. The choice of the aircraft to be inserted in the route is made randomly among those that were not inserted and whose insertion does not exceed neither the truck's capacity nor the pre-defined time window of each aircraft. If there are no aircraft satisfying these two conditions, the depot is returned, and a new route is started. The procedure comes to an end when all aircraft are inserted in some route. It can be observed that using this construction the initial solutions are always feasible and we obtain an upper limit on the number of trucks to be used.

Nearest-Neighbor Heuristic (NNH). According to Salomon [11], the nearest-neighbor heuristic starts every route by finding the unrouted customer "closest" to the depot. At every subsequent iteration, the heuristic searches for the customer "closest" to the last customer added to the route. This search is performed among all the customers who can feasibly (with respect to time windows, vehicle arrival time at the depot, and capacity constraints) be added to the end of the emerging route. A new route is started any time the search fails unless there are no more customers to schedule. The metric used in this approach tries to account for both geographical and temporal closeness of customers.

Let the last customer on the current partial route be customer i, and let j denote any unrouted customer that could be visited next. It searches for node j that minimizes a weighted cost $x = a * tempDist + b * waiting + c * urgency$, where a, b and c are parameters. The wait related to node j can be characterized by: $wait = max(a_i - (hCurrent + currentServiceTime + tempDist_{current,i}), 0)$, where a_i is the starting time of the time window of node i, $hCurrent$ is the current time (which corresponds to the start of the current node's service), $currentServiceTime$ is the time consumed at the current node to perform its service and $tempDist_{current,i}$ is the time from the current node to node i. Urgency is defined as: $urgency = (b_i - (hCurrent + currentServiceTime + tempDist_{current,i})$. The procedure comes to an end when all aircraft are inserted. It is noted that with this construction the initial solutions are always feasible.

4.3 Neighborhood Structure

A set N of seven different move types is used to make changes between customers (aircraft) of different routes and customers of the same route. *Shift* and *Swap* moves define the inter-route neighborhood structures, and *Reinsertion* and *Swap* moves define the intra-route neighborhood structures. When the algorithm is looking for the next solution, there is a certain probability of choosing one of the seven moves to improve the current solution. It can be observed that by using these moves, both feasible and non-feasible solutions are considered in the exploration of the search space.

Inter-Route Neighborhood Structures. The two structures are based on λ-*interchange* moves (Osman [9]), which consists of swapping up to λ consecutive customers between two routes. To minimize the computational effort, λ was limited to 2. These swaps are best explained as doubles (λ_1, λ_2), in which λ_1 clients are transferred from route r_1 to route r_2 and the λ_2 clients of route r_2 to route r_1. Therefore, disregarding symmetries, the following combination of *2-interchange* moves is possible: $((1;0), (1;1), (2;0), (2;1), (2;2))$. Suppose $r_1 = 0 \rightarrow 1 \rightarrow 2 \rightarrow 3 \rightarrow 4 \rightarrow 5 \rightarrow 0$ and $r_2 = 0 \rightarrow 6 \rightarrow 7 \rightarrow 8 \rightarrow 9 \rightarrow 10 \rightarrow 0$.

Shift(1,0) - $N^{(1)}$: A client i is transferred from route r_1 to route r_2. For example, client 3 is removed from route r_1 and inserted into route r_2. The new route is the sequence: $r_1 = 0 \rightarrow 1 \rightarrow 2 \rightarrow 4 \rightarrow 5 \rightarrow 0$ and $r_2 = 0 \rightarrow 6 \rightarrow 7 \rightarrow 8 \rightarrow 3 \rightarrow 9 \rightarrow 10 \rightarrow 0$.

Swap(1,1) - $N^{(2)}$: Performs a permutation between a client i of a route r_1 and a client j belonging to another route r_2. For example, client 2 is exchanged with client 7 and the new route is the sequence: $r_1 = 0 \rightarrow 1 \rightarrow 7 \rightarrow 3 \rightarrow 4 \rightarrow 5 \rightarrow 0$ and $r_2 = 0 \rightarrow 6 \rightarrow 2 \rightarrow 8 \rightarrow 9 \rightarrow 10 \rightarrow 0$.

Shift(2,0) - $N^{(3)}$: Two consecutive clients i and j are transferred from route r_1 to another r_2. Adjacent clients 2 and 3 are moved from one route to another, forming the route $r_1 = 0 \rightarrow 1 \rightarrow 4 \rightarrow 5 \rightarrow 0$ and $r_2 = 0 \rightarrow 6 \rightarrow 7 \rightarrow 8 \rightarrow 9 \rightarrow 2 \rightarrow 3 \rightarrow 10 \rightarrow 0$.

Swap(2,1) - $N^{(4)}$: Two consecutive clients, i and j, belonging to a route r_1 are exchanged with a client i' from another route r_2. Adjacent clients 1 and 2 of a route are exchanged with client 7 from another route. The new route is the sequence: $r_1 = 0 \rightarrow 7 \rightarrow 3 \rightarrow 4 \rightarrow 5 \rightarrow 0$ and $r_2 = 0 \rightarrow 6 \rightarrow 1 \rightarrow 2 \rightarrow 8 \rightarrow 9 \rightarrow 10 \rightarrow 0$.

Swap(2,2) - $N^{(5)}$: Two consecutive clients, i and j, belonging to route r_1 are exchanged with two other consecutive clients i' and j' from another route r_2. Adjacent clients 1 and 2 of one route are exchanged with adjacent clients 6 and 7 from another route, forming route $r_1 = 0 \rightarrow 6 \rightarrow 7 \rightarrow 3 \rightarrow 4 \rightarrow 5 \rightarrow 0$ and $r_2 = 0 \rightarrow 1 \rightarrow 2 \rightarrow 8 \rightarrow 9 \rightarrow 10 \rightarrow 0$.

Note that such combinations include shift $((1;0); (2;0))$ and swap $((1;1); (2;1); (2;2))$ moves.

Intra-Route Neighborhood Structures. The *Reinsertion* and *Swap* moves are defined as follows.

Reinsertion - $N^{(6)}$: A customer is removed and reinserted at another position on the route. Client 3 of the original route r_1 is relocated to another position on the route and the new route is sequence: $r_1 = 0 \rightarrow 1 \rightarrow 2 \rightarrow 4 \rightarrow 5 \rightarrow 3 \rightarrow 0$

Swap - $N^{(7)}$: It consists of swapping two customers on the same route. On route r_1, clients 2 and 5 are exchanged, forming the route $r_1 = 0 \rightarrow 1 \rightarrow 5 \rightarrow 3 \rightarrow 4 \rightarrow 2 \rightarrow 0$.

4.4 Evaluation Function

Solution s is evaluated by function f, given by equation (12), which must be minimized:

$$f(s) = Dist(s) + \alpha * f_1(s) + \beta * f_2(s) \tag{12}$$

where: $Dist(s)$ is the distance traveled by the trucks in solution s; $f_1(s)$ is the total load excess among all used vehicles; $f_2(s)$ represents the total amount of time by which the latest times to service aircraft are exceeded, and α, β are penalty weight factors. Note that when s is feasible, the value given by f will only correspond to the traveling distance, since in this case: $f_1(s) = f_2(s) = 0$. The comparison between two solutions is made based only on the value of the evaluation function, without taking into account the number of vehicles associated with each solution.

In the developed method, α equal to the value of the greatest distance between any two clients and β equal to 1000 are adopted. These values are set so that infeasible solutions have a low probability of being chosen.

4.5 Simulated Annealing

The SA algorithm is a metaheuristic that has been successfully used in several works for obtaining a good approximation of a function's optimal solution. SA is based on an analogy of an optimization problem with thermodynamics [7]. SA is presented in Algorithm 1. It has four main parameters: initial temperature (T_0), final or freezing temperature (T_c), cooling factor (α) and the maximum number of iterations at each temperature (SA_{max}).

```
input : s0, T0, Tc, α, SAmax
output: Best solution s*
numIter ← 0;
s* ← s0;
s ← s0;
T ← T0;
while T > Tc do
    while numIter < SAmax do
        numIter ← numIter + 1;
        s' ← GenerateNeighbor(s) ;
        Δf ← f(s') − f(s*) ;
        if Δf < 0 then
            s ← s';
            if f(s') < f(s*) then
                s* ← s';
            end
        end
        else
            Generate random number x ∈ [0, 1];
            if x < e^(−Δ/T) then
                s ← s';
            end
        end
    end
    T ← T * α;
    numIter ← 0;
end
```

Algorithm 1: SA algorithm pseudocode

Considering a problem of minimizing function f and an initial solution s, at each iteration, the temperature T is determined using a cooling factor $0 < \alpha < 1$. Then a new solution s' is found by performing local searches in the neighborhood of the current solution. If the delta energy level, $\Delta = f(s') - f(s)$, is negative, then the new solution is of better quality than the current solution; and s' solution is updated as the current solution. Otherwise, when the solution is of poorer quality, it can be accepted with $e^{-\Delta/T}$ probability. At each temperature SA_{max} iterations are performed where at each iteration, a new solution is found. This procedure is performed until the temperature reaches a final or freezing temperature T_c and the closer to that temperature, the less likely the algorithm will accept bad moves [7].

4.6 Iterated Local Search

The Iterated Local Search metaheuristic is simple but very effective. It starts with the initial solution s_0 and applies a local search to it, obtaining s^*. Then, the algorithm performs the following steps: it perturbs the current best solution s^*; obtains a solution s'; and performs a local search in s', reaching a local optimum s''. If the solution s'' is better than the current best solution s^* then the algorithm transforms s'' into the new current solution. Otherwise, the algorithm performs another iteration. As long as the stopping criterion is not met, the procedure is repeated. Its pseudocode is given by Algorithm 2.

```
   input : Initial solution s0
   output: Best solution s*
1  numIter ← 0;
2  s* ← LocalSearch(s0);
3  while numIter < ILSmax do
4      s' ← Pertubation(s*) ;
5      s'' ← LocalSearch(s') ;
6      numIter ← numIter + 1;
7      if f(s'') < f(s*) then
8          s* ← s'';
9          numIter ← 0;
10     end
11 end
```

Algorithm 2: ILS algorithm pseudocode

Line 4 of Algorithm 2 calls a perturbation routine that performs different moves from those used in the neighborhood generation. Similar to a 2-opt move, a customer is randomly chosen and permuted with the next customer within the route, creating a small but distinct perturbation. The local search method is as follows.

Local Search. The objective of Local Search is to find local optima, generating at each iteration, neighboring solutions from the current solution and accepting only better solutions than the current one or those that meet a certain acceptance criterion. At the end of the procedure, the best solution found is returned. In this study, the Hill Climbing local search algorithm was implemented. The algorithm ends after H iterations without improving the objective function, where H is an input parameter. Algorithm 3 shows the pseudo-code as implemented in this work.

```
input : Solution s, H
output: Best solution s*
i ← 0;
s* ← s;
while i < H do
    s' ← GenerateNeighbor(s*) ;
    Δf ← f(s') − f(s*) ;
    if Δf < 0 then
        s* ← s';
        i ← 0;
    end
    i ← i + 1;
end
```

Algorithm 3: Hill Climbing local search algorithm

5 Computational Experiments

For the experiments, a set of eight instances with six to forty aircraft and six to ten available trucks were used to represent a real airport. Let Instance W_i be associated with a pair (Number of aircraft, Number of available trucks). Then, $W_1 = (6,6)$; $W_2 = (11,6)$; $W_3 = (15,6)$; $W_4 = (18,6)$; $W_5 = (18,6)$; $W_6 = (25,7)$; $W_7 = (30,8)$; $W_8 = (40,10)$. All instances are based on the scenario of the aircraft refueling activity at medium traffic volume airports. The data used correspond to the premises observed at a real airport.

The MILP model was solved using IBM ILOG CPLEX 12.8, written at language OPL, and the proposed SA and ILS algorithms were coded in Python 3.8. The computational tests were performed on a desktop computer with Intel Core i5-8250U Processor of 1.60 GHz with 4 GB RAM, running Windows 10 64-bit. The algorithms were run 5 times, and in each run, 300 repetitions of the algorithm were performed in order to find the incumbent solution (best solution during the re-optimization process).

5.1 Definition of Parameters

To solve the MILP model, CPLEX was parameterized in the following way: maximum execution time of 2 h (7,200 s); tree memory limit of 80 GB; work memory of 10 GB and number of threads equal to 8. The reason for those parameters is to handle the out of memory situation normally found in larger models.

The implementation of SA was based on Algorithm 1. The parameters of SA are: initial temperature (T_0); cooling factor (α); the maximum number of iterations at each temperature (SA_{max}) and final or freezing temperature (T_c). The parameter SA_{max} was adopted as being equal to the number of aircraft in each instance, that is, equal to n. For the stopping criterion, a freezing temperature was considered, which by the definition of Annealing, occurs when the possibility of improving the current result is very low. In this work, $T_c = 0.001$ was adopted. Parameters T_0 and α were determined by experimentation. Five values for parameter T_0 were analyzed: $T_0 = 10; 100; 1,000; 10,000; 100,000$; and for each T_0 different cooling factors were considered, $\alpha = 0.80; 0.85; 0.9; 0.95; 0.98$.

Figure 1 shows the results obtained considering an instance of the problem for the different initial temperatures and cooling factors for the SA algorithm. The horizontal axis represents the different values of T_0 considered and the vertical axis is the solution value to the problem, that is, the route distance ($f(s)$). Note that α is represented by the bars following the colors specified in Fig. 1.

The instances used for parameter calibration (including that in Fig. 1) had n = 12 to 18 and $\bar{k} = 6$. Tests with these instances showed that the best combination of parameter values is $T_0 = 10$ and $\alpha = 0.98$.

The ILS_{max} parameter of Algorithm 2 was also defined as the total amount of aircraft ($n = |N_A|$) in each instance.

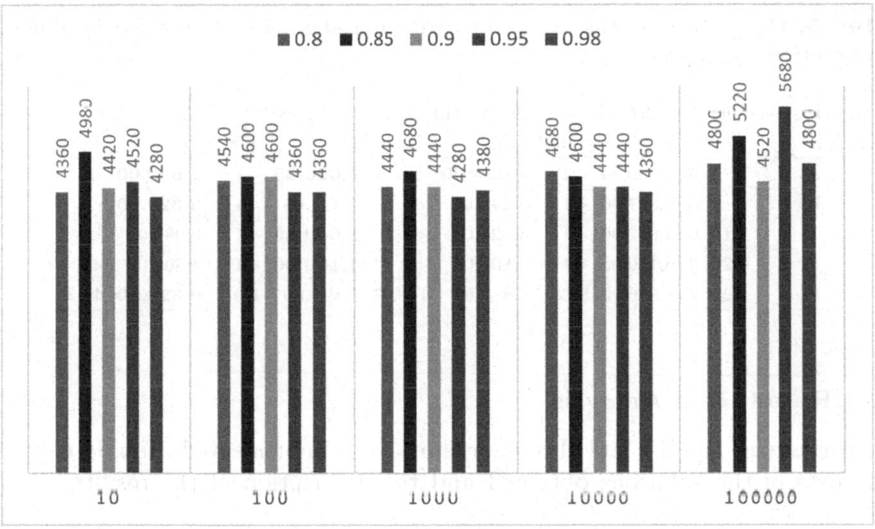

Fig. 1. Parameter analysis T_0 and α

5.2 Study of the Impact of the Initial Solution

Table 5 presents a comparison of the algorithms SA and ILS with initial solutions provided by the different construction algorithms RCH and NNH. For this comparison, five instances were considered (A, B, C, D, E) having 5 to 25 aircraft and 6 to 7 available trucks. For each instance, the algorithms were run five times. The table shows the best solution obtained among the five runs with 300 repetitions of the algorithm in each run. Columns Instance, n, $\bar{k}$, $f(s)$ and $Time$ represent the instance, the number of aircraft, the number of the available trucks, the best solution and the total execution time (in seconds) of the SA and ILS algorithm, respectively.

It can be observed that for Instances B to E, the best solution found by SA and ILS was obtained by using the initial solution given by the NNH heuristic (highlighted in bold). For Instance A, the best solution found by SA was given by the NNH heuristic and ILS found the same solution with both initial solution approaches.

Related to the execution time, observe that for Instances A to D, the solutions were found with a time under one second (< 1). For the largest instance (Instance E), the RCH heuristic takes longer to build a solution due to the fact that the nodes to be visited are chosen randomly. This random choice may lead to many poor solutions. Note that RCH - ILS spent 158s to obtain the best solution. The larger the instance, the longer the RCH heuristic will take to build a solution. Therefore, for this work we used the NNH heuristic to construct the initial solutions.

Table 5. Comparison of the algorithms with initial solutions provided by different construction algorithms.

Instance	n	$\bar{k}$	RCH - SA		RCH - ILS		NNH - SA		NNH - ILS	
			$f(s)$	Time	$f(s)$	Time	$f(s)$	Time	$f(s)$	Time
A	5	6	1,780.00	<1	**1,620.00**	<1	**1,620.00**	<1	**1,620.00**	<1
B	9	6	6,357.00	<1	5,240.00	<1	5,394.00	<1	**3,320.00**	<1
C	15	6	3,862.00	<1	3,520.00	<1	**3,000.00**	<1	3,080.00	<1
D	20	6	6,120.00	<1	5,800.00	<1	**4,100.00**	<1	4,800.00	<1
E	25	7	8,680.00	87.8	8,480.00	158.07	7,194.00	1.67	**6,820.00**	4.22

5.3 Results and Analysis

Six variants of the SA and ILS algorithms were implemented. Table 6 contains the costs of the solutions obtained and the description of the results in each column, where:

I Corresponds to the execution of the SA algorithm using the local search with a random neighborhood considering all seven proposed moves ($N^{(1)}$ to $N^{(7)}$).

II Corresponds to the execution of the ILS algorithm using the local search with a random neighborhood considering all seven proposed moves ($N^{(1)}$ to $N^{(7)}$).

III Corresponds to the execution of the SA algorithm using the local search with a random neighborhood considering only four proposed moves. We analyzed neighborhoods $N^{(1)}$, $N^{(2)}$, $N^{(4)}$ and $N^{(5)}$.

IV Corresponds to the execution of the ILS algorithm using the local search with a random neighborhood considering only four proposed moves. We analyzed neighborhoods $N^{(1)}$, $N^{(2)}$, $N^{(4)}$ and $N^{(5)}$.

V Corresponds to the execution of the SA algorithm using the local search with a random neighborhood considering four moves, which were neighborhoods $N^{(2)}$, $N^{(3)}$, $N^{(6)}$ and $N^{(7)}$.

VI Corresponds to the execution of the ILS algorithm using the local search with a random neighborhood considering four moves, which were neighborhoods $N^{(2)}$, $N^{(3)}$, $N^{(6)}$ and $N^{(7)}$.

Table 6. Result of the execution of the six variants of the SA and ILS algorithms.

W	*n*	CPLEX			Best total cost obtained					
		LB	*UB*	*GAP*(%)	*I*	*II*	*III*	*IV*	*V*	*VI*
1	6	370.00	**370.00**	0.00	**370.00**	**370.00**	**370.00**	**370.00**	**370.00**	**370.00**
2	11	1,400.00	**1,400.00**	0.00	1,760.00	**1,400.00**	1,880.00	**1,400.00**	1,880.00	**1,400.00**
3	15	828.68	**860.00**	3.64	**860.00**	**860.00**	**860.00**	**860.00**	**860.00**	**860.00**
4	18	1,588.00	**1,800.00**	11.78	2,920.00	**1,800.00**	2,660.00	**1,800.00**	2,660.00	**1,800.00**
5	18	1,588.21	1,690.00	6.02	1,690.00	**1,600.00**	1,690.00	**1,600.00**	1,730.00	1,690.00
6	25	2,598.57	**2,640.00**	1.57	3,450.00	2,840.00	3,340.00	**2,640.00**	3,940.00	3,390.00
7	30	2,477.34	3,270.00	24.24	4,050.00	3,270.00	3,960.00	**3,150.00**	4,170.00	3,230.00
8	40	3,189.94	4,850.00	34.23	7,230.00	4,880.00	6,870.00	**4,840.00**	7,370.00	5,220.00

Table 6 shows CPLEX, SA and ILS results. Column *W* indicates the instance and columm *n* the number of aircraft that requested service in each instance. Columns *UB* and *LB* show the upper bound and lower bound found by CPLEX. The *GAP* column shows the gap found by CPLEX, $GAP = (UB - LB)/UB$. The results of the six variants are shown in columns $I, II, ..., VI$. The columns indicate the best solution in the 5 runs, respectively.

Looking at the values in bold in Table 6, we can consider that the fourth variant (*IV*) produced the largest number of best solutions. The second variant (*II*) also obtained advantageous results. The other variants found solution values greater than or equal to those of CPLEX up to Instance 4. For the remainder instances, the other variants found poor solutions.

We can affirm that the variants (II, IV, VI) of the ILS algorithm obtained the best solutions compared to the SA algorithm. Therefore, considering the ILS algorithm, note that by decreasing the possibilities of the local search from seven (variant *II*) to four (variant *IV*), the quality of the solution improves. Note that variant *IV* is formed by inter-route neighborhood structures and variants *II* and *VI* by inter-route and intra-route structures. In this problem, the ILS algorithm presented greater diversity with inter-route moves.

Adopting variant *IV* of the ILS algorithm and comparing its results in detail with those obtained by the MILP model in Table 7, it is noticeable that the method proposed here made it possible to reduce the average execution time (in seconds) of the algorithm in the 5 runs.

The *Time* column shows the execution time of CPLEX. Column v shows the number of the used trucks. The columns *Best*, *Avg*, *Worst*, v_{min} and v_{max} indicate the best solution value, the average solution value, the worst solution value, the minimum number of used trucks and the maximum number of used trucks by ILS in the 5 runs, respectively. The *Dev* column represents the deviation of the solutions based on the best solution found ($Dev = 100(Worst - Best)/Best$).

Column T_{avg} designates the average execution time (in seconds) of the algorithm in the 5 runs. Table 7 shows the results.

Table 7. Comparison of CPLEX and ILS results with random neighborhood structure considering four proposed moves $N^{(1)}$, $N^{(2)}$, $N^{(4)}$ and $N^{(5)}$.

W	n	CPLEX				Algorithm ILS - Variation IV							
		LB	*UB*	*GAP(%)*	*Time*	v	*Best*	*Avg*	*Worst*	*Dev*	T_{avg}	v_{min}	v_{max}
1	6	370.00	**370.00**	0.00	<1.00	1	**370.00**	370.00	370.00	0.00	<1.00	1	1
2	11	1,400.00	**1,400.00**	0.00	<1.00	2	**1,400.00**	1,400.00	1,400.00	0.00	1.20	2	2
3	15	828.68	**860.00**	3.64	2.29	1	**860.00**	860.00	860.00	0.00	<1.00	1	1
4	18	1,588.00	**1,800.00**	11.78	6.16	2	**1,800.00**	1,808.00	1,840.00	2.22	27.56	2	2
5	18	1,588.21	1,690.00	6.02	34.05	3	**1,600.00**	1,600.00	1,600.00	0.00	30.03	3	3
6	25	2,598.57	**2,640.00**	1.57	810.11	7	**2,640.00**	2,796.00	3,000.00	13.63	100.23	7	7
7	30	2,477.34	3,270.00	24.24	7,200.00	7	**3,150.00**	3,256.00	3,350.00	6.34	144.5	7	8
8	40	3,189.94	4,850.00	34.23	7,200.00	8	**4,840.00**	4,807.00	4,970.00	2.68	1,376.00	8	9

Since the ARP is NP-hard, it is expected that the exact approach will not be able to efficiently solve medium to large instances. This indeed happened and it can be seen in Table 7, where CPLEX proved solution optimality only for Instances 1 and 2 (with 6 and 11 service requests).

For Instances 3 to 6, which ranged from 15 to 25 service requests, CPLEX was unable to find an optimal solution. For Instances 7 and 8, which ranged from 30 to 40 service requests, CPLEX did not find an optimal solution after running for 2 h (time limit) obtaining gaps of 24.24% and 34.23%, respectively. ILS found slightly better results than CPLEX for Instances 5, 7 and 8. ILS had little deviation between the results of the 5 runs for these instances, 0.00, 6.34 and 2.68 respectively.

As it can be observed in Table 7, the ILS algorithm found solutions for all instances, including the optimal solution for Instances 1 and 2. For Instances 3 and 4, the solution found by ILS was the same found by CPLEX. For the remaining instances, the solution value found by ILS was between the *LB* and the *UB* found by CPLEX with reduced execution time.

The ILS heuristic provides good results at an affordable time when compared with the 2 h of CPLEX execution. Note that the average execution time for our largest instance (Instance 8) is of about 22 min. In civil aviation, flight schedules are planned ahead, and even if they suffer adjustments during an operational period, the times required by the proposed ILS algorithm are still acceptable. The results shown here confirm that the proposed algorithm is a valuable tool to help planning daily refueling truck routes at an airport.

6 Conclusions

This article addressed a problem that often occurs at airports: the problem of refueling aircraft using tank trucks. A mixed-integer linear programming model and SA and ILS algorithms were designed for solving this problem. Variants of methods for generating initial solutions and generating neighborhoods were tested. These variants significantly affected the results. The computational experiments showed that CPLEX could solve only small instances of the problem and that the ILS algorithm is an effective approach to solve the problem. The proposed model can be used in any scenario of the aircraft refueling activity at airports and its approach is a significant advance in terms of preventing routes where flight schedule delays may occur. Moreover, the ability of considering trucks with different capacities makes ILS more applicable under real circumstances.

In future research, strategies to improve the efficiency of the presented algorithm are to be considered. Moreover, strategies can be studied to address instances that involve extremely unfeasible cases, where not all aircraft can be serviced without violating time restrictions. Meanwhile, we apply the proposed model in real practice.

Acknowledgments. This study was financed in part by the Coordenação de Aperfeiçoamento de Pessoal de Nível Superior - Brasil (CAPES) - Finance Code 001 and the Fundação de Amparo à Pesquisa e Inovação do Espírito Santo (FAPES) (Grant Number 2020-LGJV3).

References

1. Babić, O.: Optimization of refuelling truck fleets at an airport. Transp. Res. Part B Methodologica **21**(6), 479–487 (1987)
2. Braekers, K., Ramaekers, K., Nieuwenhuyse, I.: The vehicle routing problem: state of the art classification and review. Comput. Ind. Eng. **99** (2015). https://doi.org/10.1016/j.cie.2015.12.007
3. Bräysy, O., Gendreau, M.: Vehicle routing problem with time windows, part i: route construction and local search algorithms. Transp. Sci. **39**(1), 104–118 (2005)
4. Du, Y., Zhang, Q., Chen, Q.: Aco-ih: an improved ant colony optimization algorithm for airport ground service scheduling. In: IEEE International Conference on Industrial Technology, pp. 1–6 (2008). https://doi.org/10.1109/ICIT.2008.4608674
5. Gamayanti, N., Sahal, M., Wibisono, A.: Optimization of vehicle routing problem with tight time windows, short travel time and re-used vehicles (vrptsr) for aircraft refueling in airport using ant colony optimization algorithm. J. Adv. Res. Electric. Eng. **2**(1), 43–46 (2018)
6. Gendreau, M., Tarantilis, C.D.: Solving large-scale vehicle routing problems with time windows: the state-of-the-art. Montreal (2010)
7. Kirkpatrick, S.: Optimization by simulated annealing: quantitative studies. J. Stat. Phys. **34**(5–6), 975–986 (1984)
8. Lin, S.W., Ying, K.C., Lee, Z.J., Chen, H.S.: Vehicle routing problems with time windows using simulated annealing. In: 2006 IEEE International Conference on Systems, Man and Cybernetics, vol. 1, pp. 645–650 (2006). https://doi.org/10.1109/ICSMC.2006.384458
9. Osman, I.H.: Metastrategy simulated annealing and tabu search algorithms for the vehicle routing problem. Ann. Oper. Res. **41**, 421–451 (1993). https://doi.org/10.1007/BF02023004

10. Rochat, Y., Taillard, É.D.: Probabilistic diversification and intensification in local search for vehicle routing. J. Heurist., 147–167 (1995). https://doi.org/10.1007/BF02430370
11. Solomon, M.M.: Algorithms for the vehicle routing and scheduling problems with time window constraints. Oper. Res. **35**(2), 254–265 (1987)
12. Wang, Z., Li, Y., Hei, X., Meng, H.: Research on airport refueling vehicle scheduling problem based on greedy algorithm. In: Huang, D.-S., Bevilacqua, V., Premaratne, P., Gupta, P. (eds.) ICIC 2018. LNCS, vol. 10954, pp. 717–728. Springer, Cham (2018). https://doi.org/10.1007/978-3-319-95930-6_73

A Pascal-Like Triangle with Quaternionic Entries

Maria Irene Falcão[1(✉)] and Helmuth R. Malonek[2]

[1] Centro de Matemática, Universidade do Minho, Braga, Portugal
mif@math.uminho.pt
[2] CIDMA, Universidade de Aveiro, Aveiro, Portugal
hrmalon@ua.pt

Abstract. In this paper we consider a Pascal-like triangle as result of the expansion of a binomial in terms of the generators e_1, e_2 of the non-commutative Clifford algebra $\mathcal{C}\ell_{0,2}$ over $\mathbb{R}$. The study of various patterns in such structure and the discussion of its properties are carried out.

Keywords: Pascal triangle · Quaternions · Clifford algebras

1 Introduction

Over the years several authors have constructed arithmetic triangles by choosing as their elements numbers which satisfy a recurrence relation of the form

$$\mathcal{E}_{k,s} = A(k,s)\mathcal{E}_{k-1,s} + B(k,s)\mathcal{E}_{k-1,s-1}, \tag{1}$$

with appropriate coefficients $A(k,s)$ and $B(k,s)$ and initial conditions. The triangle corresponding to the choice $A(k,s) = B(k,s) = 1$, with the initial conditions

$$\mathcal{E}_{k,0} = 1,\ k = 0,1,\ldots \quad \mathcal{E}_{0,s} = 0,\ s = 1,2,\ldots \tag{2}$$

reduces to the well known Pascal triangle whereas the initial conditions $\mathcal{E}_{1,0} = 1$, $\mathcal{E}_{1,1} = 2$ and $\mathcal{E}_{k,s} = 0$, for $s < 0$ or $s > k$ leads to Lucas triangle. The Stirling triangle of the second kind corresponds to a choice of $A(k,s) = s$ and $B(k,s) = 1$ with the initial values (2). The book [2] contains several results and detailed references concerning generalized Pascal triangles and other arithmetic triangles.

In this work we consider the arithmetic triangle obtained by choosing the generators of the non-commutative Clifford Algebra $\mathcal{C}\ell_{0,2}$ as the coefficients in (1) together with the initial values (2). We study various patterns in its structure and discuss its main properties. They reveal, in a very particular form, similarities with the classic properties of the Pascal triangle with real entries and at the same time illustrate the consequences of the non-commutativity.

This work was supported by Portuguese funds through the Research Centre of Mathematics of University of Minho - CMAT, and the Center of Research and Development in Mathematics and Applications - CIDMA (University of Aveiro), and the Portuguese Foundation for Science and Technology ("FCT - Fundação para a Ciência e Tecnologia"), within projects UIDB/00013/2020, UIDP/00013/2020, and UIDB/04106/2020.

O. Gervasi et al. (Eds.): ICCSA 2021, LNCS 12952, pp. 439–448, 2021.
https://doi.org/10.1007/978-3-030-86973-1_31

2 A Pascal-Like Triangle

Let $\{e_1, e_2, \cdots, e_n\}$ be an orthonormal base of the Euclidean vector space $\mathbb{R}^n$ with a product according to the multiplication rules

$$e_k e_l + e_l e_k = -2\delta_{kl},\ k, l = 1, \cdots, n, \tag{3}$$

where δ_{kl} is the Kronecker symbol. This non-commutative product generates the 2^n-dimensional Clifford algebra $\mathcal{C}\ell_{0,n}$ over $\mathbb{R}$.

The vector space $\mathbb{R}^{n+1}$ is embedded in $\mathcal{C}\ell_{0,n}$ by the identification of the element $(x_0, x_1, \cdots, x_n)$ in $\mathbb{R}^{n+1}$ with the element

$$x = x_0 + x_1 e_1 + \cdots + x_n e_n \tag{4}$$

in $\mathcal{A}_n := \text{span}_{\mathbb{R}}\{1, e_1, \ldots, e_n\} \subset \mathcal{C}\ell_{0,n}$; such an element $x \in \mathcal{A}_n$ is usually called paravector. For a paravector x of the form (4) we define

- *scalar part* resp. *vector part* of x:

$$\text{Sc}(x) = x_0 \quad \text{and } \text{Vec}(x) = e_1 x_1 + \cdots + e_n x_n;$$

  if $\text{Sc}(x) = 0$, then x is called a *pure paravector*;

- *conjugate of* x:

$$\bar{x} = x_0 - x_1 e_1 - \cdots - x_n e_n;$$

- *norm of* x:

$$|x| = (x\bar{x})^{\frac{1}{2}} = \sqrt{x_0^2 + x_1^2 + \cdots + x_n^2}.$$

Usually $\{e_1, e_2, \cdots, e_n\}$ are called the imaginary units or *generators* of the Clifford algebra $\mathcal{C}\ell_{0,n}$. Obviously, we can identify the case $n = 1$ with the complex algebra $\mathbb{C}$ by choosing $i := e_1$. The quaternion algebra $\mathbb{H}$ can be obtained through the identification $\mathbf{i} := e_1, \mathbf{j} := e_2$ and $\mathbf{k} := e_1 e_2$. We refer the readers to the books [3,10] for details on Clifford algebras.

In this paper we consider the arithmetical triangle obtained by choosing as its elements the numbers which satisfy the recurrence relation

$$\mathcal{E}_{k,s} = e_1 \mathcal{E}_{k-1,s} + e_2 \mathcal{E}_{k-1,s-1} \tag{5}$$

with the initial conditions

$$\mathcal{E}_{k,0} = e_1^k,\ k = 0, 1, \ldots \quad \mathcal{E}_{0,s} = 0,\ s = 1, 2, \ldots \tag{6}$$

The problem (5)–(6) is equivalent to the problem (1)–(2) for the choice of the generators of the Clifford algebra $\mathcal{C}\ell_{0,2}$ as the coefficients $A(k,s)$ and $B(k,s)$.

The various elements $\mathcal{E}_{k,s}$, $(0 \leq s \leq k)$, defined by (5)–(6) can be arranged in the form of a triangular array as in the case of Pascal triangle. In Fig. 1 we present the first rows of such triangle and highlight the relationships of a given

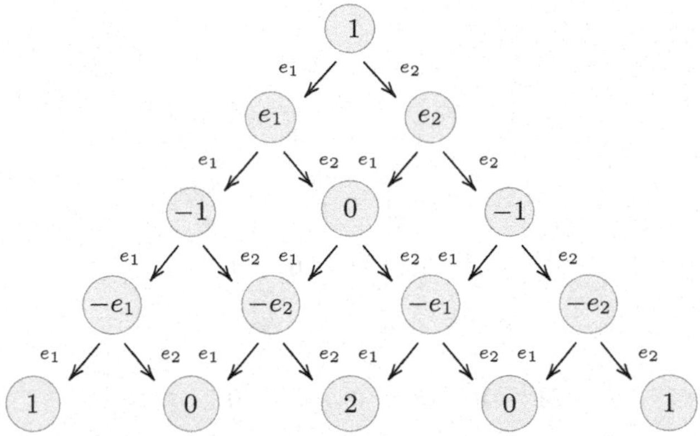

Fig. 1. First rows of the hypercomplex Pascal triangle $\mathcal{E}_{k,s}$

entry with its neighbors. It is also visible that the values of the rows change over alternately between real numbers and paravectors in $\mathcal{A}_2$.

Observe that considering the norm of each element of the triangle of Fig. 1, i.e. considering elements of the form

$$\tilde{\mathcal{E}}_{k,s} = |\mathcal{E}_{k,s}|,$$

we end up with the so-called Pauli Pascal triangle [11], a triangular array made of three copies of the Pascal triangle (see Fig. 2). It is easy to see that the entries of one of the triangles are the non-zero elements of the even rows (in green) and the other two are obtained by considering alternating elements (blue/red) of the odd rows.

Reading the entries of the triangle by rows, we obtain the sequence

$$1, 1, 1, 1, 0, 1, 1, 1, 1, 1, 1, 0, 2, 0, 1, 1, 1, 2, 2, 1, 1, 1, 0, 3, 0, 3, 0, 1, 1, 1, 3, 3, 3, 3, 1, 1 \ldots$$

listed in *The On-Line Encyclopedia of Integer Sequences* [14] (A051159).

For the above reasons the triangle corresponding to (5)–(6) will be called henceforward *quaternionic Pascal triangle* or *Pascal triangle with quaternion entries*. Along the next section we will present several other arguments supporting such designations.

Before we proceed we need to introduce some other tools from the Clifford algebra $\mathcal{C}\ell_{0,2}$, namely the embedding of the non-commutative product into an n-nary symmetric product (see [12]) defined as

$$a_1 \times a_2 \times \cdots \times a_n = \frac{1}{n!} \sum_{\pi(s_1,\ldots,s_n)} a_{s_1} a_{s_2} \cdots a_{s_n}, \tag{7}$$

where the sum runs over all permutations of all $(s_1, \ldots, s_n)$. If the factor a_j occurs μ_j-times in (7), we briefly write $a_1{}^{\mu_1} \times a_2{}^{\mu_2} \times \cdots \times a_n{}^{\mu_n}$ and set parentheses if the powers are understood in the ordinary way.

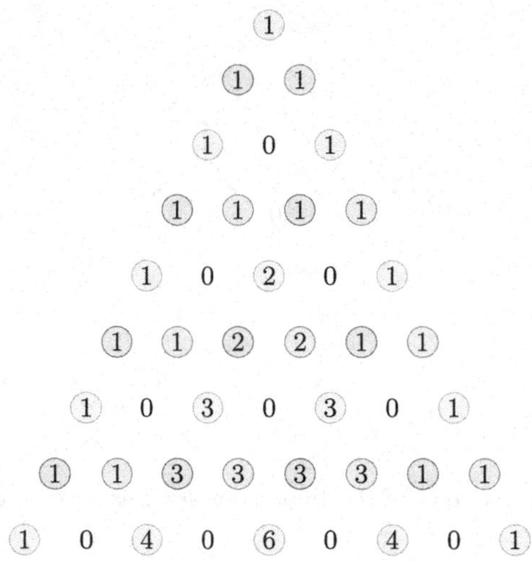

Fig. 2. Three Pascal triangles (Color figure online)

For example,

$$e_1 \times e_2 = \tfrac{1}{2}(e_1 e_2 + e_2 e_1) = 0$$

while

$$e_1^2 \times e_2 = e_1 \times e_1 \times e_2 = \tfrac{1}{3!}(2e_1^2 e_2 + 2e_1 e_2 e_1 + 2e_2 e_1^2) = -\tfrac{1}{3}e_2$$

and

$$(e_1)^2 \times e_2 = -e_2.$$

The symmetric product along with the established convention permit to deal with a polynomial formula exactly in the same way as in the case of two commutative variables. More precisely, the following relation holds (see [12,13])

$$(v_1 + v_2)^k = \sum_{m=0}^{k} \binom{k}{m} v_1^{k-m} \times v_2^m. \tag{8}$$

3 Properties of the Quaternionic Pascal Triangle

It is well known that the entries of the Pascal triangle are the coefficients in the expansion of $(x+y)^n$, while the Lucas triangle is generated by the coefficients in the expansion of $(x+y)^{n-1}(x+2y)$ [7] and the Pauli Pascal triangle is generated by the coefficients in expansion of $(x+y)^n$ where x and y anticommute [11].

We prove now that the entries of the quaternionic Pascal triangle are also the coefficients in the expansion of a particular binomial.

Theorem 1. *The entries $\mathcal{E}_{k,s}$ of the quaternionic Pascal triangle are the coefficients in the expansion of $(e_1 + te_2)^n$, $t \in \mathbb{R}$, i.e.*

$$\mathcal{E}_{k,s} = \binom{k}{s} e_1^{k-s} \times e_2^s.$$

Proof. The use of (8) leads to

$$(e_1 + te_2)^k = \sum_{s=0}^{k} \binom{k}{s} e_1^{k-s} \times e_2^s t^s.$$

Denote by $\alpha_{k,s}$ the coefficients of t^s in the right-hand side of last expression, i.e.

$$\alpha_{k,s} := \binom{k}{s} e_1^{k-s} \times e_2^s.$$

Observe that the coefficients $\alpha_{k,s}$ clearly satisfy the initial conditions (6). We are going to prove that they also satisfy the recurrence relation (5), concluding in this way that they are equal to $\mathcal{E}_{k,s}$. To prove the additive property (5) we recall the following recursive formula (see e.g. [12]):

$$v_1^{\mu_1} \times v_2^{\mu_2} = \frac{1}{\mu_1 + \mu_2} [\mu_1 v_1 ({v_1}^{\mu_1 - 1} \times {v_2}^{\mu_2}) + \mu_2 v_2 ({v_1}^{\mu_1} \times {v_2}^{\mu_2 - 1})],$$

which for $v_1 = e_1$, $v_2 = e_2$, $\mu_1 = k - s$, $\mu_2 = s$ allows to write

$$\begin{aligned}\alpha_{k,s} &= \binom{k}{s} \left[\tfrac{k-s}{k} e_1 ({e_1}^{k-s-1} \times {e_2}^s) + \tfrac{s}{k} e_2 ({e_1}^{k-s} \times {e_2}^{s-1}) \right] \\ &= e_1 \binom{k-1}{s} {e_1}^{k-s-1} \times {e_2}^s + e_2 \binom{k-1}{s-1} {e_1}^{k-s} \times {e_2}^{s-1} \\ &= e_1 \alpha_{k-1,s} + e_2 \alpha_{k-1,s-1}\end{aligned}$$

and the proof is completed. □

Theorem 2. *The entries $\mathcal{E}_{k,s}$ of the quaternionic Pascal triangle can be written explicitly as*

$$\mathcal{E}_{k,s} = (-1)^{\lfloor \frac{k}{2} \rfloor} \binom{\lfloor \frac{k}{2} \rfloor}{\lfloor \frac{s}{2} \rfloor} (\epsilon_k \epsilon_s + \epsilon_{k+1} \epsilon_s e_1 + \epsilon_{k+1} \epsilon_{s+1} e_2), \tag{9}$$

where $\epsilon_j = 0$, for odd j and $\epsilon_j = 1$, for even j.

Proof. The result follows by induction on k together with the recursive definition of $\mathcal{E}_{k,s}$. □

A similar result was proved in [4] by using the T. Abadie's formula for the derivative of a composed function. In its present form, (9) can be used to easily identify several properties of the quaternionic Pascal triangle. The first properties can be considered as hypercomplex analogues of well-known properties of the classical Pascal triangle.

Property 1 (Row sum).

$$\sum_{s=0}^{k} \mathcal{E}_{k,s} = \begin{cases} (-2)^{\frac{k}{2}}, & \text{if } k \text{ is even} \\ (-2)^{\frac{k-1}{2}}(e_1+e_2), & \text{if } k \text{ is odd} \end{cases}$$

Proof. If $k = 2m$, $m \in \mathbb{N}$, then (9) together with the well known property $\sum_{s=0}^{k} \binom{k}{s} = 2^k$ give

$$\sum_{s=0}^{2m} \mathcal{E}_{2m,s} = \sum_{s=0}^{2m} (-1)^m \binom{m}{\lfloor \frac{s}{2} \rfloor} \epsilon_s = (-1)^m \sum_{s=0}^{m} \binom{m}{s} = (-1)^m 2^m.$$

On the other hand, for odd values of k, we get

$$\sum_{s=0}^{2m+1} \mathcal{E}_{2m+1,s} = \sum_{s=0}^{m} (-1)^m \binom{m}{\lfloor \frac{s}{2} \rfloor} (\epsilon_{2s}e_1 + \epsilon_{2s+2}e_2) = (-1)^m (e_1+e_2) \sum_{s=0}^{m} \binom{m}{s}$$

and the result is proved. □

Property 2 (Row "alternating" sum).

$$\sum_{s=0}^{k} (-1)^{\lfloor \frac{s}{2} \rfloor} \mathcal{E}_{k,s} = 0, \ k \geq 2.$$

Proof. The property follows at once by combining result (9) with the property $\sum_{s=0}^{k} (-1)^s \binom{k}{s} = 0, k \geq 1$.

□

Property 3 (Central coefficients).

$$\mathcal{E}_{2k,k} = \begin{cases} \binom{k}{\frac{k}{2}}, & \text{if } k \text{ is even} \\ 0, & \text{if } k \text{ is odd} \end{cases}$$

Proof. The proof is immediate. □

Property 4 (Row sum squares).

$$\sum_{s=0}^{k} \mathcal{E}_{k,s}^2 = \begin{cases} \mathcal{E}_{2k,k}, & \text{if } k \text{ is even} \\ -2\mathcal{E}_{2k-2,k-1}, & \text{if } k \text{ is odd} \end{cases}$$

Proof. From (3) and (9) we obtain

$$\mathcal{E}_{k,s}^2 = \binom{\lfloor \frac{k}{2} \rfloor}{\lfloor \frac{s}{2} \rfloor}^2 (\epsilon_k^2 \epsilon_s^2 - \epsilon_{k+1}^2 \epsilon_s^2 - \epsilon_{k+1}^2 \epsilon_{s+1}^2),$$

or equivalently

$$\mathcal{E}_{k,s}^2 = \begin{cases} \binom{m}{\lfloor \frac{s}{2} \rfloor}^2 \epsilon_s^2, & \text{if } k = 2m \\ -\binom{m}{\lfloor \frac{s}{2} \rfloor}^2 (\epsilon_s^2 + \epsilon_{s+1}^2), & \text{if } k = 2m+1 \end{cases} \tag{10}$$

Therefore

$$\sum_{s=0}^{k} \mathcal{E}_{k,s}^2 = \begin{cases} \sum_{s=0}^{m} \binom{m}{s}^2, & \text{if } k = 2m \\ -2\sum_{s=0}^{m} \binom{m}{s}^2, & \text{if } k = 2m+1 \end{cases}$$

The results follows now from the well known fact that the sum of the squares of each element in the row k of the Pascal triangle equals the central binomial coefficient $\binom{2k}{k}$. □

Table 1 summarizes the properties here deduced, which, as already pointed out, reveal great similarities with some of the most well known properties of the Pascal triangle with real entries (see e.g. [2,9]). We now present properties intrinsic to the quaternionic nature of the structure.

Property 5. $\mathcal{E}_{k,s} = 0$ if and only if k is even and s is odd.

Proof. From (9) we know that $\mathcal{E}_{k,s} = 0$ iff

$$\begin{cases} \epsilon_k \epsilon_s = 0 \\ \epsilon_{k+1}\epsilon_s = 0 \\ \epsilon_{k+1}\epsilon_{s+1} = 0 \end{cases} \Leftrightarrow \begin{cases} k \text{ odd or } s \text{ odd} \\ k \text{ even or } s \text{ odd} \\ k \text{ even or } s \text{ even} \end{cases}$$

and the result follows. □

Property 6.

$$\sum_{s=0}^{k} \binom{k}{s}^{-1} \mathcal{E}_{k,s}^2 = \binom{k}{\lfloor \frac{k}{2} \rfloor}^{-1} (-2)^k.$$

Proof. If $k = 2m$, $m \in \mathbb{N}$, then from (10) we obtain

$$\sum_{s=0}^{k} \binom{k}{s}^{-1} \mathcal{E}_{k,s}^2 = \sum_{s=0}^{m} \binom{2m}{2s}^{-1} \binom{m}{s}^2.$$

Using the identity (cf. [8, Identity (6.11)])

$$\sum_{s=0}^{m} \frac{\binom{m}{s}^2}{\binom{2m}{2s}} = \frac{4^m}{\binom{2m}{m}}, \tag{11}$$

Table 1. Parallels between Pascal triangle with real and quaternionic entries

Properties	Pascal triangle	Quaternion triangle
Coefficients	$\mathcal{C}_{k,s}$	$\mathcal{E}_{k,s}$
Recurrence relation	$\mathcal{C}_{k,s} = \mathcal{C}_{k-1,s} + \mathcal{C}_{k-1,s-1}$ $\mathcal{C}_{k,0} = \mathcal{C}_{k,k} = 1$	$\mathcal{E}_{k,s} = e_1\mathcal{E}_{k-1,s} + e_2\mathcal{E}_{k-1,s-1}$ $\mathcal{E}_{0,0} = 1,\ \mathcal{E}_{k,0} = e_1^k,\ \mathcal{E}_{k,k} = e_2^k$
Explicit expression	$\mathcal{C}_{k,s} = \binom{k}{s} = \frac{k!}{s!(k-s)!}$	$\mathcal{E}_{k,s} = \begin{cases} (-1)^{\frac{k}{2}} \binom{\frac{k}{2}}{\frac{s}{2}}, & k \text{ even}, s \text{ even} \\ (-1)^{\frac{k-1}{2}} \binom{\frac{k-1}{2}}{\frac{s}{2}} e_1, & k \text{ odd}, s \text{ even} \\ (-1)^{\frac{k-1}{2}} \binom{\frac{k-1}{2}}{\frac{s-1}{2}} e_2, & k \text{ odd}, s \text{ odd} \\ 0, & \text{otherwise} \end{cases}$
Sum of values	$\sum_{s=0}^{k} \mathcal{C}_{k,s} = 2^k$	$\sum_{s=0}^{k} \mathcal{E}_{k,s} = \begin{cases} (-2)^{\frac{k}{2}}, & k \text{ even} \\ (-2)^{\frac{k-1}{2}} (e_1 + e_2), & k \text{ odd} \end{cases}$
Alternating sum	$\sum_{s=0}^{k} (-1)^s \mathcal{C}_{k,s} = 0,\ k \geq 1$	$\sum_{s=0}^{k} (-1)^{\lfloor \frac{s}{2} \rfloor} \mathcal{E}_{k,s} = 0,\ k \geq 2$
Central coefficient	$\mathcal{C}_{2k,k}$	$\mathcal{E}_{2k,k} = \begin{cases} \mathcal{C}_{k,\frac{k}{2}}, & k \text{ even} \\ 0, & k \text{ odd} \end{cases}$
Sum of square values	$\sum_{s=0}^{k} \mathcal{C}_{k,s}^2 = \mathcal{C}_{2k,k}$	$\sum_{s=0}^{k} \mathcal{E}_{k,s}^2 = \begin{cases} \mathcal{E}_{2k,k}, & k \text{ even} \\ -2\mathcal{E}_{2k-2,k-1}, & k \text{ odd} \end{cases}$

the results follows.

Consider now the case where $k = 2m + 1$. Then

$$\sum_{s=0}^{k} \binom{k}{s}^{-1} \mathcal{E}_{k,s}^2 = \sum_{s=0}^{2m+1} \binom{2m+1}{2s}^{-1} \binom{m}{\lfloor \frac{s}{2} \rfloor}^2 (-\epsilon_s^2 - \epsilon_{s+1}^2)$$

$$= -\sum_{s=0}^{m} \binom{m}{s}^2 \left(\binom{2m+1}{2s}^{-1} + \binom{2m+1}{2s+1}^{-1} \right).$$

From the relation

$$\binom{2m+1}{2s}^{-1} + \binom{2m+1}{2s+1}^{-1} = \frac{2m+2}{2m+1} \binom{2m}{2s}^{-1}$$

and using again (11) it follows that

$$\sum_{s=0}^{k} \binom{k}{s}^{-1} \mathcal{E}_{k,s}^2 = -\frac{2m+2}{2m+1} \frac{4^m}{\binom{2m}{m}} = \frac{m+1}{2m+1} \frac{(-2)^{2m+1}}{\binom{2m}{m}}.$$

and the result is proved, since $\frac{2m+1}{m+1}\binom{2m}{m} = \binom{2m+1}{m}$. □

It is worth to point out that Property 6 hides a sequence of real numbers which combines apparently unrelated subjects in real, complex and hypercomplex analysis [1,5,15,16].

Such sequence was mentioned for the first time in hypercomplex context in [6] and was introduced in the form

$$c_k := \left[\sum_{s=0}^{k} (-1)^k \binom{k}{s} \left(e_1^{k-s} \times e_2^{s} \right)^2 \right]^{-1}, \; k = 0, 1, \ldots. \tag{12}$$

Using Theorem 1 and Property 6, the explicit expression of c_k can be written as

$$c_k = (-1)^k \left[\sum_{s=0}^{k} \varepsilon_{k,s}^2 \binom{k}{s}^{-1} \right]^{-1} = \frac{1}{2^k} \binom{k}{\lfloor \frac{k}{2} \rfloor} \tag{13}$$

The first terms of the sequence $(c_k)_k$ are

$$1, \frac{1}{2}, \frac{1}{2}, \frac{3}{8}, \frac{3}{8}, \frac{5}{16}, \frac{5}{16}, \frac{35}{128}, \frac{35}{128}, \frac{63}{256}, \frac{63}{256}, \frac{231}{1024}, \frac{231}{1024}, \frac{429}{2048}, \frac{429}{2048}, \frac{6435}{32768} \cdots$$

4 Generalizations

The Pascal triangle obtained in last section by the use of the generators of the Clifford algebra $\mathcal{C}\ell_{0,2}$ can be extended to a n regular polytope structure by considering the generators $e_1, e_2, \ldots, e_n$ of the 2^n–dimensional Clifford algebra $\mathcal{C}\ell_{0,n}$ over $\mathbb{R}$, obtaining in this way a generalization of the Pascal n-simplex. In such case we can construct an hypercomplex Pascal n-simplex by choosing as its elements $\mathcal{E}_{k,s_1,\ldots,s_{n-1}}$, the numbers which satisfy the recurrence relation

$$\mathcal{E}_{k,s_1,\ldots,s_{n-1}} = e_1 \mathcal{E}_{k-1,s_1,\ldots,s_{n-1}} + e_2 \mathcal{E}_{k-1,s_1-1,\ldots,s_{n-1}} + \cdots + e_n \mathcal{E}_{k-1,s_1-1,\ldots,s_{n-1}-1}$$

with initial conditions $\mathcal{E}_{0,0,\ldots,0} = 1$ and $\mathcal{E}_{s_0,s_1,\ldots,s_{n-1}} = 0$, for $s_i > s_{i-1}$ or $s_i < 0$. Details on this hypercomplex n-simplex will appear in a forthcoming paper.

References

1. Askey, R., Steinig, J., Trans. AMS: Some positive trigonometric sums **187**(1), 295–307 (1974)
2. Bondarenko, B.A.: Generalized Pascal triangles and pyramids, their fractals, graphs, and applications, volume vii. CA: The Fibonacci Association, (translated from the Russian by Richard C. Bollinger), Santa Clara (1993)
3. Brackx, F., Delanghe, R., Sommen, F.: Clifford Analysis. Pitman, Boston-London-Melbourne (1982)
4. Cação, I., Falcão, M.I., Malonek, H.R.: On Vietoris' number sequence and combinatorial identities with quaternions. In: Vigo-Aguiar, J. (eds.) CMMSE 2017: 17th International Conference on Computational and Mathematical Methods in Science and Engineering, pp. 480–488. Almería (2017)
5. Cação, I., Falcão, M.I., Malonek, H.R.: Hypercomplex polynomials, vietoris' rational numbers and a related integer. Numbers Sequence. Complex Anal. Oper. Theory **11**(5), 1059–1076 (2017)

6. Falcão, M.I., Cruz, J., Malonek, H.R.: Remarks on the generation of monogenic functions. In: 17th International Conference on the Application of Computer Science and Mathematics on Architecture and Civil Engineering, Weimar (2006)
7. Feinberg, M.: A Lucas Triangle. Fibonacci Quart. **5**, 486–490 (1967)
8. Gould, H.W.: Combinatorial identities: Table I: Intermediate techniques for summing finite series, from the seven unpublished manuscripts of H. W. Gould. edited and compiled by Jocelyn Quaintance (2010)
9. Graham, R.L., Knuth, D., E., Patashnik, O.: Concrete mathematics. 2nd edn. Addison-Wesley Publishing Company, Reading, MA (1994)
10. Gürlebeck, K., Habetha, K., Sprößig, W.: Holomorphic functions in the plane and n-dimensional space, Birkhäuser Verlag, Basel (translated from the 2006 German original) (2008)
11. Horn, M.E.: Die didaktische Relevanz des Pauli-Pascal-Dreiecks, In: Dietmar Höttecke (eds.): Naturwissenschaftlicher Unterricht im internationalen Vergleich, Beiträge zur Jahrestagung der GDCP in Bern, vol. 27, pp. 557–559, LIT-Verlag Dr. W. Hopf, Berlin (2007)
12. Malonek, R.: Power series representation for monogenic functions in $\mathbb{R}^{n+1}$ based on a permutational product. Complex Variables, Theory Appl. **15**, 181–191 (1990)
13. Malonek, H.: Selected topics in hypercomplex function theory. In: Eriksson, S.-L. (eds.) Clifford algebras and potential theory, vol. 7, pp. 111–150. University of Joensuu (2004)
14. Sloane, N.J.A.: The On-Line Encyclopedia of Integer Sequences. http://oeis.org
15. Ruscheweyh, St., Salinas, L.: Stable functions and Vietoris' theorem. J. Math. Anal. Appl. **291**, 596–604 (2004)
16. Vietoris, L.: Über das Vorzeichen gewisser trigonometrischer Summen. Sitzungsber. Österr. Akad. Wiss **167**, 125–135 (1958)

Mathematica Tools for Coquaternions

Maria Irene Falcão[1], Fernando Miranda[1(✉)], Ricardo Severino[2], and Maria Joana Soares[3]

[1] CMAT and Departamento de Matemática, Universidade do Minho, Braga, Portugal
{mif,fmiranda}@math.uminho.pt
[2] Departamento de Matemática, Universidade do Minho, Braga, Portugal
ricardo@math.uminho.pt
[3] NIPE and Departamento de Matemática, Universidade do Minho, Braga, Portugal
jsoares@math.uminho.pt

Abstract. Coquaternions form a four dimensional real algebra generalizing complex numbers and were introduced by James Cockle at about the same time that Hamilton discovered the famous algebra of quaternions. Although not as popular as quaternions, in recent years one can observe an emerging interest among mathematicians and physicists on the study of these numbers. In this work we revisit a Mathematica package for implementing the algebra of coquaternions – `Coquaternions` – and discuss a set of Mathematica functions – `CoqPolynomial` – to deal with coquaternionic polynomials. These two sets of functions provide the basic tools necessary for manipulating coquaternions and unilateral coquaternionic polynomials, reflecting, in its present form, the recent interests of the authors in the area.

1 Introduction

Quaternions, introduced in 1843 by the Irish mathematician William Rowan Hamilton (1805–1865) as a generalization of complex numbers [15], have become a powerful tool for solving problems in almost all applied sciences [17], unlocking also new approaches in many branches of applied mathematics. This increasing interest in using quaternions has motivated the emergence of several software packages to perform computations in the algebra of the real quaternions (see, for example, [5,9,10,21]), or more generally, in Clifford Algebras (see [1,2] and the references therein for details).

In 1849, the English mathematician James Cockle, introduced another *system of quadruple algebra* [4] whose elements he designated by the name *coquaternions*. Although coquaternions, also known in the literature as split quaternions, are not as popular as the Hamilton's quaternions, one can say that recently they have also become an active research area [3,6,7,14,16,18,19].

Supported by FCT - Fundação para a Ciência e a Tecnologia, within the Projects UIDB/00013/2020, UIDP/00013/2020 and UIDB/03182/2020.

O. Gervasi et al. (Eds.): ICCSA 2021, LNCS 12952, pp. 449–464, 2021.
https://doi.org/10.1007/978-3-030-86973-1_32

Recently [12], we have introduced a Mathematica add-on application – `Coquaternions` – whose main purpose is to define arithmetic rules for coquaternions and have described a collection of functions – `CoqPolynomial` – for dealing with some polynomial problems over the algebra of coquaternions. As far as we know, these are the only computational tools specially designed to work with coquaternions.

In this paper we discuss a new set of functions for dealing with unilateral coquaternionic polynomials, which, in particular, contains a function implementing a recently proposed algorithm to determine and classify the zeros of such polynomials [13]. A function for computing the nth roots of a coquaternion, accordingly to [11], is also added to `CoqPolynomial`. Several examples have been designed to show clearly the use and performance of the computational tools presented in this work.

2 The Package `Coquaternions` Revisited

In this section we recall some basic definitions and results on coquaternions and we revisit the Mathematica package `Coquaternions`. We mainly follow the presentation of [12], where more details can be found.

Let $\{1, \mathsf{i}, \mathsf{j}, \mathsf{k}\}$ be an orthonormal basis of the Euclidean vector space $\mathbb{R}^4$. The algebra of real coquaternions, which we denote by $\mathbb{H}_{\text{coq}}$, is generated by the product given according to the following rules

$$\mathsf{i}^2 = -1,\ \mathsf{j}^2 = \mathsf{k}^2 = 1,\ \mathsf{ij} = -\mathsf{ji} = \mathsf{k}.$$

Given $\mathsf{q} = q_0 + q_1\mathsf{i} + q_2\mathsf{j} + q_3\mathsf{k} \in \mathbb{H}_{\text{coq}}$, its *conjugate* $\overline{\mathsf{q}}$ is defined as $\overline{\mathsf{q}} = q_0 - q_1\mathsf{i} - q_2\mathsf{j} - q_3\mathsf{k}$; the number q_0 is called the *real part* of q, denoted by $\operatorname{Re}\mathsf{q}$, and the *vector part* of q, denoted by $\underline{\mathsf{q}}$, is given by $\underline{\mathsf{q}} = q_1\mathsf{i} + q_2\mathsf{j} + q_3\mathsf{k}$. We call *trace* of q, denoted by $\operatorname{tr}\mathsf{q}$, the quantity given by $\operatorname{tr}\mathsf{q} = \mathsf{q} + \overline{\mathsf{q}} = 2\operatorname{Re}\mathsf{q}$ and call *determinant* of q, denoted by $\det\mathsf{q}$, the quantity given by $\det\mathsf{q} = \mathsf{q}\overline{\mathsf{q}} = q_0^2 + q_1^2 - q_2^2 - q_3^2$.

Unlike $\mathbb{C}$ and $\mathbb{H}$, $\mathbb{H}_{\text{coq}}$ is not a division algebra. In fact, a coquaternion q is invertible if and only if $\det\mathsf{q} \neq 0$. In that case, we have $\mathsf{q}^{-1} = \frac{\overline{\mathsf{q}}}{\det\mathsf{q}}$. Finally, we endow $\mathbb{H}_{\text{coq}}$ with the *semi-norm* $\|\mathsf{q}\| = \sqrt{|\det\mathsf{q}|}$ and call q a *unit coquaternion* if $\|\mathsf{q}\| = 1$.

In the `Coquaternions` package, a coquaternion $\mathsf{q} = q_0 + q_1\mathsf{i} + q_2\mathsf{j} + q_3\mathsf{k}$ is an object of the form `Coquaternion[q0,q1,q2,q3]`, whose entries are numeric quantities or symbols (in such case the package assumes that all symbols represent real numbers).

The package adds rules to the functions `Plus`, `Minus`, `Times`, `Power` and `NonCommutativeMultiply` to make it easy to perform basic arithmetic operations and also extends some standard functions to coquaternion objects. A summary of the functions included in the package is given in Table 1.

Table 1. Basic operations on coquaternions

Function	Description
`Abs[q]`	extends the `Abs` function to coquaternion objects
`ComplexMatrixToCoquaternion[m]`	gives the coquaternion corresponding to $\mathtt{m} \in \mathcal{M}_2(\mathbb{C})$
`ComplexToCoquaternion[{a,b}]`	gives the coquaternion $\mathsf{a} + \mathsf{bj}$, with $\mathsf{a}, \mathsf{b} \in \mathbb{C}$
`Conjugate[q]`	extends the `Conjugate` function to coquaternion objects
`Coquaternion[q0,q1,q2,q3]`	represents the coquaternion $\mathsf{q}_0 + \mathsf{q}_1\mathsf{i} + \mathsf{q}_2\mathsf{j} + \mathsf{q}_3\mathsf{k}$
`CoquaternionQ[q]`	gives `True` if q is a coquaternion and `False` otherwise
`CoquaternionToComplex[q]`	gives a list $\{q_0 + \mathsf{i}q_1, q_2 + \mathsf{i}q_3\}$ for the complex form of q
`CoquaternionToComplexMatrix[q]`	gives the complex 2×2 representation matrix of q
`CoquaternionToMatrix[q]`	gives the real 2×2 representation matrix of q
`CoquaternionTo4DMatrixL[q]`	gives the real 4×4 left representation matrix of q
`CoquaternionTo4DMatrixR[q]`	gives the real 4×4 right representation matrix of q
`Det[q]`	extends the `Det` function to coquaternion objects
`MatrixToCoquaternion[m]`	gives the coquaternion corresponding to $\mathtt{m} \in \mathcal{M}_2(\mathbb{R})$
`Norm[q]`	extends the `Norm` function to coquaternion objects
`Power[q,n]`	extends the `Power` function to coquaternion objects for integer exponents
`Re[q]`	extends the `Re` function to coquaternion objects
`ToCoquaternion[a]`	gives de coquaternion form of a when a is a real or complex number
`Tr[q]`	extends the `Tr` function to coquaternion objects
`Vec[q]`	gives the vector part of q

3 Coquaternionic Polynomials

In this section we describe a new collection of functions added to the Mathematica tool `CoqPolynomial` for dealing with some polynomial problems in $\mathbb{H}_{\text{coq}}$. The first part of the section follows mainly [12].

Let $\mathbb{H}_{\text{coq}}[x]$ denote the set of polynomials of the form

$$P(x) = \mathsf{c}_n x^n + \mathsf{c}_{n-1} x^{n-1} + \cdots + \mathsf{c}_1 x + \mathsf{c}_0, \ \mathsf{c}_i \in \mathbb{H}_{\text{coq}}, \tag{1}$$

i.e., the set of polynomials whose coefficients are only located on the left of the variable, with the addition and multiplication of such polynomials defined as in the commutative case, where the variable is assumed to commute with the coefficients. This is a ring, referred to as the ring of (left) *one-sided* or *unilateral* polynomials in $\mathbb{H}_{\text{coq}}$, or simply the ring of *coquaternionic polynomials.* We usually omit the reference to the variable and write simply P when referring to an element $P(x) \in \mathbb{H}_{\text{coq}}[x]$, since all the polynomials considered in this work are in the indeterminate x.

As usual, if $\mathsf{c}_n \neq 0$, we say that the *degree* of the polynomial P is n and refer to c_n as the leading coefficient of the polynomial. When $\mathsf{c}_n = 1$, we say that P is *monic.* If the coefficients c_i in (1) are real, then we say that P is a *real polynomial.* Given a polynomial P of the form (1), its *conjugate polynomial* is the polynomial defined by

$$\overline{P}(x) = \overline{\mathsf{c}}_n x^n + \overline{\mathsf{c}}_{n-1} x^{n-1} + \cdots + \overline{\mathsf{c}}_1 x + \overline{\mathsf{c}}_0.$$

For a coquaternionic polynomial P, the *evaluation map* at a given element $\mathsf{q} \in \mathbb{H}_{\text{coq}}$ is defined by

$$P(\mathsf{q}) = \mathsf{c}_n \mathsf{q}^n + \mathsf{c}_{n-1} \mathsf{q}^{n-1} + \cdots + \mathsf{c}_1 \mathsf{q} + \mathsf{c}_0.$$

If $P(\mathsf{q}) = 0$, then we say that q is a *zero* (or a *root*) of P.

The evaluation map is not a homomorphism from the ring $\mathbb{H}_{\text{coq}}[x]$ into $\mathbb{H}_{\text{coq}}$; given two polynomials $L, R \in \mathbb{H}_{\text{coq}}[x]$, in general, we do not have $(LR)(\mathsf{q}) = L(\mathsf{q})R(\mathsf{q})$.

Before we present some results on the structure of the sets of zeros of a coquaternionic polynomial, we first recall the concept of quasi-similarity for coquaternions; see e.g. [8,13] and references therein.

We say that two elements $\mathsf{p}, \mathsf{q} \in \mathbb{H}_{\text{coq}}$ are *quasi-similar* if and only if $\operatorname{Re}\mathsf{p} = \operatorname{Re}\mathsf{q}$ and $\det \mathsf{p} = \det \mathsf{q}$. This is an equivalence relation in $\mathbb{H}_{\text{coq}}$;[1] the class of an element $\mathsf{q} \in \mathbb{H}_{\text{coq}}$ with respect to this relation will be denoted by $[\![\mathsf{q}]\!]$ and referred to as the *quasi-similarity class* of q. Observe that

$$[\![\mathsf{q}]\!] = \{x_0 + x_1\mathsf{i} + x_2\mathsf{j} + x_3\mathsf{k} : x_0 = q_0 \text{ and } x_1^2 - x_2^2 - x_3^2 = \det \underline{\mathsf{q}}\}$$

can be identified with a hyperboloid in the hyperplane $\{(x_0, x_1, x_2, x_3) \in \mathbb{R}^4 : x_0 = q_0\}$: a hyperboloid of two sheets if $\det \underline{\mathsf{q}} > 0$, a hyperboloid of one sheet if $\det \underline{\mathsf{q}} < 0$ and a degenerate hyperboloid, i.e. a cone, if $\det \underline{\mathsf{q}} = 0$.

Given a quasi-similarity class $[\![\mathsf{q}]\!] = [\![q_0 + \underline{\mathsf{q}}]\!]$, we call *characteristic polynomial* of this class and denote by $\Psi_{[\![\mathsf{q}]\!]}$, the second degree monic polynomial with real coefficients given by

$$\Psi_{[\![\mathsf{q}]\!]}(x) = x^2 - 2q_0\, x + \det \mathsf{q}.$$

It is important to observe that any second degree monic polynomial S with real coefficients is the characteristic polynomial of a (uniquely defined) quasi-similarity class: if S has two roots $\alpha, \overline{\alpha} \in \mathbb{C} \setminus \mathbb{R}$, then $S = \Psi_{[\![\mathsf{q}]\!]}$, with $\mathsf{q} = \alpha$, and if S has real roots r_1 and r_2 (with, eventually, $r_1 = r_2$), then $S = \Psi_{[\![\mathsf{q}]\!]}$, with $\mathsf{q} = \frac{r_1+r_2}{2} + \frac{r_1-r_2}{2}\mathsf{j}$.

[1] For a discussion on how this concept relates to another well-known equivalence in $\mathbb{H}_{\text{coq}}$, the similarity relation, see e.g. [8].

We recall that in the Mathematica tool `CoqPolynomial`, introduced in [12], a coquaternionic polynomial is an object of the form `Polynomial`$[\mathsf{c}_n,\mathsf{c}_{n-1},\ldots,\mathsf{c}_1,\mathsf{c}_0]$ accordingly to (1). For such objects, several rules and functions are defined.

A function `CharacteristicPolynomial` for computing the characteristic polynomial of a (representative of a given) class was recently added to `CoqPolynomial`. We illustrate its use with three simple examples.

```
In[1]:= <<CoqPolynomial`
In[2]:= q1 = ToCoquaternion[1+2I]; ChP1 = CharacteristicPolynomial[q1]
Out[2]= Polynomial[1, -2, 5]
In[3]:= Solve[PolyForm[ChP1,x] == 0, x]
Out[3]= {{x -> 1 - 2 i}, {x -> 1 + 2 i}}
In[4]:= q2 = ToCoquaternion[2]; ChP2 = CharacteristicPolynomial[q2]
Out[4]= Polynomial[1, -4, 4]
In[5]:= Solve[PolyForm[ChP2,x] == 0, x]
Out[5]= {{x -> 2}, {x -> 2}}
In[6]:= q3 = Coquaternion[2,0,-2,0]; ChP3 = CharacteristicPolynomial[q3]
Out[6]= Polynomial[1, -4, 0]
In[7]:= Solve[PolyForm[ChP3,x] == 0, x]
Out[7]= {{x -> 0}, {x -> 4}}
```

We now present very briefly some results on the zeros of coquaternionic polynomials; more details can be seen in e.g. [13]. In what follows we restrict our attention to monic polynomials, i.e. to polynomials of the form (1) with $\mathsf{c}_n = 1$.[2]

Given a polynomial P, we denote by $Z(P)$ the *zero-set* of P, i.e. the set of all the zeros of P; we also define the *companion polynomial* of P, $\mathcal{C}_P$, as the polynomial given by

$$\mathcal{C}_P(x) = P(x)\overline{P}(x).$$

As was shown in [13], if $\mathsf{z} \in \mathbb{H}_{\rm coq}$ is a zero of P, then the characteristic polynomial of $[\![\mathsf{z}]\!]$ is a divisor of $\mathcal{C}_P$. When P is monic (or with a non-singular leading term), it can be shown easily that $\mathcal{C}_P$ is a polynomial of degree $2n$ with real coefficients and, as such, considered as a polynomial in $\mathbb{C}$, has $2n$ roots. If these roots are $\alpha_1, \overline{\alpha}_1, \ldots, \alpha_m, \overline{\alpha}_m \in \mathbb{C} \setminus \mathbb{R}$ and $r_1, r_2, \ldots, r_\ell \in \mathbb{R}$, where $\ell = 2(n-m)$, $(0 \leq m \leq n)$, then it is easy to conclude that the second-degree monic polynomials with real coefficients which divide $\mathcal{C}_P$ are the characteristic polynomials of the following quasi-similarity classes:

[2] As far as the computation of zeros is concerned, considering this type of polynomials is equivalent to considering polynomials whose leading term is invertible.

$$[\![\alpha_k]\!];\ k = 1, \ldots, m, \tag{2a}$$

$$[\![\mathsf{r}_{ij}]\!];\ i = 1, \ldots, \ell - 1,\ j = i+1, \ldots, \ell, \tag{2b}$$

with

$$\mathsf{r}_{ij} = \frac{r_i + r_j}{2} + \frac{r_i - r_j}{2}\mathsf{j}. \tag{2c}$$

We thus have the following result concerning the zero-set of P:

$$Z(P) \subseteq \bigcup_k [\![\alpha_k]\!] \bigcup_{i,j} [\![\mathsf{r}_{ij}]\!],$$

where $[\![\alpha_k]\!]$ and $[\![\mathsf{r}_{ij}]\!]$ are the quasi-similarity classes defined by (2). We call the classes given by (2) the *admissible classes* (with respect to the zeros) of the polynomial P.

Two new functions to determine, respectively, the companion polynomial and the admissible classes of a coquaternionic polynomial – `CompanionPolynomial` and `AdmissibleClasses` – are now part of `CoqPolynomial`.

```
In[8]:= P = Polynomial[1,Coquaternion[2,-1,2,-1],Coquaternion[1,1,4,1]];
        CPP = CompanionPolynomial[P]
Out[8]= Polynomial[1,4,2,-12,-15]
In[9]:= Solve[PolyForm[CPP,x] == 0, x]
```

Out[9]= $\{\{x \to -2 - \mathbb{i}\}, \{x \to -2 + \mathbb{i}\}, \{x \to -\sqrt{3}\}, \{x \to \sqrt{3}\}\}$

```
In[10]:= AdmissibleClasses[P]//TraditionalForm
```

Out[10]= $\{-2 - \mathbb{i}, \sqrt{3}\ \mathbb{j}\}$

The results given in the following theorem show how to find the zeros of a polynomial P belonging to one of its admissible classes.

Theorem 1 ([13, Theorem 3.14]). *Let $P(x)$ be a monic polynomial of the form* (1) *and let $[\![\mathsf{q}]\!] = [\![q_0 + \underline{\mathsf{q}}]\!]$ be an admissible class of $P(x)$. Also, let $\mathsf{a} + \mathsf{b}x$, with $\mathsf{b} = b_0 + b_1\mathsf{i} + b_2\mathsf{j} + b_3\mathsf{k}$, be the remainder of the right division of $P(x)$ by the characteristic polynomial of $[\![\mathsf{q}]\!]$.*

1. *If $\det \mathsf{b} \neq 0$, then $[\![\mathsf{q}]\!]$ contains only one zero of P, given by*

$$\mathsf{z} = -\mathsf{b}^{-1}\mathsf{a}.$$

2. *If $\mathsf{a} = \mathsf{b} = 0$, then $[\![\mathsf{q}]\!] \subseteq Z(P)$.*
3. *If $\mathsf{b} \neq 0$, $\det \mathsf{b} = 0$ and the equation $\mathsf{a} + \mathsf{b}x = 0$ has a real solution γ_0 satisfying*

$$(q_0 - \gamma_0)^2 = -\det(\underline{\mathsf{q}}),$$

then the zeros of P in $[\![\mathsf{q}]\!]$ form the following line in the hyperplane $x_0 = q_0$,

$$\mathcal{L} = \{q_0 + \alpha\mathsf{i} + (k_2\alpha + k_1(q_0 - \gamma_0))\,\mathsf{j} + (-k_1\alpha + k_2(q_0 - \gamma_0))\,\mathsf{k} : \alpha \in \mathbb{R}\},$$

with k_1 and k_2 given by

$$k_1 = -\frac{b_0b_2 + b_1b_3}{b_0^2 + b_1^2} \quad \text{and} \quad k_2 = \frac{b_1b_2 - b_0b_3}{b_0^2 + b_1^2}. \tag{3}$$

4. If $\mathsf{b} \neq 0, \det \mathsf{b} = 0$ *and the equation* $\mathsf{a} + \mathsf{b}x = 0$ *has a non-real solution* $\gamma = \gamma_0 + \gamma_1 \mathsf{i}$*, then the class* $[\![\mathsf{q}]\!]$ *contains only one zero of* P*, given by*

$$\mathsf{z} = q_0 + (\beta + \gamma_1)\mathsf{i} + (k_2\beta + k_1(q_0 - \gamma_0))\,\mathsf{j} + (-k_1\beta + k_2(q_0 - \gamma_0))\,\mathsf{k},$$

where

$$\beta = \frac{\det(\underline{\mathsf{q}}) + (q_0 - \gamma_0)^2 - \gamma_1^2}{2\gamma_1}$$

and k_1 *and* k_2 *are given by* (3).

5. If none of the above conditions holds, then there are no zeros of P *in* $[\![\mathsf{q}]\!]$.

In cases 1. and 4., we say that the zero z is an *isolated zero* of P; in case 2., we say that the class $[\![\mathsf{q}]\!]$ (or any of its elements) is a *hyperboloidal zero* of P and in case 3. we call the line $\mathcal{L}$ (or any of its elements) a *linear zero* of P.

With the understanding that all the zeros belonging to the same quasi-similarity class are counted as one zero, we have the following result.

Theorem 2 (**[13, Theorem 3.10]**). *A polynomial of degree* n *in* $\mathbb{H}_{\mathrm{coq}}[x]$*, has at most,* $n(2n-1)$ *zeros.*

A function `NumZeros` indicating the number of zeros of each type that a given polynomial possesses is now available in `CoqPolynomial`.

Example 1. The polynomials P and Q given by

$$\begin{aligned} P(x) &= x^4 - (\mathsf{j} + \mathsf{k})x^3 + (-8 + 4\mathsf{i} - 2\mathsf{j} - 5\mathsf{k})x^2 + (9 + 4\mathsf{i} + 7\mathsf{j} + 10\mathsf{k})x \\ &\quad - (5 + 5\mathsf{i} + 7\mathsf{j} + \mathsf{k}), \\ Q(x) &= x^5 + (2\mathsf{i} - \mathsf{j} - 4\mathsf{k})x^4 + (2\mathsf{i} - \mathsf{j} - 4\mathsf{k})x^3 + (-21 + 35\mathsf{i} - 10\mathsf{j} + 37\mathsf{k})x^2 \\ &\quad + (-63 + 7\mathsf{i} + 16\mathsf{j} + 46\mathsf{k})x + 6 - 88\mathsf{i} + 74\mathsf{j} - 48\mathsf{k} \end{aligned}$$

are examples of polynomials achieving the maximum number of zeros allowed by the respective degrees (28 for a polynomial of degree 4, and 45 for a polynomial of degree 5).

```
In[11]:= P=Polynomial[1,- Coquaternion[0,0,1,1],Coquaternion[-8,4,-2,-5]],
           Coquaternion[9,4,7,10],- Coquaternion[5,5,7,1]];

         NumZeros[P]
Out[11]= {28,0,0}
```

The output indicates that P has 28 isolated zeros, no linear zeros and no hyperboloidal zeros.

```
In[12]:= Q=Polynomial[1,Coquaternion[0,2,-1,-4],Coquaternion[-7,-8,13,5],
           Coquaternion[-21,35,-10,37],Coquaternion[-63,7,16,46],
           Coquaternion[6,-88,74,-48]];

         NumZeros[Q]
Out[12]= {45,0,0}
```

Example 2. The polynomial $R(x) = x^2 - (1 + \mathsf{j} + \mathsf{k})$ illustrates an important difference between coquaternionic polynomials and complex (or quaternionic) polynomials: there exist polynomials with no zeros, i.e., the Fundamental Theorem of Algebra is not valid in $\mathbb{H}_{\mathrm{coq}}[x]$.

```
In[13]:= R = Polynomial[1,0,-Coquaternion[1,0,1,1]];NumZeros[R]
Out[13]= {0,0,0}
```

A function to compute and classify the zeros of a coquaternion polynomial – `Zeros` – was recently added to `CoqPolynomial`. This function implements an algorithm, proposed in [13], which makes use of formulas (2) for the identification of the admissible classes, followed by the application of the results of Theorem 1 to determine and classify the zeros in each class (if existing). We now present several examples of application of this function. Note that the output of the function `Zeros` is a list composed of three lists, containing, respectively, the isolated zeros, the linear zeros and (representatives of) the hyperboloidal zeros of the input polynomial.

Example 3. We consider again the polynomials given in Example 1 and present some of their zeros.

```
In[14]:= {zIP, zLP, zHP} = Zeros[P];
         (first4zP = Take[zIP,4])//TraditionalForm
```

Out[14]= $\{-2 - \frac{7\mathrm{i}}{8} - \frac{15\mathrm{j}}{8} - \frac{\mathrm{k}}{2}, -1 + \frac{6\mathrm{i}}{7} - \frac{2\mathrm{j}}{7} + \frac{9\mathrm{k}}{7}, -\frac{1}{2} + \frac{5\mathrm{i}}{2} - \frac{3\mathrm{j}}{2} + \frac{5\mathrm{k}}{2},$
$-\frac{1}{2} + \frac{1}{46}(163 - 72\sqrt{3})\mathbb{i} - \frac{3}{46}(-13 + 8\sqrt{3})\mathbb{j} + \frac{1}{46}(-137 + 102\sqrt{3})\mathbb{k}\}$

```
In[15]:= Eval[P,first4zP]
Out[15]= {0,0,0,0}
```

```
In[16]:= {zIQ, zLQ, zHQ} = Zeros[Q];
         (first4zQ = Take[zIQ,4])//TraditionalForm
```

Out[16]= $\{-\frac{5}{2} - \frac{157\mathrm{i}}{114} + \frac{113\mathrm{j}}{114} + \frac{41\mathrm{k}}{38}, -\frac{3}{2} + \frac{31\mathrm{i}}{13} - \frac{73\mathrm{j}}{26} + \frac{3\mathrm{k}}{13},$
$-1 + \frac{7\mathrm{i}}{9} - \frac{11\mathrm{j}}{9} - \frac{\mathrm{k}}{3}, -1 - \frac{650\mathrm{i}}{159} + \frac{430\mathrm{j}}{159} + \frac{194\mathrm{k}}{53}\}$

```
In[17]:= Eval[Q,first4zQ]
Out[17]= {0,0,0,0}
```

Example 4. The three quadratic polynomials

$$S(x) = x^2 - (2 + 6\mathsf{i} + 3\mathsf{j} + 5\mathsf{k})x + 9\mathsf{i} + 4\mathsf{j} + 8\mathsf{k},$$
$$T(x) = x^2 - (2 + 2\mathsf{i} + 2\mathsf{k})x + 1 + 2\mathsf{i} + 2\mathsf{k}$$

and

$$U(x) = x^2 - 2x + 1$$

have the same companion polynomial, $(x-1)^4$, hence the same unique admissible class, $[\![1]\!]$, but different types of zeros: S has an isolated zero, T a linear zero and U a hyperboloidal zero.

```
In[18]:= S=Polynomial[1,-Coquaternion[2,6,3,5],Coquaternion[0,9,4,8]];
          T=Polynomial[1,-Coquaternion[2,2,0,2],Coquaternion[1,2,0,2]];
          U=Polynomial[1,-2,1];
In[19]:= Simplify[PolyForm[CompanionPolynomial[S],x]]
```

Out[19]= $(-1+x)^4$

```
In[20]:= AdmissibleClasses[S]//QSimplify
Out[20]= {1}
In[21]:= QSimplify[AdmissibleClasses[T]]=={1} &&
          QSimplify[AdmissibleClasses[U]]=={1}
Out[21]= True
In[22]:= {zIS, zLS, zHS} = Zeros[S]
Out[22]= {{Coquaternion[1,5,3,4]},{},{}}
In[23]:= {zIT, zLT, zHT} = Zeros[T]
```

Out[23]= {{},{Coquaternion[1, c_1, 0, c_1]},{}}

```
In[24]:= {zIU, zLU, zHU} = Zeros[U]
Out[24]= {{},{},{1}}
In[25]:= PolynomialZeroQ[S,zIS[[1]]]
Out[25]= True
In[26]:= PolynomialZeroQ[T,zLT[[1]]]
Out[26]= True
```

One can easily check that any element in the class $[\![1]\!]$ is, in fact, a zero of the polynomial U.

```
In[27]:= Assuming[Det[Coquaternion[1,C[1],C[2],C[3]]] ==
          Det[ToCoquaternion[1],
          PolynomialZeroQ[U,Coquaternion[1,C[1],C[2],C[3]]]]
Out[27]= True
```

Example 5. The five polynomials considered in this example are all polynomials of second degree and illustrate the very different behaviors that (even simple) polynomials may have, in what concerns their zero-sets.

1. *One linear zero*

```
In[28]:= Zeros[Polynomial[1,Coquaternion[0,1,1,0],0]]//TraditionalForm
```

Out[28]= {{},{$\mathbb{i}c_1+\mathbb{j}c_1$},{}}

2. *Two isolated zeros and one linear zero*

```
In[29]:= Zeros[Polynomial[1,Coquaternion[-2,1,1,0],
          Coquaternion[0,-2,-2,0]]]//TraditionalForm
```

Out[29]= $\{\{-\mathbb{i}-\mathbb{j},2\},\{1+\mathbb{i}c_1+\mathbb{j}c_1-\mathbb{k}\},\{\}\}$

3. *Two linear zeros*

```
In[30]:= Zeros[Polynomial[1,Coquaternion[0,0,2,0],
          Coquaternion[-1,0,-2,0]]]
```

Out[30]= $\{\{\},\{1+\mathbb{i}c_1-2\mathbb{j}-\mathbb{k}c_1,1+\mathbb{i}c_1+\mathbb{k}c_1\},\{\}\}$

4. *Two isolated zeros and two linear zeros*

```
In[31]:= Zeros[Polynomial[1, Coquaternion[-2,-1,1,1],
          Coquaternion[1,1,-1,-1]]]//TraditionalForm
```

Out[31]= $\{\{1,1+\mathbb{i}-\mathbb{j}-\mathbb{k}\},\{\frac{1}{2}+\mathbb{i}c_1-\frac{\mathbb{j}}{2}-\mathbb{k}c_1,\frac{3}{2}+\mathbb{i}c_1-\mathbb{j}c_1-\frac{\mathbb{k}}{2}\},\{\}\}$

5. *Two isolated zeros and one hyperboloidal zero*

```
In[32]:= Zeros[Polynomial[1,-3,2]]//TraditionalForm
```

Out[32]= $\{\{1,2\},\{\},\{\frac{3}{2}+\frac{\mathbb{i}}{2}\}\}$

The following theorem states a sufficient condition for the existence of linear zeros of a polynomial.

Theorem 3 **([13, Theorem 3.16]).** *Let $P(x)$ be a polynomial of degree n whose companion polynomial has m real simple zeros $r_1, r_2, \ldots, r_m$, $m \leq 2n$, and let $P_r(x) = P(x)(x-r)$ with $r \in \mathbb{R}$, $r \neq r_i; i = 1, \ldots, m$. Then, $P_r(x)$ has (at least) m linear zeros.*

Example 6. We illustrate the result of the previous theorem with a simple example. Consider the polynomial $P(x) = x^2 + (-1+3\mathsf{i}-2\mathsf{j}+\mathsf{k})x - 2\mathsf{i} - 2\mathsf{k}$. The companion polynomial of P has two simple real roots $r_1 = 0$ and $r_2 = 2$ (and two complex conjugate roots $\pm\sqrt{2}\mathsf{i}$). This polynomial has two isolated zeros:

```
In[33]:= Clear[P];
         P=Polynomial[1,Coquaternion[-1,3,-2,2],Coquaternion[0,-2,0,-2]];
```

```
In[34]:= Solve[PolyForm[CompanionPolynomial[P],x] == 0]
```

Out[34]= $\{\{x\to 0\},\{x\to 2\},\{x\to -\mathbb{i}\sqrt{2}\},\{x\to \mathbb{i}\sqrt{2}\}\}$

```
In[35]:= NumZeros[P]
```

Out[35]= $\{2,0,0\}$

Multiplying P by the factor $(x-1)$, we obtain a polynomial with two linear zeros (and three isolated zeros):

```
In[36]:= Clear[P1]; P1=P**Polynomial[1,-1];
```

Table 2. Some functions of `CoqPolynomial`

Function	Description
`AdmissibleClasses[P]`	gives the admissible classes of the polynomial `P`
`CharacteristicPolynomial[q]`	gives the characteristic polynomial of (the class) of the coquaternion `q`
`CompanionPolynomial[P]`	gives the companion polynomial of the polynomial `P`
`Conjugate[P]`	gives the conjugate of the polynomial `P`
`Eval[P,q]`	computes `P(q)`
`NumZeros[P]`	gives the number of each type of zeros of the polynomial `P`
`PolyForm[P,x]`	gives the standard representation of the real polynomial `P` in the variable `x`
`Polynomial[`c_n`,`c_{n-1}`,...,`c_1`,`c_0`]`	represents the polynomial $c_n x^n + c_{n-1} x^{n-1} + \cdots + c_1 x + c_0$
`PolynomialZeroQ[P,q]`	gives `True` if `q` is a zero of `P` and `False` otherwise
`PSimplify[P]`	gives the polynomial `P` with simplified coefficients
`Zeros[P]`	gives the zeros of the polynomial `P`

In[37]:= `NumZeros[P1]`

Out[37]= $\{3, 2, 0\}$

In[38]:= `Zeros[P]//TraditionalForm`

Out[38]= $\{-6\mathbb{i} + 3\mathbb{j} - 5\mathbb{k}, 1 - \mathbb{i} + \mathbb{j} - \mathbb{k}\}, \{\}, \{\}\}$

In[39]:= `Zeros[P1]//TraditionalForm`

Out[39]= $\{\{-6\mathbb{i} + 3\mathbb{j} - 5\mathbb{k}, 1, 1 - \mathbb{i} + \mathbb{j} - \mathbb{k}\},$
$\{\frac{1}{2} + \mathbb{i}\mathbb{c}_1 + \frac{\mathbb{j}}{2} + \mathbb{k}\mathbb{c}_1, \frac{3}{2} + \mathbb{i}\mathbb{c}_1 - \mathbb{j}\mathbb{c}_1 - \frac{\mathbb{k}}{2}\}, \{\}\}$

A list of functions related to `CoqPolynomial` is presented in Table 2.

Observation: For all the polynomials considered in the previous examples, it was possible to compute the roots of the corresponding companion polynomial exactly, and hence, to obtain the zeros with infinite precision. In general, however, even for a polynomial P of moderate degree n, the zeros of $\mathcal{C}_P$ (which is a polynomial of degree $2n$), may only be obtained by using a numerical method. Since the classification and determination of the zeros of the polynomial depend critically on knowing of whether or not certain quantities are zero and also on the existence or not of a real or complex solution of a linear system, having approximate values for the representatives for the admissible classes may lead, in some cases, to a miss-classification and inappropriate determination of zeros and some care has to be taken. Ways to circumvent these problems require further investigation.

4 The nth Roots of a Coquaternion

The nth roots of a coquaternion q can be obtained by solving the equation $x^n - \mathsf{q} = 0$, through the use of the algorithm described in the previous section. However, as already pointed out, this may involve a numerical method for finding the zeros of a $2n$th degree real polynomial. In order to avoid this issue and have explicit exact solutions to the problem, one can use the polar form of a non-real coquaternion q together with a De Moivre's formula. When $\mathsf{q} \in \mathbb{R}$ the technique described in Sect. 3 allows to obtain exact solutions.

This approach was used in [11], where the authors gave a complete characterization of the nth roots ($n \geq 2$) of a coquaternion, extending the results of [20].

We recall that a coquaternion q is called *space-like, light-like* or *time-like* if $\det \mathsf{q} < 0$, $\det \mathsf{q} = 0$ or $\det \mathsf{q} > 0$, respectively; the sets of such coquaternions is denoted by $\mathbb{S}$, $\mathbb{L}$ and $\mathbb{T}$, respectively. When two coquaternions belong to the same set $\mathbb{S}$, $\mathbb{L}$ or $\mathbb{T}$, we say that they have the same nature. We also adopt the notations

$$\begin{aligned}&\mathbb{T}_{\mathbb{S}} = \{\mathsf{q} \in \mathbb{T} : \underline{\mathsf{q}} \in \mathbb{S}\},\ \mathbb{T}_{\mathbb{L}} = \{\mathsf{q} \in \mathbb{T} : \underline{\mathsf{q}} \in \mathbb{L}\},\ \mathbb{T}_{\mathbb{T}} = \{\mathsf{q} \in \mathbb{T} : \underline{\mathsf{q}} \in \mathbb{T}\},\\ &\mathbb{L}_{\mathbb{S}} = \{\mathsf{q} \in \mathbb{L} : \underline{\mathsf{q}} \in \mathbb{S}\},\ \mathbb{L}_{\mathbb{L}} = \{\mathsf{q} \in \mathbb{L} : \underline{\mathsf{q}} \in \mathbb{L}\}.\end{aligned}$$

We observe that since $\det \mathsf{q} \geq \det \underline{\mathsf{q}}$, if q is space-like, $\underline{\mathsf{q}}$ is of the same nature and a light-like coquaternion can not have a time-like vector part. The function `Nature` to classify coquaternions is included in `Coquaternions` (see [12] for more details).

Any coquaternion $\mathsf{q} = q_0 + q_1\mathsf{i} + q_2\mathsf{j} + q_3\mathsf{k} \in \mathbb{S} \cup \mathbb{T}$, such that $\underline{\mathsf{q}} \notin \mathbb{L}$, has a polar representation in one of the forms

$$\mathsf{q} = \begin{cases} \|\mathsf{q}\|\big(\sinh\phi_{\mathsf{q}} + \boldsymbol{\omega}_{\underline{\mathsf{q}}}\cosh\phi_{\mathsf{q}}\big), & \text{if } \mathsf{q} \in \mathbb{S},\\ \|\mathsf{q}\|\big(\operatorname{sgn} q_0 \cosh\psi_{\mathsf{q}} + \boldsymbol{\omega}_{\underline{\mathsf{q}}}\sinh\psi_{\mathsf{q}}\big), & \text{if } \mathsf{q} \in \mathbb{T}_{\mathbb{S}},\\ \|\mathsf{q}\|\big(\cos\theta_{\mathsf{q}} + \boldsymbol{\omega}_{\underline{\mathsf{q}}}\sin\theta_{\mathsf{q}}\big), & \text{if } \mathsf{q} \in \mathbb{T}_{\mathbb{T}}, \end{cases} \tag{4a}$$

where *sgn* is the usual sign function,

$$\sinh\phi_{\mathsf{q}} = \frac{q_0}{\|\mathsf{q}\|},\quad \sinh\psi_{\mathsf{q}} = \frac{\|\underline{\mathsf{q}}\|}{\|\mathsf{q}\|},\quad \cos\theta_{\mathsf{q}} = \frac{q_0}{\|\mathsf{q}\|},\quad \sin\theta_{\mathsf{q}} = \frac{\|\underline{\mathsf{q}}\|}{\|\mathsf{q}\|},\ \theta_{\mathsf{q}} \in (0,\pi) \tag{4b}$$

and

$$\boldsymbol{\omega}_{\underline{\mathsf{q}}} = \frac{\underline{\mathsf{q}}}{\|\underline{\mathsf{q}}\|} \tag{4c}$$

is a unit coquaternion satisfying $\boldsymbol{\omega}_{\underline{\mathsf{q}}}^2 = 1$, if $\underline{\mathsf{q}} \in \mathbb{S}$ and $\boldsymbol{\omega}_{\underline{\mathsf{q}}}^2 = -1$, if $\underline{\mathsf{q}} \in \mathbb{T}$.

We recall that the polar form (4) is implemented in `Coquaternions` through the use of the function `PolarForm[q]` which gives a list of one of the forms

$$\{\text{nat} \to \text{Spacelike}, r \to \|\mathsf{q}\|, \varphi \to \phi_{\mathsf{q}}, \omega \to \boldsymbol{\omega}_{\underline{\mathsf{q}}}\},$$

$$\{\text{nat} \to \text{TimeSpacelike}, r \to \|\mathsf{q}\|, \varphi \to \psi_{\mathsf{q}}, \omega \to \boldsymbol{\omega}_{\underline{\mathsf{q}}}, \text{sgn} \to sgn q_0\},$$

$$\{\text{nat} \to \text{TimeTimelike}, r \to \|\mathsf{q}\|, \varphi \to \theta_{\mathsf{q}}, \omega \to \boldsymbol{\omega}_{\underline{\mathsf{q}}}\},$$

according to (4a)–(4c). The function `FromPolarForm` reads a list of one of the above forms and gives the corresponding coquaternion. For more details on the use of these functions we refer to the work [12].

In what follows, we use ζ_k and η_k to denote the complex nth ($n \geq 2$) roots of 1 and -1, respectively, i.e.,

$$\zeta_k = \cos\tfrac{2k\pi}{n} + \mathsf{i}\sin\tfrac{2k\pi}{n};\; k = 0, 1, 2 \ldots, n-1$$

and

$$\eta_k = \cos\tfrac{(2k+1)\pi}{n} + \mathsf{i}\sin\tfrac{(2k+1)\pi}{n};\; k = 0, 1, 2 \ldots, n-1.$$

The nth roots of a coquaternion q depend on the nature of q, on the parity of n and (eventually) on the sign of the real part of q. Since these roots are the zeros of the equation $x^n = \mathsf{q}$ and linear zeros never occur in the case of polynomials of this form, the roots of a coquaternion q are either isolated or hyperboloidal.

The new function `RootsN[q]` implements the algorithm described in [11, Theorems 3.1, 3.2, 4.3] for obtaining the nth roots of the coquaternion q. The output is a list with two lists: the first one contains the isolated roots, while the second one contains representatives of the hyperboloidal roots (compare with the function `Zeros` described in Sect. 3). To offer a glimpse of the diversity of roots that a coquaternion may have, we now present several examples.

Example 7. The coquaternion $\mathsf{q} = 1 + \mathsf{i} + \mathsf{j} + \mathsf{k}$ has a positive real part and is in $\mathbb{L}_\mathbb{S}$. Therefore its nth roots are in $\mathbb{L}_\mathbb{S}$ and the number of roots depends on the parity of n.

```
In[40]:= Nature2[q_Coquaternion]:=Nature/@{q,Vec[q]};
         SetAttributes[Nature2,Listable];

In[41]:= q=Coquaternion[1,1,1,1];Nature2[q]
Out[41]= {Lightlike, Spacelike}

In[42]:= ({iroots,hroots}=RootsN[q,2])//TraditionalForm
```

Out[42]= $\{\{-\frac{1}{\sqrt{2}}-\frac{\mathrm{i}}{\sqrt{2}}-\frac{\mathrm{j}}{\sqrt{2}}-\frac{\mathrm{k}}{\sqrt{2}}, \frac{1}{\sqrt{2}}+\frac{\mathrm{i}}{\sqrt{2}}+\frac{\mathrm{j}}{\sqrt{2}}+\frac{\mathrm{k}}{\sqrt{2}}\}, \{\}\}$

```
In[43]:= Union[iroots^2]=={q}
Out[43]= True

In[44]:= Nature2[iroots]
Out[44]= {{Lightlike, Spacelike}, {Lightlike, Spacelike}}

In[45]:= ({iroots,hroots}=RootsN[q,3])//TraditionalForm
```

Out[45]= $\left\{\left\{\frac{1}{2^{2/3}}+\frac{\mathrm{i}}{2^{2/3}}+\frac{\mathrm{j}}{2^{2/3}}+\frac{\mathrm{k}}{2^{2/3}}\right\}, \{\}\right\}$

```
In[46]:= Nature2[iroots]
Out[46]= {{Lightlike, Spacelike}}
```

Example 8. The coquaternion $\mathsf{q} = 3 + 2\mathbb{j}$ has a positive real part and is in $\mathbb{T}_{\mathbb{S}}$. The number and nature of the nth roots of q depend on the parity of n.

In[47]:= `q=Coquaternion[3,0,2,0];PolarForm[q]`

Out[47]= $\{\texttt{nat} \to \texttt{Timelike-Spacelike}, r \to \sqrt{5},$
$\psi \to \texttt{ArcSinh}\left[\frac{2}{\sqrt{5}}\right], \omega \to \texttt{Coquaternion}[0,0,1,0], \texttt{sgn} \to 1\}$

In[48]:= `({iroots,hroots}=RootsN[q,2])//TraditionalForm`

Out[38]= $\{\{\frac{1}{2}(1+\sqrt{5}) + \frac{1}{2}(-1+\sqrt{5})\mathbb{j}, \frac{1}{2}(-1-\sqrt{5}) + \frac{1}{2}(1-\sqrt{5})\mathbb{j},$
$\frac{1}{2}(-1+\sqrt{5}) + \frac{1}{2}(1+\sqrt{5})\mathbb{j}, \frac{1}{2}(1-\sqrt{5}) + \frac{1}{2}(-1-\sqrt{5})\mathbb{j}\}, \{\}\}$

In[49]:= `Tally[Nature2[iroots]`

Out[39]= `{{{Timelike, Spacelike}, 2}, {{Spacelike, Spacelike}, 2}}`

In[50]:= `Select[iroots,Nature2[#]=={Timelike,Spacelike}&]`

Out[40]= $\{\frac{1}{2}(1+\sqrt{5}) + \frac{1}{2}(-1+\sqrt{5})\mathbb{j}, \frac{1}{2}(-1-\sqrt{5}) + \frac{1}{2}(1-\sqrt{5})\mathbb{j}\}$

Example 9. The nth roots of a non-real coquaternion q are all isolated. When $\mathsf{q} \in \mathbb{R}$ the situation is quite different. Here one can also find hyperboloidal roots. We compute now some of the roots of 1 and -1.

In[51]:= `roots=Table[RootsN[ToCoquaternion[1],k],{k,2,10}];`

In[52]:= `Map[Length,roots,{2}]`

Out[42]= $\{\{2,1\},\{1,1\},\{2,2\},\{1,2\},\{2,3\},\{1,3\},\{2,4\},\{1,4\},\{2,5\}\}$

In[53]:=
```
TableForm[
  Transpose@Prepend[Transpose@Take[roots,5],Range[2,6]]//
  TraditionalForm,TableDepth→2, TableHeadings→
  {None,{"n","Isolated roots","Hyperboloidal roots"}}]
```

Out[43]/TableForm=

n	Isolated roots	Hyperboloidal roots
2	$\{-1,1\}$	$\{\mathbb{j}\}$
3	$\{1\}$	$\left\{-\frac{1}{2} + \frac{\sqrt{3}\mathbb{i}}{2}\right\}$
4	$\{-1,1\}$	$\{\mathbb{j}, \mathbb{i}\}$
5	$\{1\}$	$\left\{-\frac{1}{4} + \frac{\sqrt{5}}{4} + \sqrt{\frac{5}{8} + \frac{\sqrt{5}}{8}}\mathbb{i}, -\frac{1}{4} - \frac{\sqrt{5}}{4} + \sqrt{\frac{5}{8} - \frac{\sqrt{5}}{8}}\mathbb{i}\right\}$
6	$\{-1,1\}$	$\left\{-\frac{1}{2} + \frac{\sqrt{3}\mathbb{i}}{2}, \mathbb{j}, \frac{1}{2} + \frac{\sqrt{3}\mathbb{i}}{2}\right\}$

In[54]:= `roots=Table[RootsN[ToCoquaternion[-1],k],{k,2,10}];`

In[55]:= `Map[Length,roots,{2}]`

Out[44]= $\{\{0,1\},\{1,1\},\{0,2\},\{1,2\},\{0,3\},\{1,3\},\{0,4\},\{1,4\},\{0,5\}\}$

In[56]:=
```
TableForm[
  Transpose@Prepend[Transpose@Take[roots,5],Range[2,6]]//
```

Table 3. Functions associated with roots of a coquaternion

Function	Description
`FromPolarForm[l]`	gives the coquaternion whose "polar coordinates" are `l`
`LightlikeQ[q]`	gives `True` if `q` is light-like and `False` otherwise
`Nature[q]`	classifies `q` as space-like, light-like or time-like
`PolarForm[q]`	gives the polar form of `q` (in case of existence)
`RootsN[q,n]`	gives the `n`th roots of `q`
`SpacelikeQ[q]`	gives `True` if `q` is space-like and `False` otherwise
`TimelikeQ[q]`	gives `True` if `q` is time-like and `False` otherwise

```
TraditionalForm,TableDepth→2,TableHeadings→
{None,{"n","Isolated roots","Hyperboloidal roots"}}]
```

Out[45]/TableForm=

n	Isolated roots	Hyperboloidal roots
2	{}	$\{\mathbb{i}\}$
3	{−1}	$\left\{\frac{1}{2}+\frac{\sqrt{3}\mathbb{i}}{2}\right\}$
4	{}	$\left\{\frac{1}{\sqrt{2}}+\frac{\mathbb{i}}{\sqrt{2}},-\frac{1}{\sqrt{2}}+\frac{\mathbb{i}}{\sqrt{2}}\right\}$
5	{−1}	$\left\{\frac{1}{4}+\frac{\sqrt{5}}{4}+\sqrt{\frac{5}{8}-\frac{\sqrt{5}}{8}}\mathbb{i},\frac{1}{4}-\frac{\sqrt{5}}{4}+\sqrt{\frac{5}{8}+\frac{\sqrt{5}}{8}}\mathbb{i}\right\}$
6	{}	$\left\{\frac{\sqrt{3}}{2}+\frac{\mathbb{i}}{2},\mathbb{i},-\frac{\sqrt{3}}{2}+\frac{\mathbb{i}}{2}\right\}$

Table 3 contains a description of the functions related to the computation of the roots of a coquaternion.

5 Conclusions

This work presents a collection of Mathematica tools – `CoqPolynomial` – complementing the package – `Coquaternions` – introduced in [12]. `CoqPolynomial` contains several functions to manipulate coquaternionic polynomials, including the function `Zeros` for polynomial rootfinding. These packages are fundamental tools supporting the recent interests of the authors in the area and should be considered as work in progress; their current versions are available at the web-page http://w3.math.uminho.pt/Coquaternions.

References

1. Abłamowicz, R.: Computations with Clifford and Graßmann algebras. Adv. Appl. Clifford Algebr. **19**(3–4), 499–545 (2009)
2. Abłamowicz, R., Fauser, B.: Mathematics of Clifford - a maple package for Clifford and Graßmann algebras. Adv. Appl. Clifford Algebr. **15**(2), 157–181 (2005)
3. Brody, D.C., Graefe, E.M.: On complexified mechanics and coquaternions. J. Phys. A Math. Theory **44**, 1–9 (2011)

4. Cockle, J.: On systems of algebra involving more than one imaginary; and on equations of the fifth degree. Philos. Mag. **35**(3), 434–437 (1849)
5. Falcão, M.I., Miranda, F.: Quaternions: a Mathematica package for quaternionic analysis. In: Murgante, B., Gervasi, O., Iglesias, A., Taniar, D., Apduhan, B.O. (eds.) ICCSA 2011. LNCS, vol. 6784, pp. 200–214. Springer, Heidelberg (2011). https://doi.org/10.1007/978-3-642-21931-3_17
6. Falcão, M.I., Miranda, F., Severino, R., Soares, M.J.: Basins of attraction for a quadratic coquaternionic map. Chaos, Solitons Fractals **104**, 716–724 (2017)
7. Falcão, M.I., Miranda, F., Severino, R., Soares, M.J.: Iteration of quadratic maps on coquaternions. Int. J. Bifurcat. Chaos **27**(12), 1730039 (2017)
8. Falcão, M.I., Miranda, F., Severino, R., Soares, M.J.: Polynomials over quaternions and coquaternions: a unified approach. In: Gervasi, O., et al. (eds.) ICCSA 2017. LNCS, vol. 10405, pp. 379–393. Springer, Cham (2017). https://doi.org/10.1007/978-3-319-62395-5_26
9. Falcão, M.I., Miranda, F., Severino, R., Soares, M.J.: Computational aspects of quaternionic polynomials - Part I : Manipulating, evaluating and factoring. Math. J. **20**(4) (2018). https://doi.org/10.3888/tmj.20-4
10. Falcão, M.I., Miranda, F., Severino, R., Soares, M.J.: Computational aspects of quaternionic polynomials - Part II: root-finding methods. Math. J. **20**(5) (2018). https://doi.org/10.3888/tmj.20-5
11. Falcão, M.I., Miranda, F., Severino, R., Soares, M.J.: On the roots of coquaternions. Adv. Appl. Clifford Algebr. **28**, 97 (2018)
12. Falcão, M.I., Miranda, F., Severino, R., Soares, M.J.: Symbolic computations over the algebra of coquaternions. In: 4th International Conference on Numerical and Symbolic Computation: Developments and Applications - SYMCOMP 2019 Proceedings, pp. 141–155 (2019)
13. Falcão, M.I., Miranda, F., Severino, R., Soares, M.J.: The number of zeros of unilateral polynomials over coquaternions revisited. Linear & Multilinear Algebra **67**(6), 1231–1249 (2019)
14. Gao, C., Chen, X., Shen, Y.-G.: Quintessence and phantom emerging from the split-complex field and the split-quaternion field. Gen. Relativ. Gravit. **48**, 11 (2016)
15. Hamilton, W.R.: On a new species of imaginary quantities connected with a theory of quaternions. Proc. R. Ir. Acad. **2**, 424–434 (1843)
16. Kula, L., Yayli, Y.: Split quaternions and rotations in semi Euclidean space E_2^4. J. Korean Math. Soc. **44**, 1313–1327 (2007)
17. Malonek, H.R.: Quaternions in applied sciences. a historical perspective of a mathematical concept. In: 17th International Conference on the Applications of Computer Science and Mathematics on Architecture and Civil Engineering, Weimar (2003)
18. Özdemir, M., Ergin, A.: Some geometric applications of time like quaternions. In: Proceedings of 16th International Conference Jangjeon Mathematical Society, vol. 16, pp. 108–115 (2005)
19. Özdemir, M., Ergin, A.: Rotations with unit timelike quaternions in Minkowski 3-space. J. Geometry Phys. **56**(2), 322–336 (2006)
20. Özdemir, M.: The roots of a split quaternion. Appl. Math. Letters **22**, 258–263 (2009)
21. Sangwine, J., Le Bihan, N.: Quaternion Toolbox for Matlab (2005). http://qtfm.sourceforge.net

Aircraft Navigation Systems Safety Assessment via Probabilistic Model Checking

Gabriel Duarte Pasa[1] and Valdivino Alexandre de Santiago Júnior[2(✉)]

[1] Embraer, Avenida Brigadeiro Faria Lima, 2170, Putim, São José dos Campos, SP 12227-901, Brazil
gabriel.pasa@embraer.com.br

[2] Instituto Nacional de Pesquisas Espaciais (INPE), Avenida dos Astronautas, 1758, Jardim da Granja, São José dos Campos, SP 12227-010, Brazil
valdivino.santiago@inpe.br

Abstract. The safety assessment process is a mandatory step in the development and certification of safety-critical systems such as the ones in the aerospace industry. In this work we show how Probabilistic Model Checking, a Formal Verification method, can help to assess the safety of navigation systems for a civil commercial transport category aircraft. The process involves a top-down approach identifying functions and its respective failure modes. Each failure event is associated with a hazard level, with an inverse relationship between the maximum acceptable probability and the event severity. Fault Tree Analysis (FTA) is the most commonly used method to quantify each event's probability, but probabilistic models are also accepted as means of compliance demonstration, as per ARP-4761. Results show that the use of Probabilistic Model Checking as a means to complement non-formal methods is valuable, where we were able to evaluate the probability of several failure modes described in FAA's AC 20-138D, making use of Continuous-Time Markov Chains (CTMCs) with up 4.3 million of reachable states and 60 million of transitions.

Keywords: Safety assessment · Aerospace systems · Probabilistic model checking · Aircraft navigation

1 Introduction

The safety assessment process is part of the development of modern systems in several industries such as aerospace, biomedical, nuclear, and automotive. With the rapid advent of technology over the past years, those safety-critical systems are becoming more and more complex, which brought the industries to a collective effort to build guidelines for safe systems design. In the aeronautical industry, the Part 25 airworthiness standards introduce the fail-safe design concept which considers the effect of single and multiple failure modes and defines some basic

O. Gervasi et al. (Eds.): ICCSA 2021, LNCS 12952, pp. 465–480, 2021.
https://doi.org/10.1007/978-3-030-86973-1_33

objectives pertaining those failures, such as that a single failure, regardless of its probability, shall not prevent continued safe flight and landing [7].

The standard guidelines for conducting safety assessment on civil airborne systems is defined in the SAE ARP-4761 [15]. The methods presented in the document are considered by the major regulation authorities as accepted means of compliance with the safety related airworthiness requirements and those methods are directly related with the ones defined in the SAE ARP-4754A [16], guidelines for development of civil aircraft and systems. The process is based on a top-down approach, starting from the aircraft functions, and Failure Mode and Effect Analysis (FMEA) and Failure Hazard Analysis (FHA), assessing how the aircraft system and equipment failure modes may lead to aircraft level failure conditions. The ARP-4761 [15] suggests a few different methods for performing the safety assessment but the most widely used is the Fault Tree Analysis (FTA).

Even though the methodology presented in the ARP-4761 [15] is what is commonly accepted by the regulation authorities as means of compliance with the airworthiness requirements, this does not mean that alternative methods can not be considered. The AC 25.1309-1B [7] and ARP-4761 [15] are intended to provide guidance to the product development engineer, although they are not mandatory. As the aeronautical industry evolves with new methodologies, techniques, and tools, so does the means of compliance with the airworthiness standards. An alternative to the traditional FTA is the use of probabilistic models on the safety assessment process, and even though these methods are not yet widely applied, they are predicted in the ARP-4761 [15].

Probabilistic Model Checking is a Formal Verification method which is roughly composed of two concepts: a probabilistic model, such as Discrete-Time Markov Chain (DTMC), Continuous-Time Markov Chain (CTMC), and properties formalised via probabilistic temporal logics, such as Probabilistic Computation Tree Logic (PCTL) and Continuous Stochastic Logic (CSL) [12]. It is an interesting field which has been used to solve problems in several domains such as biology [5], power supply systems [6], communication and networks protocols [11], performance of systems [17], and many more.

When compared to the FTA methodology, a Probabilistic Model Checking analysis brings the possibility to express a temporal sequence of events or state-dependent behaviour of systems. In addition, the introduction of formal-based safety assessment methods brings the possibility of automating certain parts of the safety assessment process.

In this article, we hypothesise that Formal Verification methods can effectively contribute to the process of assessing the safety of aircraft navigation systems, providing an alternative to complement the study carried out using classic but non-formal methods. Hence, we show how Probabilistic Model Checking can help in the safety assessment for commercial transport category aircraft. Our focus is set on a subset of functions related to aircraft positioning and navigation, for which the failure modes and hazard classifications are described in the AC 20-138D [8]. We derived several CTMC models and formalised properties via CSL using the PRISM Probabilistic Model Checker tool [13].

This article is organised as follows. In Sect. 2, we present background while in Sect. 3 we show in detail the methodology we devised to address the problem stated. Results and analysis are in Sect. 4, and in Sect. 5 we present related work. Conclusions and future research directions are presented in Sect. 6.

2 Background

According to [1], "Model checking is an automated technique that, given a finite-state model of a system and a formal property, systematically checks whether this property holds for (a given state in) that model". It has been successfully used for quite some time by academia and some industry sectors. On the other hand, Probabilistic Model Checking [1,12] is an extension of Model Checking relying on probabilistic models (e.g. DTMC, CTMC) and probabilistic temporal logics (e.g. PCTL, CSL). One of the main motivations to develop Probabilistic Model Checking is to relax the rigid notions related to Functional Model Checking (a model satisfies or does not satisfy a formal property), because many systems are subject to various phenomena of a stochastic nature, and trying to figure out whether the system has a 99% chance of failing is often more realistic.

Markov Chains are used to model randomly changing processes, where transitions between the different possible states are only dependent on the current state (i.e. the system has no memory). In this article we consider CTMC as our probabilistic model. A CTMC makes transitions from state to state, independent of the past and similarly to a DTMC, but once entering a state remains in that state, independent of the past, for an exponentially distributed amount of time before changing state again. Moreover, a continuous random variable X has an exponential distribution, with parameter (event rate) λ, if its probability density function is given by ($\lambda > 0$):

$$f(x;\lambda) = \begin{cases} \lambda e^{-\lambda x}, & \text{if } x \geq 0 \\ 0, & \text{otherwise} \end{cases} \tag{1}$$

We can define a CTMC in accordance with the Formal Methods community as follows.

Definition 1: *A (labelled) CTMC is a tuple* $\mathcal{C} = (S, \iota, \mathbf{R}, L)$*, where:*

- S *is a finite set of states,*
- $\iota \in S$ *is the initial state,*
- $\mathbf{R} : S \times S \longrightarrow \mathbb{R}_{\geq 0}$ *is the transition rate matrix,*
- $L : S \rightarrow 2^{AP}$ *is a labelling function which assigns to each state* $s \in S$ *the set* $L(s)$ *of atomic propositions that are valid in the state (*AP *= set of atomic propositions).*

In the above definition, $\mathbf{R}$ assigns rates to each pair of states in the CTMC (used as parameters of the exponential distribution). A transition can only occur between states s and s' if $\mathbf{R}(s, s') > 0$ and, in this case, the probability of this transition being triggered within t time-units equals $1 - e^{-\mathbf{R}(s,s')\cdot t}$ (Cumulative Distribution Function).

The probabilistic temporal logic we selected was CSL [12]. CSL extends the classical Computation Tree Logic (CTL) [3] with two probabilistic operators: path ($\mathcal{P}$) and steady-state ($\mathcal{S}$) operators. The syntax of CSL is defined using state and path formulas.

3 Methodology

3.1 Failure Conditions and Hazard Classifications

As per AC 25.1309-1B [7], failure conditions are classified into five classes according to the criticality, ranging from "No safety effect" to "Catastrophic", as described in Table 1. The more severe a failure condition is, the lower is the acceptable probability for it to happen. When demonstrating compliance with the safety objectives, one must classify each mapped failure condition into one of those categories and then demonstrate that the probability of it occurring, per flight hour, is lower than the respective threshold.

Note that AC 25.1309-1B [7] mentions that for "Minor" failure conditions, a quantitative analysis is not required and a numerical range is provided as a reference only (and as such will not be analysed in this work). Naturally, the "No safety effect" conditions do not require a quantitative analysis either.

Table 1. Relationship between probability and severity of failure condition as per AC 25.1309-1B [7].

Failure condition classification	No safety effect	Minor	Major	Hazardous	Catastrophic
Effect on occupants	Inconvenience	Physical discomfort	Physical distress, possibly including injuries	Serious or fatal injury to a small number of passengers or cabin crew	Multiple fatalities
Allowable qualitative probability	No Probability Requirement	Probable	Remote	Extremely Remote	Extremely Improbable
Allowable quantitative probability	No Probability Requirement	$<10^{-3}$	$<10^{-5}$	$<10^{-7}$	$<10^{-9}$

The scope of this work will encompass the aircraft positioning and navigation failure conditions described in the AC 20-138D [8] (refer to Table 2), which fall into two categories: "loss of navigation" and "misleading information". Each failure condition is applicable to a certain type of operation, mostly related to approach procedures (navigation leading to landing).

Table 2. Hazard classifications for the subset of aircraft positioning and navigation functions being evaluated (adapted from FAA AC 20-138D [8]).

	Advisory Vertical Guidance	Enroute/Terminal Area/Non-precision Approach (LNAV or RNP 0.3)	Non-precision Approach with Vertical Guidance (LNAV/VNAV)	LP/LPV Approach	GLS Approach
Loss of Navigation	No Effect	Major	Major	Major	Major
Misleading Information	Minor	Major	Major	Hazardous	Hazardous

The "Advisory Vertical Guidance" function will not be evaluated since it is attributed with at most a "Minor" failure condition, which does not require a quantitative analysis.

The "Enroute/Terminal Area/Non-precision Approach" function is essentially the capacity for the aircraft to determine its lateral position (latitude and longitude) with the appropriate level of position uncertainty (which depends on the type of operation and flight phase). Lateral Navigation (LNAV) is a mode of operation where the aircraft lateral trajectory is typically controlled by the Flight Management System (FMS). Required Navigation Performance (RNP) 0.3 is a similar mode, but it has a stricter position uncertainty limit of 0.3 nautical miles.

The "Non-precision Approach with Vertical Guidance" function is a type of approach procedure with both lateral (LNAV) and Vertical Navigation (VNAV). The vertical guidance is usually a glide path from cruise altitude towards the runway, constructed by the FMS based on the barometric altitude, which is obtained from the Air Data System (ADS).

The "LP/LPV Approach" is another type of approach procedure where the guidance is provided by the Global Navigation Satellite System (GNSS). LP refers to "Localiser Performance" which provides lateral guidance only. Localiser Performance with Vertical Guidance (LPV) is similar to LP but with vertical guidance as well, both provided by the GNSS. In order to achieve the precision required for this type of operation, the GNSS system must be compatible with Satellite-Based Augmentation System (SBAS). In SBAS, geostationary satellites (in addition to the regular satellites from the GNSS constellation) broadcast augmentation information to the receivers, which improves the accuracy and integrity of the position solution.

The "GNSS Landing System" (GLS) approach is similar to LPV, and it uses the GNSS data to calculate both lateral and vertical guidance for the final approach segment. However, instead of using satellite-based, it uses ground-based augmentation to improve the positioning accuracy. A ground station located near the airport runways constantly receives the GNSS satellite signals and calculates the local position errors (it can do it well since the station is fixed at a known position). This correction information is broadcast to nearby receivers via a Very High Frequency (VHF) datalink. This datalink requires another receiver (not the GNSS receiver).

Each aircraft function relies on a specific set of equipment and as such will only be affected by failures in those equipment. The navigation failure modes are also typically attributed to specific operations and flight phases (for instance, a GLS approach failure will only occur during approach), so it is important to also model the flight phase transitions.

3.2 High-Level System Architecture

The high-level avionics system architecture considered in this work is depicted in Fig. 1.

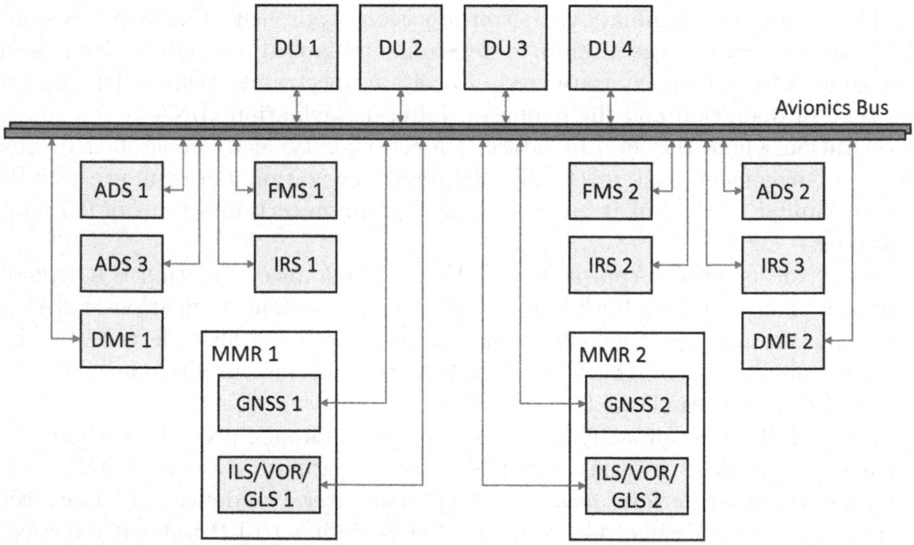

Fig. 1. High-level avionics architecture, including Display Units (DU), Air Data System (ADS), Flight Management System (FMS), Inertial Reference System (IRS), Distance Measuring Equipment (DME), Multi-Mode Receiver (MMR), Global Navigation Satellite System (GNSS), Instrument Landing System (ILS), VHF Omnidirectional Range (VOR), GNSS Landing System (GLS).

The Flight Management System (FMS) is the main navigation computer. It provides high level aircraft commands (desired heading, airspeed, vertical speed) so that the aircraft follows the flight plan (sequence of waypoints from the origin to destination). In order to navigate, the FMS reads data from several sensors, such as the GNSS, Inertial Reference System (IRS), Air Data System (ADS), Distance Measuring Equipment (DME), and Multi-Mode Receiver (MMR).

The display units (DU) are the cockpit displays which provide information for the pilots, such as altitude, airspeed, attitude (roll, pitch, and yaw angles), as well as information from the FMS. The IRS and ADS provide critical information for continued safe flight (i.e. attitude, airspeed, altitude, angle of attack) and as such are triple redundant.

In the scope of this work, only the navigation-related systems are modelled. For brevity and generality, some low-level implementation-specific failure modes are abstracted away, such as avionics bus or display failures.

3.3 Flight Phases and Exposure Times

Many failure conditions are dependent on specific flight phases (either more likely or only possible in specific conditions). This can be seen in the accident statistics shown in Fig. 2 where, for example, the final approach and landing phases combined account for 49% of fatal accidents, while only representing 4% of the total flight time, in a typical 1.5-h flight.

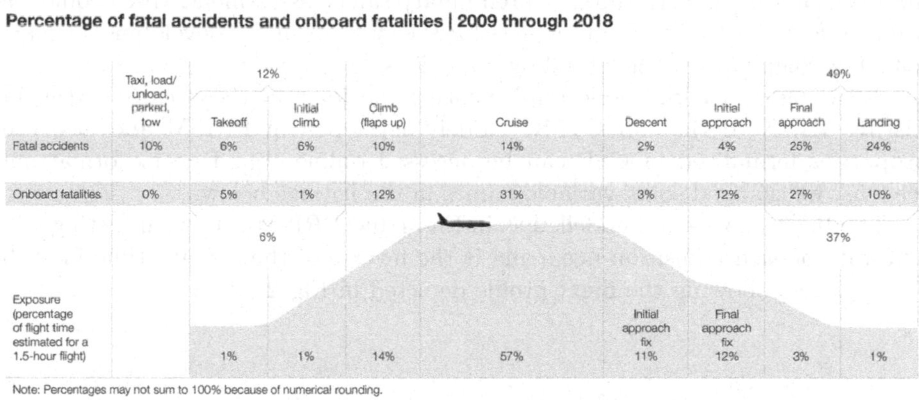

Fig. 2. Commercial airplanes statistics on fatal accidents, on-board fatalities, and exposure times per flight phase. Adapted from [2].

Since the failure conditions evaluated in this work (Table 2) are dependent on the flight phase, a typical flight is modelled based on the exposure times shown in Fig. 2.

3.4 Continuous-Time Markov Chain Models

In order to perform the quantitative safety assessment analysis, a CTMC model is used to map the relevant aircraft flight phases and behaviour of the multiple avionics systems involved in providing the selected subset of aircraft functions being evaluated. The CTMC approach is suitable for the problem at hand since safety assessment usually deals with failure rates (not static probabilities) and the safety objectives are usually expressed in terms of probability per flight hour (which is intrinsically a rate too).

The different systems depicted in the high-level avionics architecture (Fig. 1) were modelled in PRISM as per the diagram in Fig. 3. All systems start as healthy and may present one out of two possible failure modes: they may become failed (annunciated fault) or may present erroneous information (non-annunciated fault). Once failed, the system shall continue failed until the end of the flight. Once erroneous, the system may eventually transition to failed.

The failure mode rates (for annunciated and non-annunciated faults) for each system are listed in Table 3. The values used for those rates are naturally very important for the result of the safety assessment analysis. In our case they were estimated based on experience, but usually these are provided by the equipment manufacturer or, if performing a preliminary safety assessment, these could be used to define reliability requirements for the systems under development, guaranteeing compliance with the safety objectives.

A sample of PRISM code implementing the logic in Fig. 3 can be seen in Listing 1.1. Note that all CTMC models developed in PRISM and also the properties formalised in CSL can be accessed online [14]. Due to formatting reasons, we changed some variable names in the listings below.

The flight phases are modelled as in Fig. 4 and PRISM code is in Listing 1.2. The rate of each transition occurring is the inverse of the average time in each flight phase, following the flight profile depicted in Fig. 2.

Table 3. Equipment failure mode rates.

System	Failure Rate (per hour)	Erroneous Rate (per hour)
FMS	1E-6	1E-7
GNSS	1E-4	1E-6
IRS	1E-6	1E-8
DME	1E-5	1E-6
ADS	1E-6	1E-8
GLS	1E-5	1E-7

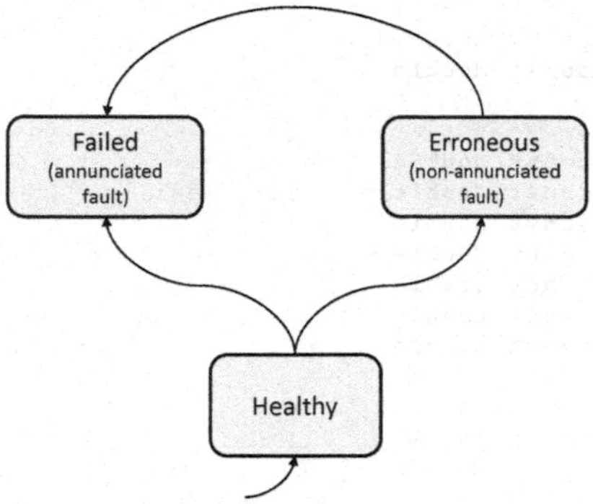

Fig. 3. Equipment state transitions.

```
// --------------------------------
// Inertial Reference System (IRS)
// --------------------------------
const double irs_failure_rate = 1E-6;
const double irs_erroneous_rate = 1E-8;

module irs1
  irs1_fail: bool init false;
  irs1_err: bool init false;

  [] true -> irs_failure_rate : (irs1_fail'=true)&(irs1_err'=false);
  [] (!irs1_fail) -> irs_erroneous_rate : (irs1_err'=true);
endmodule
module irs2 = irs1[irs1_fail=irs2_fail, irs1_err=irs2_err] endmodule
module irs3 = irs1[irs1_fail=irs3_fail, irs1_err=irs3_err] endmodule
```

Listing 1.1. Sample of PRISM code implementing the IRS. All other systems are implemented similarly.

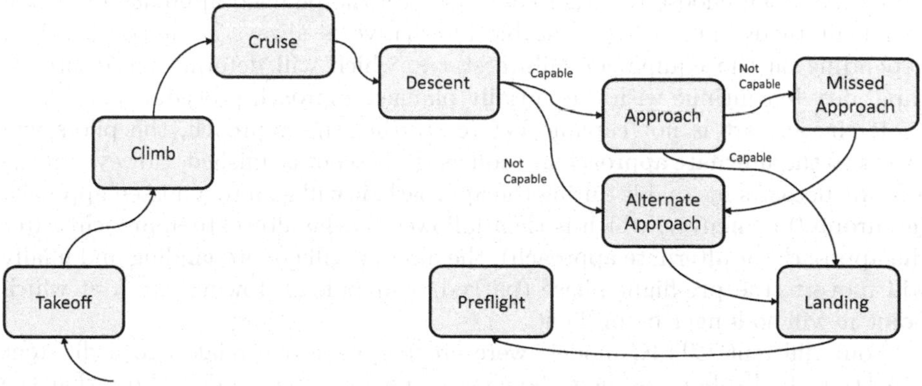

Fig. 4. Flight phases state transitions.

```
// Typical flight duration (in hours)
const double flight_duration = 1.5;

// Mean times spent on each flight phase (in hours)
const double time_in_takeoff = 0.01 * flight_duration;
const double time_in_climb = 0.15 * flight_duration;
const double time_in_cruise = 0.57 * flight_duration;
const double time_in_descent = 0.11 * flight_duration;
const double time_in_approach = 0.15 * flight_duration;
const double time_in_landing = 0.01 * flight_duration;
const double time_in_missed_approach = time_in_climb;

module flight_phase
  // Phases of flight: 0 = pre-flight; 1 = takeoff;
  // 2 = climb; 3 = cruise; 4 = descent;
  // 5 = approach; 6 = alternate approach;
  // 7 = landing; 8 = missed approach
  phase: [0..8] init 1;

  // Takeoff to climb
  [] (phase=1) -> 1/time_in_takeoff: (phase'=2);
  // Climb to cruise
  [] (phase=2) -> 1/time_in_climb: (phase'=3);
  // Cruise to descent
  [] (phase=3) -> 1/time_in_cruise: (phase'=4);
  // Descent to approach / alternate approach
  [] (phase=4) & (!loss_of_navigation) -> 1/time_in_descent: (phase'=5);
  [] (phase=4) & (loss_of_navigation) -> 1/time_in_descent: (phase'=6);
  // Approach to landing / missed approach
  [] (phase=5) & (!loss_of_navigation) -> 1/time_in_approach: (phase'=7);
  [] (phase=5) & (loss_of_navigation) -> 1E5: (phase'=8);
  // Alternate approach to landing
  [] (phase=6) -> 1/time_in_approach: (phase'=7);
  // Missed approach to alternate approach
  [] (phase=8) -> 1/time_in_missed_approach: (phase'=6);
  // Landing to pre-flight
  [] (phase=7) -> 1/time_in_landing: (phase'=0);
endmodule
```

Listing 1.2. PRISM code implementing the flight phase state transitions.

The initial state is takeoff which is followed by climb, cruise, and descent. Pilots may then choose to either continue with the planned approach or switch to an alternate approach (a suitable alternative is always assumed to exist), depending on the equipment failure states, which will determine the aircraft capability to continue with the initially planned approach procedure.

If the aircraft is not capable before starting the approach, the pilots will divert to the alternate approach as soon as the descent is finished. However, if the aircraft becomes incapable during the approach, it will go into a missed approach (go around) maneuver, which is then followed by the alternate approach. After the approach (or alternate approach), the aircraft will go into landing and finally will move to the pre-flight phase (parked, load/unload, towing, etc.), at which point it will no longer be in flight.

Four different CTMC models were created, each one related to a different operation. In Table 4, we show the characteristics of the models. Note that the CTMC model for the LNAV/VNAV operation has around 4.3 million of reachable states and about 60 million of transitions, showing the degree of detail we embedded in our solution.

Table 4. Characteristics of the CTMC models.

Operation	# Reachable states	# Transitions
LNAV/RNP 0.3	159,787	1,719,943
LNAV/VNAV	4,331,609	59,590,374
LP/LPV	16,771	146,329
GLS	158,011	1,692,511

3.5 Safety Properties

The definition of capable depends on the type of operation being performed (different types of approach procedures will require different systems to be operational). In PRISM code this is represented by the " loss_of_navigation " formula. The "misleading_information" formula will determine if the systems indications are erroneous to a point where the pilots could be mislead, which may be a more severe failure condition (refer to Table 2).

One architectural assumption is that each instance of the triple redundant systems (IRS and ADS) may be accessed by either FMS (i.e. FMS 1 and FMS 2 may use IRS 1, IRS 2, and IRS 3). The other systems (GNSS, GLS, DME) are primarily used by the FMS on the same side (i.e. FMS 1 uses GNSS 1, FMS 2 uses GNSS 2). The display unit presenting the Primary Flight Display (PFD) 1 is fed by FMS 1 and the PFD 2 is fed by FMS 2.

The "Enroute/Terminal Area/Non-precision Approach (LNAV or RNP 0.3) operation is assumed to be able to be performed with a single navigation source (valid information in a single PFD). This is expected to be viable since this operation has at most a "Major" hazard classification as per Table 2. The capability formulas for this operation mode can be seen in Listing 1.3. Note that the FMS uses the onside GNSS, onside DME or any IRS to compute the lateral guidance.

```
formula enroute_terminal_approach = (phase >= 2 & phase <=5);

// Loss of navigation
formula all_irs_fail = (irs1_fail) & (irs2_fail) & (irs3_fail);
formula pfd1_not_av = (fms1_fail) | (gnss1_fail & dme1_fail & all_irs_fail);
formula pfd2_not_av = (fms2_fail) | (gnss2_fail & dme2_fail & all_irs_fail);
formula loss_of_navigation = (pfd1_not_av) | (pfd2_not_av);

// Misleading Information
formula all_irs_err = (irs1_err) & (irs2_err) & (irs3_err);
formula pfd1_err = (gnss1_err | dme1_err | all_irs_err) | (fms1_err);
formula pfd2_err = (gnss2_err | dme2_err | all_irs_err) | (fms2_err);
formula misleading_information = (pfd1_err) | (pfd2_err);
```

Listing 1.3. PRISM code implementing the Enroute/Terminal Area/Non-precision Approach (LNAV or RNP 0.3) capability formulas.

CSL representation of the "loss of navigation" safety property for the LNAV/RNP 0.3 mode can be seen in Eq. 2, while the "misleading information" property is seen in Eq. 3:

$$\mathcal{P}_{<10^{-5}\times T}[\Diamond(\text{enroute\_terminal\_approach} \wedge \text{loss\_of\_navigation})] \quad (2)$$

$$\mathcal{P}_{<10^{-5}\times T}[\Diamond(\text{enroute\_terminal\_approach} \wedge \text{misleading\_information})] \quad (3)$$

Notice that in Eq. 2 and Eq. 3 there is a factor T which stands for the average flight time. It is included since the safety objectives are given as a probability per flight hour. Note that one can check this flight time by calculating it via cost/reward in PRISM, as shown in Listing 1.4, and via a cost/reward-based property, as shown in Eq. 4.

```
rewards "flight_hours"
    phase > 0 : 1;
endrewards
```

Listing 1.4. PRISM code implementing the flight time cost/reward.

$$T := R\{\text{“flight\_hours”}\} =?[C] \quad (4)$$

The “Non-precision Approach with Vertical Guidance (LNAV/VNAV)” operation is also assumed to be able to be performed with a single navigation source. CSL representation of the “loss of navigation” safety property for the LNAV/VNAV mode can be seen in Eq. 5, while the “misleading information” property is seen in Eq. 6:

$$\mathcal{P}_{<10^{-5}\times T}[\Diamond(\text{phase} = 8)] \quad (5)$$

$$\mathcal{P}_{<10^{-5}\times T}[\Diamond(\text{phase} = 5 \wedge \text{misleading\_information})] \quad (6)$$

The “LP/LPV Approach” operation is assumed to require independent navigation sources in both PFD 1 and PFD 2. This was a necessity since this approach type has lower minimum altitudes and as such has a more severe misleading information hazard classification (“Hazardous” instead of “Major”). In this mode, the FMS only requires the GNSS (to calculate the current position and trajectory) and the IRS (to calculate the attitude). The capability formulas are given in Listing 1.5.

```
// Loss of navigation
formula all_irs_fail = (irs1_fail) & (irs2_fail) & (irs3_fail);
formula pfd1_not_av = (gnss1_fail) | (fms1_fail) | (all_irs_fail);
formula pfd2_not_av = (gnss2_fail) | (fms2_fail) | (all_irs_fail);
formula loss_of_navigation = (pfd1_not_av) & (pfd2_not_av);

// Misleading Information
formula all_irs_err = (irs1_err) & (irs2_err) & (irs3_err);
formula pfd1_err = (gnss1_err) | (fms1_err) | (all_irs_err);
formula pfd2_err = (gnss2_err) | (fms2_err) | (all_irs_err);
formula misleading_information = (pfd1_err) & (pfd2_err);
```

Listing 1.5. PRISM code implementing the LP/LPV Approach capability formulas.

CSL representation of the “loss of navigation” safety property for the LP/LPV Approach mode can be seen in Eq. 7, while the “misleading information” property is seen in Eq. 8:

$$\mathcal{P}_{<10^{-5}\times T}[\Diamond(\text{phase} = 8)] \quad (7)$$

$$\mathcal{P}_{<10^{-7}\times T}[\Diamond(\text{phase} = 5 \wedge \text{misleading\_information})] \tag{8}$$

Similarly, the "GLS Approach" operation is assumed to require independent navigation sources in the PFDs. In this mode, the FMS requires the onside GNSS and the onside GLS (to calculate the current position and trajectory) and any IRS (to calculate attitude). CSL formulation of the "loss of navigation" safety property can be seen in Eq. 9, while the "misleading information" property is seen in Eq. 10:

$$\mathcal{P}_{<10^{-5}\times T}[\Diamond(\text{phase} = 8)] \tag{9}$$

$$\mathcal{P}_{<10^{-7}\times T}[\Diamond(\text{phase} = 5 \wedge \text{misleading\_information})] \tag{10}$$

4 Results and Analysis

In order to demonstrate compliance with the safety properties defined for each failure mode, for each type of operation, the properties were evaluated in PRISM and the results are shown in Table 5. The "Objective" column shows the maximum acceptable probability limit and it is obtained by the probability per flight hour (as defined in Table 1) multiplied by the average flight time $T = 1.5$ h.

The "Probability" column shows the probability for each property as calculated by PRISM. These values should be always lower than the objective in order to be compliant.

Table 5. Safety properties results as evaluated by PRISM.

Operation	Failure mode	Classification	Objective	Probability	Compliant
LNAV/RNP 0.3	Loss of Navigation	Major	1.5E-5	2.97E-6	✓
	Misleading Information	Major	1.5E-5	6.24E-6	✓
LNAV/VNAV	Loss of Navigation	Major	1.5E-5	4.50E-7	✓
	Misleading Information	Major	1.5E-5	6.24E-6	✓
LP/LPV	Loss of Navigation	Major	1.5E-5	6.82E-9	✓
	Misleading Information	Hazardous	1.5E-7	3.71E-12	✓
GLS	Loss of Navigation	Major	1.5E-5	8.23E-9	✓
	Misleading Information	Hazardous	1.5E-7	4.41E-12	✓

As shown in Table 5, all safety objectives were met. Note that the compliance is heavily reliant on the failure rates assumed for each system, and during development of the aircraft these values should be reassessed as changes are made to the components.

We went further in our experiments and decided to increase the flight time, T, in order to realise whether the compliance was still achieved. Figure 5 shows the results for the Loss of Navigation failure mode and considering the LNAV/RNP 0.3 operation with $T = 18$ h, which is currently considered the longest flight in the world [4]. Note that now the "Objective" probability is 18E-5 but, again, the final probability is still lower than the "Objective" and hence the compliance is still met. Due to space constraints, we omit other experiments that we have performed with different values of flight time, but the results were similar.

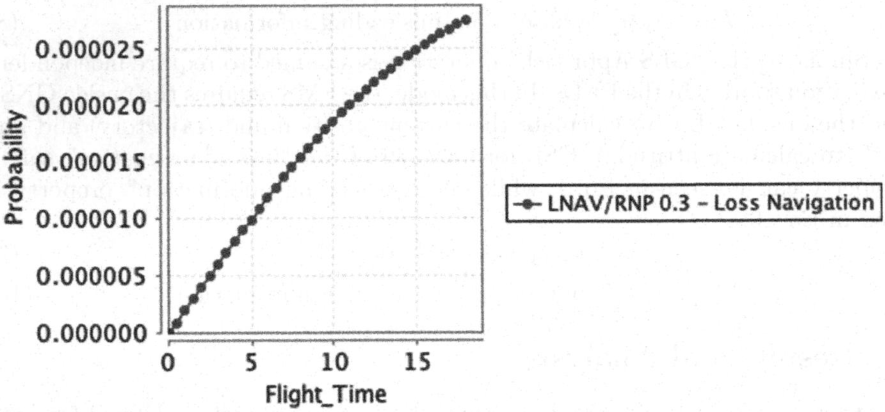

Fig. 5. LNAV/RNP 0.3: Loss of Navigation, $T = 18$ h.

5 Related Work

In this section, we present some relevant studies related to our research. Gomes et al. [9] presented an approach for systematic safety assessment using Probabilistic Model Checking. CTMC models are constructed automatically from Simulink (block) diagrams and a set of tabular data about the underlying system failure modes and hazard analysis. Their safety objectives are defined as steady-state properties, as opposed to transient, which is only viable in models with infinite paths (no terminal state). In these infinite path models, failures are introduced and must later be repaired, adding additional assumptions about the repair strategy and latent failures.

In [10], the authors show how functional models used during design or for qualitative safety assessment may be directly reused for a quantitative analysis. A simple case study is provided, using the PRISM Probabilistic Model Checker.

One major difference between our work and all these previous studies is the detail of the CTMC models. Even though we derived the models manually, the level of details of our models are considerably higher, and hence we believe that the results we obtained are more realistic.

6 Conclusions

The safety assessment process is of extreme importance to the aerospace industry, due to its safety-critical nature. This process, especially for very large and complex systems, is laborious, time-consuming, and expensive. Therefore the industry has much to gain by optimising it, for instance, by adopting formal and possibly more automated model-based methods.

In this article, we wondered whether Formal Verification methods can contribute to the process of assessing the safety of aircraft navigation systems, providing an alternative to complement the study carried out using classical but non-formal methods. By relying on Probabilistic Model Checking (CTMC models and safety properties formalised in CSL), we could validate this hypothesis with consistent results and dealing with models with up to 4.3 million of reachable states and 60 million of transitions. CTMC models can represent arbitrary asynchronous stochastic transition systems, which are very flexible (for instance, allowing for the modelling of flight phases, pilot decisions as well as multiple equipment failure modes). A Probabilistic Model Checker such as PRISM allows for the Formal Verification of the system's safety properties, which can be performed iteratively from early stages of development when the impacts of design changes are smaller.

This article does not feature a complete assessment of all aircraft functions due to the high complexity of this type of modelling. One future direction is trying to integrate classical methods, such as FTA, FMEA, with Probabilistic Model Checking where the latter participates in part of the process. Other direction is trying to address the issue of scalability related to Probabilistic Model Checking via compositional techniques.

References

1. Baier, C., Katoen, J.P.: Principles of Model Checking, p. 975. The MIT Press, Cambridge (2008)
2. Boeing: Statistical summary of commercial jet airplane accidents - Worldwide operations, 1959–2019 (2020). https://bit.ly/3cGqgfb. Accessed 14 June 2021
3. Clarke, E.M., Emerson, E.A., Sistla, A.P.: Automatic verification of finite-state concurrent systems using temporal logic specifications. ACM Trans. Program. Lang. Syst. **8**(2), 244–263 (1986)
4. CNN: The world's longest flight is back - and now it's even longer (2020). https://cnn.it/3sXBnXD. Accessed 14 June 2021
5. Dannenberg, F., Kwiatkowska, M., Thachuk, C., Turberfield, A.J.: DNA walker circuits: computational potential, design, and verification. In: Soloveichik, D., Yurke, B. (eds.) DNA 2013. LNCS, vol. 8141, pp. 31–45. Springer, Cham (2013). https://doi.org/10.1007/978-3-319-01928-4_3
6. Dioto, M., Eras, E.R., de Santiago Júnior, V.A.: On the feasibility of probabilistic model checking to analyze battery sustained power supply systems. In: Misra, S., Gervasi, O., Murgante, B., Stankova, E., Korkhov, V., Torre, C., Rocha, A.M.A.C., Taniar, D., Apduhan, B.O., Tarantino, E. (eds.) ICCSA 2019. LNCS, vol. 11620, pp. 743–757. Springer, Cham (2019). https://doi.org/10.1007/978-3-030-24296-1_59
7. FAA: AC 25.1309-1B - System Design and Analysis. Federal Aviation Administration (FAA) (2002)
8. FAA: AC 20–138D - Airworthiness Approval of Positioning and Navigation Systems. Federal Aviation Administration (FAA) (2014)
9. Gomes, A., Mota, A., Sampaio, A., Ferri, F., Buzzi, J.: Systematic model-based safety assessment via probabilistic model checking. In: Margaria, T., Steffen, B. (eds.) Leveraging Applications of Formal Methods, Verification, and Validation, pp. 625–639. Springer, Heidelberg (2010)
10. Güdemann, M., Ortmeier, F.: Probabilistic model-based safety analysis. Electron. Proc. Theoretical Comput. Sci. **28**, 114–128 (Jun 2010)

11. Konur, S., Fisher, M.: Formal analysis of a vanet congestion control protocol through probabilistic verification. In: 2011 IEEE 73rd Vehicular Technology Conference (VTC Spring), pp. 1–5 (2011). https://doi.org/10.1109/VETECS.2011.5956327
12. Kwiatkowska, M., Norman, G., Parker, D.: Stochastic model checking. In: Bernardo, M., Hillston, J. (eds.) SFM 2007. LNCS, vol. 4486, pp. 220–270. Springer, Heidelberg (2007). https://doi.org/10.1007/978-3-540-72522-0_6
13. Kwiatkowska, M., Norman, G., Parker, D.: PRISM 4.0: verification of probabilistic real-time systems. In: Gopalakrishnan, G., Qadeer, S. (eds.) CAV 2011. LNCS, vol. 6806, pp. 585–591. Springer, Heidelberg (2011). https://doi.org/10.1007/978-3-642-22110-1_47
14. Pasa, G.D., Santiago Júnior, V.A.: PRISM models and properties: Aircraft navigation systems safety assessment via probabilistic model checking (2021). https://bit.ly/3gsWons. Accessed 14 June 2021
15. SAE: ARP4761 - Guidelines and Methods for Conducting the Safety Assessment Process on Civil Airborne Systems and Equipment. SAE International (1996)
16. SAE: ARP4754A - Guidelines for Development of Civil Aircraft and Systems. SAE International (2010)
17. de Santiago Júnior, V.A., Tahar, S.: Time performance formal evaluation of complex systems. In: Cornélio, M., Roscoe, B. (eds.) SBMF 2015. LNCS, vol. 9526, pp. 162–177. Springer, Cham (2016). https://doi.org/10.1007/978-3-319-29473-5_10

Optimisation Approach for Parameter Estimation of the Generalised PTT Viscoelastic Model

M. Fernanda P. Costa(✉), C. Coelho, and L. L. Ferrás

Centre of Mathematics University of Minho, Campus de Gualtar, 4710-057 Braga, Portugal
{mfc,llima}@math.uminho.pt, cmartins@cmat.uminho.pt
https://www.cmat.uminho.pt/

Abstract. The exponential form of the original Phan-Thien and Tanner (PTT) model is often used to study complex viscoelastic fluids. Recently, a generalised version of the PTT model, that uses the Mittag-Leffler function to compute a new function of the trace of the stress tensor, was proposed. This new model adds one or two additional fitting parameters that allow for greater fitting capability. In this paper, we propose two optimisation problems for estimating the model parameters when fitting experimental data in shear (storage modulus, loss modulus, shear viscosity). We also propose a numerical sequential approach for solving one of these problems. The optimal values for the parameters produced by the optimisation approach allow the model to reproduce almost exactly the experimental data.

Keywords: Optimisation · Sequential approach · Viscoelastic models · Phan-thien and tanner · gPTT · Rheology

1 Introduction

The stress felt in our hands (σ), induced by stretching a spring is proportional to the deformation (γ_e) with G_0 the constant of proportionality. This is known as Hook's law (see the illustration in Fig. 1 - left). The stress felt by stretching a dashpot is proportional to the velocity of that deformation ($\frac{d\gamma_f}{dt}$), with η the constant of proportionality. This is known as Newton's law for fluids. In the Newton's law, a smooth stretch leads to a low stress and a rapid stretch leads to a high stress (see the illustration in Fig. 1 - centre). The Newton's law for fluids states that the faster we move our hands, the higher the resistance.

These are two *laws* universally accepted and observed experimentally (under the limitations of the experiment and the material used).

The Maxwell model of viscoelasticity can be easily obtained by combining a spring and a dashpot in series, as shown in Fig. 1.

Supported by FCT - Fundação para a Ciência e a Tecnologia, through projects UIDB/00013/2020 and UIDP/00013/2020, and CMAT - Centre of Mathematics, University of Minho.

O. Gervasi et al. (Eds.): ICCSA 2021, LNCS 12952, pp. 481–494, 2021.
https://doi.org/10.1007/978-3-030-86973-1_34

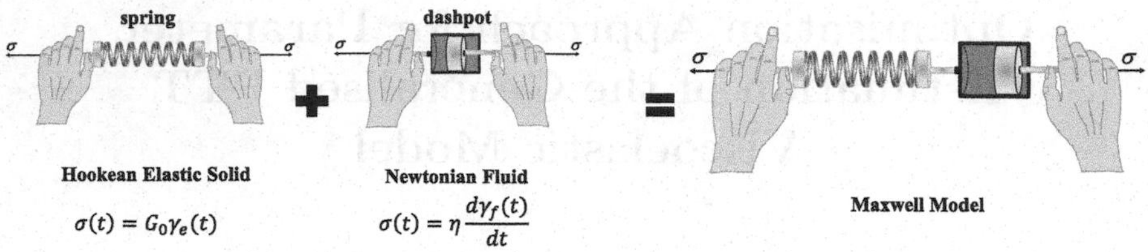

Fig. 1. The Maxwell model represented by a combination of a spring and a dashpot, in series. The subscripts e and f stand for elastic solid and fluid, respectively.

To derive the Maxwell model one assume that the total deformation, γ, is the sum of the deformation applied to the spring, γ_e, and the deformation applied to the dashpot, γ_f. That is, $\gamma(t) = \gamma_e(t) + \gamma_f(t)$. Applying the time derivative to both sides of this equation, we obtain the total rate of deformation $\frac{d\gamma(t)}{dt} = \frac{d\gamma_e(t)}{dt} + \frac{d\gamma_f(t)}{dt}$. Applying again the time derivative to both sides of Hook's law and substituting in the equation for the total rate of deformation, we arrive at the Maxwell model:

$$\sigma(t) + \lambda\frac{d\sigma(t)}{dt} = \eta\frac{d\gamma(t)}{dt},$$

with $\lambda = \frac{\eta}{G_0}$ the relaxation time of the fluid (in *seconds*), η the zero shear-rate viscosity (the viscosity obtained when $\frac{d\gamma(t)}{dt} \to 0$, in *Pascal* $\times$ *seconds*), and $\lambda,\ \eta \geq 0$. The model can also be written in integral form as:

$$\sigma(t) = \int_0^t G_0 e^{-\frac{t-t'}{\lambda}} \frac{d\gamma}{dt'} dt'. \tag{1}$$

This model is really simple and lacks a generalisation to every point in the three-dimensional (3D) space $\boldsymbol{x} = (x, y, z)$. The state of stress of a point in the 3D space can be represented by a 3×3 tensor (with 9 stress components),

$$\boldsymbol{\sigma}(t, \boldsymbol{x}) \equiv \boldsymbol{\sigma} = \begin{bmatrix} \sigma_{xx} & \sigma_{xy} & \sigma_{xz} \\ \sigma_{yx} & \sigma_{yy} & \sigma_{yz} \\ \sigma_{zx} & \sigma_{zy} & \sigma_{zz} \end{bmatrix},$$

and the rate of deformation of a body of viscoelastic material in the 3D space, $\frac{d\gamma(t)}{dt}$, is related to the way the velocity of a material point varies in that space (velocity gradient $\nabla\boldsymbol{u}$) [1] by,

$$\frac{d\gamma(t)}{dt} = 2\boldsymbol{D} = (\nabla\boldsymbol{u} + (\nabla\boldsymbol{u})^T) = \begin{bmatrix} \frac{\partial u}{\partial x} + \frac{\partial u}{\partial x} & \frac{\partial u}{\partial y} + \frac{\partial v}{\partial x} & \frac{\partial u}{\partial z} + \frac{\partial w}{\partial x} \\ \frac{\partial u}{\partial y} + \frac{\partial v}{\partial x} & \frac{\partial v}{\partial y} + \frac{\partial v}{\partial y} & \frac{\partial v}{\partial z} + \frac{\partial w}{\partial y} \\ \frac{\partial u}{\partial z} + \frac{\partial w}{\partial x} & \frac{\partial v}{\partial z} + \frac{\partial w}{\partial y} & \frac{\partial w}{\partial z} + \frac{\partial w}{\partial z} \end{bmatrix}$$

where $\boldsymbol{u} = (u, v, w)$ is the velocity vector, ∇ is the gradient operator and $\boldsymbol{D}(t, \boldsymbol{x}) \equiv \boldsymbol{D}$ is the rate of deformation tensor. Note that this derivation is not trivial. More details can be found in any classical book of fluid or solid mechanics [1].

This generalisation to the 3D space results in the Maxwell model,

$$\boldsymbol{\sigma} + \lambda \frac{d\boldsymbol{\sigma}}{dt} = 2\eta \boldsymbol{D}$$

that is only valid for *really small* deformations.

Qualitative and quantitative descriptions of physical phenomena must remain unchanged if we make any change in the point of view from which we observe them. This is called objectivity or frame-invariance. The Maxwell model is not invariant and therefore cannot be used in large deformations. This is due to the operator $\frac{d\sigma}{dt}$. This time derivative is not invariant, and therefore the term $\frac{d\sigma}{dt}$ should be replaced by some physically equivalent term. The new term should provide the time variation of the stress tensor, and also guarantee that this variation is always the same for all observers. A possible solution is to use:

1. Upper-Convected time derivative:

$$\overset{\nabla}{\boldsymbol{\sigma}} = \frac{\partial}{\partial t}\boldsymbol{\sigma} + (\mathbf{v} \cdot \nabla)\boldsymbol{\sigma} - (\nabla \mathbf{v})^T \cdot \boldsymbol{\sigma} - \boldsymbol{\sigma} \cdot (\nabla \mathbf{v}) \qquad (2)$$

with

$$\frac{D}{Dt}\boldsymbol{\sigma} = \frac{\partial \boldsymbol{\sigma}}{\partial t} + \boldsymbol{u} \cdot \nabla \boldsymbol{\sigma}$$

known as the material derivative. This derivative describes the time rate of change of some physical quantity of a material element that is subjected to a space-and-time-dependent macroscopic velocity field. In Eq. (2), the " · " represents the usual dot product and the term $(\mathbf{v} \cdot \nabla)\boldsymbol{\sigma}$ results in a tensor with entry i, j given by,

$$u\frac{\partial \sigma_{ij}}{\partial x} + v\frac{\partial \sigma_{ij}}{\partial y} + w\frac{\partial \sigma_{ij}}{\partial z}$$

where $i = x, y, z$ and $j = x, y, z$.

2. Lower-Convected time derivative:

$$\overset{\Delta}{\boldsymbol{\sigma}} = \frac{\partial}{\partial t}\boldsymbol{\sigma} + (\mathbf{v} \cdot \nabla)\boldsymbol{\sigma} + \boldsymbol{\sigma} \cdot (\nabla \mathbf{v})^T + (\nabla \mathbf{v}) \cdot \boldsymbol{\sigma}$$

3. Gordon-Schowalter time derivative:

$$\mathring{\boldsymbol{\sigma}} = \frac{\partial}{\partial t}\boldsymbol{\sigma} + (\mathbf{u} \cdot \nabla)\boldsymbol{\sigma} - (\nabla \mathbf{u})^T \cdot \boldsymbol{\sigma} - \boldsymbol{\sigma} \cdot (\nabla \mathbf{u}) + \xi(\boldsymbol{\sigma} \cdot \mathbf{D} + \mathbf{D} \cdot \boldsymbol{\sigma}), \qquad (3)$$

where ξ is a real parameter typically set in [0,1]. The ξ parameter accounts for the slip between the molecular network and the continuous medium.

Note that a combination of Upper-Convected, Lower-Convected and Gordon-Schowalter derivatives, can also be used.

The Upper-Convected Maxwell (UCM) model is therefore a generalisation of the Maxwell material for the case of large deformations using the upper-convected time derivative. Note that the Lower-Convected Maxwell model can be obtained in a similar way.

The UCM model was proposed by James G. Oldroyd, and can be written as:

$$\boldsymbol{\sigma} + \lambda \overset{\nabla}{\boldsymbol{\sigma}} = 2\eta \mathbf{D}. \tag{4}$$

This model is frame-invariant and can be used to model large deformations. The choice of derivative will influence the characteristics of the model, and its ability to model real viscoelastic materials.

The Maxwell and the UCM models were obtained mechanically from springs and dashpots but can also be derived from molecular theory.

In the recent decades, several models were developed, either based on mechanical analogues of springs and dashpots, molecular theory, or, network theories. Network theories characterise the materials as networks of entangled molecules (see Fig. 2).

In the 1970s a model was proposed in the literature that is apparently *quite* similar to the UCM model but that can better model real fluids.

It was derived from a Lodge-Yamamoto type of network theory (see Fig. 2) for polymeric fluids [2–5]. For the isothermal case, the model can be expressed by the constitutive equation

$$K(\boldsymbol{\sigma_{kk}})\boldsymbol{\sigma} + \lambda \mathring{\boldsymbol{\sigma}} = 2\eta \mathbf{D},$$

where $\boldsymbol{\sigma_{kk}}$ is the trace of the stress tensor and $K(\boldsymbol{\sigma_{kk}})$ is the network destruction function given by either a linear or an exponential function of $\boldsymbol{\sigma_{kk}}$. The *only* difference to the UCM model (Eq. (4)) is the presence of $K(\boldsymbol{\sigma_{kk}})$ and the use of the Gordon-Schowalter time derivative.

More recently (2019), a generalised Phan-Thien - Tanner constitutive equation (gPTT) was proposed [5], where $K(\sigma_{kk})$, the network destruction function is defined by,

$$K(\sigma_{kk}) = \Gamma(\beta) E_{\alpha,\beta}\left(\frac{\varepsilon\lambda}{\eta}\sigma_{kk}\right)$$

where α, β and ε are real positive parameters, being ε known by the extensibility parameter (in the classical model). Here the normalisation $\Gamma(\beta)$ is used to ensure that $K(0) = 1$ for all choices of the parameter β. $E_{\alpha,\beta}(.)$ is the generalised Mittag-Leffler function [6]

$$E_{\alpha,\beta}(z) = \sum_{k=0}^{\infty} \frac{z^k}{\Gamma(\alpha k + \beta)}$$

and Γ is the Gamma function given by

$$\Gamma(t) = \int_0^{\infty} x^{t-1} e^{-x} dx.$$

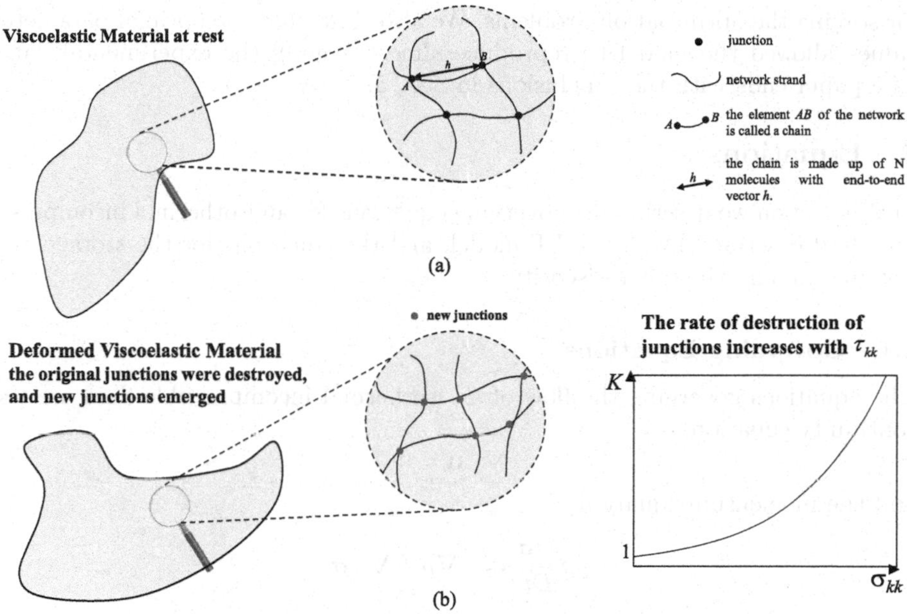

Fig. 2. The lodge-yamamoto theory. (a) The molecules entanglements are represented by a network strand connected by junctions. (b) These junctions are destroyed with deformation of the material and new junctions are created. Note that the rate of destruction of junctions ($K(\sigma_{kk})$) is represented schematically in the graph shown in the right bottom corner. K increases with the stress.

We note that, for $\alpha = \beta = 1$ the Mittag-Leffler function $E_{\alpha,\beta}(.)$ reduces to the exponential function.

The parameters α, β, ε, λ, G_0 and ξ will affect the behaviour of the constitutive model (recall that $G_0 = \eta/\lambda$). The proposed mathematical model depends on six unknown parameters that require investigation. Since the mathematical model simulates real fluids, the parameter values can be estimated based on experimental data. The aim of a parameter estimation optimisation problem is to calibrate the model so that it can reproduce the experimental data. This is performed by minimising an objective function that measures the goodness of the fit. Therefore, it is important to develop an optimisation methodology to obtain the fitting parameters correctly, considering different flows.

Since this model has only recently been proposed in the literature, there is no specific optimisation approach for this type of model. Therefore, the aim of this work is to develop a new optimisation approach that considers weak flows.

This work is organised as follows. In Sect. 2, we introduce the governing equations for an isothermal incompressible fluid described by the generalised PTT model (gPTT), and derive the equations for the storage and loss moduli and the shear viscosity. In Sect. 3, we present the optimisation problems for estimating the parameters of the model. In Sect. 4, we describe the optimisation approach for solving the optimisation problems. We also show that the optimal parameter values allowed the model to reproduce almost exactly the experimental data. The paper ends with the conclusions in Sect. 5.

2 Equations

In this section we describe the governing equations for an isothermal incompressible fluid described by the gPTT model, and the equations for the storage and loss moduli and the shear viscosity.

2.1 Governing Equations

The equations governing the flow of an isothermal incompressible fluid are the continuity equation,

$$\nabla \cdot \mathbf{u} = 0$$

and the momentum equation,

$$\rho \frac{D\mathbf{u}}{Dt} = -\nabla p + \nabla \cdot \boldsymbol{\sigma}$$

together with the constitutive equation,

$$\Gamma(\beta) E_{\alpha,\beta}\left(\frac{\varepsilon\lambda}{\eta}\sigma_{kk}\right)\boldsymbol{\sigma} + \lambda\overset{\circ}{\boldsymbol{\sigma}} = 2\eta\mathbf{D} \tag{5}$$

where p is the pressure, t the time and ρ the mass density. The Gordon-Schowalter derivative $\overset{\circ}{\boldsymbol{\sigma}}$ is given by Eq. (3).

2.2 The Storage and Loss Moduli

The storage and loss moduli [7] allow one to study how our model behaves when an oscillatory deformation is imposed. We can see how much is recovered (Hook's law) and how much is lost (Newton's law) when the deformation is applied. The storage and loss are represented by G' and G'' respectively.

The G' and G'' can be determined using Laplace Transform, $\mathcal{L}$, and the convolution theorem. Let $\bar{\sigma}(s)$ and $\bar{\gamma}(s)$ denote the Laplace transform of $\sigma(t)$ and $\gamma(t)$, respectively. For small deformations, the gPTT model reduces to the integral Maxwell model (Eq. (1)) and we have that (assuming $\sigma(t) = 0$ for $t = 0$):

$$\begin{aligned}
\bar{\sigma}(s) &= \mathcal{L}\{\sigma(t)\} \\
&= \mathcal{L}\left\{\int_0^t G_0 e^{-\frac{t-t'}{\lambda}} \frac{d\gamma}{dt'} dt'\right\} \\
&= \int_0^\infty G_0 e^{-\frac{t}{\lambda}} e^{-st} dt \int_0^\infty \frac{d\gamma(t)}{dt} e^{-st} dt \\
&= \frac{sG_0\lambda\bar{\gamma}(s)}{1+s\lambda}.
\end{aligned} \tag{6}$$

The ratio of $\bar{\sigma}(s)$ and $\bar{\gamma}(s)$ is given by:

$$\frac{\bar{\sigma}(s)}{\bar{\gamma}(s)} = \frac{sG_0\lambda}{1+s\lambda} = G^*(s)$$

where $\bar{\sigma}(s)$ and $\bar{\gamma}(s)$ are proportional, as in Hook's law, and therefore the symbol G^* is used to represent this *modulus*.

Assuming that $s = i\omega$ $(i = \sqrt{-1})$, we have that,

$$G^*(i\omega) = \frac{G_0(\lambda\omega)^2}{1+(\lambda\omega)^2} + i\frac{G_0\lambda\omega}{1+(\lambda\omega)^2} = G' + iG''.$$

2.3 Weak Steady Flows

For steady simple shear flows, the explicit expressions for viscosity are easily found. Following the work of Alves et al. [8] and considering a simple plane shear flow aligned with the x-axis, the constitutive Eq. (5) reduces to:

$$K(\sigma_{kk})\sigma_{xx} = (2-\xi)(\lambda\dot{\gamma})\sigma_{xy}, \tag{7}$$

$$K(\sigma_{kk})\sigma_{yy} = -\xi(\lambda\dot{\gamma})\sigma_{xy}, \tag{8}$$

$$K(\sigma_{kk})\sigma_{xy} = G_0\lambda\dot{\gamma} + (1-\xi/2)(\lambda\dot{\gamma})\sigma_{yy} - \frac{\xi}{2}(\lambda\dot{\gamma})\sigma_{xx}, \tag{9}$$

where $\dot{\gamma}$ is the constant shear rate $\dot{\gamma} = |du/dy|$. The division of each member of Eq. (7) by the respective member of Eq. (8) leads to the relationship $\sigma_{yy} = -\sigma_{xx}\xi/(2-\xi)$, and, its substitution in Eq. (9) together with σ_{xy} obtained from Eq. (7) and $K(\sigma_{kk}) = \Gamma(\beta)E_{\alpha,\beta}\left(\frac{\varepsilon}{G_0}(\sigma_{xx}+\sigma_{yy})\right)$ leads to the following nonlinear equation for σ_{xx}:

$$\Gamma^2(\beta)E_{\alpha,\beta}\left(\frac{\varepsilon}{G_0}\left(\frac{2-2\xi}{2-\xi}\right)\sigma_{xx}\right)^2\sigma_{xx} - (2-\xi)(\lambda\dot{\gamma})^2[G_0 - \sigma_{xx}\xi] = 0 \tag{10}$$

that can be written in a compact form as

$$h(\dot{\gamma};\sigma_{xx},\lambda,G_0,\alpha,\beta,\varepsilon,\xi) = 0.$$

The shear stress σ_{xy} as a function of $\dot{\gamma}$ is obtained from Eq. (9), and is given by:

$$\sigma_{xy}(\dot{\gamma}) = \frac{G_0\lambda\dot{\gamma} - \sigma_{xx}\lambda\dot{\gamma}\xi}{\Gamma(\beta)E_{\alpha,\beta}\left(\frac{\varepsilon}{G_0}\left(\frac{2-2\xi}{2-\xi}\right)\sigma_{xx}\right)}.$$

The steady shear viscosity, $\eta(\dot{\gamma})$, is given by:

$$\eta(\dot{\gamma}) = \frac{\sigma_{xy}(\dot{\gamma})}{\dot{\gamma}}.$$

2.4 Prony Series

Due to the different entanglement states of the molecules in the viscoelastic material, it is common to consider more than one mode to describe its behaviour. Therefore, assuming the existence of N modes, the quantities of interest presented earlier are now given by:

$$\hat{G}' = \sum_{k=1}^{N} \frac{G_{0_k}(\lambda_k \omega)^2}{1+(\lambda_k \omega)^2}$$

$$\hat{G}'' = \sum_{k=1}^{N} \frac{G_{0_k}\lambda_k \omega}{1+(\lambda_k \omega)^2}$$

$$\hat{\eta}(\dot{\gamma}) = \sum_{k=1}^{N} \frac{G_{0_k}\lambda_k\dot{\gamma} - \sigma_{xx_k}\lambda_k\dot{\gamma}\xi_k}{\dot{\gamma}\Gamma(\beta_k)E_{\alpha_k,\beta_k}\left(\frac{\varepsilon_k}{G_{0_k}}\left(\frac{2-2\xi_k}{2-\xi}\right)\sigma_{xx_k}\right)}.$$

We have defined $\boldsymbol{\alpha} = (\alpha_1, \alpha_2, ..., \alpha_N)$, $\boldsymbol{\beta} = (\beta_1, \beta_2, ..., \beta_N)$, $\boldsymbol{\lambda} = (\lambda_1, \lambda_2, ..., \lambda_N)$, $\boldsymbol{\xi} = (\xi_1, \xi_2, ..., \xi_N)$, $\boldsymbol{G_0} = (G_{0_1}, G_{0_2}, ..., G_{0_N})$, $\boldsymbol{\varepsilon} = (\varepsilon_1, \varepsilon_2, ..., \varepsilon_N)$. Note that $\boldsymbol{\sigma_{xx}} = (\sigma_{xx_1}, \sigma_{xx_2}, ..., \sigma_{xx_N})$, where each σ_{xx_k} is obtained from Eq. (10) for the given $\dot{\gamma}$.

3 Optimisation Problems

The parameters $\boldsymbol{\alpha}$, $\boldsymbol{\beta}$, $\boldsymbol{\lambda}$, $\boldsymbol{\xi}$, $\boldsymbol{G_0}$, and $\boldsymbol{\varepsilon}$ are unknown, but can be estimated by minimising two objective functions that measure the error given by the distance between experimental values and model predicted values, over the ω and the $\dot{\gamma}$ ranges.

Thus, to estimate the model parameters that come from two distinct experiments, we propose a two-step optimisation procedure.

First, we estimate $\boldsymbol{\lambda}$ and $\boldsymbol{G_0}$ parameters from the storage and loss moduli data (problem **P1**). Then, the optimal values $\boldsymbol{\lambda}^*$ and $\boldsymbol{G_0}^*$ are used in a second step to estimate $\boldsymbol{\alpha}$, $\boldsymbol{\beta}$, $\boldsymbol{\varepsilon}$ and $\boldsymbol{\xi}$ from the shear viscosity data (problem **P2**).

- **(P1):** the $\boldsymbol{\lambda}$ and $\boldsymbol{G_0}$ parameters estimation problem is formulated as:

$$\min_{\boldsymbol{\lambda},\boldsymbol{G_0} \in R^N} E_{G',G''}(\boldsymbol{\lambda}, \boldsymbol{G_0}) = \sum_{l}^{N_{G'G''}} \left(\left[\frac{\hat{G}'(\omega)_l}{G'_l} - 1\right]^2 + \left[\frac{\hat{G}''(\omega)_l}{G''_l} - 1\right]^2 \right)$$
$$\begin{aligned} \text{subject to}: \ & \lambda_k > 0, G_{0_k} > 0,\ k = 1, ..., N \\ & \lambda_k < \lambda_{k+1},\ k = 1, ..., N-1 \\ & G_{0_k} \geq G_{0_{k+1}},\ k = 1, ..., N-1 \end{aligned}$$

with $N_{G'G''}$ the number of experimental values obtained for storage (G'_l) and loss (G''_l) moduli.

- **(P2):** the $\boldsymbol{\alpha}$, $\boldsymbol{\beta}$, $\boldsymbol{\xi}$ and $\boldsymbol{\varepsilon}$ parameters estimation problem is formulated as:

$$\min_{\boldsymbol{\alpha},\boldsymbol{\beta},\boldsymbol{\varepsilon},\boldsymbol{\xi}\in R^N} E_\eta(\boldsymbol{\alpha},\boldsymbol{\beta},\boldsymbol{\varepsilon},\boldsymbol{\xi}) = \sum_l^{N_\eta} \left[\frac{\hat{\eta}(\dot{\gamma},\sigma_{xx})_l}{\eta_l} - 1\right]^2$$

$$\begin{aligned} \text{subject to}: & \ h(\dot{\gamma}_l;\sigma_{xx_{kl}},\lambda_k^*,G_{0_k}^*,\alpha_k,\beta_k,\varepsilon_k,\xi_k) = 0, \quad k=1,...,N,\ l=1,...,N_\eta \\ & \alpha_k\beta_k,\varepsilon_k, > 0,\ k=1,...,N \\ & 0 \le \xi_k < 1,\ k=1,...,N \end{aligned}$$

where we set $\boldsymbol{\lambda} = \boldsymbol{\lambda}^*$ and $\mathbf{G_0} = \mathbf{G_0^*}$. N_η is the number of experimental values obtained for shear viscosity (η_l).

4 Methodologies and Numerical Experiments

4.1 Methodologies

To solve the optimisation problem **P1** we have used the **Ipopt** solver that is available online on the NEOS servers (http://neos.mcs.anl.gov/neos/solvers). The **Ipopt** (Interior Point optimiser) is a solver for large-scale nonlinear programming (NLP) which implements an interior point line search filter method. The mathematical details of the method can be found in [10–14].

Since the problem **P2** involves $N \times N_\eta$ nonlinear equations (Eq. (10)), this problem is hard to solve. Thus, in this work we propose a Sequential Approach for solving **P2**. Using a Sequential Approach the optimisation is carried out in the space of the input parameters only. In the Sequential Approach the nonlinear equations and the optimisation problem are solved sequentially, one after the other, giving rise to the bound constrained optimisation problem **P2#**.

- **(P2#):** the new $\boldsymbol{\alpha}$, $\boldsymbol{\beta}$, $\boldsymbol{\xi}$ and $\boldsymbol{\varepsilon}$ parameters estimation problem is formulated as described next (Fig. 3). We now consider the minimisation problem:

$$\min_{\boldsymbol{\alpha},\boldsymbol{\beta},\boldsymbol{\varepsilon},\boldsymbol{\xi}\in R^N} E_\eta(\boldsymbol{\alpha},\boldsymbol{\beta},\boldsymbol{\varepsilon},\boldsymbol{\xi}) = \sum_l^{N_\eta} \left[\frac{\hat{\eta}(\dot{\gamma},\sigma_{xx})_l}{\eta_l} - 1\right]^2$$

$$\begin{aligned} \text{subject to}: & \ \alpha_k,\beta_k,\varepsilon_k, > 0,\ k=1,...,N \\ & 0 \le \xi_k < 1,\ k=1,...,N \end{aligned}$$

and the nonlinear equations are solved numerically using an iterative procedure, so that the objective function can be evaluated. Thus, the nonlinear equations are satisfied at each iteration of the optimisation process. We note this strategy may lead to a computational demanding process since the nonlinear equations are solved for each iteration of the NLP algorithm. Since the experimental data for the first and second normal stress differences were not considered, the parameters $\boldsymbol{\xi}$ were set to 0 in **P2#**.

We implement the proposed sequential approach in Matlab®, and we use the *fmincon* function [15–19], to solve the nonlinear problem **P2#**. The nonlinear equations were solved using the *fsolve* function [15]. The sequential optimisation can be described schematically as shown in Fig. 3:

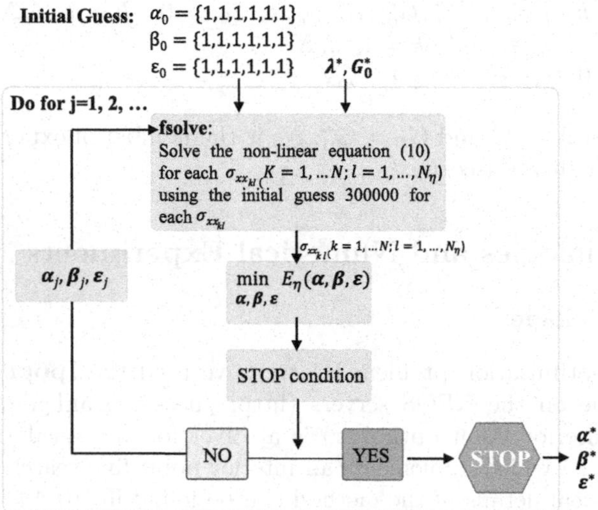

Fig. 3. Algorithm used to solve problem **P2#**.

The experimental data was obtained for a High Density Polyethylene (HDPE) at 190°C [9], and is shown in Fig. 4 (symbols) with $N_{G'G''} = 34$ and $N_\eta = 39$.

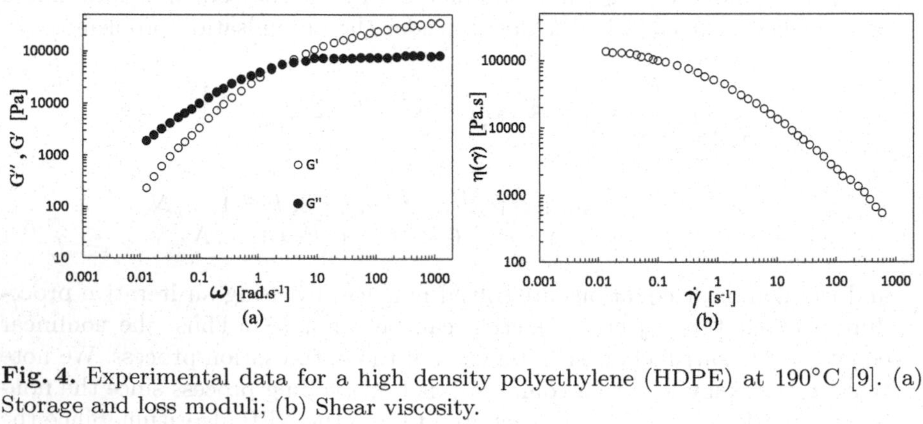

Fig. 4. Experimental data for a high density polyethylene (HDPE) at 190°C [9]. (a) Storage and loss moduli; (b) Shear viscosity.

4.2 Fit to Experimental Data (storage and loss moduli)

To obtain the optimal parameters $\boldsymbol{\lambda}^*$ and $\boldsymbol{G}_0^*$ the optimisation problem **P1** was coded in AMPL - Modelling Language for Mathematical Programming. By default, AMPL applies a presolve phase to the optimisation problem in order to reduce the size of the problem sent to the solver. Since the decisions made by the presolve phase rely on numerical computations, sometimes small differences between numbers can have a large effect on the results. Thus, to avoid this issue the presolve was disabled.

After some numerical experiments we realised that a value of $N = 6$ with initial guess:
$\boldsymbol{\lambda} = (0.005, 0.05, 0.5, 0.9, 5, 50)$,
$\boldsymbol{G_0} = (100000, 85000, 70000, 40000, 10000, 1000)$,
could provide good results. We used the IPOPT solver with the default settings and we fed the solver with these initial guess values.

The optimal parameter values $\boldsymbol{\lambda}^*$ and $\mathbf{G}_0^*$ obtained after the optimisation are:
$\boldsymbol{\lambda}^* = (0.00113292, 0.0112355, 0.0882049, 0.576664, 3.60712, 28.496)$,
$\boldsymbol{G}_0^* = (144113, 101039, 101039, 55374.8, 15286.3, 1625.3)$,
with $E^*_{G',G''} = 0.104239$. This optimal solution was obtained after 25 objective function evaluations, 25 objective gradient evaluations, 25 inequality constraint evaluations, 25 inequality constraint Jacobian evaluations and 24 Lagrangian Hessian evaluations. The total CPU seconds in IPOPT (without function evaluations) was 0.041 and the total CPU seconds in NLP function evaluations was 0.065 (these computations were performed in the free NEOS computation cloud).

From Fig. 5 we can see that a very good fit was obtained, as expected from the low error value obtained, $E^*_{G',G''} = 0.104239$.

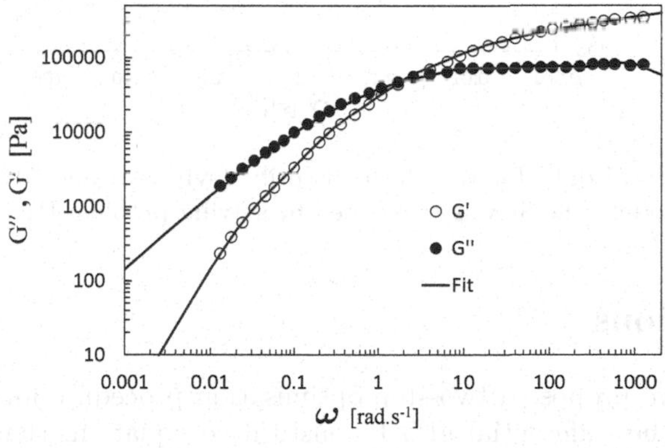

Fig. 5. Experimental data for the storage and loss moduli (symbols) and fit obtained with a 6-mode gPTT model. The fit was performed by solving problem P1.

4.3 Fit to Experimental Data (shear viscosity)

To obtain the optimal parameters $\boldsymbol{\alpha}^*$, $\boldsymbol{\beta}^*$, $\boldsymbol{\varepsilon}^*$ the optimisation problem **P2#** was solved using the sequential approach described in Fig. 3 and coded in Matlab®.

Since the Mittag-Leffler function is not available in the installation package of Matlab®, we have used the routine developed by Igor Podlubny and Martin Kacenak (2001–2012).

The *fmincon* function was used with the interior-point method, considering for stop condition the tolerance 1×10^{-9}. The remaining parameters were set to default. The *fsolve* function was used with the trust-region dogleg algorithm [15], where each iteration involves the approximate solution of a large linear system using the method of Preconditioned Conjugate Gradients.

The program stopped after 6 iterations ($j = 6$ - see Fig. 3), resulting in the following optimal parameters:

$\boldsymbol{\alpha}^* = (2.8249, 1.4277, 0.8429, 0.6087, 1.1905, 2.5488)$,

$\boldsymbol{\beta}^* = (2.8384, 2.6732, 3.8326, 3.9366, 2.9260, 3.0454)$,

$\boldsymbol{\varepsilon}^* = (3.7370, 4.0484, 2.8484, 2.1562, 3.0511, 3.3780)$.

with an error $E_\eta = 0.3814$. This error is again quite small and therefore a very good fit was obtained (Fig. 6).

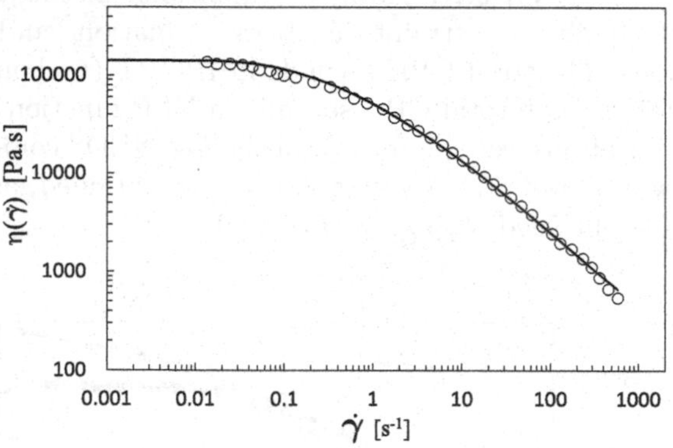

Fig. 6. Experimental data for the shear viscosity (symbols) and fit obtained with a 6-mode gPTT model. The fit was performed by solving problem P2#.

5 Conclusions

In this paper, we propose a two-step optimisation procedure for estimating the parameters of the differential gPTT constitutive equation, that better fit the experimental data obtained for an HDPE at 190°C [9].

First, we estimate $\boldsymbol{\lambda}$ and $\boldsymbol{G_0}$ parameters from the storage and loss moduli data. Then, the optimal values $\boldsymbol{\lambda}^*$ and $\boldsymbol{G_0}^*$ are used in a second step to estimate $\boldsymbol{\alpha}$, $\boldsymbol{\beta}$ and $\boldsymbol{\varepsilon}$ from the shear viscosity data.

To obtain the optimal parameter values we formulated two optimisation problems. One to fit the storage and loss moduli data, and the other to fit the shear viscosity data.

These problems were solved using the IPOPT solver and a Sequential Approach, respectively. A very good fit was obtained for both sets of experimental data.

The research group is now considering to optimise all parameters simultaneously, and using a larger set of experimental data.

References

1. Holzapfel, G.: Nonlinear Solid Mechanics. A continuum Approach for Engineering (2001)
2. Phan-Thien, N., Tanner, R.I.: New constitutive equation derived from network theory. J. Nonnewton. Fluid Mech. **2**(4), 353–365 (1977)
3. Phan-Thien, N.: A nonlinear network viscoelastic model. J. Rheol. **22**(3), 259–283 (1978)
4. Tanner, R.I., Huilgol, R.R.: On a classification scheme for flow fields. Rheologica Acta **14**(11), 959–962 (1975). https://doi.org/10.1007/BF01516297
5. Ferrás, L.L., Morgado, M.L., Rebelo, M., Mckinley, G.H., Afonso, A.: A generalized phan-thien - tanner model. J. Nonnewton. Fluid Mech. **269**, 88–99 (2019)
6. Podlubny, I.: Fractional Differential Equations: an Introduction to Fractional Derivatives, Fractional Differential Equations, to Methods of Their Solution and Some of Their Applications. vol. 198, Elsevier, San Diego (1998)
7. Huilgol, R.R., Phan-Thien, N.: Fluid Mechanics of Viscoelasticity: General Principles, Constitutive Modelling, Analytical and Numerical Techniques. Elsevier, Amsterdam (1997)
8. Alves, M.A., Pinho, F.T., Oliveira, P.J.: Study of steady pipe and channel flows of a single-mode phan-thien - tanner fluid. J. Nonnewton. Fluid Mech. **101**(1–3), 55–76 (2001)
9. Ansari, M., Hatzikiriakos, S.G., Mitsoulis, E.: Slip effects in HDPE flows. J. Nonnewton. Fluid Mech. **167**, 18–29 (2012)
10. Nocedal, J., Wächter, A., Waltz, R.A: Adaptive barrier strategies for nonlinear interior methods. SIAM J. Optim. **19**(4), 1674–1693 (2009)
11. Wächter, A., Biegler, L.T.: Line search filter methods for nonlinear programming: local convergence. SIAM J. Optim. **16**(1), 32–48 (2005)
12. Wächter, A., Biegler, L.T.: Line search filter methods for nonlinear programming: motivation and global convergence. SIAM J. Optim. **16**(1), 1–31 (2005)
13. Wächter, A., Biegler, L.T.: On the implementation of a primal-dual interior point filter line search algorithm for large-scale nonlinear programming. Math. Program. **106**(1), 25–57 (2006)
14. Wächter, A.: n interior point algorithm for large-scale nonlinear optimization with applications in process engineering. PhD thesis. Carnegie Mellon University, Pittsburgh, PA, USA (2002)
15. Coleman, T.F., Li, Y.: An interior trust region approach for nonlinear minimization subject to bounds. SIAM J. Optim. **6**(2), 418–445 (1996)
16. Gill, P.E., Murray, W., Wright, M.H.: Pract. Optim. Academic Press, London (1981)

17. Han, S.P.: A globally convergent method for nonlinear programming. J. Optim. Theory Appl. **22**(3), 297–309 (1977)
18. Powell, M.J.D.: A fast algorithm for nonlinearly constrained optimization calculations. In: Watson, G.A. (ed.) Numerical Analysis. LNM, vol. 630, pp. 144–157. Springer, Heidelberg (1978). https://doi.org/10.1007/BFb0067703
19. Powell, M.J.D., The convergence of variable metric methods for nonlinearly constrained optimization calculations. In: Nonlinear Programming, vol. 3, pp. 27–63. Academic Press (1978)

3D Simulations of Two-Component Mixes for the Prediction of Multi-component Mixtures' Macrotexture: Intermediate Outcomes

Mauro D'Apuzzo[1](✉), Azzurra Evangelisti[1], Daniela Santilli[1], and Vittorio Nicolosi[2]

[1] University of Cassino and Southern Lazio, Via G. Di Biasio 43, 03043 Cassino, Italy
{dapuzzo,daniela.santilli}@unicas.it
[2] University of Rome "Tor Vergata", via del Politecnico 1, 00133 Rome, Italy
nicolosi@uniroma2.it

Abstract. It is a consolidated knowledge that road macrotexture affects direct primary aspects related to road safety as friction or aquaplaning and secondary aspects related to environmental issues as noise or fuel consumption. These premises highlight how the prediction of road macrotexture is still an open research field for pavement designer, especially for theoretical models which would better describe the relationships with grading and volumetric properties, laying techniques and compaction energy.

In this paper intermediate outcomes about the theoretical prediction of road macrotexture are presented. In order to investigate the arrangement and compaction of a bituminous mix in a gyratory compactor, the Discrete Element Method (DEM) approach has been used to develop numerical simulations of two-component mixes. A large simulation campaign has been designed and performed and the Void Content diagram has been used for the macrotexture representation.

In analogy with the packing theory, the extension of the results obtained for the two-component mixtures into the multi-component systems, has been proposed and an effective novel theoretical method, based on a "revisiting" of the classical Void Content diagrams, for the macrotexture prediction has been performed. Finally, a numerical application of the method has been provided and the outcomes discussed.

Keywords: Discrete Element Method (DEM) · Packing model · Void Content diagram · Two-component mixes · Numerical simulation · Macrotexture · Road pavement

1 Introduction

Within scientific literature, significant association between low macrotexture and crashes risk have been found [1–3], as well as macrotexture and friction in wet conditions [4] or skid deterioration models [5]. For these reasons the road macrotexture prediction is of prominent interest for both private and public road management agencies. In the past,

O. Gervasi et al. (Eds.): ICCSA 2021, LNCS 12952, pp. 495–511, 2021.
https://doi.org/10.1007/978-3-030-86973-1_35

empirical models have been deeply analyzed, their critical issues have been brought to light and tried to overcome [6, 7]. However, further studies are necessary to deeply investigate the theoretical links between the macrotexture and the volumetric and grading characteristics of the bituminous mixtures and the compaction techniques and released energy. This work fits in this direction.

1.1 Field and Laboratory Tests Overview

Both laboratory and outdoor methods are available to measure the macrotexture and the simplest and most known method is the Sand Patch Method [8]. It is a volumetric method that, with a very simple apparatus and test process (see Fig. 1), provides the average pavement macrotexture depth, expresses by means of the Mean Texture Depth (MTD) which, according to the Standard [8] can be evaluated by means of the Eq. (1):

$$MTD = \frac{4 \cdot V}{\pi \cdot D^2} \tag{1}$$

where:

- MTD = mean texture depth of pavement macro-texture [mm];
- V = sample volume [mm^3];
- D = average diameter of the area covered by the material [mm].

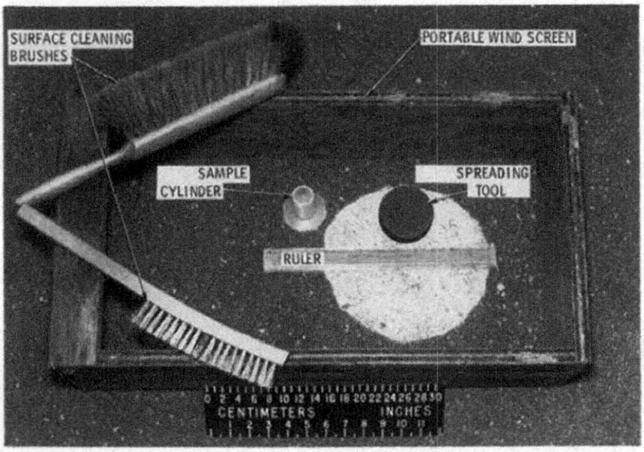

Fig. 1. Apparatus for sand patch measurement [8].

In order to simulate and reproduce the compaction technique under actual road laying operations, with the aim to analyse the final compaction condition of the asphalt in terms of void content, the gyratory compactor has been identified as adequate laboratory test [9]. In fact, the test is able to reproduce on the bituminous specimen, shearing forces similar to those performed under the action of a roller during field compaction [10].

Furthermore, the choice to use the gyratory compactor specimens, well fits with the use of the DEM simulation method, allowing to considerably reduce the computational burden.

1.2 Packing Theory Background

In a non-exhaustive way, a brief introduction on the most important basic concept of aggregate packing has been provided below.

Since the mid-1920s, several studies have been performed in order to investigate factors affecting packing and porosity of cement and asphalt concretes [11–13].

As far as two-component mixtures have been concerned, two types of particles interaction have been highlights:

- The wall effect, due to the interaction between particles and any type of boundary placed in contact with the granular mass;
- The interference effects, due to the increasing fraction of fine aggregates added to the coarse fraction, which cause the coarse-to-coarse contact.

First significant developments of the Void content diagrams have been done by Furnas [11], which on the basis of numerous experiments, produced generalized experimental curves describing the void index variation of the mix, varying both coarse aggregate proportion and diameter ratio of fine and coarse aggregates (see Fig. 2).

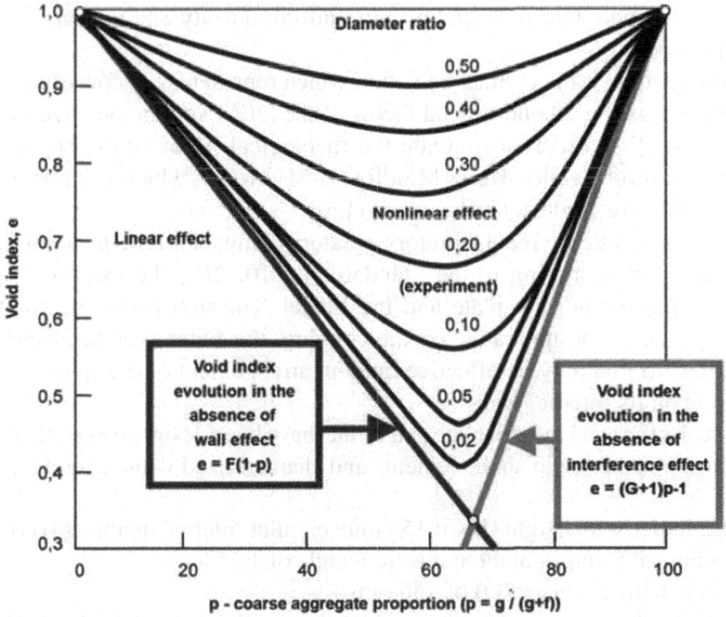

Fig. 2. Void Content diagram of a two-component system of coarse (g) and fine (f) aggregate vs. the coarse aggregate proportion for different diameter ratios [14].

As it is possible to see, according to the experimental evidences, the curves present a clear minimum and for any given proportion of fine to coarse aggregate, the voids in the mix decrease with decreasing diameter ratio.

1.3 Objective

The main aim of this paper is to introduce a novel theoretical method for the macrotexture prediction of multi-component spherical mixtures, by means of the Void Content diagram representation.

Twenty simulations of gyratory compaction specimens, of two-component spherical mixes, with five different fixed fractions of fine particles respect to the coarse particles, have been performed. The macrotexture values have been evaluated and depicted in analogy to the Void Content diagram designed for the representation of the voids ratio of two-component mixes.

Finally, a numerical application of the proposed method has been provided and the results have been discussed.

2 Design of the Virtual Experimental Campaign

2.1 Numerical Model

The Discrete Element Method (DEM) is a numerical method, introduced in 1971 by Peter Cundall [15], in which discrete spherical particles collide one each other and with other surfaces using the force-displacement law. Each particle is represented as a rigid spherical single-node with fixed radius and uniform density and is characterized by 6 degrees of freedom.

With the geometry, the contact behavior, which represents the constitutive behavior of the materials, is the second crucial factor of the DEM simulation. According to the literature [16–19], in order to simulate the rheological behavior of asphalt mixtures, the viscoelastic model called Hertz-Mindlin (H-M) Model, which is composed by two Kelvin's constitutive models, has been used [20].

In order to simulate the real laboratory gyratory compactor test, the numerical model has been designed according to the Standards [9, 10, 21]. The external geometry is composed of the mould, the plate and the funnel. The first two are actually part of the gyratory compactor apparatus, on the contrary, the funnel has been introduced in the simulation, to guaranty an effective random arrangement of the spherical particles, which impact on its internal wall.

In particular the steel mould, plate and funnel have been designed as rigid bodies, with null thickness, meshed with shell elements and characterized with different geometries:

- Mould: cylinder with height (H) of 150 mm, circular internal diameter (D) of 150 mm (inner radius of 75 mm), and compaction angle of 1.25°.
- Plate: circle with diameter (D) of 150 mm.
- Funnel: conical geometry characterized by the smaller radius of 60 mm (Rmin), the bigger radius of 1000 mm (Rmax) and height (Hf) of 1240 mm (required dimensions to guaranty a regular distance between the particles in the initial position).

Their assembly has been reported in the Fig. 3.

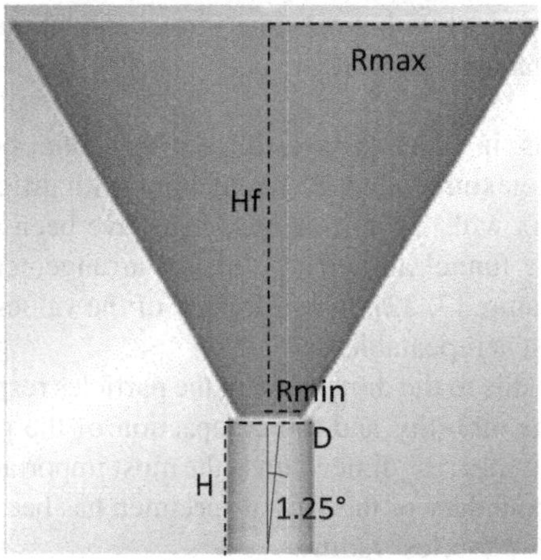

Fig. 3. Virtual model of the gyratory compactor with the funnel.

The aggregates have been represented by rigid bodies with spherical shape, which are characterized by a density of 2500·kg/m^3 and radius between 20 mm and 4 mm. The most important features have been summarized in the Table 1:

Table 1. Features of the virtual particles

Diameter [mm]	Radius [mm]	Volume [mm]	Volume [mm]	Mass [mm]
20	10	4188.79	4.18879E−06	0.010472
16	8	2144.661	2.14466E−06	0.005362
12	6	904.7787	9.04779E−07	0.002262
8	4	268.0826	2.68083E−07	0.00067
4	2	33.51032	3.35103E−08	8.38E-05

As far as the kinematics and loads are concerned, the mould is characterized by a constant rotation of 30 rev/min around the compaction axis (angle of 1.25° respect to the vertical axis), the plate, once that all the spheres have been fallen into the mould, applies a vertical pressure of 600 kPa. Finally, it should be highlighted that, in order to reduce the analysis noise, the mass proportional damping has been used and that the friction coefficient for the contact between particles has been set at 0.5 and between particles and plate/mould at 0.2.

2.2 Previous Findings

In order to establish the better simulation procedures and to calibrate the virtual model, several efforts have been spent within previous virtual and laboratory tests and the main results have been summarized below [20]:

- Repeatability analysis: in order to investigate if the initial position of each sphere, affects the final macrotexture value, 25 simulations with different initial positions of the monogranular mix with 20 mm of diameter, have been performed. It has been demonstrated that the funnel allows an effective arrangement of the particles and, according to the literature [7, 22], the variability of the values of the macrotexture is conserved and the test is repeatable.
- Wall Effect Analysis: due to the dimension of the particles respect to the mould, along the boundary line, the mobility and the compaction of the particles could be more difficult. Although the spheres' dimension is the most important affecting factor, a cut of 15 mm along the boundary of the virtual specimen has been identify to neglect the wall effect, regardless particles' radius.
- Reference Depth: the simulations on the monogranular mixes have shown that the cut at depth 'D/2', respect to the upper surface of the specimen, produces MTD values closer or belonging to the theoretical packing configurations domain (the cubical packing model and the tetrahedral packing model which represent the loose and the dense configurations respectively).

2.3 Simulation Series Design

In order to investigate the behavior of two-component mixtures, especially in terms of compaction and mutual interference, according to the packing theory [11, 13] a set of simulations, with different d/D ratio, has been performed.

With the aim to find a compromise between the results validity and the computational efforts, 20 mm for the maximum aggregate diameter and a duration of 10 s of virtual simulation have been selected and four two-component mixes have been designed, with fixed total mass and density, of about 2,86 kg and 2500 kg/m^3, respectively. For each mixture, five different percentage proportions have been defined: 0%–100%; 25%–75%; 50%–50%; 75%–25% and 100%-0%. The most important features of the mixtures have been summarized in the Table 2:

Table 2. Characteristics of the simulations of the two-component mixtures.

d/D	Incidence				
16/20	0%–100%	25%–75%	50%–50%	75%–25%	100%-0%
N° particles	273	133–204	267–136	400–68	527
N° particles ratio	0	0.651961	1.963235	5.882353	–

(continued)

Table 2. (*continued*)

d/D	Incidence				
16/20	0%–100%	25%–75%	50%–50%	75%–25%	100%-0%
Virtual duration sim. [sec]	10	10	10	10	10
Real duration sim. [h]	8	9.5	11	13	15.5
12/20	0%–100%	25%–75%	50%–50%	75%–25%	100%-0%
N° particles	273	316–204	632–136	945–68	1275
N° particles ratio	0	1.55	4.65	13.90	–
Virtual duration sim. [sec]	10	10	10	10	10
Real duration sim. [h]	8	20.5	38	54.5	70
8/20	0%–100%	25%–75%	50%–50%	75%–25%	100%-0%
N° particles	273	1063–204	2126–136	3189–68	4285
N° particles ratio	0	5.21	15.63	46.90	–
Virtual duration sim. [sec]	10	10	10	10	10
Real duration sim. [h]	8	74	131.5	182.5	238
4/20	0%–100%	25%–75%	50%–50%	75%–25%	100%-0%
N° particles	273	8531-204	17063-136	25594-68	34125
N° particles ratio	0	41.82	125.46	376.38	–
Virtual duration sim. [sec]	10	10	10	10	10
Real duration sim. [h]	8	413	645	848.5	1080

By way of example, the d4/D20 two-component mixtures with the three percentage proportions, before the compaction phase, have been showed in the Fig. 4.

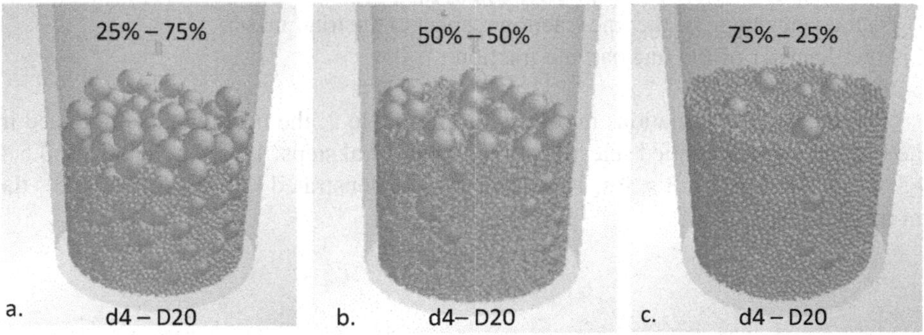

Fig. 4. Random arrangement of the two-component mixture d4/D20, before the compaction phase, with the percentage proportions: a. 25%–75%; b. 50%–50%; c. 75%-25%.

Although the entire development of the simulation has been previously detailed [20], a brief general description of the individual steps of the virtual test is provided. The simulation is composed of four phases:

1. Definition of the position of the apparatus (mould, plate and funnel) and of the particles in a regular grid;
2. Free fall of the particles into the funnel and consequently into the mould;
3. Right position of the plate into the mould;
4. Rotation of the mould around the compaction axis at 30 rev/min, and compaction of the plate to the mixture with a vertical pressure of 600 kPa.

2.4 Post Analysis of the Outputs

In order to evaluate, for each simulation, the final value of the macrotexture, in terms of MTD index, the construction of the upper surface of the virtual specimen, by means of an ad hoc code, has been performed. In particular the code allows to distinguish the size of each particle and to convert the coordinates of the node (x, y and z) into a grid-surface with a sample spacing of 0.5 mm. The flowchart of the conversion procedure has been summarized in the Fig. 5.

It must be observed that the Deq (equivalent diameter in terms of volumetric properties) can be considered a theoretical dimension of the virtual particle if the two-component mix would be composed of only one fraction. Its evaluation has been reported in the Eq. (2).

$$D_{eq} = \sqrt[3]{\%_D \cdot D^3 + \%_d \cdot d^3} \tag{2}$$

where:

D_{eq} is the equivalent diameter of the corresponding monogranular mix;
$\%_D$ is the percentage of the larger fraction respect to the total mass;
D is the diameter of the larger particle fraction;
$\%_d$ is the percentage of the fine fraction respect to the total mass;
d is the diameter of the fine particle fraction.

For all the 20 simulations introduced in the Table 2, the procedure summarized in the Fig. 5 has been applied selecting 13 fixed temporal steps: 1.5 s, 2 s, 2.5 s, 3 s, 3.5 s, 4 s, 4.5 s, 5 s, 6 s, 7 s, 8 s, 9 s, 10 s. In fact, as demonstrated [20] within 0 to 1.5 s the mixtures stabilize.

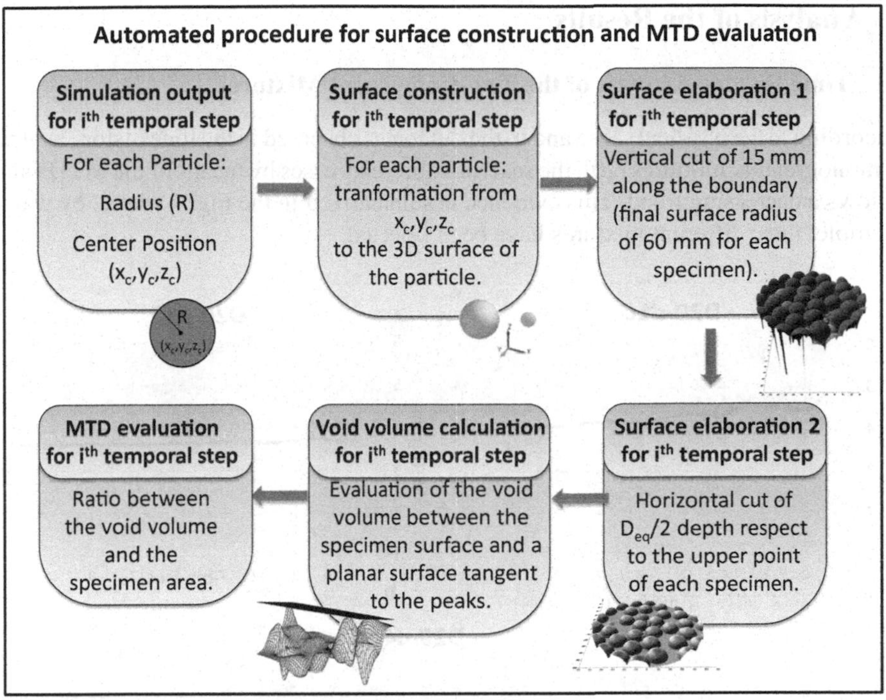

Fig. 5. Workflow of the automated procedure for the construction of the surface specimen and MTD evaluation.

By way of example, with a fixed percentage proportion of 50%–50% the final surfaces of the two-component mixtures d16-D20, d12-D20 and d8-D20, have been reported in the Fig. 6.

Finally, 260 final surfaces have been constructed and their relative MTD values have been evaluated.

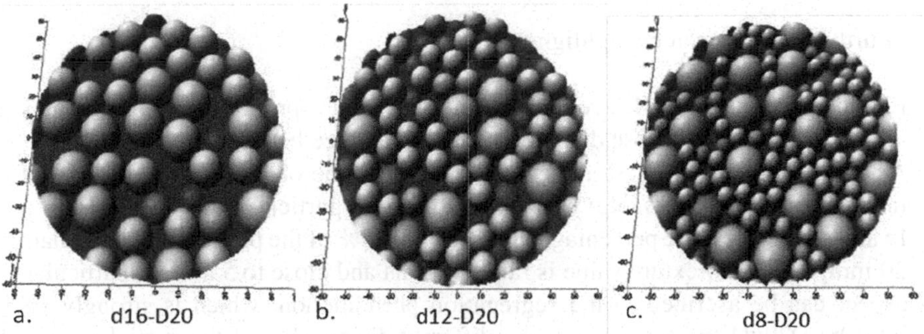

Fig. 6. Deq/2 surface with the final surface radius of 60mm of the mixtures with the percentage proportion of 50%–50% and with the d-D ratios a. 16–20; b. 12–20; c. 8–20.

3 Analysis of the Results

3.1 Time History Analysis of the Two-Component Mixtures

According to the physical sense and to the outcomes observed in the time history analysis of monogranular mixtures [20], the macrotexture, expresses by means of the MTD value, follows a decreasing trend. This evidence is summarized in the Fig. 7 where, by way of example, three different mixtures have been selected.

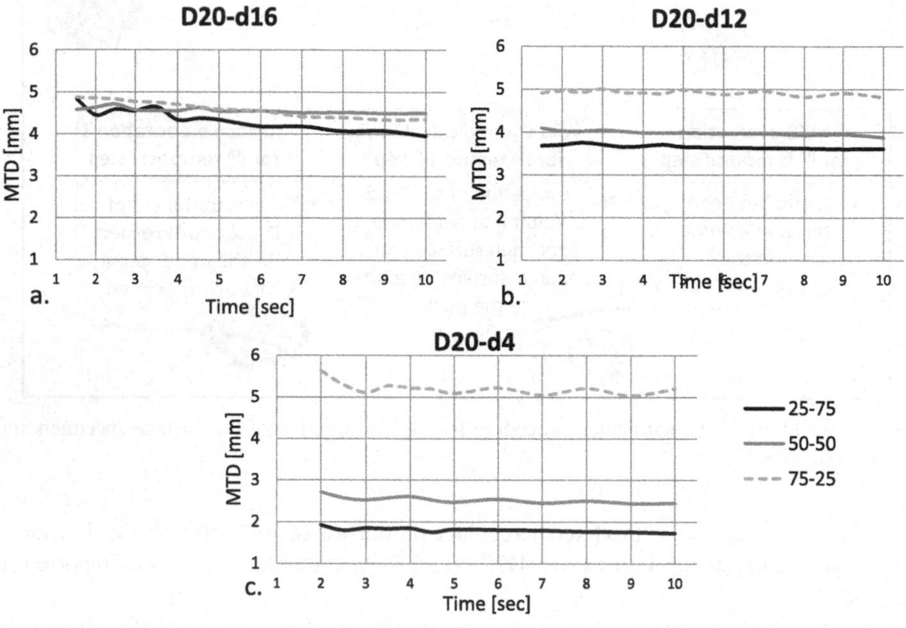

Fig. 7. Time history curves at different level of percentage proportion for the mixtures a. 16–20; b. 12–20; c. 4–20.

Further remarks can be highlighted:

- For the mixture D20-d16, regardless the percentage proportion, the macrotexture values and trends are close due to the small difference between the two radii.
- As the d/D ratio increases, a decreasing trend can be observed as a function of the incidence of fine (d variable) with respect to larger particles (D = 20 mm).
- In any case, within the percentage proportion at 75% of the particle size with diameter 20 mm, the macrotexture value is rater constant and close to 5 mm. In particular this aspect can be ascribed to the segregation phenomenon, which is strongly visible into the D20/d4 mixture, where the different dimensions of the particles are more accentuated (see Fig. 8).

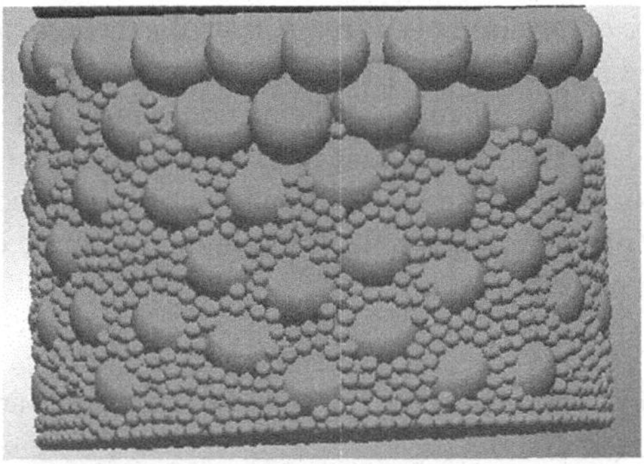

Fig. 8. Particular of the segregation phenomenon into the mixture D20/d4.

3.2 Void Content Diagram Representation of Macrotexture

In analogy with the model proposed for the representation of the voids content diagrams of two-component mixtures proposed by Furnas, the Macrotexture values of the mixes, at the fixed time of 10 s, have been arranged in the Fig. 9.

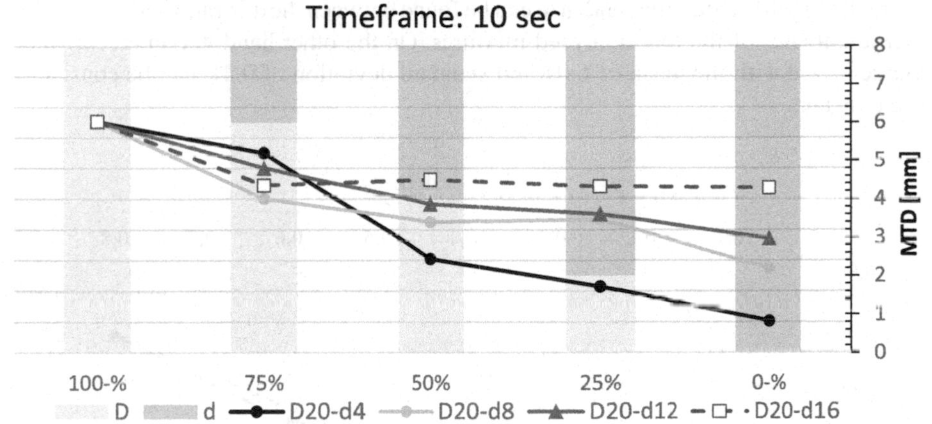

Fig. 9. Void content diagram of the macrotexture values representation.

Although the shape of the curves is different from the theoretical void ratio diagrams, even in the case of the representation of the macro texture, it can be seen that, for the same percentage, MTD values increase as the d/D ratio increases.

In particular, for each two-component mix, a decreasing trend can be seen as the diameter of the fine fraction decreases, with an increasingly accentuated slope. This concept is evident by observing the Table 3, where the summary of the regression data of each mix, has been reported.

Table 3. Summary of the regression data of the two-component analyzed mixtures.

Mixture code	d/D	Intercept	Angular coef. (Ac)	R^2
D20-D16	0.8	5.8547	−0.0201	0.65
D20-D12	0.6	6.1467	−0.0342	0.93
D20-D8	0.4	5.9527	−0.0385	0.87
D20-D4	0.2	6.3185	−0.0592	0.95

In the Fig. 10, a linear dependence can be found between the d/D ratio and the Angular coefficient (Ac) of the four analyzed mixtures. On the other hand, the intercept value, characterized with the mean of 6.07 and standard deviation of 0.21, can be considered as a constant.

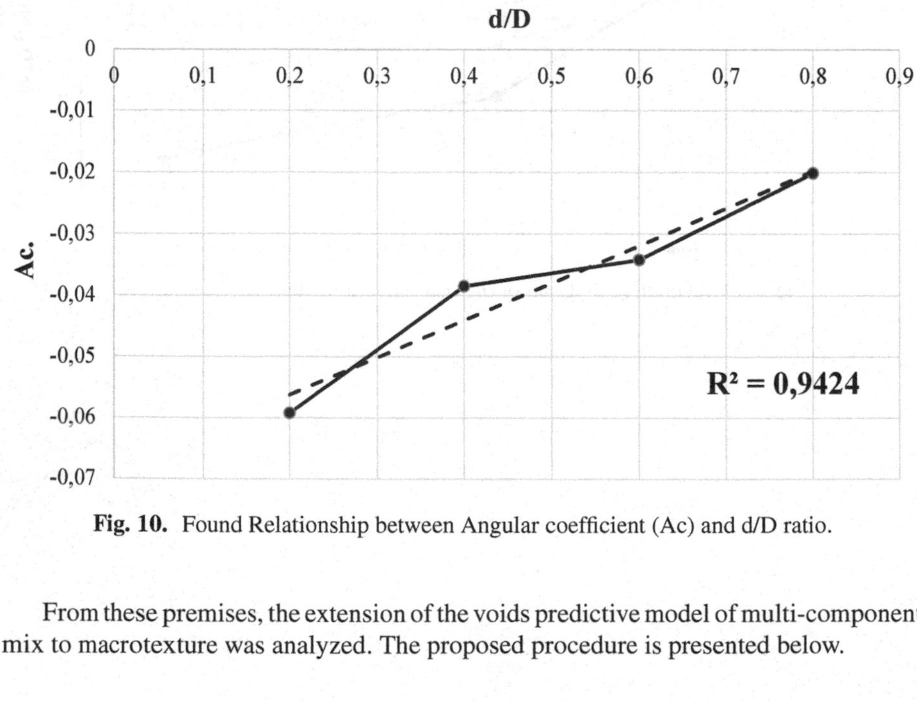

Fig. 10. Found Relationship between Angular coefficient (Ac) and d/D ratio.

From these premises, the extension of the voids predictive model of multi-component mix to macrotexture was analyzed. The proposed procedure is presented below.

4 The Power Diagram Representation for Macrotexture Prediction of Multi-component Systems

The proposed extension of the results obtained for the two-component mixture into the multi-component systems for the macrotexture prediction, has been reported in the following flowchart (Fig. 11).

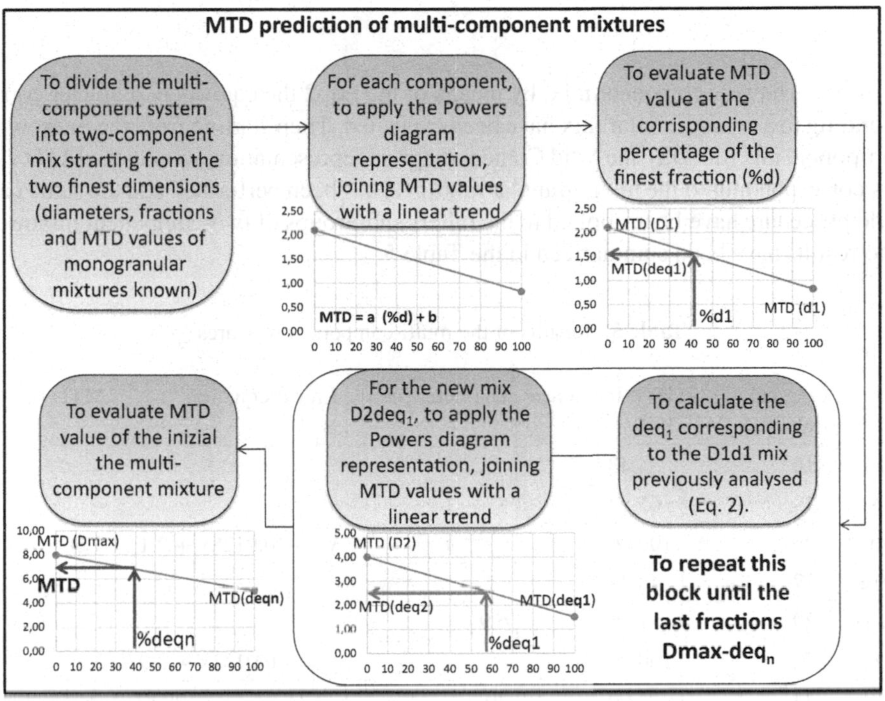

Fig. 11. Flowchart of the extension of the macrotexture evaluation from two-component to multi-component mixes.

In order to illustrate its applicability, an example has been provided below.

4.1 Example of the Proposed Method

The input data of the numerical example have been reported in the Table 4.

The first step consists into the evaluation of the incidence of the finest fraction (d) respect to the larger (D) considering the multi-component mix as a combination of three different two-component mixtures:

1. d4-D8;
2. Deq1-D12;
3. Deq2-D20.

Table 4. Input data of the numerical example.

N° fractions	Incidence [%]	Diameter [mm]	MTD monogranular [mm]
1	44	20	6.59
2	27	12	2.97
3	19	8	2.1
4	10	4	0.82

For each two-component mix, by means of the Eq. 2 the equivalent diameter corresponding to a monogranular mix have been evaluated. Then starting from the finest two-component mix (d4-D8), the Void Content diagram representation, joining the MTD values corresponding to the monogranular mixtures, has been performed and the same cascade procedure have been applied to the others sub-groups of two-component mixtures. The results have been summarized in the Table 5.

Table 5. Results of the multi-component mixtures

	Original incidence [%]	New incidence [%]	Diameter [mm]	Linear equation	MTD [mm]
d4	10	34.48	4		–
D8	19	65.52	8		–
Tot	29	100.00	–	$y = -0.0128x + 2.1$	1.66
D12	27	48.21	12		–
deq1	29	51.79	6.9		–
Tot	56	100.00	–	$y = -0.0131x + 2.97$	2.29
D20	44	44.00	20		–
deq2	56	56.00	10.0		–
Tot	100	100.00	–	$y = -0.043x + 6.59$	**4.18**

By way of example, the final Void Content diagram representation, used for the MTD evaluation of the multi-component mix, have been reported in the Fig. 12.

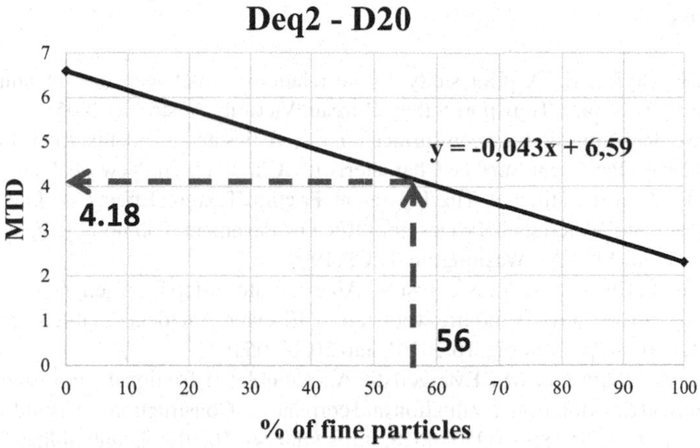

Fig. 12. Void Content diagram representation for the final MTD evaluation.

5 Conclusions

This paper presents intermediate findings obtained from the use of Void Content diagram representation for the description and prediction of the macrotexture. A simulation campaign has been performed with the aim to reproduce 20 different virtual gyratory compactor specimens with spherical particles. In particular four mixtures characterized by two different diameter dimensions (d-D) have been selected and, for each of them, five different percentage proportions have been identified.

An automated procedure for the construction of the virtual surface specimens and the related MTD values, has been proposed and the Void Content diagram representation has been applied to describe the macrotexture trend, depending on the d/D ratio.

According to the physical sense, the MTD values follow a decreasing trend as the fraction of fine particles increases respect to the course particles and this is further emphasized when the difference between the two diameters increasing (d/D ratio decreases). It can be due to the propensity of the fine fraction to occupy the interstitial voids of the coarse fraction.

Finally, a novel theoretical approach for the prediction of the macrotexture of multi-component mixtures, based on the Packing theory, has been proposed and a numerical example has been provided.

Intermediate results obtained so far, confirm that the DEM simulation can be an effective method for the macrotexture simulation also for two-component mixtures and that, although further analyses are needed, the Void Content diagram applied for the macrotexture description and prediction seems to show encouraging outcomes.

Acknowledgments. The authors would like to thank the Silesian University of Technology di Gliwice (Poland), for the use the software licence.

References

1. Cairney, P., Styles, E.: A pilot study of the relationship between macrotexture and crash occurrence. Australian Transport Safety Bureau, Victoria, Australia (2005)
2. Gothie, M.: Relationship between surface characteristics and accidents. In: 3rd International Symposium on Pavement Surface Characteristics, Christchurch, New Zealand (1996)
3. Larson, R.: Consideration of Tire/Pavement Friction/Texture Effects on Pavement Structural Design and Materials Mix Design. Office of Pavement Technology. Federal Highway Administration (FHWA), Washington, D.C. (1999)
4. D'Apuzzo M., Evangelisti A., Nicolosi V.: An exploratory step for a general unified approach to labelling of road surface and tire wet friction. Elsevier, Accident Analysis Prevention **138**, 105462 (2020). https://doi.org/10.1016/j.aap.2020.105462
5. Nicolosi, V., D'Apuzzo, M., Evangelisti, A.: Cumulated frictional dissipated energy and pavement skid deterioration: Evaluation and correlation, Construction and Building Materials, Volume 263, 120020, ISSN 0950–0618. https://doi.org/10.1016/j.conbuildmat.2020.120020 (2020)
6. D'Apuzzo, M., Evangelisti, A., Nicolosi, V.: Preliminary findings for a prediction model of road surface macrotexture. Procedia Soc. Behav. Sci. **53**, 1110–1119 (2012). https://doi.org/10.1016/j.sbspro.2012.09.960.ISSN:1877-0428
7. Evangelisti, A., D'Apuzzo, M., Nicolosi, V., Flintsch, G., De Leon Izeppi, E., Katicha, S., Mogrovejo, D.: Evaluation of Variability of Macrotexture Measurement with different Laser-based Devices. Airfield & Highway Pavement Conference (2015)
8. ASTM E965: Standard Test Method for Measuring Pavement Macrotex-ture Depth Using a Volumetric Technique. American Society for Testing and Materials In-ternational. PA, West Conshohocken: www.astm.org (2006)
9. ASTM D6925–09: Standard test method for preparation and determination of the relative density of hot mix asphalt (HMA) specimens by means of the superpave gyratory compactor. ASTM International, West Conshohocken (2009)
10. EN 12697–10: Bituminous mixtures. Test methods for hot mix asphalt. Compactibility. ISBN 0 580 38964 2 (2002)
11. Furnas, C.C.: Relations Between Specific Volume, Voids and Size Composition in Systems of Broken Solids of Mixed Sizes. U.S. Bur. of Mines, Report of lnvestigations 2894, pp. 1–10 (1928)
12. Powers, T.C.: The Properties of Fresh Concrete. Wiley, New York, 664 pages (1968)
13. Lees, D.Y.: Rational design of continuous and intermittent aggregate grading for concrete. HRR N°, pp. 441–1973 (1973)
14. Perraton, D., Meunier, M., Carter, A.: Application des méthodes d'empilement granulaire à la formulation des Stones Matrix Asphalts (SMA). Bulletin des Laboratoires des Ponts et Chaussées n°270–271, pp. 87–108 (2007)
15. Cundall, P., Strack, O.: A discrete numerical model for granular assemblies. Dans Geotechinque **29**(1), 47–65 (1979)
16. Abbas, A., Masad, E., Papagiannakis, T., Harman, T.: Micromechanical modeling of the viscoelastic behavior of asphalt mixtures using the discrete-element method. Int. J. Geomech. 7(2), 131–139 (2007)
17. Adhikari, S., You, Z.: 3D discrete element models of the hollow cylin-drical asphalt concrete specimens subject to the internal pressure. Int. J. Pavement Eng. **11**(5), 429–439 (2010)
18. Di Renzo, A., Di Maio, F.P.: Comparison of contact-force models for the simulation of collisions in DEM-based granular flow codes. Chem. Eng. Sci. **59**, 525–541 (2004)
19. Collopa, A., McDowellb, G., Lee, Y.: Modelling dilation in an idealised asphalt mixture using discrete element modelling. Granular Matter **8**(3–4), 175–184 (2006)

20. D'Apuzzo, M., Evangelisti, A., Nicolosi, V.: Preliminary investigation on a numerical approach for the evaluation of road macrotexture. In: Gervasi, O., et al. (eds.) ICCSA 2017. LNCS, vol. 10405, pp. 157–172. Springer, Cham (2017). https://doi.org/10.1007/978-3-319-62395-5_12
21. EN 12697–31: Bituminous mixtures. Test methods for hot mix asphalt. Specimen preparation by gyratory compactor. ISBN 978 0 580 50689 5, (2007).
22. D'Apuzzo, M., Evangelisti, A., Santilli, D., Nicolosi, V.: Theoretical Development and Validation of a New 3D Macrotexture Index Evaluated from Laser Based Profile Measurements. In: Gervasi, O., et al. (eds.) ICCSA 2020. LNCS, vol. 12251, pp. 367–382. Springer, Cham (2020). https://doi.org/10.1007/978-3-030-58808-3_27

Generalized Spectral Dimensionality Reduction Based on Kernel Representations and Principal Component Analysis

MacArthur C. Ortega-Bustamante[1,2], Waldo Hasperué[2], Diego H. Peluffo-Ordóñez[3,4], Juan González-Vergara[4(✉)], Josué Marín-Gaviño[4,5], and Martín Velez-Falconi[4]

[1] Universidad Técnica Del Norte, Ibarra, Ecuador
[2] III-LIDI, Facultad de Informática, Universidad Nacional de La Plata, La Plata, Argentina
[3] Modeling, Simulation and Data Analysis (MSDA) Research Program, Mohammed VI Polytechnic University, 47963 Ben Guerir, Morocco
[4] SDAS Research Group, 47963 Ben Guerir, Morocco
juan.gonzalez@sdas-group.com
[5] School of Mathematical and Computational Science, Yachay Tech, Urcuquí, Ecuador
https://www.sdas-group.com

Abstract. Very often, multivariate data analysis problems require dimensionality reduction (DR) stages to either improve analysis performance or represent the data in an intelligible fashion. Traditionally DR techniques are developed under different frameworks and settings what makes their comparison a non-trivial task. In this sense, generalized DR approaches are of great interest as they enable both to power and compare the DR techniques in a proper and fair manner. This work introduces a generalized spectral dimensionality reduction (GSDR) approach able to represent DR spectral techniques and enhance their representation ability. To do so, GSDR exploits the use of kernel-based representations as an initial nonlinear transformation to obtain a new space. Then, such a new space is used as an input for a feature extraction process based on principal component analysis. As remarkable experimental results, GSDR shows to be able to outperform the conventional implementation of well-known spectral DR techniques (namely, classical multidimensional scaling and Laplacian eigenmaps) in terms of the scaled version of the average agreement rate. Additionally, relevant insights and theoretical developments to understand the effect of data structure preservation at local and global levels are provided.

Keywords: Dimensionality reduction · Kernel representations · Principal component analysis · Spectral methods

1 Introduction

Dimensionality reduction (DR) aims to embed relevant information from high-dimensional data into a lower dimension representation, being of great use among data-related

M. Velez-Falconi—This work is supported by SDAS research group (www.sdas-group.com).

O. Gervasi et al. (Eds.): ICCSA 2021, LNCS 12952, pp. 512–523, 2021.
https://doi.org/10.1007/978-3-030-86973-1_36

areas such as big data, pattern recognition, clustering or data visualization. Many DR techniques have been extensively studied, ranging from distance-based preservation criteria, e.g. classical approaches such as classical multidimensional scaling (CMDS) [1], to graph-based approaches as Laplacian eigenmaps (LE) [2]. Given such a wide range of techniques developed under different frameworks and settings, generalized DR approaches are of great interest as it enables to contrast and enhance them in a fair, proper manner.

In this work, a generalized spectral dimensionality reduction (GSDR) approach capable of representing DR spectral techniques and exploit their representation ability is introduced. To do so, in the here-studied GSDR a new space representation is obtained through an initial nonlinear transformation employed by the use of kernel-based representations. Then, a feature extraction process based on principal component analysis is applied in such new space. Remarkable experimental results shows that in terms of the scaled version of the average agreement rate, GSDR is be able to outperform the conventional implementation of well-known spectral DR techniques -namely, classical multidimensional scaling and Laplacian eigenmaps. Additionally, aimed at better understanding the effect of data structure preservation at local and global levels simultaneously, theoretical developments and relevant insights are provided.

The remaining of this manuscript is structured as follows: Sect. 2 states the notation used throughout this work and presents a brief overview on kernels. In Sect. 3, we introduce the GSDR method. Both the nonlinear mapping and the feature extraction are explained in theoretical and computational terms. Section 4 describes the setup and parameter settings for experiments. Section 5 gathers and discusses the experimental results. Finally, conclusions and final remarks are drawn in Sect. 6.

2 Background on Kernel Functions and Notation

2.1 Notation

Let us define the input data matrix as $\mathbf{X} \in \mathbb{R}^{N \times D}$ holding N samples represented by D variables, in the form: $\mathbf{X} = (\mathbf{x}_1^\top, \ldots, \mathbf{x}_N^\top)^\top$, with $\mathbf{x}_i \in \mathbb{R}^D$ and $i \in \{1, \ldots, N\}$. Likewise, let $\mathbf{Y} \in \mathbb{R}^{N \times d}$ be the output data matrix, such that $\mathbf{Y} = (\mathbf{y}_1^\top, \ldots, \mathbf{y}_N^\top)^\top$, $\mathbf{y}_i \in \mathbb{R}^d$ and $d \leq D$. In terms of feature extraction, matrix $\mathbf{Y}$ is the embedded (also extracted, projected, or mapped) space. In such vein, it is traditionally set $d < D$ for DR purposes. That said, the aim of DR is to embed the space $\mathbf{X}$ into a lower-dimensional space $\mathbf{Y}$.

2.2 Concept of Kernel Function

Roughly speaking, the so-named kernel function can be understood as an approach that allows for estimating the similarity among input data samples [3]. In general, such similarity is calculated over samples from either independent or associated spaces [4,5]. In this work, the concept of kernel is referred to the pairwise similarity or affinity measures intended to represent the input data. Naturally, similarity measures must be ruled by a positive semi-definite function. In mathematical terms, we can express a positive semi-definite kernel function $\mathcal{K}(\cdot,\cdot)$ as follows:

$$\begin{aligned} \mathcal{K}(\cdot,\cdot) : \mathbb{R}^D \times \mathbb{R}^D &\longrightarrow \mathbb{R} \\ \mathbf{x}_i, \mathbf{x}_j &\longmapsto \mathcal{K}(\mathbf{x}_i, \mathbf{x}_j), \end{aligned} \tag{1}$$

satisfying

$$\sum_{i=1}^{N}\sum_{j=1}^{N} c_i \bar{c}_j \mathcal{K}(\mathbf{x}_i, \mathbf{x}_j) \geq 0, \tag{2}$$

for all $c_i \in \mathbb{C}$, being $\bar{c}_i$ the complex conjugate of c_i.

3 Proposed Generalized Spectral Dimensionality Reduction (GSDR) Approach

The here-proposed Generalized Spectral Dimensionality Reduction, short termed as GSDR, is based on the premise that data can be mapped onto another space $\mathbf{Z} \in \mathbb{R}^{N \times M}$ before going through a feature extraction procedure itself. In this connection and inspired by works devoted to dissimilarity-based representations [6], we alternatively propose to explore the possibility of a nonlinear mapping $\mathcal{T}\{\cdot\}$ based on pairwise similarities, such that:

$$\mathbf{Z} = \mathcal{T}\{\mathbf{X}\}, \tag{3}$$

where $z_{ij} = \mathcal{K}(\mathbf{x}_i, \mathbf{x}_j)$. Therefore, $\mathbf{Z}$ is said to be a kernel matrix as well as $M = N$. Then, a linear projection is performed over the mapped space to obtain the embedded space $\mathbf{Y}$, such that $\mathbf{Y} = \mathbf{ZR}$ where $\mathbf{R} \in \mathbb{R}^{N \times d}$ is a rotation matrix to be defined.

Figure 1 depicts a high-level outline of the proposed GSDR.

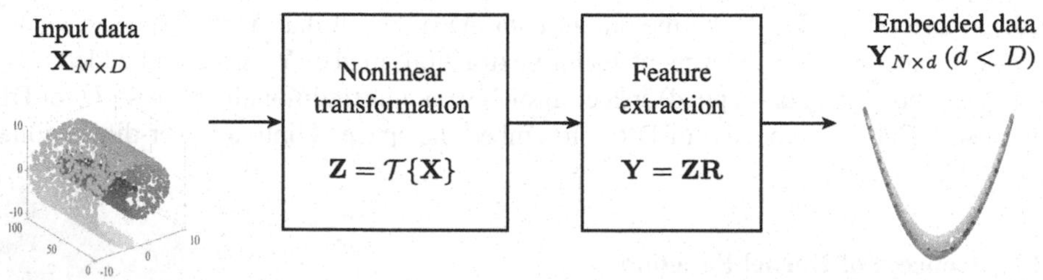

Fig. 1. Block diagram of the proposed GSDR. It mainly involves two steps: nonlinear transformation based on kernel functions (similarities) and linear feature extraction using PCA.

Notice that in this work, either an element of the space (matrix) or the space itself is indistinctly referred as space.

3.1 Nonlinear Transformation Using a Kernel Matrix

Since vectors $\mathbf{x}_i$ are assumed to be real and D-dimensional, and a collection of N vectors is available (just as stated in notation given above), a matrix $\mathbf{Z} \in \mathbb{R}^{N \times N}$ with entries $z_{ij} = \mathcal{K}(\mathbf{x}_i, \mathbf{x}_j)$ can be formed. Such a matrix is known as kernel matrix (Gram or generalized co-variance matrix as well). Therefore, a real symmetric $N \times N$ matrix $\mathbf{Z}$ whose ij entries satisfy Eq. (2) for all $c_i \in \mathbb{R}$ is also a positive semi-definite matrix.

A remarkable benefit of this property is that all eigenvalues of $\mathbf{Z}$ are ensured to be non-negative, which enables to readily carry out useful spectral developments for feature extraction purposes.

Figure 2 depicts the effect of the kernel-based data representation. By nature, a kernel entries can be understood as pairwise similarities, and therefore non-directed, weighted graph becomes a suitable geometric representation thereof.

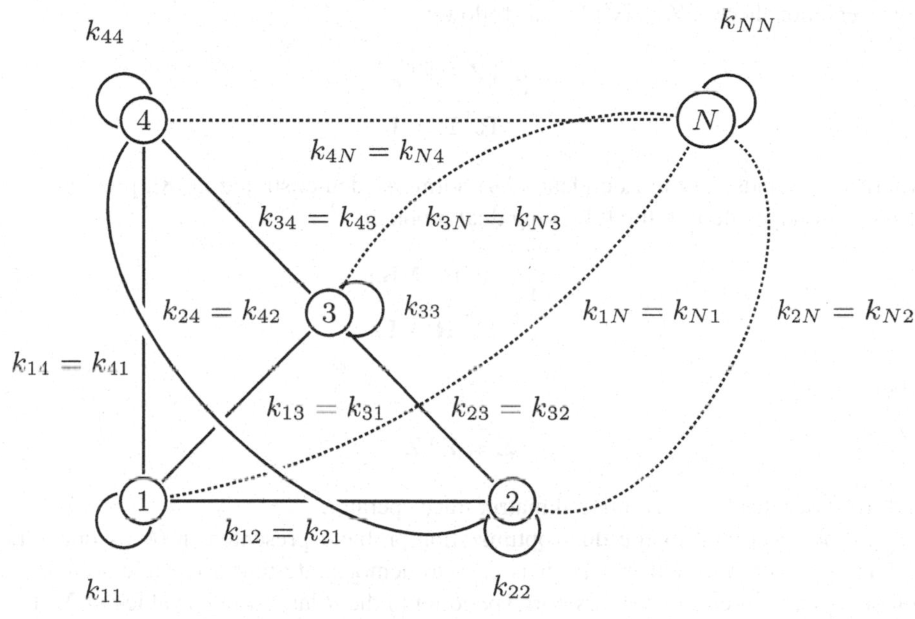

Fig. 2. An explanatory diagram depicting the relationship between the kernel entries and the weights of an N-node weighted, non-directed graph within a similarity-based representation framework.

As a matter of fact, kernel matrix entries may be related to the similarity among nodes (data points), which is in turn related to an opposite notion of distance, and therefore the concept of close neighborhood (local structure) takes place. Such a local structure of data can be preserved by a kernel function if its corresponding kernel matrix is properly tuned and selected, and subsequently used as an input to either a robust enough kernelized DR method [7] or similarity-driven generalized DR [8].

3.2 PCA-Based Feature Extraction

For the dimensionality reduction process to be carried out over the new space $\mathbf{Z}$, we use a PCA-based feature extraction approach. It works as follows: First, let us consider a linear projection in the form:

$$\mathbf{Y} = \mathbf{Z}\mathbf{R}, \tag{4}$$

where $\mathbf{R} \in \mathbb{R}^{N \times d}$ is a projection or rotation matrix. In this connection, the condition $d < D$ takes place to extract features in a lower dimensional space.

To ensure linear independence and prevent from length effects, an orthonormal rotation matrix is considered, i.e. $\mathbf{R}^\top\mathbf{R} = \mathbf{I}_d$, where $\mathbf{I}_d$ is d-dimensional identity matrix.

The estimation of $\mathbf{R}$ follows from the distance-based framework widely explained in [8].

Briefly put, this framework minimizes the distance between of $\mathbf{Z}$ and a low-rank representation thereof $\widehat{\mathbf{Z}} \in \mathbb{R}^{N \times N}$, as follows:

$$\min_{\mathbf{R}} \|\mathbf{Z} - \widehat{\mathbf{Z}}\|_2^2 \qquad \mathbf{R}^\top\mathbf{R} = \mathbf{I}_d, \tag{5}$$

where $\|\cdot\|_2$ stands for the Euclidean (L_2) norm. As demonstrated in [8], previous formulation is equivalent to the following dual problem:

$$\max_{\mathbf{R}} \operatorname{tr}(\mathbf{R}^\top\mathbf{\Sigma}\mathbf{R}) \qquad \mathbf{R}^\top\mathbf{R} = \mathbf{I}_d, \tag{6}$$

where

$$\mathbf{\Sigma} = \mathbf{Z}^\top\mathbf{Z} \tag{7}$$

and $\operatorname{tr}(\cdot)$ denotes the conventional matrix trace operator.

As the functional of the dual optimization problem presented in (6) is quadratic and $\mathbf{R}$ is an orthonormal matrix, it is easy to demonstrate that a feasible solution is selecting $\mathbf{R}$ are the eigenvectors corresponding to the d largest eigenvalues of $\mathbf{\Sigma}$. It is worth noticing that, once centered the matrix $\mathbf{Z}$ with

$$\mathbf{Z} \leftarrow \left(\mathbf{I}_N - \frac{1}{N}\mathbf{1}_N\mathbf{1}_N^\top\right)\mathbf{Z}, \tag{8}$$

being $\mathbf{1}_N$ an N-dimensional all ones vector, $\mathbf{\Sigma}$ becomes an estimation of the covariance matrix of $\mathbf{Z}$.

3.3 GSDR Algorithm

The Algorithm 1 is a pseudocode gathering the steps of the proposed GSDR.

Algorithm 1. Generalized spectral dimensionality reduction (GSDR)

$\mathbf{Y}_{N\times d} = \text{GSDR}(\mathbf{X}_{N\times D}, \mathcal{K}(\cdot,\cdot), d)$

Input: Data matrix $\mathbf{X}_{N\times D} = (\mathbf{x}_1^\top, \ldots, \mathbf{x}_N^\top)^\top$, given kernel function $\mathcal{K}(\cdot,\cdot)$, desired dimension d $(d < D)$

1: Calculate the transformation $\mathbf{Z}_{N\times N} = \mathcal{T}\{\mathbf{X}_{N\times D}\}$ as $z_{ij} = \mathcal{K}(\mathbf{x}_i, \mathbf{x}_j)$
2: Center matrix $\mathbf{Z}_{N\times N}$ with $\mathbf{Z}_{N\times N} \leftarrow \left(\mathbf{I}_N - \frac{1}{N}\mathbf{1}_N\mathbf{1}_N^\top\right)\mathbf{Z}_{N\times N}$
3: Calculate $\mathbf{\Sigma}_{N\times N}$ as $\mathbf{\Sigma}_{N\times N} = \mathbf{Z}_{N\times N}^\top \mathbf{Z}_{N\times N}$
4: Calculate the eigenvalue and eigenvector decomposition of $\mathbf{\Sigma}_{N\times N}$ as $[\mathbf{\Lambda}_N, \mathbf{V}_{N\times N}] = \text{eig}(\mathbf{\Sigma}_{N\times N})$, with $\mathbf{\Lambda}_N = (\lambda_1, \ldots, \lambda_N)$, $\mathbf{V}_N = (\mathbf{v}_1, \ldots, \mathbf{v}_N)$ and $\lambda_1 > \cdots > \lambda_N$.
5: Form $\mathbf{R}_{N\times d}$ as the eigenvectors corresponding to the first d largest eigenvalues of $\mathbf{\Sigma}_{N\times N}$ organized in decreasing order as: $\mathbf{R}_{N\times d} = (\mathbf{v}_1, \ldots, \mathbf{v}_d)$
6: Calculate $\mathbf{Y}_{N\times d} = \mathbf{Z}_{N\times N}\mathbf{R}_{N\times d}$

Output: Embedded data matrix $\mathbf{Y}_{N\times d}$

4 Experimental Setup

Kernels for DR: Two kernel approximations for spectral DR methods [9] are considered, namely CMDS and LE, as detailed in Table 1.

All previously mentioned kernels are widely described in [9].

Table 1. Brief description of the here-used kernel matrices representing dimentionality reduction.

Classical multidimentional scaling (CMDS)	Laplacian eigenmaps (LE)
CMDS kernel is the double centered distance matrix $\mathbf{D} \in \mathbb{R}^{N\times N}$, such that $\mathbf{K}_{\text{CMDS}} = -\frac{1}{2}(\mathbf{I}_N - \mathbf{1}_N\mathbf{1}_N^\top)\mathbf{D}(\mathbf{I}_N - \mathbf{1}_N\mathbf{1}_N^\top)$ where the ij entry of $\mathbf{D}$ is given by $d_{ij} = \lVert\mathbf{y}_i - \mathbf{y}_j\rVert_2^2$ and $\lVert\cdot\rVert_2$ stands for Euclidean norm.	The LE kernel can be expressed as $\mathbf{K}_{\text{LE}} = \mathbf{L}^\dagger$, where $\mathbf{L} = \mathcal{D} - \mathbf{S}$ is the graph Laplacian, $\mathbf{S}$ is a similarity matrix, $\mathcal{D} = \text{Diag}(\mathbf{S}\mathbf{1}_N)$ is the degree matrix, and $\mathbf{L}^\dagger$ stands for the pseudo-inverse of $\mathbf{L}$ Following the study done in [10], $\mathbf{S}$ is calculated by keeping the relative bandwidth parameter as $\log K$ to keep the entropy across the neighbors, being K a given number of neighbors. In this work, K is set to be 30

Performance Measure: The performance of the considered methods is quantified by the scaled version, ranged within the interval $[0, 1]$, of the average agreement rate $R_{NX}(K)$ presented in [11]. Given that $R_{NX}(K)$ is obtained at each perplexity value from 2 to $N-1$, a numerical indicator of the overall performance is acquired through calculating its area under the curve (AUC). Therefore, this AUC is an overall indicator of quality preservation of a DR approach, as it evaluates the most appropriate weights at all scales.

Both the dimensionality reduction techniques (GSDR, LE, and CMDS) and the performance measure ($R_{NX}(K)$ curve) are implemented on MATLAB Version: 9.10 (R2021a)).

Databases: Experiments are carried out over fourth conventional data sets. Figure 3 depicts examples/views of the considered data sets.

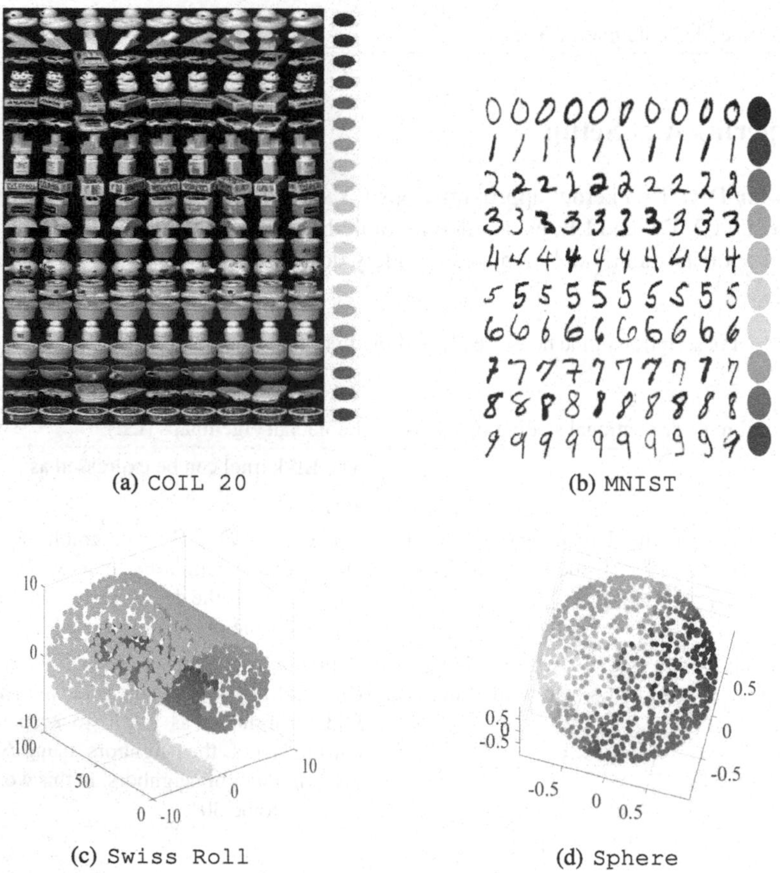

(a) COIL 20 (b) MNIST

(c) Swiss Roll (d) Sphere

Fig. 3. The four considered data sets: COIL-20, MNIST, Swiss roll and Sphere

The first data set is a randomly selected subset of the `MNIST` image bank [12], which is formed by 6000 gray-level images of each of the 10 digits ($N = 1500$ data points –150 instances for all 10 digits– and $D = 24^2$), a sample is presented in Fig. 3(b). The second one is the `COIL-20` image bank [13], which contains 72 gray-level images representing 20 different objects ($N = 1440$ data points –20 objects in 72 poses/angles– with $D = 128^2$), as seen in Fig. 3(a). The third data set (`Sphere`) is an artificial spherical shell ($N = 1500$ data points and $D = 3$), and the fourth data set is a toy set here called `Swiss roll` ($N = 3000$ data points and $D = 3$), depicted in Fig. 3(d) and 3(c), respectively.

5 Results and Discussion

The plot of the R_{NX} curve and its AUC obtained from reducing the data sets by the conventional implementation (no kernelized) of CMDS [1] and LE [2] are compared with the ones reached by GSDR $(\mathbf{X}, \mathcal{K}(\cdot,\cdot), 2)$ (according to Algorithm 1) when selecting $\mathcal{K}(\cdot,\cdot)$ as kernel functions producing respectively the kernel matrices $\mathbf{K}_{\text{CMDS}}$ and $\mathbf{K}_{\text{LE}}$. Results are shown in Fig. 4, 5, 6 and 7.

As can be observed, GSDR slightly outperforms conventional CMDS and LE in all cases. A remarkable advantage of the proposed GSDR is its ability to both unfold manifolds (as seen in Fig. 4 and 5) and reach separable-classes visualization from complex, high dimensional real data (as seen in Fig. 6 and 7).

It is also worth noticing that some rotation occurs over the embedded spaces as can be appreciated in Fig. 6(b), 6(d), 7(b) and 7(d). This fact is due to the orthogonal rotation done at the second step of GSDR procedure, which adds an effect of global structure preservation.

That said, as it performs a kernel-based representation and linearly projects the data with a PCA-based rotation, GSDR is able to preserve both the global and local structure of the input data.

Even though these preliminary results exhibit no great improvement regarding conventional DR methods, its mathematical development and versatility is highly promising as it opens possibilities to exploit simultaneously a kernel-matrix-based representation together with simple PCA.

As demonstrated in previous works [14,15], a joint formulation involving linear projections (just as PCA) and either similarity-based or kernelized representations is a suitable framework to design DR alternatives able to preserve local and global structure of the data.

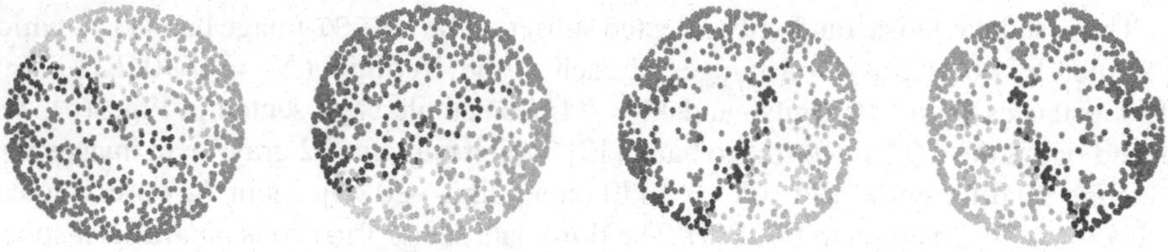

(a) CMDS (b) GSDR-CMDS (c) LE (d) GSDR-LE

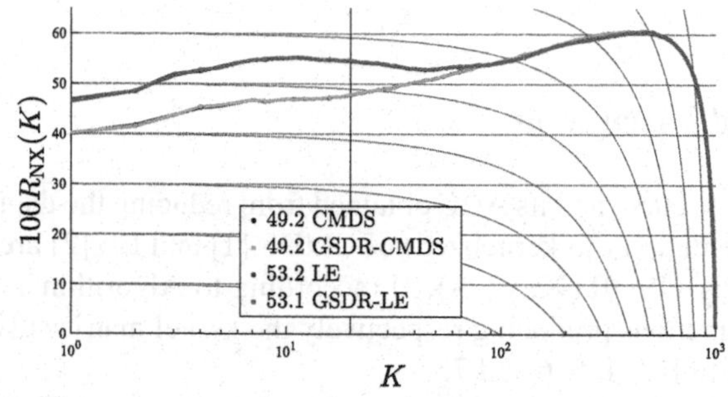

(e) R_{NX} curve

Fig. 4. Results for Sphere. Both the embedded spaces of GSDR and conventional CMDS and LE are shown. Comparison is made in terms of the R_{NX} curve

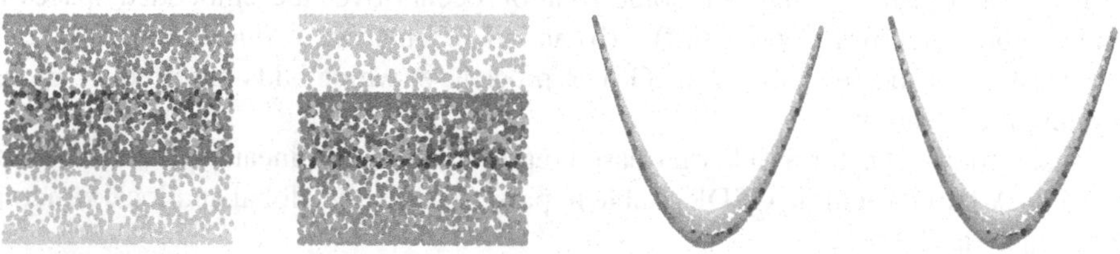

(a) CMDS (b) GSDR-CMDS (c) LE (d) GSDR-LE

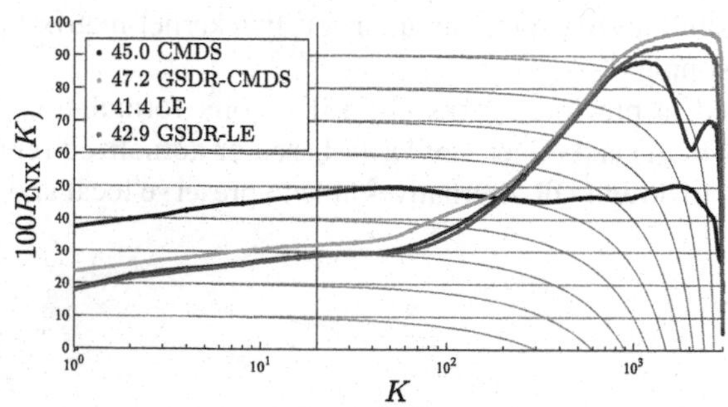

(e) R_{NX} curve

Fig. 5. Results for Swiss roll.

(a) CMDS (b) GSDR-CMDS (c) LE (d) GSDR-LE

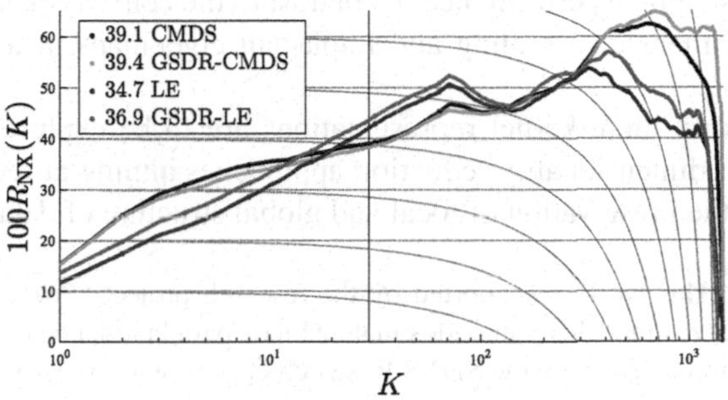

(e) R_{NX} curve

Fig. 6. Results for COIL 20.

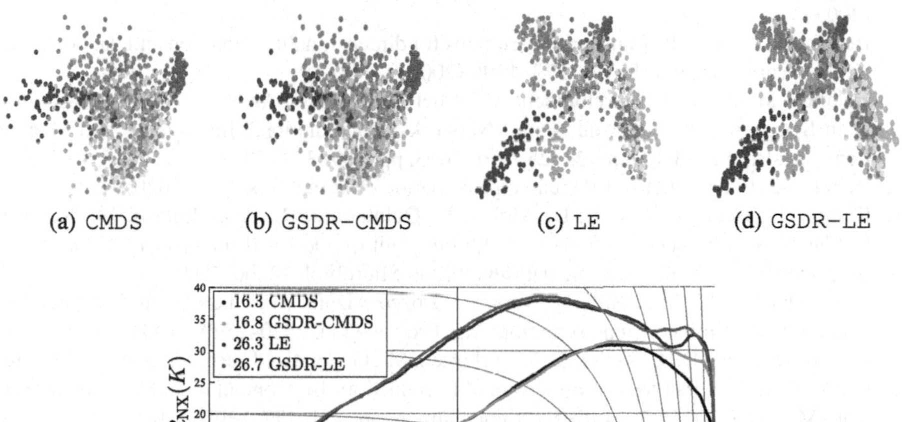

(a) CMDS (b) GSDR-CMDS (c) LE (d) GSDR-LE

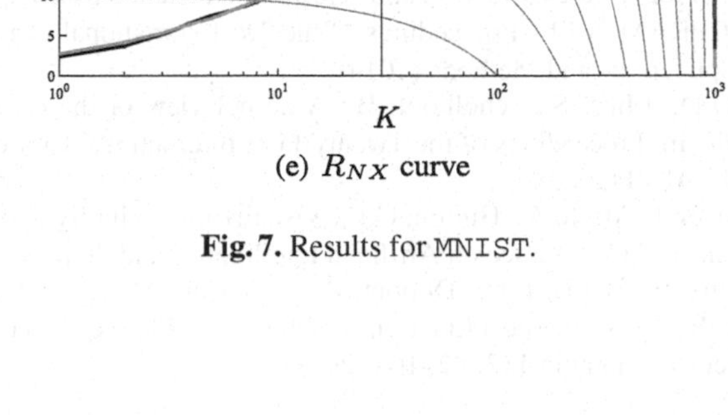

(e) R_{NX} curve

Fig. 7. Results for MNIST.

6 Conclusions and Future Work

In this work, we present a generalized spectral dimensionality reduction (GSDR) approach, which exploits simultaneously the use of kernel-based representations and a feature extraction stage. The former is an initial nonlinear transformation aimed to generate a new space wherein the local-structure attributes are captured. The latter uses that new space as an input for a principal-component-analysis-driven projection, which enables the preservation of global-structure attributes. Experimentally, we prove that proposed GSDR reaches competitive performance in contrast to the conventional implementation of classical multidimensional scaling and Laplacian eigenmaps in terms of structure preservation criteria.

As a future work, more kernel representations are to be explored, which can be plugged to spectral dimensionality reduction approaches aiming at reaching a suitable trade-off between the preservation of local and global structure of data.

Acknowledgments. This work is supported by the research project "Proyecto PN223LH010-005 Desarrollo de nuevos modelos y métodos matemáticos para la toma de decisiones". Authors thank the valuable support given by the SDAS Research Group (www.sdas-group.com).

References

1. Borg, I.: Modern Multidimensional Scaling: Theory and Applications. Springer, New York (2005)
2. Belkin, M., Niyogi, P.: Laplacian eigenmaps for dimensionality reduction and data representation. Neural Comput. **15**(6), 1373–1396 (2003)
3. Belanche Muñoz, L.A.: Developments in kernel design. In: ESANN 2013 proceedings: European Symposium on Artificial Neural Networks, Computational Intelligence and Machine Learning: Bruges (Belgium), 24–26 April 2013, pp. 369–378 (2013)
4. Bagchi, A.: Lecture notes: Efficient approximation of kernel functions (2020)
5. Ramon, E., Belanche-Muñoz, L., Molist, F., Quintanilla, R., Perez-Enciso, M., Ramayo-Caldas, Y.: kernint: a kernel framework for integrating supervised and unsupervised analyses in spatio-temporal metagenomic datasets. Front. Microbiol. **12**, 60 (2021)
6. Porro-Muñoz, D., Duin, R.P., Talavera, I., Orozco-Alzate, M.: Classification of three-way data by the dissimilarity representation. Sig. Proc. **91**(11), 2520–2529 (2011)
7. Peluffo-Ordonez, D.H., Aldo Lee, J., Verleysen, M.: Generalized kernel framework for unsupervised spectral methods of dimensionality reduction. In: Computational Intelligence and Data Mining (CIDM), 2014 IEEE Symposium on, pp. 171–177. IEEE (2014)
8. Peluffo, D., Lee, J., Verleysen, M., Rodríguez, J., Castellanos-Domínguez, G.: Unsupervised relevance analysis for feature extraction and selection: a distance-based approach for feature relevance. In: ICPRAM 2014 - Proceedings of the 3rd International Conference on Pattern Recognition Applications and Methods (2014)
9. Ham, J., Lee, D.D., Mika, S., Schölkopf, B.: A kernel view of the dimensionality reduction of manifolds. In: Proceedings of the Twenty-First International Conference on Machine Learning, vol. 47 ACM (2004)
10. Cook, J., Sutskever, I., Mnih, A., Hinton, G.E.: Visualizing similarity data with a mixture of maps. In: International Conference on Artificial Intelligence and Statistics, pp. 67–74 (2007)
11. Lee, J.A., Renard, E., Bernard, G., Dupont, P., Verleysen, M.: Type 1 and 2 mixtures of kullback-leibler divergences as cost functions in dimensionality reduction based on similarity preservation. Neurocomputing **112**, 92–108 (2013)

12. LeCun, Y., Bottou, L., Bengio, Y., Haffner, P.: Gradient-based learning applied to document recognition. Proc. IEEE **86**(11), 2278–2324 (1998)
13. Nene, S.A., Nayar, S.K., Murase, H.: Columbia object image library (coil-20). Dept. Comput. Sci. Columbia Univ. New York. **62** (1996). http://www.cs.columbia.edu/CAVE/coil-20.html
14. Rodríguez-Sotelo, J.L., Peluffo-Ordonez, D., Cuesta-Frau, D., Castellanos-Domínguez, G.: Unsupervised feature relevance analysis applied to improve ECG heartbeat clustering. Comput. Methods Programs Biomed. **108**(1), 250–261 (2012)
15. Blanco Valencia, X.P., Becerra, M., Castro Ospina, A., Ortega Adarme, M., Viveros Melo, D., Peluffo Ordóñez, D.H., et al.: Kernel-based framework for spectral dimensionality reduction and clustering formulation: a theoretical study. ADCAIJ: Adv. Distrib. Comput. Artif. Intell. J. **6**(1) (2017)

International Workshop on Computational and Applied Statistics (CAS 2021)

Time Series Forecasting: A Study on Local Urban Waste Management in a Portuguese City

A. Manuela Gonçalves[1,3](✉) and Vítor Hugo Silva[2,3]

[1] Center of Mathematics, University of Minho, Guimarães, Portugal
mneves@math.uminho.pt
[2] VITRUS AMBIENTE, EM, S.A., Guimarães, Portugal
vitor.silva@vitrusambiente.pt
[3] Department of Mathematics, University of Minho, Guimarães, Portugal

Abstract. Due to economic and social development in general and to population growth, the volume of waste, particularly municipal waste, has been significantly increasing in recent years. VITRUS AMBIENTE, EM, S.A. is a municipal company that operates at various levels in local business management, namely in Urban Waste Management (UWM), and ensures the collection of waste in the Municipality of Guimarçes (located in the northwest of Portugal). A pioneer project termed "Pay-As-You-Throw" (PAYT) was implemented in the Historic Center (HC) of this municipality and is managed by the VITRUS AMBIENTE. VITRUS is the managing entity and the Urban Hygiene Service is responsible for implementing the necessary measures to ensure the success of this project. This work focuses specifically on Urban Waste Management and aims at modeling and forecasting the behavior of urban waste production within the company's PAYT area. Time series forecasting models – Box-Jenkins SARIMA models – are applied both for the estimation and forecasting of short-term organic and recyclable intramural waste collection in the Historic Centre of Guimarçes in the PAYT system implementation pilot zone. The dataset consists of weekly measurements from 2016 to 2019. The methodologies used support the company's management and decision-making process regarding Urban Waste Management, aiming at improving the services provided to the population and having always as its cornerstone the preservation of the environment.

Keywords: Waste management · Recycling · PAYT · Modeling · Forecasting · Time series

1 Introduction

In this work, we address the issue of urban waste in the city of Guimarães located in the northwest of Portugal. An appropriate solid urban waste management

A. Manuela Gonçalves was partially financed by Portuguese Funds through FCT (Fundação para a Ciência e a Tecnologia) within the Projects UIDB/00013/2020 and UIDP/00013/2020 of CMAT-UM.

O. Gervasi et al. (Eds.): ICCSA 2021, LNCS 12952, pp. 527–538, 2021.
https://doi.org/10.1007/978-3-030-86973-1_37

becomes a local and national challenge regarding the development of legislative plans and standards set in the "Plano Estratégico da Gestão de Resíduos Urbanos" (PERSU). This plan encourages the maximization of waste potential and suggests the introduction of a tax to promote waste separation at source and collection rate increase: the Pay-As-You-Throw (PAYT) system. This system is based on the "polluter-payer" principle and on the concept of shared responsibility, according to which those who generate less waste pay less [1]. This check is carried out based on the number of bags sold, that is, citizens buy the bags of organic waste according to the capacity requested, and the bags for recycling are free of cost. This is one of the system's strengths in adopting good environmental practices. Guimarães was a pioneering city in the implementation of this system, and VITRUS AMBIENTE is a local public company that manages all the environments of the system: from waste collection to rising public awareness to this issue.

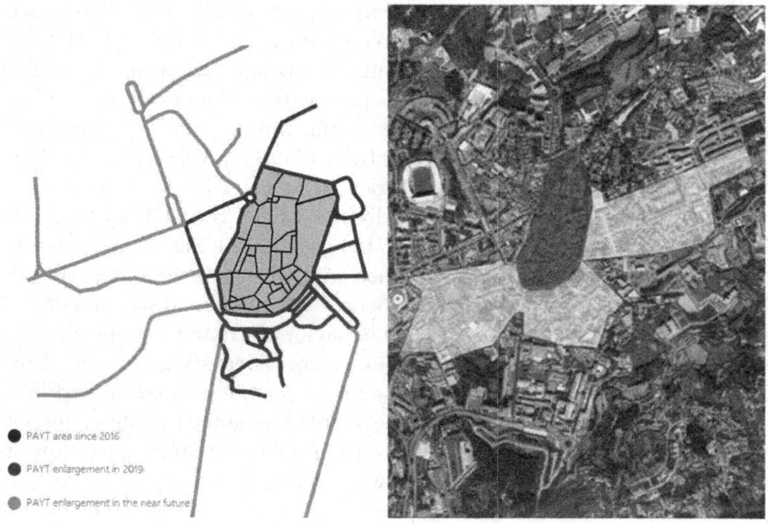

Fig. 1. Map with the PAYT system's expansion plans (left); PAYT system's current area of operation (right).

The main objective of this research is to analyze the modeling and forecasting processes of recyclable and organic waste production in the system's operation area, i.e., in the Historic Center of Guimarães, which is the PAYT system's implementation pilot zone (Fig. 1).

Predicting and forecasting environment processes - in this case, urban waste production - has always been a difficult field of research analysis, with very slow progress rate over the years. How to best model and forecast these patterns has been a long-standing issue in time series analysis. This research investigates the forecasting performances of the forecasting methods of Box-Jenkins SARIMA models [2]. These models are chosen because of their ability to model seasonal fluctuations present in this type of data, time series with seasonal patterns. Thus, statistical models are developed in this context of time series analysis to estimate and forecast, in the period from 2016 to 2019, the weekly production of waste (recyclable and organic) in the PAYT area. The validity of the modeling and forecasting models performed is judged by comparing its estimate and forecast error of the models. The smaller the error, the better the estimate and the forecast value produced by the model.

2 Methodology

2.1 SARIMA Model

A time series is an ordered sequence of values of a variable at equally spaced time intervals, in this case weekly organic and recyclable intramural waste collection in the Historic Centre of Guimarães, which is the PAYT system's implementation zone. Time series forecasting is an important area in which past observations of the same variable are collected and analyzed to develop a model describing the underlying relationship. The model is then used to extrapolate the time series into the future. Forecasting methods are a key tool in decision-making processes in many areas, such Urban Waste Management, as is the case studied in this work [3]. There are several approaches to modeling time series, but we decided to study and to compare the accuracy of the seasonal autoregressive integrated moving average models denominated by SARIMA models, because these models can increase the chance of capturing the proprieties and the dynamics in the data, in particular seasonality, and improving forecast accuracy.

The SARIMA $(p, d, q)(P, D, Q)_s$ is a short memory model and is a very flexible model, given that it accounts for stochastic seasonality, and is one of the most versatile models for forecasting seasonal time series. Such seasonality is present when the seasonal pattern of a time series changes over time. The theory of SARIMA models has been developed by many researchers and its wide application the result of the work by Box et al. [4], who developed a systematic and practical model-building method. Through an iterative three-step model-building process, model identification, parameter estimation and model diagnosis, the Box-Jenkins methodology has proven to be an effective practical time series modeling approach.

The SARIMA model has the following form

$$\Phi_p(B)N_P(B^s)(1-B)^d(1-B^s)^D Y_t = \Theta_q(B)H_Q(B^s)\epsilon_t,$$

where Y_t is the time series, with

$\Phi_p(B) = 1 - \phi_1 B - \cdots - \phi_p B^p,$
$N_P(B^s) = 1 - \nu_1 B - \cdots - \nu_P P_s,$
$\Theta_q(B) = 1 + \theta_1 B + \cdots + \theta_q B^q,$
$H_Q(B^s) = 1 + \eta_1 B^s + \cdots + \eta_Q Q_s,$

where s is the seasonal length, B is the backshift operator defined by $B^k Y_t = Y_{t-k}$, $\Phi_p(B)$ and $\Theta_q(B)$ are the regular autoregressive and moving average polynomials of orders p and q, respectively, $N_P(B^s)$ and $H_Q(B^s)$ are the seasonal autoregressive and moving average polynomials of orders P and Q, respectively, and $epsilon_t$ is a sequence of white noises with zero mean and constant variance σ^2. $(1-B)^d$ and $(1-B^s)^D$ are the nonseasonal and seasonal differencing operators, respectively.

The model with the minimum value of the AIC (Akaike's Information Criteria) is often the best model for forecasting [5]. We investigated the required transformations for variance stabilization and decided to apply logarithms to the time series under study.

Once the model has been specified, its autoregressive, moving average, and seasonal parameters (SARIMA model) need to be estimated. The parameters of SARIMA models are usually estimated by maximizing the likelihood of the model (for more details about this procedure, see [6]). The estimation is carried out in R.

2.2 Forecast Error Measures

Let's denote the actual observation for time period t by Y_t and the estimated or forecasted value for the same period by $\hat{Y}_t$ and n is the total number of observations. The most commonly used forecast error measures are the mean squared error (MSE), the root mean squared error (RMSE), the mean absolute percentage error (MAPE), the mean absolute scaled error (MASE) [7]. They are defined by the following formulas, respectively:

$$\text{RMSE} = \sqrt{\frac{1}{n}\sum_{t=1}^{n} e_t^2} = \sqrt{\frac{1}{n}\sum_{t=1}^{n}(Y_t - \hat{Y}_t)^2},$$

$$\text{MAPE} = \frac{1}{n}\sum_{t=1}^{n}\left|\frac{Y_t - \hat{Y}_t}{Y_t}\right| \times 100 \quad (\%),$$

$$\text{MASE} = \frac{1}{n}\sum_{t=1}^{n}|q_t| = \frac{1}{n}\sum_{t=1}^{n}\left|\frac{Y_t - \hat{Y}_t}{\frac{1}{n-1}\sum_{t=2}^{n}|Y_t - Y_{t-1}|}\right|.$$

When comparing the performance of forecast methods on a single dataset, there is no absolute criterion for a "good" value of the error measure: it depends on the units in which the variable is measured and on the degree of forecasting, as measured in these units, which is sought in a particular application. Frequently, different accuracy measures will lead to different results regarding the forecast method is best.

3 Solid Waste Forecasting in the PAYT Area

3.1 DATA

The urban waste data is collected weekly by the VITRUS AMBIENTE and for this study only the data collected in the city's Historic Center, in the PAYT area, is considered. The observation period was between the 9th week of 2016 and the 34th week of 2019. The time series of recyclable waste (REC) and organic waste (ORG) were analysed, in tonnes. The recyclable waste is the sum of paper, plastic/metal, and glass waste.

Table 1. Descriptive statistics of solid waste - organic, and recyclable (paper, plastic/metal, and glass) waste - in PAYT area (monthly).

	Minimum	Maximum	1st quartile	Median	Mean	3rd quartile	Standard deviation
ORG	29.34	79.44	44.88	50.06	51.63	58.64	10.21
REC	16.08	36.92	21.08	24.40	24.92	28.14	5.31
PAP	3.02	11.24	5.00	6.44	6.58	8.00	2.15
PLA	3.24	6.72	3.72	4.26	4.53	5.30	0.93
GLA	7.80	21.70	10.44	12.88	13.81	16.74	3.86

Table 1 presents descriptive statistics for the five types of waste during the observed period by month in the PAYT system. As expected, organic waste has higher statistics; in particular, the standard deviations of 10.21 tons indicate a larger variability during the observed period. Regarding the total amount of waste produced, in this system pilot zone the average amount of waste produced is equal to 76.55 tons per month and with a minimum and maximum amount equal to 45.42 tons and 103.84 tons, respectively.

In the analysis of recyclable waste, paper waste has an average production of 6.58 tons per month and, during the observed period, a production between 3.02 tons and 11.24 tons. Plastic/metal waste presents an average production of 4.53 tonnes, and during the observed period, plastic/metal production was between 3.24 tonnes and 6.72 tonnes. Finally, glass waste has an average production of 13.81 tonnes, with glass waste representing a large part of the recyclable collection, and during the observed period, glass waste production presented values between 7.80 tons and 21.70 tons monthly.

Figure 2 presents the box-plots of organic waste (ORG), and the recyclable waste (REC) (paper, plastic/metal, and glass waste), by month. The box-plots present asymmetric distributions (positive), but paper waste distribution and recyclable waste distribution are almost symmetric. It should be noted that there is a moderate outlier on the data of organic waste, which corresponds to the month of June 2018.

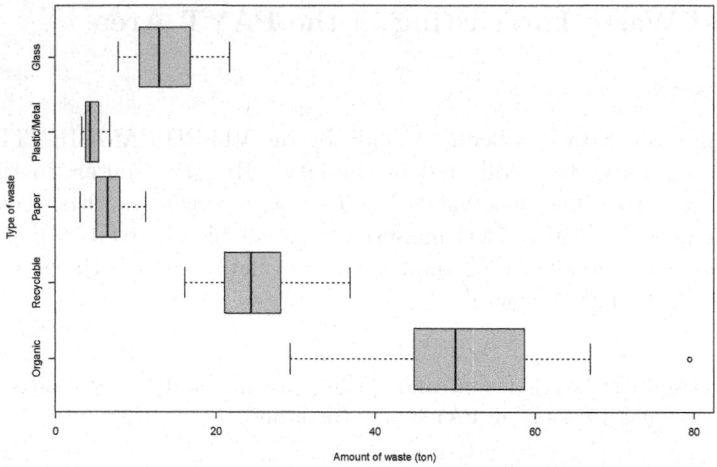

Fig. 2. Box-plots of solid waste - organic, and recyclable (paper, plastic/metal, and glass) - in PAYT area (monthly).

3.2 Results

Two time series are considered in the modeling process: recyclable waste (REC) and organic waste (ORG). The methods considered in this study are applied to two sets: training data (in-sample data) and testing data (out-of-sample data) in order to testify the accuracy of the proposed forecasting models.

For the REC and ORG waste time series, the selected training period was from the 9th week of 2016 to the 38th week of 2018 (first 134 observations) and was used to fit the models to data, and the testing period with the last 15 observations (the period from the 39th week of 2018 to the 1st week of 2019) was used to forecast. This approach allows the effectiveness of different methods of prediction.

The main task in SARIMA forecasting is to select an appropriate model order, i.e., the p, d, q, P, D, Q and s values. The modeling process follows the several steps to identify the model. Plotting the time series and choosing the proper variance-stabilizing transformation (in this case study, because the series present nonconstant variance, it was applied a logarithm transformation). Than computing and examining the ACF sample (Autocorrelation Function) and the PACF sample (Partial Autocorrelation Function) of the transformed data to further confirm a necessary degree of differencing, starting with the seasonal differencing. For seasonal modeling after analyzing the FAC, it appears that seasonality is weekly and, therefore, $s = \frac{365.25}{7} \approx 52.18 \approx 52$. This period of 52 weeks is due to the fact that there are leap years (366 d) and/or 53 weeks. In this way, this seasonality adjustment will allow a better formulation of the SARIMA model. Finally, computing and examining the ACF sample and PACF sample, we identify the properly transformed and differenced series of p, q, P, and Q by matching the patterns in the ACF sample and the PACF sample with the theoretical patterns of known models and via AICs.

After identifying an appropriate SARIMA model we have to check whether the model assumptions are satisfied. The basic assumption for both models is that ϵ_t is a zero mean Gaussian white noise process. It is considered the usual significance level of 5%. These residual analyses are not presented in this paper, but were performed. For the two final SARIMA models (recyclable waste and organic waste) all the model assumptions were verified; therefore, the diagnostics for these models leads to the conclusion that the models are adequate.

Recyclable Waste Forecasting. For the recyclable waste time series modeling process, the final SARIMA model was selected according to the procedure described earlier. Fitting the several models suggested by these observations and computing AIC for each, we obtain the results presented in Table 2. Based on the AICs, the selected model is the SARIMA $(1,0,1)(1,1,0)_{52}$.

Table 2. Parameters estimates of SARIMA models for the recyclable waste time series, and the AICs.

Model	$\hat{\phi}_1$	$\hat{\phi}_2$	$\hat{\theta}_1$	$\hat{\theta}_2$	$\hat{\nu}_1$	AIC
SARIMA(1,0,0)$(1,1,0)_{52}$	−0.393	–	–	–	−0.548	126.80
SARIMA(0,0,1)$(1,1,0)_{52}$	–	–	-0.377	–	−0.547	126.05
SARIMA(1,0,0)$(0,1,0)_{52}$	−0.354	–	–	–	–	135.66
SARIMA(2,0,1)$(1,1,0)_{52}$	−1.045	−0.234*	0.663*	–	−0.550	129.95
SARIMA(1,0,2)$(1,1,0)_{52}$	−0.734	–	0.328	−0.182	−0.557	129.31

* The parameter is not significant for a significant level of $\alpha = 0.10$.

The estimation results of the selected model can be consulted in Table 3.

Table 3. Results for the final SARIMA model for the recyclable waste time series in the historic center.

Final model: SARIMA $(0,0,1)(1,1,0)_{52}$	AIC $= 126.05$	$\hat{\sigma}^2 = 0.204$	
	θ_1	ν_1	
Estimate	−0.377	−0.547	
Standard error	0.095	0.120	

In Fig. 3 are represented the original values of recyclable waste, the estimates in the modeling period (training period), the forecasts in the forecasting period (testing period) and the forecast intervals for a confidence level of 90% by applying the SARIMA model.

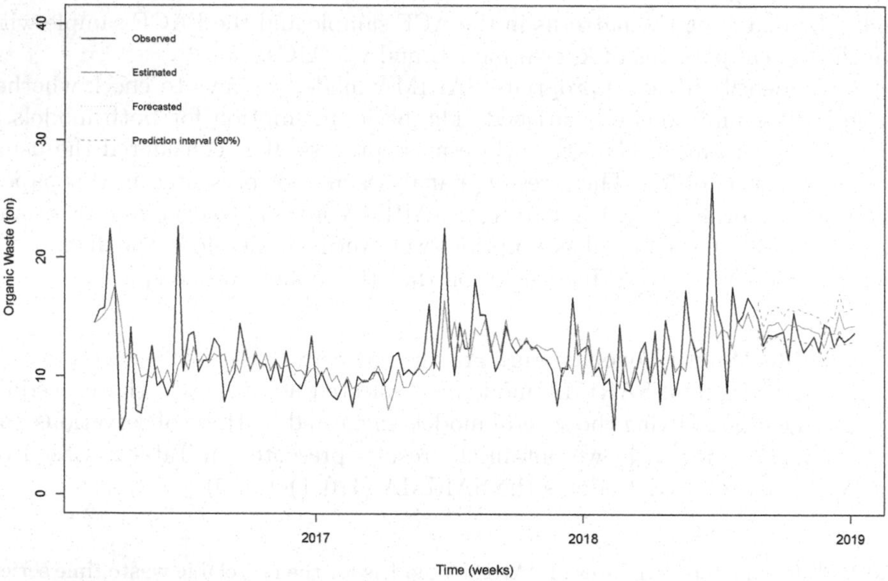

Fig. 3. Observed values, estimates and forecasts (with 90% confidence bounds) for recyclable waste time series using the final SARIMA model.

Figure 3 suggests that the model's predictive quality is better in the training series than in the testing series, since there is an atypical decrease in the amounts of recyclable waste in the original series that the model would not be able to predict given the observations of the past.

The coverage rate of empirical confidence of corrected forecasts is 40%, not similar to the confidence intervals with a confidence of 90% (6 observations of the testing series belong to the confidence interval).

Organic Waste Forecasting. The same modeling process was applied to the organic waste time series. Fitting the several models suggested by these observations and computing the AIC for each, we obtain the results presented in Table 4.

On the bases of the AICs, it is preferred the $SARIMA(1,1,2)(1,0,0)_{52}$ model. The estimation results of this model can be consulted, in more detail in Table 5.

In Fig. 4 are represented the original values of organic waste, the estimates in the modeling period (training period), the forecasts in the forecasting period (testing period) and the forecast intervals for a confidence level of 90% by applying the SARIMA model.

The confidence intervals with a 90% confidence have a coverage rate of 60% (less than 90%), since only 9 observations in the testing series belong to them.

Table 4. Parameters estimates of SARIMA models for the organic waste time series, and the AICs.

Model	$\hat{\phi}_1$	$\hat{\phi}_2$	$\hat{\theta}_1$	$\hat{\theta}_2$	$\hat{\nu}_1$	$\hat{\eta}_1$	AIC
SARIMA(0,1,1)$(1,0,1)_{52}$	–	–	−0.800	–	0.908	−0.741*	10.45
SARIMA(2,1,0)$(1,0,1)_{52}$	-0.563	-0.381	–	–	0.994	-0.931	24.41
SARIMA(0,1,0)$(1,0,1)_{52}$	–	–	–	–	0.949	-0.848	64.66
SARIMA(0,1,2)$(1,0,1)_{52}$	–	–	−0.721	−0.116*	0.875*	−0.701*	11.25
SARIMA(1,1,2)$(1,0,1)_{52}$	0.911	–	−1.719	0.719	0.896	-0.721	11.61
SARIMA(0,1,1)$(0,0,1)_{52}$	–	–	−0.810	–	–	0.221	12.24
SARIMA(0,1,1)$(1,0,0)_{52}$	–	–	−0.812	–	0.291	–	10.54
SARIMA(1,1,1)$(0,0,1)_{52}$	0.147*	–	−0.876	–	–	0.217*	12.62
SARIMA(1,1,2)$(1,0,0)_{52}$	-0.815	–	0.145	-0.822	0.280	–	4.61

* The parameter is not significant for a significant level of $\alpha = 0.10$.

Table 5. Results for the final SARIMA model for the organic waste time series in the Historic Center.

Final model: SARIMA $(1,1,2)(1,0,0)_{52}$			AIC = 4.61	$\hat{\sigma}^2 = 0.054$
	$\hat{\phi}_1$	$\hat{\theta}_1$	$\hat{\theta}_2$	$\hat{\nu}_1$
Estimate	-0.815	0.145	-0.822	0.280
Standard error	0.066	0.070	0.064	0.114

3.3 Forecasting Models Evaluation

Once established the forecasting models to the data provided, it is necessary to identify the models that best fit and (more accurately) forecast the urban waste time series. For comparative purposes, four evaluation measures are used: MSE and its corresponding on the same scale as the data, RMSE, MAPE, and MASE. In addition to these, measurements having been calculated for the testing time series, for the respective 15 observations in each time series, they are also determined for the training time series. The results can be found in Table 6.

The results in Table 6 show that the overall estimation and forecasting performance of the SARIMA models evaluated via MSE, RMSE, MAPE, and MASE are quite similar in both the training and testing periods (with the exception of the MASE measurement in each REC and ORG time series). From the analysis of Table 6, the model for recyclable waste time series in the PAYT implementation zone forecasts more accurately in the training period than in testing period. When considering the organic waste time series modeling process in the PAYT implementation area, it can be said that it has the best model adjusted to the testing time series than to the training time series.

It may be conclude that, in fact, a model that better fits the data does not necessarily forecast better, and the fit error measures should not be used to select a model for forecast.

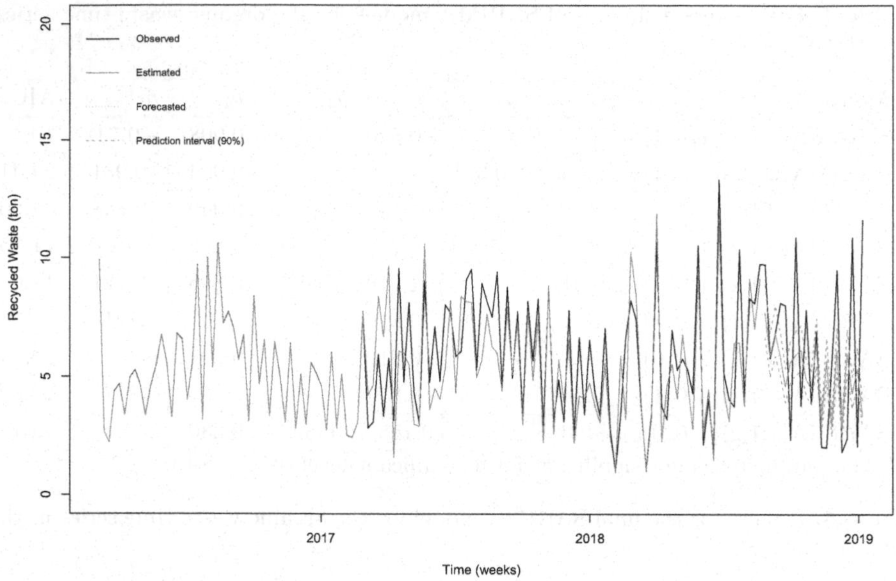

Fig. 4. Observed values, estimates and forecasts (with 90% confidence bounds) for organic waste time series using the final SARIMA model.

Table 6. Forecasting performance evaluation of the method for the training period and the testing period.

Time series	Training time series				Testing time series			
	MSE	RMSE	MAPE	MASE	MSE	RMSE	MAPE	MASE
REC	**3.202**	**1.789**	**23.473**	0.414	13.633	3.692	69.687	**0.363**
ORG	7.804	2.793	16.488	**0.579**	**1.654**	**1.286**	**7.965**	0.723

Once the forecasts' accuracy (punctual) is evaluated, it is essential to understand the effectiveness of the forecast intervals. Theoretically, the forecast intervals are calculated at 90% confidence, which means that 90% of the intervals must include the observed (real) observation. That is, it is considered that the most effective interval forecasts are those whose effective coverage rate is closer to 90%. Note that the forecast intervals are obtained based on the testing series, for each distinct series where, in this study, they contain only 15 observations and, therefore, the analysis of coverage rates must be taken care of.

In the two time series under study, REC waste and ORG waste, coverage rates of 40% and 60%, respectively, are calculated. It is notorious that the model formulated for the time series corresponding to the production of organic waste in the PAYT system's area of implementation presents better results (Table 7).

Table 7. 90% forecast confidence intervals (CI), forecasts, and observed value by using the final SARIMA for recyclable and organic waste.

REC			ORG		
Forecast CI	Forecast	Observed value	Forecast CI	Forecast	Observed value
(2.300 ; 6.667)	4.484	2.360	(12.376 ; 14.463)	13.419	13.880
(4.357 ; 8.725)	6.541	10.880	(13.072 ; 15.159)	14.115	11.520
(3.757 ; 8.124)	5.940	3.800	(12.782 ; 14.869)	13.826	15.440
(2.931 ; 7.299)	5.115	7.820	(12.972 ; 15.059)	14.015	13.420
(2.236 ; 6.604)	4.420	3.880	(12.666 ; 14.753)	13.710	12.160
(4.320 ; 8.688)	6.504	6.920	(12.649 ; 14.737)	13.693	12.740
(0.921 ; 5.288)	3.105	2.060	(12.384 ; 14.471)	13.428	13.460
(3.480 ; 7.848)	5.664	2.040	(12.249 ; 14.336)	13.293	12.180
(0.768 ; 5.135)	2.951	5.640	(10.967 ; 13.054)	12.011	14.500
(3.982 ; 8.350)	6.166	9.500	(12.303 ; 14.390)	13.347	14.240
(0.588 ; 4.956)	2.772	1.840	(12.181 ; 14.268)	13.225	12.580
(3.861 ; 8.228)	6.044	2.400	(14.008 ; 16.095)	15.052	13.540
(2.092 ; 6.460)	4.276	10.880	(12.605 ; 14.693)	13.649	13.020
(3.216 ; 7.584)	5.400	2.080	(12.796 ; 14.883)	13.839	13.340
(1.224 ; 5.591)	3.408	11.620	(12.851 ; 14.939)	13.895	13.780

In general, we find that both SARIMA models have the capability to estimate and forecast fairly well the behavior and seasonal fluctuations of the waste time series.

4 Conclusions

Due to economic and social development in general and to population growth, the amount of waste, particularly urban waste, has been significantly increasing in recent years. It is one of the major problems both at a national and global level, and action is urgently needed to ensure that waste is recovered and its volume reduced. Therefore, accurate (recyclable and organic) waste volume can have a great impact on effective local Urban Waste Management (UWM). Both established SARIMA models in this study have capabilities to enhance forecasting accuracy. Though forecasts are never totally accurate, they are the essential starting point of decision-making for any organization. Determining the expected values well ahead in time helps in fulfilling solid urban waste management orders in a municipal company as VITRUS AMBIENTE. This study will serve to draw preliminary conclusions, in order to improve management of the new PAYT system.

References

1. Reichenbach, J.: Status and prospects of pay-as-you-throw in Europe - a review of pilot research and implementation studies. Waste Manage. **28**(12), 2809–2814 (2008)
2. Navarro-Esbrí, J., Diamadopoulos, E., Ginestar, D.: Time series analysis and forecasting techniques for municipal solid waste management. Resour. Conserv. Recycl. **35**, 201–214 (2002)
3. Rimaitytė, I., Ruzgas, T., Denafas, G., Racys, V., Martuzevicius, D.: Application and evaluation of forecasting methods for municipal solid waste generation in an eastern-European city. Waste Manage. Res. **30**(1), 89–98 (2012)
4. Box, G., Jenkins, G., Reinsel, G.: Time Series Analysis, 4th edn. Wiley, Hoboken (2008)
5. Hyndman, R.J., Athanasopoulos, G.: Forecasting: Principles and Practice. Online Open-Acess Texbooks. http://otexts.com/fpp. Accessed 5 Oct 2020
6. Hyndman, R.J.: Forecast: Forecasting Functions for Time Series. R Package Version 4.06 http://cran.rstudio.com. Accessed 5 Oct 2020
7. Shumway, R.H., Stoffer, D.F.: Time series analysis and its applications: with R examples. Springer, New York (2017)

Predicting Product Quality from Operating Conditions Based on Multinomial Logistic Regression

Pedro Vaz[1(✉)], Ana Cristina Braga[1], M. Sameiro Carvalho[1], and Gerardo Menezes[2]

[1] ALGORITMI Centre, University of Minho, 4800-058 Guimarães, Portugal
{acb,sameiro}@dps.uminho.pt
[2] Bosch Car Multimedia, Braga, Portugal

Abstract. The main objective of this study is to evaluate the influence of several industrial operating conditions in the occurrence of the defect (air bubbles) in a wet bonding process of two pieces (a glass and an electronic display). The study of the influence of operating conditions in business targets is of great interest to the community of process engineers, to ensure the long-term stability of the process, as this involves complex factors. It is also relevant for the development of Data-driven approaches to support Real-Time System Monitoring.

In this work, we propose to build a multinomial logistic regression model that can assess the probability of a bonded kit (glass and electronic display) having a defect in the filling material, taking into account process operating conditions. The study was conducted in a retrospective evaluation and consisted of 659 bonded kits randomly selected from a reference period. We evaluated multiple factors in the construction of a multinomial logistic regression model with 3 logit functions. The technique used to select variables to be included in the model, was the stepwise technique by choosing the smallest p-value for the variable entering in the model.

Of the modelling process through multinomial logistic regression have resulted five operating conditions that have statistical significance and that can contribute as an auxiliary for the prediction of a defect.

Keywords: Multinomial logistic regression · Logit · Process improvement · Process monitoring

1 Introduction

In today's competitive business environment, many companies still use conventional process evaluation strategy (also named process inspection strategy), based on Sorting Out of Failure (SOF). The massive usage of this process evaluation strategy is, in many cases, associated with the incapacity to stabilize and control industrial processes, in a mass-production context, to allow the adoption of other competitive strategies different from SOF, like Process Monitoring supported by industrial statistics. The conventional SOF strategy, besides giving the safety sensation of controlling the process, in many

O. Gervasi et al. (Eds.): ICCSA 2021, LNCS 12952, pp. 539–551, 2021.
https://doi.org/10.1007/978-3-030-86973-1_38

cases, it masks the incapacity to improve the process in order to stabilize it and distracts the company, neglecting efforts to reduce variability in processes. The conventional strategy entails the costs related to 100% inspection method and is frequently associated with the higher scrap rate, which results in higher Internal Defect Costs (IDC). These costs in some cases could be higher than the ones involved in process improvements activities conducing to lower process variation.

Although, in recent years, companies are producing data exponentially, which could help in reducing variability in processes, they continue facing challenges in dealing with big data issues for rapid decision-making to achieve faster improved productivity [1]. Many manufacturing systems are not ready to manage big data due to the lack of smart analytic tools. However, the Industry 4.0 proposing the predictive manufacturing in the future industry [1] will push harder by data-driven methods.

In the era of Industry 4.0, Industrial Cyber-Physical Systems (ICPSs) are the cornerstone research subject and has become a worldwide research focus [2]. ICPSs integrate physical entities with cyber networks to build systems that can work more harmoniously, benefiting from integrated design and system-wide optimization. ICPS is a transdisciplinary subject in the infancy stage [2]. "Real-Time System Monitoring" is one of the directions of ICPS research, which in turn is also a transdisciplinary subject in its early stages. Data-driven approaches [3] are promising alternatives to simplify the design for ICPSs. According with Yin et al. [2] there are two key dimensions for data-driven approaches. The first dimension is the assumption of data structures. The second dimension is that of the estimation of undetermined parameters of data structures, using here statistical models.

The case study is a wet bonding process, which is divided in four operations. The first operation is the immobilization of a kit with display in a conveyor. The second operation is the picking up of a glass from a base. The third operation is the measurement, with a laser device integrated in the robot, of fiducial coordinates allocated at the display and the kit. Then, the measurement of distances between those fiducial and the arm of the robot, grabbing a mask with a glass. The fourth operation is the robot making the necessary movements in order to achieve the best position to assemble, through bonding, the glass with the display. Finally, at the end of the process a qualified operator controls all assembled (bonded) parts for quality reasons. In case of defect (air bubble between display, filling and glass), the operator registers the occurrence in a database. For the purpose of recording defects, process experts divided the area of the display in ten zones (A, B, C, D, 1, 2, 3, 4, 5 and 6). In Fig. 1 it is possible to observe a personal illustration of those zones in a display.

From a statistical exploratory analysis of operating conditions´ historical data in the wet bonding process, it was possible to observe that defect occurrence can vary with the type of robot where it is assembled, the spatial position of the robot, and if, during the assembly process, an error occurs at the work stations "Automatic Optical Inspection" (AOI) or "FLC". The last one is a shuttle to take out the parts that did not assemble or had some problem during the assembling.

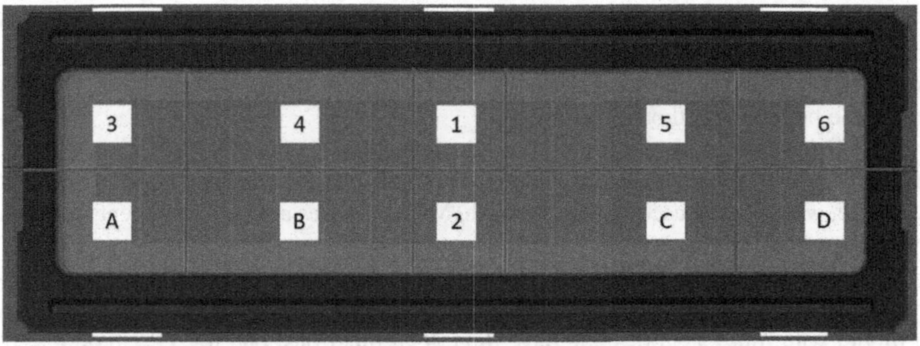

Fig. 1. Illustration of zones of the defect classification. (Source: Adapted fictitious image, for illustration purposes only).

Better understanding the operational conditions and the structures associated with them, may help the process engineers to diagnose and prevent more accurately the occurrence of operating conditions associated with the defect, thus obtaining successful stability.

In statistics, logistic regression is a type of regression analysis used for predicting the outcome of a categorical dependent variable (a dependent variable that can take on a limited number of categories) based on one or more predictor variables. Multinomial logistic regression is defined for a response variable with three or more discrete outcomes. It is an extension of logistic regression based on the binomial distribution (i.e., where the response has only two outcomes).

Like binary logistic regression, multinomial logistic regression uses maximum likelihood estimation to evaluate the probability of categorical membership [4].

In this work, multinomial logistic regression is used to predict the probability of category membership on a dependent variable based on multiple independent variables. The independent variables can be either dichotomous (i.e., binary) or continuous (i.e., interval or ratio in scale).

2 Methodology

This section presents the statistical method, the sample data, variables and model that support this work.

2.1 Statistical Method

In this work, we propose to build a multinomial logistic regression (MLR) model that could assess the association of the defect occurrence (air bubble in filling material) with process operational conditions measures and some discrete characteristics (errors occurrence in work stations "AOI" or "FLC").

Often logistic regression is referred to as a binary classifier, since there are only two outcomes [5]. In cases, where the target variable can have multiple outcomes, as the case study of this work, we face a multi-level classification problem. In these cases, MLR is often the preferred method of estimation.

MLR compares multiple groups through a combination of binary logistic regressions. The group comparisons are equivalent to the comparisons for a dummy-coded dependent variable, with a group used as the reference. MLR provides a set of coefficients for each of the two comparisons.

Adapting the example of Braga et al. [4] if the dependent variable Y has four categories, 0 is the code for the reference category, 1, 2 and 3 the remaining categories. For a model with four categories, we have three logit functions, one for Y = 1 vs Y = 0, other for Y = 2 vs Y = 0 and for Y = 3 vs Y = 0.

In other words, in the multinomial logistic regression, we develop k-1 models for k classes and a set of independent binary regression, also called logits. Essentially, in context of ordinal logistic regression we have two classes, so we develop one model.

When we extend to a multi-class problem, it means that for *k* classes, we can develop k-1 models, using multinomial logistic regression. We develop our logit functions according to Braga et al. [4].

Considering **x** to be the vector of covariates of length $p + 1$ with $x_0 = 1$ for entering with the constant term. We will designate the three logit functions by:

$$g_1(\mathbf{x}) = \ln\left(\frac{P(Y = 1|\mathbf{x})}{P(Y = 0|\mathbf{x})}\right) = \beta_{10} + \beta_{11}x_1 + \beta_{12}x_2 + \ldots + \beta_{1p}x_p = (1, \mathbf{x}')\boldsymbol{\beta}_1 \quad (1)$$

$$g_2(\mathbf{x}) = \ln\left(\frac{P(Y = 2|\mathbf{x})}{P(Y = 0|\mathbf{x})}\right) = \beta_{20} + \beta_{21}x_1 + \beta_{22}x_2 + \ldots + \beta_{2p}x_p = (1, \mathbf{x}')\boldsymbol{\beta}_2 \quad (2)$$

$$g_3(\mathbf{x}) = \ln\left(\frac{P(Y = 3|\mathbf{x})}{P(Y = 0|\mathbf{x})}\right) = \beta_{30} + \beta_{31}x_1 + \beta_{32}x_2 + \ldots + \beta_{3p}x_p = (1, \mathbf{x}')\boldsymbol{\beta}_3 \quad (3)$$

It follows that the four conditional probabilities for each category of dependent variable, given the vector of covariates, are:

$$P(Y = 0|\mathbf{x}) = \frac{1}{1 + \exp(g_1(\mathbf{x})) + \exp(g_2(\mathbf{x})) + \exp(g_3(\mathbf{x}))} \quad (4)$$

$$P(Y = 1|\mathbf{x}) = \frac{\exp(g_1(\boldsymbol{x}))}{1 + \exp(g_1(\mathbf{x})) + \exp(g_2(\mathbf{x})) + \exp(g_3(\mathbf{x}))} \quad (5)$$

$$P(Y = 2|\mathbf{x}) = \frac{\exp(g_2(\mathbf{x}))}{1 + \exp(g_1(\mathbf{x})) + \exp(g_2(\mathbf{x})) + \exp(g_3(\mathbf{x}))} \quad (6)$$

$$P(Y = 3|\mathbf{x}) = \frac{\exp(g_3(\mathbf{x}))}{1 + \exp(g_1(\mathbf{x})) + \exp(g_2(\mathbf{x})) + \exp(g_3(\mathbf{x}))} \quad (7)$$

Following the convention given to the binary model, we can do $\pi_j(\mathbf{x}) = P(Y = j|\mathbf{x})$ for j = 0, 1, 2, 3 each being a function of a vector with $3(p + 1)$ parameters, $\boldsymbol{\beta}' = \left(\boldsymbol{\beta}'_1, \boldsymbol{\beta}'_2, \boldsymbol{\beta}'_3\right)$.

A general expression for the conditional probability for a model whose dependent variable has four categories, can be given by:

$$P(Y = j|\mathbf{x}) = \frac{\exp\left(g_j(\mathbf{x})\right)}{\sum_{k=0}^{3} \exp(g_k(\boldsymbol{x}))} \tag{8}$$

where the vector $\boldsymbol{\beta}_0 = 0$ and $g_0(\mathbf{x}) = 0$.

To construct the likelihood function, it should create four binary variables coded by "0"0 and "1"1 to indicate the group member of an observation. The variables are coded as follows:

- If $Y = 0$ then $Y_1 = 0$, $Y_2 = 0$ and $Y_3 = 0$;
- If $Y = 1$ then $Y_1 = 1$, $Y_2 = 0$ and $Y_3 = 0$;
- If $Y = 2$ then $Y_1 = 0$, $Y_2 = 1$ and $Y_3 = 0$;
- If $Y = 3$ then $Y_1 = 0$, $Y_2 = 0$ and $Y_3 = 1$;

Independently of the value that Y takes, $\sum Y_i = 1$. The conditional likelihood function for an independent sample of n observations is:

$$l(\boldsymbol{\beta}) = \prod_{i=1}^{n} \left[\pi_0(\boldsymbol{x}_i)^{y_{0i}} \pi_1(\boldsymbol{x}_i)^{y_{1i}} \pi_2(\boldsymbol{x}_i)^{y_{2i}} \pi_3(\boldsymbol{x}_i)^{y_{3i}}\right] \tag{9}$$

Making the logarithm and using the fact that the $\sum y_i = 1$ for each i, the logarithm of the likelihood function is [4]:

$$L(\boldsymbol{\beta}) = \sum_{i=1}^{n} \{y_{1i} g_1(\boldsymbol{x}_i) + y_{2i} g_2(\boldsymbol{x}_i) + y_{3i} g_3(\boldsymbol{x}_i) - ln\left[1 + e^{g_1(\boldsymbol{x}_i)} + e^{g_2(\boldsymbol{x}_i)} + e^{g_3(\boldsymbol{x}_i)}\right]\} \tag{10}$$

The likelihood equations are the result of the first partial derivatives of $L(\boldsymbol{\beta})$ to thc $3(p + 1)$ unknown parameters. Using the notation $\pi_{ji} = \pi_j(\mathbf{x}_i)$, the form of these equations is:

$$\frac{\partial L(\boldsymbol{\beta})}{\partial \beta_{jk}} = \sum_{i=1}^{n} x_{ki}\left(y_{ji} - \pi_{ji}\right) \tag{11}$$

for $j = 1,2,3$ and $k = 0, 1, 2, \ldots, p$; with $x_{0i} = 1$ for each case.

The maximum likelihood estimator (MLE), $\widehat{\boldsymbol{\beta}}$ is the result of the resolution of this set of equations equal to 0 in order to $\boldsymbol{\beta}$.

2.2 Data and Sample

To analyse factors, or operating conditions that favour the absence of defects, or deliver products with the contracted customer requirements, we test aggregate data of 659 assembled units, within the three shifts in operation in the device named "AOI10_005". The sample pertains to the time interval from 20.03.2018 until 02.05.2018. In this period the internal rejection rate (IRR) of the process stayed low and with lower variation (see Fig. 2).

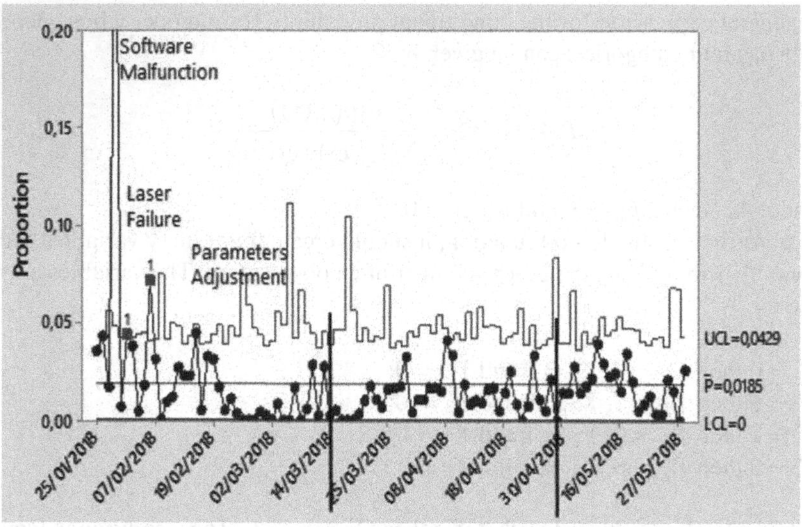

Fig. 2. AOI10_005 Minitab screen shot of Internal Rejection Rate (IRR) lowest and stable period.

2.3 Variables

In this study, the occurrence of the defect (air bubble between the sandwich composed by the display, filling and glass) was treated as the output variable. The available monitoring variables (input variables) are shown, in Table 1.

Table 1. Model variables definition.

Item	Variable	Definition	Code
1	Bubble in zone 1	Dummy variable that reflects defect (bubble) occurrence at zone 1 of the display	0 - no bubble 1 - buble
2	Bubble in zone A	Dummy variable that reflects defect (bubble) occurrence at zone A of the display	0 - no bubble 1 - buble
3	Bubble in zone D	Dummy variable that reflects defect (bubble) occurrence at zone D of the display	0 - no bubble 1 - buble
4	*AOI10_004*	The variable that reflects the unit was processed at a robot named AOI10_004	0 - no 1 - yes
5	*AOI10_005*	The variable that reflects the unit was processed at a robot named AOI10_005	0 - no 1 - yes
6	Rework	Variable indicating if the unit was submitted to recursion	0 - no 1 - yes

(*continued*)

Table 1. (*continued*)

Item	Variable	Definition	Code
7	Offset P1	The linear distance between point 1 reference at display and laser meter head included in the robot terminal that holds the tool, holding the glass to bond with the display	Milimeters (mm)
8	Offset P2	The linear distance between point 2 reference at display and laser meter head included in the robot terminal that holds the tool, holding the glass to bond with the display	mm
9	Offset P3	The linear distance between point 3 reference at display and laser meter head included in the robot terminal that holds the tool, holding the glass to bond with the display	mm
10	Offset P4	The linear distance between point 4 reference at display and laser meter head included in the robot terminal that holds the tool, holding the glass to bond with the display	mm
11	Alignment X	The linear displacement along the X-axis of the robot axis system	mm
12	Alignment Y	The linear displacement along the Y-axis of the robot axis system	mm
13	Alignment R	The linear displacement along the R axis of the robot axis system	
14	Distance display	The linear distance between display and laser meter head included in the robot terminal that holds the tool, holding the glass to bond with the display	Mm
15	AOI error	Dummy variable that reflects if, during the assembly process, occurred an error at the AOI (Automatic Optical Inspection) of particle inspection	0 - no 1 - yes
16	FLC error	Dummy variable that reflects if, during the assembly process, occurred an error at 2D reading code	0 - no 1 - yes

2.4 Model

Units with bubbles are the response or target that we wish to predict. As previously seen in the statistical method section, we generically refer to the response as *Y*. The P1 is a predictor we name as X_1. Likewise, name P2 as X_2, and so on. We can refer to the predictor vector collectively as $\mathbf{x}= (x_1 x_2 x_3 \ldots, x_p)$.

With the logit function defined in Sect. 2.1, we can make predictions of *Y* (bubbles) at new points **x** (robot offsets and process discrete characteristics).

In our case, the reference category it is a normal situation, which reflects the scenario where no bubble appears in any zone of the display. For the reference category, the variable response Y has the code 0. In terms of data set structure, it corresponds to the line where we have 0, 0, 0 for the variable Y_1 (Bubble in zone 1), Y_2 (Bubble in zone 2) and Y_3 (Bubble in Zone 3) (Table 2).

Here, the response variable can have multiple outcomes. We are facing a multi-level classification problem. Specifically, the problem is a four-level classification problem where we investigate, the response variable (Y) coded 0 = no Bubbles, 1 = Bubble in zone 1, 2 = Bubble in zone A and 3 = Bubble in Zone D. Therefore, our response variable Y has four categories. The reason we checked for defects in zones 1, A and D of the kit is because they represent the top 3 in terms of defect occurrence. This information was obtained during the statistical exploratory analysis.

Actually, the software installed at the end of line quality control workstation, only permits the operator to register, in case of bubbles, one zone of occurrence. The operator assumes as the defect occurrence zone the one with the highest incidence, in case of defect in more than one zone.

Table 2. Definition of scenarios or levels.

Scenario	Y_1(Zone 1)	Y_2(Zone A)	Y_3(Zone D)	Y
No bubble/any zone	0	0	0	0
Bubble in Zone 1	1	0	0	1
Bubble in Zone A	0	1	0	2
Bubble in Zone D	0	0	1	3

In Table 2 are exposed the scenarios defined for defect occurrence according to the operator classification at the production line aligned with each of the four model categories. For a model with four categories, we will have three logit functions.

The general model equation for each logit is expressed as:

$$\begin{aligned} &\ln[P(NS\ level = i)/P(NS\ level = 0)] = intercept_i + b_{1_i} \times AOI10_{004} + b_{2_i} \times \\ &AOI10_{005} + b_{3_i} \times \text{reworked} + b_{4_i} \times \text{offsetP1} + b_{5_i} \times \\ &b_{6_i} \times \text{offsetP3} + b_{7_i} \times \text{offsetP4} + b_{8_i} \times \text{AlignX} + b_{9_i} \times \text{AlignY} \\ &b_{10_i} \times \text{AlignR} + b_{11_i} \times \text{distdisplay} + b_{12_i} \times \text{AOIerror} \\ &b_{13_i} \times \text{FLCerror} \end{aligned} \quad (12)$$

(with $1 \leq i \leq 3$ and reference NS level = 0) and b the estimates of parameters β.

3 Results

In this section, we present the results of the computational statistical analysis. All statistical analysis were carried out in R software using package *nnet* with the function *multinom.*

To analyse the accuracy of the model we use a misclassification matrix constructed in R using the command *table* with y_actual and y_predict. The results are presented on Table 3.

Table 3. Classification table

	y_predict			
y_actual	0	1	2	3
0	508	4	3	0
1	34	15	2	0
2	28	2	19	2
3	32	0	6	4

The sum of correct classifications is 546 and the total number of classifications is 659, so the measure of accuracy is 82.8%.

Table 4 presents the results of coefficient values obtained from the application of the model to the case study.

Table 4. Coefficient estimation for multinomial logistic regression.

Logit	Component	Estimate, $\hat{\beta}$	Std. Error	*p*-value	*Signif. Level*
	Intercept	−29.608	0.786	< 2.2E−16	0.001
1	AOI10_004	−15.191	0.956	< 2.2E−16	0.001
	AOI10_005	−14.417	0.731	< 2.2E−16	0.001
	Rework	−2.118	0.685	0.002	0.01
	OffsetP1	7.254	5.932	0.221	
	OffsetP2	−10.598	6.929	0.126	
	OffsetP3	−2.468	1.614	0.126	
	OffsetP4	9.938	3.461	0.004	0.01
	AlignX	−6.136	20.870	0.768	
	AlignY	3.509	17.330	0.839	
	AlignR	108.581	48.244	0.024	0.05
	Dist. Display	2.537	0.115	< 2.2E−16	0.001

(continued)

Table 4. *(continued)*

Logit	Component	Estimate, $\hat{\beta}$	Std. Error	*p*-value	*Signif. Level*
	AOIError	3.266	0.812	5.76E−05	0.001
	FLCError	1,326	1.027	0.196	
	Intercept	23.182	2.602	< 2.2E−16	0.001
2	AOI10_004	12.409	1.415	< 2.2E−16	0.001
	AOI10_005	10.772	1.427	4.52E−14	0.001
	Rework	−1.226	0.586	0.036	0.05
	OffsetP1	−2.353	5.615	0.675	
	OffsetP2	−0.349	6.606	0.957	
	OffsetP3	−1.705	1.399	0.223	
	OffsetP4	3.570	3.349	0.286	
	AlignX	29.255	22.527	0.194	
	AlignY	−24.992	17.811	0.160	
	AlignR	107.561	39.133	0.006	0.01
	Dist. Display	−2.641	0.274	< 2.2E−16	0.001
	AOIError	3.866	0.650	2.75E−09	0.001
	FLCError	2.499	0.854	0.003	0.01
	Intercept	20.625	2.588	1.61E−15	0.001
3	AOI10_004	10.724	1.510	1.25E−12	0.001
	AOI10_005	9.902	1.512	5.82E−11	0.001
	Rework	−0.947	0.510	0.063	
	OffsetP1	5.761	5.483	0.293	
	OffsetP2	−5.549	6.488	0.392	
	OffsetP3	−1.711	1.641	0.297	
	OffsetP4	4.283	3.425	0.211	
	AlignX	34.742	22.407	0.121	
	AlignY	32.300	17.852	0.070	
	AlignR	16.595	41.904	0.692	
	Dist. Display	−2.067	0.266	8.30E−15	0.001
	AOIError	2.277	0.699	0.001	0.01
	FLCError	2.480	0.913	0.006	0.01

Source: *multinom* function of R software *nnet* package

In Table 4 it is possible to observe the statistical significance coefficients with a maximum value of 0.05, meaning a minimum confidence interval of 95%.

Taking into account the results obtained, for each logit or model equation we can interpret the estimated coefficients. Also important is the sign of the coefficient. It will tell us if it affects positively or negatively the log odds in analysis (defect occurrence). For this case study it is of relevance to know the coefficients that affect positively the log odds of defect occurrence in order to prevent it. Below are presented the statistically significant variables that affect positively the defect occurrence in a specific zone of the display.

For discrete variables:

- Errors in the AOIs impact the appearance of bubbles in the 3 zones under study, with a confidence interval of 99.9% for zones 1 and A and 99% for zone D;
- FLC error seems to favour the appearance of bubbles in zones A and D with 99% of confidence.

For continuous variables:

- Distance to the display seems to be strongly associated with the likelihood of bubbles appearing in all zones studied with 99.9% confidence for the 3 zones;
- Alignment in R appears to be associated with defects in zones 1 and A with 95% confidence interval and 99%, respectively;
- OffsetP4 seems to impact the occurrence of bubbles in zone 1 with a 99% confidence interval;

4 Discussion

As mentioned, we need to understand the inference in order to be able to understand the relationship between the independent variable and the dependent variable and that will help in policymaking, consequently taking better decisions.

From computational statistical analysis (SA) results were possible to derive a set of target conditions for the process variables, namely:

a. **Process discrete variables target conditions derived from SA results**:

   I. Application of a process reaction limit (stop process) equal one in case of AOI error or FLC error.

b. **Process continuous variables target conditions derived from SA results**:

   I. Analyse the concept of display base retention (immobilization) to reduce positional variation and expand the estimation of the robust variation for the other continuous variables (offsets) without statistical significance.
   II. Estimation of a combined robust variation range for the continuous variables with statistical significance (see Table 5).

III. Process monitoring with alarm in case of statistically significant variables laying outside the combined robust variation range.
IV. Standardized and controlled maintenance to comply with robust variation band.

Table 5. Combined robust variation range for the continuous variables in the model.

Limits	Variables			
	Offset P4	Alignment Y	Alignment R	Dist. display
Min	−1.004	−0.020	−0.013	15.290
Max	0.596	0.030	0.010	16.370

The developed statistical model with the necessary tuning can be applied to every process of the company when it is necessary to predict and monitor categorical response variables in a complex operating conditions environment. The model can also be the data structure of a "Real-Time System Monitoring" contributing to ICPS research.

5 Conclusion

This study had as its objective the analysis of the influence of several industrial operating conditions in the occurrence of the defect (air bubbles) in a wet bonding process of two pieces (a glass and an electronic display).

In this paper, we present the development and application of a multi-class classification statistical model, for predicting product quality from operating conditions, based on multinomial logistic regression. The study ran, in a real industrial process.

From data associated with 16 variables, we conceived a statistical model to estimate robust operating conditions.

According to the results obtained it was found that, to evaluate the probability of an assembled kit (glass and electronic display) having a defect (air bubble) in the filling material during the bonding process it is important to monitor the following process variables: occurrence of errors in workstations "AOI" and "FLC", distance to display, Alignment in R and OffsetP4.

This model contributes to better understanding the operating conditions of the bonding process associated with the occurrence of the defect and to estimate the robust operational conditions combination of these 5 variables. Therefore, we think that it will be a tool to predict more accurately the occurrence of a defect on the bonding process.

Furthermore, our model integrated in a "Real-Time System Monitoring" may represent an alternative to build a data-driven white-box soft-sensor [6–8], in this way contributing to future ICPS research.

Acknowledgements. This work has been supported by FCT - Fundação para a Ciência e Tecnologia within the R&D Units Project Scope: UIDB/00319/2020.

References

1. Lee, J., Kao, H., Yang, S.: Service innovation and smart analytics for Industry 4.0 and big data environment. ScienceDirect Procedia CIRP **16**(3), 3–8 (2014)
2. Yin, S., Rodríguez-Andina, J.J., Jiang, Y.: real-time monitoring and control of industrial cyber-physical systems: with integrated plant-wide monitoring and control framework. IEEE Ind. Electron. Mag. **13**(4), 38–48 (2019)
3. Kano, M., Nakagawa, Y.: Data-based process monitoring, process control, and quality improvement: recent developments and applications in steel industry. Comput. Chem. Eng. **32**, 12–24 (2008)
4. Braga, A.C., Urzal, V., Ferreira, A.P.: Orthodontics diagnostic based on multinomial logistic regression model. In: Murgante, B., et al. (eds.) ICCSA 2013. LNCS, vol. 7971, pp. 585–595. Springer, Heidelberg (2013). https://doi.org/10.1007/978-3-642-39637-3_46
5. James, L.: Logistic Regression in R Tutorial (2018). https://www.datacamp.com/community/tutorials/logistic-regression-R#rstats, Accessed 9 Apr 2021
6. Shang, C., Fang, Y., Huang, D., Lyu, W.: Data-driven soft sensor development based on deep learning technique. J. Process Control **24**, 223–233 (2014)
7. Ookita, K.: Operation and quality control for chemical plants by soft sensors (in Japanese). CICSJ Bull. **24**, 31–33 (2006)
8. Sharma, S., Tambe, S.S.: Soft-sensor development for biochemical systems using genetic programming. Biochem. Eng. J. **85**, 89–100 (2014)

Improving Short-Term Forecasts of Daily Maximum Temperature with the Kalman Filter with GMM Estimation

Marco Costa[1,3](✉), Fernanda Catarina Pereira[2,4], and A. Manuela Gonçalves[2,4]

[1] Águeda School of Technology and Management - ESTGA, University of Aveiro, Aveiro, Portugal
marco@ua.pt
[2] Department of Mathematics, University of Minho, Braga, Portugal
up202010700@edu.fe.up.pt, mneves@math.uminho.pt
[3] Centre for Research and Development in Mathematics and Applications - CIDMA, University of Aveiro, Aveiro, Portugal
[4] Center of Mathematics, University of Minho, Braga, Portugal

Abstract. Within the scope of the TO CHAIR project, a state space modeling approach is proposed in order to improve accuracy obtained from the *weatherstack.com* website with a dataset of real observations. The proposed model establishes a stochastic linear relationship between the maximum temperature observed and the h-step-ahead forecast produced from the website. This relation is modeled in a state space framework associated to the Kalman filter predictors. Since normality of disturbances was not a good assumption for this dataset, alternative Generalized Method of Moments (GMM) estimators were considered in the models parameters estimation. The results show that this approach allows reducing the RMSE of the uncorrected forecasts in 16.90% considering the 6-step-ahead forecasts and in 60.45% considering the 1-step-ahead forecasts, compared with the initial RMSE. Additionally, empirical confidence intervals at the 95% level have a coverage rate similar to this confidence level. So, this approach has proven suitable for this type of forecasts correction since it considers a stochastic calibration factor in order to model time correlation of this type of variable.

This work has received funding from FEDER/COMPETE/NORTE2020/POCI/FCT funds through grants UID/EEA/- 00147/20 13/UID/IEEA/00147/ 006933-SYSTEC, project and To CHAIR - POCI-01-0145-FEDER-028247. This work was also partially supported by the Portuguese FCT Projects UIDB/00013/2020 and UIDP/00013/2020 of CMAT-UM and the Center for Research and Development in Mathematics and Applications (CIDMA) through the Portuguese Foundation for Science and Technology (FCT - Fundação para a Ciência e a Tecnologia), references UIDB/04106/2020 and UIDP/04106/2020.

O. Gervasi et al. (Eds.): ICCSA 2021, LNCS 12952, pp. 552–562, 2021.
https://doi.org/10.1007/978-3-030-86973-1_39

Keywords: State space modeling · Kalman filter · GMM estimation · Forecasting calibration · Maximum temperature · TO CHAIR project

1 Introduction

This work is carried out in the context of project "TO CHAIR - Optimum Challenges in Irrigation" - https://systec.fe.up.pt/projects/FCT-TOCHAIR/ - and aims to understand and analyze the behavior of humidity in the soil by mathematical/statistical modeling in order to find optimal solutions to improve the efficiency of daily water use in irrigation systems [3].

In the context of the TO CHAIR project, it is necessary to improve short-term forecasts of meteorological variables. In fact, more accurate forecasts of these variables can improve the results of the optimization routines in order to obtain a more efficient use of water in irrigation systems.

In this project, the main goal of statistical modeling is to improve the accuracy of the forecast of meteorological variables obtained from the *weather-stack.com* website for the location under analysis, a farm in Portugal. However, agricultural researchers that investigate in this area know that forecasts have significant errors compared with observations obtained locally by a portable weather station. Several factors can contribute to these discrepancies. On the one hand, this farm is located in a valley in a mountainous region, and so it has a specific orography. On the other hand, the methodology adopted by the site's forecasts (which we do not know), possibly associated with the significant distance between this farm and fixed weather stations in with which forecasts are computed, can partially explain these differences.

This work intends to establish a state space framework that combines forecasts with the observations in order to correct or "calibrate" a forecast by comparing it with the knowledge from the past, namely through an estimated model based on few data. This approach has been considered in environmental problems, for instance in [1,4].

2 Exploratory Analysis of Data

The statistical analysis was performed using a dataset that includes forecasts (obtained from the weatherstack.com website) of daily maximum temperature (in Celsius degrees) for the location of the farm Senhora da Ribeira in Portugal, between February 20 and October 11, 2019. Additionally, we also use observations of daily temperatures obtained by a portable weather station installed in the farm during that period of 234 days (see Fig. 1).

In this context, we consider that Y_t is the real maximum temperature in day t with a small error associated to the measurement of the portable station. However, the forecast $W_{t:t-h}$ has an additional uncertainty associated to the interpolation methods or the methodology adopted by the website.

The data from the portable station will be used to compare with the site's forecasts and to assess their accuracy. Considering that the observations from

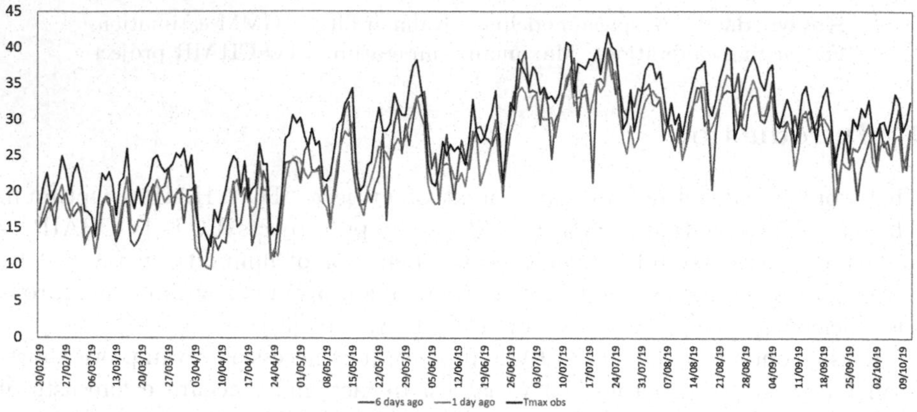

Fig. 1. Time series plots of the observed maximum temperature (in black) and the respective forecasts at 6-steps-ahead and 1-step-ahead (in blue and orange, respectively). (Color figure online)

the portable weather station are more accurate, in fact, the most accurate observations available, they will be used for correct or calibrate the site's forecasts, since the portable station was temporary installed in the farm.

The roots of the mean square error of the forecasts from the site, $W_{t:t-h}$, with $t = 1, ..., 234$ and $h = 1, ..., 6$, compared with the observations Y_t, with $t = 1, ..., 234$, computed by

$$\text{RMSE}_h = \sqrt{\frac{1}{234}\sum_{t=1}^{234}(Y_t - W_{t:t-h})^2} \tag{1}$$

where $W_{t:t-h}$ represents the h-steps-ahead forecast of the maximum temperature in day t, that is, the forecast indicated by the site h days before the day t, and Y_t is the observed maximum temperature in the farm by the portable weather station.

Table 1 presents the root mean square error, RMSE_h. Notice that, as expected, the RMSE is greater for large values of h than for forecasts obtained with few days of delay. However, all RMSE are very significant, even for forecasts obtained a day before. So, the site's forecasts are significantly inaccurate when compared with the observations collected in the farm.

Table 1. Root of the mean square error (RMSE) between the maximum temperature observed in the farm and the h-steps-ahead obtained from the site weatherstack.com, with $h = 1, ..., 6$.

h-step-ahead	6	5	4	3	2	1
RMSE	4.670	4.222	4.107	4.003	3.901	3.875

However, in spite of the website's inaccurate forecasts, forecasts and observations are linear correlated. In fact, the Pearson's correlation coefficients between observations from the portable station and the h-step-ahead forecasts show a significant linear correlation (Table 2)

Table 2. Pearson's correlation coefficients between observations from the portable station and the h-step-ahead forecasts show, with $h = 1, ..., 6$.

h-step-ahead	6	5	4	3	2	1
Correlation	0.880	0.918	0.941	0.956	0.970	0.976

3 The State Space Approach

3.1 The State Space Model

Considering that the forecasts $W_{t:t-h}$, with $t = 1, ..., 234$, are known at instant $t - h$, and the observed maximum temperature Y_t is related with forecasts, we propose a state space model composed by these two equations:

$$Y_t = \beta_t W_{t:t-h} + e_t \quad (2)$$

$$\beta_t = \mu + \phi(\beta_{t-1} - \mu) + \epsilon_t \quad (3)$$

where Eq. 2 is the observation equation and Eq. 3 is the state or transition equation. This model assumes that the maximum temperature observed in the farm at day t is linear related with the h-step-ahead forecast given by the website at day $t - h$.

The unobservable process $\{\beta_t\}$ is called the state process and must be predicted. In this case, it is be assumed that the process $\{\beta_t\}$ follows a stationary autoregressive process of order 1, that is, $\{\beta_t\} \sim$ AR(1), with mean μ and the autoregressive coefficient ϕ, such as $|\phi| < 1$.

Errors e_t and ϵ_t are assumed to be a sequence of uncorrelated variable with zero mean and variances σ_e^2 and σ_ϵ^2, respectively, and uncorrelated with each other, that is, $E(e_t\epsilon_r) = 0, \forall t, r$.

Usually, in several applications it is assumed that the disturbances e_t and ϵ_t are normally distributed, that is, $e_t \sim N(0, \sigma_e^2)$ and $\epsilon_t \sim N(0, \sigma_\epsilon^2)$, however, this assumption is not always valid with environmental data.

The model Eq. 2 - Eq. 3 assumes that the state process represents a stochastic calibration factor between the maximum temperature observation and the website's forecasts, which contain significant uncertainty. As the factor β_t is stochastic, it varies over time allowing some flexibility in the correction procedure.

3.2 Kalman Filter

The Kalman filter, proposed by Kalman (1960) and Kalman and Bucy (1961), is an iterative algorithm that produces, at each time t, an estimator of the state vector at time t. It provides optimal unbiased linear one-step-ahead and update estimators of the unobservable state β_t.

Let $\hat{\beta}_{t|t-1}$ denote the predictor of β_t based on the observations $Y_1, Y_2, \ldots, Y_{t-1}$ and $P_{t|t-1}$ be its mean square error (MSE), this is, $E[(\hat{\beta}_{t|t-1} - \beta_t)^2]$. The one-step-ahead forecast for the observable vector Y_t is given by $\hat{Y}_{t|t-1} = W_{t:t-h}\hat{\beta}_{t|t-1}$.

When, at time t, Y_t is available, the prediction error or innovation, $\eta_t = Y_t - \hat{\beta}_{t|t-1}$, is used to update the estimate of β_t (filtering) through the equation

$$\hat{\beta}_{t|t} = \hat{\beta}_{t|t-1} + K_t\eta_t, \tag{4}$$

where K_t is called the Kalman gain matrix and is given by

$$K_t = P_{t|t-1}W_{t:t-h}(W^2_{t:t-h}P_{t|t-1} + \sigma^2_e)^{-1}. \tag{5}$$

Furthermore, the MSE of the updated estimator $\hat{\beta}_{t|t}$, represented by $P_{t|t}$, verifies the relationship $P_{t|t} = P_{t|t-1} - K_tW_{t:t-h}P_{t|t-1}$.

The Kalman filter algorithm is initialized with $\hat{\beta}_{1|0}$ and $P_{1|0}$, and when the state process is stationary, it can be initialized considering that initial state vector β_1 has $\hat{\beta}_{1|0} = \mu$ and MSE $\sigma^2_\varepsilon(1-\phi^2)^{-1}$.

3.3 Parameters Estimation – A Distribution-Free Approach

When disturbances e_t and ϵ_t are normally distributed and under the independence between errors and the initial state β_1, the parameters $\Theta = (\mu, \phi, \sigma^2_e, \sigma^2_\varepsilon)$ can be estimated by the Gaussian maximum likelihood method.

The log-likelihood of a sample $(Y_1, Y_2, \ldots, Y_n)$ can be written through conditional distributions, given by

$$\log L(\Theta; Y_1, Y_2, \ldots, Y_n) = -\frac{n}{2}\log(2\pi) - \frac{1}{2}\sum_{t=1}^{n}\log(\Omega_t) - \frac{1}{2}\sum_{t=1}^{n}\eta_t^2\Omega_t^{-1}, \tag{6}$$

where

$$\Omega_t = W^2_{t:t-h}P_{t|t-1} + \sigma^2_e. \tag{7}$$

The optimization of the log-likelihood is done by numerical procedures via the Newton-Raphson method or, more often, by the EM algorithm ([6]).

However, previous modeling has shown that the normality is rejected in the residuals analysis. So, alternative methods are needed. In this context, we proposed to adapted the distribution-free estimators initially proposed in [2] and subsequently generalize them for multivariate models in [5].

Considering the model of type Eq. 2 - Eq. 3 for some h, the mean, μ, of the state $\{\beta_t\}_{t=1,2,\ldots}$, can be easily estimated by the generalized method of moments (GMM):

$$\widehat{\mu} = \frac{1}{n}\sum_{t=1}^{n} \frac{Y_t}{W_{t:t-h}}. \tag{8}$$

The autoregressive parameter ϕ is estimated by the covariance structure of process $\{Y_t W_{t:t-h}^{-1}\}_{t=1,2,\ldots}$ based on the autocovariance function of the process $\{\beta_t\}$ by

$$\widehat{\phi} = \frac{\sum_{k=1}^{\ell} \gamma(k+1)\gamma(k)}{\sum_{k=1}^{\ell} \gamma^2(k)} \tag{9}$$

where $\widehat{\gamma}(k)$ is the sample autocovariance function of the process $\{Y_t W_{t:t-h}^{-1}\}_{t=1,2,\ldots}$.

The choice of ℓ was discussed in the original work [2] and for a sample of dimension of 200, as it is approximately in this case, it is recommended the use of $\ell = 60$.

To estimate σ_ϵ^2 it is considered the distribution-free estimator

$$\widehat{\sigma}_\epsilon^2 = \frac{1-\widehat{\phi}^2}{\widehat{\phi}}\widehat{\gamma}(1). \tag{10}$$

The observation noise variance σ_e^2 is based on sample mean square error of the process $\{Y_t W_{t:t-h}^{-1}\}_{t=1,2,\ldots}$, that is, $\widehat{\gamma}_0$, defining $\widehat{\gamma}_0$ as

$$\widehat{\gamma}_0 = \frac{1}{n}\sum_{t=1}^{n}\left(\frac{Y_t}{W_{t:t-h}} - \widehat{\mu}\right)^2$$

and the estimator of σ_e^2 is given by

$$\widehat{\sigma}_e^2 = \frac{1}{n}\sum_{t=1}^{n}\left(\frac{Y_t}{W_{t:t-h}} - \widehat{\mu}\right)^2 - \frac{\widehat{\sigma}_\epsilon^2}{(1-\widehat{\phi}^2)^2}. \tag{11}$$

The estimators 8 to 11 are, under simple regularity conditions, consistent ([2]). In this sense, in this work the dataset has a high sample dimension (up to 200) which ensures the properties of the estimators.

3.4 Forecasts Correction Procedure

Once modeled the relation between the observed maximum temperature and its forecasts h-step-ahead from the website, the correction procedure for them can then be proposed.

At each day t it is available the observation Y_t and six forecasts $W_{t+1:t}$, $W_{t+2:t}$, ..., $W_{t+h:t}$, ..., $W_{t+6:t}$. The main goal is to improve these forecasts with the observations available until the present, the day t.

So, for each h-step-ahead forecast and for each day t it is possible to predict the correction factor β_{t+h} to the day $t+h$ using the Kalman filter prediction, such as

$$\widehat{\beta}_{t+h|t} = \mu + \phi^h(\widehat{\beta}_{t|t} - \mu) \tag{12}$$

with the mean square error

$$P_{t+h|t} = \phi^{2h} P_{t|t} + \phi^{2(h-1)}\sigma_\epsilon^2 + \phi^{2(h-2)}\sigma_\epsilon^2 + ... + \phi^2\sigma_\epsilon^2 + \sigma_\epsilon^2. \tag{13}$$

Thus, the corrected h-step-ahead forecast for Y_{t+h} based on data available until t is given by

$$\widehat{Y}_{t+h|t} = \widehat{\beta}_{t+h|t} W_{t+h:t} \tag{14}$$

with mean square error given by

$$\text{MSE}_{t+h|t} = W_{t+h:t}^2 P_{t+h|t} + \sigma_e^2. \tag{15}$$

Even considering the distribution-free estimators, but attending to their asymptotic properties of consistence, we can compute empirical confidence intervals with $(1-\alpha) * 100\%$ level to corrected forecasts from equations

$$Y_{t+h|t} = \widehat{Y}_{t+h|t} \pm z_{1-\frac{\alpha}{2}} \sqrt{\text{MSE}_{t+h|t}}. \tag{16}$$

where $z_{1-\alpha/2}$ is the normal quantil of probability $1-\alpha/2$.

4 Results

The modeling procedure considered two series: the training series (in-sample) and the out-sample series. The first time series comprising data between 20 February until 31 August, 2020 (193 days) is considered to estimate parameters and analyze the assumptions based on the residuals analysis; the second time series comprising data between 1 September and 11 October, 2020 (41 days), is considered to better assess the model's performance in a independent period where the models were adjusted.

Table 3. Estimates of parameters.

Parameter/h	6	5	4	3	2	1
μ	1.1650	1.1555	1.1633	1.1608	1.1658	1.1723
ϕ	0.8394	0.7857	0.8092	0.8796	0.9419	0.8888
σ_ϵ^2	0.0028	0.0032	0.0032	0.0008	0.0009	0.0011
σ_e^2	9.3464	6.0780	4.2854	3.8355	2.0164	2.2936

Table 3 presents the estimates of parameters for all six models considering $h = 1, ..., 6$. As expected, these results show that the mean of the state $\{\beta_t\}$ is greater than 1 in all models. This means that, in average, the forecasts are lower than the observations from the portable station; that is, there is a stochastic bias. However, as the state process is a factor, this bias can be interpreted in a relative way. For instance, $\widehat{\mu} = 1.1723$ for the 1-step-ahead forecasts, that is, in average, the maximum temperature observed in the farm was greater in 17.23% than the 1-step-ahead forecast. This factor does not differ much for the different values of h.

All estimates for the autoregressive parameters are less than 1, so, the state process is estimated as a stationary process, as assumed in assumptions. The error of the observation equation has a high variance in all models. However, this variability decrease as the forecasts are computed with less delay; for the 6-step-ahead forecasts the observation error was estimated in 9.3464 instead of 2.2936 for the 1-step-ahead forecasts. The error of the state equation has a low variability for all h.

In order to verify the assumptions of model, an analysis of residuals $\widehat{\eta}_{t|t-1}$ was performed. The residuals present an uncorrelated structure compatible with assumptions. Figure 2 represents histograms of the model's residuals for $h = 1$ and $h = 6$.

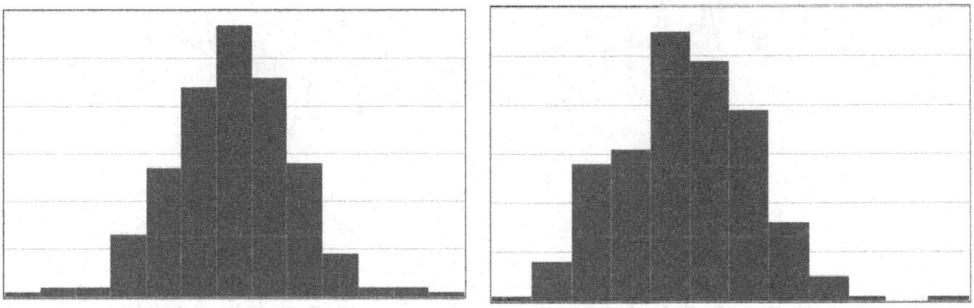

Fig. 2. Histograms of model's residuals $\widehat{\eta}_{t|t-1}$ of models for $h = 1$ and $h = 6$, for whole period under analysis.

The estimates of parameters, associated to the Kalman filter equations, allow to predict the state values, that is, the calibration factors. For instance, Fig. 3 shows the Kalman filter h-step-ahead forecasts of the calibration factors, $\widehat{\beta}_{t+h|t}$ to the model with $h = 1$ and $h = 6$. These predictions show that the calibration factor varies over time, thus showing its variability.

This approach, associated to the Kalman filter, allows to compute h-step-ahead predictions of Y_t based on Eq. 14. Figure 4 shows the observed maximum temperature in the whole period under analysis with the website's forecasts for $h = 1, 6$ and the empirical confidence intervals of the corrected forecasts by the Kalman filter.

For each h days in advance it was computed the root of the mean square error of the corrected forecasts. The RMSE of the corrected forecasts given by the Kalman filter reduced in 16.90% considering the 6-step-ahead forecasts and in

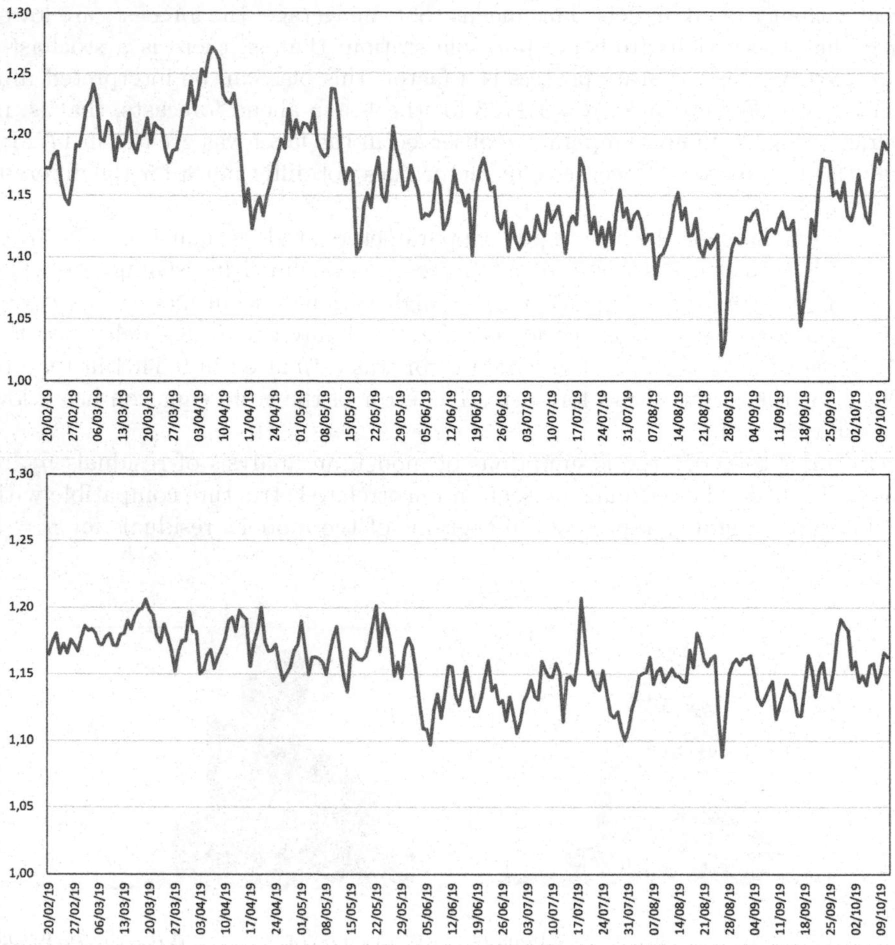

Fig. 3. Kalman filter forecasts of the calibration factor $\widehat{\beta}_{t+h|t}$ for the models with $h = 1$ (up) and $h = 6$ (down).

60.45% considering the 1-step-ahead forecasts, compared with the initial RMSE (Table 4).

These results show a big reduction in MSE considering 1 day ahead and lower reduction when h increases, as expect. Moreover, the confidence intervals with a level of 95% have a coverage rate similar to this level (Table 5). Thus, these models are well adjusted and suitable to model this type of data.

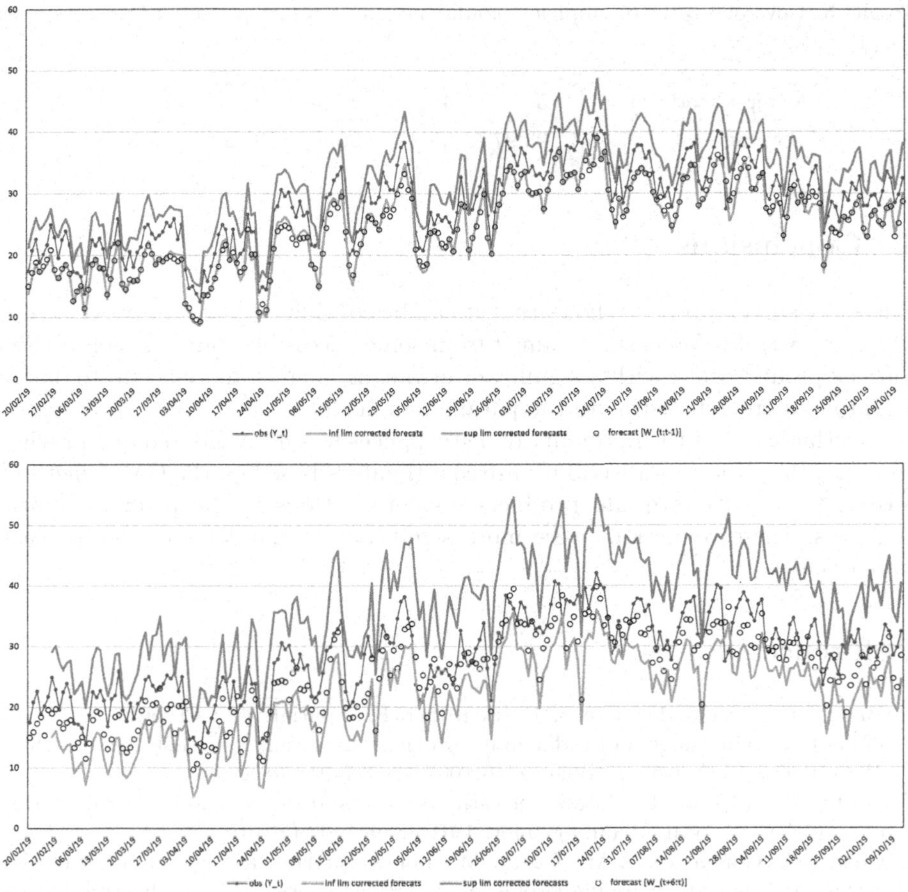

Fig. 4. Empirical confidence intervals for h-step-ahead corrected forecasts of the maximum temperature for model $h = 1$ and $h = 6$, for the whole period under analysis.

Table 4. Roots of the mean square errors before and after correction.

h	6	5	4	3	2	1
RMSE in-sample corrected	3.937	3.206	2.826	2.264	1.890	1.545
RMSE out-sample corrected	3.602	2.283	1.737	1.911	1.687	1.469
Global RMSE uncorrected	4.670	4.222	4.107	4.003	3.901	3.875
Global RMSE corrected	3.881	3.065	2.668	2.206	1.856	1.532
Reduction of global RMSE (%)	16.90%	27.41%	35.04%	44.89%	52.42%	60.45%

Table 5. Coverage rates of empirical confidence intervals of corrected forecasts, with $h = 1, ..., 6$.

h-step-ahead	6	5	4	3	2	1
Coverage rate	97.86%	93.97%	95.24%	95.65%	97.38%	95.18%

5 Conclusions

The state space approach shows that it can be considered in the improvement of weather variables forecasts obtained from some accessible sources, even if those sources produce data with a significant errors, as long as, more accurate data is available in order to estimate the parameters model.

Furthermore, as the normality of disturbances was not validated in a previous analysis, the option for distribution-free estimators based on the GMM methods proved to be adequate and produces good reductions in the RMSE of initial forecasts. These reductions were more significant as the delay of the forecasts were smaller.

References

1. Bruno, F., Cocchi, D., Greco, F., Scardovi, E.: Spatial reconstruction of rainfall fields from rain gauge and radar data. Stochast. Environ. Res. Risk Assess. **28**(5), 1235–1245 (2013). https://doi.org/10.1007/s00477-013-0812-0
2. Costa, M., Alpuim, T.: Parameter estimation of state space models for univariate observations. J. Stat. Planning Infer. **140**, 1889–1902 (2010)
3. Costa, C., Goncalves, A.M., Costa, M., Lopes, S.: Forecasting temperature time series for irrigation planning problems. In: Proceedings of the 34th IWSM International Workshop on Statistical Modelling (2019). http://hdl.handle.net/10773/26437
4. Costa, M., Alpuim, T.: Adjustment of state space models in view of area rainfall estimation. Environmetrics **22**, 530–540 (2011). https://doi.org/10.1002/env.1064
5. Gonçalves, A.M., Costa, M.: Predicting seasonal and hydro-meteorological impact in environmental variables modelling via Kalman filtering. Stoch. Environ. Res. Risk Assess **27**, 1021–1038 (2013). https://doi.org/10.1007/s00477-012-0640-7
6. Shumway, R.H., Stoffer, D.F.: Time series analysis and its applications: with R examples. Springer, New York (2011)

Exploring Methodologies for ROC Curve Covariate Study with R

Francisco Machado e Costa[1](✉) and Ana Cristina Braga[2]

[1] School of Engineering, University of Minho, Campus de Gualtar, Braga, Portugal
[2] ALGORITMI Centre, University of Minho, Campus de Azurém, Guimarães, Portugal
acb@dps.uminho.pt

Abstract. The ROC curve is a statistical tool used broadly to help professionals from several fields of study gauge the ability of a binary classifier. Recent theoretical advancements have allowed the ROC curve to better examine existing confounding variables in its analysis allowing greater calibration for markers and classifiers.

A few packages developed for the R language have already incorporated these newfound concepts and are currently available to aid users in the covariate study.

This article combines different ROC curve, adjusted ROC curve and covariate specific ROC curve methodologies across packages to study the effect of sex on the CRIB score system with a resampling strategy using parallel computing.

Results show a confounding effect on roughly 15% of cases with similar results across packages confirming a consensus among methods and providing a robust methodology for future use.

Keywords: ROC curve · AROC · Resampling

1 Introduction

The problem of assigning an object to one of two classes is limitless in application and the core concept behind decision statistics. Systems of classification are flawed however, and errors in classification can occur more often than not requiring the existence of performance classifiers such as the ROC curve.

The ROC curve, defined as a plot of False Positive Fraction (FPF), or 1-specificity and True Positive Fraction (TPF), or sensitivity, pairs obtained by varying threshold c as (x,y) axis respectively.

Defining Y_D and $Y_{\bar{D}}$ as continuous variables for diseased and non diseased groups respectively with cumulative distribution functions F_D and $F_{\bar{D}}$, we assume all test outcomes greater than c belong to the diseased group, with

This work has been supported by FCT - Fundação para a Ciência e Tecnologia within the R&D Units Project Scope: UIDB/00319/2020. The authors express their gratitude to the Portuguese National Registry for supplying the dataset used in this study.

O. Gervasi et al. (Eds.): ICCSA 2021, LNCS 12952, pp. 563–576, 2021.
https://doi.org/10.1007/978-3-030-86973-1_40

$c \in \mathbb{R}$. Subsequently, each given c will determine TPF, $TPF(c) = Pr(Y_D \geq c) = 1 - F_D(c)$ and similarly FPF, $FPF(c) = Pr(Y_{\bar{D}} \geq c) = 1 - F_{\bar{D}}(c)$.

Given the standard equation, $ROC(\cdot) = \{(FPF(c), TPF(c)), c \in \mathbb{R}\}$ [1]. By converting FPF at threshold c to t, such as, $t = FPF(c) = 1 - F_{\bar{D}}(c)$, the ROC curve is defined as $\{(t, ROC(t)) : t \in [0, 1]\}$ [2], where

$$ROC(t) = Pr\{Y_D > F_{\bar{D}}^{-1}(1-t)\} = 1 - F_D\{F_{\bar{D}}^{-1}(1-t)\}, 0 \leq t \leq 1 \quad (1)$$

To avoid bias analysis or incomplete conclusions about test accuracy covariate information must be incorporated in the ROC methodology [3]. To this goal, several mathematical approaches have been proposed in recent years to better solve this problem [1,3,4].

By denoting $\mathbf{X}_D$ and $\mathbf{X}_{\bar{D}}$ as diseased and non diseased vector of covariates of interest and a covariate value $\mathbf{x}$, the covariate-specific ROC curve is built as

$$ROC(t|\mathbf{x}) = Pr\{Y_D > F_{\bar{D}}^{-1}(1-t|\mathbf{X}_{\bar{D}} = \mathbf{x})|\mathbf{X}_D = \mathbf{x}\} \quad (2)$$

$$= 1 - F_D\{F_{\bar{D}}^{-1}(1-t|\mathbf{X}_{\bar{D}} = \mathbf{x})|\mathbf{X}_D = \mathbf{x}\} \quad (3)$$

The covariate specific ROC curve builds different curves and displays a different test accuracy for each value of $\mathbf{x}$, crucial in identifying optimal and sub-optimal populations and variable values for tests. This method, while helpful for categorical or binary variables lacked the necessary global adjustment and measurement methods for continuous variables.

To mend this issue, along with the covariate **specific** ROC, the covariate **adjusted** ROC curve, AROC [3], was defined as,

$$AROC(t) = \int ROC(t|\mathbf{x})dH_D(\mathbf{x}) \quad (4)$$

where,

$$H_D(\mathbf{x}) = Pr(\mathbf{X}_D \leq \mathbf{x}),$$

is the cumulative distribution function of $\mathbf{X}_D$. Therefore the AROC is a weighted average of covariate specific ROC curves according to the distribution of the covariates in the diseased group [2]. Janes and Pepe [3] also demonstrated that the AROC curve can also be expressed as

$$AROC(t) = Pr\{Y_D > F_{\bar{D}}^{-1}(1-t|\mathbf{X}_D)\} = Pr\{1 - F_{\bar{D}}(Y_D|\mathbf{X}_D)) \leq t\}, \quad (5)$$

proving that the AROC summarizes the covariate-specific performance of the test.

To establish a statistically significant confounding effect of a given covariate on the ROC curve we have explored the possibility of using the fit model's parameters present in both adjusted and covariate specific methodologies however another well established alternative is available in some scenarios, ROC curve comparison.

When comparing ROC curves, Area Under the Curve (AUC) is frequently used to indicate higher performance provided no curve crossing occur in areas of statistical interest. The Z-test, is often used for this comparison [5]. As long as the covariate is binary in nature, it is possible to separate the data by this covariate to detect differences of performance of the classification system which infers a confounding effect of the covariate in question.

This article will explore these different ROC curve methodologies to detect covariate effect on the CRIB score system utilizing R and recent R packages with a parallel computing and resampling strategy.

2 Methodology

2.1 Dataset

The dataset used is part of the Portuguese National Registry on low weight newborns between 2013 and 2018 and was made available for research purposes. The original data included possible confounding observations such as repeated ids and twins that were removed to ensure no unaccounted variable. After ensuring all id's were unique, these were promptly removed along with any possible identifiable features to abide by European Union's anonymity and data protection standards. The resulting dataset composed of 3823 unique entries registering gestational age in weeks, the mothers' age, in years, the biological sex of the infant (1-Male; 2-Female), CRIB score (0–21), survival (0-Survival; 1-Death) and other possibly relevant covariates were used for the remainder of the study. An abridged dataset with relevant information was published and is available for reference [6].

2.2 Resampling and Parallel Computing

Instead of using the full dataset on a single test to describe the confounding effect of the 'sex' covariate, a resampling strategy was employed to better describe the score's system accuracy and this covariate's effect.

To better represent the original data, sampling followed a 9:1 ratio of survival and death distributed equally among both sexes to ensure proportionality.

Random samples of $n = 500$, $n = 1000$, and $n = 1500$ with replacement were taken and processed through the three tests, this was done iteratively with $i = 100$ and $i = 500$, each time creating a new sample and building three distinct ROC curves.

Given the number of required iterations and high density of data, a parallel computing strategy was implemented. The package `foreach` together with the `doParallel` and `parallel` packages allow several CPU cores to calculate each process in tandem which, in practice, divides the amount of time spent on the full iteration process by the number of cores provided although diminishing returns apply due to different bottlenecks in the process. Note that the packages and code used were meant to apply to a Windows10 machine and different packages could be needed on a Linux or OSX based system due to different core processing each operating system uses.

2.3 ROC Packages

To apply the adjusted ROC and covariate specific ROC curve methodology the ROCnReg package was selected. This is a recently released package that imports some methods from a previously existing one of the same authors [7] adding to the original AROC methods, covariate specific/conditional functions. The methods used, *cROC.sp()* and *AROC.sp()*, for covariate specific and covariate adjusted ROC respectively, are both based on a semiparametric regression model to estimate $F_{\bar{D}}(\cdot|\mathbf{x})$ [4]. The covariate specific method however, does so for both healthy and diseased populations, providing two separate significance test values.

For the ROC curve and AUC comparison, the Braga methodology [5] and Comp2ROC package were selected. The method uses a collection of sampling lines similar to multi-objective distinct optimization algorithms, allowing ROC curve comparison in several regions of space evaluating statistical performance and generating confidence intervals with nonparametric bootstrap resampling method. This allows curve crossing to occur while still detecting significant differences in AUC values and ROC performance across the whole curve [5,8].

2.4 Code

Working with R and Rstudio the data and packages were imported. For replication purposes, the session info detailing the operating system and package versions will be available in Sect. 5, additionally, custom functions were built in a different file, comp2conv.R to simplify code reading but will be detailed also.

The data is imported, and the sample size is defined for this demonstration as $n = 1000$. However, and as mentioned before, values of $n = 500$, $n = 1000$, and $n = 1500$ were run through the analysis.

```
library(parallel)
library(doParallel)
library(foreach)
library(ROCnReg)
library(dplyr)
library(Comp2ROC)
set.seed('1234')
source('comp2conv.R')


neonatal <- read.csv('NeonatalPortugal2018_abridged.csv',
                     sep = ';')
neonatal$sex <- as.factor(neonatal$sex)


sample_size <- 1000
surv_sample <- sample_size * 0.9
dea_sample <- sample_size * 0.1
```

After defining the initial parameters, CPU cores are allocated, in this instance, due to machine limitations, 4 cores are allocated for the analysis. A timing function is used to detail time expenditure on the analysis however this has no bearing on the ROC analysis.

A `foreach` cycle follows, which is similar to the standard `for` however allows for parallel computing thanks to the *%dopar%* parameter. In this instance a 100 cycle is represented by $i = 1 : 100$.

A new sample is created in each cycle with *mysample()* function and be processed by each ROC curve approach in *doROCp* which builds the ROC curves and returns p-values from the fit models and Z-test, where values p-value < 0.05 point to a rejection of the null hypothesis, i.e. indicates the covariate is influencing the analysis. This function returns a list of said p-values which are recorded into the *res* dataframe object due to the *'cbind'* parameters.

After completing an i number of cycles, the parallelization is turned off and time spent on the analysis is recorded and displayed.

```

cluster <- makeCluster(4) #number of cores
registerDoParallel(cluster)

start_time <- Sys.time()

res <-
  foreach (i = 1:100, .combine = 'cbind') %dopar% {
    mysample <- makesample(neonatal, surv_sample, dea_
        sample)

    mypvalues <- doROCp(mysample)

  }

parallel::stopCluster(cluster)

end_time <- Sys.time()

print(end_time - start_time)
}
```

Finally, the p-value of each iteration and sample were analysed to reveal the rate at which the methods rejected the null hypotheses, giving the covariate 'sex' relevant weight in the outcome of the low weight infant.

```

sum(res[1,] < 0.05) / ncol(res) # AROC
sum(res[2,] < 0.05) / ncol(res) # cROC Healthy
sum(res[3,] < 0.05) / ncol(res) # cROC Diseased
sum(res[4,] < 0.05) / ncol(res) # Comp2ROC
```

Table 1. Results of the iteration process denoting H_0 hypothesis rejection.

		AROC	cROC		Comp2ROC
			Healthy	Diseased	
n = 500	r_1	0.10	0.10	0.14	0.08
i = 100	r_2	0.15	0.15	0.09	0.05
	r_3	0.06	0.06	0.08	0.06
n = 500	r_1	0.10	0.10	0.10	0.06
i = 500	r_2	0.08	0.08	0.08	0.06
	r_3	0.10	0.10	0.07	0.05
n = 1000	r_1	0.15	0.15	0.15	0.09
i = 100	r_2	0.17	0.17	0.12	0.07
	r_3	0.18	0.18	0.11	0.08
n = 1000	r_1	0.13	0.13	0.15	0.07
i = 500	r_2	0.15	0.15	0.13	0.06
	r_3	0.15	0.15	0.16	0.08
n = 1500	r_1	0.21	0.21	0.15	0.04
i = 100	r_2	0.17	0.17	0.20	0.03
	r_3	0.15	0.15	0.14	0.06
n = 1500	r_1	0.18	0.18	0.19	0.05
i = 500	r_2	0.20	0.20	0.16	0.07
	r_3	0.16	0.16	0.19	0.08

Scripts for *makesample()* and *doROCp()* are detailed in Sect. 5. This analysis was performed three times per sample size, iteration pair - $(n; i)$.

3 Results

Each $(n; i)$ pair rejection rate was recorded with triplicates (r_1, r_2, and r_3) in Table 1, and for illustration purposes one iteration of ROC curves built with each method was also recorded.

Analysing Table 1 across ROC methods we first note the same values presented across all $(n; i)$ pairs for AROC and cROC pertaining to the healthy population. This is a result of the same fit procedure being used in both methods and the adjusted ROC being a weighted average of cROC curves, which, given the 9:1 ratio of healthy and diseased sample populations heavily weighs in the calculation. Looking at the Healthy and Diseased populations of the cROC method however, also shows very slight differences between ratios of null hypothesis rejection.

The adjusted covariates method, performed with `ROCnReg` , can be seen in Fig. 1 displaying the AROC curve, AAUC and confidence intervals. Rejection rates vary between 10–20% with the increase of sample size that can be seen in Table 1. The covariate-specific method, of the same package shows similar rejection rates of 10–20% and 8–19% for surviving and deceased population respectively, the samples are separated by covariate and plotted separately as can be seen in Fig. 2 however, unlike the curve comparison method.

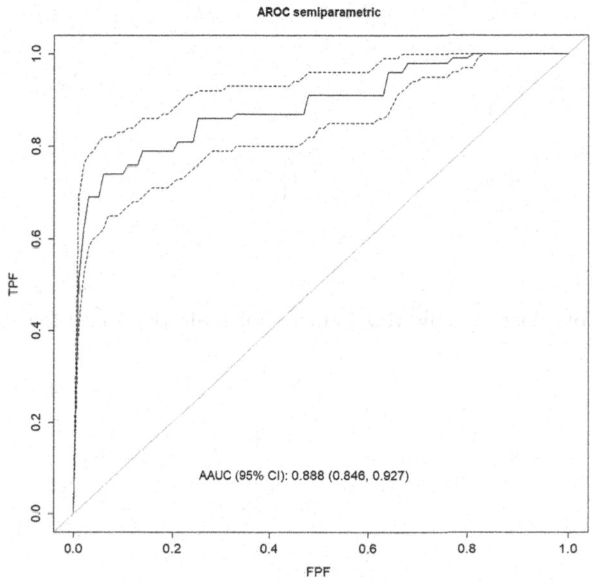

Fig. 1. AROC curve

Another global interpretation of Table 1 shows values ratios of null hypothesis rejection for the Comp2ROC method to be significantly smaller than other methods. Comp2ROC is registering H_0 rejection of Z-test rather than the fit parameters of AROC and cROC, meaning that, instead of measuring the covariate's weight in the adjustment, it records the differences of AUC and performance between covariate specific curves. These differences in global values could mean that, while the theoretical relevant weight of the covariate might be detected in the adjustment methods, the practical performance of the curve remains unchanged in a few instances. This curve comparison method generates ROC curves for both sexes as well as partial AUC performance by sampling lines and performance of sampling data and can be seen in Fig. 3. Z- statistic p-value recorded shows a rejection rate between 5–9% with an exception on r_2 of the $(n = 1500; i = 100)$ pair indicating statistical influence of the 'sex' covariate in these cases.

Results show slight differences with the increase of the sample size (n) however an iteration (i) number above 100 appears to be redundant given no large differences can be found both within or across methods.

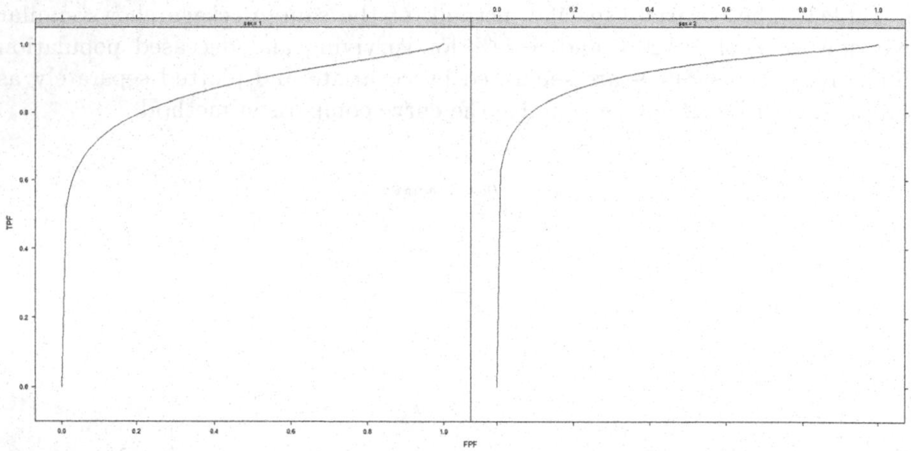

Fig. 2. Covariate specific ROC curves for male (left) and female (right)

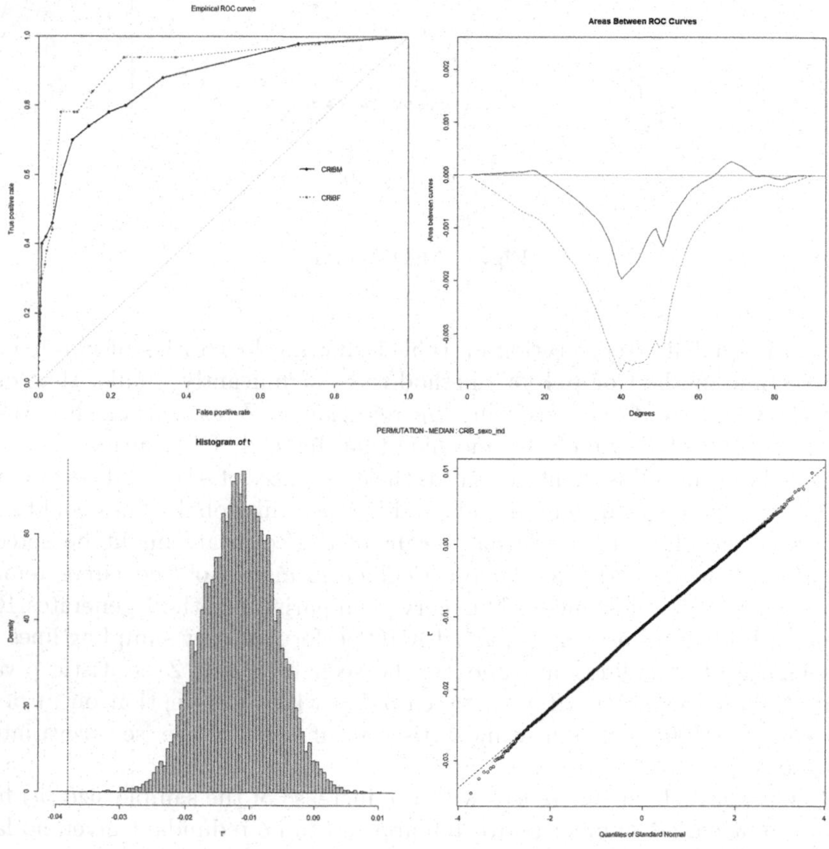

Fig. 3. Comp2ROC results

4 Discussion and Conclusion

While the curve comparison method and Z-test are known and robust procedures to analyse ROC curve and ROC curve data, the adjusted covariate and covariate specific methods are still recent methods that are slowly being implemented across software. A previous R package by the same authors was explored previously [9] however, the new `ROCnReg` shows improvements and additions to these methods keeping the same overall input-output structure as the previous one, which will allow users to transition seamlessly to the more updated version.

This computational work took the initial (null) hypothesis that the CRIB score was not influenced by the sex covariate, and explored said hypothesis by applying the newest methods for ROC curve and covariate analysis in tandem with their tried and tested counterparts and a robust resampling procedure. The results seen in Table 1, detail the rejection rates of the null hypothesis, exhibiting an influence of the covariate on the adjustment of the curve on 10–20% of cases for AROC and cROC methods, as well as a practical distinction between male and female differentiated ROC curves in 5–9% of cases in the Z-test of the `Comp2ROC` methods.

These results show a clear consensus between methods and packages of the convolution factor of the sex covariate in CRIB scores.

Applying parallel computing methods allowed for a more expedient analysis, building a more complete table of results with replicates and different combinations of $(n; i)$ pairs that show a much clearer understanding of the effects of the covariates on the CRIB score as well as how the different methods behave.

The methodology presented in this paper should provide a framework to help guide improvements to similar score systems and markers in their covariate studies that can lead to the development of better calibrated systems for healthcare and all other systems where ROC curves can be implemented.

5 Supplementary

The following code snippets detail the session info for replication purposes as well as functions used in the main article.

```
> sessionInfo()
R version 4.0.4 (2021-02-15)
Platform: x86_64-w64-mingw32/x64 (64-bit)
Running under: Windows 10 x64 (build 19041)

Matrix products: default

locale:
[1] LC_COLLATE=Portuguese_Portugal.1252  LC_CTYPE=
    Portuguese_Portugal.1252
[3] LC_MONETARY=Portuguese_Portugal.1252 LC_NUMERIC=C
[5] LC_TIME=Portuguese_Portugal.1252

```

```
attached base packages:
[1] parallel  stats     graphics  grDevices utils
    datasets  methods   base

other attached packages:
[1] Comp2ROC_1.1.4      boot_1.3-26        ROCR_1.0-7
    gplots_3.1.1        dplyr_1.0.5
[6] ROCnReg_1.0-5       doParallel_1.0.16  iterators_1.0.13
    foreach_1.5.1

loaded via a namespace (and not attached):
 [1] gtools_3.8.2          spatstat.linnet_1.65-3
 tidyselect_1.1.0      purrr_0.3.4
 [5] splines_4.0.4         lattice_0.20-41
 vctrs_0.3.6           generics_0.1.0
 [9] spatstat.utils_2.1-0  mgcv_1.8-33
 utf8_1.1.4            rlang_0.4.10
[13] spatstat.data_2.0-0   pillar_1.5.1
spatstat_2.0-1         glue_1.4.2
[17] matrixStats_0.58.0    lifecycle_1.0.0
spatstat.core_1.65-5   MatrixModels_0.5-0
[21] moments_0.14          caTools_1.18.1
codetools_0.2-18       SparseM_1.81
[25] quantreg_5.85         fansi_0.4.2
Rcpp_1.0.6             KernSmooth_2.23-18
[29] conquer_1.0.2         tensor_1.5
abind_1.4-5            deldir_0.2-10
[33] nor1mix_1.3-0         spatstat.sparse_1.2-1
polyclip_1.10-0        grid_4.0.4
[37] quadprog_1.5-8        tools_4.0.4
bitops_1.0-6           magrittr_2.0.1
[41] goftest_1.2-2         tibble_3.1.0
np_0.60-10             crayon_1.4.1
[45] pbivnorm_0.6.0        pkgconfig_2.0.3
ellipsis_0.3.1         MASS_7.3-53
[49] Matrix_1.3-2          cubature_2.0.4.1
R6_2.5.0               rpart_4.1-15
[53] spatstat.geom_1.65-5  nlme_3.1-152
compiler_4.0.4
```

The *makesample()* function, used in each iteration of the process, receives the full dataset and survival and death population sizes as inputs, with these parameters and using `dplyr` sample population are selected and bound together with *rbind()* returning a dataframe of sample population ready to be processed.

```
makesample <- function(dataframe, surv_size, dea_size) {
  surv1 <-
    dplyr::sample_n(dataframe[dataframe$survival == 0 &
```

```
                                          dataframe$sex == 1,],
                                          surv_size / 2,
                                          replace = T)
  surv2 <-
    dplyr::sample_n(dataframe[dataframe$survival == 0 &
                                          dataframe$sex == 2,],
                                          surv_size / 2,
                                          replace = T)
  dea1 <-
    dplyr::sample_n(dataframe[dataframe$survival == 1 &
                                          dataframe$sex == 1,],
                                          dea_size / 2,
                                          replace = T)
  dea2 <-
    dplyr::sample_n(dataframe[dataframe$survival == 1 &
                                          dataframe$sex == 2,],
                                          dea_size / 2,
                                          replace = T)

  nn <- rbind(surv1, surv2, dea1, dea2)
}
```

The function *doROCp()* is the main process for the article, it receives the dataframe and runs all three ROC analysis methods. Given the focus of the article on a specific covariate and dataframe, all parameters for each ROC procedure are already entered, however, one can easily generalize the function to include these parameters in the input.

As mentioned the function will compute each ROC curve and save the different p-values according to how each function records the object. Afterwards, the function returns a list of all 4 p-values ordered by function to always know which p-value relates to each method.

```
doROCp <- function(mysample) {
  # - AROC
  spCribSex <- ROCnReg::AROC.sp(
    formula.h = 'crib ~ sex',
    group = 'survival',
    tag.h = 0,
    data = mysample
  )
  spvalue <-
    signif(as.numeric(summary(spCribSex$fit)$coefficients
       [2, 4]), 4)

  #----
  # - cROC
  cspCS <- ROCnReg::cROC.sp(
    formula.h = 'crib ~ sex',
```

```
    formula.d = 'crib ~ sex',
    group = 'survival',
    tag.h = 0,
    data = mysample
  )
  pvalue_h <-
    signif(as.numeric(summary(cspCS$fit$h)$coefficients[2,
        4]), 4)
  pvalue_d <-
    signif(as.numeric(summary(cspCS$fit$d)$coefficients[2,
        4]), 4)
  #----
  # - Comp2ROC
  nnM <- mysample[mysample$sex == 1 , c('crib', 'survival'
    )]
  nnF <- mysample[mysample$sex == 2 , c('crib', 'survival'
    )]


  datafromfunc <-
    comp_converter(nnM, nnF, 'survival', 'survival', FALSE
      )
  results <-
    Comp2ROC::roc.curves.boot(datafromfunc, 1000, 0.05,
        name = 'CRIB_sexo_ind', "CRIBM", "CRIBF", FALSE)
  #----

  res <-
    c(spvalue, pvalue_h, pvalue_d, results$pvalue1) #[AROC
      ,cROC_h,cROC_d,Comp2ROC]
  res
}
```

The previous function uses the *comp_converter()* function to perform the ROC curve comparison of the `Comp2ROC` package. This function is generalized and converts the initial dataframe to the structure needed for this specific package.

```
comp_converter <- function(df1, df2, rescol1, rescol2,
    related) {
  if (length(df1) == 2 && length(df2 == 2)) {
    var1 <- names(df1)[names(df1) != rescol1]
    var2 <- names(df2)[names(df2) != rescol2]

    list1 <- df1[order(df1[[rescol1]]), ]
    list2 <- df2[order(df2[[rescol2]]), ]


    listall <- list(list1[[var1]] ,
                    list1[[rescol1]] ,
```

```
                    list2[[var2]] ,
                    list2[[rescol2]])

    var1n <- paste(var1, '1', sep = '_')
    var2n <- paste(var2, '2', sep = '_')
    rescol1n <- paste(rescol1, '1', sep = '_')
    rescol2n <- paste(rescol2, '2', sep = '_')

    names(listall) <- c(var1n, rescol1n, var2n, rescol2n)


    comp2rocdata <- read.manually.introduced(
      listall,
      modality1 = var1n,
      testdirection1 = TRUE,
      modality2 = var2n,
      testdirection2 = TRUE,
      status1 = rescol1n,
      related = related,
      status2 = rescol2n
    )


  } else {
    stop('Dataframes must have 2 columns each')
  }


}
```

References

1. Pepe, M.S.: The Statistical Evaluation of Medical Tests for Classification and Prediction. Oxford University Press, Oxford (2003)
2. Rodriguez-Alvarez, M.X., et al.: Bootstrap-based procedures for inference in nonparametric receiver-operating characteristic curve regression analysis. Stat. Methods Med. Res. **27**(3), 740–764 (2018)
3. Janes, H., Pepe, M.S.: Adjusting for covariate effects on classification accuracy using the covariate-adjusted receiver operating characteristic curve. Biometrika **96**(2), 371–382 (2009)
4. Rodriguez-Alvarez, M.X., Inacio, V.: ROCnReg: ROC Curve Inference with and without Covariates (2021). https://CRAN.R-project.org/package=ROCnReg, R package version 1.0-5
5. Braga, A.C., et al.: An alternative method for global and partial comparison of two diagnostic systems based on ROC curves. J. Stat. Comput. Simul. **83**(2), 307–325 (2013)

6. Machado e Costa, F., Braga, A.C.: NeonatalPortugal2018. Mendeley Data (2019). https://doi.org/10.17632/br8tnh3h47.1
7. Rodriguez-Alvarez, M.X., Inacio, V.: AROC: covariate-adjusted receiver operating characteristic curve inference (2018). https://CRAN.R-project.org/package=AROC, R package version 1.0
8. Braga, A.C., et al.: Comp2ROC: compare two ROC curves that intersect (2016). https://CRAN.R-project.org/package=Comp2ROC, R package version 1.1.4
9. Machado e Costa, F., Braga, A.C.: Adjusting ROC curve for covariates with AROC R package. In: Gervasi, O., et al. (eds.) ICCSA 2020. LNCS, vol. 12251, pp. 185–198. Springer, Cham (2020). https://doi.org/10.1007/978-3-030-58808-3_15

A Time Series Decomposition Algorithm Based on Gaussian Processes

Massimo Bilancia[1](✉), Fabio Manca[2], and Giovanni Sansaro[3]

[1] Ionian Department in Legal and Economic System of Mediterranean: Society, Environment, Culture (DSJGEM), Via Duomo 259, 74123 Taranto, Italy
massimo.bilancia@uniba.it

[2] Department of Education, Psychology, Communication (FORPSICOM), University of Bari Aldo Moro, Bari, Italy

[3] Graduate Program in Data Science, Department of Informatics (DIB), University of Bari Aldo Moro, Bari, Italy

Abstract. In this paper, we present an algorithm for decomposing time series based on Gaussian processes. Gaussian processes can be viewed as infinite-dimensional probability distributions over smooth functions and also provide a natural basis for additive decomposition of time series, since we can sum mutually independent Gaussian processes with a simple and elegant algebra involving covariance kernels. The component estimation algorithm we propose in this paper is general and does not depend on the number of components, nor on the correlation structure and interpretation of each component. Specifically, the proposed algorithm is based on nonparametric Bayesian Gaussian process regression, where the log-likelihood covariance is suitably structured to account for the presence of additive subcomponents. The numerical parameter estimation procedure finds MAP estimates by maximizing the unnormalized log-posterior density, with a great advantage in terms of computational cost and efficiency.

We apply our proposal to real data based on a time series of daily COVID-19 confirmed cases and daily swabs administered in Italy. The curve of daily new cases follows an oscillatory pattern, as the ratio between the number of new cases and the number of tested individuals is locally constant, while the number of daily new cases is systematically lower on some days of the week, as fewer swabs are performed. This wavelike pattern must be considered a nuisance that does not reflect the true dynamics of contagion, as it is the result of variability in human activities. We show how such a cyclic component can be successfully filtered out using the proposed algorithm.

Keywords: Time series decomposition · Gaussian processes · Bayesian hierarchical modelling · Computational methods for Bayesian statistics

1 Introduction

Real-world time series data exhibit complex patterns involving trend, oscillatory waveforms, and noise [1]. A robust decomposition of these components greatly

O. Gervasi et al. (Eds.): ICCSA 2021, LNCS 12952, pp. 577–592, 2021.
https://doi.org/10.1007/978-3-030-86973-1_41

facilitates typical time series tasks such as prediction and classification. Typical forms of fluctuations are: a) A smooth long-term tendency, the trend. b) A cyclical movement superimposed on the smooth trend. c) A less or more regular cyclical movement within a year, the seasonality. d) Residual or unexplained variation (noise). Whether or not a component is present in a particular time series depends on the human activities underlying the phenomenon and the frequency of measurement. In any case, it has often been assumed that the four components vary independently and interact on a linear additive scale. Additive time series decomposition models are an important tool in a data scientist's arsenal, and there are many ways to extract the trend and other components of a time series.

One of the first structured model-based approaches developed since the late 1970s was the LOESS (LOcal regrESSion) method for modeling trend and seasonal components using polynomial regression, which has several advantages over early decomposition methods. The STL algorithm based on LOESS is very versatile and robust, since the seasonal component is allowed to change over time and the smoothing of the trend cycle can also be controlled by the user [2]. Apart from some minor technical difficulties, the STL method is very easy to use and available on most data analysis-oriented programming platforms, such as R or Python.

However, a major drawback of classical methods based on additive decompositions is that they are rigidly bound to the subdivision into the three components trend/cycle/seasonality. Greater flexibility is only possible by introducing a new ad hoc decomposition model specific to the problem at hand. Another drawback common to all these approaches is that they are not based on stochastic processes and it is therefore impossible to determine the uncertainty associated with the subcomponent estimates. With this in mind, we have developed a decomposition algorithm based on Gaussian processes, a class of stochastic processes endowed with great modeling flexibility [3,4].

A Gaussian process can be viewed as an infinite-dimensional probability distribution over smooth functions [5]. In practice, we do not need to work with such infinite-dimensional function spaces, since it is sufficient to evaluate the probability distribution over the function at any finite collection of points. Gaussian processes also provide a natural basis for additive decomposition of time series, since we can sum mutually independent Gaussian processes with a simple and elegant algebra. The components of an additive Gaussian model can be structured very similarly to those of classical decompositions, with no restriction on their number and internal structure. Moreover, the component estimation algorithm we describe in this paper is general and does not depend on the number of components or on the correlation structure and interpretation of each component. Specifically, the proposed algorithm is based on the nonparametric Bayesian Gaussian process regression, where the log-likelihood covariance is suitably structured to account for the presence of additive subcomponents. The numerical parameter estimation procedure finds MAP estimates by maximizing the unnormalized log-posterior density, with a great advantage in terms of computational cost and efficiency.

We present a real-world experiment based on the time series of the daily total number of COVID-19 confirmed new cases and administered molecular swabs in Italy from February 21, 2020 to January 14, 2021. The curve of daily new cases follows an oscillating pattern, as the ratio of the number of new cases to that of tested subjects is locally constant, while the number of daily new cases is systematically lower on some days of the week, as fewer swabs are performed (a typical example of this pattern occurs on Monday, when most of the reported cases were tested on the previous Saturday and Sunday). This wave pattern must be considered a nuisance that does not reflect the true dynamics of contagion, as it is the result of variability in human activity, and its impact on subsequent analyses cannot be quantified. We show how the cyclic component can be successfully filtered out using the proposed algorithm.

The paper is organized as follows. Section 2 briefly recalls some alternative approaches to time series decomposition based on principal component analysis (PCA) and presents their advantages and disadvantages. Section 3 introduces the main definitions. Section 4 with the algebra of Gaussian processes and their covariance function and the way additive models can be structured. Section 5 introduces Bayesian Gaussian process regression and its approximate Bayesian inference, and provides the decomposition formula for computing the components of the additive decomposition. Section 6 presents the case study mentioned above. Section 7 draws final conclusions and suggests future research questions.

2 Related Work

Singular spectrum analysis (SSA) is a distinct technique related to additive time series decomposition, which is essentially PCA applied to lagged copies of the original data [6,7]. In the first stage, the time series is embedded in a lower-dimensional vector space of dimension M by considering M lagged copies of the data. In the second stage, the $M \times M$ lag covariance matrix estimator of the lag matrix is computed. Then, the lag-covariance matrix is diagonalized to obtain spectral information about the time series. Finally, temporal principal components are computed, and such components can be grouped to reconstruct a decomposition into a fixed number of subcomponent series. Extensions to multivariate series or 2D data (images or spatial data) are also available [8].

While SSA has significant advantages from a computational point of view, with many fast and stable programs available for extracting PCs, there are some drawbacks and differences with our approach that are worth some additional comments. From a purely algorithmic point of view, SSA is automatic and easy to use. However, the lag parameter M is a free and its choice is not obvious, and the obtained decomposition is strongly dependent on the choice of M. Finally, grouping the temporal principal components into a small number of subcomponents is not a simple task. The decomposition can be considered reasonable if each reconstructed subseries can be classified as part of either a trend or a periodic component or noise. To this end, a complete theory of SSA separability has been introduced that attempts to answer questions such as which components can be separated by SSA and how to choose M and perform proper grouping for the extraction of interpretable components [9].

Although this theory is highly developed, it is often not easy to apply in practice. The main difference with our approach is that the interpretation of the components obtained by SSA is done after the decomposition of the original time series. In our case, on the other hand, the correlation structure and the interpretation of the additive components are determined before the execution of the algorithm. In some applications this fact can be a drawback, while in others it can be useful to accurately calibrate the decomposition model to the problem at hand.

3 Gaussian Processes

Denote f a real-valued continuous-time stochastic process and $\mathcal{X} \subseteq \mathbb{R}^D$ the input space. Sequences of input data points $\mathbf{x}_1, \mathbf{x}_2, \ldots, \mathbf{x}_n \in \mathcal{X}$ are embedded in a q-dimensional space, where they may be linearly ordered since the index reflects the temporal ordering of the trajectories. A stochastic process f is said to be Gaussian if $(f(\mathbf{x}_1), f(\mathbf{x}_2), \ldots, f(\mathbf{x}_n))^\top$ is an n-dimensional Gaussian vector for all $\mathbf{x}_1, \mathbf{x}_2, \ldots, \mathbf{x}_n \in \mathcal{X}$ and all $n \geq 1$. In other words, a Gaussian stochastic process is an infinite collection of random variables such that any finite-dimensional distribution is multivariate Gaussian [10]. Each Gaussian process can be uniquely assigned by its mean function and its covariance kernel:

$$\mu(\mathbf{x}) = \mathsf{E}\left[f(\mathbf{x})\right], \quad \forall\, \mathbf{x} \in \mathcal{X}, \tag{1}$$

$$\kappa(\mathbf{x}, \mathbf{x}') = \mathsf{Cov}\left[f(\mathbf{x}), f(\mathbf{x}')\right], \quad \forall\, \mathbf{x}, \mathbf{x}' \in \mathcal{X}. \tag{2}$$

For a given mean function $\mu(\mathbf{x})$ and kernel function $\kappa(\mathbf{x}, \mathbf{x}')$, there exists a Gaussian process f whose finite-dimensional distributions are compatible with the two functions [11], which is given by:

$$f(\mathbf{x}) \sim \mathcal{GP}\left(\mu(\mathbf{x}), \kappa(\mathbf{x}, \mathbf{x}')\right). \tag{3}$$

Some examples of trajectories simulated from a Gaussian process are shown in Fig. 1. On the left side we have a set of realizations from a Gaussian process with square-exponential covariance function, while on the right side the trajectories were simulated from a Gaussian process with a periodic covariance function of period $p = 7$ (see Sect. 4 for the relevant definitions).

4 The Algebra of Covariance Functions

A time series decomposition model is based on an appropriate decomposition of the underlying data generating process into additive subcomponents. To this

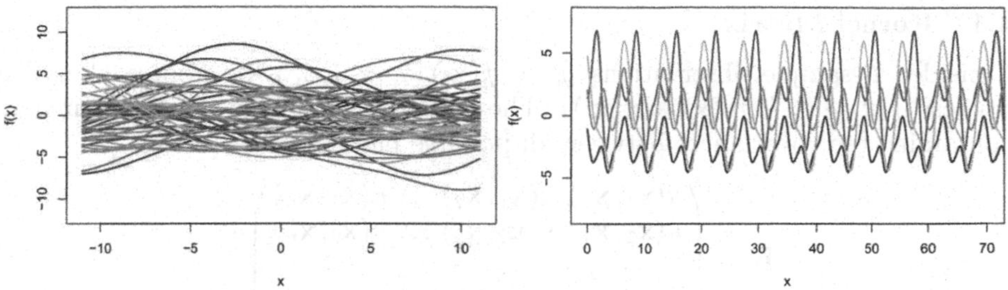

Fig. 1. Simulated trajectories from a Gaussian process.

end, let $\kappa_1(\mathbf{x}_{(1)}, \mathbf{x}'_{(1)})$ and $\kappa_2(\mathbf{x}_{(2)}, \mathbf{x}'_{(2)})$ be valid covariance functions defined on the input spaces $\mathcal{X}_1$ and $\mathcal{X}_2$, respectively. Then:

$$\kappa(\mathbf{x}, \mathbf{x}') = \kappa_1(\mathbf{x}_{(1)}, \mathbf{x}'_{(1)}) + \kappa_2(\mathbf{x}_{(2)}, \mathbf{x}'_{(2)}) \quad \text{(direct sum)}, \tag{4}$$

$$\kappa(\mathbf{x}, \mathbf{x}') = \kappa_1(\mathbf{x}_{(1)}, \mathbf{x}'_{(1)})\kappa_2(\mathbf{x}_{(2)}, \mathbf{x}'_{(2)}) \quad \text{(tensor product)}, \tag{5}$$

are valid covariance functions defined on $\mathcal{X}_1 \times \mathcal{X}_2$.

Given two independent Gaussian processes f_1 and f_2 whose covariance function is given respectively by $\kappa_1(\mathbf{x}_{(1)}, \mathbf{x}'_{(1)})$ and $\kappa_2(\mathbf{x}_{(2)}, \mathbf{x}'_{(2)})$, the additive sum:

$$f(\mathbf{x}) = f_1(\mathbf{x}_{(1)}) + f_2(\mathbf{x}_{(2)}) \tag{6}$$

is itself a Gaussian process whose covariance function is given by the direct sum (4).

We can extend this approach to define an additive model using D mutually independent Gaussian processes $f_1, \ldots, f_D$:

$$f(\mathbf{x}) = f_1(x_{(1)}) + f_2(x_{(2)}) + \cdots + f_D(x_{(D)}), \tag{7}$$

where D is the size of the input space. Each Gaussian process f_i can be defined on its own one-dimensional input space. The covariance function of the additive model is the direct sum of D covariance functions [12].

A covariance function can be further classified into the following categories:

- stationary: $\kappa(\mathbf{x}, \mathbf{x}')$ depends on the input variables only by the step size $\mathbf{x} - \mathbf{x}'$
- isotropic: $\kappa(\mathbf{x}, \mathbf{x}')$ depends on the input variables only by the Euclidean distance $r = \|\mathbf{x} - \mathbf{x}'\|$

If a covariance function does not satisfy at least the stationary condition, it is said to be nonstationary. The class of these covariance functions is invariant to translations of the coordinate system. Isotropic covariance functions are invariant to translations, rotations, and reflections (rigid motions) of the coordinate system.

4.1 Kernel Matrix

Consider T sample observations $y_i = f(\mathbf{x}_i)$, $i = 1, 2, ..., n$, from a Gaussian process $f(\mathbf{x}) \sim \mathcal{GP}(m(\mathbf{x}), \kappa(\mathbf{x}, \mathbf{x}'))$. The kernel matrix $\mathbf{K}$ is the Gram matrix containing the covariances between all possible pairs of observations:

$$\mathbf{K} = \begin{pmatrix} \kappa(\mathbf{x}_1, \mathbf{x}_1) & \kappa(\mathbf{x}_1, \mathbf{x}_2) & \dots & \kappa(\mathbf{x}_1, \mathbf{x}_n) \\ \kappa(\mathbf{x}_2, \mathbf{x}_1) & \kappa(\mathbf{x}_2, \mathbf{x}_2) & \dots & \kappa(\mathbf{x}_2, \mathbf{x}_n) \\ \vdots & \vdots & \ddots & \vdots \\ \kappa(\mathbf{x}_n, \mathbf{x}_1) & \kappa(\mathbf{x}_n, \mathbf{x}_2) & \dots & \kappa(\mathbf{x}_n, \mathbf{x}_n) \end{pmatrix}. \tag{8}$$

To be a valid covariance function, the resulting kernel matrix must be symmetric definite positive. Conversely, any symmetric definite positive matrix is the kernel matrix of a Gaussian process. Classes of valid covariance functions used to model the correlation structure of additive subcomponents are:

Squared Exponential Kernel. Squared exponential kernel (or Radial Basis Function) is an isotropic kernel having the following expression:

$$\kappa_{\mathsf{SE}}(x, x') = \sigma^2 \exp\left(-\frac{(x - x')^2}{2\ell^2}\right). \tag{9}$$

The characteristic length scale ℓ controls the smoothing of trajectories, since it can be shown that the expected value of the number of times a trajectory crosses the x-axis in the unit interval is equal to $(2\pi\ell)^{-1}$. This means that as ℓ increases, the function becomes less irregular and smoother as it wobbles less quickly above and below the x-axis. The amplitude σ determines the maximum excursion of the trajectories.

Periodic Kernel. Mapping a one-dimensional input variable $x \in \mathcal{X}$ onto the two-dimensional u-space $u(x) = (\cos(x), \sin(x))$, allows us to define a periodic stationary kernel [13,14]. Using the squared exponential kernel in u-space, we can define a periodic stationary covariance function of period 2π:

$$\kappa_{\mathsf{P}}(x, x') = \sigma^2 \exp\left(-\frac{2\sin^2(\frac{x-x'}{2})}{\ell^2}\right), \tag{10}$$

as:

$$(\cos(x_i) - \cos(x_j))^2 + (\sin(x_i) - \sin(x_j))^2 = 4\sin^2\left(\frac{x_i - x_j}{2}\right).$$

We can easily rescale the covariance function defined above to obtain the following covariance function of period p:

$$\kappa_{\mathsf{P}}(x, x') = \sigma^2 \exp\left(-\frac{2\sin^2(\frac{\pi(x-x')}{p})}{\ell^2}\right). \tag{11}$$

The parameter σ controls the amplitude of the trajectories, while ℓ controls the regularity of the waveform.

Locally Periodic Kernel. Multiplying a quadratic exponential kernel by a periodic kernel of period p can increase flexibility:

$$\kappa_{\mathsf{LP}}(x,x') = \sigma^2 \exp\left(-\frac{(x-x')^2}{2\ell_1^2}\right) \exp\left(-\frac{2\sin^2(\frac{\pi(x-x')}{p})}{\ell_2^2}\right). \tag{12}$$

The trajectories of the resulting Gaussian process are periodic time series of period p where the waveform is not stationary since its amplitude may change over time (see Fig. 2 where some synthetic trajectories are shown).

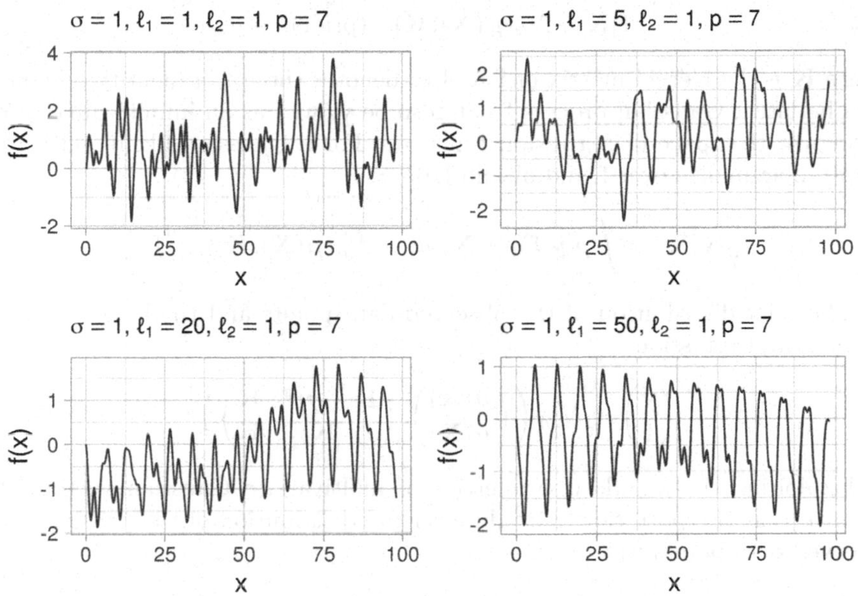

Fig. 2. Four trajectories drawn (discretized over $n = 500$ points) from a GP with locally periodic covariance function of period $p = 7$, for different values of σ, ℓ_1 and ℓ_2.

5 Gaussian Process Regression

The basic framework of our decomposition model is a noisy Gaussian process regression model, which can be expressed as $y_i = f(\mathbf{x}_i) + \epsilon_i$, $i = 1, 2, ..., n$, with $f(\mathbf{x}) \sim \mathcal{GP}(\mu(\mathbf{x}), \kappa(\mathbf{x}, \mathbf{x}'))$ and $\epsilon(\mathbf{x}) \sim \mathcal{GP}(0, \sigma_\epsilon^2 \mathbb{1}(\mathbf{x} = \mathbf{x}'))$. The Gaussian processes f and ϵ are assumed to be independent, where $\mathbb{1}(\cdot)$ denotes the indicator function. We first assume that the mean, the covariance function of f and the noise variance σ_ϵ^2 are known.

Given the design matrix $\mathbf{X} = (\mathbf{x}_1, ..., \mathbf{x}_n)^\top \in \mathbb{R}^{n \times D}$, we define:

$$\mathbf{y} = (y_1, y_2, ..., y_n)^\top, \tag{13}$$

$$\mathbf{f} = (f(\mathbf{x}_1), f(\mathbf{x}_2), ..., f(\mathbf{x}_n))^\top \tag{14}$$

$$\boldsymbol{\mu}(\mathbf{X}) = (\mu(\mathbf{x}_1), \mu(\mathbf{x}_2), ..., \mu(\mathbf{x}_n))^\top . \tag{15}$$

A nonparametric Gaussian process regression model can be formulated as the following Bayesian hierarchical model with a Gaussian likelihood and a latent Gaussian process prior [15]:

$$\begin{aligned} \mathbf{y}|\mathbf{f} &\sim \mathcal{N}_n(\mathbf{f}, \sigma_\epsilon^2 \mathbb{I}_n) \quad &\text{(likelihood)}, \\ \mathbf{f}|\mathbf{X} &\sim \mathcal{N}_n(\boldsymbol{\mu}(\mathbf{X}), \mathbf{K}) \quad &\text{(prior)}, \end{aligned}$$

where $\mathbf{K}$ is the Kernel matrix of $\mathbf{f}$ and $\mathbb{I}_n$ denotes the $n \times n$ identity matrix.

The latent Gaussian process $\mathbf{f}$ can also be viewed as an infinite-dimensional prior over the space of regression functions. For a Gaussian likelihood we can simply marginalize over $\mathbf{f}$ and obtain [16]:

$$p(\mathbf{y}|\mathbf{X}) = \int p(\mathbf{y}|\mathbf{f}) p(\mathbf{f}|\mathbf{X}) \, d\mathbf{f} \sim \mathcal{N}_n(\boldsymbol{\mu}(\mathbf{X}), \mathbf{K} + \sigma_\epsilon^2 \mathbb{I}_N) \tag{16}$$

The joint distribution of the observed data points and the latent Gaussian process has expression:

$$\begin{pmatrix} \mathbf{y} \\ \mathbf{f} \end{pmatrix} \sim \mathcal{N}_{2n} \left(\begin{pmatrix} \boldsymbol{\mu}(\mathbf{X}) \\ \boldsymbol{\mu}(\mathbf{X}) \end{pmatrix}, \begin{pmatrix} \mathbf{K} + \sigma_\epsilon^2 \mathbb{I}_n & \mathbf{K} \\ \mathbf{K} & \mathbf{K} \end{pmatrix} \right). \tag{17}$$

Exploiting the standard properties of multivariate Gaussian vectors [17], we have that the posterior finite-dimensional distribution of the process at the observed data points is:

$$\mathbf{f}|\mathbf{y}, \mathbf{X} \sim \mathcal{N}_n(\boldsymbol{\mu}_{\mathsf{post}}, \mathbf{K}_{\mathsf{post}}), \tag{18}$$

with:

$$\boldsymbol{\mu}_{\mathsf{post}} = \boldsymbol{\mu}(\mathbf{X}) + \mathbf{K}(\mathbf{K} + \sigma_\epsilon^2 \mathbb{I}_n)^{-1} (\mathbf{y} - \boldsymbol{\mu}(\mathbf{X})), \tag{19}$$

$$\mathbf{K}_{\mathsf{post}} = \mathbf{K} - \mathbf{K}(\mathbf{K} + \sigma_\epsilon^2 \mathbb{I}_n)^{-1} \mathbf{K}. \tag{20}$$

Since a Gaussian process is flexible enough to model the regression function even in the case where the mean function is identically zero, i.e. $\boldsymbol{\mu}(\mathbf{X}) \equiv \mathbf{0}$, in this case the posterior mean obviously reduces to:

$$\boldsymbol{\mu}_{\mathsf{post}} = \mathbf{K}(\mathbf{K} + \sigma_\epsilon^2 \mathbb{I}_n)^{-1} \mathbf{y}, \tag{21}$$

while the expression of the posterior covariance matrix is left unchanged. This marginal likelihood model is computationally more efficient since it uses a lower-dimensional parameter space. The latent Gaussian process formulation is useful when the dependent variable is non-Gaussian and is not pursued further.

5.1 Decomposition Formulas

If $f(\mathbf{x})$ is an additive a-Gaussian process, see Eq. (7), then each f_i is a Gaussian process with finite-dimensional posterior mean and posterior covariance matrix, given respectively by:

$$\mu_{\text{post}}(f_i) = K_i(\mathbf{K} + \sigma_\epsilon^2 \mathbb{I}_n)^{-1}\mathbf{y}, \tag{22}$$
$$K_{\text{post}}(f_i) = K_i - K_i(\mathbf{K} + \sigma_\epsilon^2 \mathbb{I}_n)^{-1} K_i, \tag{23}$$

where, for $i = 1, 2, ..., D$:

$$f_i(x_{(i)}) \overset{\text{ind.}}{\sim} \mathcal{GP}(0, \kappa_i(x_{(i)}, x'_{(i)})), \tag{24}$$

and:

$$\mathbf{K} = K_1 + K_2 + \cdots + K_D.$$

The expressions (22) and (23) fully determine a Bayesian estimate of the trajectory of the i-th component entering the additive model.

5.2 Approximate Bayesian Inference

When the covariance function depends on a vector of unknown parameters $\boldsymbol{\theta}$, we have the following extended hierarchical model:

$$\mathbf{y}|\mathbf{X}, \boldsymbol{\theta}, \sigma_\epsilon^2 \sim \mathcal{N}_n(\mathbf{0}, \mathbf{K}(\boldsymbol{\theta}) + \sigma_\epsilon^2 \mathbb{I}_n), \tag{25}$$
$$\boldsymbol{\psi} \sim \pi(\boldsymbol{\phi}). \tag{26}$$

where $\boldsymbol{\psi} = (\boldsymbol{\theta}, \sigma_\epsilon^2)^\top$ and $\pi(\boldsymbol{\phi})$ is a joint prior distribution for both kernel parameters $\boldsymbol{\theta}$ and the noise variance σ_ϵ^2, with fixed hyperparameters $\boldsymbol{\phi}$.

Combining the marginal likelihood with the prior, we get an unnormalized posterior, and inference could be done using standard Markov Chain Monte Carlo (MCMC) methods [18,19]. In principle, we could sample from the joint posterior of the parameters and the finite-dimensional distribution of the process using the factorization:

$$p(\mathbf{f}, \boldsymbol{\psi}|\mathbf{y}, \mathbf{X}) = p(\mathbf{f}|\boldsymbol{\psi}, \mathbf{X}, \mathbf{y})p(\boldsymbol{\psi}|\mathbf{y}), \tag{27}$$

and sequentially simulate $\boldsymbol{\psi}$ from $p(\boldsymbol{\psi}|\mathbf{y})$, using MCMC, and f from $p(\mathbf{f}|\boldsymbol{\psi}, \mathbf{X}, \mathbf{y})$, which is in closed form. A major problem with this approach is that its basic complexity is $\mathcal{O}(n^3)$, due to the inversion of a $n \times n$ matrix at each MCMC step, which is prohibitive for large data sets. There are quite a number of proposals to solve this problem [20–22].

In practice, we use the posterior modes $\widehat{\boldsymbol{\psi}}_{\text{MAP}}$, obtained by maximizing the unnormalized log-posterior density:

$$\widehat{\boldsymbol{\psi}}_{\text{MAP}} = \arg\max_{\boldsymbol{\psi}} \log p(\mathbf{y}|\mathbf{X}, \boldsymbol{\psi}) + \log \pi(\boldsymbol{\phi}). \tag{28}$$

Having found the MAP estimate for the hyperparameters, we can reconstruct the trajectories of each process component using (22) and (23). This solution ignores the uncertainty in posterior estimates of ψ but it can be handled appropriately using feasible iterative maximization algorithms. For example, Stan (a high-level language in which the user specifies a Bayesian hierarchical model and the posterior computations are implemented automatically) is particularly efficient at computing the gradients of the marginal likelihood as well as estimating the marginal posterior modes using a second-order iterative quasi-Netwon method, known as the Broyden-Fletcher-Goldfarb-Shanno (BFGS) algorithm, which forms an approximation of the second-order partial derivatives and the Hessian matrix by using only gradient information [23].

6 Example

The data used in this experiment are the time series of the daily total number of COVID-19 new cases and molecular swabs administered in Italy from February 21, 2020, when the first cases were officially reported, to January 14, 2021. Scraping of COVID-19 national data was performed directly from Wikipedia, using the template *COVID-19 pandemic data/Italy medical cases*, which aggregates daily data from regions and autonomous provinces (PP/AA) collected by the Ministry of Health and Istituto Superiore di Sanità (ISS) [24].

The curve of daily new cases exhibits a characteristic sawtooth pattern (see Fig. 3), as the ratio of the number of new cases to the number of subjects tested is locally constant (in the sense that it is approximately constant over short time windows), while the number of new cases is systematically lower on some days of the week, as fewer swabs are performed (a typical example of this pattern occurs on Monday, when most of the reported cases were tested on the previous Saturday and Sunday).

Such a wave pattern observed in the outcome data takes the form of a weekly cyclic oscillation with time-dependent amplitudes. This oscillatory wave exhibits phase coupling with the number of daily swabs administered, in the sense that the phase difference between the series of daily new cases and that of daily swabs remains constant for obvious reasons. However, this wave pattern must be considered a nuisance that does not reflect the actual dynamics of contagion. Rather, it is the result of variability in human activity, and its impact on subsequent analyses cannot be quantified unless different scenarios are considered for data analysis. It is therefore reasonable to construct an alternative dataset in which the periodic component is filtered out by the proposed algorithm based on Gaussian processes.

6.1 Model Setting

For time series data, we have a single common input variable $\mathbf{x} \equiv t \in \mathbb{R}$, where t is the time index. We consider the following additive model:

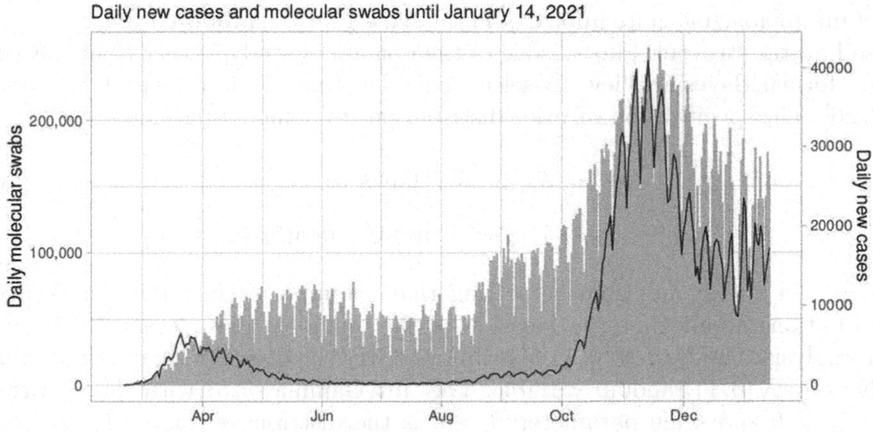

Fig. 3. Number of daily newly diagnosed cases and molecular swabs in Italy, between 21 February 2020 and 14 January 2021. Daily new cases are represented by the solid line; the bar graph shows the number of daily molecular swabs administered.

$$f(t) = f_1(t) + f_2(t) + f_3(t) + \epsilon_t, \quad t = 1, 2, \ldots, n, \tag{29}$$

where $\epsilon_t \sim \mathcal{N}(0, \sigma_\epsilon^2)$ models the Gaussian white noise. The covariance function of this Gaussian process is:

$$\kappa(t,t') = \kappa_1(t,t') + \kappa_2(t,t') + \kappa_3(t,t') + \sigma_\epsilon^2 \mathbb{1}(t = t'), \tag{30}$$

with different terms representing different scales and periodicities. In particular:

- $f_1(t)$ models the smooth long-term variation, using a Squared Exponential kernel:

$$\kappa_1(t,t') = \sigma_1^2 \exp\left(-\frac{(t-t')^2}{2\ell_1^2}\right). \tag{31}$$

- $f_2(t)$ models short-term variation, using a Squared Exponential kernel (with different parameters)

$$\kappa_2(t,t') = \sigma_2^2 \exp\left(-\frac{(t-t')^2}{2\ell_2^2}\right). \tag{32}$$

- f_3 represents the weekly periodic pattern with time-dependent amplitudes due to daily variations in the number of tests administered. In this case, the correlation structure can be conveniently described by a locally periodic kernel with period $p = 7$:

$$\kappa_3(t,t') = \sigma_3^2 \exp\left(-\frac{(t-t')^2}{2\ell_{3.1}^2}\right) \exp\left(-\frac{2\sin^2\frac{\pi(t-t')}{7}}{\ell_{3.2}^2}\right). \tag{33}$$

Our approach is quite informal, in the sense that the proposed specification is based on the structural knowledge of the domain of study, rather than insisting on a formal Bayesian view to select a model from a set of candidate models [25,26]. The specification of prior distributions over model parameters is:

$$\sigma_1, \sigma_2, \sigma_3 \overset{\text{ind.}}{\sim} \text{Half-}\mathcal{N}(0,1), \tag{34}$$

$$\ell_1, \ell_2, \ell_{3.1}, \ell_{3.2} \overset{\text{ind.}}{\sim} \text{Inv-Gamma}(5,5), \tag{35}$$

which is a weekly informative setting that attempts to introduce weak prior assumptions about the true location of the unknown parameters [27,28] into our analysis. The Half-$\mathcal{N}(0,1)$ distribution gives the distribution of the absolute value of a $\mathcal{N}(0,1)$ random variable. The Inv-Gamma $(5,5)$ with shape parameter $\alpha > 0$ and scale parameter $\beta > 0$ is the distribution of the inverse of a Gamma$(5,5)$ random variable. With the chosen setting, the latter distribution is approximately centered around 1 (the expected value is $5/4 = 1.25$) and quite diffuse, since the range between 0.025 and 0.975 percentiles is $(0.49, 3.08)$. The optimization of the unnormalized posterior (28) was performed using R 4.0.4 + rstan 2.21.2 [29].

6.2 Identifiability Issues

It is important to note that there is a fundamental ambiguity in which parameters are associated with each Gaussian process component, since the probability of the sum is invariant to each permutation of the indices. With a weakly informative prior, the posterior distribution inherits this permutational invariance. One way to resolve this ambiguity is to restrict the exploration of posterior modes to a single ordering of parameters, a trick that can be interpreted as a method of making an exchangeable prior non-exchangeable. It can be proved that the resulting inferences are correct after imposing an artificial identifiability constraint. Moreover, this approach is often able to separate the symmetric posterior modes [30,31]. The order we used for our problem can be expressed by the following restricted prior, which naturally reflects the relative weight of the additive components of the Gaussian process:

$$\pi(\sigma_1, \sigma_2, \sigma_3)\mathbb{1}(\sigma_2 < \sigma_3 < \sigma_1). \tag{36}$$

A complete decomposition of the trajectory into its component trajectories can be estimated by computing the expected value and standard deviation of the approximate posterior distribution of $f_1(t)$, $f_2(t)$, $f_3(t)$ using the expression derived for $\boldsymbol{\mu}_{\mathsf{post}}$ and $\mathbf{K}_{\mathsf{post}}$.

6.3 Results

Preliminarily, the data were standardized because in Gaussian processes it is usually assumed that the expected value function is a function of time and is identically zero. This assumption reduces the size of the parameter space, but at the same time is not a real constraint, since a Gaussian process is flexible enough to model any trajectory, even if one assumes an identically-zero expected value. The estimated components of the resulting decomposition are shown in Fig. 4. Approximate posterior confidence bands, based on the diagonal elements of the estimated $\mathbf{K}_{\text{post}}(f_i)$ matrices, have been superimposed.

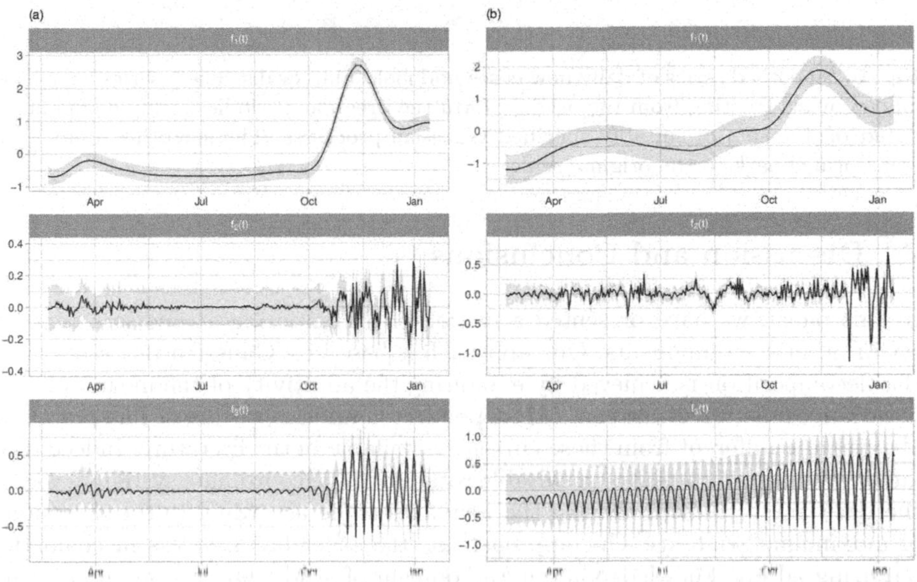

Fig. 4. Decomposition of the daily number of new cases (a) and the daily number of molecular swabs administered (b) into three linearly superimposed components, estimated using a sum of Gaussian processes. The proposed decomposition model includes: 1) Long-term trend f_1. 2) Shorter-term smooth fluctuation f_2. 3) Weekly periodic pattern with time-dependent amplitudes f_3. 4) Noise (not shown here). Gray shaded areas represent 95% posterior confidence intervals. Prior to decomposition, the original data were standardized to ensure that the empirical mean was close to zero.

The smoothed data are shown in Fig. 5. These smooth versions were obtained by subtracting the estimated periodic component from the original standardized data and then transforming back to the original scale.

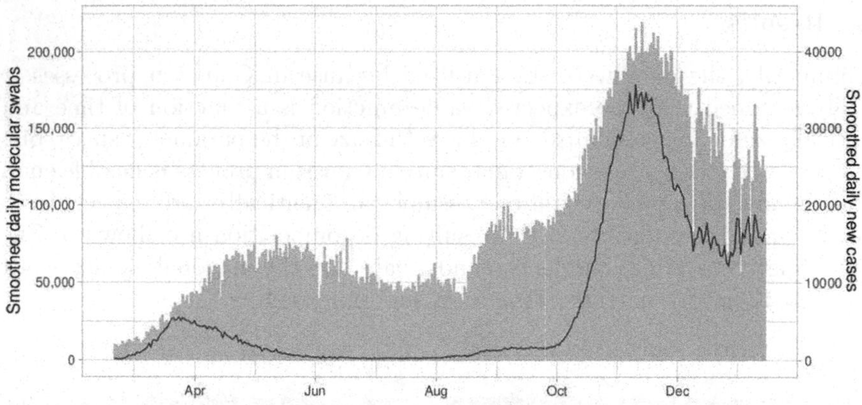

Fig. 5. Smoothed series of daily new cases and molecular swabs. These series were estimated by subtracting from the original data the irregular periodic weekly component, based on the sum of suitably specified Gaussian processes. The smoothed data were transformed back to the original scale.

7 Discussion and Conclusions

In this paper, we have presented a model for decomposing a time series into a set of additive components. Our approach is based on Gaussian processes, and the decomposition is achieved by exploiting the additivity of the mean and the covariance function of the sum of independent Gaussian processes. The proposed algorithm is different from those currently available in the literature. Indeed, the latter are generally based on a suitable rotation of the coordinate system in which the data are expressed, causing the new axes to lie according to the directions of maximum variability. Our approach, on the other hand, is less mechanistic, requiring ad hoc knowledge about the domain of study. On the one hand, this can be an advantage since the decomposition model can be calibrated accurately. From this point of view, it is obvious that the decomposition (29) is specific to the example we are dealing with and must be modified accordingly for other problems. In other contexts, the lack of an automatic procedure for determining the components of the additive decomposition may be a drawback. Whether or not the increased flexibility of our approach can be a disadvantage depends on the problem at hand.

The estimation algorithm we use does not provide a complete exploration of the posterior surface, but is limited to determining the MAP estimates of the parameters of interest. However, this approach requires caution since the target is not convex and local minima may be a problem. Sensitivity analysis to the initial conditions need to be further explored. Similarly, it is necessary to further investigate the sensitivity of the obtained results when the joint prior distribution of the parameters varies. All these problems will be addressed in future work.

References

1. Shumway, R.H., Stoffer, D.S.: Time Series Analysis and Its Applications. Springer, Heidelberg (2017). https://doi.org/10.1007/978-3-319-52452-8
2. Cleveland, R.B., Cleveland, W.S., McRae, J.E., Terpenning, I.: STL: a seasonal-trend decomposition procedure based on loess (with Discussion). J. Off. Stat. **6**, 3–73 (1990)
3. Zhang, X., et al.: Gaussian process. In: Encyclopedia of Machine Learning, pp. 428–439. Springer, US, Boston (2011). https://doi.org/10.1007/978-0-387-30164-8_324
4. Gonzalvez, J., Lezmi, E., Roncalli, T., Xu, J.: Financial applications of gaussian processes and bayesian optimization. SSRN Electron. J. (2019). https://doi.org/10.2139/ssrn.3344332
5. Roberts, S., Osborne, M., Ebden, M., Reece, S., Gibson, N., Aigrain, S.: Gaussian processes for time-series modelling. Philos. Trans. R. Soc. A Math. Phys. Eng. Sci. **371**, 20110550 (2013). https://doi.org/10.1098/rsta.2011.0550
6. Golyandina, N., Zhigljavsky, A.: Singular Spectrum Analysis for Time Series. Springer, Heidelberg (2013). https://doi.org/10.1007/978-3-642-34913-3
7. Golyandina, N., Korobeynikov, A.: Basic Singular Spectrum Analysis and forecasting with R. Comput. Stat. Data Anal. **71**, 934–954 (2014). https://doi.org/10.1016/j.csda.2013.04.009
8. Golyandina, N., Korobeynikov, A., Shlemov, A., Usevich, K.: Multivariate and 2D extensions of singular spectrum analysis with the rssa package. J. Stat. Softw. **67**, 1–78 (2015). https://doi.org/10.18637/jss.v067.i02
9. Hassani, H., Mahmoudvand, R., Zokaei, M.: Separability and window length in singular spectrum analysis. Comptes Rendus Math. **349**, 987–990 (2011). https://doi.org/10.1016/j.crma.2011.07.012
10. Rasmussen, C.E., Williams, C.K.I.: Gaussian Processes for Machine Learning. The MIT Press (2005)
11. Stein, M.L.: Interpolation of Spatial Data. Springer, New York (1999). https://doi.org/10.1007/978-1-4612-1494-6
12. Duvenaud, D.K., Nickisch, H., Rasmussen, C.: Additive gaussian processes. In: Shawe-Taylor, J., Zemel, R., Bartlett, P., Pereira, F.,Weinberger, K.Q. (eds.) Advances in Neural Information Processing Systems, pp. 226–234 (2011)
13. MacKay, D.J.C.: Introduction to gaussian processes. In: Bishop, C.M. (ed.) Neural Networks and Machine Learning, pp. 133–166. Kluwer Academic Press (1998)
14. Durrande, N., Hensman, J., Rattray, M., Lawrence, N.D.: Detecting periodicities with Gaussian processes. PeerJ Comput. Sci. **2**, e50 (2016). https://doi.org/10.7717/peerj-cs.50
15. Cheng, L., Ramchandran, S., Vatanen, T., Lietzén, N., Lahesmaa, R., Vehtari, A., Lähdesmäki, H.: An additive Gaussian process regression model for interpretable non-parametric analysis of longitudinal data. Nat. Commun. **10**, 1798 (2019). https://doi.org/10.1038/s41467-019-09785-8
16. Vanhatalo, J., Riihimäki, J., Hartikainen, J., Jylänki, P., Tolvanen, V., Vehtari, A.: GPstuff: Bayesian modeling with gaussian processes. J. Mach. Learn. Res. **14**, 1175–1179 (2013)
17. Ravishanker, N., Dey, D.K.: A First Course in Linear Model Theory. Chapman & Hall/CRC, New York (2001)
18. Robert, C.P., Casella, G.: Monte Carlo Statistical Methods. Springer, New York (2004). https://doi.org/10.1007/978-1-4757-4145-2

19. Robert, C., Casella, G.: Introducing Monte Carlo Methods with R. Springer, New York (2010). https://doi.org/10.1007/978-1-4419-1576-4
20. Neal, R.: MCMC Using Hamiltonian Dynamics. In: Brooks, S., Gelman, A., Jones, G., Meng, X.-L. (eds.) Handbook of Markov Chain Monte Carlo, pp. 116–62. Chapman and Hall/CRC (2011). https://doi.org/10.1201/b10905
21. Hoffman, M.D., Gelman, A.: The No-U-Turn sampler: adaptively setting path lengths in hamiltonian Monte Carlo. J. Mach. Learn. Res. **15**, 1593–1623 (2014)
22. Betancourt, M., Girolami, M.: Hamiltonian Monte Carlo for hierarchical models. In: Current Trends in Bayesian Methodology with Applications, pp. 79–101. Chapman and Hall/CRC (2015). https://doi.org/10.1201/b18502-5
23. Carpenter, B., et al.: Stan: a probabilistic programming language. J. Stat. Softw. **76**, 1–32 (2017). https://doi.org/10.18637/jss.v076.i01
24. Template: COVID-19 pandemic data/Italy medical cases - Wikipedia. https://tinyurl.com/njz8y89p. Accessed 04 Feb 2021
25. Vehtari, A., Ojanen, J.: A survey of Bayesian predictive methods for model assessment, selection and comparison. Stat. Surv. **6**, 142–228 (2012). https://doi.org/10.1214/12-ss102
26. Gelman, A., Hwang, J., Vehtari, A.: Understanding predictive information criteria for Bayesian models. Stat. Comput. **24**(6), 997–1016 (2013). https://doi.org/10.1007/s11222-013-9416-2
27. Gelman, A.: Prior distributions for variance parameters in hierarchical models (comment on article by Browne and Draper). Bayesian Anal. **1**, 515–534 (2006). https://doi.org/10.1214/06-BA117A
28. Gelman, A.: Prior Choice Recommendations. https://github.com/stan-dev/stan/wiki/Prior-Choice-Recommendations. Accessed 11 Feb 2020
29. R Core Team: R: A Language and Environment for Statistical Computing (2020). https://www.r-project.org/
30. Papastamoulis, P.: label.switching: an R package for dealing with the label switching problem in MCMC outputs. J. Stat. Softw. **69** (2016). https://doi.org/10.18637/jss.v069.c01
31. Betancourt, M.: Identifying Bayesian Mixture Models. https://mc-stan.org/users/documentation/case-studies/identifying_mixture_models.html. Accessed 22 Dec 2020

Shiny App to Predict the Risk of Death in Very Low Birth Weight Newborns Through a New Classifier

Claudia Rodrigues[1(✉)], Ana Rita Antunes[2], and Ana Cristina Braga[2]

[1] School of Engineering, University of Minho, Campus Gualtar, Braga, Portugal
[2] ALGORITMI Centre, University of Minho, 4800-058 Guimarães, Portugal
id9069@alunos.uminho.pt, acb@dps.uminho.pt

Abstract. Neonatal mortality is a major health concern worldwide, and one of the groups of babies that has contributed most to this outcome is the very low birth weight (VLBW) newborns. Knowing the factors that contribute to the death of these babies and having an idea of the probability of their survival can help health professionals to make important decisions. The objective of this study was to develop a classifier that predicts whether a particular newborn weighing less than 1500 g will survive or die. For this, the tools R and RStudio were used, as well as a database provided by the National Registry of Newborns of Very Low Weight from Portugal. Construction of logistic regression models were performed, and a shiny web application was created to facilitate the use of the final model by health professionals. The application is available in https://rodrigues.shinyapps.io/VLBWnewborn/. Multivariate analysis showed that gestational age, length at birth, prenatal corticosteroids, sex, average of the three Apgar scores (1st, 5th and 10th min), insufflator resuscitation, major congenital malformation, diagnosis of necrotizing enterocolitis and administration of Ibuprofen for treatment of persistent ductus arteriosus are factors responsible for neonatal mortality. This model predicts with 0.926 of certainty the real state of a VLBW newborn. Its area under the ROC curve was 0.891 and 0.797 for internal and external validation, respectively. The fact that it presents better predictive results than the CRIB and SNAPPE II indexes, when using test data, makes it a possible alternative index to be used.

Keywords: Logistic regression · ROC curve · Shiny · Classifier

1 Introduction

In the 21st century, neonatal mortality is still one of the main health concerns worldwide, where 45% of all deaths occurring in children with less than five

This work has been supported by FCT - Fundação para a Ciência e Tecnologia within the R&D Units Project Scope: UIDB/00319/2020. The authors express their gratitude to the Portuguese National Registry for supplying the dataset used in this study.

O. Gervasi et al. (Eds.): ICCSA 2021, LNCS 12952, pp. 593–608, 2021.
https://doi.org/10.1007/978-3-030-86973-1_42

years occur within the neonatal period [12]. Newborns with very low birth weight (VLBW) are one of the groups of babies that have most contributed significantly to neonatal mortality. A VLBW newborn is defined as one with a birth weight less than 1500 g and/or is born before 32 weeks of gestation [11].

The LBW has been identified as one of the most common causes of mortality in newborns. It is estimated that neonatal mortality worldwide is 20 times more likely to occur in newborns with low weight than in newborns with normal weight [14]. According to Cutland et al. (2017), newborns with low weight are more likely to present several morbidities, such as neurologic disability, increased risk of chronic diseases and exhibit also greater probability of occurrence of intracranial hemorrhage, respiratory distress, blindness, gastrointestinal disorders, among others [3]. These conditions make these babies more vulnerable to death.

However, more recent studies have been considering other variables, in addition to low weight, as possible mortality risk factors, such as male gender, congenital malformations, among others [19]. Understanding what are the factors that contribute to the mortality of VLBW newborns, among the variables that are routinely used by doctors, can help health professionals to make the best decisions in planning perinatal care and during each stage of neonatal intensive care.

Thus, severity scoring systems have been developed in order to assess mortality risk of these babies. Among the existing indexes, the most used to more objectively analyze the perspective of survival and the quality of life of very low birth weight newborns are both the CRIB (Clinical Risk Index for Babies) and the SNAPPE (Score for Neonatal Acute Physiology-Perinatal Extension) [6].

According to Medlock et al. (2011), a typical approach to estimate the risk of death of VLBW newborn and to identify the main mortality risk factors involves the use of predictive models such as logistic regression models [10]. However, before adopting the predictive model in health care units, it is necessary to determine its predictive capacity, in order to prevent it from misclassifying a particular newborn. It is usual to demonstrate the performance of a clinical classifier by analyzing the ROC curve (Receiver Operating Characteristic).

The ROC curve is defined as a plot which its axes are represented by the True Positive Fraction of a classifier (sensitivity), on the y-axis, and by the False Positive Fraction (1-specificity), on the x-axis, and where each point is generated by a different threshold value [7]. In addition, the ROC analysis also allows the visualization of several classifiers, in order to select the best predictive model based on its performance measures. One of the most used indicators in this methodology, which allows evaluate the performance of the models, is the Area Under the Curve (AUC) [5].

Nowadays, while many health professionals use analysis tools, often commercial type, to analyze ROC curves, most of them have limited analytical resources [7]. Alternatively, there are free software packages, such as R, that offer advanced analysis features, but they are more difficult to use as they require the use of a command-based user interface. This can be challenging for users who have no knowledge of the R language. In this sense, web applications based on the R language have been developed in which the end-user does not need to write any line of code. This is possible by using the shiny package available in RStudio. In a study carried out by Ribeiro (2017), a shiny application that predict the admission status of a very low birth weight newborn was constructed [15]. In this case, the factors gestational age, weight, length, administration or not of prenatal corticosteroids, the gender of the newborn, type of delivery, delivery reason, Apgar score at 1st and 10st min and the existence or not of congenital malformation were chosen to be part of the logistic regression model implemented in the application.

The objective of this article is to present a logistic regression model that can serve as a classifier that predicts whether a very low birth weight newborn will survive or die.

2 Methods

2.1 Binary Logistic Regression

Logistic regression was originally applied in the field of epidemiology, and today it is also used in other fields such as biomedical sciences, finance, criminology, ecology, engineering, biology, among others [8].

This technique is commonly used in a perspective of prediction and analyzing relationships between variables. When considering a binary logistic regression, the dependent variable can take two possible values denoted by 0 and 1, where 1 represents the occurrence of the event and 0 the absence.

Using a binary dependent variable and p independent predictors, $\mathbf{x}$, the logistic regression model, in terms of the event probability, $\pi(\mathbf{x})$, can be written as represented in Eq. 1:

$$\pi(\mathbf{x}) = \frac{e^{\beta_0+\beta_1x_1+\beta_2x_2+...+\beta_px_p}}{1+e^{\beta_0+\beta_1x_1+\beta_2x_2+...+\beta_px_p}} \tag{1}$$

where β_0, β_1, β_2, ..., β_p are coefficients of the *logit* model [8]. The *logit* is the transformation of $\pi(\mathbf{x})$, that is, the linearization of the multivariate logistic model, and is defined in terms of $\pi(\mathbf{x})$, as shown below in Eq. 2:

$$g(\mathbf{x}) = \ln\left[\frac{\pi(\mathbf{x})}{1-\pi(\mathbf{x})}\right] = \beta_0+\beta_1x_1+\beta_2x_2+...+\beta_px_p \tag{2}$$

Variable Selection Method. For the construction of the logistic regression model, the researcher must evaluate the association of each independent variable with the binary outcome. For that, some researchers opt for selection techniques like stepwise procedures. In stepwise regression, the selection procedure is automatically performed by statistical packages, in which examples of variable selection criteria are the Akaike information criterion (AIC) and the Bayesian information criterion (BIC).

This method of selecting variables can be used in three different directions, Forward, when we start with an empty model and successively add covariates, Backward, when we start with the full model and remove covariates and Both, when it is used both directions.

2.2 Diagnostic Measures of the Prediction Model

ROC Curve. The ROC curve is a graphical approach where the x-axis and y-axis represent false positive fraction, FPF (1-specificity) and true positive fraction, TPF (sensitivity), respectively, where its performance is given by the area under the curve. The analysis of these curves is considered a useful tool to visualize, organize and select classifiers according to their performance. Classifiers with AUC equal to 1 have perfect discrimination capacity, while those with an AUC of 0.5, their discrimination capacity is null [4]. For a clinical context Fan et al. (2006) indicates that ROC curves with an AUC value of 0.75 or less are not clinically useful but an AUC of 0.97 has a very high clinical value.

Sensitivity and Specificity. A good predictive model has a high value of TPF (sensitivity) and a low value of FPF (1-specificity), being considered ideal when the value of TPF is equal to one and the value of FPF is equal to zero [1]. In contrast, when the TPF and FPF values are the same, this means that the classifier is not conclusive about the prediction.

Akaike Information Criterion. AIC is a criterion widely used in the selection of the best model among a set of candidate models [21]. The selection of the best model pass by choosing the one with the lowest AIC value. The AIC criterion is defined by the following equation:

$$AIC = -2(\ln(L)) + 2k \tag{3}$$

where k represents the number of independent parameters and L represents the value obtained from the maximum likelihood function of the model.

Bayesian Information Criterion. BIC is another criterion used in the selection of the best model, and the one with the lowest BIC value will be chosen [20]. This criterion is represented by the following expression:

$$BIC = -2\log(L) + k\log(n) \tag{4}$$

where L is the likelihood function evaluated at the maximum likelihood estimate (MLE), k is the number of parameters in the model and n is the total number of observations.

Pseudo-R^2. In logistic regression, the adequacy of a model can also be assessed by the pseudo-R^2. Although there are many different statistics of R^2, none of them has been accepted as a standard.

One of the most used pseudo-R^2 in the context of logistic regression is the McFadden index. This index expresses the percentage variation between the model's Likelihood Value, which considers only the constant, and the Likelihood Value, which incorporates the explanatory variables, as is indicated in the following expression:

$$R^2 logit = \frac{[-2LLnull - (-2LLmodel)]}{(-2LLnull)} \tag{5}$$

where LL represents the logarithm of the likelihood functions. According to Hu & Lo (2007) models that present McFadden-R^2 values between 0.2 and 0.4 are considered well-adjusted models [9].

Other pseudo R^2 that are used in different studies are Cox & Snell R^2 and Nagelkerke R^2, among others. The Nagelkerke index corresponds to an improved version of Cox & Snell since it restricts its value so that it does not exceed the value of 1.

2.3 Shiny Application

Today, there are several commercial software, such as IBM® SPSS® Statistics, MedCalc, Stata® and free software, such as R, which are used in order to guide various health professionals in their decision making. However, each of these statistical analysis' tools offers different resources and some are more limited than others. Among these, R has proved to be one of the most complete, thanks to the thousands of packages it has.

One of the packages that has attracted the interest of several specialists is the shiny package. With this package it is possible to build web applications that are easy to use, quick to analyze data (such as on [2] and [13]) and they do not require great knowledge of programming language.

Regarding its structure, shiny is basically divided into two components, the user interface (UI) and the server. The user interface object is the set of code that defines the aesthetics of the application and is responsible for showing to the user the inputs to perform a certain task [18]. The server function corresponds to the code segment that decides how the inputs entered by the user will be used and how the result will be presented in the output, that is, it will be responsible for the calculations that the application will perform. As it is a tool that makes use of "reactive programming", it ensures that changes in the input are immediately reflected in the output, thus enabling the construction of a highly interactive tool [17].

To make the Shiny application accessible to other users, it is possible to put it on host platform like "Shinyapps.io" and GitHub [16].

3 Results and Discussion

All the statistical analysis performed on the data, as well as the construction of the algorithm and the web application, were made using the RStudio (version 1.3.959) and R (version 4.0.1) tools.

3.1 Database Characterization

The dataset used in this study is part of the Portuguese National Registry of Very Low Weight Newborns which include the data collected by neonatal intensive care units in the Portuguese territory between the years 2010 and 2012. All newborns registered in this database had a weight of less than 1500 g and/or gestational age of less than 32 weeks.

The original database included 3496 records and 105 variables. However, for this study, only a sample of 2306 newborns were used, in which all twins and all newborns who died in the delivery room were excluded. Of these 2306 VLBW newborns, a total of 263 (11.41%) babies ended up dying.

The age of mothers of these babies ranged from 14 to 47 years with mean of 30.25 ($\pm$6.15) years. The median age of mothers was 31. Considering the admission status of newborns, the average age of mothers for survivors and dead is 30.30 and 29.88 years, respectively. Most of these mothers had pathologies during pregnancy (66.10%) and cesarean section was the most frequent type of delivery (69.12%). Regarding the reason for the birth, spontaneous delivery was the most prevalent among mothers (44.93%), followed by fetal pathology (28.83%), voluntary terminations of pregnancy (VTP) (25.90%) and maternal pathology (0.35%).

Regarding care and treatments performed during the prenatal period, 93.40% of mothers received care before the birth of their babies and only 4.09% of mothers were subjected to medically assisted conception. Regarding the administration of corticosteroids before delivery, 12.91% of mothers did not receive corticosteroids, 25.96% of them delivered within less than 24 h after the first dose of corticosteroids or more than a week after the last dose, and finally, most mothers (61.13%) had their birth in more than 24 h and less than a week, after the administration of at least one dose of corticosteroids.

The babies in this database have an average gestational age of 207.80 ($\pm$ 18.13) weeks and a birth weight with an average of 1196 ($\pm$356.97) g. The birth weight values are ranged from 370 to 2810 g and the median is 1210 g. In this sample of newborns, 25% of them have a birth weight less than or equal to 930 g and 25% a weight greater than 1440 g. Regarding the variation in the weights of newborns according to the state of admission, survivor and dead, it was seen that, in general, survivors have a higher birth weight than newborns who end up dying. In this sample, it was also observed that it is more common for survivors to have a higher gestational age value than newborns who end up dying where 50% of the survivors had a gestational age of 212 days or less and 50% of the dead had a gestational age of 186 days or less. In addition, in this database there are no dead newborns with gestational ages higher than 268 days. Besides that, the average length at birth of newborns is 37.16 (±3.62) cm and the average head circumference at birth is 26.57 (±2.66) cm.

In this study it was also observed that the sample of 1207 (52.34%) of male babies has a slightly higher mortality rate (6.7%) compared to the sample of 1099 (47.66%) of the female gender (4.7%).

Analyzing the index that is equivalent to the average of the values of three Apgar indexes (1st min, 5th min, 10th min), it was found that its average is 7.94 and its median 8. The lowest value present in the study sample was the value 1, with three newborns having this score, and the maximum value of the index was 10 with 419 newborns. Within this scale, the value 9 was the most frequent, with 599 newborns receiving this score. Babies who were given a score of 1,2 and 4 on the Apgar index, a large part of them correspond to newborns who ended up dying with values of 66.7%, 66.7% and 51.7%, respectively. Babies that have a higher value on the Apgar index, a large part of them ended up surviving, and the score of 10 on the Apgar index is the one with the lowest number of dead newborns (2.4%). Regarding surviving newborns, 50% of them had an Apgar index equal to or less than 8, while 50% of dead newborns had a value equal to or less than 6.

Analyzing the values of the CRIB and SNAPPE II in relation to newborns for this database, it was found that the CRIB index has an average score of 2.74, a median of 1 and a final score between 0 and 20 and the SNAPPE II index has an average score of 21.64, a median of 15 and a final score ranging from 0 to 131.

Of the available resuscitation methods, the oxygen resuscitation process was the most used (60.72%). Cardiac compression and adrenaline resuscitation were the methods by which health professionals least opted, with only 4.27% and 3.70% of babies using such procedures, respectively. Among the 8 most common diseases observed in this population, the disease respiratory distress syndrome (RDS) was the most detected in these newborns (75.24%) and the least detected was gastrointestinal (GI) perforation (2.6%).

Finally, the average of hospitalization time of these babies was 49.12 (±41.00) days, and the median was 41 days. The minimum value recorded for the hospitalization time was 0 days and the maximum value was 524 days, that is, about 75 weeks.

3.2 Database Treatment

Since the main objective of this study was develop a model capable of predicting the risk of death of a very low birth weight newborn, it was necessary, in a first phase, to treat the database in order to exclude all the variables that should not be included into the model as predictor variables, as well as treat the missing values present in the database.

As mentioned before, all the data related to newborn twins and newborns who ended up dying in the delivery room were excluded from the database. In addition, 56 variables were also excluded in the first phase due to their lack of relevance to the case study. All the records with strange values and denominations have been recoded to missing values.

For this database it was decided to create a new variable "AverageApgar" that corresponds to the average of the indexes of Apgar at the 1st, 5th and 10th min.

In order to build the predictive model, it was necessary to apply a method for treating missing values in the database used in this study. In this case, the deletion method was chosen to deal with the 1.3% of missing values present in the database. Thus, the database became composed of 1535 cases and 49 variables.

3.3 Logistic Regression Model Development

To develop and validate a classifier for mortality risk, the 1535 VLBW newborns were divided into two data groups using the *caret* package (version 6.0–86), present in R, with a split of about 70:30. In this case, 70% of the data worked as the training set to train the model and the remaining 30% worked as the test set to validate the developed model. The training set consisted of 1075 records and the test set consisted of 460 records.

Before proceeding with the construction of the logistic regression model, it was necessary to choose the best set of independent variables to be introduced in the predictive model, eliminating those that did not present variability. For that, statistical and exploratory techniques were used to see which variables that a priori would not contribute mathematically to the model and could be eliminated. It started by performing a variable-to-variable univariate procedure, using logistic regression, to eliminate those that were not significant, that is, that had a p-value above 0.25. The choice of this value was based on Hosmer & Lemeshow in which they proposed this value as a criterion for choosing the variables to be implemented in the multivariate analysis [8]. Then, an exploratory analysis was carried out through simple frequency tables for all 49 variables, in order to observe the distribution of their data at each level. All the variables that showed a significant difference in the distribution of data were eliminated from the database. Finally, cross tables were built for each variable with the dependent variable, "Death", in order to analyze the correspondence of surviving and dead newborns for each variable. At the end of this analysis, a set of 18 independent variables was obtained, the possible candidates to be implemented in the model to be developed (Table 1).

In this study, different multiple logistic regression models were built. For that, the training set was used to develop different logistic regression equations having mortality as the outcome variable. All the candidate variables were included in a complete multivariate model, that is, in the first model built in this study. From this model, others were built through the application of the stepwise technique on it and by choosing variables manually that had a p-value less than a value established by us, in this case 0.050 for some models and 0.058 for others.

The model chosen for the classifier was obtained by applying the analysis of variance (ANOVA) on the complete model. This model consists of 9 independent variables corresponding to the variables that were indicated in the ANOVA analysis with a p-value less than 0.05. The statistical data related to the chosen model are shown in Table 2.

Table 1. Summary of the characteristics of the independent variables candidates to be included in the LR model.

Variable	Codes/Levels	Coefficient	p-value*
GestationalAge	–	−0.053	<0.001
WeightBirth	–	−0.002	<0.001
LengthBirth	–	−0.234	<0.001
HeadCircumferenceBirth	–	−0.313	<0.001
PrenatalCorticosteroids2	Partial	−1.352	<0.001
PrenatalCorticosteroids3	Complete	−1.006	0.001
PathologiesPregnancy1	Yes	−0.315	0.222
TypeDelivery2	Caesarean	−0.577	0.023
ReasonDelivery2	Maternal Pathology	2.478	0.015
ReasonDelivery3	Fetal Pathology	−0.501	0.112
ReasonDelivery4	VTP	−0.405	0.200
Sex2	Female	−1.301	<0.001
AverageApgar	–	−0.550	<0.001
OxygenResuscitation1	Yes	1.597	<0.001
InsufflatorResuscitation1	Yes	0.494	0.049
EtIntubationResuscitation1	Yes	1.900	<0.001
MajorCongenitalMalformation1	Yes	1.241	<0.001
DiagRds1	Yes	1.404	0.001
DiagPda1	Yes	1.252	<0.001
DiagNec1	Yes	2.004	<0.001
PdaTerapeutic1	Yes	0.616	0.040

*The p-value corresponds to Wald's statistic

Table 2. Output obtained for the final logistic regression model.

Variable	Coef.	Std. Error	z	p-value
Constant	11.400	1.970	5.811	6.20e−09**
GestationalAge	−0.019	0.012	−1.646	9.97e−02
LengthBirth	−0.149	0.054	−2.747	6.01e−03**
PrenatalCorticosteroids2	−2.053	0.485	−4.232	2.32e−05**
PrenatalCorticosteroids3	−0.981	0.379	−2.590	9.60e−03**
Sex2	−1.384	0.345	−4.016	5.93e−05**
AverageApgar	−0.482	0.092	−5.254	1.49e−07**
InsufflatorResuscitation1	−0.600	0.309	−1.938	5.26e−02
MajorCongenitalMalformation1	1.590	0.459	3.462	5.36e−04**
DiagNec1	1.930	0.353	5.481	4.22e−08**
PdaTerapeutic1	−0.332	0.365	−0.911	0.362

**p-values less than the 5% significance level, that is, they correspond to variables in the model that are statistically significant.

Results of the multiple logistic regression analysis (Table 2) revealed the impact of multiple factors on the probability of death in VLBW newborn. Gestational age, length at birth, non-administration of prenatal corticosteroids, the gender of the newborn, the average of the three Apgar scores (1st, 5th and 10th min), the non-occurrence of initial resuscitation with an insufflator, the presence of some major congenital malformation, presence of necrotizing enterocolitis (NEC), and the absence of Ibuprofen to treat ductus arteriosus (PDA) to the newborn were the risk factors for death in these babies.

3.4 Logistic Regression Model Validation

The predictive models were validated with the test set, which consisted in 460 VLBW newborn records. Some metrics chosen to help to select the most parsimonious model among of the different models developed were Akaike information criterion (AIC) and Bayesian information criterion (BIC). Pseudo-R^2 as MacFadden R^2, Cox & Snell R^2 and Nagelkerke R^2 were also chosen to assess the adequacy of a model. Furthermore, model discrimination was assessed using the area under the curve (AUC), sensitivity, specificity and predictive values. All these metrics were considered to compare the different predictive models developed. The one with the best goodness of fit, performance capacity value and a smaller number of variables was chosen to be the possible classifier (Table 3).

Table 3. Summary of model validation measures.

Model #	1	2	3	4	5	6	7	8	9	10
#var	18	11	8	9	7	9	8	9	6	8
Quality of adjustment										
AIC	378.9	367.5	388	371	396	373.5	388	371	394.2	372.4
BIC	488.5	432.2	437.8	425.8	440.9	428.3	437.8	425.8	434.1	422.2
McFadden	0.346	0.334	0.282	0.319	0.262	0.314	0.282	0.319	0.262	0.312
Cox e Snell	0.152	0.147	0.128	0.141	0.117	0.139	0.126	0.141	0.117	0.138
Nagelkerke	0.401	0.388	0.332	0.372	0.310	0.367	0.332	0.372	0.309	0.365
Predictive ability										
Acc	0.926	0.924	0.924	0.924	0.924	0.926	0.924	0.924	0.924	0.924
Se	0.932	0.932	0.926	0.934	0.926	0.930	0.926	0.930	0.926	0.930
Sp	0.500	0.429	0	0.400	0	0.500	0	0.500	0	0.400
AUCi	0.903	0.901	0.878	0.895	0.870	0.891	0.878	0.895	0.868	0.893
AUCe	0.790	0.799	0.718	0.790	0.695	0.797	0.718	0.790	0.698	0.793

The final model (# 6) seems to be parsimonious and seems to fit well with the data, showing values of 373.498, 428.279 for AIC and BIC, respectively, as well as 0.314, 0.139 and 0.367 for McFadden R^2, Cox & Snell R^2 and Nagelkerke

R^2, respectively. In addition, the model also seems to have a good discriminating power, being able to predict with 0.926 certainty the admission status of a VLBW newborn. The prediction model presented an AUC of 0.891 when it was evaluated on the training sample and an AUC of 0.797 when evaluated in the test sample.

Figure 1 shows the ROC curves obtained in the internal (A) and external (B) validation processes of the chosen model. The best cutoff value presented by the model, when performed external validation, was 0.626. This value is generated by the combination of the best values of sensitivity and specificity, and to obtain them, the *optimalCutoff* function present in R was used. In this case, the values obtained for sensitivity and specificity were 0.930 and 0.500, respectively.

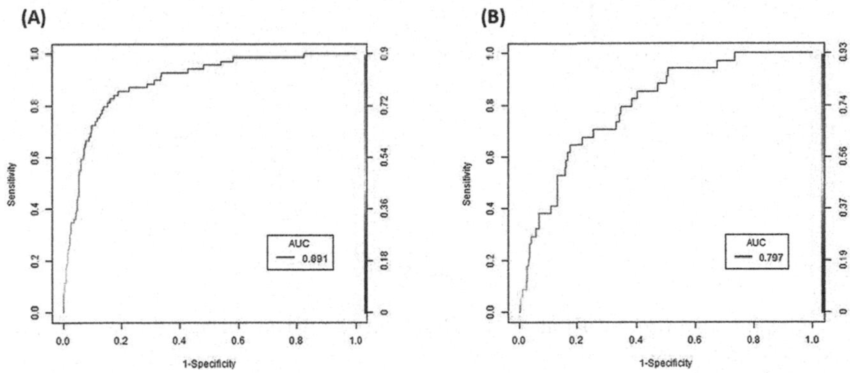

Fig. 1. ROC curves of the final model obtained in the internal validation (A) and in the external validation (B).

3.5 Comparison of the CRIB and SNAPPE II with the Developed Classifier

A comparative analysis was made between the classifier developed in this project and the mortality indexes CRIB and SNAPPE II, in order to assess whether the model developed could in fact be an alternative tool to be used in hospital units. In this case, a discriminative evaluation study was carried out, whose purpose was to estimate the predictive capacity of each indicator in predicting between two states, survival or death, of VLBW newborns. For this purpose, comparisons of ROC curves and their AUC values were made, using the *caTools* package (version 1.18.0) present in R.

Since, in the sample presented above, there are some newborns without simultaneously information referring to the CRIB and SNAPPE II indexes, for this part, a new set of test data was selected, which includes only newborns who meet these criteria. In this case, a sample of 350 records was used.

Figure 2 shows the three ROC curves for the CRIB and SNAPPE II indexes, as well as the classifier developed in this work (Model). When using the *caTools* package using the *colAUC* function, it was also possible to obtain the values of its

AUC. The AUC values presented by the built classifier, the CRIB indicator and the SNAPPE II indicator were 0.909, 0.830 and 0.794, respectively. By analyzing the ROC curves and the AUC values, it can be concluded that the developed classifier has a better predictive capacity than the other two indexes.

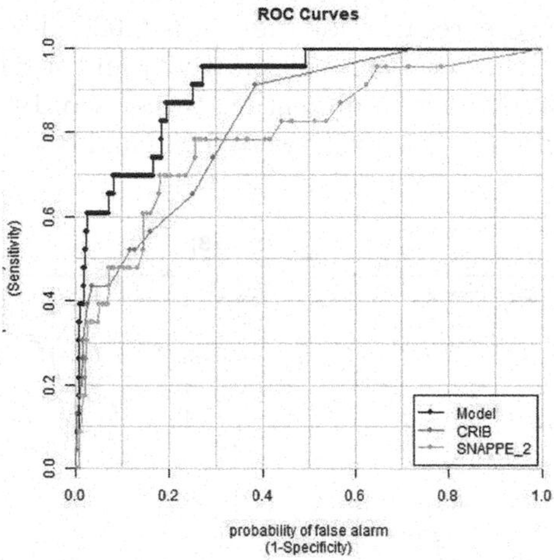

Fig. 2. Graphical representation of the ROC curves of the three indexes under study, obtained through *caTools*.

3.6 Shiny Application

Once confirmed a good predictive capacity of the developed model (final model) which will work as a classifier for the admission status of a VLBW newborn, a web application with shiny was planned, VLBWNB.

The idea of building this application arose in order to facilitate the estimation, in real time, of the probability of risk of death in these newborns, thus helping health professionals to make the best decisions in planning prenatal and postnatal care, so they can act in time. For that, the logistic regression model chosen was implemented in the built application. The application developed in this work is available for use in https://rodrigues.shinyapps.io/VLBWnewborn/.

Programming Code. For the creation of this application, we started by creating two R scripts in RStudio, the ui.R, which corresponds to the user interface object, and the server.R relating to the server function. Both files were saved in the same folder. Although shiny makes use of a template by default of Bootstrap and does not need the use of web development languages such as HTML, CSS and JavaScript for the building of the VLBWNB application, it was preferred to use the *shinythemes* package (version 1.1.2), as well as CSS, in order to customize the application in terms of its design. The code for its development can be found at https://github.com/Claudia-Rodrigues/Risk-of-death-VLBWNB.git.

The Shiny application developed for this work has an environment organized in 3 tabs, each with its own purpose. The functionalities of each section of the application will be explained as follow.

Home Page. As show in Fig. 3, the first tab of the application's navigation bar corresponds to the application's home page, which shows only the application title.

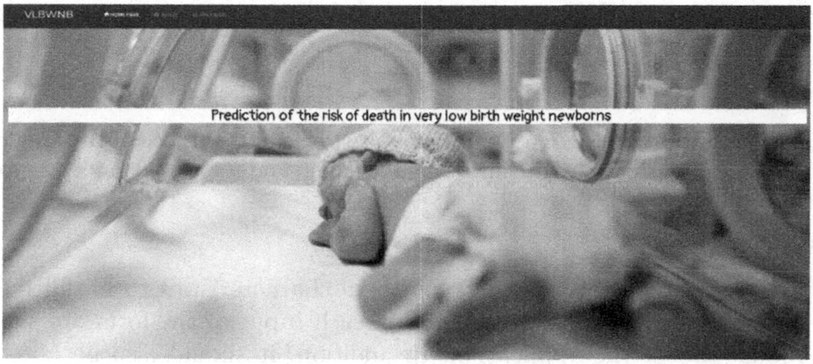

Fig. 3. Home page of the developed application.

About. As shown in Fig. 4, in the "About" tab we see explained the purpose of the application, the authors responsible for its development, the tools used for its construction, as well as, a brief description of the model/algorithm implemented on it. In the part of the model description, the accuracy of the model is presented, the AUC values for internal and external validation and the variables that are part of the model, accompanied by a short description of which values and metrics can be used for each one.

Prevision. In the "Prevision" tab of the Shiny application, the prevision x, if a particular very low birth weight newborn will survive or die is calculated in real time. Figure 5 shows the form, which is part of the "Prevision" tab, with the 9 inputs to be filled in by the user. These inputs correspond to the explanatory variables of the model implemented in the application.

After filling the form with the data of the newborn in question and pressing the calculate button, the application will indicate the probable state of admission of the newborn, as well as, the percentage of probability of dying. It should be noted that the use of this application for the calculation of the predicted risk of death of a VLBW newborn is limited to babies who present values within the

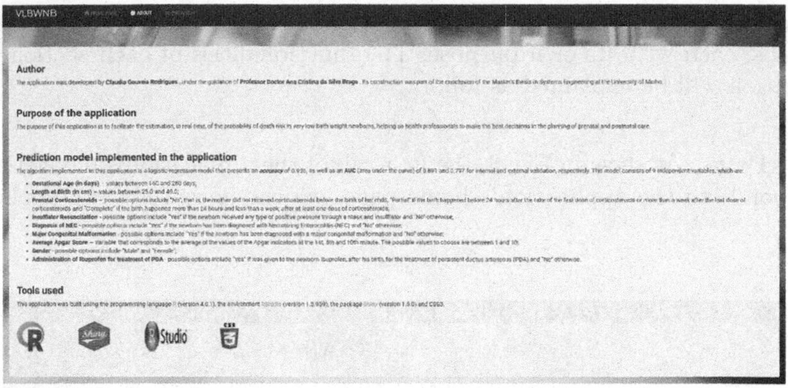

Fig. 4. Second tab of the VLBWNB application where the purpose of the application, the authors, the description of the implemented model and tools used in its construction are described.

limit presented by the application, for the 9 characteristics to be filled in the form. The possible values to be entered in each input of the form are shown in the "About" tab of the application. In addition, it should also be noted that this application is configured so that values equal to or greater than 63%, will indicate that the baby will die.

Figure 5 shows an example of an output provided by the "Prevision" tab, where the result is displayed in the right side of the application.

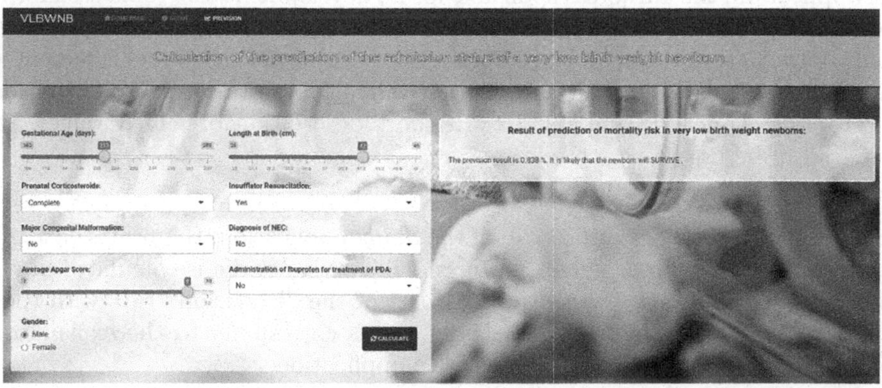

Fig. 5. Example of the output provided in the "Prevision" tab.

4 Conclusion

As mentioned before, the value of the mortality rate in VLB weight newborns is one of the main public health problems that has caused the most concerns worldwide. In this sense, it was intended with this work to develop a predictive model that was able to predict the risk of death in these kind of newborns. This model could help health professionals to understand which ones have a higher risk of death, and thus help them in making decisions about how they should act.

The model that served as basis for the construction of the classifier is a logistic regression model capable to predict with 0.926 certainty the admission status of a very low birth weight newborn. Through this model it was found that some of the factors that may contribute to the death of these babies are gestational age, length at birth, non-administration of prenatal corticosteroids, the gender of the newborn, the average of the three Apgar scores (1st, 5th and 10th min), the non-occurrence of initial resuscitation with an insufflator, the presence of some major congenital malformation, the presence of necrotizing enterocolitis (NEC), and the absence of Ibuprofen in treatment of ductus arteriosus (PDA) to the newborn.

This model presents a good fit to the data and a good predictive capacity.

Since it presented better predictive results than the CRIB and SNAPPE II indexes, which are widely used today, it leads us to believe that this classifier could be an alternative tool to be used in hospital centers. In addition, the VLBWNB web application that implements this classifier can be a more appealing and friendly tool to be used since in a few minutes it returns the probable result of a newborn's admission status. However, it should be noted that this application has limitations regard to the data that can be used to calculate the prediction of the newborn's admission status.

In a perspective of future work, it was possible to build another method of machine learning, such as, for example, Random Forest, Support Vector Machine, Artificial Neural Networks, among others.

References

1. Alonzo, T.A., Pepe, M.S.: Development and evaluation of classifiers. Topics in Biostatistics, pp. 89–116 (2007)
2. Antunes, A.R., Braga, A.C.: Shiny app to predict agricultural tire dimensions. In: Gervasi, O., Murgante, B., Misra, S., Garau, C., Blečić, I., Taniar, D., Apduhan, B.O., Rocha, A.M.A.C., Tarantino, E., Torre, C.M., Karaca, Y. (eds.) ICCSA 2020. LNCS, vol. 12251, pp. 247–260. Springer, Cham (2020). https://doi.org/10.1007/978-3-030-58808-3_19
3. Cutland, C.L., et al.: Low birth weight: case definition & guidelines for data collection, analysis, and presentation of maternal immunization safety data. Vaccine **35**(48Part A), 6492 (2017)
4. Fan, J., Upadhye, S., Worster, A.: Understanding receiver operating characteristic (roc) curves. Canadian J. Emergency Med. **8**(1), 19–20 (2006)

5. Fawcett, T.: An introduction to roc analysis. Pattern Recogn. Lett. **27**(8), 861–874 (2006)
6. Gagliardi, L., Cavazza, A., Brunelli, A., Battaglioli, M., Merazzi, D., Tandoi, F., Cella, D., Perotti, G., Pelti, M., Stucchi, I., et al.: Assessing mortality risk in very low birthweight infants: a comparison of crib, crib-ii, and snappe-ii. Archives of Disease in Childhood-Fetal and Neonatal Edition **89**(5), F419–F422 (2004)
7. Goksuluk, D., Korkmaz, S., Zararsiz, G., Karaagaoglu, A.E.: easyroc: an interactive web-tool for roc curve analysis using r language environment. R J. **8**(2), 213 (2016)
8. Hosmer, D.W., Lemeshow, S., Cook, E.: Applied Logistic Regression, 2nd edn. Wiley, New York (2000)
9. Hu, Z., Lo, C.: Modeling urban growth in Atlanta using logistic regression. Comput. Environ. Urban Syst. **31**(6), 667–688 (2007)
10. Medlock, S., Ravelli, A.C., Tamminga, P., Mol, B.W., Abu-Hanna, A.: Prediction of mortality in very premature infants: a systematic review of prediction models. PloS One **6**(9), e23441 (2011)
11. Mourão, M.F., Braga, A.C., Oliveira, P.N.: Accommodating maternal age in crib scale: quantifying the effect on the classification. In: International Conference on Computational Science and Its Applications, pp. 566–579. Springer (2014)
12. Nayeri, F., Emami, Z., Mohammadzadeh, Y., Shariat, M., Sagheb, S., Sahebi, L.: Mortality and morbidity patterns of very low birth weight newborns in eastern mediterranean region: a meta-analysis study. J. Pediatrics Rev. **7**(2), 67–76 (2019)
13. Quintas, J.P., Machado e Costa, F., Braga, A.C.: ROSY application for selecting R packages that perform ROC analysis. In: Gervasi, O., Murgante, B., Misra, S., Garau, C., Blečić, I., Taniar, D., Apduhan, B.O., Rocha, A.M.A.C., Tarantino, E., Torre, C.M., Karaca, Y. (eds.) ICCSA 2020. LNCS, vol. 12251, pp. 199–213. Springer, Cham (2020). https://doi.org/10.1007/978-3-030-58808-3_16
14. Raja, M., K, S.K., Deneshkumar, V.: Regression modeling for maternal determinants of low birth weight. Int. J. Stat. Syst. **12**(3), pp. 585–591 (2017)
15. Ribeiro, D.S.: Previsão do risco de morte de recém-nascidos prematuros de muito baixo peso. Master's thesis, University of Aveiro (2017)
16. RStudio: Share your apps. https://shiny.rstudio.com/tutorial/written-tutorial/lesson7/ (2020). Accessed 18 Mar 2021
17. Seal, A., Wild, D.J.: Netpredictor: R and shiny package to perform drug-target network analysis and prediction of missing links. BMC Bioinform. **19**(1), 1–10 (2018)
18. Sivaprakasam, B., Sadagopan, P.: Development of an interactive web application "shiny app for frequency analysis on homo sapiens genome (safa-hsg)." Interdisciplinary Sciences: Computational Life Sciences **11**(4), 723–729 (2019)
19. Vincer, M.J., Armson, B.A., Allen, V.M., Allen, A.C., Stinson, D.A., Whyte, R., Dodds, L.: An algorithm for predicting neonatal mortality in threatened very preterm birth. J. Obstetrics Gynaecology Canada **37**(11), 958–965 (2015)
20. Xi, R., Hadjipanayis, A.G., et al.: Copy number variation detection in whole-genome sequencing data using the bayesian information criterion. Proc. Natl. Acad. Sci. **108**(46), E1128–E1136 (2011)
21. Yanagihara, H., Kamo, K.I., Imori, S., Satoh, K.: Bias-corrected aic for selecting variables in multinomial logistic regression models. Linear Algebra Appl. **436**(11), pp. 4329–4341 (2012)

A Multivariate Analysis Approach to Diamonds' Pricing Using Dummy Variables in SPSS

Ana Rita Antunes[1(✉)], Cláudia Buga Buga[2], Daniel Coutinho Costa[3], José Grilo[3], Ana Cristina Braga[1], and Lino A. Costa[1]

[1] ALGORITMI Center, University of Minho, 4710-057 Braga, Portugal
id9069@alunos.uminho.pt, {acb,lac}@dps.uminho.pt

[2] DTx Digital Transformation CoLab, University of Minho, 4800-058 Guimarães, Portugal
id9400@alunos.uminho.pt

[3] Center for Micro-Electro Mechanical Systems (CMEMS), University of Minho, 4800-058 Guimarães, Portugal
{id9089,id8983}@alunos.uminho.pt

Abstract. In the present article, a distinctive methodology to predict the price of diamonds is proposed. To do so, a vast dataset was used encompassing empirical data relative to variables commonly used to assess the commercial value of diamonds. The selected dataset was retrieved from the Kaggle website [1] and includes diamonds' physical properties along with their respective price. Therefore, a data analysis based on Analysis of Variance (ANOVA) was conducted to study the diamonds' characteristics that determine their prices. It was found that the weight of the diamond (*carat*) has an impact on diamonds' price. For this reason, diamonds' price per carat was considered as a new dependent variable. Moreover, the variables diamonds' *clarity* and the width of the top of the diamond (*table*) affect the dependent variable. After applying the stepwise regression methods, it was found that the variables related to the width of the largest section of the diamond (Y), and *table* were the least significant ones. Moreover, both backward and forward selection led to the same result in terms of the predictive model. All the residuals' assumptions were validated. The adjusted coefficient of determination was 88.3%. Since multicollinearity effects can exist between the independent variables, Principal Components Analysis (PCA) can be used, as future work, to eliminate these effects.

Keywords: Diamonds' price · ANOVA · Linear regression · Stepwise methods · Dummy variables · SPSS

This work has been supported by FCT - Fundação para a Ciência e Tecnologia within the R&D Units Project Scope: UIDB/00319/2020.

O. Gervasi et al. (Eds.): ICCSA 2021, LNCS 12952, pp. 609–623, 2021.
https://doi.org/10.1007/978-3-030-86973-1_43

1 Introduction

It is common knowledge that diamonds are valuable items and often associated with elevated market values and luxury items. However, their applications go far beyond wealth and ostentation. Given their extreme mechanical hardness, stability, optical transparency, and outstanding thermal conductivity they can be applied as a valuable feedstock material in several fields [25]. Despite being a natural occurring carbon-based mineral, that can be isolated from crude oil, natural gas, and hydrocarbon materials, such as Adamantane and Diamantane, diamonds have been a research topic for a wide range of areas including geology [13], biology [25], economy [31], material and manufacturing [16]. Even though the price is influenced by three market segments (industrial, jewellery, and investment), in the past it was stated that diamond's price fluctuation is highly correlated with disposable income and inflation rate [4,24]. In 1995, the introduction of synthetic diamonds [4] offered a more economically accessible manufacturing option to the production of diamonds, which were similar in properties and aesthetics, but customizable and limited in terms of dimensions. Nonetheless, this created a steep increase in the diamond price, as well as an enlarged demand for research and development [24] as the list of diamond consumer industries grew larger [5,26]. Recently, R. Bedoui et al. conducted studies on the diamond investing potential [3], concluding that even though diamond tends not to function as a safe haven and hedge for USD (United States Dollar) movement, it should still be used as an effective diversified to mitigate market volatility.

As previously mentioned, the main goal is to find the factors that influence the diamonds' price and the relationship between the independent variables with diamonds' price.

This paper is organized as follows. In Sect. 2, the methodology used in this work is described. The case study and the results obtained are presented and discussed in Sect. 3. Finally, some conclusions and future work are drawn in Sect. 4.

2 Methodology

In this section, the statistical techniques used to analyse the dataset are described, namely analysis of variance, multiple linear regression and variables selection methods.

2.1 Analysis of Variance

The Analysis of Variance (ANOVA) technique uses the variance to compare means and it is an inferential test that can be used when there are factors to be explored [22,23]. Therefore, ANOVA analyzes, through the sample variance, if there are differences between the mean of different levels in each factor or treatment.

In order to accurately assess how the levels differ, for example, to check if in each level there are in fact significant differences, it is necessary to use post hoc analysis, like Tukey's procedure [23,28]. Furthermore, different research areas use ANOVA to answer the research questions to extract more information about the data in the study [22].

Thus, One-way ANOVA is a technique that compares the means of more than two groups (independent variables). It takes into account the variability between groups and the variability within groups, where an F-statistic is produced. It is required that the dependent variable follows a normal distribution, the samples must be independent, the errors must be also independent and normally distributed. Furthermore, the variance must be equal between the groups, also known as homoscedasticity. If the normality assumption is violated, ANOVA is still robust [18,27].

Using ANOVA, it is expected to understand if there are differences between the diamonds' price mean of the different levels of each qualitative variable. This analysis can provide useful information about which qualitative variables can be a potential factor to influence the diamonds' price.

2.2 Multiple Linear Regression

Regression analysis is a statistical method that allows building a model for one quantitative dependent variable (y_i) as a function of one or more other independent variables ($x_i = 1, ..., p$). Its purpose is to infer the causal relationship of data obtained from correlational or non-experimental research. Multiple linear regression is employed to assess the significance of the independent variables on the diamond's price. Thus, the linear model is defined as

$$y_i = \beta_0 + \beta_1 x_{i1} + \beta_2 x_{i2} + \ldots + \beta_p x_{ip} + \epsilon_i$$

where β_0 represents the additive constant, $\beta_1, \beta_2, \ldots, \beta_p$ the coefficients of the independent variables; ϵ_i the random error component of the model.

Model validation is performed by analyzing the Gauss Markov conditions for residuals [8], which includes verifying zero mean condition and homoscedasticity of the errors as well as normality and independence hypothesis. Additionally, influence diagnostics is carried out through outlier detection, Leverage values, and Cook's distance. Leverage values (h_i) are calculated from the values of the independent variable, which assesses the distance of observed response from the point average of all independent variables. In this context, a Leverage value is identified as an outlier under the following condition: $h_i > 2(p+1)$ [17]. Cook's distance (D_i) is the squared distance between the least square estimated based on all observations n points $\hat{\beta}$ and the estimate obtained from eliminating the ith point $\hat{\beta}_{(i)}$ and it is used to measure the influence of removing an observation [20]. Such distance measure can be expressed as,

$$D_i = \frac{(\hat{\beta}_{(i)} - \hat{\beta}_{(i)})'\mathbf{X}'\mathbf{X}(\hat{\beta}_{(i)} - \hat{\beta}_{(i)})}{pMSE}$$

Using regression analysis, it is expected to establish a relationship between the diamonds' price and its independent variables through means of a linear function. From the resulting analysis, conclusions can be drawn regarding the significance of the independent variables towards the dependent variables.

2.3 Variables Selection

To select the variables that should enter the predictive models, stepwise selection methods were frequently used, thanks to their reliability [14]. Simultaneously, the value of Akaike Information Criterion (AIC), associated with the obtained models, can be used to estimate the prediction error and analyze the quality of several predictive models comparatively [12,15].

The stepwise methods are used to limit the number of possible regressions evaluated by the software during the process of creating a multivariate linear regression. They evaluate a limited array of independent variables at a time and define which ones fit the dependent variable data better. Depending on the way those independent variables are selected they can be categorized into the forward selection, backward elimination, or stepwise regression method [19].

To select the independent variables for the final model through the stepwise regression method, the selection process is repeated until a maximum number of steps, or until none of the remaining variables is eligible to be entered or removed [14]. The stepwise method is based upon two defining algorithms that rely on probability (P) and F values, and all eligible variables are considered for removal and entry at each step [14].

In the case of the forward selection, only the entry phase of the stepwise method is performed. The test begins with no predictor variables and they are progressively added one at a time. The first added variable is the independent variable that presents the highest correlation with the dependent variable. Then, the variable with the highest correlation with the residuals from the previous model is chosen and this procedure is repeated until the required F ratio is met [11]. During this process, the coefficient of determination (R^2) should be monitored as a way of uncovering how much predictive capability each step iteration provides [21]. On the other hand, the backward stepwise regression begins with the entire set of independent variables and progressively eliminates them using the removal algorithm of the stepwise regression, until a satisfactory model is achieved [19].

Despite the importance of these methods for the creation and simplification of predictive models, some limitations are associated, which often lead to an unsatisfactory final model. This happens because the act of selecting a subset of independent variables, relying solely on mathematical algorithms, might cause the removal of variables that have critical importance to the study. One example occurs when two variables present almost the same predictive ability. Faced with this issue, the software might end up adding or removing the wrong variable, since it lacks the previous critical knowledge held by the user [21]. This means that even though these methods are very convenient, especially in predictive studies that encompass a large array of independent variables, ignoring the authors' knowledge about the variables' importance might lead to poor and not generalizable models [29]. Hence, the AIC value can serve as an important tool to further evaluate the resulting models from a comparative stance. This value helps to predict which fitted candidate model best suits the data [7].

In this work, stepwise procedures are used to develop an encompassing multivariate predictive model. Nonetheless, the added/removed variables will be critically analyzed at each step and their predictive value will be assessed taking into account all the information gathered, specifically during the descriptive analysis, ANOVA, and correlation steps, that will map the importance of each independent variable and uncover relationships between them. Moreover, after obtaining the models through the different stepwise regression methods, the model with the smallest associated AIC value will be selected.

3 Case Study

The presented methodology was applied to the diamonds' dataset. Firstly, a descriptive analysis is performed. Then, the relationship between the independent qualitative variables, with the diamonds' price, is tested using ANOVA. For the independent quantitative variables it was used Spearman's correlation. Multiple linear regression encompasses the model construction routine and the analysis of a multiple predictive regression model for the prediction for the diamonds' price based on its attributes. All results were obtained using IBM® SPSS® Statistics, version 27.

3.1 Descriptive Analysis

The diamonds' dataset [1] includes several variables concerning the diamonds characteristics and price. In Table 1, all variables and the respective description are presented.

Table 1. Diamonds dataset information [6,10].

	Name	Description	Measure
Independent	Carat	Weight of the diamond	Quantitative
	Clarity	A measurement of how clear the diamond is	Qualitative
	Color	Diamond color (colorless and near colorless)	Qualitative
	Cut	Quality of the cut	Qualitative
	Table	Width of top of the diamond relative to the widest point	Quantitative
	X	Length (in mm)	Quantitative
	Y	Width (in mm)	Quantitative
	Z	Depth (in mm)	Quantitative
Dependent	Price	Diamonds' price (in US dollars)	Quantitative

In this dataset, there are nearly 54,000 rows of data sampling regarding the diamonds' information. Since the number of observations is too high, 2% of them were randomly selected (approximately 1,073 diamonds). This was done due to the high computational cost involved when handling this much data. The selected sample size guarantees a good representation of the sample for the analysis and predictive model construction.

Carat, *cut*, *color*, and *clarity* are usually known as the four Cs and are the most commonly laboratory-studied variables when it comes to diamonds' price estimation [9,30]. The *clarity* variable has five groups: seriously flawed, slightly included, very slightly included, very slightly included, and internally flawless. The color variable has near colorless and colorless groups and the cut variable has fair, good, very good, premium, and ideal levels. *Cut*, *color*, and *clarity* groups are not balanced, since it was extracted only 2% of the data sampling.

After a brief data analysis, twenty outliers were found and removed. Additionally, the variable *table* was coded into two different levels since it only has 25 different values, where level one represents the *table* values less than or equal to 57 (*table* mean). Otherwise, the measurements belong to the second level.

To assure the symmetry of the distribution of the quantitative variables, another transformation was required. Thus, the natural logarithm was applied to these variables, since their distribution was asymmetrical. Moreover, it is required that the residuals follow a normal distribution. Using this transformation can help to validate this assumption. Regardless of this transformation, these variables will be referred to the "new" variables *log(X)* as *LX*, *log(Y)* as *LY*, and *log(Z)* as *LZ*. It was found that the *carat* variable has a considerable impact on the diamonds' price. Hence, the dependent variable was changed to diamonds' price per carat (*dpc*). To assure symmetric distribution of the *dpc* variable, the logarithmic transformation was also applied (*ldpc*).

3.2 Analysis of Variance

In order to evaluate which qualitative variables affect the dependent variable (*ldpc*), one-way ANOVA was used considering four factors: *clarity*, *color*, *cut*, and *table*.

The hypotheses being tested are similar where it is intended to evaluate if the factors affect the diamonds' price per carat, individually. Considering $i = \{cut, color, clarity, table\}$, the hypotheses are:

H_0: The $factor_i$ does not significantly affect the diamonds' price per carat;
H_1: The $factor_i$ significantly affects the diamonds' price per carat.

In Table 2 the results using one-way ANOVA are presented since the dependent variable follows a normal distribution.

The variables *table* and *clarity* affect the diamonds' price per carat since the $p-value$ is less than the level of significance ($\alpha = 0.05$). In contrast, the variables *cut* and *color* do not affect the diamonds' price per carat, where the $p-value$ is greater than the level of significance.

Table 2. One-way ANOVA results.

Source	Df	F	P-value
Table	1	8.901	0.003
Cut	4	0.558	0.693
Color	1	1.650	0.199
Clarity	4	2.988	0.018

In order to evaluate the homogeneity of variance and randomness of residuals, Levene's test was performed. The $p - value$ is equal to 0.061, which means the variance of the diamonds' price per carat is equal across groups. Therefore, the assumption for homoscedasticity is validated. Figure 1 presents the Normal Q-Q Plot to evaluate the normality assumption and most of the values are according to the diagonal. That means, the residuals follow a normal distribution. The same conclusion can be made using the Kolmogorov-Smirnov test of normality, in which the $p - value$ is equal to 0.067. In addition, the residuals' mean is equal to zero. All assumptions for the residuals are satisfied.

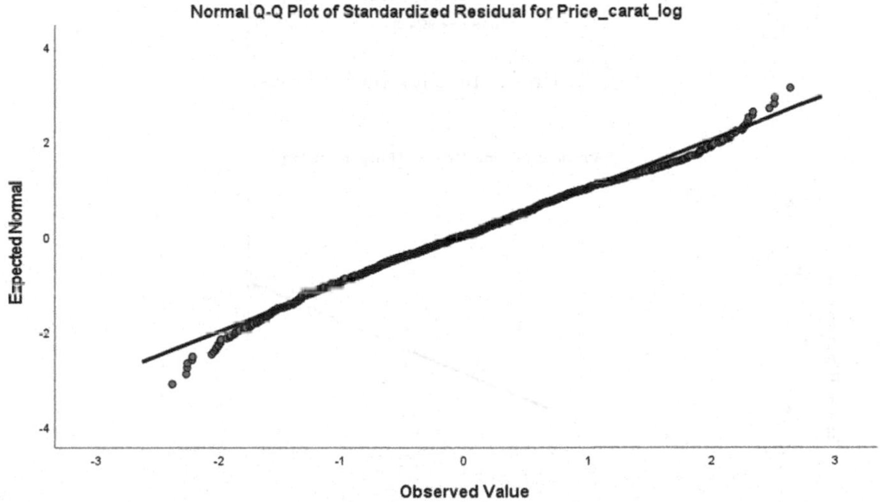

Fig. 1. Normal Q-Q Plot for the ANOVA residuals.

The Tukey HSD method was used for multiple comparisons between groups. It was only necessary to produce multiple comparisons for the variable *clarity* since it was more than two groups. Therefore, the groups seriously flawed and sightly inclusions have differences in the diamonds' price per carat ($p - value = 0.009$). The groups seriously flawed and very, very slightly included also have differences in the dependent variable ($p - value = 0.028$).

Figure 2 and Fig. 3 allow visualizing the average values for the levels of factors *clarity* and *table*, respectively. It is possible to conclude that the group seriously flawed has the lowest impact on the diamonds' price per carat when compared with the other *clarity* groups. Conversely, the second *table* group ($Table > 57$) has a greater impact, on the diamonds' price per carat, than the first level ($Table <= 57$).

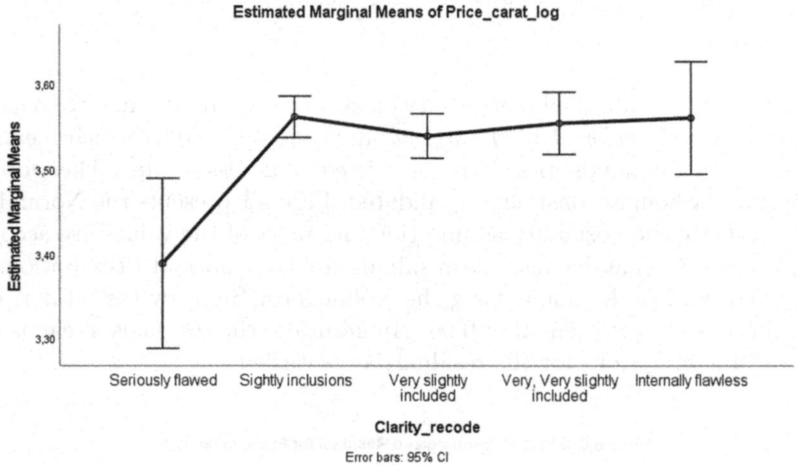

Fig. 2. Profile plot for clarity levels.

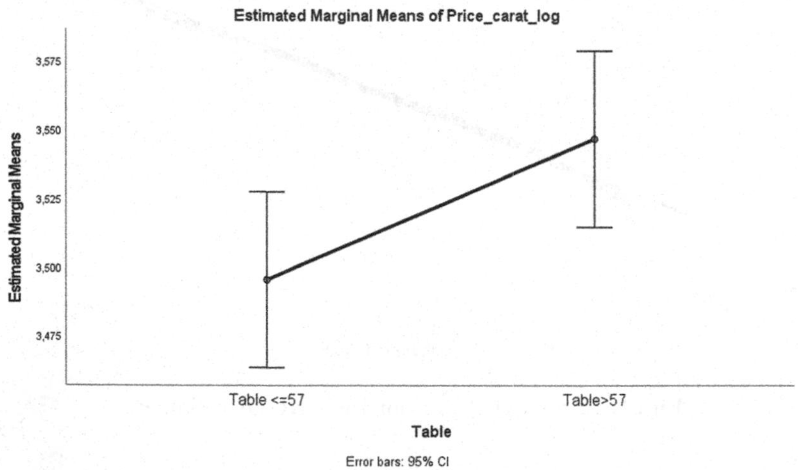

Fig. 3. Profile plot for table levels.

To analyze the relationship between the independent quantitative variables (measures *LX*, *LY*, and *LZ*) and the dependent variable of the sample, the diamonds' price, correlations were computed. Firstly, the normality of the variables *ldpc* and *LX*, *LY*, and *LZ* was assessed, by the Kolmogorov-Smirnov test. All obtained $p - values$ were less than 0.001 which allows the rejection of the null hypothesis. Thus, the variables do not follow a normal distribution. Hence, the non-parametric Spearman's correlation coefficients (r_s) were computed for the diamonds' dimensions and the diamonds' price (Table 3).

Table 3. Spearman's correlation coefficients for *LX*, *LY*, *LZ*, and *ldpc*.

	LX	*LY*	*LZ*
Correlation coefficient (r_s)	0.858	0.857	0.851
2-tailed $p - value$	<0.001	<0.001	<0.001

It can be assumed that *LX*, *LY* and *LZ* have a strong positive linear relationship with the *ldpc* since r_s was positive and near to the value of 1, with a significance value inferior to $\alpha = 0.01$. However, it is suspected that there exists multicollinearity between the independent variables *LX*, *LY* and *LZ*, which means that they could be related to one another, which indicates that if one of them has a high correlation with the dependent variable the others would have as well.

3.3 Multiple Linear Regression

The diamonds are characterized by their dimensions which are quantitative variables, but *cut*, *color*, *clarity*, and *table* are qualitative variables. By default, SPSS does not automatically consider qualitative variables as dummy variables, impairing its use in linear regression methods. Therefore, the qualitative variables were converted into dummy variables as an intermediate step. Meaning that they were coded into numerical data, enabling the accurate building of the model. The importance of each one of those variables to influence the diamonds price was assessed through multiple linear regression, using stepwise selection methods.

Table 4 shows the results of the multiple linear regression of the selected independent variables (see Table 1), taking into consideration their individual coding. The variable selection techniques considered were the enter method, forward selection, and backward elimination. The models were assessed according to their adjusted coefficient of determination (R_a^2), Akaike Information Criterion (AIC) along with analysis of the resulting residuals assumptions and Cook's distance.

After iteratively conducting changes to the sequentially created multiple linear regression models, a satisfactory solution was obtained. The final model (indicated in the last row of Table 4), obeyed every assumption and had an R_a^2 of 88.3%, thus successfully explained the dependent variable behavior (*ldpc*).

Table 4. Model regression summary.

Model	R_a^2	AIC	Residuals	Outliers	Cooks distance
Enter	0.877	−5549.771	✓	6	0.064
Backward/Forward	0.877	−5551.375	✓	6	0.069
Backward (Final model)	0.883	−5564.973	✓	0	0.055

Two variables were eliminated from the final model. The first one to be cut off from the equation was *table*, which every model identified as not significantly contributing to the model and was removed in the forward and backward methods. The elimination of this variable improved the AIC and maximum Cook's distance value (decreased), but outliers were encountered nonetheless. More iterations were conducted, and the outliers were identified and removed from the dataset. Additionally, the variable (LY) was removed based on the previous knowledge gathered from the exploratory analysis, in which a strong and positive correlation was identified amongst the quantitative variables, related to the size of the diamonds. This strong correlation led to suspected multicollinearity among them, which in turn destabilizes the model [2]. This is also perceived in the results of the previous models, where the coefficient for the LY variable exhibited a negative tendency, contrary to its expected tendency. Once again, this result is incoherent and thus, it is assumed that this variable contributes to the destabilization of the model.

The analysis of residuals assumptions was conducted. Figure 4 is a Normal Q-Q Plot to validate the normality assumption. Most of the values are according to the diagonal. Thus, this assumption is satisfied.

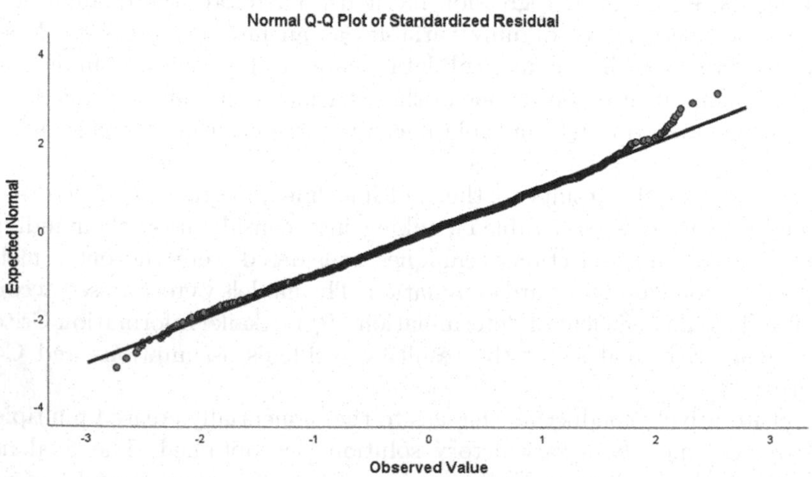

Fig. 4. Normal Q-Q Plot for the regression analysis residuals.

The homoscedasticity assumption was also validated by plotting the residuals (Fig. 5). It can be seen that does not exist any pattern and the values are randomly distributed.

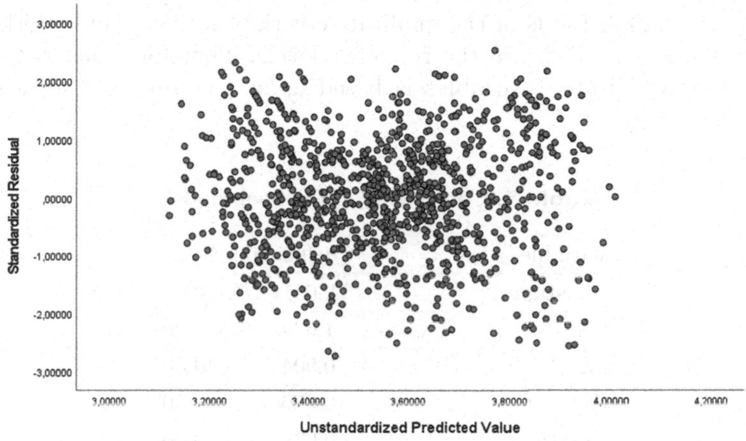

Fig. 5. Residuals plot.

In Fig. 6, it is presented the boxplot for residuals and no outliers are identified. Using the residuals descriptive statistics, the mean is equal to zero. Thereby, all the residuals assumptions were successfully validated.

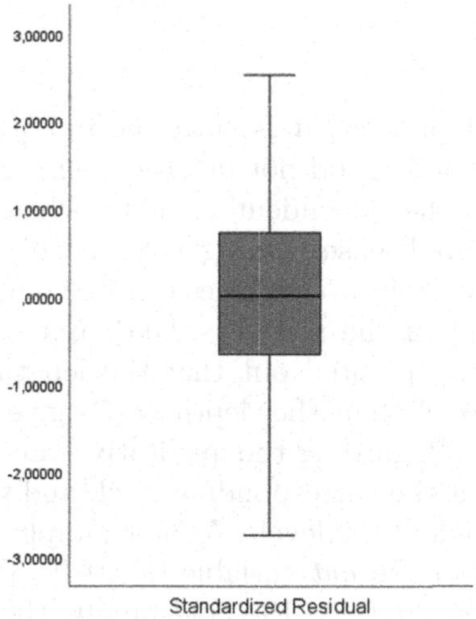

Fig. 6. Boxplot for residuals.

Having removed both *table* and *LY* variables along with the validation of all the assumptions of the final model, the backward and forward methods were both equally successful. The AIC value was the lowest reported one and the Cook's distance values did not surpass 0.06.

The coefficients and significance values of each variable are present in Table 5, except for the higher levels of the qualitative variables (ideal cut, colorless, and internally flawless), which are the reference levels. Therefore, the coefficient of the remaining qualitative variables is based upon a comparison against these reference levels.

Table 5. Coefficients of the final model.

Variable	Coefficient	P-value
Constant	2.051	<0.001
LX	1.629	<0.001
LZ	0.904	<0.001
Fair cut	−0.079	<0.001
Good cut	−0.032	<0.001
Very good cut	−0.019	0.001
Premium cut	−0.012	0.037
Near Colorless	−0.080	<0.001
Seriously flawed	−0.449	<0.001
Slightly included	−0.227	<0.001
Very slightly included	−0.128	<0.001
Very slightly included	−0.038	0.002

From a critical point of view, it is clear the importance of the *carat* variable. While the other variables did not behave as expected when the price was individually analyzed as the dependent variable, when *ldpc* is considered, the remaining variables acquired sense. Taking a closer look at the coefficients of the final model, exhibited in Table 5 tendencies can be identified.

The additive constant of the model is 2.051 and, in terms of the physical dimensions, it can also be pointed out that the length of the diamond (LX) weights more in this model than the depth (LZ), given the magnitude of the standardized coefficients. Regarding the qualitative variables, the negative coefficient is higher, the lower the corresponding level, and this is coherent with the relative importance of each of the levels. As an example, the *fair cut* is the most negatively affected level of the *cut* variable (−0.079), followed by the *good cut* (−0.032), then *very good cut* (−0.019), and finally, the *premium cut*, which is only affected by a coefficient of −0.012 in comparison with the *Ideal cut*. Moreover, it is worth noting that the lowest level of the cut variable (−0.079) is in the same range as the lowest *Color* level (−0.080) which means they negatively affect the dependent variable within these limits: [0, −0.080]. On the other hand, the variable *Clarity*, which includes the remaining levels, affects the dependent variable in a more negative manner: [0, −0.449].

4 Conclusions

In the current study, the analysis of influential factors on the diamond's price was carried out along with the proposal of an appropriate multiple linear regression model. To avoid high computational strain when processing data, a randomized sample was selected for analysis. In agreement with the established literature, the quantitative variables were transformed, which allowed a more accurate and balanced result. Moreover, it was necessary to transform the qualitative variables into dummy variables since it is a shortcoming of SPSS when the linear regression is performed.

It was possible to conclude that the variables *table* and *clarity* affect the dependent variable. Moreover, the quantitative variables have a strong positive linear relationship with the diamonds' price per carat. Stepwise selection models were conducted to evaluate which independent variables should be included in the model. As a result, the variable *table* was deemed not-significant by the selection models, and the LY was related to model destabilization. After removing them, the model was validated with an adjusted coefficient of determination of 88.3%. Besides, the final model was compliant with all the residuals' assumptions and encompassed all the remaining variables. The AIC value was reported as the lowest when compared to the other generated models and the tendencies experienced by the coefficients of the levels of the qualitative variables were coherent with the quality/price assumptions reviewed in the literature. The multiple linear regression helped define the importance of each set of variables in the final dependent variable. The variables *clarity* and length were identified as the most significant ones, in terms of qualitative and quantitative variables, respectively.

As far as future studies are concerned, the current study can be expanded upon by applying the Variance Inflation Factor (VIF), as a way of providing further insights into the multicollinearity issue that occurs among the quantitative variables. To address the identified constraints, Principal Components Analysis (PCA) can be applied to eliminate the multicollinearity effects. In addition, dividing the dataset into training and test sets can also be suggested as future work to evaluate the performance of the model to predict the diamonds' price.

References

1. Agrawal, S.: Diamond's price and atributes dataset (2007). https://www.kaggle.com/shivam2503/diamonds/metadata. Accessed 06 Oct 2020
2. Antunes, A.R., Braga, A.C.: Shiny app to predict agricultural tire dimensions. In: Gervasi, O., et al. (eds.) ICCSA 2020. LNCS, vol. 12251, pp. 247–260. Springer, Cham (2020). https://doi.org/10.1007/978-3-030-58808-3_19

3. Bedoui, R., Guesmi, K., Kalai, S., Porcher, T.: Diamonds versus precious metals: what gleams most against USD exchange rates? Finance Res. Lett. **34**, 101253 (2020). https://doi.org/10.1016/j.frl.2019.08.001
4. Bundy, F.P., Hall, H.T., Strong, H.M., Wentorfjun., R.H.: Man-Made Diamonds. Nature **176**(4471), 51–55 (1955). https://doi.org/10.1038/176051a0
5. Busch, J.V., Dismukes, J.P.: Trends and market perspectives for CVD diamond. Diamond Related Mater. **3**(4), 295–302 (1994). https://doi.org/10.1016/0925-9635(94)90175-9
6. Cardoso, M.G., Chambel, L.: A valuation model for cut diamonds. Int. Trans. Oper. Res. (2005). https://doi.org/10.1111/j.1475-3995.2005.00516.x
7. Cavanaugh, J.E., Neath, A.A.: The Akaike information criterion: background, derivation, properties, application, interpretation, and refinements. WIREs Comput. Stat. **11**(3), e1460 (2019). https://doi.org/10.1002/wics.1460
8. Chatterjee, S., Simonoff, J.S.: Handbook of Regression Analysis. Wiley, Hoboken (2012). https://doi.org/10.1002/9781118532843
9. Chu, S.: Pricing the C's of Diamond Stones. J. Stat. Educ. **9**(2) (2001). https://doi.org/10.1080/10691898.2001.11910659
10. Falls, S.: Clarity, cut, and culture: The many meanings of diamonds (2014). https://doi.org/10.5860/choice.186333
11. Forthofer, R.N., Lee, E.S., Hernandez, M.: Linear Regression. In: Forthofer, R.N., Lee, E.S., Hernandez, M. (eds.) Biostatistics (Second Edition), pp. 349–386. Academic Press, San Diego, second edi edn. (2007). https://doi.org/10.1016/B978-0-12-369492-8.50018-2
12. Glatting, G., Kletting, P., Reske, S.N., Hohl, K., C, R.: Choosing the optimal fit function: comparison of the Akaike information criterion and the F-test. Med. Phys. **34**(11), 4285–4292 (2007). https://doi.org/10.1118/1.2794176
13. Harris, J.W.: Diamond. In: Encyclopedia of Geology, pp. 455–472. Elsevier (2021). https://doi.org/10.1016/B978-0-12-409548-9.12083-4
14. IBM Corp.: Ibm spss statistics 27 documentation (2020). https://www.ibm.com/support/pages/ibm-spss-statistics-27-documentation. Accessed 03 Feb 2021
15. Kimura, K., Waki, H.: Minimization of Akaike's information criterion in linear regression analysis via mixed integer nonlinear program. Optim. Methods Softw. **33**(3), 633–649 (2018). https://doi.org/10.1080/10556788.2017.1333611
16. Li, G., Rahim, M.Z., Pan, W., Wen, C., Ding, S.: The manufacturing and the application of polycrystalline diamond tools - a comprehensive review. J. Manuf. Processes **56**, 400–416 (2020). https://doi.org/10.1016/j.jmapro.2020.05.010
17. Mason, R.L., Gunst, R.F., Hess, J.L.: Statistical Design and Analysis of Experiments, 2nd edn. Wiley, New York (2003)
18. McKnight, P.E., Najab, J.: Mann-Whitney U Test. The Corsini Encyclopedia of Psychology (2010). https://doi.org/10.1002/9780470479216.corpsy0524
19. Montgomery, D.C., Peck, E.A., Vining, G.G.: Introduction to linear regression analysis. Int. Stat. Rev. **81** (2013). https://doi.org/10.1111/insr.12020_10
20. Montgomery, D.C.: Design and Analysis of Experiments, 8th edn. Wiley
21. Riffenburgh, R.H.: Statistical Prediction. In: Riffenburgh, R.H. (ed.) Statistics in Medicine, 2nd edn., pp. 125–136. Academic Press, Burlington (2006). https://doi.org/10.1016/B978-012088770-5/50047-2
22. Rutherford, A.: ANOVA and ANCOVA: A GLM Approach: Second Edition (2013). https://doi.org/10.1002/9781118491683
23. Salkind, N.J.: Statistics for people who (think they) hate statistics: Excel 2007 edition (2010)

24. Schwander, M., Partes, K.: A review of diamond synthesis by CVD processes. Diamond Related Mater. **20**(9), 1287–1301 (2011). https://doi.org/10.1016/j.diamond.2011.08.005
25. Schwertfeger, H., Fokin, A.A., Schreiner, P.R.: Diamonds are a chemist's best friend: diamondoid chemistry beyond adamantane. Angewandte Chemie Int. Edition **47**(6), 1022–1036 (2008). https://doi.org/10.1002/anie.200701684
26. Tillmann, W.: Trends and market perspectives for diamond tools in the construction industry. Int. J. Refractory Metals Hard Mater. **18**(6), 301–306 (2000). https://doi.org/10.1016/S0263-4368(00)00034-2
27. Verma, J.P.: Data analysis in management with SPSS software (2013). https://doi.org/10.1007/978-81-322-0786-3
28. Wilcox, R.R.: Understanding the practical advantages of modern ANOVA methods. J. Clin. Child Adolescent Psychol. (2002). https://doi.org/10.1207/S15374424JCCP3103_12
29. Wilcox, R.R.: 14 - MORE REGRESSION METHODS. In: Wilcox, R.R. (ed.) Applying Contemporary Statistical Techniques, pp. 517–555. Academic Press, Burlington (2003). https://doi.org/10.1016/B978-012751541-0/50035-3
30. Zhang, C.Y., Oh, S., Park, J.: State-of-the-Art Diamond Price Predictions using Neural Networks
31. Zimper, A.: On the welfare equivalence of asset markets and banking in Diamond Dybvig economies. Econ. Lett. **121**(3), 356–359 (2013). https://doi.org/10.1016/j.econlet.2013.09.023

On Discovering Treatment-Effect Modifiers Using Virtual Twins and Causal Forest ML in the Presence of Prognostic Biomarkers

Erik Hermansson and David Svensson(✉)

AstraZeneca R&D Gothenburg, Gothenburg, Sweden
david.j.svensson@astrazeneca.com

Abstract. The recent years have seen a rapid development in the general Machine Learning area and a similar strong trend has taken place within the drug development domain, known as Precision Medicine. Traditionally, the main focus in clinical trials has been to estimate the overall treatment effect, but the reality of treatment effect heterogeneity has led to an interest in data-driven approaches for automatically identifying treatment effect modifiers and subgroups with enhanced treatment effect. These techniques are different from general purpose supervised learning due to its causal inference flavour and the notorious presence of prognostic effects in clinical trials. In this work, we focus on the popular method `Virtual Twins`; despite being among the earliest method, relatively little attention has been paid to the specifics of its implementation, in particular to the relative merits of arm-specific modelling versus a 'common-surface' approach. Since `Virtual Twins` is a generic algorithm (and not limited to any specific predictive base model such as the originally proposed `Random Forest`) we choose to base it on `XGboost`. We also study the forest-based `Causal Forest`, recently popular due to its (by-design) unbiased estimates of individual treatment effects. We compare the performance of these methods regarding their ability to disentangle prognostic and predictive effects. This is of critical importance in precision medicine, since only the latter are related to enhanced treatment effects; also a certain tendency to mistakenly declare prognostic biomarkers as predictive has been reported in the ML literature.

Keywords: Treatment effect heterogeneity · Precision medicine · Individual Treatment Effects (ITE) · Machine learning · Prognostic and predictive biomarkers

1 Introduction

A key step in the review of clinical trial data is to assess to potential presence of treatment effect heterogeneity. This arise in different ways in drug development, and one is the routine regulatory assessment of pivotal Phase III trials known as

The original version of this chapter was revised: The typographical error has been corrected in the abstract. The correction to this chapter is available at https://doi.org/10.1007/978-3-030-86973-1_51

O. Gervasi et al. (Eds.): ICCSA 2021, LNCS 12952, pp. 624–640, 2021.
https://doi.org/10.1007/978-3-030-86973-1_44

consistency assessment. This is conducted along the lines described in [1,10] and aims to assess a pre-defined set of subgroups, with the aim to identify if some patient groups lacks a proper response to the novel treatment and subsequently should be excluded when the drug is approved. The subgroups are agreed upon beforehand and are defined in terms of baseline characteristics (such as age, gender, medical history, key laboratory variables, etc.) and it is standard practice to dichotomize continuous variables (cuts decided prospectively).

In this work, we look at the more 'agnostic' approach to subgroups where machine learning (ML) is applied for discovering heterogeneous treatment effects and novel subgroups: while consistency assessment might be said to be a 'regulatory perspective', this is more the 'sponsor's perspective' [19]. The key difference is to go beyond inspection of pre-specified subgroups which normally excludes the possibility of higher order interactions.

The need for such analyses is motivated, e.g., by failed trials (where the overall result did not meet the expectations) where there is medical reasons to believe that some patients are likely to respond better than average and it was not captured by the simpler univariate, pre-specified, subgroup analysis. Different level of rigour of such ML approaches might exist, ranging from strictly aiming to define a biomarker signature (with an honest treatment effect estimate associated to the subgroup, as the basis for another trial investment) to merely short-listing the most likely effect modifying biomarkers (facilitating the scientific understanding of the drug's mechanism), see [27] for further details. We focus here on the latter aspect, which arguably is one core aspect in the practice; not all methods in the area automatically define a novel biomarker signature (e.g., Causal Forest and regression-based methods do not [19]) whereas most methods provide some quantification of importance of biomarkers.

2 Setting

We focus on parallel Randomized Clinical Trials (RCT), a standard design for Phase III drug development and implying that the 'ground truth' (individual response to each treatment) cannot be directly observed (e.g., [3]). This leads to a causal inference flavour and the concept of potential outcome; more formally, we observe data $\{(Y_i, \mathbf{x}_i, T_i)\}_i^n \sim \mathbb{P}$ where i is index for patient, $\mathbf{x}_i \in \mathbb{R}^p$ is the patient's baseline data, $T_i \in \{0, 1\}$ is the binary randomized treatment allocation (with $T_i = 0$ and $T_i = 1$ representing the control and active drug, respectively), and $Y_i \in \mathbb{R}$ is the outcome (i.e., assumed continuous). From now, we drop index i for patient. As standard in causal inference [24], let $Y^{(0)}$ and $Y^{(1)}$ denote the *potential* outcomes for a given patient on treatments 0 and 1, respectively; one will be factual and one counterfactual, due to the randomization. The target of interest [5] is then to estimate the Conditional Average Treatment Effect (**CATE**)):

$$\tau(\mathbf{x}) = \mathbf{E}[(Y^{(1)} - Y^{(0)})|X = \mathbf{x}], \tag{1}$$

which is the expected treatment effect for a patient with covariates $\mathbf{x}$, also known as the *individual treatment contrast.* The core aspect in precision medicine is to characterize $\tau(\mathbf{x})$ across the covariate space. See [22] for the nuances of such analyses and their slightly different purposes. Regardless of exact purpose, it is of practical high importance to understand if only a subset of the p variables drive $\tau(\mathbf{x})$; these are the *predictive* variables, modifying the treatment effect.

2.1 Prognostic and Predictive Effects in Clinical Trials, and Potential Confounding Issues in the ML Analysis

A general form for a linear model is

$$Y_i = h(\mathbf{x}_i) + g(\mathbf{x}_i) \cdot (T_i - \pi) + \epsilon_i \tag{2}$$

where $\epsilon_i \sim N(0, \sigma^2)$ i.i.d, π treatment probability assignment to active arm ($= 0.5$ if 1:1 randomization), and with $g()$ and $h()$ unspecified [12]. For this class of models, the treatment effect for a patient with covariates $\mathbf{x}_i$ is $g(\mathbf{x}_i)$, i.e., independent of $h(\mathbf{x}_i)$; the latter only influences the outcome y_i (identically on both arms) and is said to be prognostic. The $g(\mathbf{x}_i)$ is the predictive part, and it is possible that not all p covariates contribute to it. Since this is of key importance in our further investigations, we illustrate the concepts using the following simple model: $Y = T + x_1 + x_3 + x_2 * T + x_3 * T + \epsilon$. Here x_1 is prognostic (predicting Y); x_2 is predictive since it modifies the treatment contrast; x_3 is both prognostic and predictive; if another variable x_4 was measured in the trial it is non-informative variable.

Handling of prognostic effects in causal inference ML is a key aspect and a number of issues has been noted in the literature. It has been noted [25] that ML methods sometimes tend to confound prognostic variables with predictive ones, i.e., assigning high ranking to biomarkers which are not truly involved in any treatment interaction. In the practice of drug development, prognostic effects are often present (e.g., age, gender, disease severity are often prognostic for a given disease). These effects are typically of a stronger magnitude than treatment effects, and issues arise (revolving around prognostic effects overshadowing predictive effects) if a straightforward supervised regression approach is taken (see [19]). It is demonstrated in e.g., [21] that prognostic effects can be confounded with treatment effects in subgroups: while all prognostic baseline variables are expected to be balanced across arms due to the randomization, this does not necessarily holds in local areas of the covariate space. This is particularly an inherent problem with tree-based methods; assume x is a prognostic variable and positively correlated with the endpoint. It is expected to be evenly distributed across treatment arms in the full population, but in a (data-driven) tree-node x can now have different distributions. Since x is prognostic, it translates to a confounding with the treatment effect (e.g., [15,21]); in the node, the arm with higher x, the endpoint now (in distribution) is higher, and a naive analysis in the node would now render an artefact estimate. This is similar to inherent issues in observational data. In [25] a clear tendency of mistake prognostic effects for predictive was reported for methods (where the CRAN version of Virtual Twins was among the methods studied, [34]).

2.2 Methodology for Heterogeneous Treatment Effect ML

The literature has seen a multitude of proposed methods (e.g., [6,36,38]) and already in the 2016 paper [19] a long list of methods were described, ranging from penalized regression techniques to tree-ensemble methods. A common denominator is the current paradigm [8] to treat subgroup detection as a special case of model selection. As a background, we here only mention some well-known methods in this area before focusing in on two specific ones. The method `SIDES` [18] is a local method in the sense that it only models $\tau(\mathbf{x})$ in a sub-region of the covariate space, and has operator-choice complexity control regarding how complex a subgroup is allowed to be; `IT` [28] is an early method in this area, tree-based via interaction-test p-values; `GUIDE` [21] is also tree-based and fits local GLM models in nodes aiming to adjust for local imbalances of prognostic effects; it uses a split selection that is by design unbiased. Model-based recursive partitioning `MOB` is also tree-based and fits local models but uses a different splitting process than GUIDE's based on fluctuation tests [37], and has e.g., proposed for dose-finding trials [31]. QUINT [9] seeks qualitative interactions (i.e., with some sub-regions where the active drug might be harmful).

In this work, we compare two popular ensemble-based approaches; the 'notable' [11] **Virtual Twins** (VT) was originally proposed in 2011 [13] and became a popular choice in this area (e.g., [4,16,17,19,20,25,26,33,36,38,39]). It is a two-step approach where a supervised learning model learns to predict the outcome in the first step, then relying on factual and counterfactual predictions that renders prediction of individual treatment effects explored in a second modelling step. It is worth mentioning that this scheme is a general one in ITE modelling and not specific to VT (discussed in e.g., [3]), and we speculate that this fact has contributed to its popularity in the data science community, where the knowledge of fitting general purpose supervised learners is high. Recently, a generalized version of Random Forest has emerged, the **Causal Forest** (CF) [35] which uses a certain splitting of the training data such that the same data does not enter the tree building process and the estimation process. This is known to render unbiased estimation of individual treatment effects. Both VT and CF constructs variable importance of all predictors, offering a ranking of most important features, see next section for further details.

3 The ML Methods Compared

Before describing details of the methods we first make some general remarks: VT is a two-step procedure where the first step involves fitting a supervised learning model to the training data simply for learning to predict the outcome. This modelling then is applied for estimating the individual treatment contrasts $\tau(\mathbf{x})$. Since it appears reasonable to expect that the highest possible accuracy[1] in Step 1 would improve the overall performance of VT, we think it makes much sense to consider the XGboost rather than Random Forest. The XGboost

[1] In a cross-validation or test-data sense, but not in an overfitting sense.

[29] is arguably among the strongest general-purpose algorithms for supervised learning for tabular data (e.g., *'Undoubtedly, the reigning champions of learning from tabular currently are decision tree-based algorithms. Gradient boosted trees are often the tool of choice, evidenced from their popularity in Kaggle contests'*, [32]). It is also stressed in the recent book [11] that other base models can be used for VT. While our modernized VT is boosting-based, CF is bagging-based, i.e., based on Random Forest but with the twist that allows it to estimate individual treatment effects honestly due to separating the construction of trees from the estimation process. Another motivation to look at CF is its off-the-shelf nature; given almost non-existing practical risks of commit model fitting errors, one can consider the inclusion of CF as also offering a kind of validation of the results from the more tuning-heavy VT. For the above reasons we think it makes sense to contrast these methods. There is a practical consideration too - does it pay off to perform all the computationally optimization of the Boosting models (for VT) or will CF by default give comparable or even better results?

There is one further largely unexplored aspect that motivates our simulation study: what are the relative merits of using one- or two models in Step 1 in VT? This is elaborated on in the next section, and is related to a general modeling strategies in causal inference ML (e.g., S-learners, T-learners and hybrids [7]).

3.1 Virtual Twins Implementation and Inherent Modelling Choices; Separate Models or Shared Representation

VT is a two-step algorithm, schematically consisting of the following steps (but see the specifics further below):

- `STEP 1`: Fitting supervised regression (**F**) for predicting potential outcomes $y^{(0)}$ and $y^{(1)}$; the difference of predictions $z = \hat{\mathbf{F}}(\mathbf{x}, T = 1) - \hat{\mathbf{F}}(\mathbf{x}, T = 0)$ represents predictions of individual treatment effects,
- `STEP 2`: Use another supervised regression (**G**) modelling z as the response against the predictors $\mathbf{x}$; i.e., explore if baseline data $\mathbf{x}$ can predict the z. (Discussed below).

In `STEP 1`, the treatment variable T enters either via splitting the training data according to arm and fit separate models, or fitting a single model to the data where treatment assignment is present as a feature. This is a key aspect in this paper, further discussed in Sect. 3.2. In [13], the choice for **F** was Random Forest. Note that the treatment variable is not explicitly present as a feature in `STEP 2` since the focus there is to identify trends in z against the baseline predictors.

The modelling approach **G** in the `STEP 2` can be different from the one in `STEP 1`, e.g., $\mathbf{G}$ = CART was proposed in [13], when an explicit subgroup definition is sought; the union of tree nodes with better than average response then defines a subgroup with enhanced effect. If instead a ranking via Variable Importance (VIP) is the aim of the analysis (aiming to identify predictive x), any suitable supervised learner can be considered. Given the general inferiority of single trees versus tree ensembles, it makes sense to use more modern approaches, e.g., $\mathbf{G}$ = XGboost (see [11]), which is our choice.

3.2 A Key Modeling Choice: Arm-Specific or Single-Surface?

We think the following consideration is somewhat overlooked in the literature: originally, when VT emerged in 2011 [13] the recommendation was to not base the Step 1 on the training data *as given* (which is (Y, X, T)) but on an 'enriched' data set where certain pre-computed treatment-covariate interactions were manually entered as additional columns to the data set:

$$W = (Y, X, T, X \cdot I_{T=0}, X \cdot I_{T=1}) \tag{3}$$

where I_B denotes an indicator function (= 1 if B holds, otherwise zero). This may not be of obvious value, but the authors had noted that it improved numeric stability; they gave no further quantitative motivation. We now refer to this latter choice as 'expanded' training data. An intuition behind it (loosely speaking) may be that prognostic effects tend to be stronger than predictive ones in clinical trials, and by introducing new candidate treatment-related columns the ML is offered more chances to strike on the right path. (See e.g., [19] for illustrations of how prognostic effects tend to dominate the model fit if a standard tree-based ML approach is used, Sect. 5, and similar aspects are discussed in [7], Sect. 4). Note that in this formulation, a *single* Random Forest model is fitted to the expanded training data W. In the vignette of the `CRAN` package `aVirtualTwins` [34] it is explained that the user has modelling freedom: specifying base model of choice and, in particular, decide regarding the training data: arm-specific or expanded? The arm-specific option in Step 1 may be considered as the most natural starting point and we speculate that this sometimes (for that reason) is used in the practice.

The above considerations are generally known in causal inference ML (e.g., 'separate models', 'augment feature space', and 'shared representation' in [23]). In a recent paper [3], section 'Modeling choices and methods for individualized treatment effects' some principled pros and cons were discussed (although the explicit expansion (3) was not covered).

In this paper we look at the special case of these general considerations for the Virtual Twins method, and how this impacts the performance in terms of handling prognostic effects. We use notation **VT1** for the version based on training data W (a single surface approach), and **VT2** for arm-specific modelling.

3.3 Fitting Boosting Models

Regarding fitting Boosting models, efforts were made to avoid over-fitting and optimization was performed over a grid of hyper-parameters using cross validation (CV). (In the analysis of clinical trials, it is sometimes not feasible to split data into training, test and validation; the data is too expensive, the data sets are too small). The maximal number of trees considered was 1000 (preliminary experimental runs indicated that considerably fewer trees often were sufficient).

3.4 Causal Forest Implementation

We relied on the CRAN package `grf` [30] and treated CF as the 'off-the-shelf' option, using it based on `num_trees` = 10000 (Bagging-based methods allow a larger no. of trees without risking overfitting [35], and some preliminary runs confirmed that larger ensembles did not make a notable difference on the performance).

4 Simulation Experiments

We performed a simulation experiment were RCTs were simulated under two assumptions regarding total *trial size* ($N = 800$ and $N = 5000$), representing smaller and larger clinical trials. The number of *candidate biomarkers* were fixed to $p = 20$, a realistic and typical number (e.g., see [6,19,20,38]). (Smaller p is sometimes in the practice considered (e.g., [14]). Regarding larger, we stress that clinical trial data is not really 'Big Data', neither in n (trial size) or p (no. of covariates), and, hence, very large p (e.g., 1000) is outside the scope here). The x_j were i.i.d. standard normal ($\sim N(0,1)$), and the motivation for uncorrelated biomarkers is to enable to clearest possible interpretation of the results. However, we also included runs with a compound symmetry correlation structure (rendering $\text{corr}(x_j, x_k) = 0.3$) for all $j \neq k$. We generated *continuous endpoints* from models in Table 1.

Table 1. Simulation models. All models except model **M4** contain true predictive effects. Two models (**M7**, **M8**) deviate from having 5 prognostic variables.

Case:	Model:
M1	$y = -1 + 3 \cdot (x_1+x_2+x_3+x_4+x_5) + T \cdot I_{(X_7>0, X_8>0)} + \epsilon$
M2	$y = -1 + 3 \cdot (x_1+x_2+x_3+x_4+x_5) + T \cdot I_{(X_1>0)} + \epsilon$
M3	$y = -1 + 3 \cdot (x_1+x_2+x_3+x_4+x_5) + T \cdot I_{(X_{20}>0)} + \epsilon$
M4	$y = -1 + 3 \cdot (x_1+x_2+x_3+x_4+x_5) + \epsilon$
M5	$y = -1+3\cdot(x_1+x_2+x_3+x_4+x_5)+T\cdot(x_{10}+x_{11}+x_{12}+x_{13}+x_{14}+x_{15})+\epsilon$
M6	$y = -1+3(I_{(X_1>0)}+I_{(X_2>0)}+I_{(X_3>0)}+I_{(X_4>0)}+I_{(X_5>0)})+T\cdot I_{(X_5>0)}+\epsilon$
M7	$y = -1+3\cdot(x_1+x_2+x_3+x_4+x_5+x_6+x_7+x_8+x_9+x_{10})+I_{(X_{20}>0)}\cdot T+\epsilon$
M8	$y = -1+3\cdot(x_1+x_2+x_3+x_4+x_5+x_6+x_7+x_8+x_9+x_{10})+I_{(X_1>0)}\cdot T+\epsilon$
M9	$y = -1 + 3\cdot(x_1+x_2+x_3+x_4+x_5) + \sin(X_1) \cdot T + \epsilon$
M10	$y = -1 + 10 \cdot (x_1+x_2+x_3+x_4+x_5) + T \cdot I_{(X_1>0)} + \epsilon$
M11	$y = -1 + (x_1+x_2+x_3+x_4+x_5)^3 + X_1^3 \cdot T + \epsilon$

Other types of endpoints commonly seen in clinical trials were excluded due to the current implementation of Causal Forest is restricted to numeric ones. Another reason is that the continuous case is an informative start case and if methods have difficulties here, the problems are not likely to diminish for other endpoints (e.g., due to [2]). It is furthermore not uncommon to make comparisons in the continuous case (e.g., [6, 18, 36]). All simulations contained ≥5 *prognostic variables* with varying prognostic strength. Including many prognostic reflects reality in clinical trials, where (by design) one includes variables known to influence at least the outcome; due to limited scientific knowledge in the drug development some variables will by necessity be non-informative, and such were included too.

We vary from model to model how many variables were truly predictive (effect modifying); some scenarios were simple (making sure such are easily detected by the machines) and some more complex. One model lacked true predictive effects (**M4**). Some models have variables with both predictive and prognostic properties (e.g., (**M2**). The predictive effects were designed to be of lesser magnitude than the prognostic effects, again to reflect reality. Most models had a linear additive structure, representing simpler cases and if these already present difficulties for the ML, more complex cases will be at least as hard. The *predictive effects* were either introduced as the presence of a true subgroup via dichotomization (a true planted subgroup, e.g., (**M2**)) or as gradual covariate-treatment interactions (no clear splits involved, e.g., (**M5**)). The focus here is simply to identify these variables rather than to define novel subgroups; this is not atypical for practical applications where an understanding of drivers often is a key consideration.

Each model scenario was iterated $k = 100$ times, and for each replicate the resulting Variable Importance was tracked (from each of the VT, and CF). For clarity, the VIP for Virtual Twins is derived from the 2nd step in the algorithm. The VIPs are not directly comparable across models, but within each it is informative to compare the relative ranking of the $x_1, \ldots, x_{20}$. We define `Power` as the proportion simulation iterations when a truly predictive (treatment-effect modifying) variable was top ranked, and `Type-1-Error` as the number of iterations when a none-predictive variable was top-ranked. This is non-standard terminology in ML, e.g., no formal statistical test is actually conducted on some nominal significance level, but the terminology captures the risk of getting a false positive result. We furthermore look at to what extent this Type-1-Error-rate is driven by prognostic variables.

Another key aspect is the individual treatment effects themselves and how the ability to top-rank predictive variables correlates with estimation accuracy. We hence tracked (for each of VT1, VT2 and CF) the Root Mean Square Error (`RMSE`) of z and $\hat{z}$ in each simulation iteration, where the former here denotes is the theoretical true ITE and the latter the estimated ITE. The z are known in simulations (e.g., for model **M2** it is $z = I(x_1 > 0)$). We then average over the 100 iterations. We are focusing on the *relative performance* of VT1, VT2 and CF *within* each simulation scenario (i.e., RMSE and VIP for a fixed ML method is not directly comparable across simulation models).

5 Results

Before summarizing results across the landscape of models and iterations, we first discuss some specific results. In Fig. 1 we see how the VIP distribute across the $x_1, ..., x_{20}$ for simulation model **M1**. In this specific case, it is clear that only the single-surface VT (VT1) had some success in identifying the true predictive variables x_7 and x_8; arm-specific VT (VT2) was much worse and consistently claimed prognostic variables as predictive (i.e., the box-plots for x_j, $j = 1, ..., 5$ are clearly located far above all other boxplots). VT1 had some tendency to top rank the prognostic $x_1, x_2, ..., x_5$. (How often all this happened is summarized in Fig. 2, and described further below). Causal Forest was between VT1 and VT2 in terms of performance in this example.

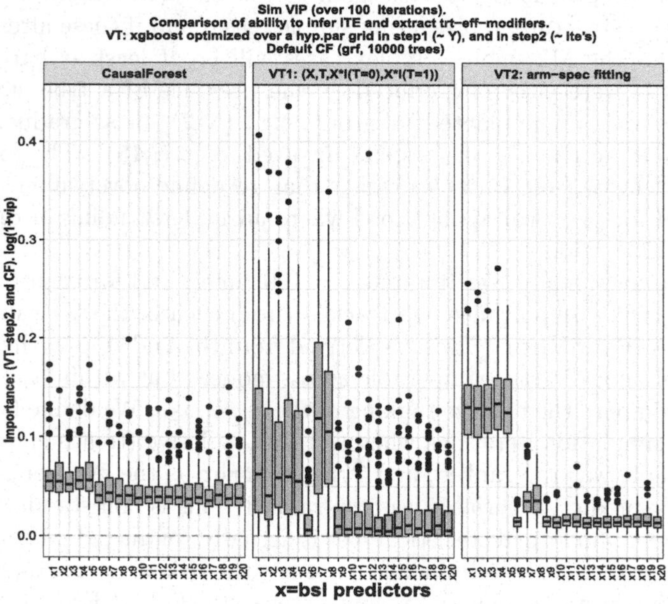

Fig. 1. Variable Importance (VIP) results for simulation model **M1**, 100 iterations (trial size 800).

Another case is displayed in Fig. 6, simulation model **M7** with rather many (ten) prognostic effects present. Then, both CF and VT2 often mistakenly top-ranked prognostic effects; this is in contrast to the single-surface VT. Furthermore the case (**M11**, $N = 5000$) is displayed in Fig. 5 where x_1 was both prognostic and predictive; here CF and VT1 performed well, whereas VT2 did (to a substantial degree) top-rank purely prognostic variables. However, the performance was very similar between VT1 and VT2 when $N = 800$ (and the same for a few other cases, e.g. **M5**, **M6**, **M9**).

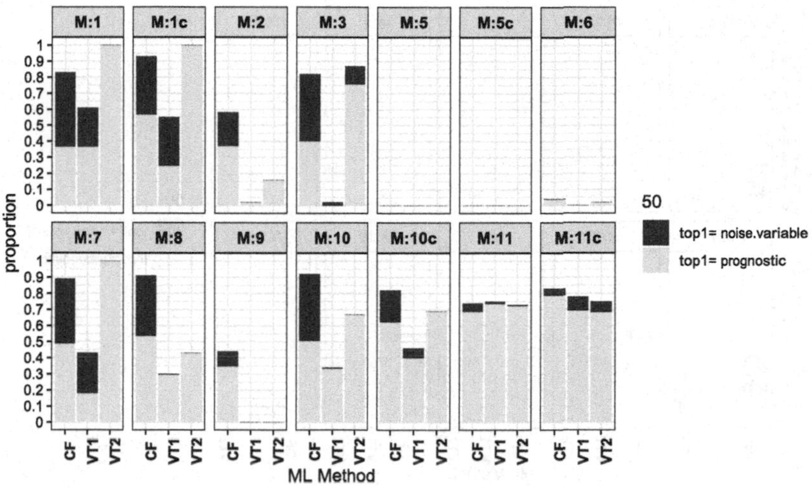

Fig. 2. Type-1-Error rates: Proportions incorrect top-ranking over 100 simulation iterations (trial size 800); total bar height displays the proportion of runs when a non-predictive variable was ranked as the most important one, with light colour scheme displaying how often this is due to a prognostic variable. (**CF** = Causal Forest, **VT1** = single-surface Virtual Twins, **VT2** = arm-specific Virtual Twins. 'c' = cases with correlation 0.3 between predictors).

The above mentioned results were typical in the sense that (1) non-informative variables were seldom top-ranked, and (2) the prognostic variables tended to drive the Type-1-Error rate (see also the Appendix for further examples). All this is summarized in what now follows.

The results regarding Type-1-Error and, in particular, how prognostic variables drive this error rate, is summarized in Fig. 2 (for trial size = 800). In that graph, the total height of a bar displays the Type-1-Error (e.g., for CF and simulation model **M1** the Type-1-Error was 0.83). The light colour scheme displays

Table 2. Simulation Result regarding Power: Proportion of simulations over 100 runs when a truly predictive variable had highest VIP. (Abbreviations: **CF** = Causal Forest, **VT1** = single-surface Virtual Twins, **VT2** = arm-specific Virtual Twins). The results for the simulation cases with correlation gave similar results to their non-correlation counterpart. Our definition of Power lacks meaning if no true predictive variables are present, hence the NA for model **M4** .

ML approach	N	M:1	M:2	M:3	M:4	M:5	M:6	M:7	M:8	M:9	M:10	M:11
CF	800	0.17	0.42	0.18	NA	1	0.96	0.11	0.09	0.56	0.08	0.26
VT1	800	0.39	0.98	0.98	NA	1	1	0.57	0.70	1	0.66	0.25
VT2	800	0.00	0.84	0.13	NA	1	0.98	0.00	0.57	1	0.33	0.27
CF	5000	0.74	1	1	NA	1	1	0.55	0.43	1	0.46	0.66
VT1	5000	1	1	1	NA	1	1	1	1	1	1	0.81
VT2	5000	0.00	1	1	NA	1	1	0.8	1	1	0.83	0.37

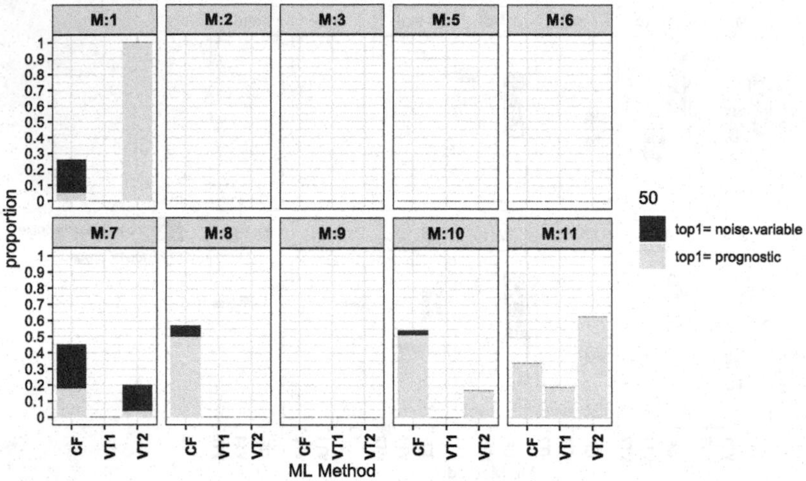

Fig. 3. Error rates: Proportions incorrect top-ranking over 100 simulation iterations for the 'ANTI-NULL' simulation models (with a true predictive effect present). Trial size was $n = 5000$. (Cases with correlation not displayed due to identical with their corresponding non-correlation results.

how the error was due to an incorrect top-1-ranking of a prognostic variable (e.g., for (CF, **M1**) it was 44% indicated by yellow. This is not directly matching the scale of the y axis, since it is a proportion of a proportion). A clear trend across the landscape of simulations is how the prognostic variables are the dominating driving factor behind the error rate (e.g., case **M11**), in particular, prominently dominating over contributions from truly non-informative variables. The corresponding results for trial size 5000 is found in Fig. 3.

Results regarding *power* are found in Table 2. The RMSE estimation accuracy is summarized in Table 3, and the relative performance of VT2 versus VT1 (in RMSE) is summarized in Fig. 4.

Table 3. Simulation results for accuracy of estimating individual treatment effects: RMSE(truth, estimated) averaged over over 100 iterations (case $N = 800$ and $N = 5000$), for each method. (Abbreviations: **CF** = Causal Forest, **VT1** = single-surface Virtual Twins, **VT2** = arm-specific Virtual Twins). The results for the simulation cases with correlation gave identical results to their non-correlation counterpart.

ML approach	N	M1	M2	M3	M4	M5	M6	M7	M8	M9	M10	M11
CF	800	0.44	0.76	0.75	0.29	1.47	0.47	0.71	0.68	0.48	0.99	4.44
VT1	800	0.43	0.82	0.80	0.30	1.45	0.48	0.62	0.63	0.49	0.73	12.12
VT2	800	1.13	1.38	1.37	1.09	1.82	0.66	1.88	1.87	1.16	2.92	21.43
CF	5000	0.33	0.79	0.81	0.12	1.28	0.49	0.52	0.51	0.40	0.64	4.83
VT1	5000	0.34	0.83	0.82	0.12	1.53	0.49	0.43	0.44	0.44	0.47	7.52
VT2	5000	0.71	1.04	1.05	0.62	1.69	0.53	1.13	1.13	0.75	1.68	14.38

6 Discussion

The literature has seen some simulation benchmarking of competing methods, such as [20,36,38], but their focus tended to be on other metrics such as accuracy of estimation of treatment effect in the identified subgroup, probability of first tree split being on a predictive variable, and selection bias regarding predictors. Albeit clearly important, there are also other important aspects that have received relatively little attention in the literature: the ability to disentangle prognostic and predictive variables, and the relative efficiency of ways of implementing VT (arm-specific versus one-surface approaches). Some of this was the topic of [25] where the default VT (single model, Random Forest-based) was among the evaluated methods, but the question from Sect. 3.2 was not explicitly addressed.

While we looked at two ways of implementing VT using the modern XGboost, we also compared to the recently proposed Causal Forsest which acted as the off-the-shelf choice (lacking the considerable tuning steps required for VT). Given that CF is known to provide unbiased ITE estimates by design, it is of interest to compare if VT would be far behind CF in accuracy.

We gave partial empirical answers regarding the implementation aspect of VT and saw that the expansion of training data as (3) indeed have clear benefits. This latter approach (combined with a 'common-surface' version of VT) strongly outperformed the arm-specific version across most simulation models regarding VIP. The latter was highly sensitive to prognostic variables and struggled with detecting the truly predictive ones. Generally, across all scenarios, the runs confirm a clear tendency of prognostic effects driving the Type-1-Error (see Figs. 2 and 3).

In terms of RMSE, VT1 outperformed the arm-specific VT considerably, see Fig. 4.

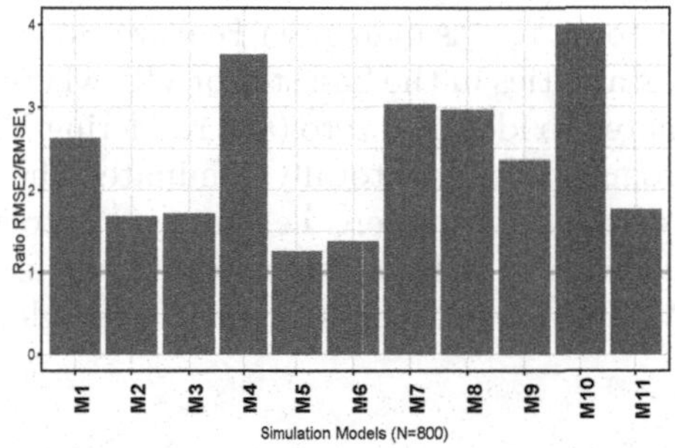

Fig. 4. *Relative performance of Arm-specific Virtual Twins (VT2) and one-surface VT (VT1). The y-axis shows* $RMSE_{\mathbf{VT2}}/RMSE_{\mathbf{VT1}}$*, where RMSE were averaged across the* 100 *iterations. Bars above* 1 *favours the version of Virtual Twins based on* $(Y, X, T, X{\cdot}I_{T=0}, X{\cdot}I_{T=1})$ with a single Boosting model fitted in Step 1. In no scenario did VT2 perform equal or better than VT1.

It was also striking that CF was relatively non-robust to prognostic variables, in the sense that it often did not rank the predictive over the prognostic ones (e.g., **M1**, **M3**, **M7**, **M8**, **M10**, **M11**). To our knowledge, this has not been investigated in any papers. Causal Forest has been proposed for Real World Evidence data, where one might assume rather large number of observations, and it is possible that the strength of CF lies more in such settings rather than in more limited RCTs; this is also in line with the $N = 5000$ results in Fig. 3. Having said that, VT1 might have a practical advantage over CF for of allowing for other types of endpoints in contrast to the current implementation of CF (restricted to continuous endpoints)

One notable conclusion from the simulations is that VT1 (extended training data, one model in Step 1) outperformed CF across the landscape of simulations in terms of both power and VIP: **M1**, **M2**, **M3**, **M7**, **M10** (with a stronger advantage to VT1 when the trial size was smaller).

It is interesting to contrast the results from models **M2** and **M10**; these are structurally identical but with higher prognostic strength in the latter case. When the RCT was smaller ($N = 800$), Causal Forest performed surprisingly bad in terms of ranking, and its power did deteriorate when the prognostic strength increased. However when the data sets were larger ($N = 5000$) CF performed perfect for the moderate prognostic strength (**M2**) but with a 54.0% Type-1-Error for the higher prognostic strength (**M10**).

Scenario (**M5**) is notable: when many (six) predictive effects were present, all models performed very well and the VIP for the predictive x did stand out strongly. This might be considered as one of the simpler simulation cases due to mutually exclusive prognostic and predictive effects, and it is relieving to see that all methods performed well here. (Still, VT1 outperformed VT2 in terms of estimating ITEs, see Table 3).

In our empirical comparisons, we have here excluded another possible implementation of VT, where a single Boosting model is fitted to the training data 'as is', i.e., (Y, T, X), without any treatment-covariate column extensions. This is sometimes referred to as the 'Augmented Feature Space' approach [23]. We noted model fitting instabilities in the 2nd step of VT, where often the individual differences were estimated to identical zero (and rendering VIP meaningless). We speculate that the prognostic effects totally dominated the model fit, suppressing the impact of treatment allocation, i.e., running into the issues discussed in [19]. Hence, our conclusion is that the extended single-surface VT is superior to arm-specific VT, which in turn is superior to single-surface VT without extensions.

A future direction of this research involves simulation comparisons regarding other types of endpoints commonly seen in clinical trials (at least regarding the implementations of VT, since Boosting models are not restricted to continuous response variables); furthermore, a larger set of simulation models might be considered, and the inclusion of other types of performance metrics (e.g., accuracy of estimating effect in planted subgroups). Also, other types of ML/ITE methods might be considered, such as Penalized Regression techniques, Model-Based Recursive Partitioning and GUIDE. This is in particular interesting in settings with more than one active treatment arm, where VT is currently only applicable to pairwise comparisons whereas some other techniques allow a single model fit to the entire data set.

7 Appendix

Here we add some additional plots (referred to in the result section). These cases are qualitatively different in the sense that one model has mutually exclusive prognostic and predictive effects whereas the other one has not. Furthermore one model has non-linear effects.

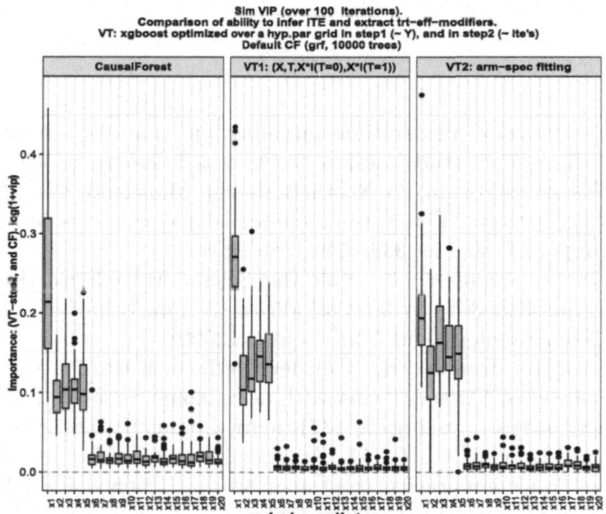

Fig. 5. Variable Importance (VIP) results for simulation model **M11**, 100 iterations with trial size $N = 5000$. The x_1 the only predictive variable, and $x_1, ..., x_5$ were prognostic.

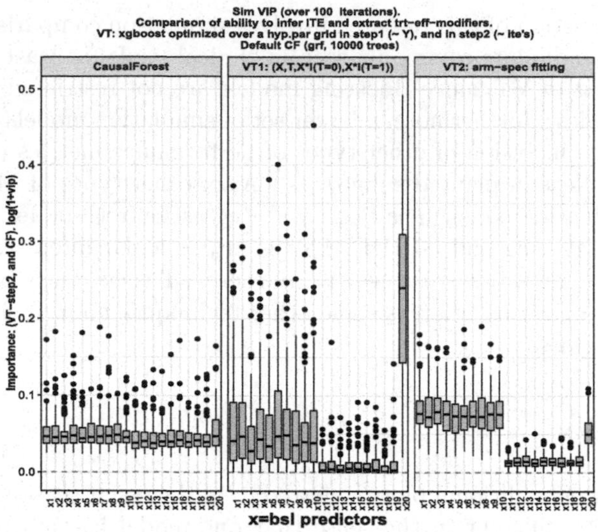

Fig. 6. Variable Importance (VIP) results for **M7**, 100 iterations with trial size $N = 800$, x_{20} predictive, $x_1, ..., x_{10}$ prognostic. It is notable that both VT2 and CF performed poorly.

References

1. Alosh, M.: Statistical Considerations on Subgroup Analysis: Interpretation of clinical trial findings and study design for targeted subgroup. Conference paper, FDA/DIA Statistics Forum, At North Bethesda, Maryland, US, (2014)
2. Altman, D., Royston, P.: The cost of dichotomising continuous variables. BMJ 332. https://doi.org/10.1136/bmj.332.7549.1080(2006)
3. Bica, I., Alaa, A., Lambert, C., Van Der Schaar M.: Clinical Pharmacology & Therapeutics published by Wiley Periodicals LLC on behalf of American Society for Clinical Pharmacology and Therapeutics (2020)
4. Bul, K., Doove, L., Franken, H., Van der Oord, S., Kato, P., Maras, A.: Results of the application of Virtual Twins with as outcome Social Skills Rating System (SSRS) (2018). https://doi.org/10.1371/journal.pone.0193681.g004
5. Chen, S., Tian, L., Cai, T., Yu, M.: A general statistical framework for subgroup identification and comparative treatment scoring. Biometrics **73**(4), 1199–1209 (2017). https://doi.org/10.1111/biom.12676
6. Chen, Y., Markatou, M.: A comparative study of subgroup identification methods for differential treatment effect: Performance metrics and recommendations. Statistical Methods in Medical Research (2017)
7. Curth, A., Van Der Schaar, M.: Nonparametric Estimation of Heterogeneous Treatment Effects: From Theory to Learning Algorithms. arXiv:2101.10943. [stat.ML] (2021)
8. Dmitrienko, A., Muysers, C., Fritsch, A., Lipkovich, I.: General guidance on exploratory and confirmatory subgroup analysis in late-stage clinical trials. J. Biopharmaceutical Stat. **26**, 71–98 (2016)

9. Dusseldorp, E., Doove, L., Mechelen, I.: Quint: An R package for the identification of subgroups of clients who differ in which treatment alternative is best for them. Behav. Res. Methods **48**(2), 650–663 (2015). https://doi.org/10.3758/s13428-015-0594-z
10. European Medicines Agency. Guideline on the investigation of subgroups in confirmatory clinical trials (2014)
11. Fang, L., Su, C.: Statistical Methods in Biomarker and Early Clinical Development. Springer. https://doi.org/10.1007/978-3-030-31503-0 (2020)
12. Foster, J.C., Nan, B., Shen, L., Kaciroti, N., Taylor, J.M.G.: Permutation testing for treatment–covariate interactions and subgroup identification. Stat. Biosci. **8**(1), 77–98 (2015). https://doi.org/10.1007/s12561-015-9125-9
13. Foster, J.C., Taylor, J.M.C., Ruberg, S.J.: Subgroup identification from randomized clinical trial data. Stat. Med. **30**, 2867–2880 (2011)
14. Gottlow, M., et al.: Application of structured statistical analyses to identify a biomarker predictive of enhanced tralokinumab efficacy in Phase III clinical trials for severe, uncontrolled asthma. BMC Pulmonary Medicine 19–129 (2019)
15. Hemmings, R., Koch, A.: Commentary on: Subgroup analysis and interpretation for phase 3 confirmatory trials: White Paper of the EFSPI/PSI working group on subgroup analysis by Dane, Spencer, Rosenkranz, Lipkovich, and Parke. Wiley (2019). https://doi.org/10.1002/pst.1935
16. Hou, J., et al.: Subgroup identification in personalized treatment of alcohol dependence. Alcohol Clin. Exp. Res. **39**(7), 1253–1259 (2015)
17. Jia, J., Tang, Q., Xie, W., Rode, R.: A Novel Method of Subgroup Identification by Combining Virtual Twins with GUIDE (VG) for Development of Precision Medicines. arXiv: Applications 167–180 (2020)
18. Lipkovich, I., Dmitrienko, A.: Strategies for identifying predictive biomarkers and subgroups with enhanced treatment effect in clinical trials using SIDES. J. Biopharmaceutical Stat. **24**, 130–153 (2014)
19. Lipkovich, I., Dmitrienko, A., D'Agostino, R., Sr.: Tutorial in biostatistics: data-driven subgroup identification and analysis in clinical trials. Stat, In Medicine (2016)
20. Loh W., Cao L., Zhou P. Subgroup identification for precision medicine: A comparative review of 13 methods. Data Mining Knowl Discov. (2019)
21. Loh, W., Man, M., Wang, S.: Subgroups from Regression Trees with adjustment for Prognostic effects and post-selection inference. Statistics in Medicine (2018)
22. Marchenko, O.V., Katenka, N.V. (eds.) Quantitative Methods in Pharmaceutical Research and Development, Chap. 6. Springer Nature Switzerland AG (2020). https://doi.org/10.1007/978-3-030-48555-9_6
23. Research Pillar: Individualized treatment effect inference. Webpage. https://www.vanderschaar-lab.com/individualized-treatment-effect-inference/
24. Rubin, D.B.: Causal inference using potential outcomes: design, modeling, decisions. J. Am. Stat. Assoc. **100**(469), 322–331 (2005)
25. Sechidis, K., Papangelou, K., Metcalfe, P.D., Svensson, D., Weatherall, J., Brown, G.: Distinguishing prognostic and predictive biomarkers: an information theoretic approach. Bioinformatics 1 **34**(23), 4139 (2018) https://doi.org/10.1093/bioinformatics/bty515
26. Sharmin Akter, S.: Subgroup identification with Virtual Twins and Guide algorithms - an application to adult fitness data. Thesis, Ball State University (2020). https://cardinalscholar.bsu.edu/handle/123456789/202449

27. Ting, N., et al. (eds.): Design and Analysis of Subgroups with Biopharmaceutical Applications, Emerging Topics in Statistics and Biostatistics. Springer Nature Switzerland AG 2020 (2020). https://doi.org/10.1007/978-3-030-40105-4_3
28. Su, X., Zhou, T., Yan, X., Fan, J., Yang, S.: Interaction trees with censured survival data. Int. J. Biostat. **4**, 1–26 (2008)
29. Chen, T., Guestrin, C.: XGboost: A Scalable Tree Boosting System. arXiv:1603.02754v3 [cs.LG]
30. Tibshirani, J.: Generalized Random Forest, CRAN package (2018). https://cran.r-project.org/web/packages/grf/index.html
31. Thomas, M., Bornkamp, B., Seibold, H.: Subgroup identification in dose-finding trials via model-based recursive partitioning. Stat. Med. **37**, 1608–1624 (2018)
32. Tune, P.: Towards Data Science Blogpost: The unreasonable in effectivness of Deep Learning on Tabular Data (2020). https://towardsdatascience.com/the-unreasonable-ineffectiveness-of-deep-learning-on-tabular-data-fd784ea29c33
33. Turner, E.: Predictive Variable Selection For Subgroup Identification. Thesis, University of Manchester, Faculty of Science and Enginering, School of Computer Science (2017). https://www.research.manchester.ac.uk/portal/files/63667893/FULL_TEXT.PDF
34. Vieille, F., Foster, J.: aVirtualTwins: Adaptation of Virtual Twins Method from Jared Foster. R package version 1.0.1 (2018). https://CRAN.R-project.org/package=aVirtualTwins
35. Wager, S., Athey, A.: Estimation and inference of heterogeneous treatment effects using random forests. J. Am. Stat. Assoc. **113**(523), 1228–1242 (2018). https://doi.org/10.1080/01621459.2017.1319839
36. Yang, et al.: Look before you leap: systematic evaluation of tree-based statistical methods in subgroup identification. J. Biopharm. Statistics (2019)
37. OI Zeileis, A., Hornik, K.: Generalized M-Fluctuation Tests for Parameter Instability. Stat. Neerland. 61. https://doi.org/10.1111/j.1467-9574.2007.00371.x (2003)
38. Zhang, Z., Seibold, H., Vettore, M., Song, W., François, V.: Subgroup identification in clinical trials: an overview of available methods and their implementations with R. Annal. Translational Med. **6**(7) (2018). https://doi.org/10.21037/atm.2018.03.07
39. Zink, R.C., Shen, L., Wolfinger, R.D., Showalter, H.D.H.: Assessment of methods to identify patient subgroups with enhanced treatment response in randomized clinical trials. In: Chen, Z., Liu, A., Qu, Y., Tang, L., Ting, N., Tsong, Y. (eds.) Applied Statistics in Biomedicine and Clinical Trials Design. IBSS, pp. 395–410. Springer, Cham (2015). https://doi.org/10.1007/978-3-319-12694-4_24

Change Point Detection in a State Space Framework Applied to Climate Change in Europe

Magda Monteiro[1,2](✉) and Marco Costa[1,2]

[1] Águeda School of Technology and Managment, University of Aveiro, Aveiro, Portugal
{msvm,marco}@ua.pt

[2] CIDMA – Center for Research and Development in Mathematics and Applications University of Aveiro, Aveiro, Portugal

Abstract. This work presents the statistical analysis of time series of monthly average temperatures in several European locations using a state space approach, where it is considered a model with a deterministic seasonal component and a stochastic trend. Temperature rise rates in Europe seem to have increased in the last decades when compared with longer periods, hence change point detection methods were applied to residuals state space models in order to identify these possible changes in the monthly temperature rise rates. In Northern Europe the change points were, almost all, identified in the late 1980s while in Central and Southeastern Europe was, for the majority of cities, in the 1990s and later.

Keywords: Air temperature · Climate change · State space models · Change point detection

1 Introduction

Global warming and climate change are in the scientific agenda. The increase of droughts, floods, severe storms, and other weather catastrophes are putting vulnerable human and biological populations at risk. Nevertheless, global warming effects vary around the world, therefore this phenomenon must be monitored at a smaller scale, for instance at a European cities level. Statistical analysis of the evolution of climate variables can contribute to a more efficient identification and monitoring of patterns of change. In particular, the study of long temperature series is of particular interest in understanding climate dynamics at smaller scales, allowing efficient monitoring of environmental processes.

This work was partially supported the Center for Research and Development in Mathematics and Applications (CIDMA) through the Portuguese Foundation for Science and Technology (FCT - Fundação para a Ciência e a Tecnologia), references UIDB/04106/2020 and UIDP/04106/2020.

O. Gervasi et al. (Eds.): ICCSA 2021, LNCS 12952, pp. 641–652, 2021.
https://doi.org/10.1007/978-3-030-86973-1_45

The application of state space models to long temperature time series in Lisbon, Coimbra, and Porto, in [6], allowed us to conclude that the latter city has a very different growth rate per century than the others. In [5], the application of state space models to long series of air temperature, together with cluster procedures, let the identification of temperature growth rates patterns in several cities in Europe. This work allowed us to conclude that temperature rates have been increasing in the last decades when compared to longer periods. Following this work, we will analyze, in a state space framework, monthly temperature averages in these European cities aiming to identify the change points from which the pattern growth has changed and use them to accurately estimate growth rates for the forthcoming decades. A state space model comprises two equations, the state equation that translates the system dynamics, regulated by a latent process (the state), and the observation equation that establishes the link between the unobservable states and the observations. This class of models allows the description of both univariate and multivariate time series, stationary or not, that can present data irregularities such as interventions and missing data, reveling to be a flexible class. Moreover, this class has the advantage, in most cases, of detecting the temporal dynamics of the process more accurately when compared to other models. State space models have been successfully used in several research areas such as environment ([4,7]), insurance ([3]), Finance ([22]) and animal ecology ([13]). Regarding structural breaks detection, there is a vast literature on the subject (see [2,20] and [23], including the references therein). Much of the methodology was first developed for a sequence of independent and identically distributed (i.i.d.) random variables and a large part of the literature is devoted to CUSUM -type and likelihood ratio procedures based on distributional assumptions (usually Gaussian) to test for a change in the mean and or in variance. When no knowledge about the distributional form of the sequence under analysis is available, nonparametric change detection methods can be used in order to identify these changes. The works of [9] and [19] consider methods that have into account well established nonparametric tests for location and scale comparisons and [18] developed an R package ([15]) with the implementation of several change points detection methods. The existence of serial dependence in many applications led to the development of methodologies to deal with change points in time series. Several approaches can be used in this context, for example one can apply test statistics developed for the independent setting to the underlying innovation process or one can try to quantify the effect of dependence on these test statistics depending on the model structure that is considered. There are several works on change point detection in climate or environmental settings. For instance, [16] makes a review of this topic in the climate context and [10] applied several change points procedures to Klementinum temperature. In line with this work, it is considered parametric and nonparametric statistical tests with the application of maximum type statistics to the the innovation processes predictions obtained by the Kalman filter algorithm for the temperature time series in Europe.

2 Data Description

The Data is available at the Climate Data Online [12] and comprises the period between January 1900 and December 2017, making a total of 1416 observations. The location of the cities and data descriptive statistics can be found in Fig. 1 and Table 1 respectively. Table 1 presents the minimum, maximum and average temperature for all period and also the same statistics for period under the year 2000 and for the second millennium. The cutoff point was chosen in order to separate centuries. The global minimums are, with the exception of Ireland, in the first period and the global maximums were reached in the second period in two thirds of the series. For all the cities analyzed, the increase in average temperatures in recent years is quite evident.

Table 1. Characterization of time series data set.

City (Country)	Min	Max	Min	Max	Min	Max	Average	Average	Average	Missing
	1900 to 2017		1900 to 1999		2000 to 2017		1900 to 2017	1900 to 1999	2000 to 2017	Values (%)
Berlin (Germany)	−10.7	23.0	−10.7	22.5	−4.8	23.0	8.7	8.5	9.9	2.3
Bucharest (Romania)	−11.5	27.5	−11.5	27.5	−6.6	26.5	10.1	9.8	11.1	2.6
Copenhagen (Denmark)	−6.7	21.6	−6.7	21.6	−3.1	21.6	8.6	8.4	9.6	0.4
Dublin (Ireland)	0.0	17.1	0.4	17.1	0.0	17.0	9.2	9.2	9.6	2.2
Kiev (Ukraine)	−15.3	26.0	−15.3	26.0	−10.0	24.7	8.1	7.9	9.4	0.9
Lisbon (Portugal)	8.0	25.1	8.0	25.1	9.4	25.1	16.9	16.8	17.4	3.4
Minsk (Belarus)	−16.8	22.6	−16.8	22.0	−11.1	22.6	6.1	5.8	7.4	1.8
Nantes (France)	−1.2	23.3	−1.2	23.2	2.5	23.3	12.0	11.9	12.5	0.4
Prague (Czech Rep.)	−13.1	22.0	−13.1	21.7	−5.5	22.0	7.9	7.6	9.1	8.2
S. Petersburg (Russia)	−18.3	24.4	−18.3	22.4	−12.1	24.4	5.3	5.1	6.5	0.0
Talin (Estonia)	−15.5	21.5	−15.5	21.2	−11	21.5	5.3	5.1	6.5	5.4
Vienna (Austria)	−9.5	24.4	−9.5	24.4	−3.4	24.1	10.1	9.9	11.3	0.2
Vilnius (Lithuania)	−17.1	21.8	−17.1	20.4	−10.4	21.8	5.8	5.6	7.3	2.6
Zagreb (Croatia)	−7.0	25.9	−7.0	25.9	−2.5	25.7	11.8	11.6	13.0	1.4
Zurich (Switzerland)	−8.7	22.4	−8.7	21.8	−3.6	22.4	8.7	8.5	9.8	0.0

3 Model and Change Point Methods Descriptions

3.1 Model

Assuming that there are no change-points, the model is defined, for all time sequence, by

$$Y_t = \tau_t + \sum_{i=1}^{12} \beta_{i;0} S_{t,i} + e_{1,t} \tag{1}$$

$$\tau_t = \mu_0 + \phi_0(\tau_{t-1} - \mu_0) + e_{2,t} \tag{2}$$

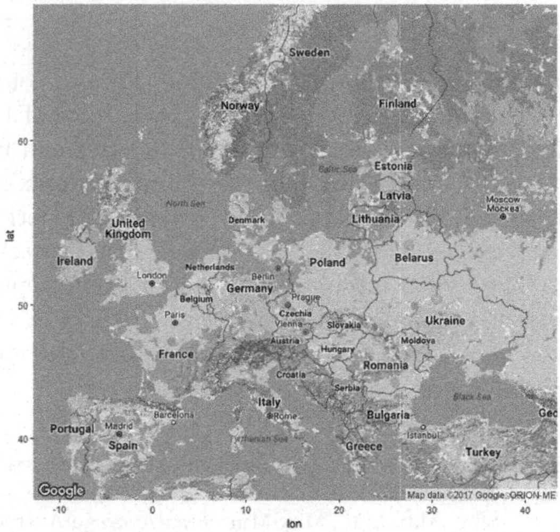

Fig. 1. Station locations (Adapted from google earth)

where Y_t represents the monthly average air temperature in the month t, with $t = 1, ..., n$, and $\beta_{i;0}$ with $i = 1, 2, ..., 12$ is the seasonal coefficient associated to the month $t = i + 12k$, for some $k = 0, 1, 2, ...$, $S_{t,i}$ is an indicative function defined such that

$$S_{t,i} = 1 = \begin{cases} 1 \text{ if } t = i + 12k, \text{ for some } k = 0, 1, 2, ... \\ 0 \quad \text{otherwise.} \end{cases} \tag{3}$$

$\{\tau_t\}$ is the trend component that follows a stationary autoregressive process with mean μ_0 with autoregressive parameter $|\phi_0| < 1$; the error $e_{i,t}$, with $i = 1, 2$, follows a white noise process ($E(e_{i,t}) = 0$, $var(e_{i,t}) = \sigma^2_{i;0}$ and $E(e_{i,t}e_{i,r}) = 0$, for $t \neq r$), and are uncorrelated errors, that is $E(e_{1,t}e_{2,r}) = 0$, $\forall t, r$.

The error $e_{1,t}$ is called the observation error and it can be seen as a measure error, whereas the error $e_{2,t}$ is called the state error and translates the randomness of the trend component. Note that state τ_t is an unobservable process and its predictions must be obtained. Kalman filter algorithms provides optimal unbiased estimators for the state τ_t; $\widehat{\tau}_{t|t-1}$ for one-step-ahead prediction, $\widehat{\tau}_{t|t}$ for Kalman filter update and $\widehat{\tau}_{t|n}$ for Kalman smoother predictions ([8]).

It is noted that no assumptions are made to distributional form of both errors, although in many situations the Gaussian distribution is considered.

3.2 Change Point Detection

In order to discover an abrupt change in the behavior of the temperature rise rates, a basic statistical tests applying maximum type statistics to detect a change in location are performed. If there are no structural changes in the temperature trend, it is expected that τ_t has no changes over time in its mean. If no change point exists, the one-step-ahead forecast residuals are independent and identically. If a change point exists at some time t^*, the one-step-ahead forecast innovations can be used to detect and estimate it [19], and it is assumed that after that time point the parameters of model 1–2 change to $\beta_{i;1}$, $i = 1, \cdots, 12$, μ_1, ϕ_1 and $\sigma^2_{j;1}$, $j = 1, 2$. We used *Maximum type* tests for both parametric and nonparametric techniques.

First, consider that it is intended to test if the change point occurs at the known time point k. The statistical hypotheses are

$$\begin{aligned} &H_0 : X_t \sim F_0(x; \theta_0) \text{ for } \forall t = 1 \cdots, n \\ &vs \\ &H_1 : X_t \sim F_0(x; \theta_0) \text{ for } t \leq k \text{ and } X_t \sim F_1(x; \theta_1), \text{ for } t > k. \end{aligned}$$

Under the non existence of change points hypothesis, it can be applied a, parametric or a nonparametric, two-sample comparison test. If the statistic test exceeds some appropriately chosen threshold then the null hypothesis that the two samples have identical distributions is rejected, and we conclude that a change point has occurred immediately after k time. Since it is not known in advance where the change point occurs, the k time is unknown and the statistic test is evaluated at every value $1 < k < n$, and the maximum value is used.

***Maximum Type* T Test.** Under normality assumption, with no changes in σ^2 which is assumed to be unknown, the test statistic $T(n)$ is the maximum of the absolute values of two sample t-test statistics

$$T(n) = \max_{1 \leq k < n} |T_k| = \max_{1 \leq k < n} \sqrt{\frac{(n-k)k}{n}} \frac{\left|\overline{X}_k - \overline{X}^*_k\right|}{s_k}$$

where

$$\overline{X}_k = \frac{1}{k} \sum_{i=1}^{k} X_i, \; \overline{X}^*_k = \frac{1}{n-k} \sum_{i=k+1}^{n} X_i$$

and

$$s_k = \sqrt{\frac{1}{n-2} \left[\sum_{i=1}^{k} \left(X_i - \overline{X}_k\right)^2 + \sum_{i=k+1}^{n} \left(X_i - \overline{X}^*_k\right)^2 \right]}.$$

The null hypothesis can be rejected if the statistic $T(n)$ is greater than the critical value. The exact distribution of $T(n)$, for independent variables, is very complex and [21] was able to calculate the true critical values only for the number of observations n less than 10. Alternatively, approximate critical values can be computed by other methods as the Bonferroni inequality, simulation or the asymptotic distribution.

When random variables X_1, X_2, ..., X_n are not independent but form an ARMA process then the asymptotic critical values of the test statistics considering independence have to be multiplied by $\sqrt{2\pi f(0)/\gamma}$, where $\gamma = var(X_t)$

and $f(\cdot)$ denotes the spectral density function of the corresponding ARMA process ([1]). Especially for an AR(1) sequence, the critical values should be multiplied by $\left[(1+\phi)(1-\phi)^{-1}\right]^{1/2}$ where ϕ is the first autoregressive coefficient, [11].

***Maximum Type* Mann-Whitney test.** In the nonparametric setting, at each k point, $1 < k < n$, the two-sample Mann-Whitney test statistic $D_{k;n}$ can be computed. The variance of $D_{k;n}$ depends on the value k, so the test statistic is obtained through the maximization of the standardized $D_{k,n}$ to have mean 0 and variance 1 (see [18]),

$$D_n = \max_{k=2,\cdots,n-1} \widetilde{D}_{k,n} = \left| \frac{D_{k,n} - \mu_{D_{k,n}}}{\sigma_{D_{k,n}}} \right|. \tag{4}$$

The null hypothesis of no change is then rejected if $D_n > h_n$ for some appropriately chosen threshold h_n. This distribution does not have an analytic finite-sample form and for the case of the Mann-Whitney statistics the asymptotic distribution of D_n can be written ([14]). However, these asymptotic distributions may not be accurate when considering finite length sequences, and so numerical simulation may be required in order to estimate the distribution ([17,18]). The best estimate of the change point location will be immediately following the value of k which maximized $\widetilde{D}_{n,k}$.

4 Results

The parameters of model 1–2 were estimated in a classical decomposition approach combining the least squares estimation of the seasonal parameters $\beta_{0;i}$, with $i = 1, ..., 12$, with a distribution-free estimators developed to state space models (see [7]) in order to estimate the remaining parameters. The results of the estimation procedure are presented in Table 2.

Table 2. Parameter estimates of model 1–2

City	$\widehat{\beta}_0$												$\widehat{\mu}_0$	$\widehat{\phi}_0$	$\widehat{\sigma}^2_{0;e_1}$	$\widehat{\sigma}^2_{0;e_2}$	$\widehat{\sigma}^2_{0;Y_t}$
	Jan.	Feb.	Mar.	Apr.	May	Jun.	Jul.	Aug.	Sep.	Oct.	Nov.	Dec.					
Berlin	−1.2	−0.4	3.0	7.6	12.7	15.8	17.5	16.6	12.9	8.1	3.2	0.1	0.709	0.576	1.937	1.319	3.912
Bucharest	−3.9	−1.7	3.6	9.9	15.3	19.1	21.3	20.7	16.0	9.8	3.8	−1.4	0.611	0.537	1.989	1.653	4.311
Copenhagen	0.0	−0.2	1.9	6.1	11.2	14.9	16.9	16.4	13.0	8.7	4.5	1.7	0.655	0.711	1.128	0.836	2.815
Dublin	4.4	4.5	5.6	7.3	9.9	12.7	14.5	14.2	12.3	9.6	6.3	5.0	0.383	0.521	0.704	0.484	1.369
Kiev	−5.5	−4.7	0.2	8.0	14.6	17.9	19.6	18.7	13.7	7.4	1.4	−3.1	0.732	0.583	2.735	1.893	5.601
Lisbon	10.9	11.6	13.4	14.9	17.0	19.9	21.8	22.3	20.9	17.9	14.0	11.6	0.510	0.771	0.859	0.179	1.299
Minsk	−7.1	−6.4	−2.1	5.3	11.8	15.4	17.0	16.0	11.1	5.2	−0.3	−4.6	0.954	0.679	3.377	1.299	5.788
Nantes	5.2	5.7	7.9	10.2	13.6	16.6	18.6	18.3	16.0	12.2	8.0	5.8	0.478	0.439	1.385	0.785	2.357
Prague	−2.8	−1.8	2.0	6.7	11.9	15.1	16.9	16.2	12.3	7.1	1.9	−1.4	0.797	0.701	2.506	0.674	3.831
S. Petersburg	−7.5	−7.5	−3.4	3.3	9.9	14.8	17.7	15.9	10.7	4.8	−0.6	−4.9	0.843	0.607	3.232	2.100	6.560
Talin	−5.5	−6.0	−2.8	2.7	8.6	13.2	16.0	15.0	10.5	5.3	0.5	−3.0	0.800	0.648	2.181	1.844	5.360
Vienna	−1.0	0.5	4.6	9.5	14.3	17.5	19.4	18.7	14.7	9.4	4.3	0.6	0.710	0.559	2.043	1.086	3.624
Vilnius	−6.7	−5.9	−2.3	4.5	11.0	14.3	16.2	15.1	10.4	4.9	−0.4	−4.3	1.132	0.821	3.487	0.782	5.889
Zagreb	0.3	2.4	6.9	11.5	16.0	19.4	21.4	20.8	16.7	11.4	6.2	1.9	0.572	0.606	2.258	1.044	3.907
Zurich	−1.2	0.0	3.8	7.5	11.9	15.1	16.9	16.3	13.1	8.2	3.1	−0.1	0.763	0.653	2.302	0.591	3.331

All ϕ estimates verifies the stationary condition of the AR(1) process and the smallest estimate of the mean of the stochastic trend level is 0.383 in Dublin (Ireland) whereas the largest is 1.132 in Vilnius (Lithuania). The residuals analysis showed that, for the majority of cities, there is no serial correlation up to lag 10 when considering a significance of 1% (see Fig. 2). The exception is the city of Lisbon which presents no serial correlation only up to lag 3.

Although no assumption was made to the distribution of the errors in the model under study, the normality was tested through the application of Jarque-Bera test to standard residuals which lead to the rejection of this assumption in the majority of the cities. This situation is not unusual, since the length of the series is quite long, and in this situations tests tend to reject quite often.

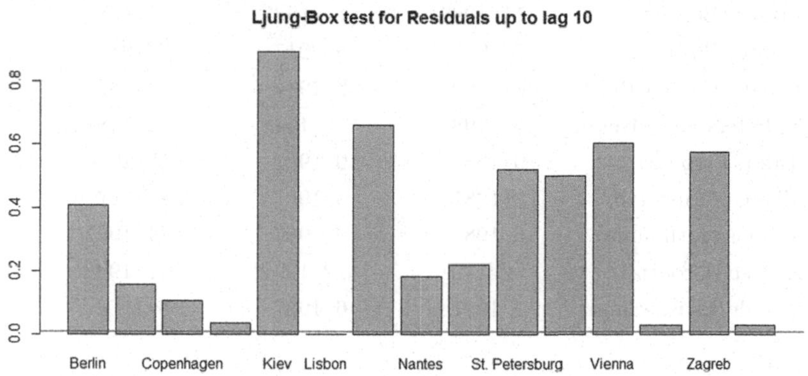

Fig. 2. Ljung-Box p-values residuals tests. $\alpha = 1\%$ in red. (Color figure online)

This is an ongoing work and we only used the at most one change point approach. For each city we have considered three situations: the maximum-type test using Mann-Whitney tests and also T test applied to the residuals; the application of the maximum-type T test applied to smoother predictions of the latent process τ_t which represents the trend of the temperature. Since τ_t has an autoregressive structure of order 1, it was necessary to adjust, for each series, the critical value of the test using the estimates of the autoregressive parameters. Results of the change point detection are presented in Table 3.

There are several cities whose change points obtained by the three methods are very similar. In most of these cities the change points are identified in the late eighties or in the early nineties of the last century, with the exception of Bucharest which was identified in 2006. Although normality assumption was rejected, the results based on the T-tests do not differ substantially from the results obtained in the nonparametric case.

We highlight Kiev, Prague and Zurich as cities where the nonparametric method identifies a change point about ten years later than the other two methods. In Lisbon case the nonparametric method identifies a change point about

Table 3. Change point time for each city;

City (Country)	M-W test change point month/year	T-test change point month/year	t-test change point month/year (smoother)
Berlin (Germany)	8/1987	8/1987	9/1987
Bucharest (Romania)	9/2006	12/2007	9/2006
Copenhagen (Denmark)	8/1987	8/1987	9/1987
Dublin (Ireland)	9/1987	9/1988	10/1988
Kiev (Ukraine)	12/1999	11/1988	12/1989
Lisbon (Portugal)	1/1945	6/1978	7/1978
Minsk (Belarus)	11/1988	11/1987	11/1987
Nantes (France)	7/1981	8/2017	7/1987
Prague (Czech Rep.)	11/1997	8/1987	8/1987
S. Petersburg (Russia)	12/1987	12/1988	12/1988
Talin (Estonia)	9/1987	9/1987	12/1988
Vienna (Austria)	8/1987	9/1987	8/1987
Vilnius (Lithuania)	6/1982	9/1987	11/1987
Zagreb (Croatia)	12/1991	12/1992	12/1992
Zurich (Switzerland)	7/1997	6/1987	8/1987

thirty years early than the other methods. Analysing the values of the statistical tests involved there is two local maximums indicating the possibility of the existence of more than one change point (Fig. 3). Note that in Lisbon the residuals show significant correlation after lag 3, so in this case the tests validity are compromised and is necessary further model investigation in order to have non correlated residuals.

Table 3 presents discrepant values in Nantes. The nonparametric method points for a change point in July 1981 and the T test applied to smoother predictions points for a change point six years later. The T test applied to the residuals presents a change point almost at the end of the period under analysis. The first difference can be explained by the fact that between 1981 and 1987 there are two local maximums in the test statistics. In the nonparametric case the global maximum occur in july 1981 but the difference for the other value is rather small, 0.08 (see Fig. 4). In july 2017 there is a spike in all test statistics, nevertheless only in the T test applied to the residuals this value exceeds all other values. Note that in the test statistic, T_k, the mean of the second segment is calculated with only 5 observations. We highlight the fact that the residuals from July 2017 are very high compared to the other values of the series which may justify the discrepancy with the other methods.

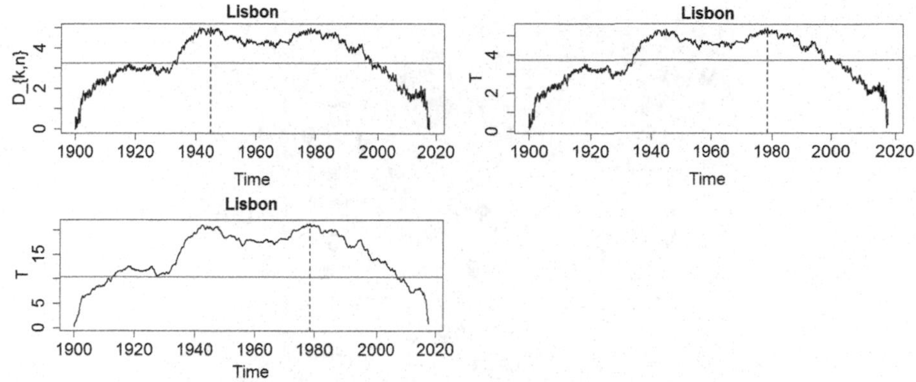

Fig. 3. Values of $\widetilde{D}_{k,n}$ for residuals , T_k for residuals and T_k for smoother predictions in Lisbon.

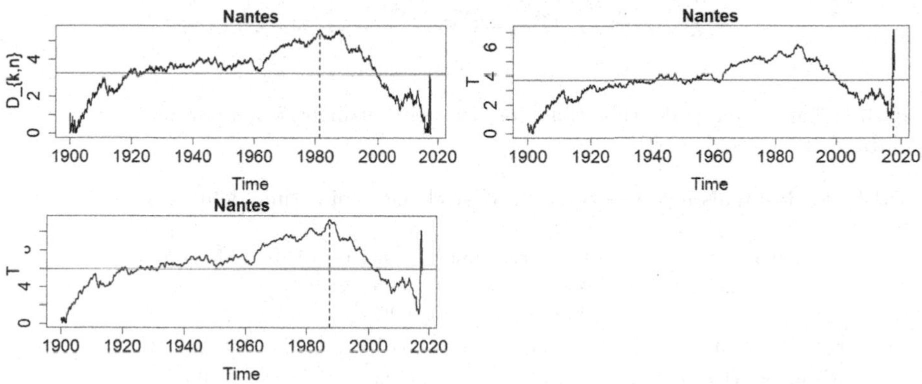

Fig. 4. Values of $\widetilde{D}_{k,n}$ for residuals , T_k for residuals and T_k for smoother predictions in Nantes.

In order to analyze the existence of a geographical pattern in the detection of change points, Fig. 5 presents, for each city and the nonparametric method, the time (in terms of early or late decade) identified as a change point. In Northern Europe the change points were, with the exception of Vilnius , identified in the late 1980s while in Central and Southeastern Europe, with Vienna one exception, this identification was in the 1990s and later. As mentioned before Lisbon case, in southwestern Europe, presents a change point much earlier than the other cities. Table 4 presents the residuals means before and after the detection of the change points using the nonparametric approach with the M-W tests. One can see, together with Table 3 and Fig. 5, that the biggest differences occur almost always for later detections and that the smaller changes occur in western Europe.

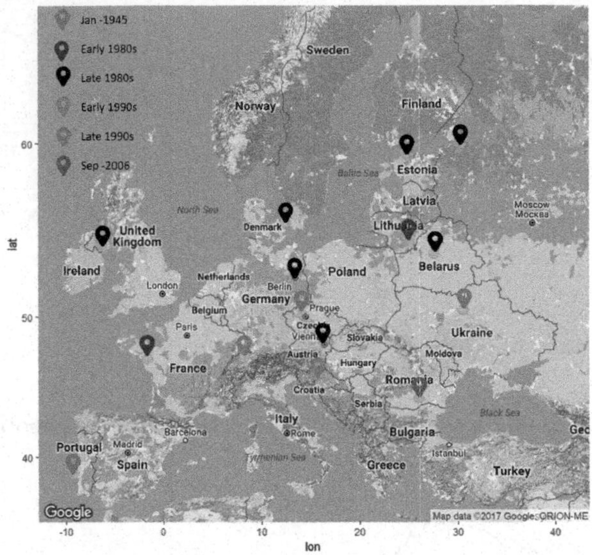

Fig. 5. Change point identification, for each city, using the nonparametric approach (adapted from google earth)

Table 4. Residuals mean before and after change point time defined by M-W test

City (country)	Mean residuals before change point	Mean residuals after change point	Mean difference
Berlin (Germany)	–0.172	0.573	0.745
Bucharest (Romania)	–0.075	0.93	1.005
Copenhagen (Denmark)	–0.121	0.371	0.492
Dublin (Ireland)	–0.092	0.305	0.397
Kiev (Ukraine)	–0.131	0.756	0.887
Lisbon (Portugal)	–0.188	0.126	0.314
Minsk (Belarus)	–0.215	0.635	0.850
Nantes (France)	–0.15	0.353	0.503
Prague (Czech Rep.)	–0.144	0.693	0.837
S. Petersburg (Russia)	–0.199	0.598	0.797
Talin (Estonia)	–0.175	0.475	0.650
Vienna (Austria)	–0.173	0.54	0.713
Vilnius (Lithuania)	–0.212	0.491	0.703
Zagreb (Croatia)	–0.157	0.609	0.766
Zurich (Switzerland)	–0.133	0.685	0.818

5 Conclusions

By applying methodologies to detect at most one change point in the residuals of the state space models applied to monthly average temperatures of European cities, it was possible to conclude that they exist and are different, in time and magnitude, for these different cities of Europe.

From this detection, and for each city, it is important to use it in the estimation of the parameters before and after the change point in order to assess the existence or not of more change points and, in a final stage, to use the most appropriate model to predict the temperature rise rates in European cities. This is a topic of future research.

References

1. Antoch, J., Huškova, M., Prášková, Z.: Effect of dependence on statistics for determination of change. J. Stat. Plan. Infer. **60**(2), 291–310 (1997)
2. Aue, A., Horváth, L.: Structural breaks in time series. J. Time Ser. Anal. **34**(1), 1–16 (2013)
3. Chukhrova, N., Johannssen, A.: State space models and the kalman-filter in stochastic claims reserving: forecasting, filtering and smoothing. Risks **5**(2) (2017). https://doi.org/10.3390/risks5020030, https://www.mdpi.com/2227-9091/5/2/30
4. Costa, M., Goncalves, A.: Clustering and forecasting of dissolved oxygen concentration on a river basin. Stoch. Environ. Res. Risk Assess. **25**, 151–163 (2011). https://doi.org/10.1007/s00477-010-0429-5
5. Costa, M., Monteiro, M.: Statistical modeling of an air temperature time series of European cities. In: Advances in Environmental Research, pp. 213–236. Nova Science (2017)
6. Costa, M., Monteiro, M.: A periodic mixed linear state space model to monthly long-term temperature data. In: Environmetrics, pp. 1–20 (2018). https://doi.org/10.1002/env.2550
7. Costa, M., Alpuim, T.: Parameter estimation of state space models for univariate observations. J. Stat. Plan. Infer. **140**(7), 1889–1902 (2010)
8. Harvey, A.: Forecasting Structural Time Series Models and the Kalman Filter. Cambridge University Press, Cambridge (2006)
9. Hawkins, D.M., Deng, Q.: A nonparametric change-point control chart. J. Qual. Technol. **42**(2), 165–173 (2010)
10. Jarušková, D., Antoch, J.: Changepoint analysis of klementinum temperature series. Environmetrics **31**(1), e2570 (2020)
11. Jarušková, D.: Some problems with application of change-point detection methods to environmental data. Environmetrics **8**(5), 469–483 (1997). https://doi.org/10.1002/(SICI)1099-095X(199709/10)8:5469::AID-ENV2653.0.CO;2-J
12. National Centers for Environmental Information: Climate Data Online. https://www.ncdc.noaa.gov/cdo-web, Accessed 10 Jan 2019
13. Patterson, T.A., Thomas, L., Wilcox, C., Ovaskainen, O., Matthiopoulos, J.: State-space models of individual animal movement. Trends Ecol. Evol. **23**(2), 87–94 (2008)
14. Pettitt, A.N.: A non-parametric approach to the change-point problem. J. Roy. Stat. Soc. Ser. C (Appl. Stat.) **28**(2), 126–135 (1979). http://www.jstor.org/stable/2346729

15. R Core Team: R: A Language and Environment for Statistical Computing. R Foundation for Statistical Computing, Vienna, Austria (2013), http://www.R-project.org/
16. Reeves, J., Chen, J., Wang, X.L., Lund, R., Lu, Q.Q.: A review and comparison of changepoint detection techniques for climate data. J. Appl. Meteorol. Climatol. **46**(6), 900–915 (2007)
17. Ross, G.J.: cpm: Sequential and Batch Change Detection Using Parametric and Nonparametric Method (2015). r package version 2.2
18. Ross, G.J.: Parametric and nonparametric sequential change detection in R: the cpm package. J. Stat. Softw. **66**(3), 1–20 (2015). http://www.jstatsoft.org/v66/i03/
19. Ross, G.J., Tasoulis, D.K., Adams, N.M.: Nonparametric monitoring of data streams for changes in location and scale. Technometrics **53**(4), 379–389 (2011)
20. Shao, X., Zhang, X.: Testing for change points in time series. J. Am. Stat. Assoc. **105**(491), 1228–1240 (2010)
21. Worsley, K.J.: On the likelihood ratio test for a shift in location of normal populations. J. Am. Stat. Assoc. **74**(366), 365–367 (1979). http://www.jstor.org/stable/2286336
22. Zandonade, E., Morettin, P.A.: Wavelets in state space models. Appl. Stoch. Models Bus. Ind. **19**(3), 199–219 (2003). https://doi.org/10.1002/asmb.496
23. Zou, C., Yin, G., Feng, L., Wang, Z.: Nonparametric maximum likelihood approach to multiple change-point problems. Ann. Stat. **42**(3), 970–1002 (2014)

Conditioning by Projection for the Sampling from Prior Gaussian Distributions

Alsadig Ali[1], Abdullah Al-Mamun[2], Felipe Pereira[1], and Arunasalam Rahunanthan[3](✉)

[1] Department of Mathematical Sciences, The University of Texas at Dallas, Richardson, TX 75080, USA
[2] Institute of Natural Sciences, United International University, Dhaka, Bangladesh
[3] Department of Mathematics and Computer Science, Central State University, Wilberforce, OH 45384, USA
aRahunanthan@centralstate.edu

Abstract. In this work we are interested in the (ill-posed) inverse problem for absolute permeability characterization that arises in predictive modeling of porous media flows. We consider a Bayesian statistical framework with a preconditioned Markov Chain Monte Carlo (MCMC) algorithm for the solution of the inverse problem. Reduction of uncertainty can be accomplished by incorporating measurements at sparse locations (static data) in the prior distribution. We present a new method to condition Gaussian fields (the log of permeability fields) to available sparse measurements. A truncated Karhunen-Loève expansion (KLE) is used for dimension reduction. In the proposed method the imposition of static data is made through the projection of a sample (expressed as a vector of independent, identically distributed normal random variables) onto the nullspace of a data matrix, that is defined in terms of the KLE. The numerical implementation of the proposed method is straightforward. Through numerical experiments for a model of second-order elliptic equation, we show that the proposed method in multi-chain MCMC studies converges much faster than the MCMC method without conditioning. These studies indicate the importance of conditioning in accelerating the MCMC convergence.

Keywords: Conditioning · Predictive simulations · Bayesian framework · MCMC

1 Introduction

Subsurface formations have spatial variability in their hydraulic properties in multiple length scales. It has been established that such variability plays an important role in determining fluid flow patterns in heterogeneous formations [4,18,24,25]. The characterization of such formations is essential for predictive

O. Gervasi et al. (Eds.): ICCSA 2021, LNCS 12952, pp. 653–669, 2021.
https://doi.org/10.1007/978-3-030-86973-1_46

simulations of multiphase flows in problems such as oil recovery, CO_2 sequestration, or contaminant transport. Procedures for characterization, such as a Bayesian framework using the Markov chain Monte Carlo (MCMC) algorithm, entails the solution of an ill-posed inverse problem. From static and dynamic data, the unknown coefficients of a governing system of partial differential equations that model fluid flow have to be recovered. In the inversion process, the available static data (for instance, measured absolute permeability values at sparse locations) have to be incorporated in the sampling of the (unknown) permeability field so that uncertainty is reduced as much as possible. This way, a conditioning procedure has to be applied such that all samples considered by the inversion method honor available measurements.

MCMC methods have been applied in several areas of science and engineering, and have attracted the attention of many research groups [19,33]. There are many recent and important developments related to gradient-based MCMC procedures. We mention, among many others, the Hamiltonian Monte Carlo [8], and the active subspace methods [10]. There are also Hessian-based procedures [34]. However, for subsurface flow problems gradient and Hessian calculations are computationally very expensive. Thus, for the problems we have in mind we consider the preconditioned (or two-stage) MCMC introduced in [9,16]. Some developments of this method include the multi-physics version [23], the parallelization in multi-core devices [21] and its extension to deformable subsurface formations [5]. This procedure has also been successfully applied in geophysics [44]. The Bayesian framework for inversion that we will use in this work has been carefully discussed in [1].

Our focus in this work is the conditioning of samples to sparse measured data. The importance of conditioning in reservoir simulation has been recognized for many years (see, for instance, [26]). The sequential Gaussian simulation (SGS) [13] has been widely used for this purpose. More recently a truncated Karhunen-Loève expansion (KLE) [16,22,29] has been applied both for dimensional reduction of the (computationally infeasible) large stochastic dimensions of fine grid discretizations of subsurface flow problems as well as for conditioning. In [37] one can find a discussion of the advantages of the KLE over the SGS. There are two lines of work for the conditioning of samples using the KLE. In [30] the basic KLE construction is altered to incorporate static data. In another line of work the vector of independent, identically distributed (i.i.d.) $\mathcal{N}(0,1)$ Gaussian variables that enter the KLE construction is modified to take data into account while keeping the KLE eigenvectors unaltered. This approach can be seen in [36] where a search through a set of matrices of size determined by the number of measurements is performed, and they take the one with the best condition number. In [37] the authors use the expressions for conditional means and covariances of Gaussian random variables [46] that require the inversion of a data covariance matrix.

The method that we introduce here does not alter the basic KLE construction and is computationally very inexpensive. By using the measured data in the KLE we define a data matrix that models Gaussian perturbations on top of a surface defined by kriging [12] of the available data. The proposed procedure consists of replacing the vectors of i.i.d., $\mathcal{N}(0,1)$ Gaussian variables by the closest vector to them (in the least-squares sense) in the nullspace of the data matrix. This way, the Gaussian fields produced by the KLE honor exactly all the data available. We remark that all one needs to implement the proposed method is a basis for the nullspace of the data matrix. Such a basis is used to construct the projection onto the nullspace of the data matrix. Besides introducing this new method, we also present multi-chain MCMC studies for a model elliptic equation. We show convergence of this method for large dimensional problems. Moreover, these studies are used to illustrate the importance of conditioning for the convergence of MCMC methods. Although outside the scope of this work we believe the method presented here can also be applied to other sampling strategies such as the hierarchical method discussed in [6]. This topic is currently being considered by the authors.

This work is organized as follows. In Sect. 2 we discuss the model problem, kriging and dimensional reduction. Section 3 introduces the new method for conditioning by projection. In Sect. 4 we explain the Bayesian framework for inversion. We describe the preconditioned MCMC method with and without conditioning for the construction of permeability fields. Also, the method we use for convergence assessment of MCMC methods is presented. Section 5 is dedicated to a discussion of numerical results from our experiments. Conclusions and some remarks appear in Sect. 6.

2 Model Problem and Dimensional Reduction

2.1 The Model Problem

In the modeling of incompressible subsurface flow problems, such as in two-phase flows in oil reservoirs [14,38], the system of governing partial differential equations consists of a second order elliptic equation coupled to a hyperbolic dominated equation that describes fluid transport. In this work, we illustrate the proposed method for conditioning Gaussian fields in terms of the elliptic equation that enters in this system.

Let us consider $\Omega \subset \mathbb{R}^2$, a bounded domain with Lipschitz boundary, let $\boldsymbol{v}(\boldsymbol{x})$ and $p(\boldsymbol{x})$ denote the Darcy velocity and the pressure of the fluid, respectively, where $\boldsymbol{x} \in \Omega$, and $k(\boldsymbol{x})$ is the absolute permeability. Using Darcy's law, we have the following model elliptic problem:

$$\begin{aligned} \boldsymbol{v}(\boldsymbol{x}) \quad &= -k(\boldsymbol{x})\nabla p(\boldsymbol{x}), \\ \nabla \cdot \boldsymbol{v}(\boldsymbol{x}) &= f, \quad \boldsymbol{x} \in \Omega, \end{aligned} \tag{1}$$

where $f \in L^2(\Omega)$ is a given source term, together with appropriate Dirichlet and Neumann type boundary conditions $p = g_p \in H^{\frac{1}{2}}(\partial\Omega_p)$ and $\boldsymbol{v} \cdot \hat{\boldsymbol{n}} = g_v \in H^{-\frac{1}{2}}(\partial\Omega_v)$, the pressure boundary data and normal velocity data, respectively, with $\partial\Omega = \overline{\partial\Omega_p} \cup \overline{\partial\Omega_v}$ and $\overline{\partial\Omega_p} \cap \overline{\partial\Omega_v} = \varnothing$, $\hat{\boldsymbol{n}}$ is the exterior unit normal vector.

The numerical approximation of the above elliptic problem is derived from the weak formulation of the velocity-pressure system. The weak formulation can be found in [17].

2.2 Kriging

Kriging is a type of interpolation method, which uses a local estimation technique that gives the best linear unbiased estimator of unknown values [12,27]. The main idea of kriging is to estimate the values of a function (or random field) in a domain by calculating a weighted average of a given point in some neighborhood. The kriging takes into account (i) the distances between the estimated points in the domain and the given data points, and (ii) the distances between the given data points themselves. Thus, the kriging gives more weights to the nearest data points. When a point $\boldsymbol{x}_0$ coincides with a given data point $\boldsymbol{x}_i$, the kriging gives the exact value and the variance is zero. In the following subsection, we discuss the KLE, and in Sect. 3, we combine both kriging and KLE.

2.3 Dimensional Reduction

We use the KLE to reduce the large dimensional uncertainty space describing the permeability field $k(\boldsymbol{x})$. In this subsection, we present a brief description of the KLE [20,29]. Let $\boldsymbol{x} \in \Omega$, and suppose $\log[k(\boldsymbol{x})] = Y^k(\boldsymbol{x})$ is a Gaussian field. Also, let us assume $Y^k(\boldsymbol{x})$ is a second-order stochastic process, that is $Y^k(\boldsymbol{x}) \in L^2(\Omega)$ with a probability one. Set $E[(Y^k)^2] = 0$. Thus, for a given orthonormal basis $\{\varphi_i\}$ in $L^2(\Omega)$, $Y^k(\boldsymbol{x})$ can be written as the following:

$$Y^k(\boldsymbol{x}) = \sum_{i=1}^{\infty} Y_i^k \varphi_i(\boldsymbol{x}), \quad \text{with random coefficients} \quad Y_i^k = \int_\Omega Y^k(\boldsymbol{x})\varphi_i(\boldsymbol{x})d\boldsymbol{x}, \tag{2}$$

where $\varphi_i(\boldsymbol{x})$ is an eigenfunction satisfying

$$\int_\Omega R(\boldsymbol{x}_1, \boldsymbol{x}_2)\varphi_i(\boldsymbol{x}_2)d\boldsymbol{x}_2 = \lambda_i \varphi_i(\boldsymbol{x}_1), \quad i = 1, 2, ..., \tag{3}$$

with $\lambda_i = E[(Y_i^k)^2] > 0$ and $R(\boldsymbol{x}_1, \boldsymbol{x}_2)$ is the covariance function, $\mathrm{Cov}(Y^k(\boldsymbol{x}_1), Y^k(\boldsymbol{x}_2))$. Letting $\theta_i^k = Y_i^k/\sqrt{\lambda_i}$, the KLE in Eq. (2) can be written as

$$Y^k(\boldsymbol{x}) = \sum_{i=1}^{\infty} \sqrt{\lambda_i}\theta_i^k \varphi_i(\boldsymbol{x}), \tag{4}$$

where λ_i and φ_i satisfy Eq. (3). We arrange the eigenvalues in the descending order. The infinite series in Eq. (4) is called the Karhunen-Loève expansion. In general, we only need first n dominating terms such that the energy E is more than 95% [28], i.e.

$$E = \frac{\sum_{i=1}^{n} \lambda_i}{\sum_{i=1}^{\infty} \lambda_i} \geq 95\%. \tag{5}$$

Then, a truncated KLE is defined by

$$Y_n^k(\boldsymbol{x}) = \sum_{i=1}^{n} \sqrt{\lambda_i}\theta_i^k \varphi_i(\boldsymbol{x}). \tag{6}$$

From now on we will use $Y(\boldsymbol{x})$ instead of $Y_n^k(\boldsymbol{x})$ for samples generated by the truncated KLE.

3 Conditioning by Projection

Suppose the Gaussian field $Y(\boldsymbol{x})$ defined in Eq. (6) is a Gaussian perturbation on top of a kriged field $\hat{Y}(\boldsymbol{x})$ discussed in Sect. 2.2. That is,

$$Y(\boldsymbol{x}) = \hat{Y}(\boldsymbol{x}) + \sum_{i=1}^{n} \sqrt{\lambda_i}\varphi_i(\boldsymbol{x})\theta_i \ . \tag{7}$$

This can also be written as

$$\begin{aligned} Y(\boldsymbol{x}) - \hat{Y}(\boldsymbol{x}) &= \sum_{i=1}^{n} \sqrt{\lambda_i}\varphi_i(\boldsymbol{x})\theta_i \\ &= \boldsymbol{\phi}^T(\boldsymbol{x})\sqrt{D}\boldsymbol{\theta}, \end{aligned} \tag{8}$$

where D is a diagonal matrix of the dominating n eigenvalues and $\boldsymbol{\theta} = (\theta_1, \theta_2, \ldots, \theta_n)$. For each $\boldsymbol{x}$, $\boldsymbol{\phi}(\boldsymbol{x}) \in \mathbb{R}^n$. Furthermore, assume that m measured data values $Y^1, Y^2, \ldots, Y^m$ of $Y(\boldsymbol{x})$ are given at sparse locations $\hat{\boldsymbol{x}} = (\hat{\boldsymbol{x}}_1, \hat{\boldsymbol{x}}_2, \ldots, \hat{\boldsymbol{x}}_m)$ in the domain Ω such that

$$Y(\hat{\boldsymbol{x}}_i) = Y^i, \quad i = 1, 2, \ldots, m \tag{9}$$

are known. Thus, by substituting (9) in Eq. (8) we have

$$\begin{aligned} \boldsymbol{\phi}^T(\hat{\boldsymbol{x}})\sqrt{D}\boldsymbol{\theta} &= Y(\hat{\boldsymbol{x}}) - \hat{Y}(\hat{\boldsymbol{x}}) \\ &= \mathbf{0}. \end{aligned} \tag{10}$$

This honors m data values at the corresponding sparse locations $\hat{\boldsymbol{x}}$. We can rewrite (10) as follows

$$A\boldsymbol{\theta} = \mathbf{0} \tag{11}$$

where $A = \boldsymbol{\phi}^T(\hat{\boldsymbol{x}})\sqrt{D} \in \mathbb{R}^{m \times n}$ is our data matrix. The solution of this homogeneous system of Eqs. (11) is the nullspace $N(A)$, a subspace of $\mathbb{R}^n$. Given an arbitrary vector $\boldsymbol{\theta} \in \mathbb{R}^n$ of i.i.d., $\mathcal{N}(0, 1)$ Gaussian variables that would be used in the KLE (7), in order to honor the given m data we select the closest vector to $\boldsymbol{\theta}$ in the subspace $N(A)$. This vector is obtained by projecting $\boldsymbol{\theta}$ onto the nullspace of the data matrix A.

Assume that A has rank r, we can easily find an orthonormal basis $\beta = \{\boldsymbol{q}_1, \boldsymbol{q}_2, \ldots, \boldsymbol{q}_{n-r}\}$ for the nullspace of A. We assume that $r < n$, so that A has a non-trivial nullspace. The projection matrix P onto the nullspace of A is given by [43]

$$P = QQ^T, \tag{12}$$

where Q is a matrix that has $\boldsymbol{q}_1, \boldsymbol{q}_2, \ldots, \boldsymbol{q}_{n-r}$ as columns. The projection vector of $\boldsymbol{\theta}$ onto the nullspace of the data matrix A is given by

$$\hat{\boldsymbol{\theta}} = P\boldsymbol{\theta}. \tag{13}$$

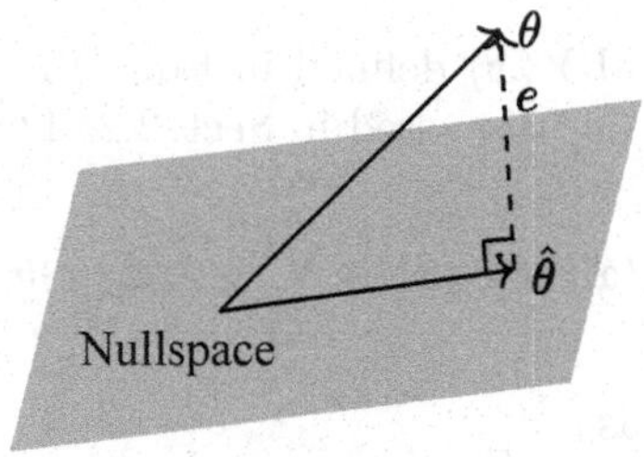

Fig. 1. Projection of the i.i.d., $\mathcal{N}(0,1)\,\boldsymbol{\theta}$ showing the closet vector $\hat{\boldsymbol{\theta}}$ in the nullspace.

Figure 1 illustrates the projection of the i.i.d., $\mathcal{N}(0,1)$ Gaussian variables $\boldsymbol{\theta}$ vector onto the nullspace of the data matrix A. The error vector defined as $\boldsymbol{e} = \boldsymbol{\theta} - \hat{\boldsymbol{\theta}}$ is minimized in the least squares sense. It is perpendicular to the projection vector $\hat{\boldsymbol{\theta}}$. Finally, we can rewrite Eq. (7) as

$$Y(\boldsymbol{x}) = \hat{Y}(\boldsymbol{x}) + \sum_{i=1}^{n} \sqrt{\lambda_i}\varphi_i(\boldsymbol{x})\hat{\theta}_i, \tag{14}$$

where $\hat{\theta}_i, i = 1, \ldots, n$ are the components of $\hat{\boldsymbol{\theta}}$ in Eq. (13). If $\boldsymbol{x} = \hat{\boldsymbol{x}}_i, i = 1, 2, \ldots, m$, in Eq. (14), the second term on the right-hand side is zero. This leads to $Y(\boldsymbol{x}_i) = \hat{Y}(\hat{\boldsymbol{x}}_i)$, and thus, we honor the exact values of the permeability field at the known locations $\hat{\boldsymbol{x}}_1, \ldots, \hat{\boldsymbol{x}}_m$.

4 The Bayesian Framework

4.1 Posterior Exploration

Our primary interest in this article is to characterize the permeability field of our domain of study. Here, we discuss the characterization of the permeability field conditioned on available pressure data. We use half (in a chessboard pattern) of the total pressure data in the discretized domain [45]. We denote the (log of the) permeability field and the reference pressure data by $\boldsymbol{\eta}$ and R_p, respectively. A Bayesian statistical approach along with a preconditioned MCMC method with and without conditioning is used to solve the inverse problem. The posterior probability is calculated using the Bayes' theorem with respect to R_p as follows:

$$P(\boldsymbol{\eta}|R_p) \propto P(R_p|\boldsymbol{\eta})P(\boldsymbol{\eta}), \tag{15}$$

where $P(\boldsymbol{\eta})$ represents the Gaussian prior distribution. The normalizing constant is disregarded in this investigation as we do an iterative search in our MCMC method. We construct the permeability field $\boldsymbol{\eta}(\boldsymbol{\theta})$ using the KLE, where $\boldsymbol{\theta}$ is generated by the MCMC method. The likelihood is considered to be a Gaussian function as in [16], and as a result of that we have our likelihood function as

$$P(R_p|\boldsymbol{\eta}) \propto \exp\Big(-(R_p - R_{\boldsymbol{\eta}})^{\top}\Sigma(R_p - R_{\boldsymbol{\eta}})\Big), \tag{16}$$

where $R_{\boldsymbol{\eta}}$ denotes the simulated pressure data. We set the covariance matrix Σ as $\Sigma = \boldsymbol{I}/2\sigma_R^2$, where $\boldsymbol{I}$ and σ_R^2 represents the identity matrix and the precision parameter, respectively.

We use a MCMC algorithm to sample from the posterior distribution (15). In the MCMC algorithm, we have an instrumental distribution $I(\boldsymbol{\eta}_p|\boldsymbol{\eta})$ by which we propose $\boldsymbol{\eta}_p = \boldsymbol{\eta}(\boldsymbol{\theta}_p)$ at every iteration, where $\boldsymbol{\eta}$ represents the previously accepted state. We solve the forward problem for a given permeability field on the numerical simulator and compute the acceptance probability of a proposed proposal using

$$\alpha(\boldsymbol{\eta}, \boldsymbol{\eta}_p) = \min\left(1, \frac{I(\boldsymbol{\eta}|\boldsymbol{\eta}_p)P(\boldsymbol{\eta}_p|R_p)}{I(\boldsymbol{\eta}_p|\boldsymbol{\eta})P(\boldsymbol{\eta}|R_p)}\right). \tag{17}$$

Below we describe the preconditioned MCMC method with and without conditioning.

4.2 MCMC Algorithms with and Without Conditioning

In our study, we use the MCMC method with and without conditioning. The following random walk sampler (RWS) [11] is used for both MCMC cases:

$$\boldsymbol{\theta}_p = \sqrt{1-\beta^2}\,\boldsymbol{\theta} + \beta\,\boldsymbol{\epsilon}, \tag{18}$$

where $\boldsymbol{\theta}_p$ denotes the current proposal and $\boldsymbol{\theta}$ represents the previously accepted proposal. The symbol β denotes the tuning parameter and $\boldsymbol{\epsilon}$ represents $\mathcal{N}(0,1)$-random variable.

We first discuss the algorithm of the MCMC method without conditioning [9,16]. The filtering step of this method is based on a coarse-scale model approximation of the governing Eq. (1). The coarse-scale discretization is similar to the fine-scale discretization and the permeability field $\boldsymbol{\eta}(\boldsymbol{\theta})$ is projected on the coarse-scale. An upscaling procedure [15] is used to set an effective permeability field on a coarse-grid that provides a similar average response as that of the underlying fine-scale problem. The numerical simulator is run on the coarse-scale model and produces the coarse-grid pressure field R_c. The coarse-scale and fine-scale acceptance probabilities are estimated as

Algorithm 1. MCMC with conditioning

For a given covariance function R generate KLE.
for $i = 1$ to M_{mcmc} **do**
    At $\boldsymbol{\eta}(\boldsymbol{\theta})$generate $\boldsymbol{\theta}_p$ using equation (18).
    Project $\boldsymbol{\theta}_p$ to the nullspace using (13) to get $\hat{\boldsymbol{\theta}}_p$.
    At $\hat{\boldsymbol{\theta}}_p$ construct $\boldsymbol{\eta}_p$ using equation (14).
    Compute the upscaled permeability on the coarse-scale using $\boldsymbol{\eta}_p$.
    Solve the forward problem on the coarse-scale to get R_c.
    Compute the coarse-scale acceptance probability $\alpha_c(\boldsymbol{\eta}, \boldsymbol{\eta}_p)$.
    if $\boldsymbol{\eta}_p$ is accepted **then**
        Use $\boldsymbol{\eta}_p$ in the fine-scale simulation to get R_f.
        Compute the fine-scale acceptance probability $\alpha_f(\boldsymbol{\eta}, \boldsymbol{\eta}_p)$.
        if $\boldsymbol{\eta}_p$ is accepted **then** $\boldsymbol{\eta} = \boldsymbol{\eta}_p$.
        end if
    end if
end for

$$\begin{aligned} \alpha_c(\boldsymbol{\eta}, \boldsymbol{\eta}_p) &= \min\left(1, \frac{I(\boldsymbol{\eta}|\boldsymbol{\eta}_p) P_c(\boldsymbol{\eta}_p|R_p)}{I(\boldsymbol{\eta}_p|\boldsymbol{\eta}) P_c(\boldsymbol{\eta}|R_p)}\right), \text{ and} \\ \alpha_f(\boldsymbol{\eta}, \boldsymbol{\eta}_p) &= \min\left(1, \frac{P_f(\boldsymbol{\eta}_p|R_p) P_c(\boldsymbol{\eta}|R_p)}{P_f(\boldsymbol{\eta}|R_p) P_c(\boldsymbol{\eta}_p|R_p)}\right), \end{aligned} \tag{19}$$

where P_c and P_f represent the posterior probabilities computed at coarse- and fine-scale, respectively. In the MCMC method with conditioning, we construct the permeability field $\boldsymbol{\eta}(\boldsymbol{\theta})$ using Eq. (14). The algorithm of the MCMC method without conditioning is described in [2] and the algorithm of the MCMC method with conditioning is presented in Algorithm 1.

4.3 Convergence Assessment

In this subsection, we discuss the convergence of the MCMC methods for a reliable characterization of the permeability field. Determining the stopping criterion in the MCMC simulations is a challenging task. For this reason, researchers use several MCMC convergence diagnostics to decide when it is safe to stop the simulations. Different diagnostic measures are discussed in [31,35,40,41]. A common approach is to start more than one MCMC chain using distinct initial conditions. In this paper, we study the convergence of the proposed MCMC methods using the Potential Scale Reduction Factor (PSRF) and its multivariate extension MPSRF [7]. Note that the PSRF does not take all the parameters into account and thus may not provide a very reliable indicator of the convergence of the parallel chains. However, the MPSRF takes all the parameters and their interactions into consideration. Therefore, the MPSRF is a better measure to determine the convergence of several chains that explore a high dimensional parameter space.

Let us consider l posterior draws of $\boldsymbol{\theta}$ (dimension n) for each of the $k > 1$ parallel chains. Let $\boldsymbol{\theta}_j^c$ be the generated samples at iteration c in jth chain of k parallel MCMCs. Then, the posterior variance-covariance matrix is computed by

$$\widehat{\mathbf{V}} = \frac{l-1}{l}\mathbf{W} + \left(1 + \frac{1}{k}\right)\frac{\mathbf{B}}{l}. \tag{20}$$

The within-chain covariance matrix $\mathbf{W}$ and between-chain covariance matrix $\mathbf{B}$ are defined by

$$\mathbf{W} = \frac{1}{k(l-1)}\sum_{j=1}^{k}\sum_{c=1}^{l}\left(\boldsymbol{\theta}_j^c - \bar{\boldsymbol{\theta}}_{j.}\right)\left(\boldsymbol{\theta}_j^c - \bar{\boldsymbol{\theta}}_{j.}\right)^T, \tag{21}$$

and

$$\mathbf{B} = \frac{l}{k-1}\sum_{j=1}^{k}\left(\bar{\boldsymbol{\theta}}_{j.} - \bar{\boldsymbol{\theta}}_{..}\right)\left(\bar{\boldsymbol{\theta}}_{j.} - \bar{\boldsymbol{\theta}}_{..}\right)^T, \tag{22}$$

respectively. $\bar{\boldsymbol{\theta}}_{j.}$ and $\bar{\boldsymbol{\theta}}_{..}$ represent the mean within the chain and the mean of the k combined chains, respectively, and T stands for transpose. The PSRFs are computed by

$$\mathrm{PSRF_i} = \sqrt{\frac{\mathrm{diag}(\widehat{\mathbf{V}})_i}{\mathrm{diag}(\mathbf{W})_i}}, \quad \text{where } i = 1, 2, ..., n. \tag{23}$$

The maximum of PSRF values, which is closer to 1, indicates that MCMC proposals sample from approximately the same posterior distribution. The MPSRF is defined as [32]

$$\mathrm{MPSRF} = \sqrt{\left(\frac{l-1}{l} + \left(\frac{k+1}{k}\right)\lambda\right)}, \tag{24}$$

where λ is the largest eigenvalue of the positive definite matrix $\mathbf{W}^{-1}\mathbf{B}/l$. If the proposals in k chains are sampled from almost the same distribution, the between chain covariance matrix becomes zero. Consequently, λ and the MPSRF approach to 0, and 1, respectively, for sufficiently large l. Thus, we achieve the required convergence of the chains.

5 Numerical Results

5.1 Setup of the Problem

In this subsection, we present the details of the simulation of our problem of interest. We consider a unit square-shaped physical domain and solve the elliptic Eq. (1) in the domain. The simulated elliptic solutions are used in the MCMC algorithms. We then present a comparative study between the MCMC methods with and without conditioning. In the MCMC method with conditioning, we include the prior measurement of the permeability field at nine specific sparse locations. This permeability field is constructed using the KLE in which we consider the covariance function as

$$R(\boldsymbol{x}_1, \boldsymbol{x}_2) = \sigma_Y^2 \exp\left(-\frac{|x_1 - x_2|^2}{2L_x^2} - \frac{|y_1 - y_2|^2}{2L_y^2}\right), \tag{25}$$

where $L_x = 0.4$ and $L_y = 0.8$ are the correlation lengths and $\sigma_Y^2 = \mathrm{Var}[(Y^k)^2] = 1$. Figure 3 illustrates the decay of the eigenvalues for these values. Considering the fast decay of the eigenvalues, in this paper, we take the first twenty dominating eigenvalues in the KLE, which preserves almost 100% (using the Eq. (5)) of the total variance or energy of Y in the Eq. (6). We set the source term $f = 0$ and impose Dirichlet boundary conditions, $p = 1$ and $p = 0$, on the left and right boundaries, respectively. We set a Neumann-type boundary condition to zero (i.e., no-flow) everywhere else on the domain boundaries. In our study, we use a synthetic reference permeability field that is generated on a fine-grid of size 16×16. We then run the forward problem using the numerical simulator and generate the corresponding reference pressure field. See Fig. 2 for both fields.

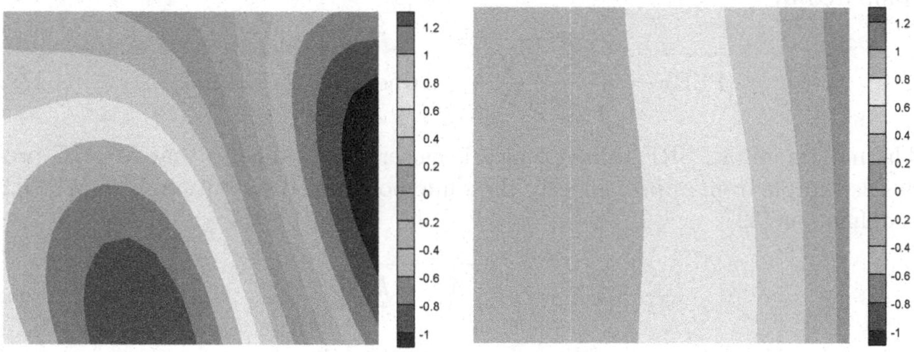

Fig. 2. Reference log permeability field (left) and the corresponding reference pressure field (right).

We take the tuning parameter $\beta = 0.85$ in (18) for both MCMC methods. As a screening step in the MCMC algorithm, we introduce a coarse-scale filter of size 8×8. The coarse-scale simulation runs almost two times faster than the corresponding fine-scale simulation while maintaining the general trend of the fine-scale simulation. We change one stochastic parameter at every iteration to construct a new permeability field for both MCMC studies.

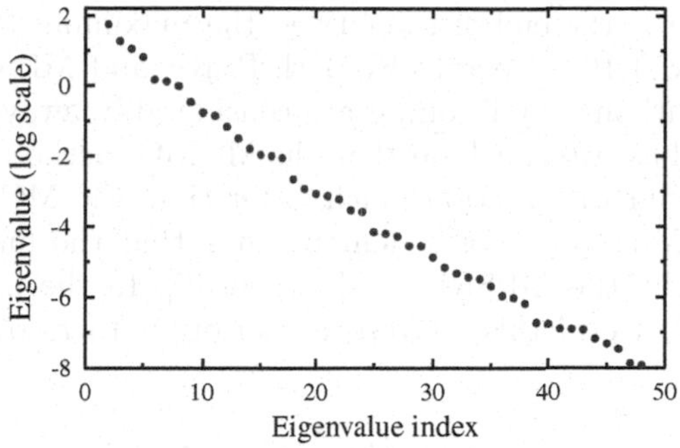

Fig. 3. Decay of eigenvalues in KLE.

5.2 Convergence Analysis of the MCMC Method

We analyze here the convergence of the MCMC algorithm for both studies in terms of the maximum of PSRFs and MPSRF. We run four MCMCs starting from distinct initial seeds for the MCMC method without conditioning. We also run another four chains, but using the same corresponding initial seeds in the former runs, for the MCMC method with conditioning. In Table 1 we show the acceptance rates for these two MCMC studies. We take $\sigma_F^2 = 10^{-4}$ and $\sigma_C^2 = 5 \times 10^{-3}$ for coarse- and fine-scale precisions, respectively, in Eq. (16).

Table 1. A comparison of acceptance rates for the MCMC with and without conditioning.

	MCMC without conditioning	MCMC with conditioning
σ_F^2	10^{-4}	10^{-4}
σ_C^2	5×10^{-3}	5×10^{-3}
Acceptance rate	53%	60%

We observe from the Table 1 that the MCMC method with conditioning has a better acceptance rate than the MCMC method without conditioning. In the calculation of the PSRFs and MPSRF, we take into account the $\boldsymbol{\theta}$ values that are accepted on the fine-scale. If there is no change in the theta values from one state to another in the Markov chain, the repetition of the accepted theta values on the fine-scale is considered in the calculation. Note that a MCMC method converges to the target distribution if both PSRFs and MPSRF values are below 1.2 [42]. Figure 4 depicts the maximum of the PSRFs and MPSRF for both cases with the same number of proposals, 26000, after burn-in. In each chain, 6500 proposals are considered. We observe that the MCMC with conditioning achieves a full convergence. Towards the end of the curves, the maximum PSRF and MPSRF values are 1.14 and 1.16, respectively. Both PSRF and MPSRF curves for the MCMC method without conditioning are considerably away from the numerical value of 1.2. Thus, we conclude that the MCMC method with conditioning explores the posterior distribution much faster than the MCMC method without conditioning. Moreover, Fig. 4 demonstrates that the maximum of PSRFs is bounded above by the MPSRF as shown in [7]. In the next paragraph, we discuss the importance of this convergence in order to recover the underlying permeability field.

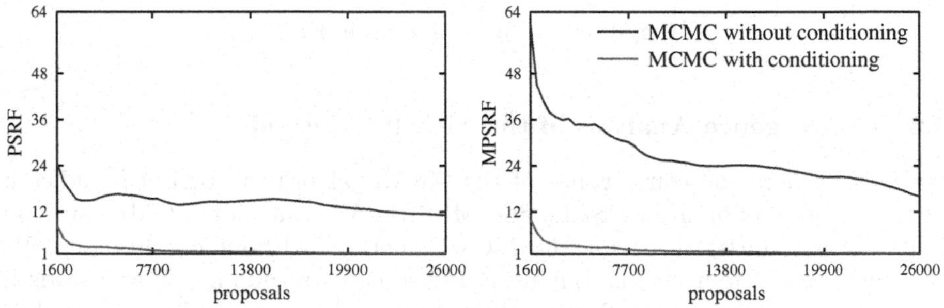

Fig. 4. The maximum of PSRFs and MPSRF for the MCMC method with and without conditioning on measured data.

Now, we discuss the permeability fields that are accepted in the MCMC methods. In Fig. 5 we show twelve permeability fields (three per chain) at 40, 5000, and 10000 iterations, respectively, in four chains for the MCMC method without conditioning. In Fig. 6 we present the corresponding permeability fields in four chains obtained from the MCMC method with conditioning. The process of constructing the permeability fields for this MCMC method with conditioning has two steps: In the first step, we create a permeability field using the KLE in which we provide the projected proposal as an input. Then we add the kriging data obtained from the measurements at nine locations (See Sect. 3). We observe that the MCMC method with conditioning recovers the reference permeability field in Fig. 2 much better than the MCMC method without conditioning. This result is consistent with the MCMC convergence discussed in the above paragraph. Thus, we conclude that the MCMC method with conditioning shows a better performance for the characterization of the permeability field in our problem.

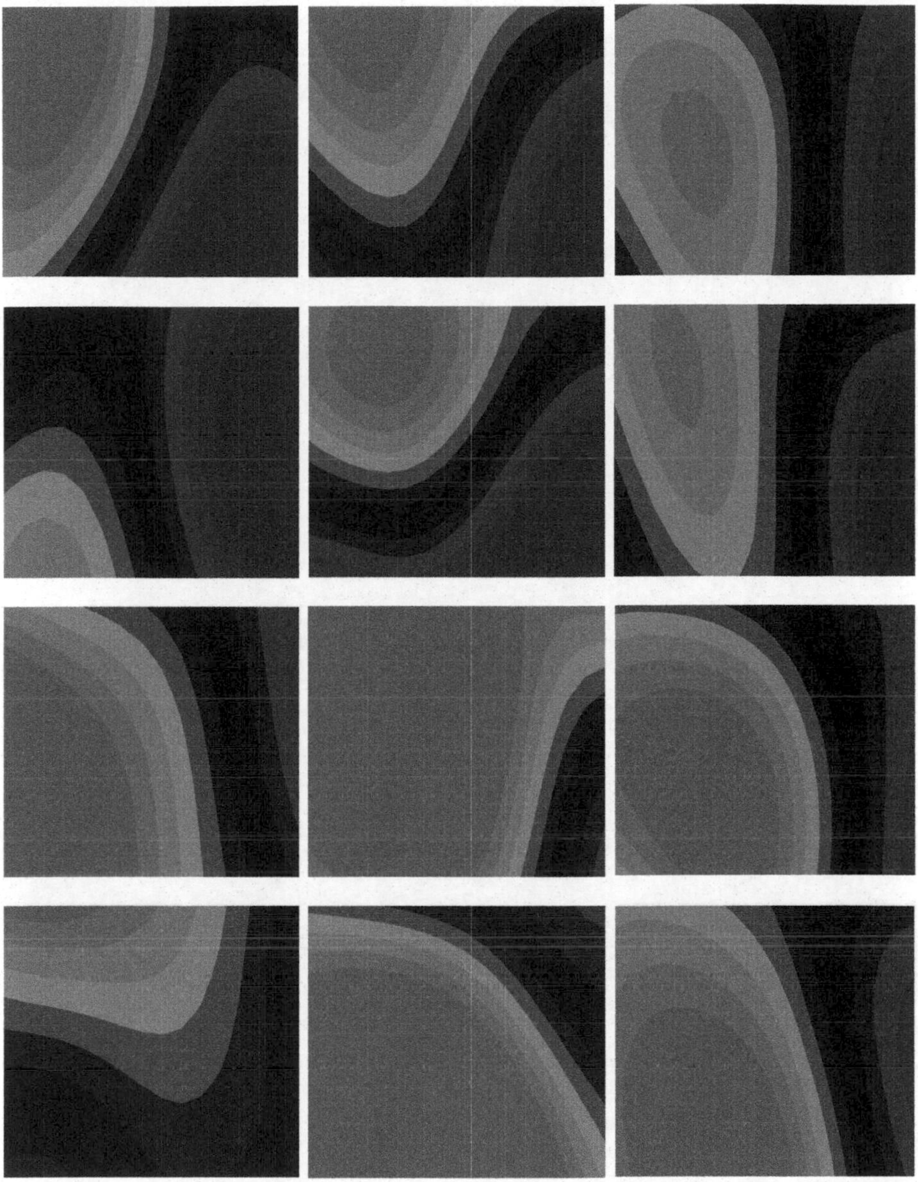

Fig. 5. Log permeability fields recovered in the MCMC without conditioning. Rows refer to four consecutive chains and columns refer to iterations 40, 5000 and 10000, respectively.

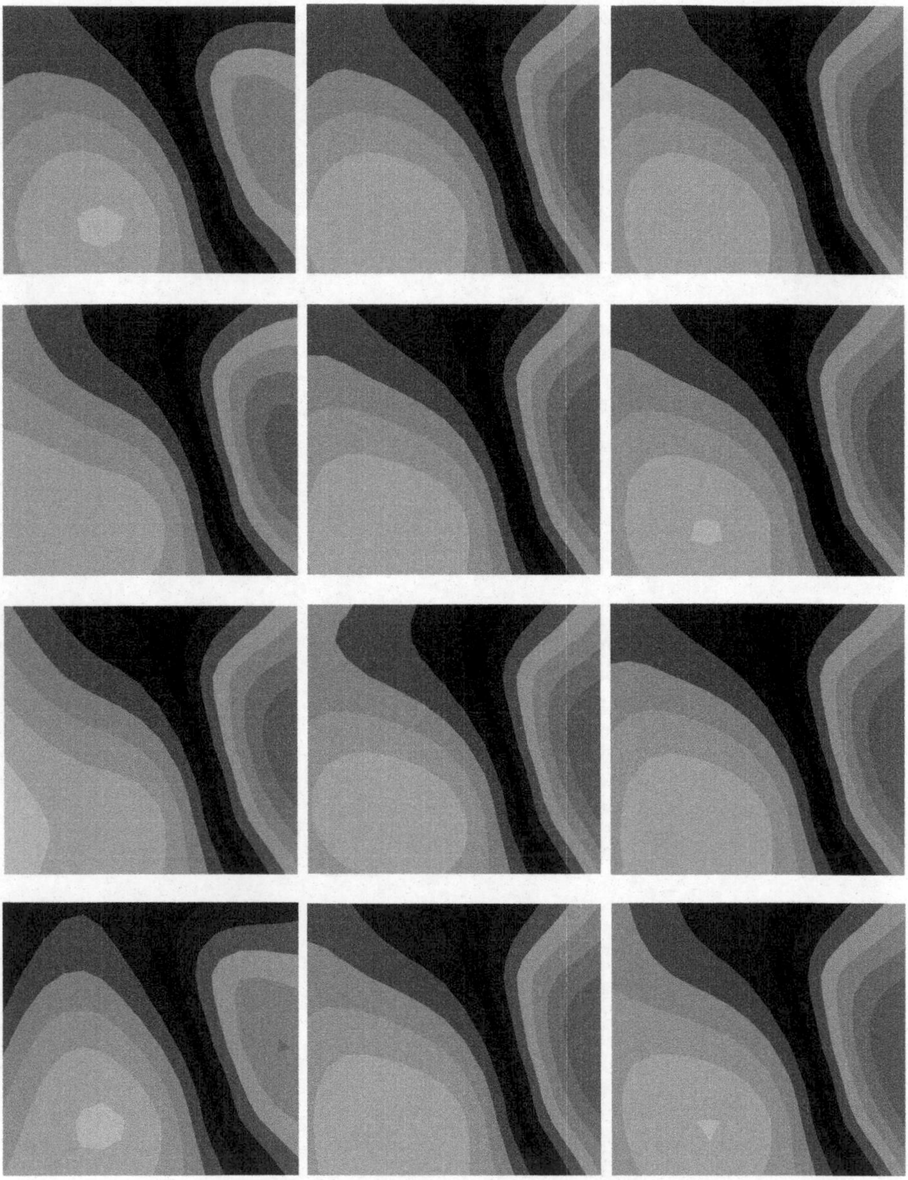

Fig. 6. Log permeability fields recovered in the MCMC with conditioning. Rows refer to four consecutive chains and columns refer to iterations 40, 5000 and 10000, respectively.

6 Conclusions

In this work, we considered the use of MCMC methods for the characterizations of subsurface formations. Usually, sparse measurements of quantities of interest (such as the permeability field) are available in several field locations and they have to be incorporated in the characterization procedure to reduce uncertainty as much as possible.

We introduced a computationally efficient method for conditioning (the log of) permeability fields. The method is based on a projection onto the nullspace of a data matrix defined in terms of a KL expansion. We also presented multi-chain studies that illustrate the importance of conditioning in accelerating the MCMC convergence.

The authors and their collaborators are currently applying the Multiscale Perturbation Method [3,39] to further speed up MCMC studies.

Acknowledgment. A. Rahunanthan was supported by grants from the National Science Foundation (Grant No. HRD–1600818), and NIFA/USDA through Central State University's Evans-Allen Research Program (Fund No. NI201445XXXXG018-0001).

All the numerical simulations presented in this paper were performed on the GPU Computing cluster housed in the Department of Mathematics and Computer Science at Central State University.

References

1. Al-Mamun, A., Barber, J., Ginting, V., Pereira, F., Rahunanthan, A.: Contaminant transport forecasting in the subsurface using a bayesian framework. Appl. Math. Comput. **387**, 124980 (2020)
2. Ali, A., Al-Mamun, A., Pereira, F., Rahunanthan, A.: Markov chain monte carlo methods for fluid flow forecasting in the subsurface. In: Krzhizhanovskaya, V.V., et al. (eds.) ICCS 2020. LNCS, vol. 12143, pp. 757–771. Springer, Cham (2020). https://doi.org/10.1007/978-3-030-50436-6_56
3. Ali, A., Mankad, H., Pereira, F., Sousa, F.S.: The multiscale perturbation method for second order elliptic equations. Appl. Math. Comput. **387**, 125023 (2020)
4. Borges, M.R., Furtado, F., Pereira, F., Amaral Souto, H.P.: Scaling analysis for the tracer flow problem in self-similar permeability fields. Multiscale Model. Simul. **7**(3), 1130–1147 (2008)
5. Borges, M.R., Pereira, F.: A novel approach for subsurface characterization of coupled fluid flow and geomechanical deformation: the case of slightly compressible flows. Comput. Geosci. **24**(4), 1693–1706 (2020)
6. Borges, M.R., Pereira, F., Amaral Souto, H.P.: Efficient generation of multi-scale random fields: a hierarchical approach. Int. J. Numer. Methods Biomed. Eng. **26**(2), 176–189 (2010)
7. Brooks, S., Gelman, A.: General methods for monitoring convergence of iterative simulations. J. Comput. Graph. Stat. **7**, 434–455 (1998)
8. Brooks, S., Gelman, A., Jones, G., Meng, X.L.: Handbook of Markov chain Monte Carlo. CRC Press, Boca Raton (2011)
9. Christen, J.A., Fox, C.: Markov chain Monte Carlo using an approximation. J. Comput. Graph. Stat. **14**(4), 795–810 (2005)
10. Constantine, P.G., Kent, C., Bui-Thanh, T.: Accelerating Markov chain Monte Carlo with active subspaces. SIAM J. Sci. Comput. **38**(5), A2779–A2805 (2016)
11. Cotter, S.L., Roberts, G.O., Stuart, A.M., White, D.: MCMC methods for functions: modifying old algorithms to make them faster. Stat. Sci. **28**(3), 424–446 (2013)

12. Delhomme, J.P.: Kriging in the hydrosciences. Adv. Water Resour. **1**(5), 251–266 (1978)
13. Deutsch, C.V., Journel, A.G., et al.: Geostatistical software library and user's guide. New York **119**(147) (1992)
14. Douglas, J., Furtado, F., Pereira, F.: On the numerical simulation of waterflooding of heterogeneous petroleum reservoirs. Comput. Geosci. **1**(2), 155–190 (1997)
15. Durlofsky, L.: Numerical calculation of equivalent grid block permeability tensors for heterogeneous porous media. Water Resour. Res. **27**(5), 699–708 (1991)
16. Efendiev, Y., Hou, T., Luo, W.: Preconditioning Markov Chain Monte Carlo simulations using coarse-scale models. SIAM J. Sci. Comput. **28**, 776–803 (2006)
17. Francisco, A., Ginting, V., Pereira, F., Rigelo, J.: Design and implementation of a multiscale mixed method based on a nonoverlapping domain decomposition procedure. Math. Comput. Simul. **99**, 125–138 (2014)
18. Furtado, F., Pereira, F.: Crossover from nonlinearity controlled to heterogeneity controlled mixing in two-phase porous media flows. Comput. Geosci. **7**(2), 115–135 (2003)
19. Ginting, V., Pereira, F., Rahunanthan, A.: Multiple Markov chains Monte Carlo approach for flow forecasting in porous media. Procedia Comput. Sci. **9**, 707–716 (2012)
20. Ginting, V., Pereira, F., Rahunanthan, A.: A multi-stage Bayesian prediction framework for subsurface flows. Int. J. Uncertain. Quantif. **3**(6), 499–522 (2013)
21. Ginting, V., Pereira, F., Rahunanthan, A.: A prefetching technique for prediction of porous media flows. Comput. Geosci. **18**(5), 661–675 (2014)
22. Ginting, V., Pereira, F., Rahunanthan, A.: Rapid quantification of uncertainty in permeability and porosity of oil reservoirs for enabling predictive simulation. Math. Comput. Simul. **99**, 139–152 (2014)
23. Ginting, V., Pereira, F., Rahunanthan, A.: Multi-physics Markov chain Monte Carlo methods for subsurface flows. Math. Comput. Simul. **118**, 224–238 (2015)
24. Glimm, J., Lindquist, W.B., Pereira, F., Peierls, R.: The multi-fractal hypothesis and anomalous diffusion. Mat. Aplic. Comp. **11**(2), 189–207 (1992)
25. Glimm, J., Lindquist, W.B., Pereira, F., Zhang, Q.: A theory of macrodispersion for the scale-up problem. Comput. Geosci. **13**(1), 97–122 (1993)
26. Hewett, T.A., Behrens, R.A.: Conditional simulation of reservoir heterogeneity with fractals. SPE Form. Eval. **5**(03), 217–225 (1990)
27. Journel, A.G.: Huijbregts: Mining eostatistics. Academic Press, Technical report (1978)
28. Laloy, E., Rogiers, B., Vrugt, J., Mallants, D., Jacques, D.: Efficient posterior exploration of a high-dimensional groundwater model from two-stage Markov chain Monte Marlo simulation and polynomial chaos expansion. Water Resour. **49**(5), 2664–2682 (2013)
29. Loève, M.: Probability Theory. Springer, Berlin (1997). https://doi.org/10.1007/978-1-4684-9464-8
30. Lu, Z., Zhang, D.: Conditional simulations of flow in randomly heterogeneous porous media using a KL-based moment-equation approach. Adv. Water Resour. **27**(9), 859–874 (2004)
31. Cowles, M.K., Carlin, B.P.: Markov chain Monte Carlo convergence diagnostics: a comparative review. J. Am. Stat. Assoc. **91**, 883–904 (1996)
32. Malyshkina, N.: Markov Switching Models: An Application to Roadway Safety. Ph.D. thesis, Purdue University (2008)

33. Mamun, A., Pereira, F., Rahunanthan, A.: Convergence analysis of MCMC methods for subsurface flow problems. In: Gervasi, O., Murgante, B., Misra, S., Stankova, E., Torre, C.M., Rocha, A.M.A.C., Taniar, D., Apduhan, B.O., Tarantino, E., Ryu, Y. (eds.) ICCSA 2018. LNCS, vol. 10961, pp. 305–317. Springer, Cham (2018). https://doi.org/10.1007/978-3-319-95165-2_22
34. Martin, J., Wilcox, L.C., Burstedde, C., Ghattas, O.: A stochastic Newton MCMC method for large-scale statistical inverse problems with application to seismic inversion. SIAM J. Sci. Comput. **34**(3), A1460–A1487 (2012)
35. Mengersen, K.L., Robert, C.P., Guihenneuc-Jouyaux, C.: MCMC convergence diagnostics: a review. In: Bernardo, M., Berger, J.O., Dawid, A.P., Smtith, A.F.M. (eds.) Bayesian Statistics, vol. 6, pp. 415–440. Oxford University Press, Oxford (1999)
36. Mondal, A., Efendiev, Y., Mallick, B., Datta-Gupta, A.: Bayesian uncertainty quantification for flows in heterogeneous porous media using reversible jump Markov chain Monte Carlo methods. Adv. Water Resour. **33**(3), 241–256 (2010)
37. Ossiander, M., M.Peszynska, Vasylkivska, V.: Conditional stochastic simulations of flow and transport with Karhunen-Loève expansions, stochastic collocation, and sequential Gaussian simulation. J. Appl. Math. **2014** (2014)
38. Pereira, F., Rahunanthan, A.: A semi-discrete central scheme for the approximation of two-phase flows in three space dimensions. Math. Comput. Simul. **81**(10), 2296–2306 (2011)
39. Rocha, F.F., Mankad, H., Sousa, F.S., Pereira, F.: The multiscale perturbation method for two-phase reservoir flow problems. arXiv preprint arXiv:2103.11050 (2021)
40. Roy, V.: Convergence diagnostics for Markov chain Monte Carlo. Ann. Rev. Stat. Appl. **7**, 387–412 (2019)
41. Brooks, S.P., Roberts, G.O.: Convergence assessments of Markov chain Monte Carlo algorithms. Stat. Comput. **8**, 319–335 (1998)
42. Smith, B.J.: boa: An R package for MCMC output convergence assessment and posterior inference. J. Stat. Softw. **21**, 1–37 (2007)
43. Strang, G.: Linear Algebra and Learning from Data. Wellesley-Cambridge Press, Cambridge (2019)
44. Stuart, G.K., Minkoff, S.E., Pereira, F.: A two-stage Markov chain Monte Carlo method for seismic inversion and uncertainty quantification. Geophysics **84**(6), R1003–R1020 (2019)
45. Tong, X.T., Morzfeld, M., Marzouk, Y.M.: MALA-within-Gibbs samplers for high-dimensional distributions with sparse conditional structure. SIAM J. Sci. Comput. **42**(3), A1765–A1788 (2020)
46. Tong, Y.L.: The Multivariate Normal Distribution. Springer Series in Statistics, Springer, New York (1990). https://doi.org/10.1007/978-1-4613-9655-0

International Workshop on Computerized Evaluation of Economic Activities: Urban Spaces (CEEA 2021)

Territorial Disparities in Tuscan Industrial Assets: A Method to Assess Average Firm-Size Spatial Distribution

Diego Altafini(✉) and Valerio Cutini

Dipartimento di Ingegneria dell'Energia, dei Sistemi, del Territorio e delle Costruzioni, Università di Pisa, Largo Lucio Lazzarino, 1, 56122 Pisa, PI, Italy
diego.altafini@phd.unipi.it

Abstract. In economics, firm-size can is an important marker for economic activities' dynamism. It indicates the scale of operation and conditions regarding production and profitability, hence, the overall economic soundness of a sector or industry. Several variables can be employed for assessing firm-size, categorized in input factors – capital, labour, net-worth and total assets; output factors – volume of production, value added; and factors related to space, such as market size and presence of transportation. From a spatial perspective, addressing firm-size remains a challenge, as in-detail surveys of these variables are difficult due to the limited breakdown of economic data. However, regional characteristics of firm-size distribution can reveal several logics about territorial disparities, that ought to be considered in policies for economic recovery. This paper objective is to propose a method to estimate average firm-size throughout the Tuscany region territory, based on the variables of number of local units (firms) and number of employees, and evaluate its spatial distribution evolution between two periods of time Industrial Census data will be compared to industrial assets locational data to individuate production-oriented – spaces dedicated to manufacture – and administrative-oriented areas in the Tuscany Region. Organized in a GIS-based environment, the results assessment provides an in-detail view of spatial information regarding territorial disparities in industrial distribution, which can be compared to other territorial endowments that exist within the region, thus, being a complementary analysis for urban and regional planning.

Keywords: Firm-size · Regional planning · Tuscany

1 Introduction

Firm-size has been an extensively discussed topic in economics' theory of firm since its introduction as a rationale by Ronald Coase in the late 1930's [1]. Albeit thought by Coase as being derived from the quantity of internal and external *contractual relations* that a corporation had [1], firm-size matured as a measure which, in nowadays, encompass several aspects about the economic activities' scale. Its evaluation allows to assess firms' organizational characteristics, their financial soundness, their productivity along the

O. Gervasi et al. (Eds.): ICCSA 2021, LNCS 12952, pp. 673–687, 2021.
https://doi.org/10.1007/978-3-030-86973-1_47

overall dynamism of the sector. When related to space, it reveals aspects about firms' spatial distribution patterns along attributes regarding countries and regions economic structures [2, 3]. Nevertheless, the discussion of what are the factors that can indeed determine firm-size, is still a point of debate among economists.

Coase's interpretation of firm-size was established as part of the analysis regarding the nature of *transaction costs*. In this context, it was thought that firms that are better equipped to handle those costs would be able to have more trade contracts in the market, therefore diminishing their production costs through outsourced inputs; hence the number of contracts a firm has will be proportional to their operation size [1]. While influential, this analysis was limited by its scope, not considering other aspects that may inform firm-size. Lucas [4], in his neoclassical firm model, addressed several absent points, and introduced capital and labour as determinants of size. For Lucas, *managerial talent* is unevenly distributed among agents, so firms must reach an equilibrium ratio of managers and employees in their organizational structure. As a firm increases its capital, this cause changes in the managers-employees equilibrium ratio, that leads to alterations in total firm-size [4]; in this aspect, while capital intensive firms tend to be larger, it can be stated that the number of employees is a fundamental determinant of size. Labour (number of employees) and capital (machinery) are often referred in economics as *input factors* – being in close relation with production – and were the main elements used to assess operations' scale until the late 1990's [2, 4].

It was not until the maturation of organizational theories in the early 2000's that *output factors* were considered as determinants of firm-size [3]. *Outputs*, in economics, are interpreted as production results, such as productivity, added value, sales and profits, and can inform aspects that, when compared amid firms, cam be indicative of their relative scale and size. Other factors – some also related to spatial or territorial endowments – can also influence in the maximum firm-sizes, such as R&D intensity, sector and market size, and the presence of utilities and transportation networks [3].

Despite the remarkable advances in the theoretical comprehension of what are the determinants of firm-size, problems remain on how to address them from a spatial perspective. The limited breakdown of economic data – as surveys are often available just at national, or at best, at regional scales – creates several issues for an in-detail evaluation of territorial disparities in the firms' operation sizes. In turn, the absence of such spatial data may hinder the effectiveness of economic recovery policies, as no clear picture of the regional industrial assets location and dimensions is readily available. With these issues in consideration, this paper objective is to propose a method to assess the average firm-size distribution within the Tuscany region – as well as understand the data limitations in this assessment. Organized in a GIS-based environment, average firm-sizes are estimated based on input variables of number of local units (firms) and number of employees, available in the Italian Industrial and Services Census for two periods of time (2001 and 2011), that are spatialized according to survey (census) zones to reveal their territorial density. Data is also compared to the location of the industrial assets – built-structures dedicated to manufacture – hence, individuating where *productive* and *administrative-oriented* territories are predominant in Tuscany. The spatial information results from this assessment can be further compared to other territorial endowments of the region, thus, being, beyond an economic analysis, a source of complementary data for urban and regional planning policies.

2 Datasets Construction and Methods

Datasets used to assess industrial distribution territorial disparities within Tuscany are obtained from the 8th and 9th Italian Industrial and Services Census (*Censimenti ISTAT dell'industria e servizi*) [5, 6]. This database describes the total number of local units (firms) and the number of employees in the industrial and service sectors for a determined census zone, being periodic, as spans from 2001 to 2011, and methodologically homogeneous, hence allowing comparisons between periods [7]. Since the data tables (.csv) and their spatial data counterparts (.xls) are placed in different files, a spatial join is performed in QGIS [8] using the *section* variable to assemble the table datum to its respective spatial position, allowing variables' spatialization and categorization.

ISTAT data tables have local units and employees' variables described as absolute values, with any mention to their territorial area dimension being absent. The same occurs for the census zones' data as, despite being a localized spatial dataset, no variable for area is present [7]. With this in consideration, area values are independently processed in QGIS [8] for each census zone. Once calculated and converted from m^2 to km^2, those areas divide their respective variables for number of local units and employees' that results in their average density (Eq. 1 and 2). When spatialized, their distribution patterns can be visualised across the Tuscan territory.

$$D_{localunits} = \frac{N_{localunits}}{A_{censuszone}} \quad (1)$$

$$D_{employees} = \frac{N_{employees}}{A_{censuszone}} \quad (2)$$

The spatial dataset construction follows the same rules and principles applied in the *Censimento ISTAT della Popolazione e dell'industria anni 2001–2011,* a QGIS project elaborated by the *Regione Toscana* [9] with the same ISTAT dataset. Still, the analysis dataset fundamentally differs from the *Regione's* construction in two points: the numerical ranges that established for each variable in categorization – which are standardized between the different periods of time; and the presence of a categorization, that specifies, for each census zone, the density degree of each variable, that can range from *very low* to *very high; no data* encompasses "0" and Null values (Table 1).

Table 1. Local units and employees data distribution according to density for 2001 and 2011

		Local units		Employees	
Ranges	Values	2001	2011	2001	2011
Very high density	>1,000	4,108	3,566	7,678	6,724
High density	<= 1,000 > 500	2,601	2,484	3,032	2,755
Medium density	<= 500 > 100	8,094	7,488	6,104	5,983
Low density	<= 100 > 20	3,886	4,188	2,243	2,739
Very low density	<= 20 > 0	3,476	3,730	3,088	3,255
No data	0 or Null	6,808	7,378	6,808	7,378
Total census zones		28,953	28,834	28,953	28,834

The average firm-size density in a census zone is then calculated through the ratio between the density of employees and the density of local units [3] (Eq. 3).

$$D_{firmsize} = \frac{D_{employees}}{D_{localunits}} \tag{3}$$

While this variable represents the ratio between the average number of employees and the average number of local units (firms), thus, informing the average operation size of an area, it provides no distinction regarding which kind of activity is present, nor where *productive spaces* and *administrative spaces* are prevalent within the territory. ISTAT local units' data does not contain countable information about function that allows these precise assessments [7]. With this issue in consideration, it is proposed the inclusion of another dataset that can partially address these absences: the Tuscany Region built-structures data (*Edificato 2k,10k 1988–2013*) [10]. This dataset outlines the location of all built-structures within the Tuscan territory, represented by volumetric units (polygons), and categorized according to their main urban function. For this analysis, only production-oriented buildings are considered, as services often are located on mixed-use structures, which are not individuated on the dataset. Hence, the data extraction encompasses solely the built-structures that are categorized under "Industrial" (*Industriale*) or "Technological Plant" (*Impianto Tecnologico*).

Since volumetric units can overlap two census zones, the built-structures centroids – the polygon central point – are extracted. Being punctual elements, it is assured that centroids lie within a sole census zone. For each of these areas, the data regarding the total number of production-oriented buildings is joined to the average firm-size dataset (Fig. 1a, 1b), in order to assess if productive or administrative areas are predominant, as well as their distribution across the territory.

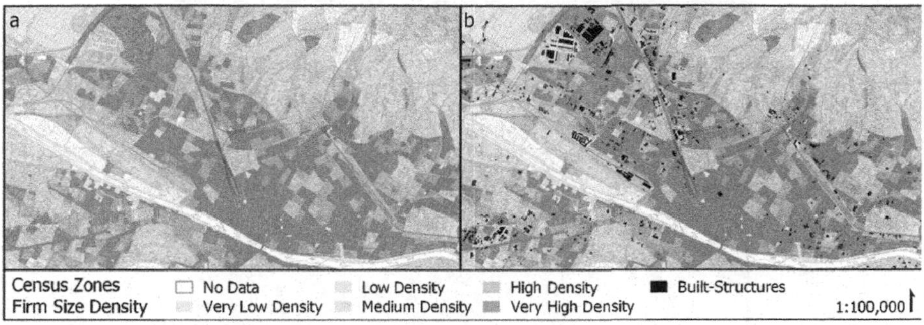

Fig. 1. Datasets of average firm-size (a) and industrial built structures (b) superimposition; data are joined for the *administrative* and *productive* areas distribution assessment.

The relation between firm-size density and presence of built-structures with industrial function can indicate if the area is predominantly oriented to the industrial sector manufacture activities – due to a significant presence of industrial plants; to the industrial firms' administrative activities or to services – if no industrial plants are present; or if the area has no defined orientation, as plants may be present but in no significant quantities when compared to the number of firms, hence limiting the possibilities of a detailed assessment that distinguish *administrative/services* and *productive* activities. This constructed dataset is spatialized to depict the differences between administrative and manufacture areas' distribution within the Tuscan Territory.

3 Results and Discussion

Spatial data distribution for average local units and employees' densities, both in 2001 and 2011, follows the same general territorial patterns depicted in the spatialization of average firm-size (2011 – Fig. 2). It can be observed that densities degrees tend to be higher near Tuscany's main urban centres, as it would be expected. However, it is also verified a clear pattern of *high* and *medium* densities alongside the main regional highways that establish the linkages between major cities. This suggests that the relationship amid economic activities location and road-circulation network *preferential routes*, addressed in previous studies [11], can be also associated to firm-size.

Although the spatialization implies territorial relations amid firms' placement and the road-infrastructure, the patterns are, nonetheless, distinctive to septentrional and, to a lesser degree, central Tuscany. Their diminished occurrence in meridional Tuscany can be explained by two reasons: its sparser road-circulation network – and consequently its lower overall regional hierarchy when compared to northern Tuscany [12]; and the lack of larger urban settlements near the highways (Fig. 2). Both characteristics aid to describe another noticeable distinction amid north and south, that concerns the firms' presence in hinterlands. Northern Tuscany has a greater number of hinterlands zones with *very low* average firm-sizes (thus, at least one local unit and employee), whereas in the south, several hinterland zones have no firm presence whatsoever *(no data)*. This is a distinguishable feature in the *Maremma* area, in-between the cities of *Siena* and *Grosseto*, which is focused primarily on agricultural activities (Fig. 2).

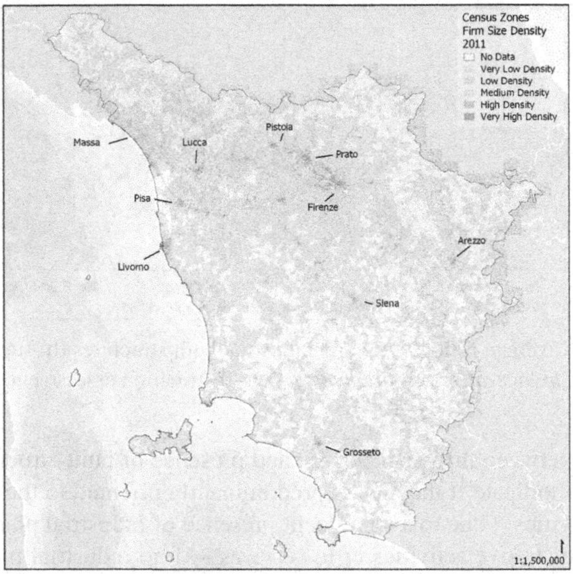

Fig. 2. Spatial distribution of average firm-size in Tuscany (2011).

From a regional standpoint, even though overall territorial patterns are maintained, the distribution of average local units and employees' densities across census zones, for certain ranges, presents significant changes between 2001 and 2011 (Table 2).

Table 2. Census zones' average local units and employees' densities variation - 2001 to 2011

	Local units			Employees		
	2001	2011	Δ%	2001	2011	Δ%
Very high density	4,108	3,566	−13.19	7,678	6,724	−12.42
High density	2,601	2,484	−4.50	3,032	2,755	−9.13
Medium density	8,094	7,488	−7.48	6,104	5,983	−1.98
Low density	3,886	4,188	7.71	2,243	2,739	22.11
Very low density	3,476	3,730	7.30	3,088	3,255	5.40

The data overview demonstrates that, in 2001–2011 interval, there was a decrease in the number of census zones categorized under *medium, high* and *very high* density ranges, accompanied by an increase in *low* and *very low* ranges, a trend noted for both variables. Sizeable variations are observed in the *very high* range, as decrements of 13.19% and 12.42% happen for, respectively, average local units and employees'; and in the *low* range, that, despite a comparably smaller increase on average local units (7.71%), presents a significative increase on the average employees (22.11%).

A similar behaviour is observed for average firm-size, as significative changes in census zones quantities are also verified for the same ranges (Table 3).

Table 3. Census zones' average firm-size variation - 2001 to 2011

Ranges	Values	Firm-size		
		2001	2011	Δ%
Very high density	>100	8,282	7,000	−15.48
High density	<= 100 > 50	3,599	3,516	−2.30
Medium density	<= 50 > 10	6,297	6,601	4.83
Low density	<= 10 > 5	883	1,039	17.67
Very low density	<= 5 > 0	3,084	3,300	7.00

In the interval of 2001 to 2011, average firm-size maintains variation arrangements similar to those observed in the previous variables, as there are decreases in the number of census zones within the *very high* (15.48%) and *high* (2.30%) ranges, while increments are verified for the *low* (17.67%) and *very low* (7.00%) ranges. However, when the number of census zones categorized as *medium* is considered, it is verified instead a slight increase, an opposite trend when compared to both average local units and average number of employees (Table 2).

Observed under a same context, these results suggest that several territorial shifts occurred in the Tuscan economic structure during the period 2001–2011, which ought to be reflected in changes on the spatial patterns of these variables. Tabular data demonstrates that average firm-sizes tend to decrease, as there are less census zones within *very high* and *high* ranges (Table 3). Still, no alterations can be seen in the overall distribution patterns, as *very high* and *high* ranges are still concentrated in the same places: the main urban settlements (Fig. 2). Given this unchanged distribution at regional scale, and with the increases in *medium, low* and *very low* density ranges in consideration, this suggests that firms are not being displaced to different areas in the regional space – as would be inferred from tabular data – but towards the fringes or hinterlands near the main urban centres or to areas that already possess significative densities, thus increasing the overall firm-size in the urban settlements boundaries.

To explore this assumption, an in-depth analysis of the spatial structure of the areas with higher densities is needed, since are these local shifts in distribution patterns that can reveal additional information about the evolution dynamics in Tuscan economic structures. In this aspect, evaluating changes in the area that concentrate most census zones with ranges between *low, medium, high* and *very high,* given that the regional scale distribution patterns are assumed to remain similar, yields a clearer explanation about how these tendencies repeat across other urban settlements within the region.

Located throughout the provinces of *Pisa, Lucca, Pistoia, Prato* and *Firenze*, the highlighted area, henceforth referred as *Valdarno* (Fig. 3), encompasses:

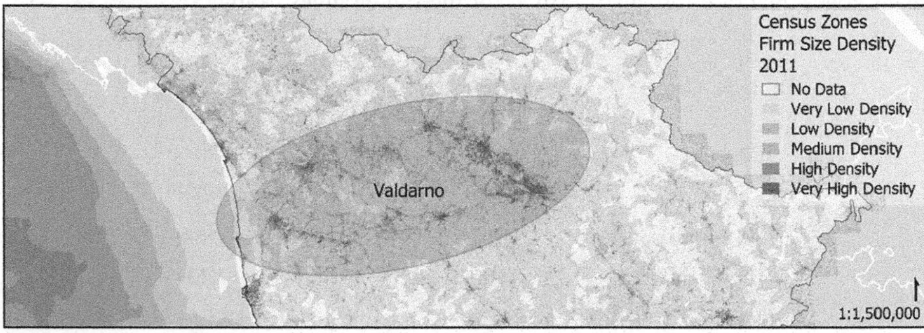

Fig. 3. Position and extents of the *Valdarno* area relative to the Tuscany Region.

- 51.24% (2001) and 50.21% (2011) of the average number of local units;
- 51.12% (2001) and 50.38% (2011) of the average number of employees;
- 51.02% (2001) and 50.36% (2011) of the average firm-size total number of census zones within ranges between *low* and *very high.*

The evolution of the average local units' densities patterns in the period 2001–2011 in the *Valdarno* area (Fig. 4) reveals several assumed particularities of the economic structures territorial shift. In the spatialization it is possible to highlight that several census zones in the boundaries of *Firenze* that in 2001 are categorized in the *very low* range (grey) become, in 2011, areas within the *low* range (green), thus an indicative of a firm presence increase. The same spatial behaviour can be observed in some areas once categorized as *no data,* which in 2011 appear instead in the *very low* range.

Even though those shifts in distribution patterns are more distinguishable around *Firenze,* due to their greater occurrence, they are not particular to it. Similar patterns can be also verified around smaller urban areas such as *Empoli,* or throughout the conurbations within *Pisa, Lucca* and *Prato* areas. This redistribution is also not exclusive to the lesser density ranges, as territorial distribution shifts may be observed, as well, for the *high* and *very high* categories, especially around *Prato* and *Pistoia.*

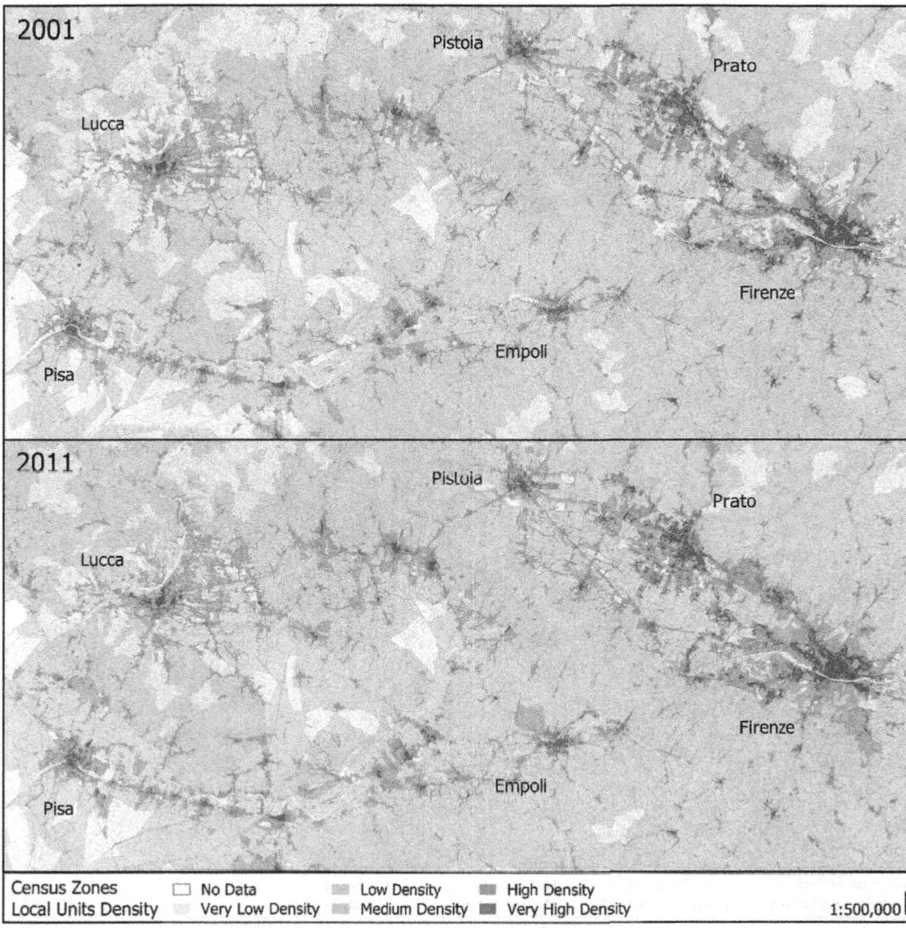

Fig. 4. Average local units' densities – census zones territorial distribution shifts in the period between 2001 and 2010 within the *Valdarno* area. (Color figure online)

Although the average number of employees' densities possess a broader territorial distribution within the *Valdarno* area when compared to the average local units, its spatialization identifies several similarities in the economic structures' territorial shift tendencies (Fig. 5). For the interval between 2001 and 2011, it is observed that certain areas – throughout the *Firenze* metropolitan region and around *Empoli* urban area – present a slight decrease in the number of census zones with *high* and *very high* densities (Fig. 5 – 2001), in accordance with the verified in the regional data (Table 2). In the same manner, the number of census zones categorized as *very low*, but, above all, in the *low* density range, demonstrate a relevant increase across the cities' boundaries (Fig. 5 – 2011). Still, *low* density shifts are also verified, as some areas in the borders of *Pisa* metropolitan area transition from *low* to *very low*. Overall, these results, once again, corroborate with the assumption of the firm displacement trend, as movements from consolidated centres towards the urban fringes are observed during the period.

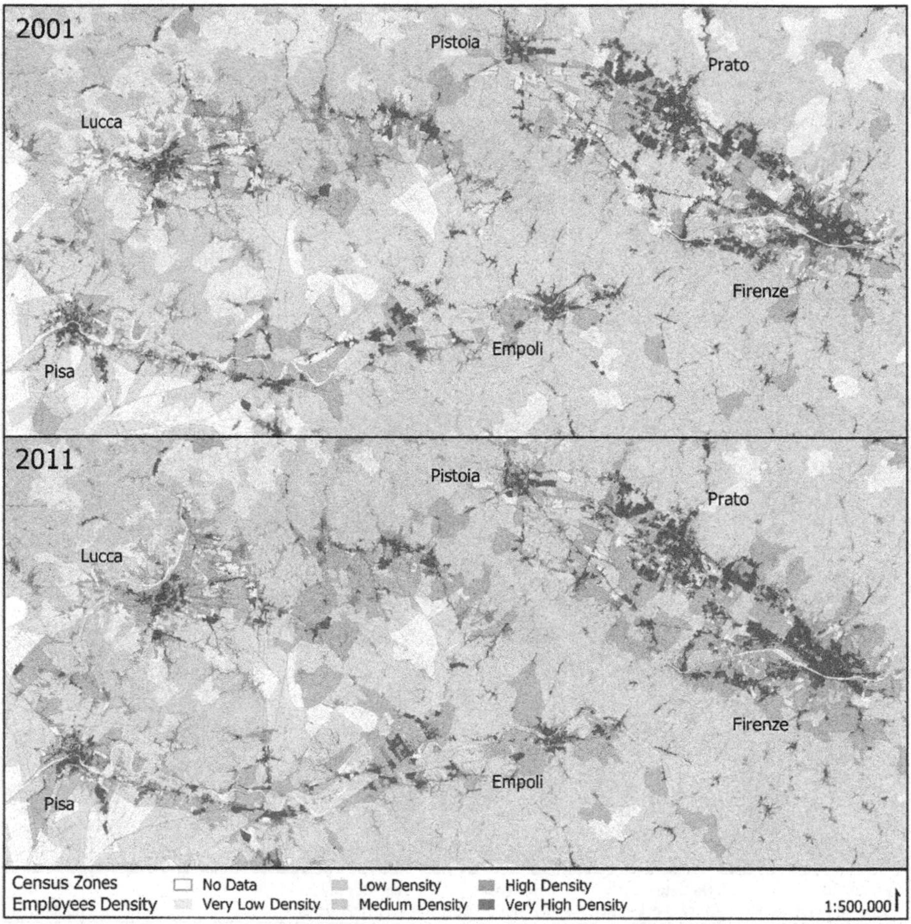

Fig. 5. Average number of employees' densities – census zones territorial distribution shifts in the period between 2001 and 2010 within the *Valdarno* area. (Color figure online)

Another distinguishable pattern highlighted in the average number of employees spatialization, regards the increases in the number of census zones categorized in the *low* density range. Those are not restricted to the urban areas' boundaries, but also can be seen around hinterland areas that already exhibited *low* densities (Fig. 5 – 2011). Associated to these increases, several areas categorized in 2001 as *low*, had their values shifted to *medium* density ranges in 2011, as observed around *Empoli* and *Lucca* urban areas. Nevertheless, these increases in employees are not always accompanied by an equivalent growth in the average number of local unts (Fig. 4 – 2011), as observed in *Empoli* (Fig. 4, Fig. 5 – 2011), which suggest that although the overall operations' size in those census zones is increasing, no additional firms are being placed in the area, therefore, not resulting in the average firm-size density increase.

The spatialization of average firm-sizes densities for the *Valdarno* area (Fig. 6) can precise where the less evident shifts in distribution patterns occur, therefore informing about the firms' disposition and economic structure evolution in the period.

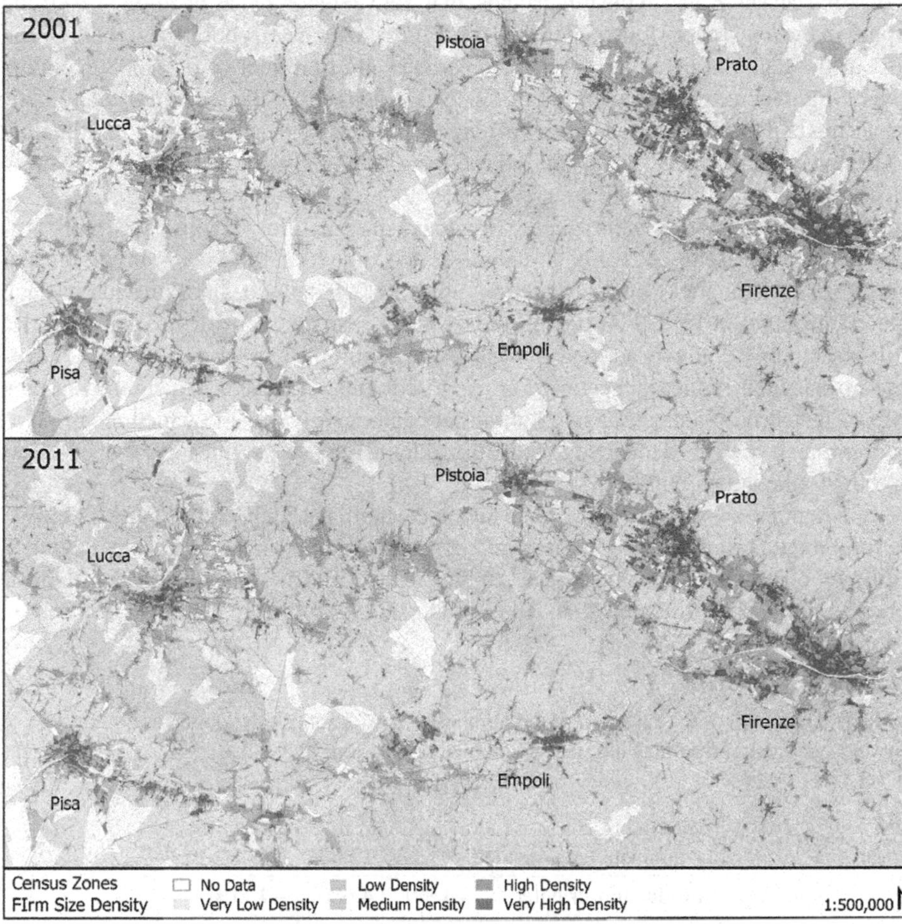

Fig. 6. Average firm-size densities – census zones ranges territorial distribution shifts in the period between 2001 and 2010 within the *Valdarno* area. (Color figure online)

Since average firm-size density (Fig. 6) is a ratio between the average number of employees (Fig. 5) and the average number of local units (Fig. 4) densities, alterations will occur only if proportional shifts take place in both variables, a situation that does not happen in the aforementioned areas around *Empoli* (Fig. 4, Fig. 5 – 2011). Still, the average form-size allows to identify spaces where an overall growth or shrinking of the productive sector happen. This may be observed, once again, in the shifts in density around the urban centres' boundaries. Taking the case of *Firenze*, it is noticeable that these areas verified an increase in the number of census zones categorized as *low* density. Another distinctive trend is the slight decrease in the number of *high* and *very high* density areas within the urban centre – given the patterns verified for local units and employees – that gave place to areas with *medium* average firm-size densities, in accordance to the verified data (Tables 2 and 3). This dynamic of decrease on concentrations can also be identified throughout smaller urban settlements in-between *Lucca* and *Pistoia*, as well as in some census zones in the hinterlands, that were categorized as *medium* in 2001, but appear in the *low* or *very low* ranges in 2011 (Fig. 6), which corroborates with the overall shift in the regional economic structure, perhaps an aftereffect of the 2008 economic crisis. Slight increases in the number of census zones within the *medium* density range are verified on the fringe areas of the *Firenze* and *Prato* provinces, but, above all, along the highways that connect *Pisa, Empoli* e *Firenze*. Being also an indicative of the firms' relocation dynamic within the area.

Even though evaluating the average firm-sizes changes allows to observe significative changes in the Tuscan economic structure, it does not reveal the shifts in the disposition of areas dedicated to the production, since ISTAT data does not provide in-detail spatial information [5, 6]. Apposing the average firm size densities to the industrial built-structures [9] allows address this issue and distinguish which census zones have a predominance of industrial sector *productive* activities – possessing a significant presence of industrial plants alongside a minimal number of firms; and which areas have a predominance of firms dedicated to industrial administrative activities or services – since no industrial plants are present.

In a regional overview (Table 4), results indicate that 45.93% (2001) and 43.82% of the total number of census zones are *administrative*-oriented areas, therefore, having no industrial plants within their confines. 16.86% (2001) and 16.49% (2011) of the census zones are *productive*-oriented areas, thus, possessing a significative number of firms and industrial structures.

Table 4. Distribution and variation of the number of census zones categorized as administrative-oriented, production-oriented and with no defined orientation - 2001–2011

	2001	2011	Δ%
Administrative-oriented	13,297	12,437	−6.46%
Production-oriented	4,881	4,680	−4.11%
No defined orientation	3,967	3,889	−1.96%
No data	6,808	7,378	8.37%

Nevertheless, in terms of absolute numbers, both administrative and productive-oriented areas have a decrease between 2001 and 2011, decurrent of the increase in the number census zones with *no data* (0 or Null), informing a general decrease in activities and corroborating the supposition that average firm-size decreases are related with the 2008 economic crisis. Regarding the number of areas with no defined orientation – identified as so, since the presence of firms and structures presents no sufficient proportion to precisely define an orientation – albeit also experiencing an absolute decrease, has maintained its proportion (13.70%) in the 2001–2011 interval.

Data spatialization reveals an important distributional pattern distinction regarding *aministrative*-oriented and *productive* oriented areas (Fig. 7). *Administrative*-oriented is predominantly located in urban centres, while *productive*-oriented areas are mainly located in urban fringes, or, along the road-infrastructure throughout the hinterlands (Fig. 7), supporting the relationship between road-network and industrial location.

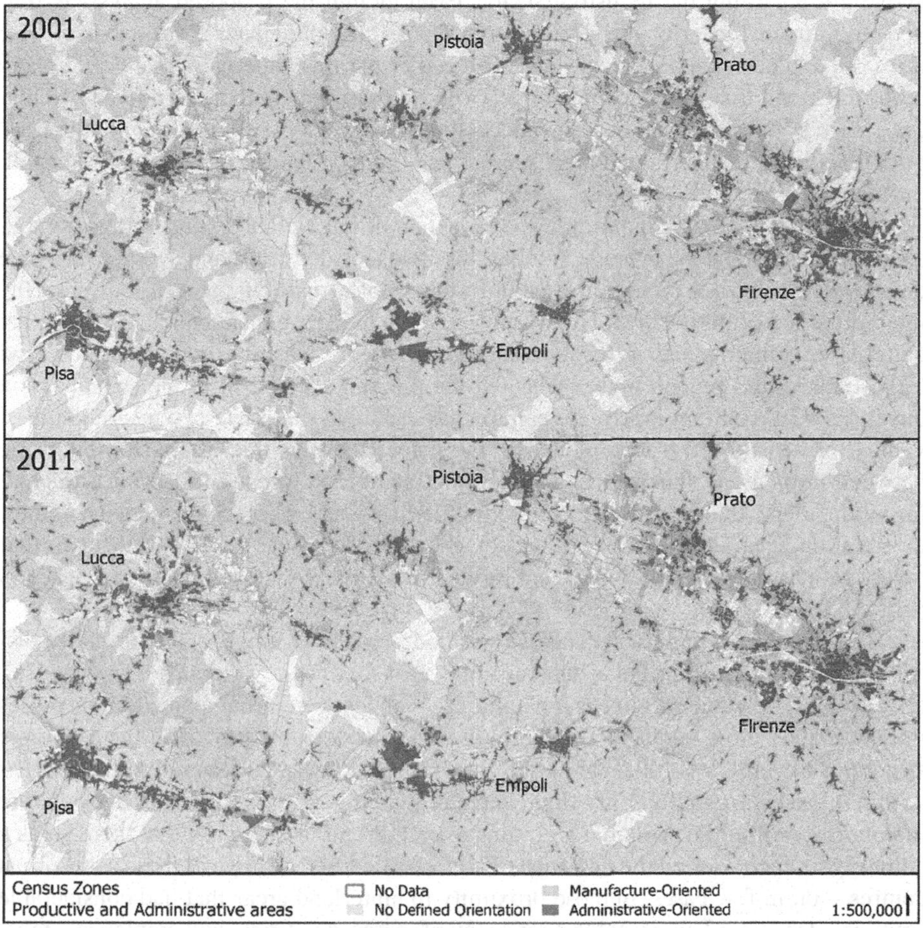

Fig. 7. Comparison between *administrative* and *productive-oriented* areas – census zones territorial distribution shifts in the period between 2001 and 2010 within the *Valdarno* area. (Color figure online)

Comparing the disposition of *administrative* and *productive-oriented* spaces (Fig. 7) and the average firm-size densities spatialization (Fig. 6), it can be observed that most of the census zones that in 2001 were marked as *no definite orientation* due to a very low average firm-size density, in 2011, now categorized under *medium* densities (Fig. 6 – 2001, 2011), turned out to be predominantly *productive-oriented* areas (Fig. 7). Therefore, it can be stated that the increments on firm-size, for the *Valdarno* area, are mostly related to an increase in Tuscany *productive-oriented* areas, while *administrative-oriented* areas are those subjected to greater decreases in firm-size.

4 Concluding Remarks

Firm-size is an important indicator of the economic activities scale and dynamism, above all, regarding the industrial sector. Even though the proposed analysis is limited one dimension – labour – of the many possible approaches to assess firm-size, it revealed, when spatialized, several territorial disparities patterns within the Tuscany region. Beyond that, accompanied by an evolution assessment that considered two distinct periods, the spatial analysis unveiled subtle changes in the regional economic structure, that would be interpreted in a different and limited manner, or not perceived at all, through a usual tabular analysis.

From a regional standpoint, the spatialization of the variables for: average number of local units' densities; average number of employees densities; and average firm-size densities, revealed that no significative shifts in territorial distribution occurred during the interval period of 2001–2011. Non significative, in the sense that general distributional patterns were maintained, as local units and employees' densities, in both periods, tend to be located and remain higher near the main urban centres. Still, the spatialization unveils several relevant locational patterns, as excluded the urban centres, the highest values for density are placed alongside the main highways that establish the linkage between those areas, thus suggesting a strong relation between the road-infrastructure importance and the industrial location. While this was explored in previous studies, the relation between road-circulation networks and firm-size is still worth of further investigation, as transportation availability is deemed as a factor that have influence in firm-size.

Even though regional scale analysis yielded very few distinguishable firm-size distribution pattern shifts, tabular data still indicated that those variations happened. For all variables, decrements in *very high* and *high* ranges were accompanied by increases in *low* and *very low* ranges, thus suggesting that alterations occurred in the economic structure. Nevertheless, those are only observable at local scale, as only certain areas within urban centres suffer only slight decreases – while the overall higher densities are maintained within the settlements. In this aspect, it can be observed that there is, as a counterpart, increases on the densities of areas located in the fringe of these same urban centres – or, in few cases, in close proximity to hinterland areas that had considerable firm-size densities. This revealed a tendency of increase in firms' and employees' presence on the boundaries of the inhabited centres, which is barely visible at a regional scale, and may be consequence of a territorial shift caused by the 2008 economic crisis. It is also observed, when comparing the *administrative* and *productive-oriented* areas disposition, that most of these fringe density increases can be attributed to industrial expansion, given that *administrative-oriented* areas tend to be located at urban centres. *Administrative-oriented* areas, nonetheless, are the ones that verify greater decrements in activities presence.

While the average firm-size densities – constructed using only labour data – can indicate a spatial dimension regarding the operation sizes, as well as the territorial disparities in this context, being limited to the simple ratio between average number of employees and average local units limits the analysis. Labour data captures a single dimension regarding firm-size and, while it is one of the most relevant, other variables such as added value, productivity or profits can indicate other territorial disparities when considered. Here, however, the in-detail spatial-economic analysis incur in the economic data breakdown limitations, as while aggregated values may be available for regions, localizing data such as added value and profits within these regions often requires the use of classified information – addresses – that is not available in Census or surveys, but still present on governmental databases. Nevertheless, instruments exist to handle and generalize information at a spatial level – such as the categorization within average values in census zones – that are not yet commonplace in the tabular analysis focused economics and statistics. With this in consideration, further studies ought to focus on overcoming those hindrances for spatial analysis, as well as to propose a shift on how economic data is made available.

References

1. Coase, R.: The nature of the firm. Economica **4**(16), 386–405 (1937). https://doi.org/10.1111/j.1468-0335.1937.tb00002.x.
2. Bernardt, Y., Muller, R.: Determinants of firms size: a survey of literature. EIM - Small Bus.Res. Consultancy, Research Report 9913/A, 77 (2000)
3. Kumar, K., Rajan, R., Zingales, L.: What determines firm size? SSRN Electron. J. 7208 (2001). https://doi.org/10.2139/ssrn.170349
4. Lucas, R.: On the size distribution of business firms. Bell J. Econ. **9**, 508–523 (1978)
5. ISTAT, 8° Censimento ISTAT dell'industria e servizi. Istituto Nazionale di Statistica, Roma (2001). https://www.istat.it/it/archivio/104317
6. ISTAT, 9° Censimento ISTAT dell'industria e servizi. Istituto Nazionale di Statistica, Roma (2011). https://www.istat.it/it/archivio/104317
7. ISTAT, Descrizione dei dati geografici e delle variabili censuarie delle Basi territoriali per i censimenti: anni 1991, 2001, 2011. Istituto Nazionale di Statistica, Roma (2016)
8. QGIS, Hannover, version 3.16 (2020). http://www.qgis.org/en/site/index.html
9. Regione Toscana, Direzione Urbanistica e Politiche Abitative - Sistema Informativo Territoriale e Ambientale – SITA: Censimento ISTAT della popolazione e dell'industria anni 2001–2011 (2019a). http://www502.regione.toscana.it/geoscopio/cartoteca.html
10. Regione Toscana, Direzione Urbanistica e Politiche Abitative - Sistema Informativo Territoriale e Ambientale – SITA.: Edificato 2k, 10k 1988–2013. (2019b). http://www502.regione.toscana.it/geoscopio/cartoteca.html
11. Altafini, D., Braga, A., Cutini, V.: Planning sustainable urban-industrial configurations: relations among industrial complexes and the centralities of a regional continuum. Int. Plann. Stud. (2021). https://doi.org/10.1080/13563475.2021.1875810
12. Altafini, D., Cutini, V.: Homothetic behavior of betweenness centralities: a multiscale alternative approach to relate cities and large regional structures. Sustainability **12**(19), 7925 (2020). https://doi.org/10.3390/su12197925

Modelling Spatial Centrality of Logistics Activities: Study in the Porto Alegre Metropolitan Region, Brazil

Clarice Maraschin[1](✉), Ana Luisa Maffini Machado[1], and Renato Maciel Damiani[2]

[1] Urban and Regional Planning Graduate Program (PROPUR), Federal University of Rio Grande Do Sul (UFRGS), Porto Alegre, Brazil
{clarice.maraschin,analuisamaffini}@ufrgs.br
[2] School of Architecture, Federal University of Rio Grande Do Sul (UFRGS), Porto Alegre, Brazil

Abstract. Recent transformations in the sphere of production and consumption have created a wide market for the logistics activities. Beyond economic development, such activities can also trigger spatial impacts becoming an urban planning concern. The purpose of this article is: a) to present a methodology for analyzing spatial distribution of logistics activities based on configurational models; b) apply this methodology to the Porto Alegre Metropolitan Region, Brazil. We propose a synthetic measure of the centrality of logistics activities, conceptualized as a hierarchy or locational advantage, and related to access to transportation routes, potential for movement and agglomeration economies. We question: How is this centrality of logistical activities spatially distributed? Is there spatial concentration or decentralization? The regional spatial system is modeled as a network of road segments and we apply Freeman-Krafta Centrality model, weighted by the amount of logistics employees. Empirical data come from RAIS (Annual Census of Social Information), provided by the Ministry of Labor, year 2019. The results show that the proposed methodology is able to identify the spatial distribution of centrality and its irregular pattern over the region. The conclusions point to the relevance of configurational approaches for logistic space studies, as well as potentialities and limits of this methodology.

Keywords: Logistics activities · Spatial centrality · Porto Alegre · Brazil

1 Introduction

Logistics activities include those related to storage, transportation, and product distribution services. Recent transformations in the sphere of production and consumption are restructuring the supply chain and creating a strong market for the logistics sector. The original development foundation of the logistics sector comes from the demand generated by the manufacturing industry [1]. The transfer of logistics functions to other

O. Gervasi et al. (Eds.): ICCSA 2021, LNCS 12952, pp. 688–703, 2021.
https://doi.org/10.1007/978-3-030-86973-1_48

companies allows manufacturing industries to focus more on their core activities, seeking efficiency and competitiveness. In the commercial sector, there is also an important transfer of the amount of activities from retailing to logistics sector. According to Coquillat [2], the rapid development of e-commerce tends to eliminate the last link of the supply chain, consisting of the physical spaces of the stores, transferring their functions to other links behind the chain, now absorbed by the logistics sector. The COVID-19 pandemic and the imposition of social distancing tend to further accelerate the transition to trade headed by the logistic sector.

Logistics activities generate economic and spatial development in cities and regions as well as increase jobs and tax revenues; however, such activities can also trigger spatial impacts. Studies are showing that warehouses and distribution centers tend to move away from urban areas towards more suburban and exurban ones, offering lower land prices and good access to highway networks [3]. This sprawling can have negative consequences such as expansion over rural areas, attraction of new residential developments, increasing traffic, pollution, among others, becoming an urban planning concern. Studies in Europe and North America have detected a tendency towards the concentration of the logistics activities at the macro-scale (national, regional) accompanied by a dispersion at smaller scales (intra-regional, metropolitan). In Brazil, there are few studies on this theme, and they focus mainly on the macro scale (country).

The purpose of this article is: a) to present a methodology for analyzing spatial distribution of logistics activities based on configurational models; b) apply this methodology to the Metropolitan Region of Porto Alegre (MRPA), Brazil. We apply a quantitative approach, based on urban network analysis [4]. The intention is to add in the literature by analyzing a case in Brazil, on a metropolitan region scale. This study may be helpful to urban and regional planners providing a better understanding of the spatial relations of logistics activities.

The paper is organized as follows. Section 2 presents a brief review of the location of the logistics activities while also focusing on the configurational approach. Section 3 describes the methodology, empirical data, and the modeling process. Section 4 presents the results and discussion. The last section brings some conclusions, potentials and limitations of the adopted methodology and future research directions.

2 Logistics Activities on Urban and Regional Space

2.1 Location of the Logistics Activities

The problem of the location of activities is of the utmost importance having a significant impact on the operating costs and competitiveness of a business as well as on the price of its goods or services. For logistics enterprises, the transportation of goods is at the core of their business, so accessibility plays a major role in the location decision. Highly accessible areas tend to attract logistics enterprises and employment. Accessibility can be understood as way of overcoming the effect of space (distance, time) in the movement of people and goods, as well as in the exchange of products, services, and information. It is the transport availability that helps to reduce spatial friction on the movement of goods. The location of logistics activities is therefore very sensitive to the quality of the highway network and the fluidity of traffic; but it fears the bottlenecks that contribute to traffic congestion [5].

The logic for the logistics enterprise's location lies between that of industries and services [6]. Factors bringing logistics locations closer to that of industry are: close links with transport infrastructure, the needs for large amounts of space, and the negative externalities generated. Some factors, on the other hand, bring together the logistics locations to that of services: the close ties with the market demand and the weight of land prices in the location choice. Government policies are also relevant, such as infrastructure provision, zoning, and incentives.

The presence of several of these factors in a region promotes the concentration of logistics activities. Spatial concentration is favored by agglomeration economies related to labor market (specialized labor), inputs sharing (combining transport flows, reducing transportation costs) and knowledge spillovers (cooperation between enterprises). This polarization of logistics facilities towards large urban regions at the relative expense of smaller areas has been noted in several world regions [6]. In the case of Brazil, Catapan and Luna [7] identified concentrations of logistics activities in some southern and southeastern states of the country. In the capitals of these states, which are large consumption centers, there is a greater concentration of logistics activities, aimed at serving the consumer market. Concentrations of logistics activities associated with industrial activities were also identified. In these cases, factors related to the availability of transport infrastructure (highways, multimodal terminals, and ports) and the supply of production factors (specialized labor, government incentives) are preponderant.

On a smaller scale, 'sprawling' patterns have been identified for logistics firms in some urban regions. In a study in North America, Woudsma et al. [3] find that warehouses and distribution centers are sprawling within the core urban area of Toronto and also the exurban area, offering lower land prices and good access to highway networks. However, negative consequences of this sprawl are additional truck-miles traveled and subsequent emissions and congestion, causing concern among city managers.

The driving forces of logistics activities spatial evolution can be seen as centripetal (agglomeration) and centrifugal (dispersion) provided by land price, market demand, traffic accessibility, agglomeration advantages and government policies [8]. These forces act at different spatial scales and may change over time.

2.2 Logistic Space and Urban Configuration

An interesting way to understand logistic space is considering it as a spatial system composed of logistics enterprises, logistics nodes and logistics infrastructure [1]. In general terms, a system can be conceived as a set of interrelated components, where changes in one element may affect the entire system [9]. Studies of the urban form as a spatial system – network analyses - have been developed in geographic studies since the 1960's [10]. More recently, the availability of the necessary tools and data have spread network analysis for urban and regional studies.

Configurational studies were first developed by Hillier and Hanson [11] applying network analysis to urban planning and design, known as Space Syntax analysis. They propose a relationship between the hierarchy of the street grid and other urban features as pedestrian movement, land uses, density, land prices, and so on. Several others approaches to graph analysis of street network have emerged since then [12–14].

Porta et al. [12] present a set of centrality indices for network analysis, being the main ones: closeness (relative distances), betweenness (importance in the shortest paths) and straightness (efficiency in the nodes communication). Each centrality captures a different aspect of one place as "being central" in geographic space. The authors find good correlations between densities of retail and service activities and betweenness centrality in studies in Bologna and Barcelona.

Broadly speaking, betweenness centrality is the property of a node (space) being along the shortest path that connects two other nodes, and their hierarchy is given by the total number of times this node appears in the paths connecting all pairs of a system [15]. Krafta [14] proposes an adaptation of betweenness centrality, named Freeman-Krafta Centrality, introducing the notions of tension and distance: the tension reflects the relationship between two nodes expressed by the product of its contents; the distance refers to the extension of the shortest path between each pair of nodes. The tension generated by each pair of nodes will be "dissipated", in other words, it will be distributed among all nodes that are part of the shortest paths. The method is capable of capturing the spatial differentiation resulting from the extension of paths. Freeman-Krafta (FK) centrality for a node k is defined as a three-step calculation (Eqs. 1, 2 and 3).

$$\text{Tension} : t_{ij} = a_i a_j \tag{1}$$

$$\text{Dissipation} : t_{ij}(k) = \frac{a_i a_j}{d} \tag{2}$$

$$\text{Centrality} : C(k) = \sum\nolimits_{i,j}^{n} t_{ij}(k) \tag{3}$$

Where tij is the tension between two nodes i and j, ai and aj are the attributes respectively in i and j, tij(k) is the portion of tension between i and j attributed to k, where k is a node belonging to the shortest path(s) between i and j, d is the number of nodes in the shortest path. Finally, C(k) is the centrality of k given after the computation of all possible pairs of the system.

When compared to the original Freeman model, the FK centrality acquires new variables (activities and interaction between them) and new features (potential tension and extension of shortest paths). The model captures the essence of location advantages in urban or regional areas, and its values should be reflected in the intensity of movement (pedestrians, vehicles) and land uses, for example, densities of services benefiting from that movement. As can be inferred, the model contains both vectors of agglomeration and dispersion [14]. The agglomeration presents itself in the form of attractiveness of the more central locations in the system; dispersion is underlying the accumulation of activities, tensions and flows that can act as potential generators of congestion, costs of displacement and competition by location. The model captures a synthesis of both forces.

In this paper, we propose applying FK centrality model weighted by the amount of logistics activities in each space (node). We conceptualized it as a hierarchy, or locational advantage, related to access to transportation routes, potential for movement and agglomeration economies. In the literature, several methods are used by researchers to assess spatial patterns of concentration and dispersion of establishments including average distance to the mean location or Gini indices to determine whether establishments are concentrated in particular areas. In this paper, we will explore a configurational method and a systemic measure, considering jointly the locational advantages of the street network and the concentration of firms expressing agglomeration economies.

3 Data and Methods

3.1 Dataset of Logistics Activities

The selection of logistics activities refers to CNAE 2.0 (IBGE) [16], a national classification of economic activities. Based on the literature [7, 17] 13 classes were selected and included as logistics activities, as shown in Table 1.

Table 1. Activities related to the transport and logistics sectors. Source: authors based on CNAE 2.0 (IBGE) [16]

Class from CNAE 2.0	Business description
49.11-6	Rail cargo transportation
49.30-2	Road freight transport
49.40-0	Pipeline transport
50.11-4	Inland shipping
50.12-2	Sea shipping
50.21-1	Transport by inland cargo shipping
51.20-0	Air cargo transport
51.11-7	Warehouse and storage
52.12-5	Loading and unloading
52.22-2	Road and rail terminals
52.32-0	Shipping agency services
52.50-8	Organization of cargo transport services
53.20-2	Mail and delivery services

Database on logistics activities comes from the national base of RAIS Microdata [18] available online. The database refers to the year 2019 and contains the following information about each registered business: activity classification, number of employees, city, and Zip Code. This data source is well documented and the methodology of collecting businesses is consolidated. Unfortunately, because of requirements for maintaining the anonymity of individual records, it is not possible to identify the exact location of the businesses, only the Zip Code is provided.

To localize each logistics firm, we used a Python code to convert the Zip Codes into geographic coordinates by converting them into addresses and them into "x,y" coordinates. With the geographic coordinates for each establishment, we were able to locate them in a GIS (Geographic Information System) environment [19]. It is important to clarify that, according to the Brazilian post system; cities under 50,000 inhabitants have only one Zip Code for the entire municipality. In our case, from the total of 34 MRPA municipalities, 14 are in this category having only one generic ZIP Code. In these 14 cases, we located the logistics firms in each city center not to lose their registries. The same method was used for some incorrect Zip Codes that could not be identified by our procedure, only the city. The original dataset contained 7,121 logistics firms' registers and 7,115 were successfully located.

3.2 The Process of Modelling MRPA Spatial System

The first step in the modelling the spatial system is to define the spatial representation of the road network. This representation allows defining the discrete unit of urban space to be used according to the study goals. We adopted a simplified version of the "road segment" representation where the spatial units (nodes) are the center portions of the roads between two intersections and the links are the connections between the roads.

We opted for using a simplified version of the road segment representation for three main reasons: a) we were interested in the results in the macro scale for the Metropolitan Area; b) the simplified version generates a lighter file, making the computer processing faster; c) the data of the logistics firms had a low level of spatial disaggregation, not requiring a network as disaggregated as the road segment representation.

The network simplification was based on the idea that urban streets are hierarchically organized in the sense that most streets are trivial, while a minority of streets is vital [20]. This hierarchy can be characterized by the 80/20 principle, where 80% of streets are less connected (below the average) in the system, while 20% of streets are well connected (above the average). Following this, we adopted a three-step simplification procedure.

First, we generate a complete network of the Metropolitan region based on OSMnx tool [21]. The second step was to calculate the frequency distribution of betweenness centrality and, as this distribution follows a power law, we selected only the streets in the head (20%) in two recursive rounds [22]. We then verified the results to check for the presence of all the highways (State and Federal), the urban main roads (arterials) inside each municipality and the paved roads relevant to the integration between MRPA municipalities. These procedures were developed in the software QGIS and were based on the official state road network shapefiles [23], as well as the limits of urbanized areas of the state, provided by IBGE [24]. The street hierarchy was checked using OpenStreetMap (OSM) and satellite imagery from Google Earth and Google Street View. The third step was to simplify the geometry of the network, directly connecting the remaining intersections with straight line segments, which is suitable for using topological distances in the model. Also, we defined a buffer of about 30 km around the limits of MRPA and included the connections to external municipalities to avoid the edge effect [25].

The final model, consisting of 3,111 road segments, was imported into GAUS (Graph Analysis of Urban Systems) software [26] a Python script developed as a QGIS plug-in. We then relate the points of each logistic establishment to the nearest road segment.

For that, the "Snap Points to Lines" feature in QGIS was used and then with the "Spatial Join" feature we were able to transfer the data from the logistics establishment's shapefile to the road segment one. The total amount of logistic employees in each road segment was included in the attribute table as a load. The software GAUS performed the configurational analysis, applying weighted FK centrality model and topological distances processed at global scale (radius n). The results obtained (tables and maps) were analyzed and evaluated, which are presented in the next section.

4 Results and Discussion

4.1 Brief Contextualization of MRPA and Logistics Activities

The MRPA) is the most densely populated area in the Rio Grande do Sul State (Fig. 1). In 2020, according to Population Estimates, it concentrated 4.4 million inhabitants or 38.2% of the total population of the State. From the 19 municipalities in the State above 100 thousand inhabitants, 9 are inside the MRPA, and the average demographic density in the region is 421.8 inhabitants/km^2 [27].

The MRPA was officially created in 1973 and was initially composed of 14 municipalities. The demographic growth of the Metropolitan Region is mainly the result of internal migrations, the interconnection of urban networks and the successive emancipations that occurred over the years. This caused new areas to be integrated into the Region, currently adding up 34 municipalities. Such municipalities have very contrasting socioeconomic indicators, reflecting an uneven distribution of economic resources and urban services and equipment such as transportation, health, education, housing, and sanitation.

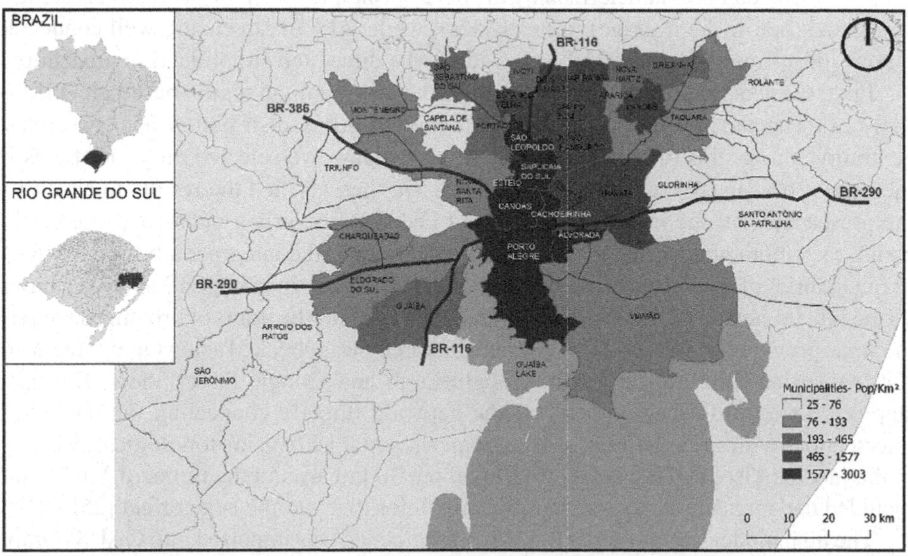

Fig. 1. Location of the Metropolitan Region of Porto Alegre, population density and main road system. Source: authors based on IBGE [24]

The Region is also a pole of attraction and functional complementarity, exhibiting an intense movement of people, attracted by the offer of services and jobs, becoming an area of intense economic expansion in the State. In 2002, industrial sector was responsible for 48% of the Region GVA (Gross Value Added), services sector was responsible for 51% and agriculture for only 1% [28]. The MRPA concentrates some important manufacturing industries, such as vehicle assemblers, petrochemicals, auto parts, plastics, food products, etc. The region is also located in a strategic position in reference to MERCOSUL (Southern Common Market), with Salgado Filho International Airport being the main gateway for passengers from countries in the Southern Cone.

Rio Grande do Sul has a relatively well-structured multimodal transport network; largely based on road transportation. In 2017 highways were responsible for 88% of the total transported, while in Brazil the share of this transport reached 65% [29]. There are also inland waterway routes and important ports, such as in Porto Alegre.

Figure 2 shows the number of logistics companies in the MRPA from 2006 to 2019. The graphic shows that the number of companies grows in both, State and MRPA until 2014, when national economic and political crisis impacted this performance. The variation in the number of companies (2006–2019) was +28% for the State and only +1% in the MRPA. This data reveals a decentralization process also occurring in the State scale.

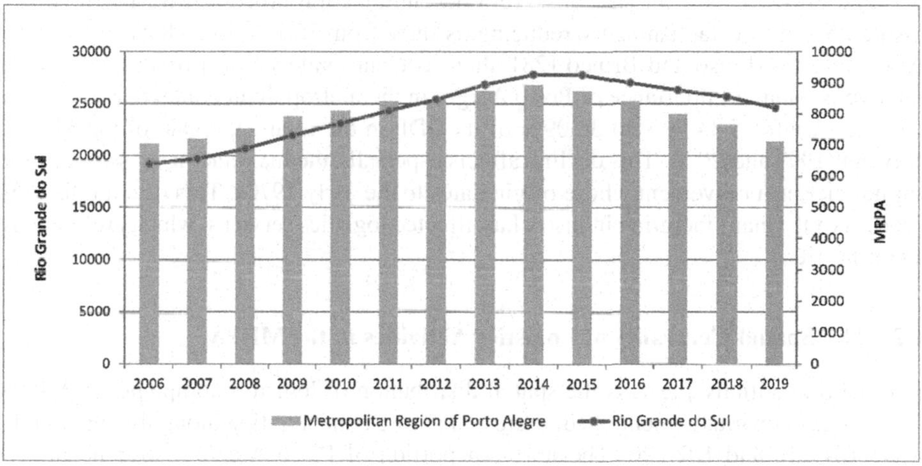

Fig. 2. Evolution on the total number of logistics companies in the MRPA and Rio Grande do Sul State, from 2006 to 2019. Source: authors, based on data from [30].

As seen in Fig. 2, the total number of logistics companies remains almost constant in the MRPA; however, the situation inside the region shows a different picture. Figure 3 shows the changes in the number of companies in each of the 34 municipalities of MRPA.

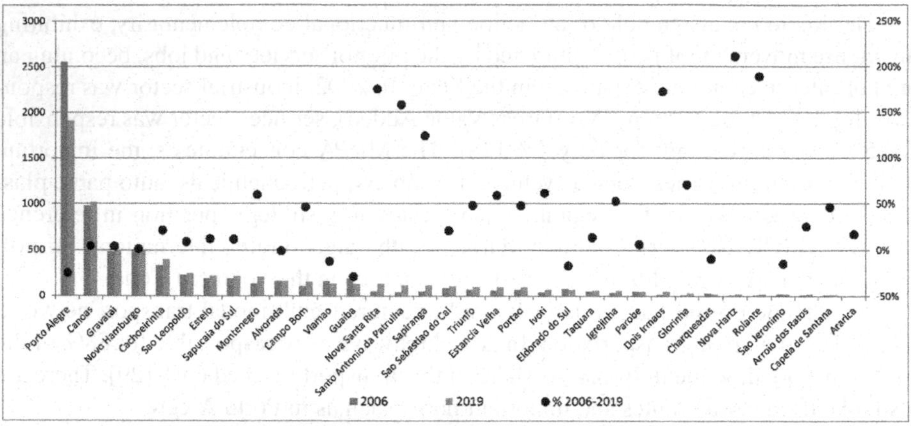

Fig. 3. Total number of logistics companies by the 34 municipalities in the MRPA 2006–2019. Source: authors, based on data from [30].

We can observe that logistics companies are concentrated in a few cities, mainly at the capital, Porto Alegre. The first eight cities make up 70.33% of MRPA companies in 2019. All these eight cities are connected by two important federal highways, BR-116 and BR-290. We can also observe a decentralization process, with Porto Alegre losing 25% of its establishments, reducing its share from 36.19% to 26.84% in 13 years. According to Alonso and Brinco [28], there is clear evidence of a process of loss of relative economic importance of Porto Alegre in the metropolitan context, as shown by the decrease from 34.70% to 30.09% of its GDP in the total aggregate of the MRPA, between 1999 and 2002. This decline affects especially the manufacturing sector of the capital city, in a movement whose origin dates to the early 1970s. This decentralization process of the manufacturing industry has affected logistics services, which are showing a similar trend.

4.2 The Spatial Centrality of Logistics Activities in the MRPA

This section initially presents the spatial distribution of logistics companies in MRPA (Fig. 4). As previously mentioned, there is a strong concentration along the main highways BR-116 and BR-290. The northern portion of Porto Alegre also concentrates logistics activities and is conceived as a Development Corridor by the local Masterplan. This area is in direct interface with the Metropolitan Region and the main highways, receiving incentives for the location of large-scale investments, including logistic ones.

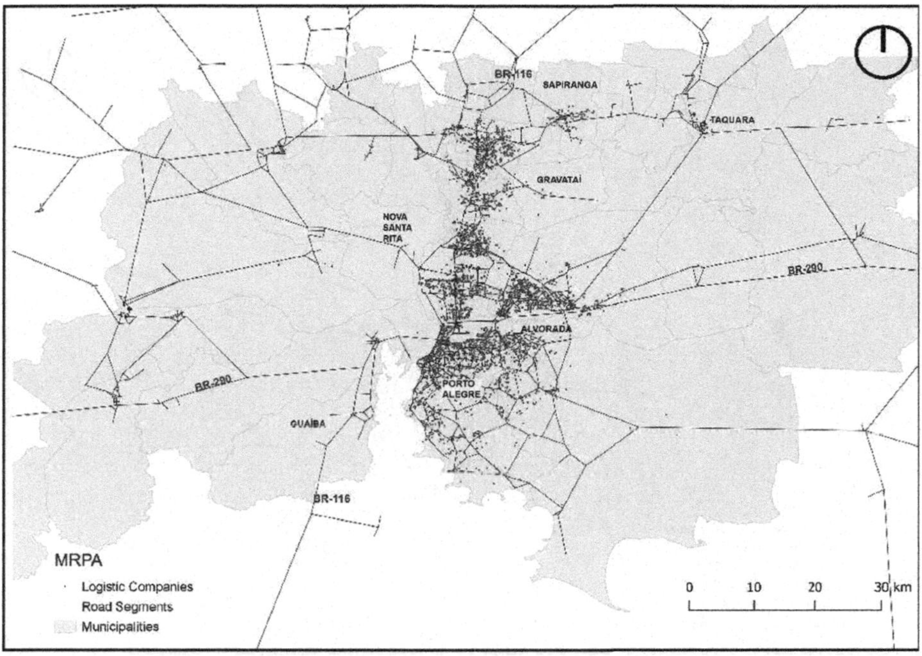

Fig. 4. Spatial distribution of the logistics companies in the MRPA in 2019 over the road segment model. Source: authors, based on data from [18].

In the historical process of urbanization of the metropolitan territory, the municipalities with the greatest economic development and population growth tend to have a more consolidated spatial structure with greater density of the road network and shortest paths. Small municipalities, on the other hand, often have only one road connection with the rest of the MRPA and, depending on their location, can be very isolated from the point of view of the global system. The metropolitan road network shows this asymmetry (Fig. 4). The weighted logistic centrality measure captures this asymmetry in the network and associates it with the uneven distribution of logistics companies, resulting in a measure that expresses this spatial differentiation (Fig. 5).

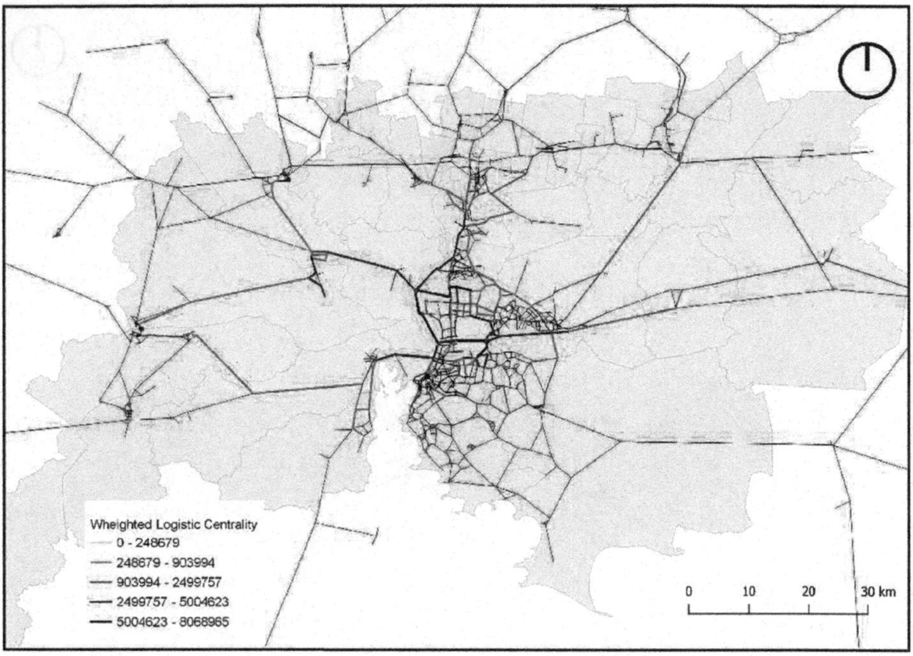

Fig. 5. Logistic centrality in the MRPA - weighted by the number of employees (5 classes, natural breaks). Source: authors.

Logistic centrality is concentrated in the region around the crossing of the main highways (BR-116 and BR-290). Another highway in the northwest (BR-386) connects industrial areas and shows high centrality values.

As previously mentioned, this hierarchical distribution can be characterized by the 80/20 principle, where 80% of streets are less connected, while 20% of streets are well connected; out of the 20%, there is 1 percent of streets that are extremely well connected [20]. Figure 6 shows that the ranking of the logistic centrality values follows a power law, with few road segments having extremely high values.

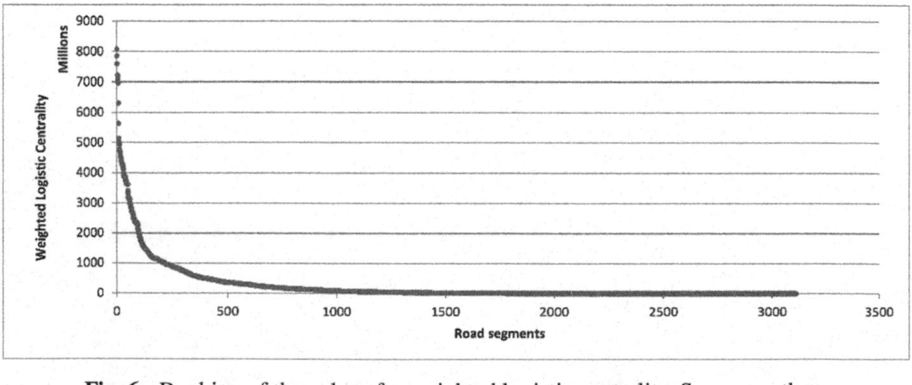

Fig. 6. Ranking of the values for weighted logistic centrality. Source: authors.

Figure 7 highlights the road segments with 1% and 20% highest values of this centrality. We observe that these very high values of centrality cover an area that goes from Porto Alegre to the north, east northwest.

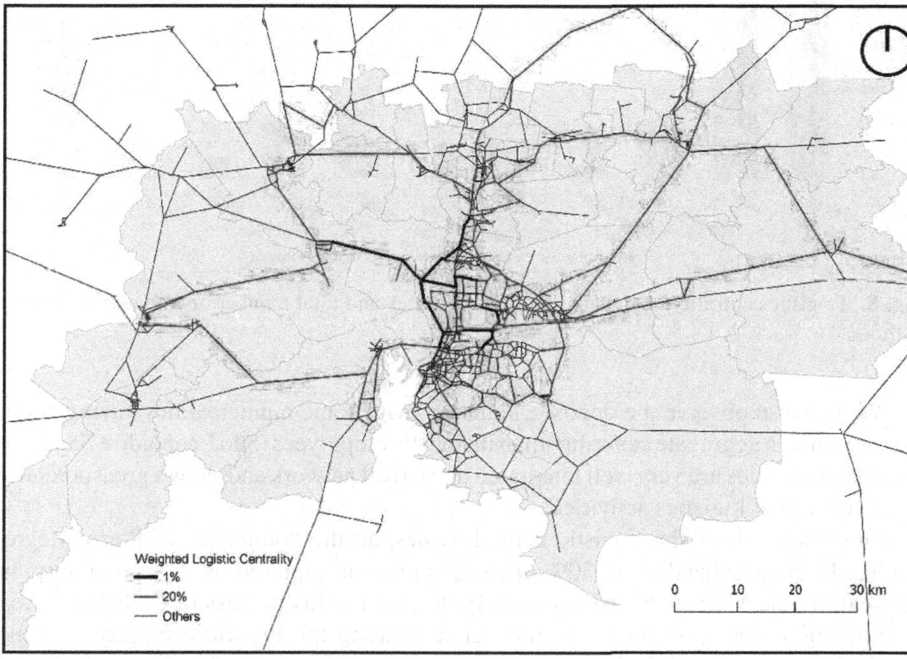

Fig. 7. Selected highest values of weighted logistic centrality in the MRPA (1% and 20%). Source: authors.

In order to analyze the share of this centrality, Fig. 8 shows the calculation for the aggregate logistic centrality by each municipality. Porto Alegre captures 32% of the total Logistic Centrality and Canoas, its neighbor to the north, captures 20%. Together, both cities are responsible for half of all centrality.

Figure 8 also shows the number of logistic employees, used as our indicator to weight the centrality. This comparison allows us to discuss losses and gains in centrality, due to the regional road network configuration. Cities like Novo Hamburgo, Triunfo e Guaíba have better performance in logistic employees than in aggregate centrality. This indicates that their location in the road network is not so strategic but, other reasons may justify their attraction of logistics activities. Triunfo, for example, hosts a large petrochemical complex having its own river port, which connects with Lake Guaíba and the southernmost sea port. Guaíba is a similar case, having an important pulp and paper industry complex and its production is also drained by the Guaíba Lake. Novo Hamburgo has a consolidated industrial park, focused on the production of shoes for export, but from the point of view of the metropolitan region, its location is more distant (far north) and its performance on the road network is weaker.

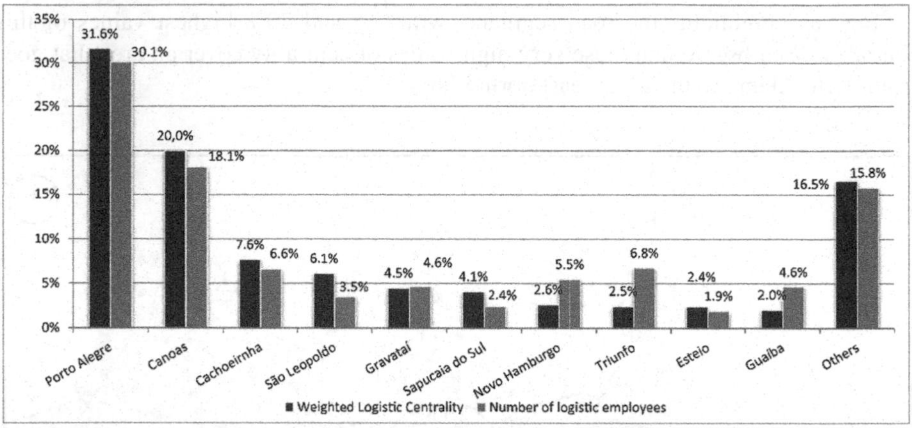

Fig. 8. Logistic centrality aggregated by municipalities and total number of employees. Source: authors.

We can also observe the opposite situation, with some municipalities having better performance in aggregate centrality than in logistic employees (São Leopoldo e Sapucaia do Sul). Both cities are very well integrated in the road network and show a great potential of the growth of logistics activities.

Our results show that logistic centrality, despite the dominance of Porto Alegre, is already decentralized; only 30% of the centrality is captured by the capital city. In the scale of the Metropolitan Region of Porto Alegre, this process of decentralization is showing a more polycentric pattern, concentrating the logistic centrality in some specific areas and corridors. In this sense, our findings converge to the studies of Masson and Petiot [6] about the trend of polarization and clustering of logistics activities. The location of the logistics activities tends to be close to market cities with the greatest demand, but external to them in search of large areas of land at low cost. An example of this decentralization can be seen in Nova Santa Rita, in MRPA, where an Amazon Distribution Center was opened in a logistic park in the margins of BR-386 in 2020. The park is about 24 km from central area of Porto Alegre, but it is strongly connected with the most populated cities of the region.

One important issue to be considered is the fact that this process of decentralization transfers the territorial effects of development of large logistics structures to small municipalities in the metropolitan suburban crowns. Coquillat [2] states that the greater territorial complexity generated by the disorder of logistics dispersion will have to be added to the attraction-inducing effects of new residential developments. The presence of large investments that requalify the suburban areas and improve the infrastructure produces, as an indirect effect, the increase of the centrality factor, and the attraction of new uses for these areas, mainly the residential one. In Brazil, the territorial planning in the metropolitan scale is not well established, raising questions about these issues in the future.

5 Conclusion

This paper presented an application of configurational models to perform a spatial analysis of the logistics activities. One positive aspect of the methodology is to be flexible; it and can be applied to the spatial analysis of other types of economic activities, for example, retail trade, industries in different sectors, among others. Also, the methodology is based on open and available data. An advantage of weighted spatial networks models is to bring together spatial and functional particularities of urban structure. These models allow to compute geometric or topological distances, and also to consider impedance effects to generate shortest paths in the street grid (not used in this work).

However, it should be noted that some simplifications were adopted in the methodology. We modelled a simplified road network of the region due to the limitations of the companies' database. Also, the network model considers only the road transportation system, not including other infrastructures, such as railways or waterways, since in our case, the highways covers the large majority of the total transported. Other studies should consider the share of transportation modals and include these networks as different layers of the basic road network. Our centrality analysis was developed only at the global scale (radius n), from the point of view of all the metropolitan system. The model also allows the exploration of intermediate scales in metropolitan networks [31]. Future studies could also focus on temporal dynamic of logistic centrality by analyzing different time periods, with different spatial configurations and distributions and intensities of logistics activities. Understanding this dynamic is crucial to planning and control.

Network analysis is on the base of several methodologies that can support public policies as they are systemic and allow the production of "what-if" scenarios. The opening of new roads or highways can be simulated, as well as the development of new logistics zones or companies and assessing their impact on the centrality of the system, both on a local or global scale. Finally, we highlight the potential of this methodology in unveiling the spatial patterns of economic activities. We expect to continue this research and develop models that consider different infrastructures with different time frames databases and network representations to get a more complete comprehension of the spatial patterns of logistics activities in the Metropolitan Region of Porto Alegre.

Acknowledgments. The authors would like to acknowledge CAPES-BRASIL (Coordination for the Improvement of Higher Education Personnel) for financial support during the development of this study, through a scholarship for doctoral degree.

References

1. He, M., Shen, J., Wu, X., Luo, J.: Logistics space: a literature review from the sustainability perspective. Sustainability, MDPI **10**, 2815 (2018)
2. Coquillat Mora, P.: Reequilíbrios na Cadeia de Suprimento. Blucher Engineering Proceedings VII CINCCI – Colóquio Internacional sobre Comércio e Cidade. Fortaleza, Nov. (2020). https://www.proceedings.blucher.com.br/article-details/reequilbrios-na-cadeia-de-suprimento-34916. Accessed 1 May 2021
3. Woudsma, C., Jacubicek, P., Dablanc, L.: Logistics sprawl in North America: methodological issues and a case study in Toronto. Transp. Res. Procedia **12**(2016), 474–488 (2016)

4. Sevtsuk, A.: Analysis and planning of urban networks. In: Alhajj, R; Rokne, J. (eds.), Enciclopedia of Social Network Analysis and Mining. Springer, New York (2018). https://doi.org/10.1007/978-1-4939-7131-2_43
5. Mérenne-Schoumaker, B.: La Localisation des Grandes Zones de Logistique. Bulletin de la Société géographique de Liège **49**, 31–40 (2007)
6. Masson, S., Petiot, R.: Concentration spatiale et activités logistiques. In: 8èmes Rencontres Internationales de la Recherche en Logistique. Bordeaux, França (2010)
7. Catapan, A., Luna, M.M.M.: Localização e Concentração de Atividades Logísticas no Brasil. J. Transp. Lit. **10**(2), 35–39 (2016)
8. Fujita, M; Krugman, P; Venables, A. J. Economia Espacial. Ed. Futura, São Paulo (2002)
9. Echenique, M.: Modelos Matemáticos de la Estructura Espacial Urbana, Aplicaciones en América Latina. Ediciones SIAP/Ediciones Nueva Visión, Buenos Aires, Argentina (1975)
10. Haggett, P., Chorley, R.J.: Network Analysis in Geography. Edward Arnold, London (1969)
11. Hillier, B., Hanson, J.: The Social Logic of Space, p. 296. Cambridge University Press, Cambridge (1984)
12. Porta, S., Crucitti, P., Latora, V.: Multiple centrality assessment in Parma: a network analysis of paths and open spaces. Urban Des. Int. **13**(1), 41–50 (2008)
13. Sevtsuk, A.: Path and Place: A Study of Urban Geometry and Retail Activity in Cambridge and Somerville, MA, p. 216. Massachusetts Institute of Technology (2010)
14. Krafta, R.: Modelling intraurban configurational development. Environ. Plann. B **21**, 67–82 (1994)
15. Freeman, L.C.: A set of measures of centrality based on betweenness. Sociometry **40**(1), 35–41 (1977)
16. Brasil. Instituto Brasileiro de Geografia e Estatística (IBGE). CNAE 2.0 - Classificação Nacional de Atividades Econômicas, versão 2.0. (2019) https://concla.ibge.gov.br/documentacao/cronologia/204-concla/classificacao/por-tema/1365-cnae-2-0.html. Accessed 1 May 2021
17. Fernandes da Costa, M. Localizações dos Prestadores de Serviço da Cadeia Logística no Brasil: um estudo de ocorrência de aglomeração. Programa de Pós Graduação em Administração de Empresas, Universidade Presbiteriana Mackenzie, São Paulo (2009)
18. Brasil. Ministério do Trabalho e Emprego. Microdados RAIS e CAGED. (2021). http://pdet.mte.gov.br/microdados-rais-e-caged. Accessed 1 May 2021
19. QGIS r2.18. Sistema de Informações Geográficas do QGIS. Projeto Código Aberto Geospatial Foundation. (2019). http://qgis.osgeo.org. Accessed 1 May 2021
20. Jiang, B.: Street hierarchies: a minority of streets account for a majority of traffic flow. Int. J. Geogr. Inf. Sci. **23**(8), 1033–1048 (2008)
21. Boeing, G.: OSMnx: new methods for acquiring, constructing, analyzing, and visualizing complex street networks. Comput. Environ. Urban Syst. **65**, 126–139 (2017)
22. Jiang, B., Liu, X., Jia, T.: Scaling of geographic space as a universal rule for map generalization. Ann. Assoc. Am. Geogr. **103**(4), 844–855 (2013).
23. Rio Grande do Sul - Fundação Estadual de Proteção Ambiental Henrique Luiz Roessler (FEPAM). Biblioteca Digital. Base Cartográfica Digital do RS. (2015). http://www.fepam.rs.gov.br/biblioteca/geo/bases_geo.asp. Accessed 1 May 2021
24. Brasil. Instituto Brasileiro de Geografia e Estatística (IBGE). Malhas Municipais. (2019) https://www.ibge.gov.br/geociencias/organizacao-do-territorio/malhas-territoriais/15774-malhas.html?edicao=30138&t=o-que-e. Accessed 1 May 2021
25. Gil, J.: Street network analysis "'edge effects"': Examining the sensitivity of centrality measures to boundary conditions. Environ. Plann. B. Plann. Des. **44**(5), 1–18 (2016)
26. Krafta, R., Dalcin, G.: GAUS (Graph Analysis of Urban Systems). Universidade Federal do Rio Grande do Sul, Software (2020)

27. Rio Grande do Sul – Atlas Socioeconômico do Rio Grande do Sul. (2020). https://atlassocioeconomico.rs.gov.br/inicial. Accessed 1 May 2021
28. Alonso, J.A.F; Brinco, R. Caracterização geral da Região Metropolitana de Porto Alegre (RMPA). Fundação de Economia e Estatística (FEE). Textos para Discussão N 112. (2009). http://cdn.fee.tche.br/tds/112.pdf. Accessed 30 Apr 2021
29. Rio Grande do Sul - Plano Estadual de Logística de Transportes -PELT-RS. (2018). https://transportes.rs.gov.br/pelt-rs. Accessed 1 May 2021
30. Brasil. Ministério do Trabalho e Emprego. Programa de Disseminação de Estatísticas do Trabalho. Acesso On-Line. (2021). http://pdet.mte.gov.br/acesso-online-as-bases-de-dados. Accessed 1 May 2021
31. Serra, M., Pinho, P.: Tackling the structure of very large spatial systems - space syntax and the analysis of metropolitan form. J. Space Syntax **4**(2), 179–196 (2013)

Form, Function and Acoustics: Productive Assets Placement and Relationship Between the Urban Soundscape Patterns and Configuration

Okba Benameur[1(✉)], Diego Altafini[2], and Valerio Cutini[2]

[1] University of Mostaganem, NR 11, Kharouba, 2700 Mostaganem, Algeria
okba.benameur@univ-mosta.dz
[2] University of Pisa, Lungarno Antonio Pacinotti, 43, 56126 Pisa, PI, Italy

Abstract. Urban acoustics is influenced by several noise sources and propagation effects, a multitude of factors that make sound-based analysis a rather complex endeavor. Nevertheless, the soundscape is an important feature in cities' environments, as noise pollution affects spaces' usage and quality of life. Computational methods have been used for soundscape analysis, however a combined evaluation of the relationships between acoustics, urban form, functions and movement logics is still in demand for urban planning. This paper summarizes the different computational methods used for soundscape analysis and focuses on the use of Geographic Information Systems to construct a comparative analysis, apposing spatial information of the acoustic maps, built-structures placement and distribution, and road networks configuration, of a productive agglomerate that extends throughout the provinces of *Firenze* (Florence) and Prato. The main objective is to unearth correlations between urban design, movement dynamics and the different noise pollution classes, highlighting the soundscape patterns in the built environment, with specific reference to the distribution of productive activities. Results aim for the creation of more detailed acoustic maps, improving spatial knowledge of this productive area for urban planning purposes.

Keywords: Acoustics · Geographic information systems · Urban planning · Noise pollution

1 Introduction

Soundscape design is a paradigm shift in environmental acoustics since it incorporates spatial, social and psychological variables [1]. Understanding and defining the different forms of soundscape can assist in decision-making towards better urban reorganization and modernization [2]. In this context, several computational methods to evaluate it has been developed throughout the last decades. These methods aim to model the acoustic phenomenon, even they remain with limitations [3], as they take into account multiple parameters at once, such as road traffic [4], building attributes, and even weather conditions. The urban form and density of a defined area, also determine the ambient noise

O. Gervasi et al. (Eds.): ICCSA 2021, LNCS 12952, pp. 704–718, 2021.
https://doi.org/10.1007/978-3-030-86973-1_49

level [5–7]. Several parameters, such as porosity, permeability, compactness, occupation and fractal indexes, also may have a direct impact [8].

In the second half of the 20th century, the Tuscany region has seen profound landscape changes, distinguished by a shift in its agricultural environment, that shifted socioeconomic and spatial patterns from compact to scatter in some areas [9]. That, coupled with the urbanization and industrialization that were intensified during this period, shifted the urban context and had a significant effect on the region's acoustic environment, prompting constant reviews and updates of the Municipal Acoustic Classification Plans.

This paper is organized in two distinct sections, one summarizing a background of the computational methods that traditionally are used to analyze and model the urban soundscape, and a second section, that proposes an analysis apposing spatial information about the soundscape to the configuration of the foreground – built structures and background – road-circulation networks – of the urban settlements. The objective is to unearth correlations between urban design, movement dynamics and the different noise pollution classes, highlighting the soundscape patterns of the built environment. The study will focus on an important productive area in Tuscany, that comprises two provinces, which are: *Firenze* (Florence), and Prato. Results indicate a significant correlation between movement – especially in the residential and mixed-use areas – and the presence of productive activities with noise pollution.

2 Computational Urban Acoustics

Various sound field prediction methods have been established over the past few decades. According to studies, these methods can be classified into Geometrical Acoustics methods and Wave-based and diffuse methods, while others predicting analysis use Hybrid Methods [10, 11] (Fig. 1). Some reviewers also include, Acceleration and Non-graphic techniques [12].

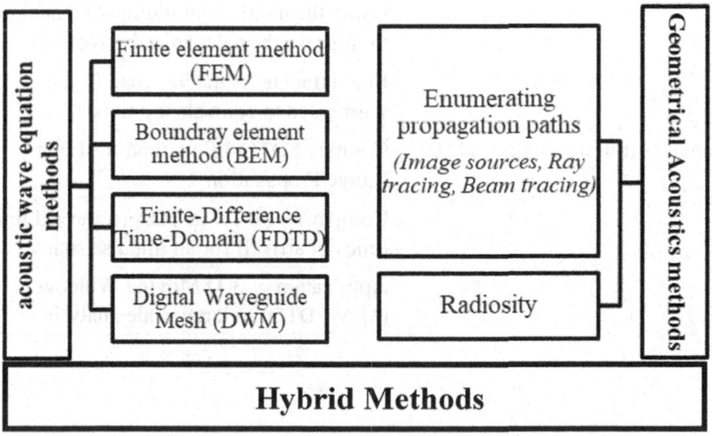

Fig. 1. Outdoor noise propagation computational methods (Source: according to [10])

It is crucial to emphasize, however, that experimental measurements are required to ensure the accuracy of digital predictions [3]. Acoustic urban analysis relies primarily on (L_{den} and L_{night}), recommended by the Environmental Noise Directive (END) [13].

Table 1 summarizes these approaches and establish a classification of past research according to their calculation methods of the environments' sound field.

Table 1. Overview of urban acoustics computational methods.

Method *(Acronym)*	Objectives	*Ref.*
Boundary element method *(BEM)*	Numerical analysis of Noise barrier using 2.5-D BEM	[14]
	Combining BEM to other methods to solve coupled vibro-acoustic problems	[15]
	Solve large acoustics problems by 3D BEM, including Fast Multipole Method	[16]
Digital waveguide mesh *(DWM)*	2-D modeling, application and limitations	[17]
	Coupled DWM-FEM for modeling wave propagation in irregularly shaped streets	[18]
Discontinuous Galerkin *(DG)*	Hybrid approach using DG-PSTD to compute arbitrary boundary conditions and complex geometries	[11]
	ExWave code based on DG method for modeling complex geometries	[19]
	DG for solving the AwRascle traffic system of hyperbolic partial differential equations	[20]
Equivalent source method *(ESM)*	2.5-D ESM for modeling an exposed and sheltered urban canyons	[21]
	Using the multi-point multipole technique, to improve the calculation's precision	[22]
	Beam tracing to analyze road traffic segmented to equivalent points	[23]
Finite-differences times-domain *(FDTD)*	Coupled FDTD-PE method for Long Range Propagation	[14]
	Comparing FDTD to TOA (observed first times of arrival) for an impulse source	[24]
	Application of 3-D Moving Window (MW-FDTD) to large-scale analysis	[25]

(*continued*)

Table 1. *(continued)*

Method *(Acronym)*	Objectives	*Ref.*
Finite element method *(FEM)*	Using FEM to predict sound propagation in buildings with a periodic distribution	[26]
	Introduction meteorological effects by Linearized Euler equation (LEE) provided by a CFD software (Open FOAM)	[14]
	Insertion loss measurements of noise barriers using FEM in 2-D	[27]
Lattice Boltzmann method *(LBM)*	Application of LBM used for incompressible flows in outdoor acoustic propagation	[28]
	Determine the numerical dissipation and dispersion resolution dependency	[29]
	LBM as a performant Bottom-up method to compute micro and macroscale algorithms	[30]
Parabolic equation *(PE)*	3-D wide angle PE to model low frequency propagation in irregular urban canyons	[31]
	Wind's speed and height effect on outdoor noise propagation	[14]
	Coupled FDTD-PE for modeling acoustic reduction through vegetation	[32]
Pseudo-spectral time-domain *(PSTD)*	Modeling scattering of a small tree geometry using PSTD	[33]
	Analysis of noise sources directivity and physical properties	[11]
	Comparing Fourier PSTD domain to DG boundaries for wave propagation in cities	[34]
*Waveguide Web *(WGW)*	Second-order accuracy in modeling sparsely reflecting outdoor acoustics	[35]

*Waveguide Web is reverberator design for outdoor, it differs from Digital Waveguide Method.

The complementarity of these numerical methods aids in the modeling of realistic acoustic scenes. The majority of these studies were conducted on the micro scale, nevertheless, few equations were developed to significantly comprehend and manage the macro scale.

3 Soundscape Environment and Geographic Information System

The use of geographic information systems (GIS) has proven its potential in various fields of applications including transportation, urban, regional planning and cartography as a key element for decision-making [36]. In the Acoustics field, early studies in 1990's aimed to create a two-dimensional cartography in GIS, in order to develop a prototype visualization system to understand the sound behavior of different urban configurations. This requires the collection of different quantitative and qualitative information on traffic and human activities [37, 38].

Given the variety of subjects studied, these methods have progressed significantly since their inception. Several studies are attempting to model acoustic maps to locate causes of sound emission and perhaps predict future potential problems [39–42].

A significant number of studies in this field have focused on the analysis of vehicular traffic since this modal is regarded as a primary source of noise. While numerical solutions are often used to resolve the noise problem, as shown in the previous section, researchers tried to develop several plugins on GIS software for modeling the vehicle traffic according to the available data [43]. In a recent study, GIS was used as a tool to help address the parameters related to the design of buildings (type, height) that play a role in the problem of urban nuisance [44]. Bello et al., 2019 on the other hand, used a GIS software called "URBANE" for 3-D visualization after developing an innovative noise-detecting device that combines learning machines and human interactions in New York City's neighborhoods [45]. With these studies in consideration, in the last years, GIS-based sound analyses have become reliable in apposing infrastructural data to the soundscape, yet some aspects about configuration still merit further exploration.

4 Methodology

This investigation aims to analyze the soundscape and spatial forms using an Opensource GIS Software – QGIS [46]. A preliminary step consists of geometry preparation after delimiting our study area which comprises six municipalities in the provinces of *Firenze* and *Prato*. These areas form a continuous productive area that comprises the largest industrial agglomeration in Tuscany. Infrastructural data comprises the built-structures, derived from the Tuscany Region Built-Structure's dataset *(Edificato 2k,10k 1988–2013*) [47], and the road-circulation network, obtained from the Tuscany Region Road Graph (*Grafo Itnet)* [48]. In order to understand the urban structure and movement dynamics among the elements that make up the studied area, the sectioned graph was modeled using the Space Syntax's Angular Analysis [49] measures of Normalized Angular Integration (NAIN) and Normalized Angular Choice (NACH) which possess a good correspondence regarding vehicular traffic and movement potentials – both regarding accessibility – NAIN; and preferential routes within the System - NACH [50, 51]. For the acoustic analysis, the Municipal Acoustic Classification Plans *(Piani Comunali di Classificazione Acustica - PCCA*) for the Tuscany Region, established on December 5, 2012. These plans specify six acoustic groups that are recommended by the Environmental Noise Directive (END [52] and were used to determine the limits in noise pollution for each area. With the road-circulation network modeled it is possible to focus on the complex relationship between the studied area's forms and functions of the background and foreground, and the acoustic environment, through the correlation between the acoustic classes, roads that present a greater degree of movement potential and buildings typologies.

5 Results and Discussion

The research area encompasses six municipalities, distributed in-between the *Firenze* and *Prato* provinces: *Calenzano, Campi Bisenzio, Firenze, Sesto Fiorentino and Signa,* that are part of the metropolitan city of *Firenze*, while *Prato* is the capital city of its homonymous province (Fig. 2). This region covers an area of 373.34 Km^2 and is well-known for its appeal as a touristic destination. Still, this territorial extent also possesses a substantial importance within Tuscany as a productive and industrialized area [9].

From an urban morphology standpoint, it is possible to observe that the analysis area, is rather compact in form, exhibiting a distinguishable conurbation that extends across the six municipalities (Fig. 3). The area locates the largest concentration of industrial-dedicated buildings and industrial land use within the region, with those productive spaces being characterized by the orthogonal-based configuration of its road-circulation network. Residential presence is also extensive throughout the area, with a cohesive distribution. The road-infrastructure in the boundary areas, especially around the municipalities of *Calenzano* and *Sesto Fiorentino* exhibit, instead, a radicle-based organization, around the main roadway, and have a productive land-use mainly dedicated to agricultural production, or as natural protected areas (Fig. 3).

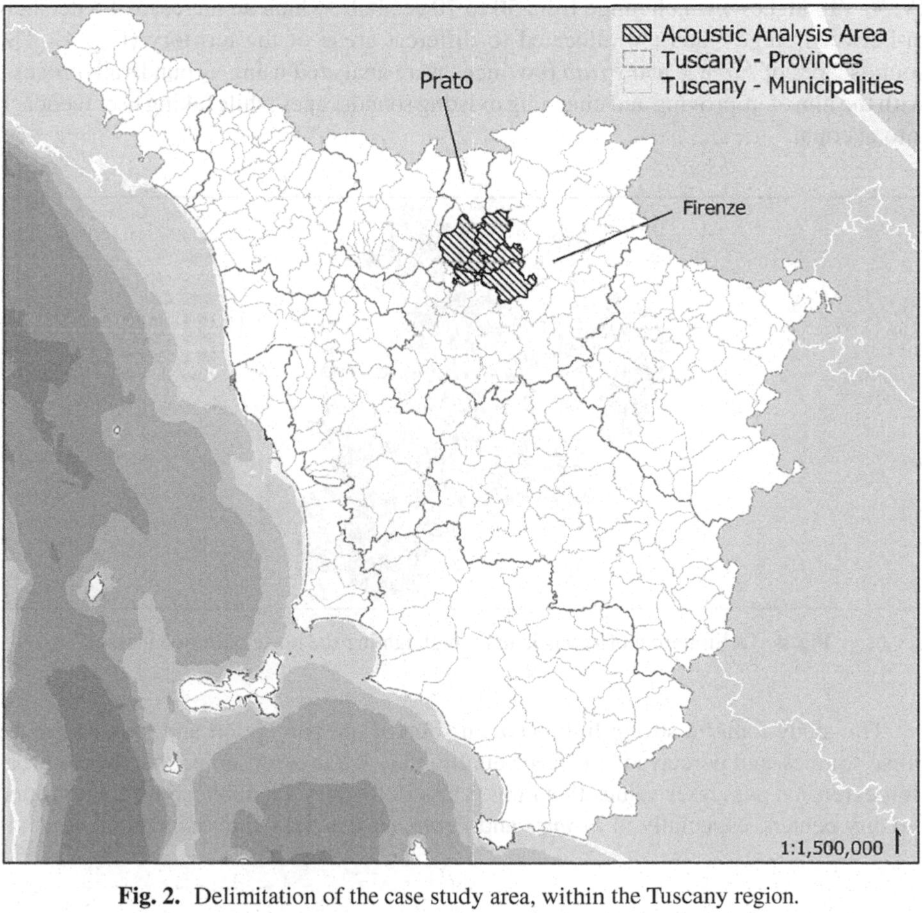

Fig. 2. Delimitation of the case study area, within the Tuscany region.

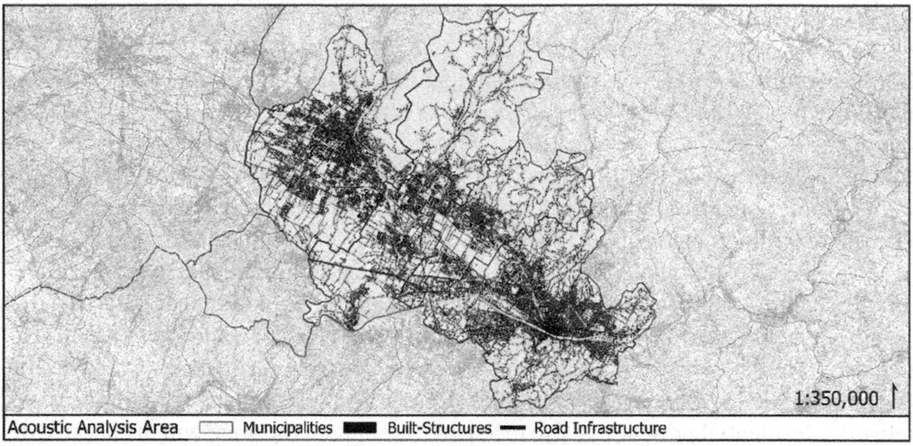

Fig. 3. Delimitation of the case study area, with the disposition of municipalities, built-structures and road-infrastructure.

The acoustic data from the PCCA specifies six acoustic groups (I - lowest, II, III, IV, V, VI - highest) which range from 50 to 70 decibels, which an increase of 5 decibels in-between ranges, and are allocated to different areas of the territory (Fig. 4). The soundscapes of *Firenze* and *Prato* provinces were analyzed using a soundwalk process, with the aim of improving and changing existing soundscapes while taking user feedback into account.

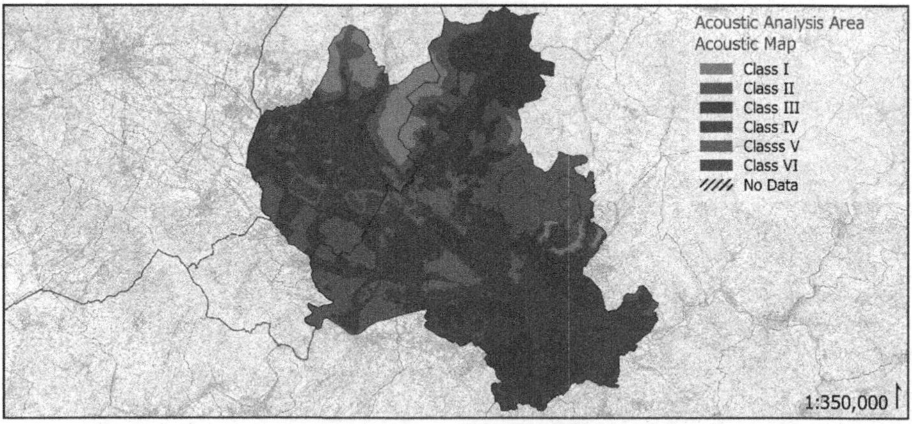

Fig. 4. Delimitation of acoustic map, highlighting the noise pollution classes

The study found a strong link between soundscape perception and measurements, noise sources, and perceived landscape quality [53]. It can be observed that the conurbation extension possesses values that range class III to class VI, albeit some areas around the city centers, especially in *Firenze* and *Prato*, have a class II classification, which is the minimal for both urbanized and rural areas. Class I is only found in the mountain area in-between *Calenzano* and *Prato*, a non-urbanized site (Fig. 4).

It can be noticed that the areas with compact urban fabric have higher noise characters, due to the intensity of human activities in the area – predominantly made of residential and mixed-uses, that are categorized mostly in the classes III and IV (Fig. 5).

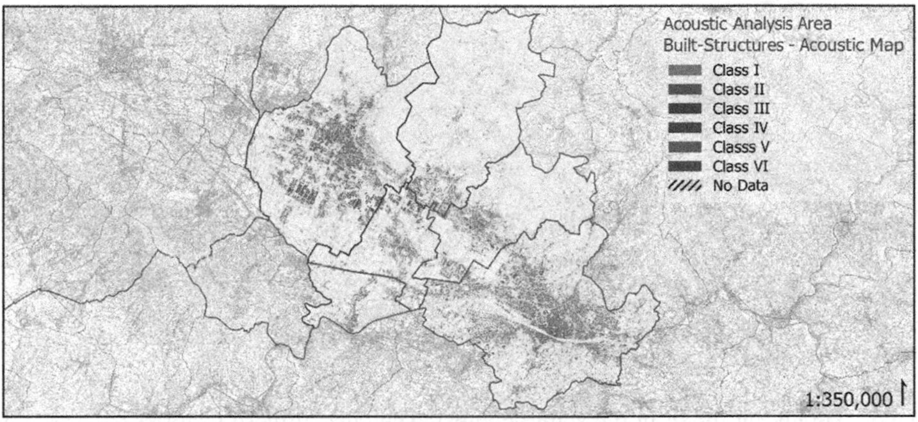

Fig. 5. Built-structures apposition with the acoustic map noise classes.

Industrial-dedicated areas, however, are included in the classes V and VI. These sites are predominant on *Prato*, that locates most of the areas categorized under the highest class (VI). In that aspect, it is highlighted that only the municipalities *Prato, Calenzano, Campi Bizenzio* and *Signa* possess buildings included in the highest class (VI), while buildings categorized under in the class V are present in all municipalities. Few small and isolated rural estates are included in the class I, placed in-between *Calezano* and *Prato* (Fig. 5).

The percentual distribution of the built-structures located within each sound character class is depicted in Table 2, while the Fig. 6 establishes the relation between the soundscape classes and the urban functions – allocating the number of buildings that have a determined urban function within each acoustic category.

Table 2. Percentual distribution of built-structures according to the acoustic classes

Class I	Class II	Class III	Class IV	Class V	Class VI
0.1%	3%	27.3%	65.1%	3.8%	0.6%

Residential buildings represent the main bulk of the noise sources with a high rate of 25.8% registered in class III and 70.6% registered in Class IV. Albeit their little impact on daily sound quality, rural and unidentified areas remain an important source too, accounting for 37.5% and 70.6 if Class III and IV, respectively. Industrial buildings also

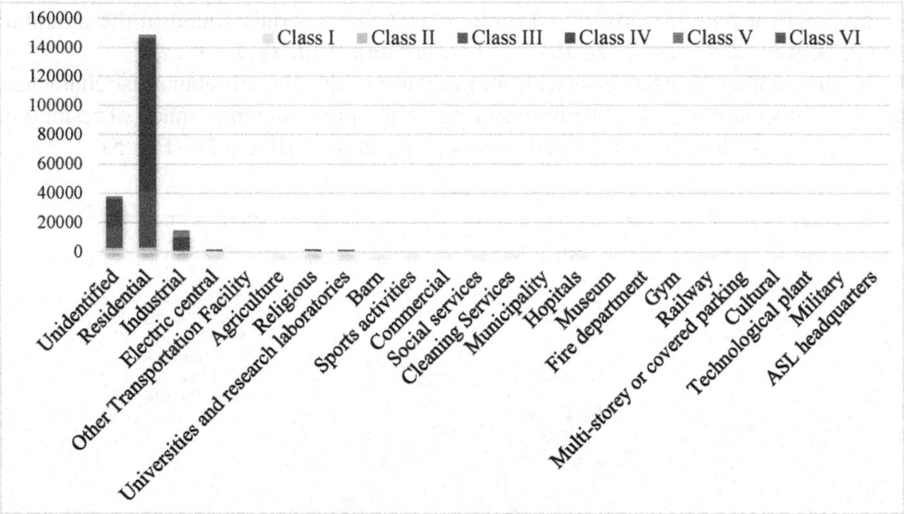

Fig. 6. Relationship between noise classes and built structures.

have a significant effect in the sound context. The bulk of these factories are based in the municipalities of Prato, Calenzano, Signa – with sources arriving at the VI class, and in a lesser degree, Sesto Fiorentino and Firenze. Industrial buildings are disposed as follows: 54.7% in the class IV and 27.1% in the class V. Other activities, such as cultural and military functions, are characterized by a medium-low-noisy environment (Class III) and, due to their limited presence contribute less to the overall acoustic landscape. Hospitals tend to be located within areas within Class II.

The road-circulation network in the study area is dense and structured in a conurbation, where the main connection in-between the municipalities is made through urban highways (Fig. 7) These structures are listed on the classes IV and V, meaning that vehicular traffic represents the main noise source within the region, and has a direct impact on the daily life of residents and on their health.

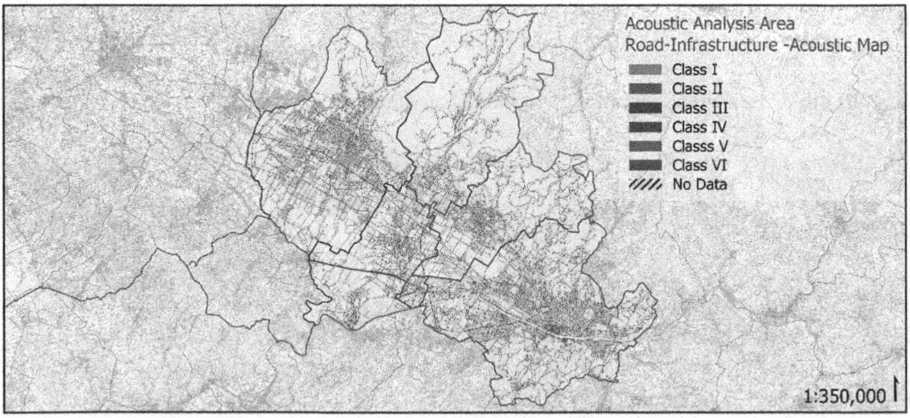

Fig. 7. Road-circulation network apposition to the acoustic map noise classes

The Angular Segment Analysis shows an aggregated urban fabric, where Normalized Angular Integration (NAIN) measures were calculated independently for each one of the six municipalities and apposed to compose the whole system (Fig. 8a). In this aspect it is possible to highlight the local centers for each municipality, as well as have an idea of where the interactions between local and global road-circulation networks occur. These are depicted when NAIN values are restricted to their highest values – 90° and 100° deciles (Fig. 8b) – that represent the centrality cores of each urban settlement, or the places with the highest accessibility. When observed alongside the Normalized Angular Choice (NACH), calculated at global scale for the whole system, and establish the internal hierarchies regarding the preferential routes within the system (Fig. 8a). As observed in previous studies, betweenness centralities (the mathematical component of NACH) possess a homothetic behavior [54], which justify its modeling as a whole region, unlike the integration that varies according to depth.

Through the restriction of the global NACH - 90° and 100° deciles – it is possible assess the road-segments that structure the paths across the region and establish the linkages among the Integration cores (Fig. 9b).

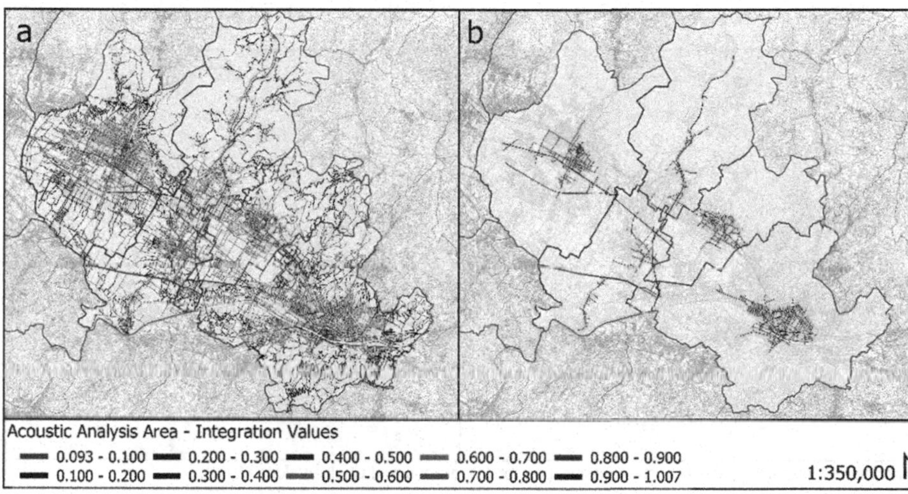

Fig. 8. Normalized Angular Integration (NAIN) values for each municipality (a) and Integration Cores restricted to the 90° and 100° deciles (b).

Angular Analysis models (NAIN and NACH), where then correlated to the noise classes, in order to highlight if movement potentials – that are a representation of the expected movement, had a correspondence with the degree of noise identified in each space (Fig. 10).

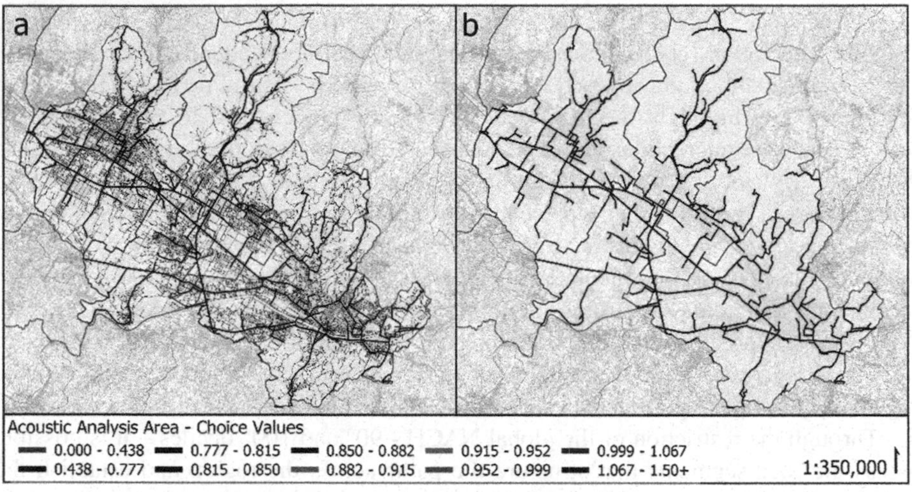

Fig. 9. Normalized Angular Integration (NACH) values for the region-wide system (a) and *Preferential Routes* restricted to the 90° and 100° deciles (b).

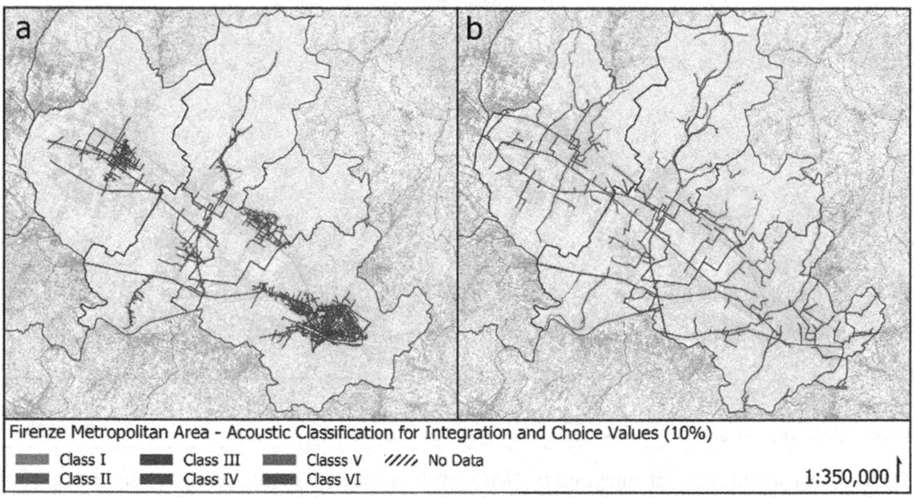

Fig. 10. Acoustic classification and correlation for normalized angular integration (NAIN) and normalized angular choice (NACH) values (90° and 100° deciles)

Correlations demonstrate that 85.61% of the road-elements within highest NAIN values (integration cores) belongs to class IV, whereas 66.98% of the most sought *preferential routes* (NACH) is included in this same class, which demonstrate a significative relation between movement and noise levels. It is important to highlight that class V and VI are mostly restricted to the industrial areas (Fig. 11).

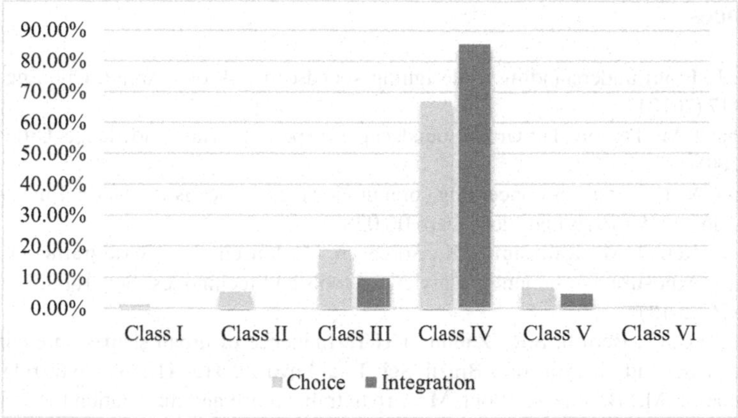

Fig. 11. Restricted normalized angular integration (NAIN) and normalized angular choice (NACH) – 90° and 100° deciles – distribution in relation to acoustic classes.

Road-elements in the Classes I and II are restricted to the *preferential routes*, given that these extend towards the municipalities' borders, where the suburban condition reflects a lower noise level. Classes III, IV and V have a better distribution regarding the number of road elements: while Class III has a predominance of *preferential routes*, Integration has a predominance on Class IV, explained, as the most road-elements are located within central urban areas – especially in *Firenze*, which has a considerable tourism activity, thus, pedestrian movement, in its historical center. Class V, in the other hand, presents an equilibrium between Integration and Choice, and mostly indicates that the industrial activities are integrated within the system, as well as placed near the preferential routes. Being Class IV the dominant noise class in the urban system it explains the assumed relationship between the movement and noise levels.

6 Conclusions

Results showed considerable impact of the form function and spatial configuration on the acoustic environment. It is highlighted that vehicular traffic and the concentration of pedestrians, motivated by tourism and commercial activities are the main source of noise pollution in Firenze city center. In the other parts of its metropolitan area, however, while vehicular movement still contributes to the acoustic environment, productive activities – mainly industrial – are the main sources of noise pollution in the region, with the higher classes being mostly concentrated at the city of Prato. Highest values of global measures of the Angular Segment Analysis have the ability to provide a clear overview of the acoustic phenomenon.

The relation between road-circulation network configuration – movement potentials, the background; and the built-structures – the foreground can serve as a helpful planning instrument for updating the Municipal Acoustic Classification Plan, since it introduces variables that can produce a finer detail regarding the noise sources and their distribution.

References

1. Kang, J.: From understanding to designing soundscapes. Front. Archit. Civ. Eng. China **4**, 403–417 (2010)
2. Raimbault, M., Dubois, D.: Urban soundscapes: experiences and knowledge. Cities **22**, 339–350 (2005)
3. Hornikx, M.T.: questions concerning computational urban acoustics. Build. Environ. (2016). https://doi.org/10.1016/j.buildenv.2016.06.028
4. Khan, J., Ketzel, M., Kakosimos, K., Sørensen, M., Jensen, S.S.: Road traffic air and noise pollution exposure assessment – a review of tools and techniques. Sci. Total Environ. **634**, 661–676 (2018)
5. Guedes, I.C.M., Bertoli, S.R., Zannin, P.H.T.: Influence of urban shapes on environmental noise: a case study in Aracaju - Brazil. Sci. Total Environ. **412–413**, 66–76 (2011)
6. Salomons, E.M., Berghauser Pont, M.: Urban traffic noise and the relation to urban density, form, and traffic elasticity. Landscape Urban Plann. **108**, 2–16 (2012)
7. Tang, U.W., Wang, Z.S.: Influences of urban forms on traffic-induced noise and air pollution: results from a modelling system. Environ. Model. Softw. **22**, 1750–1764 (2007)
8. Oliveira, M.F., Silva, L.T.: How urban noise can be influenced by the urban form. 6th WSEAS International Conference on Cellular and Molecular Biology, Biophysics and Bioengineering, BIO 2010, 8th WSEAS International Conference on Environmental Ecosystems and Development, EED 2010, International Conference on Biosciences and Bioinformatics, ICBB 2010 I, pp. 31–36 (2010)
9. Zullo, F., Paolinelli, G., Valentina, F., Fiorini, L., Romano, B.: Urban development in Tuscany. Land uptake and landscapes changes. TeMA J. Land Use Mob. Environ. **8**, 183–202 (2015)
10. Lakka, E., Malamos, A., Pavlakis, K.G., Ware, J.A.: Spatial sound rendering – a Survey. Int. J. Interact. Multimedia Artif. Intell. **5**, 33 (2018)
11. Georgiou, F., Munoz, R.P., Rietdijk, F., Zachos, G.: Prediction and auralisation of urban sound environments. In: Urban Sound Planning - the Sonorus project 118 (DanagardLiTHO, 2016)
12. Charalampous, P., Michael, D.: Sound propagation in 3D spaces using computer graphics techniques. In: Proceedings of the 2014 International Conference on Virtual Systems and Multimedia, VSMM 2014, pp. 43–49 (2014) https://doi.org/10.1109/VSMM.2014.7136674
13. European Parliament and Council of the European Union. Assessment and management of environmental noise (EU Directive). Official J. Eur. Commun. (2002). http://eur-lex.europa.eu/legal-content/EN/TXT/PDF/?uri=CELEX:32002L0049&from=EN%5Cn, http://eur-lex.europa.eu/legal-content/EN/TXT/?uri=celex:32002L0049. https://doi.org/10.1016/j.jclepro.2010.02.014
14. Toyoda, M. et al. Noise propagation Simulation. In: Sakuma T., Sakamoto S., Otsuru T. (eds.) Computational Simulation in Architectural and Environmental Acoustics, pp. 179–242. Springer, Tokyo (2014). https://doi.org/10.1007/978-4-431-54454-8
15. Kirkup, S.: The boundary element method in acoustics: a survey. Appl. Sci. **9**, 48 (2019)
16. Bashir, I., Carley, M.: Development of 3D boundary element method for the simulation of acoustic metamaterials/metasurfaces in mean flow for aerospace applications. Int. J. Aeroacoustics **19**, 324–346 (2020)
17. Murphy, D., Kolloniemi, A., Mullen, J., Shelley, S.: Acoustic modeling using the digital waveguide mesh. IEEE Signal Process. Mag. **24**, 55–66 (2007)
18. Pelat, A., Felix, S., Pagneux, V.: A coupled modal-finite element method for the wave propagation modeling in irregular open waveguides. J. Acoust. Soc. Am. **129**, 1240–1249 (2011)
19. Schoeder, S., Wall, W.A., Kronbichler, M.: ExWave: a high performance discontinuous galerkin solver for the acoustic wave equation. SoftwareX **9**, 49–54 (2019)

20. Buli, J., Xing, Y.: A discontinuous galerkin method for the aw-rascle traffic flow model on networks. J. Comput. Phys. **406**, 109183 (2020)
21. Hornikx, M., Forssén, J.: The 2.5-dimensional equivalent sources method for directly exposed and shielded urban canyons. J. Acoust. Soc. Am. **122**, 2532 (2007)
22. Gounot, Y.J.R., Musafir, R.E.: Simulation of scattered fields: some guidelines for the equivalent source method. J. Sound Vib. **330**, 3698–3709 (2011)
23. Wang, H., Cai, M., Cui, H.: Simulation and analysis of road traffic noise among urban buildings using spatial subdivision-based beam tracing method. Int. J. Environ. Res. Public Health **16**(14), 2491 (2019)
24. Cheinet, S., Ehrhardt, L., Broglin, T.: Impulse source localization in an urban environment: time reversal versus time matching. Acoust. Soc. Am. **139**, 128–140 (2016)
25. Oikawa, T., Sonoda, J., Honma, N., Sato, M.: Analysis of lighting electromagnetic field on numerical terrain and urban model using three-dimensional MW-FDTD parallel computation. Electron. Commun. Japan **100**, 76–82 (2017)
26. Molerón, M., Félix, S., Pagneux, V., Richoux, O.: Sound propagation in periodic urban areas. J. Appl. Phys. **111**, 114906 (2012)
27. Papadakis, N.M., Stavroulakis, G.E.: Finite element method for the estimation of insertion loss of noise barriers: comparison with various formulae (2D). Urban Sci. **4**, 77 (2020)
28. Fraser, N., Hall, R.: Simulating acoustic propagation using a lattice boltzmann model of incompressible fluid flow, pp. 42–47 (2006)
29. Viggen, E.M.: The lattice Boltzmann method with applications in acoustics. Master's thesis, Norwegian University of Science, pp. 1–5 (2009)
30. Brès, G.A., Pérot, F., Freed, D.: Properties of the Lattice-Boltzmann method for acoustics. In: 15th AIAA/CEAS Aeroacoustics Conference (30th AIAA Aeroacoustics Conference), pp. 11–13 (2009). https://doi.org/10.2514/6.2009-3395
31. Doc, J.-B., Lihoreau, B., Félix, S., Faure, C., Dubois, G.: Three-dimensional parabolic equation model for low frequency sound propagation in irregular urban canyons. J. Acoust. Soc. Am. **137**, 310–320 (2015)
32. Ow, L.F., Ghosh, S.: Urban cities and road traffic noise: reduction through vegetation. Appl. Acoust. **120**, 15–20 (2017)
33. van Renterghem, T., Botteldooren, D., Verheyen, K.: Road traffic noise shielding by vegetation belts of limited depth. J. Sound Vib. **331**, 2404–2425 (2012)
34. Muñoz, R.P., Hornikx, M.: Hybrid fourier pseudospectral/discontinuous galerkin time-domain method for wave propagation. J. Comput. Phy. **348**, 416–432 (2017). https://doi.org/10.1016/j.jcp.2017.07.046
35. Stevens, F., Murphy, D.T., Savioja, L., Valimaki, V.: Modeling sparsely reflecting outdoor acoustic scenes using the waveguide web. IEEE/ACM Trans. Audio Speech Lang. Process. **25**, 1566–1578 (2017)
36. Malczewski, J.: GIS-based multicriteria decision analysis: a survey of the literature. Int. J. Geogr. Inf. Sci. **20**, 703–726 (2006)
37. Servigne, S., Laurini, R., Kang, M.-A., Li, K.J.: First specifications of an information system for urban soundscape. In: Proceedings IEEE International Conference on Multimedia Computing and Systems, vol. 2, pp. 262–266 (1999)
38. Krygier, J.B.: Sound and geographic visualization. In: Modern Cartography Series, vol. 2 (Elsevier Science Ltd, 1994)
39. Zannin, P.H.T., de Sant'Ana, D.Q.: Noise mapping at different stages of a freeway redevelopment project - A case study in Brazil. Appl. Acoust. **72**, 479–486 (2011)
40. Hossam Eldien, H.: Noise mapping in urban environments: application at Suez city center. In: 2009 International Conference on Computers and Industrial Engineering, CIE 2009, pp. 1722–1727 (2009). https://doi.org/10.1109/iccie.2009.5223696

41. Bilaşco, Ş, Govor, C., Roşca, S., Vescan, I., Filip, S., Fodorean, I.: GIS model for identifying urban areas vulnerable to noise pollution: case study. Front. Earth Sci. **11**(2), 214–228 (2017). https://doi.org/10.1007/s11707-017-0615-6
42. Garcia, J.S., et al.: Spatial statistical analysis of urban noise data from a WASN gathered by an IoT system: application to a small city. Appl. Sci. (Switzerland) **6**(12), 380 (2016)
43. Cai, M., Zou, J., Xie, J., Ma, X.: Road traffic noise mapping in Guangzhou using GIS and GPS. Appl. Acoust. **87**, 94–102 (2015)
44. Huang, B., Pan, Z., Liu, Z., Hou, G., Yang, H.: Acoustic amenity analysis for high-rise building along urban expressway: modeling traffic noise vertical propagation using neural networks. Transp. Res. Part D **53**, 63–77 (2017)
45. Bello, J.P., et al.: Sonyc. Commun. ACM **62**, 68–77 (2019)
46. QGIS, Hannover, version 3.16 (2020). http://www.qgis.org/en/site/index.html
47. Regione Toscana, Direzione Urbanistica e Politiche Abitative - Sistema Informativo Territoriale e Ambientale – SITA.: Edificato 2k, 10k 1988–2013. (2019b). http://www.502.regione.toscana.it/geoscopio/cartoteca.html
48. Toscana, R.: (2019b) Direzione Urbanistica e Politiche Abitative - Sistema Informativo Territoriale e Ambientale – SITA.: Grafo stradario e ferroviario della Regione Toscana - Itnet. http://www.502.regione.toscana.it/geoscopio/cartoteca.html
49. Turner, A.: Angular Analysis. In: Proceedings of the 3rd International Symposium on Space Sy*ntax,* pp. 7–11. Georgia Institute of Technology, Atlanta, Georgia (2001)
50. Turner, A.: From axial to road-centre lines: a new representation for space syntax and a new model of route choice for transport network analysis. Environ. Plann. B. Plann. Des. **34**, 539–555 (2007)
51. Hillier, B., Yang, T., Turner, A.: Normalising least angle choice in depthmap - and how it opens up new perspectives on the global and local analysis of city space. J. Space Synt. **3**(2), 155–193 (2012)
52. Toscana, R.: Direzione Urbanistica e Politiche Abitative - Sistema Informativo Territoriale e Ambientale – SITA.: Piano Comunale di Classificazione Acustica - PCCA; art 4 l.r. 89/98 - http://www.502.regione.toscana.it/geoscopio/cartoteca.html(2019c)
53. Luzzi, S., Bartalucci, C., Radicchi, A., Brusci, L., Brambilla, G. Participative soundscape projects in Italian contexts. In: Inter-Noise 2019 MADRID - 48th International Congress and Exhibition on Noise Control Engineering (2019)
54. Altafini, D., Cutini, V.: Homothetic behavior of betweenness centralities: a multiscale alternative approach to relate cities and large regional structures. Sustainability **12**(19), 7925 (2020). https://doi.org/10.3390/su12197925

Syntactic Study of the Correlation Between Urban Spatial Configuration and Use of Streets in the City of Bejaia

Safia Mahfoud(✉) and Yassine Bada

Lacomofa Lab, University of Biskra, Biskra, Algeria

Abstract. The city is a coherent whole with a structure and a meaning, and streets play a very important role in its functioning and represent its framework. Unfortunately, some cities, such as Bejaia, are facing many problems such as the disparities in the use of urban spaces like streets, and this between different parts of the city. The questions which then arise are the following: What is the main cause of this disparity of use between the streets of the different parts of the city of Bejaia? And what is the impact of the resulting consequences on the functioning of the city and on urban life?

The present work examines the correlation between the spatial configuration of the city and the use of streets. The investigation implemented is based on Space Syntax as a theory and analysis approach using Depthmap software. Thus, the syntactic analysis is concretized on two scales: at the scale of the city (macro) to capture the connectivity of the spatial configuration of the city combining the street network and urban entities, and at the scale of a street crossing different parts of the city (micro), and this to compare its syntactic properties with its intensities of use resulting from behavioral analysis.

The results of this investigation indicate that there is a strong correlation between the intensity of use of streets, the syntactic properties and functional ones such as activities and services present at their walls.

Keywords: Spatial configuration · Streets · Use · Space syntax · Depthmap software

1 Introduction

Cities are formed mainly by blocks, a framework that represents the organization of its spatial structure. Within a single city or a single block, it is possible to find a variety of urban fabrics and functions. The streets in this spatial structure have, as their main function, the service and circulation of individuals, thus structuring the connections within the urban space. Therefore, circulation can then be considered as a reflection of this spatial structure [1]. Urban public spaces are characterized by a circulation dynamic whose type and intensity of flow differs from one place to another, with these flow patterns being also related to time and day-period.

O. Gervasi et al. (Eds.): ICCSA 2021, LNCS 12952, pp. 719–731, 2021.
https://doi.org/10.1007/978-3-030-86973-1_50

The creation of cities takes place through a dual process, "generative" and "conservative" [2], which takes into consideration the existing relationship between physical space and the movement that takes place there [3]. From a "generative" standpoint [2], the process aims to maximize the use of spaces by promoting movement and human co-presence -the shared use of space-, and it is mainly influenced by economic activities side such as commerce. It is this process that leads to the formation of the global structure of the city called "foreground" [4]. As for the "conservative" process, which is also called "residential spatial process" [2], the aim is to minimize or control local movement according to the needs of a particular residential culture, thus conservative process are linked to individual aspects of local culture, while structuring the relationships between its different members.

The movement of people within the urban spatial structure is done by imagining a series of successive spaces leading them to their destination [5]. Kurt Lewin defined this by introducing the term "hodological space", from the Greek "hodos" which means path, and which is a "possible space of movement" [6]. According to Lewin, the hodological space "consists of 'preferred path' according to many objectives such as 'short distance', 'safety', 'minimum work', 'maximum experience' etc" [6]. Paths are one of the five elements of the city that contribute to its imageability, as defined by Kevin Lynch in his book "The Image of the City" [7]. According to the author: "Paths whose origins and destinations are well known had stronger identities, helped connect the city and gave the viewer an idea of his landmarks each time he crossed them" [7].

Hence, the paths are spaces of connection between the various parts of the city and serving various activities, a support for circulation and movement, but also a place of exchange and meeting thus ensuring a social function. The use of paths is linked to several physical factors that must be taken into consideration when planning the urban spaces, such as user density, land-use mix, pedestrian-vehicle interaction, configuration and context [8, 9].

The term "spatial configuration" is used to refer to the structure accommodating movement dynamics and human co-presence, and which is determined by the presence of boundaries between different areas and the connection and disconnection of these spaces [10]. Urban networks are characterized by very important configurational properties that are associated with functional structure from the foreground, such as movement potentials or relative accessibility (to-movement) which create a certain "spatial hierarchy" [11, 12]. By having a relation with the movement and by impacting the latter, the configuration properties have a role in the distribution of activities which are closely linked to the human presence and the use of space. These activities are considered as attractive elements at the level of the urban fabric, and which can also influence the movement by an equivalence relation, or by having a multiplier effect on the latter if it is already influenced by the configuration [13, 14]. Hillier et al. clarified the relationship between the three parameters as follows: "Attractors and movement can influence each other, but the other two relationships are asymmetric. The configuration can influence the location of the attractors, but the location of the attractors cannot influence the configuration. Likewise, the configuration can influence the movement, but the movement cannot influence the configuration. If strong correlations are found between movement and configuration and attractors, the only logically possible lines of influence are from configuration to movement and attractors, the last two influencing each other" [11].

The configuration of the urban spatial structure is, therefore, a fundamental generator of pedestrian movement, which in turn influences the distribution of attractors within the urban space. These attractors can also have a multiplier effect on movement [13, 14], and it sometimes happens that the rate of movement generated by these attractors is higher than that generated by the configuration of the space.

Each city is characterized by two dimensions: the physical and the social; this latter being related to how the physical city is conceived and arranged. As discussed, there is a strong relationship between the configuration of the urban network, the movement flows generally determined by this configuration, and the use of space, i.e. human co-presence. The spatial networks' configuration then has a considerable impact on human co-presence, intensity and disparities in the use of spaces [12–15]. Hence, this relationship is considered to be a "basic urban relationship" [3] which significantly influences the shape and the functioning of the cities, and what called "the theory of natural movement"– the foundation of the Space Syntax methodologies [3–11].

Street networks then play a very important role within the urban space, because in addition to being the support of movement and circulation, they create links between the different spaces by offering several choices of routes leading to the same places, and this to promote permeability and readability for all users of public space [16].

Based on these considerations about city structure, configuration, and their relation with urban functions, what is proposed is the study of the correlation between urban spatial configuration and the use of streets in the city of Bejaia. Bejaia is a Mediterranean city located in the northeast of Algeria, 250 km east of the capital Algiers. Its urban area has undergone an evolution by stratification, which gave as result a continuous urban fabric. However, despite its evolution in continuity, and the fact that all its parts are cohesive, certain parts of the city and urban spaces, even though possessing similar functions, are not used in the same way. In this aspect, some urban streets are heavily used, while others are not. This prompts a question: what are the causes of these disparities in use and their consequences on the functioning of the city and on urban life within it? Therefore the objective is to investigate the correlation between the spatial configuration of the city of Bejaia and the use of its streets, and this in two scales: at the scale of the city (macro) to capture the connectivity of its spatial configuration combining the street network and urban entities, and at the scale of a street crossing different parts of the city (micro), and this to compare its syntactic properties with its intensities of use resulting from behavioral analysis.

The use of urban public spaces such as streets, according to Hillier [11], is linked to the spatial configuration and the presence of attracting elements such as the presence of activities at the level of their walls and within the district where they are located, hence the need to study the correlation between these three parameters (use of streets, spatial configuration and presence of attracting elements) by relying on in-situ observation and on the method of space syntax; which considers as a theory that every activity, mobility or occupation of space is influenced by the spatial configuration [12–15], and this in order to highlight the causes of disparities in the use of streets between the different parts of the city.

2 Methods

In order to investigate the questions posed in the introduction and to be able to make a comparison, the city of Bejaia was divided into zones, using as a criterion, the urban functions predominance – or their vocation. With this in consideration, three different zones were chosen for the study: a housing zone – the "ZHUN of Sidi Ahmed" (ZHUN) as a new urban residential zone (Zone 1); the Old City and Plain (OCP) – a heritage zone with mixed-use function (Zone 2), and the Bejaia Industrial Zone (BIZ) (Zone 3). From these three areas is highlighted a street path, the "Aurès Street" that establishes the linkage between all zones (Fig. 1).

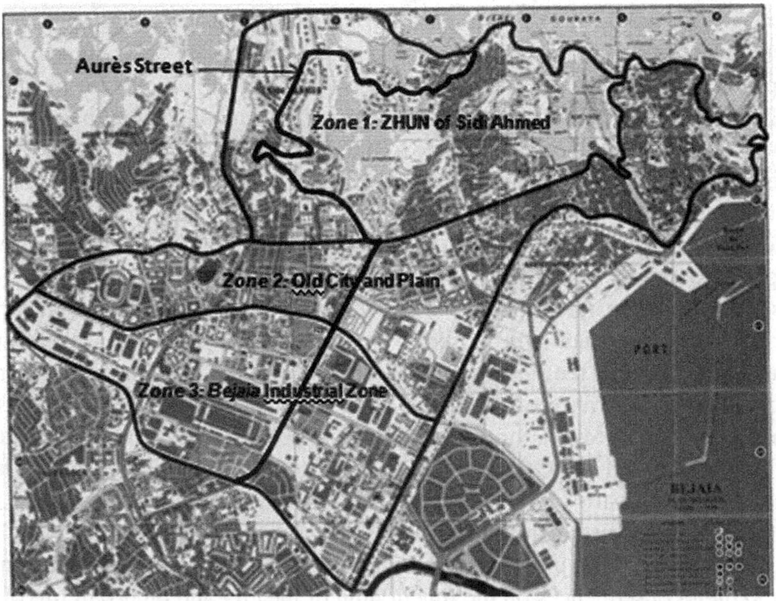

Fig. 1. Location of the study street at the level of the three study zones. **Source.** Direction of town planning, Architecture and Construction, wilaya of Bejaia - DUAC. Elaborated by Mahfoud, 2021.

The ZHUN of Sidi Ahmed is a mainly residential area, characterized by a network of winding streets, which are mostly secondary roads used by the area's inhabitants. The Old City and the Plain are characterized by a distinct morphology, with the historical center being comprised by a series of irregular streets with mixed-use, while the Plain expansions possess a more regular morphology. The highlighted street in this area is a point of encounter for its inhabitants due to its commercial and services presence, being also a strategic location in relation to the whole city – connected to all parts. The Industrial Zone instead is entirely regular, possessing a usual orthogonal grid morphology. The highlighted street establishes the connection between the productive area and the suburbs.

The methodology for analyzing these areas consist of the use of two quantitative methods with overlap of the results. The first method consists of the in-situ observation with people counting "gate counts". As for the second, it employs Space Syntax

Axial [12] and Segment [17] analysis, as a method of evaluating public space with the generation of axial graphs and the calculation of the syntactic values of Integration (Mathematical Closeness) and Choice (Mathematical Betweenness). Axial graphs are modeled through the Depthmap X 0.50 [18]. The second set of methods is used at two different scales: at the macro scale within a radius of 800 m (R800), that uses both axial and axial-segment analysis, and at the micro scale within a radius of 200 m (R200), which uses only the axial-segment analysis. Second order measures of Intelligibility – integration-connectivity correlation – and Synergy – local and global integration correlation – are also estimated. The syntactic results (numerical and graphical) will be overlapped and compared to the results of the use of space.

Although the public urban space extends to a multitude of spaces (streets, plazas, squares, etc.), the present analysis addresses only the streets, to assess their importance within the city. In that sense, it is limited – on the gate counts – to the analysis of one street that crosses the three study zones (Fig. 1), with the aim of being able to carry out a comparison of the use of the same street by pedestrians between the three zones. The "Aurès Street" (Fig. 1), is one of the main linkages within the city, considered to be a very important axis of transport in Bejaia. It is characterized by a sinuous shape at Zone 1 (ZHUN) that becomes linear once it enters at the Zones 2 (OCP) and 3 (BIZ). The street about 15 m wide, with a length of 3270 m at Zone 1, 500 m at Zone 2 and 1105 m at Zone 3.

The "gate counts" method based on pedestrian observation only, was made at the same time for the three study zones, on a weekday (29/03/2021) and a weekend (02/04/2021). The observation considered only moving (walking) people in the two opposite directions and was taken from five different stations placed on the street belonging to each zone. The gate count was established by drawing a fictive line of view across the width of the street from an observation point located at the level of one of the walls of the street. The gate count observations lasted each 10 min, being repeated five times a day between morning and afternoon.

Regarding the Space Syntax methods, the three study zones were analyzed together, with the creation of an axial map. Connectivity and Integration measures were modelled to estimate intelligibility and synergy correlations.

Intelligibility represents the correlation between the connectivity of the axial lines and their integration HH, and it refers to the capacity of a structure to provide information at the local level on the structuring role of spaces at the global one. This would show how easy is to read the urban space, to move and to get the space in question. As for synergy, correlating the Local Integration HH (R3) and the Global Integration HH (Rn) informs the link of the local structure to the global level, and it is a measure of how local dynamic relations are kept intact by global dynamics.

At the macro scale, an axial-segment map is then generated in order to assess the Normalized Integration Values (NAIN) for the studied street. At a micro-scale, the axial-segment maps were generated individually for each zone, in order to analyze both Normalized Angular Integration at this scale, as well as the values for Normalized Angular Choice (NACH). The normalization of measures, introduced by Hillier, Yang and Turner [19], allows to compare between several study objects of different sizes and depth as is the case with the three parts of the street. Therefore, the normalization was done to avoid the depth influence on the analysis.

3 Results and Discussion

The results of the in-situ observation and the "gate counts" method show that the aggregate number of people crossing the control gates is 6.670. The Zone 2, that comprise the Old City and Plain area recorded the highest number of people, with 3.910, followed by the Zone 1 (ZHUN) with 2.045, and then the Zone 3, the Industrial Zone, with the least counts – 715. These results are in accordance with the expected movement, since the Zone 2 possesses the greater number of functional attractors – commerce and services – when compared to the other zones. The results are shown in the table below (Table 1).

Table 1. The aggregate number of people crossing the gates in each zone on both days.

Zone	Zone 1	Zone 2	Zone 3
Aggregate number of people crossing the gates on both days	2.045	3.910	715

From the syntactic and axial analysis of the three studied zones taken together, it can be noticed, from the scatter diagrams, that the reading of the urban space is not easily done and that movements are made with some difficulty, and this according to the value of intelligibility which is lower than 0.5 (intelligibility = 0.25), while the local structure is well linked to the global level according to the synergy value which is upper than 0.5 (synergy = 0.58) (Fig. 2; Fig. 3).

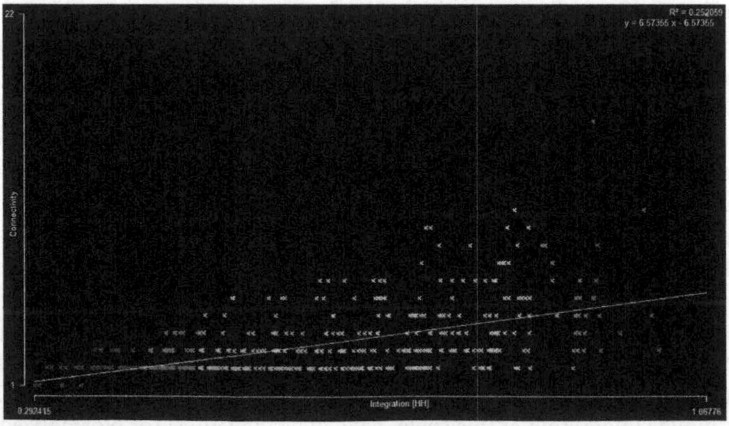

Fig. 2. Scatter plot showing the correlation between connectivity and global integration (intelligibility).

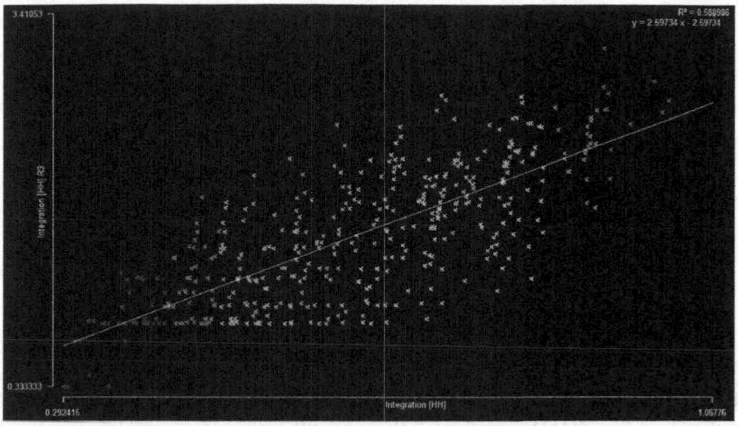

Fig. 3. Scatter plot showing the correlation between local and global integration (synergy).

The axial-segment map established at the same scale, demonstrates that on a global scale, the part of the street located at the level of Zone 2 is the most integrated with a value of 0.021, revealing a good correspondence with the movement. The Zone 3 presents a value of 0.016, and represents the Industrial Zone, where pedestrian movement is uncommon, thus explaining the lower values for gate count. NAIN values of 0.010 are found for the Zone 1, which are the lowest from the three areas at a global level (Fig. 4, Table 2). All zones, comprised the analyzed street, demonstrate NAIN values lower than the historical center area comprehending the Old City.

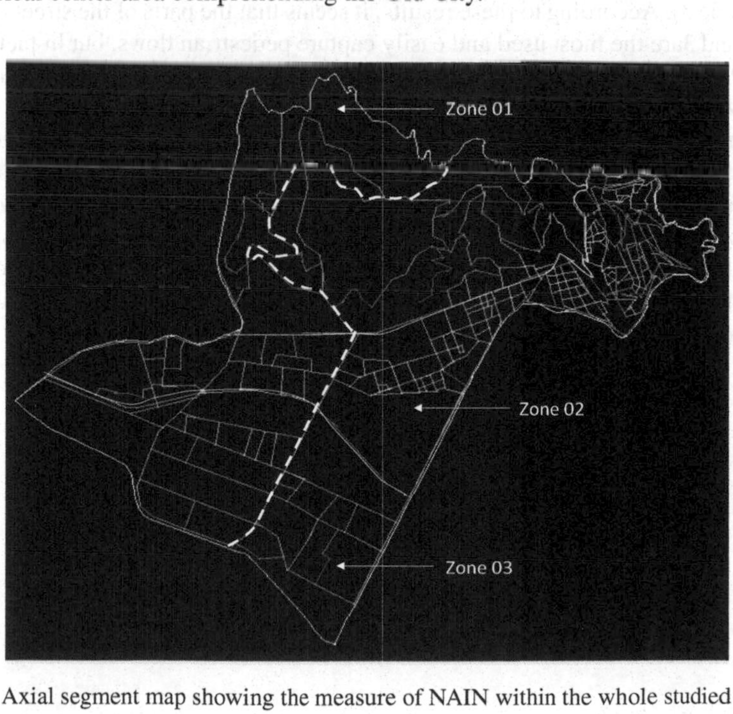

Fig. 4. Axial segment map showing the measure of NAIN within the whole studied system.

Table 2. The average NAIN values of the three parts of the studied street within the whole studied system.

Part of the street	Average value of NAIN
Zone 1	0.010
Zone 2	0.021
Zone 3	0.016

Regarding the axial segment analysis on a smaller scale, the representations of NACH (Fig. 5) and NAIN (Fig. 6), informs the dynamics at a local level for each part of the studied street. For NACH values, the higher results are observed on the part of the street located at the Zone 1 (ZHUN) with a value of 1.897, therefore explaining the high gate count – deriving from flows at local scale, since it is a street that collects movement from the local roads and private accesses. The Industrial Zone (Zone 3) demonstrates NACH values of 1.890 – also high, since it collects the roads from the orthogonal grid structure. The Zone 2 (OCP) possesses lower values when compared to the rest, with 1.875. NAIN results demonstrate that both Zones 1 and 3 have equal values for integration (0.034), where the NAIN value for Zone 2 is slightly lower (0.03) (Table 3).

For the combination of the two measures of normalized choice and integration to better reveal human movement (Fig. 7), the results show that the parts of the street located at Zones 1 and 3 always come in first position with a value of these two combined measures of 0.020, then come the part of the street situated in Zone 2 with a value of 0.018 (Table 3). According to these results, it seems that the parts of the street located in Zones 1 and 3are the most used and easily capture pedestrian flows, but in fact it is not.

A comparison between the results of the different methods and analyzes, is summarized in Table 4.

By superimposing all these results for each zone, and which are not in compliance with Space Syntax theory, we note that the good use of the street at the level of Zone 2 despite its low local syntactic properties compared to the two other zones, as well as the low use of the same street at Zone 3 despite its good local syntactic properties; this can be related to global syntactic properties such as global integration, or to functional ones such as the urban vocation of the zone, since Zone 2 is a zone with a functional mixing, while Zone 3 is an industrial one.

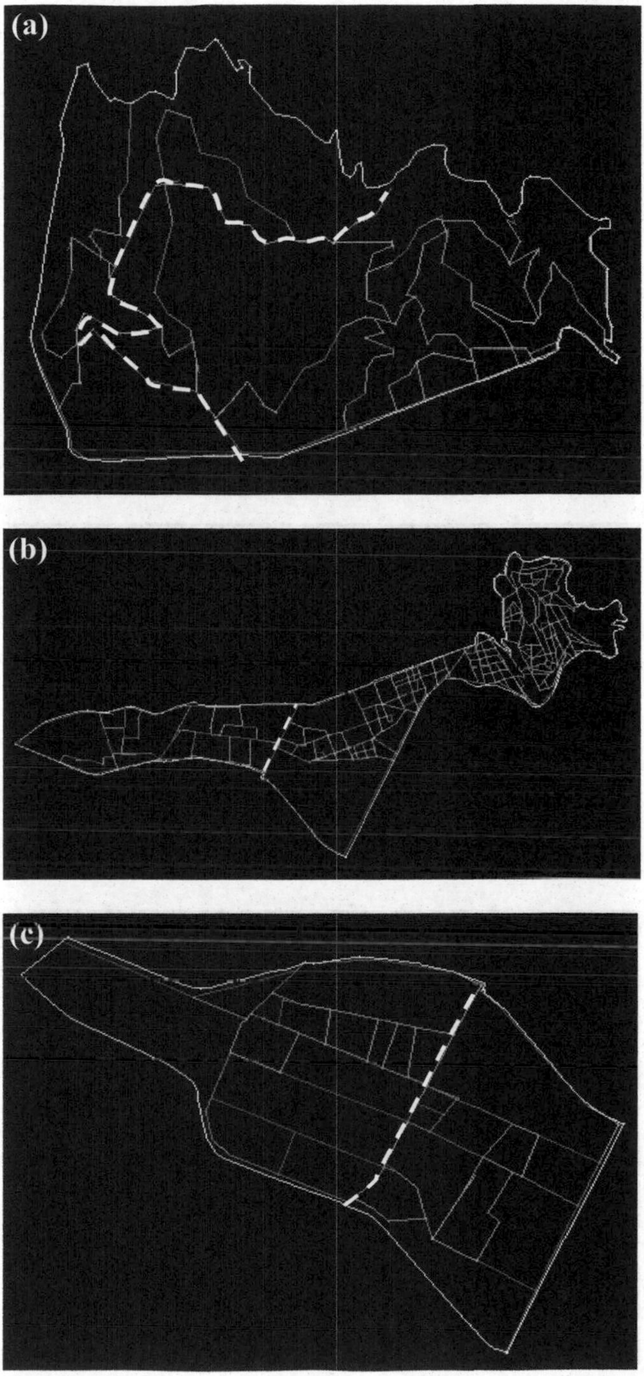

Fig. 5. Axial segment maps showing the measure of NACH within each study zone: Zone 1 (a), Zone 2 (b) and Zone 3 (c).

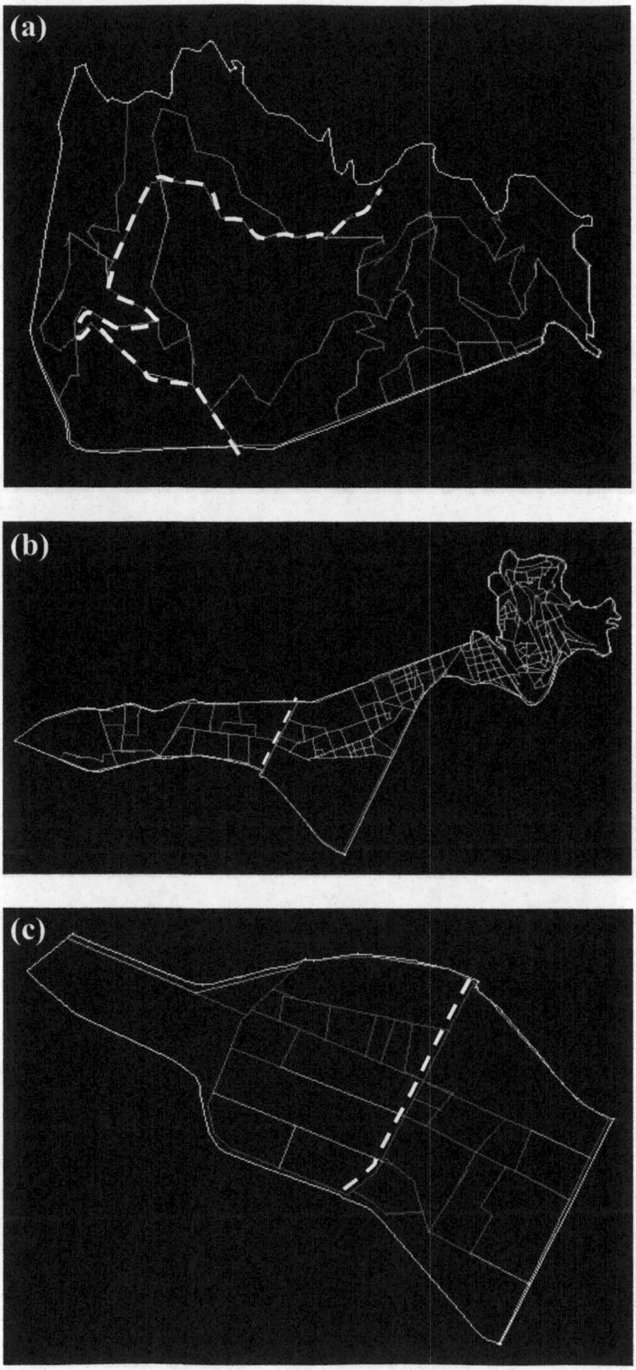

Fig. 6. Axial segment maps showing the measure of NAIN within each study zone: Zone 1 (a), Zone 2 (b) and Zone 3 (c).

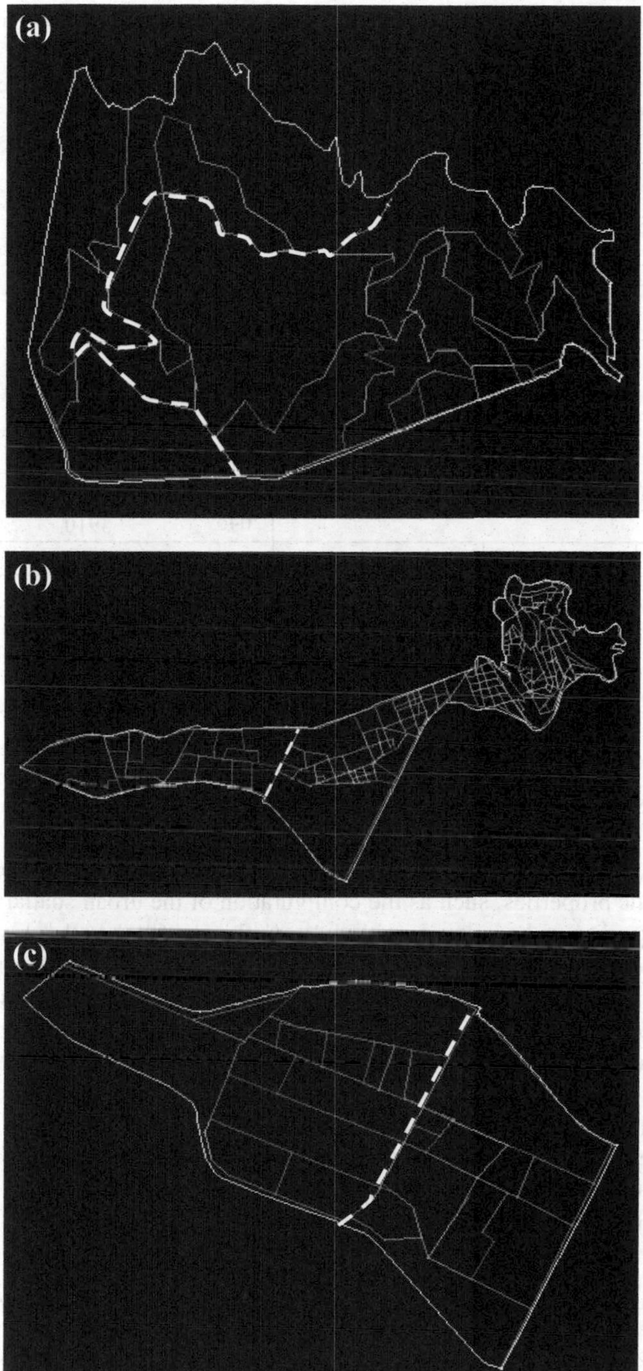

Fig. 7. Axial segment maps showing the measure of combined NACH and NAIN within each study zone: Zone 1 (a), Zone 2 (b) and Zone 3 (c).

Table 3. The average values of NACH, NAIN and of these two combined measures at the level of the three parts of the studied street.

Part of the street	Average value of NACH	Average value of NAIN	Average value of combined NACH and NAIN
Zone 1	1.897	0.034	0.020
Zone 2	1.875	0.03	0.018
Zone 3	1.890	0.034	0.020

Table 4. Table summarizing the results of the different methods and analyzes.

Methods and measures \ Part of the street			Zone 1	Zone 2	Zone 3
Gate counts			2045	3910	715
Space Syntax	Macro scale	NAIN	0.010	0.021	0.016
	Micro scale	NACH	1.897	1.875	1.890
		NAIN	0.034	0.03	0.034
		Combined NACH and NAIN	0.020	0.018	0.020

4 Conclusion

The attendance and use of the streets in the city of Bejaia depend on the one hand, on the global syntactic properties, such as the configuration of the urban spatial structure and the good integration of these streets within the whole city. On the other hand, functional properties also play a very important role in the use of streets, such as the urban vocation of the area where they are located, the land use pattern and the activities and services present at their walls. These activities have a multiplier effect on the attractiveness of streets and participate in urban life, thus affecting the proper functioning of the city of Bejaia.

The identified limit of this research is the fact that we didn't have enough time to conduct the observation for people counting for several days and to use multiple observation stations in order to have more detailed results, but that didn't prevent us to have sufficiently relevant results.

References

1. Bastié, J., Désert, B.: Urban Space. Masson, Paris (1980)
2. Hillier, B.: The art of place and the science of space. Word Arch. **11**(185), 96–102 (2005)
3. Hillier, B., Vaughan, L.: The city as one thing. Prog. Plan. **67**(3), 205–230 (2007)

4. Hillier, B.: Studying cities to learn about minds: how geometric intuitions shape urban space and make it work. In: Proceedings of the Workshop held in Bremen-Space Syntax and Spatial Cognition, pp. 11–31. Hölscher, C. & al., Bremen (2006)
5. Bada, Y.: The Impact of Visibility on Visual Perception and Space Use: The Case of Urban Plazas in Biskra. PhD thesis. University of Biskra, Algeria (2012).
6. Lewin, K.: Field theory in social science: selected theoretical papers. Dorwin Cartwright (1951)
7. Lynch, K.: The Image of the City. The MIT Press, Cambridge (1960)
8. Moughtin, C.: Urban Design, Street and Square. Routledge, Abingdon (2003)
9. Schumacher, T.: Buildings and streets: notes on configuration and use. On Streets, 133–149 (1986)
10. Peponis, J.: Geometries of architectural description: shape and spatial configuration. In: 1st International Space Syntax Symposium Proceedings, pp. 34.1–34.8. London (1997)
11. Hillier, B., Penn, A., Hanson, J., Grajewski, T., Xu, J.: Natural movement: or, configuration and attraction in urban pedestrian movement. Environ. Plann. B. Plann. Des. **20**, 29–66 (1993)
12. Hillier, B.: Space is the Machine: A Configurational Theory of Architecture. Cambridge University Press, Cambridge (1996)
13. Hillier, B.: Cities as movement economies. Urban Des. Int. **1**(1), 41–60 (1996)
14. Cutini, V.: Configuration and Centrality some evidences from two Italian case studies. In: 3rd International Space Syntax Symposium Proceedings. Georgia Institute of Technology, Atlanta (2001)
15. Hillier, B., Hanson, J.: The Social Logic of Space. Cambridge University Press, Cambridge (1984)
16. Lahart, J., et al.: Design Manual for urban roads and streets. Technical Paper. Department of Transport, Tourism and Sport of Ireland, Dublin, Ireland (2013)
17. Turner, A.: Getting serious with depthmap: segment analysis and scripting. Bartlett School of Graduate Studies, UCL, pp. 18–25. London (2008)
18. Varoudis, T.: DepthmapX 0.5. https://varoudis.github.io/depthmapX/, Accessed 01 Apr 2020
19. Hillier, B., Yang, T., Turner, A.: Normalising least angle choice in Depthmap - and how it opens up new perspectives on the global and local analysis of city space. J. Space Synt. **3**(2), 155–193 (2012)

Correction to: Computational Science and Its Applications – ICCSA 2021

Osvaldo Gervasi, Beniamino Murgante, Sanjay Misra, Chiara Garau, Ivan Blečić, David Taniar, Bernady O. Apduhan, Ana Maria A. C. Rocha, Eufemia Tarantino, and Carmelo Maria Torre

Correction to:
O. Gervasi et al. (Eds.): *Computational Science and Its Applications – ICCSA 2021*, LNCS 12952, https://doi.org/10.1007/978-3-030-86973-1

Chapter "Automated Housing Price Valuation and Spatial Data" was previously published non-open access. It has now been changed to open access under a CC BY 4.0 license and the copyright holder updated to 'The Author(s)'.

Chapter "Solving Differential Equations Using Feedforward Neural Networks" was previously published open access. It now has been changed to non-open access and the copyright holder updated to "Springer Nature Switzerland AG".

The originally published version of chapter 44 contained a typographical error in the abstract. The typographical error has been corrected in the abstract.

The updated version of these chapters can be found at
https://doi.org/10.1007/978-3-030-86973-1_26
https://doi.org/10.1007/978-3-030-86973-1_27
https://doi.org/10.1007/978-3-030-86973-1_44

O. Gervasi et al. (Eds.): ICCSA 2021, LNCS 12952, p. C1, 2021.
https://doi.org/10.1007/978-3-030-86973-1_51

Author Index

Printed in the United States
by Baker & Taylor Publisher Services